Fodor's 2020

ESSENTIAL
IRELAND

D0252076

Welcome to Ireland

It's a Celtic mystery: how can a country as small as Ireland be packed with so much majestic history, natural beauty, vibrant culture, and, of course, fun? Norman castles overlook wild, empty beaches, Georgian Country houses host impromptu traditional music sessions, excited theatergoers spill out into bustling Dublin pubs. Drama and spectacle lie at every turn, with a pint of Guinness to toast it all. But the real Irish secret is the people: their unique blend of warmth, humor, and irreverence will ensure your trip to the Emerald Isle is a true adventure.

TOP REASONS TO GO

★ **Untamed Nature:** From rugged marshlands to glacial lakes, wild Ireland blows the mind.

★ **Living History:** Neolithic Knowth, Celtic Cashel, Christian Glendalough, and more.

★ **Perfect Pubs:** A fire, some chowder, and a pint of stout—the Irish pub is a slow, sacred space.

★ **Festivals:** Oysters in Galway, jazz in Cork, St. Paddy in Dublin; celebrate year-round.

★ **Cracking Culture:** Every second native's a poet or a fiddle player—it's in the air.

★ **Hidden Treasures:** Empty islands, silent forests, untouched beaches: serenity abounds.

Contents

Fodor's Features

MAPS

Chapter 1

EXPERIENCE IRELAND

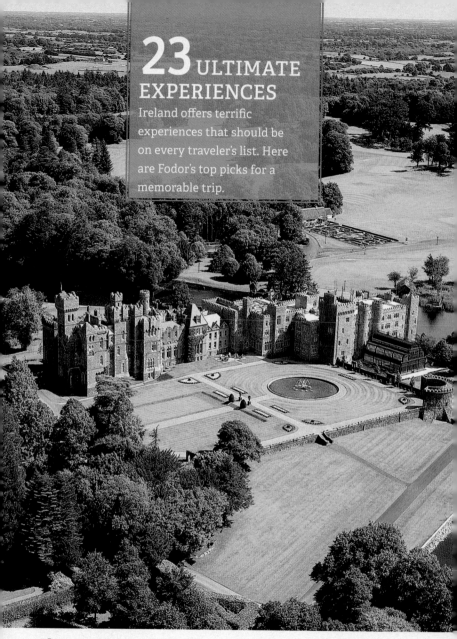

23 ULTIMATE EXPERIENCES

Ireland offers terrific experiences that should be on every traveler's list. Here are Fodor's top picks for a memorable trip.

1 A Castle Stay

Enjoy the royal treatment and your fill of history, luxury, adventure, and charm with a stay in an Irish castle-hotel. Ashford Castle, set on 350 stunning acres and hugging Lake Corrib, offers a fairy-tale feel. *(Ch. 10)*

2 The Giants Causeway

A UNESCO World Heritage Site, the Giant's Causeway was created either by erupting lava 60 million years ago or a mighty Irish giant in love. Decide for yourself! *(Ch. 12)*

3 James Joyce

Visit the James Joyce Centre or join the Bloomsday celebrations in June for readings, performances, and pub crawls as you follow Joyce's footsteps around Dublin. *(Ch. 3)*

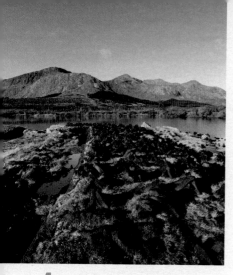

4 A Connemara Hike

With some of the finest rugged scenery and dramatic coastline in all of Ireland, a hike or guided walk in Connemara National Park is a must for lovers of the outdoors. *(Ch. 10)*

5 Grafton Street

Dublin's pedestrian-only street bustles with shoppers, world-famous buskers, and flower vendors. Smaller side streets offer boutiques with Irish crafts and fashion. *(Ch. 3)*

6 The East Coast

There's much to discover along Waterford's coast, including seaside towns like Tramore, Ardmore, and the unspoiled Gaeltacht area An Rinn (Ring). *(Ch. 6)*

7 Guinness

The Guinness Brewery and Storehouse tells the history, and the brewing process, of Guinness—Dublin's black blood. The top-floor bar offers city views and a free pint. *(Ch. 3)*

8 Monastic Sites

The round tower of St Kevin's monastic settlement at Glendalough ("Glen of Two Lakes")
deep in the Wicklow Mountains, is an iconic feature of Ireland's monastic ruins. *(Ch. 4)*

9 Belfast/Titanic Experience

The impressive Titanic Visitor Center presents the tragic story of the biggest ocean liner
ever built and commemorates Belfast's connection and industrial heritage. *(Ch. 12)*

10 Derry/Londonderry

Take in Derry's long history, its murals, and the 17th-century town as you stroll its ramparts and then cross the modern Peace Bridge, a symbol of unity. *(Ch. 12)*

11 Trad Music

Ennis is a great place to hear music at any time, but especially during the Fleadh in late August. Singers, musicians, and dancers compete, and much of the music is free. *(Ch. 9)*

12 Killarney National Park

Hike, bike, or hire a car to explore Killarney National Park with its blue lakes, purple mountains, and red deer. Highlights include the ruins of Muckross Friary and Torc Waterfall. *(Ch. 8)*

13 Skellig Ring

The drive from Waterville to Portmagee is a popular extension to the Ring of Kerry; the narrow road cannot handle tour buses and the coastal scenery is glorious. *(Ch. 8)*

14 National Gallery

The National Gallery is one of Europe's finest smaller art museums with a collection of paintings by Irish artists. *(Ch. 3)*

15 Wild Atlantic Way

Whether you tour it from end-to-end, or just enjoy sections, the Wild Atlantic Way is an epic driving, biking, or hiking journey along Ireland's stunning west coast. *(Ch. 11)*

16 Golfing

From renowned courses designed by celebrated golf architects to welcoming local clubs in every corner of the country, Ireland is a golfer's paradise.

17 Artisanal Cheeses

The revival of Irish Farmhouse Cheeses was pioneered in Cork: look for pungent Milleens, milder Durrus and Coolea, Gouda-like Gubbeen, and Fermoy Natural Cheese. *(Ch. 7)*

18 Galway

Enjoy the buskers, bookshops, boutiques, festivals, and lively pub culture of Ireland's liveliest city, a university town and favorite weekend getaway for the Irish. *(Ch. 9)*

19 Irish Design

Home to the Crafts Council of Ireland, the Kilkenny Design Centre, and a craft trail that includes Nicholas Mosse pottery, hit Kilkenny for contemporary Irish design. *(Ch. 6)*

20 Dingle

Sample seafood and music in Dingle Town before heading out on the peninsula to Slea Head. Stop along the coast to investigate the ancient stone beehive huts. *(Ch. 8)*

21 Trinity College

Founded in 1592 to "civilize Ireland," Trinity is best known for its noted alumni and its Old Library, which houses the exquisite illuminated manuscript, the *Book of Kells. (Ch. 3)*

22 Croagh Patrick

Join the 30,000 pilgrims, some barefoot, who climb Croagh Patrick on the last Sunday in July, or walk it solo for serene views of Clew Bay and its 365 islands. *(Ch. 10)*

23 The Cliffs of Moher

Rising dramatically out of the Atlantic Ocean, these cliffs are one of Ireland's most breathtaking natural sights, best viewed from a cruise or on a trail from Doolin. *(Ch. 9)*

The Best Historical Sights to Visit in Ireland

CÉIDE FIELDS, COUNTY MAYO

Located in a remote coastal region of north Mayo on the Wild Atlantic Way, Céide (pronounced Kay-jeh) is a historical bogland and unique ecosystem on which barley was once grown in its cultivation ridges. The fields are among the most extensive Stone Age monuments in the world.

SKELLIG MICHAEL, COUNTY KERRY

Two stark and bare islands of old red sandstone lie 13 km (8 miles) off the southwest Irish coast. An early Christian hermitage, Skellig is on the UNESCO World Heritage list.

CLONMACNOISE, COUNTY OFFALY

Clonmacnoise, which translates from the Irish as "Meadow of the Sons of Nóis," is a monastic site, founded by St. Ciarán in the 6th century.

KILMAINHAM GAOL, COUNTY DUBLIN

With its tiers of cells, overhead catwalks, and grim corridors, Kilmainham prison—where the leaders of the 1916 Easter Rising as well as other Irish revolutionaries were executed by the British—evokes a chilling period in the past.

GLENDALOUGH, COUNTY WICKLOW

In the heart of the Wicklow mountains, Glendalough is a captivating valley carved by Ice Age glaciers lays claim to some of the best-preserved monastic sites in Ireland's heritage. It was here that St. Kevin founded his 6th-century settlement, a peaceful place where he retreated to pray.

HILLSBOROUGH CASTLE, COUNTY DOWN

Dating from the 1770s, Hillsborough Castle is the only royal palace in Ireland and it is still used by the British royal family on state visits to Northern Ireland. This Georgian beauty sits 19 km (12 miles) south of Belfast, and was given new life as part of a £16 million renovation completed in 2018.

BRÚ NA BÓINNE, NEWGRANGE, COUNTY MEATH

The Newgrange passage grave known as Brú na Bóinne is one of the most celebrated prehistoric sites in Ireland. Dating to about 3200 BC, Newgrange, a UNESCO World Heritage site, is an enormous mound made of layers of earth and stone.

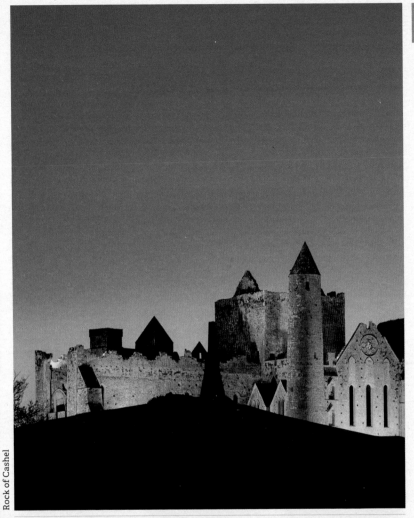

Rock of Cashel

ROCK OF CASHEL, COUNTY TIPPERARY

Perched high on a solitary lump of gray limestone, the Rock was originally a ceremonial center and home to the kings of Munster, known as the Eóganacht, and it remains a potent symbol.

KILKENNY MEDIEVAL MILE, COUNTY KILKENNY

Labeled by tourism gurus as the Medieval Mile, this trail runs through Kilkenny's city center, linking a 13th-century cathedral with a hulking, 800-year-old, creeper-clad castle alongside a potpourri of other ancient buildings.

DÚN AENGUS, INISHMORE, ARAN ISLANDS, COUNTY GALWAY

Far and away the most thrilling ancient site on the three sea-battered Aran Islands, Dún Aengus is a dramatic semicircular fort perched against sheer, 90-meter-high cliffs on the edge of the Western world.

Ireland's Top 10 Natural Wonders

BEN BULBEN , COUNTY SLIGO

Seen from a distance, the striking, flat-topped profile of Ben Bulben resembles the capsized hull of a ship. This is the best-known Irish mountain because it is inextricably linked to W. B. Yeats, the country's most illustrious poet.

KILLARNEY LAKES, COUNTY KERRY

They say that the best things come in threes, and aside from seeing the last remnants of ancient Irish trees, the chief reason to visit this area is for the stunning trio of Killarney's famed lakes: Lough Leane (lower), Muckross (middle), and the Upper Lake.

THE BURREN, COUNTY CLARE

Catch a clear spring evening and you will be enchanted by one of the strangest of all effects that the Burren affords: a delicate, pale-pink hue creeping imperceptibly across the rocks, rouging them with sunset.

GIANT'S CAUSEWAY, COUNTY ANTRIM

In the eyes of the 18th-century writer Dr. Samuel Johnson, the Giant's Causeway was "worth seeing ... but not worth going to see." Despite the dis, hundreds of thousands of visitors make the trek each year to the north Antrim coast to explore the phenomenon of a UNESCO World Heritage site where history and folklore coalesce.

SLIEVE LEAGUE CLIFFS, COUNTY DONEGAL

Imagine a remote hilltop where you humble yourself before the ocean and sky. Such a place is Slieve League, home to the highest cliffs in Ireland and one of the west coast's most spectacular sights.

HILL OF TARA, COUNTY MEATH

Long, undulating lines of earthworks, grassy banks, and ditches make up the fascinating Hill of Tara. It's unspectacular at first sight, but you will soon discover a landscape of myth and legend overlapping with history and archaeology. Tara is a many-sided place scrutinized by antiquarians, with monuments, including a passage tomb, a henge, and standing stones, ranging in date from 3500 BC to AD 400.

CLEW BAY, COUNTY MAYO

The island-studded Clew Bay, sitting hard by the Atlantic coastline, is made up of scores of tiny dots, which from a distance look like sleeping whales,

Slieve League cliffs, Donegal

snakes, dragons, or an upturned curragh (a traditional boat with a wooden frame). The best place to get a feel for the scale of the bay and its reputed 365 islands is from the Great Western Greenway walking and cycling route along the line of an old railway track.

MACGILLYCUDDY'S REEKS, COUNTY KERRY

At the heart of the ancient yet newly christened Reeks district of Kerry is Carrauntoohil, the highest point in Ireland and part of the oldest red sandstone mountains in Europe. It is a truly magical experience to get up close to these jagged peaks, glacial lakes, babbling streams, and fields ablaze with yellow gorse and wildflowers. The best way to tackle the Reeks is to hire a guide or join a walking tour from Killarney.

POWERSCOURT WATERFALL, COUNTY WICKLOW

Awe-inspiring Powerscourt, the biggest waterfall in Ireland (England, too), is a dazzling sight, leaping and splashing in a frenzy across the rock face. At nearly 398 feet, it stands in a valley on the River Dargle near the foot of the Wicklow Mountains, and through the centuries has inspired writers and painters. Pack a picnic and keep an eye out for finches, warblers, red squirrels, and Sika deer.

DÚN BRISTE SEA STACK, DOWNPATRICK HEAD, BALLYCASTLE, COUNTY MAYO

The squabbling of thousands of seabirds who make their nest on Dún Briste's ragged limestone sea stack, which separated from the mainland in 1393, is reminiscent of children in a playground.

Ireland's Top Castles and Manor Houses

HAYFIELD MANOR, CORK CITY
A redbrick charmer, this family-run period house is a hidden bolt-hole within a leafy, 5-meter-high walled garden, a 20-minute stroll from the center of Cork City. White-sash windows and quirky dormers bring radiance to the exterior of this neo-Georgian building that was originally owned by the Musgrave family, a dynasty of Cork merchants.

ADARE MANOR, COUNTY LIMERICK
Dating to the 1830s and set on an immaculate 842-acre estate shaded by some 19,000 trees, this Limerick property was home to the earls of Dunraven and one of the finest private homes in Ireland.

DROMOLAND CASTLE, NEWMARKET-ON-FERGUS, COUNTY CLARE
For more than 400 years Dromoland Castle, the ancestral home of the O'Briens, barons of Inchiquin and descendants of Brian Boru, the High King of Ireland, has played host to guests who wish to savor its mix of supreme luxury and history.

ASHFORD CASTLE, CONG, COUNTY MAYO
From the moment you enter the stone gates, this stately castle is the stuff of fairy tales, oozing luxury and contemporary cool after a €25 million restoration. Originally built in the 13th century, it was the former hunting lodge of the Guinness family during the 1800s.

LOUGH ESKE CASTLE, DONEGAL TOWN, COUNTY DONEGAL

In a remote setting close to the shores of Lough Eske, this eponymous Tudor-style baronial castle is approached by a drive through ancient woodland. The clans of Donegal, the O'Donnells, had their seat on the lake here in the 1470s.

BALLYNAHINCH CASTLE, CONNEMARA, COUNTY GALWAY

A venerable house with impeccable historical cachet, Bally-nahinch Castle is set on 700 acres of private woodlands and stands harmoniously in a landscape overlooking a salmon fishery.

BELLINGHAM CASTLE, CASTLEBELLINGHAM, COUNTY LOUTH

At the end of tree-lined drive and on the banks of a crystal river, Bellingham Castle is exactly what you imagine when you think "gloriously romantic Irish castle."

PARKNASILLA RESORT, COUNTY KERRY

Built in 1897 and set on the Ring of Kerry looking across Kenmare Bay and the country's highest mountains, Parknasilla has hosted artists and royalty who enjoy the unhurried hospitality for which the "Kingdom" (of Kerry) is famed.

CABRA CASTLE, COUNTY CAVAN

If you are more drawn to the evil witch than the princess in fairy tales, you can get castle feels of the goosebumps-inducing variety at Cavan's Cabra Castle, which dates to 1820.

DELPHI LODGE, COUNTY GALWAY

Snuggling amidst the starkly beautiful wides-creen wilderness of high mountains, Delphi is a spectacularly sited 200-year-old chic country house.

WATERFORD CASTLE, COUNTY WATERFORD

Few, if any, other Irish castles can point to such seclusion as 16th-century Waterford Castle, magnifi-cently secreted away on its own 310-acre wooded island and accessible only by private ferry.

What to Eat and Drink in Ireland

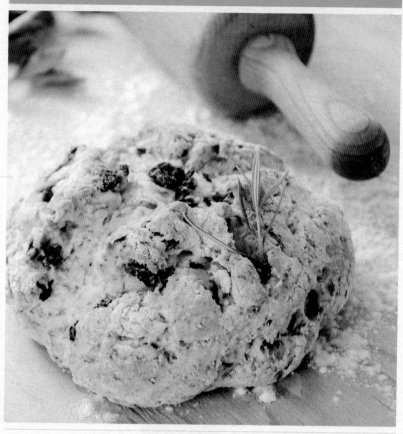

Soda Bread

BOXTY

Boxty is a blend of mashed potatoes and raw grated potato bulked up with the addition of ingredients like flour, eggs, and milk.

CHIPS

Humble "chipper" vans roam the villages of Ireland plying a bounty of fresh, crispy chips (which Americans know as French fries).

SMOKED SALMON

You'll find smoked salmon all over Ireland, but a visit to Burren Smokehouse gives you a chance to learn about how the products are made.

OYSTERS

You'll find oysters all over the country, but County Galway is renowned for its bivalves, with the native oysters being a particular specialty.

PERIWINKLES AND SEAWEED

Periwinkles are traditionally boiled in seawater and then eaten out of paper bags using a pin to fish out the meat, while seaweed appears in numerous dishes.

Oysters

IRISH BREAKFAST
Specific items in a full breakfast may vary, but core cast members include black and white pudding, browned mushrooms, sausages, eggs, at least one tomato, and either soda bread or a potato farl).

SODA BREAD
It's hard to say why soda bread in Ireland is so dramatically different from its sad American iteration. Whatever the case, soda bread, with its tender crumb, crusty exterior, and slightly sweet flavor, is better in Ireland.

TEA AND SCONES
You'll find that teatime can come with different food options, governed in part by the time of day you're taking your tea.

POITÍN
In Tunisia it's called boukha. In Italy, grappa. In the United States, moonshine. In Ireland, this beast is called poitín and—once illegal—it's making a comeback.

WHISKEY
Jamesons and Bushmills are fine examples of Irish whiskey, but Ireland has a number of newer craft distillers. Look for Dingle, the Connacht Whiskey Company, Knappogue Castle, and Proper No. Twelve.

CIDER
While you can find cider in a variety of styles, and with varying levels of sweetness and fermented funk, it's said that the apples of County Armagh are of particularly high quality.

CRAFT BEERS
Craft beer is finding fans across the globe and Ireland is no exception. Ireland's craft-beer scene is small, but growing interest helps provide a counterpoint to the behemoth that is Guinness.

GUINNESS
Guinness is ubiquitous, omnipresent, and an easy choice for those disinclined to roll the dice on the undulating flavor wheel that modern craft beer represents.

COLCANNON
Colcannon is a traditional dish of mashed potatoes mixed with kale or cabbage. It's simple, hearty, and a good match for Ireland's frequently blustery weather.

What to Buy in Ireland

MOURNE TEXTILES

Using traditional weaving techniques and custom-made handlooms, Irish heritage brand Mourne Textiles. is based in a workshop at the foot of the Mourne mountains in Co. Down. Look for wide scarves in earthy tones.

IRISH POTTERY

A visit to one of Ireland's ceramics studios will have you wondering why people focus on Waterford Crystal when there are so many incredible Irish potters and ceramicists producing cool, contemporary designs. Look for work by Nicholas Mosse, Paul Maloney, and Shanagarry Potters who produce handmade and hand-decorated pottery that follows a 250-year-old tradition of handcrafted pottery in East Cork.

FRAGRANCE

Located in the heart of Co. Clare's Burren, the Burren Perfumery creates small-batch perfumes and cosmetics inspired by the beautiful surrounding landscape. Visit the store to check out the herb garden and tea room, and to test fragrances, creams, and other products.

KNITWEAR

Specializing in detailed graphic knitwear with contemporary illustrations and bold patterns, Irish knitwear label Electronic Sheep's quirky, unisex sweaters and scarves are everything Grandma's Aran isn't.

JEWELRY

Designed and handcrafted in a seaside village in West Cork, Enibas Jewellery's single or interlocked infinite circles are inscribed " Croí álainn," Irish for "beautiful heart," which makes for a simple, but still sentimental alternative to the ubiquitous Claddagh ring gift. Also, look for Liwu Jewellery by designer Áine Breen whose work is inspired by the ancient meaning and beauty of Celtic symbols. Delicate necklaces with Celtic symbols for growth, serenity, eternity, and progress make lovely gifts.

CANDLES

Candle making is a traditional craft and for many hundreds of years candles were the primary means of providing light after darkness fell. Rathbornes candles—which traces its origins back to Dublin, circa 1488—lays claim to the title of "world's oldest candle company" and continues to make a wide range of fine products with captivating scents.

BLANKETS

Originally founded by an Irish Sister of Charity in 1892, Foxford Woollen Mill in County Mayo sources its wool from local sheep, its power from the River Moy, and its talent from local weavers. The high-quality woven rugs, blankets, and tweeds that have been made here more than 100 years, in the timeless designs of plaid, herringbone, and houndstooth, are available shades that reflect the earthy colors of the surrounding landscape.

WHISKEY

You don't have to spend much time in Ireland to discover there's a range

Whiskey

of craft distilleries, as well as distillery-only special blends such as the Glendalough Distillery Triple Barrel, which uses bourbon, Oloroso sherry, and canteiro-aged Madeira barrels to finish the whiskey. For some of these blends, such as the Triple Barrel, you'll need to buy them on-premise, but keep an eye open in the duty free airport shops as well for Ireland-only selections.

TWEED CAPS

County Donegal's traditional craft of tweed goes back centuries, and is both iconically Irish and easy to find. While we highly endorse head-to-toe Donegal tweed, a Donegal tweed cap from Hanna Hats is definitely easier on the wallet (and perhaps, the eye). Designed and made in Donegal since 1924 this third-generation company's hats are local, made from the finest Donegal tweed (pure new wool), and

stylish, too. Ps. they're also waterproof, which comes in handy in Ireland.

AVOCA THROWS

Known for its signature colorful woolen throws, which are woven at one of the oldest mills in Ireland, Avoca throws are every bit as comfortable as they are cheerful. Visit their flagship store to see the mill in action in the hills of Wicklow.

BODHRÁN

Among the rocky isles and bays of western Ireland in a Franciscan Monastery in the village of Roundstone, Malachy Kearns, known as "Malachy Bodhrán," has been building and stretching traditional goatskin drums known as a bodhráns (bow-rawns) for 35 years. Widely used by Irish folk musicians, bodhráns are a beautiful and historically significant musical instrument, and

Kearns makes some of the best available. These make a great gift for a musician but also a unique souvenir, especially if you have yours personalized with a family crest or other artwork.

SMOKED SALMON

Chance are you ate smoked salmon on your visit to Ireland, and chances are you'll want to continue eating it when you return home. Fortunately, there are a number of award-winning smokehouses located around the country offering vacuum packed salmon. Notables include Frank Hederman, the Burren Smokehouse, Ballyhack Smokehouse, and Shanagarry, all of whom use Irish salmon (mostly organic, farmed salmon). Also, while U.S. Customs is notoriously persnickity about travelers bringing food back to the States, fish is generally exempt.

Top Festivals and Events in Ireland

MIDSUMMER FESTIVAL

Every June, Cork City struts its artistic stuff with the Midsummer Festival (⊕ *www.corkmidsummer.com*), a mix of music, film, and theater. It runs on consecutive weekends in June leading up to the 21st.

ALL IRELAND HURLING FESTIVAL

Usually the first Sunday in September, the All-Ireland Hurling Final (⊕ *www.gaa. ie*), at Dublin's Croke Park, features the country's two top teams who chase down a heavy leather ball, or *sliothar*, with their ash hurleys at warp speeds.

PUCK FAIR

Puck Fair (⊕ *www.puckfair. ie*) in Kerry is the oldest festival in Ireland, dating back to pagan times, where a goat is made king for three days of drinking, dancing, and general abandon. Held on the second weekend in August, it's truly one of Ireland's most unusual festivals.

KINVARA CUCKOO FLEADH

Happening on the May bank-holiday weekend, the Kinvara Cuckoo Fleadh (⊕ *www.kinvara.com/ cuckoo*) is perfectly timed to welcome in the warmer evenings of early summer. A well-established and richly deserved reputation has ensured that the *fleadh* has become a showcase for the best in traditional music.

LISTOWEL WRITER'S WEEK

Listowel Writer's Week (⊕ *writersweek.ie*) is a chaotic and seriously democratic gathering devoted to all things literary. It takes place all over the town of Listowel on the first weekend in June.

TULLAMORE SHOW

Ireland's biggest agricultural gathering, Tullamore Show (⊕ *www.tullamoreshow.com*), attracts 60,000 people annually in mid-August for cattle contests, sheep-shearing competitions, Irish Axe Men demonstrations, exhibits of local artisanal produce, fashion shows, displays of vintage farm machinery, and more.

BLOOMSDAY

Even though it is now reckoned that more Americans and Japanese attend the events surrounding Bloomsday (⊕ *jamesjoyce.ie*) than Irish people, it hasn't taken away a jot from an event that continues to grow regardless. Bloomsday is June 16.

Cork Jazz Fest

THE OULD LAMMAS FAIR

Running for nearly 400 years, on the last Monday and Tuesday of August, this harvest fair in the seaside town of Ballycastle in County Antrim features traditional snacks, entertainers, and stalls selling local crafts and specialities.

CROAGH PATRICK

On the last Sunday in July, join the thousands of pilgrims and adventurers who climb Mayo's Croagh Patrick (⊕ www.croagh-patrick.com)—in your bare feet, for the full purging of your misdeeds.

CRUÍNNIU NA MBÁD

August's Cruínniu na mBád (⊕ irelandsmaritimefestivals.com/cruinniu-na-mbad-festival/), or the Gathering of the Boats, is basically a big booze-up and regatta to celebrate the unique and beautiful boat that is the Galway hooker.

KINSALE GOURMET FESTIVAL

Long noted for its cuisine innovations, the Kinsale Gourmet Festival (⊕ www.kinsalerestaurants.com) is all about the happy pursuit of great food and wine plus the excitable bravado of this infectious coastal town. It takes place on the second weekend in October.

CORK JAZZ FEST

For jazz lovers, the Cork Jazz Festival (⊕ www.guinnessjazzfestival.com) on the second-to-last weekend in October is a perfect antidote to the approaching winter.

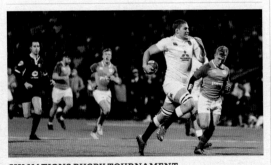

SIX NATIONS RUGBY TOURNAMENT

Every spring rugby fever grips the country as the Six Nations Tournament (⊕ www.rbs6nations.com) begins. The beloved Irish team takes on the might of Wales, France, Scotland, Italy, and its old enemy England in a series of bone-crunching encounters.

WHAT'S WHERE

1 Dublin. A transformed city since the days of O'Casey and Joyce, Ireland's capital may have replaced its legendary tenements with modern high-rises but its essential spirit remains intact. One of Europe's most popular city-break destinations, it has art, culture, Georgian architecture, and, of course, hundreds of pubs where conversation and vocal dexterity continue to flourish within an increasingly multicultural mix. Get spirited at the Guinness Brewery, stroll through teeming Temple Bar, and be illuminated by the *Book of Kells* at Trinity College's great library.

2 Dublin Environs. The counties outside the Pale are a treasure trove of history, monastic settlements, ancient tombs, battlefields, and peaceful valleys only an hour from the hubbub of the capital's center. From the lush greenery of Kildare and Wicklow, to the mythology and traditions of Meath and Louth, the historic time line encompasses many of the pivotal pre-Christian and early church locales of Ireland's past. Listen for ancient echoes at the Hill of Tara, hike into prehistory at Newgrange, and opt for opulence at Castletown House.

3 The Midlands. Overlooked by many visitors due to the region's relative absence of wow-factor attractions, this verdant oasis of bog and lake harks back to the simpler, and slower, life of Ireland 40 years ago. Friendly, almost shy natives, old-style pubs, unspoiled vistas and walks, plus a wealth of historic ruins make for a relaxing adventure into the way we were. Tree-hug one of the great yews at Tullynally Gardens, lift your spirits at Clonmacnoise, and take a river cruise down the Shannon.

4 The Southeast. Ireland's sunniest corner (with almost double the national average), the coastal counties have long been the favored hideaway of Dublin folk on vacation. Quiet seaside villages, country houses, and some of the nation's best land all offer delightful reasons to tarry. Inland, counties like Kilkenny and Tipperary offer a lion's share of history and important monuments in the main towns, Wexford and Waterford. Follow in the footsteps of St. Patrick at the Rock of Cashel and dig the ducal lifestyle at Lismore.

5 County Cork. After exploring the delights of Cork City—museums, lively pubs, quirky cafés, and lots of good music, trad and otherwise—use it as a base to explore Ireland's largest county, as nearly everyone heads to get the gift of gab by kissing the famous Blarney Stone. Get your fill of five-star scenery by traveling east to Shanagarry, and teach yourself good taste at Ballymaloe House, pioneer of the New Irish cuisine. Due south is the "Irish St-Tropez," fashionable Kinsale, while westward lies Bantry, one of Ireland's finest stately homes, which sits atop a breathtaking bluff over Bantry Bay. From here a cliff-top road with stunning views leads to ruggedly beautiful Glengarriff.

MAYO

Achill Island

Clare Island

Clew Bay

Inishturk

Inishbofin

Lough Corrib

Oileáin Árainn (Aran Islands)

Mouth of the Shannon

Tralee

Corca Dhuibhne (Dingle Peninsula)

Blasket Islands

Dingle Bay

KERRY

Iveragh Peninsula

Skellig Rocks

Beara Peninsula

Kenmare Bay

Bantry Bay

Mizen Head

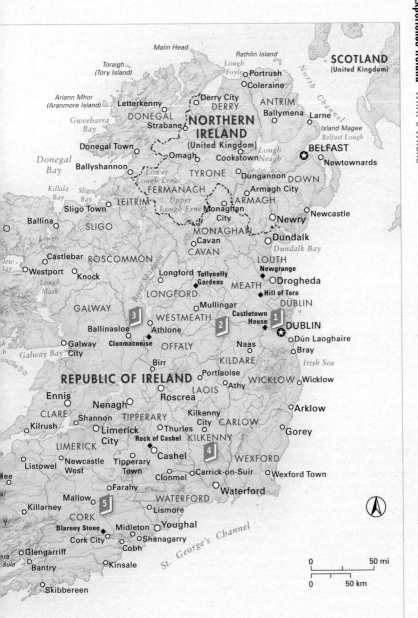

Malin Head

Toraigh
(Tory Island)

Rathlin Island

Lough
Foyle

Portrush

Coleraine

North Channel

SCOTLAND
(United Kingdom)

Ariann Mhor
(Aranmore Island)

Letterkenny

Derry City

DERRY

ANTRIM

Ballymena

Larne

Gweebarra
Bay

DONEGAL

Strabane

NORTHERN
IRELAND

Island Magee

Belfast Lough

Donegal Town

(United Kingdom)

Omagh

Cookstown

Lough
Neagh

BELFAST

Newtownards

Donegal
Bay

Ballyshannon

Lower
Lough Erne

TYRONE

Dungannon

DOWN

Killala
Bay

Sligo
Bay

LEITRIM

FERMANACH

Upper
Lough Erne

Monaghan
City

Armagh City

ARMAGH

Newry

Newcastle

Ballina

Sligo Town

SLIGO

MONAGHAN

Dundalk

Lough
Conn

Castlebar

ROSCOMMON

Cavan

CAVAN

Dundalk Bay

lew
ay

Westport

Knock

LOUTH

Newgrange

Lough
Mask

Longford

Tullynally
Gardens

MEATH

Drogheda

GALWAY

LONGFORD

Mullingar

Hill of Tara

River Shannon

WESTMEATH

Castletown
House

DUBLIN

Ballinasloe

Athlone

3

DUBLIN

Galway
City

Clonmacnoise

OFFALY

2

1

Galway Bay

Naas

Dún Laoghaire

h
b

Birr

KILDARE

Bray

REPUBLIC OF IRELAND

Portlaoise

Irish Sea

Ennis

Nenagh

Roscrea

LAOIS

Athy

WICKLOW

Wicklow

CLARE

Shannon

TIPPERARY

Kilkenny
City

CARLOW

Arklow

Kilrush

Limerick
City

Thurles

Gorey

LIMERICK

Rock of Cashel

KILKENNY

4

Listowel

Newcastle
West

Tipperary
Town

Cashel

WEXFORD

ee
)

Farahy

Clonmel

Carrick-on-Suir

Wexford Town

Mallow

Lismore

WATERFORD

Waterford

ā
sula

5

CORK

Youghal

Killarney

Blarney Stone

Midleton

Shanagarry

St. George's Channel

y

Glengarriff

Cork City

Cobh

Bantry

Kinsale

Skibbereen

0		50 mi
0		50 km

WHAT'S WHERE

6 The Southwest. The counties of Kerry and Limerick have sights that top every tourist's must-see list. The most brazenly scenic coastal drive in the land, the Ring of Kerry, will use up your entire flash card in a jiffy! While there, take a wet-and-wonderful ride out to the Skellig Islands, whose twin peaks rise out of the sea. The Gap of Dunloe lets you walk through the heart of Killarney's purple mountains and cross the glittering blue lake of Killarney. And don't forget to have your Nikon handy for Ireland's prettiest village, Adare. Everywhere, the glories of Ireland's coastline combine to paint a canvas that still casts a potent spell upon the stranger.

7 County Clare, Galway, and the Aran Islands. Set with postcard-perfect villages like Doolin, the lunar landscape of the Burren, and the towering Cliffs of Moher—they'll give you a new understanding of the word *awesome*—County Clare is pure tourist gold. As is nearby Galway City: one of Ireland's liveliest, it has a compact historic center bursting with artistic energy, and a lively pub culture. For a complete change of pace, head to the three Aran Islands, with their singular Irish heritage, miles of low stone walls, and car-free lanes.

8 Connemara and County Mayo. With the most westerly seaboard in Europe, this region remains a place apart—the most Irish part of Ireland. Connemara is an almost uninhabited landscape of misty bogland, studded with deep blue lakes under huge Atlantic skies, and distant purple hills: painters and photographers have strived for generations to capture the ever-changing light. Nearby is the delightful village of Cong, setting for *The Quiet Man*, where fetching ivy-covered thatched cottages contrast with the baronial splendor of Ashford Castle. For bright lights, head to Clifden and Westport, both lively small towns of great charm.

9 The Northwest. Sligo, Leitrim, and Donegal are homelands of rugged, self-sufficient people and roads where wandering sheep and cows are still the norm. Weatherwise, the area gets more than its fair share of the elements—a condition more than compensated for in its warm welcomes. Take a poetry break beside W.B. Yeats's grave near Ben Bulben, discover hidden Glencolumbkille, and immerse yourself in Irish in Sligo Town.

10 Northern Ireland. This region has positively bloomed since the peace dividend of recent times. From the beauty of Antrim's coastline to the vibrant cultural renaissance of Derry and Belfast, Northern Ireland has finally emerged from the yoke of its sectarian past into a present full of promise and possibility. Cross the Giant's Causeway, relive the glory and tragedy of the world's most famous ship at the stunning Titanic Belfast, and trail after the island's ancient Celtic mysteries in the shimmery Glens of Antrim.

MAYO

Achill Island

Clare Island

Clew Bay

Inishturk

Inishbofin

Clifden

CONNEMARA

Lough Corrib

Oileáin Árainn (Aran Islands)

Mouth of the Shannon

Tralee

Corca Dhuibhne (Dingle Peninsula)

Blasket Islands

Dingle Bay

Gap of Dunloe

Iveragh Peninsula

KERRY

Skellig Islands

Ring of Kerry

Beara Peninsula

Kenmare Bay

Bantry Bay

Mizen Head

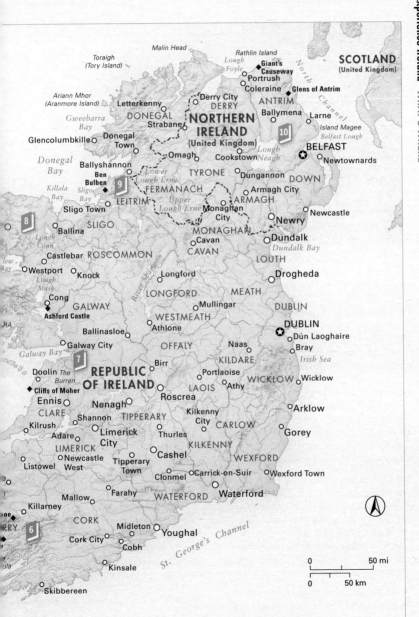

Malin Head

Toraigh
(Tory Island)

Lough
Foyle

Rathlin Island

Giant's
Causeway

Portrush

Coleraine

Glens of Antrim

SCOTLAND
(United Kingdom)

North

Channel

Arionn Mhor
(Aranmore Island)

Letterkenny

Derry City

DERRY

ANTRIM

Ballymena

Larne

Gweebarra
Bay

DONEGAL

Strabane

NORTHERN
IRELAND

Island Magee
Belfast Lough

Glencolumbkille

Donegal
Town

(United Kingdom)

Omagh

Cookstown

Lough
Neagh

10

BELFAST

Newtownards

Donegal
Bay

Ballyshannon

Ben
Bulben

Lower
Lough Erne

TYRONE

Dungannon

DOWN

Killala
Bay

Sligo
Bay

9

LEITRIM

Upper
Lough Erne

FERMANACH

Monaghan
City

Armagh City

ARMAGH

Newcastle

Sligo Town

SLIGO

MONAGHAN

Newry

8

Ballina

Cavan

Dundalk

Lough
Conn

CAVAN

LOUTH

Dundalk Bay

lew
ay

Castlebar

ROSCOMMON

Westport

Knock

Longford

Drogheda

Lough
Mask

LONGFORD

MEATH

Cong

GALWAY

Mullingar

DUBLIN

Ashford Castle

WESTMEATH

Ballinasloe

Athlone

DUBLIN

Galway City

OFFALY

Naas

Dún Laoghaire

Galway Bay

7

Birr

KILDARE

Bray

Irish Sea

Doolin The
Burren

REPUBLIC
OF IRELAND

Portlaoise

WICKLOW

Wicklow

Cliffs of Moher

LAOIS

Athy

Ennis

Nenagh

Roscrea

Arklow

CLARE

Shannon

TIPPERARY

Kilkenny
City

CARLOW

Gorey

Kilrush

Limerick
City

Thurles

KILKENNY

Adare

LIMERICK

Cashel

WEXFORD

Newcastle
West

Tipperary
Town

Clonmel

Carrick-on-Suir

Wexford Town

Listowel

Mallow

Farahy

WATERFORD

Waterford

Killarney

CORK

RY

6

Midleton

Youghal

St. George's Channel

Cork City

Cobh

Kinsale

0   50 mi

0   50 km

Skibbereen

Ireland Today

Navigating a good conversation in Ireland can be as tricky as driving its winding coastal lanes, but armed with these pointers it can be equally as rewarding.

Crime

The U.S. Overseas Security Advisory Council cites Ireland as a low-risk country when it comes to crime. Violent crime is rare and it is largely confined to rival drug gangs in the capital and other metropolitan areas. Sensible precautions mitigate any risk. Dial ☎ 999 or ☎ 112 for emergency.

Ireland's police force, the Garda Síochána, employ a predictably good-humored approach to their Twitter feed (@ gardainfo).

Culture

Ireland's emergence as a European technology hub hasn't dented the nation's fondness for the written word. Although there have been few to match the talent of Shaw, Wilde, and Joyce, the huge-selling works of Donal Ryan, Roddy Doyle, Colum McCann, Colm Tóibín, Anna Burns, and Maeve Binchy underline the country as one of the biggest book-buying populations in Europe. In the theater, playwrights like Conor McPherson and Enda Walsh tell Irish stories to a world audience.

In the movies, time and tide have taken us a long way from John Wayne in *The Quiet Man* to the modern romance of *Once*, the warts-and-all visions of modern Ireland from writer-directors like Lenny Abrahamson (*Garage*) and award-winning, high-tech animation like *The Song of The Sea*.

For the latest in all things Irish culture, follow Hugh Linehan, the arts and culture editor for The Irish Times, on Twitter @ hlinehan.

Economics

With its seductive corporate tax rate and its educated, English-speaking workforce, Ireland has continued to lure multinationals and tech companies to its small, open-trading nation, and is currently benefiting from the most sustained expansion in the global economy in a decade. That said, the growing possibility of a disorderly Brexit has sent a chill through the country's business sector. Studies have shown that Ireland is the country with the most to lose from Brexit—even more than the United Kingdom itself. Irish exporters hurt as the U.K.'s economy slows and sterling weakens, and it could get worse if exit negotiations result in tariffs on trade with Britain.

While the demise of the Celtic Tiger economy was no laughing matter, the Irish have since kept a watchful eye on the state's financial system with an annual festival that, in typical Irish fashion, paradoxically combines stand-up comedy with the serious topic of economics, to create the successful Kilkenomics (⊕ www.kilkenomics.com) event.

David McWilliam, an economist of legendary status in Ireland and founding member of Kilkenomics has an excellent Twitter feed (@davidmcw) with a unique and independent take on the nation's finances.

HUMOR

Tongue-in-cheek banter and self-deprecating humor accompanies most social gatherings, regardless of context or company. Throughout turbulent centuries of its history, this characteristic evolved in Irish DNA and can always be counted on to stand up in times of excitement or alarm like the quills on a porcupine.

Waterford Whispers Twitter account (@ WhispersNewsLTD) offers a snapshot of that humor with its cynical take on national and international news.

Media

The three bastions of Irish daily news are the *Irish Times* (⊕ *www.irishtimes.com*), the *Irish Independent* (⊕ *www.independent.ie*), and the *Irish Examiner* (⊕ *www.irishexaminer.com*). Raidió Teilifís Éireann (RTE) is the state-controlled and publicly subsidized national broadcaster. Newstalk is a populist, 24-hour current affairs and opinion radio station.

Online media such as the Journal.ie, national newspapers' social media feeds, and gender-targeted Joe.ie and Her.ie are very influential.

Politics

Just as the Irish economy is roaring again, the threat of Brexit and its fallout looms on the political horizon. At the time of publishing, it threatens to derail not just the booming GDP but also the fragile peace that has reigned in Northern Ireland for the last two decades. The current, center-right coalition government has had success with its liberal social agenda including same-sex marriage, but is struggling with a critical housing crisis and archaic health system, giving the left opposition parties plenty of floor time during Dáil (Parliamentary) sessions. The Irish are fascinated by American politics, so expect to hear as much about U.S. goings-on as Irish.

Harry McGee from the Irish Times has a Twitter account (@harrymcgee) that provides an impartial news feed on Irish politics.

Religion

When Ireland became the first country in the world to legalize same-sex marriage by popular vote (as necessitated by its constitution), it became clear that the Catholic Church had lost its firm grasp on society. A liberalization of the strict abortion laws quickly followed. While the majority of the population still identify as Catholic, weekly church attendance and strict adherence to its doctrine are dwindling. Another example of its declining influence? For almost a century every pub closed on Good Friday; this ban was lifted by legislation without a whimper of protest.

Sports

Depending on what county you are in, and the time of year, soccer, rugby, Gaelic football, or hurling talk can dominate any social gathering. Katie Taylor's surge to the top of the boxing world lifted the nation's spirits, just as the national soccer team's continued failures sent us all to cry into our pints. On a local level, Gaelic football and hurling are still the sports that really matter. With parish (neighborhood) pitted against parish and county against county, the passions run deep, with every victory or defeat a personal experience. Horse racing also holds a special place in Irish hearts—note the bookie's shop on every main street—and we seem to have the uncanny knack for breeding some of the best Thoroughbreds on the planet.

Follow Irish sports journalist Vincent Hogan's colorful commentary on Twitter (@vincent_hogan).

If You Like

CHARMING VILLAGES

Adare, Co. Limerick. Right out of a story-book, this celebrated village of low-slung Tudor cottages is adorned with ivied churches and a moated castle from the days when knighthood was in flower.

Birr, Co. Offaly. The epitome of Georgian perfection, with a layout that curls along the contours of its famous castle to the west and enough asymmetrical quirks to make it interesting.

Cong, Co. Mayo. John Ford's *The Quiet Man* introduced this charmer to the world and the singular beauty of its whitewashed single-story cottages with tied-on thatched roofs.

Dunmore East, Co. Waterford. With a streetscape that snakes along its cove, Dunmore East has a mishmash of traditional architecture from thatched cottages to slated town houses that nestle together in a crimson cliff-side setting.

Glengarriff, Co. Cork. Set in a lush valley where the Caha Mountains vanish into the ocean, this comely village has lured visitors for centuries.

Inistioge, Co. Kilkenny. If you think Inistioge, with its perfect Irish village square and meandering pathways along the River Nore, looks like it was peeled straight from a movie set, you'd be right. Its streetscape was filmed in major movies, including *Circle of Friends* and *Widow's Peak*.

Kinvara, Co. Galway. This village is picture-perfect, thanks to its gorgeous bayside locale, great walks, and numerous pubs. North of the town is spectacularly sited Dunguaire Castle, noted for its medieval-banquet evenings.

Lismore, Co. Waterford. Set within some of Ireland's lushest pasturelands and lorded over by the Duke of Devonshire's castle, dreamy Lismore is popular with both romantic folk and anglers (the sparkling Blackwater here teems with salmon).

Roundstone, Co. Galway. Framed by the Twelve Bens mountains, with a pastel-color streetscape that faces the Atlantic Ocean, Roundstone is the most alluring village in Connemara.

Westport, Co. Mayo. On an inlet of Clew bay, this lively little town's scenic setting includes a charming main street complete with cute painted pubs, Georgian buildings, and a triple-arched stone bridge in the middle of town all festooned with flowers and plants. Add Croagh Patrick Mountain in the background and Clew Bay with its hundreds of islands and you can see why this was once a vacation destination for the 18th-century gentry.

MOVIE LOCATIONS

The Cliffs of Moher. In *Harry Potter and the Half-Blood Prince,* Harry and Dumbledore are perched on County Clare's famous cliffs, facing giant waves and an impenetrable coastline.

Connemara. Brendan Gleeson's portrayal of flawed Sergeant Gerry Boyle unleashing his caustic manner against the beautifully brooding backdrop of Connemara earned him a Golden Globe nomination for *The Guard.*

Co. Antrim. Strictly speaking, not a movie, but HBO's *Game of Thrones* has plucked out as many scene locations from Northern Ireland as it has characters, from the King's Road (the Dark Hedges) to Winterfell (Castle Ward and Shane's Castle).

Curracloe Beach. This County Wexford strand took on a French role as the scene for the U.S. arrival to World War II on D-Day in Steven Spielberg's epic war movie, *Saving Private Ryan.*

Dublin. Neil Jordan's biopic *Michael Collins* stages Dublin beautifully, earning it a cinematography Oscar nomination, with backdrops of Trinity College, the Ha'apenny Bridge and, of course, Kilmainhain Goal, which also appeared in the original *Italian Job,* starring Michael Caine.

Grafton Street, Dublin. One of Dublin's main shopping streets, Grafton Street has served as a backdrop for several music videos but it is best known for its supporting role in Indie film, *Once,* with Irish musician Glen Hansard.

Skellig Michael. Ahch-To (to *Star Wars* fans), Skellig Michael in County Kerry features throughout *Star Wars: The Force Awakens,* and its stubbornly present puffins inspired the entire species of Porgs.

Trim Castle. County Meath's castle doubled as York in *Braveheart,* the biopic of Scottish freedom fighter William Wallace, starring Mel Gibson.

Trinity College. Dublin became Liverpool in multi-award-winning movie, *Educating Rita,* where Ireland's most famous college took central stage.

Yeats Tower (Thoor Ballylee), Connemara, and Cong. Galway's and Mayo's appearances in John Ford's classic, *The Quiet Man,* turned the town of Cong into a tourist attraction (still visited by fans today) and, no doubt, helped the movie earn an Oscar for cinematography in 1953.

LITERARY HAUNTS

Aran Islands, Co. Galway. See what inspired the dark genius of Synge's *The Playboy of the Western World* and the black comedy of Martin McDonagh's *The Cripple of Inishmaan.*

Bellaghy, Co. Derry. Located in the heart of the landscape that shaped his life and work, HomePlace visitor and arts center celebrates the life, inspiration, literature, and legacy of one of Ireland's greatest writers, the late Seamus Heaney.

The Burren, Co. Clare. Walk the actual road through the Burren that is the setting, and title, of Man Booker Prize–winning author Anne Enright's 2015 novel, *The Green Road.* JRR Tolkien visited the West of Ireland on many occasions and spent considerable time in the Burren's fantastical landscapes. An underground lake called Pol na Gollum (or Cave of Gollum) is often held up by fans as evidence that Middle-Earth, at least partly, is descended from here.

Enniscorthy, Co. Wexford. Acclaimed Irish author Colm Tóibín was born and raised in this small town in the east of Ireland that would come to form the backdrop to many of Tóibín's novels, among them *Nora Webster* and *Brooklyn.*

Limerick City, Co. Limerick. Frank McCourt's *Angela's Ashes* had thousands heading here to tour Angela's city and partake of the tearfulness of it all.

Sligo Town, Co. Sligo. Take in the town where William Butler Yeats grew up, then visit his grave in Drumcliff to view his beloved mountain, Ben Bulben.

Thoor Ballylee, Co. Galway. This restored 16th-century Norman tower house in Gort, just south of Galway City, was the summer home of W.B. Yeats. Yeats described the house as "a tower set by a stream's edge," and it served as the inspiration for his poems "The Winding Stair" and "The Tower."

Trinity College, Co. Dublin. Founded by Queen Elizabeth I, this university provided the greats—Beckett, Wilde, Stoker—with 30 acres of stomping grounds.

Irish Music and Dance

When the eye-popping spectacle of *Riverdance* first "tapped" its way into the Irish psyche in 1995 by jazzing up traditional step dancing and moving it from the local parish hall to the stages of Dublin's Point Theatre, it immediately sent its audiences reeling. The first show to introduce the Irish jig to world theaters, it has since been seen by 18 million people and taken in more than $1 billion at the box office. Along the way, it gave the once-languishing, "old-fashioned" arts of Ireland's folkloric music and dance a modern chic—today, thousands of young Irish are learning to play hornpipes, sing the old chanties, and dance the old jigs.

A Gaelic Rebirth

Irish dancing has always been popular in American-Irish communities, as the first *Riverdance* stars proved: Jean Butler was born on Long Island to a mother from Mayo, while Michael Flatley was born in Chicago to immigrant parents. In 1995 Flatley founded his own triumphant show, *Lord of the Dance,* which inspired international troupes and, in turn, was followed by *Feet of Flames,* with more than 100 dancers.

Thanks to these shows, the world has fallen in step—literally—as the passion for Irish dancing has taken hold. Intenrational competitions now attract thousands of dancers and tens of thousands of spectors.

Going "Trad"

Competitors, indeed: Irish dancing is now also a competitive sport, with thousands of passionate devotees (see its social networking site ⊕ *www.diddlyi. com*) attending *feis* (festivals). Thousands of dollars are invested in costumes, wigs (you thought all those ringlets were

real?) and, last but not least, shoes. Irish dancers are now found in far-off lands like Japan and Estonia. Whatever accounts for trad's continuing enormous crossover success—does it appeal because it is a return to a simpler time, or remains a dazzling slice of national culture in a blandly homogeneous age?—it certainly keeps growing more popular.

Traditional Irish music and dance have taken the world by storm—but you need to journey to the West of Ireland to really get in step.

Irish Dance Revival

Before *Riverdance,* Irish dancing was something schoolchildren performed chiefly for competitions, and sometimes on civic occasions, with their arms rigidly held by their sides (only the legs would move—a holdover from religious teachings that felt that dancing was sinful), and an expression of grave concentration on their faces. Today, it's a big thing for young people and also, due to those glitzy costumes and contests, a very expensive hobby.

FANCY FOOTWORK

Because there were no accompanying drums, the sound of the feet on wooden floors has always been an important element in Irish dancing. When dancing really took off in the 18th century, many cabins only had earth floors, so the custom was to remove the top half of the half-door, and dance on that. Dancing masters used to display their prowess on fair days by dancing on soapy barrel lids, so they developed the ability to vary their steps in a confined space. From this came the tradition of dancing solos on one spot.

SET DANCING

Set dancing is also the name given to social dancing in which four couples face one another in a square in dances based on the French cotillion and the quadrilles. Nearly every town in Ireland once again has dancing at least one evening a week.

STEPS AND SETS

Ireland has a long tradition of solo dancing, first introduced by the jigs, reels, and hornpipes that traveling dancing masters taught in the 18th century. Some are performed in hard shoes, with the dancer beating out rhythms on the floor to complement the music, while others are danced with soft shoes to emphasize their graceful, airborne nature. In both cases, the main interest of the dance is in the foot and lower leg. Some solo dances have specific patterns of steps and are only danced to one tune and are known as "set dances"—in some places, set dances are known as "table dances," because the dancer often jumped up on the table to display his or her skills.

Traditional Irish Musical Instruments

Irish traditional music is very much the music of the people, played on relatively simple, portable instruments: fiddle, flute, tin whistle, accordion, handheld drum, and, recent additions, guitar or banjo.

BODHRÁN

The bodhrán (pronounced "bow-rawn") is a simple goatskin drum played with the back of the hand or a small wooden stick. When played well, by Mel Mercier, John Joe Kelly, or Tommy Hayes, it makes an exciting addition to the running rhythms of trad music. They make it look easy, but in the hands of an untrained amateur, a badly played bodhrán can wreck a session.

FIDDLE

The classical violin in all but name, this is the most popular instrument in trad music for its singing, swooping versatility, its portability, and its relative affordability. Local fiddle styles still persist—especially in Donegal, Sligo, and the Sliabh Luachra region of Cork and Kerry—and virtuosos such as Frankie Gavin of Dé Dannan, Martin Hayes, Tommy Peoples, and Liz Doherty are famed for their rhythm, color, and ornamentation.

FLUTE AND WHISTLE

The tin whistle is the ideal beginner's instrument, but be sure to buy one in the key of D. It is still called the "penny whistle," because it costs so little to buy. But the flute used in Irish music is usually a simple wooden flute—hear it at its best in the hands of Matt Molloy and Paddy Moloney of The Chieftains, Mary Bergin, and Olcan Masterson.

IRISH HARP

Ireland is the only country to have a musical instrument as its national emblem. The harp appears on *garda* (police) caps, Irish euro coins, and government stationery. The original Irish harp was a small, triangular instrument designed to be held on the knee (not the large version of today's concert halls). The harp was first used as a logo for Guinness stout in 1850. The Guinness harp faces right, while the national emblem faces left.

UILLEANN PIPES

The *uilleann* (pronounced "illun") pipes, literally "elbow" pipes, are a quieter indoor version of bagpipes. The player sits with a bag under one arm, the bellows under the other, and the "chanter," which plays the melody, on the thigh. A temperamental instrument, it can be heartrenderingly beautiful in the hands of a master like Liam O'Flynn or Paddy Keenan of The Bothy Band.

SQUEEZE-BOXES AND ACCORDIONS

Squeeze-box is a generic term for a variety of melodeons, accordions, and concertinas. The concertina is a small, hexagonal-shape button-key instrument. The simplest accordion is the one-row button accordion, usually called a melodeon. Styles of playing can vary enormously. Sharon Shannon is rooted in the highly rhythmic East Clare style, but can veer into swing and Cajun styles as she plays her wildly energetic dance music.

Traditional Music Happenings

If you're interested in trad music, the beat of a bodhrán or the tap of a shoe will likely lead you to Galway and County Clare's great folk fleadhs (festivals) and pub *seisúns* (sessions).

If you happen on a pub session, there are a few ground rules. Don't talk during the solo, and don't stare at the singer; most people look at the floor. Buy the musicians a drink if it's a small session, and if at all possible, have a party piece to contribute yourself. It's the gesture that counts.

THE BIGGEST FLEADH

The biggest festival of all is a three-day event called the All-Ireland finals of **Fleadh Cheoil na hÉireann** (pronounced "*flah-kyole*," meaning "festival of music" ⊕ *www.fleadhcheoil.ie*). The 2015 event was held in Sligo and was attended by nearly 10,000 musicians and 200,000 visitors, many of them second-generation Irish from overseas. This noncommercial festival of traditional music takes over a whole town, whose pubs become

centers for casual music making. The All-Ireland rotates to different towns every year, much to the delight of the pub owners in the chosen town.

THE ENNIS BLOW-OUT

During the last week in May, the pleasant country town of Ennis hosts the **Fleadh Nua** (⊕ *www.fleadhnua.com*), a massive eight-day-long celebration of dancing and song, with concerts, workshops, competitions, and *céilithe*. Many of the events are open-air and free, and there is a great festive buzz. Ennis is home to a growing cadre of musicians: the Custys, Siobhán and Tommy Peoples, flute player Kevin Crawford, and accordion whiz kid Murty Ryan. Check out **Knox's Pub** (✉ *Abbey St.* ☎ *065/682–9264*) and **Cruise's Bar** (✉ *Abbey St.* ☎ *065/684–1800*) for lively evening sessions.

TOE-TAPPING IN MILTOWN

Held during the first week in July, the **Willie Clancy Summer School** (⊕ *www. scoilsamhraidhwillieclancy.com*) is Ireland's biggest traditional-music summer school. Classes, lectures, and recitals attract around 1,500 students from 42 countries to this tiny village on the west coast of Clare near Spanish Point. Set dancing is a big draw here, and a surefire way to make friends.

Great Outdoors in Ireland

Top Boating Trips

Imagine the scene: gentle waves lap at the edges of your boat as it heads for open water, drawing a perfect silver line across the tranquil, mirror-flat surface. Every sound is crystal clear—a dog barks, a kingfisher whirrs past flying low across the water, and fellow sailors shout a hearty welcome. This magical moment can easily be yours in Ireland, thanks to the wealth of possibilities for either guided tours or private hires.

COAST OR INLAND

Ireland's indented western seaboard from Donegal to Cork has many first-class sailing opportunities. The main towns have sailing clubs in scenic areas. The best option is to choose an area such as West Cork and spend a week sailing from port to port. If you want to enjoy the very heart of Ireland, the River Shannon offers an unequaled choice of boating trips from the Northern Midlands down to Killaloe in County Clare. Cruisers can be hired at Carrick-on-Shannon, Banagher, and Portumna. Crossing the Irish border, the Shannon–Erne Waterway has opened up a little-known area of untamed beauty, and the renaissance of Ireland's canals is a regeneration success.

THE FIVE BEST BOATING TRIPS

Fermanagh Lakes: With 700 km (430 miles) of rivers, lakes, and canals, Fermanagh is tops. Upper and Lower Lough Erne are dotted with islands topped with castles or Round Towers ideal for exploring.

River Barrow: Hire a traditional steel canal boat at Rathangan in County Kildare for a 120-km (75-mile) trip along the idyllic Barrow—Ireland's oldest navigation—passing through a Chaucerian landscape and dropping anchor at Graiguenamanagh (pronounced "*grayg-na-mana*" and

known as Graig); en route, sign up for a canalways pub crawl.

River Shannon Cruising: One of the best places to hire from is the delightful boating town of Carrick-on-Shannon—putter your leisurely way down to Lough Ree or as far as the Lower Shannon.

Royal Canal: With its reconstructed locks and bridges, the 145-km (90-mile) canal is perfect for those on narrow boats, and in 2010 it became fully navigable from Dublin to Richmond Harbor in County Longford. Towpaths run from the Liffey all the way to the Shannon.

West Cork Sailing: The harbors of the ports of call along this coast, such as Kinsale, Glandore, Baltimore, and Bantry, offer delightful overnight stays.

GUIDED TOURS OR PRIVATE HIRE

A first-time boater? Get some courses under your belt by contacting the International Sailing Schools Association. If you want to sit back and have it all done for you, book half-day or full-day guided pleasure cruises. ⇨ *For more info, see "Cruising on the Shannon" in the Midlands.*

INFORMATION

The best resources about boating in Ireland include: ⊕ *www.sailing.ie*; ⊕ *www.issa-schools.org*; ⊕ *www.discoverireland.ie/lakelands*; ⊕ *www.waterwaysireland.org*; ⊕ *www.iwai.ie*; Canalways Ireland (⊕ *www.canalways.ie*); Cruise Ireland (⊕ *www.cruiseireland.com*); Emerald Star Cruisers (⊕ *www.emeraldstar.ie*); and Riversdale Barge Holidays (⊕ *www.riversdalebargeholidays.com*).

Best Walks and Hikes

Catch the right day and an Irish hilltop can seem like a slice of heaven. The country is laced with 33 well-marked walking trails. If you're not feeling adventurous, strolls through a forest park or a lakeside wander are wonderful options. If you're going for bragging rights, consider walking the extension to the world-renowned International Appalachian Trail. The two best websites for hiking information are ⊕ *www.discoverireland.ie/walking* and ⊕ *www.walkni.com.*

THE TOP FIVE HIKING REGIONS

Ballyhoura Country: Whether it's mountain biking or hiking through a lesser-known portal of Irish countryside, Ballyhoura's Mesolithic past comes alive across lakelands, parks, and the ancient Lough Gur in counties Limerick and Cork.

The Reeks of Kerry: Munster, in the southwest of the country, has Ireland's biggest mountains with MacGillycuddy's Reeks in Kerry (3,414 feet) leading the way in the hierarchy of height. They attract serious hill walkers and serious gongoozlers (those who like to gaze up at the peaks).

Ulster Way: Relaunched in 2009, the 1,000-km (625-mile) circular Ulster Way crosses the most stunning upland areas of Northern Ireland including the impressive Mountains of Mourne.

West Is Best: Many of Ireland's west-coast walking routes are framed by spectacular Atlantic scenery: Connemara, Sligo, and Donegal are renowned for the allure of their hills with thrilling views.

The Wicklow Way: Starting in the suburbs of Dublin, 137 km (85 miles) of trails take you through the heart of the spectacular Wicklow Mountains. Check out some of the gorgeous villages along the way.

THE TOP FIVE WALKS

The Barrow Way, Co. Carlow. Follow the Barrow River on a 113-km (70-mile) meander through the forgotten Midlands, where countless historical sights pepper the pastoral landscape. It's a feast for wildlife lovers as well.

Burren, Co. Clare. An unforgettable trip into an otherworldly place, this lunar landscape is threaded with looped walks, rare flowers, and ancient ruins, many with a backdrop of unbeatable views across Galway Bay. The entire Burren Way is a 123-km (76-mile) pleasure-filled walk.

Glendalough, Co. Wicklow. The gentle, three-hour circular Spink Walk takes you across a wooden bridge, along a boardwalk, through conifer woodland, and alongside the Upper Lake, with sweeping views over the valley.

Silent Valley, Co. Down. Catch a bus from Newcastle and, after a two-hour (undemanding) walk around this idyllic place, you will realize why it was so named.

Slievenamon, Co. Tipperary. An unmistakable landmark famed in song, there is an easy track to the top where a burial cairn reputedly contains the entrance to the Celtic underworld.

WEATHER OR NOT

Irish weather is fickle, mist comes down quickly, and it's easy to get lost. Check the forecast and leave word with someone at your hotel about where you are going. Layers of waterproof gear and fleeces are a good bet so you can strip off when the sun comes out. Even though signposting is generally good in hill areas, bring a map: free walking guides are available from regional tourism offices, but invest in Ordnance Survey Discovery Maps, available at newsagents for €8.

Ancestor-Hunting in Ireland

More than 39 million Americans claim Irish ancestry, and the desire to trace those long-lost roots back to the "auld sod" can run deep. Here are some pointers for how you can make your trip to Ireland a journey into your past.

The first port of call is a visit to Ireland's online national archives (⊕ *www. nationalarchives.ie*), which has volumes of information and is constantly releasing genealogy records with an extensive search function through the census of 1901 and 1911, which may help you trace your relations before you leave home.

BEFORE YOU GO

The more you can learn about your ancestors, the more fruitful your search is going to be once you're on Irish soil. Crucial facts include:

■ The name of your ancestor

■ Names of that ancestor's parents and spouse

■ His or her date of birth, marriage, or death

■ County, parish, and townland of origin in Ireland

■ Religious denomination

The first place to seek information is directly from members of your family. A grandparent or a great-aunt with a story to tell can be the source of important clues. And relatives may have documents stored away that can help with your sleuthing—old letters, wills, diaries, birth certificates, and photos.

ON THE GROUND IN IRELAND

General Register Office. Civil records—dating back to 1865—are available at the General Register Office. Records for Anglican marriages date from 1845. ⊠ *Werburg St., Dublin* ☎ *01/863–8200* ⊕ *www.groireland.ie*.

The Mellon Centre for Migration Studies. For Northern Ireland, you can find information at the Mellon Centre for Migration Studies at the Ulster American Folk Park. ⊠ *Ulster American Folk Park, 2 Mellon Rd., Omagh* ☎ *028/8225–6315* ⊕ *www.qub.ac.uk/cms*.

National Archives. These extensive archives include census records and, like the National Library, they provide free genealogy consultations on weekdays from 10 to 1:30. A lot of the archives are now online. ⊠ *Bishop St., Dublin* ☎ *01/407–2300* ⊕ *www.nationalarchives. ie*.

National Library of Ireland. Ancestor hunters have long traveled throughout Ireland to comb parish church records, but most of these records are now available on microfilm in Dublin at the National Library of Ireland and increasingly through their online service. The library is a great place to begin your hunting; you can consult a research adviser there free of charge. ⊠ *Kildare St., Dublin* ☎ *01/661–2523* ⊕ *www.nli.ie*.

Public Record Office. ⊠ *2 Titanic Blvd., Queen's Island, Titanic Quarter* ☎ *028/9053–4800* ⊕ *www.nidirect.gov. uk/proni*.

If you'd rather not spend your vacation in a records hall, you can hire a professional to do your spadework. The **Association of Professional Genealogists** in Ireland (⊕ *www.irishgenealogy.ie*) will present you with a "package of discovery" upon your arrival.

The *Irish Times* newspaper also has ancestor-hunting resources (⊕ *www.john-grenham.com*), and the National Library provides references for professionals.

IRISH FAMILY NAMES

Antrim
Lynch
McDonnell
McNeill
O'Hara
O'Neill
Quinn

Armagh
Hanlon
McCann

Carlow
Kinsella
Nolan
O'Neill

Cavan
Boylan
Lynch
McCabe
McGovern
McGowan
McNally
O'Reilly
Sheridan

Clare
Aherne
Boland
Clancy
Daly
Lynch
McGrath
McInerney
McMahon
McNamara
Molon(e)y
O'Brien
O'Dea
O'Grady
O'Halloran
O'Loughlin

Cork
Barry
Callaghan
Cullinane
Donovan
Driscoll
Flynn
Hennessey
Hogan
Lynch
McCarthy
McSweeney
Murphy
Nugent
O'Casey

O'Cullane
(Collins)
O'Keefe
O'Leary
O'Mahony
O'Riordan
Roche
Scanlon
Sheridan

Derry
Cahan
Hegarty
Kelly
McLaughlin

Donegal
Boyle
Clery
Doherty
Friel
Gallagher
Gormley
McGrath
McLoughlin
McSweeney
Mooney
O'Donnell

Down
Lynch
McGuinness
O'Neil
White

Dublin
Hennessey
O'Casey
Plunkett

Fermanagh
Cassidy
Connolly
Corrigan
Flanagan
Maguire
McManus

Galway
Blake
Burke
Clery
Fah(e)y
French
Jennings
Joyce
Kelly
Kenny
Kirwan
Lynch

Madden
Moran
O'Flaherty
O'Halloran

Kerry
Connor
Fitzgerald
Galvin
McCarthy
Moriarty
O'Connell
O'Donoghue
O'Shea
O'Sullivan

Kildare
Cullen
Fitzgerald
O'Byrne
White

Kilkenny
Butler
Fitzpatrick
O'Carroll
Tobin

Laois
Dempsey
Doran
Dunn(e)
Kelly
Moore

Leitrim
Clancy
O'Rourke

Limerick
Fitzgerald
Fitzgibbon
McKeough
O'Brien
O'Cullane
(Collins)
O'Grady
Woulfe

Longford
O'Farrell
Quinn

Louth
O'Carroll
Plunkett

Mayo
Burke
Costello
Dugan

Gormley
Horan
Jennings
Jordan
Kelly
Madden
O'Malley

Meath
Coffey
Connolly
Cusack
Dillon
Hayes
Hennessey
Plunkett
Quinlan

Monaghan
Boylan
Connolly
Hanratty
McKenna
McMahon
McNally

Offaly
Coghlan
Dempsey
Fallon
Malone
Meagher
(Maher)
Molloy
O'Carroll
Sheridan

Roscommon
Fallon
Flanagan
Flynn
Hanley
McDermot
McKeogh
McManus
Molloy
Murphy

Sligo
Boland
Higgins
McDonagh
O'Dowd
O'Hara
Rafferty

Tipperary
Butler
Fogarty
Kennedy

Lynch
Meagher
(Maher)
O'Carroll
O'Dwyer
O'Meara
Purcell
Ryan

Tyrone
Cahan
Donnelly
Gormley
Hagan
Murphy
O'Neill
Quinn

Waterford
Keane
McGrath
O'Brien
Phelan
Power

Westmeath
Coffey
Dalton
Daly
Dillon
Sheridan

Wexford
Doran
Doyle
Hartley
Kavanagh
Keating
Kinsella
McKeogh
Redmond
Walsh

Wicklow
Cullen
Kelly
McKeogh
O'Byrne
O'Toole

Best Irish Greens

The wonderfully alive, challenging natural terrain is one of the things that makes Irish golf so remarkable. In a country where mountains and sea so often meet, scraggly coastline and rolling hills of heather dominate the courses here, not the other way around. Real golfers are challenged, rather than deterred, by the vagaries of the elements—the wind, rain, and mist—and by the lack of golf carts on courses in rougher terrain. Naturally, links courses tend to be more prevalent in the coastal regions, while parkland courses are found inland. Of the estimated 150 top-quality links courses in the world, 39 of them are in Ireland. Most of these leading courses were designed by celebrated golf architects, such as Tom Morris, James Braid, Harry Colt, and Alister MacKenzie, who capitalized on spectacular landscapes. Others—such as Jack Nicklaus, with his course at Killeen Castle in County Meath—will continue in their footsteps.

PLANNING AHEAD

The top links courses can book up in summer, so if you're after a prime-time slot you might want to book well in advance. At other times you shouldn't have too much problem with a late reservation; pretty much every course in the country now has its own online booking facility. Keep an eye out for the Irish Tourism Quality Assurance Shamrock when choosing a course. Ireland is such a small country that you can easily sample courses of very different topographies in one visit without feeling like you're rushing around. Pack for smart-casual dress and for staying dry. Soft spikes are advised, and don't forget to bring your handicap certificate where possible. A shirt and tie may be needed in a few of the posher club dining rooms.

KEEPING THE COST DOWN

While golf in Ireland couldn't be called cheap, it's often a great value when contrasted with that other links haven, Scotland. There are great savings to be had if you're prepared to come off-season or if you avoid playing weekends on the expensive courses. Focusing on the lesser-known, but equally spectacular, links courses can also cut your costs dramatically. For example, Donegal is a county full of overlooked links golf. You can also save by booking in a group, or buying a golf pass for a number of courses.

THE WEATHER FACTOR

You see all kinds of weather in Ireland—driving winds, rain, sleet, and sunshine—and you may see it all in one round. There are no rain checks here. You play unless there's lightning, so pack your sweaters, waterproof shoes, and rain gear, especially if you're planning your trip between fall and spring.

THE SUNDAY BAG FACTOR

If you don't have a golf bag that's light enough for you to carry for 18 holes, invest in one before your trip. Electric carts are generally available only at the leading venues, so you usually have the option of using a caddy or caddy car (pull cart)—or of carrying your own bag. Many courses have caddies but don't guarantee their availability, because they're not employed by the course, so you may have to tote your bag yourself. Be prepared with a carryall or a Sunday bag.

THE PRIVATE CLUB FACTOR

Unlike those in America, most private golf clubs in Ireland are happy to let visitors play their courses and use their facilities. It's important to remember, however, that such clubs place members first; guests come second. In some, you'll need a letter of introduction from your club in America to secure your playing privilege. There are often preferred days for visitors; call in advance to be sure that a club can make time for you.

THE PERFECT LINKS

Ballybunion Golf Club, Co. Kerry. On the Old Course, one of the country's classics, each and every hole is a pleasure to play. Set on the shore of the Atlantic at the southern entrance to the River Shannon, Ballybunion is famed for tough but pleasant golf, epitomized by the huge dunes—great for a stroll but hellish to play out of.

Donegal Golf Club, Co. Donegal. This wild and wonderful course sits between the shores of beautiful Donegal Bay and the shadow of the majestic Blue Stack Mountains. From the 5th to the 9th you enter the "Valley of Tears," a fearsome challenge of four perilous holes made all the more challenging by feisty winds.

The K Club, Co. Kildare. You'd have to be a nongolfer and a hermit not to have heard of this course, one of the country's most prestigious and demanding. Arnold Palmer designed the main course, famed for its water obstacles and inland-links feel. The on-site facilities are the best in Ireland.

Lahinch, Co. Clare. Lahinch's old golf course constantly ranks in the world's top 100 because of its spectacular setting and its master architects over the last 126 years, Old Tom Morris and Alister MacKenzie. Goats have full right of access.

Old Head, Co. Cork. Set on a spectacular peninsula jutting out into the wild Atlantic below, the Old Head is the romantic favorite of Irish golf lovers. Often compared to the Pacific sections of Pebble Beach, expect your pulse to race at the stunning views and wildlife.

Portmarnock Golf Club, Co. Dublin. One of the nation's "Big Four" golf clubs (along with Ballybunion, Royal County Down, and Royal Portrush), Portmarnock is a links course near Dublin. Located on a sandy peninsula, it has hosted regular Irish Opens with its 100-plus bunkers ready to trap amateur and pro alike.

Royal County Down, Co. Down. A lunar landscape makes this course as beautiful as it is difficult. It has recently ousted St. Andrews as *Golf Digest's* best course outside the United States. The sea of craterlike bunkers and the long rough reward the straight and punish the proud.

Royal Portrush, Co Antrim. This grand old course has made it into *Golf Digest's* top-10 courses outside the United States. It's a sea of sand hills and curving fairways, with the White Rocks par-5 5th set on the edge of a cliff. Word has it (okay, Royal Portrush recommends) that a long carry over the mounds to the right of the white stone will be rewarded with a much shorter approach to the green.

Ballyliffin Golf Club, Co. Donegal. Designed around imposing dunes and often described as "the Ballybunion of the North," the Glashedy Links at the world-famous Ballyliffin Golf Club has earned notoriety for its devilish bunkers. Running high above both the sea and the club's Old Links, the views from Ballyliffin's Glashedy Links are spectacular, especially from the par-3 7th tee. Designed by Ireland's own Pat Ruddy, Glashedy Links is one of the finest courses in all of Ireland.

What to Read Before Your Trip

Angela's Ashes by Frank McCourt. Frank McCourt's memoir, which begins in Brooklyn and progresses to Limerick, is a tale driven by familial loss, tragedy, and the challenges of intensive poverty. Throughout this book McCourt recounts his experiences being a member of a large family and touches on subjects such as illness, hunger, religion, and the impact his alcoholic father had on both himself and his family. Despite having been written in the relatively recent mid-1990s, *Angela's Ashes* is considered a classic and is a good choice for those looking for insight into what it meant to be an Irish immigrant in the early 1900s.

Are You Somebody? The Accidental Memoir of a Dublin Woman by Nuala O'Faolain. Nuala O'Faolain's reputation as a powerful, respected writer who never minces words is clearly on display in this memoir about her own life. The second of nine children, O'Faolain writes about her family (and particularly her hard-drinking, neglectful mother), her time at a convent school, and her university studies, relationships, and work in compelling, beautiful, and painfully honest stories.

The Country Girls by Edna O'Brien. The fact that this trilogy was banned after publication tells you a bit about how leery Ireland was of material that questioned the status quo. While these books are about the relationship of two young female friends who decide to move to the city together, it was the focus on sensitive issues such as gender inequality and sexual taboos—and the fact that they were at times sexually explicit and critical of Irish culture—which led to them being banned and the subject of book burnings. Today this trilogy is an example of the barriers female Irish authors faced, but also is a vital story about personal exploration and fulfillment.

Death of a Naturalist by Seamus Heaney. The 34 poems that make up Heaney's first major volume of poetry are largely autobiographical but speak volumes about what life was like on farms across rural Ireland. The Nobel Prize-winning Irish author, poet, and translator recalls a boyhood spent searching for tadpoles in a muddy pond; digging for potatoes; the death of his younger brother. Life as portrayed by Heaney is beautiful but hard, and this collection of poems draws you into those experiences.

Dubliners by James Joyce. By telling stories about what everyday life was like in the early 1900s for middle-class residents of Dublin, James Joyce spoke both directly and indirectly about class and national identity, topics that were roiling Ireland. Even today, just more than a century later, these issues remain far from settled, particularly as Ireland and Northern Ireland grapple with the potential ramifications of Brexit. For these reasons, and simply as a piece of classic literature, *Dubliners* remains an essential read for anybody interested in what it meant to be Irish at the turn of the 20th century.

Foster by Claire Keegan. Set in Wexford, a village on the coast of southeast Ireland, Foster tells the story of a young girl sent to temporarily live with a foster family while her mother prepares to give birth. Not only is this novella brilliantly written (and available to read for free via the New Yorker, where it was published), its importance has been cemented in Ireland, where it is now a part of the curriculum for the Irish Leaving Certificate (the test that determines whether a student can progress to university).

The Gathering by Anne Enright. It's only after her brother Liam Hegarty drowns himself that Veronica, Liam's dearest sibling, begins to consider whether events that unfolded earlier in their life might have contributed to his alcoholism and eventual suicide. While *The Gathering*'s focal point is Liam's death and his wake in Dublin, the Man Booker Prize–winning novel is truly about the cost of untold secrets and hidden trauma, the pain of absent parents, and what it's like to grow up in a large family.

***The Green Road* by Anne Enright.** Anne Enright has shown a proclivity toward examining the more challenging side of family life, and *The Green Road* is no exception. Devoted to telling the story of the Madigan family from each member's viewpoint, the novel deftly weaves together individual narratives while also portraying a whole, fractured family unit. This is one of Enright's most beloved novels, a story that's comedic while being largely dark and which shows how familial obligation can be a heavy weight to bear.

***How the Irish Saved Civilization* by Thomas Cahill.** Stereotypes about the Irish erode one of history's great truths: that Ireland is not just a great center of culture, learning, and the arts, but that it was also instrumental in keeping civilization from falling completely apart during the Middle Ages. Thomas Cahill's historical text focuses on how Irish monks helped to preserve knowledge and promote learning during a bleak time in human history. The next time you're thinking about the fact that it's a miracle we're still here at all, pick up this book and give thanks to the Irish.

***The Immortal Irishman: The Irish Revolutionary Who Became an American Hero* by Timothy Egan.** The term "badass" gets thrown around with impunity these days, but Thomas Francis Meagher deserves the title. During Ireland's Great Famine he planned an uprising against the British and—when that didn't work out—was

sentenced to death, but ultimately was exiled to the penal colony on Tasmania, an island off the coast of Australia. From there he escaped to the United States, married, worked as a journalist, joined the army, and generally lived a life of drama, adventure, and derring-do. Irish history, while important, is typically a bit of a bummer, but this volume definitely is not.

***Irish Fairy and Folk Tales* by William Butler Yeats.** It might seem a bit clichéd to say that Ireland is a mystical country, but the idea that there's a fairy around every corner truly is something many people embrace, and particularly in the country. William Butler Yeats's collection of Irish stories, songs, and poems taps into the island's substantial history of folklore and provides a glimpse of the magical, untamed side of Ireland. Plus, if we're being honest, Ireland's cliffs, deep forests, and fog-shrouded bogs might have you looking over your shoulder for fairies anyway, so at the very least this collection will have you better prepared for the magic that is to come.

***Milkman* by Anna Burns.** Set during the Troubles of the 1970s, Burns' book *Milkman* follows an unnamed young woman who attracts the eye of a paramilitary officer named only as "Milkman," who in short order begins following her and interrupting her life. It's a challenging read noteworthy not only for the tension present within the storyline but also its rambling, stream-of-consciousness style. If you traverse the tangled lanes of this Man Booker Prize–winning novel, you'll find it lives not only in the period of Ireland's most challenging modern-day struggle, but also in the commonplace terror experienced by any person who finds themselves in the crosshairs of unwelcome advances.

Say Nothing: A True Story of Murder and Memory in Northern Ireland by Patrick Radden Keefe. A great many lives were damaged or destroyed during the period known as the Troubles, but few stories are as shocking as that of Jean McConville, a 38-year-old widowed mother of 10 who on a frigid December night was abducted from her Belfast apartment by masked assailants, never to be seen alive again. McConville's death serves as the centerpiece of this book, which in itself is part detective story, part historical period piece.

The Sea by John Banville. When Max, a recently widowed art historian, returns to the seaside house he knew as a child, he finds himself caught up in a rush of tangled memories, reliving the loves and losses he experienced across his life. This novel, which tells Max's story in the form of a journal, is the 13th from author John Banville. It also won the Man Booker Prize in 2005, a decision that proved to be controversial both because it beat out Kazuo Ishiguro's stellar *Never Let Me Go,* and because of the author's lack of decorum after accepting the award. Said Banville: "The kind of novels that I write very rarely win the Man Booker Prize, which in general promotes good, middlebrow fiction."

The Wonder by Emma Donoghue. When the story gets out that an 11-year-old girl named Anna appears to be living solely on "manna from heaven," a nurse named Lib travels to rural Ireland from England to aid a nun in helping to determine whether Anna is either a genuine manifestation of the divine, or part of an elaborate con. This novel from the acclaimed writer of *Room* speaks about both Irish faith and a belief in miracles, but also uses Lib's deep yet casual hatred of the Irish to discuss the prejudice the Irish have faced for far too long.

The Spinning Heart by Donal Ryan. This slim volume explores Ireland's devastating financial collapse of 2008 and how a small Irish town comes violently unglued in the aftermath.

Skippy Dies by Paul Murray. This tragicomedy follows super-awkward fourteen year old Skippy on his bumbling exploits through his expensive prep school and explores how and why he dies and what happens next. It's smart, hilarious, and heartbreaking.

In The Woods by Tana French. French's Dublin Murder Squad series is an Irish literary hat trick: it's a page turner, has a complex and sympathetic main character, and delivers a liberal does of dark Irish family dynamics.

What to Watch Before Your Trip

***The Crying Game* directed by Neil Jordan.** Set in Northern Ireland during the Troubles, this film centers on a member of the IRA who becomes close with a captured British soldier and develops a friendship that causes him to question his loyalty. This film earned fans in both the United Kingdom and the United States, and won a BAFTA Award for Best British Film and an Academy Award for Best Original Screenplay.

Derry Girls. *Derry Girls* straddles kind of a funny line, in the sense that it's both an ensemble sitcom about a group of adolescent schoolgirls and a period piece about Northern Ireland during the Troubles. That unusual combination helps to keep it lively, though, as it gives you an idea of what it was like to lead a normal life in Northern Ireland, without getting hung up on the legitimately grim details that define so many stories from the era. It also helps that it's both funny and ridiculous, making it a lighter choice and suitable for bingeing.

***The Field* directed by Jim Sheridan.** When a curmudgeonly Irish farmer unceremoniously dumps a murdered donkey in a lake it sets off a complicated feud centered on land rights, encroaching commercial development, and unresolved family trauma. Incredibly, none of these issues were particularly unusual during the 1930s in Ireland, when questions about the country's future, and who was entitled to its land and heritage, were very much in flux. While the subject matter is vital, the film's all-star cast (including John Hurt, Sean Bean, Richard Harris, Brenda Fricker, and Tom Berenger) has also helped to cement it as a classic.

***The Guard* directed by John Michael McDonagh.** *The Guard* is as Irish as a police buddy comedy can be: funny, but also decidedly grim. In this film, an unhappy, irresponsible sergeant (Brendan Gleeson) partners with a straight-man FBI investigator (Don Cheadle) to try to get to the bottom of a murder potentially connected to several wanted Irish drug runners. Gleeson and Cheadle play off each other marvelously, and the performances and twisting plot helped it become the single most commercially successful independent Irish film in history.

***The Irish Pub* directed by Alex Fegan.** This friendly documentary from director Alex Fegan centers on that most famous of Irish institutions: the humble pub. Watching this film impresses upon the viewer that one of the great treats of visiting Ireland isn't just a chance to drink in an honest-to-goodness Irish pub, but is really about spending some time in a friendly place where you'll be treated well. If you're looking for a movie to get you ready for a trip to Ireland, this is the perfect choice.

***My Left Foot* directed by Jim Sheridan.** Daniel Day-Lewis built his reputation by being a committed (if somewhat insane) character actor, and nowhere is this more evident than in *My Left Foot*. In a truly remarkable, award-winning performance, Day-Lewis portrays a young man from a poor, working-class Irish family with severe cerebral palsy. While his condition greatly limits his ability to move, he learns to express himself creatively using only his left foot, an act which helps him more deeply integrate with his family, and later, his community.

***Michael Collins* directed by Neil Jordan.** Michael Collins's role in Irish history, both as a politician and as a violent revolutionary, cannot be overstated. This film, which stars Liam Neeson in the title role, delves into the violence and intrigue that defined the final years of England's rule over Ireland. It's a top-notch action-oriented drama and, while it takes some liberties with the actual history of the time, it's still well worth watching.

Philomena directed by Stephen Frears.
When an Irish teenager named Philomena Lee becomes pregnant, her father forces her to move to a convent in Roscrea. There, after being forced to work as an indentured servant for several years, the nuns abruptly give her son up for adoption without her consent. Nearly 50 years later British journalist Martin Sixsmith embarks on a journey with Philomena to find her son and discover why things unfurled the way they did. This extremely well-received movie is billed as a comedic drama, but it's also heartwarming and blood-curdling, and the fact that it's based on a true story only enhances how you'll feel about the secrets it uncovers.

The Quiet Man directed by John Ford.
John Ford is a legendary director, and this film, a romantic comedy from the 1950s, is one of his lesser-known gems. Filmed in a village by Ashford Castle, The Quiet Man sees John Wayne play an Irish-American man from Pittsburgh who returns to purchase the farm that is his family's ancestral home. The pastoral setting, and the performances of both Wayne and Maureen O'Hara, also helped Ford earn his fourth Academy Award for Best Director.

Rebellion. This miniseries (which is currently available on Netflix) is a lush period piece set around the Easter Rising in 1916, which saw Irish Republicans stage an armed insurrection during the height of World War I in order to break away from British rule. It's a gorgeously shot, meticulously crafted show that portrays the uncertainty and chaos that ruled during this time in Ireland's history. The second season—originally called Resistance—is set during the Irish War of Independence, and is also available

on Netflix, which is great because when you finish the first season you'll want to move straight into the second.

The Secret of Kells directed by Tomm Moore and Nora Twomey. While the real Book of Kells—a highly ornate illuminated manuscript—is on display at Trinity College Library in Dublin, this animated film is about its creation and importance to the monks who kept it safe. The telling of the story might not be entirely historically accurate (there are bloodthirsty Vikings and fairies in equal supply), but it is a spectacular and beautiful movie about a real piece of art that, if you find yourself in Dublin, you absolutely should see in person.

The Wind That Shakes The Barley directed by Ken Loach. Set during the Irish Civil War in the early 1920s, this film centers on two brothers from County Cork who have joined the Irish Republican Army in order to repel British forces. For many years it was the highest-grossing independent film in Ireland's history (The Guard now holds that honor), a testament to its popularity. Cillian Murphy's performance is particularly noteworthy, and this film was made during the height of his acting career in the mid-2000s.

The Young Offenders directed by Peter Foott. Shot in Cork, The Young Offenders follows two thickheaded youths who—after hearing about a cocaine-filled ship that has capsized off the coast—decide to try earn their fortune by recovering a bale that has reportedly not yet been found. While the main characters are as dense as they are unlucky, this comedy has developed a bit of a cult following both because the characters are remarkably likeable and the story is as funny as it is lively.

TRAVEL SMART IRELAND

Updated by
Vic O'Sullivan
and Jacob Dean

★ **CAPITAL:**
Dublin

👫 **POPULATION:**
4,803,000

💬 **LANGUAGE:**
Irish and English

$ **CURRENCY:**
Euro

☎ **COUNTRY CODE:**
353

⚠ **EMERGENCIES:**
999

🚗 **DRIVING:**
On the left

⚡ **ELECTRICITY:**
230 volts/50 cycles; electrical plugs have three prongs

🕐 **TIME:**
5 hours ahead of New York

🌐 **WEB RESOURCES:**
www.discoverireland.ie
www. tourismni.com
www.irelands-blue-book.ie

Atlantic Ocean

Belfast

Dublin

IRELAND

Irish Sea

10 Things You Need to Know Before You Go

YOU'LL BE GRAND

Much of the fun—and some of your best memories—will involve just winging it in Ireland, wandering off the beaten path in Ireland, getting stuck in traffic behind a herd of cows or sheep, and interacting with locals.

PEOPLE DRIVE ON THE LEFT SIDE OF THE ROAD

This is a simple one, but essential to remember—in Ireland, as in England, people drive on the left-hand side of the road, which any local will tell you is the "right" side of the road. This means that when you rent a car, yes, the driver's seat will be on the right-hand side, and the clutch will be on the driver's left. It also means that many ingrained behaviors are going to fail you, such as making sure you look the correct direction when you cross the street, remembering which side of the street you use to board a bus going in the direction you want, and so on. You may have to do a few rounds of the first roundabout as you leave the airport while your brain adjusts, but you'll get the hang of it soon enough.

ONE ISLAND, SEPARATE COUNTRIES

Due to the Government of Ireland Act 1920, the Republic of Ireland and Northern Ireland are actually separate countries. They share the same history and in most ways the same culture, but they have their own currencies and differences in language. There's also a border between the two countries, but border crossings are inconspicuously labeled and you won't be stopped at a checkpoint or asked for a passport. This ease of travel is one of the most contentious parts of Brexit, which has the potential to close the border (something neither Ireland wants).

PUBS ARE FAMILY-FRIENDLY

If you think Irish pubs outside Ireland are authentic, you're in for a huge surprise. Not only do most international Irish pubs get their stuff from a kitschy prepackaged kit, they lack true pub culture, which emphasizes socializing with family and friends (including children), live music, watching a soccer match (or hurling), and eating hearty grub while enjoying a pint (or two). They're also a welcoming environment for strangers, so don't be surprised if people start chatting with you and buying you drinks—just keep in mind you're expected to return the favor.

YOU DON'T NEED TO BE A LORD OR LADY TO STAY IN A CASTLE

While Ireland has its share of trendy new hotels with slick lobbies and amenities, this country's incredible history, and care in preserving it, means that there are a number of castles and estates all over the country that offer lodging. For at least one or two special nights on your trip, splurge to stay in a historic mansion or castle where you can enjoy a prim and proper afternoon tea with hot scones in the wood-paneled salon of a storied estate, or gaze over the ramparts of an honest-to-goodness 15th-century castle. If you've ever had *Downton Abbey*–esque daydreams, this is the way to go.

DON'T TIP THE BARMAN

While it's true tipping isn't required or customary in many European countries, a tipping custom does exist in Ireland. If you're in a restaurant leave a tip of 10%—or more if you had great service—but also make sure to check your bill before you do, as the service charge may have already been added for you. You do not need to tip in bars, unless you get food service. Rounding up your bill up at the end of a round of drinks, or offering to buy the bartender a drink, is a nice gesture if you feel like showing your appreciation.

A HERITAGE CARD IS A MUST

Ireland's National Monuments and National Historic Properties are run by the government and many charge an entry fee. By purchasing a flat-rate Heritage Card you gain access to all of these sites (minus one, Muckross Traditional Farms in Killarney). This includes more than 75 heritage sites all over the country, some of which are among the most popular places to visit in Ireland, like Kilmainham Jail, the Rock of Cashel, Muckross House, Kilkenny Castle, Glendalough, Brú na Bóinne, and Clonmacnoise. Plus you can get a discounted rate on the card if you're a senior, a child, a student (make sure to bring a valid student ID), or if you buy a family card. If you plan to visit a number of historic sites this is a great option, but do bear in mind that not every site charges admission, so you should plan your visits in advance to make sure this represents a good savings. Heritage Cards can be purchased at many historic sites, or you can order one by mail, fax, or phone.

IT'S JUST RAIN AND IT WILL PASS

It's not exactly news that it rains in Ireland—hence the lush green valleys and meadows—but it may be a surprise that the weather can be so changeable. Ireland's weather is generally temperate, but stormy weather can roll in and out without warning, and foggy, chilly conditions are common all year round. Watch the morning weather forecast and you will be none the wiser. In fact, you may laugh to see every weather possibility proposed for your day, from hail, a "chance of showers,"

and treacherous roads due to frost, to "sunny spells" and sun showers. You can get four seasons in one day, sometimes in one hour. All you need to know is that you should not let the weather interfere with your plans, because it will pass. There may be a monsoon as you set out for the Cliffs of Moher in the morning, but there's a good chance the clouds will part and the sun will be shining gloriously as you arrive—or it will still be raining. Either way, it doesn't really matter. Pack accordingly with layers, a waterproof jacket regardless of the season, and good waterproof shoes or boots. Don't bother with an umbrella—its resistance is futile. Ireland has some of the most skilled weavers in the entire world, so if you find yourself in need of new layers, you have a good excuse to shop for tweed caps and cable-knit sweaters.

SUMMER DAYS ARE 18 HOURS LONG

Ireland's location in the northern hemisphere means that at the height of the summer the sun sets after 11 pm, providing a total of about 18 hours of daylight. Conversely, during the winter the sun sets in the early afternoon, around 4 pm. Obviously, it is more expensive to visit Ireland in summer, but you really do get bang for your buck with long, leisurely evenings to enjoy the bounty of summer festivals, prolonged sightseeing, and long walks in the beautiful countryside. If you visit in winter, plan your schedule so that your walks and

outdoor sightseeing happen in the earlier part of the day, and fill the darker evenings with museums, cultural events, and pubs.

THERE'S MORE TO IRISH FOOD THAN MEAT AND POTATOES

Stereotypes that Irish food is largely centered on potatoes, beef, and lamb are actually pretty fair, but keep in mind that Ireland is an island surrounded by cold Atlantic waters, which means it's a wonderland for certain types of seafood. Smoked fish such as salmon, trout, and mackerel are delicious and easy to find, as is bread made with seaweed (laver), and beautiful oysters. There are 16 Michelin-starred restaurants in Ireland: 15 are one-star restaurants and Dublin's Restaurant Patrick Guilbaud is the only one with two-star status. The Michelin list in 2019 included three new restaurants, all in County Cork: Ichigo Ichie offers a no-choice *kaiseski*, a Japanese tasting menu of 12 courses; Restaurant Chestnut, in a former pub in Ballydehob village; and Mews, a restaurant in Baltimore, Cork, with a focus on seasonal Irish cuisine.

SUNDAYS ARE SLOW DAYS

Ireland doesn't exactly shut down on Sunday as it did in days of old, but it is a day when many businesses (including restaurants) are either closed or have shortened hours, especially outside major cities. Sunday is a great day for sports, and you can always stop by a pub.

Getting Here

✈ Air Travel

Flying time to Ireland is 6½ hours from New York, 7½ hours from Chicago, 10 hours from Los Angeles, and 1 hour from London.

Flying into Ireland involves few hassles, although an increase in traffic in the last decade has caused a slight increase in flight delays and time spent waiting for baggage to clear customs. There are few domestic flights within Ireland. Government subsidies were withdrawn following the completion of the highway (motorway) system, and an increase in express train services. The only survivor is the Kerry-to-Dublin route and the short flights to the Aran Islands. Checking in and boarding an outbound plane tends to be civilized. Security is professional but not overbearing, and airport staffers are usually helpful and patient. In the busy summer season the lines can get long, and you should play it safe by arriving a couple of hours before your flight.

AIRPORTS
The major gateways to Ireland are Dublin Airport (DUB) on the east coast, 10 km (6 miles) north of the city center, and Shannon Airport (SNN) on the west coast, 25 km (16 miles) west of Limerick. Two airports serve Belfast: Belfast International Airport (BFS) at Aldergrove, 24 km (15 miles) from the city, handles local and U.K. flights, as well as international traffic; George Best Belfast City Airport (BHD), 6½ km (4 miles) from the city, handles local and U.K. flights only. In addition, the City of Derry Airport (LDY) receives flights from Liverpool, London Stansted, and Glasgow in the United Kingdom. If you plan to visit mainly the Southwest of Ireland, use Cork Airport (ORK), which handles flights from the United Kingdom, as well as from Boston, Paris, Malaga, and Rome.

FLIGHTS
From North America and the United Kingdom, Aer Lingus, the national flag carrier, has the greatest number of direct flights to Ireland.

Aer Lingus flies to Shannon and Dublin from New York's JFK (John F. Kennedy Airport), Chicago's O'Hare, Boston, San Francisco, and Orlando. Delta has a daily departure from New York's JFK to Dublin, and American Airlines flies to Dublin from New York's JFK and Chicago. United flies direct to Dublin, Shannon, and Belfast, departing daily from Newark Liberty International Airport in New Jersey. Norwegian Airlines flies to Shannon, Cork (summer only), and Dublin from Boston, New York, and Los Angeles. Except for special offers, prices for the airlines tend to be similar. London to Dublin is one of the world's busiest international routes. Aer Lingus, British Airways, and CityJet all have several daily flights. Ryanair—famous for its cheap, no-frills service—runs several daily flights from London Gatwick, Luton, and Stansted airports to Dublin, Kerry, Shannon, Cork, and Ireland West Airport Knock. With such healthy competition, bargains abound. British Airways, Flybe, and EasyJet run regularly scheduled flights to Belfast from Birmingham, Manchester, London Gatwick, Luton, and Stansted airports.

Within Ireland, Aer Lingus Regional provides service from Dublin to Kerry. Flybe flies from Dublin to Donegal.

⚓ Boat Travel

TO AND FROM IRELAND
Ferries are a convenient way to travel between Ireland and elsewhere in Europe, particularly the United Kingdom. There are four main ferry ports in Ireland—two in the republic at Dublin Port

and Rosslare, and two in Northern Ireland at Belfast and Larne. The cost of your trip can vary substantially, so compare prices carefully. Bear in mind, too, that flying can be cheaper, so look into all types of transportation before booking.

Irish Ferries operates the *Ulysses,* the world's largest car ferry, between Dublin and Holyhead, Wales (3 hours, 15 minutes); there's also a swift service (1 hour, 50 minutes) between these two ports. There are several trips daily. The company also runs between Rosslare and Pembroke, Wales (four hours), and has service to France. Stena Line sails several times a day between Dublin and Holyhead (3 hours, 15 minutes). The company also runs a fast craft (two hours) and a superferry (three hours) between Belfast and Stranraer, Scotland, as well as a fast craft (two hours) between Rosslare and Fishguard, Wales. There are several trips daily on both routes.

P&O Irish Sea vessels run between Larne and Troon, Scotland (two hours), a couple of times a day. The company also sails from Dublin to Liverpool twice daily (eight hours), with a choice of daytime or overnight sailings.

Brittany Ferries offers an overnight service from Cork to Roscoff in France and Santander in northern Spain.

WITHIN IRELAND

There is regular service to the Aran Islands from Ros an Mhíl (Rossaveal) in County Galway and Doolin in County Clare. Ferries also sail to Inishbofin (off the Galway coast) and Arranmore (off the Donegal coast), and to Bere, Whiddy, Sherkin, and the Cape Clear Islands off the coast of County Cork. Bere and Whiddy have a car ferry, but the other islands are all small enough to explore on foot, so the ferries are for foot passengers and bicycles only. Other islands—the Blaskets and the Skelligs in Kerry, Rathlin in Antrim, and Tory, off the Donegal coast—have seasonal ferry services between May and September, less frequently the rest of the year. Fáilte Ireland publishes a free guide and map with ferry details.

🚌 Bus Travel

In the Republic of Ireland, long-distance bus service is operated by Bus Éireann, which also provides local service in Cork, Galway, Limerick, and Waterford. There's only one class, and prices are similar for all seats. Note, though, that outside of the peak season, service is limited; some routes (e.g., to the Ring of Kerry) disappear altogether.

Bus Éireann's Expressway buses go directly, in the straightest available line, from one biggish town to another, stopping at a limited number of designated places. There's sometimes only one trip a day on express routes.

A round-trip from Dublin to Cork costs €27, and a Dublin-to-Galway City round-trip is €22.

■ TIP→ **Prepaid tickets don't apply to a particular bus time, just a route, so show up at least 30 minutes early to get a seat.**

Rural bus service, which rambles around the countryside passing through as many villages as possible, shuts down at around 7 or 8 pm. To ensure that a bus journey is feasible, check online or ask at the nearest bus station. Many of the destination indicators are in Irish (Gaelic), so make sure you get on the right bus.

Citylink, a Galway-based company, has service between Galway, Limerick, Cork, Clifden, and Dublin, as well as Cork and Dublin airports. Prices are competitive, with the two-hour, 45-minute journey

Getting Here

from Dublin Airport to Galway costing no more than €16.50 one-way. This can be cut to two hours, 30 minutes by using the Citylink's Eireagle service, which travels direct to the airport, bypassing the city center. All buses have complimentary Wi-Fi.

Aircoach operates a similar service, with Wi-Fi on most buses, between Dublin, Cork, and Belfast and their respective airports. The three-hour journey from Cork to Dublin costs €16 one-way. Online fares can be cheaper, and booking online guarantees you a seat and priority boarding, ahead of those paying in cash.

IN NORTHERN IRELAND

All buses in Northern Ireland are operated by the state-owned Translink. Goldline is the long-distance bus division, while Ulsterbus runs local services. Service is generally good, with particularly useful links to towns not served by train. Ulsterbus also runs tours. Eurolines buses run from London and from Birmingham, making the Stranraer–Port of Belfast crossing.

FARES AND PASSES

You can buy tickets online, at tourist offices, at bus stations, or on buses (though it's cash-only for the latter option).

You can save money with multiday passes, some of which can be combined with rail service. Consider the Irish Explorer Rail and Bus Pass, which gives you five days out of 15 of bus and rail travel for €160. An iLink Card costs £60 for seven days of unlimited bus and rail travel in Northern Ireland—a great deal when you consider that a one-day ticket costs £16.50.

Some cost-cutting passes include both Northern Ireland and the Republic of Ireland. An Irish Rover bus ticket for travel on Ulsterbus and Bus Éireann covers Ireland, north and south. It also includes

city-center bus travel in Cork, Waterford, Limerick, Galway, and on the Metro services in Belfast—but not Dublin.

Car Travel

U.S. driver's licenses are recognized in Ireland.

Roads in the Irish Republic are generally good, with four-lane highways, or motorways, connecting Dublin with Waterford, Cork, Limerick, Shannon Airport, Galway, and Newry on the border with Northern Ireland. Service areas with restrooms and food are gradually being added; meanwhile, you may have to leave the motorway for comfort stops, usually located in gas stations. National routes and minor roads are slower, but much more scenic. On rural roads, watch out for cattle and sheep.

ROAD SIGNS

Road signs in the republic are generally posted in both Irish and English; destinations in which Irish is the spoken language are signposted only in Irish. The most important one to know is "An Daingean," which is now the official name of Dingle Town. ■TIP➜ **Get a good bilingual road map, and know the next town on your itinerary; neither the signposts nor the locals refer to roads by official numbers.** Traffic signs are the same as in the rest of Europe. On the newer green signposts, distances are in kilometers; on some of the old white signposts they're still miles. Most important, speed limits are posted in the republic (but not in Northern Ireland) in kilometers.

There are no border checkpoints between the Irish Republic and Northern Ireland, where the road network is excellent and, outside Belfast, uncrowded. Road signs and traffic regulations conform to the British system.

CAR FERRIES

All ferries on both principal routes to the Irish Republic welcome cars. Fishguard and Pembroke are relatively easy to reach by road. The car trip to Holyhead, on the other hand, is sometimes difficult: delays on the A55 North Wales coastal road aren't unusual.

ROAD CONDITIONS

Most roads are paved and make for easy travel. Roads designated with an *M* for "motorway" are double-lane divided highways with paved shoulders; *N,* or "national," routes are generally undivided highways with shoulders; and *R,* or "regional," roads tend to be narrow and twisty.

Rush-hour traffic in Dublin, Cork, Limerick, Belfast, and Galway can be intense. Rush hours in Dublin run 7 to 9:30 am and 5 to 7 pm; special events such as soccer matches also tie up traffic in and around the city, as does heavy rain.

🚆 Train Travel

Irish Rail trains are generally reliable, reasonably priced, and comfortable. You can easily reach all the principal towns from Dublin, though service between provincial cities can be roundabout. To get to Cork City from Wexford, for example, you have to go via Limerick Junction. It's often quicker, though perhaps less comfortable, to take a bus. Most mainline trains have one standard class. Round-trip tickets are usually cheapest. The best deals are available online, booking at least one week in advance.

Northern Ireland Railways has three main rail routes, all operating out of Belfast's Central Station: north to Derry via Ballymena and Coleraine, east to Bangor along the shores of Belfast Lough, and south to Dublin and the Irish Republic.

Note that Eurail Passes aren't valid in Northern Ireland.

There's only one class of train travel in Ireland (with the exception of the express trains between Dublin and Belfast, which have first-class and standard-class tickets). Seat reservations are part of the package if you book online on Dublin–Cork and Dublin–Belfast routes, but otherwise it's first-come, first-served. ■ TIP→ **Get to the station at least 30 minutes ahead to ensure a seat. It's not uncommon on busier routes to find all the seats are occupied.**

Before You Go

🌐 Passports

All U.S. citizens, even infants, need a valid passport to enter Ireland for stays of up to 90 days. Citizens of the United Kingdom, when traveling on flights departing from Great Britain, do not need a passport to enter Ireland, but it's advisable to carry some form of photo ID. Passport requirements for Northern Ireland are the same as for the republic.

📅 When to Go

High Season: June through August is the most expensive and popular time to visit, and the major tourist spots can be quite crowded then. Famously fickle weather means you should always have a light rain jacket handy.

Low Season: The post-Christmas months of January and February are the quietest, but they are vibrant times in the cities, with shows opening for the new theater season. These are also the prime months for cheap hotels (be prepared to haggle for a killer price). But expect rain, and plenty of it.

Value Season: September is actually the driest month in Ireland. Saner airfares and a host of cultural events also make it a very attractive time to visit. Mid-March to May is another great shoulder season—before the masses arrive, but when cafés are abuzz and the students are still in town.

📷 What to Pack

In Ireland you can experience all four seasons in a day. There can be damp, chilly stretches even in July and August, the warmest months of the year. Layers are the best way to go. Pack several long- and short-sleeve T-shirts (in winter, some should be thermal or silk), a sweatshirt, a lightweight sweater, a heavyweight sweater, and a hooded, waterproof windbreaker that's large enough to go over several layers if necessary. A portable umbrella is absolutely essential, and the smaller and lighter it is, the better, as you'll want it with you every second. You should bring at least two pairs of walking shoes; footwear can get soaked in minutes and take hours to dry.

The Irish are generally informal about clothes. In the more expensive hotels and restaurants, people dress up for dinner, but very few places operate a strict dress policy. Old or tattered blue jeans and running shoes are a no-no in certain bars and dance clubs.

If you're used to packing things or stowing dirty clothes in plastic shopping or drawstring bags, bring your own. About the only place you can find the latter here is in the closets of better hotel rooms (for on-site dry cleaning and laundry). Plastic bags carry a 22¢ government levy and can be sold by supermarkets, but it's illegal to give them away. Most stores use paper bags or recycle boxes.

Essentials

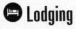 Lodging

In Dublin and other cities, boutique hotels blend luxury with contemporary (and often truly Irish) design. Manors and castles boast a unique combination of luxury and history. Less impressive, but equally charming, are the provincial inns and country hotels with simple but adequate facilities.

Fáilte Ireland has a grading system and maintains a list of registered hotels, guesthouses, B&Bs, farmhouses, hostels, and campgrounds. For each accommodation, the list gives a maximum charge that can't be exceeded without special authorization. Prices must be displayed in every room; if the hotel oversteps its limit, don't hesitate to complain.

■TIP→ Don't depend on the address used on your accommodation provider's website. Request an Eircode (⊕ www.eircode.ie), which gives the exact location of every property in Ireland.

BED-AND-BREAKFASTS

B&Bs are classified either as town homes, country homes, or farmhouses. Most B&Bs have private bathrooms for most bedrooms, but don't expect this as a matter of course. Some B&Bs are on farms, but the "farmhouses" are more likely to be modern bungalows or undistinguished two-story houses than creeper-clad Georgian mansions. However, there *are* some mansions offering B&B rooms, and they are priced accordingly.

At the lower end of the price scale, expect to pay an average of €30–€40 per person per night. Ask for a reduction if staying more than one night. Many travelers don't bother booking a B&B in advance. They are so plentiful in rural areas that it's often more fun to leave the decision open, allowing yourself a choice of final destinations for the night. Long holiday weekends are the exception to this rule, with B&Bs often getting booked up far in advance, so keep an eye on the calendar. If you want to be sure of staying in a family home, check out the places listed by Family Homes of Ireland.

CASTLES AND MANORS

In line with the overall recovery in the hotel industry, Ireland's luxury heritage hotels like Adare Manor (County Limerick), Dromoland Castle (County Clare), and Ashford Castle (County Mayo) have undergone significant restorations recently. Smaller manor houses set on private estates still retain the essence of their original purpose and can be booked through Ireland's Blue Book of Country Houses & Restaurants or Hidden Ireland.

🍽 Dining

MEALS AND MEALTIMES

Breakfast is served from 7 to 10, lunch runs from 12:30 to 2:30, and dinners are usually midevening occasions with last orders at 9 pm. Unless otherwise noted, the restaurants listed are open daily for lunch and dinner.

Pubs are generally open Monday through Thursday 10:30 am–11:30 pm and Friday and Saturday 10:30 am–12:30 am. On Sunday, pubs are open 12:30 pm–11 pm or later on certain Sundays. All pubs close on Christmas Day, but hotel bars are open for guests.

Pubs in Northern Ireland are open 11:30 am–11 pm Monday–Saturday and 12:30–2:30 pm and 7–10 pm on Sunday (note that Sunday hours are at the owner's or manager's discretion).

Children under the age of 18 cannot enter a pub after 9 pm (or 10 pm May to September).

Essentials

Guided Tours

GENERAL TOURS

CIE Tours International is one of the biggest and longest-established tour operators in the Irish market. It runs a selection of fully inclusive, escorted bus tours, or independent fly-drive vacations. An eight-day itinerary with car rental and confirmed hotel bookings starts at €1,549 per person. Starting in Dublin, the Heritage Tour is a seven-day bus tour that takes in Blarney Castle, the Cliffs of Moher, the Skellig Experience, and the Giant's Causeway, among other attractions, with accommodations in superior hotels.

Discovering Ireland Vacations, a young company set up by three friends, aims to create the best holiday experience by using enthusiastic local guides. A customized, eight-day self-driven "Highlight of Ireland" tour starts at €730 per person. The price includes seven nights at a B&B, car rental, and toll-free calls to your vacation specialist. Escorted bus tours include the Irish Spirit 8 Days, which includes one day in Dublin, a drive to Blarney Castle via the Rock of Cashel, Killarney, the Ring of Kerry, and the Cliffs of Moher. Rates start at €2,349 per person.

Vagabond Small-Group Tours of Ireland specializes in off-the-beaten-track tours of Ireland, with small group sizes that allow for a more personal experience, smaller buses, and smaller hotel and guesthouse options. Tours visit the essential, iconic sites such as Blarney Castle, the Cliffs of Moher, and the Ring of Kerry, along with less-trafficked gems like the Beara Peninsula and wild Donegal. Vagabond Adventure tours offer a more active experience (with hiking, horse riding, cycling, and kayaking) while the Driftwood tours are geared to visitors looking for a more relaxed, less active experience. Rates start at €1,699 per person.

SPECIAL-INTEREST TOURS

Irish Cycling Safaris pioneered cycling holidays in Ireland and offers easygoing to moderate cycling trips along rural back roads with luggage transfer and accommodations in small family-run hotels and guesthouses. A week-long off-peak tour of West Cork and Kerry, including Killarney, costs €830 per person. Tour groups are accompanied by a local guide who drives the support van. Alternatively, you can opt for a self-guided tour that includes bike rental, itinerary, luggage transfer, and prebooked accommodations for the same price.

Iron Donkey guided group tours have something for all levels here, from novices to hammerheads. The 10-day West of Ireland itinerary sets out from Ennis and passes through Kilkee, the Cliffs of Moher, the Burren coastline, Connemara, Clifden, and Westport (cost is about €2,250 per person). Superthorough and well-run custom tours will meet you at the first lodging (all great options, incidentally), size your bike, review the route, and prep you for the ride.

Golfbreaks.com can customize a golf getaway for you and also has tours of different regions of Ireland. Its Northern Ireland and the Northwest package include rounds at the legendary Royal County Down and Royal Portrush courses.

A long-established company with self-drive holidays and escorted tours, Isle Inn also has an interesting range of activity holidays and escorted hiking holidays averaging 16–19 km (10–12 miles) a day. You stay in family-run guesthouses and characterful small hotels while walking through scenic areas, including the

Donegal coast, the Glens of Antrim, Achill Island, and Mayo. Escorted hiking holiday options (prices vary) include a chauffeur-driven itinerary of the Wild Atlantic Way combines culture and cuisine with seven nights at four- and five-star hotels, gourmet dinners, and a driver to escort you.

$ Taxes

When leaving the Irish Republic, U.S. and Canadian visitors get a refund of the value-added tax (V.A.T.), which currently accounts for a hefty 23% of the purchase price of many goods and 13.5% of those that fall outside the luxury category. Accommodations and restaurants charge 9% V.A.T., while most items of interest to visitors, right down to ordinary toilet soap, are rated at 23%. Value-added tax is not refundable on accommodations, car rental, meals, or any other form of personal services received on vacation.

$ Tipping

In some hotels and restaurants, a service charge of around 10%—rising to 15% in plush spots—is added to the bill. If in doubt, ask whether service is included. If there's no service charge, add a minimum of 10% to the total. Taxi drivers or hackney cab drivers, who make the trip for a prearranged sum, don't expect tips. Tip hotel porters at least €1 per suitcase. You don't tip in pubs, but for table service in a bar, a hotel lounge, or a Dublin lounge bar, leave about €1.

Tipping Guidelines for Ireland

Bellhop	€1–€2, depending on the level of the hotel
Hotel Concierge	€5 or more if he or she performs a special service for you
Hotel Doorman	€1–€2 if he helps you get a cab
Hotel Maid	€1–€3 per day (either daily or at the end of your stay, in cash)
Hotel Room-Service Waiter	€1–€2 per delivery, even if a service charge has been added
Restroom Attendant	Restroom attendants in more expensive restaurants expect some small change or €1
Taxi Driver	10%, or just round up the fare to the next euro amount
Tour Guide	10% of the cost of the tour
Valet Parking Attendant	€1–€2, but only when you get your car
Waiter	Just small change (up to a euro or two) to round out your bill if service is already included; otherwise, add 10%

Great Itineraries

The Best of Ireland in a Week

Ireland might be a small island, but it's packed with things to do and see, so a bit of planning goes a long way. If this is your first trip to the Emerald Isle, then Dublin, Galway, and Kerry have to be top of the list. But what else? You can use Dublin as a base for all of the east coast and the Midlands. And from Galway you can take in all the wilds of the West and even some of the Atlantic islands. This weeklong itinerary should help make sure you don't miss out on any of the must-sees. If it's not your first trip, you might find some more unusual options in the extension itineraries that follow.

Dublin, Galway City, and Killarney (County Kerry) are three of the most vibrant, fun places for any visitor, but they also make great base camps for exploring the wild, ancient, and stunning parts of this rugged and beautiful island. From these hubs you can opt for day trips into the countryside or choose to overnight in a more rural country house or B&B. Either way, the days are very long in summer, and driving times should be comfortable.

DAY 1: DUBLIN

Fly into Dublin and use one of its elegant Georgian hotels as your luxurious base, with **Number 31** a great option. Start the day with a trip to **Trinity College**, Beckett's old stomping ground, and its legendary *Book of Kells*. Take in the elegant architecture of Georgian Dublin with a visit to beautiful **Merrion Square**, with the **National Museum** a definite highlight. After lunch at **Fallon & Byrne**, pay your respects to Dublin's favorite tipple by taking a tour of the impressive **Guinness Storehouse.** As evening falls head to cobblestoned **Temple Bar**, Dublin's party zone, and join locals in this city-of-1,000-pubs for a foamy pint with traditional dinner at **Gallagher's Boxty House.** For your first night in the city catch a show at W.B. Yeats's old haunt, the **Abbey Theatre,** or listen to a traditional music session at the wild and wonderful **Cobblestone** pub.

DAY 2: EXCURSIONS FROM DUBLIN

First drive to the Boyne Valley, a short trip north of the capital. Spend the morning walking among the Iron Age ruins of the rolling **Hill of Tara.** After a picnic lunch on top of the hill, drive through ancient **Kells**—one of the centers of early Christianity in Ireland—and then to **Newgrange,** famous for its ancient passage graves. One thousand years older than Stonehenge, the great white-quartz structure merits an hour or two at least. Next take the M50 ring road south around Dublin for a spectacular drive through the County Wicklow mountains. You might want to stop in one of the small, quiet towns along the **Wicklow Way** hiking trail and go for a short hike. Drive on to stately **Powerscourt House,** whose gardens epitomize the glory and grandeur of the Anglo-Irish aristocracy. From the profane to the sacred, head next to the "monastic city" of **Glendalough** and the medieval monastery of the hermit St. Kevin. Repair to Ireland's highest village, Roundwood, for dinner at the town's 17th-century inn. Head back to Dublin for the night.

DAYS 3 AND 4: WEST CORK AND KERRY

An early-morning departure from Dublin and a 3½-hour drive southwest takes you to **Killarney,** at the heart of glorious Kerry and West Cork. The **Cahernane House Hotel** is the ideal refuge from the touristy buzz. Although it has been almost transformed into a Celtic theme park by a flood of visitors, Killarney is a good base for exploring your pick of two great Atlantic-pounded peninsulas: the strikingly scenic **Ring of Kerry** and the beloved **Dingle Peninsula.**

Both offer stunning ocean views, hilly landscapes (like the Macgillycuddy's Reeks mountains), and welcoming towns with great bed-and-breakfasts. Both drives can be done in a day, or you might choose to focus on one and stop off in the villages along the way or go for a hike. To avoid the crowds in Killarney you could head to serene **Kenmare** for a spot of dinner and some toe-tapping music and dancing, before an overnight in the magnificent **Park Hotel.** The next morning, a beautiful hour-long drive through the mountains and along the coast takes you to the small towns of **West Cork** and the kind of landscape that inspired Ireland's nickname, the Emerald Isle. **Skibbereen, Clonakilty,** and **Glengarriff** are all magical places to spend a few hours and maybe do a little crafts shopping. Finish your drive at picture-perfect **Bantry House and Gardens** where you can splurge on authentic 18th-century room with stunning views of the bay. Alternatively, head back to Killarney for the night.

DAYS 5–7: THE WEST

An almost three-hour drive north from Killarney will take you straight to **Galway City,** the urban center of the wild and ancient West. But don't make the mistake of rushing through the wonders of County Clare. Take a detour straight for the jaw-dropping 710-foot-high **Cliffs of Moher,** perhaps the single most impressive sight in Ireland. After lunch in the waterside village of **Ballyvaughan** spend a couple of hours exploring the lunar landscape of the harsh, limestone **Burren.** In spring it becomes a mighty rock garden of exotic colors. If you still have time you could take in the 2-million-year-old **Ailwee Cave** and the picture-perfect village of **Kinvara** before you hit Galway. An evening out in that city is a must, as it's always brim full of music, theater, and truly great seafood. Next morning head northwest to the tiny village of **Clifden,** with some of the country's best Atlantic views. From here, head east through one of the most beautiful stretches of road in Connemara—through Kylemore Valley, home of **Kylemore Abbey,** a huge Gothic Revival castle. After seeing the castle and its grounds, head north through tiny **Leenane** (the setting of the hit Broadway play, *The Beauty Queen of Leenane*) and on to the most attractive town in County Mayo, **Westport.** It's the perfect spot to spend the night: the 18th-century planned town is on an inlet of Clew Bay, and some of the west coast's finest beaches are nearby. The cozy and spectacularly located **Knockranny House Hotel & Spa** is a great hotel option. Day 7

Great Itineraries

is one of real adventures as you drive an hour south to Rossaveal and take a small boat to the unique and beautiful Aran Islands. The 20-minute boat ride carries you to a quintessential Irish experience. If possible, head for **Inis Meáin,** the middle island, which still looks and feels much as it did a hundred years ago. It's perfect for walking (there's no traffic) and you'll most likely have the ancient tombs and Christian ruins all to yourself. Enjoy a bit of sweater shopping at **Inis Meáin Knitting** before you head back to the boat. Once back on the mainland it's time for the drive back to Dublin. The Georgian luxury and comfort of the **Merrion Hotel** should make your last night in Ireland memorable.

Ireland In Depth

If you have more than a week, these easy add-ons will help you prioritize your time.

COUNTY CORK EXTENSION, 2 DAYS
Follow Day 1 of the "Best of Ireland" Itinerary. Days 2 and 3. On your way from Dublin to West Cork, detour for **Cork City,** a great walking city of bridges and winding hilly streets. A visit to the colorful **English Market** can be combined with a hearty Irish lunch. A few miles outside Cork sits the 15th-century **Blarney Castle,** where you can kiss the famous stone. After your visit, drive to the foodie paradise that is **Kinsale.** Try to take in a serene harbor cruise to help build an appetite. Spend the night at the Georgian **Friar's Lodge.** In the morning on your way out of town, stop off at the unique **Charles Fort,** one of Europe's best-preserved star forts situated atop a sheer cliff face. *Titanic* history buffs will want to stop off at **The Queenstown Story of Cobh Heritage Centre,** which tells the story of the great transatlantic liners. The nearby **Titanic Experience** allows visitors to literally follow in the footsteps of embarking passengers. From Cobh it's only 1½ hours to Killarney where you can pick up Days 2 and 3 of the "Best Of Ireland" Itinerary.

NORTHWEST EXTENSION, 2 DAYS
Follow Days 1–7 of the "Best of Ireland" Itinerary, including the 2-day County Cork Extension. Days 10 and 11. Instead of heading back to Dublin after visiting the Aran Islands (Day 7 of the "Best Of Ireland" Itinerary), drive north through the heart of **Yeats Country** in Sligo. Just north of cozy **Sligo Town** is the stark outline of a great hill, **Ben Bulben,** in whose shadow poet W.B. Yeats wanted to be buried. South of town, follow the signposted Yeats Trail around woody, gorgeously scenic **Lough Gill.** Continuing north, you pass W.B.'s simple grave in unassuming **Drumcliff,** a 3000 BC tomb in **Creevykeel,** and small but vibrant **Donegal Town.** Eat some local seafood then spend the night at the **Central Hotel,** and the next morning head north along the tight, meandering roads of the stunning Donegal coastline. Two wild, breathtaking natural wonders are must-sees on this stretch of coastline. First, the tiny hamlet of **Glencolumbkille** clings dramatically to the rock-bound harbor of Glen Bay. The cliffs surrounding the tiny village rise up to 700 feet and are awash with prehistoric cairns. Keep driving north through the Gaeltacht (Irish-speaking) region and head inland for the mountains, lakes, and moorlands of glorious **Glenveagh National Park.** A beautiful drive through the mountains and past serene **Gartan Lough** will take you to Derry and a night at the Victorian **Merchant's House.** This is ideal for the start of the Northern Ireland Extension below.

NORTHERN IRELAND EXTENSION
Days 12 and 13. Begin exploring the province in historic, divided **Derry City** (called Londonderry by unionists), Northern

Ireland's second city. A few hours are sufficient to take in the views from the old city walls and the fascinating murals of the Catholic Bogside district. Continue on to two of the region's main attractions, the 13th-century Norman fortress of **Dunluce Castle** and the **Giant's Causeway,** shaped from volcanic rock some 60 million years ago. Heading south, sticking to coastal roads for the best scenery, you'll soon pass through the **Glens of Antrim,** whose green hills roll down into the sea. Tucked in the glens are a number of small, unpretentious towns with great hotels. Spend the night in the traditional inn that is the **Londonderry Arms Hotel** in serene Carnlough. Early in the morning, head straight to Northern Ireland's capital, **Belfast.** The old port city, gray and often wet, is a fascinating place, recovering from years of strife. A **Black Taxi Tour** is a brilliant way to get to the heart of this old city. Follow this with a visit to the hugely impressive **Titanic Belfast Visitor Centre** before you start heading back to Dublin. If you're ahead of schedule, take the longer route that passes through the glorious **Mountains of Mourne** and around icy-blue **Carlingford Lough.** Arrive back in Dublin for a final night at the luxurious **Merrion Hotel** before flying home in the morning.

By Car: Some Tips

Road signs are generally posted in both Irish and English, although in Gaeltacht areas new laws mandate signs in Irish only (most such regions are located in the counties along the western coast of the country—Donegal and Connemara, in particular). If traveling in these areas, invest in a detailed map with both Irish and English names.

Another new law has mandated that all speed-limit signs be posted in kilometers—not miles—per hour. Slow down on smaller, countryside lanes and roads: traffic jams can sometimes be caused by flocks of sheep and herds of cattle, not cars.

New divided highways are the fastest way to get from one point to another, but use caution: highways sometimes end as abruptly as they begin.

Contacts

✈ Air Travel

AIRPORTS Belfast International Airport. ☎ 028/9448–4848 ⊕ www.belfastairport.com. **City of Derry Airport.** ☎ 028/7181–0784 ⊕ www.cityofderryairport.com. **Cork Airport.** ☎ 021/431–3131 ⊕ www.corkairport.com. **Dublin Airport** (DUB). ☎ 01/814–1111 ⊕ www.dublinairport.com. **George Best Belfast City Airport.** ☎ 028/9093–9093 ⊕ www.belfastcityairport.com. **Shannon Airport** (SNN). ☎ 061/712–000 ⊕ www.shannonairport.ie.

⛴ Boat/ Ferry Travel

Brittany Ferries. ☎ 021/427–7801 in Ireland ⊕ www.brittanyferries.ie. **P&O Ferries.** ☎ 01/686–9467 in Ireland, 0800/130–0030 in U.K. ⊕ www.poferries.com. **Stena Line.** ☎ 01/907–5555 in Ireland, 028/9074–7747 in Northern Ireland, 0844/770–7070 in U.K. ⊕ www.stenaline.ie.

🚌 Bus Travel

Aircoach. ☎ 01/844–7118 ⊕ www.aircoach.ie. **Bus Éireann.** ☎ 1850/836–6111 in Republic of Ireland ⊕ www.buseireann.ie. **Citylink.** ☎ 091/564–164 within Ireland ⊕ www.citylink.ie.

Dublin Coach. ☎ 353/465–9972 ⊕ www.dublincoach.ie. **Eurolines.** ☎ 08717/818–178 in U.K. ⊕ www.eurolines.co.uk. **Translink Goldline.** ☎ 028/9033–7002 in Northern Ireland ⊕ www.translink.co.uk. **Ulsterbus.** ☎ 028/9066–6630 in Northern Ireland ⊕ www.translink.co.uk.

🚆 Train Travel

TRAIN STATIONS Belfast Central Station. ✉ East Bridge St., Belfast ☎ 028/9089–9400 ⊕ www.translink.co.uk. **Connolly Station.** ✉ Amiens St., Dublin ☎ 01/703–2358 ⊕ www.irishrail.ie. **Galway Station.** ✉ Station Rd., Galway City ☎ 091/564–222 ⊕ www.irishrail.ie. **Heuston Station.** ✉ St. John's Rd. W (N4), Dublin ☎ 01/703–2132 ⊕ www.irishrail.ie. **Kent Station.** ✉ Lower Glanmire Rd., City Center North ☎ 021/450–4777 ⊕ www.irishrail.ie.

RAIL COMPANIES Irish Rail (Iarnrod Éireann). ☎ 01/836–6222 ⊕ www.irishrail.ie. **Northern Ireland Railways.** ☎ 028/9066–6630 ⊕ www.translink.co.uk/services/ni-railways.

🚶 Guided Tours

GENERAL TOURS CIE Tours International. ☎ 888/996–0017 from U.S. ⊕ www.cietours.com. **Discovering Ireland Vacations.** ☎ 800/963–9260 ⊕ www.discoveringireland.com. **Vagabond Small-Group Tours of Ireland.** ☎ 1/563–4358 in Ireland, 833/230–0288 toll-free from U.S. ⊕ www.vagabondtoursofireland.com.

SPECIAL INTEREST TOURS Irish Cycling Safaris. ✉ Belfield Bike Shop, UCD, Dublin ☎ 01/260–0749 ⊕ www.cyclingsafaris.com. **Iron Donkey.** ☎ 029/2089–1650 ⊕ www.irondonkey.com. **Isle Inn Hiking Tours.** ☎ 800/237–9376 ⊕ www.isleinntours.com.

📍 Visitor Information

INFORMATION Discover Ireland. ☎ 800/242–473 ⊕ www.discoverireland.ie. **Discover Northern Ireland.** ✉ 59 North St., Belfast ☎ 028/9024–6609 ⊕ www.discovernorthernireland.com. **Tourism Ireland.** ⊕ www.ireland.com. **Tourism Ireland New York Office.** ✉ 345 Park Ave., 17th fl., New York ☎ 212/418–0800 ⊕ www.ireland.com. **Tourism NI** (NITB). ✉ 59 North St., Belfast ☎ 028/9023–1221 ⊕ www.discovernorthernireland.com.

Chapter 3

DUBLIN

Updated by
Anto Howard

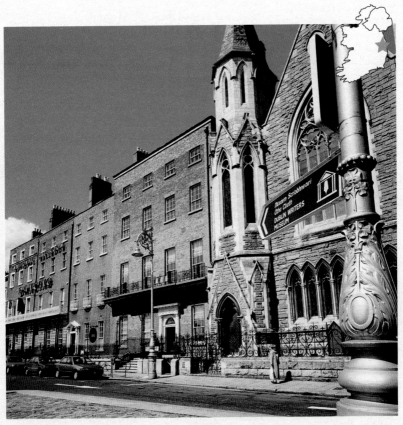

⊙ Sights	🍴 Restaurants	🛏 Hotels	🛍 Shopping	🍸 Nightlife
★★★★★	★★★★★	★★★★★	★★★★★	★★★★★

WELCOME TO DUBLIN

TOP REASONS TO GO

★ **Georgian Elegance:** Dublin's signature architectural style makes its most triumphant showing in Merrion, Fitzwilliam, Mountjoy, and Parnell Squares.

★ **The Guinness Brewery and Storehouse:** A high-tech museum tells the story of Guinness, Dublin's black blood. At the top, the Gravity Bar has the city's best views.

★ **Destination Dining:** An explosion of inventive new restaurants, alongside an array of classy old favorites, has made Dublin the place to be for dinner.

★ **Magnificent Museums:** From the Renoirs at the Hugh Lane to the Tara Brooch at the National Museum and the first editions of Joyce at the Dublin Writers Museum, Dublin is one big treasure chest.

★ **Trinity College:** An oasis of books, granite, and grass sits at the heart of the city. Highlights are the exquisitely illustrated Book of Kells and the ornate Long Room.

Despite the seismic changes of the infamous boom-and-bust-and-boom economy, Dublin happily remains an intimate capital that mixes elegant Georgian buildings, wrought-iron bridges, a battalion of booksellers, and more than 1,000 pubs. The heart of the city is the River Liffey, which runs east to west, splitting Dublin neatly in two. The more affluent Southside has a greater concentration of sights, and it can seem a world apart from the more working-class Northside. North or south, Dublin is compact and easily navigated, making it a great walking city.

1 Southside. Between Christ Church Cathedral and Trinity College lies a heavy concentration of famous sights. From St. Stephen's Green to the stylish shopping stretch of Grafton Street and west to bustling Georges Street, this is the heart of Dublin.

2 Georgian Dublin. The streets around Merrion Square and southeast of Trinity form the city's most important Georgian district; to the west of the square four major museums sit side by side. Farther south lies the

Grand Canal and more Georgian splendor in upmarket Ballsbridge.

3 Temple Bar. The cobblestone streets and small lanes bounded by Wellington Quay and Dame Street make up Dublin's trendiest—and liveliest—neighborhood. On weekends, the streets are packed with young people from all over Europe. The retractable, giant "umbrella" canopies that shelter Meeting House Square make it a year-round hive of activity.

4 Northside. Less affluent but more eloquent than the Southside, this neighborhood was once home to James Joyce; today it's the site of the Dublin Writers Museum and the James Joyce Centre. Other highlights are the grand Custom House, historic O'Connell Street, and Dublin's two

great theaters, the Abbey and the Gate.

5 Dublin West. This former industrial district stretches from Christ Church west to that other Dublin shrine, the Guinness Brewery. Imposing Dublin Castle houses the Chester Beatty Library—arguably the most impressive museum in Ireland.

6 Phoenix Park and Environs. Only a 20-minute walk from the city center, Phoenix Park, Europe's largest public city park, hugs the north bank of the Liffey. It's home to Dublin Zoo, and perfect for a stroll or cycle. A handful of other cultural attractions near the park also merit a visit.

DUBLIN'S SEAFOOD BOUNTY

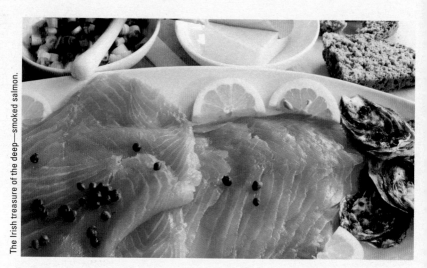

The Irish treasure of the deep—smoked salmon.

Clarenbridge oysters, Carlingford Lough mussels, Ballina wild smoked salmon, Donegal crab—the menus of the top restaurants in Dublin are now full of some of the most flavorsome seafood on the planet.

A somewhat apocryphal story about Ireland joining the EEC (European Economic Community) in 1973 has the government being given a stark choice: you can farm or you can fish, but you can't do both. They chose to protect farming, and the result was the massive overfishing by giant Spanish factory ships off Irish waters. This fact may, in part, explain why Ireland—a relatively pollution-free, sea-surrounded nation—is not one of the first places gourmands think of for great seafood. Historically, there was also a certain snobbery about eating fish, as it was seen as peasant food only suitable for fasting Fridays. Well, things have certainly changed in the last two decades.

TOP FISHY JOINTS

Some standout joints in Dublin go that extra mile. The oyster stall at the Temple Bar Farmers' Market every Saturday is something of a Dublin institution, where affordable Atlantic oysters and white wine are downed alfresco. The West Pier in Howth has become a hive of buzzing, quality seafood eateries. Fish Shop has taken the traditional Dublin chipper to a whole new culinary level.

SMOKED SALMON

From all corners of Ireland small producers are now making some of Europe's finest smoked salmon. Obviously, and perhaps unfortunately, the wild Atlantic salmon still has a richer, more piquant taste than its farmed cousin. The word "wild" in the description will tell you the fish isn't farmed. The traditional smoking method uses only Irish oak, which gives it a very distinctive, subtle flavor, and deep orange color. The best way to enjoy smoked salmon is over some toasted Dublin brown bread with a simple squeeze of lemon and some coarse black pepper to add that little extra tang.

IRISH CHOWDER

It's the pint of heavy cream and density of mussels tossed into the mix that makes Irish seafood chowder such a great snack on the run. It's also a dish that even the most humble of eateries doesn't usually mess up, although the general rule still applies: the nearer to the coast the eatery is located, the better its chowder. Regular fish stock is often used but clam juice—an Irish specialty—also adds to the unique flavor. Outside of the capital enjoy chowders at Ireland's great seafood festivals: the Galway Oyster Festival, the event in Baltimore in West Cork, and the Killybegs festival.

Seaweed is a chic new condiment.

When it comes to fish-and-chips, some say the greasier the better.

FISH-AND-CHIPS

Every Dubliner will argue about the best place to get their favorite fast-food dish of fish-and-chips, but few will quarrel with the fact that cod, ray, and haddock are the top three battered delights to go for. Interestingly, the descendants of 1950s Italian immigrants—with names like Macari and Borza—are the recognized masters of the battering art, and you'll find one of their eponymously named shops in almost every neighborhood. Tip: a single portion is usually enough to feed two!

SEAWEED

Yes, the Irish are slowly discovering the delights of farming native seaweed for use in the kitchen and elsewhere. Irish seaweed is usually gathered along the western seaboard, dried, and then sold in small packets, a bit like herbs. Look closely at restaurant menus and you'll find dulse, carrageen moss, and various kelps and wracks all turning up to add spice to risottos, salads, soups, breads, and even ice cream. The local spa industry has cottoned on, developing "algotherapies," including wraps, antiaging creams, and even full-on seaweed baths.

Dublin is back, or in local lingo, "sucking diesel," having undergone a phenomenal turnaround in the 10 years since the capital city hit rock bottom with the collapse of the economic boom nicknamed the Celtic Tiger. The economy is thriving, construction cranes are everywhere, and every corner of the city is buzzing with new life and business. For visitors, Dublin has once again become one of western Europe's most popular and delightful urban destinations. Whether you're out to enjoy the old or new Dublin, you'll find it a colossally entertaining city, all the more astonishing considering its intimate size.

It is ironic and telling that James Joyce chose Dublin as the setting for his famous *Ulysses, Dubliners,* and *A Portrait of the Artist as a Young Man* because it was a "center of paralysis" where nothing much ever changed. Which only proves that even the greats get it wrong sometimes. Indeed, if Joyce were to return to his once-genteel hometown today—disappointed with the city's provincial outlook, he left it in 1902 at the age of 20—and take a quasi-Homeric odyssey through the city (as he so famously does in *Ulysses*), would he even recognize Dublin as his "Dear Dirty Dumpling, foostherfather of fingalls and dotthergills"?

For instance, what would he make of Temple Bar—the city's erstwhile down-at-the-heels neighborhood, now crammed with cafés and trendy hotels and suffused with a nonstop international-party atmosphere? Or the simple sophistication of the open-air restaurants of the tiny Italian Quarter (named Quartier Bloom after his own creation), complete with sultry tango lessons? Today, Ireland's capital is packed with elegant shops and hotels, theaters, galleries, coffeehouses, and a stunning variety of new, creative little restaurants can be found on almost every street in Dublin, transforming the provincial city that suffocated Joyce into a place almost as cosmopolitan as the Paris to which he fled. And the locals are a hell of a lot more fun!

Now that the economy is very much on the upswing, Dublin citizens can cast a cool eye over the last 20 crazy years. Some argue that the boomtown transformation of their heretofore-tranquil city has permanently affected its spirit and character. These skeptics (skepticism long being a favorite pastime in the capital city) fear the possibility that the tattered old lady on the Liffey has become a little less unique, a little more like everywhere else. Yet, the fundamentals—the Georgian elegance of Merrion Square, the Norman drama of Christ Church Cathedral, the foamy pint at an atmospheric pub—are still on hand to gratify. And most of all, there are the locals themselves: the nod and grin when you catch their eye on the street, the eagerness to hear half your life story before they tell you all of theirs, and their paradoxically dark but warm sense of humor.

Planning

When to Go

When is it best—and worst—to pay a call on the Irish capital? The summer offers a real lift, as the natives spill out of the pubs into the slew of sidewalk cafés and open-air restaurants. The week around St. Patrick's Day (March 17) is, naturally, a nonstop festival of parades, cultural happenings, and "hooleys" (long nights of partying) throughout the city. Christmas in Dublin seems to last a month, and the city's old-style illuminations match the genteel, warm mood of the locals. The newly launched New Year's Festival Dublin (NYF) is an organized three days of music, spectacle, and *craic* to see in the first day of the new year. The downside quickly follows, however, for January and February are damp hangover months, but there are plenty of hotel and restaurant bargains to be found. A warm sweater is a must year-round, as even summer nights can occasionally get chilly. Dublin gets its share of rain (though a lot less than other parts of Ireland), so an umbrella is a good investment—and best to make it a strong one, as the winds show no mercy to cheaper models.

Planning Your Time

IF YOU HAVE ONE DAY

Begin with Trinity College—the oldest seat of Irish learning and home to the Old Library, the staggering Long Room, and Ireland's greatest art treasure, the *Book of Kells,* one of the world's most famous illuminated manuscripts. Leave the campus and take a stroll along Grafton Street, Dublin's busiest shopping street and the pedestrian spine of the Southside. Take in a few shops and entertaining buskers on the street; at the end of Grafton you will find yourself at the northwest corner of St. Stephen's Green, Dublin's favorite relaxation spot. Head over to the northeast corner of the park to find ground zero for the city's cultural institutions. Here, surrounding the four points of Leinster House (built by the earl of Kildare, Ireland's first patron of Palladianism), are the National Museum, replete with artifacts and exhibits dating from prehistoric times; the National Gallery of Ireland (don't miss the Irish collection and Caravaggio's *The Taking of Christ*); the National Library; and the Natural History Museum.

For a lovely lunch, head back to St. Stephen's Green and the Victorian-era Shelbourne—the lobby salons glow with Waterford chandeliers and blazing fireplaces. From St. Stephen's Green walk west for 10 minutes to pay your respects to "St. Paddy" (St. Patrick's Cathedral).

Dublin Past and Present

Early Days

Until AD 500, Dublin was little more than a crossroads for four of the main thoroughfares that traversed the country. It had two names: Baile Átha Cliath, meaning Town of the Hurdled Ford, bestowed by Celtic traders in the 2nd century AD; and Dubhlinn, or "dark pool," after a body of water believed to have been where Dublin Castle now stands.

In 837, Norsemen carried out the first invasion of Dublin, to be followed by new waves of warriors staking their claim to the city—from the 12th-century Anglo-Normans to Oliver Cromwell in 1651.

Not until the 18th century did Dublin reach a golden age, when the patronage of wealthy nobles turned the city into one of Europe's most prepossessing capitals. But the era of "the glorious eighteenth" was short-lived; in 1800, the Act of Union brought Ireland and Britain together into the United Kingdom, and power moved to London.

Political Turmoil

The 19th century proved to be a time of political turmoil, although Daniel O'Connell, the first Catholic lord mayor of Dublin, won early success with the introduction of Catholic Emancipation in 1829.

The city entered another period of upheaval in the first decades of the 20th century, marked by the Easter Rising of 1916. A war for independence from Britain began in 1919, followed by establishment of the Irish Free State in December 1921 and subsequent civil war. In its aftermath Dublin entered an era of political and cultural conservatism, which continued until the late 1970s. A major turning point occurred in 1973, when Ireland joined the European Economic Community.

Boom and Bust

The 1990s and first years of the 21st century were truly Ireland's boom time, set in motion to a great extent by the country's participation in the European Union. When Ireland approved the new EU treaty in 1992, it was one of the poorest member nations, qualifying it for grants of all kinds.

Ireland quickly transformed itself into the economic envy of the world, propelled by massive investment from multinational corporations. In 2000 the government announced that Ireland was the world's largest exporter of software. But the later years of the Tiger were fueled by a monumental property bubble, and Dublin, like most of the world, suddenly woke up with one doozy of an economic hangover.

Dublin Today

Less than a decade after the bottom fell out of its economy, Ireland is again Europe's fastest growing economy and the natives hope they have learned their lesson. More than a third of the Irish Republic's 4.8 million people live in Dublin and its suburbs. It's a city of young people, astonishingly so: students from all over Ireland—and the world—attend Trinity College and the city's dozen other universities.

If, instead, the Dublin of artists and poets is more your speed, hop a double-decker bus and head north of the Liffey to the Dublin Writers Museum. End the day with a performance at the nearby Gate Theatre, another Georgian stunner, or spend the evening exploring the cobbled streets and the many cafés and shops of Dublin's bohemian quarter, the compact Temple Bar area, back on the south bank of the Liffey.

IF YOU HAVE THREE DAYS

Dedicate your second day to the areas north and west of the city center. In the morning, cross the Liffey via O'Connell Bridge and walk up O'Connell Street, the city's widest thoroughfare, stopping to visit the General Post Office—the besieged headquarters of the 1916 rebels—on your way to the Dublin Writers Museum (if you didn't have a chance to visit on your first day) and the Dublin City Gallery, the Hugh Lane. Be sure to join the thousands of Dubliners strolling down Henry, Moore, and Mary Streets, the Northside's pedestrian shopping area. In the afternoon, head back to the Liffey for a quayside walk by Dublin's most imposing structure, the Custom House; then head west to the Guinness Brewery and Storehouse. Hop a bus or catch a cab back into the city for a blowout dinner at Restaurant Patrick Guilbaud at the Merrion Hotel. Spend the evening on a literary pub crawl to see where the likes of Beckett and Behan held court, perhaps joining a special guided tour. On the third day tour the northern and western outskirts of Dublin from Glasnevin Cemetery and the National Botanic Gardens across to the majestic Phoenix Park and the quaint fishing village of Howth. Back in the city, have tea at Bewley's and catch a musical performance at the Olympia Theatre or a play at the Abbey Theatre.

IF YOU HAVE FIVE DAYS

Follow the two itineraries above and then head west to start your fourth day at Dublin's dawn—a living history of Dublin can be seen at medieval Dublinia, across the street from ancient Christ Church Cathedral, whose underground crypt is Dublin's oldest structure. Head north, jumping across the Liffey to the Four Courts, James Gandon's Georgian masterpiece and until recently the home of the Irish judiciary. Recross the river to the Southside and go west again to visit the Royal Hospital Kilmainham, which houses the Irish Museum of Modern Art, and Kilmainham Gaol, where the leaders of the Easter Rising were executed following their capture. Return via Dublin Castle—residence of British power in Ireland for nearly 800 years, and star of Neil Jordan's film *Michael Collins*—and then move on to the Chester Beatty Library, which connoisseurs prize because of its Chinese and Turkish treasures. On your fifth and final day, explore the northern suburbs of Dublin, home to two architectural jewels: picturesque Malahide Castle and Newbridge House, famed for its gorgeous 18th-century salons. The beautiful, buzzing coastal town of Howth is also worth a visit. Back in Dublin, have a final farewell dinner, hopefully at your "local": your favorite neighborhood pub.

Getting Here and Around

AIR TRAVEL

Dublin Airport, 10 km (6 miles) north of the city center, serves international and domestic flights.

AIRPORT CONTACTS Dublin Airport.
☎ 01/814–1111 ⊕ www.dublinairport.com.

AIRPORT TRANSFERS: BUSES AND TAXIS

Dublin Bus operates the Airlink shuttle service between Dublin Airport and the city center, with departures outside the arrivals gateway. Journey time from the airport to the city center is normally 30 minutes, but it may be longer in heavy traffic. The single fare is €7 and round-trip is €12; pay the driver inside the bus or purchase a one-day bus pass for the same price. If you have time, you can save money by taking a regular bus for €3.30. Aircoach's comfortable coaches run from the airport to the city center 24 hours a day for €7 one-way and €12 round-trip. ■TIP→ **Book airport buses in advance for discounts.** The service stops at major hotels. A taxi is a quicker alternative than the bus to get from the airport to Dublin center. A line of taxis waits by the arrivals gateway; the fare for the 30-minute journey to any of the main city-center hotels is about €23 to €26 plus tip (tips don't have to be large). Ask about the fare before leaving the airport.

BOAT AND FERRY TRAVEL

Irish Ferries runs a regular high-speed car and passenger service into Dublin port from Holyhead in Wales. The crossing takes one hour and 50 minutes on the faster *Dublin Swift* and three hours and 15 minutes on the bigger cruise ships. Stena Line has services to Dublin port from Holyhead (3½ hours). Prices and departure times vary according to season, so call to confirm. In summer, reservations are strongly recommended; book online or through a travel agent. Dozens of taxis wait to take you into town or you can take a bus to the city center.

CONTACTS Irish Ferries. ⊠ *Box 19, Alexandra Rd., Ferryport, Dublin North* ☎ *0818/300–400, 01/607–5700* ⊕ *www. irishferries.com.* **Stena Line.** ⊠ *Dublin Port, Dublin South* ☎ *01/204–7777* ⊕ *www.stenaline.ie.*

BUS TRAVEL

Busáras, just behind the Custom House on the Northside, is Dublin's main station for buses to and from the city. Dublin Bus runs the city's regular buses. Bus Éireann is the main intercity bus company, with service throughout the country. Aircoach has direct bus connections to Cork and Belfast, and is usually a bit cheaper than Bus Éireann.

In town, there's an extensive network of buses, most of which are yellow and blue double-deckers.

Some bus services run on cross-city routes but most buses start in the city center.

Buses to the north of the city begin in the Lower Abbey Street–Parnell Street area, while those to the west begin in Middle Abbey Street and in the Aston Quay area. Routes to the southern suburbs begin at Eden Quay and in the College Street area. Several buses link to the DART and LUAS stations, and another regular bus route connects the two main provincial railway stations, Connolly and Heuston. If the destination board indicates "an lár," that means that the bus is going to the city center.

BUS FARES AND SCHEDULES

In the city, fares begin at €2.15 and are paid to the driver, who will accept cash but can't give any change. Ticket buying and the city's heavy traffic can slow service considerably. Most bus lines run until 11:30 at night, but some Nitelink buses run Friday to Saturday until 4:30 am on some major routes; the fare is €6.60. You can save a lot of money by buying a Leap Card, which works for the bus, DART, and LUAS (trams). You can even order your Leap Card online (⊕ *www.leapcard.ie*) before coming to Ireland. Otherwise you can get a card at shops throughout the city.

CONTACTS Aircoach. ☎ *01/844–7118* ⊕ *www.aircoach.ie.* **Bus Éireann.** ☎ *01/836–6111* ⊕ *www.buseireann. ie.* **Busáras.** ⊠ *Store St., Dublin North* ☎ *01/836–6111.* **Dublin Bus.** ⊠ *59 Upper O'Connell St., Dublin North* ☎ *01/873– 4222* ⊕ *www.dublinbus.ie.*

CAR TRAVEL

Renting a car in Dublin is very expensive, with high rates and a 13.5% local tax. Gasoline is also expensive by U.S. standards, at around €1.30 a liter. Peak-period car-rental rates begin at around €220 a week for the smallest stick models, like a Ford Fiesta. Dublin has many car-rental companies, and it pays to shop around. A dozen car-rental companies have desks at Dublin Airport; all the main national and international firms also have branches in the city center.

Traffic in Ireland has increased exponentially in the last few years, and nowhere has the impact been felt more than in Dublin, where the city's complicated one-way streets are congested not only during the morning and evening rush hours but also often during much of the day. If possible, avoid driving a car except to get in and out of the city (and be sure to ask your hotel or guesthouse for clear directions to get you out of town).

TAXI TRAVEL

There are taxi stands beside the central bus station, and at train stations, O'Connell Bridge, St. Stephen's Green, College Green, and near major hotels; the Dublin telephone directory has a complete list. The initial charge is €3.80 (€4 after 8 pm and on Sunday), with an additional charge of about €1.14 (€1.45 after 8 pm and on Sunday) per kilometer thereafter. The fare is displayed on a meter (make sure it's on). You may, instead, want to phone a taxi company and ask for a cab to meet you at your hotel, but this may cost up to €2 extra. There is no charge for luggage. Uber is not widely available in Dublin, but Mytaxi (⊕ www.mytaxi.com) and Lynx (⊕ www.lynx.ie) are two online services used by a lot of licensed Dublin taxi drivers and hackney cabs.

Hackney cabs, which also operate in the city, have neither roof signs nor meters and will sometimes respond to hotels' requests for a cab.

Although the taxi fleet in Dublin is large, the cabs are nonstandard, and some cars are neither spacious nor in pristine condition. NRC Taxis has a reliable track record. Global Taxis (☎ 01/872–7272) is one of the city's biggest but also the busiest. SCR Taxis has some of the friendliest drivers.

CONTACTS NRC Taxies. ☎ 01/677–2222 ⊕ www.nrc.ie. **SCR Taxis.** ☎ 01/473–1166.

TRAIN AND TRAM TRAVEL

As a delightfully compact city, Dublin does not have—or need—a subway system. But its LUAS trams and DART electric railway are great ways to get around the city center and beyond. The DART (Dublin Area Rapid Transit) connects Dublin with the fishing village of Howth to the north and the seaside resort of Bray to the south on a fast, efficient, superscenic train line that hugs the coastline, providing one spectacular view after another. But this line also runs through the center city with three convenient stations and then continues to such seaside destinations as Dun Laoghaire, Dalkey, and Bray.

As for the LUAS tram service, its two lines are connected and run right through the heart of the city, facilitating easy access to sights like the Guinness Storehouse (James Street stop), O'Connell Street (the Northside Abbey Street stop), and St. Stephen's Green.

Tickets can be bought at stations, but it's also possible to buy weekly rail tickets, as well as weekly or monthly rail-and-bus tickets, from the Irish Rail Travel Centre. Leap Cards work on the buses, DART, and LUAS.

CONTACTS Connolly Station. ✉ Amiens St., Dublin North. **DART.** ☎ 01/836–6222 ⊕ www.irishrail.ie/dart. **Heuston Station.** ✉ End of Victoria Quay, Dublin West. **Irish Rail–Iarnod Éireann.** ☎ 01/836–6222 ⊕ www.irishrail.ie. **LUAS.** ☎ 1800/300–604 ⊕ www.luas.ie. **Pearse Station.** ✉ Westland Row, Dublin South.

TRAIN AND TRAM FARES AND SCHEDULES

DART service starts at 6:10 am and runs until 11:55 pm; at peak periods—8 to 9:30 am and 5 to 7 pm—trains arrive every five minutes. At other times of the day, the intervals between trains are 15 to 25 minutes. Individual fares begin at €2.25 and range up to €6.20 one-way. You'll pay a heavy penalty for traveling the DART without a ticket. LUAS trams run from 5:30 am until 12:43 am Monday to Saturday and 7 am until 11:30 pm on Sunday. They come every 7 to 10 minutes at peak times and every 15 to 20 minutes after that. Fares range from €2.10 to €3.20 according to the number of zones traveled. Once again, using a Leap card will save you a lot of money.

TRAINS TO AND FROM DUBLIN

Irish Rail (Iarnród Éireann) runs intercity trains connecting Dublin with the rest of Ireland. Connolly Station provides train service to and from the east coast, Belfast, the north (with stops in Malahide, Skerries, and Drogheda), the northwest, and some destinations to the south, such as Wicklow. Heuston Station is the place for trains to and from the south and west including Galway, Limerick, and Cork. Trains also run from here to Kildare Town, Newbridge, and other west-of-Dublin stops.

Hotels

Despite a flurry of new construction, Dublin hotel prices remain in line with the best hotels of any major European or North American city. Service charges range from 15% in expensive hotels to zero in moderate and inexpensive ones. Be sure to inquire when you make reservations.

As a general rule of thumb, lodgings on the north side of the River Liffey tend to be more affordable than those on the south. Bed-and-breakfasts charge as little as €50 a night per person, but they tend to be in suburban areas—generally a 15-minute bus ride from the center of the city. This is not in itself a great drawback, and savings can be significant. Many hotels have a weekend, or "B&B," rate

that's often 15% to 25% cheaper than the ordinary rate; some hotels also have a midweek special that provides discounts of up to 25%. *Hotel reviews have been shortened. For full information, visit Fodors.com.*

Restaurants

With the Irish food revolution long over and won, Dublin now has a city full of fabulous, hip, and suavely sophisticated restaurants. The rapidly growing economy has seen a new cohort of upstart, adventurous eateries crop up alongside award-winning Euro-toques and their sous chefs, who continue to come up with new and glorious ways to abuse your waistline. Instead of just spuds-glorious-spuds, you'll find delicious new entries to New Irish cuisine like roast scallops with spiced pork belly and cauliflower au gratin topped with a daring caper-and-raisin sauce or sautéed rabbit loin with Clonakilty black pudding. Okay, there's still a good chance spuds will appear on your menu—and most likely offered in several different ways.

Dubliners dine later than the rest of Ireland. They stay up later, too, and reservations are usually not booked before 6:30 or 7 pm and up to around 10 pm. Lunch is generally served from 12:30 to 2:30 pm. Pubs often serve food through the day—until 8:30 or 9 pm. Most pubs are family-friendly and welcome children until 7 pm, and the quality of the cuisine they offer is a different world from what it was even five years ago. The Irish are an informal bunch, so smart-casual dress is typical. *Restaurant reviews have been shortened. For full information, visit Fodors.com.*

What It Costs in Euros			
$	$$	$$$	$$$$
RESTAURANTS			
under €19	€19–€24	€25–€32	over €32
HOTELS			
under €140	€140–€200	€201–€270	over €270

Tours

Dublin is a walker's city, and it's a city full of storytellers. Put two and two together, and it's little surprise that Dublin is a particularly good place for guided walking tours.

BUS TOURS
Dublin Bus
BUS TOURS | Three- and four-hour tours of the north and south coastlines take in sights such as the James Joyce Tower and the Casino at Marino. The one-hour city tour takes in Trinity College, the Royal Hospital Kilmainham, Phoenix Park, and other city-center sights. The one-hour city tour, with hourly departures, allows you to hop on and off at any of the main stops. Tickets are available from the driver or Dublin Bus. There's also a continuous, guided, open-top bus tour, which allows you to hop on and off the bus as often as you wish and visit some 23 sights along its route. The company also goes to Glendalough on a day trip, and conducts a north-city coastal tour, going to Howth, and a south-city tour, traveling as far as Enniskerry. ☎ 01/873–4222 ⊕ www.dublinsightseeing.ie ✉ From €20.

Love Ireland
BUS TOURS | City-center tours cover the main Dublin itineraries. ☎ 01/898–0700 ⊕ www.loveireland.com ✉ From €22.

Viking Splash Tours
SPECIAL-INTEREST | This is a big hit with kids. The amphibious ex–U.S. military vehicle tours the city center before launching onto the water by the IFSC (International Financial Service Center, near the Custom House). Kids get a helmet to wear and love terrifying native pedestrians with the "Viking roar." It runs year-round (less frequently from November to January). ☎ 01/707–6000 ⊕ www.vikingsplash.com ✉ From €20.

PUB AND MUSICAL TOURS
Dublin Discover Ireland Centre (⇨ see Visitor Information below) has a booklet on its self-guided Rock 'n' Stroll trail, which covers 16 sights with associations to such performers as Bob Geldof, Christy Moore, Sinéad O'Connor, and U2. Most of the sights are in the city center and Temple Bar.

Dublin Literary Pub Crawl
SPECIAL-INTEREST | Loveable rogue Colm Quilligan arranges a highly enjoyable evening Dublin Literary Pub Crawl, where "brain cells are replaced as quickly as they are drowned." ☎ 01/670–5602 ⊕ www.dublinpubcrawl.com ✉ From €14.

Traditional Musical Pub Crawl
SPECIAL-INTEREST | Led by two professional musicians who perform songs and tell the story of Irish music, the tour is given April through October, daily at 7:30 pm, and from Thursday to Saturday, at 7:30 pm, the rest of the year. It begins at the Oliver St. John Gogarty and moves on to other famous Temple Bar pubs. ✉ 20 Lower Stephens St., Dublin South ☎ 01/478–0191 ⊕ www.discoverdublin.ie ✉ From €16.

WALKING TOURS
Historical Walking Tours of Dublin
WALKING TOURS | Run by Trinity College history graduate students, these are excellent two-hour introductions to the city. The Tourism Ireland–approved tours take place from May to September, starting at the front gate of Trinity College, daily at 11 am and 3 pm, with an extra tour on weekends at noon.

These tours are also available October and April daily at 11 am and November to March, Friday through Sunday at 11 am. ☎ 087/688–9412 ⊕ www.historicaltours.ie ✉ From €14.

1916 Rebellion Walking Tour

WALKING TOURS | This exciting walk outlines the key areas and events of the violent Dublin rebellion that began Ireland's march to independence. The guides are passionately political and the two-hour tour never flags. They meet at the International Bar on Wicklow Street and operate March through October, Monday to Saturday at 11:30 am and Sunday at 1 pm. In February and November tours run Friday to Sunday. ☎ 086/858–3847 ⊕ www.1916rising.com ✉ From €15.

Trinity Tours

WALKING TOURS | This company organizes walks of the Trinity College campus daily from February to early December. The half-hour tour includes the *Book of Kells* exhibit; tours start at the college's main gate every 40 minutes from 10:15 am. There are generally nine tours a day. ⊕ www.tcd.ie/visitors/tours ✉ From €15.

Visitor Information

The main Fáilte Ireland tourism center (known as Visit Dublin) is on Suffolk Street and is open July and August, Monday–Saturday 9–7, Sunday 10:30–3, and September to June, Monday–Saturday 9–5:30, Sunday 10:30–3. There is a smaller Northside branch on O'Connell Street that is open Monday–Saturday 9–5.

CONTACTS Dublin Discover Ireland Centre O'Connell Street. ✉ 14 Upper O'Connell St., Dublin North ☎ 01/605–7700, 1850/230–330 ⊕ www.visitdublin.com. **Visit Dublin.** ✉ 25 Suffolk St. off Grafton St., Dublin South ☎ 1850/230–330 ⊕ www.visitdublin.com.

DUBLIN PASS

Like many tourist capitals around the world, Dublin now features a special pass to help travelers save on admission prices. In conjunction with Fáilte Ireland (Suffolk Street office and at many other Irish tourist offices throughout Ireland), the Dublin Pass is issued for one, two, three, or five days, and allows free—or, rather, reduced (the cards do cost something)—admission to 30 sights, including the Guinness Brewery, the Dublin Zoo, the Dublin Writers Museum, and Christ Church Cathedral. It also includes an airport transfer. Prices are €62 for one day, €83 for two days, €92 for three days, and €128 for five days; children's prices are much lower (only €33 for one day). You can buy your card online and have it waiting for you at one of Dublin's tourist information offices when you arrive. Another plus: you can jump to the head of any line at participating museums and sights. Get your passes online at ⊕ www.dublinpass.ie.

Southside

The River Liffey provides useful orientation, flowing as it does through the direct middle of Dublin. If you ask a native Dubliner for directions—from under an umbrella, as it will probably be raining in the approved Irish manner—he or she will most likely reply in terms of "up" or "down," meaning up and away from the river, or down and toward it. Until recently, Dublin's center of gravity was O'Connell Bridge, a diplomatic landmark in that it avoided locating the center either north or south of the river—strong local loyalties still prevailed among "Northsiders" and "Southsiders," and neither group would ever accept that the city's center lay elsewhere than on their own side. The 20th century, however, saw diplomacy fall by the wayside—Dublin's heart now beats loudest southward across the Liffey, due in part to a large-scale refurbishment and pedestrianization of Grafton Street, which made this already upscale shopping address the main street on which to shop, stop, and be seen. At the top of Grafton Street is the city's most famous and recognizable landmark, Trinity College; at the foot of it is Dublin's most popular strolling retreat, St. Stephen's Green, a 22-acre landscaped park with flowers, lakes, bridges, and Dubliners enjoying their leisure time.

 ## Sights

Bank of Ireland

BANK | Across the street from the west facade of Trinity College stands one of Dublin's most striking buildings, formerly the original home of Irish Parliament. A pedimented portico fronted by six massive Corinthian columns dominates the grand facade, which follows the curve of Westmoreland Street as it meets College Green, once a Viking meeting place and burial ground. Inside, stucco rosettes adorn the coffered ceiling in the pastel-hue, colonnaded, clerestoried main banking hall, at one time the Court of Requests, where citizens' petitions were heard. Just down the hall is the original House of Lords, with an oak-panel nave, a 1,233-drop Waterford glass chandelier, and tapestries depicting the Battle of the Boyne and the Siege of Derry; ask a guard to show you in. Visitors are welcome during normal banking hours. The bank has long-term plans to build a heritage center. ✉ *2 College Green, Dublin South* ☎ *01/677–6801* ⊕ *www.visitdublin. com* ✆ *Free* ☉ *Closed weekends.*

The Douglas Hyde Gallery of Modern Art

MUSEUM | Trinity College's starkly modern Arts and Social Sciences Building, with an entrance on Nassau Street, houses the Douglas Hyde Gallery, which concentrates on contemporary art exhibitions and has its own bookstore. Also in the building, down some steps from the gallery, is a snack bar serving coffee, tea, and sandwiches, where students willing to chat about life in the old college frequently gather. ✉ *Nassau St., Dublin South* ☎ *01/896–1116* ⊕ *www.douglashydegallery.com* ✆ *Free* ☉ *Closed Sun.*

George's Street Arcade

MARKET | This Victorian covered market fills the block between Drury Street and South Great George's Street. Around two dozen stalls sell books, prints, clothing (new and secondhand), local foodstuffs, and trinkets. ✉ *S. Great George's St., Dublin South* ⊕ *www.georgesstreetarcade.com.*

Grafton Street

NEIGHBORHOOD | It's no more than 200 yards long and about 20 feet wide, but Grafton Street, open only to pedestrians, can claim to be the most humming street in the city, if not in all of Ireland. It's one of Dublin's vital spines: the most direct route between the front door of Trinity College and St. Stephen's Green, and the city's premier shopping street, with Dublin's most distinguished department store, Brown Thomas, as well as tried and trusted Marks & Spencer. Grafton Street and the smaller alleyways that radiate off it offer independent stores, a dozen or so colorful flower sellers, and some of the Southside's most popular watering holes. In summer, buskers from all over the world line both sides of the street, pouring out the sounds of drum, whistle, pipe, and string.

★ Iveagh Gardens

CITY PARK | Dublin's best-kept secret has to be this 1865 Ninian Niven–designed "English Landscape" walled garden that shockingly few natives seem to even know about. The architect showed off his dramatic flair in the rustic grotto and cascade, the sunken panels of lawn with their fountains, the blooming rosarium, and wonderful little wooded areas. This public park has no playground, but kids really love the "secret garden" feel to the place and the fact that the waterfall

G H I

Surface Tram
Spencer Dock
The Point

Dublin Southside and Georgian Dublin

Sir John Rogerson's Quay

Hanover Quay

Pearse Street

Bridge St.

South Dock Street

Gordon Street

Barrow Street

South Lotts Road

Bath Avenue

Lansdowne Park

Lansdowne Road

Lansdowne Road

Baggot Lane

Pembroke Road

Haddington Rd.

Mary's Road

Elgin Road

Raglan Road

Elgin Road

Clyde Road

Pembroke Park

Herbert Park

Herbert Park

Shelbourne Road

Anglesea Road

Merrion Road

Morehampton Road

0   250 m
0   1,000 ft

Sights ▼

1	Bank of Ireland	B2
2	The Douglas Hyde Gallery of Modern Art	C3
3	George's Street Arcade	B3
4	Government Buildings	D4
5	Grafton Street	B3
6	Irish Jewish Museum	A7
7	Iveagh Gardens	B5
8	Little Museum of Dublin	C4
9	Merrion Square	E4
10	National Gallery of Ireland	D3
11	National Library	D3
12	National Museum of Archaeology	C4
13	National Museum of Natural History	D4
14	Neary's Pub	B4
15	The Old Library and the Book of Kells	C2
16	Powerscourt Townhouse Centre	B3
17	Royal Hibernian Academy	D5
18	Royal Irish Academy	E3
19	Sandymount Strand	I7
20	The Shelbourne Hotel	C4
21	St Ann's Church	C3
22	St Stephen's Green	C4
23	Trinity College Dublin	D2

Restaurants ▼

1	Busyfeet & Coco Café	B3
2	Cafe Joly	D3
3	Cake Café	A6
4	Chai-Yo	E5
5	Dax	D5
6	Dunne and Crescenzi	C3
7	Ely Winebar	D4
8	Fade Street Social	B3
9	Fallon & Byrne	B3
10	Forest Avenue	D7
11	The French Paradox	I7
12	The Good World	A3
13	The Green Hen	B3
14	The Greenhouse	C4
15	La Maison	B3
16	L'Gueuleton	A3
17	One Pico	C4
18	The Pepper Pot	B3
19	Restaurant Patrick Guilbaud	D4
20	Roly's Bistro	H7
21	Shanahan's on the Green	B4
22	Unicorn	D4
23	Wagamama	B4
24	Yamamori Noodles	A3

Hotels ▼

1	Ariel Guest House	I5
2	Brooks Hotel	B3
3	Central Hotel	A3
4	Clayton Hotel Burlington Road	E7
5	Conrad Dublin International	C5
6	Dawson Hotel and Spa	C4
7	The Dean	B5
8	The Devlin	E9
9	Dylan Hotel	F6
10	Grafton Guest House	A3
11	Herbert Park Hotel	I8
12	InterContinental Dublin	I7
13	Iveagh Garden Hotel	B5
14	Kellys Hotel	A3
15	Kilronan House Hotel	C6
16	The Marker	G2
17	The Merrion Hotel	D4
18	Number 31	D6
19	Pembroke Townhouse	G6
20	Premier Suites Dublin	C5
21	Schoolhouse Hotel	G4
22	The Shelbourne Dublin, Renaissance	C4
23	Westbury Hotel Dublin	B3
24	The Westin Dublin	C2

Dublin Quick Bites

Bewley's Oriental Café. The grand-daddy of the capital's cafés, and an essential part of the character of Grafton Street, Bewley's Oriental Café has served coffee and sticky buns to Dubliners since its founding by the Quakers in 1840. A major renovation has brought back some of the old grandeur associated with Bewley's, including the exotic picture wallpaper and trademark stained-glass windows, designed by the distinguished early-20th-century artist Harry Clarke. ⊠ *78/79 Grafton St., Dublin South* ☎ *01/672–7720* ⊕ *bewleys.com/bewleys-grafton-street-cafe.*

Long Hall Pub. With its mahogany bar, mirrors, and plasterwork ceilings, the Long Hall Pub is one of Dublin's most ornate traditional taverns. It's a good place to take a break for a cup of tea or a cheeky daytime pint of Guinness. ⊠ *51 S. Great George's St., Dublin South* ☎ *01/475–1590* ⊟ *No credit cards.*

has rocks from every one of Ireland's 32 counties. Restoration of the gardens began in 1995 and has left the city with a Victorian treasure complete with a perfect box hedge and a working sundial. Access is from Hatch Street. ⊠ *Clonmel St., Dublin South* ☎ *01/475–7816* ⊕ *www.iveaghgardens.ie* ⊠ *Free.*

★ Little Museum of Dublin
MUSEUM | This clever, eclectic little museum, one of Dublin's best, sets out to tell the history of Dublin in the last hundred years through changing exhibitions of the objects and stories of its citizens. The collection includes art, photography, ads, letters, objects, and ephemera relating to life in the capital since 1900. Housed in the first floor of a Georgian building, it even has an interesting section on U2 and how the city shaped them. There's a slightly informal, hodgepodge feel to the place, but that just adds to the pleasure of strolling around and taking it all in. The museum has regular, free guided tours for visitors and holds fascinating talks. ⊠ *15 Stephen's Green, Dublin South* ☎ *01/661–0000* ⊕ *www.littlemuseum.ie* ⊠ *€10.*

Neary's Pub
RESTAURANT—SIGHT | The exotic, Victorian-style interiors here were once haunted by Dublin's literary set, most notably the master bar raconteur Brendan Behan. ⊠ *1 Chatham St., Dublin South* ☎ *01/677–7371.*

★ The Old Library and the *Book of Kells*
LIBRARY | Home to Ireland's largest collection of books and manuscripts, the Old Library's principal treasure is the *Book of Kells,* generally considered to be the most striking manuscript ever produced in the Anglo-Saxon world and one of the great masterpieces of early Christian art. The book, which dates to the 9th century, was re-bound in four volumes in 1953, two of which are usually displayed at a time, so you typically see no more than four original pages. However, such is the incredible workmanship of this illuminated version of the Gospels that one folio alone is worth the entirety of many other painted manuscripts. The most famous page shows the "XPI" monogram (symbol of Christ), but if this page is not on display, you can still see a replica of it, as well as many other lavishly illustrated pages, in the library's exhibition *Turning Darkness into*

Light—dedicated to the history, artistry, and conservation of the book—through which you must pass to see the originals.

Because of the fame and beauty of the *Book of Kells,* it's all too easy to overlook the other treasures in the library. Highlights include the spectacular Long Room, the narrow main room of the library and home to approximately 200,000 of the 3 million volumes in Trinity's collection, including one of the remaining copies of the 1916 Proclamation of the Irish Republic; a grand series of marble busts, of which the most famous is Roubiliac's depiction of Jonathan Swift; the carved Royal Arms of Queen Elizabeth I, the only surviving relic of the original college buildings; a beautiful early Irish harp; the *Book of Armagh,* a 9th-century copy of the New Testament that also contains St. Patrick's Confession; and the legendary *Book of Durrow,* a 7th-century Gospel book from County Offaly. You may have to wait in line to enter the library if you don't get here early in the day, and tickets are less expensive off-peak ⊠ *Front Sq., Trinity College, Dublin South* ☎ *01/896–2320* ⊕ *www.tcd.ie/visitors/book-of-kells* ⊠ *From €11, includes Book of Kells.*

Powerscourt Townhouse Centre

STORE/MALL | One of the finest 18th-century mansions in Dublin, the Powerscourt Townhouse Centre has magnificent architecture, quality shopping, and an Irish dancing museum and show. Designed by Robert Mack in 1771, it's a massive edifice that towers over the little street it sits on (note the top story, framed by large volutes, which was intended as an observatory). Inside, there are rococo salons designed by James McCullagh, splendid examples of plasterwork in the Adamesque style, and a shopping atrium filled with high-quality Irish crafts shops, installed in and around the covered courtyard. The mall exit leads to St. Teresa's Carmelite Church and Johnson's Court. Beside the church, a pedestrian lane leads onto Grafton Street. There's also a small museum and performance space that often features Irish dance. Check the website for details. ⊠ *59 S. William St., Dublin South* ☎ *01/611–1060* ⊕ *www. powerscourtcentre.com.*

Royal Irish Academy

LIBRARY | The country's leading learned society houses important documents in its 18th-century library, including a large collection of ancient Irish manuscripts, such as the 11th- to 12th-century *Book of the Dun Cow,* and the library of the 18th-century poet Thomas Moore. ⊠ *19 Dawson St., Dublin South* ☎ *01/676–2570* ⊕ *www.ria.ie* ⊠ *Free* ☉ *Closed weekends.*

Sandymount Strand

BEACH—SIGHT | South of the city center, a few blocks west of the Sydney Parade DART station, Sandymount Strand stretches for 5 km (3 miles) from Ringsend to Booterstown. It was cherished by James Joyce and his beloved Nora Barnacle from Galway, and it figures as one of the settings in *Ulysses;* it's also a popular spot with strolling Dubliners today. (The beach is "at the lacefringe of the tide," as Joyce put it.) When the tide recedes, the beach extends for 1½ km (1 mile) from the foreshore, but the tide sweeps in again very quickly. A sliver of a park lies between Strand Road and the beach, the water of which is not suitable for swimming. At the end of the strand there's a wonderful walk out along the south harbor wall to the Poolbeg Lighthouse, which has eye-popping views of Dublin Bay. ⊠ *Sandymount, Dublin South.*

The Shelbourne Hotel

HOTEL—SIGHT | The iconic, redbrick, white-wood-trim Shelbourne hotel commands "the best address in Dublin" from the north side of St. Stephen's Green, where it has stood since 1865. You don't have to stay to take advantage of the gorgeous location; stop in for afternoon tea in the very opulent Lord Mayor's Lounge, a true Dublin treat, and bask in the history, grandeur, and other tasty dining options available at Dublin's most iconic hotel. In 1921 the Irish Free State's constitution was drafted here, in a first-floor suite. Elizabeth Bowen wrote her novel *The Hotel* about this very place. ⊠ *27 St. Stephen's Green, Dublin South* ☎ *01/676–6471* ⊕ *www.marriott.co.uk.*

St. Ann's Church

RELIGIOUS SITE | A plain, neo-Romanesque granite exterior, built in 1868, belies the rich Georgian interior of this church, which Isaac Wills designed in 1720. Highlights of the interior include polished-wood balconies, ornate plasterwork, and shelving in the chancel dating from 1723—and still in use for organizing the distribution of food to the parish's poor. ⊠ *Dawson St., Dublin South* ☎ *01/676–7727* ⊕ *www.stann.dublin. anglican.org* ⊠ *Free* ☉ *Closed Sat.*

★ St. Stephen's Green

CITY PARK | Dubliners call it simply Stephen's Green, and green it is (year-round)—a verdant, 27-acre Southside square that was used for the public punishment of criminals until 1664. After a long period of decline, it became a private park in 1814—the first time in its history that it was closed to the public. Its fortunes changed again in 1880, when Sir Arthur Guinness paid for it to be laid out anew. Flower gardens, formal lawns, a Victorian bandstand, and an ornamental lake with lots of waterfowl are all within the park's borders, connected by paths guaranteeing that strolling here or just passing through will offer up unexpected delights (such as palm trees). Among the park's many statues are a memorial to W.B. Yeats and another to Joyce by Henry Moore. A large outdoor market springs up around the park at Christmastime. ⊠ *Southside, Dublin* ⊠ *Free.*

★ Trinity College Dublin

COLLEGE | Founded in 1592 by Queen Elizabeth I to "civilize" (Her Majesty's word) Dublin, Trinity is Ireland's oldest and most famous college. The memorably atmospheric campus has housed Jonathan Swift, Oscar Wilde, Bram Stoker, and Samuel Beckett. The college was founded on the site of the confiscated Priory of All Hallows. For centuries Trinity was the preserve of the Protestant Church; a free education was offered to Catholics—provided that they accepted the Protestant faith. Trinity's grounds cover 40 acres, and most buildings date from the 18th and early 19th centuries. On the right side of the cobblestone quadrangle of **Parliament Square** (commonly known as Front Square) is Sir William Chambers's theater, or Examination Hall, dating from the mid-1780s, which contains the college's most splendid Adamesque interior, designed by Michael Stapleton. The looming campanile, or bell tower, is the symbolic heart of the college; erected in 1853, it dominates the center of the square. ⊠ *Trinity College, Dublin South* ☎ *01/896–1000* ⊕ *www. tcd.ie.*

Restaurants

Busyfeet & Coco Café

$ | **CAFÉ** | One of the city center's best-situated spots for a bit of people-watching, this bustling, bohemian café emphasizes good, wholesome food. Organic ingredients play a prominent role on a menu that's laden with delicious salads and sandwiches. **Known for:** grilled goat-cheese salad; ideal location for people-watching; bohemian buzz. ⑤ *Average main: €9* ⊠ *41–42 S. William St., Dublin South* ☎ *01/671–9514* ▭ *No credit cards.*

★ Cake Café

$ | **CAFÉ** | At Michelle Darmody's dreamy little Cake Café local, organic, and seasonal are the words to live by, where you can chow down on simple savory and sweet delights, all made with a loving, homey touch. The plant-filled courtyard is also the perfect summer spot for a daytime glass of prosecco and small bites. **Known for:** pitch-perfect cakes; personal touches; slow-food philosophy.

Dublin's Gorgeous Georgians

"Extraordinary Dublin!" sigh art lovers and connoisseurs of the 18th century. It was during the glorious 18th that this duckling of a city was transformed into a preening swan, largely by the Georgian style of art and architecture that flowered between 1714 and 1820 during the reigns of the four English Georges.

Today Dublin remains in good part a sublimely Georgian city, thanks to enduring grace notes: the commodious and uniformly laid-out streets, the genteel town squares, the redbrick mansions accented with demilune (half-moon) fan windows. The great 18th-century showpieces are **Merrion, Fitzwilliam, Mountjoy**, and **Parnell Squares. Merrion Square East**, the longest Georgian street in town, reveals scenes of decorum, elegance, polish, and charm, all woven into a "tapestry of rosy brick and white enamel," to quote the 18th-century connoisseur Horace Walpole.

Setting off the facades are fanlighted doors (often lacquered in black, green, yellow, or red) and the celebrated "patent reveal" window trims—thin plaster linings painted white to catch the light. These half-moon fanlights— as iconic of the city as clock towers are of Zurich—are often in the Neoclassical style known as Adamesque (which was inspired by the designs of the great English architect Robert Adam).

Many facades appear severely plain, but don't be fooled: just behind their stately front doors are entry rooms and stairways aswirl with tinted rococo plasterwork, often the work of *stuccadores* (plasterers) from Italy (including the talented Lafranchini brothers). Magnificent **Newman**

House (✉ *85–86 St. Stephen's Green, Southside* ☎ *01/477–9810* ⊕ *www. visitdublin.com*) , one of the finest of Georgian houses, is currently closed to tours as it is transformed into a museum of literature.

The Palladian style—as the Georgian style was then called—began to reign supreme in domestic architecture in 1745, when the Croesus-rich Earl of Kildare returned from an Italian grand tour and built a gigantic Palladian palace called **Leinster House** in the seedy section of town.

"Where I go, fashion will follow," he declared, and indeed it did. By then, the Anglo-Irish elite had given the city London airs by building the **Parliament House** (now the Bank of Ireland), the **Royal Exchange** (now City Hall), the **Custom House**, and the **Four Courts** in the new style.

But this phase of high fashion came to an end with the Act of Union: according to historian Maurice Craig, "On the last stroke of midnight, December 31, 1800, the gaily caparisoned horses turned into mice, the coaches into pumpkins, the silks and brocades into rags, and Ireland was once again the Cinderella among the nations."

It was nearly 150 years before the spotlight shone once again on 18th-century Dublin. In recent decades, the conservation efforts of the **Irish Georgian Society** (✉ *74 Merrion Sq., Southside* ☎ *01/676–7053* ⊕ *www.igs.ie*) have done much to restore Dublin to its Georgian splendor. Thanks to its founders, the Hon. Desmond Guinness and his late wife, Mariga, many historic houses have been saved and preserved.

Trinity College's Front Square is paved with cobblestones and dotted with statues of its famous alumni, including Oliver Goldsmith and Samuel Beckett.

$ *Average main: €12* ✉ *The Daintree Bldg., Pleasants Pl., Dublin South* ☎ *01/478–9394* ⊕ *www.thecakecafe.ie* ⏰ *Closed Sun. No dinner.*

★ Dunne and Crescenzi

$ | ITALIAN | The unpretentious brilliance of this husband-and-wife restaurant and deli just off Nassau Street is what makes the classy little Italian joint so popular. The menu is extensive but simple: panini, a horde of antipasti, a few choice pasta specials, and some evening meat dishes and desserts. **Known for:** Italian wine cellar; killer antipasti; great for large groups. $ *Average main: €18* ✉ *14 S. Fredrick St., Dublin South* ☎ *01/677–3815* ⊕ *www. dunneandcrescenzi.com.*

Fade Street Social

$$$ | MODERN IRISH | Former Michelin-star celebrity chef Dylan McGrath has another hit on his hands with Fade Street Social, a cavernous tapas bar, restaurant, and pub all rolled into one. At 8,000 square feet, the place can seem a bit overwhelming, but if you want a busy, fun, all-in-one dining-and-drinking experience, this place is ideal. **Known for:** celebrity chef; brash, busy atmosphere; inventive tapas. $ *Average main: €30* ✉ *4 Fade St., Dublin South* ☎ *01/604–0066* ⊕ *www.fadestreetsocial.com.*

★ Fallon & Byrne

$$$ | FRENCH | This fresh, one-stop shop for everything organic and delicious in Dublin combines a huge deli with a cozy cellar wine bar and expansive second-floor French brasserie. Located on the top floor of a beautiful old telephone exchange building, the high-ceiling, light-filled dining room is always bustling. **Known for:** hearty brasserie menu; bustling city-center vibe; elegant dining room. $ *Average main: €27* ✉ *11–17 Exchequer St., Dublin South* ☎ *01/472–1010* ⊕ *www.fallonandbyrne.com.*

The Good World

$ | CHINESE | When Dublin's growing Chinese population wants a big, uptown night out, they come here. The surroundings are modest, with large round tables (ideal for groups) in a somewhat dark but comfortable room. **Known for:**

top dim sum; large group gatherings; authentic menu. $ *Average main: €17* ✉ *18 S. Great George's St., Dublin South* ☎ *01/677–5373* ⊕ *goodworldchineserestaurant.goldenpages.ie.*

The Green Hen

$$$ | FRENCH | It can be hard to re-create that classic bistro feel outside France, but this intimate spot at the heart of busy Dublin has managed to get the mix of bustle and tranquillity just right. A quick glance at the gilt-framed, mirrored menu reveals that this kitchen is all about rich, evocative French fare—two winners are the rib eye and the panfried bass. **Known for:** best confit in town; adventurous plats du jour; informal bistro vibe. $ *Average main: €25* ✉ *33 Exchequer St., Dublin South* ☎ *01/670–7238* ⊕ *www.thegreenhen.ie* ▭ *No credit cards.*

★ The Greenhouse

$$$$ | FRENCH | The elegant dining room of this Michelin-starred restaurant is a touch posh, with turquoise velvet seats and white tablecloths, but the food of one of Ireland's hottest and most creative chefs, County Clare man Mikael Viljanen, deserves its stage. The four-course, fixed-price menu is proud of its French influences, but constantly surprises with starters like a whipped foie gras topped with Granny Smith apple gel, walnut, and smoked eel. **Known for:** Michelin star; creative twists on French classics; luxurious lunches. $ *Average main: €45* ✉ *21 Dawson St., Dublin South* ☎ *01/676–7015* ⊕ *www.thegreenhouserestaurant.ie* ☺ *Closed Sun. and Mon.*

La Maison

$$$ | FRENCH | This Breton-inspired, unpretentious eatery has one of the most inviting and good-value menus in the city. The look is very much "casual bistro," a satisfying backdrop for starters like the beetroot risotto with winter truffles, and such mouthwatering mains as the loin of venison with red cabbage and celeriac paste. **Known for:** quality wine list; intimate atmosphere; irresistible chocolate

fondant. $ *Average main: €25* ✉ *15 Castle Market, Dublin South* ☎ *01/672–7258* ⊕ *www.lamaisondublin.com.*

L'Gueuleton

$$$ | FRENCH | This exceptional eatery just off George's Street lost a little of its intimacy when it expanded, but the crowds still come for authentic French food at a fair price. Start with 12 snails, fresh herbs, garlic, and pastis butter. **Known for:** decadent desserts; great people-watching; tip-top service. $ *Average main: €27* ✉ *1 Fade St., Dublin South* ☎ *01/675–3708* ⊕ *www.lgueuleton.com.*

★ One Pico

$$$$ | MODERN IRISH | Chef-owner Eamonn O'Reilly cuts quite a dash, but it's his sophisticated, daring, contemporary cuisine that tends to seduce visitors to his little restaurant tucked away in a quiet lane only a few minutes from Stephen's Green. As is usual with Dublin's luxe eateries, the fixed-price lunch and pretheater menus offer great value. **Known for:** gregarious chef-host; daring ingredient combinations; passion-fruit soufflé. $ *Average main: €35* ✉ *5–6 Molesworth Pl., off Schoolhouse La., Dublin South* ☎ *01/676–0300* ⊕ *www.onepico.com* ☺ *Closed Sun.*

The Pepper Pot

$ | CAFÉ | The hodgepodge collection of old tablecloths, cutlery, and cups creates a warm, family atmosphere in this sweet little café on the balcony level of the Powerscourt Town House Centre. Weary shoppers resuscitate with the simple menu, fresh-baked goods, TLC, and wonderful people-watching. **Known for:** homey vibe; best salads in the city; divine sponge cake. $ *Average main: €11* ✉ *Powerscourt Town Centre, 1st fl. balcony, S. William St., Dublin South* ☎ *01/707–1610* ⊕ *www.thepepperpot.ie* ▭ *No credit cards* ☺ *Closed Sun. No dinner.*

Shanahan's on the Green

$$$$ | **AMERICAN** | Glowing with gilded chandeliers and graced with a few marble fireplaces, this American-style steak house in a restored Georgian town house offers a sleekly elegant setting in which to chow down on some of the most tender Irish Angus beef this side of the Atlantic (they cook it in a special high-temperature oven, searing the outside to keep the inside good and juicy). If steak doesn't float your boat, they also do a mean baked turbot with mussels, clams, and creamed fennel and leek. **Known for:** expertise with steak; sumptuous surroundings; deep wine list. ⑤ *Average main: €45* ⊠ *119 St. Stephen's Green, Dublin South* ☎ *01/407–0939* ⊕ *www.shanahans.ie* ⊘ *No lunch Sat.–Thurs.*

Wagamama

$ | **JAPANESE** | Modeled on a Japanese canteen, Wagamama, with its long wooden tables and benches and high ceilings with exposed metal piping, attracts a young, loud crowd and has a fun, city-center buzz. Formal courses aren't acknowledged—food is served as soon as it's ready, and appetizers and main courses arrive together. **Known for:** young, lively crowd; great chili beef ramen; good beer selection. ⑤ *Average main: €16* ⊠ *S. King St., Dublin South* ☎ *01/478–2152* ⊕ *www.wagamama.ie.*

Yamamori Noodles

$$ | **JAPANESE** | The open plan and family-style tables have kept Yamamori popular with noodle addicts and the younger, hipster crowd. The meals-in-a-bowl are a splendid slurping experience, and although you'll be supplied with a small Chinese-style soup spoon, the best approach is with chopsticks. **Known for:** bento box; hip crowd; efficient service. ⑤ *Average main: €21* ⊠ *72 S. Great George's St., Dublin South* ☎ *01/475–5001* ⊕ *www.yamamori.ie/yamamori-noodles.*

Hotels

Brooks Hotel

$$$ | **HOTEL** | It has nearly 100 rooms, but this hotel—minutes from Grafton Street—likes to describe itself as a boutique property, and it does manage to convey the personal touch of a much smaller establishment. **Pros:** next to Grafton Street; live piano music in bar; rooms refurbished every six years. **Cons:** office-block exterior; business clientele makes for slightly flat atmosphere; standard rooms on small side. ⑤ *Rooms from: €250* ⊠ *Drury St., Dublin South* ☎ *01/670–4000* ⊕ *www.brookshotel.ie* ⌁ *98 rooms* ⦿ *No meals.*

★ Central Hotel

$$ | **HOTEL** | Established in 1887, this grand, old-style redbrick spot is just steps from Grafton Street and Temple Bar, but also has the little oasis every city center needs: a book-and-armchair-filled Library Bar, warmed by a Victorian fireplace. **Pros:** central location; original 1887 facade; old-fashioned feel. **Cons:** rooms on the small side; street noise in some rooms; you have to prepay up front. ⑤ *Rooms from: €200* ⊠ *1–5 Exchequer St., Dublin South* ☎ *01/679–7302* ⊕ *www.centralhoteldublin.com* ⌁ *70 rooms* ⦿ *No meals.*

Clayton Hotel Burlington Road

$$ | **HOTEL** | The days when Irish and international celebrities partied the nights away at the Burlington hotel might be gone, but this Dublin institution is convenient to St. Stephen's Green and Grafton Street and home to a lively bar and restaurant so it's still a focal point for social events and gatherings. **Pros:** a Dublin institution; large, light-filled rooms; happening cocktail bar. **Cons:** looks a little bit like a parking garage; popular with conferences; rooms are a little basic and bland. ⑤ *Rooms from: €197* ⊠ *Upper Leeson St., Georgian Dublin* ☎ *01/618–5600* ⊕ *www.claytonhotelburlingtonroad.com* ⌁ *501 rooms* ⦿ *No meals.*

Conrad Dublin International

$$$$ | HOTEL | The best thing about the ugly-on-the-outside, seven-story, red-brick, and smoked-glass Conrad is the spectacular views out over the city, so ask for—no, insist on—a room on one of the top three floors. **Pros:** just off St. Stephen's Green; great views on higher floors; top-class concierge. **Cons:** drab 1970s-style exterior; slightly cramped standard rooms; poor views on lower floors. ⑤ *Rooms from: €365* ⊠ *Earlsfort Terr., Dublin South* ☎ *01/602–8900* ⊕ *www.conradhotels.com* ⤸ *192 rooms* ⦵ *No meals.*

Dawson Hotel and Spa

$$ | HOTEL | Overlooking the Mansion House and 50 yards from Trinity College, this intimate town house is one of the classiest boutique hotels on the Dublin scene. **Pros:** great luxury for the price; choice of three restaurants; spa oasis in the city. **Cons:** small, so fills up quickly; no parking; one could overdose on the Asian theme. ⑤ *Rooms from: €178* ⊠ *35 Dawson St., Dublin South* ☎ *01/672–7900* ⊕ *www.thedawson.ie* ⊟ *No credit cards* ⤸ *36 rooms* ⦵ *Free breakfast.*

The Dean

$$$ | HOTEL | This urbane and boldly designed new hotel a few minutes from Grafton Street is truly boutique with a unique mix of Georgian and modern architecture and an unusual selection of room sizes and shapes. **Pros:** stunning views from rooftop bar; varied room-size options; Irish art on show. **Cons:** tries a little too hard to be cool; rooms aren't huge; noisy nightlife nearby. ⑤ *Rooms from: €225* ⊠ *33 Harcourt St., Dublin South* ☎ *01/607–8110* ⊕ *deandublin.ie* ⤸ *52 rooms* ⦵ *No meals.*

The Devlin

$$$ | HOTEL | Located in trendy Ranelagh village, just outside the city center, this boutique property refers to its compact rooms as "pods," and offers a rooftop restaurant and terrace, ground-floor bar and coffee shop, and subterranean 42-seat cinema and bar, making it one of the coolest places to stay in Dublin right now. **Pros:** cool, contemporary design; rooftop restaurant has great city views; good variety of room sizes. **Cons:** outside city center; no parking; small rooms. ⑤ *Rooms from: €227* ⊠ *119 Ranelagh Rd., Dublin South* ☎ *01/406–6550* ⊕ *www.thedevlin.ie* ⤸ *40 rooms* ⦵ *No meals.*

Grafton Guest House

$ | HOTEL | A stone's throw from the famous shopping street that gave it its name, this Victorian Gothic–style building has been tastefully transformed into one of central Dublin's best bargains. **Pros:** best value in city center; warm, unfussy service; simple but cool design. **Cons:** some rooms are cramped; can suffer from street noise; no elevator. ⑤ *Rooms from: €139* ⊠ *26–27 S. Great George's St., Dublin South* ☎ *01/648–0010* ⊕ *www.graftonguesthouse.com* ⤸ *16 rooms* ⦵ *Free breakfast.*

Iveagh Garden Hotel

$$$ | HOTEL | Housed in an elegant four-story Georgian terrace just a five-minute walk from St. Stephen's Green, this contemporary-luxe hotel is decorated with rich wallpapers, touches of brass, gleaming mirrors, stylish tiled floors, lots of Navan-manufactured furniture—and it is fully powered by an underground river. **Pros:** Ireland's only sustainable hotel; overlooks gardens in back; excellent location. **Cons:** no gym, pool, or spa; eco ethos does not extend to room amenities; parking is limited. ⑤ *Rooms from: €220* ⊠ *72–74 Harcourt St., Dublin South* ☎ *01/568–5500* ⊕ *www.iveaghgardenhotel.ie* ⤸ *145 rooms* ⦵ *No meals.*

★ Kellys Hotel

$$ | HOTEL | With buzzing Hogan's bar and the classy L'Gueuleton restaurant right downstairs, this cool little hotel, situated in an original Victorian redbrick, is at the epicenter of trendy Dublin. **Pros:** killer city-center location; relaxed vibe;

authentic-Dublin feel. **Cons:** some rooms are small; can suffer noise from bar below; no elevator. ⑤ *Rooms from: €155* ✉ *36 S. Great George's St., Dublin South* ☎ *01/648-0010* ⊕ *www.kellysdublin.com* ⥎ *15 rooms, 1 suite* ⎮◉⎮ *Free breakfast.*

The Marker

$$$$ | HOTEL | The checkerboard facade and sloping, honeycomb ceilings of the Marker make a bold architectural statement, while the view of the docklands from the stunning rooftop bar has quickly become a top Dublin delight. **Pros:** roof garden and bar; impressive room design; attracts the in crowd. **Cons:** design-heavy in the public spaces; not all rooms have views; a little outside the city center. ⑤ *Rooms from: €320* ✉ *Grand Canal Sq., Docklands, Dublin South* ☎ *01/687-5100* ⊕ *www.themarkerhoteldublin.com* ⥎ *187 rooms* ⎮◉⎮ *No meals.*

★ The Shelbourne Dublin, Renaissance

$$$$ | HOTEL | Paris has the Ritz, New York has the St. Regis, and Dublin has the Shelbourne—resplendent in its broad, ornamented, pink-and-white mid-Victorian facade right off Grafton Street. **Pros:** afternoon tea in Lord Mayor's Lounge; no-expense-spared renovations; spa and wellness center. **Cons:** some noise in front rooms; feels a little stuffy at times; pricey. ⑤ *Rooms from: €370* ✉ *27 St. Stephen's Green, Dublin South* ☎ *01/663-4500, 800/543-4300 in U.S.* ⊕ *www.marriott.co.uk/hotels/travel/ dubbr-the-shelbourne-dublin-a-renaissance-hotel* ⥎ *265 rooms* ⎮◉⎮ *No meals.*

★ Westbury Hotel Dublin

$$$$ | HOTEL | This luxurious, chandelier-filled, modern hotel just off Grafton Street is a favorite with elegantly dressed Dubliners who stop for afternoon tea in the Gallery, the spacious mezzanine-level main lobby, furnished with a grand piano and a grand view out onto the bustling streets. **Pros:** great service; prime people-watching; convenient location; the Art Deco glamour of the Marble bar. **Cons:** tries a little too hard to be posh;

pricey. ⑤ *Rooms from: €430* ✉ *Grafton St., Dublin South* ☎ *01/679-1122* ⊕ *www. doylecollection.com* ⥎ *205 rooms* ⎮◉⎮ *No meals.*

The Westin Dublin

$$$$ | HOTEL | Reconstructed from three 19th-century landmark buildings opposite Trinity College, the Westin is all about location, but the marble pillars, tall mahogany doorways, blazing fireplaces, Palladian marble busts, and period details also set it apart. **Pros:** beside Temple Bar but not in Temple Bar; in-room spa treatments; some rooms overlook Trinity College. **Cons:** on a busy traffic corner; windowless bar; not cheap. ⑤ *Rooms from: €415* ✉ *College Green, Dublin South* ☎ *01/645-1000* ⊕ *www.thewestin-dublin.com* ⥎ *163 rooms* ⎮◉⎮ *No meals.*

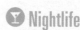 # Nightlife

IRISH CABARET, MUSIC, AND DANCING

Bewley's Café Theatre

CABARET | With its intimate nights in this small, Victorian venue, Bewley's Café Theatre has become the atmospheric cabaret hot spot in Dublin. Set in the Oriental Room on the second floor above the glorious, stained-glass jewel that is the Grafton Street restaurant, the unique lunchtime performances here—a one-act play by O'Casey or Wilde with a bowl of soup and soda bread—are also noteworthy. ✉ *78–79 Grafton St., 2nd fl., Dublin South* ☎ *086/878-4001* ⊕ *www. bewleyscafetheatre.com.*

The Sugar Club

MUSIC CLUBS | There's a touch of Vegas about this landmark venue with the tables and chairs on tiered levels that look down on the stage. The Sugar Club has regular music and performance (some touted as "burlesque") nights. ✉ *8 Lower Leeson St., Dublin South* ☎ *01/678-7188* ⊕ *www.thesugarclub. com.*

JAZZ
Ha'penny Bridge Inn
MUSIC CLUBS | In its tiny but buzzing upstairs room, the Ha'penny Bridge regularly hosts blues and jazz nights and has good comedy on Thursday. ⊠ *42 Wellington Quay, Dublin South* ☎ *01/677–0616* ⊕ *www.hapennybridgeinn.com.*

The Mint Bar
MUSIC CLUBS | A basement venue set in a former bank vault, the Mint Bar is a classic cocktail bar presenting live jazz, lounge, and swing music Thursday, Friday, and Saturday. ⊠ *Westin Hotel, College Green, Dublin South* ☎ *01/645–1000* ⊕ *www.themintbar.ie.*

NIGHTCLUBS
★ Lillie's Bordello
DANCE CLUBS | Once the hot spot for celebs, Lillie's Bordello is now more for regular Joes: a popular hangout for a young late-night crowd. Hot or not, the decor remains a knockout: Victorian brocaded velvets and gilded frames plus pink and purple neon lasers. Take a rest from the dance floor in the gorgeous Library room or one of the two cinema rooms. ⊠ *Grafton St., Dublin South* ☎ *01/679–9204* ⊕ *www.lilliesbordello.ie.*

PUBS
★ Cafe en Seine
BARS/PUBS | Dublin's first superpub received a €4 million face-lift and reopened in late 2018 with three floors of opulent Art Nouveau style à la grand Parisian brasserie, an extensive food menu, and a spectacular enclosed garden terrace with a retractable glass roof. One of Dublin's more elegant places to socialize. ⊠ *40 Dawson St., Dublin South* ☎ *01/677–4567* ⊕ *www.cafeenseine.ie.*

Cassidy's
BARS/PUBS | Once a quality neighborhood pub with a tasty pint of stout, Cassidy's has morphed into an often overcrowded but very popular spot with a young clientele. ⊠ *42 Lower Camden St., Dublin South* ☎ *01/475–6540.*

Davy Byrnes
BARS/PUBS | A noted pilgrimage stop for Joyceans, Davy Byrnes is where Leopold Bloom stops in for a glass of Burgundy and a Gorgonzola-cheese sandwich in *Ulysses* (and ruminates before helping a blind man cross the road). The decor—with leather seats and dramatic art on the walls—is more decadent than in Joyce's day ("He entered Davy Byrnes. Moral pub."), but it still serves some fine pub grub. ⊠ *21 Duke St., Dublin South* ☎ *01/677–5217* ⊕ *www.davybyrnes.com.*

Doheny & Nesbitt
BARS/PUBS | A traditional spot with snugs, dark wooden furnishings, and smoke-darkened ceilings, Doheny & Nesbitt has hardly changed over the decades. ⊠ *4–5 Lower Baggot St., Dublin South* ☎ *01/676–2945* ⊕ *www.dohenyandnesbitts.ie.*

Doyle's In Town
BARS/PUBS | A cozy pub, Doyle's is a favorite with journalists from the *Irish Times* and Trinity students. ⊠ *9 College St., Dublin South* ☎ *01/671–0616* ⊕ *www.doylesintown.com.*

The George
BARS/PUBS | Dublin's two-floor main gay pub, the George draws an almost entirely male crowd; its nightclub stays open until 2:30 am nightly except Tuesday. The "alternative bingo night," with star drag act Miss Shirley Temple Bar, is a riot of risqué fun. SaturGays are always packed. ⊠ *89 S. Great George's St., Dublin South* ☎ *01/478–2983* ⊕ *www.thegeorge.ie.*

The Globe
BARS/PUBS | The Globe draws hipster Dubliners who sip espresso drinks by day and enjoy its late opening and DJs at night. They do a mean wood-fired pizza and specialize in cocktails. ⊠ *11 S. Great George's St., Dublin South* ☎ *01/671–1220* ⊕ *www.theglobe.ie.*

★ Grogan's
BARS/PUBS | Also known as the Castle Lounge, Grogan's is a small place packed

with creative folk. Owner Tommy Grogan is known as a patron of local artists, and his walls are covered with their work. There's no music or TV, so you can have a proper chat with your pint and toastie. ✉ *15 S. William St., Dublin South* ☎ *01/677–9320.*

Hogan's

BARS/PUBS | A huge space on two levels, Hogan's gets jammed most nights with a cool, college crowd. But in the afternoons it's a quieter spot and perfect for people-watching out the large windows. ✉ *35 S. Great George's St., Dublin South* ☎ *01/677–5904.*

★ Horseshoe Bar

BARS/PUBS | The who's who of city society have always been drawn to the elegance of this glorious Dublin institution at the Shelbourne hotel. There's comparatively little space for drinkers around the famous semicircular bar—but this does wonders for making friends quickly. ✉ *Shelbourne, 27 St. Stephen's Green, Dublin South* ☎ *01/676–6471* ⊕ *www.shelbournedining.ie/the-horseshoe-bar.*

Kehoe's

BARS/PUBS | Popular with Trinity students and local hipsters, Kehoe's has a tiny back room that is nice and cozy, while the upstairs is basically the owner's old living room, open to the public. ✉ *9 S. Anne St., Dublin South* ☎ *01/677–8312* ⊕ *www.kehoesdublin.ie.*

★ Library Bar

BARS/PUBS | The place to go when you're ready to get away from all the madness, the Library has book-lined shelves, big armchairs and sofas, and a blazing fireplace—all in all, this first-floor hideaway is one of the most serene nighttime spots in Dublin. ✉ *Central Hotel, 1–5 Exchequer St., Dublin South* ☎ *01/679–7302* ⊕ *www.centralhoteldublin.com/library-bar.html.*

The Little Pig

BARS/PUBS | This hidden speakeasy is a fabulous spot for a late-night cocktail with its luxurious red velvet walls, polished bronze roofing, dark velvet seating, and dimmed tassled lamps. The martinis are said to be the best in town, and the sublime Italian dishes (some served in porcelain teacups) are a delightful surprise. ✉ *Wicklow St., Dublin South* ☎ *01/565–4398* ⊕ *www.thelittlepig.ie.*

The Long Hall

BARS/PUBS | One of Dublin's most ornate traditional taverns, the Long Hall has Victorian lamps, a mahogany bar, mirrors, chandeliers, and plasterwork ceilings, all more than 100 years old. The pub serves sandwiches and an excellent pint of Guinness. ✉ *51 S. Great George's St., Dublin South* ☎ *01/475–1590.*

McDaid's

BARS/PUBS | A landmark that once attracted boisterous Brendan Behan and other leading writers in the 1950s, McDaid's wild literary reputation still lingers, although the bar has been discreetly modernized and is altogether quieter. ✉ *3 Harry St., Dublin South* ☎ *01/679–4395.*

Mulligan's

BARS/PUBS | Synonymous in Dublin with a truly perfect pint of Guinness, Mulligan's started life as a *shebeen* (unlicensed drinking venue) and then, pub lore tells us, was listed as "legal" in 1782. Today, locals and students flock here for a good pint. ✉ *8 Poolbeg St., Dublin South* ☎ *01/677–5582* ⊕ *www.mulligans.ie.*

Neary's

BARS/PUBS | With an exotic, Victorian-style interior, Neary's was once the haunt of music-hall artists and a certain literary set, including Brendan Behan. Join the actors from the adjacent Gaiety Theatre for a good pub lunch. ✉ *1 Chatham St., Dublin South* ☎ *01/677–7371.*

No Name

BARS/PUBS | Considering itself too cool to even have a name when it opened, the Secret Bar/No Name Bar eventually decided to play on its hidden-away vibe. Above L'Gueuleton restaurant, the open-plan, buzzing bar even has a cute little covered patio. ⊠ *1 Fade St., Dublin South* ☎ *01/675–3708* ⊕ *www.kellysdublin.com.*

The Odeon

BARS/PUBS | The converted main building of Harcourt Street's old railway station houses this large, modern cocktail bar. Both the lunch and dinner menus include fish-and-chips, burgers, and good salads. Sunday brunch is served between noon and 5. ⊠ *57 Harcourt St., Dublin South* ☎ *01/478–2088* ⊕ *odeon.ie.*

O'Donoghue's

BARS/PUBS | A cheerful, tourist-friendly hangout, O'Donoghue's has impromptu musical performances that often spill out onto the street. ⊠ *15 Merrion Row, Dublin South* ☎ *01/676–2807* ⊕ *www.odonoghues.ie.*

The Old Stand

BARS/PUBS | One of the oldest pubs in the city, the Old Stand is named after the now demolished Old Stand at Lansdowne Road stadium, home to Irish rugby and football. The pub is renowned for great pints and fine steaks. ⊠ *37 Exchequer St., Dublin South* ☎ *01/677–7220* ⊕ *www.theoldstandpub.com.*

★ Peruke & Periwig

BARS/PUBS | This stylish, three-floor cocktail bar, named for the wigmakers once located here, has cutting-edge cocktails, plush velvet banquettes, wood panels, and baroque portraits and wigs on the walls. The food is decent, too. ⊠ *31 Dawson St., Dublin South* ☎ *01/672–7190* ⊕ *www.peruke.ie.*

Peter's Pub

BARS/PUBS | The epitome of the cozy little boozer, Peter's Pub hugs a busy corner where people-watching becomes an art at the outside tables in summer. ⊠ *Johnson Pl., Dublin South* ☎ *01/679–3347.*

★ Stag's Head

BARS/PUBS | A Victorian beaut, the Stag's Head dates from 1770 and was rebuilt in 1895. Theater people from the nearby Olympia and Trinity students gather around the unusual Connemara red-marble bar, study their reflections in the many mirrors, and drink in all the oak carvings. They host a great traditional-music session on the last Wednesday of the month. ⊠ *1 Dame Ct., Dublin South* ☎ *01/679–3701* ⊕ *www.stagshead.ie.*

🎭 Performing Arts

CLASSICAL MUSIC AND OPERA

Bord Gáis Energy Theatre

MUSIC | Housed in a brash, Daniel Liebskind–designed building in the growing docklands area of the city, this theater has a 2,000-plus capacity, making it Ireland's biggest theater space. Its calendar includes the best of international ballet, classical music, pop gigs, and even Broadway musicals. ⊠ *Grand Canal Sq., Dublin South* ☎ *01/677–7999* ⊕ *www.bordgaisenergytheatre.ie.*

St. Stephen's Church

MUSIC | Under its glorious "pepper canister" cupola, St. Stephen's Church stages a tempting program of choral and orchestral events. ⊠ *Upper Mount St., Dublin South* ☎ *01/288–0663* ⊕ *www.peppercanister.ie.*

ROCK AND CONTEMPORARY MUSIC

International Bar

MUSIC | A long-established, tiny, get-close-to-the-band venue upstairs, the International also hosts theater in the afternoon and comedy on weekends. ⊠ *Wicklow St., Dublin South* ☎ *01/677–9250* ⊕ *www.international-bar.com.*

Opium Rooms

MUSIC | Set in a striking, glass-front building, the Opium Rooms is a new take on an old favorite music spot, with regular rock gigs or bass-thumping international DJ sets. There's a pan-Asian restaurant out front if you get peckish. ⊠ *26 Wexford St., Dublin South* ☎ *01/475–8555* ⊕ *opium.ie.*

Whelan's

MUSIC | It might look a bit shabby around the edges, but Whelan's is one of the city's best—and most popular—music venues. Well-known performers play everything from rock to folk to traditional music. ✉ *25 Wexford St., Dublin South* ☎ *01/478–0766* ⊕ *www.whelanslive.com.*

FILM

★ The Stella

FILM | This gorgeous Art Deco cinema has been restored to all its 1920s glory. Enjoy a cocktail while watching old classics or new releases in the sumptuous leather seats. ✉ *207–209 Rathmines Rd. Lower, Dublin South* ☎ *01/496–7014* ⊕ *stellatheatre.ie.*

THEATER

★ Gaiety Theatre

THEATER | When this shimmering red-and-gold 19th-century theater is not showing musical comedy, drama, and revues, the sumptuous Gaiety is taken over by Opera Ireland for one of their big shows. ✉ *S. King St., Dublin South* ☎ *01/677–1717* ⊕ *www.gaietytheatre.ie.*

Samuel Beckett Centre

THEATER | Home to Trinity College's drama department and the student Players group, as well as visiting European companies, the Samuel Beckett Centre also hosts dance performances by visiting troupes; the theater was built in 1992 and stands near the center of Trinity's campus. ✉ *Trinity College, Dublin South* ☎ *01/608–2266* ⊕ *www.tcd.ie/ beckett-theatre.*

🛍 Shopping

BOOKS

Books Upstairs

BOOKS/STATIONERY | An excellent selection of special-interest books is available here, including Irish literature, gay and feminist literature, psychology, and self-help books. There's a cool café upstairs. ✉ *17 D'Olier St., Dublin South* ☎ *01/679–6687.*

Easons

BOOKS/STATIONERY | This Northside Dublin institution has opened a branch in the Stephen's Green shopping center with a strong focus on best sellers, travel, and Irish interest. ✉ *St. Stephen's Green Centre, Dublin South* ☎ *01/478–3060* ⊕ *www.easons.com.*

★ Hodges Figgis

BOOKS/STATIONERY | Dublin's leading independent bookstore, Hodges Figgis stocks 1½ million books on three floors. Once considered Ireland's oldest, its "independent" claim is a bit bogus, as a giant chain bought it some years ago. That noted, it has a stock, staff, look, and even aroma of an independent bookstore, and might even still please James Joyce (who alludes to it in his *Ulysses*). ✉ *56–58 Dawson St., Dublin South* ☎ *01/677–4754* ⊕ *www.waterstones. com/bookshops/hodges-figgis.*

★ Stokes Books

BOOKS/STATIONERY | A gem of an antique bookstore, Stokes has a great used-book section and specializes in Irish history and literature. While on the small side, Stokes is a treasure trove that will turn on most book lovers. ✉ *George's Street Arcade, Dublin South* ☎ *01/671–3584* ⊕ *www.georgesstreetarcade.ie.*

★ Ulysses Rare Books

BOOKS/STATIONERY | Head here for a fine array of first editions of Irish literature and many other books of Irish interest, plus old maps of Dublin and Ireland. ✉ *10 Duke St., Dublin South* ☎ *01/671–8676* ⊕ *www.rarebooks.ie.*

CHINA, CRYSTAL, CERAMICS, AND JEWELRY

Appleby Jewellers

JEWELRY/ACCESSORIES | This is the best known of the several classy, old-style jewelry shops that line tiny Johnson's Court, a delightful little lane off busy Grafton Street. ✉ *Johnson's Ct., Grafton St., Dublin South* ☎ *01/679–9572* ⊕ *www.appleby.ie.*

Dublin Shopping Streets

Southside

Dawson Street. Just east of Grafton Street between Nassau Street to the north and St. Stephen's Green to the south, Dawson Street is full of lively cafés and bars. It's also the address of Hodges Figgis, the best bookstore in the country.

Francis Street. Part of the Liberties, the oldest part of the city and the hub of Dublin's antiques trade, Francis Street and surrounding areas, such as the Coombe, have plenty of shops where you can browse. If you're looking for something in particular, dealers will gladly recommend the appropriate store to you. It's also home to a couple of hot new galleries.

Grafton Street. Dublin's bustling pedestrian-only main shopping street, Grafton Street has two department stores: down-to-earth Marks & Spencer and très chic Brown Thomas. The rest of the street is taken up by shops, many of them branches of international chains, such as the Body Shop and Next, and many British chains. This is also the spot to buy fresh flowers, available at reasonable prices from outdoor stands. On the smaller streets off Grafton Street—especially Duke Street, South Anne Street, and Chatham Street—are worthwhile crafts, clothing, and designer housewares shops.

Nassau Street. Dublin's main tourist-oriented thoroughfare, Nassau has some of the best-known stores selling Irish goods, but you won't find many locals shopping here. Still, if you're looking for classic Irish gifts to take home, you should be sure at least to browse along here.

Temple Bar

Temple Bar. Once dubbed Dublin's hippest neighborhood, Temple Bar is still dotted with small, precious boutiques—mainly intimate, quirky shops that traffic in a small selection of trendy goods, from vintage clothes to some of the most avant-garde Irish garb anywhere in the city.

Northside

Henry Street. Running westward from O'Connell Street, Henry Street is where cash-conscious Dubliners shop. Arnotts department store is the anchor here. Henry Street's continuation, Mary Street, has a branch of Marks & Spencer and the Jervis Shopping Centre.

O'Connell Street. The city's main thoroughfare, O'Connell Street is more downscale than Southside city streets (such as Grafton Street), but it is still worth a walk. One of Dublin's largest department stores, Clery's, is across from the GPO. On the same side of the street is Eason's, a large book, magazine, and stationery store.

★ **Barry Doyle Design**
JEWELRY/ACCESSORIES | A true original with his Celtic modern jewelry, Barry Doyle is a master who allows you to watch him at work in his adjoining studio as he fashions beautiful wedding rings and his lovely Lilac Collection baubles. It was chosen as one of the top 50 shops in Ireland by *Irish Times* readers. ✉ *George's Street Arcade, Upstairs, Dublin South* ☎ *01/671–2838* ⊕ *www. barrydoyledesign.com.*

House of Ireland
CERAMICS/GLASSWARE | For Irish goods and crafts, this is a great one-stop-shopping

resource with an extensive selection of crystal, jewelry, tweeds, sweaters, and other upscale goods. ⊠ *114 Grafton St., Dublin South* ☎ *01/671–1111* ⊕ *www. houseofireland.com.*

Industry & Co
HOUSEHOLD ITEMS/FURNITURE | An intimate space curating and showcasing the very best of Irish furniture, jewelry, and ceramic design—a one-stop shop to support Irish makers. Be sure to leave time to visit the popular on-site Middle Eastern café. ⊠ *41 Drury St., Dublin South* ☎ *01/613–9111* ⊕ *www.industry-andco.com.*

Irish Design Shop
JEWELRY/ACCESSORIES | Two young jewelers got together to open this exciting shop dedicated to the best in Irish design and designers. They sell woolen accessories, kitchen stuff, jewelry, and assorted other treasures. ⊠ *41 Drury St., Dublin South* ☎ *01/679–8871* ⊕ *www.irishde-signshop.com.*

Kilkenny Shop
CERAMICS/GLASSWARE | Specializing in contemporary Irish-made ceramics, pottery, and silver jewelry, Kilkenny Shop regularly holds exhibits of exciting new work by Irish craftspeople and has a wide array of gifts fashioned by Orla Kiely and other top Irish designers. ⊠ *6–15 Nassau St., Dublin South* ☎ *01/677–7066* ⊕ *www. kilkennyshop.com.*

★ Momuse
JEWELRY/ACCESSORIES | Bespoke jewelry maker Margaret O'Rourke fills this wonderful little shop with her own contemporary, subtle pieces, plus select work from other up-and-coming Irish designers. ⊠ *Ground fl., Powerscourt Townhouse Centre, Dublin South* ☎ *01/707–1763* ⊕ *www.momuse.ie.*

Sweater Shop
CERAMICS/GLASSWARE | They might sell sweaters and scarves but Trinity Woollen Mills is also your one-stop shop for everything kitschy Irish, such as trashy treasures like "the leprechauns made me do it" mugs and Guinness-logo underwear. ⊠ *30 Nassau St., Dublin South* ☎ *01/672–5663* ⊕ *www.sweatershop. com.*

CLOTHING STORES
★ Atrium
CLOTHING | It's about more than the clothes at this self-styled "concept shop," which specializes in contemporary Irish designers including Electronic Sheep and Emma Manely. You can also pick up the newest trends in local jewelry, bags, and scarves. ⊠ *Top fl., Powerscourt Townhouse Centre, Dublin South* ☎ *01/555–4644* ⊕ *www.atriumdublin.com.*

Carousel
CLOTHING | If cute vintage clothing is your thing, husband-and-wife-operated Carousel has a great selection of dresses, skirts, knitwares, and accessories. ⊠ *20 Exchequer St., Dublin South* ☎ *01/677–8713* ⊕ *www.ilovecarousel.com.*

★ Costume
CLOTHING | A classy boutique for Dubliners with fashion sense and money, Costume showcases local designers such as Leigh Tucker and Helen Steele. Temperley and Preen are among the international designers featured among the rails of colorful, stylish clothes. ⊠ *10 Castel Market, Dublin South* ☎ *01/679–4188* ⊕ *www.costumedublin.ie.*

DEPARTMENT STORES
★ Brown Thomas
DEPARTMENT STORES | Dublin's most exclusive department store, Brown Thomas stocks the leading designer names (including top Irish designers) in clothing and cosmetics, plus lots of stylish accessories. There's also a good selection of crystal. Their January sales are a big draw. ⊠ *Grafton St., Dublin South* ☎ *01/605–6666* ⊕ *www.browntho-mas.com.*

Dunnes Stores
DEPARTMENT STORES | Ireland's largest chain of department stores, all Dunnes

Dublin à la Mode

The success of shops such as Costume has given young Irish designers the confidence to produce more original and impressive work. One of Dublin's most popular designers, **Helen James** graduated from the National College of Art and Design in textile design. She went straight to New York, where she worked for Donna Karan, among others. She returned to Ireland and developed her line of unique, hand-printed textile accessories. She now specializes in home-ware design; her Considered line is carried nationally by Dunnes. Check out her work at ⊕ *helenjamesdesign.blogspot.com.*

A star of Irish fashion, **Simone Rocha** gained international acclaim for her elegant, classic evening wear with some daring twists. She has already expanded into furniture and recently opened stores in London and New York.

The Tucker family has been a key player in Irish fashion for a long time, and **Leigh Tucker** has quickly established herself as one of Dublin's classiest young designers. Fine tailoring is her trademark—the finish on her evening wear is nonpareil—and beaded French lace and draped jersey are her favorite materials. She is now designing women's wear and kids' clothing for Dunnes Stores in the city center under her Willow label.

branches stock fashion (including the exciting Savida range), household (try the new Considered line), and grocery items, and have a reputation for value and variety. Other branches can be found on Henry Street and in the Ilac Centre on Mary Street. ⊠ *St. Stephen's Green Centre, Dublin South* ☎ *01/478–0188* ⊕ *www. dunnesstores.com.*

Marks & Spencer

DEPARTMENT STORES | More affordable than high-end Grafton Street competitor Brown Thomas, Marks & Spencer stocks everything from fashion (including lingerie) to tasty, unusual groceries. ⊠ *Grafton St., Dublin South* ☎ *01/679–7855* ⊕ *www.marksandspencer.com.*

MUSIC
Gael Linn

MUSIC STORES | A specialist in traditional Irish music and Irish-language recordings, Gael Linn is where the aficionados go. ⊠ *35 Dame St., Dublin South* ☎ *01/675– 1200* ⊕ *www.gael-linn.ie.*

McCullogh Piggott

MUSIC STORES | This is the best place in town to buy instruments, sheet music, scores, and books about music. ⊠ *11 S. William St., Dublin South* ☎ *01/670–6702* ⊕ *www.mcculloughpigott.com.*

Tower Records

MUSIC STORES | With the demise of HMV, Tower is the last big mainstream music store in Dublin. It carries all the latest CDs, DVDs, music books, vinyl, and music merchandise. ⊠ *7 Dawson St., Dublin South* ☎ *01/671–3250* ⊕ *www. towerrecords.ie.*

OUTDOOR MARKETS
George's Street Arcade

SHOPPING CENTERS/MALLS | Opened in 1881 as South City Markets, this classic Victorian market right in the heart of town is home to a small but eclectic collection of clothes, books, food, and jewelry stalls. It's covered, but feels outdoors, and open every day. ⊠ *S. Great George's St., Dublin South* ⊕ *www. georgesstreetarcade.ie.*

SHOPPING CENTERS

Powerscourt Centre

SHOPPING CENTERS/MALLS | Once the regal former town home of Lord Powerscourt (built in 1771), this was largely gutted two decades ago to make room for an interior roofed-over courtyard and a space shared by a mix of restaurants, cafés, antiques stores, and boutiques of original Irish fashions by young designers. A pianist often plays on the dais at ground-floor level. ⊠ *59 S. William St., Dublin South* ☎ *01/679–4144* ⊕ *www.power-scourtcentre.com.*

Royal Hibernian Way

SHOPPING CENTERS/MALLS | On the former site of the two-centuries-old Royal Hibernian Hotel, a coaching inn that was demolished in 1983, this complex is home to pricey, stylish shops—about 20 or 30, many selling fashionable clothes and accessories—including Clarke Irish and Celtic Jewellers. ⊠ *Off Dawson St., between S. Anne and Duke Sts., Dublin South* ☎ *01/679–5919.*

St. Stephen's Green Centre

SHOPPING CENTERS/MALLS | Dublin's city center's largest and most ambitious shopping complex, St. Stephen's Green Centre resembles a giant greenhouse, with Victorian-style ironwork. On three floors overlooked by a giant clock, the 100 mostly small shops sell crafts, fashions, and household goods. ⊠ *Northwest corner of St. Stephen's Green, Dublin South* ☎ *01/478–0888* ⊕ *www.stephens-green.com.*

Westbury Mall

SHOPPING CENTERS/MALLS | An upmarket shopping mall, the Westbury is where you can buy a stylish range of designer jewelry, antique rugs, and decorative goods. ⊠ *Westbury Hotel, off Grafton St., Dublin South.*

SWEATERS AND TWEEDS

Avoca

CLOTHING | A beautiful store with an eclectic collection of knitwear, jewelry, ceramics, and housewares from contemporary Irish designers. There's an artisanal food market in the basement and a fantastic café on the top floor with unmissable cakes. ⊠ *11–13 Suffolk St., Dublin South* ☎ *01/274–6900* ⊕ *www.avoca.ie.*

★ Kevin and Howlin

CLOTHING | A quintessential Irish store, Kevin and Howlin stocks spiffy fashions, with lots of stylish handwoven tweed men's jackets, suits, and hats, along with an array of treasures woven from tweedy fabrics. All in all, a fabulous, one-stop shop for traditional clothes with flair. Wait until you see the whole wall devoted to headgear—eat your heart out, Ralph Lauren! ⊠ *31 Nassau St., Dublin South* ☎ *01/677–0257* ⊕ *www.kevinandhowlin.com.*

Monaghan's

CLOTHING | If you're into cashmere, you should get yourself into Monaghan's. ⊠ *21 S. Anne St., Dublin South* ☎ *01/677–0823* ⊕ *monaghanscashmere.ie.*

Georgian Dublin

If there's one travel poster that signifies "Dublin" more than any other, it's the one that depicts 50 or so Georgian doorways—door after colorful door, all graced with lovely fanlights upheld by columns. Today, heading south from Merrion Square all the way to Ballsbridge, visitors can enjoy perfectly planned, tree-lined Georgian streets with some of the most elegant 18th-century buildings in Europe. Included in these are four of the most fascinating and glamorous museums in Ireland, sitting cheek by jowl: the National Gallery, National Library, National Museum of Natural History, and best of all, keeper of the Celtic treasures of ancient Ireland, the National Museum of Archaeology. No part of the city is more uniquely and gloriously Dublin. For convenience we have included the areas slightly farther south, around the Grand Canal and in the heart of the leafy suburb of Ballsbridge, in this section, as they have their own Georgian delights.

◉ Sights

Government Buildings

GOVERNMENT BUILDING | The swan song of British architecture in the capital, this enormous complex, a landmark of Edwardian Baroque, was the last Neoclassical edifice to be erected by the British government. It was designed by Sir Aston Webb, who did many of the similarly grand buildings in London's Piccadilly Circus, to serve as the College of Science in the early 1900s. Following a major restoration, these buildings became the offices of the Department of the *taoiseach* (the prime minister, pronounced *tea*-shuck) and the *tánaiste* (the deputy prime minister, pronounced *tawn*-ish-ta). Fine examples of contemporary Irish furniture and carpets populate the offices. A stained-glass window, known as "My Four Green Fields," was made by Evie Hone for the 1939 New York World's Fair. It depicts the four ancient provinces of Ireland: Munster, Ulster, Leinster, and Connacht. The government offices are accessible only via 35-minute guided tours; phone for details. They are dramatically illuminated every night. ⊠ *Upper Merrion St., Georgian Dublin* ☎ *01/619–4249* ⊕ *www.taoiseach.gov. ie* ✉ *Free; pick up tickets from National Gallery on day of tour.*

Irish Jewish Museum

MUSEUM | Roughly 5,000 European Jews fleeing the pogroms of Eastern Europe arrived in Ireland in the late 19th and early 20th centuries. Today the Jewish population hovers around 1,800. The museum, opened in 1985 by Israeli president Chaim Herzog (himself Dublin educated), includes a restored synagogue and a display of photographs, letters, and personal memorabilia culled from Dublin's most prominent Jewish families. Exhibits trace the Jewish presence in Ireland back to 1067. In homage to Leopold Bloom, the Jewish protagonist of Joyce's *Ulysses*, every Jewish reference in the novel has been identified. The museum is a 20-minute-or-so walk southwest from St. Stephen's Green. ⊠ *3–4 Walworth Rd., Georgian Dublin* ☎ *085/706–7357* ⊕ *www.jewishmuseum.ie* ✉ *Free* ⊘ *May–Sept., closed Fri. and Sat.; Oct.– Apr., closed Mon.–Sat.*

★ Merrion Square

PLAZA | Created between 1762 and 1764, this tranquil square a few blocks east of St. Stephen's Green is lined on three sides by some of Dublin's best-preserved Georgian town houses, many of which have brightly painted front doors crowned by intricate fanlights. Leinster House, the National Museum of Natural History, and the National Gallery line the west side of the square. It's on the other sides, however, that the Georgian terrace streetscape comes into its own—the finest houses are on the north border. Even when the flower gardens here are not in bloom, the vibrant, mostly evergreen grounds, dotted with sculpture and threaded with meandering paths, are worth strolling through. Several distinguished Dubliners have lived on the square, including Oscar Wilde's parents, Sir William and "Speranza" Wilde (No. 1); Irish national leader Daniel O'Connell (No. 58); and authors W.B. Yeats (Nos. 52 and 82) and Sheridan LeFanu (No. 70). Until 50 years ago the square was a fashionable residential area, but today most of the houses serve as offices. At the south end of Merrion Square, on Upper Mount Street, stands the Church of Ireland St. Stephen's Church. Known locally as the "pepper canister" church because of its cupola, the structure was inspired in part by Wren's churches in London. An open-air art gallery featuring the works of local artists is held on the square on Sunday. ⊠ *Georgian Dublin* ⊕ *www.merrionart. com.*

Reflected in the waters of the Liffey, the Custom House is just one of the many famed Dublin landmarks spectacularly illuminated at night.

★ National Gallery of Ireland

MUSEUM | Established in 1864, and designed by Francis Fowke (who also designed London's Victoria & Albert Museum), the National Gallery of Ireland is one of Europe's finest smaller art museums. But unlike most, the National Gallery can be thoroughly covered in a morning or afternoon without inducing exhaustion. A highlight of the museum is the major collection of paintings by Irish artists from the 17th through 20th centuries. The Yeats Museum section contains works by members of the Yeats family, including Jack B. Yeats, the brother of writer W.B. Yeats. The collection also claims exceptional paintings from the 17th-century French, Dutch, Italian, and Spanish schools, and works by French impressionists Monet, Sisley, and Renoir. Highlights include Caravaggio's *The Taking of Christ* (1602), Van Gogh's *Rooftops of Paris* (1886), and Vermeer's *Lady Writing a Letter with Her Maid* (circa 1670). ■TIP➜ **Free guided tours are available on Saturday at 12:30 and on Sunday at 12:30 and 1:30.** ✉ *Merrion Sq. W, Georgian Dublin*

☎ *01/661–5133* ⊕ *www.nationalgallery.ie* ✉ *Free; special exhibits €10.*

National Library

LIBRARY | Along with works by W.B. Yeats, George Bernard Shaw, Samuel Beckett, and Seamus Heaney, the National Library contains first editions of every major Irish writer, including Jonathan Swift, Oliver Goldsmith, and James Joyce. In addition, almost every book ever published in Ireland is kept here, along with an unequaled selection of old maps and an extensive collection of Irish newspapers and magazines. The stiff Neoclassical building is no showpiece, but the main Reading Room, opened in 1890 to house the collections of the Royal Dublin Society, has a dramatic dome ceiling, beneath which countless authors have researched and written. The personal papers of greats such as W.B. Yeats are also on display. ■TIP➜ **The library has a free genealogical consultancy service that can advise you on how to trace your Irish ancestors.** ✉ *Kildare St., Georgian Dublin*

01/603–0200 ⊕ www.nli.ie ⊠ Free
⊗ Closed Sun.

★ National Museum of Archaeology

MUSEUM | Ireland's National Museum of Archaeology, one of four branches of the National Museum of Ireland, is home to a fabled collection of Irish artifacts dating from 7000 BC to the present. The museum holds the largest collection of Celtic antiquities in the world, including gold jewelry, carved stones, bronze tools, and weapons. The Treasury collection, including some of the museum's most renowned pieces, is open on a permanent basis. Among the priceless relics on display are the 8th-century Ardagh Chalice, a two-handled silver cup with gold filigree ornamentation; the bronze-coated iron St. Patrick's Bell, the oldest surviving example (5th–8th century) of Irish metalwork; the 8th-century Tara Brooch, an intricately decorated piece made of white bronze, amber, and glass; and the 12th-century bejeweled oak Cross of Cong, covered with silver and bronze panels. Other exhibits are devoted to Irish goldwork, "Viking Ireland," and preserved bodies that have been found in Ireland's peat bogs. ⊠ Kildare St. Annex, 7–9 Merrion Row, Georgian Dublin ☎ 01/677–7444 ⊕ www.museum.ie ⊠ Free ⊗ Closed Mon.

National Museum of Natural History

MUSEUM | **FAMILY** | One of four branches of the National Museum of Ireland, this museum is little changed from Victorian times and remains a fascinating repository of mounted mammals, birds, and other flora and fauna. Locals still affectionately refer to the place as the "Dead Zoo." The Irish Room houses the most famous exhibits: skeletons of the extinct, prehistoric, giant Irish elk. The International Animals Collection includes a 65-foot whale skeleton suspended from the roof. Another highlight is the very beautiful Blaschka Collection, finely detailed glass models of marine creatures, the zoological accuracy of which has never

been achieved again in glass. Exhibitions include *Mating Game* and *Taxonomy Trail*. Built in 1856 to hold the Royal Dublin Society's rapidly expanding collection, it was designed by Frederick Clarendon to sit in harmony with the National Gallery on the other side of Leinster Lawn. When it was completed, it formed an annex to Leinster House and was connected to it by a curved, closed Corinthian colonnade. In 1909 a new entrance was constructed at the east end of the building on Merrion Street. ⊠ Merrion St., Georgian Dublin ☎ 01/677–7444 ⊕ www.museum.ie ⊠ Free ⊗ Closed Mon.

Royal Hibernian Academy

MUSEUM | The Royal Hibernian Academy, an old Dublin institution, is housed in a well-lighted building, one of the largest exhibition spaces in the city. The gallery holds adventurous exhibitions of the best in contemporary art, both from Ireland and abroad. ⊠ 15 Ely Pl., off St. Stephen's Green, Georgian Dublin ☎ 01/661–2558 ⊕ www.rhagallery.ie ⊠ Free.

🍴 Restaurants

Café Joly

$ | **IRISH** | The National Library's light-filled tearoom, Café Joly is usually one of the city's more serene lunchtime spots. There's a light, French-country influence to the fare, with top specials including smoked fish plates and charcuterie boards. "Cup and Crust" (small soup, half a sandwich) is a lunchtime favorite. $ Average main: €12 ⊠ Kildare St., Georgian Dublin ☎ 01/603–0257 ⊕ www.nli.ie/ en/cafe-and-shop.aspx ⊟ No credit cards.

Chai-Yo

$$ | **ASIAN** | The Japanese teppanyaki area at this classy Pan-Asian restaurant on bustling Baggot Street, where the chef cooks your food right on your tabletop, is a feast for the eye as well as the palate. The simplicity of the white walls and dark lacquered furnishings are enhanced by the delicate glassware and

Continued on page 116

LITERARY DUBLIN

A PLAYWRIGHT ON EVERY CORNER

As any visit to the Dublin Writers Museum will prove, this city packs more literary punch per square foot than practically any other spot on the planet. While the Irish capital may be relatively small in geographic terms, it looms huge as a country of the imagination. Dubliners wrote some of the greatest works of Western literature, including these immortal titles: *Ulysses,* *Gulliver's Travels, Dracula, The Importance of Being Earnest, and Waiting for Godot.* Today Dublin is a veritable literary theme park: within a few minutes' walk you can visit the James Joyce Centre, visit the Abbey Theatre, and pop into the pub where Brendan Behan loved to get marinated.

Above, Long Gallery library at Trinity College; Left and right, first editions of Joyce, Swift, Behan, and O'Casey

Dubliners

by JAMES JOYCE

THE ALBATROSS

Ulysses, First American Edition

Dublin Writers Museum, Gallery of Writers

A WAY WITH WORDS

As tellers of the tallest tales, speakers of Gaelic (reputedly the world's most perfect medium for prayers, curses, and seduction), and the finest practitioners of the art of blarney, it's little surprise that the Hibernian race produced no fewer than four Nobel prize winners: Shaw, W. B. Yeats, Samuel Beckett, and Seamus Heaney. But what is surprising is that this tiny, long-colonized island on the outskirts of Europe somehow managed to maneuver itself to the very heart of literature in the language of the invader itself, English. And at that heart's core lies Dublin.

A ramble through literary Dublin is a crash course in Irish soul.

FOR BETTER OR VERSE

By the 18th century, the Gaelic tradition was trumped by the boom of literature written in English, often by second- or third-generation descendants of English settlers, such as William Congreve, Richard Brinsley Sheridan, and Oliver Goldsmith. With the establishment of the Irish Free State in 1922, so many Irish writers found themselves censored that "being banned" became a matter of prestige (it also did wonders for book sales abroad, with a smuggled copy of *Ulysses* becoming the ultimate status symbol). Sadly, many writers became exiles; most famously, Joyce was joined in Paris by Beckett in 1932.

DUBLIN B(U)Y THE BOOK

Book lovers know that a guidebook to this city is an anthology of Irish literature in itself. Dublin's Northside is studded with landmarks immortalized in James Joyce's novels. A stone's throw from the Liffey is the Abbey Theater, a potent symbol of Ireland's great playwrights. To the south lies Trinity College, alma mater of Jonathan Swift, Bram Stoker, Oscar Wilde, and Samuel Beckett. And scattered around the city are hundreds of pubs where storytelling evolved as the incurable Irish "disease." They are the perfect places to take a time-out while touring Dublin's leading literary shrines and sites.

THE TRAIL OF TALES

Allowing you to turn the pages of the city, as it were, with your feet, a literary ramble through Dublin is a magical mystery tour through more than 400 years of Irish history.

The view from Front Square, Trinity College

DUBLIN WRITERS MUSEUM. The best place to start any literary tour of the city, this gloriously restored 18th-century mansion was once the home of the Jameson Whiskey family (booze and writers are never too far apart in Dublin). Its Edwardian rooms are filled with inky treasures like the 1804 edition of Swift's *Gulliver's Travels* and the 1899 first edition of Stoker's *Dracula*. ✉ *18 Parnell Sq. N.*

GATE THEATRE. Landmarked by its noble Palladian portico, this magnificent Georgian theater (built 1784) today sees the premieres of some of Ireland's most talked-about plays. Orson Welles and James Mason got their starts here. ✉ *Cavendish Row.*

JAMES JOYCE CENTRE. Now an extensive library dedicated to arguably the greatest novelist of the 20th century, this sumptuously decorated 18th-century town house was featured in *Ulysses* as a dancing academy. Letters from Beckett, Joyce's guitar and cane, and a Joyce edition illustrated by Matisse are collection highlights. ✉ *35 N. Great George's St.*

ABBEY THEATRE. Hard to believe this 1950s modernist eyesore is the fabled home of Ireland's national theater company, established on a wave of nationalist passion by Yeats and his patron, Lady Gregory, in 1904. Here premiered J. M. Synge's scandalous *Playboy of the Western World* and the working-class plays of Sean O'Casey. The foyer and bar display mementos of the theater's fabled "Abbeyists." ✉ *Lower Abbey St.*

TRINITY COLLEGE DUBLIN. This 400-year-old college has an incredible record for turning out literary giants like Swift, Goldsmith, Wilde, Synge, Stoker, and Beckett. Majestically presiding over its famous library is the 9th-century Book of Kells, mother of all Irish tomes.

NATIONAL LIBRARY. Joyce used the 1890 Main Reading Room, with its dramatic domed ceiling, as the scene of the great literary debate in *Ulysses*. At No. 30 Kildare Street a plaque marks a former residence of *Dracula's* creator, Bram Stoker. ✉ *Kildare St.*

MERRION SQUARE. An elegant mansion, which can be toured, No. 1 Merrion Square is the former Oscar Wilde family residence. A statue of Oscar reclines in the park opposite. Around the square, note the plaques

Neary's Pub

that indicate former residents, including W. B. Yeats and Sheridan le Fanu, Dublin's most famous ghost-story teller.

ST. STEPHEN'S GREEN. This pretty, flower-filled park is home to a wonderful statue of Joyce.

NEARY'S PUB. The Victorian-style interiors here were once haunted by Dublin's literary set, most notably the raconteur Brendan Behan. ⊠ 1 Chatham St.

THE WINDING STAIR. Long known as a meeting place for generations of Dublin writers, this bookstore and restaurant makes a perfect pitstop on your literary ramble. ⊠ 40 Ormond Quay Lower.

A DUBLIN PANTHEON

JONATHAN SWIFT

"Where fierce indignation can no longer tear his heart": Swift, one of the great satirists in the English language, willed these words be carved on his tomb at Dublin's St. Patrick's Cathedral. Swift was born on November 30, 1667, in the Liberties area of Dublin. Life would deal him many misfortunes, but he gave as good as he got, venting his great anger with a pen sharper than any sword. His rage at the British government's mistreatment of the Irish was turned into the brilliant satire *A Modest Proposal* where he politely recommends a solution to the dual problems of hunger and overpopulation: breed babies for meat. Best remembered for the brilliant moral fable *Gulliver's Travels*, he died on October 19, 1745, and is buried in Dublin's St. Patrick's Cathedral, where he was dean.

OSCAR WILDE

The greatest wit of his age and arguably any other, Wilde was born on October 16, 1834, at 21 Westland Row in Dublin, the son of an eminent eye doctor. He was educated at Trinity College, where he was a promising boxer and was quoted as saying his greatest challenge was learning to live up to the blue china he had installed in his rooms. Wilde moved to London in 1879, where he married, had children, and became celebrated for the plays *The Importance of Being Earnest* and *Salome* and his titillating novel *The Picture of Dorian Gray*. But his life was always more famous than his work and a scandalous affair with the aristocratic Alfred Douglas finally led to his ruin and imprisonment.

W. B. YEATS

Poet, dramatist, and prose writer, Yeats—winner of the Nobel Prize for Literature in 1923—stands as one of the greatest English-language poets of the 20th century. And yet in Ireland itself he is best remembered for his key role in the struggle for Irish freedom and the revival of Irish culture, including his part in forming the Abbey Theatre (National Theatre). Born in the seaside suburb of Sandymount in Dublin in 1865, his fascination with Celtic folklore and the stories of Cuchulainn can be seen throughout his early poems and plays. But many of his greatest poems are haunted by the dashing figure of Maud Gonne, actress, revolutionary, and unrequited love. He died in 1939 in Paris but his body was buried in Drumcliffe, at the foot of Ben Bulben mountain in his beloved County Sligo.

GEORGE BERNARD SHAW

G. Bernard Shaw—he hated George, and never used it either personally or professionally—was born in Dublin in 1856. His father was a boozing corn merchant and his mother a professional singer. When Shaw was a boy his mother ran away with her voice coach, and it may be no coincidence that his plays are dotted with problem child/parent relationships. In 1886 he went to London where plays such as *Pygmalion* and *Saint Joan* helped propel him to international stardom. Pacifist, socialist, and feminist, Shaw was a true original; a radical in the real sense of the word, his work always challenged the norms of his day. He lived to the ripe old age of 94 and died in 1950 after falling off a ladder while trimming trees outside his house.

SEAN O'CASEY

The first working-class Irish literary great, dramatist O'Casey was born at 85 Upper Dorset Street in the inner-city Dublin slums in 1880. Problems with his eyes as a child kept him indoors where he gleaned a love of reading. An early advocate of Yeats's Celtic Revival, he later found his true faith in the socialism of union leader Jim Larkin. His trilogy of great tragicomedies—*Shadow of a Gunman, Juno and the Paycock,* and *The Plough and the Stars*—all deal with ordinary families caught up in the maelstrom of Irish politics and were performed at Yeats's Abbey in the 1920s. Their playful language and riotous action have made them classics ever since. He spent his later life in England and died in Devon in 1964.

BRENDAN BEHAN

Writer, fighter, drinker, and wit, Brendan Francis Behan was born in Dublin's Holles Street Hospital in 1923 into an educated, political working-class family. Urged on by his fiercely patriotic grandmother, he joined Fíanna Eireann, the youth wing of the IRA and in 1939 was jailed for three years for possessing explosives. In prison he began to write but it wasn't until the 1950s that he hit it big with *The Quare Fellow,* a play based on his prison experiences, and later works *The Hostage* and *Borstal Boy*. But it was in the bars of Dublin that the "demon drinker" Behan delivered many of his greatest lines—alas, lost now forever. A self-proclaimed "drinker with a writing problem," he died in 1964 at the age of only 41.

REJOICE!: The Darlin' Dublin of James Joyce

If Joyce fans make one pilgrimage in their lives, let it be to Dublin on June 16th for Bloomsday. June 16th, of course, is the day Leopold Bloom toured Dublin in Ulysses, and commemorative events take place all week long leading up to the big day (and night).

Grown men and women stroll the streets attired in black suits and carrying fresh bars of lemon soap in their pockets, imitating the unassuming hero of what is arguably the 20th century's greatest novel. Denounced as obscene, blasphemous, and unreadable when it was first published in 1922 (and then banned in the U.S. until 1933), this 1,000-page riff on Homer's *Odyssey* portrays three characters—Leopold Bloom, a Jewish ad salesman, his wife, Molly, and friend Stephen Dedalus—as they wander through Dublin during the span of one day, June 16th, 1904. Dedicated Joyceans flock to the weeklong event, now called "Bloomstime," for Bloomsday breakfasts (where they can enjoy, like Bloom himself, "grilled mutton kid- neys . . . which gave to his palate a fine tang of faintly scented urine"), readings, performances, and general merriment.

But don't despair if you miss Bloomsday, because you can experience the Dublin that inspired the author's novels year-round. James Joyce (1882–1941) set all his major works—*Dubliners, A Portrait of the Artist as a Young Man, Ulysses,* and *Finnegans Wake*—in the city where he was born and spent the first 22 years of his life. Joyce knew and remembered Dublin in such detail that he bragged (and that's the word) that, if the city were destroyed, it could be rebuilt in its entirety from his written works.

Left, Joyce Statue, Earl Street;
Top left, a portrait of James Joyce, 1915
Top right, Bloomsday celebrations

IN THE FOOTSTEPS OF A POET: A James Joyce Walk

Begin in the heart of the Northside, on Prince's Street, next to the GPO (General Post Office), where the office of the old and popular *Freeman's Journal* newspaper (published 1763–1924) was once located and where Bloom once worked.

Head north up O'Connell Street down Parnell Square before turning right onto Dorset Street and then left onto Eccles Street. Leopold and Molly Bloom's fictional home stood at 7 Eccles Street, north of Parnell Square.

Head back to Dorset Street and go east. Take a right onto Gardiner Street and then a left onto Great Denmark Street and Belvedere College. Between 1893 and 1898, Joyce studied at Belvedere College under the Jesuits; it's housed in a splendid 18th-century mansion. The **James Joyce Centre**, a few steps from Belvedere College on North Great George's Street, is the hub of Bloomsday celebrations.

Go back to Gardiner Street and then south until you come to Railway Street on your left. The site of **Bella Cohen's Brothel** (✉ *82 Railway St.*) is in an area that in Joyce's day had

many houses of ill repute. A long walk back down O'Connell Street to the bridge and then a right will take you to Ormond Quay. On the western edge of the Northside, the (closed) **Ormond Quay Hotel**,

under threat by developers, was an afternoon rendezvous spot for Bloom.

Across the Liffey, walk up Grafton Street to **Davy Byrne's Pub.** Here, Bloom comes to settle down for a glass of Burgundy and a Gorgonzola cheese sandwich, and meets his friend Nosey Flynn. Today, the pub has gone very upscale from its pre–World War II days, but even Joyce would have cracked a smile at the sight of the shamrock-painted ceiling and the murals of Joycean Dublin by Liam Proud.

After a stop at Davy Byrne's, proceed via Molesworth Street to the **National Library**— where Bloom has a near meeting with Blazes Boylan, his wife's lover. Walk up Molesworth Street until you hit Trinity. Take a right and walk to Lincoln Place. No establishment mentioned by Joyce has changed less since his time than **Sweny's Pharmacy** (✉ *Lincoln Pl.*). Today volunteers maintain the shop as it was in Joyce's time.

Map labels

7 Eccles
Eccles St. Lower Dorset St.
Upper Gardiner St.
Mountjoy Square
Belvedere College
Great Denmark St.
Upper Dorset St.
George's St. N. Great
James Joyce Centre
Parnell Square
Summerhill
Gardiner St.
Bella Cohen's Brothel
Railway St.
Parnell St.
O'Connell St.
Earl St. N. Talbot St.
Prince's St. General Post Office
New Ormond Hotel
Bachelor's Walk
River Liffey
Aston Quay
Anglesea St.
College Green
Grafton St.
Trinity College
College Park
Duke St.
Davy Byrne's Pub
Molesworth St.
Leinster St. Lincoln Place
Sweny's Pharmacy
National Library
Leinster Lawn

0   1,000 ft
0   300 m

fine green-washed porcelain. **Known for:** food prepared at the table; Asian tapas; bustling atmosphere. ⑤ *Average main: €22* ⊠ *100 Lower Baggot St., Georgian Dublin* ☎ *01/676–7652* ⊕ *www.chaiyo.ie* ⊘ *No lunch weekends.*

Dax

$$$ | FRENCH | When is a wine bar not just a wine bar? When it's also one of the city's most talked-about restaurants where you can drink or dine (tapas-style) at the bar, in the lush armchairs of the open-plan lounge, or in the more formal, restrained-modern dining room. **Known for:** impressive by-the-glass wines; relaxed atmosphere; great bar-food options. ⑤ *Average main: €30* ⊠ *23 Pembroke St., Georgian Dublin* ☎ *01/676–1494* ⊕ *www.dax.ie* ⊘ *Closed Sun. and Mon. No lunch Sat.*

Ely Winebar

$$$ | IRISH | Almost equidistant from the twin dames of Dublin hotel elegance, the Shelbourne and the Merrion, Ely started out as a mere wine bar—and oh, what a selection of wines they have—but it has quickly grown into a wonderful little eatery with organic meat and vegetables from the owner's family farm in County Clare. Dishes such as Burren beef carpaccio with pine nuts and arugula are simple but incredibly fresh and succulent. **Known for:** endless wine list; organic local ingredients; sumptuous cheese board. ⑤ *Average main: €25* ⊠ *22 Ely Pl., Georgian Dublin* ☎ *01/676–8986* ⊕ *www.elywinebar.ie* ⊘ *Closed Sun. No lunch Sat.*

★ Forest Avenue

$$$ | CONTEMPORARY | Named after the street in Queens where chef-owner Sandy Wyer grew up, Forest Avenue is a rising star on the Dublin food stage. The menu is a five-course taster, and while choice is limited, quality and value are off the charts. **Known for:** warm, friendly vibe; daring tasting menu; pairing wine with food. ⑤ *Average main: €32* ⊠ *8 Sussex Terr., Georgian Dublin* ☎ *01/667–8337*

⊕ *www.forestavenuerestaurant.ie* ⊘ *Closed Sun.–Tues. No Lunch Wed.*

★ The French Paradox

$$ | FRENCH | Relaxed, simple, but chic would best describe this little restaurant above a wineshop in the heart of Balls-bridge; it also describes the people of the south of France who inspired the place. Wine buffs, Francophiles, and gourmets flock here for the hearty traditional fare and Mediterranean ambience. **Known for:** ground-floor wineshop; charcuterie; trendy crowd. ⑤ *Average main: €20* ⊠ *53 Shelbourne Rd., Georgian Dublin* ☎ *01/660–4068* ⊕ *www.thefrenchpara-dox.com* ⊘ *Closed Sun.*

★ Restaurant Patrick Guilbaud

$$$$ | FRENCH | Also known as "Dublin's finest restaurant," this do-be-impressed place on the ground floor of the Merrion Hotel boasts a menu described as French, but chef Guillaume Lebrun's genius lies in his occasional daring use of traditional Irish ingredients—so often taken for granted—to create the unexpected. The ambience is just as delicious, if you're into lofty, minimalist dining rooms and Irish modern art (the Roderic O'Conors and Louis le Brocquys are all from the owner's private collection). **Known for:** award-winning chef; Annagassan blue lobster; Irish modern art collection. ⑤ *Average main: €60* ⊠ *21 Upper Merrion St., Georgian Dublin* ☎ *01/676–4192* ⊕ *www.restaurantpatrick-guilbaud.ie* ⊘ *Closed Sun. and Mon.*

Roly's Bistro

$$$ | BISTRO | While the bistro food at this Ballsbridge stalwart is always top-class, it's the jovial atmosphere and superb service that keep locals coming back. It's famed for the wine list, with great options by the glass, and that certainly helps to explain the wonderful buzz that always seems to be about this popular neighborhood place. **Known for:** wine list; jovial vibe; seafood. ⑤ *Average main: €26* ⊠ *7 Ballsbridge Terr., Georgian Dublin*

Topped by half-moon fanlights, the brightly hued doorways of Merrion Square are icons of Dublin's 18th-century Georgian style.

☎ 01/668–2611 ⊕ www.rolysbistro.ie
▤ No credit cards.

Unicorn

$$$ | MEDITERRANEAN | In the art of creating the perfect place to get slightly sozzled over some quality eats, the Unicorn is a master. Posh locals love to head here when they want to let their hair down in some wine-fueled, late-evening craic: the atmosphere is loose and relaxed, especially on the little terrace overlooking Merrion Court, and the menu is scrumptious Italian. **Known for:** a lively clientele; terrace eating in summer; antipasti. ⑤ *Average main: €30* ⊠ *12B Merrion Ct., Georgian Dublin* ☎ *091/5998–4874* ⊕ *www.theunicorn.restaurant* ⊘ *Closed Sun. No lunch Sat.*

 Hotels

Ariel Guest House

$$ | B&B/INN | The homemade preserves and oven-warm scones are reason enough to stay at this redbrick 1850 Victorian guesthouse, in one of Dublin's poshest tree-lined suburbs and a 15-minute walk from St. Stephen's Green. **Pros:** four-poster beds in larger rooms; fantastic collection of Victoriana throughout the house; good price for smaller rooms. **Cons:** no elevator; a good walk to the city center. ⑤ *Rooms from: €179* ⊠ *52 Lansdowne Rd., Georgian Dublin* ☎ *01/668–5512* ⊕ *www.ariel-house.net* ⇋ *37 rooms* ⦿⧉ *No meals.*

Dylan Hotel

$$$$ | HOTEL | Formerly a Victorian-era nurses' boardinghouse, then the dreary Hibernian Hotel, the Dylan, with a recent refurbishment of its previous vampy Victorian decor, has sharpened its style with a focus on contemporary Irish design rich in tones and textures that make this boutique property a more refined, opulent option. **Pros:** a quiet side street but still close to bars and restaurants; great bar and restaurant on-site; modern rooms and amenities. **Cons:** business-heavy area; breakfast is extra; no gym or spa. ⑤ *Rooms from: €330* ⊠ *Eastmoreland Pl.,*

Georgian Dublin ☎ *01/660–3000* ⊕ *www. dylan.ie* 🛏 *72 rooms* ⦿ *No meals.*

Herbert Park Hotel

$$ | HOTEL | Only a short distance from the city, this hotel nestled next to leafy Herbert Park and the doddering Dodder River feels pleasantly secluded—to maximize enjoyment, you'll want to secure a room overlooking the park, or go for one of the two suites with balconies. **Pros:** independently owned hotel; terrace dining in summer; secluded city setting. **Cons:** looks a little like an office block; rooms not too exciting; outside the city center. $ *Rooms from: €190* ⊠ *Merrion Rd., Georgian Dublin* ☎ *01/667–2200* ⊕ *www.herbertparkhotel.ie* 🛏 *153 rooms* ⦿ *No meals.*

★ Intercontinental Dublin

$$$$ | HOTEL | Set within the show grounds of the Royal Dublin Society, this Victorian-Georgian hybrid—topped by gigantic eaves and a lovely cupola—has an impressive 4 acres of gardens; a big effort has been made to ensure that a bit of greenery can be seen from most rooms. **Pros:** one of the country's top spas; full range of facilities; Lobby Lounge great for afternoon tea. **Cons:** a bit of an architectural mishmash; room design not the most inventive. $ *Rooms from: €300* ⊠ *Simmonscourt Rd., Georgian Dublin* ☎ *01/665–4000* ⊕ *www. intercontinental.com/dublin* 🛏 *197 rooms* ⦿ *No meals.*

Kilronan House Hotel

$$ | B&B/INN | Just a five-minute walk from St. Stephen's Green, this mid-19th-century terraced guesthouse, with its elegant white facade and cozy sitting-room fire, will welcome you home at the end of a long day's sightseeing. **Pros:** great price for location; beautiful, calming facade; cozy sitting room. **Cons:** public areas a bit worn; uncreative room furnishings; no elevator. $ *Rooms from: €180* ⊠ *70 Adelaide Rd., Georgian Dublin* ☎ *01/475–5266* ⊕ *www.kilronanhouse. com* 🛏 *14 rooms* ⦿ *Free breakfast.*

What a Character!

Check out one of the National Gallery's most eye-catching paintings, Sir Joshua Reynolds's *First Earl of Bellomont* (1773). Depicted in pink silks and ostrich plumes, Charles Coote was a notorious womanizer and was shot in the groin for his troubles by rival Lord Townshend. Famously, Coote gave his inaugural speech as quartermaster general of Ireland in French, continually referred to his County Cavan neighbors as "Hottentots," and wound up marrying the daughter of the super-rich Duke of Leinster.

★ The Merrion Hotel

$$$$ | HOTEL | Stately and spiffy, and splendidly situated directly across from the Government Buildings between St. Stephen's Green and Merrion Square, this luxurious hotel actually comprises four exactingly restored Georgian town houses. **Pros:** Michelin-starred restaurant; infinity pool; city-center location. **Cons:** you'll pay extra for a room in the original house; some rooms are overdecorated. $ *Rooms from: €440* ⊠ *Upper Merrion St., Georgian Dublin* ☎ *01/603–0600* ⊕ *www.merrionhotel.com* 🛏 *142 rooms* ⦿ *No meals.*

★ Number 31

$$$$ | B&B/INN | Whether your lodging style is sublime Georgian elegance or cool modern, this one-in-a-million guesthouse, a short walk from St. Stephen's Green, serves up both—as well as the best made-to-order breakfast in town. **Pros:** the king and queen of guesthouse hosts; serene decor and art; fantastic breakfasts. **Cons:** a few rooms can be a little noisy; no elevator; minimum two-night stay on summer weekends. $ *Rooms from: €290* ⊠ *31 Leeson Close,*

Georgian Dublin ☎ *01/676–5011* ⊕ *www.
number31.ie* 🛏 *21 rooms* ⍾⊙⍾ *Free
breakfast.*

★ Pembroke Townhouse

$$ | B&B/INN | "Townhouse" does not do
justice to the splendor of the place, but
it does hint at the cozy, relaxed atmosphere of the Pembroke, a superb example of classic 18th-century grandeur. **Pros:**
a Georgian wonderland; big, airy rooms;
privately owned. **Cons:** 15-minute trip to
the city center; often books up early; no
a/c. ⑤ *Rooms from: €180* ✉ *90 Pembroke
Rd., Georgian Dublin* ☎ *01/660–0277*
⊕ *www.pembroketownhouse.ie* 🛏 *48
rooms* ⍾⊙⍾ *No meals.*

Premier Suites Dublin

$$ | HOTEL | FAMILY | Get a top-floor suite
at this modernized Georgian town house
just off St. Stephen's Green and lord it
over the whole Southside. **Pros:** spectacular city views; ground-floor suites have
private entrances; good family option.
Cons: decor is "motel functional"; lacks
facilities; rooms vary in quality. ⑤ *Rooms
from: €195* ✉ *14–17 Lower Leeson St.,
Georgian Dublin* ☎ *01/638–1111* ⊕ *www.
premiersuitesdublinleesonstreet.com*
🛏 *37 rooms* ⍾⊙⍾ *No meals.*

★ Schoolhouse Hotel

$$ | HOTEL | Pardon the pun, but this con-
verted Victorian parochial school just off
the Grand Canal really is A-plus—set in a
gorgeous example of 19th-century architecture complete with turrets and soaring
nave (now the setting for the restaurant),
this may be the most uniquely up-cycled
hotel in Ireland. **Pros:** unique building;
top-class Irish restaurant; in-room spa
treatments. **Cons:** a trip to the city center;
fills up quickly; no elevator. ⑤ *Rooms
from: €199* ✉ *2–8 Northumberland Rd.,
Georgian Dublin* ☎ *01/667–5014* ⊕ *www.
schoolhousehotel.com* 🛏 *31 rooms*
⍾⊙⍾ *No meals.*

�)| Nightlife

PUBS

Cellar Bar

BARS/PUBS | An 18th-century wine vault
with bare brick walls and vaulted ceilings,
this spot at the superstylish Merrion
Hotel tends to draw a well-heeled crowd.
✉ *24 Upper Merrion St., Georgian Dublin*
☎ *01/603–0600* ⊕ *www.merrionhotel.
com.*

The 51 Bar

BARS/PUBS | Famous for its collection of
whiskeys from around the world, the 51
has a beer garden that is always buzzing
with activity in fine weather. ✉ *51 Haddington Rd., Ballsbridge* ☎ *01/660–0150*
⊕ *www.the51bar.com.*

The Horse Show House

BARS/PUBS | A Ballsbridge institution, the
Horse Show House is a favorite of the
boisterous but welcoming rugby and
show-jumping set. A great spot to watch
sports of any kind. They have a full à la
carte menu. ✉ *32 Merrion Rd., Georgian
Dublin* ☎ *01/668–9424* ⊕ *www.madigan.
ie.*

Leeson Lounge

BARS/PUBS | This has the look of a classic
old Dublin "boozer," with one notable
exception: it has a television. The Leeson
is known as a place to watch televised
sports of all kinds, and it's always
pleasant and inclusive. There's often
live music; Tuesday is popular for jazz.
✉ *148 Upper Leeson St., Georgian Dublin*
☎ *01/660–3816.*

Toner's

BARS/PUBS | Though billed as a Victorian
bar, Toner's actually goes back 200 years,
with an original flagstone floor to prove
its antiquity, as well as wooden drawers
running up to the ceiling—a relic of the
days when bars doubled as grocery
shops. Oliver St. John Gogarty, who was
the model for Buck Mulligan in James
Joyce's *Ulysses,* accompanied W. B.
Yeats here, in what was purportedly the

latter's only visit to a pub. ✉ *139 Lower Baggot St., Georgian Dublin* ☎ *01/676–3090* ⊕ *www.tonerspub.ie.*

 Performing Arts

CLASSICAL MUSIC AND OPERA
The National Concert Hall
MUSIC | Just off St. Stephen's Green, the National Concert Hall is Dublin's main theater for classical music of all kinds, from symphonies to chamber groups. The slightly austere Neoclassical building was transformed in 1981 into one of Europe's finest medium-size concert halls. It houses the cream of Irish classical musicians, the National Symphony Orchestra of Ireland. A host of guest international conductors and performers—Maxim Vengerov, Radu Lupu, and Pinchas Zukerman are just a few of the soloists who have appeared—keep the standard very high, and performances continue throughout the year. The concert year picks up speed in mid-September and sails through to June; July and August also get many dazzling troupes. The smaller, more intimate John Field and Carolan rooms are perfect for chamber music. ✉ *Earlsfort Terr., Georgian Dublin* ☎ *01/417–0000* ⊕ *www.nch.ie.*

 Activities

HORSE RACING
Leopardstown Racecourse
HORSE RACING/SHOW | The hub of horse racing in Dublin is Leopardstown, an ultramodern course that in February hosts the Hennessey Gold Cup, one of Ireland's most prestigious steeplechases. Summertime is devoted to flat racing, and the rest of the year to racing over fences. You can also nip in for a quick meal at the restaurant. ✉ *Leopardstown Rd., Georgian Dublin* ☎ *01/289–3600* ⊕ *www.leopardstown.com.*

RUGBY
For many years rugby was a "garrison sport" in Ireland, the preserve of "West Brits" and private-school boys. The success of the Irish team internationally, and Ulster, Leinster, and Munster in European club competitions, has changed that somewhat, and you might see an oval ball being tossed around by kids in any area of the country.

Aviva Stadium
SOCCER | The home ground of Irish rugby and soccer, Aviva's state-of-the-art arena opened in 2010 (on the site of the old Lansdowne Stadium) and can accommodate 50,000 fans. ✉ *62 Lansdowne Rd., Georgian Dublin* ☎ *01/238–2300* ⊕ *www.avivastadium.ie.*

 Shopping

CLOTHING
Cleo
CLOTHING | Hand-knit sweaters and accessories made only from natural fibers are a specialty at Cleo. ✉ *18 Kildare St., Georgian Dublin* ☎ *01/676–1421* ⊕ *www.cleo-ltd.com.*

Temple Bar

Locals complain about the late-night noise, and visitors sometimes say the place has the feel of a Dublin theme park, but a visit to Dublin wouldn't be complete without spending some time in the city's most famously vibrant area. More than any other neighborhood in the city, Temple Bar represents the dramatic changes (good and bad) and ascending fortunes of Dublin that came about in the last few decades. The area, which takes its name from one of the streets of its central spine, was targeted for redevelopment in 1991–92 after a long period of neglect, having survived widely rumored plans to turn it into a massive bus depot or a giant parking lot. Temple Bar took off as Dublin's version of New

York's SoHo, Paris's Bastille, or London's Notting Hill—a thriving mix of high and alternative culture distinct from what you'll find in any other part of the city. Dotting the area's narrow cobblestone streets and pedestrian alleyways are apartment buildings (inside they tend to be small and uninspired), vintage-clothing stores, postage-stamp-size boutiques selling overpriced gewgaws, art galleries, roaring traditional-music bars aimed at tourists, a hotel resuscitated by U2, hip restaurants, pubs, clubs, European-style cafés, and a smattering of cultural venues.

Temple Bar's regeneration was no doubt abetted by that one surefire real-estate asset that appealed to the Viking founders of the area: location. The area is bordered by Dame Street to the south, the Liffey to the north, Fishamble Street to the west, and Westmoreland Street to the east. In fact, Temple Bar is situated so perfectly between everywhere else in Dublin that it's difficult to believe this neighborhood was once largely forsaken. It's now sometimes called the "playing ground of young Dublin," and for good reason: on weekend evenings and daily in summer it teems with young people—not only from Dublin but from all over Europe—drawn by its pubs, clubs, and lively scene.

Sights

The Ark
ARTS VENUE | FAMILY | A self-described cultural center for children, The Ark engages and inspires young imaginations through a variety of creative endeavors and activities like music, poetry readings, film, dance, painting, interactive exhibitions, and more. Its theater opens onto Meeting House Square for outdoor performances in summer. A gallery and workshop space host ongoing activities. ⊠ *11a Eustace St., Temple Bar* ☎ *01/670–7788* ⊕ *www.ark.ie* 🎟 *Free.*

Blackrock Market

Held every weekend just off the Main Street in Blackrock Village (take the DART to Blackrock), the mostly covered Blackrock Market is one of the oldest markets in the country and offers a classic, eclectic assortment of bric-a-brac with rare objects, furniture, books, crystals, herbs, and just about everything else. With more than 50 vendors in attendance, this market has a vibrant European-flea-market feel and is a great spot for bargain hunting, souvenir shopping, or just wandering. ⊕ *www.blackrockmarket.com*

Gallery of Photography
MUSEUM | Dublin's premier photography gallery has a permanent collection of early-20th-century Irish photography and also puts on monthly exhibitions of work by contemporary Irish and international photographers. The gallery is an invaluable social record of Ireland. The bookstore is the best place in town to browse for photography books and to pick up arty postcards. ⊠ *Meeting House Sq. S, Temple Bar* ☎ *01/671–4654* ⊕ *www.galleryofphotography.ie* 🎟 *Free.*

Ha'penny Bridge
BRIDGE/TUNNEL | Every Dubliner has a story about meeting someone on this cast-iron Victorian bridge, a heavily trafficked footbridge that crosses the Liffey at a prime spot—Temple Bar is on the south side, and the bridge provides the fastest route to the thriving Mary and Henry Streets shopping areas to the north. Until early in the 20th century, a halfpenny toll was charged to cross it. Congestion on the Ha'penny was relieved with the opening of the Millennium Footbridge a few hundred yards up the river. A

Temple Bar

Westmoreland Street

Surface Tram

Westmoreland

Trinity

Trinity College

Grafton Street

College Green

College Green

Suffolk Street

Price's Lane

Fleet Street

Aston Place

Aston Quay

Bedford Row

Anglesea Street

Asdill's Row

Fleet Street

Crown Alley

Fownes Street Upper

Temple Bar

TEMPLE BAR

Cope Street

Cecilia St.

Crow Street

Temple Lane S.

Curved St.

Eustace St.

Meeting House Square

Sycamore Street

Dame Street

Dame Lane

Dame Court

S. Great George's St.

Saint Andrew's St.

Trinity Street

Dame Street

Barnardo Square

Dublin Castle

Essex Street East

Essex Street Lower

Parliament Street

Exchange St. Upper

River Liffey

Ormond Quay Lower

Millennium Bridge

Swift's Row

Wellington Quay

Grattan Bridge

Capel Street

Great Strand St.

Little Strand St.

Ormond Quay Upper

Ormond Square

Essex Quay

Exchange Street Lower

Essex Street West

Cow's Lane

Fishamble Street

Lord Edward Street

Castle Street

100 m

250 ft

0

0

Sights ▶

1	The Ark	E2
2	Gallery of Photography	D2
3	Ha'penny Bridge	F1
4	Irish Film Institute (IFI)	E2
5	Meeting House Square	E2
6	National Library Photographic Archive	D2
7	Olympia Theatre	D2
8	Wall of Fame	E2

Restaurants ▶

1	Elephant & Castle	F1
2	Montys Of Kathmandu	E2
3	Toscana	C3

Hotels ▶

1	The Clarence	D2
2	Handel's Hotel Temple Bar	B3
3	The Morgan	G1
4	Paramount Hotel	C2

KEY

1 Exploring Sights

1 Restaurants

1 Hotels

refurbishment, including new railings, a return to the original white color, and tasteful lighting at night, has given the bridge a new lease on life.

Irish Film Institute (IFI)

ARTS VENUE | The opening of the IFI in a former Quaker meetinghouse helped to launch the revitalization of Temple Bar. It has three comfortable art-house cinemas showing revivals and new independent films, the Irish Film Archive, a bookstore for cineastes, and a popular bar and restaurant-café, all of which make this one of the neighborhood's most vital cultural institutions and *the* place to be seen. On Saturday nights in summer, films screen outdoors on Meeting House Square. ✉ *6 Eustace St., Temple Bar* ☎ *01/679–5744* ⊕ *www.ifi.ie* ✉ *Event ticket prices vary.*

Meeting House Square

PLAZA | A spectacular retractable canopy of four 70-foot "umbrellas" has turned this already vibrant square into a year-round playground for Dubliners. The square, which is behind the Ark children's center and accessed via Curved Street, takes its name from a nearby Quaker meetinghouse. Today it's something of a gathering place for Dublin's youth and artists. Numerous cultural events—classic movies, theater, games, and family programs—take place here. (Thankfully, seats can be installed for screenings.) The square is also a favorite site for the continuously changing street sculpture that pops up all over Temple Bar (artists commissioned by the city sometimes create oddball pieces, such as half of a Volkswagen protruding from a wall). The square is also a great spot to sit, people-watch, and take in the sounds of the performing buskers who swarm to the place. There's also an organic food market here every Saturday all day. ⊕ *www. meetinghousesquare.ie.*

National Library Photographic Archive

MUSEUM | This important photographic resource holds regular exhibitions in its stylish modern building in Temple Bar.

Too Great a Toll

William Butler Yeats was one of many Dubliners who found the halfpenny toll of Ha'penny Bridge too steep. He detoured to O'Connell Bridge instead.

The collection comprises approximately 600,000 photographs, most of which are Irish, making up a priceless visual history of the nation. Although most of the photographs are historical, dating as far back as the mid-19th century, there's also a large number of contemporary pictures. Subject matter ranges from topographical views to studio portraits, from political events to early tourist photographs. You can also buy a print of your favorite photo. ✉ *Meeting House Sq., Temple Bar* ☎ *01/603–0200* ⊕ *www. nli.ie/en/national-photographic-archive. aspx* ✉ *Free.*

Olympia Theatre

ARTS VENUE | One of the most atmospheric places in Europe to see musical acts, the Olympia is Dublin's second-oldest theater, and one of its busiest. This classic Victorian music hall, built in 1879, has a gorgeous red wrought-iron facade. The Olympia has brought numerous musical performers to Dublin, and the theater has also seen many notable actors strut across its stage, including Alec Guinness, Peggy Ashcroft, Noël Coward, and even the old-time Hollywood team of Laurel and Hardy. Big-name performers like Van Morrison often choose the intimacy of the Olympia over larger venues. It's really a hot place to see some fine performances, so if you have a chance, by all means, go. Conveniently, there are two pubs here—through doors directly off the back of the theater's orchestra section. Their Christmas Pantomime is a Dublin tradition and great for younger kids. ✉ *72 Dame*

St., Temple Bar ☎ 01/679–3323 ⊕ www. olympia.ie ✉ Event ticket prices vary.

Wall of Fame

PUBLIC ART | If you're strolling through Temple Bar and suddenly come upon a group of slack-jawed young people staring wide-eyed at a large wall, then you've probably stumbled upon the Wall of Fame. The whole front wall of the Button Factory music venue has become a giant tribute to the giants of Irish rock music. Twelve huge photos adorn the wall, including a very young and innocent U2, a very beautiful Sinead O'Connor, and a very drunk Shane McGowan. ✉ Curved St., Temple Bar ☎ 01/607–9202.

Restaurants

Elephant & Castle

$$ | **AMERICAN** | The Elephant was long established in Temple Bar before the Tiger (Celtic, that is) came and went and changed the neighborhood forever. Large windows are great for people-watching in the city's trendiest area, but "nothing fancy" would be a good motto for the traditional American food. **Known for:** generous portions; family-friendly vibes; bustling Sunday brunch. ⑤ Average main: €20 ✉ 18 Temple Bar, Temple Bar ☎ 01/679–3121 ⊕ www.elephantandcastle.ie.

Montys of Kathmandu

$$ | **ASIAN** | You might not expect to come to Dublin for fabulous Nepalese cuisine, but this place is a real standout. The decor is nothing to write home about, but the food at this little eatery in the middle of bustling Temple Bar is as authentic as it is unique. *Kachela*, raw minced lamb with garlic, ginger, herbs, and spices, served with roti bread (a delicacy among the Newars of Kathmandu) or a shot of whiskey, is a more adventurous starter. **Known for:** traditional Kathmandu dishes; momos, dumplings served with chutney; celiac-friendly menu. ⑤ Average main: €22 ✉ 28 Eustace St., Temple Bar ☎ 01/670–4911 ⊕ www.montys.ie ⊘ No lunch Sun.

Toscana

$ | **ITALIAN** | A genuine trattoria in the heart of crazy Temple Bar, Toscana buzzes with chatter all evening long and offers a popular pretheater menu. A Mediterranean slant to the simple dining room includes plenty of Italian landscapes, cream tones, and wood. **Known for:** quality pizza; seafood; Bailey's cheesecake. ⑤ Average main: €18 ✉ 3 Cork Hill, Dame St., Temple Bar ☎ 01/670–9785 ⊕ www. toscanarestaurant.ie.

Hotels

The Clarence

$$$ | **HOTEL** | Temple Bar's most prestigious hotel, and occasional home to your potential new best friends/elevator buddies, co-owners Bono and the Edge of U2, this renovated 1852 grand old hotel is the place to sample Temple Bar's nightlife, even if your pals are too busy rocking to hang. **Pros:** stylish Octagon Bar; the owners might be on-premises; Cleaver East restaurant. **Cons:** rooms a bit small; some rooms suffer from street noise; paying a premium for "cool". ⑤ Rooms from: €242 ✉ 6–8 Wellington Quay, Temple Bar ☎ 01/407–0800 ⊕ www.the-clarence.ie ⤳ 50 rooms ⦿ No meals.

Handel's Hotel Temple Bar

$$ | **HOTEL** | Right in the heart of Temple Bar, this basic but well-run hotel somehow manages to feel like something of an oasis from the hustle of this lively neighborhood. **Pros:** ideal location for nightlife; cleverly designed rooms; option of interconnecting rooms. **Cons:** rooms are small; noisy neighborhood; a little short on amenities. ⑤ Rooms from: €189 ✉ 16–18 Fishamble St., Temple Bar ☎ 01/670–9404 ⊕ www.thekeycollection.ie ▭ No credit cards ⤳ 40 rooms ⦿ No meals.

The Morgan

$$$ | **HOTEL** | A sparkling gem among a lot of very drab hotels in Temple Bar, the Morgan boasts about its chic design and decor, and the excitingly designed bedrooms and luxurious bathrooms are indeed pleasing to the many fashionistas and photographers who love this place. **Pros:** heated outside courtyard; great cocktail bar; extended-stay apartments are a good value. **Cons:** a little overdesigned in places; no parking; no restaurant. $ *Rooms from: €255 ☒ 10 Fleet St., Temple Bar ☎ 01/643–7000 ⊕ www.themorgan.com ⇨ 121 rooms* ⦿| *No meals.*

Paramount Hotel

$$ | **HOTEL** | Classic 1930s American movies seem to have been the inspiration for the interior of this medium-size hotel in the heart of Temple Bar—dark woods, leather, and subtle colors decorate the bedrooms, continuing the sleek, elegant look. **Pros:** stylish, integrated design; great location; midweek prices are good. **Cons:** street noise can be a problem; no a/c; fills up on weekends. $ *Rooms from: €145 ☒ Parliament St. and Essex Gate, Temple Bar ☎ 01/417–9900 ⊕ www.paramounthotel.ie ⇨ 64 rooms* ⦿| *No meals.*

Nightlife

NIGHTCLUBS

Button Factory

DANCE CLUBS | A happening music venue, the Button mixes top DJs and up-and-coming live acts. The place tends to be on the cutting edge of the Irish dance-music scene. ☒ *Curved St., Temple Bar ☎ 01/670–9202 ⊕ www.buttonfactory.ie.*

Club M

DANCE CLUBS | Club M is a large, old-school disco-type venue, popular with the suburban crowd in town for the night. It gets loud and sweaty but everyone seems to have fun. They only open Friday and Saturday night. ☒ *Cope St., Temple Bar ☎ 01/671–5274 ⊕ clubm.ie.*

The Turk's Head

DANCE CLUBS | The Turk's Head pub-nightclub is known for its extravagant mosaics, Moroccan woodwork, bits of Arabian Nights decor, and its world-culture (Latin,

reggae, funk, and flamenco) late nights. They also have live bands. ☒ *Paramount Hotel, 27–30 Parliament St., Temple Bar ☎ 01/679–9701 ⊕ www.paramounthotel.ie/dine-drinks.*

The Workman's Club

MUSIC CLUBS | Housed in a former workingman's club, this no-frills, hip spot specializes in indie club nights and attracts an artistic and hipster crowd. It has three floors of music and live gigs. Check the website for upcoming nights. ☒ *10 Wellington Quay, Temple Bar ☎ 01/670–6692 ⊕ www.theworkmansclub.com.*

PUBS

The Liquor Rooms

BARS/PUBS | This quality cocktail joint under the Clarence Hotel consists of individually designed rooms and a huge list of expertly made cocktails. ☒ *5 Wellington Quay, Temple Bar ☎ 087/339–3688 ⊕ www.theliquorrooms.com.*

Oliver St. John Gogarty

BARS/PUBS | A lively bar that attracts all ages and nationalities, the Oliver St. John Gogarty overflows with patrons in summer. On most nights there's traditional Irish music upstairs. ☒ *57 Fleet St., Temple Bar ☎ 01/671–1822 ⊕ www.gogartys.ie.*

Palace Bar

BARS/PUBS | Established in 1823, and scarcely changed since the 1940s, the Palace Bar is tiled and rather barren looking, but is popular with journalists and writers (the *Irish Times* used to be nearby). The walls are lined with cartoons drawn by newspaper illustrators. ☒ *21 Fleet St., Temple Bar ☎ 01/677–9290.*

The Porterhouse

BARS/PUBS | One of the few bars in Ireland to brew its own beer, the Plain Porter has won the best stout award at the "Brewing Oscars," beating out the mighty Guinness. The tasteful interior is all dark woods and soft lighting. ☒ *16–18 Parliament St., Temple Bar ☎ 01/679–8847 ⊕ www.theporterhouse.ie.*

Some Dubliners now give the Temple Bar district the brush-off; others still find it the pulsing aorta of the city's nightlife.

The Wild Duck

BARS/PUBS | Filled to the brim with the owner's wonderful collection of art and retro furniture, this eclectic bar hosts jazz, drama, and pretty much anything else you fancy in its small theater space. The piano player in the corner keeps the place hopping at nights. ✉ *17/22 Sycamore Street, Temple Bar* ☎ *01/535–6849* ⊕ *www.thewildduck.ie.*

Performing Arts

CLASSICAL MUSIC AND OPERA

Opera Theatre Company

MUSIC | Ireland's only touring opera company, the Opera Theatre company performs at venues in Dublin and throughout the country. ✉ *Temple Bar Music Centre, Curved St., Temple Bar* ☎ *01/679–4962* ⊕ *www.opera.ie.*

ROCK AND CONTEMPORARY MUSIC

Olympia Theatre

MUSIC | Everything from rock tribute bands to country greats is presented at the Olympia, which is noted for its intense atmosphere and great acoustics. ✉ *72 Dame St., Temple Bar* ☎ *01/679–3323* ⊕ *www.olympia.ie.*

THEATER

The New Theatre

THEATER | A troupe with a political agenda, the New Theatre often favors productions by Irish working-class writers like Sean O'Casey and Brendan Behan in its renovated Temple Bar space. ✉ *43 E. Essex St., Temple Bar* ☎ *01/670–3361* ⊕ *www.thenewtheatre.com.*

Olympia Theatre

THEATER | Dublin's oldest and premier multipurpose theatrical venue, the Olympia hosts drama, pantomime, and live comedy in addition to its high-profile musical performances. ✉ *72 Dame St., Temple Bar* ☎ *01/677–7744* ⊕ *www.olympia.ie.*

Project Arts Centre

THEATER | A theater and performance space in an ugly modern building at the center of Temple Bar, the Project Arts

Center premiers a lot of new Irish theater talent as well as contemporary music and experimental art events. ⊠ *39 E. Essex St., Temple Bar* ☎ *01/881–9613* ⊕ *www.projectartscentre.ie.*

Smock Alley Theatre

THEATER | Smock Alley is a wonderfully atmospheric theater space tucked down a little lane. Now housed in a lovely 19th-century Irish neo-Gothic structure, it stands on the site of a famous 17th-century Dublin theater. ⊠ *6/7 Lower Exchange St., Temple Bar* ☎ *01/677–0014* ⊕ *www.smockalley.com.*

Shopping

CLOTHING

Indigo and Cloth

CLOTHING | This has become the place where Irish men with a bit of taste come for quality, slightly edgy clothing. Designers like Oliver Spencer and Velour dominate, and they also have a small, but classy, women's section. ⊠ *9 Essex St. E, Temple Bar* ☎ *01/670–6403* ⊕ *indigoandcloth.com.*

MUSIC

Claddagh Records

MUSIC STORES | Head here for a good selection of traditional and folk music. They have another shop on Westmoreland Street. ⊠ *2 Cecilia St., Temple Bar* ☎ *01/677–0262* ⊕ *www.claddagh-records.com.*

OUTDOOR MARKETS

Meeting House Square Market

OUTDOOR/FLEA/GREEN MARKETS | Held Saturday from 10 am to 4:30 pm in the heart of Temple Bar, this is a good place to buy homemade foodstuffs: cheeses, breads, chocolate, and organic veggies. ⊠ *Temple Bar* ⊕ *www.meetinghousesquare.ie/events.*

Northside

If you stand on O'Connell Bridge or the pedestrian-only Ha'penny span, you'll get excellent views up and down the River Liffey, known in Gaelic as the *abha na life,* transcribed phonetically as Anna Livia by James Joyce in *Finnegans Wake.* Here, framed with embankments like those along Paris's Seine, the river nears the end of its 128-km (80-mile) journey from the Wicklow Mountains to the Irish Sea. And near the bridges, you begin a pilgrimage into James Joyce country—north of the Liffey, in the center of town—and the captivating sights of Dublin's Northside, a mix of densely thronged shopping streets and genteelly refurbished homes.

For much of the 18th century, the upper echelons of Dublin society lived in the Georgian houses in the Northside—around Mountjoy Square—and shopped along Capel Street, which was lined with stores selling fine furniture and silver. But development of the Southside—the Georgian Leinster House in 1745, Merrion Square in 1764, and Fitzwilliam Square in 1825—changed the Northside's fortunes. The city's fashionable social center crossed the Liffey, and although some of the Northside's illustrious inhabitants stuck it out, the area gradually became run-down. The Northside's fortunes have now changed back, however. Once-derelict swaths of buildings, especially on and near the Liffey, have been rehabilitated, and large shopping centers bring the crowds to Mary and Jervis Streets and the "Italian Quarter." The LUAS Red Line links the Northside inner city and the Docklands area, east of the Custom House, which is packed with modern high-rise apartments. In addition, a little Chinatown has formed on Parnell Street, while a swing bridge has been added between City Quay and the Northside. O'Connell Street itself has been partially pedestrianized, and most impressive of all is the Spire, the street's 395-foot-high stainless-steel monument.

Sights

Abbey Presbyterian Church

RELIGIOUS SITE | Built on the profits of sin—well, by a generous wine merchant actually—and topped with a soaring Gothic spire, this church anchors the northeast corner of Parnell Square, an area that was the city's most fashionable address during the gilded days of the 18th-century Ascendancy. Popularly known as Findlater's Church, after the merchant Alex Findlater, the church was completed in 1864 with an interior that has a stark Presbyterian mood despite stained-glass windows and ornate pews. For a bird's-eye view of the area, climb the small staircase that leads to the balcony. ⊠ *Parnell Sq., Dublin North* ☎ *01/837–8600* ⊕ *www.abbeychurch.ie* ⊡ *Free.*

Custom House

GOVERNMENT BUILDING | Seen at its best when reflected in the waters of the Liffey during the short interval when the high tide is on the turn, the Custom House is the city's most spectacular Georgian building. Extending 375 feet on the north side of the river, this is the work of James Gandon, an English architect who arrived in Ireland in 1781, when the building's construction commenced (it continued for 10 years). Note the exquisitely carved lions and unicorns supporting the arms of Ireland at the far ends of the facade. After Republicans set fire to the building in 1921, it was completely restored and reconstructed to house government offices. A visitor center traces the building's history and significance and the life of Gandon. ⊠ *Custom House Quay, Dublin North* ☎ *01/888–2000* ⊕ *www.visitdublin.com.*

Dublin City Gallery The Hugh Lane

MUSEUM | The Francis Bacon studio, reconstructed here exactly as the artist left it on his death, makes this already impressive gallery a must-see for art lovers and fans of the renowned British artist. Built as a town house for the Earl of Charlemont in 1762, this residence was so grand that the Parnell Square street on which it sits was nicknamed "Palace Row" in its honor. It is named after Sir Hugh Lane, who collected both impressionist paintings and 19th-century Irish and Anglo-Irish works. A complicated agreement with the National Gallery in London stipulates that a portion of the 39 French paintings amassed by Lane shuttle between London and here; the group includes Pissarro's *Printemps,* Manet's *Eva Gonzales,* Morisot's *Jour d'Été,* and Renoir's *Les Parapluies.* Irish artists are also represented, including Roderic O'Conor, William Leech, Sean Scully, and the most famous of the group, Jack B. Yeats (W.B.'s brother). ⊠ *Parnell Sq. N, Dublin North* ☎ *01/222–5550* ⊕ *www.hughlane.ie* ⊡ *Free* ⊙ *Closed Mon.*

Dublin Writers Museum

MUSEUM | "If you would know Ireland—body and soul—you must read its poems and stories," wrote W.B. Yeats in 1891. Further investigation into the Irish way with words can be found at this unique museum, in a magnificently restored 18th-century town house on the north side of Parnell Square. The mansion, once the home of John Jameson, of the Irish whiskey family, centers on the Gallery of Writers, an enormous drawing room gorgeously decorated with paintings, Adamesque plasterwork, and a deep Edwardian lincrusta frieze. Rare manuscripts, diaries, posters, letters, limited and first editions, photographs, and other mementos—and there are many of them, so leave plenty of time—commemorate the lives and works of the nation's greatest writers, including Joyce, Shaw, J. M. Synge, Lady Gregory, W.B. Yeats, Beckett, and others. The bookshop and café make this an ideal place to spend a rainy afternoon. ⊠ *18 Parnell Sq.*

N, Dublin North ☎ 01/872–2077 ⊕ www. writersmuseum.com ⊠ €8.

EPIC Irish Emigration Museum

MUSEUM | It's fitting that Ireland's emigration museum should be housed near the Dublin docks where so many said goodbye to their island home forever. Deep in the redbrick vaults of the CHQ building, each visitor gets a symbolic "passport" before touring the 20 educational and interactive galleries. The focus is on digitally retelling the moving, human stories of the people who were forced to leave, the adventures and struggles they had, and the huge diaspora they left all over the world. There's a gallery dedicated to famous folk who claim Irish heritage, including numerous U.S. presidents such as Barack Obama, and outlaws like Billy the Kid. ⊠ Customs House Quay (CHQ), Dublin North ☎ 01/531–3688 ⊕ www. epicirelandchq.com ⊠ €15.

GAA Museum

MUSEUM | **FAMILY** | The Irish are sports crazy and reserve their fiercest pride for their native games. In the bowels of Croke Park, the main stadium and headquarters of the GAA (Gaelic Athletic Association), this museum gives you a great introduction to native Irish sport. The four Gaelic games (football, hurling, camogie, and handball) are explained in detail, and if you're brave enough you can have a go yourself. High-tech displays take you through the history and highlights of the games. National Awakening is a really smart, interesting short film reflecting the key impact of the GAA on the emergence of the Irish nation and the forging of a new Irish identity. The exhilarating A Day in September captures the thrill and passion of All Ireland finals day—the annual denouement of the intercounty hurling and Gaelic football seasons—which is every bit as important to the locals as the Super Bowl is to sports fans in the United States. Tours of the stadium, one of the largest in Europe, are available. ⊠ St. Joseph's Ave., Croke Park Stadium, Dublin North ☎ 01/819–2300 ⊕ www.crokepark.ie/gaa-museum ⊠ Museum €7, museum and stadium tour €14.

Garden of Remembrance

NATIONAL/STATE PARK | Opened 50 years after the Easter Rising of 1916, the garden in Parnell Square commemorates those who died fighting for Ireland's freedom. At the garden's entrance is a large plaza; steps lead down to the fountain area, graced with a sculpture by contemporary Irish artist Oisín Kelly, based on the mythological Children of Lír, who were turned into swans. The garden serves as an oasis of tranquility in the middle of the busy city. ⊠ Parnell Sq., Dublin North ☎ 01/821–3021 ⊕ www. heritageireland.ie ⊠ Free.

Gate Theatre

ARTS VENUE | The show begins here as soon as you walk into the auditorium, a gorgeously Georgian masterwork designed by Richard Johnston in 1784 as an assembly room for the Rotunda Hospital complex. The Gate has been one of Dublin's most important theaters since its founding in 1929 by Micheál MacLiammóir and Hilton Edwards, who also founded Galway City's An Taibhdhearc as the national Irish-language theater. The Gate stages many established productions by Irish as well as foreign playwrights—and plenty of foreign actors have performed here, including Orson Welles (his first paid performance) and James Mason (early in his career). ⊠ Cavendish Row, Dublin North ☎ 01/874–4045 ⊕ www.gatetheatre.ie ⊠ Event ticket prices vary ⊙ Closed Sun.

General Post Office (GPO)

MUSEUM | The GPO's fame is based on the role it played in the fateful 1916 Easter Rising. The building, with its impressive Neoclassical facade, was designed by Francis Johnston and built by the British between 1814 and 1818 as a center of communications. This gave it great strategic importance—and was

Dublin Northside

Sights ▼

1. Abbey Presbyterian Church....... E3
2. Custom House...................... G5
3. Dublin City Gallery The Hugh Lane.................... D3
4. Dublin Writers Museum E3
5. EPIC Irish Emigration Museum.............. H5
6. GAA Museum G1
7. Garden of Remembrance......... E3
8. Gate Theatre E4
9. General Post Office (GPO)........ E5
10. James Joyce Centre E3
11. Mountjoy Square F3
12. O'Connell Street F4
13. Rotunda Hospital E4
14. Sean O' Casey House E1
15. The Spire E5
16. St Francis Xavier Church E2
17. St Mary's Pro Cathedral......... F4

Restaurants ▼

1. Brother Hubbard.................. D6
2. Chapter One...................... D3
3. Enoteca delle Langhe D6
4. Hop House......................... E4
5. Kingfisher......................... E4
6. L. Mulligan Grocer................ A5
7. Mr Fox............................. D4
8. Musashi Noodle and Sushi Bar D6
9. 101 Talbot......................... F5
10. Soup Dragon D6
11. The Winding Stair E6

Hotels ▼

1. Academy Plaza Hotel E4
2. Charleville Lodge Hotel A2
3. Dublin Skylon Hotel.............. E1
4. The Gibson Hotel J5
5. The Gresham Hotel............... E4
6. The Morrison, a DoubleTree by Hilton Hotel D6
7. The Spencer....................... I5
8. Wynn's Hotel F5

Dublin NORTHSIDE — 3

KEY

- ● Exploring Sights
- ● Restaurants
- ● Hotels

0 — 250 m
0 — 1,000 ft

one of the reasons it was chosen by the insurgent forces in 1916 as a headquarters. Here, on Easter Monday, 1916, the Republican forces, about 2,000 in number and under the guidance of Pádraig Pearse and James Connolly, stormed the building and issued the Proclamation of the Irish Republic. After a week of shelling, the GPO lay in ruins; 13 rebels were ultimately executed, including Connolly, who was dying of gangrene from a wound in a leg shattered in the fighting and had to be propped up in a chair in front of the firing squad. Most of the original building was destroyed, though the facade survived, albeit with the scars of bullets on its pillars. Rebuilt and reopened in 1929, it is now home to **GPO Witness History,** an impressive interactive museum that brings to life the glory and horror of that violent uprising and the part this famous building played in it. It includes an original copy of the Proclamation of Independence. There's also a café. ⊠ *O'Connell St., Dublin North* ⊕ *www.gpowitnesshistory.ie* ⊠ *€14.*

James Joyce Centre

LIBRARY | Few may have read him, but everyone in Ireland has at least heard of James Joyce (1882–1941)—especially since owning a copy of his censored and suppressed *Ulysses* was one of the top status symbols of the early 20th century. Joyce is, of course, now acknowledged as one of the greatest modern authors, and *Dubliners, Finnegan's Wake,* and *A Portrait of the Artist as a Young Man* can even be read as quirky "travel guides" to Dublin. Open to the public, this restored 18th-century Georgian town house, once the dancing academy of Professor Denis J. Maginni (which many will recognize from a reading of *Ulysses*), is a center for Joycean studies and events related to the author. It has an extensive library and archives, exhibition rooms, a bookstore, and a café. The collection includes letters from Beckett, Joyce's guitar and cane, and a celebrated edition of *Ulysses* illustrated by Matisse. The

The Scars of History

Look for the bullet marks on the pillars of the General Post Office— they're remnants of the 1916 Easter Rising.

interactive exhibition *James Joyce and Ulysses* allows you to delve into the mysteries and controversies of the novel. The center is the main organizer of "Bloomstime," which marks the week leading up to the Bloomsday celebrations. (Bloomsday, June 16, is the single day *Ulysses* chronicles, as Leopold Bloom winds his way around Dublin in 1904.) ⊠ *35 N. Great George's St., Dublin North* ☎ *01/878–8547* ⊕ *jamesjoyce.ie* ⊠ *€5, guided tour €10* ⊗ *Closed Mon. in Oct.–Mar.*

Mountjoy Square

PLAZA | Irishman Brian Boru, who led his soldiers to victory against the Vikings in the Battle of Clontarf in 1014, was said to have pitched camp before the confrontation on the site of Mountjoy Square. Playwright Sean O'Casey lived here, at No. 35, and used the square as a setting for *The Shadow of a Gunman.* Built over the course of the two decades leading up to 1818, this Northside square was once surrounded by elegant terraced houses. Today only the northern side remains intact. The houses on the once derelict southern side have been converted into apartments.

O'Connell Street

NEIGHBORHOOD | Dublin's most famous thoroughfare, which is 150 feet wide, was once known as Sackville Street, but its name was changed in 1924, two years after the founding of the Irish Free State. After the devastation of the 1916 Easter Rising, the Northside street had to be almost entirely reconstructed, a task that took until the end of the 1920s. At one time the main attraction of the street was Nelson's Pillar, a Doric column towering over the city center and a marvelous vantage point, but it was blown up in 1966, on the Rising's 50th anniversary. A major cleanup and repaving have returned the street to some of its old glory. The large monument at the south end of the street is dedicated to Daniel O'Connell (1775–1847), "The Liberator," and was erected in 1854 as a tribute to the orator's achievement in securing Catholic Emancipation in 1829. Look closely and you'll notice that O'Connell is wearing a glove on one hand, as he did for much of his adult life, a self-imposed penance for shooting a man in a duel. But even the great man himself is dwarfed by the newest addition to O'Connell Street: the 395-foot-high Spire was built in Nelson's Pillar's place in 2003, and today this gigantic, stainless-steel monument dominates the street. ⊠ *Dublin North.*

Rotunda Hospital

HOSPITAL—SIGHT | Founded in 1745 as the first maternity hospital in Ireland and Britain, the Rotunda was designed on a grand scale by architect Richard Castle (1690–1751), with a three-story tower and a copper cupola. It's now mostly worth a visit for its chapel, which has elaborate plasterwork and, appropriately, honors motherhood; it was built by Bartholomew Cramillion between 1757 and 1758. The Gate Theatre, in a lavish Georgian assembly room, is on the O'Connell Street side of this large complex. ⊠ *Parnell St., Dublin North* ☎ *181/71700* ⊕ *www.rotunda.ie.*

Sean O'Casey House

HOUSE | A onetime construction laborer, O'Casey became Ireland's greatest modern playwright, and this is the house where he wrote all his famous Abbey plays, including *Juno and the Paycock*

and *The Plough and the Stars.* ⊠ *422 N. Circular Rd., Dublin North.*

The Spire

MEMORIAL | Christened the "Stiletto in the Ghetto" by local smart alecks, this needlelike monument is the most exciting thing to happen to Dublin's skyline in decades. The Spire, also known as the Monument of Light, was originally planned as part of the city's millennium celebrations. But Ian Ritchie's spectacular 395-foot-high monument wasn't erected until the beginning of 2003. Seven times taller than the nearby General Post Office, the stainless-steel structure rises from the spot where Nelson's Pillar once stood. Approximately 10 feet in diameter at its base, the softly lighted monument narrows to only 1 foot at its apex—the upper part of the Spire sways gently when the wind blows. The monument's creators envisioned it serving as a beacon for the whole of the city, and it will certainly be the first thing you see as you drive into Dublin from the airport. ⊠ *O'Connell St., Dublin North.*

St. Francis Xavier Church

RELIGIOUS SITE | One of the city's finest churches in the classical style, the Jesuit St. Francis Xavier's was begun in 1829, the year of Catholic Emancipation, and was completed three years later. The building is designed in the shape of a Latin cross, with a distinctive Ionic portico and an unusual coffered ceiling. The striking, faux-marble high altarpiece, decorated with lapis lazuli, came from Italy. The church appears in James Joyce's story "Grace." ⊠ *Upper Gardiner St., Dublin North* ☎ *01/836–3411* ⊕ *www. gardinerstparish.ie* ⊠ *Free.*

St. Mary's Pro-Cathedral

RELIGIOUS SITE | Dublin's principal Catholic cathedral (also known as St. Mary's) is a great place to hear the best Irish male voices: a Palestrina choir, in which the great Irish tenor John McCormack began his career, sings in Latin here every Sunday morning at 11. The cathedral, built between 1816 and 1825, has a classical church design—on a suitably epic scale. The church's facade, with a six-Doric-pillared portico, is based on the Temple of Theseus in Athens; the interior is modeled after the Grecian-Doric style of St. Philippe du Roule in Paris. But the building was never granted full cathedral status, nor has the identity of its architect ever been discovered; the only clue to its creation is in the church ledger, which lists a "Mr. P." as the builder. ⊠ *83 Marlborough St., Dublin North* ☎ *01/874–5441* ⊕ *www.procathedral.ie* ⊠ *Free.*

🍴 Restaurants

Brother Hubbard

$ | MIDDLE EASTERN | A delightful slow-food sanctuary within the Dublin dining scene, Brother Hubbard is a cozy, elegantly designed Northside café with a stripped-down but standout menu. The healthy emphasis is on fresh salads and soups with delicious twists; dishes tend to have a Middle Eastern feel, with an Irish touch here and there. **Known for:** meze; guilty-pleasure cakes; great coffee. ⑤ *Average main: €16* ⊠ *153 Capel St., Dublin North* ☎ *01/441–1112* ⊕ *www.brotherhubbard.ie* ⊗ *No dinner Sun. and Mon.*

★ Chapter One

$$$$ | MODERN IRISH | This wonderful, culture-vulture favorite gets its name from its location, downstairs in the vaulted, stone-wall basement of the Dublin Writers Museum; the natural stone-and-wood setting makes it cozily cavelike. The contemporary French eatery is currently the culinary king of the Northside. **Known for:** pretheater crowd; award-winning chef; cozy setting. ⑤ *Average main: €38* ⊠ *18–19 Parnell Sq., Dublin North* ☎ *01/873–2266* ⊕ *www.chapteronerestaurant.com* ⊗ *Closed Sun. and Mon. No lunch Sat.*

★ Enoteca delle Langhe

$ | ITALIAN | Situated in the self-styled Italian Quarter, this Italian eatery serves up the full *enoteca* experience: quality, affordable Italian wines (more than 75% are sourced from the Langhe district); a limited but enticing selection of appetizers; and friendly, family-style service. In summer, tango dancers perform outside in the square that has become a charming little (very little) Italian quarter just off Ormond Quay. **Known for:** authentic Italian ambience; strong wine list; lively buzz in summer. ⑤ *Average main: €18* ⊠ *Blooms La., Dublin North* ☎ *01/888–0834* ⊕ *www.wallacewinebars.ie* ⊗ *Closed Mon.*

★ Hop House

$ | KOREAN FUSION | A unique Korean-Japanese standout in the slew of cheap and cheerful Chinese eateries on Parnell Street (the closest Dublin comes to a Chinatown), Hop House is a restaurant and pub in one. Part of the old Shakespeare pub has been transformed into one of the friendliest, best-value restaurants in the city. **Known for:** kimchi; bright and busy dining room; great music from the bar next door. ⑤ *Average main: €13* ⊠ *160 Parnell St., Dublin North* ☎ *01/872–8318* ⊕ *www.hophouse.ie.*

Kingfisher

$ | IRISH | Don't let the down-at-heel canteen decor put you off—this place has been around for a long time and is a master of the art of fish-and-chips. Their mammoth-value menu is full of seafood surprises like such Dublin favorites as cod and ray (or more unusual choices like mackerel) and you can even order a whole sea bass and rainbow trout. **Known for:** fish-and-chips; award-winning Irish breakfast; popularity with the locals. ⑤ *Average main: €15* ⊠ *166–168 Parnell St., Dublin North* ☎ *01/872–8732* ⊕ *www.kingfisherdublin.com.*

L. Mulligan Grocer

$$ | IRISH | This gem of an old Dublin boozer—which was once also the local grocer—has been turned into a gastropub and world-beer emporium, without losing too much of its real Dublin feel.

Did You Know?

The pinlike Spire on busy O'Connell Street has several nicknames including "the Nail in the Pale" and "the Pin in the Bin."

It's the perfect spot for a quick pint of ale and a plate of black pudding (with pear relish and red chard) if you don't feel like a full sit-down meal. **Known for:** huge beer selection; popularity with hipsters; rib eye with whiskey butter. $ *Average main: €21* ✉ *18 Stoneybatter, Dublin North* ☎ *01/670–9889* ⊕ *www.lmulligan-grocer1.weebly.com* ▭ *No credit cards* ⊘ *No lunch weekdays.*

Mr Fox

$$$ | FRENCH | The stuffed fox on the wall with the pistol in his hand inspired the name of this warm, gamy, stylish new eatery in a Georgian basement conveniently near the Gate Theatre. The chef-owner graduated from a Michelin-star kitchen and he brings that elevated standard to dishes like venison with parsnip, black pudding, chestnut, and blackberries. **Known for:** classical French-Irish food with modern touches; sister restaurant of the Pig's Ear; pig's head croquettes. $ *Average main: €26* ✉ *38 Parnell Sq. W, Dublin North* ☎ *01/874–7778* ⊕ *www.mrfox.ie* ⊘ *Closed Sun. and Mon.*

★ Musashi Noodles and Sushi Bar

$ | SUSHI | This hot sushi bar on suddenly hip Capel Street has given birth to a Dublin franchise because it's finally made the Japanese staple affordable. Japanese owned and run, the restaurant serves fresh and flavorful dishes—all the sushi standards you'd expect but better than anything else in the city. The interior is simple and unfussy; a long, narrow room with dark wood floors and rows of pinewood tables and seats dotted with red cushions. **Known for:** affordable, quality sushi; tempura; BYOB policy. $ *Average main: €17* ✉ *15 Capel St., Dublin North* ☎ *01/532–8068* ⊕ *www.musashidublin.com* ▭ *No credit cards.*

101 Talbot

$ | MEDITERRANEAN | Close to the Abbey and Gate theaters, so there's no danger of missing a curtain call, this creative eatery focusing on contemporary food—with eclectic Mediterranean and Eastern influences—uses fresh local ingredients. It's very popular with the artistic and literary set. **Known for:** artsy clientele; pretheater options; strong vegetarian choices. $ *Average main: €17* ✉ *101 Talbot St., Dublin North* ☎ *01/874–5011* ⊕ *www.101talbot.ie* ⊘ *Closed Sun. and Mon.*

Soup Dragon

$ | IRISH | This tiny café and takeout shop serves an astonishing array of fresh soups daily. They come in three sizes, and you can get vegetarian soup or soups with meat- or fish-based broth; best bets include pumpkin chili and coconut; fragrant Thai chicken; beef chili; and hearty mussel, potato, and leek. **Known for:** endless variety of soups; smoothies; breakfast and lunch to go. $ *Average main: €7* ✉ *168 Capel St., Dublin North* ☎ *01/872–3277* ⊕ *www.soupdragon.com* ⊘ *Closed weekends. No dinner.*

The Winding Stair

$$ | IRISH | Once Dublin's favorite second-hand bookshop–café, the Winding Stair now houses an atmospheric, buzzing little restaurant, with old wooden floors, simple decor, a downstairs bookshop, and grand views of the Ha'penny Bridge and the River Liffey. Hearty portions of upmarket traditional Irish food rely on Irish-only ingredients; the pork chop with crispy pigs' ears and hispi cabbage is a standout. **Known for:** views of the River Liffey; historic location; Irish produce–inspired cooking. $ *Average main: €24* ✉ *40 Ormond Quay, Dublin North* ☎ *01/872–7320* ⊕ *www.winding-stair.com.*

Hotels

Academy Plaza Hotel

$$ | HOTEL | This modern, architecturally uninspired hotel is centrally located just off O'Connell Street and offers lots of comfort at an affordable, slightly unfashionable-neighborhood price. **Pros:** soundproof windows; tripple and quad

rooms great value; choice of restaurants. **Cons:** unfashionable location; rooms are not huge; bland exterior. $ *Rooms from: €190* ⊠ *10–14 Findlater Pl., Dublin North* ☎ *01/878–0666* ⊕ *www.academyplazahotel.ie* ⥱ *304 rooms* ⦶ *No meals.*

Charleville Lodge

$ | **B&B/INN** | There's a slightly funky feel to this Georgian wonder. **Pros:** Victorian elegance; near Phoenix Park; public transport nearby. **Cons:** outside the city center; two-night minimum on some rooms on summer weekends; no elevator. $ *Rooms from: €139* ⊠ *268–272 N. Circular Rd., Phibsborough, Dublin North* ☎ *01/838–6633* ⊕ *www.charlevillelodge. ie* ⥱ *30 rooms* ⦶ *Free breakfast.*

Dublin Skylon Hotel

$ | **HOTEL** | Location, location, and spacious rooms: the three reasons for choosing the Skylon. **Pros:** located between the airport and city center; big rooms suitable for families; prices stable year-round. **Cons:** basic room furnishings; mediocre restaurant; mainly business clientele. $ *Rooms from: €138* ⊠ *Upper Drumcondra Rd., Drumcondra, Dublin North* ☎ *01/884–3900* ⊕ *www.dublinskylonhotel.com* ⥱ *126 rooms* ⦶ *No meals.*

★ The Gibson Hotel

$$$ | **HOTEL** | The terrace bar at the tastefully modern Gibson Hotel has to be the dream spot to view the impressive skyline and shimmering waterways of Dublin's trendy docklands area. **Pros:** stunning views from terrace bar; impressive Nordic design; light-filled rooms, some with private courtyards. **Cons:** slightly off the beaten track; can get busy on concert nights. $ *Rooms from: €210* ⊠ *Point Village, Dublin North* ☎ *01/681–5000* ⊕ *www.thegibsonhotel. ie* ▤ *No credit cards* ⥱ *252 rooms* ⦶ *No meals.*

The Gresham Hotel

$$$ | **HOTEL** | Opened in 1817, it's been a while since this was *the* place to stay for visiting dignitaries and local celebs, but the Gresham remains a solid city-center option without the astronomical expense. **Pros:** good price for city center; great views down O'Connell Street; ample facilities. **Cons:** bar and public areas can get busy; room design unexciting; it can bump prices on busy weekends. $ *Rooms from: €230* ⊠ *23 Upper O'Connell St., Dublin North* ☎ *01/874–6881* ⊕ *www.gresham-hotels-dublin.com* ⥱ *323 rooms* ⦶ *No meals.*

The Morrison, A DoubleTree by Hilton Hotel

$$$$ | **HOTEL** | Showcasing new Irish talent in everything from the textiles to the art on the walls and the sculptures in public spaces—there are even famous Irish song lyrics on the walls in some bedrooms—this sleek, trendy spot remains top of the Northside lodging charts. **Pros:** people-watching in cocktail bar; intensely designed rooms; near O'Connell Bridge. **Cons:** tries a little too hard to be cool; located on busy road; some may find design over-the-top. $ *Rooms from: €330* ⊠ *Ormond Quay, Dublin North* ☎ *01/887–2400* ⊕ *www.morrisonhotel.ie* ⥱ *145 rooms* ⦶ *No meals.*

The Spencer

$$$ | **HOTEL** | Built with business guests in mind, this high-rise hotel in the middle of the International Financial Services Centre has been a surprise hit with all travelers interested in the business of good value and clean, quiet rooms with good amenities. **Pros:** weekend bargains available; front rooms have River Liffey views; little nocturnal street noise. **Cons:** room design pretty functional; business clientele; no buzz at night. $ *Rooms from: €226* ⊠ *IFSC, Dublin North* ☎ *01/433–8800* ⊕ *www.thespencerhotel. com* ⥱ *187 rooms* ⦶ *No meals.*

Wynn's Hotel

$$ | **HOTEL** | A few doors down from the Abbey Theatre, Wynn's began its life as a Dublin boardinghouse in 1845, and its beautiful stained-glass awning has become something of a landmark as a romantic meeting spot for locals. **Pros:**

great location for theater fans; feels like a genuine full-service hotel; a touch of history about the place. **Cons:** decor can fell a bit hodgepodge; rooms are on the small side; can be some noise from ballroom downstairs. $ *Rooms from: €160* ✉ *35–39 Lower Abbey St., Dublin North* ☎ *01/874–5131* ⊕ *www.wynnshotel.ie* ▬ *No credit cards* ⇨ *65 rooms* ⦿ *No meals.*

Nightlife

NIGHTCLUBS
The Academy
DANCE CLUBS | A music hub with four floors of entertainment of every kind, the Academy is anchored by big-name local and international DJs and gigs. It attracts a young, dance-crazy crowd who like to party until the wee hours. ✉ *57 Middle Abbey St., Dublin North* ☎ *01/877–9999* ⊕ *www.theacademydublin.com.*

PUBS
The Big Romance
BARS/PUBS | This new, cool bar for lovers of electronic music is based around a custom-made sound system and an envious vinyl collection… oh, and they specialize in craft bears and daring cocktails, too. ✉ *98 Parnell St., Dublin North* ☎ *01/598–4117* ⊕ *www.thebigromance. ie.*

The Flowing Tide
BARS/PUBS | Directly across from the Abbey Theatre, the Flowing Tide draws a lively pre- and posttheater crowd. No TVs, quality pub talk, and a great pint of Guinness make it a worthwhile visit (although the decor won't win any prizes). ✉ *Lower Abbey St., Dublin North* ☎ *01/874–4108.*

Paddle and Peel
BARS/PUBS | Dublin hipsters are flocking to this new craft beer oasis where a wide variety of selections from Ireland and the wider world are served up, along with quality pizza with interesting toppings. ✉ *199 King St., Dublin North*

☎ *01/534–4584* ⊕ *www.galwaybaybrewery.com/paddleandpeel/.*

Pantibar
BARS/PUBS | Fronted by the infamous Dublin drag queen Panti, this amusingly named gay bar has loud music at night but is pretty chilled-out during the day. ✉ *7–8 Capel St., Dublin North* ☎ *01/874–0710* ⊕ *www.pantibar.com.*

Quay 14
BARS/PUBS | This latest incarnation of the bar at the Morrison Hotel is an uberhip cocktail joint that is trying (perhaps a little too hard) to attract the cool crowd. Still, the bar staff are inventive with their cocktails, and aficionados of Irish whiskeys will be thrilled with the selection. ✉ *Morrison Hotel, Lower Ormond Quay, Dublin North* ☎ *01/887–2400* ⊕ *www. morrisonhotel.ie.*

Performing Arts

Dublin City Gallery The Hugh Lane
CONCERTS | One of the city's most distinctive art museums, the Dublin City Gallery The Hugh Lane is a serene home to Sundays@Noon, a series of free Sunday concerts featuring some top Irish and international talent. Concerts attract a full house, so get there early. ✉ *Parnell Sq. N, Dublin North* ☎ *01/222–5550* ⊕ *www. hughlane.ie* ⦿ *€2.*

ROCK AND CONTEMPORARY MUSIC
3Arena
MUSIC | Home to the grandest, big-gig concerts by rock stars and dance luminaries, the 3Arena is a high-tech, 14,500-capacity venue. ✉ *Northwall Quay, Dublin North* ☎ *01/819–8888* ⊕ *www.3arena.ie.*

THEATER
★ Abbey Theatre
THEATER | One of the most fabled theaters in the world, the Abbey is the home of Ireland's national theater company. In 1904 W.B. Yeats and his patron, Lady

Gregory, opened the theater, which became a major center for the Irish literary renaissance—the place that first staged works by J. M. Synge and Sean O'Casey, among many others. Plays by recent Irish drama heavyweights like Brian Friel, Tom Murphy, Hugh Leonard, and John B. Keane have all premiered here, and memorable productions of international greats like Mamet, Ibsen, and Shakespeare have also been performed. You should not, however, arrive expecting 19th-century grandeur: the original structure burned down in 1951. A starkly modernist auditorium was built in its place—but what it may lack in aesthetics it makes up for in space and acoustics. Some say the repertoire is still overly reverential and mainstream, but the Abbey is not afraid to put a new spin on old Irish classics, and a second stage offers more experimental drama. But the Abbey will always be relevant since much of the theatergoing public still looks to it as a barometer of Irish culture. ⊠ *Lower Abbey St., Dublin North* ☎ *01/878–7222* ⊕ *www.abbeytheatre.ie.*

Gate Theatre

THEATER | An intimate 371-seat theater in a jewel-like Georgian assembly hall, the Gate produces the classics and contemporary plays by leading Irish writers, including Beckett, Wilde (the production of *Salome* was a worldwide hit), Shaw, and the younger generation of dramatists, such as Conor McPherson. ⊠ *Cavendish Row, Parnell Sq., Dublin North* ☎ *01/874–4045* ⊕ *www.gatetheatre.ie.*

 ## Shopping

BOOKS

Eason

DEPARTMENT STORES | Known primarily for its large selection of books, magazines, and stationery, Eason also sells an array of toys and audiovisual goodies at its main O'Connell Street branch; all in all, it has about 50 bookstores throughout

Antiques

Dublin is one of Europe's best cities in which to buy antiques, largely due to a long and proud tradition of restoration and high-quality craftsmanship. The Liberties, Dublin's oldest district, is, fittingly, the hub of the antiques trade, and is chockablock with shops and traders. Bachelor's Walk, along the quays, also has some decent shops. It's quite a seller's market, but bargains are still possible.

Ireland. ⊠ *O'Connell St., Dublin North* ☎ *01/873–3811* ⊕ *www.easons.com.*

CHINA, CRYSTAL, CERAMICS, AND JEWELRY

McDowells

JEWELRY/ACCESSORIES | Popular with Dubliners, this jewelry shop has been in business for more than 100 years. ⊠ *3 Upper O'Connell St., Dublin North* ☎ *01/874–4961* ⊕ *www.mcdowellsjewellers.com.*

DEPARTMENT STORES

Arnotts

DEPARTMENT STORES | Fully filling three floors, Arnotts stocks a wide selection of clothing, household accessories, and sporting goods. It is known for matching quality with value. There is a Gap section downstairs. ⊠ *Henry St., Dublin North* ☎ *01/805–0400* ⊕ *www.arnotts.ie.*

 ## Activities

FOOTBALL

Soccer—called football in Europe—is very popular in Ireland, largely due to the euphoria resulting from the national team's underdog successes since the late 1980s.

Football Association of Ireland

SOCCER | League of Ireland matches take place throughout the city on Friday evening or Sunday afternoon from March to November. For details, contact the Football Association of Ireland. ⊠ *National Sports Campus, Snugborough Rd., Dublin North* ☎ *01/899–8500* ⊕ *www. fai.ie.*

GAELIC GAMES

Gaelic Athletic Association (*GAA*)

LOCAL SPORTS | The traditional games of Ireland, Gaelic football and hurling, attract a huge following, with roaring crowds cheering on their county teams. Games are held at Croke Park, the stunning, high-tech national stadium for Gaelic games, just north of the city center. For details of matches, contact the Gaelic Athletic Association. ⊠ *Croke Park, Dublin North* ☎ *01/836–3222* ⊕ *www.gaa.ie.*

Dublin West

A cornucopia of things quintessentially Dublin, this area is studded with treasures ranging from the opulent 18th-century salons of Dublin Castle to time-burnished St. Patrick's Cathedral, and from the Liberties neighborhood—redoubt of the city's best antiques stores—to the Irish Museum of Modern Art (housed at the strikingly renovated Royal Hospital Kilmainham). You can time-travel from the 10th-century crypt at Christ Church Cathedral—the city's oldest surviving structure—to the modern plant of the Guinness Brewery and its storehouse museum. You can also cross the Liffey for a visit to Smithfield, Dublin's old (but recently revitalized) market area where flowers, fruit, vegetables, and even horses have been sold for generations. Traditional-music bars sit side by side here with modern hotels and the newly refurbished Old Jameson Distillery museum.

Keep in mind that Dublin is compact. The following sights aren't far from those in the other city-center neighborhoods. In fact, City Hall is just across the street from Temple Bar, and Christ Church Cathedral is a short walk farther west. The westernmost sights covered here—notably the Royal Hospital and Kilmainham Gaol—are, however, at some distance, so if you're not an enthusiastic walker, you may want to drive or catch a cab, bus, or LUAS tram to them.

◉ Sights

★ Chester Beatty Library

LIBRARY | A connoisseur's delight, this "library" is considered one of the overlooked treasures of Ireland. After Sir Alfred Chester Beatty (1875–1968), an American mining millionaire and a collector with a flawless eye, assembled one of the most significant collections of Islamic, early Christian, and Far Eastern art in the Western world, he donated it to Ireland. Housed in the gorgeous clock-tower building of Dublin Castle, exhibits include clay tablets from Babylon dating from 2700 BC, Japanese woodblock prints, Chinese jade books, early papyrus bibles, and Turkish and Persian paintings. The second floor, dedicated to the major religions, houses 250 manuscripts of the Koran from across the Muslim world, as well as one of the earliest Gospels. The first-floor *Arts of the Book* exhibition looks at the different origins and finest examples of books throughout the world. Guided tours of the library are available on Wednesday at 1 pm and Sunday at 3 pm and 4 pm. On sunny days the garden is one of the most tranquil places in central Dublin. ⊠ *Castle St., Dublin West* ☎ *01/407–0750* ⊕ *www. cbl.ie* ⊡ *Free* ⊘ *Closed Mon. Nov.–Feb.*

★ Christ Church Cathedral

RELIGIOUS SITE | From its exterior, you'd never guess that the first Christianized Danish king built a wooden church at this site in 1038; because of the extensive

19th-century renovation of its stone-work and trim, the cathedral looks more Victorian than Anglo-Norman. Construction on the present Christ Church—the flagship of the Church of Ireland and one of two Protestant cathedrals in Dublin (the other is St. Patrick's just to the south)—was begun in 1172 by Strongbow, a Norman baron and conqueror of Dublin for the English Crown, and continued for 50 years. By 1875 the cathedral had deteriorated badly; a major renovation gave it much of the look it has today, including the addition of one of Dublin's most charming structures: a Bridge of Sighs–like affair that connects the cathedral to the old Synod Hall, which now holds the Viking multimedia exhibition, Dublinia. Strongbow himself is buried in the cathedral, beneath an impressive effigy. The vast, sturdy **crypt,** with its 12th- and 13th-century vaults, is Dublin's oldest surviving structure and the building's most notable feature. The exhibition *Treasures of Christ Church* includes manuscripts, various historic artifacts, and the tabernacle used when James II worshipped here. But the real marvels are the mummified bodies of a cat and rat—they were trapped in an organ pipe in the 1860s—who seem caught in a cartoon chase for all eternity. At 6 pm on Wednesday and Thursday and 3:30 pm on Sunday, you can enjoy the glories of a choral evensong, and the bell ringers usually practice on Friday at 7 pm. ✉ *Christ Church Pl. and Winetavern St., Dublin West* ☎ *01/677–8099* ⊕ *www.christchurchdublin.ie* 💶 *€7.*

City Hall

GOVERNMENT BUILDING | Facing the Liffey from Cork Hill at the top of Parliament Street, this grand Georgian municipal building (1769–79), once the Royal Exchange, marks the southwest corner of Temple Bar. Today it's the seat of Dublin Corporation, the elected body that governs the city. Thomas Cooley designed the building with 12 columns that encircle the domed central rotunda,

which has a fine mosaic floor and 12 frescoes depicting Dublin legends and ancient Irish historical scenes. The 20-foot-high sculpture to the right is of Daniel O'Connell, "The Liberator." He looks like he's about to begin the famous speech he gave here in 1800. The building houses a multimedia exhibition—with artifacts, kiosks, graphics, and audiovisual presentations—tracing the evolution of Ireland's 1,000-year-old capital. ✉ *Dame St., Dublin West* ☎ *01/222–2204* ⊕ *www.dublincity.ie/dublincityhall* 💶 *Free* 🕐 *Closed Sun.*

Dublin Castle

CASTLE/PALACE | As seat and symbol of the British rule of Ireland for more than seven centuries, Dublin Castle figured largely in Ireland's turbulent history early in the 20th century. It's now mainly used for Irish and EU governmental purposes. Highlights include the sprawling Great Courtyard, the reputed site of the Black Pool (Dubh Linn, pronounced "*dove-lin*") from which Dublin got its name; the Record Tower, the largest remaining relic of the original Norman buildings that were built by King John between 1208 and 1220; the clock-tower building, which houses the fabulous Chester Beatty Library; the State Apartments—now used by the president of Ireland

Dublin West and Phoenix Park

Sights ▼

1 Arbour Hill Cemetery **F3**
2 Chester Beatty Library **J5**
3 Christ Church Cathedral **I5**
4 City Hall **J5**
5 Dublin Castle **J5**
6 Dublin Zoo **B1**
7 Dublinia **I5**
8 Farmleigh **A2**
9 Guiness Storehouse **F6**
10 Irish Museum of Modern Art **C6**
11 Kilmainham Gaol **A6**
12 Marsh's Library **I7**
13 The National College of
   Art & Design **H5**
14 National Museum of
   Decorative Arts and History **F3**
15 Old Jameson Distillery **H4**
16 Phoenix Park **B3**
17 Royal Hospital Kilmainham **C5**
18 Smithfield **G4**
19 St Michan's Church **H4**
20 St Patrick's Cathedral **I6**
21 Teeling's Whiskey **H7**
22 Vaults Live **H5**

Restaurants ▼

1 Bastible **I9**
2 Bibi's **I8**
3 Fish Shop **G4**
4 The Fumbally **I7**
5 Leo Burdock **I5**
6 Lovin Catering **I6**
7 Nancy Hands Bar & Restaurant . **D4**
8 Phoenix Café **A2**

Hotels ▼

1 Hilton Dublin Kilmainham **A6**
2 Jurys Inn Christchurch **I5**
3 Maldron Hotel
   Newlands Cross **A8**
4 Radisson Blu Royal Hotel,
   Dublin **J6**

to host visiting heads of state and EU ministers; and Bermingham Tower, where numerous Irish leaders were imprisoned in the tower from the 16th century to the early 20th century. Enter the castle through the Cork Hill Gate, just west of City Hall. One-hour guided tours are available throughout the day. ✉ *Castle St., Dublin West* ☎ *01/645–8813* ⊕ *www. dublincastle.ie* 🎫 *State Apartments €8 (€12 with tour).*

Dublinia

MUSEUM | FAMILY | Ever wanted a chance to put your head in the stocks? Dublin's Medieval Trust has set up an entertaining and informative reconstruction of everyday life in medieval Dublin. The main exhibits use high-tech audiovisual and computer displays; you can also see a scale model of what Dublin was like around 1500, a medieval maze, a life-size reconstruction based on the 13th-century dockside at Wood Quay, and a fine view from the tower. Dublinia is in the old Synod Hall (formerly a meeting place for bishops of the Church of Ireland), joined via a covered stonework Victorian bridge to Christ Church Cathedral. An exhibition on "Viking Dublin" consists of a similar reconstruction of life in even earlier Viking Dublin, including a Viking burial. There's a guided tour at 2:30 pm every day. ✉ *St. Michael's Hill, Dublin West* ☎ *01/679– 4611* ⊕ *www.dublinia.ie* 🎫 *Exhibit €10.*

★ Guinness Storehouse

MUSEUM | Ireland's all-dominating brewery—founded by Arthur Guinness in 1759 and at one time the largest stout-producing brewery in the world—spans a 60-acre spread west of Christ Church Cathedral. The brewery itself is closed to the public, but the Guinness Storehouse is a spectacular attraction, designed to woo—some might say brainwash—you with the wonders of the "dark stuff." In a 1904 cast-iron-and-brick warehouse, the museum display covers six floors built around a huge, central glass atrium, which is shaped like a giant pint glass.

Beneath the glass floor of the lobby you can see Arthur Guinness's original lease on the site, for a whopping 9,000 years. The exhibition elucidates the brewing process and its history and offers a chance to pull your own perfect pint. The star attraction is undoubtedly the top-floor **Gravity Bar,** with 360-degree floor-to-ceiling glass walls that offer a nonpareil view out over the city at sunset while you sip your free pint. ✉ *St. James' Gate, Dublin West* ☎ *01/408–4800* ⊕ *www. guinness-storehouse.com* 🎫 *From €19.*

Irish Museum of Modern Art

MUSEUM | Housed in the Royal Hospital Kilmainham, the Irish Museum of Modern Art concentrates on the work of contemporary Irish artists along with regular international exhibitions. Artists such as Richard Deacon, Richard Gorman, Dorothy Cross, Sean Scully, Matt Mullican, Louis le Brocquy, and James Coleman are included in the collection. The museum also displays works by some non-Irish 20th-century greats, including Picasso and Miró, plus recent hotshots like Damien Hirst, and regularly hosts touring shows from major European museums. The café serves light fare including soups and sandwiches, and has a cool kids play area. It's a short ride by taxi or bus from the city center and there is a LUAS stop nearby. ✉ *Kilmainham La., Dublin West* ☎ *01/612–9900* ⊕ *www. imma.ie* 🎫 *Free* ⊙ *Closed Mon.*

★ Kilmainham Gaol

MUSEUM | Leaders of many failed Irish rebellions spent their last days in this grim, forbidding structure, and it holds a special place in the myth and memory of the country. The 1916 commanders Pádraig Pearse and James Connolly were held here before being executed in the prison yard. Other famous inmates included the revolutionary Robert Emmet and Charles Stewart Parnell, a leading politician. You can visit the prison only as part of a very moving and exciting guided tour, which leaves every hour on the hour. The cells are a chilling sight, and the guided tour and a 30-minute audiovisual presentation relate a graphic account of Ireland's political history over the past 200 years—from an Irish Nationalist viewpoint. A newer exhibition explores the history of the prison and its restoration. A small tearoom is on the premises. ■TIP→ It is almost essential to book ahead for the guided tour, especially during high season. You really don't want to chance a three-hour wait. ⊠ Inchicore Rd., Dublin West ☎ 01/453–5984 ⊕ kilmainhamgaol-museum.ie ⊠ €8.

Marsh's Library
LIBRARY | When Ireland's first public library was founded and endowed in 1701 by Narcissus Marsh, the archbishop of Dublin, it was made open to "All Graduates and Gentlemen." The two-story brick Georgian building has remained virtually the same since then. It houses a priceless collection of 250 manuscripts and 25,000 15th- to 18th-century books. Many of these rare volumes were locked inside cages, as were the readers who wished to peruse them. The cages were to discourage the often impecunious students, who may have been tempted to make the books their own. The library has been restored with great attention to its original architectural details, especially in the book stacks. It's a short walk west from St. Stephen's Green and is accessed through a charming little cottage garden. ⊠ St. Patrick's Close off Patrick St., Dublin West ☎ 01/454–3511 ⊕ www.marshlibrary.ie ⊠ €3 ⊙ Closed Sun. and Tues.

The National College of Art & Design
COLLEGE | The delicate welding of glass and iron onto the redbrick Victorian facade of this onetime factory makes this school worth a visit. A walk around the cobblestone central courtyard often gives the added bonus of viewing students working away in glass, clay, metal, and stone. The glass-fronted new gallery combines work by local, national, and international avant-garde artists. ⊠ 100 Thomas St., Dublin West ☎ 053/1636–4200 ⊕ www.ncad.ie ⊠ Free ⊙ Closed weekends.

Old Jameson Distillery
WINERY/DISTILLERY | Founded in 1791, this distillery produced one of Ireland's most famous whiskeys for nearly 200 years, until 1966, when local distilleries merged to form Irish Distillers and moved to a purpose-built, ultramodern distillery in Middleton, County Cork. A major recent renovation has turned this original distillery into a state-of-the-art museum and whiskey experience to rival Guinness's storehouse. In fact, Jameson claims to be the most visited distillery in the world. Tours focus on either exploring the history of the old place, blending your own whiskey, or honing your whiskey-cocktail-making skills. Tours include a complimentary tasting; four attendees are invited to taste different brands of Irish whiskey and compare them against bourbon and Scotch. If you have a large group and everyone wants to do this, phone in advance to arrange it. You can also get tutored—complete with certification—in whiskey tasting. ⊠ Bow St., Dublin West ☎ 01/807–2348 ⊕ www.jamesonwhiskey.com ⊠ From €19.

Royal Hospital Kilmainham
BUILDING | This replica of Les Invalides in Paris is regarded as the most important 17th-century building in Ireland. Commissioned as a hospice for disabled and veteran soldiers by James Butler—the Duke of Ormonde and viceroy to King Charles II—it was completed in 1684, making it the first building erected in Dublin's golden age. It survived into the 1920s as a hospital, but after the founding of the Irish Free State in 1922, the building fell into disrepair. The entire edifice has since been restored. The architectural highlight is the hospital's Baroque chapel, distinguished by its extraordinary plasterwork ceiling and fine wood carvings. The hospital also houses the Irish Museum

of Modern Art. ✉ *Kilmainham La., Dublin West* ☎ *01/612–9900* ⊕ *www.rhk.ie.*

Smithfield

MARKET | Bordered on the east by Church Street, on the west by Blackhall Place, to the north by King Street, and to the south by the Liffey, Smithfield is Dublin's old market area where flowers, fruit, vegetables, and even horses have been sold for generations. Chosen as a flagship for north inner-city renovation during the boom, the area saw a major face-lift—with mixed reactions from the locals. Some of the beautiful cobblestones of its streets have been taken up, refinished, and replaced, and giant masts topped with gaslights used to send 6-foot-high flames over Smithfield Square. Unfortunately they don't light the gas anymore, and there's the air of a white elephant about the whole thing. But the area is still worth a visit, especially in the early morning, as the wholesale fruit and vegetable sellers still ply their trade in the wonderful 19th-century covered market. It's also home to the Lighthouse cinema and a twice-yearly horse-trading market. ✉ *Smithfield, Dublin West.*

St. Michan's Church

RELIGIOUS SITE | However macabre, St. Michan's main claim to fame is down in the vaults, where the totally dry atmosphere has preserved several corpses in a remarkable state of mummification. They lie in open caskets. Most of the resident deceased are thought to have been Dublin tradespeople (one was, they say, a religious crusader). Except for its 120-foot-high bell tower, this Anglican church is architecturally undistinguished. The church was built in 1685 on the site of an 11th-century Danish church (Michan was a Danish saint). If preserved corpses are not enough of a draw, you can also find an 18th-century organ, which Handel supposedly played for the first performance of *Messiah*. Don't forget to check out the Stool of Repentance—the only one still in existence in

the city. Parishioners judged to be "open and notoriously naughty livers" used it to do public penance. ✉ *Lower Church St., Dublin West* ☎ *01/872–4154* ⊕ *www. visitdublin.com* ✇ *Crypts €6.*

★ St. Patrick's Cathedral

RELIGIOUS SITE | The largest cathedral in Dublin and also the national cathedral of the Church of Ireland, St. Patrick's was built in honor of Ireland's patron saint, who—according to legend—baptized many converts at a well on this site in the 5th century. The original building, dedicated in 1192 and early English Gothic in style, was an unsuccessful attempt to assert supremacy over the capital's other Protestant cathedral, Christ Church Cathedral. At 305 feet, this is the longest church in the country. Make sure you see the gloriously heraldic Choir of St. Patrick's, hung with colorful medieval banners, and find the tomb of Jonathan Swift, most famous of St. Patrick's many illustrious deans and immortal author of *Gulliver's Travels*. Swift's tomb is in the south aisle, not far from that of his beloved "Stella," Mrs. Esther Johnson. ■**TIP**➔ **If you're a music lover, matins (9:40 am) and evensong (5:45 pm) are still sung on many days.** ✉ *Patrick St., Dublin West* ☎ *01/453–9472* ⊕ *www.stpatrickscathedral.ie* ✇ *€8.*

Teelings Whiskey

FACTORY | While this state-of-the-art whiskey distillery in Dublin's historic Liberties neighborhood is new, it's only a stone's throw from the 1782 site of the original Teelings. Part of the modern Irish renaissance in whiskey making, this pot-still operation offers one of the best and most inclusive whiskey tours in the country. You get to see the nuts and bolts of how the *uisce beatha* or "water of life" is made, and there's a delicious tasting waiting for you at the end. The little café out front is usually lively. ■**TIP**➔ **Price of tours vary greatly depending on the quality of the whiskey you will be tasting at the end.** ✉ *13–17 Newmarket Sq., The*

Liberties ☎ *01/531–0329* ⊕ *www.teeling-whiskey.com* ✉ *From €15.*

★ **Vaults Live**

TOUR—SIGHT | FAMILY | Dublin's newest sensation is a whirlwind immersive experience with Irish actors bringing local history to life, with plenty of laughs and a few scares along the way. In this state-of-the-art venue, you can visit a Viking settlement, Cromwellian torture chamber, medieval apothecary, and Dublin's Victorian red-light district re-created with clever scripts and great performances. Interaction is encouraged here, so don't be surprised if you're accosted by Dracula, Molly Malone, Viking Ikea, or any of the other host of characters. There's also a surprisingly good café and gift shop. ⊠ *John's La. W, Dublin West* ☎ *01/541–1485* ⊕ *www.vaults.live* ✉ *€25* ⊗ *Closed Mon. and Tues.*

🍴 Restaurants

★ **Bastible**

$$$ | BISTRO | Even with its location in a relatively unfashionable corner of the city, this high-end bistro has the natives traveling miles to get a treasured table. The five-course set menu manages to be daring and traditional at the same time, with game and fish transformed in particularly ingenious ways. **Known for:** trendy crowd; booking up; ample wines by the glass. ⑤ *Average main: €28* ⊠ *111 S. Circular Rd., Dublin West* ☎ *01/473–7409* ⊕ *www.bastible.com* ⊗ *Closed Mon. and Tues. No lunch Wed. and Thurs. No dinner Sun.*

Bibi's

$ | CAFÉ | The small menu at this tiny café in the middle of a quiet, off-the-beaten-track residential street emphasizes creative breakfasts and lunch (and brunch on the weekend) with a local twist. It's a good spot to sit and watch locals go about their everyday lives as you eat black rice quinoa porridge with coconut milk, miso, and banana or their wonderful spicy cannellini beans with chorizo,

crème fraîche, and thyme. **Known for:** great people-watching; healthy breakfasts; delicious cakes. ⑤ *Average main: €10* ⊠ *14b Emorville Ave., Dublin West* ☎ *01/454–7421* ⊕ *www.bibis.ie* ⊟ *No credit cards* ⊗ *No dinner.*

★ **Fish Shop**

$$$ | SEAFOOD | Irish seafood is finally getting the royal treatment it deserves at this simple but brilliant new eatery in the old market, Smithfield district. The award-winning kitchen serves up inventive treasures like whipped hake and dillisk (native seaweed) on sourdough, but don't expect a choice in seafood: you're served a three-course menu focused on what was caught that morning. **Known for:** elevated fish-and-chips; fun, casual atmosphere; three-course menu focused on fresh catches. ⑤ *Average main: €27* ⊠ *6 Queen St., Dublin North* ☎ *01/430–8594* ⊕ *fish-shop.ie* ⊗ *Closed Sun. and Mon. No lunch Wed. and Thurs.*

★ **The Fumbally**

$ | MODERN IRISH | FAMILY | Opened by a group of friends, the Fumbally started out with a market stall but quickly become the vanguard of true slow food in Dublin, finding its roots in a spacious, light-filled space smack in the middle of the Liberties area, the heart of the old city. Menus are simple but clever, with the Fumbally eggs, lightly scrambled with Gubeen cheese and sautéed kale, a classic. **Known for:** local produce; great eggs; slow-food attitude. ⑤ *Average main: €12* ⊠ *Fumbally La., Dublin West* ☎ *01/592–8732* ⊕ *www.thefumbally.ie* ⊗ *Closed Mon. No dinner.*

Leo Burdock

$ | IRISH | Old man Burdock has moved on and the place hasn't been the same since, but the hordes still join the inevitable queue at Dublin's famous 100-year-old takeout fish-and-chips shop. You can't eat here, but why would you anyway, when you can sit in the gardens of St. Patrick's Cathedral a few minutes away. **Known for:** fresh cod and chips; battered sausage;

a line outside. $ Average main: €12 ⊠ 2 Werburgh St., Christchurch, Dublin West ☎ 01/454–0306 ⊕ www.leoburdock.com.

Lovin Catering

$ | CAFÉ | This unassuming little shop on Francis Street conjures up some of the best pastries in town. There's no seating in this powerhouse patisserie, but long counters allow space for perching your coffee and tucking into the finest sweet and savory treats. **Known for:** great quiches and pastries; quality coffee; fast service. $ Average main: €9 ⊠ 49 Francis St., Dublin West ☎ 01/454–4912 ⊕ www. lovincatering.com ⊘ Closed Sun. No dinner.

 ## Hotels

Hilton Dublin Kilmainham

$$ | HOTEL | While the exterior of this no-nonsense chain hotel in the historic Kilmainham district is distinctly function-al, the higher-floor rooms have some of the most stunning panoramas in the whole city. **Pros:** stunning city views; close to Heuston train station; large rooms. **Cons:** uninspiring exterior; outside city center; attracts a business crowd. $ Rooms from: €199 ⊠ Kilmainham, Dublin West ☎ 01/420–1800 ⊕ www. hiltondublinkilmainham.com ⤴ 120 rooms ⥠ No meals ▬ No credit cards.

Jurys Inn Christchurch

$$$ | HOTEL | Expect few frills at this functional budget (at least, budget by city center standards) hotel, on a hill facing Christ Church Cathedral and within walk-ing distance of most city-center attrac-tions. **Pros:** large rooms; views of Christ Church; near Temple Bar. **Cons:** ugly build-ing; basic, functional room design; tends to be popular with bachelor(ette) parties. $ Rooms from: €210 ⊠ Christ Church Pl., Dublin West ☎ 01/454–0000 ⊕ www. jurysinn.com ⤴ 182 rooms ⥠ No meals.

Maldron Hotel Newlands Cross

$$ | HOTEL | This four-story franchise hotel on the southwest outskirts of the city is cheap, cheerful, and especially ideal if you're planning to travel to the west or southwest of Ireland and you don't want to deal with Dublin's crazy morning traf-fic. **Pros:** flat rates for up to three adults or two adults and two children; good location for further travels; delicious Bew-ley's coffee in the morning. **Cons:** mainly business clientele; not convenient to the city center; overlooks the expressway. $ Rooms from: €156 ⊠ Newlands Cross at Naas Rd., Dublin West ☎ 01/464–0140 ⊕ www.maldronhotelnewlandscross.com ⤴ 299 rooms ⥠ No meals.

Radisson Blu Royal Hotel, Dublin

$$$ | HOTEL | The sleek glass-and-concrete Radisson, just off South Great George's Street, offers to-the-point business accommodations with a dash of cool contemporary style, proof positive that it is possible to be elegant and functional at the same time. **Pros:** right in the heart of "real Dublin"; stylish, understated decor; landscaped rooftop terrace. **Cons:** looks out over a block of flats; restaurant is hit-or-miss; mostly business clientele. $ Rooms from: €260 ⊠ Golden La., Dublin West ☎ 01/898–2900 ⊕ www. radissonblu.com ⤴ 150 rooms ⥠ No meals.

 ## Nightlife

PUBS

Brazen Head

BARS/PUBS | Reputedly Dublin's oldest pub (the site has been licensed since 1198), the Brazen Head doesn't have much of a time-burnished decor, except for one big exception: an enchanting stone courtyard that is intimate, charming, and delightful. The front is a faux one-story castle, complete with flambeaux, while the interior looks modern-day (except for the very low ceilings). People love to jam the place not for its history but for its traditional-music performances and lively sing-along sessions on Sunday evening. On the south side of the Liffey quays, it's a little difficult to find—turn down Lower

Bridge Street and make a right onto the old lane. ⊠ *20 Lower Bridge St., Dublin West* ☎ *01/677–9549* ⊕ *www.brazenhead.com.*

★ **Cobblestone**

BARS/PUBS | A glorious house of ale in the best Dublin tradition, the Cobblestone is popular with Smithfield Market workers. Its chatty imbibers and high-quality, nightly live traditional music are attracting a more varied, younger crowd from all over town. ⊠ *N. King St., Dublin West* ☎ *01/872–1799* ⊕ *www.cobblestonepub.ie.*

Dice Bar

BARS/PUBS | Cool students and twenty-somethings pack this East Village–style, dark, loud, and lively spot at the heart of Smithfield. DJs keep the crowd happy most nights. ⊠ *79 Queen St., Dublin West* ☎ *01/633–3936* ⊕ *www.thatsitdublin.com.*

★ **Fallons**

BARS/PUBS | Somehow you always get a seat in this tiny sliver of a pub—a warm, old-school boozer at its best—tucked away on a corner near St. Patrick's Cathedral. Pure Dublin class. ⊠ *129 The Coombe, Dublin West* ☎ *01/454–2801.*

★ **Ryan's Pub**

BARS/PUBS | One of Dublin's last genuine, late-Victorian-era pubs, Ryan's has changed little since its last (1896) remodeling. There is a steak house upstairs. ⊠ *28 Parkgate St., Dublin West* ☎ *01/677–6097* ⊕ *www.fxbuckley.ie/ryans-victorian-pub.*

🎭 Performing Arts

St. Patrick's Cathedral

CONCERTS | Along with some regular concert performances, you can catch some beautiful church singing at evensong at St. Pat's most weekdays around half past 5 pm. ⊠ *Saint Patrick's Close, Dublin West* ☎ *01/453–9472* ⊕ *www.stpatrickscathedral.ie* 🎟 *€6.*

ROCK AND CONTEMPORARY MUSIC

Vicar Street

MUSIC | Across from Christ Church Cathedral, Vicar Street is a venue for intimate concerts. It often plays host to folk music, jazz, and comedy, as well as rock performances. ⊠ *58–59 Thomas St., Dublin West* ☎ *01/775–5800* ⊕ *www.vicarstreet.com.*

🛍 Shopping

ANTIQUES

Christy Bird

ANTIQUES/COLLECTIBLES | Dublin's oldest furniture shop, Christy Bird was recycling household items before anyone else dreamed of it. You have to hunt for anything that is true quality and most of the goods here are now repro and mass-market. ⊠ *32 S. Richmond St., Dublin West* ☎ *01/475–4049* ⊕ *www.christybird.com.*

Martin Fennelly Antiques

ANTIQUES/COLLECTIBLES | A stalwart of Dublin's traditional antiques quarter around Francis Street, Fennelly's specializes in early furniture and decorative items like candlesticks, tea caddies, and fitted jewelry caskets. ⊠ *60 Francis St., Dublin West* ☎ *01/473–1126* ⊕ *www.fennelly.net.*

★ **O'Sullivan Antiques**

ANTIQUES/COLLECTIBLES | Specializing in 18th- and 19th-century furniture, with a high-profile clientele (including Mia Farrow and Liam Neeson), the O'Sullivan "look" has been so successful that it now runs a full-time sister shop in New York. ⊠ *43–44 Francis St., Dublin West* ☎ *01/454–1143, 01/453–9659* ⊕ *www.osullivanantiques.com.*

CHINA, CRYSTAL, CERAMICS, AND JEWELRY

Jam Art Factory

ART GALLERIES | This independent gallery shop is a one-stop option for finding cool young Irish designers in print, ceramics, textiles, and jewelry. It's the perfect spot for a more unusual gift. There is a second outlet in Temple Bar. ⊠ *64/65 Patrick St., Dublin West* ☎ *01/616–5671* ⊕ *www.jamartfactory.com.*

OUTDOOR MARKETS
Liberty Market
OUTDOOR/FLEA/GREEN MARKETS | Just minutes from Christ Church Cathedral, this working-class favorite is a great place to get a feel for Dubliners at play. The stalls vary from knickknacks to children's clothing and candy. Open Thursday to Saturday. ⊠ *Meath St., Dublin West.*

Activities

GOLF
Hermitage Golf Club
GOLF | Set in a part of the Liffey Valley idyllically titled the Strawberry Beds, this rolling parkland course has been a feature of West Dublin golf since 1905. The gentle terrain of the front nine stands in start contrast to the stern, water-featured test that awaits you on the way home. The signature hole is the picturesque 10th, which looks down on the river as it winds through a spectacular treescape. The course has seen some big personalities walk its fairways over the years, including Bing Crosby, Seve Ballesteros, and Colin Montgomerie. A sense of history pervades the place. ⊠ *Lucan* ☎ *01/626–8491* ⊕ *www.hermitagegolf.ie* 🚮 *Weekdays €45, weekends €50* 🏌 *18 holes, 6596 yards, par 71.*

Phoenix Park and Environs

Far and away Dublin's largest park, Phoenix Park (the name is an anglicization of the Irish *Fionn Uisce,* meaning "clear water") is a vast, green, arrowhead-shape oasis north of the Liffey, about a 20-minute walk from the city center. It's the city's main escape valve and sports center (cricket, soccer, Gaelic games, and polo), and the home of the noble creatures of the Dublin Zoo. A handful of other cultural sights near the park also merit a visit.

Sights

Arbour Hill Cemetery
CEMETERY | All 14 Irishmen executed by the British following the 1916 Easter Rising are buried here, including Pádraig Pearse, who led the rebellion; his younger brother Willie, who played a minor role in the uprising; and James Connolly, a socialist and labor leader wounded in the battle. Too weak from his wounds to stand, Connolly was tied to a chair and then shot. The burial ground is a simple but formal area, with the names of the dead leaders carved in stone beside an inscription of the proclamation they issued during the uprising. ⊠ *Arbour Hill, Dublin West* ☎ *01/821–3021* ⊕ *www.heritageireland.ie/en/dublin/arbourhill-cemetery* 🚮 *Free.*

Dublin Zoo
ZOO | **FAMILY** | Founded in 1830, Dublin Zoo may be the third-oldest public zoo in the world but the modern incarnation is an exciting, humane, and well thought out wildlife adventure. Animals from tropical climes are kept in unbarred enclosures, and Arctic species swim in the lakes close to the reptile house. Some 700 lions have been bred here since the 1850s, one of whom became familiar to movie fans the world over when MGM used him for its trademark. (As they will tell you at the zoo, he is in fact yawning in that familiar shot: an American lion had to be hired to roar and the "voice" was dubbed.) The African Plains section houses the zoo's larger species; the Nakuru Safari is a 25-minute tour of this area. Sea Lion Cove is one of the most popular destinations, especially at feeding time. In summer the Lakeside Café serves ice cream and drinks. ⊠ *Phoenix Park, Dublin West* ☎ *01/474–8900* ⊕ *www.dublinzoo.ie* 🚮 *€18.*

Farmleigh

FARM/RANCH | This 78-acre Edwardian estate, situated northwest of Phoenix Park and accessed via the main park road, includes Farmleigh House (which is full of antique furnishings and historic art, now used to accommodate visiting dignitaries), a working farm, walled and sunken gardens, wonderful picnic-friendly grounds, a regular organic food market, and a restaurant in the boathouse. Guided tours of the house last 45 minutes and are offered hourly on a first-come, first-served basis but are limited in size; moreover, the house may be closed on short notice if it is in use by the government. ⊠ *Castleknock, Dublin West* ☎ *01/815–5900 for hrs, 01/815–7255* ⊕ *www.farmleigh.ie* 🎫 *Free, €8 guided tour.* 🕙 *Closed Jan. and Feb.*

★ National Museum of Decorative Arts and History

MUSEUM | Here, in one gigantic treasure chest, is the full panoply of the National Museum's collection of glass, silver, furniture, and other decorative arts, along with some items from the country's military history. The setting is spectacular: the huge Collins Barracks, named for the assassinated Irish Republican leader Michael Collins (1890–1922). Built in the early 18th century, and designed by Captain Thomas Burgh, these erstwhile "Royal Barracks" were stylishly renovated to become a showcase for the museum, which opened in September 1997. The displays are far ranging, covering everything from one of the greatest collections of Irish silver in the world to Irish period furniture—you'll see that the country's take on Chippendale was far earthier than the English mode. *Soldiers and Chiefs: The Irish at War* and a thousand years of Irish coins are other highlights. Headlining the collections are some extraordinary objects, including the Fonthill Vase, the William Smith O'Brien Gold Cup, and the Lord Chancellor's Mace. There is also a small military museum. ⊠ *Benburb St., Phoenix Park*

and Environs ☎ *01/677–7444* ⊕ *www.museum.ie* 🎫 *Free* 🕙 *Closed Mon.*

★ Phoenix Park

CITY PARK | **FAMILY** | Europe's largest public park, which extends about 5 km (3 miles) along the Liffey's north bank, encompasses 1,752 acres and holds a lot of verdant green lawns, woods, lakes, and playing fields. Sunday is the best time to visit: games of cricket, football (soccer), polo, baseball, hurling (a traditional Irish sport the resembles a combination of lacrosse, baseball, and field hockey), and Irish football are likely to be in progress. Old-fashioned gas lamps line both sides of Chesterfield Avenue, the main road that bisects the park for 4 km (2½ miles), which was named for Lord Chesterfield, a lord lieutenant of Ireland, who laid out the road in the 1740s. The beautiful, pristine 1896 Victorian Tea Rooms near the Avenue still serve dainty dishes for the park visitors. To the right as you enter the park is the People's Garden, a colorful flower garden designed in 1864. Rent bikes (including tandems) at the main gate to get the most from the park's hidden corners. Within Phoenix Park is a visitor center, in the 17th-century fortified Ashtown Castle; it has information about the park's history, flora, and fauna. Admission to the center is free, and it runs guided tours of the park throughout the year. They also have the wonderful Phoenix Cafe beside the old walled garden. ☎ *01/677–0095 visitor center* ⊕ *www.phoenixpark.ie* 🕙 *Closed Mon. and Tues. in Jan. and Feb.*

 Restaurants

Nancy Hands Bar & Restaurant

$$ | **ECLECTIC** | There's a fine line between re-creating tradition and looking like a theme bar, but Nancy Hands just about pulls it off. A galleylike room juxtaposes old wood, raw brick, and antiques with contemporary art to create a convivial, cozy dining area. **Known for:** pub grub; hearty Irish dishes; famed spirit selection. $ *Average main: €23* ✉ *30–32 Parkgate St., Phoenix Park and Environs* ☎ *01/677–0149* ⊕ *www.nancyhands.ie.*

Phoenix Cafe

$ | **CAFÉ** | **FAMILY** | A pastry-laden café in the middle of a huge park and next door to a playground—it's no wonder kids love the Phoenix Cafe. This gem is overlooked by a lot of locals, but when the sun is shining and you can sit outdoors there are few more tranquil and idyllic spots in the capital. **Known for:** popularity with families; salads and cakes; outdoor grazing in summer. $ *Average main: €11* ✉ *Ashtown Castle, Phoenix Park Visitors Centre, Phoenix Park and Environs* ☎ *01/677–0090* ⊕ *www.phoenixcafe.ie* ⊘ *No dinner.*

Side Trips: North County Dublin

Dublin's northern suburbs remain largely residential, but there are a few places worth the trip, such as the historic Glasnevin Cemetery. As with most suburban areas, walking may not be the best way to get around. It's good, but not essential, to have a car. Buses and trains serve most of these areas.

Glasnevin

Drive from north city center by Lower Dorset St., as far as bridge over Royal Canal. Turn left; go up Whitworth Rd., by side of canal, for 1 km (½ mile); at its end, turn right onto Prospect Rd. and then left onto Finglas Rd. (N2). You can also take Bus 40 or Bus 40A from Parnell St., next to Parnell Sq., in northern city center.

Need A Break?

Ryan's Pub. One of Dublin's last remaining genuine late–Victorian era pubs, Ryan's has changed little since its last remodeling—in 1896. It's right near the entrance to Phoenix Park. ✉ *28 Parkgate St., Dublin West* ☎ *01/677–6097* ⊕ *www. fxbuckley.ie/ryans-victorian-pub* ⊟ *No credit cards.*

◉ Sights

Glasnevin Cemetery and Museum

CEMETERY | Glasnevin Cemetery, on the right-hand side of Finglas Road, is the best-known burial ground in Dublin. It's the site of the graves of many distinguished Irish leaders, including Eamon de Valera, a founding father of modern Ireland and a former Irish *taoiseach* (prime minister) and president, and Michael Collins, the celebrated hero of the Irish War of Independence. Other notables interred here include the late-19th-century poet Gerard Manley Hopkins and Sir Roger Casement, a former British consul turned Irish nationalist, hanged for treason by the British in 1916. The large column to the right of the main entrance is the tomb of "The Liberator" Daniel O'Connell, perhaps Ireland's greatest historical figure, renowned for his nonviolent struggle for Catholic emancipation, achieved in 1829. The cemetery is freely accessible 24 hours a day. An impressive museum has a *City of the Dead* permanent exhibition that covers the burial practices and religious beliefs of the 1.5 million people buried in Glasnevin. The Milestone Gallery has exhibits on key historical figures buried here. They also run great tours of the cemetery itself. ✉ *Glasnevin* ☎ *01/882–6550* ⊕ *www.glasnevintrust.ie* ⌨ *Museum €7, tour €14.*

National Botanic Gardens

GARDEN | The National Botanic Gardens, on the northeastern flank of Glasnevin Cemetery and the south bank of the Tolka River, date from 1795 and have more than 20,000 varieties of plants, a rose garden, and a vegetable garden. The main attraction is the beautifully restored Curvilinear Range—400-foot-long greenhouses designed and built by a Dublin ironmaster, Richard Turner, between 1843 and 1869. The Great Palm House, with its striking double dome, was built in 1884 and houses orchids, palms, and tropical ferns. Inspiring free guided tours are offered Sunday at noon and 2:30. ⊠ *Glasnevin Rd.* ☎ *01/804–0300* ⊕ *www. botanicgardens.ie* ⌧ *Free.*

 Activities

GOLF
Island Golf Club

GOLF COURSE | Talk about exclusive—until 1960, the only way to reach this club was by boat. It was about as remote as you could get and still be only 24 km (15 miles) from Dublin. But things have changed. The Island has opened its doors to reveal a fine links course with holes that force you to navigate between spectacular sand dunes toward small, challenging greens. ⊠ *Corballis, Donabate* ☎ *01/843–6205* ⊕ *www.theislandgolfclub.com* ⌧ *Nov.–Mar. daily €80; Apr.–Oct. Mon.–Thurs. €150, Fri.–Sun. €175* 🏌️ *18 holes, 6902 yards, par 71.*

Portmarnock Golf Club

GOLF | The hoo-ha and court battles over Portmarnock's refusal to admit women as full members often overshadows the club's position as the most famous of Ireland's "Big Four" (Ballybunion, Royal County Down, and Royal Portrush are the others). This links course, on a sandy peninsula north of Dublin, has hosted numerous major championships and Tom Watson often used it as a preparation for the Open. Known for its flat fairways and greens and its 100-plus bunkers, it provides a fair test for any golfer who can keep it out of the heavy rough. Greens fees include lunch. ⊠ *Portmarnock* ☎ *01/846–2968* ⊕ *www.portmarnock-golfclub.ie* ⌧ *Nov.–Mar. daily €145; Apr.–Oct. weekdays €225, weekends €250* 🏌️ *Championship Course: 18 holes, 7382 yards, par 72; Yellow Course: 9 holes, 3449 yards, par 37.*

★ The Royal Dublin Golf Club

GOLF | Links courses are usually in remote, even desolate areas, but this captivating example is only 6 km (4 miles) from the center of Dublin—on Bull Island, a bird sanctuary. Ireland's third-oldest club has always been challenging, but Martin Hawtree's ongoing redesign is making things even trickier. Watch out for the 5th, the 13th, and the infamous 18th—a par-4 dogleg with plenty of opportunities to shoot out-of-bounds. ⊠ *Dollymount* ☎ *01/833–6346* ⊕ *www.theroyaldublingolfclub.com* ⌧ *Nov.–mid-Mar., Mon.–Thurs. €100, Fri.–Sun. €115; mid-Mar.–Oct., Mon.–Thurs. €150, Fri.–Sun. €175* 🏌️ *18 holes, 7296 yards, par 72.*

North Bull Island

From Dublin's north city center, take Clontarf Rd. for 4 km (2½ miles) to causeway.

A 5-km-long (3-mile-long) island created in the 19th century by the action of the tides, North Bull Island is one of Dublin's wilder places—it's a nature conservancy with a vast beach and dunes that attract thousands of varied seabirds year-round. The island is linked to the mainland via a wooden causeway that leads to Bull Wall, a 1½-km (1-mile) walkway that stretches as far as the North Bull Lighthouse. The island is also accessible via a second, northerly causeway, which takes you to Dollymount Strand. (The two routes of entry don't meet at any point on the island.) You can reach this causeway from the mainland via James Larkin Road.

Sights

St. Anne's Park

CITY PARK | On the mainland directly across from North Bull Island is St. Anne's Park, a public green with extensive rose gardens (including many prize hybrids), woodland walks, a farmers' market, and a scrumptious café. ✉ James Larkin Rd. and Mt. Prospect Ave., Dublin North.

Howth

From Dublin, take DART train, or Bus 31B from Lower Abbey St. in city center. Or, by car, take Howth Rd. from north city center for 16 km (10 miles).

A quick DART ride from the city takes you the vibrant, upmarket coastal town of Howth. A fishing village at the foot of a long peninsula, Howth (rhymes with "both," and derived from *hoved,* Norse for "head") was an island inhabited as long ago as 3250 BC. Between 1813 and 1833, Howth was the Irish terminus for the sea crossing to Holyhead in north Wales, but it was then superseded by the newly built harbor at Kingstown (now Dun Laoghaire). Today, its harbor, which supports a large fishing and sailing fleet, includes a marina. Both arms of the harbor pier form extensive walks with lots of great seafood options along the way.

Sights

Baily Lighthouse

LIGHTHOUSE | At the King Sitric restaurant on the East Pier, a 2½-km (1½-mile) cliff walk begins, leading to the white Baily Lighthouse, built in 1814. In some places, the cliff path narrows and drops close to the water, but the views out over the Irish Sea are terrific. Some of the best views in the whole Dublin area await from the parking lot above the lighthouse, looking out over the entire bay as far south as Dun Laoghaire, Bray, and the north Wicklow coast. You can also see quite a bit of Dublin. ✉ Howth Summit ⊕ www.cil.ie.

Howth Castle Gardens

GARDEN | The Howth Castle Gardens, next door to the Transport Museum and accessible from the Deer Park Hotel, were laid out in the early 18th century. The many rare varieties in the fine rhododendron garden are in full flower April through June; there are also high beech hedges. The rambling castle, built in 1654 and considerably altered in the following centuries, is not open to the public, but you can access the ruins of a tall, square, 16th-century castle and a Neolithic dolmen. ✉ Deer Park Hotel ☎ 01/832–2624 ⌨ Free.

Ireland's Eye

ISLAND | Separated from Howth Harbour by a channel nearly 1½ km (1 mile) wide is Ireland's Eye, with an old stone church on the site of a 6th-century monastery, and an early-19th-century Martello tower. In calm summer weather, local boatmen make the crossing to the island from the East pier in Howth Harbour. Check the notice board in the harbor for the number of a boat owner willing to do the trip. ✉ Howth.

National Transport Museum Of Ireland

MUSEUM | FAMILY | Until 1959 a tram service ran from the railway station in Howth over Howth Summit and back down to the station. One of the open-top Hill of Howth trams that plied this route is now the star at the National Transport Museum, a short, 800-yard walk from Howth's DART station. Volunteers spent several years restoring the tram, which stands alongside other unusual vehicles, including horse-drawn bakery vans. ✉ Heritage Depot, Howth Demense ☎ 01/832–0427 ⊕ www.nationaltransportmuseum.org ⌨ €3 ⊙ Closed weekdays.

Restaurants

Aqua

$$$ | SEAFOOD | Stunning views over Howth Harbor are your first reward for choosing this impressive seafood restaurant located in the old yacht club building only a few yards from where local fishermen still land their catch. The open, modern interior is awash with light that pours in the huge windows—definitely get a seat beside one of these. **Known for:** fresh crab spring roll with tuna tataki; Castletownbere seared scallops; Harbor views. ⑤ *Average main: €31* ✉ *1 West Pier* ☎ *01/832–0690* ⊕ *www.aqua. ie* ⊗ *Closed Mon.*

King Sitric

$$$ | SEAFOOD | Joan and Aidan MacManus's well-known seafood restaurant down by the harbor attracts many contemporary visitors to the old town. It's in a Georgian house, with the yacht marina and port on one side and sea views from which you can watch the boats land the very fish that might be tomorrow's special. **Known for:** sea views; fillet of turbot with crab mash and caviar cream sauce; fresh lobster. ⑤ *Average main: €28* ✉ *East Pier* ☎ *01/832–5235* ⊕ *www. kingsitric.ie* ⊗ *Closed Mon. and Tues. No lunch Wed.–Sat. No dinner Sun.*

Malahide

By car, drive from north city center on R107 for 14½ km (9 miles). Or catch hourly train from Connolly Station. Or board Bus 42 to Malahide, which leaves every 15 mins from Beresford Place behind Custom House.

👁 Sights

Malahide Castle

CASTLE/PALACE | FAMILY | This township is chiefly known for its glorious Malahide Castle, a picture-book castle occupied by the Talbot family from 1185 until 1976,

when it was sold to the local County Council. The great expanse of parkland around the castle has more than 5,000 different species of trees and shrubs, all clearly labeled. The castle itself combines styles and crosses centuries; the earliest section, the three-story tower house, dates from the 12th century. The stunning walled gardens are now open to the public, with a fairy trail for kids and a butterfly house. Hung with many family portraits, the medieval great hall is the only one in Ireland that is preserved in its original form. Authentic 18th-century pieces furnish the other rooms. An impressive new addition includes a visitor center, the Avoca restaurant, and a shop. ✉ *10 km (6 miles) north of Howth on Coast Rd.* ☎ *01/846–2184* ⊕ *www. malahidecastleandgardens.ie* 🎫 *€13.*

★ Newbridge House and Farm

HOUSE | FAMILY | One of the greatest stately homes of Ireland, Newbridge House, in Donabate, was built between 1740 and 1760 for Charles Cobbe, archbishop of Dublin. A showpiece in the Georgian and Regency styles, the house is less a museum than a home because the Cobbe family still resides here, part of a novel scheme the municipal government allowed when they took over the house in 1985. The sober exterior and even more sober entrance hall—all Portland stone and Welsh slate—don't prepare you for the splendor of Newbridge's Red Drawing Room, perhaps Ireland's most sumptuous 18th-century salon. Cobbe's son, Thomas, and his wife, Lady Betty Beresford, sister of the marquess of Waterford, had amassed a great collection of paintings and needed a hall in which to show them off, so they built a back wing on the house to incorporate an enormous room built for entertaining and impressing others. That it does, thanks to its crimson walls, fluted Corinthian columns, dozens of Old Masters, and glamorous rococo-style plaster ceiling designed by the Dublin stuccadore Richard Williams. Beyond the house's walled garden are 366 acres of parkland and a restored 18th-century animal farm. The coffee shop is renowned for the quality and selection of its homemade goods. You can travel from Malahide to Donabate by train, which takes about 10 minutes. From the Donabate train station, it's a 15-minute walk to the Newbridge House grounds. ✉ *Donabate, 8 km (5 miles) north of Malahide, signposted from N1* ☎ *01/843–6534* ⊕ *www.newbridgehouseandfarm. com* 🎫 *House €7, farm €6, combined €10* 🕑 *Closed Mon. Oct.–Mar.*

Chapter 4

DUBLIN ENVIRONS

4

Updated by
Anto Howard

 Sights
★★★★★

 Restaurants
★★★★☆

 Hotels
★★★★☆

 Shopping
★★★☆☆

 Nightlife
★★★☆☆

WELCOME TO DUBLIN ENVIRONS

TOP REASONS TO GO

★ **Newgrange:** Just standing amid these 5,000-year-old tombs (which predate the pyramids), you'll wonder: how did they build them?

★ **A Day at the Races:** The Irish may be known to enjoy a sociable drink, but they really love to gamble, as you'll discover in Kildare, center of the Irish bloodstock world. Punchestown in spring and the Curragh in summer are both unique, passionate racecourse experiences.

★ **Spectacular Georgian Country Houses:** Modesty was not a feature of the Anglo-Irish class, whose propensity to flaunt their riches led to such over-the-top stately homes as Castletown, Russborough, and Powerscourt.

★ **Wicklow Is for Walkers:** There's no better way to meet the locals and see the land than trekking out on the 137-km-long (85-mile-long) Wicklow Way, Ireland's most popular trail.

★ **Early Morning at Glendalough:** Channel the spirit of the 6th-century, isolation-seeking St. Kevin.

The Dublin environs include the heart of Ireland's Ancient East trail and can be divided into three main regions: the Boyne Valley, County Wicklow's coast and mountains, and County Kildare. The Boyne Valley includes much of counties Meath and Louth to the north and east of Dublin. Wicklow and Kildare are to the southeast and south of the capital. Tour this small region, or opt for day trips from Dublin, especially to the Wicklow Mountains, which rise up suddenly at the fringes of the city.

1 Hill of Tara. Unassuming but incredibly important, this hill and its ancient monuments were the seat of power for ancient High Kings.

2 Kells. While the *Book of Kells* no longer sleeps in this area's bogs, this town has High Crosses, a Round Tower, and lots of history.

3 Newgrange. A Neolithic burial ground and solar observatory still evocative of the mysteries of pre-Celtic civilization.

4 Slane. Slane Castle is the main draw in this small Georgian village.

5 Drogheda. Georgian architecture, a medieval town gate, and lots of churches are the draw to this riverside town.

6 Mellifont Abbey. The first Cistercian monastery in Ireland.

7 Dundalk. The main town of Ireland's smallest county is a perfect base for exploring both north and south of the border.

8 Glendalough. This 6th-century monastic site is so serene you may be tempted to renounce the profane world.

NORTHERN
IRELAND

ARMAGH   DOWN

MONAGHAN
Annayalla
Castleblayney

Omeath   Carlingford Lough

N53   **7**   Dundalk

Inniskeen   Dundalk
                        Bay

CAVAN

N2

Cavan

New Inn

Ardee   LOUTH

N3   M1

N52   N2

Mellifont Abbey ◆ **6**

Kells   BOYNE VALLEY   **5**

2   **4** ◆   Drogheda

N3   Slane ○ **3**

N52   Newgrange ◆   M1

N51   Navan ○

WESTMEATH   Hill of Tara ◆

Cloghan ○   **1**   N2

MEATH   DUBLIN

M3

Kinnegad ○   N4   Swords ○

Lambay
Island   M1

Tyrrellspass ○

OFFALY   DUBLIN   Drumleck Point

KILDARE   ★ DUBLIN   Dublin
                                Bay
Castletown ◆
House   N81

Russborough ◆   M11
House
Naas ○   Bray ○

M7   Powerscourt ◆
Punchestown ◆
racecourse
Cherryville ○   Kilmacanogue ○

N7   The Curragh ◆   WICKLOW

Kildare ○   N11

Kilcullen ○

N78   Wicklow Way ◆

Ballinalea ◆

Mountrath ○   Athy ○   Glendalough ◆ **8**   Wicklow ○

M9   Wicklow
                                          Head
LAOIS

Abbeyleix ○

CARLOW

Durrow ○   N11

Arklow ○

WEXFORD

I r i s h   S e a

0   10 mi

0   10 km

THE RIVER BOYNE VALLEY: IRELAND'S HISTORIC HEART

Newgrange is a spectacular passage tomb.

Stone Age, Celtic, early Christian, and Norman: the country is scattered with sites that act as signposts in the long and twisting story called "Ireland." But by circumstance of geography and mystical significance many of the great stone ghosts of ancient Ireland are concentrated in the counties immediately surrounding Dublin.

Here, often so closely thrown together as to make a mockery of the vastness of time and history, stand the man-made wonders that are impressive but slightly melancholic reminders of more heroic and more savage ages. In fact, a tour down the valley of the River Boyne is a trip into the past, back beyond history, to the Neolithic tombs of Newgrange, the Druidic holy place of the Hill of Tara, the monasteries of early Christianity, and the Norman castles of the chain-mailed invaders who brought a bloody end to so much of Celtic Ireland. Not far from Dublin, chart the rise and fall of Irish culture at their glorious monuments.

THE HIGH CROSS

The Celtic High Cross is an endearing symbol of Ireland, and Monasterboice has more of them than anywhere in Ireland. Dating to AD 923, the 20-foot-high Muireadach Cross is the best preserved, as its panels depicting the slaying of Abel, David and Goliath, and the Last Judgment prove. The nearby 110-foot Round Tower gives you a view of the once-glorious monastic site.

NEWGRANGE

Built in the fourth millennium BC, a thousand years before Stonehenge, Newgrange is not only one of the world's pristine surviving passage tombs but also a great granite reminder of the ingenuity, spirituality, and perseverance of modern Ireland's Neolithic ancestors. How did they move 250,000 tons of stone? How did they align it to perfectly capture the first rays of the dawn sun on the winter solstice? The thrill of visiting and entering the somber tomb at Newgrange lies not only in what you discover but in the awesome mysteries that can only be answered by the imagination.

GLENDALOUGH

A single early-morning hour spent in the isolated and serene Glendalough Valley—a green jewel in the Wicklow Mountains—should be enough to convince you that St. Kevin made the perfect choice when he was searching for 6th-century solitude and peace. The simplicity, separation, and sparseness that were at the heart of early Christianity in Ireland are sublimely apparent in the hermit's cave called St. Kevin's Bed and the ruins of the tiny Church of the Oratory.

The Stone of Destiny rests on the Hill of Tara.

HILL OF TARA

First-timers are sometimes disappointed when they finally see the mythical Hill of Tara, spiritual and regal heart of Celtic and Druidic Ireland. It is now just a hill: 300 feet high, with awesome views out over the flat central plains of Ireland and all the way to Galway in the west. But with a little reading at the interpretive center and a lot of imagination, you can picture the Iron Age fort that once stood here and the huge *feis,* or national assembly, where Celtic Ireland passed its laws and settled its tribal disputes. It is a place that is both beyond history and made of it.

MELLIFONT ABBEY

As well as war, the Normans brought great stone-church building to Ireland; one of their greatest religious monuments is Mellifont Abbey. Founded in 1142 by St. Malachy, the main parts of the abbey were built a little later in the Norman style, including the two-story chapter house and the octagonal lavabo, where the monks used to wash. Although much of the abbey is in ruins, it still manages to illustrate the medieval church's rise to wealth and power in Ireland. Incidentally, the term "Celtic" is derived from the tribes that arrived on Irish shores around 700 BC, first called Galli by the Romans and then named Gaels in Ireland.

Graves and High Crosses hallow the grounds of Glendalough.

Walt Disney himself couldn't have planned it better. The small counties immediately north, south, and west of Dublin—historically known as the Pale—seem expressly designed to entertain and enchant sightseers. The entire region is rich with legendary Celtic sites, gorgeous gardens, and the most elegant Palladian country estates in Ireland.

Due to its location on the Irish Sea, facing Europe, the region was the first to attract the earliest "tourists"—conquerors and rulers—and the first over which they exercised the greatest influence. Traces of each new wave remain: the Celts chose Tara as the center of their kingdom; the Danes sailed the Rivers Boyne and Liffey to establish many of today's towns; and the region's great Protestant-built houses of the 18th century remind us that the Pale (originally the area of eastern Ireland ruled directly by the Normans) was the starting point and administrative center for the long, violent English colonization of the whole island.

The Dublin environs include three basic geographical regions. North of Dublin lies the Boyne Valley, with its abundant ruins of Celtic Ireland extending from counties Meath to Louth. In pagan times this area was the home of Ireland's High Kings and the center of religious life. All roads led to Tara, the fabled Hill of Kings, the royal seat, and the place where the national assembly was held. Today, time seems to stand still—and you should, too, for it's almost sacrilegious to introduce a note of urgency here.

South of the capital is the mountainous county of Wicklow, where the gently rounded Wicklow Mountains contain the evocative monastic settlement at Glendalough, many later abbeys and churches, and the great 18th-century estates of the Anglo-Irish aristocracy, such as Castletown, Powerscourt, and Russborough.

Southwest of Dublin are the pastoral plains of County Kildare, which stretch between the western Midlands and the foothills of the Dublin and Wicklow mountains—both names refer to the same mountain range, but each marks its county's claim to the land. Kildare is the flattest part of Ireland, a natural playing field for breeding, training, and racing some of the world's premier Thoroughbreds.

Rapid, omnivorous expansion of the capital city in the last 30 years has seen its suburban limits spread deep into the once-bucolic areas of Meath and Kildare, so don't be surprised to hear Dublin accents starting to dominate in towns like Navan and Naas. The recent upturn in the economy and the parallel hike in house prices have been strongly felt in these satellite towns so dependent on the economy of Dublin.

MAJOR REGIONS

Set 48 km (30 miles) north of Dublin, this entire area is packed with prehistoric and pagan sites. You don't have to be an Indiana Jones to be awed by the Hill of Tara or Newgrange, a Neolithic burial ground and solar observatory still evocative of the mysteries of pre-Celtic civilization.

The Boyne Valley. For every wistful schoolchild in Ireland, the River Boyne is a name that resonates with history and adventure. It was on the banks of that river in 1014 that the Celtic chieftain Brian Boru defeated the Danish in a decisive battle that returned the east of Ireland to native rule. It was also by this river that Protestant William of Orange defeated the Catholic armies of exiled James II of England in 1690. In fact, this whole area, only 48 km (30 miles) north of cosmopolitan Dublin, is soaked in stories and legends that predate the pyramids. You can't throw a stick anywhere in the valley without hitting some trace of Irish history. The great prehistoric, pagan, and Celtic monuments of the wide arc known as the Boyne Valley invariably evoke a sense of wonder. You don't have to be an archaeologist to be awed by **Newgrange** and Knowth—set beside the River Boyne—or the **Hill of Tara**, **Mellifont Abbey**, or the High Cross of Monasterboice. One way to explore this area is to start at Trim, the town closest to Dublin, and work your way north. Keep in mind that Omeath and the scenic Cooley Peninsula are on the border of Northern Ireland.

County Kildare. Horse racing is a passion in Ireland—just about every little town has at least one betting shop—and County Kildare is the country's horse capital. Nestled between the basins of the River Liffey to the north and the River Barrow to the east, its gently sloping hills and grass-filled plains are perfect for breeding and racing Thoroughbreds.

For some visitors, the fabled National Stud Farm just outside Kildare Town provides a fascinating glimpse into the world of horse breeding. And don't forget the Japanese Gardens, adjacent to the National Stud, which are among Europe's finest. You may want to head to this area from Glendalough—the spectacular drive across the Wicklow Gap, from Glendalough to Hollywood, makes for a glorious entrance into Kildare.

County Wicklow. Make your way to the fourth or fifth story of almost any building in Dublin that faces south, and you can see off in the distance—amazingly, not *that* far off in the distance—the green, smooth hills of the Dublin and Wicklow mountains. On a clear day, the mountains are even visible from some streets in and around the city center. If your idea of solace is green hills, and your visit to Ireland is otherwise limited to Dublin, County Wicklow—or Cill Mhantáin (pronounced "kill *wan*-tan"), as it's known in Irish—should be on your itinerary.

Not that the secret isn't out; rugged and mountainous with dark, wooded forests, central Wicklow, known as the "garden of Ireland," is a popular picnic spot among Dubliners. It has some of Ireland's grandest 18th-century mansions, including Russborough and Powerscourt, and cradles one of the country's earliest Christian retreats: Glendalough. Nestled in a valley of dense woods and placid lakes, Glendalough and environs can seem (at least during the off-season) practically untouched since their heyday 1,000 years ago. The granite mountains that have protected Glendalough all these years run into the sea along the east coast, which has several popular sandy beaches.

Planning

When to Go

While certainly not the wettest part of Ireland (the West gets that dubious distinction), the counties around Dublin do get their fair share of rain. June, July, August, and September tend to be the driest months, and the good news is that the summer showers are usually light and short-lived. Wicklow, with all its hills and valleys, seems to have an obscure microclimate of its own, so don't rely too much on the weather forecast to get it right.

Planning Your Time

Most people who explore Dublin Environs base themselves in the capital and sample the very different landscapes on day trips. Driving distances from downtown are less than two hours (in decent traffic). Just don't plan on visiting both the north and south of Dublin in the same day—each region is worth its own day or half-day trip.

Visits to Newgrange and Glendalough are musts, and the latter could be combined with a country house visit to Powerscourt. For more active visitors, a one-day walk along the Wicklow Way might pair best with an overnight stay in the cozy Hunter's Hotel.

Getting Here and Around

BUS TRAVEL

Bus Éireann links Dublin with towns in the area. Dublin Bus serves some towns and estates in the region as well. All buses for the region depart from Dublin's Busáras, the central bus station, at Store Street. St. Kevin's Bus Services offers regular trips from Dublin to numerous towns and sights in Wicklow, including Glendalough, Roundwood, Laragh, and Bray.

CONTACTS Bus Éireann. ☎ 01/836–6111 ⊕ www.buseireann.ie. **Dublin Bus.** ☎ 01/873–4222 ⊕ www.dublinbus.ie. **St. Kevin's Bus.** ☎ 01/281–8119 ⊕ www. glendaloughbus.com.

CAR TRAVEL

The easiest and best way to tour Dublin's environs is by car, because many sights are not served by public transportation. What service there is, especially to outlying areas, is infrequent. To visit destinations in the Boyne Valley, follow N3, along the east side of Phoenix Park, out of the city and make Trim and Tara your first stops. Alternatively, leave Dublin via N1/M1 toward Belfast. To reach destinations in County Kildare, follow the quays along the south side of the River Liffey (they are one-way westbound) to St. John's Road West (N7/M7); in a matter of minutes you're heading for open countryside. Avoid traveling this route during the evening rush hour, especially on Friday, when Dubliners are making their weekend getaways. To reach destinations in County Wicklow, N11/M11 is the fastest and most clearly marked route. The two more scenic routes to Glendalough are R115 to R759 to R755, or R177 to R755. All major roads can be congested during rush hours, and like most major cities, Friday afternoon is a busy time to leave the city.

TRAIN TRAVEL

Irish Rail (Iarnród Éireann) trains run the length of the east coast, stopping at towns between Dundalk to the north in County Louth to Arklow along the coast in County Wicklow. From Heuston Station, the Arrow, a commuter train service, runs westward to Celbridge, Naas, Newbridge, Athy, and Kildare Town.

CONTACTS Irish Rail–Iarnód Éireann. ☎ 01/836–6222 in Dublin, 041/983–8749 in Drogheda ⊕ www.irishrail.ie.

Hotels

When exploring the region around Dublin, many people opt to stay in the capital and take day trips. The city center is obviously a favorite option, but does leave you subject to some heavy rush-hour traffic; in general, you can still get in and out of Dublin quite quickly. A hotel on the Southside of the city or in South County Dublin might be a good idea if you're planning to spend time in Wicklow or East Kildare. For Meath and Louth, a hotel on the Northside or to the west of the city might work better.

If you don't want to "commute" from the city, the noted country-house hotels around Kildare and Wicklow are great options. They are a surprisingly good value given their unique, luxurious atmospheres. Bed-and-breakfasts are another good option, and although those in this region tend to be a little more expensive than in other parts of Ireland, they also are more stylish. Like in Dublin, hotel prices have increased over the last few years, but less dramatically. *Hotel reviews have been shortened. For full information, visit Fodors.com.*

Restaurants

Dining out in the area is usually a casual affair, but Dublin's top restaurateurs are influencing the cooking—and the prices—at the finer establishments outside the capital. The recent economic downturn also encouraged smaller, innovative, and, above all, good-value restaurants like Las Rada to spring up in unlikely places like Naas. Chefs hereabouts have a deep respect for fresh, locally grown and raised produce. You'll find everything from Continental-style meals to hearty ploughman's lunches. *Restaurant reviews have been shortened. For full information, visit Fodors.com.*

What It Costs in Euros

	$	$$	$$$	$$$$
RESTAURANTS				
	under €19	€19–€24	€25–€32	over €32
HOTELS				
	under €120	€120–€170	€171–€210	over €210

Tours

Loveireland.com
BUS TOURS | Guided bus tours throughout the region around Dublin are offered by this company between May and September, including day trips to Wicklow and to Newgrange and Mellifont Abbey. ☎ 01/898–0700 ⊕ www.loveireland.com ⌨ *From €33.*

Railtours Ireland
BUS TOURS | Take a half-day ride through the Wicklow Mountains with Railtours Ireland. The train stops at Arklow, where a bus takes you through Avoca and on to Glendalough. ☎ 01/856–0045 ⊕ www.railtoursireland.com ⌨ *From €69.*

Tourism Ireland
DRIVING TOURS | The website for Tourism Ireland has a Grand Tour section that outlines a number of cleverly themed driving tours in the area. ☎ 800/242–473 ⊕ www.ireland.com.

Wild Wicklow Tours
BUS TOURS | For smaller groups, Wild Wicklow Tours' buses try to take you off the beaten track. Day trips to Glendalough also take in Avoca Handweavers and a Dublin coastal drive. ☎ 01/280–1899 ⊕ www.wildwicklow.ie ⌨ *From €33.*

Visitor Information

You're likely to encounter signs and other promotional materials for the country's newest tourism initiative, "Ireland's

Boyne Valley

Ancient East," which is designed to link many of the great sites in this half of the country. Like the hugely successful "Wild Atlantic Way" initiative before it, the resources developed to promote and support the campaign are a huge benefit to visitors. Be sure to check the Ireland's Ancient East website as it is a great source for current events and suggested stops. County Kildare, County Louth, and County Meath all have offices that offer year-round tourism advice. Some are run by Tourism Ireland while others are locally operated. In summer, temporary offices are open in such towns as Trim in County Meath, Drogheda and Dundalk in County Louth, and Kildare Town in County Kildare.

CONTACTS County Kildare Tourism.
☎ *045/898–888* ⊕ *www.intokildare.ie.*
County Louth Tourism. ☎ *042/933–5457*
⊕ *www.visitlouth.ie.* **County Meath Tourism.** ☎ *046/909–7060* ⊕ *www. meath.ie/tourism.* **Ireland's Ancient East.** ☎ *1850/230–330* ⊕ *www.ire- landsancienteast.com.* **Wicklow Tourism.** ☎ *0404/69118* ⊕ *www.visitwicklow.ie.*

Hill of Tara

40 km (25 miles) northwest of Dublin.

In legends and in the popular imagination, the "seat of the High Kings of Ireland" has taken on mythic proportions. As with much of the Celtic past, it was the 19th-century revival led by W.B. Yeats and Lady Gregory that was responsible for the near-religious veneration of this site, set at the junction of the five ancient roads of Ireland. Today, its ancestral banqueting hall and great buildings (one was the former palace of the *Ard Rí*, or High King) have vanished except for a few columns. Still, the site is awe-inspiring.

GETTING HERE AND AROUND

An hour's drive from Dublin, the Hill of Tara is just off the N3/M3 motorway. From Belfast it's a 1½-hour drive; take the M1 and connect with the N51 at Drogheda. There's ample parking near the site. You can also take a Navan-bound Bus Éireann, which passes within 2 km (1 mile) of the site and walk; ask the driver to drop you at the Tara Cross and follow the signs. A taxi from Navan to Tara costs about €18.

TOURS

Newgrange Tours

Bus tours run from Dublin Monday through Saturday. The company charges €40, which includes admission to the Hill of Tara and Newgrange. Tours depart from outside the Visit Dublin Centre on Suffolk Street, as well as from some major hotels. ☎ *086/335–1355* ⊕ *www. newgrangetours.com.*

 Sights

★ **Hill of Tara**

HISTORIC SITE | One of the most sacred places in pre-Christian Ireland, and the seat of power for ancient High Kings, the Hill of Tara is at the nexus of Celtic myth and history. You are free to roam across the site, but it might require a little research and imagination to bring it all to life. From the top of the Hill—it rises more than 300 feet above sea level—you can see across the flat central plain of Ireland, with the mountains of east Galway visible from a distance of nearly 160 km (100 miles). At the summit you will also find an oval Iron Age hilltop enclosure, a massive "hill fort," which became known as the Fort of the Kings (Ráith na Ríogh). Within the fort are further earthworks, a ring fort and a ring barrow—Cormac's House (Teach Chormaic) and the Royal Seat (Forradh).

In the middle of the Forradh you'll notice a solitary standing stone. This is believed to be the Stone of Destiny (Lia Fáil), the ancient crowning place of the High Kings. Wander further to find further earth-works, a massive ring fort known as Rath Maeve, and a Holy Well. The legend of St. Patrick claims he came to the Hill of Tara to confront the ancient pagan religion at its most important site. In the mid-19th century, the nationalist leader Daniel O'Connell staged a mass rally here that supposedly drew more than a million people. ■ **TIP→ Before you wander, stop at the Interpretive Center, housed in an old church on the hillside, where you can learn the story of Tara and its legends and watch a short movie showing stunning aerial views. Without this background it will be difficult to get your bearings or to identify many of the earthworks outside.** After systematic excavations in the 20th century, archaeologists have concluded that the Iron Age fort was ruined in the 19th century by religious zealots searching for the Ark of the Covenant. The Mound of the Hostages, a Neolithic passage grave, most likely gave the place its sacred air. ⊠ *Navan* ✛ *12 km (7 miles) south of Navan off N3* ☎ *046/902–5903* ⊕ *www. heritageireland.ie/en/midlands-eastcoast/ hilloftara* 🎫 *€5* 🕑 *Visitor center closes early Sept.–late May.*

 Restaurants

Eden

$$$ | MODERN IRISH | Located in the impressive vaulted cellar of Bellinter House, Eden sticks strictly to a season-al ethos with menus based on locally sourced produce. Oenophiles rave about the value-for-money wine list. The Eden smokies is the signature starter with smoked haddock, cherry tomatoes, scallions, crème fraîche, and a cheddar gratin, and the sea bass with cauliflower and cumin puree, baby potato cakes, anchovies, and lemon crème fraîche is a standout main. **Known for:** modern Irish bistro fare; Georgian manor-house setting; impressive wine cellar. $ *Average main: €31* ✉ *Bellinter House, Navan ✛ 4 km (2½ miles) northwest of Hill of Tara* ☎ *046/903–0900* ⊕ *www.bellinterhouse. com.*

Hotels

★ Bellinter House

$$$ | **B&B/INN** | Surrounded by 12 acres on the banks of the Boyne, this splendid 1750 country house retains the glories of the original architecture while adding a few modern twists. **Pros:** stunningly authentic original rooms; impressive spa; relaxing atmosphere. **Cons:** newer rooms not as grand; some areas of the house require TLC; service can be inconsistent. $ *Rooms from: €209* ✉ *Navan ✛ 4 km (2½ miles) northwest of Hill of Tara* ☎ *046/903–0900* ⊕ *www.bellinterhouse. com* ⮌ *34 rooms* ⊙ *Free breakfast.*

Activities

GOLF

Killeen Castle Golf Club

GOLF | The great Jack Nicklaus had a hand in the design and construction of this championship-level course and golf school set in the serene woodlands of Norman Killeen Castle in Meath. Covering twice the acreage of an average championship course—you might need a buggy to get around—Nicklaus really had room to let his imagination run free, and the natural water features and stonework are a special treat. ■ **TIP→ Check out the wonderful Paul Ferriter sculpture of the great man himself near the first tee box.** ✉ *1 Loughmore Ave., Dunsany* ☎ *01/689–3000* ⊕ *www.killeencastle.com* 🗓 *May– Sept. €70–€90, Apr. and Oct. €60–€70, Nov.–Mar. €50–€70* 🏌 *18 holes, 7700 yards, par 72.*

Kells

67 km (41 miles) northwest of Dublin.

In the 9th century, a group of monks from Scotland took refuge at Kells (Ceanannus Mór), where St. Columba had founded a monastery 300 years earlier. Although some historians think it was indigenous monks who wrote and illustrated the *Book of Kells*—the Latin version of the four Gospels, and one of Ireland's greatest medieval treasures— most now believe that the Scottish monks brought it with them. Reputed to have been fished out of a watery bog at Kells, the legendary manuscript was removed for safekeeping during the Cromwellian wars to Trinity College, Dublin, where it remains.

GETTING HERE AND AROUND

Kells is a 50-minute drive northwest of Dublin on the M3 motorway. There is ample parking in and around the town. Bus Éireann has regular service from Dublin; the trip takes one hour and 25 minutes.

◉ Sights

Kells Tourist Office

INFO CENTER | Located in Kells Town Hall, the office is also home to a brilliant copy of the *Book of Kells*—it's a more pleasant, less rushed, and less expensive way to see this medieval masterpiece compared with the madness of Trinity College in high season. They also have a diorama of Kells Town around AD 815. ⌧ *Headfort Pl.* ☎ *046/924–8856* ⊕ *www. meath.ie* ⌧ *Free* ⊘ *Closed weekends.*

Round Tower

MILITARY SITE | The nearly 100-foot-high Round Tower, adjacent to St. Colmcille's House, dates back to 1076 and is in almost perfect condition. The tower was likely used as a defensive hideout by local monks during an invasion; they would climb up the rope ladder with their valuables and pull it up after them. Its top story has five windows, not the usual four, each facing an ancient entrance into the medieval town. You can't go inside, but just standing beside it gives a real sense of the inventiveness and desperation of the Viking-fearing monks. ⌧ *R163, west of intersection of N3 and N52.*

St. Colmcille's House

RELIGIOUS SITE | Similar in appearance to St. Kevin's Church at Glendalough and Cormac's Chapel at Cashel, St. Colmcille's House is an 11th-century church on a much older site. It measures about 24 feet square and nearly 40 feet high, with a steeply pitched stone roof. It's well worth going inside and getting a feel for what the ancient monastic life was like. ⌧ *R163, west of intersection of N3 and N52.*

St. Columba's

RELIGIOUS SITE | Four elaborately carved High Crosses stand in the church graveyard; you'll find the stump of a fifth in the marketplace—it was used as a gallows during the 1798 uprising against British rule. ⌧ *Off Cannon St. and Church St.*

Winter Solstice ◉ at Newgrange

A visit to Newgrange's passage grave during the winter solstice is a memorable experience. You'll have to get on the nine-year waiting list to reserve one of the 24 places available on each of the five mornings (December 19–23). And then pray that no clouds obscure the sun and ruin the light show the Bronze Age builders intended.

Newgrange

21 km (13 miles) east of Kells, 28 km (17 miles) northwest of Dublin.

★ Expect to see no less than one of the most spectacular prehistoric tombs in Europe when you come to Newgrange. Built in the 4th millennium BC—which makes it roughly 1,000 years older than Stonehenge—Newgrange was constructed with some 250,000 tons of stone, much of which came from the Wicklow Mountains, 80 km (50 miles) to the south. The Brú na Bóinne (loosely translated as "Palace of the Boyne") Visitor Centre, near the village of Donore, is the starting point for all visits to Newgrange and Knowth. Newgrange often sells out in high season.

GETTING HERE AND AROUND

From Dublin it's about a 50-minute drive to Newgrange: take the M1 motorway north to the Donore exit before Drogheda; Brú na Bóinne is clearly signposted before the exit. Drive about 6 km (4 miles) to the village of Donore, turn right and travel about half a mile to the visitor center. There is ample parking at the center. The Bus Éireann route from Dublin to Drogheda stops at Newgrange, and Newgrange Tours combines a visit to this site with the Hill of Tara on its bus tour.

Built between 3100 and 2900 BC, Newgrange is strikingly adorned with boulders carved with Neolithic triple spirals and diamonds.

VISITOR INFORMATION

CONTACTS Brú na Bóinne Visitor Centre.
☒ Off Staleen Rd., near Donore Village,
Slane ☎ 041/988–0300 ⊕ www.heritage-ireland.ie.

 Sights

★ Knowth

ARCHAEOLOGICAL SITE | Under excavation since 1962, the prehistoric site of Knowth is comparable in size and shape to Newgrange, standing at 40 feet and having a diameter of approximately 214 feet. Some 150 giant stones, many of them beautifully decorated, surrounded the mound. More than 1,600 boulders, each weighing from one to several tons, were used in the construction. The earliest tombs and carved stones date from the Stone Age (3000 BC); and in the early Christian era (4th–8th centuries AD), it was the seat of the High Kings of Ireland. Much of the site is still under excavation, and you can often watch archaeologists at work. Tours of the site depart from the Brú na Bóinne Visitor Centre. ☒ Off N2,

near Donore Village, Slane ☎ 041/988–0300 for Brú na Bóinne Visitor Centre ⊕ www.heritageireland.ie ☒ €6.

★ Newgrange

MEMORIAL | One of the most spectacular prehistoric sites in the world, Newgrange's Neolithic tomb inexplicably remains something of a hidden gem when compared with less-ancient Stonehenge. The wondrous site is shrouded in myth and mystery, including how the people who built Newgrange transported the huge stones to the spot. The mound above the tomb measures more than 330 feet across and reaches a height of 36 feet. White quartz was used for the retaining wall, and egg-shape gray stones were studded at intervals. The passage grave may have been the world's earliest solar observatory. It was so carefully constructed that, for five days on and around the winter solstice, the rays of the rising sun still hit a roof box above the lintel at the entrance to the grave. The rays then shine for about 20 minutes down the main interior passageway to illuminate the burial chamber. The geometric designs on some stones at the center of the burial chamber continue to baffle experts. Tours of the site depart from the Brú na Bóinne Visitor Centre. ■TIP→ **Reserving tickets in advance is a must. Walk-in tickets are rarely available.** ⊠ *Off N2, 2 km (1 mile) west of Donore Village, Slane* ☎ *041/988–0300 for Brú na Bóinne Visitor Centre* ⊕ *www.heritageire-land.ie* ⌨ *€7.*

Slane

2½ km (1½ miles) north of Newgrange, 46 km (29 miles) northwest of Dublin.

Slane Castle is the draw at this small Georgian village, built in the 18th century around a crossroads on the north side of the River Boyne.

GETTING HERE AND AROUND
Slane is 46 km (29 miles) northwest of Dublin on the N2 major road. There is plenty of parking around the town and at the castle. Bus Éireann runs a regular service from Dublin; it takes about an hour and 10 minutes.

◉ Sights

Hermitage
BUILDING | The 16th-century Hermitage was constructed on the site where St. Erc, a local man converted to Christianity by St. Patrick himself, led a hermit's existence. All that remains of his original monastery is the faint trace of the circular ditch, but the ruins of the later church include a nave and a chancel with a tower in between, and a stroll through them can evoke a little of the atmosphere of medieval Ireland. ⊠ *Slane Castle Demesne.*

Newgrange Farm
FARM/RANCH | FAMILY | A two-hour tour of farmer Willie Redhouse's fully function-ing farm includes feeding the ducks, bottle-feeding the lambs, a visit to

aviaries stocked with exotic birds, and a straw maze and go-karts for the kids. A blacksmith gives demonstrations of his ancient art, and there's a nice tractor ride around the farm. Every Sunday at 3 pm the Sheep Derby takes place, with teddy bears tied astride the animals in the place of jockeys. ⊠ *N51* ✛ *3 km (2 miles) east of Slane* ⊕ *www.newgrangefarm. com* ⌨ *€9* ⊘ *Closed early Sept.–mid-Mar.*

★ Slane Castle
CASTLE/PALACE | The stately 18th-century Slane Castle overlooks a natural amphi-theater, a bowl-shape hollow formed by surrounding hills. In 1981 the castle's owner, Anglo-Irish Lord Henry Mount Charles, staged the first of what have been some of Ireland's largest outdoor rock concerts; up to 100,000 fans have gathered to watch stars including U2, Bob Dylan, and the Rolling Stones. A tour of the Gothic-style castle includes the main hall, with its delicate plasterwork and beautiful stained glass, and the dazzling neo-Gothic ballroom completed in 1821 for the visit of King George IV. The stunning parklands were laid out by Capability Brown, a famous 18th-cen-tury landscape gardener. Slane Castle produces its own whiskey and has fun tasting tours. ⊠ *Off N51* ☎ *041/988–4477* ⊕ *www.slanecastle.ie* ⌨ *Castle €12, Whiskey Tour €18* ⊘ *Castle: closed Sept. 2–Apr., and Fri. and Sat. May–Aug.*

Slane Hill
VIEWPOINT | North of Slane is the 500-foot-high Slane Hill, where St. Patrick proclaimed the arrival of Christianity in 433 by lighting the Paschal fire. From the top you have sweeping views of the Boyne Valley. On a clear day, the panora-ma stretches from Trim to Drogheda, a vista extending 40 km (25 miles). ⊠ *Off N2* ✛ *1½ km (1 mile) northeast of Slane Castle.*

Hotels

★ **Tankardstown House**

$$$$ | B&B/INN | A sumptuous Georgian-era manor house with a classic walled garden and 80 acres of breathtaking parkland, no expense was spared in the loving restoration of what is often lauded as Ireland's best private house hotel. **Pros:** authentic Georgian exterior and interiors; idyllic setting; great restaurant. **Cons:** some rooms a bit small; limited facilities; cottages lack style of house rooms. $ *Rooms from: €251* ✉ *Slane* ✛ *2½ km (1½ mile) from gates of Slane Castle* ☎ *041/982–4621* ⊕ *www.tankardstown.ie* ⊗ *Closed Mon. and Tues.* ↩ *7 rooms, 7 cottages* ♖ *Free breakfast.*

Drogheda

15½ km (9 miles) east of Slane, 45 km (28 miles) north of Dublin.

Drogheda (pronounced "*dra-he-da*") is one of the most enjoyable and historic towns on the east coast of Ireland—and a setting for one of the most tragic events in Irish history, the siege and massacre wrought by Oliver Cromwell's English army. The town was colonized in 911 by the Danish Vikings; two centuries later, it was taken over by Hugh de Lacy, the Anglo-Norman lord of Meath, who was responsible for fortifying the towns along the River Boyne. At first, two separate towns existed, one on the north bank, the other on the south. In 1412, already heavily walled and fortified, Drogheda was unified, making it the largest English town in Ireland. Today, 18th-century warehouses line the northern bank of the Boyne. The center of town, around West Street, is the historic heart of Drogheda.

GETTING HERE AND AROUND

Thanks to the M1 motorway, Drogheda is a 45-minute trip north of Dublin. Paid parking is available throughout the town.

Bus Éireann operates express and regular service connecting Drogheda to Dundalk (30 minutes), Dublin (40 minutes), Navan (40 minutes), and Belfast (1 hour, 30 minutes), while Irish Rail connects the town to Hueston Station in Dublin (51 minutes), Belfast (1 hour, 40 minutes), and Dundalk (20 minutes) on the same line. The bus station is south of the river on the corner of John Street and Donore Road, and the train station is south of the river and east of the town center on the Dublin Road.

VISITOR INFORMATION

CONTACTS Drogheda Tourist Office. ✉ *The Tholsel, West St.* ☎ *041/987–2843* ⊕ *www.drogheda.ie.*

 Sights

Butler's Gate

BUILDING | One of the city's original 11 entrances, Butler's Gate predates St. Laurence's Gate by 50 years or more, making it one of the country's oldest surviving Norman urban structures. It's near the Drogheda Museum Millmount. ✉ *Off Mount Saint Oliver, Millmount.*

★ **Drogheda Museum Millmount**

MUSEUM | It was in Millmount that the townsfolk made their last stand against the bloodthirsty Roundheads of Cromwell. Perhaps in defiance of Cromwell's attempt to obliterate the town from the map, the museum contains relics of eight centuries of Drogheda's commercial and industrial past, including painted banners of the old trade guilds and a circular willow-and-leather coracle (the traditional fishing boat on the River Boyne). Most moving are the mementos of the infamous 1649 massacre of 3,000 people by Cromwell. The exhibit inside the Martello Tower, adjacent to the museum, focuses on the town's military history. The museum shares space in a renovated British Army barracks with several crafts workshops. ✉ *Off Mount Saint Oliver, Millmount* ✛ *Off N1, south of Drogheda*

☎ *041/983–3097* ⊕ *www.millmount.net*
✉ *€6.*

St. Laurence's Gate

BUILDING | There were once 11 passages through the city walls, but the 13th-century St. Laurence's Gate is one of the last that remains. With two four-story drum towers, it's one of the most perfect examples in Ireland of a medieval town gate. ⊠ *Saint Laurence St.*

St. Peter's

RELIGIOUS SITE | A severe church within an enclosed courtyard, the 18th-century Anglican St. Peter's is rarely open except for Sunday services. It's worth a peek for its setting and for the fine views of the town from the churchyard. ⊠ *Peter St. off Fair St.* ⊕ *drogheda.armagh.anglican.org/.*

St. Peter's Church

RELIGIOUS SITE | The Gothic Revival Roman Catholic St. Peter's Church houses the preserved head of St. Oliver Plunkett. Primate of all Ireland, he was martyred in 1681 at Tyburn in London; his head was pulled from the execution flames. ⊠ *West St.* ⊕ *www.saintpetersdrogheda. ie.*

Tholsel

BANK | This bank building has an 18th-century square granite edifice with a cupola. ⊠ *West St. and Shop St.*

Victorian Railway Viaduct

BUILDING | Among the town's landmarks is its long railway viaduct, which towers over the river. Built around 1850 as part of the railway line from Dublin to Belfast, it's still in use and is a splendid example of Victorian engineering. Its height above the River Boyne makes the viaduct Drogheda's most prominent landmark. ⊠ *Drogheda* ✛ *Crosses Marsh Rd. on south side of river, and N. Strand on north side of river.*

Hotels

Boyne Valley Hotel and Country Club

$$ | B&B/INN | Once owned by a Drogheda brewing family, this 19th-century mansion has been restored in period fashion with Neoclassical pillars, intricate plasterwork, and crystal chandeliers. **Pros:** great facilities; lovely grounds; renowned breakfast. **Cons:** newer building a touch functional; can attract a business crowd; some rooms can be noisy. ⑤ *Rooms from: €140* ⊠ *Dublin Rd.* ☎ *041/983–7737* ⊕ *www.boyne-valley-hotel.ie* ⇄ *71 rooms* ⦿| *Free breakfast.*

The D Hotel

$$ | HOTEL | A dramatic location on the south bank of the Boyne easily makes up for the slightly functional exterior of this trendy hotel in the center of medieval Drogheda. **Pros:** dramatic riverside location; modern room design; great terrace for people-watching. **Cons:** only some rooms have great views; restaurant is nothing special; attracts a business crowd. ⑤ *Rooms from: €155* ⊠ *Marsh Rd.* ☎ *041/987–7700* ⊕ *www.thedhotel. com* ⇄ *111 rooms* ⦿| *Free breakfast.*

Activities

GOLF
County Louth Golf Club

GOLF | How do they keep this links treasure such a secret? Covering 190 acres by the Irish Sea at the mouth of the River Boyne, this wonderful links course really has flown under the radar of the golfing world, which means smaller crowds in summer. Long hitters will love the atypical layout, a par-72 that features five par-5s, but beware the well-protected, undulating greens. ⊠ *Off R167, Baltray* ✛ *8 km (5 miles) east of Drogheda* ☎ *041/988–1530* ⊕ *www.countylouth-golfclub.com* ✉ *Nov.–Mar. €80; Apr. and Oct. €120; May–Sept. Mon.–Thurs. €160, Fri.–Sun. €175* ⚐ *18 holes, 6936 yards, par 72.*

Mellifont Abbey

10 km (8 miles) northwest of Drogheda.

On the eastern banks of the River Mattock, which creates a natural border between Counties Meath and Louth, lie the remains of Mellifont Abbey, the first Cistercian monastery in Ireland.

GETTING HERE AND AROUND

The abbey is a 13-km (8-mile) drive northwest of Drogheda off the R168. There is ample parking at the site. There is no public transport to the abbey, but you can get a taxi from Drogheda.

 ## Sights

★ Mellifont Abbey

RELIGIOUS SITE | Founded in 1142 by St. Malachy, Mellifont Abbey was inspired by the formal structure surrounding a courtyard of St. Bernard of Clairvaux's monastery, which St. Malachy had visited. Among the substantial ruins are the two-story chapter house, built in 12th-century English–Norman style and once a daily meeting place for the monks; it now houses a collection of medieval glazed tiles. Four walls of the 13th-century octagonal lavabo, or washing room, still stand, as do some arches from the Romanesque cloister. At its peak, Mellifont presided over almost 40 other Cistercian monasteries throughout Ireland, but all were suppressed by Henry VIII in 1539 after his break with the Catholic Church. Adjacent to the parking lot is a small architectural museum depicting the history of the abbey and the craftsmanship that went into its construction. ⊠ *Off Old Mellifont Rd., off N2, Collon* ⊕ *www.heritageireland.ie* 🖾 *€5* 🕓 *Closed Sept.–June.*

Dundalk

80 km (53 miles) north of Dublin.

Perfectly positioned as a hub to explore the region north and south of the border, Dundalk—only 9½ km (6 miles) from Northern Ireland—is the main town of County Louth, Ireland's smallest county. Its earliest settlement dates from the early Christian period, around the 7th century. In May the town hosts an avant-garde "fringe" drama and visual arts festival that includes a nice schedule of children's events.

GETTING HERE AND AROUND

From Dublin, take the M1 north and exit at junction 16 onto the roundabout. Take the first exit onto the N52 to Dundalk. Bus Éireann runs regular buses from Dublin to the town's bus station on Long Walk; the trip takes one hour and 30 minutes. Routes from Belfast and Drogheda also connect to Dundalk. Serviced by Irish Rail, Clarke Train Station is on Carrickmacross Road. There are daily trains from Dublin (1 hour, 20 minutes); Belfast (1 hour, 20 minutes); and Drogheda (20 minutes).

VISITOR INFORMATION

CONTACTS Dundalk Tourist Office.
⊠ *Market Sq.* ☎ *042/935–2111* ⊕ *www.dundalktown.ie.*

 ## Sights

Bell Tower

BUILDING | This bell tower of a Franciscan monastery dates back to the 13th century. Keep an eye out for the lovely Gothic windows. ⊠ *Mill St.*

County Museum Dundalk

MUSEUM | Set in a beautifully restored 18th-century warehouse, this museum is dedicated to preserving the history of the dying local industries, such as beer brewing, cigarette manufacturing, shoe

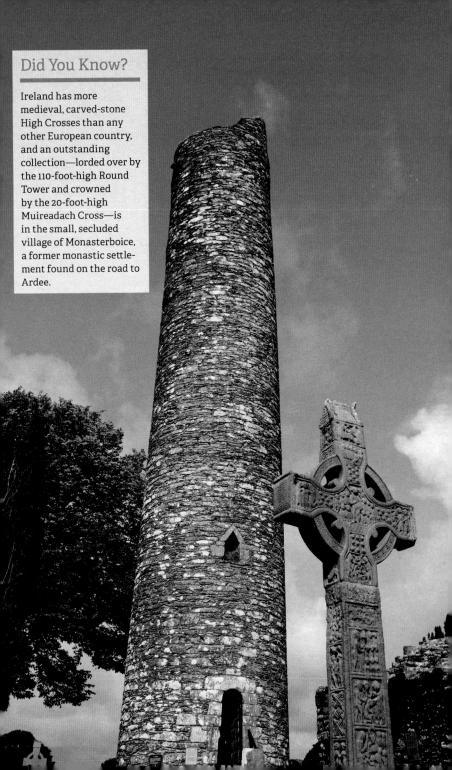

Did You Know?

Ireland has more medieval, carved-stone High Crosses than any other European country, and an outstanding collection—lorded over by the 110-foot-high Round Tower and crowned by the 20-foot-high Muireadach Cross—is in the small, secluded village of Monasterboice, a former monastic settlement found on the road to Ardee.

and boot making, and railway engineering. Other exhibits deal with the history of Louth from 7500 BC to the present, and include Oliver Cromwell's shaving mirror. ⊠ *Carroll Centre, Joycelyn St.* ☎ *042/932–7056* ⊕ *www.dundalkmuseum.ie* ⊠ *€2* ⊘ *Closed Sun. and Mon.*

St. Patrick's Cathedral

RELIGIOUS SITE | Built between 1835 and 1847, this grand cathedral was designed when the Gothic Revival was at its height. With its buttresses and mosaics lining the chancel and the side chapels, it was modeled on the 15th-century King's College Chapel at Cambridge, England. The fine exterior was built in Newry granite, and the high altar and pulpit are of carved Caen stone. ⊠ *Roden Pl.* ☎ *042/933–4648* ⊕ *www.stpatricksdundalk.com.*

Restaurants

Riva

$ | **EUROPEAN** | Much beloved by locals, Riva magically transforms over the course of the day from a bustling café and breakfast joint to a stylish, intimate restaurant and cocktail bar. The Irish breakfasts are legendary, but in the evening the baby back ribs and the roasted rabbit are favorite starters and mains. Located right in the center of Dundalk, the interior is a large open space dominated by an impressive chandelier, with a cool little cocktail bar tucked in the back. To complete the fully indulgent experience, try the bread-and-butter pudding with crème anglaise. **Known for:** local favorite; excellent Irish breakfast; great cocktails. ⓢ *Average main: €18* ⊠ *3 Earl St.* ☎ *042/935–4578* ⊕ *www.riva.ie* ⊘ *No dinner Mon.*

The Legendary Cuchulainn

The area around Dundalk is closely connected with Cuchulainn (pronounced "coo-chu-lain")—"a greater hero than Hercules or Achilles," as Frank McCourt, in *Angela's Ashes*, quotes his father. Cuchulainn, the warrior of the Irish epic *Táin Bó Cuailnge* (Cattle Raid of Cooley), heroically defended this area of ancient Ulster against invaders.

🛏 Hotels

Ballymascanlon House Hotel

$$$ | **HOTEL** | Just north of Dundalk, this Victorian mansion with a slightly severe but elegant modern addition sits on 130 acres on the scenic Cooley Peninsula. **Pros:** guest rooms big enough to get lost in; discount golf for guests; good weekend deals. **Cons:** a little pricey for the area; in-room facilities sparse; sometimes crowded with wedding parties. ⓢ *Rooms from: €175* ⊠ *Off R173, 3 km (2 miles) north of Dundalk* ☎ *042/935–8200* ⊕ *www.ballymascanlon.com* ⇆ *97 rooms* ⦿ *Free breakfast.*

Innisfree House

$ | **B&B/INN** | An early-20th-century redbrick gem in the heart of Dundalk, Innisfree House is a shockingly good value considering the genteel, stylish atmosphere created by the beautiful Edwardian furniture and antiques throughout. **Pros:** genuine afternoon tea served; option of evening dining; authentic Edwardian furnishings. **Cons:** not in the most picturesque area; maybe a little overdecorated; short on facilities. ⓢ *Rooms from: €79* ⊠ *Carrickmacross Rd.* ☎ *042/933–4912* ⊕ *www.innisfreehouse.ie* ⇆ *9 rooms* ⦿ *Free breakfast.*

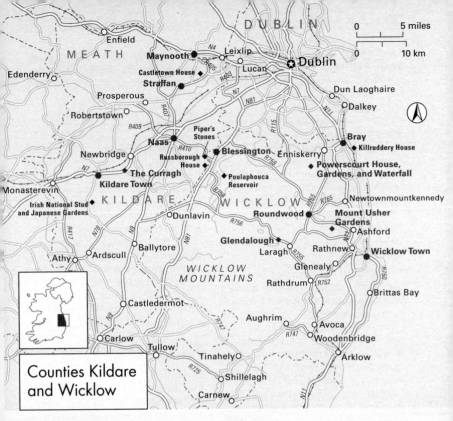

Counties Kildare and Wicklow

Blessington

23 km (14 miles) southwest of Dublin.

With its wide main street lined on both sides by tall trees and Georgian buildings, Blessington is one of the most charming villages in the area. It was founded in the late 17th century, and was a stop on the Dublin–Waterford mail coach service in the mid-19th century. Until 1932, a steam train ran from here to Dublin. Just outside the village are two of the marvels of Ireland: 18th-century Russborough House and the adjacent Poulaphouca Reservoir.

GETTING HERE AND AROUND

You can reach Blessington by car from Dublin via the N81; the drive takes half an hour. Dublin Bus runs a daily service to Blessington.

◉ Sights

Poulaphouca Reservoir

BODY OF WATER | Known locally as the Blessington Lakes, Poulaphouca (pronounced "pool-a- *fook*-a") is a large, meandering reservoir that provides Dublin's water supply. You can drive around the entire perimeter of the artificial lake on minor roads; on its southern end lies Hollywood Glen, a particularly beautiful natural spot. The whole area is great for a walk or a picnic. ⊠ *R758 ✛ 6½ km (4 miles) southwest of Blessington* ⊕ *www. coillte.ie/our-forests/explore.*

Russborough House

HOUSE | FAMILY | A conspicuously grand house rising seemingly in the middle of nowhere—actually the western part of County Wicklow—Russborough was an extravagance paid for by the wages of beer. In 1741, a year after inheriting a vast fortune from his brewer father, Joseph Leeson commissioned architect Richard Castle to build him a home of palatial stature, and was rewarded with this slightly over-the-top house, whose monumental 700-foot-long facade one-upped every other great house in Ireland. Today, the house serves as a showcase for the celebrated collection of Old Master paintings of Sir Alfred Beit, a descendant of the De Beers diamond family, who had bought and majestically restored the property in 1952. A 3-D exhibition of his amazing photos from the 1920s and 1930s is a highlight.

The first sight of Russborough draws gasps from visitors: a mile-long, beech-lined avenue leads to a distant embankment. Constructed of silver-gray Wicklow granite, the facade encompasses a seven-bay central block, from either end of which radiate semicircular loggias connecting the flanking wings—the finest example in Ireland of Palladio's "winged device." The interiors are full of grand period rooms that were elegantly refurbished in the 1950s under the eye of the legendary 20th-century decorator, Lady Colefax. The Hall is centered on a massive black Kilkenny marble chimney-piece and has a ceiling modeled after one in the Irish Parliament. Four 18th-century Joseph Vernet marine landscapes grace the glorious stucco moldings created to frame them in the Drawing Room. The grandest room, the Saloon, is famed for its 18th-century stucco ceiling by the Lafranchini brothers; fine Old Masters hang on walls covered in 19th-century Genoese velvet. The views out the windows take in the foothills of the Wicklow Mountains and the famous Poulaphouca Reservoir in front of the house. Kids will love getting lost in the huge hedge maze on the grounds. Additional attractions include a tearoom, gift shop, sheepdog demonstrations, and a National Bird of Prey center. ■ TIP→ **You can only see the house on a guided tour, but the guides are** **good storytellers and bring the old place to life.** ⊠ *N81* ☎ *045/865–239* ⊕ *www.russboroughhouse.ie* ☎ *€12* ⊙ *Closed Jan. and Feb.*

Hotels

★ Rathsallagh House

$$$$ | HOTEL | A lovely hotel set on more than 50 acres of parkland, Rathsallagh House first came into being when the low-slung, ivy-covered Queen Anne stables were converted into a farmhouse in 1798. **Pros:** luxurious rooms; superb dining room; sumptuous walled garden. **Cons:** books up quickly; some variance in room quality; expensive food. ⑤ *Rooms from: €220* ⊠ *Church Rd., Dunlavin* ⊹ *5 km (3 miles) southwest of Dunlavin* ☎ *045/403–112* ⊕ *www.rathsallagh.com* ⌂ *29 rooms* ⦿ *Free breakfast.*

Activities

HIKING
Church Mountain

HIKING/WALKING | You can take in splendid views of the Blessington Lakes from the top of Church Mountain, which you reach via a vigorous walk through Woodenboley Wood, at the southern tip of Hollywood Glen. Follow the main forest track for about 20 minutes, and then take the narrow path that heads up the side of the forest to the mountaintop for about another half hour. ⊠ *R756* ⊹ *19 km (12 miles) southwest of Poulaphouca Reservoir.*

Bray

22 km (14 miles) south of Dublin on N11, 8 km (5 miles) east of Enniskerry on R755.

One of Ireland's oldest seaside resorts, Bray is a trim town known for its summer cottages and sand-and-shingle beach, which stretches for 2 km (1 mile). When the trains first arrived from Dublin in

1854, Bray became the number one spot for urban vacationers and subsequently took on the appearance of an English oceanfront town. Some Dubliners still flock to the faded glory of Bray's boardwalk to push baby carriages and soak up the sun. Uncrowded trails for hiking and mountain biking crisscross the mountains bordering Bray to the south.

GETTING HERE AND AROUND

From Dublin, take the N81 south to the M50 southbound. Exit onto the M11, and at junction 5 take the second exit at the roundabout to the R761 (signposted "Bray"). The drive takes about half an hour. The DART train runs regularly from Dublin to Bray, as do a number of city buses. There is plenty of parking around the town. St. Kevin's Bus from Dublin also stops in Bray.

Sights

★ Killruddery House

HOUSE | FAMILY | The 17th-century formal gardens at Killruddery House are precisely arranged, with fine beech hedges, Victorian statuary, and a parterre of lavender and roses. The Brabazon family, the earls of Meath, have lived here since 1618. In 1820 they hired William Morris to remodel the house as a revival Elizabethan mansion. The estate also has a Crystal Palace conservatory modeled on those at the botanic gardens in Dublin. Killruddery Arts organizes year-round events including an old-fashioned Easter egg hunt. You have to take one of the twice-daily tours to see the house itself, but the real draw are the gardens, which you are free to roam at your leisure. The teahouse in the old dairy is a perfect spot for a light snack and kids will love watching the sheep shearing and the chickens being fed on the adjoining farm. There's a wonderful farmers' market every Saturday. ⊠ *Bray–Greystones Rd.* ✛ *3 km (2 miles) south of Bray, off R768* ☎ *01/286–3405* ⊕ *www. killruddery.com* 🎫 *Gardens €9, house and gardens €16* ☉ *Gardens closed*

Nov.–Mar., and weekdays in Apr. and Oct. House closed Oct.–June.

National SEA LIFE

ZOO | FAMILY | Dedicated to the creatures of the sea, National SEA LIFE emphasizes those that occupy the waters around Ireland. Besides massive tanks that contain all manner of swimming things, there are major conservation projects focusing on breeding sea horses and stingrays. FinZone is an undersea adventure trail perfect for kids. Touch-screen computers and video games give the place a high-tech feel. There are also regular feeding demonstrations during the day. In winter, call ahead to confirm opening times. ⊠ *Strand Rd.* ☎ *01/286–6939* ⊕ *www.visitsealife.com/bray* 🎫 *€14.*

Restaurants

Campo de Fiori

$ | ITALIAN | The old posters, fishing nets, and wine bottles on display might suggest imitation Italian, but this award-winning eatery is introducing locals to the delights of hearty, authentic Italian cuisine. The pizza and pasta specials are always worth checking out, especially the spaghetti with lobster. Owners Laura and Marco Roccasalvo (he's also the chef) and their Italian staff give this little place a warm, informal vibe. The wine list is large, and the staff loves to help you match your vino to your food. **Known for:** authentic Italian food; wine by the glass; pizza and pasta specials. $ *Average main: €17* ⊠ *1 Albert Ave.* ☎ *01/276–4257* ⊕ *www.campodefiori.ie* 🖃 *No credit cards.*

★ The Hungry Monk

$$ | SEAFOOD | The cloisters-and-refectory-style decor is definitely tongue-in-cheek at this upbeat, fun restaurant in sleepy Greystones, an old-fashioned seaside resort a couple of miles south of Bray. Dinner is served by candlelight and the menu specializes in uncluttered seafood dishes in summer and wild

The Wicklow Way

Whether you're a novice or veteran hiker, Wicklow's gentle, rolling hills are a terrific place to begin an Irish walking vacation. Devoted hikers come from all over the world to traverse the 137-km (85-mile) **Wicklow Way** (⊕ *www.wicklowway. com*), the first long-distance trail to open in Ireland and still one of the best. Wicklow is Ireland's little Alps, with bracing fresh air guaranteed among the (hopefully) blue skies and mountain heather and gorse. Much of the route lies above 1,600 feet and follows rough sheep tracks, forest firebreaks, and old bog roads (rain gear, windproof clothing, and sturdy footwear are essential). The trail starts in the outskirts of Dublin suburbs, in Marlay Park, just south of Dublin city center, then ascends into the Wicklow mountain foothills, before passing glens, farms, and historic sights such as Rathgall, home to the Kings of Leinster, and the Mill of Purgatory—a venerated "wardrobe" in Aghowle Church—before finishing up in Clonegal. It's a great way to see some of the more scenic villages of County Wicklow, and also a good excuse to sit down for a hearty lunch or dinner at some of their fine eateries—you will have earned it. You'll most likely run into fellow hikers, make new friends, and maybe even walk a few miles together. If you're going to spend a couple of days on the Way it's wise to plan out your accommodations in advance, as it can get busy in peak season. Overall the trail is wild and secluded enough to give you the sense of proper hiking and self-orienteering, but it's also established enough to suit even the first-timer. Consider participating in one of the walking festivals held at Easter, in May, and in autumn. If your feet are less than bionic, you might opt for biking, another excellent way to see the area.

The autumn **Wicklow Walking Festival** (☎ 0404/45152 ⊕ *www. walkinghikingireland.com*) is a three-day event based in the Glenmalure area. It costs around €60 for three days' walking, or you can just pay for individual walks.

game on cold winter nights. Owner Pat Keown is a great host, and his laughter and love of good food and fine wine are contagious. The Seafood Symphony is a particular favorite, as is the roast haunch of Wicklow venison with red cabbage roulade. Sunday lunches, in the bar area, are famous for their length (they often last into the early evening) and for the lively atmosphere. **Known for:** fresh seafood; candlelight dinners; leisurely Sunday lunches. ⑤ *Average main: €22* ✉ *1 Church Rd., Greystones* ☎ *01/287–5759* ⊕ *www.thehungrymonk. ie* ⊗ *Closed Wed. No lunch Thurs.–Sat. No dinner Sun.*

Activities

HIKING
Bray Head

HIKING/WALKING | A well-marked path leads from the beach to the 10-foot-tall cross that crowns the spiny peak of Bray Head, a rocky outcrop that rises 791 feet from the sea. The fairly difficult one-hour climb affords stunning views of Wicklow Town and Dublin Bay. ✉ *Bray* ✛ *South end of Bray, off Raheen Park.*

★ **Wicklow Way**

HIKING/WALKING | Devoted hikers come from all over the world to traverse the

137-km (85-mile) Wicklow Way, the first long-distance trail to open in Ireland, and still one of the best. Much of the route lies above 1,600 feet and follows rough sheep tracks, forest firebreaks, and old bog roads, so rain gear, windproof clothing, and sturdy footwear are essential. The trail starts in Marlay Park, just south of central Dublin, then ascends into the Wicklow mountain foothills, before passing glens, farms, and historic sights like Rathgall, home to the Kings of Leinster, and the Mill of Purgatory—a venerated "wardrobe" in Aghowle Church—before finishing up in Clonegal. If your feet are less than bionic, you can opt for any number of the short walks, or hop on a bike. ☎ 0404/45152 ⊕ www.wicklowway.com.

Powerscourt House, Gardens, and Waterfall

25 km (16 miles) south of Dublin on R117, 22 km (14 miles) north of Glendalough on R755.

One of the grandest estates and gardens in Ireland, Powerscourt is one of the main reasons that people head to Enniskerry. Within the shadow of the Great Sugar Loaf Mountain, Enniskerry remains one of the prettiest villages in Ireland. It's built around a sloping central triangular square with a backdrop of the wooded Wicklow Mountains. But the real draw is the majesty of Powerscourt.

GETTING HERE AND AROUND
Powerscourt is about a half-hour drive from Dublin. Head south from Dublin on the N81 to the M50 southbound. Take the exit for the M11, which becomes the N11; then take the R117 for Enniskerry and continue on to Powerscourt House and Gardens. You can also take the bus from Dublin to Enniskerry and walk the mile to Powerscourt. Alternatively, you can take the Irish Rail's DART train line from Dublin to Bray and then take Dublin Bus 185c (€1.80) to Powerscourt. Not all No. 185 buses go to Powerscourt, only the 185c buses; ask the driver whether you have the right bus.

Sights

★ Powerscourt House & Gardens
GARDEN | FAMILY | At more than 14,000 acres, including stunning formal gardens and a 400-foot waterfall, Powerscourt was truly one of the great houses of Ireland and Britain in its day. The grounds were originally granted to Sir Richard Wingfield, the first viscount of Powerscourt, by King James I of England in 1609. Richard Castle (1690–1751), the architect of Russborough House, was hired to design the great house. His was an age not known for modesty, and he chose the grand Palladian style. The house took nine years to complete and was ready to move into in 1740.

Unfortunately, you won't be able to see much of it. A terrible fire almost completely destroyed the house in 1974, cruelly on the eve of a huge party to celebrate the completion of a lengthy restoration. The original ballroom on the first floor—once "the grandest room in any Irish house," according to historian Desmond Guinness—is the only room that still gives a sense of the place's former glory. It was based on Palladio's version of the "Egyptian Hall" designed by Vitruvius, architect to Augustus, emperor of Rome.

The real draw here is not the house but Powerscourt Gardens, considered among the finest in Europe. They were laid out from 1745 to 1767, following the completion of the house, and radically redesigned in the Victorian style from 1843 to 1875 by Daniel Robertson. The Villa Butera in Sicily inspired him to set these gardens with sweeping terraces, antique sculptures, and a circular pond and fountain flanked by winged horses. The grounds include many specimen trees (plants grown for exhibition), an avenue of monkey puzzle trees, a parterre of brightly colored summer flowers, and a Japanese garden. The kitchen gardens, with their modest rows of flowers, are a striking antidote to the classical formality of the main sections. A cute café, crafts and interior design shops, a garden center, and a children's play area are also in the house and on the grounds. Kids love Tara's Palace, a 22-room Georgian-style dollhouse. ⊠ *Enniskerry* ⊹ *Off R760* ☎ *01/204–6000* ⊕ *www.powerscourt.com* ⊠ *€10.*

Powerscourt Waterfall

BODY OF WATER | One of the most inspiring sights to the writers and artists of the Romantic generation, the 400-foot Powerscourt Waterfall is the highest in Ireland or Britain. ⊠ *Enniskerry* ⊹ *5 km (3 miles) south of Powerscourt Gardens* ☎ *01/204–6000* ⊠ *€6* ☙ *Closed mid-Dec.*

 Restaurants

Poppies Country Cooking

$ | IRISH | This cozy café—with a pine-panel ceiling, farmhouse furniture, and paintings of poppies on the walls— is a great place for breakfast, lunch, or late-afternoon tea. Expect potato cakes, shepherd's pie, lasagna, vegetarian quiche, house salads, and soups. The most popular dishes are Poppies chicken (a casserole-like concoction) and beef and Guinness pie. For dessert try the apple pie or the rhubarb crumble, which is so good that the Irish rugby team stops by after practice. **Known for:** farm-fresh produce; irresistible desserts; healthy choices. $ *Average main: €10* ⊠ *The Square, Enniskerry* ☎ *01/282–8869* ⊕ *www.poppies.ie* ☙ *No dinner.*

Sika

$$$ | FRENCH | Local produce and stunning views are the stars of this hotel restaurant, with the Wicklow lamb a thrilling house specialty in season. Low ceilings give the very formal dining room

a slightly overbearing feel, but floor-to-ceiling windows look out onto the serene Sugar Loaf mountain. The food focuses on Wicklow produce with a twist, and a favorite starter is the quail breast. You can follow that with the Challans duck breast with savoy cabbage, beetroot, and picked garlic jus. As a treat you can book the chef's table in the kitchen and watch the team at work as you sample a tasting menu. **Known for:** quail breast; Sugar Loaf mountain views; local produce. $ *Average main: €32* ⊠ *Powerscourt Hotel, Powerscourt Estate, Enniskerry* ☎ *01/274–9377* ⊕ *www.powerscourthotel.com* ☙ *No lunch.*

 Hotels

★ Powerscourt Hotel

$$$$ | RESORT | The gargantuan Palladian-style exterior of this Xanadu may seem out of place in the bucolic surroundings, but luxury always makes itself at home, and the views of the fabled Sugar Loaf peak outside the soaring windows are breathtaking. **Pros:** sumptuous pool and spa; excellent dining options; beautiful setting in Powerscourt grounds. **Cons:** over-the-top exterior is not for everyone; garden rooms don't have a great view; can get very busy. $ *Rooms from: €280* ⊠ *Powerscourt Estate, Enniskerry* ☎ *01/274–8888* ⊕ *www.powerscourthotel.com* ⇥ *194 rooms* ⫧ *Free breakfast.*

 Activities

GOLF

★ Druids Glen Resort

GOLF | Known in golfing circles as the "Augusta of Europe," the beautiful Druids Glen Golf Course has hosted the Irish Open on four occasions since it opened in 1995. The wonderful landscaping and the extensive use of water in the layout explain the comparisons to the home of the Masters. It's essentially an American-style target course incorporating some delightful changes in elevation, and its forbidding, par-3 17th has an island green, like the corresponding hole at the Tournament Players Club at Sawgrass. A second course, Druids Heath, is a marvelous attempt to combine the best of links, heathland, and parkland golf. ⊠ *Newtownmountkennedy* ☎ *01/287– 3600* ⊕ *www.druidsglenresort.com* ⚐ *€60–€125* ⚲ *Glen Course: 18 holes, 7046 yards, par 71; Heath Course: 18 holes, 7434 yards, par 71.*

Powerscourt Golf Club

GOLF | This pair of courses is nestled in the foothills of the Wicklow Mountains on the grounds of the legendary 18th-century stately home and garden. Panoramic views to the sea and Sugar Loaf Mountain—and all those 200-year-old trees—give the impression that the course has been here for years. The older East Course is a parkland course, but some holes have certain links characteristics. The course's tiered greens test even the best golfers. The newer West Course is even more challenging and is designed with top-class tournament play in mind. ⊠ *Enniskerry* ☎ *01/204–6033* ⊕ *www. powerscourt.ie* ⚐ *Apr.–Oct. €65–€75; Nov.–Mar. €40–€55* ⚲ *East Course: 18 holes, 7022 yards, par 72; West Course: 18 holes, 6938 yards, par 72.*

Roundwood

18 km (11 miles) south of Enniskerry on R755.

At 800 feet above sea level, Roundwood is the highest village in Ireland. It's also surrounded by spectacular mountain scenery. The Sunday afternoon market in the village hall, where cakes, jams, and other homemade goods are sold, livens up what is otherwise a sleepy place. From the broad main street, a minor road leads west for 8 km (5 miles) to two lakes, Lough Dan and Lough Tay, lying deep between forested mountains like Norwegian fjords.

GETTING HERE AND AROUND

Drive south from Dublin on the N81 to the M50 southbound, then take the exit for the M11, which becomes the N11. At junction 12, exit onto the R772 into Newtownmountkennedy. Turn right onto the R765 for Roundwood. St. Kevin's Bus runs here from Dublin.

 Restaurants

★ **Roundwood Inn**

$ | IRISH | Travel back to the 17th century at this evocatively furnished inn, distinguished by its wooden floors, dark furniture, and diamond-shape windows. The place is best known for its wonderful, hearty game and seafood lunches and dinners that are served in a nook of the bar—try the glorious cream of seafood soup. They also do a mean Sunday lunch. The menu blends Continental and Irish cuisines, reflecting the traditions of the German proprietor, Jurgen Schwalm, and his Irish wife, Aine. Highlights include an excellent seafood platter of salmon, oysters, lobster, and shrimp, along with a rich Hungarian goulash. **Known for:** hearty Sunday lunch; historic setting; game and seafood dishes. Ⓢ *Average main: €18* ⊠ *Main St.* ☎ *01/281–8107* ⊕ *www. roundwood.ie.*

Glendalough

9 km (6 miles) southwest of Roundwood via R755 and R756.

One of Ireland's best monastic sites, Glendalough also has a stunningly photogenic lakeside setting. It's a popular destination for day trips.

GETTING HERE AND AROUND

If you're driving, consider taking the scenic route along R115, but be prepared for awesome, austere mountain passes. Don't take this route if you're in a hurry—it takes about an hour and 45 minutes, compared to an hour on the N11—and

Did You Know?

While the palatial house of Powerscourt was devastated by fire after a 1974 renovation, its gardens remain as one of the finest examples of the Victorian style. Designed by the often-drunk Daniel Robertson, his creation remains a marvel of order cut from chaos. Nature, as if in approval, supplies the stunning backdrop of the famed Sugar Loaf Mountain.

don't expect a lot of signposting. Just concentrate on the nifty views.

St. Kevin's Bus has daily service between Dublin and Glendalough, with a stop in Bray. The trip takes 1½ hours. There is no direct train to Glendalough, but you can take the Irish Rail train from Dublin as far as Rathdrum (1 hour, 20 minutes) and then take a taxi (approximately €10) the 11 km (7 miles) from there to Glendalough.

Sights

★ Glendalough
ARCHAEOLOGICAL SITE | Nestled in a lush, quiet valley deep in the rugged Wicklow Mountains, among two lakes and acres of windswept heather, Gleann dá Loch ("glen of two lakes") is one of Ireland's premier monastic sites. The hermit monks of early Christian Ireland were drawn to the Edenic quality of some of the valleys in this area, and this evocative settlement remains to this day a sight to calm a troubled soul. Stand here in the early morning (before the crowds and the hordes of students arrive), and you can appreciate what drew the solitude-seeking St. Kevin to this spot.

Glendalough's visitor center is a good place to orient yourself and pick up a useful pamphlet. Many of the ruins are clumped together beyond the visitor center, but some of the oldest surround the Upper Lake, where signed paths direct you through spectacular scenery devoid of crowds. Most ruins are open all day and are freely accessible.

Probably the oldest building on the site, presumed to date from St. Kevin's time, is the **Teampaill na Skellig** (Church of the Oratory), on the south shore of the Upper Lake. A little to the east is **St. Kevin's Bed,** a tiny cave in the rock face, about 30 feet above the level of the lake, where St. Kevin lived his hermit's existence. It's not easily accessible; you approach the cave by boat, but climbing the cliff to the

Genius in a Bottle

Powerscourt's grand Victorian gardens were designed by an eccentric boozer, Daniel Robertson, who liked to be tooled around the gardens-in-progress in a wheelbarrow while taking nips from a bottle of sherry.

cave can be dangerous. At the southeast corner of the Upper Lake is the 11th-century **Reefert Church,** with the ruins of a nave and a chancel. The saint also lived in the adjoining, ruined beehive hut with five crosses, which marked the original boundary of the monastery. You get a superb view of the valley from here.

The ruins by the edge of the Lower Lake are the most important of those at Glendalough. The **gateway,** beside the Glendalough Hotel, is the only surviving entrance to an ancient monastic site anywhere in Ireland. An extensive **graveyard** lies within, with hundreds of elaborately decorated crosses, as well as a perfectly preserved six-story **Round Tower.** Built in the 11th or 12th century, it stands 100 feet high, with an entrance 25 feet above ground level. ⊠ *Glendalough* ✛ *Visitor center car park off R757* ☎ *040/445–325* ⊕ *www.heritageireland.ie* ✉ *Ruins free, visitor center €5.*

Hotels

Tudor Lodge
$ | B&B/INN | This 1990s lodge may not be genuine Tudor, but it's a wonderfully cozy and serene B&B only half a mile from the entrance to Glendalough. **Pros:** very close to Glendalough; walking trails all around; great hosts. **Cons:** not cheap for a B&B; limited facilities; limited Wi-Fi available. ⑤ *Rooms from: €90* ⊠ *Tudor Lodge, R755* ✛ *3 km (2 miles west) of*

Even though destroyed by Viking raids and then disbanded as a monastery by the Reformation, medieval Glendalough remains magical and magnificent.

Glendalough visitor center ☎ *040/445–554* ⊕ *www.tudorlodgeireland.com* ⊙ *Closed weekdays in Jan.* ↰ *8 rooms* ⍼ *Free breakfast* ▭ *No credit cards.*

Nightlife

Wicklow Brewery
BREWPUBS/BEER GARDENS | Located a few miles southeast of Glendalough in Redcross, this little brewery and beer hall is the home of St. Kevin's Red Ale and a great place to hear traditional and folk music on the weekend. They also have regular tastings and you can call in advance to book a brewery tour. ⊠ *Mick Finn's Pub, Redcross* ☎ *040/441–661* ⊕ *www.wicklowbrewery.ie* ⊠ *Tour €15.*

Mount Usher Gardens

18 km (11 miles) east of Glendalough via R755 and R763.

Close to both Ashford and Rathnew villages, these extensive gardens are a popular day trip from Dublin. The excellent café is run by Avoca, and shouldn't be missed on a visit here.

GETTING HERE AND AROUND
From Dublin, Mount Usher Gardens is less than an hour's drive. Take the N81 to the M50 southbound and exit onto the M11. At junction 15, exit onto the R772 to Ashford and turn left to the signposted Mount Usher Gardens. Bus Éireann runs regular service to Ashford from Dublin.

Sights

Mount Usher Gardens
GARDEN | Covering more than 20 acres on the banks of the River Vartry, the gardens were first laid out in 1868 by textile magnate Edward Walpole. Succeeding generations further planted and maintained the grounds, which today include more than 5,000 types of native and nonnative plants. The gardener has made the most of the riverside locale by planting eucalyptus, azaleas, camellias, and rhododendrons. The river is visible

from nearly everywhere in the gardens; miniature suspension bridges bounce and sway underfoot as you cross the river. Near the entrance, you'll find a cluster of crafts shops (including a pottery workshop) as well as a country clothing shop and café. The twin villages of Ashford and Rathnew are to the south and east, and Newtownmountkennedy is to the north. ⊠ *Ashford* ✛ *Off R772* ☎ *404/40205* ⊕ *www.mountushergardens.ie* ⬚ *€8.*

Hotels

★ Hunter's Hotel

$$ | **HOTEL** | On 2 acres of flower gardens (the Knot Garden is an award winner) beside the Vartry River, the beautiful white Hunter's Hotel is the oldest coaching inn in Ireland. **Pros:** pleasing period atmosphere; enchanting gardens; fine restaurant. **Cons:** books up easily; bedrooms aren't huge. ⑤ *Rooms from: €165* ⊠ *Newrath Bridge, Rathnew* ☎ *404/40106* ⊕ *www.hunters.ie* ⇆ *16 rooms* ⑩ *Free breakfast.*

Wicklow Town

26 km (16 miles) east of Glendalough, 51 km (32 miles) south of Dublin.

At the entrance to the attractive, tree-lined Main Street of Wicklow Town sprawl the extensive ruins of a 13th-century Franciscan friary. Wicklow, from the Danish *wyking alo,* means "Viking meadow," testifying to the region's very ancient roots.

The streets of Wicklow ran with blood during the 1798 rebellion when Billy Byrne, member of a wealthy local Catholic family, led rebels from south and central Wicklow against the forces of the Crown. Byrne was eventually captured and executed at Gallow's Hill just outside town. There is a memorial to him in the middle of Market Square.

GETTING HERE AND AROUND

A 50-minute drive south on the N81 and then the N11/M11 takes you from Dublin straight into Wicklow Town. Parking is available throughout the town. There are also daily trains and buses from Dublin.

VISITOR INFORMATION

CONTACTS Wicklow Tourist Office. ⊠ *Railto House, Fitzwilliam Sq., Wicklow* ☎ *040/469–117* ⊕ *www.visitwicklow.ie.*

Sights

Black Castle

ARCHAEOLOGICAL SITE | Immediately south of the harbor, perched on a promontory that has good views of the coastline, are the ruins of the Black Castle. This structure was built in 1169 by Maurice Fitzgerald, an Anglo-Norman lord who arrived with the English invasion of Ireland. The freely accessible ruins extend over a large area; with some difficulty, you can climb down to the water's edge. ⊠ *Off South Quay, Wicklow Head.*

Friary

ARCHAEOLOGICAL SITE | Closed down during the 16th-century dissolution of the monasteries, the Friary is a reminder of Wicklow's stormy past, which began with the unwelcome reception given to St. Patrick on his arrival in AD 432. Inquire at the nearby priest's house to see the ruins. ⊠ *Abbey St., NW corner of Wicklow Town, across road from Old Forge Pub, Wicklow* ☎ *040/467–196* for priest's house.

St. Thomas Church

RELIGIOUS SITE | Between the River Vartry and the road to Dublin stands the Protestant church, which incorporates various unusual details: a Romanesque door, 12th-century stonework, fine pews, and an atmospheric graveyard. The church is topped by a copper, onion-shape cupola, added as an afterthought in 1771. ⊠ *Church Hill, off Dublin Rd., Wicklow* ⊡ *Free.*

Wicklow Harbour

BEACH—SIGHT | The town's most appealing area is Wicklow Harbour. Take South Quay down to the pier; Bridge Street leads you to a bridge across the River Vartry leading to a second, smaller pier at the northern end of the harbor. From this end, follow the shingle beach, which stretches for 5 km (3 miles); behind the beach is the Broad Lough, a lagoon noted for its wildfowl. ⊠ *South Quay, Wicklow.*

Wicklow's Historic Gaol

MUSEUM | Just above Market Square, the town's old jail has been converted into a museum and heritage center where it's possible to trace your genealogical roots. The "gruff gaoler" escorts you to your prison cell before computer displays, actors, and life-size models tell the gruesome history of the prison, from the 1798 rebellion to the late 19th century. ⊠ *Market Sq., Wicklow* ☎ *404/61599* ⊕ *www.wicklowshistoricgaol.com* ⊡ *€10.*

🍴 Restaurants

★ The Strawberry Tree

$$$$ | **FRENCH** | Claiming to be Ireland's first "certified organic restaurant," this idyllic spot is tucked away in a rural valley as part of the BrookLodge Hotel. Grilled mackerel with smoked-chili yogurt, carrot-and-orange sorbet, and wood pigeon with crispy coppa and white tomato foam are part of the feast. The glossy decor—midnight-blue walls, mirrored ceiling, and gleaming mahogany furniture—comes as a surprise, but cues you to the creative menu that awaits. The Big Table, which seats up to 40, is perfect for large parties or people who want to eat family-style. After dessert, check out the spectacular wine cellar. **Known for:** serene rural setting; creative menu; great for groups. ⑤ *Average main: €38* ⊠ *BrookLodge*

Hotel, Macreddin Rd., Macreddin ☎ *040/236–444* ⊕ *www.brooklodge.com* ⊘ *Closed Mon. No lunch.*

Hotels

BrookLodge

$$$ | **HOTEL** | Located in a spectacular valley, 30 km (18 miles) from Wicklow Town, this serene country house has a get-away-from-it-all feel, but that doesn't mean it skimps on the luxury. **Pros:** great amenities; stunning views; excellent dining options. **Cons:** a little out of the way; can get very busy; popular with weddings. ⑤ *Rooms from: €178* ⊠ *Off Aughrim Oaks Rd., Macreddin* ☎ *040/236–444* ⊕ *www.brooklodge.com* ⟳ *86 rooms* ⑩ *Free breakfast.*

★ Wicklow Head Lighthouse

$$$$ | **RENTAL** | This 95-foot-high stone tower—first built in 1781—once supported an eight-sided lantern, and has been renovated by the Irish Landmark Trust as a delightfully quirky lodging. **Pros:** unique octagonal bedrooms; stunning views; great for groups. **Cons:** a lot of stairs; books up quickly; minimum stay is two nights. ⑤ *Rooms from: €255* ⊠ *Dunbar Head, Wicklow Head* ☎ *01/670–4733* ⊕ *www.irishlandmark.com* ⟳ *2 rooms* ⑩ *No meals.*

Maynooth

21 km (13 miles) west of Dublin.

Maynooth itself is a serene university town named for a pre-Christian king of Ireland. The mighty Fitzgerald family inherited the local manor in the 12th century and founded the original Catholic college. A few minutes south of the tiny Georgian town is the hamlet of Celbridge, official address to Ireland's largest country house, Castletown.

GETTING HERE AND AROUND

From Dublin take the N4/M4 in the direction of Galway/Sligo, then exit at junction 7 and take the R406 to Maynooth. The drive takes around half an hour. Dublin Bus serves Maynooth from Merrion Square in the city center, and there is a regular train service from Connolly Station in Dublin.

 Sights

★ Castletown House

HOUSE | In 1722, William Conolly (1662–1729) decided to build himself a house befitting his new status as the speaker of the Irish House of Commons and Ireland's wealthiest man. On an estate 20 km (12 miles) southwest of Dublin, he began work on Castletown, designed in the latest Neoclassical fashion by the Florentine architect Alessandro Galilei. As it turns out, a young Irish designer and Palladian-style aficionado by the name of Sir Edward Lovett Pearce (1699–1733) was traveling in Italy, met Galilei, and soon signed on to oversee the completion of the house. Inspired by the use of outlying wings to frame a main building—the "winged device" used in Palladio's Venetian villas—Lovett Pearce added Castletown's striking colonnades and side pavilions in 1724. It is said that between them a staggering total of 365 windows were built into the overall design of the house. Conolly died before the interior of the house was completed, and work resumed in 1758 when his great-nephew Thomas and his 15-year-old wife, Lady Louisa Lennox, took up residence there. Little of the original furnishings remain today, but there is plenty of evidence of the ingenuity of Louisa and her artisans, chief among whom were the Lafranchini brothers, master craftsmen who created the famous wall plasterwork, considered masterpieces of their kind. Rescued in 1967 by Desmond Guinness of the brewing family, Castletown was deeded to the Irish state and remains the headquarters for the Irish Georgian Society.

Studded with 17th-century hunting scenes painted by Paul de Vos, the soaring **Entrance Hall** showcases one of Ireland's greatest staircases. Also extraordinary are the walls festooned with plasterwork sculpted by the Brothers Lafranchini, famous for their stuccoed swags, flora, and portraits. Upstairs at the rear of the house, the **Long Gallery**—almost 80 feet by 23 feet—is the most notable of the public rooms. Hued in a vibrant cobalt blue and topped by a coved ceiling covered with Italianate stuccowork and graced by three Venetian Murano glass chandeliers, it is a striking exercise in the antique Pompeian style. ✉ Celbridge ⊕ Exit 6 off M4 ☎ 01/628–8252 ⊕ www.castletownhouse.ie 🖾 €8 🕘 Closed Nov.–Feb.

St. Patrick's College

BUILDING | What was once a center for the training of Catholic priests is now one of Ireland's most important lay universities. The visitor center chronicles the college's history and that of the Catholic Church in Ireland. Stroll through the university gardens—the Path of Saints or the Path of Sinners. At the entrance to St. Patrick's College are the ruins of Maynooth Castle, the ancient seat of the Fitzgerald family. The Fitzgeralds' fortunes changed for the worse when they led the ill-fated rebellion of 1536. The castle keep, which dates from the 13th century, and the great hall are still in decent condition. ✉ Main St. ☎ 01/628–5222, 01/628–6744 for castle tours ⊕ www.nuim.ie 🖾 Free.

 Restaurants

Celbridge Canteen

$$$ | EUROPEAN | Hidden away in nearby, sleepy Celbridge town, this buzzy little eatery turns local produce into some of the most daring and original dishes outside the capital. Try the poached Carlingford oysters, with leek and watercreess

Continued on page 196

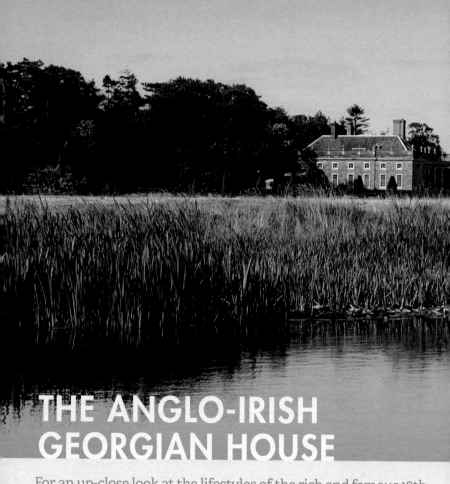

THE ANGLO-IRISH GEORGIAN HOUSE

For an up-close look at the lifestyles of the rich and famous, 18th-century style, nothing beats a visit to the great treasure houses of Castletown and Russborough. Set just a half-hour south of Dublin and located only 20 miles apart, they offer a unique peek through the keyhole into the extravagant world of Ireland's "Princes of Elegance and Prodigality."

Castletown House and its impressive grounds.

When the Palladian architectural craze swept across England, the Anglo-Irish—determined not to be outdone—set about building palaces in their own domain that would be the equal of anything in the mother country. Both Castletown House and Russborough House set new benchmarks in symmetry, elegance, and harmony for the Georgian style, which reigned supreme from 1714 to 1830 and was named after the four Georges who successively sat on the English throne.

This style was greatly influenced by the villa designs of the 16th-century Italian architect Andrea Palladio.

Although Castletown remains the largest private house in Ireland, and Russborough has the longest façade of any domicile in the country, Georgian groupies know that the real treasures lie inside: ceilings lavishly worked in Italianate stuccowork, priceless Old Master paintings, and an intimate look at the glory and grandeur of the Anglo-Irish lords.

CASTLETOWN: A GEORGIAN VERSAILLES

Reputedly the inspiration for a certain building at 1600 Pennsylvania Avenue, Castletown remains the finest example of an Irish Palladian–style house.

In 1722, William Conolly (1662–1729) decided to build himself a house befitting his new status as the speaker of the Irish House of Commons and Ireland's wealthiest man. On an estate 20 km (12 miles) southwest of Dublin, he began work on Castletown, designed in the latest Neoclassical fashion by the Florentine architect Alessandro Galilei. As it turns out, a young Irish designer and Palladian aficionado by the name of Sir Edward Lovett Pearce (1699–1733) was traveling in Italy, met Galilei, and soon signed on to oversee the completion of the house. Inspired by the use of outlying wings to frame a main building—the "winged device" used in Palladio's Venetian villas—Lovett Pearce added Castletown's striking colonnades and side pavillons in 1724. It is said that between them a staggering total of 365 windows were built into the overall design of the house—legend has it that a team of four servants were kept busy year-round keeping them all clean.

Conolly died before the interior of the house was completed, and work resumed in 1758 when his great nephew Thomas, and more importantly, his 15-year-old wife, Lady Louisa Lennox, took up residence there. Luckily, Louisa's passion for interior decoration led to the creation of some of Ireland's most stunning salons, including the Print Room and the Long Gallery. Little of the original furnishings remain today, but there is plenty of evidence of the ingenuity of Louisa and her artisans, chief among whom were the Lafranchini brothers, master craftsmen who created the famous wall plasterwork, considered masterpieces of their kind. Rescued in 1967 by Desmond Guinness of the brewing family, Castletown was deeded to the Irish state and remains the headquarters for the Irish Georgian Society.

Above left: Castletown House facade
Above right: The family crest of William Conolly.

THE ENTRANCE HALL

Studded with 17th-century hunting scenes painted by Paul de Vos, this soaring white-on-white entryway showcases one of Ireland's greatest staircases. Also extraordinary are the walls festooned with plasterwork sculpted by the Brothers Lafranchini, famous for their stuccoed swags, flora, and portraits.

THE LONG GALLERY

Upstairs at the rear of the house, this massive room—almost 80 feet by 23 feet—is the most notable of the public rooms. Hued in a vibrant cobalt blue and topped by a coved ceiling covered with Italianate stuccowork and graced by three Venetian Murano glass chandeliers, it is a striking exercise in the antique Pompeian style.

THE PRINT ROOM

Smaller but even more memorable is the Print Room, the only example in Ireland of this elegant fad. Fashionable young women loved to glue black-and-white prints—here, looking like oversize postage stamps in a giant album—onto salon walls. This was the 18th-century forerunner of today's teens covering their walls with posters of rock-star icons.

Above left: The Grand Staircase. Upper right: 18th-century Italian engravings decorate the Print Room. Bottom right: A marble statue within the Long Gallery. Far right: Mahogony bureau made for Lady Louisa, circa 1760.

WHAT A WAY TO GO

"I do not get any idea of the beauty of my house if I live in it . . . only if I can gaze upon the house from far off," proclaimed Lady Louisa in 1821 of her beloved Castletown. In her late seventies, she had a tent built on the front lawn so she could study the house at her leisure. After one evening on the lawn she caught a chill and promptly died.

OTHER GREAT GEORGIAN HOUSES

Newbridge, County Dublin

Emo Court, County Laois

Westport House, County Mayo

Florence Court, County Fermanagh

Castle Coole, County Fermanagh

Ballyfin Demesne, County Laois

Bellinter House, County Meath

Carton House, County Kildare

Farnham House, County Cavan

RUSSBOROUGH: A TEMPLE TO ART

An Irish Xanadu, Russborough House pulls out all the stops to achieve Palladian perfection.

Another conspicuously grand house rising seemingly in the middle of no-where—actually the western part of County Wicklow—Russborough was an extravagance paid for by the wages of beer. In 1741, a year after inheriting a vast fortune from his brewer father, Joseph Leeson commissioned architect Richard Castle to build him a home of palatial stature, and was rewarded with this slightly over-the-top house, whose monumental 700-foot-long façade one-upped every other great house in Ireland. Following Castle's death, the project was taken over and completed by his associate, Francis Bindon. Today, the house serves as a showcase for the celebrated collection of Old Master paintings of Sir Alfred Beit, a descendant of the De Beers diamond family, who had bought and majestically restored the property in 1952.

PRINCELY MAGNIFICENCE
The first sight of Russborough draws gasps from visitors: a mile-long, beech-lined avenue leads to a distant embankment on which sits the longest house frontage in Ireland. Constructed of silver-gray Wicklow granite, the façade encompasses a seven-bay central block, from either end of which radiate semicircular loggias connecting the flanking wings—the finest example in Ireland of Palladio's "winged device."

The interiors are full of grand period rooms that were elegantly refurbished in the 1950s by their new, moneyed owner under the eye of the legendary 20th-century decorator, Lady Colefax. The Hall is centered around a massive black Kilkenny marble chimneypiece and has a ceiling modeled after one in the Irish Parliament. Four 18th-century Joseph Vernet marine landscapes—once missing but found by Sir Alfred—once again grace

Top left: A look at the 700–foot façade of Russborough House. Bottom left: The grand Saloon. Above right: The Hall. Opposite, top: Drawing Room. Opposite: Vermeer's *Lady Writing a Letter*.

the glorious stucco moldings created to frame them in the Drawing Room. The grandest room, the Saloon, is famed for its 18th-century stucco ceiling by the Lafranchini brothers; fine Old Masters hang on walls covered in 19th-century Genoese velvet. The views out the windows take in the foothills of the Wicklow Mountains and the famous Poulaphouca reservoir in front of the house.

VERMEER, DIAMONDS, AND GANGSTERS

If it can be said that beer paid for the house, then diamonds paid for the paintings. Russborough House is today as famed for its art collection—and the numerous attempts, some successful, to steal it—as for its architecture. Credit for this must go to Sir Alfred Beit (1903—1994), nephew of the cofounder of De Beers Diamonds. One evening in 1974 while Alfred was enjoying a quiet dinner with his wife, the door burst open and in marched Rose Dugdale, an English millionaire's daughter turned IRA stalwart. Her gang "liberated" 19 of the Beit masterpieces, including Vermeer's fabled *Lady Writing a Letter*, hopefully to bargain for the release of two IRA members jailed in London. Once the paintings were recovered a week later, Sir Alfred decided to donate 17 works to the National Gallery of Ireland. Alas, a week before the handing-over ceremony in 1986, Sir Alfred and his wife were again settling down to dine when in marched Martin Cahill, a.k.a. "The General," Dublin's most notorious underworld boss (and subject of three major movies). He made off with the Vermeer and 16 other paintings. They were returned and now sit safely (we hope) in the National Gallery.

RENEWED ELEGANCE

The first phase of a major refurbishment project was completed in 2018, and the ornately fitted and furnished house is now resplendent with sparkling chandeliers and restored tapestries. As well as essential improvements to infrastructure and security, Beit paintings have been taken out of storage and re-hung including *Grand Canal* and *Palazzo Grimani, Venice* by Francesco Guardi (18th century Italian) and *Country Road and Cottages* by Jan van Goyen (17th Century Dutch). Also back in the house, after more than a century in the National Gallery, are furniture, silver, and art from the original Milltown Collection (named for the original owners, the Leeson family who were ennobled with the Earldom of Milltown), including paintings by Sir Joshua Reynolds, George Barrett, Agostino Masucci, Girolamo Troppa, and Jan Baptist Bosschaert.

LOOK UP

The elaborate ceilings in the Music Room and Library were executed by celebrated stuccadores the Brothers Lafranchini but they pale in comparison to the the plasterwork done by an unknown artisan in the Staircase Hall --an extravaganza of whipped cream moldings, cornucopias, and Rococo scrolls.

Reputedly the inspiration for a certain building at 1600 Pennsylvania Avenue, Castletown remains the finest example of the Irish Palladian-style house.

velouté, followed by wild brill with buckwheat and violet artichoke. The wine list is small but eclectic. **Known for:** performing miracles with potatoes; big-city quality at country prices; well-chosen wine list. $ *Average main: €27* ✉ *4 Main St., Celbridge* ☎ *01/627–4967* ⊕ *www. canteencelbridge.com* ⊘ *Closed Sun. and Mon. No lunch Tues.–Fri.*

 Activities

GOLF

Carton House Golf Club

GOLF | This just-outside-of-Dublin estate has quickly become one of the brightest stars in the Irish golfing universe. The parkland Mark O'Meara course makes use of the estate's rolling hills, specimen trees, and the River Rye. The stretch of the 14th, 15th, and 16th holes is a highlight: a pair of classy par-3s wrapped around a heroic par-5. The second 18 holes, created by Colin Montgomerie, are an inland links-style course that is flatter and virtually treeless. There's a good mix of long par-4s backed up with tricky

short ones. Recessed pot bunkers lie in wait to pick up off-line shots. ✉ *Off R148* ☎ *01/651–7720* ⊕ *www.cartonhouse. com/golf.html* ✉ *May–Sept., weekdays €75, weekends €85; Oct.–Apr. daily €65* ⅄ *O'Meara Course: 18 holes, 7006 yards, par 72; Montgomerie Course: 18 holes, 7301 yards, par 72.*

Straffan

5 km (3 miles) southwest of Castletown House, 25½ km (16 miles) southwest of Dublin.

Its attractive location on the banks of the River Liffey, its unique butterfly farm, and the Kildare Hotel and Country Club—where Arnold Palmer designed the K Club, one of Ireland's most renowned 18-hole golf courses—are what make Straffan so appealing.

GETTING HERE AND AROUND

To get here by car from Dublin, take the N4/M4 toward Galway and exit at junction 7 to the R406 (toward Naas). At the roundabout take the second exit onto Barberstown Road (signposted "Straffan"). Bus Éireann runs a regular service here from Dublin.

Sights

The Steam Museum
MUSEUM | This museum covers the history of Irish steam engines, handsome machines used both in industry and agriculture—for churning butter or threshing corn, for example. There's also a fun collection of model locomotives. Engineers are present on "live steam days" every Sunday and on bank holidays. The adjoining Lodge Park Walled Garden is included in the price and is perfect for a leisurely summer stroll. ⊠ *Lodge Park, off Baberstown Rd.* ☎ *01/627–3155* ⊕ *www. steam-museum.com* ✉ *€8* ⊘ *Closed Oct.–Apr.; June–Aug., closed Mon.–Thurs.; May and Sept., closed weekdays.*

Hotels

Barberstown Castle
$$$$ | HOTEL | With a 13th-century castle keep at one end, an Elizabethan section in the middle, a large Georgian country house at the other end, and a modern wing, Barberstown Castle represents 750 years of Irish history. **Pros:** 20 acres of serene gardens; real fires in public spaces. **Cons:** prices still a little inflated; newer wings have less charm. ⑤ *Rooms from: €260* ⊠ *Baberstown Rd.* ☎ *01/628–8157* ⊕ *www.barberstowncastle.ie* ⟿ *55 rooms* ⦿ *Free breakfast.*

★ Kildare Hotel and Country Club
$$$$ | RESORT | Manicured gardens and the renowned Arnold Palmer–designed K Club golf course surround this mansard-roof country mansion. **Pros:** lovely views; luxurious spa; championship golf course. **Cons:** attracts golf crowd; rooms vary in quality; can get very busy in summer. ⑤ *Rooms from: €324* ⊠ *Off Baberstown Rd.* ☎ *01/601–7200* ⊕ *www.*

kclub.ie ⟿ 69 rooms, 23 apartments ⦿ Free breakfast.

Activities

GOLF
★ The K Club
GOLF | "Home to the 2006 Ryder Cup" says all a golfer needs to know about the pedigree of the K Club. The Ryder Cup Course (formerly the Palmer Course) was designed by the legendary Arnold Palmer, and offers a round of golf in lush, wooded surroundings bordered by the River Liffey. The generous fairways and immaculate greens are offset by formidable length, which makes it one of the most demanding courses in the Dublin vicinity. The Smurfit Course is essentially an "inland links" course. The signature 7th hole wows visitors with its water cascades and rock-quarry feature. ⊠ *Kildare Country Club, off Baberstown Rd.* ☎ *01/601–7321* ⊕ *www.kclub.ie* ✉ *May–Sept. €250; Jan.–Mar. €120; Apr. and Oct. €180* ⚓ *Palmer Course: 18 holes, 7350 yards, par 72; Smurfit Course: 18 holes, 7277 yards, par 72.*

Naas

13 km (8 miles) south of Straffan, 30 km (19 miles) southwest of Dublin.

The seat of County Kildare and a thriving market town in the heartland of Irish Thoroughbred country, Naas (pronounced "nace") is full of pubs with high stools where short men (apprentice jockeys) discuss the merits of their various stables.

GETTING HERE AND AROUND
To get here from Dublin, take the N81 to the N7 toward Limerick. Exit at junction 9 to the R445 (signposted Naas). The drive takes about 35 minutes. Bus Éireann runs a regular service from Dublin. Parking is available throughout the town.

Restaurants

Las Rada

$ | **WINE BAR** | Experienced foodies Jules and Joanne Bradbury have taken a creative approach to tapas adding local flavor to their Moorish-inspired, brightly colored bar and restaurant. Tapas choices include wonderful sweet potatoes with truffle mayo and cheese, and roasted red peppers stuffed with salmon and crab. The wine list always offers something out of the ordinary. **Known for:** original tapas; lively atmosphere; roasted red peppers stuffed with salmon and crab. $ Average main: €17 ⊠ New Row ☎ 045/879–978 ⊕ www.lasradatapas.ie ▭ No credit cards ⊗ No lunch.

Activities

HORSE RACING

Punchestown Racecourse

HORSE RACING/SHOW | A wonderful setting amid rolling plains distinguishes the Punchestown Racecourse, with the Wicklow Mountains providing a spectacular backdrop. Horse races are held regularly, but the most popular event is the Punchestown National Hunt Festival in April, a real pilgrimage for fans of steeplechase racing. ⊠ R411 ✛ 3 km (2 miles) south of Naas ☎ 045/897–704 ⊕ www. punchestown.com.

The Curragh

8 km (5 miles) southwest of Naas, 25½ km (16 miles) west of Poulaphouca Reservoir.

The broad plain of the Curragh, bisected by the main N7 road, is the biggest area of common land in Ireland, encompassing about 31 square km (12 square miles) and devoted mainly to grazing.

Activities

HORSE RACING

★ **Curragh Racecourse**

HORSE RACING/SHOW | A day out at the Curragh, especially on Derby day, is a Irish summer ritual. The area is Ireland's major racing center, and the Curragh Racecourse is its main showplace. It's a flat racing mecca for enthusiasts from all over the world, and the Irish Derby and other international horse races are run here. ⊠ N7, Naas ☎ 045/441–205 ⊕ www.curragh.ie ▭ €18.

Kildare Town

5 km (3 miles) west of the Curragh, 51 km (32 miles) southwest of Dublin.

Horse breeding is the cornerstone of County Kildare's thriving economy, and Kildare Town is the place to come if you're crazy about horses. But, in addition to all things equine, Kildare boasts other stellar attractions, including the famous Japanese Gardens.

GETTING HERE AND AROUND

Kildare Town is about 45 minutes from Dublin; take the N81 south to the N7/M7, exit at junction 13, and take the third exit at the roundabout to the R415 (signposted "Kildare"). Parking is available throughout the town. Kildare Town is a major junction stop for Irish Rail, which has trains to Dublin (45 minutes), Cork (2 hours, 25 minutes), Limerick (1 hour, 45 minutes), and Galway (2 hours). The town's train station is just outside town, but a free bus service drops you into the center of town. Bus Éireann travels here from Dublin.

VISITOR INFORMATION

CONTACTS Kildare Tourist Office.
⊠ Heritage Centre, Market Sq., Kildare ☎ 045/521–240 ⊕ www.kildare.ie.

Sights

Irish National Stud

FARM/RANCH | If you're a horse aficionado, or even just curious, check out this stud farm, a main center of Ireland's racing industry. The Stud was founded in 1900 by brewing heir Colonel William Hall-Walker. It's here that breeding stallions are groomed, exercised, tested, and bred. Spring and early summer, when mares have foals, are the best times to visit. The **National Stud Horse Museum,** also on the grounds, recounts the history of horses in Ireland. Its most outstanding exhibit is the skeleton of Arkle, the mighty Irish racehorse that won major victories in Ireland and England during the late 1960s. The museum also contains medieval evidence of horses, such as bones from 13th-century Dublin, some early examples of equestrian equipment, and "Living Legends" or retired equine stars of the racing game. ⊠ *Tulley Rd., Kildare* ✛ *1½ km (1 mile) south of Kildare Town* ☏ *045/521–617* ⊕ *irishnationalstud. ie* ✉ *€13, includes Japanese Gardens* ☉ *Closed Jan.–mid-Feb.*

Japanese Gardens

GARDEN | Adjacent to the Irish National Stud, the Japanese Gardens were created between 1906 and 1910 by the horse breeder's founder, Colonel Hall-Walker, and laid out by a Japanese gardener, Tassa Eida, and his son Minoru. Although quite small and cramped, the gardens are recognized as among the finest Asian gardens in the world, although they're more of an East–West hybrid than authentically Japanese. The Scots pines, for instance, are an appropriate stand-in for traditional Japanese pines, which signify long life and happiness. The gardens symbolically chart the human progression from birth to death, although the focus is on the male journey.

A series of landmarks runs along a meandering path: the Tunnel of Ignorance (No. 3) represents a child's lack of understanding; the Engagement and Marriage bridges (Nos. 8 and 9) span a small stream; and from the Hill of Ambition (No. 13), you can look back over your joys and sorrows. It ends with the Gateway to Eternity (No. 20), beyond which lies a Zen Buddhist meditation sand garden. Spring and fall are when the gardens are at their best. ⊠ *Tully Rd., Kildare* ✛ *About 2½ km (1½ miles) south of Kildare Town* ☏ *045/521–617* ⊕ *irishnationalstud.ie* ✉ *€13, includes Irish National Stud* ☉ *Closed Jan.–mid-Feb.*

Round Tower

MILITARY SITE | The 108-foot-high Round Tower, dating from the 12th century, is the second-highest in Ireland (the highest is in Kilmacduagh in County Galway). Extraordinary views across much of the Midlands await if you're energetic enough to climb to the top. ⊠ *St. Brigid's Cathedral, off Market Sq.* ☏ *045/521–229* ⊕ *www.kildare.ie* ✉ *€6* ☉ *Closed Oct.–Apr.*

St. Brigid's Cathedral

RELIGIOUS SITE | The Church of Ireland St. Brigid's Cathedral is where the eponymous saint founded a religious settlement in the 5th century. The present cathedral, with its stocky tower, is a restored 13th-century structure. It was partially rebuilt around 1686, but restoration work wasn't completed for another 200 years. The stained-glass west window of the cathedral depicts three of Ireland's greatest saints: Brigid, Patrick, and Columba. In pre-Christian times Druids gathered around a sacred oak that stood on the grounds and from which Kildare (*Cill Dara*), or the "church of the oak," gets its name. Also on the grounds is a restored fire pit reclaimed from the time of Brigid, when a fire was kept burning—by a chaste woman—in a female-only temple. Interestingly, Brigid started the place for women, but it was she who asked monks to move here as well. ⊠ *Off Market Sq., Kildare* ⊕ *www.kildare.ie* ☉ *Closed Oct.–Apr.*

Restaurants

★ The Green Barn

$$ | MODERN IRISH | FAMILY | Look out the floor-to-ceiling windows and see the veggies that you're about to eat growing in front of you at this family-run, organic café in a revamped barn on the rolling grounds of gorgeous Burtown House. Fresh and homegrown are the buzzwords on the menu, where the organic chicken, leek, and kale pie is melt-in-the-mouth perfect. The dark chocolate and orange mousse is the pick of the desserts. Burtown House is a small trip out of town on the way to Athy. **Known for:** stunning setting; family-friendly; organic chicken, leek, and kale pie. ⑤ *Average main: €19* ⊠ *Burtown House, Kildare* ☎ *059/862–3865* ⊕ *www.burtownhouse. ie* ☉ *Closed Jan., and Mon. and Tues. No dinner Wed.–Fri. and Sun.*

 Hotels

Keadeen Hotel

$$ | HOTEL | The luxurious spa and health center are the big attractions at this family-owned hotel on 10 acres of flower-filled gardens. **Pros:** good spa and pool; light-filled rooms. **Cons:** uninspired architecture; crowded with weddings; can feel very busy at times. ⑤ *Rooms from: €150* ⊠ *Off Ballymany, Newbridge* ☎ *045/431–666* ⊕ *www.keadeenhotel.ie* ⇥ *71 rooms* ⑩ *Free breakfast.*

THE MIDLANDS

Updated by
Paul Clements

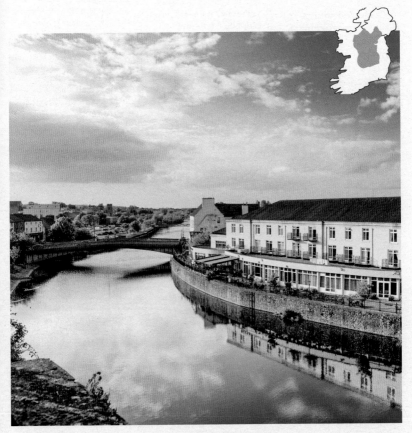

👁 **Sights**
★★★★★

🍴 **Restaurants**
★★★★☆

🛏 **Hotels**
★★★☆☆

🛍 **Shopping**
★★☆☆☆

🍸 **Nightlife**
★★☆☆☆

WELCOME TO THE MIDLANDS

TOP REASONS TO GO

★ **Stately Clonmacnoise:** Atmospheric and still spirit-warm, this great early Christian monastery survived Viking, Norman, and English invaders over the centuries.

★ **Castles:** While known for its rich farmlands, the Midlands is also home to stately homes and gardens, including fairy-tale Tullynally Castle and Birr Castle.

★ **Hiking the Slieve Bloom Mountains:** Dip in and out of the 32-km (20-mile) Slieve Bloom Trail, ideal hiking country for those with a yen to rise above their surroundings.

★ **Athlone:** The restored 13th-century castle along with the quirky shops and Europe's oldest pub are worth taking time to visit, as is the Luan Gallery.

★ **The Treasure House of Emo:** A quintessential landmark of 18th-century Palladian elegance, Emo—the former home of the Earl of Portarlington—has a spectacular rotunda inspired by Rome's Pantheon.

Perfect for the relaxed visitor who values the subtle over the spectacular, the flat, fertile plain at the center of Ireland is full of relatively undiscovered historic towns, abbey ruins, and grand houses.

1 **Abbeyleix.** An elegant tree-lined town with original shop fronts and Georgian stone buildings.

2 **Portlaoise.** The busy county town of Laois with historic architecture stands at a crossroads linking major cities.

3 **Portarlington.** A delightful riverside town set amidst rich agricultural hinterland.

4 **Tullamore.** A vibrant place and county town of Offaly, noted for its whiskey making.

5 **Kilbeggan.** A small town founded on a 6th-century monastery and the home of a major whiskey distiller.

6 **Mullingar.** One of the biggest towns in Westmeath, pleasantly sited on the Grand Canal and famed for its cattle trade.

7 **Castlepollard.** A village laid out around a triangular green and renowned for its colorful shop fronts.

8 **Fore.** Lying in a valley between two hills, the village is an example of an early Christian settlement.

9 **Cavan.** The county town, which boasts some fine sandstone buildings, is an ideal base for exploring the lakelands.

10 **Longford Town.** A market town known for its literary associations and its historic cathedral restored after being destroyed by fire.

11 **Anthony Trollope Trail.** A trail with 27 locations celebrating the English author who introduced pillar boxes to Ireland.

12 **Athlone.** A thriving town on the River Shannon, its imposing castle is a major attraction.

13 **Clonmacnoise.** One of Ireland's most important ecclesiastical sites set in an atmospheric landscape.

14 **Banagher.** A small crossroads town on the river with a busy marina.

15 **Birr.** An outstanding heritage town dating from the 6th century where exquisite Georgian buildings are the main feature.

16 **Roscrea.** The past is all around you in this Tipperary town of ancient castles, towers, and churches.

Sligo
Balladrihid
SLIGO
Boyle
N61
LEITRIM
NORTHERN
IRELAND
Upper
Lough Erne
Armagh
N2
N12
Monaghan
N54
Clones
N3
MONAGHAN
N2
Butler's Bridge
9 Cavan Town
Bellananagh
CAVAN
N55
N3
Ardee
Slane
N4 11
Strokestown
House
Tulsk
ROSCOMMON
N60
LONGFORD
10 Longford
Center Parcs,
Longford Forest
Roscommon
Edgeworthstown
Castlepollard
N55
MEATH
Tullynally
Castle
7
Fore
Abbey
8 Fore
WESTMEATH
Balrath
Mullingar
6
The Old
Rail Trail
Moate
N6
0   25 mi
0   25 km
N61
ALWAY
Athlone
12
N6
13 Clonmacnoise
N62
OFFALY
5 Kilbeggan
Distillery
Belvedere
House
N80
4 Tullamore
KILDARE
Banagher 14
Birr Castle
15 Birr
SLIEVE BLOOM
MOUNTAINS
N80
3 Portarlington
Naas
Kilcullen
Emo Court
Borrisokane
Portlaoise
2
N7
LAOIS
CLARE
Roscrea
16
Abbeyleix
1
Nenagh
N7
N62
TIPPERARY
N8
KILKENNY
N80

CRUISING ON THE SHANNON

A great vacation along the Shannon River.

Whether you opt for a one-hour or one-week journey—and choose either a guided boat tour or private boat hire—cruising on the River Shannon is a never-to-be-forgotten experience, giving a new perspective on ole Ireland.

Think of blissful, relaxing times on the river, mooring for lunch at a quayside inn, or sampling traditional culture with gregarious lockkeepers. Along the Shannon's 334-km (207-mile) length you can head to major boating hubs like Athlone, or to historic stretches where it meanders past ancient settlements (such as Clonmacnoise), or to lakes aplenty. The biggest is Ireland's "inland sea," Lough Derg, bordered by easygoing villages like Terryglass and Mountshannon that offer appealingly quiet streets, stone-built cottage restaurants, and rustic harborside bars with picnic tables (many with evening music or Irish dancing sessions). Remember, the motto of Shannon cruising is "There's no hurry": the boats travel at only 11 kph (7 mph), so a river journey is a slow affair with time to drink in the history, wildlife, and inland gems of an older Ireland many thought had disappeared.

WHEN TO GO

Good times to cruise are in May through early June. Rentals are cheaper, the waterways are less crowded, the weather is generally favorable, and daylight stretches well into late evening. Whenever you go, get the scoop on permits, moorings, and river bylaws from Waterways Ireland (⊕ www.waterwaysireland.org).

A WONDERFUL DAY ON THE WATER

On the map, the scale of the Shannon may look daunting—it *is* the longest river in Ireland or Britain—but that's one reason why many people opt for an idyllic daylong exploration. If you only have time for a short guided journey, then one of the best is upriver from Athlone to Lough Ree on a three-hour trip on board the *Viking* boat (€10–€20). Or opt to go downriver to magnificent Clonmacnoise. You can also board pleasure cruisers at Killaloe and Dromineer. If you're feeling romantic, try an evening cruise with the Moon River company, which operates a luxurious 100-seater from Carrick-on-Shannon. A detailed commentary is provided on these cruises.

GUIDED CRUISES Moon River. ⊠ *Marina, Carrick-on-Shannon waterfront* ☎ *071/962–1777* ⊕ *www.moonriver. ie.* **Silver Line Cruisers.** ⊠ *The Marina, Banagher* ☎ *057/915–1112* ⊕ *www. silverlinecruisers.com.* **The Spirit of Killaloe.** ⊠ *The Quay, Lakeside Dr., Killaloe* ☎ *086/814–0559* ⊕ *www.killaloerivercruises.com.* **Viking Ship Cruises.** ⊠ *The Quay at Athlone Castle, Athlone* ☎ *086/262–1136* ⊕ *www.vikingtoursireland.ie.*

Many travelers opt to boat 'n' bike downriver to the boating hub of Athlone.

GOING WITH THE SHANNON FLOW

As the Shannon has its own slow-paced signature—a place where you are alive to the layers of history along the riverside and sequestered villages, which are a joy to explore—why not consider your own boat hire? The beauty of a personal cruise is that you can concoct your own itinerary, moving at your own speed and stopping off where the notion, and the motion, takes you.

There are four main boating towns for hiring cruisers: Carrick-on-Shannon, Portumna, Banagher, and Williamstown. From luxury cabin cruisers to barges or smaller boats, a glittering array of vessels is available for rent. Prices range from €650 for a two- to four-berth cruiser for one week in the quieter off-season, and from €1,550 in the more expensive summer months. With most companies, you can also rent for three-night/four-day short breaks. In addition to guided tours, Silver Line Cruisers offers boat rentals.

BOAT HIRES Carrick Craft. ⊠ *The Marina, Carrick-on-Shannon* ☎ *071/962– 1777* ⊕ *www.carrickcraft.com.* **Emerald Star.** ☎ *071/962–3711* ⊕ *www.emeraldstar.ie.* **Silver Line Cruisers.** ⊠ *The Marina, Banagher* ☎ *057/915–1112* ⊕ *www. silverlinecruisers.com.*

Ireland's "inland sea," Lough Derg.

During the boom years of economic growth in Ireland, from the mid-1990s to 2008, newly built motorways bypassed many small Midlands towns. But for a slice of authentic Ireland, this region is worth lingering in. That's not to say its pleasures are all workaday; visitors can sample first-class food and rural peace in spa hotels or farmhouses, experience festivals, walk or cycle through lush countryside, and follow well-developed tourist trails—all in an area where life moves at a different pace.

The flat plains of the center of Ireland are made up of elegant places rich in delights that attract the culturally curious. Art galleries and heritage museums cluster around the town centers of Birr, Athlone, Tullamore, and Cavan. You won't find many international coffee chains or behemoth brands, but you will discover age-old industries such as lace making, crystal making, and whiskey making. Slow down and appreciate the gentle pace of time-burnished G&G (Grocery & Guinness) pubs, old-school barbers, or hardware and drapery stores complete with high shelves, long counters, and garrulous owners. With blink-and-you'll-miss-them one-tractor villages, half the fun is in driving down a back road and stumbling on a teddy-bear shop or craft workers sculpting wood. Spend enough time in the region and you might even get to recognize the difference between a Cavan twang and a Tipperary brogue.

The big set pieces are here, too. Among them are Clonmacnoise, Ireland's most important monastic ruins; the gorgeous gardens of Birr Castle, now open to the public for tours for the first time in its history; and some of Ireland's finest Anglo-Irish houses, including Strokestown Park House and Emo Court. As for scenic pleasures, this region has its fair share of Ireland's 800 bodies of water, and much of the landscape is blanket bog. The River Shannon, one of the longest rivers in Europe and the longest in Britain or Ireland, bisects the Midlands from north to south, piercing a series of loughs (lakes): Lough Allen, Lough Ree, and Lough Derg. The Royal Canal and the Grand Canal cross the Midlands from east to west, ending in the Shannon north and south of Lough Ree.

The Midlands comprises nine counties: Tipperary, Laois (pronounced "leash"), Offaly, Westmeath, Longford, Roscommon, Leitrim, Cavan, and Monaghan.

Tourism authorities have hatched a plot to entice more visitors to the Midlands with the launch by Fáilte Ireland of a new €2 million program called Ireland's Hidden Heartlands. The campaign, which extends through all the Midland counties, is a major drive to help promote the region's natural delights through what marketing gurus describe as "the power of quiet," "slow tourism," and "great escapes." Newly opened cycle routes, scenic walkways, forest paths, and horseback riding on Celtic trails have been put in place to tap into the relaxed rhythm of this oft-neglected area. Center stage is the vital "Broad Majestic Shannon" (as the Pogues had it in their song), whether through cruising, swimming, fishing, kayaking, or stand-up paddleboarding.

MAJOR REGIONS

The Eastern Midlands. Just an hour from Dublin, this region is essentially rich farmland but is studded with even richer sights: grand homes such as Emo Court, Belvedere House, and Tullynally Castle; once-upon-a-time villages such as Abbeyleix; and the historic treats of Fore Abbey and Kilbeggan Distillery. Leaving the ancient kingdom of Leinster, you come to two counties of Ulster: Cavan and Monaghan. Beyond Cavan Town you enter the heart of the Northern Lakelands, dotted with hundreds of beautiful lakes.

The Western Midlands. One of the corners of "hidden Ireland," this region is unblighted by crowds—although if the tourist board has its way, this may soon change. This section of the Midlands covers the area's western fringe, making its way from the heart of the region, the town of Longford, and skirting the hilly landscape of County Leitrim, dappled with lakes and beloved of anglers for its fish-filled waters. Moving south through Roscommon, western Offaly, and the northern part of Tipperary, the scenery is generally low on spectacle but high on unspoiled, lush, and undulating countryside. The towns are small and undistinguished, except Birr and Strokestown, both designed to complement the "big houses" that share their names. The historic highlight of this region is the ancient site of Clonmacnoise, an important monastery of early Christian Ireland, while Birr Castle, opened in 2013 to the public for the first time in 400 years, is an essential part of any visitor's itinerary.

Planning

Getting Here and Around

AIR TRAVEL
Dublin Airport is the principal international airport that serves the Midlands; car-rental facilities are available here.

BIKE TRAVEL
One of the best ways to immerse yourself in the Midlands is to meander through the region on a bike. Although the area may not offer the spectacular scenery of the more hilly coastal regions, its level, Netherlands-like terrain means a less strenuous ride. New cycling blueways and greenways capitalize on this, as does the recent opening of the Old Rail Trail as a major cycle route leading from Athlone to Mullingar.

The twisting roads are generally in good (well, good enough) condition. There are picnic spots galore in the many state-owned forests just off the main roads. The more rural regions of Laois allow you to spend days exploring beautiful glens, waterfalls, nature trails, and wooded regions around the Slieve Bloom Mountains. Try to avoid the motorways that bisect the region—after all, this is an area that deserves thorough and leisurely

Walk the Slieve Bloom Mountains

Crystal clear freshwater streams, gushing waterfalls, lush forests, and no fewer than 27 glens are all part of the Slieve Bloom Mountains experience. The mountains stretch across the southern end of Offaly and are shared with neighboring County Laois. At one time, the summit—Arderin—was considered to be the highest point in Ireland. Whether you come for serious hiking, a gentle stroll, or just to drink in the spectacular views, you won't be disappointed. Looped walks, some led by guides, range from 4 km (2.5 miles) to 15 km (9 miles). Popular trailheads start from the villages of Kinnitty, Cadamstown, and Clonaslee, or you can make your base in the beautiful heritage town of Birr. Information and guided walking leaflets are available from the tourist information offices in Birr and Tullamore.

exploration. Contact the regional and township tourist offices for all the details.

BUS TRAVEL

With a much more extensive network than trains, buses are a better bet for exploring much of the Midlands. Most small towns and villages are serviced by at least one bus per day, while trains are generally limited to towns on main lines linking cities. Bus Éireann runs express buses from Dublin to many Midlands towns, and regular-speed buses connect others. The train stations for Athlone and Longford also act as their bus depots, while Cavan's bus station is at Farnham Street.

CAR TRAVEL

The roads of the Midlands offer an easier intro to Irish driving than the hairpin bends of West Cork and Connemara. Because the area has a decent network of main arteries and off-the-beaten-track byroads, a car may be your best option for covering the widest itinerary.

Don't be surprised to round a bend only to confront a herd of sheep idly grazing with little hurry about them—do what the locals do, slow to a stop and wait for an opening in the woolly mass to occur. The same goes for cows. Refrain from honking your horn on these occasions—it will only confirm your status as an impatient tourist, and, besides, the cows won't take a bit of notice.

TRAIN TRAVEL

All trains are run by Irish Rail. The main Midlands towns that have train connections lie on cross-country routes linking the cities, either east–west or north–south. Intercity trains make only a few stops at smaller towns, while slower trains stop at small towns and some villages. You can connect from one Midlands town to another by train, but check in advance on the regularity of services. There are no exclusively local train services—they all continue on to cities.

CONTACTS Sligo Railway Station. ✉ *Lord Edward St., Sligo* ☏ *071/916–9888* ⊕ *www.irishrail.ie.*

Hotels

As commercial progress has blossomed in the Midlands, so, too, have the options in hotels, country houses, and cottage rentals. There is an acute lack of hotel accommodation in the smaller

Shannon-side towns, but on the plus side, the Irish bed-and-breakfast offers great value in the Midlands—farmhouses and homes geared to paying guests provide direct contact with local families and the lore of their area. Good beds, decent heating, en suite bathrooms, and the legendary Irish breakfast are the norm. *While most properties have Internet access, Wi-Fi is not a given at B&Bs in the Midlands.*

From June to early September, tourism gets into serious stride, bolstered by the many Irish families using their holiday homes and getaway cottages in the region. Finding accommodations is never a major problem—except for those weekends when a town is holding an annual music festival. *Hotel reviews have been shortened. For full information, visit Fodors.com.*

Restaurants

The Midlands town of Birr is known as the "belly button of Ireland" because of its central location, not because this region is regarded as one of the cuisine centers of Ireland. No matter that Ireland's best restaurant (according to some)—Neven Maguire's MacNean's, near Cavan town—is in the Midlands, nor the fact that the region is also home to Wineport Lodge, Ireland's first "wine hotel," you'll find that most restaurants here are simple eateries, ranging in price from inexpensive to moderate.

Nevertheless, there are those restaurants that will entice you right in off the street, especially those offering beef—Mullingar, in the center of the Midlands—is the beef capital of Ireland—and fish specialties, as the many lakes and rivers of the region provide an abundance of fresh salmon and trout (in fact, since no place is more than an hour and a half from the sea, expect to find lots of fresh ocean fish). *Restaurant reviews have been shortened. For full information, visit Fodors.com.*

What It Costs in Euros			
$	$$	$$$	$$$$
RESTAURANTS			
under €19	€19–€24	€25–€32	over €32
HOTELS			
under €120	€120–€170	€171–€210	over €210

Planning Your Time

The Midlands is a slice of old Ireland. Spend a few days traveling around the unspoiled countryside with its traditional hay meadows and you will come across ancient humped bridges, handsome square tower-houses, and curious-looking castles.

IF YOU HAVE THREE DAYS

If you come from the Greater Dublin area (the Midlands is easily accessible from the city in less than two hours) or surrounding counties such as Wicklow and Kildare, then a grand kickoff to a tour is at Portarlington to visit the nearby Emo Court and Gardens, a large country house designed by James Gandon, the architect responsible for much of Georgian Dublin. Head on to Tullamore, stopping at the elegantly restored 19th-century bonded warehouse of Tullamore Dew Irish Whiskey Distillery (based in the heritage center). Consider an overnight in Tullamore, which has a good selection of hotels and bed-and-breakfasts.

On Day 2 drive across to Birr for a morning's exploration of its Georgian architecture and a wander around the castle grounds. The formal gardens contain the tallest box hedges in the world; in spring you will see a dazzling display of flowering magnolias, cherries, crab apples, and naturalized narcissi. Guided tours of the Gothic Revival castle, opened to the public in 2013 for the first time in its 400-year history, take place in the summer, pulling back a curtain into a previously unseen world.

A half-hour drive takes you to Clonmacnoise, Ireland's most important monastic settlement, where it's worthwhile to join a guided tour that will give you a sense of the place and its past in less than an hour. The next day head for Athlone on the River Shannon and walk around the quirky Left Bank, full of crafts and antiques shops as well as secondhand-book shops, cafés, and Sean's Bar (which lays claim, sometimes disputed, to be Ireland's oldest). You could easily spend an hour or two touring the exhibits in the wonderfully restored Athlone Castle as well as visiting the nearby Luan Gallery. Make time for a two-hour cruise along the Shannon to get a different perspective on the Midlands.

Festivals and Events

JULY

Percy French Summer School

During the first week of July, one of Ireland's best-loved songwriters, Percy French, is celebrated in Roscommon town and at Castlecoote House with a summer school, complete with concerts and lectures. French was born at Cloonyquinn House near Elphin; his best-known songs include "Are Ye Right There, Michael?" and "Phil the Fluter's Ball." ⊠ *Castlecoote House, Castlecoote, Elphin* ☎ *090/666–3794* ⊕ *www.percy-french.ie.*

AUGUST

Castle Palooza Festival

Started in 2006, this annual arts and music festival takes place over a three-day weekend in early August (a bank holiday in Ireland) around the 17th-century Charleville Castle and its grounds, surrounded by ancient oak woods. Ticket holders are welcome to explore the castle and take in the art exhibits, games, restored rooms, and a myriad of other creative offerings. Music is mainly by

John McGahern

Until his death in 2006, the Midlands was the home of one of Ireland's leading writers, John McGahern; at the end of July, the John McGahern International Seminar and Summer School—a series of lectures, workshops, and tours—is held in Carrick-on-Shannon in his honor.

Irish artists. ⊠ *Charleville Castle, Tullamore* ⊕ *www.castlepalooza.com.*

★ **Tullamore Show**
Ireland's biggest agricultural gathering (and one of its longest established) attracts 60,000 annually in mid-August, when the largest assembly of cattle anywhere in the country compete in 1,000 classes for 42 national titles. Apart from the many different breeds of cows, there are also sheep-shearing competitions, cooking demonstrations, exhibits of local artisanal produce, displays of vintage farm machinery, and fashion shows. An international visitor center caters to the huge crowds of overseas tourists who flock to the show, which appeals to all generations. Scores of trade stands encourage you to spend money, and an art and photography section features the work of local artists. ⊠ *Butterfield Estate, Birr Rd., near Blueball, Tullamore* ⊹ *Free shuttle buses to venue run from Tullamore train station every hr from 9 am* ☎ *057/935–2141* ⊕ *www.tullamore-show.com.*

Visitor Information

Four Midlands Tourist Information Offices (TIOs) are open all year: Cavan, Monaghan, Mullingar, and Portlaoise. The Mullingar TIO has information on

Counties Westmeath, Offaly, Monaghan, Cavan, Longford, and Laois. Another two Midlands TIOs are open seasonally: Athlone (April–October) and Birr (June–September), and Longford (all year).

Find tourist office contact info listed under the main town sections throughout this chapter.

Abbeyleix

99 km (61 miles) southwest of Dublin.

★ One of the most elegant small towns in Ireland, Abbeyleix has retained its Georgian feel and its broad main street, which is lined with well-appointed stone-cut buildings and original shop fronts in the traditionally ornate Irish style. The entire tree-lined village was built in the 18th century, on the orders of the Viscount de Vesci, to house servants and tradesmen working on his nearby estate. Many town houses and vernacular buildings date from the 1850s, but more recent buildings, including the Market House, erected in 1906, and the Hibernian Bank, from 1900, contribute greatly to the town's refined character.

GETTING HERE AND AROUND

Drivers between Cork and Dublin can now bypass Abbeyleix via the N8, which has partially alleviated the town's traffic problems. However, on busy summer holiday weekends, congestion still occurs, so add a little extra time in case of delays. Allow 75 minutes driving time to Dublin or 90 minutes to Dublin Airport. The nearest large town is Portlaoise, a 10-minute drive, while Kilkenny is 30 minutes south on the N77. Free on-street car parking and several car parks are available in town. Daily buses connect Abbeyleix to Dublin or Cork; the former is just less than two hours away, the latter a 2¾-hour trip.

⊙ Sights

Heritage House

HOUSE | Also known as the former North Boys School, the Heritage House has fascinating informative displays on Laois life from the Stone Age to the present as well as the history of Abbeyleix and the de Vescis, an Anglo-Norman family who, in 1699, came to live at an estate nearby. They were instrumental in building and developing the new town of Abbeyleix in 1770. The school was originally constructed for the education of Catholics (at the other end of the town you'll find the South School, built for Protestants). Also accessible through the Heritage House is the original Sexton's House (no extra charge), which boasts a stylish interior from the turn of the 19th century. ✉ *Main St.* ☎ *057/873–1653* ⊕ *www.abbeyleix-heritage.com* ✉ *€3* ⊘ *Closed Sun. and Mon.*

Heywood Gardens

GARDEN | The pretty Georgian village of Ballinakill contains the Heywood Gardens, which were designed by the English architect Sir Edwin Lutyens in the early 20th century within an existing 18th-century park. The Lutyenses' house burned down, but the gardens, with landscaping most likely attributable to the famed Gertrude Jekyll, are worth a detour. Guided one-hour tours by prior booking (Monday–Thursday) are available through this gardener's paradise, where a formal lawn flanked by traditional herbaceous borders leads to a sunken Italian garden. Highlights include a rose called Natalie Naples and Johnston's Blue geraniums. ✉ *About 5 km (3 miles) south of Abbeyleix* ☎ *057/873–3563* ⊕ *www.heritageireland.ie* ✉ *Free.*

★ Morrissey's Pub

HISTORIC SITE | Don't miss Morrissey's. A working public house since 1775, this is one of Ireland's best-loved drinking emporiums and has a dark, wood-panel interior furnished with antique bar

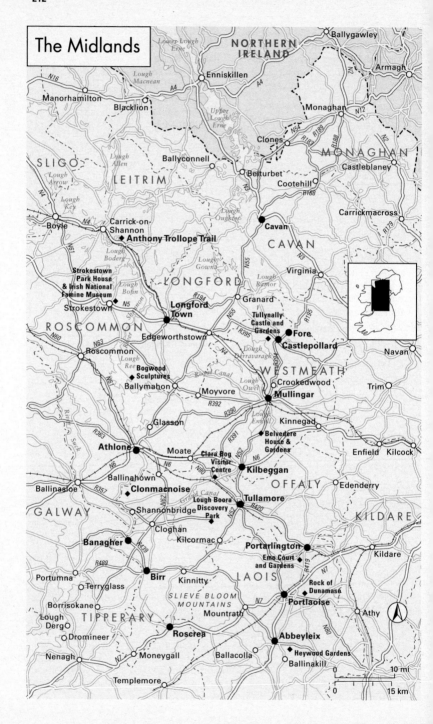

The Midlands

fittings. Customers can warm themselves by an ancient potbelly stove. Until 2005 this establishment still functioned as a shop, and while it retains its stocks of groceries, they are no longer for sale. An evocative time capsule, it serves as a reminder of times when you could purchase a pound of butter, the newspaper, and cattle feed while enjoying the obligatory pint of Guinness. They serve sandwiches in the afternoon, which you can enjoy alfresco at picnic tables at the front of the bar, and pizzas are available into the late evening. ⊠ *10 Main St.* ☎ *057/873–1281.*

Hotels

The Foxrock Inn

$ | B&B/INN | The main attraction of this modest 200-year-old guesthouse, set in the tiny village of Clough right in the heart of the County Laois countryside, is the genuinely warm welcome extended by its owners, Sean and Marian Hyland, one that is delightfully seconded by a friendly springer by the name of Jill and a terrier called Marley. **Pros:** ideally situated for exploring Slieve Bloom Mountains; close to golf and fishing activities; traditional music nights in summer. **Cons:** no frills; rooms are rather bland; well off the tourist track. ⑤ *Rooms from: €80* ⊠ *12 The Limekiln ⊹ 12 km (8 miles) west of Abbeyleix (signposted off R434 road to Borris-in-Ossory)* ☎ *086/128–6838* ⊕ *www.foxrockinn.com* ⤳ *5 rooms* ⏹ *Free breakfast.*

Portlaoise

14 km (9 miles) north of Abbeyleix.

Near the heart of County Laois, the rich farmland south and west of Portlaoise is one of Ireland's undiscovered gems. Golf, fishing, hiking, and horseback riding are traditional sports here, and the development of the Grand Canal for recreational purposes is adding to the area's attractions. Explore the pretty villages and romantic, ivy-covered ruins by car, follow one of the many hiking trails, or drive the Garden Trail.

Portlaoise's name is derived from the Irish for "Fort of Laois" and refers to the town's strife-filled history. In terms of its architecture, it's rather eclectic—it feels as if bits of other towns were picked up and dropped randomly onto the site. Once best known for having Ireland's highest-security prison, which housed the IRA's most notorious members during the 1970s and '80s and still looms over the town, Portlaoise is undergoing a renaissance. The main street, which once formed part of the main Dublin–Cork road, is now largely given over to pedestrians; pubs and restaurants are flourishing; and the thriving Dunamaise Arts Centre adds an extra dash of culture.

GETTING HERE AND AROUND

Portlaoise is an hour by train, bus, or car from Dublin. Kilkenny is 45 minutes south on the N8 and then N77. Roads from Portlaoise also lead south and west to Cork, Galway, and Limerick. There is no free parking anywhere in town; paid parking is available on James Fintan Lalor Avenue, next to County Hall, and at shopping centers.

Portlaoise has several daily Irish Rail trains to the capital and is on the main line linking it with Cork, Limerick, and Tralee. The small station is five minutes from the town center. Bus routes leading to Ireland's three main cities—Dublin, Cork, and Limerick—converge at Portlaoise. In addition to Bus Éireann, an independent operator, J. J. Kavanagh & Sons, serves the town, and Dublin Coach offers a route to Dublin Airport. ■**TIP→ Staying in Portlaoise gives you a good base from which to explore the surrounding countryside and helps you avoid the heavy traffic that can clog the main N7 Dublin road.**

CONTACTS Dublin Coach. ⊠ *James Fintan Lalor Ave. ⊹ Pickup/drop-off at bus* *shelter* ☏ *01/465–9972* ⊕ *www.dublin-coach.ie.* **J. J. Kavanagh.** ✉ *James Fintan Lalor Ave.* ⊹ *Buses stop and pick up at bus shelter* ☏ *056/883–1106* ⊕ *www.jjkavanagh.ie.*

VISITOR INFORMATION

CONTACTS Portlaoise Tourist Office. ✉ *James Fintan Lalor Ave.* ☏ *057/862–1178* ⊕ *www.laoistourism.ie.*

 Sights

Laois Garden Trail

GARDEN | Connecting 10 of the county's celebrated formal gardens and expertly maintained privately owned ones, this driving route promotes the area's horticultural heritage. There's no set order for visiting the gardens; start the trail wherever you wish—although Portlaoise is a good base from which to begin—and spend as long as you'd like in each garden. To do unhurried justice to all 10 gardens, it'll take you at least two days, better still three if time permits. Stops include the state-run gardens at Emo Court and Heywood House, as well as Gash Gardens in Castletown, which offers a delightful river walk along the banks of the Nore; the demesne gardens of Castle Durrow, with its glorious scented roses; and the organically managed potager-style kitchen garden of Dunmore Country School, just outside Durrow. There is a charge for only one garden, at Ballintubbert (€5); admission to the others is free. ■TIP→ **Maps of the trail are available in Portlaoise Tourist Office.** ✉ *Portlaoise* ⊕ *www.laoistourism.ie.*

Laois Heritage Trail

SCENIC DRIVE | Stop by the Portlaoise Tourist Office to pick up a map of the Laois Heritage Trail, a signposted, daylong drive on quiet back roads that takes in 13 heritage sites, ranging from Abbeyleix to Emo Court. The circular trail starts in Borris-in-Ossory on the N7. ■TIP→ **Some sites along the trail charge an admission fee.** ✉ *Portlaoise Tourist Office, James Fintan Lalor Ave.* ⊕ *www.laoistourism.ie.*

Rock of Dunamase

ARCHAEOLOGICAL SITE | A dramatic 150-foot-high limestone outcrop, the famous Rock of Dunamase dominates the landscape east of Portlaoise. For this reason, it was used as a military stronghold. As far back as AD 140, its occupants kept watch against marauders, and it was fought over in turn by the Vikings, Normans, Irish, and English. Today it's crowned by the ruins of a 12th-century castle, once home to Diarmuid MacMurrough, king of Leinster, who precipitated the Norman invasion when he invited the famed and feared Norman leader Strongbow to Ireland to marry his daughter. Some of the castle's thick walls still stand. ■TIP→ **The main reason for visiting the Rock today is to take the short walk to its summit to enjoy the view of the Slieve Bloom Mountains to the north and the Wicklow Mountains to the south.** ✉ *N80 (Stradbally Rd.)* ⊹ *5 km (3 miles) east of Portlaoise.*

 Restaurants

Kelly's Steakhouse

$$$ | STEAKHOUSE | Just across the road from the Midlands Park Hotel, Kelly's Steakhouse expertly prepares cuts of Irish beef in all shapes and sizes, from a 20-ounce porterhouse T-bone to a more modest 10-ounce rib eye. The chef knows a thing or two about gradations, but if you want to try your own hand, the steak house offers the unique chance to cook the meat yourself over a volcanic black rock hot stone. **Known for:** prime cuts of Irish meat; cooking your own steak over a black rock hot stone; Ma Kelly's cheesecake. $ *Average main: €26* ✉ *Jessop St.* ⊹ *Opposite Midlands Park Hotel* ☏ *057/867–8588* ⊕ *www.midlandspark-hotel.com/kellys-steakhouse* ☉ *Closed Mon. No lunch.*

Hotels

★ The Heritage Killenard

$$$$ | RESORT | This hotel's spacious, light-filled atrium with its touches of marble, cherrywood, and mahogany is as elegant as its guest rooms, which look out over the parkland setting of an 18-hole course and across to the Slieve Bloom Mountains. **Pros:** a haven of peace, calm, and elegance; 5 km (3 mile) walking trail with exercise stations; the smoked haddock at breakfast is a winner. **Cons:** the grass cutters start early so prepare for a lawn-mower wake-up call around 6:30; isolated from any nearby towns; five-minute walk to the spa. ⑤ *Rooms from: €239* ✉ *Killenard* ⊕ *5 km (3 miles) south of Portarlington* ☎ *057/864–5500* ⊕ *www.theheritage.com* ➵ *98 rooms* ⑩ *Free breakfast.*

Ivyleigh House

$$ | B&B/INN | "The best of everything" is the maxim of affable owners Dinah and Jerry Campion and that is certainly evident the minute you step inside this elegant Georgian town house next to the Portlaoise train station—open fires, antiques, and sumptuously cozy sofas await you in the beige-on-brown, wood-accented sitting room. **Pros:** lavish breakfasts; luxury linens; convenient location for town. **Cons:** no baths, so it's a power shower only; pricey for this area; few extra frills. ⑤ *Rooms from: €125* ✉ *Intersection of Bank Pl. and Church St.* ☎ *057/862–2081* ⊕ *www.ivyleigh.com* ➵ *6 rooms* ⑩ *Free breakfast.*

Nightlife

Ramsbottom's Bar

BARS/PUBS | For a glimpse of old Ireland, call into Ramsbottom's in Lower Main Street where a log fire burns brightly beside comfy settees. This former grocery-cum-bar now sells only alcohol but reminders of its past are all around. The original bacon-slicing machine from the grocery shop is on display; walls are adorned with sepia-tinted photographs, whiskey and cigarette signs, and record sleeves featuring John McCormack and Bing Crosby, and bank notes from around the world are pinned to the bar. For €2 you can select your own five tunes from the jukebox, sit back, and enjoy a flawless pint. ✉ *101 Lower Main St.* ☎ *057/866–1298.*

Performing Arts

Dunamaise Arts Centre

ARTS CENTERS | This lively arts center has a 240-seat theater, an art gallery, and a friendly coffeehouse (closed Sunday). You may catch a professional production on tour or a local amateur show. The exhibition space displays the work of contemporary Irish artists. It's built into the back of the 18th-century stone courthouse on Church Street in a space that used to be the town jail. Caffe Latte serves sandwiches and salads at lunch, and afternoon tea. ✉ *Church St.* ☎ *057/866–3355* ⊕ *www.dunamaise.ie.*

Activities

GOLF
Heath Golf Club

GOLF | From early spring the dazzling blaze of yellow furze—also known as gorse—decorates the open heathland at this 18-hole course. The area has a colorful history, too, as the popular Irish politician Daniel O'Connell held meetings here in the mid-1830s. They've been playing golf on the Heath since the 1890s and the club dates from 1930. The course, open to the public, incorporates three natural lakes and is referred to as an "inland links." Good-value deals for visitors include special rates combining golf with a meal; or you can settle for a drink in the friendly "19 Hole" bar. ✉ *The Great Heath of Maryborough* ⊕ *5 km (3 miles) northeast of Portlaoise on main Dublin Rd.* ☎ *057/864–6533* ⊕ *www.theheathgc.ie* ⌚ *Feb.–July, Oct., and Nov., weekdays*

€15, weekends €20; Aug., Sept., Dec., and Jan., weekdays €17, weekends €22 ⚡ *18 holes, 6120 yards, par 72.*

★ Heritage Golf Resort

GOLF | Millions of dollars were spent on developing this 18-hole championship course—and it shows. A challenge for the pros but somehow forgiving to the amateur at the same time, Heritage has second-to-none facilities including a 38,000-square-foot clubhouse. A life-size bronze of Seve Ballesteros (by the renowned sports sculptor Paul Ferriter) greets you at the entrance to the course he designed here, which is noted for its mix of challenging doglegs and water traps (including five on-course lakes). Add four demanding par-5s to the mix and the result is a truly world-class parkland course. The development of luxury on-site accommodations has also increased the club's attractiveness to the visiting golfer. ⊠ *Killenard* ✛ *5 km (3 miles) south of Portarlington* ☎ *057/864–2301* ⊕ *www.heritageresort.ie* ✉ *Apr.–Oct., weekdays €45–€60, weekends €65–€80; Nov.–Mar., weekdays €40, weekends €45* ⚡ *18 holes, 7319 yards, par 72.*

Portarlington

13 km (8 miles) northeast of Portlaoise.

Built on the River Barrow in the late 17th century, Portarlington was originally an English settlement. Later, a Huguenot colony developed here, and French surnames are still common in the area. Some good examples of Georgian architecture can be seen in the town.

GETTING HERE AND AROUND

On the road between Mullingar and Portlaoise, Portarlington is a small crossroads town relatively free of traffic—it's well clear of the N7 so it misses out on the motorway trade. Tullamore is a 30-minute drive away, Portlaoise is 20 minutes, and Dublin is a 45-minute drive. There are several free parking lots in town. The Dublin–Cork train stops at Portarlington and there are regular Bus Éireann connections to the bigger towns and to Dublin.

Sights

Coolbanagher Church

RELIGIOUS SITE | Coolbanagher Church, the familiar name for the exquisite Church of St. John the Evangelist, was, like Emo Court and Gardens, designed by James Gandon. On view inside are Gandon's original 1795 plans and an elaborately sculpted 15th-century font from an earlier church that stood nearby. Adjacent to the church is Gandon's mausoleum for Lord Portarlington, his patron at Emo. The church is open only by advance telephone arrangement. ⊠ *Portarlington* ✛ *8½ km (5 miles) south of Portarlington on R419* ☎ *057/862–4143* ⊕ *www.mountmellickgroupofparishes.ie* ✉ *Free.*

★ Emo Court and Gardens

HOUSE | A quintessential landmark of Irish Palladian elegance, Emo Court is one of the finest large-scale country houses near Dublin that is open to the public. To come upon the house from the main drive, an avenue lined with magisterial Wellingtonia trees, is to experience one of Ireland's great treasure-house views. Begun in 1790 by James Gandon, architect of the Custom House and the Four Courts in Dublin, Emo is thought to be Gandon's only domestic work matching the grand scale of his Dublin civic buildings.

The ground-floor rooms have been beautifully restored and decorated and are prime examples of life on the grand scale. Among the highlights are the entrance hall, with trompe-l'oeil paintings in the apses on each side, and the library, which has a carved Italian-marble mantel. But the showstopper, and one of the finest rooms in Ireland, is the dome rotunda, inspired by the Roman Pantheon.

Marble pilasters with gilded Corinthian capitals support the rotunda's blue-and-white coffered dome. For the first time, several upstairs rooms are now open to the public following renovation during 2019. These include bedrooms with original features such as sash-style windows, cornice, and ceiling rose, while another room contains the architectural archives. One room has been turned into a gallery and is used to exhibit work from local and visiting artists. Guided tours are held every hour in summer. Emo's 55 acres of grounds include a 20-acre lake, lawns planted with yew trees, a small garden (the Clocker) with Japanese maples, and a larger one (the Grapery) with rare trees and shrubs. ■TIP➔ **Make time for a 3 km (2 mile) stroll around the attractive lake walkway. Afterward, visit the tearoom serving tasty snacks and light lunches.** ✉ *Emo* ⊹ *7 km (4½ miles) south of Portarlington* ☎ *057/862–6573* ⊕ *www.heritageireland. ie* 🎟 *Gardens free, house €8* ⊙ *House closed Oct.–Mar.*

Hotels

★ Roundwood House

$$ | B&B/INN | There's a dreamy beauty to this château-like mansion set on the slopes of the Slieve Bloom Mountains—as you arrive, a dark tree-lined avenue suddenly opens up to reveal a dramatically gorgeous Palladian villa, while some ducks, hens, and a Labrador called Rococo often form the welcoming party. **Pros:** characterful house filled with history; mature woodland is ideal for walks; elegant and airy rooms in the main house. **Cons:** dinner sometimes served at a communal table; no TVs; so many books, so little time. 💲 *Rooms from: €160* ✉ *Mountrath* ⊹ *5 km (3 miles) from Mountrath on scenic road to Kinnitty* ☎ *057/873–2120* ⊕ *www.roundwood-house.com* ↪ *10 rooms, 2 self-catering cottages* 🍴 *Free breakfast.*

Tullamore

27 km (17 miles) northwest of Portarlington.

The county seat of Offaly, Tullamore is a bustling market town that thrived during Ireland's economic boom that lasted from the mid-1990s until 2008; like many parts of Ireland it has suffered in the downturn, but the general feeling is that things are improving. The town's historical success was based on its location on the Grand Canal, one of Ireland's most important trading links during the 18th and 19th centuries.

GETTING HERE AND AROUND

A medium-size Midlands town, Tullamore is a transportation hub. Six roads converge here, meaning that market days at the end of the week are especially busy and free street parking is first-come, first-served. Dublin is just over an hour's drive, while the neighboring towns of Athlone, Mullingar, and Portlaoise are approximately 30 minutes away. Travelers are reasonably well served by Bus Éireann; routes connect to Dublin (two hours east) as well as towns north, south, and west of Tullamore. By train, Tullamore is 70 minutes from Dublin, 90 minutes from Galway, and two hours from Sligo. Train and bus services coalesce at Cormac Street in town.

Sights

Charleville Castle

CASTLE/PALACE | One relic of Tullamore's former splendor is found on the southwestern edge of town, where, if you take the road heading to Birr from the center of Tullamore, you'll find a storybook vision: Charleville Castle. Perhaps the finest neo-Gothic, British-style 19th-century castle in Ireland, its Flag Tower and turrets rise above its domain of 30 acres of woodland walks and gardens. The Georgian–Gothic Revival house was built as a symbol of English might triumphing over French force (the French revolutionary forces, to be exact, who had become a little too cozy with the Irish locals). In fact, the floor plan is even modeled on the Union Jack. Commissioned by Baron Tullamore and dating from 1812, the castle is a rural example of the work of architect Francis Johnston, who was responsible for many of Dublin's stately Georgian buildings. The interiors are somewhat the worse for wear—most are gigantic chambers with a few sticks of furniture—but the William Morris–designed dining room still has its original stenciled wallpaper.

Descended through the Bury family, who eventually lost their fortune and left no heirs, the castle became an orphan in the 1960s and is being slowly restored. Some parts of the building, such as the cantilevered oak staircase and the adjoining chapel, are in need of extensive repairs. Fund-raisers include open-air festivals on the grounds. The surrounding forest is said to be haunted by the spirits of the ancient Druids. The castle is open all year. In the summer guided tours leave every 40 minutes between 11 and 5, and in the winter at noon, 2, and 4. ⊠ *Tullamore* ⊕ *1½ km (1 mile) outside Tullamore on N52 to Birr* ☎ *057/932–3040* ⊕ *www.charlevillecastle.ie* ☑ *Tour from €20.*

Clara Bog Visitor Centre

NATURE PRESERVE | **FAMILY** | As one of the best remaining examples of an intact raised bog in western Europe, Clara Bog is home to protected wildlife species, including the rare dark tussock moth, the keeled skimmer, a powder-blue dragonfly, as well as two rare midges and a click beetle. Unique bog plants, such as sphagnum mosses and the pink rosemary (Offaly's county flower), can be seen. Clara Bog's visitor center—based in Clara library—provides unique insights into bog ecology and 10,000 years of natural and social history through touchscreen, text, and audiovisuals. The center is staffed seasonally by education guides (call in advance to check on opening hours). A five-minute walk from Clara railway station, Clara Bog is a wet environment (deep pools and quaking surfaces), so dress appropriately and stay on the boardwalk. ⊠ *Clara, Ballycumber Rd.* ⊕ *2 km (1 mile) southeast of Clara town* ☎ *093/68878* ⊕ *www.npws.ie* ⊗ *Closed Nov.–Apr.; May–Sept., closed weekends.*

★ Lough Boora Discovery Park

CITY PARK | **FAMILY** | This open expanse of once commercial, now exhausted, bog has been restored for a variety of leisure activities, from hiking and cycling to coarse angling and bird-watching (more than 150 species make their home here). When it was first established as a sanctuary in 2001 there were just 11 breeding pairs of gray partridge in the parkland—now there are several hundred of these ground-nesting birds, the last remaining population of them in Ireland. You're unlikely to see them, however, as they spend only one minute of each day in the air. Best of all, Lough Boora is home to one of Ireland's most unique sculpture parks. Along the **Sculpture Walk**, where golden plovers, lapwings, and starlings may accompany you, 24 large-scale sculptures made from local materials (including glacial stone, water, and willow) have been created by artists influenced by the legacy of the bogs. The result is some of the most creative environmental outdoor artwork anywhere in Ireland. To cite one example, the installation artist Mike Bulfin has turned a rusty old bog train into a cartoonish curve whose image will remain imprinted in your mind long after your visit to this magical place. The most recent sculpture, the *Gathering of Stones*, features a different type of stone from each of the four provinces in Ireland, creating a ring fort and circular wall. It reflects the Irish diaspora through "emigrant stones" laid out in a cruciform shape embracing people from all corners of the world. A café serves snacks from 10 am to 6 pm.

In the spring, the gardens at Emo Court rival the splendor of its Neoclassical-style salons—here, a section of parkland abloom with bluebells.

An off-road bike trail runs for 22 km (13 miles). You can choose from five different looped color-coded walks, while guided walking tours run April–September. ■TIP→ **Bring your binoculars: bird hides are located throughout the park to provide the opportunities to spy on birds such as golden plover and lapwing.** ⊠ *Boora, 3 km (2 miles) north of Kilcormac* ⊕ *Turn off R537; Lough Boora is in townland of Leabeg* ☎ *057/934–5978* ⊕ *www.lough-boora.com* ✉ *Free; bike rental €5 per hr, parking €4 full day* ⊘ *Closed weekdays Oct.–Mar.*

★ **Tullamore Dew Visitor Centre**
WINERY/DISTILLERY | Along the banks of the Grand Canal, Tullamore Dew Visitor Centre—in a 19th-century bonded warehouse—trades heavily on its historic Irish identity. Highlights include whiskey tours, tasting sessions, and a whiskey master class. In 2014, a €35 million distillery opened at Clonminch on the outskirts of town, bringing whiskey production back to the area after a gap of 60 years. The company embarked on a €10 million global marketing campaign, and today it's the world's second-largest and fastest-growing Irish whiskey brand—just behind Jameson. It's all a far cry from humble beginnings in 1829 when Tullamore Distillery was founded. It was greatly expanded under the aegis of Daniel E. Williams, whose family became joint shareholders, and his own initials (D.E.W.) were added to the whiskey's name, inspiring the slogan "Give every man his Dew" (which appeared on the bottles for many years). Triple distilled, and made from a unique blend of single malt, pot still, and grain whiskey, it is regarded by connoisseurs as exceptionally smooth. Guided tours include the Curious Taster's Journey (€16), which includes a triple tasting, a Whiskey Wise master class (€29) with six tastings of rare whiskeys, and the Ultimate Distillery Experience (€90) lasting three hours, where you can create your own unique whiskey and sample some exclusive blends. ■TIP→ **For an extra-special tipple ask for a bottle of the limited-edition Old Bonded Warehouse whiskey,**

sold exclusively on-site and priced at €58. Check the website for tour and tasting schedules. ⊠ *Bury Quay* ☎ *057/932–5015* ⊕ *www.tullamoredew.com* ✉ *Free entry to shop.*

Hotels

Annaharvey Farm

$ | B&B/INN | Dedicated to all things equestrian, this family farmhouse, now in the fifth generation of the same family, was once an old-world grain barn but has been converted into elegant accommodations, with pitch-pine floors, massive roof beams, and open fireplaces. **Pros:** secluded location; horse-riding packages; convenient to Clonmacnoise and Birr Castle. **Cons:** bathrooms are small; neighing horses may disturb your slumber; meals must be booked in advance. ⑤ *Rooms from: €90* ⊠ *Tullamore* ⊹ *6 km (4 miles) outside of Tullamore town on the Portarlington road* ☎ *057/934–3544* ⊕ *www.annaharveyfarm.ie* ⊘ *Closed Nov.–mid-Mar.* ⇆ *7 rooms* ⦿� *Free breakfast.*

Activities

GOLF

Esker Hills Golf Club

GOLF | Studded with natural lakes and woodlands, as well as excellent sand-based greens and valleys, Esker Hills is an 18-hole championship course. Masterfully designed by Christy O'Connor Jr., it is regarded as one of Ireland's leading inland links–type courses. It is playable all year round and welcomes visitors. The club takes its name from eskers, or mounds of sand or gravel left by streams of melted ice, which provide the dramatic undulations, never mind the challenges, of the course. ⊠ *N52, Esker Hills* ⊹ *5 km (3 miles) north of Tullamore* ☎ *057/935–5999* ⊕ *www.eskerhillsgolf.com* ✉ *Weekdays €30, weekends €35* ⚐ *18 holes, 6626 yards, par 71.*

Kilbeggan

11 km (7 miles) north of Tullamore.

GETTING HERE AND AROUND

The small town of Kilbeggan is on the main M6 Dublin–Athlone route; the nearest large town is Tullamore, 15 minutes south on the N52. There is free parking in town. Regular buses serving the busy Dublin–Galway route stop at Kilbeggan. Athlone is a 15-minute journey by bus, and Dublin is an 80-minute ride.

Sights

Kilbeggan Distillery Experience

WINERY/DISTILLERY | It's the whiskey (the Irish spell their traditional tipple with an "e") that brings most people to the unassuming little town of Kilbeggan, home of the Kilbeggan Distillery Experience, the oldest pot-still distillery in the world and the last of its type in Ireland. Established in 1757, it closed as a functioning distillery in 1954, but has since found new life as a museum of industrial archaeology, illustrating the process of Irish pot-whiskey distillation and the social history of the workers. The glorious timber waterwheel has been restored and repainted, and is now creaking again. Four different types of tours are available. The one-hour Apprentice tour (€14) includes tasting three whiskeys; on the 90-minute Distillers tour (€30), you get to taste all four Kilbeggan core brands: Kilbeggan single grain, Kilbeggan Irish whiskey, Tyrconnell single malt, and Connemara peated single malt. The Artisan tour (€65), which lasts 2½ hours, is sensory and focuses on an enticing mix of cheese pairings, essential oils, and premium whiskeys. For the serious whiskey lover, the Connoisseur Experience tour, costing €85 and lasting 3½ hours, includes tasting all the whiskeys in the Kilbeggan portfolio and bottling your own sample from an aging cask to take home. ⊠ *Lower Main St.* ☎ *057/933–2134* ⊕ *www.kilbegganwhiskey.com* ✉ *Free for shop and bar.*

Mullingar

24 km (15 miles) northeast of Kilbeggan.

The Irish are great ones for wrapping an insult up in a lyrical turn of phrase. Rather than describe a woman as overweight they'll say with a wink that she's "beef to the heels, like a Mullingar heifer." Of course, the phrase also illustrates Mullingar's role as Ireland's beef capital, a town surrounded by rich countryside where cattle trading has historically been one of the chief occupations. It's also County Westmeath's major town—a busy commercial and cattle-trading center on the Royal Canal, midway between two large, attractive lakes, Lough Owel and Lough Ennel. Although best used as a base to tour the surrounding countryside, Mullingar has some sights worthy of your time.

GETTING HERE AND AROUND

Mullingar is a busy town on the N4 Longford–Dublin route. Although it is bypassed by the highway, traffic in town can still come to a standstill at certain times of the day. The Dublin–Sligo train stops at Mullingar, and buses run to Athlone (one hour) and Dublin (90 minutes).

VISITOR INFORMATION

CONTACTS Mullingar Discover Ireland Centre. ⊠ *Market Sq.* ☎ *044/934–8650* ⊕ *www.discoverireland.ie/lakelands.*

 ## Sights

Belvedere House & Gardens

HOUSE | FAMILY | A stately mid-18th-century hunting lodge with extensive gardens, Belvedere House occupies a beautiful spot on the northeast shore of Lough Ennel. Access to the mansion is through the servants' entrance—so you can see what life behind the scenes was like back then. The interiors are a quirky mix of Georgian stateliness and Victorian charm. The noted bow and Palladian windows have great parkland views sloping down to the lake and its islands.

It was built in 1740 by architect Richard Cassels for Robert Rochfort, 1st Earl of Belvedere, and his wife, Mary. She was accused of having an affair with Robert's brother Arthur, which was denied, but she was locked away in the Rochfort's ancestral home at Gaulstown House for 31 years on a charge of adultery. During this time, Robert had considerable work carried out on Belvedere House to make it more homey; one of the most impressive features he commissioned was the rococo plasterwork ceiling by the renowned stucco artist Bartholomew Cramillion. He spent much of his family fortune dotting the gardens of the estate with "follies," including the Jealous Wall, a gigantic mock-castle ruin that served to cover up a view of the adjoining estate, owned by another brother, also hated.

You can walk around the 160 acres of the estate and 10 km (6 miles) of woodland trails; some walks take you past the Gothic arch folly. Also on the grounds are a café and three children's play areas, which include a zipline. At the back of the house look out for the new sculpture of King Malachy, the last High King of Ireland, made from the stump of an old oak tree. ⊠ *N52 ⊕ 5 km (2½ miles) south of Mullingar* ☎ *044/933–8960* ⊕ *www.belvedere-house.ie* ⌛ *House and parkland €8.*

Cathedral of Christ the King

RELIGIOUS SITE | The town's largest structure is the Renaissance-style Catholic Cathedral of Christ the King, completed in 1939. Note the facade's finely carved stonework, and the mosaics of St. Patrick and St. Anne by the Russian artist Boris Anrep in the spacious interior. There's a museum in the cathedral, and tours are available in the spring and summer by appointment (call for times). Otherwise, wander through anytime the doors are open, knowing you will be restricted when mass is in session. ⊠ *Mary St.* ☎ *044/934–8338* ⊕ *www.mullingarparish.ie.*

Hotels

Mullingar Park Hotel

$$ | HOTEL | On the outskirts of Mullingar, this stylish hotel has built up a solid reputation, both for its inviting accommodations and the high quality of its cuisine. **Pros:** amenities including gym, pool, and sauna; free car parking; conveniently situated. **Cons:** business conferences can take over; popular with weddings; twins rooms are small. $ *Rooms from: €155* ✉ *Dublin Rd.* ☎ *044/933–7500* ⊕ *www.mullingarparkhotel.com* ➾ *95 rooms* ⦾ *Free breakfast.*

Activities

GOLF

Mullingar Golf Club

GOLF | Mullingar Golf Club is a demanding—some say roller-coaster—18-hole course designed by James Braid. Mature oak, beech, and ash trees surround the idyllic course in undulating parkland, making precision a priority with every shot. Many holes have special features but the trees are common to all of them, presenting an old-style arboreal challenge, which visiting golfers enjoy. You can book your tee time online. The club is open to visitors from Monday to Saturday and is noted for the warmth of its welcome. ✉ *Belvedere* ✛ *Take Exit 15 off M4 and follow signs for Belvedere House along R400; club is 7 km (4 miles) along this road on right* ☎ *044/934–8366* ⊕ *www.mullingargolfclub.ie* ⌚ *Mon. €20, Tues.–Fri. €35, Sat. €45* ↟ *18 holes, 6685 yards, par 72.*

Castlepollard

21 km (13 miles) north of Mullingar.

A pretty village of multihue 18th- and 19th-century houses laid out around a large, triangular green, Castlepollard is also home to Tullynally Castle and Gardens, the largest castle in Ireland that still functions as a family home.

GETTING HERE AND AROUND

The small rural town of Castlepollard sits at a crossroads between Cavan and Mullingar, which is the nearest large town, 20 minutes south on the narrow R394. Free parking is available in the Square or on side streets. There is a daily bus service to Dublin (the trip takes two hours), and a route once a week to Mullingar.

Sights

★ Tullynally Castle and Gardens

CASTLE/PALACE | It's hard to figure out which is more famous: Tullynally's storybook castle or the magical parklands that surround this fabled family seat. And this is not just any family: the Pakenhams are the famous Irish tribe that has given us Elizabeth Longford (whose biography of Queen Victoria is in most libraries) and Antonia Fraser, wife of the late playwright Harold Pinter and best-selling biographer of Mary, Queen of Scots, among others. In fact, Tullynally—the name, literally translated, means "Hill of the Swans"—has been the home of 10 generations of the family, which also married into the earldom of Longford.

As a result of an 18th-century "Gothicization," the former Georgian house was transformed into a faux castle by architect Francis Johnston. The resulting 600 feet of battlements were not just for show, as the earls were foes of Catholic emancipation. Inside, the family has struggled to make the vast salons warm and cozy—a bit of a losing battle. The house really comes into its own as a stage set for the surrounding park—the gray-stone structure is so long and has so many towers it looks like a miniature town from a distance. The total circumference of the building's masonry adds up to nearly ½ km (¼ mile) and includes a motley agglomeration of towers, turrets, and crenellations.

Today, more attention is given to the beautiful parkland, in part due to the passion of Thomas Pakenham, a tree-hugger extraordinaire who founded the Irish Tree Society in 1992 and authored several books, his most famous being *Meetings with Remarkable Trees* (1996). The estate's rolling parkland was laid out in 1760, much along the lines you see today, with fine rhododendrons, numerous trees (oak, ash, sycamore, Scots pine, beech, silver fir, larch, and spruce, among others), and two ornamental lakes. A garden walk through the grounds in front of the castle leads to a spacious flower garden, a pond, a grotto, and walled gardens. You'll also find a Tibetan garden, a Chinese garden, and a kitchen garden, one of the largest in Ireland, with a row of old Irish yew trees. ■ TIP➜ Don't miss the forest path, which takes you around the perimeter of the parkland and affords excellent views of the romantic castle. After your walk, enjoy a visit to the Tullynally Tea Rooms in a renovated Georgian stable block, which serves lunches such as lasagna, quiche, and preconcert supper roasts. ⊠ *Castlepollard* ⊹ *1½ km (1 mile) west of Castlepollard on R395 road to Granard* ☎ *044/966–1159* ⊕ *www.tullynallycastle.com* ✉ *Garden only €7. House tours must be prebooked, minimum 20 people, and cost €14, includes entry to garden* ⊘ *Closed Oct.–Mar., and Mon.–Wed.*

Fore

5 km (3 miles) east of Castlepollard.

You've heard of the seven wonders of the ancient world, but here in the heart of the Irish Midlands is a tiny village with seven wonders all to itself! According to Irish myth, this is the place where water runs uphill, where there's a tree that will not burn and water that will not boil,

among other fantastical occurrences. The village is known not only for its legend, but also for its medieval church and the remains (supposedly the largest in Ireland) of a Benedictine abbey.

GETTING HERE AND AROUND

Fore is on a quiet country road between Castlepollard and Oldcastle on the R195. The nearest main town is Mullingar, a 30-minute drive. There's free parking in the village. Fore cannot be reached by train or bus.

 Sights

Fore Abbey

RELIGIOUS SITE | The spectacular remains of Fore Abbey dominate the simple village—its structure is massive and its imposing square towers and loophole windows make it resemble a castle rather than an abbey. This site is now part of the newly designated Ireland's Ancient East. It is worth taking time to explore the 3 km (2 mile) looped walk, St. Feichin's Way, and ponder the Seven Wonders of Fore, which include water flowing uphill, a tree that will not burn, and a mill without a millrace. ⊠ *Fore* ⊹ *From Castlepollard take R195 eastbound and 4 km (2½ miles) along this road take minor road signposted to Fore and follow it for 3 km (2 miles)* ⊕ *www. voicesfromthedawn.com.*

Cavan

36 km (22 miles) north of Fore, 114 km (71 miles) northwest of Dublin.

Like all the larger towns of the region, Cavan is growing and prosperous. It is perhaps best known for its crystal factory. But as one of the main transportation hubs of the Midlands, Cavan has also attracted an impressive array of restaurants and hotels, so this is a fine base for exploring this region, which lies near the border to Northern Ireland. There are two central streets: Main Street is like many other streets in similar Irish towns, with its pubs and shops; Farnham Street has Georgian houses, churches, a court-house, and a bus station.

GETTING HERE AND AROUND

Cavan is a thriving market town on the main N3 from Navan to Enniskillen in Northern Ireland. There is metered pay-parking in the town center. The town and surrounding south Ulster area, including neighboring Monaghan, relies on an extensive bus network for public transport. Cavan is equidistant from Belfast and Galway with a three-hour travel time to both cities by bus. Bus Éireann serves Cavan on Galway–Belfast, Athlone–Belfast, and Dublin–Donegal Expressway routes, and there is week-day service to small towns throughout Cavan and Monaghan.

CONTACTS Cavan Bus Office. ✉ Farnham St. ☎ 049/433–1709.

VISITOR INFORMATION

CONTACTS Cavan Tourist Office. ✉ Farnham St. ☎ 049/433–1942 ⊕ www.thisiscavan.ie.

Sights

Bear Essentials Ireland

MUSEUM | FAMILY | Relive your childhood at this fun stop for all ages where you can view the largest collection of teddy bears in Ireland. Each bear is handcrafted in the workshop from the finest mohair. The Silver Bear Centre and gift shop is next door. There's a "Teddy Bear Hospital" on-site, where you can bring your damaged teddy for repair or redesign, and the shop also sells "My First Teddy," a baby bear for infants. Free 30-minute tours of the visitor center must be prebooked. ✉ Tirnawannagh, Bawnboy ✛ 23 km (18 miles) northwest of Cavan town ☎ 049/952–3461 ⊕ www.bearessentials.ie ✆ Free.

Restaurants

★ MacNean's House & Restaurant

$$$$ | IRISH | Run by Neven Maguire, one of Ireland's top chefs, MacNean's is one of the best restaurants in the country; in fact, there's a waiting list of up to two years for weekends. The Menu Prestige, at €89 (€139, including wine), delivers a staggering eight courses. **Known for:** delicious local duck; eight-course dinner menu; very difficult to get a table. ⑤ Average main: €89 ✉ Main St., Blacklion ☎ 071/985–3022 ⊕ www.nevenmaguire.com ⊘ Closed Mon. and Tues. No lunch Wed.–Sat. ⋔ Jacket required.

★ The Olde Post Inn

$$$$ | IRISH | A restored, stone former post office in an elegantly landscaped garden, the Olde Post Inn has won a clutch of awards and, as a result, is often booked solid. Sea bass, steak, game, and bacon and cabbage terrine are main-course favorites and highlight local and seasonal ingredients. **Known for:** outstanding venison; impressive wine selection; dreamy rural location. ⑤ Average main: €49 ✉ Cloverhill, N54 ✛ 11 km (8 miles) north of Cavan town ☎ 047/55555 ⊕ www.theoldepostinn.com ⊘ Closed Mon. and Tues. No lunch Wed.–Sat.

🛏 Hotels

Cabra Castle

$$$ | HOTEL | With its collection of mock-Gothic towers, turrets, and crenellations, along with rumors of paranormal activity, Cabra Castle has been deemed one of the world's scariest hotels; the Irish Ghosthunters Association has confirmed that it was indeed a place visited by spirits. **Pros:** stunning views of the countryside; superb range of rooms; Victorian Gothic charm. **Cons:** emphasis on weddings; rumors of ghostly goings-on; some rooms in castle are small. ⑤ Rooms from: €198 ✉ Carrickmacross Rd., Kingscourt ✛ 45 km (27 miles) south of Cavan, on R179 ☎ 042/966–7030

Tullynally Castle, the largest in Ireland—just a small portion is shown here—is surrounded by spectacular parkland, forest paths, and kitchen gardens.

⊕ www.cabracastle.com ⇌ 105 rooms ⦾ Free breakfast.

★ Farnham Estate Spa and Golf Resort

$$$ | HOTEL | A blend of stone, wood, and glass, the Farnham Estate—one of the top spots in the Midlands to detox and purify—exudes the promise of contentment over its 1,300 acres, as well as offering a superb choice of dining options. **Pros:** revitalizing spa; cathedral-like silences of the grounds; nature trails. **Cons:** slow service at peak times; spa gets very busy; weddings and conferences can take over. Ⓢ *Rooms from: €179* ✉ *Farnham Estate, Killashandra Rd., Farnham* ☎ *049/437–7700* ⊕ *www.farnhamestate.ie* ⚐ *Reservations essential* ⇌ *158 rooms* ⦾ *Free breakfast.*

Slieve Russell Hotel Golf and Country Club

$$ | HOTEL | Outdoors types, especially golfers, prick up their ears when they hear of the facilities on offer at this modern country hotel set on 300 acres—apart from two golf courses, it also has an excellent health club. **Pros:** opulent rooms, all with large beds; excellent

dining options; convenient place to break up a journey between Dublin and Sligo. **Cons:** busy with families during school breaks; unimpressive exterior; late-night noise in some areas. Ⓢ *Rooms from: €165* ✉ *Off N87, 26 km (16 miles) west of Cavan, Cranaghan* ✛ *Take N3 to Belturbet, then take left turn for Ballyconnell and hotel is 8 km (5 miles) along this road* ☎ *049/952–6444* ⊕ *www.slieverussell.ie* ⇌ *222 rooms* ⦾ *Free breakfast.*

 Activities

GOLF

County Cavan Golf Club

GOLF | Visitors are welcome at this beautifully manicured 18-hole course, set amid parkland in the heart of the southern Ulster lakelands. The Cavan Club has a long pedigree stretching back to 1894; it moved to its present location in 1920. The visual reshaping included work on the fairways lined with mature trees and present a challenge, especially on holes 14–18. The 197-yard 10th is difficult from a tee-box in front of the clubhouse to a new green under an old chestnut tree. The club pro, Bill Noble, holds regular lessons. Golfers can sharpen their pitching, chipping, bunker, and putting techniques in a top-notch practice area. ⊠ *Arnmore House, Drumelis* ☎ *049/433–1541* ⊕ *www.cavangolf.ie* ✉ *Mon. and Tues. €10, Wed.–Sun. €25* 🏌 *18 holes, 6164 yards, par 70.*

Longford Town

37 km (23 miles) southwest of Cavan, 124 km (77 miles) northwest of Dublin.

Longford, the seat of County Longford and a typical, small, market-town community, is rich in literary associations, though after Oliver Goldsmith, the names in the county's pantheon of writers may draw a blank from all but the most dedicated Irish literature enthusiasts. Longford town provides a good base for exploring the countryside surrounding it. A day trip to the pretty heritage village of Ardagh (10 km [7 miles] southeast of Longford town), with its quaint houses and village green, is a popular option. Tours of the village may be booked through Ardagh Heritage Centre (☎ *086/302–7602*). The talk of the county, however, has been the opening of the glitzy new Center Parcs near Ballymahon, which has turned a forest into a playground and has the potential to revolutionize tourism in this quiet backwater.

GETTING HERE AND AROUND

Longford is on the N4 linking Mullingar and Carrick-on-Shannon. It's easily accessible by car, and town parking is generally not a problem. Shop around, as some parking is free, while other streets are metered. Unlike many Midlands towns, Longford is doubly blessed with both train and bus links. Convenient for making connections, buses stop outside Longford train station. Bus Éireann routes fan out in all directions. Dublin

Airport and the city are 2¼–2½ hours away, and Belfast is a four-hour ride. There's also a cross-border bus from Longford to Derry operated in conjunction with Ulsterbus; journey time is four hours. The town is on the main Irish Rail Dublin–Sligo railway line: Dublin is 1¾ hours away and Sligo is 1¼ hours.

CONTACTS Longford Railway Station. ⊠ *Convent Rd., Longford* ☎ *043/334–5208.*

VISITOR INFORMATION

CONTACTS Longford Tourism Office. ⊠ *Market Sq., Longford* ☎ *043/334–2577.*

 Sights

Casey's Bogwood Sculptures

MUSEUM | A lovely spot near Longford Town is Newtowncashel, on the banks of Lough Ree, where you can visit Casey's Bogwood Sculptures, a fascinating workshop and showroom run by sculptors Michael and Kevin Casey. The center displays sculptures and keepsakes made from bog oak and bog yew, which is hewn from the 5,000-year-old trees submerged and ultimately preserved by the area's ancient peatlands. Their handiwork includes birds and fish, while other pieces furnish churches and sanctuaries. The owners will tell you the story of how they re-created froglike creatures called the *lucht na fathi* (the swamp people), inspired by a mix of local tales and Celtic mysticism. ⊠ *Barley Harbour, Newtowncashel* ✛ *From Longford, drive 14 km (9 miles) on N63 to Lanesborough, then take R392 for 2 km (1 mile) and follow signs for Turreen–Newtowncashel* ☎ *043/332–5297* ⊕ *www.bogoak.ie* ✉ *Free* ☉ *Closed Sun.*

Strokestown Park House & Irish National Famine Museum

MUSEUM | The highlight of a trip to Strokestown in County Roscommon is the Irish National Famine Museum in the stable yard of Strokestown Park House. The museum tells the story of the devastating Irish potato blight in the 1840s, which is now regarded as one of the greatest social disasters in 19th-century Europe. Two million people—about a quarter of the population of Ireland—either died or emigrated and their harrowing story is well worth exploring. Museum exhibits include original famine documents found during the restoration of the house; it's a remarkable contrast to the opulent surroundings of the Georgian Palladian mansion and its 6 acres of restored garden, which includes a fernery, rose garden, and lily pond representative of horticultural practices and garden architecture from the 1740s. The Strokestown Park House landlord, Major Denis Mahon, was assassinated in November 1847 at the height of the famine. A poignant glass memorial wall bears the names of 1,492 tenants from the estate who boarded famine ships to Quebec. Almost half died on their way to Canada. Guided tours of the house are held three times daily in the main tourist season, and once in winter. ■TIP→ It **is not possible to tour the house on your own—all visitors must join a guided tour.** ✉ *Strokestown* ✛ *30-min drive west of Longford Town on N5* ☎ *071/963–3013* ⊕ *www.strokestownpark.ie* 🎫 *House, museum, and gardens from €10.*

🍴 Restaurants

★ The Purple Onion

$$ | IRISH | Originally a standard public house with low ceilings, this Shannon-side resting place on the main street of a tiny village to the west of Longford Town has been transformed into a gourmet's delight—a special gastropub, abustle with locals and tourists alike. Specialties include Thornhill duck, baked sea bream, and renowned John Stone steaks from an artisanal butcher specializing in Irish grass-fed beef. **Known for:** duck and artisanal-butcher steaks; delicious Toblerone cheesecake; good-value early-bird menu. ⑤ *Average main: €24*

✉ *Main St., Tarmonbarry* ✛ *From Longford Town drive 10 km (6 miles) west on N5* ☎ *043/335–9919* ⊕ *www.purpleonion. ie* ⊗ *Closed Mon. No lunch Tues.–Thurs.*

Hotels

Center Parcs Longford Forest

$$$$ | RESORT | Rising out of the flat bogland and forest, Center Parcs is a huge new family-friendly resort that may have been developed for the Irish family travel market, but its wide variety of accommodations, amenities, and activities makes it a great option for visiting families with kids who might want a break from the typical castles-and-cliffs Irish vacation. **Pros:** luxury accommodation; biggest water park in Ireland; wide range of activities. **Cons:** minimum three-night stay; restaurant reservations essential; many activities cost extra. ⑤ *Rooms from: €299* ✉ *Center Parcs, Newcastle Rd, Ballymahon, Longford* ✛ *3 km (2 miles) east of Ballymahon on Newcastle Rd.* ☎ *1890/995–588* ⊕ *www. centerparcs.ie* 🛏 *466 cottages, 30 apartments* ¶⃝ *No meals.*

Keenan's Boutique Hotel

$$ | HOTEL | Barry Keenan is the fifth generation of his family since 1838 to run this first-rate hotel overlooking the Shannon, with a quality restaurant perfectly capable of challenging the Purple Onion next door for culinary polish and panache. **Pros:** hospitable family-run operation; great tree-lined walks along the riverbank; good bar and restaurant. **Cons:** Tarmonbarry is best for just one night on your way east or west; a long way from the bright lights; rooms are on the small side. ⑤ *Rooms from: €120* ✉ *On main N5, Tarmonbarry* ✛ *8 km (5 miles) west of Longford Town* ☎ *043/332–6052* ⊕ *www.keenanshotel.ie* 🛏 *12 rooms* ¶⃝ *Free breakfast.*

Viewmount House

$$ | B&B/INN | The exquisite 400-year-old house, once owned by the Earl of

Longford, has been restored to its former charm; the bedrooms are full of character and have impressive period wallpapers and antique mahogany wardrobes and beds. **Pros:** antique charm with modern luxuries; lovely gardens; restaurant with good-value multicourse dinners. **Cons:** 20-minute walk into town; bland suburban location; expensive for this area. *⑤ Rooms from: €170 ✉ Dublin Rd., Longford ⊹ 2 km (1 mile) outside Longford Town, just off old Dublin road (R393) ☎ 043/334–1919 ⊕ www.viewmounthouse.com ⊃ 12 rooms ⏐◎⏐ Free breakfast.*

Performing Arts

Backstage Theatre
DANCE | This theater, the center of a thriving local arts scene, is on the grounds of the local Gaelic Athletic Association club. Catch a local match before heading into the theater for a dose of drama, dance, classical music, or opera. The theater and club are located a mile outside Longford on the road to Athlone. *✉ Farneyhoogan, Longford ☎ 043/334–7888 ⊕ www.backstage.ie.*

Anthony Trollope Trail

Trail starts in the village of Drumsna, 16 km (10 miles) north of Longford Town.

GETTING HERE AND AROUND
The Trollope Trail is centered in Drumsna, a village 10 minutes from Carrick-on-Shannon and 30 minutes from Longford Town. Dublin is a two-hour drive along the N4. Sligo lies 30 minutes north on the N4. Head west across the Plains of Mayo and two hours' driving will take you to Galway.

Sights

Anthony Trollope Trail
TRAIL | This trail, created to honor the celebrated English Victorian novelist Anthony Trollope (1815–82), takes in 27 locations throughout Leitrim and incorporates many fascinating topographical spots, including an area along the River Shannon known as Flaggy Bottoms. Trollope, a senior civil servant, was sent to Drumsna in 1843 to investigate the financial affairs of the postmaster. While living there he wrote his first novel, *The Macdermots of Ballycloran,* drawing inspiration from the nearby ruin of Headford House. A leaflet and information on the trail is available from the tourist office in Carrick-on-Shannon (*☎ 071/962–0170*). A series of events was held in 2015 to mark his bicentenary and helped rekindle interest in the man who introduced pillar boxes to both Ireland and Britain.

Athlone

34 km (21 miles) southwest of Longford Town, 127 km (79 miles) west of Dublin, 121 km (75 miles) east of Limerick.

★ The mighty Shannon flows majestically through the heart of Athlone, yet for years it seemed as if the town was happy to turn its back on one of Europe's great waterways. That trend has been well and truly reversed, and there is a real buzz of regeneration. The area around Athlone Castle has been transformed into a veritable "Left Bank," with the Luan Gallery attracting culture vultures from all over Ireland. On both sides of the Shannon, new restaurants and stylishly modern architecture have sprung up on streets lined with 200-year-old buildings that have been given some imaginative repurposing alongside one of Ireland's most architecturally dazzling churches. Look out, too, for the stunning sculpture of the singer John Count McCormack, a famous Athlonian. Once upon a time, tourists were few and far between in what was cuttingly termed the "dead center" of Ireland, but the renaissance has made Athlone an increasingly attractive destination.

GETTING HERE AND AROUND

Athlone is one of the Midlands' largest towns and on busy days its long main street can take 30 minutes to drive end to end. Although the main Dublin N6 motorway has considerably eased congestion, this is still a place where delays are inevitable. Parking is available on the street, in paid lots, and at shopping centers. The drive to Dublin takes two hours, while Galway is 90 minutes west.

With its central location, Athlone is an important Bus Éireann hub with connecting expressway services to more than 20 principal towns and cities as well as dozens of smaller destinations across Ireland. Some routes are operated in conjunction with Ulsterbus. Trains branch out in three main directions from Athlone: southwest to Galway, west to Westport, and east to Dublin. The east–west intercity Irish Rail Galway–Dublin service takes 1¾ hours to reach Dublin.

CONTACTS Athlone Railway Station. ⊠ Southern Station Rd. ☎ 090/647–3300.

VISITOR INFORMATION

CONTACTS Athlone Tourist Office. ⊠ Athlone Castle, Castle St. ☎ 090/649–4630 ⊕ www.athlone.ie.

 ## Sights

Athlone Castle
CASTLE/PALACE | FAMILY | Bold and imposing, Athlone Castle stands beside the River Shannon. A raft of dazzling exhibitions are housed inside this 13th-century Norman stronghold. After their defeat at the Battle of the Boyne in 1691, the Irish retreated to Athlone and made the river their first line of defense. The castle,

which is now more than 800 years old, has played a strategic role in Irish history. Eight exhibition spaces—in the main building as well as the keep and the armory—detail this enthralling chronological story and that of the town from the earliest settlement up to modern trading times. Sculptural forms convey human figures that bring the characters of Athlone to life in an engaging way. They sit cheek by jowl with 3-D maps, audiovisuals, and weapons, like a bow and arrow, that allow hands-on experiences for both children and adults. You will feel right at the center of things with the 360-degree view of events of the Siege of Athlone in 1690. It's not your typical Irish fairy-tale castle, but it is fun, and kids especially love the interactive game "How to Capture a Castle." It's hard to beat on a wet day in the Midlands. A fascinating permanent exhibition focuses on the life of the singer John Count McCormack, who was born in Athlone in 1884. Programs from the Dublin Amateur Operatic Society, his Papal Chain presented to him in 1928, a montage of photographs, and HMV records with his signature song, "I Hear you Calling Me," are on show. Cabinets contain a silver cup from his admirers in Philadelphia and a cup presented by the Friendly Sons of St. Patrick, New York. McCormack sang in the Metropolitan Opera House in New York opposite Dame Nellie Melba in 1910 and continued to sing at the Met until 1918. The castle gatehouse serves as the town's tourist office. ■ TIP→ **You can save up to 10% on the admission charge by prebooking tickets online.** ⊠ St. Peter's Square ☎ 090/644–2130 ⊕ www.athlone-castle.ie ⊠ €8 ⊗ Closed Mon. and Tues. Nov.–mid-Mar.

Luan Gallery
MUSEUM | The Luan Gallery has created a much-needed municipal space to showcase the work of local artists from throughout the Midlands. Since its opening in 2012, Athlone's cultural status has risen a few notches, and this

A Great Irish Tenor

John Count McCormack (1884–1945) was perhaps the finest lyric tenor Ireland has produced. Born in Athlone, he recorded 600 records from 1914 to 1918 and made the Hollywood film *Song of My Heart*. A magnificent bronze sculpture of McCormack stands as the centerpiece of a civic park dedicated as a permanent memorial to him in 2014 beside Athlone Civic Centre. Created by the Irish artist Rory Breslin and designed in a relaxed pose, the sculpture stands atop a 4-ton plinth. It marks the starting point of a self-guided walking trail covering 12 stops including the house in which he was born and his old school. It also takes in a memorial bust on Grace Road by the Shannon unveiled in 1970.

contemporary visual-arts gallery, idyllically sited on the River Shannon, has been well supported by both townspeople and tourists. While it organizes exhibitions and guided tours featuring both emerging and established local artists, the Luan also draws on the national and international permanent collection of the Irish Museum of Modern Art in Dublin. ⊠ *Grace Rd.* ☎ *090/644–2154* ⊕ *www. athloneartsandtourism.ie* ⊘ *Closed Mon.*

St. Peter and St. Paul Catholic Church
RELIGIOUS SITE | Sparkling with its restored granite walls, St. Peter and St. Paul Catholic Church is a striking Baroque ecclesiastical landmark that many come to see. Built in a completely different style from that generally adopted in Ireland, the church opened on June 29, 1937 (the feast day of the patron saints of St. Peter and St. Paul). Repair work on the impressive interior included redecoration of the vaulted ceiling, walls, floors, and pews. Dominating the skyline for many miles around, the twin campaniles symbolize the saints, while the squat copper dome adds to the overall grace of this much-loved building. Look out for the six fine stained-glass windows from the famed Harry Clarke Studios in Dublin. The tribute window to St. Patrick is a riot of glorious color. ⊠ *Market Sq.* ☎ *090/649–2171* ⊕ *www.sspeterandpaulsparishathlone.com.*

Restaurants

The Fatted Calf
$$ | IRISH | One of the Midlands food heroes, chef-owner Feargal O'Donnell uses fresh, locally sourced ingredients at his popular, contemporary Irish restaurant in the town center, where you can sink into comfortable orange chairs made of cowhide leather for signature dry-aged steak. Typical main courses may include panfried cod fillet, 30-day dry-aged beef tenderloin, or a Black Island lamb with chantenay carrots and salsa verde. **Known for:** John Stone dry-aged Irish steaks; Young Buck blue cheese; calm, contemporary atmosphere. ⓢ *Average main: €24* ⊠ *Church St.* ☎ *090/643–3371* ⊕ *www. thefattedcalf.ie* ⊘ *Closed Sun. and Mon.*

Kin Khao Thai Restaurant
$ | THAI | Many regard this as the leading Thai restaurant in the Midlands, if not all of Ireland. Adam Lyons runs a slick first-floor operation in a 650-year-old building on the west bank where the extensive menu features dishes from the Isaan region of northeast Thailand, including the Crying Tiger (grilled fillet of beef on a sizzling hot platter with a hot chili sauce). **Known for:** flaming curries; extensive menu of authentic dishes; best Thai food in the Midlands. ⓢ *Average main: €16* ⊠ *1 Abbey La.* ☎ *090/649–8805* ⊕ *www.*

kinkhaothai.ie ⊘ *No lunch Mon., Tues., and Sat.*

★ The Left Bank Bistro

$$ | ASIAN | One of Athlone's culinary highlights, this bistro is noted for its early-bird menu, which runs through the evening (except Saturday, when it ends at 6 pm), filled with such delights as bacon and colcannon mash with cider sauce, or chargrilled pork fillet. Later on, the beige-on-brown dining room fills up for the main dinner menu, which favors steaks, fish, duck, and rack of lamb. **Known for:** value early-bird menu; innovative food; minimalist style. ⑤ *Average main: €23* ✉ *Fry Pl.* ☎ *090/649–4446* ⊕ *www.left-bankbistro.com* ⊘ *Closed Sun. and Mon.*

 Hotels

The Bastion

$ | B&B/INN | An inviting glow hits you as you step into the long, narrow corridor of this unconventional B&B, all nooks and little staircases, an easygoing place to chill for a few days. **Pros:** minimalist chic and no clutter; excellent value; great pubs and restaurants nearby. **Cons:** bathrooms are small; no phones, TVs, or elevators; no breakfast. ⑤ *Rooms from: €65* ✉ *2 Bastion St.* ☎ *090/649–4954* ⊕ *www.thebastion.net* ⇆ *7 rooms* ⑩ *No meals.*

★ Glasson Country House Hotel and Golf Club

$$ | HOTEL | With views extending out to Hare Island and beyond to Lough Ree, this 1780 stone manor house has seen its popularity rise with golfers every year since 1993, when the welcoming hosts Tom and Breda Reid turned a 70-acre field into a challenging course. **Pros:** family-run; woodland walks and boat trips nearby; great on-site restaurant. **Cons:** strong winds whip in off the lake; bunker discussions dominate at breakfast; exterior is strange mix of old and new. ⑤ *Rooms from: €120* ✉ *Glasson* ✛ *7 km (4 miles) north of Athlone on N55 Cavan–Longford road* ☎ *090/648–5120* ⊕ *www.glassongolfhotel.ie* ⇆ *65 rooms* ⑩ *Free breakfast.*

Radisson Blu Hotel, Athlone

$$$ | HOTEL | In a prime location on the banks of the Shannon, this property has a distinctive water theme; not surprising, as more than half the bedrooms have superb views of the meandering river with a lovely look at Sts. Peter and Paul across the way. **Pros:** stunning views; great location for exploring the town, castle, and left bank; rooms are clean and modern. **Cons:** precooked breakfasts are mediocre; good pool but no spa; can be noisy during family communion and confirmation lunches. ⑤ *Rooms from: €180* ✉ *Northgate St.* ☎ *090/644–2600* ⊕ *www.radissonblu.ie/hotel-athlone* ⇆ *128 rooms* ⑩ *Free breakfast.*

★ Sheraton Athlone Hotel

$$$ | HOTEL | Right in the heart of town, this distinctive 12-story tower hotel comes not only with outstanding comfort but also top-class views of the Midlands, making it one of the highest points in Westmeath—a county not noted for many mountains. **Pros:** central location with parking; rooms with inspiring views; luxurious spa and swimming pool. **Cons:** temptingly close to shopping center; easy to lose yourself in complex of corridors; less intimate than some Midland boutique hotels. ⑤ *Rooms from: €200* ✉ *Gleeson St., beside Athlone Shopping Center* ☎ *090/645–1000* ⊕ *www.sheratonathlonehotel.com* ⇆ *167 rooms* ⑩ *Free breakfast.*

★ Wineport Lodge

$$$ | HOTEL | Ireland's first "wine hotel" began life as a humble boathouse, but today it is one of Ireland's most enchanting hideaways—stylishly modern and light filled, with rooms opening out onto the placid waters of Killinure Lough. **Pros:** magical lake and forest setting; underfloor bathroom heating; water views.

Cons: serenity is occasionally broken by Jet Skis on the lake; restaurant service can be slow; only some rooms have balconies. 💲 *Rooms from: €210* ⊠ *Glasson* ✛ *5 km (3 miles) north of Athlone* ☎ *090/643–9010* ⊕ *www.wineport.ie* 🛏 *29 rooms* �‖ *Free breakfast.*

Nightlife

★ Sean's Bar

BARS/PUBS | In Athlone's buzzing Left Bank sector, Sean's Bar styles itself as the world's oldest pub (a claim some cynics dispute, although a framed certificate from *Guinness World Records* says otherwise), dating to AD 900. This date has inspired the house beer, AD 900, a pale lager brewed in County Carlow. In 2018, Sean's produced two new whiskies specially blended for the bar: one is dedicated to Luain, the first innkeeper, and is a blend of grain and malt, while the other is a malt whiskey called Clonmacnoise, a tribute to the monks who perfected the art of distillation. Sawdust on the floor of this dimly lighted, low-ceiling, long, narrow bar helps give it a rustic look and soaks up spills. Framed pictures and prints line the walls alongside maps of the Shannon navigation system, and the beer garden stretches almost down to the water. There's traditional music—or on Wednesday bluegrass and folk—most nights of the year. ⊠ *13 Main St.* ☎ *090/649–2358* ⊕ *www.seansbar.ie.*

🛍 Shopping

The Left Bank district is a jumble of lanes and small streets lined with pubs, antiques shops, bookstores, and one of the few surviving Irish bookbinders.

Bastion Gallery

GIFTS/SOUVENIRS | An Aladdin's cave of a place in which to browse, the funky Bastion Gallery sells quirky gifts, books, and toys. The owner, Katie McCay, designs and handcrafts jewelry designed with ogham, the first written form of Gaelic, sculpting words onto chains, pendants, and earrings. ⊠ *6 Bastion St.* ☎ *090/649–4948* ⊕ *www.thebastiongallery.com.*

Celtic Roots Studio

CRAFTS | Combining a workshop and gallery, the Celtic Roots Studio in Ballinahown specializes in hand-carved sculptures and personalized jewelry from 5,000-year-old bogwood in the nearby Lough Boora bog, where the wood was preserved in the peat. The owner engraves her work, creating wish stones and all manner of carvings evocative of the natural world and Irish mythology, which make special keepsakes. Ballinahown is the last village in Westmeath as you travel to Clonmacnoise. ⊠ *N62, south from Athlone to Limerick* ✛ *Ballinahown is 12 km (7½ miles) south of Athlone* ☎ *090/643–0404* ⊕ *www.celticroots.ie.*

John's Bookshop

BOOKS/STATIONERY | Owned and run since 1997 by the affable John Donohoe, this bookshop is exactly the way a second-hand bookstore should be: cluttered, disorganized, and heaving with rare and signed Irish-related and general books (up to 10,000 titles at any one time). ⊠ *9 Main St.* ☎ *090/649–4151* ⊕ *www.johnsbookshop.com.*

Activities

BICYCLING
Buckleys Cycles

BICYCLING | A combination of unfrequented back roads, lakeside scenery, and flatlands makes this attractive biking country, so head to this place to rent a bike. ⊠ *Kenna Centre, Dublin Rd.* ☎ *090/647–8989* ⊕ *www.buckleycycles.ie.*

BOATING

A boat trip reveals the importance of Athlone's strategic location on the River Shannon as well as the beauty of the region. *For the complete scoop on*

Goldsmith Country

All that glitters may not be Goldsmith, but that hasn't prevented the Irish tourist board from promoting the Northern Lakelands to the burgeoning literary tourism market as "Goldsmith Country."

Yes, this is the region that gave birth to the writer Oliver Goldsmith (1728–74), celebrated for his farcical drama *She Stoops to Conquer* and his classic novel *The Vicar of Wakefield.* Goldsmith left his homeland as a teenager and returned rarely. However, he is thought to have drawn on memories of his native Longford for his most renowned poem, "The Deserted Village." At Goldsmith's childhood home in Lissoy in County Longford, only the bare walls of the family house remain standing. At Pallas, near Ballymahon in County Longford, his birthplace, there's a statue in his memory but little else. The plot of *She Stoops to Conquer* involves a misunderstanding in which a traveler mistakes a private house for an inn. This actually happened to Goldsmith at Ardagh House, now a college, in the center of the village of Ardagh (just off N55) in County Longford. In the same play the character Tony Lumpkin sings a song about a pub called the Three Jolly Pigeons; today the pub of the same name, on the Ballymahon road (N55) north of Athlone, is the headquarters of the Oliver Goldsmith International Literary Festival.

Every year on the first weekend in June, leading academics from around the world speak on Goldsmith at this pub and other venues, and there are readings by the best of Ireland's contemporary poets and evening traditional-music sessions in the tiny, atmospheric, country pub. Call the Athlone Tourist Office (☎ 090/649–4630) for more information, or visit the website (⊕ www.olivergoldsmithfestival.com).

getting out on the water, see our special section on "Cruising on the Shannon."

Viking Tours

BOATING | For a unique way to cruise the Shannon, take a ride on the *Viking*. A replica of a Viking longboat, it travels upriver to nearby Lough Ree. Originally built in 1923, it's the longest-serving timber passenger boat in Ireland or the United Kingdom. The cost is €16 for a 75-minute round-trip sailing; they take place March through October. You can also sail southbound from Athlone to the ecclesiastical site of Clonmacnoise for €20; it takes 90 minutes one-way, with return by bus. Check the website for schedules. ✉ The Quay at Athlone Castle ☎ 086/262–1136 ⊕ www.vikingtoursireland.ie.

GOLF
Athlone Golf Club
GOLF | An 18-hole parkland course, founded in 1892, Athlone is one of Ireland's oldest clubs. The course stretches along the shores of Lough Ree at Hodson Bay with stunning views of the Shannon. Tree-lined fairways, sandy greens, and undulating terrain make for an idyllic location that visitors hold in high regard. A new fertilizer program has improved the quality of the fairway and rough by producing a thicker sward—resulting in a much more playable course. The club hosts national and provincial competitions, and the resident head pro, Irish golfer Kevin Grealy, offers lessons to players of all abilities and specializes in tuition on the short game. ■TIP➔ Every Wednesday, throughout the year, the club

One of Ireland's greatest monastic settlements, Clonmacnoise was nearly leveled in places—including the Norman Castle seen above—but has other ruins that still inspire awe.

holds popular "Open Wednesday" competitions, as well as open competitions on bank holiday weekends. ✉ *Hodson Bay* ☎ *090/649–2073* ⊕ *www.athlonegolfclub. ie* ⌚ *Weekdays €30, weekends €35* 🏌 *18 holes, 6001 yards, par 72.*

HIKING AND WALKING
The Old Rail Trail

BICYCLING | FAMILY | Westmeath's Old Rail Trail is a newly established off-road route through the heart of the Midlands, ideal for cyclists and walkers. In the days of the Midland Great Western Railway, the line linked Dublin to both Galway and Sligo. Now the 40-km (25-mile) journey running between Athlone and Mullingar has been converted into a popular flat rural trail—with just a few gentle slopes—forming part of a proposed Galway-to-Dublin cycleway. Starting at Garrycastle on the eastern edge of Athlone, the trail leads through Moate and Castletown Station, as well as arched bridges, a tunnel, and farmland to Mullingar, where you can continue your journey by joining the Royal Canal. ✉ *Starting point:*

Garrycastle, Athlone ☎ *044/932–2000* ⊕ *www.greenway.westmeathcoco.ie.*

Shannon Banks Nature Trail

HIKING/WALKING | Along the newly established Shannon Banks color-coded nature trail, wildflowers such as herb Robert, stitchwort, speedwell, and silverweed are all prominent. The looped, bidirectional trail starts at the main bridge of the Shannon at the back of Athlone castle. To the west, follow the promenade that runs parallel with Grace Road and you will come across a park filled with multilimbed trees such as silver birch, horse chestnut, red oak, common limes, and Norway maple, all of which attract rich birdlife. The other direction leads along the quay to Athlone docks. Along the way, signposts detail flora, fauna, wildlife, and fish to look for. The route takes about 45 minutes in either direction. ✉ *Athlone* ⊕ *www.athlone.ie/visit/ shannon-banks-nature-trail.*

Clonmacnoise

20 km (12 miles) south of Athlone, 93 km (58 miles) east of Galway.

Many ancient sites dot the River Shannon, but Clonmacnoise is early Christian Ireland's foremost monastic settlement and, like Chartres, a royal site. The monastery was founded by St. Ciarán between 543 and 549 at a location that was not as remote as it now appears to be, near the intersection of what were then two of Ireland's most vital routes: the Shannon River, running north–south, and the Eiscir Riada, running east–west. Like Glendalough, Celtic Ireland's other great monastic site, Clonmacnoise benefited from its isolation; surrounded by bog, it's accessible only via one road or via the Shannon.

GETTING HERE AND AROUND

It takes dedication to get here. As the easiest way to Clonmacnoise is by car, it can be crowded in high season, although many visitors also arrive on tour buses. Get here early—the main parking lot fills up quickly. The site is 20 minutes south of Athlone; take the N62 then turn off onto the narrow R444 in the direction of Shannonbridge. Birr is 35 minutes by car south along the R357 and then the N52. Parking here is free.

Clonmacnoise is well-nigh impossible to reach by public transport. If you don't have a car, it's best to book a trip with companies such as CIE Tours, Paddywagon, Shamrocker, or Midlands Tours. Or opt to board a boat in Athlone for a 90-minute journey to the jetty beside Clonmacnoise visitor center. Trips are run on the *Viking*, and advance booking is necessary. The round-trip is €15.

◉ Sights

★ **Clonmacnoise**

RELIGIOUS SITE | Thanks to its location, this legendary monastery survived almost everything thrown at it, including raids by feuding Irish tribes, Vikings, and Normans. But when the English garrison arrived from Athlone in 1552, they ruthlessly reduced the site to ruin. Still, with a little imagination, you can picture life here in medieval times, when the nobles of Europe sent their sons to be educated by the local monks. The monastery was founded on an esker (natural gravel ridge) overlooking the Shannon and a marshy area known as the Callows.

Numerous buildings and ruins remain. The small **cathedral** dates as far back as the 10th century but has additions from the 15th century. It was the burial place of kings of Connaught and of Tara, and of Rory O'Conor, the last High King of Ireland, who was buried here in 1198. The two Round Towers include **O'Rourke's Tower,** which was struck by lightning and subsequently rebuilt in the 12th century. There are eight **smaller churches,** the littlest of which is thought to be the burial place of St. Ciaran. The Nun's Church's chancel arch and doorway is a fine example of Romanesque architecture.

Clonmacnoise has always been a prestigious burial place. Among the ancient stones are many other graves dating from the 17th to the mid-20th century. The whole place is time-burnished, though in midsummer it can be difficult to avoid the throngs of tourists. There are 30-minute tours every hour during the summer season. ⊠ *5 km (3 miles) north of Shannonbridge, 21 km (13 miles) south of Athlone* ⊹ *Take N62 from Athlone and turn off at Doon Cross Roads on to R444 following signposts* ☎ *090/967–4195, 090/967–4134 for Shop at Clonmacnoise* ⊕ *www.heritageireland. ie* ⊠ *€8 (under 12 free).*

The Boglands

The natives of the Midlands retain a historic attachment to their vast boglands and will extol their virtues at length if prompted by a stranger.

In rural parts, turf (peat) still accounts for much of the winter fuel supply and locals can always be counted upon to discuss in great detail the quality and consistency of this uniquely native resource.

"Grand year for the turf" will generally indicate a sunny August—key drying time when the "sods" are cut and allowed to dry along the banks. Conversely, "wicked bad turf" denotes a typically soft Irish summer with poor drying.

Along country lanes, the sight of reeks of cut turf is still commonplace. If you're tired of using the weather as a conversational icebreaker, try turf as an alternative and virtually guaranteed discourse igniter.

No matter that from a distance an Irish peat bog looks like a flat, treeless piece of waterlogged land. A close-up view shows a much more exciting landscape.

Bogs support an extraordinary amount of wildlife, including larks and snipe, pale-blue dragonflies, and Greenland white-fronted geese. Amid the pools and lakes of the peat bog, amazing jewel-like wildflowers thrive, from purple bell heather to yellow bog asphodel, all alongside grasses, lichens, and mosses.

As you pass through the small town of Shannonbridge, 10 km (6 miles) south of Clonmacnoise, on either side of the road are vast stretches of chocolate-brown boglands and isolated industrial plants for processing the area's natural resource.

Bord na Móna, the same government agency that makes commercial use of other boglands, has jurisdiction over the area.

Banagher

31 km (19 miles) south of Clonmacnoise.

"Well, that beats Banagher!" This small Shannon-side town is best known in Ireland because of this common phrase, which dates from the 19th century when the town was the very worst example of a "rotten borough"—a corrupt electoral area controlled by the local landed gentry. In short, if something "beats Banagher" it's either pretty bad or rather extraordinary. Nowadays, Banagher is a lively marina town that is a popular base for water-sports enthusiasts. Charlotte Brontë (1816–55) famously spent her honeymoon here. On the second Sunday in September each year one of Ireland's oldest horse fairs takes over the town. Buyers and sellers come from all over the country to take part in the horse trading that gives the town a raffish air thick with the fragrance of horse odor and horse leather. ■TIP→ **Pick up a copy of the Banagher Heritage Trail, available in shops, pubs, and B&Bs. It will guide you around 17 buildings, sculptures, and sites of interest in the town and along the riverside, including places with a Brontë connection.**

GETTING HERE AND AROUND
Midway between Athlone and Roscrea, Banagher is a small crossroads town. Athlone and Birr are both a 40-minute drive, and although the town is busy in summer, parking is generally not a

problem. Kearns Transport operates daily services with links from Banagher to Birr (15 minutes), Tullamore (35 minutes), and Dublin (three hours).

CONTACTS Kearns Transport. ⊠ *Harper Rd.* ✥ *Pickup and drop-off is at Corrigan's Corner on main street* ☎ *057/912–0124* ⊕ *www.kearnstransport.com.*

Sights

The River Queen
BODY OF WATER | If you happen to be in Banagher in summer, consider taking a cruise along the Shannon aboard *The River Queen,* an enclosed launch run by Silver Line Cruisers Ltd. that seats 50 passengers and has a full bar on board. ■ **TIP→ Call to book in advance; seats aren't guaranteed to those who turn up on a day-of.** ⊠ *The Marina* ☎ *057/915–1112* ⊕ *www.silverlinecruisers.com* 💶 *€12* 🕙 *Closed Sept.–June.*

Restaurants

Flynn's Bar & Lounge
$ | MODERN IRISH | FAMILY | In the center of town, Flynn's is worth visiting to appreciate its light and spacious Victorian-style design. The lunch menu includes sandwiches, salad platters, and dishes such as red Thai curry, chicken Milanese, or Irish lamb stew. **Known for:** quality roast beef; scrumptious apple pie; Irish coffees. ⑤ *Average main: €13* ⊠ *Commercial House, Main St.* ☎ *057/915–1312.*

🛏 Hotels

Charlotte's Way
$ | B&B/INN | The sweet aroma of turf smoke percolates in the living room of this historic B&B, where the delightful Nicola Daly welcomes guests to her "home from home," an 18th-century house that has a connection to Charlotte Brontë, whose husband lived here after her death. **Pros:** Victorian history seeps from its pores; homemade jams from the

property; countryside views. **Cons:** quiet; short walk into town; no credit cards. ⑤ *Rooms from: €80* ⊠ *Birr Rd., Kylebeg* ☎ *057/915–3864* ⊕ *www.charlottesway. com* 🚫 *No credit cards* 🕙 *Closed Nov.– mid-Mar.* 🛏 *6 rooms* ⑩ *Free breakfast.*

Nightlife

J. J. Hough's
BARS/PUBS | Travelers love Hough's, where on spring and summer nights there's usually a sing-along around the German piano. Try the cocktails or the house special, Shakalaka Boom, a mix of Irish whiskey and Bailey's cream liqueur. Note the walls decorated with business cards, testifying to the pub's popularity the world over. Side rooms lead to a beer garden with wooden chairs and tables. You can also join in card games with the locals, and there's generally traditional music on Saturday night. The owner, Mick Hough, has been known to launch into song himself on occasion. ⊠ *Main St.* ☎ *057/915–1893.*

Birr

12 km (7 miles) southeast of Banagher, 130 km (81 miles) west of Dublin.

Beautifully reminiscent of an English country town with its tree-lined malls and well-preserved houses, the heritage town of Birr has roots that date to the 6th century. Still, the mid-18th-century Georgian buildings set the tone. Birr Castle is the pièce de résistance and an ideal place to while away a morning on a guided tour or spend the afternoon in an idyllic setting. For those who enjoy a riparian ramble, head to the Camcor River Walk. Birr is also noted for its variety of festivals throughout the year, including the longest-running hot-air-balloon championships in the world, held at the end of September.

GETTING HERE AND AROUND

Six main roads meet at Birr. Limerick is 90 minutes south on the N52 and then the N7, while Athlone is 30 minutes north on the N52. There may be traffic delays along the town's narrow central streets. Several paid lots and on-street metered spaces provide parking. Buses leave from Emmet Square for Dublin (3½ hours away) and west for Limerick (75 minutes).

 Sights

★ **Birr Castle Gardens and Science Centre**
CASTLE/PALACE | FAMILY | Summer visitors can join a guided tour of one of Ireland's most elegant stately homes and peer behind the scenes of a previously closed-off world. The Gothic Revival castle (built around an earlier 17th-century castle that was damaged by fire in 1823) is still the home of the earls of Rosse. Castle tours, usually given by family members, bring you through the spectacular Gothic music saloon from 1810 (said by many to be the most beautiful room in Ireland), the library, the yellow drawing room, and reception rooms. Held only in the mornings in May, July, and August, the tours last around 75 minutes. Note that the castle has more than 100 rooms and the tour takes in just a small number of them. The present Earl and Countess of Rosse continue the family tradition of making botanical expeditions for specimens of rare trees, plants, and shrubs to fill the demesne's 150 acres. The formal gardens contain the tallest box hedges in the world (at 32 feet) and vine-sheltered hornbeam allées. In spring, check out the wonderful display of flowering magnolias, cherries, crab apples, and naturalized narcissi; in autumn, the maples, chestnuts, and weeping beeches blaze red and gold.
■ TIP→ **If you are joining a house tour, book in advance; allow at least three hours to see everything in the demesne—there are 3,400 plants and 3,860 varieties of trees from 40 countries (including the largest gray poplar**

in the world). ✉ Rosse Row ☎ 057/912–0336 ⊕ www.birrcastle.com ✍ Castle tour, gardens, and science center €18, gardens €10 ⊗ Castle closed Sept.–Apr. and Sun.

Birr Library
BUILDING | Based in a former convent, this 19th-century library has an exquisite Gothic-style stained-glass windows. Upstairs you will find a facsimile of an early Christian illuminated manuscript, the *Gospel Book of MacRegol*, also known as the *Book of Birr* and the *Rushworth Gospels*, on permanent display. MacRegol was a scribe, bishop, and abbot in Birr. The original manuscript, which is now in Oxford's Bodleian Library, was produced around AD 800 and consists of 169 vellum folios or leaves. The library also offers Internet service. ✉ Wilmer Rd. ☎ 057/912–4950 ⊗ Closed Sun. and Mon.

 Restaurants

Emma's Café and Deli
$ | IRISH | A tempting array of both savory and sweet delights are on display at this central daytime café and deli counter. Nourishing soups at lunchtime, such as colcannon (cabbage and potato) or mushroom come with freshly baked brown bread. **Known for:** colcannon soup; meat-filled sandwiches; superfresh scones. ⑤ Average main: €10 ✉ 31 Main St ☎ 057/912–5678.

The Thatch Bar
$ | IRISH | Imaginative food and a warm welcome await at this 300-year-old bar and restaurant, its thatched roof (completely redone in 2017), exposed wooden beams, and brick walls adding to the intimate country atmosphere. Inexpensive meals are available at lunchtime (Friday to Sunday only) and early evening (4 to 7:30); later at night the restaurant offers a two- or three-course Hidden Heartlands dinner menu for €26 or €32. **Known for:** steaks; huge portions; flawless service.

Presidential Roots

The village of Moneygall (population 320) is an unassuming place on the main N7 Dublin–Limerick road, but it was thrust into the spotlight in 2011 when President Barack Obama paid a visit to check on his ancestors and since then, Moneygall has forced itself onto the map as the ancestral homeland of the 1/32nd-Irish former president. His great-great-great grandfather came from the village and his maternal ancestors lived and worked in the Moneygall area more than 160 years ago. Ollie Hayes' Bar on the main street has an "Obama Corner," and on a Thursday evening you may see the Obama Set Dancers strutting their

Cashel and Ballycommon sets and practicing a mix of jigs, reels, polkas, and hornpipes. In 2014 the President Barack Obama Visitor Centre was opened, which explores the links between the village and the president. It's based in Barack Obama Plaza, a service station at junction 23 of the M7. Tour companies passing through from Dublin stop here regularly to offer an opportunity to drink at the pub where the former president took a healthy swig of Guinness, and, of course, shop the presidential plaza for Obama swag. Kitsch-factor alone makes this a worthy stop if you happen to be driving through.

⑤ *Average main: €18* ⊠ *Military Rd., Crinkill* ⊹ *2 km (1 mile) south of Birr, just off N62 Roscrea road* ☎ *057/912–0682* ⊕ *www.thethatchcrinkill.com* ⊗ *No lunch Mon.–Thurs.*

 ## Hotels

Dooly's Hotel

$$ | HOTEL | Originally a coach house, this unpretentious country hotel in Birr's central square, just a five-minute walk to Birr Castle, began life in 1747 and has retained its old-style homeliness with well-appointed rooms decorated with neutral furnishings. **Pros:** huge rooms; a handy Midlands stopover, if you're on your way to the west coast; short walk to Birr Castle. **Cons:** attached nightclub can be noisy; stairs can be difficult for the disabled or elderly; no pool. ⑤ *Rooms from: €120* ⊠ *Emmet Sq., O'Connell St.* ☎ *057/912–0032* ⊕ *www.doolyshotel.ie* ⇶ *17 rooms* †⊚† *Free breakfast.*

The Maltings

$ | B&B/INN | FAMILY | Sheltered beneath the eaves of Birr Castle on a riverbank, this converted cut-stone storehouse—built to store malt for Guinness in 1810—is a good option for families and offers special rates for children. **Pros:** idyllic location; attractive rooms; great breakfasts. **Cons:** showing signs of wear and tear; no dinner available, but there are several restaurants in the area; not many frills. ⑤ *Rooms from: €90* ⊠ *Castle St.* ☎ *057/912–1345* ⊕ *the-maltingsbirr.com* ⇶ *6 rooms* †⊚† *Free breakfast.*

Roscrea

19 km (12 miles) south of Birr.

★ Every corner you turn in this charming town will offer reminders of its rich and sometimes turbulent past. Ancient castles, towers, and churches dot the skyline, proof of a rich heritage that dates to the 7th century. The road through town cuts right through the remains of a monastery founded by St. Cronan. It also passes the west facade of a 12th-century Romanesque church that now forms an entrance gate to a modern Catholic church. Above the structure's rounded doorway is a hood mold enclosing the figure of a bishop, probably St. Cronan.

GETTING HERE AND AROUND

Roscrea is on the main N7 road between Dublin and Cork, making it ideal as a stopover en route to the south. Limerick is one hour south on this route, and roads from the town lead to all points of the Midlands compass. Cars park free on the main streets, and there is ample parking on side streets and in designated areas.

The Bus Éireann Expressway from Dublin to Limerick stops in Roscrea, a 2½-hour journey. The Roscrea–Limerick leg of the route is 70 minutes. From Roscrea you can also catch a bus south to Cashel (2¼ hours) and Cork (three hours) as well as north to Athlone (70 minutes) or as far northwest as Sligo, a journey of nearly five hours. The Irish Rail Dublin–Limerick train stops in Roscrea as well; the town is 90 minutes from each city.

 Sights

Roscrea Castle

CASTLE/PALACE | In the very center of town is Roscrea Castle, a Norman fortress dating from 1314, given by King Richard II to the Duke of Ormonde. Inside are vaulted rooms graced with tapestries and 16th-century furniture. A ticket to the castle gains entry to the adjacent **Damer House,** a superb example of an early-18th-century town house on the grand scale. It was built in 1725 within the curtain walls of the castle, at a time when homes were often constructed beside or attached to the strongholds they replaced. The house has a plain, symmetrical facade and a magnificent carved-pine staircase inside; on display are exhibits about local history. The Damer Art Gallery is on the second floor while on the third the Kelly Exhibition showcases furniture and farm implements donated from a local farmhouse. Guided 45-minute tours are held in

spring and summer. Your ticket also includes entry to the restored **Black Mills** in Church Street, a small museum with local artifacts, of which the star attraction is St. Cronan's High Cross. ⊠ *Castle St.* ⊹ *To get here, start with your back to St. Cronan's Monastery, turn left, and then turn right onto Castle St.* ☎ *0505/21850* ⊕ *www.heritageireland.ie* ⊠ *€5* ⊗ *Closed Oct.–Easter.*

 Shopping

Roscrea Country Market

MARKET | For a real taste of some honest-to-goodness Tipperary home baking, try to catch the Roscrea Country Market, held every Friday 10–1 at the Abbey Hall, for whole-grain scones and breads, apple and rhubarb tarts, fruit and sponge cakes, and homemade jams. Potatoes, vegetables, eggs from free-range chickens, and flowers are also on offer. The market has been running since 1962. ⊠ *Roscrea.*

THE SOUTHEAST

Updated by
Anto Howard

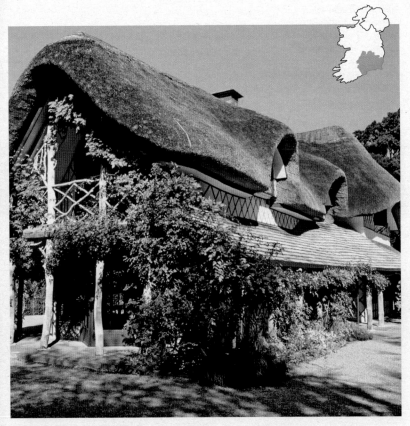

👁 **Sights**   🍴 **Restaurants**   🛏 **Hotels**   🛍 **Shopping**   🍸 **Nightlife**

★★★★★   ★★★★★   ★★★★★   ★★★★★   ★★★★★

WELCOME TO
THE SOUTHEAST

TOP REASONS TO GO

★ **Sacred Ardmore:** St. Declan founded Ireland's first Christian settlement near this beautifully situated fishing village on the Waterford coast.

★ **Kilkenny, Ireland's Medieval Capital:** With its famous 14th-century "witch," Petronilla, Camelot-worthy Black Abbey, and fairy-tale Kilkenny Castle, the city still conjures up the days of knights and damsels.

★ **Pretty-as-a-Postcard Lismore:** Presided over by the neo-baronial castle of the Dukes of Devonshire, this storybook village has attracted visitors ranging from Sir Walter Raleigh to Fred Astaire.

★ **Cashel of the Kings:** Ireland's "Rock of Ages," this spectacular 200-foot-tall rock bluff was the ancient seat of the Kings of Munster.

★ **Wexford and Waterford:** Big-city lights shine brightest here, thanks to such attractions as the famed Wexford Opera Festival and the reborn House of Waterford Crystal factory and visitor center.

Set around Tipperary—Ireland's largest inland county—the Southeast is a vast region that stretches from the town of Carlow near the border of County Wicklow in the north to Ardmore near the border of County Cork in the south. Although main towns can be packed with camera-wielding tourists, you can easily escape the tour buses thanks to endless expanses of tranquil countryside.

1 **Kilkenny City.** A picturesque city with a medieval castle, a lively pub scene, and quality Irish crafts.

2 **Thomastown.** This pretty riverside village is known for Jerpoint Abbey and Mount Juliet Golf Course.

3 **Enniscorthy.** On the road between Dublin and Wexford with an imposing Norman castle worth visiting.

4 **Wexford Town.** A compact coastal town famous for its opera festival and beautiful Johnstown Castle Gardens.

5 **Rosslare.** A seaside town and port for the ferry to Wales and France.

6 **Kilmore Quay.** This quiet and pretty fishing village has thatch cottages and the Saltee Islands.

7 **Ballyhack.** A picturesque village with a square castle keep, thatch cottages, and one of Ireland's finest country houses.

8 **Waterford City.** Ireland's oldest city offers preserved city walls, the

Waterford Crystal factory, and a fairy-tale castle.

9 Tramore. The most popular beach in the "sunny Southeast."

10 Dungarvan. A great base for climbers and hikers and a must-visit for the new Waterford Greenway and one of Ireland's top restaurants.

11 Ardmore. A picture-postcard little town with

an award-winning restaurant and a famous Irish pottery studio and shop.

12 Lismore. Highlights here include the Knockmealdown Mountains and Lismore Castle and Gardens.

13 Cahir. A compact and attractive town with a beautiful castle.

14 Cashel. Home to one of Ireland's top attractions, the Rock of Cashel.

15 Bansha. Great for mountain walking, fishing, horseback riding, and generally soaking in the Glen of Aherlow.

16 Birdhill. A charming little town on the shores of Lough Derg.

Going to Ireland for the sunshine might sound like a joke, but not if you head to the golden beaches and blue surf of the "Sunny Southeast." While not exactly California, the shore resorts here receive almost double the rays found in some less fortunate parts of the country, and buzz with activity from May to October. Little wonder the outdoors-loving Irish have made the Southeast's coast a popular warm-weather vacation destination. The counties Wexford, Carlow, Kilkenny, Tipperary, and Waterford are also packed with enough history, culture, food, and festivals to satisfy the most demanding visitor.

Thousands of families take their annual summer holidays here, where picnics and barbecues—often a rain-washed fantasy elsewhere in Ireland—are a golden reality.

The entire Southeast is rich with natural beauty—not the rugged and wild wonders found to the north and west, but a coast that alternates between long, sandy beaches and rocky bays backed by low cliffs, and an inland landscape of fertile river valleys and lush, undulating pastureland. The landscape of the region is diverse, the appeal universal: you'll find seaside fishing villages with thatched cottages, and Tipperary's verdant, picturesque Golden Vale. The region doesn't lack for culture, either. History-rich Ardmore, Carlow Town, the cities of Kilkenny and Waterford, and Wexford Town have retained traces of their successive waves of invaders—Celt, Viking, and Norman.

The most important of these destinations is Kilkenny City, a major ecclesiastic and political center until the 17th century and now a lively market town. Its streets still hold remnants from medieval times—most notably St. Canice's Cathedral—and a magnificent 12th-century castle that received a sumptuous Victorian makeover. Wexford's narrow streets are built on one side of a wide estuary, giving it a delightful maritime air. Waterford, although less immediately attractive than Wexford, is also built at the confluence of two of the region's rivers, the Suir and the Barrow. It offers a rich selection of Viking and Norman remains, some attractive Georgian buildings, and the visitor center and shop at the famed House of Waterford Glass Factory.

Deeper into the countryside, rustic charms beckon. The road between Rosslare and Ballyhack passes through quiet, atypical, flat countryside dotted with thatched cottages. In the far southwest of County Waterford, near the Cork border, Ardmore presents early Christian ruins on an exposed headland, while, in the wooded splendor of the Blackwater Valley, the tiny cathedral town of Lismore has a hauntingly beautiful fairy-tale castle.

MAJOR REGIONS

Kilkenny City. Creativity is evident in every aspect of this town, from its medieval stonework to its array of modern and traditional craft and design found in galleries and studios. Many festivals and events are held here year-round.

Southeast Inlands. North of Kilkenny City is a region notably rich in historical sights. Travel through the farmlands of the Barrow Valley to the small county seat of Carlow Town, with scenic detours to **Leighlinbridge's** picturesque castle and **Old Leighlin's** time-stained cathedral.

The Southeast Coast. This journey takes you along mainly minor roads through the prettiest parts of the coast in counties Wexford and Waterford, pausing midway to explore **Waterford City**—home of the dazzling cut glass—on foot. Along the way expect to see long golden beaches, quaint fishing villages like **Kilmore Quay** and **Ballyhack,** some of the country's best nature reserves, and the family seaside resort of **Tramore.** If you're coming from the Continent or England, chances are

you'll end up on a ferry bound for **Rosslare Harbour,** one of Ireland's busiest ferry ports.

County Tipperary and Around. "It's a long way to Tipperary ..." So run the words of that famed song sung all over the world since World War I. Actually, Tipperary is *not* so far to go, considering that, as Ireland's biggest inland county, it's within easy striking distance of Waterford and Cork. Moving in from the coastline, you can travel through some of Ireland's lushest pasturelands and to some of its most romantic sights, such as Lismore Castle in the enchanting town of **Lismore.** The Blackwater Valley is renowned for its peaceful beauty and excellent fishing. Some of the finest racehorses in the world are raised in the fields of Tipperary, which is also where you can find the Rock of Cashel—the greatest group of monastic ruins in all Ireland.

Planning

Getting Here and Around

BOAT AND FERRY TRAVEL

If you are coming to Ireland from England, chances are you'll end up on a ferry bound for Rosslare Harbour, 19 km (12 miles) south of Wexford, one of Ireland's busiest ferry ports. There are two main companies that service Rosslare. Irish Ferries connects Rosslare to Pembroke, Wales (four hours). Stena Line sails directly between Rosslare Ferryport and Fishguard, Wales (three hours), and to Cherbourg in France (19½ hours). They both have small information kiosks in the ultramodern terminal, which also has lockers and a sprawling waiting room. Passage East Car Ferry is a shortcut across the Suir Estuary, connecting Ballyhack in Wexford with Passage East in Waterford.

You can purchase ferry tickets at the terminal, but try to reserve a space in advance online to avoid the frequent sell-outs, particularly in summer and anytime the Irish soccer team is playing in a major tournament abroad.

Reservations are a must if you're traveling by car or motorcycle because onboard parking space is at a premium. Eurail Pass holders get a discount on ferries from France. Departure times vary from season to season, so call ahead.

CONTACTS Irish Ferries. ⊕ *www.irish-ferries.com.* **Passage East Ferry Company.** ⊕ *www.passageferry.ie.* **Stena Line.** ⊕ *www.stenaline.ie.*

BUS TRAVEL

Bus Éireann runs frequent buses between Waterford and Dublin, Limerick, Cork, and Rosslare. J. J. Kavanagh & Sons runs daily buses from Dublin to Carlow, Waterford, and Kilkenny.

CONTACTS Bus Éireann. ⊕ *www.buseireann.ie.* **J. J. Kavanagh & Sons.** ⊕ *jjkavanagh.ie.*

CAR TRAVEL

With recently completed highways to Waterford and Kilkenny, a car is the best option for covering ground quickly and easily. Waterford City, the regional capital, is easily accessible from all parts of Ireland.

From Dublin, take M7 southwest, change to the M9, and continue along as it bypasses Carlow Town and Thomastown until it ends in Waterford. N25 travels east–west through Waterford City, connecting it with Cork in the west and Wexford Town in the east. From Limerick and Tipperary Town, N24 stretches southeast until it, too, ends in Waterford City.

For the most part, the main roads in the Southeast are of good quality and are free of congestion. Side roads are generally narrow and twisting, and you should keep an eye out for farm machinery and animals on country roads.

TAXI TRAVEL

It costs €3.80 to hire a taxi on the street (€4.20 by night) in the larger towns: add €2 to book by phone, and €1.14 per kilometer or part of a kilometer for the first 15 km (9 miles). Reputable companies include Celtic Cabs in Wexford, Rapid-cabs in Waterford, and Kilkenny Taxi.

CONTACTS Celtic Cabs. ☎ *085/808–20404.* **Kilkenny Taxi.** ☎ *056/772–2224* ⊕ *www.kilkennytaxi.com.* **Rapidcabs.** ☎ *051/858–585* ⊕ *www.rapidcabs.com.*

TRAIN TRAVEL

Waterford City is linked by daily Irish Rail service to Dublin, with trains making stops at Thomastown, Kilkenny, Bagenalstown, and Carlow Town. The daily train between Waterford City and Limerick makes stops at Carrick-on-Suir, Clonmel, Cahir, and Tipperary Town. The daily trail from Dublin to Rosslare port travels through Wexford.

CONTACTS Irish Rail. ⊕ *www.irishrail.ie .* **MacDonagh Station.** ✉ *St. John's St., Kilkenny.* **O'Hanrahan Station.** ✉ *Redmond Pl., Wexford.* **Plunkett Station.** ✉ *Dock Rd., Waterford.*

Hotels

Festivals, the good weather, and commerce make the Southeast popular, so plan way ahead for a stay in any of the main towns (or in many country manors, which usually have fewer than six bedrooms and fill up fast). As always, the local tourist offices can offer assistance if you arrive without reservations. *Hotel reviews have been shortened. For full information, visit Fodors.com.*

Restaurants

Food is usually prepared in a simple, country-house style, though pleasant surprises abound. A number of ambitious Irish chefs are at work in the Southeast's restaurants and hotels, and at newer joints with inventive offerings that offer a great value. The best of the region's cuisine rests on modern, international interpretations of classic Irish dishes. Leading lights in the area include chef Kevin Dundon at Dunbrody Country House, Paul Flynn of the Tannery, and Martjin Kajuiter at the Michelin-starred Cliff House in Ardmore.

Other than its fabled strawberries, the Southeast is probably best known for its rich seafood, especially Wexford mussels, crabs, and locally caught salmon. Kilmore Quay, noted for lobster and deep-sea fishing, hosts an annual Seafood Festival the second week of July. Many restaurants serve local lamb, beef, and game in season. *Restaurant reviews have been shortened. For full information, visit Fodors.com.*

Tune In to the Southeast

If you want to feel the true pulse of the nation, check out any of RTÉ Radio 1's morning and afternoon shows. In a country still reeling from the government mismanagement and social damage of the great economic crash, the radio has become Ireland's modern confessional and a serious insight into what makes the Irish tick. Waterford Local Radio (95.1/97.5 FM) and South East Radio (95.6/96.4 FM) are the popular options around Waterford and Wexford, respectively.

What It Costs In Euros			
$	$$	$$$	$$$$
RESTAURANTS			
under €19	€19–€24	€25–€32	over €32
HOTELS			
under €120	€120–€170	€171–€210	over €210

Tours

Burtchaell Tours of Waterford City

WALKING TOURS | The knowledgeable and delightful Jack Burtchaell leads a Waterford City walk daily at noon and 2 pm from mid-March through mid-October. Tours depart from the Granville Hotel. ☎ 051/873–711 ⊕ www.jackswalkingtours.com ⊠ From €7.

A Rural Experience

GUIDED TOURS | This outfit runs day excursions and extended private chauffeur tours all over the Southeast, and the County Kilkenny tour is especially popular. ☎ 056/772–7590 ⊕ www.aruralexperience.com ⊠ From €220.

Tynan Tours of Kilkenny City

WALKING TOURS | These walking tours of Kilkenny take place Monday to Saturday, April through October, and by appointment November to March. ☎ 087/265–1745 ⊕ www.kilkennywalkingtours.ie ⊠ From €10.

Wexford Walking Tours

WALKING TOURS | Walking tours of historic Wexford Town can be prebooked for groups through town tourist offices from mid-March to October. There's also a daily tour that you can join in Monday through Saturday at 11 am from tourist office. ☎ 086/107–9497 ⊕ www.wexfordwalkingtours.net ⊠ From €7.

When to Go

As well as having some of the richest land in the country, the Southeast is the envy of all Ireland for that most elusive element—sunshine. The region is also one of the driest in Ireland, which is saying something in a country where seldom do more than three days pass without some rain. Compared with an average of 80 inches on parts of the west coast, the Southeast gets as little as 40 inches of rainfall per year, varying from the finest light drizzle (a soft day, thank goodness!) to full-blown downpours.

Festivals and Events

With practically every hamlet and village across the country glorying in its own festival (excuse for keeping pubs open later), the Southeast delivers some of Ireland's most popular gatherings. Check with the tourist boards for listings and dates of all events, big and small.

JUNE

Carlow Arts Festival

The Carlow Arts Festival (also sometimes referred to as Éigse) is a five-day celebration of visual arts held every June. ☎ 059/917–2400 ⊕ www.carlowartsfestival.com.

AUGUST

Kilkenny Arts Festival

Every August, Kilkenny becomes the focus for Ireland's culture vultures when the Kilkenny Arts Festival takes over the city for about two weeks. Street theater, elaborate parades, and even a rock concert set the mood. ⊠ Kilkenny ☎ 056/775–1704 ⊕ www.kilkennyarts.ie.

Spraoi

Every August, the Spraoi street arts festival presents an exuberant display of music, theater, and other entertainment in Waterford City. You'll find it around the city's extensive pedestrian areas. ⊠ Waterford ⊕ www.spraoi.com.

OCTOBER

Wexford Fringe Festival

Running alongside the opera festival from late October to early November, the chaotic and theatrical Wexford Fringe Festival is an eclectic mix of theater, literature, music, dance, and street events. ⊠ Wexford ⊕ www.wexfordfringe.ie.

Wexford Opera Festival

From late October to early November, the two-week-long Wexford Opera Festival is the biggest social and artistic event in the entire Southeast. From mid-September until the final curtain comes down, Wexford becomes home to a colorful cast of international singers, designers, and musicians as they prepare for the annual staging of three grand operas at the Wexford Opera House. Along with an ever-expanding offering of more populist fare performed in small venues and pubs, the festival supplies a feast of concerts and recitals that start at 11 am and continue until midnight. The bad news: nearly every single bed within miles is booked during the festival, and usually for months ahead of time. ⊠ Wexford ⊕ www.wexfordopera.com.

Planning Your Time

IF YOU HAVE THREE DAYS

Distances are not great, but if you are here for a short stay—three days or fewer—you might want to base yourself in one of the region's cities or larger towns: Waterford, Kilkenny, or Wexford. All three are historic locations with plenty of places of cultural and historical interest accessible on foot. They are also growing shopping destinations. Day trips from Waterford and Wexford could include idyllic coastal villages like Ardmore, Dunmore East, and Kilmore Quay. From Kilkenny and Waterford the mountains, glens, and lakes of Tipperary are only a short drive away. Spend a night at a coastal hotel like the Cliff House in Ardmore or the country manor of Ballyduff House in Thomastown.

IF YOU HAVE FIVE DAYS

If you have more time in the region, you might want to drive the whole of the scenic coast from Wexford down around spectacular Hook Head to Waterford and on to the winding road to Ardmore and Dungarvan. Take your time, avoid the motorway, and stop off at any village or watering hole that takes your fancy. You'll still have plenty of time for a detour north into Tipperary along some beautiful mountain back roads and on to the historic town of Cashel to see the legendary Rock. From there, head northwest for a touch of water sports on Lough Derg or take the short, scenic hop back to medieval Kilkenny City.

Visitor Information

Eight tourist information offices of varying quality in the Southeast are open all year. They are in Carlow Town, Dungarvan, Gorey, Kilkenny, Lismore, Waterford City, Tramore, and Wexford Town. Another four TIOs are open seasonally: Cahir (April–October); Cashel (April–September); Rosslare (April–September); and Tipperary Town (May–October). If traveling extensively by public transportation, be sure to load up on information (schedules, the best taxi companies, etc.) upon arriving at the train and bus stations in Kilkenny City, Wexford Town, and Waterford City.

Kilkenny City

101 km (63 miles) southwest of Dublin.

Dubbed "Ireland's Medieval Capital" by its tourist board, and also called "the Oasis of Ireland" for its many pubs and watering holes, Kilkenny is one of the country's most alluring destinations. It demands to be explored by foot or bicycle, thanks to its easily circumnavigated town center, a 900-year-old Norman citadel that is now a lovely place of Georgian streets and Tudor stone houses. The city (population 24,500) is impressively preserved and attractively situated on the River Nore, which forms the moat of the magnificently restored Kilkenny Castle. In the 6th century, St. Canice (known as "the builder of churches") established a

large monastic school here. The town's name reflects Canice's central role: Kil Cainneach means "Church of Canice." Kilkenny did not take on its medieval look for another 400 years, when the Anglo-Normans fortified the city with a castle, gates, and a brawny wall. Kilkenny City's central location means that it's not too far from anywhere else in Ireland.

GETTING HERE AND AROUND

From Dublin, take the N7/M7 to the M9 and exit at junction 8 for the N10 to Kilkenny. These are major motorways, so the 101-km (62-mile) trip takes only an hour and a half. Cork is a two-hour drive, while Waterford City is only a 40-minute hop. There is plenty of paid parking around the town.

The bus stop is a bit down from the train station on St. John's Street, and Bus Éireann runs eight buses a day from Dublin, but you have to change at Carlow. Prices vary but the three hour, 10-minute trip generally costs around €12 one-way, €17 round-trip. J. J. Kavanagh & Sons runs five buses a day from Dublin city center and airport. The two-hour journey costs €9 one-way, €18 round-trip.

MacDonagh Station, the city train station, is a short walk from the city center at the top of St. John's Street. The station is on the Dublin–Waterford City line, which also serves Athy, Carlow, Bagenalstown, and Thomastown. Irish Rail runs six trains a day from Dublin, and the trip takes about one hour, 45 minutes and costs approximately €15 each way if you book online. There is no direct train from Cork, but five trains a day arrive via Newbridge, a nearly five-hour journey that costs a ridiculous €31 each way.

VISITOR INFORMATION

CONTACTS Kilkenny Tourist Office. ✉ *Shee Alms House, Rose Inn St., Kilkenny* ☎ *056/775–1500* ⊕ *www.visitkilkenny.ie.*

◉ Sights

Kilkenny's city center is small, and despite the large number of historic sights and picturesque streets—in particular, Butter Slip and High Street—you can easily cover it in less than three hours. One of the most pleasant cities south of Dublin (and one of its most sports-minded—from July to September practically the only topic of conversation is the fate of the city's team at the All-Ireland Hurling Championship), Kilkenny City has become in recent years something of a haven for artists and craft workers seeking an escape from Dublin. At such venues as the Kilkenny Design Centre, you can find an array of quality Irish crafts.

The city has more than 60 pubs, many of them on Parliament and High Streets, which also support a lively music scene. Many of the town's pubs and shops have old-fashioned, highly individualized, brightly painted facades, created as part of the town's 1980s revival of this Victorian tradition. So after taking in Kilkenny Castle and the Riverfront Canal Walk—an overgrown pathway that meanders along the castle grounds—mosey down High and Kieran Streets. These parallel avenues, considered the historic center of Kilkenny, are connected by a series of horse cart–wide lanes and are fronted with some of the city's best-preserved pubs and Victorian flats. Be sure to look up over the existing modern storefronts to catch a glimpse of how the city looked in years past, as many of the buildings still have second-floor facades reflecting historic decorative styles.

Black Abbey

RELIGIOUS SITE | With a stained-glass, carved-stone interior that seems right out of the musical *Camelot,* the 13th-century Black Abbey is one of the most evocative and beautiful Irish medieval structures. Note the famous 1340 five-gabled Rosary Window, an entire wall agleam with ruby and sapphire glass, depicting the life of Christ. Home to a Dominican order of monks since 1225, the abbey was restored as a church by the order, whose black capes gave the abbey its name. Interestingly, it's also one of the few medieval churches still owned by the Roman Catholic Church, as most of the oldest churches in Ireland were built by the Normans and reverted to the Church of Ireland (Anglican) when the English turned to Protestantism. Nearby is the Black Freren Gate (14th century), the last remaining gateway to the medieval city. ⊠ *South of St. Canice's Cathedral, Kilkenny* ☎ *056/772–1279* 🖾 *Free.*

★ Kilkenny Castle

CASTLE/PALACE | Built in 1172 and set amid 50 acres of rolling lawns beside the River Nore, Ireland's most recognizable castle is a bewitching marriage of Gothic and Victorian styles. It conjures images of knights and damsels, dukes and duchesses. For more than 500 years, beginning in 1391, Kilkenny Castle served as the seat of one of the more powerful clans in Irish history, the Butler family, members of which were later designated earls and dukes of Ormonde. Around 1820, William Robert, son of the 1st Marquess of Ormonde, overhauled the castle to make it a wonderland in the Victorian Feudal Revival style. In 1859, John Pollen was called in to redo the aptly named Long Gallery—a refined, airy hall with dazzling green walls hung with a vast collection of family portraits and frayed tapestries, and a marvelously decorated ceiling, replete with oak beams carved with Celtic lacework and brilliantly painted animal heads. The main staircase was also redone in the mid-1800s to become a showpiece of Ruskinian Gothic.

The castle's Butler Gallery, formerly the servants quarters, houses a superb collection of Irish modern art, including examples by Nathaniel Hone, Jack B. Yeats, Sir John Lavery, Louis Le Brocquy, and James Turrell. Be sure to stroll the

While studded with plenty of historic sights, Kilkenny also welcomes the traveler with traditional and "characterful" pubs.

grounds, and the Celtic cross–shape rose garden, after a spot of tea in the old Victorian kitchen. ⊠ *The Parade, Kilkenny* ☎ *056/770–4100* ⊕ *www.kilkennycastle. ie* ⊠ *€8*.

Kyteler's Inn

RESTAURANT—SIGHT | The oldest inn in town, Kyteler's is notorious as the place where Dame Alice Le Kyteler, a member of a wealthy banking family and an alleged witch and "brothel keeper," was accused in 1324 of poisoning her four husbands. So, at least, said the enemies of this apparently very merry widow. The restaurant retains its medieval aura, thanks to its 14th-century stonework and exposed beams down in the cellar, built up around Kieran's Well, which predates the house itself. Food and drink in this popular pub are as simple and plentiful as they would have been in Dame Alice's day—minus her extra ingredients. ⊠ *Kieran St., Kilkenny* ☎ *056/772–1064* ⊕ *www. kytelersinn.com*.

Rothe House

HOUSE | There's a feeling of time travel as you step off the busy main street and into one of Ireland's finest examples of a Tudor-era merchant's house. Built by John Rothe between 1594 and 1610, this medieval complex with stone-wall court-yards (one of which houses a medieval well) is owned by the Kilkenny Archaeological Society and houses a collection of Bronze Age artifacts, ogham stones (carved with an early Celtic alphabet), and period costumes. The Burgage Garden re-creates, down to the plant types themselves, a typical 17th-century Irish merchant's garden. There's also a genealogical research facility to help you trace your ancestry. ⊠ *Parliament St., Kilkenny* ☎ *056/772–2893* ⊕ *www.rothehouse. com* ⊠ *€7, garden only €4* ⊙ *Closed Nov.–Mar., closed Sun*.

★ St. Canice's Cathedral

RELIGIOUS SITE | In spite of Cromwell's defacements, this is still one of the finest cathedrals in Ireland and the country's second-largest medieval church, after St.

Kilkenny City

KEY

1 *Exploring Sights*

1 *Restaurants*

1 *Hotels*

0 ———— 1/8 mile

0 ———— 200 meters

Patrick's Cathedral in Dublin. Behind the massive walls of this 13th-century structure (restored in 1866) is an exuberant Gothic interior, given a somber grandeur by the extensive use of a locally quarried black marble. Many of the memorials and tombstone effigies represent distinguished descendants of the Normans, some depicted in full suits of armor. Look for a female effigy in the south aisle wearing the old Irish, or Kinsale, cloak; a 12th-century black-marble font at the southwest end of the nave; and St. Ciaran's Chair in the north transept, also made of black marble, with 13th-century sculptures on the arms.

In recent years, St. Canice's has achieved notoriety as the resting place of President Obama's great-great-great uncle, the Bishop of Ossory. The biggest attraction on the grounds is the 102-foot-high Round Tower, which was built in 847 by King O'Carroll of Ossory; if you have the energy, climb the tower's 167 steps for the tremendous 360-degree view from the top, as well as for the thrill of mounting 102 steps on makeshift wooden stairs. Next door is St. Canice's Library, containing some 3,000 16th- and 17th-century volumes. ✉ *Dean St., Kilkenny* ☎ *056/776–4971* ⊕ *www.stcanices-cathedral.ie* ✉ *From €4.*

Tholsel

GOVERNMENT BUILDING | With its distinctive clock tower and grand entrance portico, this limestone-marble building on Parliament Street stands on the site of the execution of poor Petronilla, the "witch" burned at the stake in the 14th century in lieu of her mistress, Dame Alice Le Kyteler. Built in 1761, burned down in 1985, and then completely rebuilt, Tholsel now houses the city's municipal archives and council offices. But musicians often busk in the portico, and city walking tours are sometimes allowed inside to explore. Adjacent to the Tholsel is Alice's Castle, a town jail rather grandly fitted out in 18th-century architectural ornamentation. ✉ Parliament St., Kilkenny.

🍴 Restaurants

★ Campagne

$$$ | FRENCH | When Garrett Byrne, the former head chef of Dublin's celebrated Chapter One, returns home and opens a restaurant, people take notice, and the awards—and diners from all of Ireland—start flooding in. The menu is a work of art, with common French themes toyed with and expanded. **Known for:** modern French cuisine; destination dining; relaxed contemporary setting. ⑤ Average main: €32 ✉ 5 The Arches, Gashouse La., Kilkenny ☎ 056/777–2858 ⊕ www.campagne.ie ▭ No credit cards ⊗ Closed Mon. and Tues. No dinner Sun. No lunch Wed. and Thurs.

★ Langton's

$$ | IRISH | A landmark since the 1940s, Langton's is a labyrinth of interconnected bars and eateries. Up front is one of Ireland's most famous "eating pubs," often crammed to the rafters of its low ceiling with a lively crowd. **Known for:** variety of seating options; Irish stew; lively scene. ⑤ Average main: €20 ✉ 69 John St., Kilkenny ☎ 056/776–5133 ⊕ www.langtons.ie.

Ristorante Rinuccini

$$$ | ITALIAN | A warm glow emanates from this Georgian town-house restaurant, where owner-chef Antonio Cavaliere is intensely involved in preparing such luscious Italian dishes as rigatoni all' arrabbiata (tubes of homemade egg pasta in a fresh tomato sauce with chili and garlic). Other specialties, such as Silver Hill Irish duckling in a fresh orange juice and Aurum liquor sauce, go particularly well with Antonio's garlic roasted potatoes—highly recommended as a side dish. **Known for:** best Italian in town; excellent Italian wine list; Silver Hill Irish duckling. ⑤ Average main: €28 ✉ 1 The Parade, across from Kilkenny Castle, Kilkenny ☎ 056/776–1575 ⊕ www.rinuccini.com.

Hotels

Butler House

$$$ | HOTEL | Who needs Kilkenny Castle when you can stay at the Dowager Duchess of Ormonde's 18th-century town house, a charming piece of Georgian grandeur with an ivy-covered three-bay facade and an elegant walled garden? (There's even a private entrance to Kilkenny Castle.) Inside, the reception salon has a magnificent plaster ceiling and marble fireplaces. **Pros:** classic castle feel; serene walled garden; breakfast in the old stables of Kilkenny Castle. **Cons:** books up quickly; no restaurant or bar; some rooms a lot smaller than others. ⑤ Rooms from: €200 ✉ 16 Patrick St., Kilkenny ☎ 056/776–5707 ⊕ www.butler.ie ↩ 14 rooms ⦿ Free breakfast.

Zuni Townhouse and Restaurant

$$ | HOTEL | This popular family-owned hotel in the center of Kilkenny boasts the gloss of a big-city boutique lodging but not the icy-cool reception you get in some fashionable joints. **Pros:** in the heart of the city; family-owned and-run; tasty eatery. **Cons:** books up quickly; limited one-night stays in summer; can get noisy outside on weekends. ⑤ Rooms from: €140 ✉ 26 Patrick St., Kilkenny ☎ 056/772–3999 ⊕ www.zuni.ie ↩ 13 rooms ⦿ Free breakfast.

Nightlife

John Cleere's

BARS/PUBS | If you're craving a pint, you have a choice of pubs along Parliament and High Streets. John Cleere's is the best in town for a mix of live traditional music, poetry readings, and theatrical plays. ✉ *22 Parliament St., Kilkenny* ☎ *056/776–2573.*

Lenehan's

BARS/PUBS | A pristine, classic Irish pub that dates back to the 18th century, Lenehan's has been at the heart of Kilkenny social life for generations. Settle into the private snug in the front bar section and enjoy the view. ✉ *10 Castlecomer Rd., Kilkenny* ☎ *056/772–1621.*

★ Tynan's Bridge House

BARS/PUBS | Set on one of Kilkenny's famous "slips," Tynan's Bridge House was first used as an exercise run for dray horses. Inside, you can guess that the pub is more than 200 years old from all the gas lamps, silver tankards, and historic teapots on display. Behind the horseshoe-shape bar, you'll find antiquities from its time as a grocery and pharmacy, but it's best known these days for its Guinness and good conversation. ✉ *2 Horseleap Slip, Kilkenny* ☎ *056/772–1291.*

🎭 Performing Arts

Watergate Theatre

THEATER | With a roster of operas, plays, concerts, and comedy shows, the Watergate hosts affordable local, national, and international productions. ✉ *Parliament St., Kilkenny* ☎ *056/776–1674* ⊕ *www. watergatetheatre.com.*

🛍 Shopping

Kilkenny is a byword for attractive, original crafts that combine traditional arts with modern design elements.

CLOTHING

Sweater Shop

CLOTHING | You'll find a great selection of Irish knitwear and accessories for men, women, and children at this popular shop. ✉ *81 High St., Kilkenny* ☎ *056/776–3405* ⊕ *www.sweatershop.ie.*

CRAFTS

Jerpoint Glass Studio

CRAFTS | You can see glass being blown at this noted family-run studio, where the glass is heavy, modern, uncut, and hand-finished using traditional tools and methods. The studio's factory shop, 16 km (10 miles) south of Kilkenny, is a good place to pick up a bargain. ✉ *Main St., Stoneyford* ☎ *056/772–4350* ⊕ *www. jerpointglass.com.*

★ Kilkenny Design Centre

CRAFTS | One of Ireland's favorite sources for Irish handicrafts, the Kilkenny Design Centre sells ceramics, jewelry, sweaters, and handwoven textiles. This spot in the old stable yard opposite the castle has a restaurant specializing in hearty Irish fare. ✉ *Opposite Kilkenny Castle, Kilkenny* ☎ *056/772–2118* ⊕ *www.kilkennydesign. com.*

★ Nicholas Mosse Pottery

CERAMICS/GLASSWARE | One of the best-known names in Irish ceramics, Mosse first set up his potter's wheel in an old flour mill in 1975. Since then, the shop's rustic floral-pattern pottery has become instantly recognizable for its "spongeware" designs. A visit to the shop, in a quiet village 16 km (10 miles) south of Kilkenny, allows you to see the pottery being made, and the adjoining factory shop often has good bargains. ✉ *Off Annamult Rd., Bennettsbridge* ☎ *056/772–7505* ⊕ *www.nicholasmosse. com.*

JEWELRY

Murphy Jewellers

JEWELRY/ACCESSORIES | This county favorite specializes in silver and diamond jewelry. ✉ *85 High St., Kilkenny* ☎ *056/772–1127* ⊕ *murphyjewellers.ie.*

Rudolf Heltzel

JEWELRY/ACCESSORIES | German-born but living in Kilkenny since the 1960s. Rudolf Heltzel is known for striking, modern designs and mostly showcases gold and silver jewelry. ✉ *10 Patrick St., Kilkenny*

Extending 150 feet, Kilkenny Castle's Long Gallery is lined with family portraits and has a hammer-beam ceiling supported on carved stone corbels with gilded animal and bird heads on the crossbeams.

☎ *056/772–1497* ⊕ *www.rudolfheltzel. com.*

🏃 Activities

HURLING

★ Kilkenny GAA Grounds

LOCAL SPORTS | The 1366 Statutes of Kilkenny expressly forbade the ancient Irish game of hurling. No matter: today, Kilkenny is considered one of the great hurling counties. Like its neighbor and archenemy, Wexford, Kilkenny has a long history of success in hurling, and as the annual All-Ireland Hurling Championships draws to its final stages during July and August, interest in the county's team runs to fever pitch. Catch the home team at matches held at Kilkenny GAA Grounds. ⊠ *Nowlan Park, Kilkenny* ☎ *056/776–5122* ⊕ *www.kilkennygaa.ie.*

Thomastown

14½ km (9 miles) south of Kilkenny.

Originally the seat of the kings of Ossory (an ancient Irish kingdom), Thomastown is a pretty, stone-built village on the River Nore. It takes its name from Thomas FitzAnthony of Leinster, who encircled the town with a wall in the 13th century. Fragments of this medieval wall remain, as do the partly ruined 13th-century church of St. Mary. Mullins Castle sits adjacent to the town bridge.

GETTING HERE AND AROUND

From Kilkenny, take the N77 to Thomastown exit. The 14½-km (9-mile) trip should take 20 minutes. Bus Éireann runs regular services from Dublin and Kilkenny. There is also regular train service from Dublin, Kilkenny, and Waterford.

Hurling: A Fast and Furious Sport

Get chatting with the locals in almost any pub across the Southeast, mention the sport of hurling, and an enthusiastic and often passionate conversation is bound to ensue. The region is the heartland of this ancient sport, whose followers have an almost religious obsession with the game.

Hurling is a kind of aerial field hockey with players wielding curved sticks. Its history comes from Ireland's Celtic ancestors, but it bears about the same relation to field hockey as ice hockey does to roller-skating. It's no accident that prowess on the hurling field is regarded as a supreme qualification for election to public office. A man who succeeds at hurling is eminently capable of dealing with anything that fate and the spite of other politicians can throw at him. Hurling is also an extremely skillful sport. A player must have excellent hand-eye coordination combined with an ability to run at high speeds while balancing a small golf-ball-size ball on his *camán* (hurling stick). Fans will proudly tell you it's also the world's fastest team sport.

Ireland's other chief sporting pastimes, including soccer and hurling's cousin, Gaelic football, take a backseat in this part of the country. Stars like Kilkenny's TJ Reid, rather than professional soccer players, are sporting icons for local kids. Counties Tipperary, Wexford, and Waterford are among the top teams in the region, but Kilkenny (nicknamed "The Cats") dominated the national scene over the last two decades before a dip in form in recent years. It won 11 of the last 18 All-Ireland Hurling Championships and is considered one of the best teams in history.

There's an intense rivalry between the counties, especially between old foes Tipperary and Kilkenny. When it gets down to club level, passions run even higher. Almost every parish in the region has a hurling club, and a quick inquiry with locals will usually be enough to find out when the next game is on. Even for the uninitiated, hurling is a great spectator sport. Sporty types wishing to give it a go, be warned; it's fast, furious, and entails more than a hint of danger, as players flail the air to capture the bullet-fast *sliotar* (hurling ball).

◉ Sights

★ **Jerpoint Abbey**

ARCHAEOLOGICAL SITE | Known for its rearing and massive 15th-century tower, Jerpoint Abbey is one of the most notable Cistercian ruins in Ireland, dating from about 1160. The church, tombs, and the restored cloister are must-sees for lovers of the Irish Romanesque. The vast cloister is decorated with affecting carvings of human figures and fantastical mythical creatures, including knights and knaves (one with a stomachache) and the assorted dragon or two. Dissolved in 1540, Jerpoint was taken over, as was so much around these parts, by the earls of Ormonde. The one part of the abbey that remains alive, so to speak, is its hallowed cemetery—the natives are still buried here. Guided tours are available or you can just wander at your leisure. ✉ *N9, 2 km (1 mile) south of Thomastown* ☎ *056/772–4623* ⊕ *www.heritageireland. ie/en/south-east/jerpointabbey* 💶 *€5* 🕓 *Closed Dec.–Feb.*

Hotels

Ballyduff House

$ | B&B/INN | As the clematis-clad mansion comes into view at the top of a gently curving driveway you can understand why this wonderfully picturesque house was used as a location in the 1990s movie adaptation of Maeve Binchy's *Circle of Friends*. **Pros:** great river views from some rooms; stunningly authentic mansion; guests can use kitchen to prepare a picnic. **Cons:** fills up fast; few modern facilities; can attract a mostly golf crowd. $ *Rooms from: €100 ✉ Off R700 ☎ 056/775–8488 ⊕ www.ballyduffhouse. ie ⇨ 5 rooms ❖ Free breakfast.*

★ Mount Juliet

$$$$ | HOTEL | For many, the Jack Nicklaus–designed golf course—which has hosted the Irish Open on three occasions—is the main draw, but this lush 1,500-acre estate beside the beautiful River Nore offers so much more. **Pros:** great golf on your doorstep; period elegance with modern amenities; Michelin-starred restaurant. **Cons:** rooms outside main house a little inferior; some charm sacrificed for modern comfort; restaurant books up quickly. $ *Rooms from: €275 ✉ Off L4206 ☎ 056/777–3000 ⊕ www.mountjuliet.ie ⇨ 125 rooms ❖ Free breakfast.*

Activities

GOLF

★ Mount Juliet Golf Course

GOLF | Attached to a magisterial country-house hotel, this Jack Nicklaus–designed championship parkland course, 19 km (11 miles) from Kilkenny Town, includes practice greens, a driving range, and, for those who feel a little rusty, a David Leadbetter golf academy. The heavily forested course has eight holes that play over water, including the wonderful 3rd hole—a par-3 over a stream from an elevated tee. The back nine present a series of difficult bunker shots. Greens fees are above average, and although visitors are always welcome, a weekday round is best, since it's often crowded with members on weekends. ✉ *Mount Juliet Estate, Off L4206 ☎ 056/777–3010 ⊕ www.mountjuliet.ie ✉ May–Sept., daily €95–€115; Nov.–Mar., daily €50–€60; Apr. and Oct., daily €75–€90 ⅄ 18 holes, 7264 yards, par 72.*

Enniscorthy

32 km (20 miles) east of Graiguenamanagh.

On the sloping banks of the River Slaney and on the main road between Dublin and Wexford to the south of the popular resort of Gorey, Enniscorthy is a thriving market town that is rich in history.

GETTING HERE AND AROUND
From Wexford, take the N1 to the N30; the 32-km (20-mile) trip takes about half an hour. From Dublin, take the N11/M11 all the way to Enniscorthy; the trip takes about 90 minutes. There is regular bus and train service from Wexford and Dublin.

Sights

★ Enniscorthy Castle

CASTLE/PALACE | The town is dominated by Enniscorthy Castle, built in the first quarter of the 13th century by the Prendergast family. The imposing Norman castle was the site of fierce battles against Oliver Cromwell in the 17th century and during the Rebellion of 1798. The castle has reopened after extensive renovations, with an exhibition exploring the development of the building and the town. Exhibits also explore the 1916 Rising in Enniscorthy and the work of furniture designer and architect Eileen Gray, who was born in 1878 just outside town. Gray went on to become one of the founding designers of the Modernist movement in the 1920s and now enjoys

Southeast Inlands

worldwide fame at staggering prices (one chair she designed brought $22 million at auction). The guided tour is a real treat, with a trip to the dungeon followed by a walk on the roof with impressive views out over the town and beyond. ✉ *Castle Hill* ☎ *053/923–4699* ⊕ *www.enniscorth-ycastle.ie* 🎟 *€5* ⏱ *Closed Nov.*

National 1798 Centre

MUSEUM | This small museum tells the tale of the United Irishmen and the ill-fated 1798 rebellion. ✉ *Arnold's Cross* ☎ *053/923–7596* ⊕ *www.1798centre.ie* 🎟 *€7* ⏱ *Closed weekends Sept.–May.*

St. Aidan's Cathedral

RELIGIOUS SITE | Standing on a command-ing site overlooking the Slaney, the Gothic Revival structure of St. Aidan's was built in the mid-19th century under the direction of Augustus Welby Pugin, famed architect of the Houses of

Parliament in London. ✉ *Cathedral St.* ☎ *053/923–5777* ⊕ *www.staidanscathe-dral.ie* 🎟 *Free.*

 ## Shopping

Kiltrea Bridge Pottery

CRAFTS | Garden pots and country kitchen crocks are just a few of the goodies at this pottery studio and shop just west of Enniscorthy. ✉ *Kiltealy Rd.* ☎ *053/923–5107* ⊕ *www.kiltreapottery.com.*

Wexford Town

19 km (12 miles) south of Enniscorthy, 62 km (39 miles) northeast of Waterford City, 115 km (72 miles) southwest of Dublin.

This coastal town is most famed for the Wexford Opera Festival, usually held in October, which has been seducing the world with wonderful productions of rare opera for more than 50 years. The warm and vivacious welcome, the narrow streets, and the atmospheric Theatre Royal add to the pleasure of this event and to any visit to Wexford Town.

From its appearance today, you would barely realize that Wexford is an ancient place, but in fact the Greek cartographer Ptolemy mapped it as long ago as the 2nd century AD. Its Irish name is Loch Garman, but the Vikings called it Waesfjord (the harbor of the mudflats), which became Wexford in English. Wexford developed into an English garrison town after it was captured by Oliver Cromwell in 1649.

Rising above the town's rooftops are the graceful spires of two elegant examples of 19th-century Gothic architecture. These twin churches have identical exteriors, their foundation stones were laid on the same day, and their spires each reach a height of 230 feet. The Church of the Assumption is on Bride Street. The Church of the Immaculate Conception is on Rowe Street.

GETTING HERE AND AROUND
From Dublin take the N11/M11 all the way to Wexford Town; the trip takes about two hours and 10 minutes.

Intercity buses arrive at O'Hanrahan Train Station on Redmond Place. Fares are approximate as prices vary depending on season and day of week. Bus Éireann has nine buses a day from Dublin (three hours; around €19 one-way, €27 round-trip), nine from Rosslare (30 minutes; around €8 one-way, €10 round-trip), and six (three on Sunday) from Waterford City (three hours; around €12 one-way, €19 round-trip).

Irish Rail trains arrive at O'Hanrahan Train Station, at the northern end of town on Redmond Place. Wexford is on the Dublin–Roslare line and three trains a day arrive from Dublin; the 2½-hour trip costs approximately €17 one-way, €33 round-trip. The short hop to Rosslare costs €5 one-way, €10 round-trip, and takes 25 minutes. There are no direct trains to Cork or Waterford.

VISITOR INFORMATION
CONTACTS Wexford Tourist Office. ✉ Crescent Quay, Wexford ☎ 053/912–3111 ⊕ www.visitwexford.ie.

Sights

The River Slaney empties into the sea at Wexford Town. The harbor has silted up since the days when Viking longboats docked here; nowadays only a few small trawlers fish from here. Wexford Town's compact center is on the south bank of the Slaney. Running parallel to the quays on the riverfront is the main street (the name changes several times) and its pleasant mix of old-fashioned bakeries, butcher shops, stylish boutiques, and a share of Wexford's many pubs. It can be explored on foot in an hour or two. Allow at least half a day in the area if you also intend to visit Irish National Heritage Park at nearby Ferrycarrig, and a full day if you want to take in Johnstown Castle Gardens or walk in the nature reserve at nearby Curracloe Beach.

Franciscan Friary
RELIGIOUS SITE | While Oliver Cromwell made a bonfire of the original 13th-century Friary, this rebuilt 19th-century landmark has a ceiling worth noting for its fine, locally crafted stuccowork and a relic and wax effigy of St. Adjutor—a young martyr slain by his own father. ✉ School St., Wexford ☎ 053/912–2758 💷 Free.

Irish National Heritage Park
MUSEUM | FAMILY | A 35-acre, open-air, living-history museum beside the River Slaney, this is one of Ireland's most successful and enjoyable family attractions. In about 90 minutes, a guide takes you

260

Sights ▼

1 Franciscan
   Friary **B6**

2 Irish National
   Heritage
   Park **A2**

3 Johnstown
   Castle
   Gardens..... **A7**

4 Westgate
   Tower **C2**

5 Wexford Bull
   Ring.......... **C4**

6 Wexford Opera
   House **C5**

7 Wexford
   Wildfowl
   Reserve **D3**

Resturants ▼

1 Cistín Eile ... **C7**

2 D'Lush
   Cafe **C4**

3 Reeds
   Restaurant.. **A2**

Hotels ▼

1 Ferrycarrig
   Hotel......... **A2**

2 Riverbank
   House
   Hotel......... **D3**

Wexford Town

KEY

1 *Exploring Sights*

1 *Restaurants*

1 *Hotels*

through 9,000 years of Irish history—from the first evidence of humans on this island, at around 7000 BC, to the Norman settlements of the mid-12th century. Full-scale replicas of typical dwellings illustrate the changes in beliefs and lifestyles. Highlights include a prehistoric homestead, a *crannóg* (lake dwelling), an early Christian *rath* (fortified farmstead), a horizontal water mill, a Viking longhouse, and a Norman castle. There are also examples of pre-Christian burial sites and a stone circle. Most of the exhibits are "inhabited" by students in appropriate historic dress who will answer questions. The riverside site includes several nature trails and there's a family restaurant. ⊠ *N11, 5 km (3 miles) north of Wexford Town, Ferrycarrig* ☏ *053/912–0733* ⊕ *www.inhp.com* ☏ *€11.*

★ Johnstown Castle Gardens

MUSEUM | Set in a beautiful garden estate, this Victorian Gothic castle looks like it was designed for a Disney movie but it was in fact built for the Grogan-Morgan family between 1810 and 1855. The magnificent parklands—with towering trees and ornamental gardens—offer a grand frame to the castle. Unfortunately, you can't tour the building (it houses an agricultural college) other than its entrance hall, but the well-maintained grounds are open to the public. The centerpiece is the 5-acre lake, one side of which has a statue-lined terrace where you can take in the panorama of the mirrored castle. Because there's such a variety of trees—Japanese cedars, Atlantic blue cedars, golden Lawson cypresses—there's color through much of the year. Nearby are the Devil's Gate walled garden—a woodland garden set around the ruins of the medieval castle of Rathlannon—and the Irish Agricultural Museum. The latter, housed in the quadrangular stable yards, shows what life was once like in rural Ireland. It also contains a 5,000-square-foot exhibition on the potato and the Great Famine (1845–49). ⊠ *Off N25, 6 km (4 miles) southwest of Wexford Town,*

Wexford ☏ *053/914–2888* ⊕ *www.irish-agrimuseum.ie* ☏ *Gardens and museum €8, museum €6, gardens €3. Gardens free Nov.–Feb.*

Westgate Tower

MILITARY SITE | Of the five fortified gateways through the Norman and Viking town walls, Westgate is the only one remaining. The early-13th-century tower has been sensitively restored. Keep an eye out as you wander this part of town for other preserved segments of the old town walls. ⊠ *Westgate, Wexford.*

Wexford Bull Ring

HISTORIC SITE | Once the scene of bull baiting, a cruel medieval sport that was popular among the Norman nobility, this arena was sad witness to other bloody crimes. In 1649, Cromwell's soldiers massacred 300 panic-stricken townspeople who had gathered here to pray as the army stormed their town. The memory of this heartless leader has remained a dark folk legacy for centuries and is only now beginning to fade. ⊠ *Quay St., Wexford.*

Wexford Opera House

ARTS VENUE | Wexford's grand and hoary landmark, the Theatre Royal, has been entirely rebuilt to serve as the Wexford Opera Theatre for the world-famous Wexford Opera Festival, held here during the last two weeks of October and the beginning of November. The strikingly modern, Keith Williams–designed building is custom-built for opera and offers fabulous views out over Mt. Lenister to the northwest and Tuskar Rock lighthouse to the southeast. The surprisingly large main auditorium seats 749 with a smaller second space for 172. Year-round, touring companies and local productions are also seen at these venues. ⊠ *27 High St., Wexford* ☏ *053/912–2144* ⊕ *wexfordopera.com.*

Wexford Wildfowl Reserve

NATURE PRESERVE | A nature lover's paradise, Wexford Wildlife Reserve is just a short walk across the bridge from

Viking longboats once docked where fishing trawlers now berth in Wexford's busy harbor.

the main part of town. It shelters a third of the world's Greenland white-fronted geese. As many as 10,000 of them spend their winters on the mudflats (known locally as "slobs"), which also draw ducks, swans, and other waterfowl. Observation hides are provided for bird-watchers, and an audiovisual show and exhibitions are available at the visitor center. ⊠ *Wexford Harbour, Wexford* ☎ *053/912–3406* ⊕ *www.wexfordwild-fowlreserve.ie* 🎫 *Free.*

🍴 Restaurants

★ Cistín Eile

$ | MODERN IRISH | Proud of its modern Irishness, Cistín Eile takes the produce of local farmers and applies a simple but stunning brand of culinary magic. The menu changes depending on what's good in the local market. **Known for:** inventive Irish cuisine; cozy atmosphere; black-and-white pudding with cabbage salad. 💲 *Average main: €12* ⊠ *80 S. Main St., Wexford* ☎ *053/912–1616* 💳 *No credit cards* 🕐 *Closed Sun. No dinner Mon. and Tues.*

D'Lush Cafe

$ | CAFÉ | Locals swear this cute little joint at the back of the Arts Centre is the home of Wexford's best coffee. The interior is simple but cozy with creative touches like local artwork visible throughout. **Known for:** quality snacks; delicious desserts; arty crowd. 💲 *Average main: €11* ⊠ *Wexford Arts Centre, Cornmarket, Wexford* ☎ *053/912–3795* ⊕ *www. dlushcafe.ie.*

Reeds Restaurant

$$ | IRISH | Fresh-off-the-boat fish is the big draw at this restaurant at the family-friendly Ferrycarrig Hotel. Seafood from Kilmore Quay is a favorite, but the Killurin lamb is just as local and tasty, as is the rib-eye steak with smoked garlic mash and blue cheese butter. **Known for:** seafood selection; riverfront views; extensive wine list. 💲 *Average main: €24* ⊠ *Ferrycarrig Hotel, off N11, 4 km (2½ miles) outside Wexford Town, Wexford* ☎ *053/912–0999* ⊕ *www. ferrycarrighotel.ie.*

Off The Beaten Path

Curracloe Beach. Steven Spielberg filmed the terrifyingly gory D-Day landing scenes from his blockbuster *Saving Private Ryan* along this beautiful, soft, white-sand strand. In real life it's a popular swimming place in summer and a quiet home to many migratory birds in winter. It's 9 km (5½ miles) long, with a 1-km (½-mile) nature trail in the seashore sand dunes. There are 500 parking spaces at the White Gap entrance. Amenities are minimal, with lifeguards on duty only in summer on one stretch of the beach. **Amenities:** lifeguards; parking; showers. **Best for:** solitude in winter; swimming; walking; windsurfing. ⊠ *R742, 11 km (7 miles) northeast of Wexford Town, Wexford* ⊕ *www. wexford.ie.*

🛏 Hotels

Ferrycarrig Hotel

$$ | HOTEL | FAMILY | A favorite with families, this spot offers a swimming pool for kids, a peaceful and tranquil riverside location for parents, and a well-equipped health center for both. **Pros:** family-friendly; good restaurant; riverside location. **Cons:** can get a bit hectic in summer; a little overpriced; some rooms better than others. ⑤ *Rooms from: €161* ⊠ *Off N11, 4 km (2½ miles) outside Wexford Town, Wexford* ☎ *053/912–0999* ⊕ *www. ferrycarrighotel.ie* ⮑ *102 rooms* ⦿ *Free breakfast.*

Riverbank House Hotel

$ | HOTEL | Located across a bridge from the center of town, with stunning views of the River Slaney, the Riverbank's perfectly manicured gardens and original Victorian furnishings add to the romantic vibe of this boutique hotel. **Pros:** stunning riverside location; comfortable public areas; minutes from town center. **Cons:** popular with weddings; some noise from town. ⑤ *Rooms from: €115* ⊠ *The Bridge, Wexford* ☎ *053/912–3611* ⊕ *www.riverbankhouse-hotel.com* ⮑ *23 rooms* ⦿ *Free breakfast.*

🍸 Nightlife

Centenary Stores

BARS/PUBS | As the saying goes, if you can find a street without at least one bar on it, you've left Wexford. Centenary Stores is a Victorian-style pub with an adjoining nightclub that makes it popular with the young crowd. Lunch is served daily, and there's traditional music every Sunday morning. ⊠ *Charlotte St., Wexford* ☎ *053/912–4424* ⊕ *www.thestores.ie.*

The Sky & the Ground

BARS/PUBS | One of the best pubs in town, the Sky & the Ground is a hub for Irish music sessions, which pack in the crowds from Monday through Thursday. ⊠ *112 S. Main St., Wexford* ☎ *053/912–1273.*

★ Thomas Moore Tavern

BARS/PUBS | Dating to the 13th century, the Thomas Moore Tavern is Wexford's oldest pub, named after the renowned Irish poet whose parents lived here. The pub has its original medieval walls and fine old beams along the ceiling, and a spot by the roaring fire is the perfect place for a quiet drink. There's a restaurant attached, and pub-grub dinners are served in the bar. ⊠ *Cornmarket, Wexford* ☎ *053/917–4688* ⊕ *www.thomasmoore-tavern.com.*

Shopping

Barkers

CRAFTS | Established in 1848, Waterford crystal, Belleek china, local pottery, linens, and crafts are found here in tempting array. ⊠ *36 S. Main St., Wexford* ☎ *053/912–3159* ⊕ *www.barkers.ie.*

Martin's Jewellers

CRAFTS | This popular shop specializes in bespoke Celtic jewelry. Have it made before your eyes in the attached workshop. ⊠ *Lower Rowe St., Wexford* ☎ *053/912–2635* ⊕ *www.martinsjewellers.ie.*

Westgate Design

CRAFTS | A good selection of quality Irish crafts, clothing, pottery, candles, and jewelry is found at Westgate Design. There's also a restaurant and deli. ⊠ *22A N. Main St., Wexford* ☎ *053/912–3787* ⊕ *www.westgatedesign.ie.*

Activities

GAELIC FOOTBALL
Wexford Park GAA

LOCAL SPORTS | Wexford is mostly a hurling county, but you can watch both Gaelic football and hurling at the Wexford Park GAA. ⊠ *Clonard Rd., Wexford* ☎ *053/914–4808* ⊕ *www.wexfordgaa.ie.*

Rosslare

16 km (10 miles) southeast of Wexford Town.

Sometimes called Ireland's sunniest spot, the village of Rosslare is a seaside getaway with an attractive beach. Many vacationers head here to hike, golf, sun, and swim. But the truth is that most visitors are only here to take the ferry from the Rosslare Europort terminal, the only reason (some point out) you should find yourself in this otherwise dull little town.

GETTING HERE AND AROUND

As Rosslare is so well connected to the ferry port, the roads to major cities to and from here are very good: N81, N11, and N25. Rosslare is 16 km (10 miles) southeast of Wexford Town on the R470. The trip from Dublin takes around two hours, 12 minutes.

Bus Éireann has service from many cities and towns in Ireland, including Waterford City (around €18 one-way, €34 round-trip; 1½ hours) and Dublin (around €20 one-way, €27 round-trip; three hours). Irish Rail runs three trains daily on the Dublin–Rosslare Europort line via Wexford Town. The trip to Dublin takes three hours (around €18 one-way, €35 round-trip) and to Wexford Town only 25 minutes (around €4.50 one-way, €9 round-trip).

Stena Line Express sails May to September between Rosslare Harbour and Fishguard in Wales (3½ hours; two sailings per day) year-round. The fare in summer starts from €39, or €132 for a car and driver. Irish Ferries sails to Pembroke in Wales (3¾ hours, twice daily). Single summer fares start at €39 for a foot passenger, €149 for a car and driver. There are also daily ferries to Cherbourg, France (19½ hours, up to three a week). ■ **TIP➔ Ferries to and from Rosslare sometimes sell out, so reserve your space in advance.**

Sights

Rosslare Harbour

TRANSPORTATION SITE (AIRPORT/BUS/FERRY/TRAIN) | The end of the line for car ferries to and from Fishguard (3½ hours) and Pembroke (3¾ hours) in Wales and Cherbourg (19½ hours) in France, Rosslare Harbour, is 8 km (5 miles) south of the village. Irish Ferries and Stena Sealink have small kiosks in the ultramodern terminal, which also has lockers, a café, and a sprawling waiting room. You can purchase ferry tickets at the terminal, but reservations are also a must if you're traveling by car, because space is at a premium. Connecting bus and rail stations are also here. ⊠ *Rosslare* ⊕ *rosslareeuroport.irishrail.ie.*

Hotels

Kelly's Resort Hotel & Spa
$$$ | **HOTEL** | **FAMILY** | A local institution, Kelly's has been consistently entertaining families since 1895 with its winning formula of a stunning beachfront location, excellent entertainment and leisure facilities, a child-friendly approach, and a reputation for good food. **Pros:** great Irish art collection; ample on-site family activities; relaxing spa. **Cons:** lots of kids make it hectic; fairly basic amenities in rooms; one-week minimum stay in summer. ⑤ *Rooms from: €198* ⊠ *Strand Rd.* ☎ *053/913–2114* ⊕ *www.kellys.ie* ⊗ *Closed Dec.–mid-Feb.* ⤵ *118 rooms* ⦿⊙⦿ *Free breakfast.*

Nightlife

Portholes Bar
BARS/PUBS | A trendy spot with designer decor, the Portholes Bar is the main hangout at the Hotel Rosslare. It's particularly popular for live music on weekends. ⊠ *Hotel Rosslare, Rosslare Harbour* ☎ *053/913–3110* ⊕ *www.hotel-rosslare.ie.*

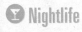 Activities

GOLF
Rosslare Golf Club
GOLF | Opened in 1905, this 30-hole championship links sits on a narrow peninsula with the harbor on one side and the Irish Sea on the other. On the 18-hole Old Course, the "Barber's Pole" is the devilishly tricky par-4 11th hole. The 12-hole Burrow Course was designed by Irish legend Christy O'Connor Junior. The course is famous for its stunning flora and birdlife. ⊠ *Rosslare Strand* ☎ *053/913–2203* ⊕ *www.rosslaregolf.*

com ✉ *May–Sept., weekdays €35, weekends €50; Mar. and Apr., weekdays €30, weekends €35; Oct.–Dec., weekdays €25, weekends €30* ⦁ *Old Course: 18 holes, 6786 yards, par 72; Burrow Course: 12 holes, 3956 yards, par 48.*

St. Helens Bay Golf Resort
GOLF | With panoramic views of the south Wexford coastline and Tuskar Rock, 18-hole St. Helens Bay, a relatively new course, is a classic Irish golf experience. Designed by Irish Ryder Cup hero Philip Walton, it's famous for its challenging but stunning final two holes. There's a fun 9-hole golf course right next door if you feel like extending your day. ⊠ *Off St. Helen's Dr., Kilrane* ☎ *053/913–3234* ⊕ *www.sthelensbay.ie* ✉ *Apr.–Oct., weekdays €25, weekends €30; Nov.–Mar., weekdays €20, weekends €25* ⦁ *18 holes, 6715 yards, par 72.*

Kilmore Quay

22 km (14 miles) south of Rosslare.

Noted for its fishing industry, this quiet, old-fashioned seaside village of thatched and whitewashed cottages is also popular with recreational anglers and bird-watchers. From the harbor there's a pleasant view to the east over flat coast that stretches for miles. Recent development has turned the harbor into a popular leisure marina.

Sights

★ Ballyteigue Burrow
NATURE PRESERVE | Nature lovers and walkers flock to the 8-km-long (5-mile-long) Ballyteigue Burrow, one of the finest sand-dune systems in Europe. It runs all the way from Kilmore Quay to Cullenstown, and is perfect for a long summer stroll and a picnic, with trails through the rolling dunes or along the beautiful beach. The western end is an important

The Southeast Coast

KEY
Ferry lines
Rail lines

St. George's Channel

TO WALES, FRANCE →

Celtic Sea

Blackwater
Enniscorthy
Ferns
Oilgate
Curracloe
Wexford Town see detail map
Irish National Heritage Park
Rosslare
Rosslare Harbour
Wexford Harbour
Lady's Island
Tomhaggard
Kilmore Quay
Saltee Islands
Piercetown
Duncormick
Forlorn Pt.
Ballyteige Burrow
Fethard-on-Sea
Wellington Bridge
Carrick
Churchtown
Hook Peninsula
Duncannon
Ballyhack
Cheekpoint
Passage East
Dunmore East
Clonroche
WEXFORD
R. Slaney
Clonroche
St. Mullins
Graiguenamanagh
Borris
New Ross
John F. Kennedy Arboretum
Dunganstown
R. Barrow
R. Nore
Inistioge
Thomastown
Bennettsbridge
KILKENNY
Waterford City see detail map
Tramore
Annestown
Portlaw
Callan
Stoneyford
Knocktopher
Ahenny
Mullinavat
Waterford Harbour
Stradbally
Clonea
Bunmahon
Kilmacthomas
Lemybrien
Ballinagarry
Killenaule
Fethard
Windgap
SLIEVENAMON MOUNTAIN
Carrick-on-Suir
TIPPERARY
WATERFORD
Ballymacarbry
The Nire Valley
Clonmel
Ring (An Rinn)
Dungarvan
Ardmore

0   10 miles
0   10 km

nature reserve rich in butterflies, flowers, and wading birds. ⊠ *Kilmore Quay*.

Kehoe's Pub and Parlour
RESTAURANT—SIGHT | The hub of village activity, Kehoe's Pub has a collection of maritime artifacts as interesting as that of many museums. ⊠ *Kilmore Quay* ☏ *053/671–0338*.

Kilmore Quay Seafood Festival
FESTIVAL | For three days in early July, Kilmore Quay hosts a lively Seafood Festival with a parade, live music, seafood barbecues, guided walks, and other events. ⊠ *Kilmore Quay* ⊕ *www.kilmorequayseafoodfestival.com*.

Saltee Islands
NATURE PRESERVE | Ireland's largest bird sanctuary, the Saltee Islands make a fine day trip from Kilmore Quay. You can see kittiwakes, puffins, guillemots, cormorants, gulls, and petrels, especially in late spring and early summer when several million seabirds nest among the dunes and rocky scarp on the southernmost of the two islands. From mid-May to mid-September, look for boats at the village waterfront or on the marina to take you to the islands, weather permitting. ⊠ *Kilmore Quay* ⊕ *www.discoverireland.ie*.

Restaurants

The Silver Fox Seafood Restaurant
$$ | SEAFOOD | Given its quayside location, seafood is the specialty at this busy family-run seafood restaurant. Fisherman's pie is a real favorite—scrumptious freshly caught prawns, monkfish, salmon, and cod in a dill and Pernod cream sauce topped with a mashed-potato crust. **Known for:** fisherman's pie; good value lobster; waterside location. $ *Average main: €24* ⊠ *Kilmore Quay* ☏ *053/912–9988* ⊕ *www.silverfox.ie* ⊗ *Closed Dec.–Easter, and Mon.–Thurs. No lunch Fri.*

Hotels

Quay House
$ | B&B/INN | A perfect base for those interested in boating or fishing, this family-run guesthouse is a three-minute walk from the pier. **Pros:** great angling and diving spot; nonguests can join you for the tranquil breakfast; nautical decor. **Cons:** rooms are not huge; few facilities; fills up in fishing and diving seasons. $ *Rooms from: €90* ⊠ *Kilmore Quay* ☏ *053/912–9988* ⊕ *www.quayhouse.net* ⇥ *10 rooms* ⦿| *Free breakfast*.

Ballyhack

39 km (24 miles) west of Kilmore Quay, 54 km (33 miles) west of Rosslare.

★ On the upper reaches of Waterford Harbour, this pretty village with a square castle keep, thatch cottages, and a green, hilly background is admired by painters and photographers.

GETTING HERE AND AROUND
A small car ferry makes the five-minute crossing from Passage East in County Waterford. Driving from Wexford, take the N25 west to the R373. The 48-km (30-mile) trip takes about an hour on these relatively narrow roads. There is regular bus service from Wexford Town.

Sights

Ballyhack Castle
CASTLE/PALACE | The gray-stone keep of Ballyhack Castle dates from the 16th century. It was once owned by the Knights Templar of St. John of Jerusalem, who held the ferry rights by royal charter. The first two floors now house local-history exhibits. Guided tours are available by appointment. ⊠ *Ballyhack* ☏ *051/389–468* ⊕ *www.heritageireland.ie/en/south-east/ballyhackcastle* ⊠ *Free* ⊗ *Closed Sept.–early May*.

John F. Kennedy Arboretum

GARDEN | About 12 km (8 miles) to the north of Ballyhack lies the John F. Kennedy Arboretum, with more than 600 acres of forest, nature trails, and gardens, plus an ornamental lake. The grounds contain some 4,500 species of trees and shrubs and serve as a resource center for botanists and foresters. The top of the park offers fine panoramic views. The arboretum is clearly signposted from New Ross on R733, which follows the banks of the Barrow southward for about 5 km (3 miles). The cottage where the president's great-grandfather was born is in Dunganstown; Kennedy relatives still live in the house. About 2 km (1 mile) down the road at Slieve Coillte you can see the entrance to the arboretum. ⊠ *Off R733, Dunganstown* ☎ *051/388–171* ⊕ *www.heritageireland.ie/en/south-east/ thejohnfkennedyarboretum/* ⊠ *€5.*

🍽 Restaurants

★ Harvest Room

$$$$ | CONTEMPORARY | Gourmands come in droves to the ruby-red dining room at Dunbrody House, where celebrity-chef Kevin Dundon serves up foie gras with toasted brioche and balsamic-marinated strawberries, suckling pig with artichoke, girolles, and pearl onion, and a chocolate "selection of indulgences." The weekend eight-course tasting menu is a parade of culinary delights. If you're a hands-on type, you can learn how to cook the Harvest Room's delights yourself; Dundon runs a cooking school on weekends. **Known for:** culinary reputation; legendary Sunday lunch; cooking school. $ *Average main: €35* ⊠ *Dunbrody House, Off L4052, Arthurstown* ☎ *051/389–600* ⊕ *www.dunbrodyhouse.com* ☉ *Closed Mon. and Tues. No lunch Wed.–Sat.*

🛏 Hotels

★ Dunbrody Country House

$$$$ | HOTEL | One of Ireland's finest country houses, Dunbrody is a sprawling, two-story 1830s Georgian manor house with beautiful gardens, cooking classes with an Irish celeb chef, guest rooms that charm with a judiciously luxe combination of period antiques and fine reproductions, and restful views over the Barrow Estuary. **Pros:** authentic Georgian feel; ideally positioned for exploring Wexford and the Hook Peninsula; great restaurant and lively bar. **Cons:** expensive for this region; spa is small; quality of rooms can vary. $ *Rooms from: €250* ⊠ *Off L4052, Arthurstown* ☎ *051/389– 600* ⊕ *www.dunbrodyhouse.com* ⇗ *22 rooms* ⊚ *Free breakfast.*

★ Kilmokea Country Manor & Gardens

$$ | B&B/INN | Originally an 18th-century stone rectory, the authentic Georgian-country-house experience is promised and more than delivered at luxurious Kilmokea, known for its award-winning gardens. **Pros:** award-winning gardens; authentic Georgian experience; rooms boast gorgeous garden views. **Cons:** a little out of the way; occasionally booked up for private parties; expensive for the region. $ *Rooms from: €160* ⊠ *Great Island, Campile, Wexford* ☎ *051/388–109* ⊕ *www.kilmokea.com* ⇗ *7 rooms, 1 cottage* ⊚ *Free breakfast* ⊟ *No credit cards.*

Waterford City

10 km (6 miles) west of Ballyhack by ferry and road, 62 km (39 miles) southwest of Wexford Town, 158 km (98 miles) southwest of Dublin.

The largest town in the Southeast and Ireland's oldest city, Waterford was founded by the Vikings in the 9th century and was taken over by Strongbow, the Norman invader, with much bloodshed in 1170. The city resisted Cromwell's

1649 attacks but fell the following year. It did not prosper again until 1783, when George and William Penrose set out to create "plain and cut flint glass, useful and ornamental," and thereby set in motion a glass-manufacturing industry long without equal. The famed glass-works closed in 2008, but Waterford Crystal has triumphantly risen from the flames in a smaller, leaner version that opened in 2010.

GETTING HERE AND AROUND

From Dublin, take the N7/M7 to the N9/M9 and all the way to Waterford City. This motorway is often quiet, and the trip takes only two hours. The city is only 45 minutes from Kilkenny via the N9 and N10.

It can be a long drive around the coast from Wexford to Waterford and the Passage East Car Ferry Company operates year-round from Passage East in Wexford to Ballyhack, near Waterford City. The five-minute crossings are continuous from 7 am until 10 pm, April through September, and until 8 pm the rest of the year (with first sailing on Sunday at 9:30 am). The cost is €8 one-way and €12 round-trip for a car and passengers and €1.50 one-way, €2 round-trip for a foot passenger.

Bus Éireann has a station on the waterfront at Merchant's Quay and runs regular buses to cities and towns all over the country, including Tramore (around €4 one-way, €7 round-trip; 30 minutes); Dungarvan (around €7 one-way, €10 round-trip; 50 minutes); Wexford (around €13 one-way, €20 round-trip; 1½ hours); Cork (around €17 one-way, €23 round-trip; 2¼ hours); and Dublin (around €18 one-way, €23 round-trip; three hours). Bus Éireann also runs a local city bus service in Waterford City, with five routes that cover the city center.

On the north side of the river, Plunkett Station receives Irish Rail trains from Kilkenny (€9 one-way, €15 round-trip;

45 minutes); Dublin (€20 one-way, €32 round-trip; 2¾ hours); and Limerick (€22 one-way, €43 round-trip; 2¾ hours). Note: bus and rail fares fluctuate depending on when you travel.

VISITOR INFORMATION
CONTACTS Waterford City Tourist Office. ✉ *120 Parade Quay, Waterford* ☎ *051/875–823.*

Sights

Waterford has better-preserved city walls than anywhere else in Ireland besides Derry. ■ TIP➔ **You can spot one of the remaining portions of the city walls along Spring Garden Alley, off Colbeck Street.** Initially, the slightly run-down commercial center doesn't look promising. You need to park your car and proceed on foot to discover the city's proudly preserved heritage, in particular the grand 18th-century Georgian buildings that Waterford architect John Roberts (1714–96) built, including the town's Protestant and Catholic cathedrals.

Waterford's compact town center can be visited in a couple of hours. Most visitors consider the Waterford Glass Visitor Centre and the impressive pair of history museums as must-sees in any city tour.

Bishop's Palace
HOUSE | Among the most imposing of the city's remaining Georgian town houses, the Bishop's Palace is the home to the Georgian part of the Waterford Treasures exhibition, mapping the history of what was Ireland's second city from 1700 to 1790. The most impressive part of the collection is the elegant silverware and, of course, fine glassmaking, including the oldest piece of Waterford crystal on the planet—a decanter from the 1780s. Try to catch one of the regular tours, where local actors play some well-known scenes from Waterford history. ✉ *The Mall, alongside Waterford City Hall, Waterford* ☎ *051/304–500* ⊕ *www.*

Waterford City

River Suir

PEOPLE'S PARK

KEY

- ① Exploring Sights
- ① Restaurants
- ① Hotels

0 — 200 m
0 — 1/8 mile

Court House

Fire Station

City Wall

City Wall

Browne's Lane

Tourist Information Office

Arts Centre

Government Offices

Mayors Walk

Sights

1 Bishop's Palace	**F2**
2 Blackfriars Abbey	**F1**
3 Christ Church Cathedral	**F2**
4 French Church (Greyfriars)	**F1**
5 House of Waterford Crystal	**F2**
6 Medieval Museum	**F1**
7 Reginald's Tower	**F1**
8 St. Olaf's Church	**E2**
9 Waterford City Hall	**F2**

Restaurants ▶

1 Bodega Restaurant & Wine Bar	**E3**
2 La Boheme	**C1**
3 Munster Room	**H2**

Hotels ▶

1 Dooley's Hotel	**C1**
2 Waterford Castle Hotel & Golf Resort	**H2**

waterfordtreasures.com/bishops-palace
⊠ *From €7.*

Blackfriars Abbey

RELIGIOUS SITE | While you can't go inside, you can get close to the remains of this genuinely medieval abbey and get a sense of how impressive it once was. This ruined tower belonged to a Dominican abbey that was founded in 1226 and returned to the Crown in 1541 after the dissolution of the monasteries. It was used as a courthouse until Cromwellian forces destroyed most of it in the 17th century. ⊠ *High St., Waterford.*

Christ Church Cathedral

RELIGIOUS SITE | Lovers of Georgian decorative arts will want to visit this late-18th-century Church of Ireland cathedral, the only Neoclassical Georgian cathedral in Ireland, designed by local architect John Roberts. Inside, all is elegance—yellow walls, white-stucco florets and laurels, grand Corinthian columns—and you can see why architectural historian Mark Girouard called this "the finest 18th-century ecclesiastical building in Ireland." It stands on the site of a great Norman Gothic cathedral, which a bishop authorized knocking down after rubble fell in his path a few times (with a little help from potential builders). Medievalists will be sad, but those who prize Age of Enlightenment high style will rejoice. Try to catch one of the regular choral concerts to get the full atmospheric reward. ⊠ *Henrietta St., Waterford* ☏ *051/858–958* ⊕ *www.christchurchwaterford.com* ⊠ *€3* ⊙ *Closed Sun. (except for normal services).*

French Church (Greyfriars)

ARCHAEOLOGICAL SITE | Roofless ruins are all that remain of French Church, a 13th-century Franciscan abbey. The church, also known as Greyfriars, was given to a group of Huguenot refugees (hence the "French") in 1695. A splendid east window remains amid the ruins. The key is available at Reginald's Tower. ⊠ *Greyfriars St., Waterford.*

★ House of Waterford Crystal

FACTORY | Iconic Waterford crystal is once again being produced in the city, albeit on a much smaller scale than before. The factory tour, which includes the blowing, sculpting, and cutting departments, is a must for anyone who appreciates timeless craftsmanship and unique design. After watching a team of glassworkers create a twinkling masterpiece from a molten blob, you may have trouble resisting the retail store, where you can select from the world's largest collection of Waterford crystal. You can have your purchase engraved on the spot. ⊠ *The Mall, Waterford* ☏ *051/317–000* ⊕ *www.waterfordvisitorcentre.com* ⊠ *Tour €15* ⊙ *Nov.–Feb., closed weekends.*

Medieval Museum

MUSEUM | Waterford's newest museum cleverly incorporates two medieval-era structures within its walls. Inside, the focus is on Waterford's rich Norman history. A collection of rare and beautiful artifacts includes the Charter Roll of 1372, a list of all charters granted to Waterford up to that time, written in Latin. Also here you'll find the sword of King Edward IV and 15th-century "Cloth of Gold" religious vestments—a true work of art. There's a detailed audiovisual display to add to the experience. ⊠ *The Mall, Waterford* ☏ *051/304–500* ⊕ *www.waterfordtreasures.com/medieval-museum* ⊠ *From €7.*

★ Reginald's Tower

BUILDING | Restored to its original medieval appearance, Reginald's Tower—a circular structure on the east end of Waterford's quays—is a striking setting for a museum on Waterford's Viking history. Built by the Vikings for the city's defense in 1003, it has 80-foot-high, 10-foot-thick walls; an interior stairway leads to the top. The tower served in turn as the residence for a succession of Anglo-Norman kings (including Henry II, John, and Richard II), a mint for silver coins, a prison, and an arsenal. It's said that Strongbow's

The circular Reginald's Tower, originally built by the Vikings, is one of the eye-catching sights along Waterford's Merchant's Quay, long the center of the city's social and economic scene.

marriage to Eva, the daughter of Dermot MacMurrough, took place here in the late 12th century, thus uniting the Norman invaders with the native Irish. The impressive exhibits include the full weapon kit of a local Viking leader. On the top floor there's an audiovisual display and objects to represent every century since the tower was built. ⊠ *The Quay, Waterford* ☎ *051/304–500* ⊕ *www.waterfordtreasures.com/reginalds-tower* 🎫 *€5* ⊘ *Closed mid-Dec.–Jan 6., and Mon. and Tues. Jan. 7–mid-Mar.*

St. Olaf's Church

ARCHAEOLOGICAL SITE | Built, as the name implies, by the Vikings in the mid-11th century, this church has one sole extant remnant: its original door, which has been incorporated into the wall of a meeting hall. ⊠ *St. Olaf's St., Waterford.*

Waterford City Hall

GOVERNMENT BUILDING | One of Waterford's finest Georgian buildings, Waterford City Hall dates from 1783 and was designed by native son John Roberts. The arms of Waterford hang over the entrance, which leads into a spacious foyer that originally served as a town meeting place and merchants' exchange. The building contains an enormous 1802 Waterford glass chandelier, which hangs in the Council Chamber (a copy hangs in Independence Hall in Philadelphia). The Victorian horseshoe-shape Theatre Royal is the venue for the annual Festival of Light Opera in September. ⊠ *The Mall, Waterford* ☎ *051/309–900* 🎫 *Free* ⊘ *Closed weekends.*

Restaurants

Bodega Restaurant & Wine Bar

$ | MODERN IRISH | A casual, modern Irish eatery, Bodega Restaurant is known as the fun place to eat in town. Everything is prepared with locally sourced ingredients, with the Kilmore Quay haddock bake a hearty favorite, along with chicken with wild mushrooms and Gubbeen-chorizo potatoes. **Known for:** Kilmore Quay haddock bake; good wine menu; great live music. ⑤ *Average main: €18* ⊠ *54 John's St., Waterford*

Waterford Crystal

Silica sand + potash + litharge = Waterford crystal. It reads like cold science, but something magical happens when the craftsmen of Waterford produce arguably the top crystal in the world (although France's Baccarat might have something to say about that).

When the Waterford Glass Factory opened in 1783, it provided English royalty and nobility with a regular supply of ornate handcrafted stemware, chandeliers, and decorative knickknacks. Since then, Waterford crystal has graced the tables of heads of state the world over, and Waterford's earlier pieces have become priceless heirlooms.

The best Waterford glass was produced from the late 18th century to the early 19th century. This early work, examples of which can be found in museums and public buildings all over the country, is characterized by a unique, slightly opaque cast that is absent from the modern product.

Crystal glass is not cheap: each piece is individually fashioned by almost two dozen pairs of hands before it passes final inspection and receives the discreet Waterford trademark.

The first thing on the itinerary of any visitor to Waterford was for many years a tour of the glass factory, a buzzing hive of master craftspeople. But the global downturn saw the landmark factory close. Happily, Waterford Crystal arose from the ashes in 2010 and now offers a smaller specialist facility at the Mall (⊕ *www.waterfordvisitorcentre.com*). The adjoining visitor center is already a must-see.

☎ *051/844–177* ⊕ *www.bodegawaterford.com* ☽ *Closed Sun.*

La Boheme

$$$ | FRENCH | In the historic Port of Waterford building, this intimate eatery offers an authentic taste of France and plenty of old-world charm. Popular dishes include a starter of beef carpaccio with a black peppercorn crust, white truffle oil, and rocket (arugula) leaves, followed by Dunmaore East monkfish with cocoa bean and bell pepper fricassee. **Known for:** historic location; elegant setting and cuisine; excellent service. ⑤ *Average main: €27* ⊠ *2 George's St., Waterford* ☎ *051/875–645* ⊕ *www.labohemerestaurant.ie* ☽ *Closed Sun. and Mon. No lunch Sat.–Thurs.*

★ Munster Room

$$$$ | FRENCH | Inside the Waterford Castle Hotel, the Munster Room's luxe decor—with oak paneling darkened with age and ancestral portraits in gilt frames—hints at one of the most sophisticated menus around. Options include a fixed-price, three-course menu featuring adventurous starters such as ballotine of quail with celeriac foam, winter slaw, and cinnamon and apple jelly. **Known for:** elegant dining; extensive wine cellar; smart dress code. ⑤ *Average main: €35* ⊠ *Waterford Castle Hotel, The Island, 2 km (1 mile) south of Waterford, Ballinakill* ☎ *051/878–203* ⊕ *www.waterfordcastleresort.com/munster-room-restaurant.html* ☽ *No lunch.*

Hotels

Dooley's Hotel

$$ | HOTEL | A short stroll from all the main attractions, this unpretentious hotel on the banks of the River Suir is popular both with families and business travelers, while the traditional bar is packed with locals. **Pros:** downtown location; large guest rooms; excellent service. **Cons:** attracts a business clientele; you can get more for same price elsewhere; can be a little noisy. $ *Rooms from: €162* ✉ *30 The Quay, Waterford* ☎ *051/873–531* ⊕ *www.dooleys-hotel.ie* ⮑ *112 rooms* ⦿ *Free breakfast.*

★ **Waterford Castle Hotel & Golf Resort**
$$$$ | HOTEL | Not only does this fairy-tale castle come with an 800-year history, its own 310-acre island, a private ferry, and a highly rated 18-hole golf course, it also caters to lucky guests with the best of Irish service and the grandest of Irish style. **Pros:** historic building; great golf course; awe-inspiring Great Hall. **Cons:** expensive for this region; books up quickly in summer; popular with weddings. $ *Rooms from: €298* ✉ *The Island, 2 km (1 mile) south of Waterford, Ballinakill* ☎ *051/878–203* ⊕ *www.waterfordcastleresort.com* ⮑ *19 rooms* ⦿ *No meals.*

Nightlife

Geoffs
BARS/PUBS | A dimly lighted pub, Geoffs is frequented by a mixed crowd including students and locals. Big flagstones cover the floors, and seating is on old wooden benches. An outdoor area is available for smokers. A wide selection of food is served until 9 pm every night. ✉ *9 John St., Waterford* ☎ *051/874–787.*

The Gingerman
BARS/PUBS | Glass, brass, and dark wood identify this city-center hostelry as a genuine old-school classic. Great place to meet locals at rest and the pub-grub menu is an excellent value. ✉ *6 Arundel La., Waterford* ☎ *051/879–522.*

Jack Meades
BARS/PUBS | Known to locals as "Meades under the Bridge," this place is indeed set beneath a time-stained stone bridge. In centuries past it was a stop on the coach road from Waterford to Passage East. There's a solid pub menu, and sing-along sessions on Saturday. In

winter the fireplaces roar, illuminating the wood beams and bric-a-brac. ✉ *Halfway House, Cheekpoint Rd., Dunmore East* ☎ *051/873–187* ⊕ *www.jackmeades.com.*

Old Ground
BARS/PUBS | Housed in an 800-year-old building, this pub is highly popular with locals. Lunch is served daily, and it's a cozy spot on a rainy day. ✉ *10 The Glen, Waterford* ☎ *051/852–283.*

Performing Arts

Garter Lane Arts Centre
ARTS CENTERS | Culture buffs shouldn't miss the Garter Lane Arts Centre, which has a schedule filled with concerts, exhibits, and theater productions. ✉ *22A O'Connell St., Waterford* ☎ *051/855–038* ⊕ *www.garterlane.ie.*

Theatre Royal Waterford
THEATER | One of the oldest theaters in Ireland, the elegant Theatre Royal is devoted to large-scale theater and musical productions as well as live music. ✉ *Waterford City Hall, The Mall, Waterford* ☎ *051/874–402* ⊕ *www.theatreroyal.ie.*

Shopping

Penrose Crystal
CERAMICS/GLASSWARE | Check out the quality goods at the town's hand-made-crystal factory. With a little notice, Penrose can have a personally engraved piece waiting for you when you arrive. ✉ *32 John St., Waterford* ☎ *051/876–537* ⊕ *www.penrosecrystal.com.*

Tower Gift Shop
GIFTS/SOUVENIRS | You'll find a mix of local arts and crafts and kitschy souvenirs, along with insights into what's going on around the city, in this fun little gift shop. ✉ *128 Parade Quay, Waterford* ☎ *086/407–3191* ⊕ *www.towergiftshop.com.*

🏃 Activities

GAELIC FOOTBALL

Waterford GAA Grounds

LOCAL SPORTS | Watch exciting and spectacular Gaelic football and hurling at the Waterford GAA Grounds. ⊠ *Walsh Park, Waterford* ☎ *051/591–5544* ⊕ *www.waterfordgaa.ie*.

GOLF

Faithlegg Golf Club

GOLF | A perfectly manicured, 20-year-old, 18-hole parkland course, Faithlegg is set in the mature landscape of a 200-acre estate on the banks of the River Suir. Problematic doglegs, blind shots, and nasty sand traps make it a lot trickier than it seems on first glance. The difficult finishing stretch, with Faithlegg House as the backdrop, can catch out the overambitious golfer. ⊠ *Faithlegg House, Checkpoint* ☎ *051/380–587* ⊕ *www.faithlegg-golfclub.com/* ✉ *Nov.–Mar., weekdays €30, weekends €40; Oct., weekdays €35, weekends €50; Apr.–Sept., weekdays €40, weekends €50* ⅃ *18 holes, 6674 yards, par 72*.

Waterford Castle Hotel & Golf Club

GOLF | Claiming to be Ireland's only true island course, Waterford Castle is completely detached from the mainland on a privately owned 310-acre island. Designed by Irish golfing great Des Smyth, the tricky but playable 18-hole course winds through mature woodland and features four internal water features in addition to the encroaching sea. There are plenty of opportunities to hit one into the drink. ⊠ *The Island, 2 km (1 mile) south of Waterford, Ballinakill* ☎ *051/871–633* ⊕ *www.waterfordcastleresort.com* ✉ *Nov.–Mar., weekdays €25, weekends €30; Apr. and Sept., weekdays €35, weekends €45; May–Aug., weekdays €45, weekends €50* ⅃ *18 holes, 6372 yards, par 72*.

Tramore

11 km (7 miles) south of Waterford City on R675, 4 km (2½ miles) west of Dunmore East.

Tramore's 5-km-long (3-mile-long) beach is a popular escape for families from Waterford and other parts of the Southeast, as the many vacation homes indicate. The beach is adjacent to the giant Tramore Amusement Park, which features all the usual rides, including a Ferris wheel, roller coaster, and old-fashioned dodgems. Kiddie heaven, in other words.

GETTING HERE AND AROUND

From Waterford City, take the R675 south to Tramore. The trip takes about 15 minutes. Bus Éireann runs frequent service from Waterford City (around €4 one-way, €7 round-trip; 30 minutes). The Bus Éireann bus stop is outside the tourist office near Splashworld.

VISITOR INFORMATION

CONTACTS Tramore Tourist Office. ⊠ *Railway Sq.* ☎ *051/381–572* ⊕ *www.tramore.ie*.

Restaurants

The Copper Hen

$ | **MODERN IRISH** | Located in a village just outside Tramore, this unassuming, family-run eatery above a pub is home to award-winning chef Eugene Long and his inventive twists on modern Irish cuisine. Local produce dominates, as in the belly of Crowe's free-range pork, white onion and potato puree, wilted summer spinach, and veal jus. **Known for:** countryside gem; cozy setting; quality food and experience. ⑤ *Average main: €18* ⊠ *Fenor* ☎ *051/330–300* ⊕ *www.thecopperhen.ie* ⊙ *Closed Mon. and Tues. No lunch Wed. and Thurs.*

Dungarvan

42 km (26 miles) southwest of Tramore, 44 km (27 miles) southwest of Waterford.

With their covering of soft grasses, the lowlands of Wexford and eastern Waterford gradually give way to heath and moorland. The mountains responsible for the wetter climate rise up behind Dungarvan, the largest coastal town in County Waterford. This bustling fishing and resort spot sits at the mouth of the River Colligan where it empties into Dungarvan Bay. It's a popular base for climbers and hikers.

GETTING HERE AND AROUND

From Waterford, take the N25 west to Dungarvan. The trip takes 45 minutes. Bus Éireann drops off passengers on Davitt's Quay. It has regular daily services from Waterford (around €7 one-way, €10 round-trip; 1 hour); Cork (around €8 one-way, €11 round-trip; 1½ hours; 13 daily); and Dublin (around €20 one-way, €27 round-trip).

VISITOR INFORMATION

CONTACTS Dungarvan and West Waterford Tourism. ⊠ *Main St.* ☎ *058/41741* ⊕ *www.dungarvantourism.com.*

Sights

★ Ring (An Rinn)

TRAIL | FAMILY | Unusual in the south and east of the country, Ring (An Rinn) is an unspoiled Gaeltacht area on Dungarvan Bay where you will find the Irish language still in daily use. Courses in Irish have been taught at Coláiste na Rinne, a language college, since 1909. It's a lovely spot for bikers, walkers, and bird-watchers—the area includes An Cuinigear, a long, thin peninsula that thousands of seabirds call home. Helvic, a tiny fishing village, commands great views over the Waterford coastline, with the Comeragh Mountains as a backdrop. ⊠ *Off N674F, 7 km (4½ miles) southeast of Dungarvan.*

★ The Waterford Greenway

TRAIL | FAMILY | Running along a converted railway track between Dungarvan and Waterford City, the 46 km (29 miles) of the Waterford Greenway has quickly become a must-do destination for walkers and off-road cyclists. Passing through some of the regions most spectacular countryside, and crossing no fewer than three tall viaducts, you'll lose yourself in the natural surroundings. The flat, paved path is perfect for families, and you can take on the whole route or just do one of the many small sections. Bikes can be rented all along the way, and new, funky eateries are opening all the time. ⊠ *Waterford Greenway, Dungarvan* ☎ *053/58–41741* ⊕ *www.visitwaterford-greenway.com.*

🍴 Restaurants

★ The Tannery

$$$ | ECLECTIC | Local culinary wizard Paul Flynn whets quite an appetite in the flocks of Dubliners who besiege every weekend what is commonly regarded as one of Ireland's leading restaurants. The menu is rustic but whimsical and always seasonal. **Known for:** celebrity chef; award-winning cuisine; culinary school. ⑤ *Average main: €32* ⊠ *10 Quay St.* ☎ *58/45420* ⊕ *www.tannery.ie* ⊗ *Closed Mon. and 2 wks in Jan. No dinner Sun. Sept.–May. No lunch Tues.–Thurs. and Sat.*

🛏 Hotels

Gold Coast Golf Hotel

$ | HOTEL | FAMILY | Overlooking Dungarvan Bay, this hotel is part of a family-run and family-friendly property that includes self-catering holiday cottages and golf villas on the edge of a woodland course on a links setting. **Pros:** great location; owners love kids; great value even in high season. **Cons:** can be hectic and noisy; guest rooms are a little mundane; limited facilities. $ *Rooms from: €119* ✉ *Off Clonea Rd.* ☎ *058/42249, 058/42416* ⊕ *www.goldcoastgolfresort. com* ⇨ *37 rooms, 16 cottages, 12 villas, 27 lodges* ⭐ *Free breakfast.*

🆕 Performing Arts

Coláiste na Rinne
DANCE | A few miles outside Dungarvan, you can sit/join in on a *ceilí* (traditional Irish dance), held most nights in summer at Coláiste na Rinne, the school in this Irish-speaking community known for its strong tradition in Irish language, heritage, and culture. ✉ *Ring* ☎ *058/46104* ⊕ *www.anrinn.com.*

Ardmore

29 km (18 miles) southwest of Dungarvan.

★ Historic spiritual sites, white beaches, dramatic cliff walks, local fishermen—little Ardmore is a picture-postcard Irish town that packs a whole lot of wonder into a small peninsula at the base of a tall cliff. With a few notable exceptions—including John F. Kennedy and Gregory Peck—the cute but very real village, with a highly lauded restaurant, is often overlooked by most overseas tourists.

GETTING HERE AND AROUND
From Waterford, take the N25 west and exit left onto the R673. The trip takes about an hour, with the last part traveled on a small country road. There are a few buses a day from Dungarvan and Youghal. Parking can be a problem in the high season.

👁 Sights

Cathedral of St. Declan and Round Tower
ARCHAEOLOGICAL SITE | There's a story behind every ruin you pass in Ireland; behind many, there's a truly ancient story.

Inside the ruined 12th-century Cathedral of St. Declan are some pillar stones decorated with ogham script (an ancient Irish alphabet) as well as weathered but stunningly abstract biblical scenes carved on its west gable. St. Declan is reputed to have disembarked here in the 5th century—30 years before St. Patrick arrived in Ireland—and founded a monastery. The saint is said to be buried in St. Declan's Oratory, a small early Christian church that has been partially reconstructed.

On the grounds of the ruined cathedral is the 97-foot-high Round Tower, which is in exceptionally good condition. Round Towers were built by the early Christian monks as watchtowers and belfries, but came to be used as places of refuge for the monks and their valuables during Viking raids. This is the reason the doorway is 15 feet above ground level—once inside, the monks could pull the ladder into the tower with them. ✉ *Off Tower Hill.*

🍴 Restaurants

★ The Cliff House Restaurant
$$$$ | ECLECTIC | Celebrated Dutch chef Martjin Kajuiter presides over the compact, award-winning dining room of the Cliff House. The food is locally sourced and innovatively prepared—think traditional Irish cuisine with flourish. **Known for:** cliff setting; award-winning chef; creative menu. $ *Average main: €41* ✉ *Cliff House, Cliff Rd.* ☎ *024/87800* ⊕ *www.thecliffhousehotel.com* ⊙ *No lunch weekdays.*

🛏 Hotels

★ Cliff House
$$$$ | HOTEL | Tucked into the cliffs overlooking the fishing village of Ardmore, ageless nature confronts Modernist design at Cliff House—and this luxury hotel and spa remains one of the most innovative additions to Irish accommodations in the last two decades. **Pros:** the

Did You Know?

One of the earliest landmarks of Christianity in Ireland, St. Declan's Cathedral stands on a cliff top settled by the saint between 350 and 420—decades before St. Patrick arrived. On St. Declan's Day, July 24, pilgrims walk along the 80-km (50-mile) St. Declan's Way to the Rock of Cashel.

sea is everywhere; great spa and pool; up the road from the wonderful Ardmore Pottery shop. **Cons:** pricey for the region; sometimes has two-day minimum in summer; younger staff still learning the trade. ⑤ *Rooms from: €350* ✉ *Cliff Rd.* ⊕ *www.thecliffhousehotel.com* ⇥ *39 rooms* ⟊ *No meals.*

Shopping

★ Ardmore Pottery & Craft Shop
CRAFTS | Home to potter Mary Lincoln, a poll of *Irish Times* readers a few years back agreed this is one of the most beloved, creative, and cleverly stocked craft shops in the country, with everything from Alan Ardiff gold jewelry to Veronica Molloy's famed homemade jams. You can even watch Mary work at the wheel and purchase some of her own beautiful, delicate designs. ✉ *The Cliff* ☎ *024/94152* ⊕ *www.ardmorepottery.com.*

🏃 Activities

Ardmore Adventures
WATER SPORTS | Ardmore and other nearby beaches have become meccas for water-sports lovers, and this shop organizes snorkeling, kayaking, powerboating, and anything else that involves fun and the sea. There's also some rock climbing on local cliffs. ✉ *Main St.* ☎ *083/374–3889* ⊕ *www.ardmoreadventures.ie.*

Lismore

20 km (13 miles) northwest of Dungarvan.

★ Lismore is one of Ireland's grandest places to get lost in. Popular with both anglers and romantics, the enchanting little town is built on the banks of the Blackwater, a river famous for its trout and salmon. From the 7th to the 12th century it was an important monastic center, founded by St. Carthac (or Carthage), and it had one of the most renowned universities of its time. The village has two cathedrals: a soaring Roman Catholic one from the late 19th century, and the Church of Ireland's St. Carthage's, which dates from 1633 and incorporates fragments of an earlier church.

Glamour arrived in the form of the dukes of Devonshire, who built their Irish seat here, Lismore Castle (their main house is Chatsworth in England); in the 1940s, Fred Astaire, whose sister, Adele, had married Lord Charles Cavendish, younger son of the ninth duke, would bend the elbow at the town's Madden's Pub. Other architectural jewels include a quaint library funded by Andrew Carnegie and the Ballysaggartmore "folly," a Gothic-style gateway to a 19th-century house that was so costly the house itself was never erected.

GETTING HERE AND AROUND
From Waterford take the N25 west to the N72. The trip takes about 55 minutes. There are regular buses from Dungarvan. In summer, parking spots are at a premium around the small town.

VISITOR INFORMATION
CONTACTS Lismore Tourist Office. ✉ *Lismore Heritage Centre, West St. and Chapel St.* ☎ *058/54975* ⊕ *www.discoverlismore.com.*

Sights

Knockmealdown Mountains
MOUNTAIN—SIGHT | Leaving Lismore, head east on N72 for 6½ km (4 miles), then north on R669 into the Knockmealdown Mountains. From the summit, called Vee Gap, you'll have superb views of the Galtee Mountains in the northwest and a peak called Slievenamon in the northeast. If the day is clear, you should be able to see the Rock of Cashel, ancient seat of the Kings of Munster, some 32 km (20 miles) away. Just before you enter the Vee Gap, look for a 6-foot-high mound

The Duke of Devonshire's Lismore Castle once sheltered Edmund Spenser when he was writing *The Faerie Queene;* today, his parklands are home to avant-garde artworks.

of stones beside the road. It marks the grave of Colonel Grubb, a local landowner who liked the view so much that he arranged to be buried here standing up so that he could look out over the scene for all eternity. ⊠ *Vee Gap Rd.*

★ **Lismore Castle and Gardens**
CASTLE/PALACE | As you cross the bridge entering Lismore, you spot the magnificent Lismore Castle, a vast, turreted building atop a rock overhanging the River Blackwater. There has been a castle here since the 12th century, but the present structure, built by the 6th Duke of Devonshire, dates from the mid-19th century. The house remains the estate of the Cavendish family, and most of it is not open to the public. You can see the contemporary-art gallery, designed by Cork architect Gareth O'Callaghan, in the west wing, as well as the upper and lower gardens, which consist of woodland walks, including an unusual yew walk said to be more than 800 years old (Edmund Spenser is said to have written parts of *The Faerie Queene* here),

certain months of the year. The gardens have an impressive display of magnolias, camellias, and shrubs, and are adorned with examples of contemporary sculpture. ⊠ *Off N72* ☎ *058/54424* ⊕ *www. lismorecastle.com* ✉ *€8* ⊘ *Closed mid-Oct.–mid-Mar.*

Lismore Heritage Center
INFO CENTER | In the former town courthouse, Lismore Heritage Center and its exhibits focus on the town's Celtic origins and its links to famous people from Sir Walter Raleigh to Prince Charles to Fred Astaire. "Lismore Experience," an impressive video presentation, charts the history of the town from its monastic 7th-century origins up to the present day. The center also has a large crafts shop. ⊠ *West St. and Chapel St.* ☎ *058/54975* ⊕ *www.discoverlismore.com* ✉ *€5 for Lismore Experience* ⊘ *Nov.–Mar., closed weekends.*

Mount Melleray Abbey
RELIGIOUS SITE | The first post-Reformation monastery, Mount Melleray Abbey was founded in 1832 by the Cistercian Order

in what was then a barren mountainside wilderness. Over the years the order has transformed the site into more than 600 acres of fertile farmland. The monks maintain strict vows of silence, but you're welcome to join in services throughout the day and are permitted into most areas of the abbey. It's also possible to stay in the guest lodge. There's a small heritage center about the history of Irish monasticism with a few ogham stones and a short film. ⊠ *Off R669, 13 km (8 miles) from Lismore, Cappoquin* ☎ *058/54404* ⊕ *www.mountmellerayabbey.org* ⊠ *Free.*

 ## Hotels

Richmond House
$$ | **B&B/INN** | It's been 300 years since the Earl of Cork and Burlington built this handsome country house, and it still retains its imposing aura of courtly elegance, thanks to owners Claire and Paul Deevy. **Pros:** excellent restaurant; enchanting gardens. **Cons:** limited facilities; place is a little tattered around the edges. ⑤ *Rooms from: €170* ⊠ *Off N72, Cappoquin* ☎ *058/54278* ⊕ *www.richmondhouse.net* ⊗ *Closed late Dec.–mid-Jan.* ⋑ *10 rooms* ⑩ *Free breakfast.*

Cahir

37 km (23 miles) north of Lismore.

Cahir (pronounced "care") is a busy but easygoing market town with a pleasant Georgian square at its heart. It is built on the River Suir at the eastern end of the Galtee mountain range. The Suir is known for its good salmon and trout fishing, as is the Aherlow River, which joins it above town.

GETTING HERE AND AROUND
From Dublin, take the N7/M7 south to junction 19 and the N24. At junction 10, take the R670 to Cahir. The trip takes just over two hours. There is regular bus service from Kilkenny and Waterford, as well as train service from Dublin and Kilkenny.

VISITOR INFORMATION
CONTACTS Cahir Tourist Office. ⊠ *Castle Car Park* ☎ *052/744–1453.*

 ## Sights

Cahir Castle
CASTLE/PALACE | The unavoidable focal point of the town, Cahir Castle is dramatically perched on a rocky island on the River Suir. Once the stronghold of the mighty Butler family and one of Ireland's largest and best-preserved castles, it retains its dramatic keep, tower, and much of its original defensive structure. An audiovisual show and guided tour are available upon request. ⊠ *Castle St.* ⊕ *www.heritageireland.ie* ⊠ *€5.*

★ Swiss Cottage
CASTLE/PALACE | If there's little storybook allure to the brute mass of Cahir Castle, fairy-tale looks grace the 1st Earl of Glengall's 1812 Swiss Cottage, a dreamy relic from the days when Romanticism conquered 19th-century Ireland. A mile south of town on a particularly picturesque stretch of the River Suir, this "cottage *orné*" was probably designed by John Nash, one of the Regency period's most fashionable architects. Half thatch-roof cottage, half mansion, it was a veritable theater set that allowed the lordly couple to fantasize about being "simple folk" (secret doorways allowed servants to bring food without being noticed). Inside, some of the earliest Dufour wallpapers printed in Paris charm the eye. A pleasant way to get here is to hike from Cahir Castle on a footpath along the river. In peak season, crowds can be fierce. ⊠ *Off R670* ⊕ *www.heritageireland.ie* ⊠ *€5* ⊗ *Closed late Oct.–Mar.*

Hotels

★ Aherlow House Hotel & Lodges

$ | HOTEL | Built in 1928 to replace a house destroyed in Ireland's Civil War, Aherlow is set on the slopes of Sliabh na Muc (Mountain of the Pigs), and comes with its own private forest and incredible views of the magnificent Galtee Mountains and the ancient Glen of Aherlow. **Pros:** rooms are big; families will love the lodges; stunning natural surroundings. **Cons:** popular with local weddings and parties; gets booked up summer weekends. ⑤ *Rooms from: €85* ✉ *Off R663, Aherlow* ⊕ *www.aherlowhouse.ie* ⌁ *29 rooms, 15 lodges* ⫶⊙⫶ *No meals.*

Cashel

17 km (11 miles) northeast of Tipperary Town.

Cashel is a market town on the busy Cork–Dublin road, with a lengthy history as a center of royal and religious power. From roughly AD 370 until AD 1101, it was the seat of the Kings of Munster, and it was probably at one time a center of Druidic worship. Here, according to legend, St. Patrick arrived in about AD 432 and baptized King Aengus, who became Ireland's first Christian ruler. One of the many legends associated with this event is that St. Patrick plucked a shamrock to explain the mystery of the Trinity, thus giving a new emblem to Christian Ireland.

GETTING HERE AND AROUND

Cashel is on the busy N8/M8 motorway between Dublin and Cork. Dublin is 162 km (100 miles) northeast of Cashel on the N8/M8 and N7/M7. Cork City is 97 km (60 miles) or one hour and 10 minutes south of Cashel on the N8/M8 and the N74. Bus Éireann runs buses from Dublin (around €17 one-way, €29 round-trip; three hours; six daily), Cork (around €16 one-way and €27 round-trip; 1½

hours) via Cahir (around €7 one-way and €12 round-trip; 15 minutes) and Fermoy (around €14 one-way and €26 round-trip; 1 hour, 20 minutes). The bus stop for Cork is outside the Bake House on Main Street. The Dublin stop is directly opposite.

To head to the Rock of Cashel directly from Dublin, many travelers use the Irish Rail route that heads to the small town of Thurles, then take a 20-minute bus or taxi ride to Cashel.

VISITOR INFORMATION

CONTACTS Cashel Tourist Office. ✉ *Cashel Heritage Centre, Main St.* ☎ *062/62511* ⊕ *www.cashel.ie.*

 Sights

The awe-inspiring, often mist-shrouded **Rock of Cashel** is one of Ireland's most visited sites.

Cashel Heritage Centre

INFO CENTER | In the same building as the tourism office, the Cashel Heritage Centre explains the historic relationship between the town and the Rock and includes a scale model of Cashel as it looked during the 1600s. ✉ *City Hall, Main St.* ☎ *062/62511* ⊕ *www.cashel.ie* ⫷ *Free* ⊙ *Closed weekends Nov.–Feb.*

★ The Rock of Cashel

RELIGIOUS SITE | Seat of the Kings of Munster and the hallowed spot where St. Patrick first plucked a shamrock to explain the mystery of the Trinity, the Rock of Cashel is Ireland's greatest group of ecclesiastical ruins. Standing in the middle of a sloped, treeless valley, the Rock's titanic grandeur and majesty creates what one ancient scribe called "a fingerpost to Heaven." Today, the great limestone mass still rises 300 feet to command a panorama over all it surveys—fittingly, the name derives from the Irish *caiseal,* meaning "stone fort," and this gives a good idea of its strategic importance.

Continued on page 289

THE ROCK
OF
CASHEL

Haunt of St. Patrick, Ireland's "rock of ages" is a place where history, culture, and legend collide.

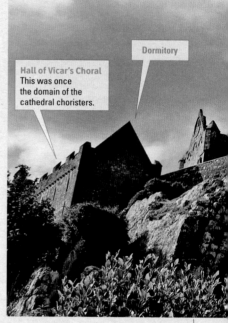

Dormitory

Hall of Vicar's Choral This was once the domain of the cathedral choristers.

Seat of the Kings of Munster and the hallowed spot where St. Patrick first plucked a shamrock to explain the mystery of the Trinity, the Rock of Cashel is Ireland's greatest group of ecclesiastical ruins. Standing like an ominous beacon in the middle of a sloped, treeless valley, the Rock has a titanic grandeur and majesty that create what one ancient scribe called "a fingerpost to Heaven."

Historians theorize the stupendous mass was born during the Ice Age. This being Ireland, however, fulsome myths abound: There are those who believe it was created when the Devil himself took a huge bite of the Slieve Bloom Mountains only to spit it out right in the middle of the Golden Vale. Today, the great limestone mass still rises 300 feet to command a panorama over all it surveys—fittingly, the name derives from the Irish *caiseal*, meaning stone fort, and this gives a good idea of the strategic importance of Cashel in days of yore.

For centuries, Cashel was known as the "city of the kings"—from the 5th century, the lords of Munster ruled over much of southern Ireland from here. In 1101, however, they handed Cashel over to the Christian fathers, and the rock soon became the center of the reform movement that reshaped the Irish Church. Along the way, the church fathers embarked on a centuries-long building campaign that resulted in the magnificent group of chapels, round towers, and walls you see

at Cashel today. View them from afar on the N8 highway and the complex looks so complete you're surprised upon arriving to discover guides in modern dress and not knights in medieval uniform.

■TIP➔ **You have to stay at the Cashel Palace Hotel on Main St. to enjoy the best approach to the rock; along the Bishop's Walk, a 10-minute hike that begins outside the drawing room.**

Cormac's Chapel
The finest example of Hiberno-Romanesque architecture.

The Choir
Look for the Tomb of Myler McGrath.

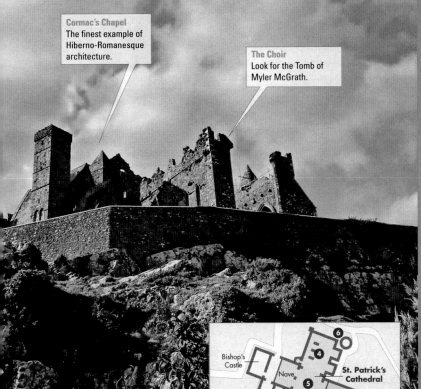

Bishop's Castle

Nave

St. Patrick's Cathedral

South Transept

Tickets

Dormitory

❶ HALL OF THE VICAR'S CHORAL

Built in the 15th century—though topped with a modern reconstruction of a beautifully corbeled medieval ceiling—this was once the domain of the cathedral choristers.

The Museum Located in the hall's undercroft, this collection includes the original St. Patrick's Cross and fast-forwards you to the present thanks to a striking audiovisual display on the Rock entitled the "Stronghold of the Faith."

❷ CORMAC'S CHAPEL

The real showpiece of Cashel is this chapel, built in 1127 by Cormac McCarthy, King of Desmond and Bishop of Cashel. A rare jewel in gleaming red sandstone, it is the finest example of Hiberno-Romanesque architecture. The entry archway carries a tympanum featuring a centaur in a helmet with a bow and arrow aimed at a lion, perhaps a symbol of good over evil. Such work was rare in Irish architecture and points to possible European influence. Preserved within the chapel is a splendid but broken sarcophagus, once believed to be Cormac's final resting place. At the opposite end of the chapel is the nave, where you can look for wonderful medieval paintings now showing through old plasterwork.

ST. PATRICK'S CATHEDRAL

With thick walls that attest to its origin as a fortress, this now-roofless cathedral is the largest building on the site. Built in 1169, it was dedicated on March 17th—St. Patrick's Day. On the theory that ancient churches were oriented to the sunrise on the feast day of their dedicated saint, the cathedral points east, a direction agreeing closely with March 17th. The original cathedral, constructed in a flamboyant variation on Irish Romanesque style, was destroyed by fire in 1495. In ❸ **The Choir**, look for the noted Tomb of Myler McGrath. Note the tombs in the ❹ **North Transept** whose carvings—of the apostles, other saints, and the Beasts of the Apocalypse—are remarkably detailed. The octagonal staircase turret that ascends the cathedral's central tower leads to a series of defensive passages built into the thick walls—from

North Transept

the top of the tower, you'll have wonderful views. At the center of the cathedral is the area known as ❺ **The Crossing**, a magnificently detailed arch where the four sections of the building come together.

COMING OF AGE

AD 450—St. Patrick comes to Cashel, bringing the advent of Christianity when King Aengus accepts baptism from Ireland's patron saint.

990—Cashel is fortified by King Brian Boru, the legendary figure who broke the stranglehold of the Danes at the Battle of Clontarf in 1014.

1101—King Murtagh O'Brien, grandson of Brian Boru, proclaims the royal fortress "for God, St. Patrick, and St. Ailbe," making Cashel center of the Irish Church.

1317—The arrival of the Scots: Edward Bruce, brother of Robert I, is inaugurated king of Ireland, and attends Mass on the Rock where he later holds a parliament.

1749—Protestant archbishop Price earns undying infamy by pulling down the roof of the cathedral to rebuild his own church.

Detail of wooden ceiling in the Vicar's Choral, Rock of Cashel

NORTHERN VIEW OF THE ROCK

Bishop's Castle

Central Tower

❻ THE ROUND TOWER

As the oldest building on the Rock, the Round Tower rises 92 feet to command a panoramic view of the entire Vale of Tipperary. Dating back to 1101, its construction followed the grim reality of the Viking invasions. A constant lookout was posted here to warn of any advancing armies, and food was always provisioned in the tower so as to outlast any prolonged siege. Note the door 10 feet from the ground, allowing ladders to be pulled up to thwart attackers, some of whom attempted to chip the rock at the base, to little effect.

❼ ST. PATRICK'S CROSS

Directly beyond the Rock's main entrance is this 7-foot-tall High Cross carved from one large block and resting upon what is said to have been the original coronation stone of the Munster kings. The cross was erected in the saint's honor to commemorate his famous visit to Cashel in 450. Upon both sides carved in high relief are two figures—the face of Christ crucified and a robed St. Patrick with his feet resting upon an ox head. Unique among High Crosses, this one has vertical supports on either side, perhaps allusions to the crosses of the good and bad thieves. A sort of early Irish bible class, these large stone crosses (which were sculpted from the 9th to the 12th centuries) were perfect teaching tools for a population that was largely illiterate. This cross is a faithfully rendered replica—the original now rests in the site museum.

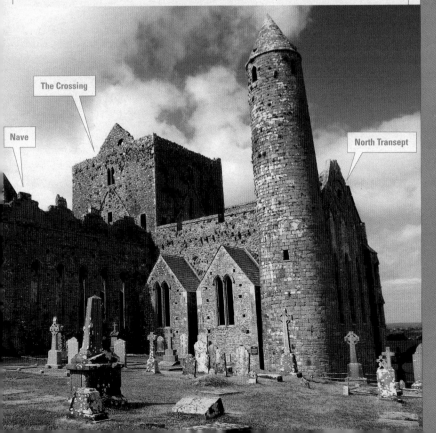

The Crossing

Nave

North Transept

THE ST. PATRICK CONNECTION

While many legends surround Saint Patrick, he was an actual historical figure—his writings, a Latin text dating from the 5th century AD, yield the few undisputed facts about him. Born into a wealthy family in Roman-occupied Britain, he was kidnapped as a young man by Irish marauders and enslaved for six years as a sheepherder on the slopes of Slemish in County Antrim. He escaped, and returned to Britain, but a vision called him back to Ireland to convert the people to Christianity. Arriving in 433, he defied the pagan priests of Tara by kindling the Easter fire on Slane but went on in a peaceful conversion of Ireland to Christianity— not a drop of blood was shed—until his death in AD 460.

St. Patrick's conversion of Ireland was characterized by clever diplomacy: his missionaries were careful to combine elements of then-current druidic ritual with new Christian practice. For example, the Irish Christian church popularized the Feast of all Saints, and arranged for it to be celebrated on November 1, the same day as the great Celtic harvest festival, Samhain. Today's Halloween evolved from this linking of Celtic and Christian holidays.

Clearly a skilled negotiator as well as missionary, St. Patrick wisely preserved the social structure of Ireland, converting the people tribe by tribe. He first attempted to establish the Roman system of dioceses and bishops, but—since Ireland had never been conquered by the Romans—this arrangement did not suit a society without large cities. Instead, the Celts preferred a religious institution introduced by the desert fathers: the monastery, an idea of a "family" of monks being easy to grasp in a tribal society. Over 70 monasteries were founded in the 5th and 6th centuries, and by AD 700 abbots had replaced bishops as the leaders of the Catholic church.

In 457 St. Patrick retired to Saul, where he died. The only relic that can be tied to him is the famous 5th-century iron bell in Dublin's National Museum. Even if it was not, as is traditionally believed, used by the saint, he carried one very like it, and used it to announce his approach.

Above: Dublin, St. Patrick's Day parade

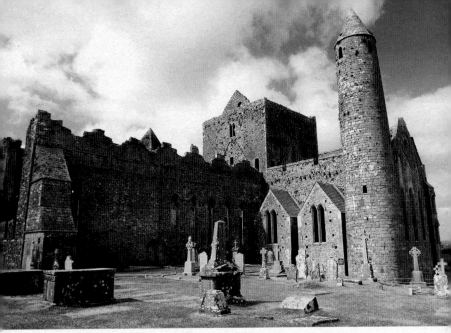

Dating to 1101, the Round Tower is the oldest building on the Rock, rising to 92 feet and providing a panoramic view of the entire Vale of Tipperary.

For centuries, Cashel was known as the "city of the kings"—from the 5th century, the lords of Munster ruled over much of southern Ireland from here. In 1101, however, they handed Cashel over to the Christian fathers, and the rock soon became the center of the reform movement that reshaped the Irish Church. Along the way, the church fathers embarked on a centuries-long building campaign that resulted in the magnificent group of chapels, Round Towers, and walls you see at Cashel today.

Built in the 15th century—though topped with a modern reconstruction of a beautifully corbelled medieval ceiling—the **Hall of the Vicar's Choral** was once the domain of the cathedral choristers. Located in the hall's undercroft, the museum includes the original St. Patrick's Cross.

The real showpiece of Cashel is **Cormac's Chapel,** completed in 1134 by Cormac McCarthy, King of Desmond and Bishop of Cashel. It is the finest example of Hiberno-Romanesque architecture. Preserved within the chapel is a splendid but broken sarcophagus, once believed to be Cormac's final resting place. At the opposite end of the chapel is the nave, where you can look for wonderful medieval paintings now showing through old plasterwork.

With thick walls that attest to its origin as a fortress, the now roofless **St. Patrick's Cathedral** is the largest building on the site. In the choir, look for the noted tomb of Myler McGrath. Note the tombs in the north transept, whose carvings—of the apostles, other saints, and the beasts of the Apocalypse—are remarkably detailed. The octagonal staircase turret that ascends the cathedral's central tower leads to a series of defensive passages built into the thick walls—from the top of the tower, you'll have wonderful views. At the center of the cathedral is the area known as **The Crossing,** a magnificently detailed arch where the four sections of the building come together.

Directly beyond the Rock's main entrance is the 7-foot-tall **High Cross,** carved from one large block and resting upon what is

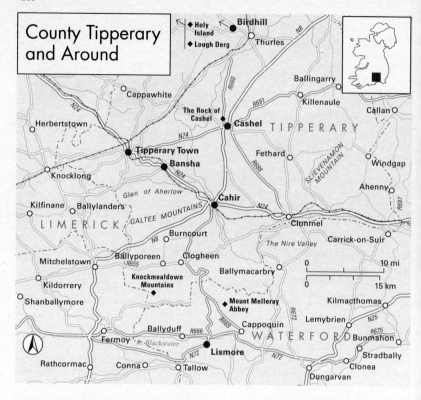

County Tipperary and Around

said to have been the original coronation stone of the Munster kings. The cross was erected in St. Patrick's honor to commemorate his famous visit to Cashel in AD 450. This cross is a faithfully rendered replica—the original now rests in the Rock's museum. As the oldest building on the Rock, the **Round Tower** rises 92 feet to command a panoramic view of the entire Vale of Tipperary. A constant lookout was posted here to warn of any advancing armies. ⊠ *Rock of Cashel* ☎ *062/61437* ⊕ *www.heritageireland.ie* 📷 *€8.*

🍴 Restaurants

★ Chez Hans
$$$ | MODERN IRISH | It's rather fitting that this restaurant is in a converted church, as it's become something of a shrine for foodies. Jason Matthia's cuisine is classic French with contemporary twists. The seafood cassoulet—half a dozen varieties of fish and shellfish with a delicate chive velouté—is legendary. **Known for:** popular with foodies; seafood cassoulet; stunning dining room. ⑤ *Average main: €30* ⊠ *Moore La.* ☎ *062/61177* ⊕ *www. chezhans.net* ⊘ *Closed Mon., and late Jan.–early Feb. No lunch Tues.–Sat. No dinner Sun.*

🎭 Performing Arts

Brú Ború Cultural Centre
ARTS CENTERS | Enjoy folksinging, storytelling, trad music, and dancing at the Brú Ború Centre at the foot of the Rock of Cashel. The center also has the "Sounds of History" audiovisual exhibition open all day, and regular arts and music events throughout the year. ⊠ *Rocklane* ⊕ *www. bruboru.ie.*

Bansha

16 km (10 miles) south west of Cashel.

This prosperous little farming town at the foot of the Galtee Mountains is really of interest as a base for the beautiful Glen of Aherlow. The glen itself is a lush valley formed where the River Aherlow runs between the Galtees and the tree-covered ridge of Slievenamuck. Historically, it was a key passageway for the native Irish between Tipperary and Limerick.

GETTING HERE AND AROUND

From Dublin take the N7/M7 toward Cork. Exit onto the M8 and get off on the N24 to Bansha. From Cashel take the N74 west, then the N24 to Bansha. There are regular bus services from Dublin, Limerick, and Waterford.

 Sights

The Glen of Aherlow is a hiking and horse-riding paradise, with a feast of national trails ranging from gentle loops to some serious climbs. The rewards for mountain walking are great, with Lough Curra and Lake Muskry, two stunning corrie lakes with views overlooking the whole of central and southern Ireland. The Glen hosts two walking festivals on the last weekend in January and the first weekend in June. For history buffs, the Tipperary Heritage Way (based on ancient pilgrim walks) from Cashel to Ardmore also passes through here. The walks will take you past a number of ancient sites, from St. Pecaun's Holy Well at the eastern end of the Glen to the fascinating and overlooked Darby's Bed passage tomb on the west side of Slievenamuck hill near the village of Galbally. This is also prime horse country, and the same trails can often be taken on a locally hired mount with an experienced guide to help along the way. Hillcrest Riding Centre (☎ *062/37915*) in nearby Galbally can organize treks, including a picnic lunch. For details of walks, activities, and events

in the Glen, see the very helpful site ⊕ *aherlow.com.*

 Hotels

Foxford Farmhouse B&B

$ | B&B/INN | FAMILY | Honora and Philip Russel clearly love having visitors to their modern, simple house—a classic Irish B&B—on their family farm at the entrance to the hiker's paradise that is the Glen of Aherlow. **Pros:** family-run; great value; perfect hiking base. **Cons:** only three rooms; limited amenities. ⑤ *Rooms from: €80* ✉ *Foxford* ☎ *062/54552* ⊕ *www.foxfordfarmhouse. net* 🛏 *3 rooms* ⧖ *Free breakfast* 🚫 *No credit cards.*

Birdhill

62 km (38 miles) north of Bansha, 24 km (15 miles) northeast of Limerick City.

It's no coincidence that this picturesque little village in undiscovered north Tipperary always does well in the national "Tidy Towns" competition, a village beauty contest that the Irish take very seriously. But the real charm of this cute hamlet is its proximity to the majestic Lough Derg with the mysterious Holy Island at its center.

GETTING HERE AND AROUND

From Bansha take the N24 north to the R455. From Dublin take the N7/M7 south and exit at junction 21 to the R445.

VISITOR INFORMATION

CONTACTS Tipperary Tourist Information.
⊕ *www.tipperary.com.*

 Sights

Lough Derg is the third-largest lake in Ireland and actually borders three counties: Clare, Tipperary, and Galway. The lake area near Birdhill is some of its least explored territory. It's a haven for anglers and water-sports enthusiasts, including wind surfers, sailors, and relaxed cruisers. The Lough Derg Drive is another undiscovered treasure of the area. It meanders around the lake, through gorgeous little villages in all three counties. You can pull over at numerous lookout points to appreciate the unique setting of the monastic settlement at the center of the lake. The Lough Derg section of ⊕ *www.discoverireland.ie* has a list of the best providers for waterskiing, wakeboarding, sailing, and other activities. The Watermark Ski Club (based in Terryglass) is one of the best places on the lake to get started and meet fellow water sporters.

Holy Island

RELIGIOUS SITE | The 6th-century monastic settlement of Holy Island (*Inis Cealtra* in Irish) sits in the middle of Lough Derg, slightly closer to the western shore. Around the year AD 520, St. Columba, seeking the type of solitude only an island can offer, founded his small monastery here. It was later expanded into a serious seat of Christian learning. The Vikings arrived in 836 and killed many of the monks before making off with most of their treasures, but the monastery survived in different forms until the Reformation. The ruins on the island include a Round Tower, St. Caimin's Romanesque church, and the Saints' Graveyard, which includes 11th-century grave markers in Irish, and one headstone for Cosrach, "the miserable one," who died in 898. Access to the island is via boats that leave from Mountshannon, on the western side of the lake.

 ## Hotels

Coolbawn Quay

$$ | **HOTEL** | The main appeal of this collection of cottages built in the style of a 19th-century Irish village is the magical setting between Lough Derg and the surrounding rolling hills and forests. **Pros:** incredible natural setting; great choice of accommodations types; high-quality

spa. **Cons:** can book up on weekends; popular for weddings. $ *Rooms from: €170* ⊠ *Coolbawn Quay, Lough derg* ☏ *067/28158* ⊕ *www.coolbawnquay.com* ⊟ *No credit cards* ⊷ *17 cottages* ⦿ *Free breakfast.*

 ## Activities

BOATING

Killaloe River Cruises

BOATING | A cute, 12-seater passenger boat takes you on a serene, one-hour cruise of Lough Derg and into the River Shannon. It's a great chance to take in the unique wildlife and natural beauty of the region. Boats leave from the lakeshore at Killaloe, on the Clare bank of the lake. ⊠ *Killaloe* ☏ *086/814–0559* ⊕ *www.killaloerivercruises.com.*

COUNTY CORK

Updated by
Alannah Hopkin

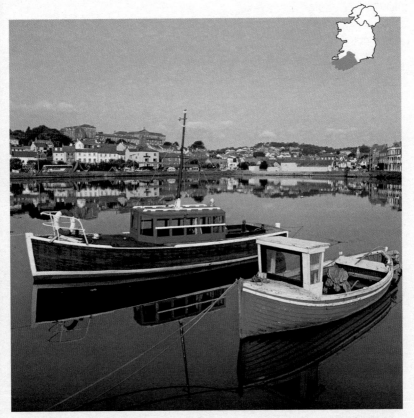

👁 Sights	🍴 Restaurants	🛏 Hotels	🛍 Shopping	🍸 Nightlife
★★★★★	★★★★★	★★★☆☆	★★★★★	★★★★☆

WELCOME TO COUNTY CORK

TOP REASONS TO GO

★ **Blarney Castle:** Visitors line up to kiss the Blarney Stone and acquire the gift of gab. This is an impressive 15th-century tower-house castle with unusual gardens, at their best in daffodil season (early to mid-March).

★ **Cobh:** If you have Irish roots, chances are your ancestors left from Cobh. Exhibits in "The Queenstown Story" at Cobh Heritage Centre commemorate the 2½ million emigrants who sailed from here.

★ **Kinsale:** This picturesque port, long a favored haven of sailors, is famed for its fine dining in tiny front-parlor eateries. It's also a chic place to see and be seen—the Irish St-Tropez.

★ **The Cork Coastline:** On the drive from Kinsale to Skibbereen, one of the less rugged stretches of the Wild Atlantic Way, you'll encounter charming little villages.

★ **Bantry House:** One of Ireland's finest stately homes, packed with treasures from all over Europe, stands on a breathtaking bluff.

1 Cork City. Identifying Cork as Ireland's second-largest city is misleading—it has just one-tenth the population of Dublin, and its character is more along the lines of a college town—which it is—than a metropolis. That means lively pubs, quirky cafés, and lots of good music, trad and otherwise.

2 Blarney. Blarney is now a suburb, but the village green is still there, outside the castle gates, a short walk from Blarney Woollen Mills, a huge emporium where Irish crafts and fashion are a magnet for visitors.

3 Cork Harbour. This wide expanse of sea is bordered by the botanical gardens and parkland of Fota Island and the historic transatlantic port of Cobh.

4 Midleton. A lively market town with some attractive 18th- and 19th-century stone buildings, it is dominated by its whiskey distillery.

5 Shanagarry. Long associated with the Quakers, this tiny village has a huge reputation among food lovers, being the home base of Ballymaloe, once just a farm, now a byword for culinary excellence.

6 Fermoy. A quiet country town on the scenic Blackwater River,

famous among fly-fishermen.

7 Kinsale. Just a half-hour drive south of Cork City, this historic small town on a picturesque harbor has a reputation for fine dining and attracts visitors year-round.

8 Clonakility and Nearby. The gateway to west Cork, this picture-book pretty market town has charming hand-painted shop fronts and a growing reputation for crafts and artisanal food.

9 **Skibbereen.** The practical hub for west Cork's scenic coast, Skib's Saturday market is a must in summer, while its Heritage Centre will put Ireland's Great Famine of the mid-19th century in perspective.

10 **Castletownshend.** A contender for the title of Ireland's prettiest village, its one street leads downhill past lovingly restored 19th-century houses and a famous pub to the water's edge.

11 **Bantry.** The chief market town of the region, its best features are its location at the head of Bantry Bay and its imposing landmark, Bantry House.

12 **Glengarriff.** A small village with an island-studded harbor, its subtropical climate and sheltered location give rise to lush vegetation, while its landward aspect is less charming, with a busy main road and a string of souvenir shops.

CORK'S FOOD MARKETS

Long known as "the belly of Ireland," West Cork is celebrated for its rich fishing and even richer farming. Like a world-class picnic, this cook's tour is the tastiest recipe for a day trip through the region.

FINDING THE FEAST

The best places to track down top temptations from Cork's gastronomic cornucopia are the area's food markets, often set in small villages and averaging only about a dozen stalls, and held one morning a week. Low overhead means bargains for the buyers, who enjoy an amazing array of artisanal foodstuffs. And the markets' festive atmosphere is complemented by the camaraderie of the stall-holders—this is often their main contact with the buying public. Check out ⊕ *www.westcorkmarkets. com* for up-to-date information.

MARKETS

Bantry, Main Square, Friday 9:30 am to 1 pm. This traditional street market has a strong presence of growers of organic plants and vegetables.

Skibbereen, Saturday 9 am to 2 pm. The Saturday market, one of the biggest around, takes over Fairfield off Bridge Street, offering organic fruit and vegetables, excellent coffee, cut flowers, and crafts. It's also a great place to people-watch.

Kinsale, Market Square, Wednesday 9 am to 2:30 pm. Snack on a Breton crepe while stocking up on chutneys, smoked salmon, farmhouse cheeses, fresh fish, and organic fruit and vegetables at this cute piazza market.

Midleton, Saturday 9:30 am to 1 pm. One of the liveliest farmers' markets, it's held in a small parking lot, with buskers creating a festive vibe.

Schull, Sunday 9:30 am to 2 pm, Easter to December. At its best in summer and at Christmas, this foodie's market showcases superb products from local bakers, fish smokers, and cheese makers, and Gubbeen smoked pork products.

The English Market, Monday to Saturday 8 am to 6 pm. Today this famous city-center covered market is a thriving hub of artisanal bakers, butchers, fishmongers, and greengrocers selling organic fruit and vegetables, top-quality meat and fresh fish, imported coffees and teas, locally made charcuterie, farmhouse cheeses—and even a champagne from the local wine merchant, Bubble Brothers.

OTHER FOODIE FAVES

The Irish deli is unlike any other, perhaps because there is no indigenous tradition of specialty-food shops, so those that do exist tend to be one-off expressions of their owners' personalities.

In Clonakilty head for **The Lettercollum Kitchen Project.** Both talented chefs and dedicated vegetable gardeners, Con McLaughlin and Karen Austin are masters of the vegetarian and ethnic repertory (and also offer cooking

classes). Their bakery sells specialist breads, cooks' ingredients, sandwiches, and savory tarts.

Mannings' Emporium, with its open-air display of vegetables and outdoor picnic tables, looks as if it belongs on a Southern Italian roadside, rather than at Ballylickey, on the road between Bantry and Glengarriff. Val Manning has long championed West Cork's artisanal food producers, home bakers, and confectioners, and what was once a corner store selling milk and bread is now a renowned gastronomic outpost. Try the house-made charcuterie or cheese platters to get acquainted with local fare, including pungent Mileens, Ardsallagh goat's cheese, Knockalara sheep's milk cheese, and two local hard cheeses, Gabriel and Desmond.

SUPERMARKETS

In West Cork, local supermarkets make a point of supporting small, local food producers, and local people enjoy the chance to support their friends and neighbors by buying their produce. **Scally's** of Clonakilty and **Field's** of Skibbereen, both trading under the **SuperValu** logo, are prime examples of this trend.

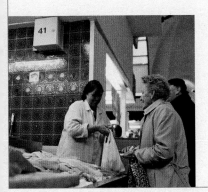

With its deep-rooted rebel history, a landscape dotted with small farms and charming towns, and a gently lilting up-and-down accent that flows like the green hills that lead to its famous Blarney Castle, the county of Cork and its abundance of character—and characters—is the essence of what makes Ireland special. Known locally as The People's Republic of Cork, Ireland's largest county is also home to the country's second-biggest city, and while you'll find huge festivals, a vibrant culinary scene, and big, breathtaking scenery, it feels small and friendly. The city is pleasantly compact and walkable, while the outlying towns are tiny and within easy reach along narrow, winding roads.

But as you look over the fuchsia-laden hedges that ring thriving dairy farms or stop at a wayside restaurant to sample locally sourced beef, it's difficult to imagine that a century and a half ago this area was decimated by famine. Thousands perished in fields and workhouses, and thousands more took "coffin ships" from Cobh in Cork Harbour to the New World. The region was battered again during both the War for Independence and the civil war that were fought with intensity in and around "Rebel Cork" between 1919 and 1921. Most Cork families have relatives who left for the USA on an emigrant liner back in the 1950s and '60s, and memories of the civil war years are kept alive, fueled by memorial events.

Cork City's locals will immediately charm you, as will the generally festive air that prevails in its streets, where many visitors assume that some kind of festival is going on, even on those rare occasions when it is not.

MAJOR REGIONS

The major metropolis of the South, **Cork City and its Environs** makes a great base from which to explore the whole southern region. Though it's Ireland's second-largest city, it runs a distant second, with a population of 123,000, roughly one-tenth the size of Dublin. In the last decade, with high prices and overcrowding in Dublin, Cork became the new hot spot for short city breaks. Groups of Europeans frequently pop over for a weekend of partying, as the city is a spirited place, with a formidable pub culture, a lively traditional-music scene, a respected and progressive university, attractive art galleries, and offbeat cafés. Nearby Blarney, northwest of Cork City on R617, makes a perfect day trip. **Blarney's** attractions are Blarney Castle and the famous Blarney Stone.

East Cork. The county's eastern portions—Cork Harbour, Midleton, and Shanagarry—are less frequented by visitors to Cork but worth exploring. Products of the rich farming land east of Cork City used to include whiskey: see how it was made at the Jameson Experience in Midleton, just a short drive from Ballymaloe House, pioneer of the New Irish cuisine. The long, flat, sandy beaches here—a summertime favorite with Irish holiday-makers—are great for windswept walks year-round.

West Cork. The historic old port—and now booming seaside town—of **Kinsale** is the perfect place to begin the 136-km (85-mile) trip, via Bantry Bay and through a variety of seascapes, to the lush vegetation of Glengarriff. If you tackle this scenic West Cork coastal route nonstop, the drive takes less than two hours, but the whole point of this journey is to linger in

places that tickle your fancy. Must-sees include the famed 18th-century manse of Bantry House and the romantic island gardens of Ilnacullin.

Between 9½ and 13 km (6–8 miles) wide, **Bantry Bay** is one of the largest natural harbors in the world. It was here that the French attempted to land a force of some 14,000 men in 1796, during the Napoleonic Wars. A combination of foul winds and naval incompetence proved their undoing. The chief market town for this part of Cork is Bantry, which lies at the head of Bantry Bay. This is a quiet rural area where small family farms, fishing, and shellfish farming are the main industries besides tourism.

Planning

Getting Here and Around

AIR TRAVEL

Cork Airport, 5 km (3 miles) south of Cork City on the Kinsale road, has direct flights daily to London (Heathrow, Gatwick, and Stansted), Manchester, East Midlands, Paris, and Malaga, and direct flights to many other European cities. There are up to three transatlantic flights a week from Providence/Boston–T. F. Green. There are no flights connecting Dublin to Cork. Shannon Airport, 26 km (16 miles) west of Limerick City, is the point of arrival for many transatlantic flights, including direct flights from Atlanta, Chicago, Philadelphia, Toronto (summer only), and New York City (from both JFK and Newark). It also has regular flights from the United Kingdom and many European cities.

AIRPORTS Cork Airport. ☎ 021/431–3131 ⊕ www.corkairport.com. **Shannon Airport.** ☎ 061/712–000 ⊕ www.shannonairport.ie.

AIRPORT TRANSFERS

Bus Éireann has a bus link between Cork Airport and the Cork Parnell Place Bus Station about every 30 minutes, and a route between the airport and Kinsale roughly every hour. Tickets for both destinations can be bought on the bus.

SHUTTLES Bus Éireann. ☎ *021/450–8188* ⊕ *www.buseireann.ie.*

BUS TRAVEL

Bus Éireann and Aircoach operate express buses from Dublin, Galway, Shannon Airport, Limerick, Tralee, and Killarney to Cork City. Be warned: some so-called express buses from Dublin make up to four off-motorway stops en route, so the journey takes four hours and 15 minutes, and more, if the traffic is heavy. To travel direct from Dublin to Cork with Bus Éireann, use its GoBe service, run with Galway-based Go Bus, which takes three hours nonstop from Dublin to Cork and has Wi-Fi, charging points, and onboard toilets. The bus starts at Dublin Airport, and has a city-center pickup point (Busáras). Citylink buses serve many Irish cities, including Cork City; book online for the best prices. Local buses tend to stop running in the early evening, which rules out many day trips—unless you want to spend most of the day on the bus. As a general rule, the smaller and more remote the town, the less frequent its bus service. Consult with hotel concierges, tourist board staffers, or the bus lines' websites for schedules.

CONTACTS Aircoach. ☎ *01/844–7118* ⊕ *www.aircoach.ie.* **Bus Éireann.** ☎ *01/836–6111 in Dublin, 021/450–8188 in Cork* ⊕ *www.buseireann.ie.* **Citylink.** ☎ *091/564–164* ⊕ *www.citylink.ie.* **Cork Bus Station Parnell Place.** ✉ *Parnell Pl. and Merchant's Quay, City Center South* ☎ *021/450–8188.* **Go Bus.** ✉ *Unit 1, Forster Ct., Galway City* ☎ *091/564–600* ⊕ *www.gobus.ie.*

CAR TRAVEL

Scenery is the main attraction in County Cork, and unless you're a biker or hiker, the best option for taking it in is to rent a car, although regional buses do run on main roads. Once behind the wheel, plan to adopt the local pace: slow. Covering about 100 km (60 miles) a day is ideal, with many stops along the way. Speed is dictated to some degree by the roads—most are small, with one lane in each direction and plenty of bends and hills.

The main driving route from Dublin is the M7 motorway, connecting with the M8 in Portlaoise to continue 257 km (160 miles) on to Cork City. The journey from Dublin to Cork takes less than three hours. A car is the ideal way to explore this region's scenic routes and attractive but remote towns. Except for Cork City, where you're best off using a garage, parking is relatively easy to figure out.

TAXI TRAVEL

Taxis at Shannon and Cork airports connect with Limerick and Cork respectively. Shannon to Limerick City costs about €40; from Cork to Cork City Railway Station, about €15. The National Transport Authority website has a fare estimator tool.

CONTACTS Cork Taxi Co-op. ☎ *021/427–2222* ⊕ *www.corktaxi.ie.* **National Transport Authority.** ☎ *01/879–8300* ⊕ *www.transportforireland.ie/taxi.*

TRAIN TRAVEL

Irish Rail–Iarnród Éireann runs direct hourly trains from Dublin Heuston Station to Cork's Kent Station; the trip takes just under three hours. Suburban trains serve Fota Island, Midleton, and Cobh. The journey time to Midleton or Cobh is about 25 minutes.

CONTACTS Irish Rail–Iarnód Éireann. ☎ *01/836–6222 for inquiries and booking, 01/836–6222 in Ireland, 021/450–4777 in Cork* ⊕ *www.irishrail.ie.*

Hotels

County Cork's great country-house accommodations include Ballymaloe House in East Cork, along with the guest wing at magnificent Bantry House. There are many excellent family-owned and-run traditional hotels, such as the Blarney Castle Hotel on Blarney's village green and the Seaview in Ballylickey on Bantry Bay. *Hotel reviews have been shortened. For full information, visit Fodors.com.*

Restaurants

County Cork, home of the famous Slow Food Ireland movement, has become one of Ireland's top foodie destinations. The mecca: Ballymaloe House, where Myrtle Allen pioneered New Irish cuisine and her daughter-in-law, the celebrated cookbook author Darina Allen, learned her trade. Adventurous, well-traveled chefs throughout County Cork make the most of the first-rate local specialties: succulent beef and lamb, game in the winter, fresh seafood, and farmhouse cheeses. The best restaurants are not all in towns: even tiny villages might boast a gastropub. *Restaurant reviews have been shortened. For full information, visit Fodors.com.*

What It Costs in Euros

	$	$$	$$$	$$$$
RESTAURANTS				
	under €19	€19–€24	€25–€32	over €32
HOTELS				
	under €120	€120–€170	€171–€210	over €210

Tours

Adams & Butler
SPECIAL-INTEREST | Self-driven or chauffeur-driven group tours with accommodations in private country houses and castles are available. The company also conducts special-interest tours; topics include gardens, architecture, ghosts, and golf. ☎ 01/288–9355 ⊕ *www.adamsandbutler.com* ✉ *From $1900.*

Ireland Walk Hike Bike
SPECIAL-INTEREST | Themed walks and bike routes take you along the coast of West Cork, around the Sheep's Head and Beara peninsulas in Bantry Bay. ⊠ *Collis Sandes House, Tralee* ☎ *066/718–6181* ⊕ *www.irelandwalkhikebike.com* ✉ *From €345.*

Irish Cycling Safaris
BICYCLE TOURS | Group and self-guided cycling tours are offered on the Beara Way and the Sheep's Head Peninsula, plus other areas of Ireland. Tours include accommodations, some meals, and support van with local guide. ⊠ *Belfield Bike Shop, University College, Dublin* ☎ *01/260–0749* ⊕ *www.cyclingsafaris.com* ✉ *From €730.*

Kinsale Pottery & Arts Centre
SPECIAL-INTEREST | Adrian Wistreich of the Kinsale Pottery & Arts Centre puts together bespoke vacation packages for corporate groups or private parties that include multidestination tours, hands-on pottery, jewelry-making, stained-glass, and other workshops. Tours can include workshops, accommodations, and studio visits. ⊠ *Olcote, Kinsale* ☎ *021/477–7758* ⊕ *www.kinsaleceramics.com* ✉ *From €420.*

Top of the Rock Pod Páirc
WALKING TOURS | FAMILY | The Ross family operates an accommodations center on the family farm for walkers in innovative sleeping pods, and has 15 km (9 miles) of walkways. Tailor your own package in consultation with David Ross. Sleeping

pods with en suite facilities are from €59 for two. They will provide transport back to the farm for the night if you choose the very popular two-day walk on St. Finbarr's Pilgrim Path, a 37-km (23-mile) cross-country route. ⊠ *Top of the Rock (Ard na Carraig), Drimoleague* ☎ *086/173–5134* ⊕ *www.topoftherock.ie* ✉ *From €59 for two.*

When to Go

The best times to visit County Cork are from mid-March to June and in September and October. July and August are the peak holiday periods. Roads are more crowded, prices are higher, and the best places are booked in advance. March can be chilly, with daily temperatures in the 40s and 50s. The average high in June is 65°F (18°C). May and June are the sunniest months, while May and September are the driest ones. From November to March, daylight hours are short, the weather is damp, and many places close.

Festivals and Events

Cork is known as Ireland's festival city, with a busy calendar of events, including a number of high-profile festivals. Elsewhere in the county there are annual festivals that are well worth planning your trip around, along with small community events that portray local heritage, local passions, and the character of the local people. These are just a selection.

JUNE AND JULY
West Cork Chamber Music Festival
Internationally renowned musicians perform in the library of Bantry House for nine days in late June–early July. ⊠ *Bantry* ☎ *027/527–889* ⊕ *www.westcorkmusic.ie.*

AUGUST
Masters of Tradition
One very good reason to visit County Cork at any time is to hear authentic traditional music, but time your trip to coincide with this mid-August five-day festival in Bantry and you'll hear some of the finest. ⊠ *Bantry* ☎ *027/527–889* ⊕ *www.westcorkmusic.ie.*

SEPTEMBER
Cork International Short Story Festival
Readings, author interviews, workshops, and award presentations are highlights of this four-day literary event in mid-September. ⊠ *Cork City* ☎ *021/431–2955* ⊕ *www.munsterlit.ie.*

A Taste of West Cork
A 10-day food festival in a region famed for its artisanal foods and top-class organic meat and seafood, it programs over 230 events in 36 towns, and on eight islands. These range from lectures and symposia by foodie-celebs like Darina Allen of Ballymaloe, to cheese-making workshops, farm tours, and guest chefs cooking up a feast in local restaurants. ⊠ *Skibbereen* ☎ *087/665–5567* ⊕ *www. atasteofwestcork.com.*

OCTOBER
Guinness Cork Jazz Festival
Late October brings an international lineup of jazz and soul musicians to the city, for four days of concerts in the big venues—Opera House, Everyman, Triskel Auditorium, and Triskel Christchurch— bands in pubs and hotels, street music, and various fringe events. ⊠ *Cork City* ⊕ *www.guinnessjazzfestival.com.*

NOVEMBER
Cork Film Festival
In the second week of November, this nine-day festival puts on a lively program of world cinema at several city venues, and includes feature films, documentaries, shorts, and other events. ⊠ *Cork City* ☎ *021/427–1711* ⊕ *www.corkfilmfest.org.*

Planning Your Time

When you plan a trip to County Cork, you'll need to make a pick of the ports. The biggest one, Cobh, to the east of the Cork City, was the point of embarkation for most 19th-century Irish transatlantic passengers and it retains a strong whiff of nostalgia. Dominated by its tall-spired cathedral, the town, filled with 19th-century buildings, climbs vertiginously up- and downhill and faces southward out to sea. Kinsale is more of a village than a town, built beside a hill at one end of an unspoiled fjordlike harbor. With its yacht marinas and tempting restaurants, Kinsale has a cosmopolitan air, but it also offers serious history at Charles Fort. Timoleague is a sleepy hamlet, nestled beside the romantic ruins of its abbey. Many visitors regard Castletownshend as the prettiest village, while others prefer the sheltered waters of subtropical Glengarriff.

IF YOU HAVE THREE DAYS

If you're here for a short stay—three days or fewer—you'd do well to base yourself in Cork City, which is easy to explore on foot. Allow a day to take in the sights of the city center, including the Crawford Art Gallery, the indoor English Market, and the boutiques along St. Patrick's Street (also called Patrick Street). On the second day, visit Blarney Castle; from there it's a half-hour drive to Cork Harbour, where you can visit Fota Island and Cobh. On the third day head for Kinsale, worth a day itself, or you can head to the scenic coast of West Cork, which can be comfortably driven in a day. The narrow roads here meander through attractive waterside villages to the splendid prospect of Bantry Bay, overlooked by the stately Bantry House. A few miles farther west is another highlight of the Wild Atlantic Way, the sheltered inlet of Glengarriff. Return that night to Kinsale or Cork, both handy for the airport.

Visitor Information

Fáilte Ireland tourist information offices are open year-round in Bantry, Clonakilty, Cobh (Cork Harbour), Cork Airport (Arrivals), Cork City, and Skibbereen. Those in Blarney, Glengarriff, Kinsale, and Midleton are open from mid-March to mid-September or the end of October. Fáilte Ireland's Discover Cork website page has details about locations and hours.

CONTACTS Cork Tourist Office. ⊠ *125 Patrick St., City Center South* ☎ *021/425–5100* ⊕ *www.discoverireland.ie/places-to-go/cork.*

Cork City

253 km (157 miles) southwest of Dublin.

Cork City received its first charter in 1185 from Prince John of Norman England, and it takes its name from the Irish word *corcaigh*, meaning "marshy place." The original 6th-century settlement was spread over 13 small islands in the River Lee. Major development occurred during the 17th and 18th centuries with the expansion of the butter trade, and many attractive Georgian-design buildings with wide bowfront windows were constructed during this time. As late as 1770 Cork's present-day main streets—Grand Parade, St. Patrick's Street, and the South Mall—were submerged under the Lee. Around 1800, when the Lee was partially dammed, the river divided into two streams that now flow through the city, leaving the main business and commercial center on an island, not unlike Paris's Île de la Cité. As a result, the city has a number of bridges and quays, which, although initially confusing, add greatly to the port's unique character.

Corkonians—as Cork City people are known—are famed for loyalty to their city, which has its own national newspaper, *The Irish Examiner;* its own stout, Murphy's; a lively artistic and literary community; and famous offspring, from the labor organizer Mother Jones (1837–1930) to rock guitarist Rory Gallagher (1948–95), actor Cillian Murphy, and soccer manager Roy Keane. But depending on what part of town you're in, Cork can also be distinctly itself—the sort of place where hipsters, accountants, and farmers drink at the same pub.

PLANNING YOUR TIME

You can tour the city's center in a morning or an afternoon, depending on how much you plan to shop along the way. To really see everything, however, allow a full day, with a break for lunch at the Farmgate Café in the English Market. Note that the Crawford Art Gallery and the English Market are closed on Sunday.

GETTING HERE AND AROUND

The drive from Dublin to Cork City on the M7/M8 motorway takes just less than three hours. The drive from Shannon Airport to Cork takes less than two hours, with motorway for some stretches. Use the tunnel (toll €1.80) to avoid traveling through the center of Limerick. Cork is about a 1½-hour drive from Killarney. Cork is well served by express buses. Irish Rail–Iarnród Éireann direct trains from Dublin Heuston Station to Cork's Kent Station run hourly. The trip takes just less than three hours.

If you're driving within Cork City, it's advisable to use a multistory parking garage, as on-street parking can be hard to find and the process of paying for it can be difficult to master. Cork's city center is compact and walkable, but if you want to bus the mile to the university campus, pick up a No. 8 outside Debenham's department store on St. Patrick's Street. A great introductory tour is the hop-on, hop-off Cork City Tour, a double-decker bus that departs (March–October, €14) from the tourist information office on Saint Patrick's Street between 9:30 am and 5 pm.

CONTACTS Cork Bus Station Parnell Place. ⊠ *Parnell Pl. and Merchant's Quay, City Center South* ☎ *021/450–8188.* **Cork City Tour Bus.** ☎ *021/430–9090* ⊕ *www. corkcitytour.com.* **Kent Station.** ⊠ *Lower Glanmire Rd., City Center North* ☎ *021/836–6222* ⊕ *www.irishrail.ie.*

 Sights

Cork City Gaol

MUSEUM | FAMILY | This castlelike building contains an austere, 19th-century prison. Life-size wax figures occupy the cells, and realistic sound effects illustrate the appalling conditions that prevailed into the 20th century. Also here, in the Governor's House, the **Radio Museum Experience** exhibits genuine artifacts from a 1923 radio station, 6CK, and tells the story of radio broadcasting in Cork. ⊠ *Sunday's Well Rd., Sunday's Well* ☎ *021/430–5022* ⊕ *www.corkcitygaol. com* ⊴ *€8.*

★ Crawford Art Gallery

MUSEUM | The large redbrick building was built in 1724 as the customs house and is now home to Ireland's leading provincial art gallery. An imaginative expansion has added gallery space for visiting exhibitions and adventurous shows of modern Irish artists. The permanent collection comprises more than 2,000 works and includes landscape paintings depicting Cork in the 18th and 19th centuries as well as contemporary video installations. Take special note of works by Irish painters William Leech (1881–1968), Daniel Maclise (1806–70), James Barry (1741–1806), and Nathaniel Grogan (1740–1807). The café, run by the renowned Allen family of Ballymaloe, is a good place for a light lunch or a house-made sweet. ⊠ *Emmet Pl., City Center South* ☎ *021/480–5042* ⊕ *www. crawfordartgallery.ie* ⊴ *Free.*

★ English Market

MARKET | Fetchingly housed in an elaborate, brick-and-cast-iron Victorian building,

As the River Lee flows through Cork's center, delightful bridges and quays add to the city's unique character.

such is the fame of this famous foodie mecca that Her Majesty Queen Elizabeth insisted on an impromptu walkabout here on her historic first visit to Ireland in 2011. Among the 140 stalls, keep an eye out for the Alternative Bread Company, which produces more than 40 varieties of handmade bread every day. Tom Durcan's Meats Limited sells vacuum-packed local specialties including spiced beef and dry-aged beef. The Olive Stall sells olive oil, olive-oil soap, and olives from Greece, Spain, France, and Italy. Kay O'Connell's Fish Stall, in the legendary fresh-fish alley, purveys local smoked salmon. O'Reilly's Tripe and Drisheen is the last existing retailer of tripe, a Cork specialty, and *drisheen* (blood sausage). Upstairs is the Farmgate, an excellent café. ✉ Entrances on Grand Parade and Princes St., City Center South ⊕ www.englishmarket. ie ⊗ Closed Sun.

Fitzgerald's Park

CITY PARK | FAMILY | This picture-perfect riverside park a short walk west of the city center is accessed along The Mardyke, a tree-lined walkway overlooking a pitch where cricket is still played. Like the cricket pitch, the park is a remnant of Cork's Victorian past, and was the site of the 1902 Cork Exhibition. Its best-loved feature is the "Shakey Bridge," a famously unstable pedestrian suspension bridge linking the north and south banks of the Lee. The park is a popular venue for outdoor entertainment during the Midsummer Festival, and contains the **Cork Public Museum,** a Georgian mansion with displays of the city's history. ✉ *Western Rd., Western Road* ☎ *021/427–0679* ⊕ *www. discoverireland.ie/Arts-Culture-Heritage/ fitzgerald-park/44826* ✉ *Free* ⊗ *Museum closed Mon. and Sun. Oct.–Apr.*

Nano Nagle Place

BUILDING | Nano Nagle (1718–84) founded the Presentation order of nuns, and was a pioneer in the education of the poor. The convent that was her Cork headquarters has been transformed into a delightful heritage center and provides a welcome oasis of calm in the city center. Visit her tomb, with its water fountain, graveyard, and garden before discovering the ornate Victorian Gothic Revival chapel ("The Goldie Chapel"), a popular new venue for readings and other events. The oldest buildings on-site, dating from the early 18th century, including Miss Nagle's parlor, can be visited only on guided tours, which depart daily at 11 am and 3 pm. ⊠ *60–61 Douglas St., City Center South* ⊕ *A short walk from Grand Parade or South Mall, across Nano Nagle Bridge and up Mary St.* ☎ *021/419–3580* ⊕ *www.nanonagleplace.ie* ☞ *Garden and graveyard free, heritage center €8.*

Patrick's Bridge

BRIDGE/TUNNEL | From here you can look along the curve of Patrick Street and north across the River Lee to St. Patrick's Hill, with its tall Georgian houses. The hill is so steep that steps are cut into the pavement. Tall ships that served the butter trade used to load up beside the bridge at Merchant's Quay before heading downstream to the sea. The design of the large, redbrick shopping center on the site evokes the warehouses of old. ⊠ *St. Patrick's St., City Center South.*

Paul Street

PLAZA | A narrow stretch between the River Lee and St. Patrick's Street and parallel to both, Paul Street is the backbone of the trendy shopping district that now occupies Cork's old French Quarter. The area was first settled by Huguenots fleeing religious persecution in France. Musicians and other street performers often entertain passersby in the Rory Gallagher Piazza, named for the late rock guitarist, whose family was from Cork. There are some offbeat specialty stores including high fashion, books, and a wide choice of cafés and inexpensive eating places. ⊠ *City Center South.*

St. Anne's Church

RELIGIOUS SITE | The church's pepper-pot steeple, which has a four-sided clock and is topped with a golden, salmon-shape weather vane, is visible from throughout the city and is the chief reason why St.

Anne's is so frequently visited. The Bells of Shandon were immortalized in an atrocious but popular 19th-century ballad of that name. Your reward for climbing the 120-foot-tall tower is the chance to ring the bells out over Cork, with the assistance of sheet tune cards. Beside the church, **Firkin Crane,** Cork's 18th-century butter market, houses two small performance spaces. ⊠ *Church St., Shandon* ☎ *021/450–5906* ⊕ *www.shandonbells.ie* ☞ *Church free, tower €5.*

St. Fin Barre's Cathedral

RELIGIOUS SITE | On the site that was the entrance to medieval Cork, this compact, three-spire Gothic cathedral, which was completed in 1879, belongs to the Church of Ireland and houses a 3,000-pipe organ. According to tradition, St. Fin Barre established a monastery on this site around AD 650 and is credited with being the founder of Cork. ⊠ *Bishop St., City Center South* ☎ *021/496–3387* ⊕ *corkcathedral.webs.com* ☞ *€6.*

St. Patrick's Street

NEIGHBORHOOD | Extending from Grand Parade in the south to Patrick's Bridge in the north, Panna (as it's known locally—also commonly referred to as Patrick Street) is Cork's main shopping thoroughfare. It has been designed as a pedestrian-priority area with wide walks and special streetlights. A mainstream mix of department stores, boutiques, pharmacies, and bookshops lines the way. If you look above some of the plate-glass storefronts, you can see examples of the bowfront Georgian windows that are emblematic of old Cork. The street saw some of the city's worst fighting during the War of Independence. ⊠ *City Center South.*

★ University College Cork

COLLEGE | The Doric-porticoed gates of UCC stand about 2 km (1 mile) from the city center. The college, which has a student body of roughly 10,000, is a constituent of the National University of Ireland. The main quadrangle is a fine example of

Cork City

Sights ►

1 Cork City Gaol....................C1
2 Crawford Art Gallery.........E2
3 English Market...................E2
4 Fitzgerald's Park...............A2
5 Nano Nagle Place...............F3
6 Patrick's Bridge.................F2
7 Paul Street........................E2
8 St Anne's Church...............E1
9 Saint Fin Barre's
  Cathedral........................C3
10 Saint Patrick's Street.......F2
11 University
   College Cork...................A3

Restaurants ►

1 Elbow Lane Brew and
  Smoke House...................F2
2 The Electric.......................E3
3 Farmgate Cafe..................E2
4 Flemings Restaurant.........H1
5 Greenes Restaurant..........G1
6 Isaacs...............................G1
7 Ivory Tower.......................E3
8 Jacques............................F3
9 L'Atitude 51
  Wine Cafe.......................G3
10 Liberty Grill
   Restaurant.....................D2
11 Market Lane
   Restaurant & Bar............G1
12 Paradiso...........................B2
13 Strasbourg Goose
   Restaurant.....................E2

Hotels ►

1 Ambassador Hotel.............H1
2 Clayton Hotel Cork City....G2
3 Gabriel House...................H1
4 Garnish House...................F2
5 Hayfield Manor.................B3
6 Hotel Isaacs Cork.............G1
7 Imperial Hotel...................F3
8 Lancaster Lodge................C3

KEY

1 Exploring Sights
1 Restaurants
1 Hotels

19th-century university architecture in the Tudor-Gothic style, reminiscent of many Oxford and Cambridge colleges. Several ancient ogham stones are on display in the North Quadrangle (near the visitor center), and the renovated Crawford Observatory's 1860 telescope can be visited. The Honan Collegiate Chapel, east of the quadrangle, was built in 1916 and modeled on the 12th-century Hiberno-Romanesque style, best exemplified by the remains of Cormac's Chapel at Cashel. The UCC chapel's stained-glass windows, as well as its collection of art and crafts, altar furnishings, and textiles in the Celtic Revival style, are noteworthy. Three large, modern buildings have been successfully integrated with the old, including the Boole Library, named for mathematician George Boole (1815–64), who was a professor at the college, and whose bicentenary was celebrated in 2015. Both indoors and out the campus is enhanced by works of contemporary Irish art. The **Lewis Glucksman Gallery,** a striking new building adjacent to the college's entrance gates, displays works from the college's outstanding collection and hosts cutting-edge contemporary-art exhibitions. ⊠ *College Rd., Western Road* ☎ *021/490–1876* ⊕ *www.ucc.ie* ✉ *Free; guided tours €4* ☽ *Visitor center closed Sun., and Dec. and Jan.*

🍴 Restaurants

Elbow Lane Brew and Smoke House
$$ | IRISH | The small, dark, L-shape room (hence the name) on the ground floor of a handsome town house is dominated by a blue-tiled chimney with a wood-smoke grill, whose aroma pervades the room. There's a masculine ambience here, as befits a brewery and smokehouse renowned for hearty portions of grilled food and triple-cooked chips. **Known for:** slow-smoked pork ribs with smokehouse sauce and house brews; grilled whole fish of the day; no reservations, creating a wait at peak times. ⑤ *Average main:*

€20 ⊠ *4 Oliver Plunkett St., City Center South* ☎ *021/439–0479* ⊕ *www.elbow-lane.ie* ☽ *No lunch.*

The Electric
$ | **MODERN IRISH** | In front of a fast-flowing, urban stretch of the River Lee, the neon-clad exterior of a snazzy Art Deco building announces a casual city-center venue that combines a sense of dining as theater with a friendly staff that puts everyone at ease. The ground floor has a square bar with booths and dining niches around the perimeter, while upstairs is a more conventional dining room. **Known for:** hearty lunchtime stews: local, fresh, and made to order; good range of simply prepared seafood; river view with seats outside in summer. ⑤ *Average main: €15* ⊠ *41 South Mall, City Center South* ☎ *021/422–2990* ⊕ *www.electriccork. com* ▭ *No credit cards.*

Farmgate Café
$ | IRISH | One of the best—and busiest—informal lunch spots in town is on a terraced gallery above the fountain at the Princes Street entrance to the atmospheric English Market. All ingredients used at the café are purchased in the market below. **Known for:** delicious traditional Irish comfort food like corned beef

and colcannon; an artistic clientele including many poets; good people-watching. $ *Average main: €14* ✉ *English Market, Princes St., City Center South* ☎ *021/427–8134* ⊕ *www.farmgate.ie* ⊗ *Closed Sun. No dinner.*

★ **Flemings Restaurant**

$$$ | FRENCH | On a hillside overlooking the river on the eastern edge of the city, this restaurant is in a stately Georgian house with extensive grounds, including a kitchen garden that supplies the restaurant. The food is classical French, and it's served, appropriately, in a dining room decorated in the French Empire style. **Known for:** romantic country-house location; elegant Louis XV–style dining room; panfried foie gras with black pudding and glazed apple starter. $ *Average main: €32* ✉ *Silver Grange House, Lower Glanmire Rd., Tivoli* ☎ *021/482–1621* ⊕ *www.flemingsrestaurant.ie* ⊗ *Closed Mon. No lunch Wed.–Sat., except by reservation.*

★ **Greenes Restaurant**

$$$ | FUSION | Tucked away on a cobbled patio, this surprising haven is part of a Victorian warehouse conversion that houses Hotel Isaacs. Stone and redbrick walls are the backdrop to a minimalist modern interior, while out back a gigantic rock-wall waterfall makes a stunning backdrop to the dining area. **Known for:** creative cuisine using local produce; seven- and nine-course tasting menus; buzzy atmosphere. $ *Average main: €26* ✉ *Hotel Isaacs, 48 MacCurtain St., City Center North* ☎ *021/455–2279* ⊕ *www.greenesrestaurant.com* ⊗ *No lunch Mon.–Wed.*

Isaacs

$ | CONTEMPORARY | Cross Patrick's Bridge to the River Lee's north side and turn right to reach this large, atmospheric brasserie in a converted 18th-century warehouse—a true Cork institution. Modern art, muted jazz, high ceilings, and well-spaced tables with colored wooden tops create an easygoing ambience. **Known for:** group gathering spot;

East-meets-Mediterranean fusion menu; fresh-baked bread. $ *Average main: €18* ✉ *48 MacCurtain St., City Center North* ☎ *021/450–3805* ⊕ *www.isaacsrestaurant.ie* ⊗ *No lunch Sun.*

Ivory Tower

$$$$ | CONTEMPORARY | Don't be put off by the seedy-looking street entrance to this second-floor restaurant: Seamus O'Connell, the American-born owner-chef here, is one of the stars of the Irish culinary scene, describing his approach as "transethnic fusion." Imaginative presentation, including a surprise taster to set the mood, compensates for the stark interior of the dining room, as does the tradition that the maestro himself often serves the dishes he has created. **Known for:** eclectic dishes combining Mexican, Japanese, and French influences; a new menu every weekend; tasting menus. $ *Average main: €35* ✉ *35 Princes St., Washington Village* ☎ *021/427–4665* ⊕ *www.ivorytower.ie* ⊟ *No credit cards* ⊗ *Closed Sun.–Wed. No lunch.*

★ **Jacques**

$$$ | EUROPEAN | Tucked away near the GPO is one of Cork's favorite restaurants approached through a carefully lighted, curved Art Deco–style bar, that combines with exposed brick walls and leather banquettes to create a soothing respite from the city center. Food is always sourced from local artisanal producers, and the seafood as fresh as it gets, while the imaginative, well-judged cooking allows the flavor to shine through. **Known for:** elegant, intimate dining; the great value, €26 two-course dinner menu; tapas and side plates menu. $ *Average main: €26* ✉ *23 Oliver Plunkett St., City Center South* ☎ *021/427–7387* ⊕ *www.jacques-restaurant.ie* ⊗ *Closed Sun. and Mon.*

L'Atitude 51 Wine Cafe

$ | EUROPEAN | Formerly a pub, this informal riverside venue is now a sunny wine and tapas bar with large, often shared tables, where an imaginative selection of small plates featuring local, artisanal

Great resources like the English Market have made Cork a foodie mecca. Her Majesty Queen Elizabeth II's walkabout here was a highlight of her first visit to Ireland, in 2011.

food is served to accompany the wines. It is an informal "canteen" for the Cork School of Music around the corner, and a venue beloved of Cork's many artists and writers, who find it an agreeable place to while away the hours. **Known for:** more than 50 wines by the glass; unusual tapas like roast bone marrow; popular with local artists and musicians. $ *Average main: €16* ⊠ *1 Union Quay, South Docklands* ⊹ *To west of City Hall, corner with Anglesea St.* ☎ *021/239–0219* ⊕ *www.latitude51.ie* ⊙ *Closed Sun. No lunch Sat. No dinner Mon.*

Liberty Grill Restaurant

$ | **AMERICAN | FAMILY** | This busy eaterie with a plain decor—black leather banquettes, plain white walls, and a wood-plank floor—is popular with families. It may primarily be a burger joint, but it's a burger joint with a difference—all the food is freshly prepared and locally sourced, the classic burger really tastes of beef, and there are also lamb, crab, and tuna varieties. **Known for:** excellent burgers; locally sourced produce; can

be very busy. $ *Average main: €15* ⊠ *32 Washington St., Washington Village* ☎ *021/427–1049* ⊕ *www.libertygrill.ie* ⊙ *Closed Sun.*

Market Lane Restaurant & Bar

$ | **MODERN IRISH** | All that remains of this building's former identity as a pub is the long mahogany bar; today, it is a bustling bistro-style restaurant serving robust, freshly prepared food from an open kitchen. Art Deco touches and a predominantly black-and-white theme set a Parisian mood, and light floods in from two walls of large windows on summer evenings. **Known for:** Irish comfort food; homemade sausages with colcannon; variety of vegetarian options. $ *Average main: €16* ⊠ *5–6 Oliver Plunkett St., City Center South* ☎ *021/427–4710* ⊕ *www. marketlane.ie.*

Paradiso

$$$$ | **VEGETARIAN** | Irish owner-chef Denis Cotter has won awards for his cookbooks, which have added greatly to the fame of this simple, café-style restaurant. The Mediterranean–Eastern fusion-style

food is locally grown, and is known for its imaginative combinations, so tasty that even dedicated meat eaters forget that it's vegetarian. **Known for:** risottos of seasonal vegetables; attractively plated combinations; local cheeses and vegetables. $ *Average main: €33* ⊠ *16 Lancaster Quay, Western Road* ☎ *021/427–7939* ⊕ *paradiso.restaurant* ☉ *Closed Sun. and last 2 wks of Aug. No lunch weekdays and Jan.–Mar.*

Strasbourg Goose Restaurant

$ | IRISH | Tucked away in a pedestrian alley, this is the kind of personable restaurant you dream of finding on vacation and turning into a culinary home away from home. It's cheerful, bustling, basic, and—like its name—a little odd. **Known for:** unpretentious comfort food; friendly, efficient service; good value. $ *Average main: €18* ⊠ *17–18 French Church St., City Center South* ☎ *021/427–9534* ▭ *No credit cards* ☉ *Closed Mon. No lunch.*

 ## Hotels

★ Ambassador Hotel

$$ | HOTEL | An imposing redbrick and cut-limestone Victorian-era nursing home is now a comfortable hotel, which might not be the fanciest or hippest in Cork, but it has the most character and the best view, encompassing the city and surrounding hills. **Pros:** patronized by lively clientele; amazing views from its hilltop perch over the river and docks; generous-size bedrooms. **Cons:** steep hike up from city; in a residential area with few other pubs or cafés; decor fusty and unadventurous. $ *Rooms from: €140* ⊠ *Military Hill, St. Luke's, City Center North* ☎ *021/453–9000* ⊕ *www.ambassadorhotelcork.ie* ⤴ *70 rooms* ¡○¡ *Free breakfast.*

Clayton Hotel Cork City

$$$ | HOTEL | Occupying a corner block beside the River Lee, the Clayton is a pioneer of Cork's docklands development—as you enter you'll spot black-clad

receptionists standing behind simple wooden desks at the far end of the vast, marble-floor lobby, the first indication that this place aspires to boutique-hotel chic. **Pros:** short stroll from shopping and entertainment; stylish rooms; good spa, pool, and leisure facilities. **Cons:** limited parking; neighborhood is quiet after dark; some rooms overlook the atrium. $ *Rooms from: €180* ⊠ *Lapp's Quay, City Center South* ☎ *021/422–4900* ⊕ *www.claytonhotelcorkcity.com* ⤴ *201 rooms* ¡○¡ *Free breakfast.*

Gabriel House

$$ | B&B/INN | On a bluff high above the train station and the docks, this huge Victorian house is in Cork's boho north-side quarter among fine 19th-century homes, many of which have seen better days. **Pros:** young, enthusiastic staff; quiet location; oodles of character; rock-bottom prices. **Cons:** nearly hostel-like; some rooms very small; a long hike uphill. $ *Rooms from: €120* ⊠ *Summerhill N, St. Luke's Cross, Montenotte* ☎ *021/450–0333* ⊕ *www.gabriel-house.com* ⤴ *28 rooms* ¡○¡ *Free breakfast.*

Garnish House

$ | B&B/INN | At this pair of large Victorian town houses near the university, owner-manager Johanna Lucey will be offering you tea and homemade cake before you have even crossed the threshold—the kind of old-fashioned hospitality that's fast disappearing in modern Ireland. **Pros:** delicious breakfasts; genuine Irish experience; short walk from town center. **Cons:** main house clean but dated in style; on a busy road; rooms book up well in advance. $ *Rooms from: €110* ⊠ *Western Rd., Washington Village* ☎ *021/427–5111* ⊕ *www.garnish.ie* ⤴ *21 rooms* ¡○¡ *Free breakfast.*

★ Hayfield Manor

$$$$ | HOTEL | An elegant Georgian-style house, its red brick brightened by white-sash windows, the exterior hints at the comfy luxury that lies within, and the location—off College Avenue in an

undistinguished suburb—is forgotten as soon as you enter the walled gardens. **Pros:** modern country-house style; a good value for luxury accommodations; great dining options. **Cons:** a taxi or 15-minute walk to city center; nearby streets busy with students by day. ⑤ *Rooms from: €320* ✉ *Perrott Ave., Western Road* ☎ *021/484–5900* ⊕ *www.hayfieldmanor. ie* ↵ *88 rooms* ⦿*Ⓘ Free breakfast.*

Hotel Isaacs Cork

$ | HOTEL | A stylish renovation transformed an old, city-center warehouse into a contemporary boutique hotel, which is accessed via a cobblestone arch and includes original features like exposed stone walls as well as a courtyard patio with a waterfall. **Pros:** convenient location; courtyard dining; historic hotel. **Cons:** heavy through-traffic outside; parking is not on-site; breakfast not included. ⑤ *Rooms from: €110* ✉ *48 MacCurtain St., City Center North* ☎ *021/450–0011* ⊕ *www.hotelisaacscork. com* ↵ *47 rooms, 11 apartments* ⦿*Ⓘ No meals.*

Imperial Hotel

$$ | HOTEL | Though it cannot compete in size with the grande-dame hotels of bigger cities, the Imperial, which dates to 1813, plays the part with conviction, with its marble lobby, opulent finishes, and traditional concierge. **Pros:** central location; genuine Cork character; elegant dining options. **Cons:** some standard bedrooms are very small; quiet rooms have no view; popular venue for wedding receptions. ⑤ *Rooms from: €160* ✉ *South Mall, City Center South* ☎ *021/427–4040* ⊕ *www. flynnhotels.com/imperial_hotel_cork* ↵ *126 rooms, 1 suite* ⦿*Ⓘ Free breakfast.*

Lancaster Lodge

$$ | B&B/INN | Free city-center parking, a great location midway between the shopping district and the university, and good value are the main reasons to stay at this modern, four-story inn. **Pros:** central location; spacious and stylish rooms; good value. **Cons:** no bar or wine license.

⑤ *Rooms from: €125* ✉ *Lancaster Quay, Western Road* ☎ *021/425–1125* ⊕ *www. lancasterlodge.com* ↵ *48 rooms* ⦿*Ⓘ Free breakfast.*

 Nightlife

The Abbey Tavern

BARS/PUBS | Just across the road from St. Fin Barre's Cathedral and a short walk from University College, this traditional and cozy pub has rock memorabilia throughout, a beer garden, and a Monday evening Full Moon Club with live music. If you're hungry, the bartenders will order in pizza from an artisanal place around the corner. ✉ *54 Gilabbey St., City Center South* ☎ *087/673–8307.*

Bierhaus

BARS/PUBS | The huge world-beer selection, poker on Tuesday, and a DJ on Saturday lure a young, hip crowd here. ✉ *Pope's Quay, Shandon* ☎ *021/455–1648* ⊕ *www.thebierhauscork.com.*

Charlies Bar

BARS/PUBS | This traditional "early bar" is open Monday through Saturday from 7 am, Sunday from 12:30 pm; nightly music sessions are held here, with traditional Irish showcased on Sunday from 3 pm. ✉ *2 Union Quay, South Docklands* ☎ *021/431–8342* ⊕ *www.charliesbarcork. com.*

Corner House

BARS/PUBS | This popular bar, Cork's best local in the opinion of many regulars, is open daily and hosts Cajun, folk, or Irish music from Thursday to Sunday. ✉ *7 Coburg St., City Center North* ☎ *021/450–0655.*

Counihan's

BARS/PUBS | On Sunday evening this popular music bar features Arundo, with their blend of traditional Irish and Latin-rhythm music, while on Monday from 9:30 pm Ricky Lynch's folk-blues guitar session is legendary. ✉ *3 Pembroke St., City*

Thanks to streets lined with cafés, pubs, and shops, a simple stroll around Cork can be a delightful way to while away the hours.

Center South ☎ *021/427–7850* ⊕ *www. counihans.ie.*

Cyprus Avenue

MUSIC CLUBS | This is the hippest nightclub among younger Corkonians, featuring new local bands and DJs, and visiting talent, including leading reggae artists. It's open Thursday to Sunday from 9 pm till late. ⊠ *Caroline St., City Center South* ☎ *021/427–6165* ⊕ *www.cyprusavenue. ie.*

★ Fionbarra

BARS/PUBS | Across the road from the Nano Nagle Center on Douglas Street, this hidden gem has a quirky (and heated) beer garden, a traditional feel with eclectic upcycled furniture and original murals, and more than 20 beers on tap, 70 whiskeys, and a large selection of rum and tequila. Excellent grub offerings include pizzas, wraps, baked potato with fillings, and daily specials from midday to 9 pm. ⊠ *73 Douglas St., City Center South* ☎ *021/484–7543.*

Franciscan Well Brewery

BREWPUBS/BEER GARDENS | This lively, award-winning microbrewery, on the site of an ancient Franciscan monastery, has a heated beer garden and an atmospheric candlelit bar, open daily from 3 pm. Share a pizza fresh from the wood-burning oven. ⊠ *North Mall, Shandon* ☎ *021/439–3434* ⊕ *www.franciscanwell-brewery.com.*

The Oliver Plunkett

MUSIC CLUBS | You can hear live music here nightly—trad, blues, rock, swing, and soul. ⊠ *116 Oliver Plunkett St., City Center South* ☎ *021/422–2779* ⊕ *www. theoliverplunkett.com.*

Sin é

MUSIC CLUBS | Pronounced "*shin*-ay" (Irish for "that's it"), this is the place for live Irish music—fiddles, flutes, banjos, and bodhráns. Sessions are Friday and Sunday at 6:30 and Tuesday at 9:30. ⊠ *8 Coburg St., City Center North* ☎ *021/450–2266.*

Performing Arts

Cork Opera House

MUSIC | The city's major hall for touring productions also presents dance, theater, comedy, and music events. ✉ *Lavitt's Quay, City Center South* ☎ *021/427–0022* ⊕ *www.corkoperahouse.ie.*

Everyman Palace Theatre

THEATER | Modest-size theatrical productions are staged at this theater, which has an ornate Victorian interior. ✉ *15 MacCurtain St., City Center North* ☎ *021/450–1673* ⊕ *www.everymancork. com.*

Triskel Arts Centre

ARTS CENTERS | The popular venue presents live music, classic and contemporary films, and readings in the former Christchurch (dating from 1717), and hosts art exhibitions. ✉ *Tobin St., off S. Main St., Washington Village* ☎ *021/427–2022* ⊕ *www.triskelartscentre.ie.*

👜 Shopping

CLOTHING

Carousel

CLOTHING | Look for Carousel's Irish-designed and-manufactured vintage-inspired range, Circus. ✉ *26 Oliver Plunkett St., City Center South* ☎ *021/427–9619* ⊕ *www.ilovecarousel.com.*

Elverys

CLOTHING | This is where Cork's many hikers and runners buy their gear. There's a large stock of shoes, clothing, and equipment, including local teams' sports gear. ✉ *120 Oliver Plunkett St., City Center South* ☎ *021/424–8776* ⊕ *www.elverys.ie.*

Salinger's Bespoke

CLOTHING | "Original, contemporary, affordable" is the mantra at this men's outfitters, offering made-to-measure and off-the-peg shirts and suits designed in-house, as well as some very stylish accessories. ✉ *19, Drawbridge St., City Center South* ☎ *021/427–8496* ⊕ *www.salingers.ie.*

GALLERIES

Lavit Gallery

ART GALLERIES—ARTS | This ground-floor space exhibits works by members of the long-established Cork Arts Society and others. ✉ *Wandesford Quay, Clarkes Bridge, Washington Village* ☎ *021/427–7749* ⊕ *www.lavitgallery.com.*

JEWELRY

Designworks Studio

JEWELRY/ACCESSORIES | A local favorite, this store is not only a showcase for imaginative, modern Irish jewelry but home to a thriving open-view workshop with three full-time goldsmiths. ✉ *Cornmarket St., City Center South* ☎ *021/427–9420* ⊕ *www.corkjewellery.ie.*

Silverwood

JEWELRY/ACCESSORIES | A large selection of Celtic-inspired silver jewelry is sold here, including traditional claddagh rings. ✉ *84a Oliver Plunkett St., City Center South* ☎ *021/427–8150* ⊕ *www.silverwoodjewellery.com.*

Blarney

10 km (6 miles) northwest of Cork City.

"On Galway sands they kiss your hands, they kiss your lips at Carney, but by the Lee they drink strong tea, and kiss the stone at Blarney." This famous rhyme celebrates one of Ireland's most noted icons—the Blarney Stone, which is the main reason most people journey to this small community built around a village green.

GETTING HERE AND AROUND

Blarney is about a 20-minute drive west of Cork City, midway between the N22 Killarney road and the N20 to Limerick. Local buses that depart from Cork Bus Station Parnell Place drop you at the Village Green, adjacent to the castle and

East Cork

Mitchelstown

WATERFORD

Castletownroche

Kanturk

River Blackwater

Mallow   Fermoy   Lismore

Dungarvan

Rathcormac

CORK

◆ Fota House, Arboretum
& Gardens
◆ Fota Island Wildlife Park

Blarney

Cork

Youghal

Macroom

Cork
Harbour   Midleton

Cloyne   Shanagarry

Cobh   Ballycotton

Cork City
see detail
map

Cork Airport
(ORK)

*Cork
Harbour*

Bandon   Kinsale

Kilbrittain

Celtic Sea

Timoleague

Clonakilty   Courtmachsherry

Rosscarbery

the crafts shops. There is a large parking lot (no fee). Taxis are available from Castle Cabs by phone reservation.

CONTACTS Castle Cabs. ☎ *021/438–2222.*

VISITOR INFORMATION
CONTACTS Blarney Tourist Office. ✉ *Blarney Woolen Mills entrance, The Square* ☎ *021/438–1624.*

👁 Sights

★ Blarney Castle
CASTLE/PALACE | In the center of Blarney, the ruined central keep is all that's left of this mid-15th-century stronghold. The castle contains the famed **Blarney Stone**; kissing the stone, it's said, endows the kisser with the fabled "gift of the gab." It's 127 steep steps to the battlements. To kiss the stone, you must lie down on the battlements, hold on to a guardrail,

and lean your head way back. It's good fun and not at all dangerous. Expect a line from mid-June to early September; while you wait, you can admire the views of the wooded River Lee valley and chuckle over how the word "blarney" came to mean what it does. As the story goes, Queen Elizabeth I wanted Cormac MacCarthy, Lord of Blarney, to will his castle to the Crown, but he refused her requests with eloquent excuses and soothing compliments. Exhausted by his comments, the queen reportedly exclaimed, "This is all Blarney. What he says he rarely means."

You can take pleasant walks around the castle grounds; Rock Close contains oddly shaped limestone rocks landscaped in the 18th century, and a grove of ancient yew trees that is said to have been a site of Druid worship. In early March there's a wonderful display of daffodils. ✉ *Village Green* ☎ *021/438–5252* ⊕ *www.blarney-castle.ie* 💰 *€18.*

 Restaurants

Blairs Inn

$ | EUROPEAN | Surrounded by woods just five minutes' drive from Blarney, Blair's Innis the perfect retreat from Blarney's tour-bus crowds. This is a real "local," run by genial owner-hosts and their sons, who serve generous portions of tradition-al Irish fare made from fresh local pro-duce. **Known for:** Irish stew; hot gratin of prawns, crab, and salmon; beer garden. ⑤ *Average main: €18* ✉ *R579, Cloghroe* ☎ *021/438–1470* ⊕ *www.blairsinn.ie.*

 Hotels

Blarney Castle Hotel

$$ | HOTEL | Set on the village green only a minute's walk from the famed castle, this 1837 hotel occupies a traditional gabled building, with guest rooms on two stories above the bar and a quiet residents' lounge on the first floor. **Pros:** ideal touring base; good alternative to Cork City (8 km [5 miles]); restaurant on premises. **Cons:** bar can get busy on Sunday night; no elevator; some rooms overlook parking lot and yard. ⑤ *Rooms from: €120* ✉ *Village Green* ☎ *021/438–5116* ⊕ *www.blarneycastlehotel.com* ⇱ *13 rooms* ⦿| *Free breakfast.*

The White House Blarney

$ | B&B/INN | On an elevated site on the main road between the N20 and Blarney village (a five-minute walk from the latter), this hacienda-style bungalow has a distant view of the castle from its front door. **Pros:** good value; quiet and comfortable; professional and hospitable hosts. **Cons:** won't win any style awards. ⑤ *Rooms from: €80* ✉ *Shean Lower* ☎ *021/438–5338* ⊕ *www.thewhite-houseblarney.com* ⇱ *6 rooms* ⦿| *Free breakfast.*

 Shopping

Blarney Woollen Mills

CRAFTS | With the largest stock and the highest turnover of Blarney's crafts shops, this noted emporium sells everything from Irish-made high fashion to Aran hand-knitted items to leprechaun key rings. ✉ *The Square* ☎ *021/451–6111* ⊕ *www.blarney.com.*

Cork Harbour

16 km (10 miles) east of Cork City.

Cork City's nearby harbor district has seen plenty of history. Cork Harbour's draws include Fota Island—with an arboretum, a wildlife park, and the Fota House ancestral estate—and the fishing port of Cobh.

GETTING HERE AND AROUND
Cobh lies 16 km (10 miles) east of Cork City, and is signposted from the N25 (fol-low signs for Waterford). A suburban train from Cork's Kent Station stops at Fota Island and Cobh, and offers better harbor views than the journey by road.

TOURS
★ **Spike Island**
WALKING TOURS | FAMILY | Call it Ireland's Alcatraz. A scenic 15-minute boat ride from Cobh, Spike Island was originally the site of a 6th-century monastery, then a British artillery fortification in the 18th century, and a holding for convicts awaiting deportation to Australia in the mid-19th century. Ten times the size of Alcatraz, it remained a prison until the late 20th century, and now contains interpretive displays and a café. The island itself has plenty to see, from the abundant wildlife to the museum build-ing, gun store, and observation bunker, as well as the tunnels and punishment block. The island also offers great views of Cork Harbour, especially lovely when the weather cooperates. The regular tour takes 3½ hours including boat trips,

but there are shorter "after dark" tours, fully guided, with no costumed actors or forced scares, just the grim reality of the island fortress prison to strike a chill in your soul. ✉ *Cobh* ⚓ *Kennedy Pier is in center of Cobh's waterfront, below cathedral* ☎ *085/851–8818* ⊕ *www.spikeisland-cork.ie* ✉ *From €20.*

The Titanic Trail

WALKING TOURS | A 60-minute guided walking tour of Cobh by local historian and author, Dr. Michael Martin, covers Titanic sites and history. The tour departs daily at 11 am from the Commodore Hotel. No advance booking required. ✉ *Cobh* ☎ *087/276–7218* ⊕ *www.titanic.ie* ✉ *From €13.*

VISITOR INFORMATION

CONTACTS Cobh Tourist Office. ✉ *Sirius Arts Centre, Lower Rd., Cobh* ☎ *021/481–3301* ⊕ *www.visitcobh.com.*

Sights

Fota House, Arboretum & Gardens

GARDEN | The name of the Smith-Barry ancestral estate is derived from the Irish *Fód te,* which means "warm soil," a tribute to the unique tidal estuary microclimate here and the reason why one of Ireland's most exotic botanical gardens was established here. The original lodge house was built in the mid-18th century for the family, which owned vast tracts of land in South Cork, including the whole of Fota Island. The next generation of the powerful family employed the renowned architects Richard and William Vitruvius Morrison to convert the structure into an impressive Regency-style house that has now been painstakingly restored. The symmetrical facade is relatively unadorned and stands in contrast to the resplendent Adamesque plasterwork of the formal reception rooms (somewhat denuded of furniture). The servants' quarters are almost as big as the house proper. Fota's glories continue in the gardens, which include an arboretum,

a Victorian fernery, an Italian garden, an orangerie, and a special display of magnolias. You can also (for an extra charge) visit the Victorian working garden. There's a tearoom, and the house hosts a program of concerts and exhibitions: see the website for details. ✉ *Fota Island* ☎ *021/481–5543* ⊕ *www.fotahouse.com* ✉ *From €5; gardens and arboretum free* ⊘ *House closed Oct.–Feb.*

Fota Wildlife Park

ZOO | FAMILY | The 70-acre park is 12 km (7 miles) east of Cork via N25 and R624, the main Cobh road, and also accessible by rail from Cork's Kent Station. It's an important breeding center for cheetahs and wallabies, and also is home to monkeys, zebras, giraffes, ostriches, flamingos, emus, and kangaroos. ✉ *Fota Island* ☎ *021/481–2678* ⊕ *www.fotawildlife.ie* ✉ *€17.*

★ The Queenstown Story at Cobh Heritage Centre

MUSEUM | Many of the people who left Ireland on immigrant ships for the New World departed from Cobh, which was formerly known as Queenstown. The exhibit, in the old Cobh train station, re-creates the experience of the 2½ million emigrants who left from here between 1848 and 1960. It also tells the stories of great transatlantic liners, including the ill-fated *Titanic,* whose last port of call was Cobh, and the *Lusitania.* ✉ *Lower Rd., Cobh* ☎ *021/481–3591* ⊕ *www.visitcobh.com* ✉ *€10* ⊘ *Closed Dec. 23–27 and Dec. 31–Jan. 7.*

St. Colman's Cathedral

RELIGIOUS SITE | The best view of Cobh, well worth the uphill stroll, is from St. Colman's Cathedral, an exuberant neo-Gothic granite church designed by the eminent British architect E. W. Pugin in 1869, and completed in 1919. Inside, granite niches portray scenes of the Roman Catholic Church's history in Ireland, beginning with the arrival of St. Patrick. ✉ *Cathedral Close, Cobh*

The Sinking of the Lusitania

On May 7 every year an event is held on the quayside in Cobh at the *Lusitania* Peace Memorial to commemorate the 1,198 innocent civilians lost at sea on May 7, 1915. The Cunard liner *Lusitania* was torpedoed off the Old Head of Kinsale, 40 km (25 miles) west of Queenstown (as Cobh was then known). This attack on a nonmilitary target was a major factor in the decision by the United States to declare war in 1917.

The *Lusitania* was the pride of the Cunard fleet. It had set a record in 1907, crossing the Atlantic in four days, 19 hours, 52 minutes, and the transatlantic service continued, despite the outbreak of war in 1914. The vessel was on a voyage from New York to Liverpool when it was struck by a torpedo from the German submarine U20 shortly after 2 pm. It quickly listed to one side, making it difficult to launch the lifeboats, and 18 minutes later, the mighty liner had sunk, leaving hundreds struggling in the water. A flotilla of local boats, tenders, tugs, and fishing vessels rushed to the rescue, while those onshore worked tirelessly to cope with the sudden disaster. Of the 1,959 passengers and crew aboard, only 761 survived. Of the 289 bodies recovered, 169 are buried in Cobh, 45 of them unidentified.

☎ *021/481–3222* ⊕ *www.cobhcathedralparish.ie.*

The Titanic Experience Cobh

MUSEUM | Cobh was the last port of call for the ocean liner *Titanic*. At 1:30 pm on April 11, 1912, tenders carried 123 passengers out to the ship from the offices of the White Star Line. These offices have now been converted into an interactive exhibition (cinema, holographs, touchscreen displays), allowing visitors to follow, literally, in the footsteps of the passengers as they embarked on the fateful voyage. ✉ *The Promenade, Cobh* ☎ *021/481–4412* ⊕ *www.titanicexperiencecobh.ie* 🎟 *€10.*

 Restaurants

Gilbert's Bistro in the Square

$$ | CONTEMPORARY | Just below Cobh's cathedral, a short step from the waterfront, this handsome cut-stone house dates to 1824. Locals can be seen lingering over coffee and newspapers through the street-front windows of the café and bar area, and the elegant bistro-style restaurant, with bentwood chairs and contemporary art, has an equally relaxed Continental atmosphere. **Known for:** tempura cod and chips; good selection of salads; lively bistro. $ *Average main: €19* ✉ *11 Pearse Sq., Cobh* ☎ *021/481–1300* ⊕ *www.gilbertsincobh.com* ⊗ *Restaurant closed Jan.–mid-Mar.*

Midleton

12 km (8 miles) east of Cork City.

Midleton is famous for its school, Midleton College, founded in 1696, and its distillery, founded in 1825 and modernized in 1975, which manufactures spirits—including Irish whiskey—for distribution worldwide. A pleasant market town set at the head of the Owenacurra River estuary, near the northeast corner of Cork Harbour, Midleton has many gray-stone buildings dating mainly from the early 19th century.

GETTING HERE AND AROUND

Midleton is 12 km (8 miles) east of Cork City on the main N25. It also has regular bus and train connections with the city. If you're going to visit the Jameson distillery, it runs a daily shuttle, April through October, from St. Patrick's Quay in Cork. In other months, Bus Éireann's daily service from Cork Bus Station Parnell Place is the best option because it stops right outside the distillery (€9 round-trip, 30 minutes). Many trains run from Cork's Kent Station every day (€6.50 round-trip); the Midleton train station is about 25 minutes' walk from the distillery.

CONTACTS Bus Éireann. ✉ *Parnell Pl., City Center South* ☎ *021/450–8188* ⊕ *www.buseireann.ie.* **Irish Rail.** ✉ *Kent Station, City Center North* ☎ *021/450–6766 for timetable* ⊕ *www.irishrail.ie.*

 Sights

Jameson Experience

WINERY/DISTILLERY | On a tour of the Old Midleton Distillery, you'll learn how this now world-renowned whiskey (*uisce beatha*, or "the water of life") was made in the old days. The old stone buildings are excellent examples of 19th-century industrial architecture, the impressively large old waterwheel still operates, and the pot still—a copper dome that can hold 32,000 imperial gallons of whiskey—is the world's largest. ■ **TIP→ Early in the tour, requests are made for a volunteer "whiskey taster," so be alert if this option appeals.** Tours end with a complimentary glass of Jameson's Irish whiskey (or a soft drink). A gift shop and café are also on the premises. From April to October there is a daily shuttle bus service from St. Patrick's Quay Cork; inquire when booking. ✉ *Old Midleton Distillery, Old Distillery Walk* ☎ *021/461–3594* ⊕ *www.jamesonwhiskey.com* 🎟 *€22.*

 Hotels

Castlemartyr Resort

$$$$ | RESORT | FAMILY | A gracious 18th-century manor house is the centerpiece of this resort overlooking ancient pastures grazed by Kerry Bog ponies, and adjacent to a 12th-century castle. **Pros:** luxurious period-style suites; excellent spa and golf course; 220-acre grounds include a lake and woodland paths. **Cons:** a bit off the beaten track; popular as a wedding and conference venue; some of the new bedrooms are a bit far from main amenities. ⑤ *Rooms from: €309* ✉ *Castlemartyr* ☎ *021/421–9000* ⊕ *www. castlemartyrresort.ie* 🛏 *103 rooms, 45 lodges* ¶⚪ *Free breakfast.*

Shanagarry

15 km (8 miles) southeast of Midleton, 17 km (11 miles) southeast of Cork Harbour.

There are three reasons to come to Shanagarry, a farming village known chiefly for its Quaker connections: Ballymaloe House, one of Ireland's first and still most famous country-house hotels; Ballymaloe Cookery School Gardens, a top destination for chefs-in-training; and the gallery and shop of Stephen Pearce, a leading designer of earthenware pottery. All three enterprises are run by Quaker families, testimony to the religious roots of this community.

GETTING HERE AND AROUND

Shanagarry, on a rural back road, is about an hour's drive from Cork City or Cork Harbour on the N25 to the R632; from Midleton, take the R629. Or take the Ballycotton bus (there are five runs daily) from Cork Bus Station Parnell Place. The trip takes an hour and a quarter. The last bus back to Cork leaves Shanagarry at 4:45 pm.

Sights

Ballymaloe Cookery School and Gardens

GARDEN | FAMILY | While the late, lamented Myrtle Allen reigned supreme at Ballymaloe House, her daughter-in-law Darina, Ireland's most famous celebrity chef and slow-food advocate, rules at the Ballymaloe Cookery School, 3 km (2 miles) east. The school offers 12-week residential courses for aspiring professional chefs, and day and half-day courses with famous visiting chefs (including Darina's daughter-in-law, Rachel Allen). The extensive organic gardens here provide herbs and vegetables for the school and the restaurant, and visitors can ramble through wildflower meadows and admire herbaceous borders leading to an ornately crafted shell house, the potager vegetable garden, rustic tree house, and a Celtic maze. A farm walk visits cows in their clover field, rare-breed pigs, and some 400 hens. Conclude your visit in the Farm Shop, open the same hours as the garden. ⊠ Kinoith House ☎ 021/464–6785 ⊕ www.cookingisfun.ie/gardens/our-gardens ⊠ €6 ⊗ Closed Sun.

Shanagarry Design Centre

STORE/MALL | Run by the Kilkenny Shop, the spacious gallery and showroom (with scrumptious home baking in the café) is in the village center. On display are high-end Irish-made crafts including Newbridge silverware, Orla Kiely handbags, and potter Louis Mulcahy's huge bowls and lamps, as well as Irish-made clothing, woolen goods, Irish linen, and jewelry. Several artists and craft makers have studios in the basement, where their work is also for sale. ⊠ Next to Shanagarry Parish Church ☎ 021/464–5838 ⊕ www.kilkennyshop.com/shanagarrydesigncentre ⊠ Free.

★ Stephen Pearce Pottery

STORE/MALL | Now returned to the village where he grew up, potter Stephen Pearce has reopened the traditional craft pottery that launched his career in the late 1960s. The showroom sells his distinctive, contemporary hand-thrown black-and-cream earthen tableware and the terra-cotta–and-white line, made from organic local clay and both beloved of collectors. The tearoom opens daily from May to September, weekends only in winter. Book a pottery tour in advance, and ask about workshops. ■ TIP➔ Pearce's simple, practical, but beautiful pottery makes for great, contemporary Irish gifts and souvenirs. U.S. shipping is available if you can't limit yourself to something packable! ⊠ The Old Pottery ☎ 021/464–6807 ⊕ www.shanagarrypotters.com.

Hotels

★ Ballymaloe House

$$$$ | B&B/INN | FAMILY | This Georgian manor is a symphony of whites and beiges, its drawing room beckoning with fine modern Irish paintings—a lovely touch for what is basically a farmhouse family home, albeit a world-famous one: Ballymaloe is the fountainhead of New Irish cuisine. **Pros:** run by Ireland's food royalty; country-house charm; quiet rural location. **Cons:** advance booking essential; village not in walking distance. $ Rooms from: €280 ⊠ Off R629 ☎ 021/465–2531 ⊕ www.ballymaloe.ie ⤶ 29 rooms ❢❂❢ Free breakfast.

Kinsale

29 km (18 miles) southwest of Cork City.

Foodies flock to Kinsale, a picturesque port that pioneered the Irish small-town tradition of fine dining in unbelievably small restaurants. In the early 1980s, Kinsale had a village-size population of 2,000 and at least a dozen top-grade restaurants, mostly run by enthusiastic owner-chefs. Things have leveled out since then—the town has grown, while the number of restaurants has remained nearly the same, and most of the original chefs have moved on—but there is still a great choice of places to eat. Year-round, head to Market Square (Wednesday 10–1) to find Kinsale Market, a cute piazza market where you can snack on a Breton crepe while stocking up on chutneys, smoked salmon, farmhouse cheeses, fresh fish, and organic goodies.

In Kinsale's town center, at the tip of the wide, fjordlike harbor that opens out from the River Bandon, upscale shops and eateries with brightly painted facades line small streets. Kinsale has two yacht marinas, and skippers with deep-sea angling boats offer day charters. The Kinsale Yacht Club hosts racing and cruising events during the sailing season, which runs from March to October for hardy souls and from June to August for everyone else.

GETTING HERE AND AROUND
Kinsale is 29 km (18 miles) southwest of Cork City on the R600, a half-hour drive, and is only a 15-minute drive from Cork Airport. Ground-level parking is easily available. Buses from Cork City stop at the airport and run every hour. Kinsale's town center is compact, and there is no public transport, but taxis can be booked from Kinsale Cabs.

CONTACTS Kinsale Cabs. ✉ *Market Sq.* ☎ *021/477–2642* ⊕ *www.kinsalecabs. com.*

TOURS
Don & Barry's Kinsale Historic Stroll
GUIDED TOURS | On this tour of Old Kinsale you'll learn about the town's links to "Man Friday" and the truth about Kinsale Hookers pirates. It departs from the town's tourist office daily at 11:15; there's an additional tour at 9:15 Monday to Saturday from May to September. ✉ *Kinsale* ☎ *021/477–2873* ⊕ *www.historicstrollkinsale.com* ✐ *€8.*

Kinsale Harbour Cruises
BOAT TOURS | **FAMILY** | For an overview of Kinsale's great natural harbor, take an hour-long cruise on the *Spirit of Kinsale,*

offered by Kinsale Harbour Cruises. You'll hear informative commentary and view wildlife, including herons, seals, and otters. ✉ *Pier Rd.* ☎ *086/250–5456* ⊕ *www.kinsaleharbourcruises.com* ✐ *€13.*

Kinsale Heritage Town Walks
GUIDED TOURS | Dermot Ryan, a native of Kinsale and a local-history enthusiast, leads guided town walks daily at 10:30 am and 3 pm. ✉ *Kinsale* ☎ *021/477–2729* ⊕ *www.kinsaleheritage.com* ✐ *€5.*

VISITOR INFORMATION
CONTACTS Kinsale Tourist Office. ✉ *Pier Rd.* ☎ *021/477–2234* ⊕ *www.kinsale.ie.*

 ## Sights

★ Charles Fort
MILITARY SITE | **FAMILY** | The British built Charles Fort on the east side of the Bandon River estuary in the late 17th century, after their defeat of the Spanish and Irish forces. One of Europe's best-preserved "star forts" encloses some 12 cliff-top acres and is similar to Fort Ticonderoga in New York State. If the sun is shining, take the footpath from Kinsale signposted Scilly Walk; it winds along the harbor's edge under tall trees and then through the village of Summer Cove. ✉ *3 km (2 miles) east of town* ☎ *021/477–2263* ⊕ *www.heritageireland.ie* ✐ *€5.*

Kinsale Museum
MUSEUM | Memorabilia from the wreck of the *Lusitania* are among the artifacts in this museum, housed in a 17th-century, Dutch-style courthouse. The 1915 inquest into that ship's sinking took place in the wood-paneled courtroom. Downstairs is a fascinating collection of antique tradesman's tools. Because the staff consists of volunteers, it's best to call to confirm opening times. ✉ *Old Courthouse, Market Sq.* ☎ *021/477–2234* ⊙ *Closed Nov.–Mar.*

West Cork
and Bantry Bay

Spaniard Inn

RESTAURANT—SIGHT | The inn looks over the town and harbor from a hairpin bend on the road to Charles Fort. Inside, sawdust-covered floors and a big open fireplace make this onetime fishermen's bar a cozy spot in winter. In summer you can take a pint to the veranda and watch the world go by on land and sea. ⊠ *Lower Rd., Scilly* ☎ *021/477–2436* ⊕ *www. thespaniard.ie.*

 Restaurants

Bastion

$$$ | **CONTEMPORARY** | Prosecco on tap sets the tone for fun at this wine bar and restaurant in the heart of Kinsale. There's a bar in the funky front parlor, along with some tables beside its street windows, supplemented by a more private back room. **Known for:** experimental small plates; more than 100 wines; range of prix-fixe and tasting menus. $ *Average main: €26* ⊠ *5 Main St.* ☎ *021/470–9696* ⊕ *www.bastionkinsale.com.*

The Black Pig

$ | **WINE BAR** | A small 18th-century coach house on a backstreet was an unlikely candidate to become the hottest place in a town famed for sophisticated eateries, but that's what happened here, and the uncluttered, minimalist premises positively buzz with life. Reserve and your name is chalked on the wall beside your table, but the tall squeaky bar stools are just as popular. **Known for:** up to 40 wines available by the glass; daily hot special; local coffee and chocolates. $ *Average main: €14* ⊠ *66 Lower O'Connell St.* ☎ *021/477–4101* ⊟ *No credit cards* ⊙ *Closed mid-Jan.–Mar. No lunch.*

★ The Bulman Bar and Toddies

$ | **CONTEMPORARY** | Kinsale has other pub-restaurants, but none with such an idyllic waterside location. In summer, bar food is served on the big stone quay right beside the ocean. **Known for:** half-grilled lobster in summer months; slow-cooked pork ribs with house barbecue sauce; deep-fried calamari salad. *$ Average main: €16 ⊠ Summercove ☎ 021/477–2131 ⊕ www.thebulman.ie ⊗ No food Mon.*

★ Finns' Table

$$$$ | **CONTEMPORARY** | Since opening in 2013, Finns' has become Kinsale's undisputed crown jewel of fine dining and one of the very best examples of its front-parlor restaurants. Talented owner-chef John Finn runs the restaurant with his wife, Julie, and John's parents' butchery supplies the meat. **Known for:** roast rack of lamb; crab tasting-plate starter; excellent wine list. *$ Average main: €34 ⊠ 6 Main St. ☎ 021/470–9636 ⊕ www.finnstable.com ⊗ Closed Nov.; Dec. 26–Mar., Sun.–Wed.; Apr. and May, Wed. and Sun.; June–Oct., Wed.*

★ Fishy Fishy Café

$$$ | **SEAFOOD** | **FAMILY** | Originally a café in a fish shop, this place has moved up in the world, with sumptuous two-story premises in the town park. TV chef Martin Shanahan, who trained in San Francisco, brings California pizzazz to his dishes. **Known for:** surf 'n' turf of scallops and black pudding on parsnip puree; "fishy fish pie" served with mash au gratin in a hot cream sauce; spicy seafood chowder. *$ Average main: €25 ⊠ Crowley's Quay ☎ 021/470–0415 ⊕ www.fishyfishy.ie ⊗ No dinner Sun.–Wed., Nov.–Feb.*

Jim Edwards

$$ | **EUROPEAN** | One of Ireland's original bar-restaurants, this is a Kinsale institution that serves local steak, lamb, duck, and fresh seafood. Choose from the inexpensive daily specials in the busy bar, or have a more leisurely meal among the mahogany tables and dark-red decor of the somewhat baronial restaurant. **Known for:** generous portions of fresh seafood; top-quality local steak; good-value set menu. *$ Average main: €22 ⊠ Market Quay ☎ 021/477–2541 ⊕ www.jimedwardskinsale.com.*

Max's

$$$ | **FRENCH** | Polished antique tables, a large stone chimney, and bay windows lend considerable charm to the open-plan ground floor of this double-fronted town house. At dinner, owner-chef Olivier Queva's classical French background is evident in his treatment of the daily catch, including fresh grilled lobster in the summer, and clever ways with unusual cuts of meat. **Known for:** good value early-bird menu; excellent seafood; reservations required on summer weekends. *$ Average main: €28 ⊠ 48 Main St. ☎ 021/477–2443 ⊕ www.maxs.ie ⊗ Closed Jan.–mid-Mar.*

 ## Hotels

★ Friar's Lodge

$ | **B&B/INN** | A large Georgian town house has been tastefully converted into this cheerful guesthouse, with an array of amenities that would do a hotel proud. **Pros:** quiet location yet close to town; pleasant, spacious rooms; private parking. **Cons:** no restaurant; no bar. *$ Rooms from: €118 ⊠ Friar's St. ☎ 021/477–7384 ⊕ www.friars-lodge.com ⊗ Closed Christmas wk ⇩ 18 rooms ⦿ Free breakfast.*

★ Giles Norman Gallery Townhouse

$$ | **B&B/INN** | The gallery sells striking black-and-white photos, so it's fitting that the rooms in this carefully restored Victorian house are decked out in black, white, and gray contemporary furnishings, with large photo murals on the walls. **Pros:** town-center location; comfortable, spacious rooms; sea views. **Cons:** no breakfast; up two or three flights of stairs and no elevator; no dedicated parking. *$ Rooms from: €160 ⊠ 45 Main St. ☎ 021/477–4373*

⊕ *www.gilesnorman.com* ♥ *Closed mid-Dec.–Feb.* � *4 rooms* ⊙ *No meals.*

Innishannon House

$$ | HOTEL | A pretty country house, built in the château style in 1720 on the banks of the Bandon, Innishannon retains plenty of casual character. **Pros:** scenic riverside location; highly romantic; private car parking. **Cons:** a mile from nearest village; often hosts wedding parties; new rooms lack the charm of those in original house. ⑤ *Rooms from: €135* ⊠ *Innishannon* ☎ *021/477–5121* ⊕ *www.innishannon-hotel.ie* ♥ *Closed mid-Feb.–mid-Mar., Oct.–mid-Dec., and mid-Jan.–mid-Feb., closed Mon.–Thurs.* ➥ *23 rooms* ⊙ *Free breakfast.*

Trident Hotel

$$ | HOTEL | The modern three-story building may lack old-world charm, but the waterfront location—built around three sides of a former dockyard on the edge of Kinsale's magnificent harbor—more than compensates. **Pros:** great sea views; working harbor setting; lively tavern. **Cons:** bland interiors; pool and spa are at a sister hotel a five-minute walk away. ⑤ *Rooms from: €142* ⊠ *Pier Rd., World's End* ☎ *021/477–9300* ⊕ *www.tridenthotel.com* ➥ *75 rooms* ⊙ *Free breakfast.*

Nightlife

The Folk House

BARS/PUBS | This friendly pub presents live music on weekends year-round, and also midweek from May through October. ⊠ *Guardwell* ☎ *021/477–2382* ⊕ *folkhousevenue.com.*

Spaniard Inn

MUSIC CLUBS | Check out the Spaniard Inn for rock and folk groups. There's a traditional Irish session on Wednesday from 10 pm year-round. ⊠ *Scilly* ☎ *021/477–2436.*

Shopping

ART

The Boathouse Gallery

ART GALLERIES | Many of the works by locally based contemporary artists sold here are small enough to carry home. ⊠ *60 Main St.* ☎ *021/470–9981.*

Giles Norman Photography Gallery

ART GALLERIES | Black-and-white photographs of Irish scenes are featured at this local gallery. ⊠ *44 Main St.* ☎ *021/477–4373* ⊕ *www.gilesnorman.com.*

BOOKS

bookstór

BOOKS/STATIONERY | This popular local hangout stocks new and vintage books, and a great selection of local interest reads. They've won awards for their children's section, and the staff has plenty of helpful tips. ⊠ *1 Newman's Mall* ☎ *021/477–4966.*

HOUSEWARES

Granny's Bottom Drawer

TEXTILES/SEWING | A selection of fine Irish linen and hand weaving, in classic and contemporary styles, is carried at this shop, together with Irish-made luxury knitwear in cashmere and silk. ⊠ *53 Main St.* ☎ *021/477–4839* ⊕ *www.grannysbottomdrawer.com.*

Hilary Hale

HOUSEHOLD ITEMS/FURNITURE | This wood turner uses storm-felled, locally grown timber to make lamps, bowls, and platters. ⊠ *Rincurran Hall, Summercove* ☎ *021/477–2010* ⊕ *www.hilaryhale.com.*

Kinsale Crystal

CERAMICS/GLASSWARE | This family-run studio sells handblown, hand-cut Irish crystal. ⊠ *Market St.* ☎ *21/477–4493* ⊕ *www.kinsalecrystal.ie.*

JEWELRY

Kinsale Silver

JEWELRY/ACCESSORIES | Dominic Dolan is the silversmith who crafts fine jewelry

Thanks to locals painting their houses with bright colors, the historic seaside village of Kinsale has become one of Ireland's most picturesque photo ops.

on the premises here. ✉ *Pearse St.* ☎ *021/477–4359* ⊕ *www.kinsalesilver.ie.*

 Activities

GOLF
★ Old Head Golf Links

GOLF | Golf doesn't get much more spectacular than this. On a celebrated 215-acre peninsula, which juts out into the wild Atlantic nearly 300 feet below, you can find an awe-inspiring spectacle that defies comparison. The only golfing stretches that could be likened to it are the 16th and 17th holes at Cypress Point and small, Pacific sections of Pebble Beach, from the 7th to the 10th, and the long 18th. Even if your golf is moderate, expect your pulse to race at the stunning views and wildlife. They've added 15 suites and a spa, so you can now stay at the course for a few days. ✉ *Old Head, off R604* ☎ *021/477–8444* ⊕ *www.old-head.com* ✉ *€350 May–mid-Oct.; €200 mid-Apr. and late Oct.* ⚑ *18 holes, 7215 yards, par 72.*

Clonakilty and Nearby

28 km (19 miles) west of Kinsale.

Clonakilty is a small market town to the west of Kinsale on a scenic, largely coastal road that passes through the village of Timoleague. Many of the storefronts in Clonakilty have charmingly traditional hand-painted signs and wooden facades. Clonakilty marks the western edge of the Seven Heads Peninsula, which stretches back eastward to Timoleague, whose ruined abbey dominates the view. Timoleague sits on the Argideen River estuary, renowned for its birdlife, especially great flocks of wintering migrants. From the abbey, you can see the road to Courtmacsherry, across the water. The sandy beach of this postcard-pretty village attracts many vacationers.

GETTING HERE AND AROUND
Clonakilty is 28 km (19 miles) west of Kinsale on the R600, Timoleague 19 km (12 miles). Follow the signposts from Timoleague to reach Courtmacsherry.

Parking is easy in all three towns. There is no public transit between Kinsale and Clonakilty, but you can take a bus (about an hour) from Cork City.

VISITOR INFORMATION

CONTACTS Clonakilty Tourist Information Office. ✉ *25 Ashe St., Clonakilty* ☎ *023/883–3226* ⊕ *www.clonakilty.ie.*

 Sights

Inchydoney Beach

BEACHES | The beach is on an island connected to the mainland by causeways, and accessible by car. It consists of two flat, wide stretches of fine white sand divided by a rocky promontory. The east side is the most sheltered and has dunes that can be walked. The slope to the sea is so gentle, that at low tide it's a long walk to find deep water. Busy in July and August, its vast expanses offer exhilarating walks the rest of the year. **Amenities:** lifeguards; parking (no fee); toilets; water sports. **Best for:** surfing; swimming; walking. ✉ *Inchydoney Island, 3 km (2 miles) south of town, Clonakilty.*

Timoleague Abbey

RELIGIOUS SITE | A mid-13th-century Franciscan abbey at the water's edge is Timoleague's most striking monument. The abbey was built before the estuary silted up, and its main business was the importing of wine from Spain. A tower and walls with Gothic-arch windows still stand, and you can trace the ground plan of the old friary—chapel, refectory, cloisters, and the extensive wine cellar. The English sacked the abbey in 1642, but like many other ruins of its kind it was used as a burial place until the late 20th century, hence the modern gravestones. ■**TIP→ Walk around the back to find the entrance gate. The view of the sea framed by the structure's ruined Gothic windows is a don't-miss photo op.** ✉ *The Quay, Timoleague* ⊕ *www.timoleague.ie.*

 Restaurants

The Pink Elephant

$ | EUROPEAN | FAMILY | The legendary Pink Elephant looks out to sea and across the bay to wooded slopes. Huge windows frame the stunning view, and in good weather there is seating outside. **Known for:** local meat, fresh fish, organic produce; traditional Sunday lunch; served in a room with a great view. ⑤ *Average main: €16* ✉ *R600 between Kinsale and Timoleague, Harbour View, Kilbrittain* ☎ *023/884–9608* ⊕ *www.pinkelephant. ie* ▭ *No credit cards* ⊗ *No dinner Mon.–Wed. No lunch weekdays Sept.–June.*

Shopping

Edward Twomey

FOOD/CANDY | This butcher's shop is known the world over (at least with Irish expats) for its Clonakilty Black Pudding, a breakfast product that's prominently featured on the shop's T-shirts—the ultimate West Cork souvenir. ✉ *16 Pearse St., Clonakilty* ☎ *023/883–4835* ⊕ *www. clonakiltyblackpudding.ie.*

Etain Hickey Collection

CRAFTS | Etain Hickey is one of Ireland's leading ceramic artists, and her shop stocks the best of contemporary crafts from local artists, including her partner Jim Turner of Rossmore Pottery, and fairtrade sources. ✉ *40 Ashe St., Timoleague* ☎ *023/883–8875* ⊕ *www.rossmorepottery.com.*

Lettercollum Kitchen Project

FOOD/CANDY | Owners Con McLaughlin and Karen Austin are masters of the vegetarian and ethnic repertory. Their bakery and deli sells specialty breads, cooks' ingredients, sandwiches, and savory herb tarts. You can assemble a superior picnic here. ✉ *22 Connolly St., Clonakilty* ☎ *023/883–6938* ⊕ *www.lettercollum.ie.*

Spiller's Lane Gallery

JEWELRY/ACCESSORIES | Set in a converted grain store at a pretty mews, this shop sells Irish-made jewelry, cutlery, pottery, and paintings. ✉ *Spiller's La., Bridge St., Clonakilty* ☎ *023/883–4815.*

Urru

FOOD/CANDY | After taking the Ballymaloe certificate cookery course, Ruth Healy left the corporate treadmill behind to open the ultimate cooks' shop, which aims to bring urban chic to rural Ireland. It's worth a stop en route if you're driving from Cork or Kinsale to Clonakilty. Sip a latte while browsing among locally made foodstuffs, including pâtés and patisserie, and a tempting range of cookbooks, cookware, and chocolates. ✉ *The Mill, MacSwiney Quay, Bandon* ☎ *023/885–4731* ⊕ *www.urru.ie.*

Skibbereen

33 km (20 miles) west of Clonakilty.

Skibbereen is the main market town in this neck of southwest Cork. The Saturday country market and the plethora of pubs, punctuated by bustling shops, supermarkets, and coffeehouses, keep the place jumping year-round.

GETTING HERE AND AROUND

Skibbereen is 85 km (53 miles) southwest of Cork City, a drive of an hour and 20 minutes on the N71, the main Bantry road. The town lies 33 km (20 miles) west of Clonakilty, about a half-hour drive. There is free parking on the street and in several parking lots. Buses depart from Cork Bus Station Parnell Place, but there's no local public transportation. For local excursions, contact Long's Taxis. Skibbereen is a designated hub of the National Cycle Network, with three signposted routes of one-day and half-day trips. Book a bike in advance from Roycroft Cycles.

CONTACTS Roycroft Cycles. ✉ *Ilen St.* ☎ *028/21235* ⊕ *www.westcorkcycles. ie.* **Skibbereen Cabs & Taxi Service.** ✉ *55 Bridge St.* ☎ *028/21258.*

VISITOR INFORMATION

CONTACTS Skibbereen Tourist Office. ✉ *North St.* ☎ *028/21766* ⊕ *www.skibbereen.ie.*

 ## Sights

★ Mizen Vision Visitor Centre

MUSEUM | Travel to this visitor center, set in a lighthouse at the tip of the Mizen Head (follow the R591 through Goleen to the end of the road), and you'll wind up reaching the Irish mainland's most southerly point. The lighthouse itself is on a rock at the tip of the headland; to reach it, you must cross a dramatic 99-step suspension footbridge. The lighthouse was completed in 1910; the Engine Room and Keepers' House have been restored by the local community. The exhilaration of massive Atlantic seas swirling 164 feet below the footbridge and the great coastal views and scenic drive here guarantee a memorable outing. ✉ *Harbour Rd., Goleen* ☎ *028/35115* ⊕ *www.mizenhead.ie* ✉ *€8* ⊗ *Nov.–Feb., closed weekdays.*

Nic Slocum Whale Watch West Cork

SPORTS—SIGHT | More than 24 species of whale and dolphin have been spotted off the coast of West Cork. Trips to see at least some of them last three–four hours, with commentary on other local bird- and wildlife, and leave from the harbor at Baltimore, about 13 km (8 miles) southwest of Skibbereen. Reservations are recommended in peak season. ✉ *Baltimore* ☎ *086/120–0027* ⊕ *www.whalewatchwestcork.com* ✉ *€50* ⊗ *Closed Sept.–Mar.*

Skibbereen Heritage Centre

MUSEUM | A thoughtful renovation of a stone gasworks building has created an attractive, architecturally appropriate home for the Skibbereen Heritage Centre. An elaborate audiovisual exhibit on the Great Famine presents dramatized firsthand accounts of what it was like to live in this community when it was hit hard by hunger. Other attractions include displays on area marine life, walking tours, access to local census information, and a varying schedule of special programs. ⊠ *Upper Bridge St.* ☎ *028/40900* ⊕ *www.skibbheritage.com* 🎫 *€6* ⊗ *Closed Nov.–mid-Mar.; mid-Mar.– Apr. and Oct., closed Sun. and Mon.; May–Sept. closed Sun.*

Restaurants

Heron's Cove

$$$ | SEAFOOD | Although only minutes by foot from the main road and Goleen's village center, this harborside retreat is a peaceable kingdom—expect to see herons outside the window. "Fresh fish and wine on the harbour" is the motto here. The restaurant, in Sue Hill's modern house (she also offers bed and breakfast) is well run and extremely civilized. **Known for:** fresh, local seafood served by the waterside; lobster from the harbor; an interesting selection of wine, chosen from bottles on wall racks. $ *Average main: €28* ⊠ *The Harbour, Goleen* ☎ *028/35225* ⊕ *www.heronscove.com.*

Island Cottage

$$$$ | EUROPEAN | On Heir Island—a four-minute ferry ride—this unlikely venture is a pilgrimage spot for food lovers, who praise the high standard of cooking and the location. The five-course set menu (no choices) focuses on local produce, some of it picked in the wild on the island. **Known for:** five-course menu; served in the chef's home on an offshore island; excellent desserts. $ *Average main: €45* ⊠ *Heir Island* ⚓ *Ferry departs from Cunnamore, about 15 km (9 miles) west of Skibbereen; follow signs on Ballydehob road* ☎ *028/38102* ⊕ *www. islandcottage.com* ⊗ *Closed mid-Sept.– mid-June, and Sun.–Tues. mid-June–mid-Sept. No lunch (except for groups).*

Shopping

Gubbeen Farmhouse Products

OUTDOOR/FLEA/GREEN MARKETS | About 27 km (17 miles) west of Skibbereen, farmer Tom Ferguson tends a herd of prize cows, whose rich milk is made into creamy cheese by his wife, Giana. The fresh-straw piggery allows its lucky pigs to have a view of Roaring Water Bay, one of the most scenic corners of Ireland. Tom and Giana's son, Fingal, runs the smokehouse (great smoked bacon, chorizo, and salamis), while daughter Clovisse grows organic fruit, vegetables, and herbs. Products are sold at Neal's Yard in London and West Cork's Farmers' Markets, and can also be bought direct from the farm. Order produce in advance via the website to make sure of getting what you want. ⊠ *Gubbeen, Schull* ⚓ *From Skibbereen, take N71 west to Ballydehob, then R592 to Schull. Beyond Schull center, fork left, signposted "Coast Road L4406," and continue to Gubbeen* ☎ *028/28231* ⊕ *www.gubbeen.com.*

Castletownshend

8 km (5 miles) southeast of Skibbereen.

Castletownshend has an unusual number of large, stone houses, most of them dating from the mid-18th century, when it was an important port. The main street runs steeply downhill to the 17th-century castle (built by the Townshends, a noted family in the region) and the sea. The sleepy town awakens in July and August, when its sheltered harbor bustles. Sparkling views await from cliff-top St. Barrahane's Church, which has a medieval oak altarpiece and three stained-glass windows by early-20th-century Irish artist Harry Clarke.

GETTING HERE AND AROUND

Castletownshend lies southeast of Skibbereen on R596. The best way to get here and around is by car. The 8-km (5-mile) drive takes about 10 minutes.

 Restaurants

★ Mary Ann's

$$ | EUROPEAN | Irish writer Edna O'Brien calls this low-beamed pub—one of Ireland's oldest—her favorite in the world. Visitors mingle happily with the few locals left in the village in the front barroom or the large garden. **Known for:** baked avocado stuffed with crabmeat; local farmhouse cheeses and home-baked brown bread; platter of Castlehaven Bay shellfish and seafood. $ *Average main: €23 ✉ Main St. ☎ 028/36146 ✺ Nov.–Mar., no bar food Mon., closed weekdays 2:30–6.*

Bantry

25 km (16 miles) northwest of Skibbereen.

The town of Bantry is at the head of Bantry Bay, between the Sheep's Head Peninsula to the southwest and the Beara Peninsula to the northwest. A somewhat unprepossessing town at first sight, Bantry is centered on a large square that attracts artisans, craftspeople, and musicians to its Friday-morning market in summer. If you approach Bantry heading west on the seaside road, before you reach town you'll spot the parking lot and visitor's entrance to the area's big attraction, Bantry House and Gardens.

GETTING HERE AND AROUND

Bantry is on the N71, midway between Skibbereen and Kenmare, a 1½-hour drive from Cork and an hour from Killarney. There is a large parking lot (free) in the main square. Buses from Cork Bus Station Parnell Place continue on to Glengarriff *(see Glengarriff).* There is no other local public transportation.

VISITOR INFORMATION

Ireland can be expensive, but in this part of the country many of the best things are free. Ask at tourist information offices about the many coves and small beaches or the looped walks along sections of the Sheep's Head Walking Route. Information on looped walks in Bantry Town can be found in local bars and hotels and on ⊕ *www.bantry.ie.*

CONTACTS Bantry Tourist Office. ✉ *Wolfe Tone Sq.* ☎ *027/50229* ⊕ *www.bantry.ie.*

 Sights

★ Bantry House and Gardens

GARDEN | One of Ireland's most famed manors is noted for its picture-perfect perch, on a hillock above the south shore of Bantry Bay. The fine Georgian mansion is surrounded by a series of stepped gardens and parterres that make up "the stairway to the sky." Spreading out below lies the bay and, in the far distance, the spectacular range of the Caha Mountains—one of the great vistas of Ireland. Built in the early 1700s and altered and expanded later that century, the manor is the ancestral seat of the White family. The house is largely the vision of Richard White, 1st Earl of Bantry, who traveled extensively through Europe and brought a lot of it back with him: fabulous Aubusson tapestries said to have been commissioned by Louis XV adorn the Rose Drawing Room, while state portraits of King George III and Queen Charlotte glitter in floridly rococo gilt frames in the hypertheatrical, Wedgwood blue–and-gold dining room. An antique or two is thought to have belonged to Marie Antoinette.

Outside, the drama continues in the garden terraces, set with marble statues, framed by stone balustrades, and showcasing such delights as an embroidered parterre of dwarf box trees.

The tearoom serves light lunches, and features local artisanal foods. In summer the house hosts concerts in the grand library, notably the West Cork Chamber Music Festival (held during the first week of July). ⊠ N71 ☎ 027/50047 ⊕ www.bantryhouse.com ✉ €11 house and garden, €5 garden only ⊗ House closed Nov.–Mar.

Restaurants

O'Connors Seafood Restaurant

$$ | SEAFOOD | On Bantry's main square, this restaurant is a stone's throw from the sea that provides for the bulk of its menu. The chef has a way with fish, but meat eaters have ample choices, too, including steak from a local herd of Black Angus cattle. **Known for:** beer-battered fish-and-chips; monkfish and smoked salmon risotto; local scallops with black pudding topping. ⑤ Average main: €24 ⊠ Wolfe Tone Sq. ☎ 027/55664 ⊕ www.oconnorseafood.com ⊗ No lunch Mon.–Thurs.

Hotels

★ Bantry House

$$$ | B&B/INN | When the day-trippers leave, you can play lord and lady of this celebrated manor for the night, thanks to six guest bedrooms, set in a self-contained wing off a long corridor with views over the famous garden. **Pros:** a genuine heritage experience; unique location amid lovely gardens; underfloor heating and modern bathrooms. **Cons:** a longish walk (or a short drive) into town; worth the premium only if you are into history and heritage; no public bar or coffee shop on-site after gardens close. ⑤ Rooms from: €179 ⊠ N71 ☎ 027/50047 ⊕ www.bantryhouse.com ⌁ 6 rooms ❑ Free breakfast.

★ The Maritime Hotel

$$ | HOTEL | FAMILY | A legacy of Ireland's boom years, this gleaming, modern, waterfront hotel recalls times when building budgets were lavish, and it's a superstylish addition to the town, with state-of-the-art leisure facilities that make it a good all-weather touring base. **Pros:** great location; most rooms have stunning views; high comfort levels. **Cons:** long, dimly lit internal corridors; some rooms accessible only via two elevators with a longish walk in between; rates shoot up when there's a festival in town (July and August). ⑤ Rooms from: €120 ⊠ The Quay ☎ 027/54700 ⊕ www.themaritime.ie ⌁ 110 rooms ❑ Free breakfast.

Seaview House Hotel

$$ | HOTEL | Among private, wooded grounds overlooking Bantry Bay, this large, three-story, 19th-century country house is an oasis of calm, nestled in its own gardens well away from the main road. **Pros:** sea views; unostentatious comfort; good food. **Cons:** make your own entertainment; the "village" is more a suburb of Bantry, with only one pub. ⑤ Rooms from: €140 ⊠ N71, Ballylickey ☎ 027/50073 ⊕ www.seaviewhousehotel.com ⊗ Closed Nov.–mid-Mar. ⌁ 25 rooms ❑ Free breakfast.

Shopping

Dunbeacon Pottery

CERAMICS/GLASSWARE | Europe's most southwesterly pottery workshop can be found on the scenic Durrus–Mizen Head road just west of Bantry. Helen Ennis produces handmade ceramic tableware in a variety of glazes. ⊠ R591 ☎ 027/61036 ⊕ www.dunbeaconpottery.com.

★ Forest and Flock

ART GALLERIES | A group of local artists and craftspeople sell their wares at this large retail premises in the town center. Wood turning from storm-felled timber, knitwear, local ceramics, small artworks, candles, and jewelry are among the handcrafted items on offer. ⊠ New St. ☎ 087/386–1799.

Divided by the Hundred Steps, the gardens of Bantry House are adorned with exotic plants due to the microclimate of its bay setting.

Manning's Emporium
FOOD/CANDY | On the road between Bantry and Glengarriff, this deli (and wine bar) is a showcase for locally made farmhouse cheeses, pâtés, and salamis, served on attractive sampling platters. It's also an excellent place to assemble a picnic or just to browse. ⊠ *Ballylickey* ☎ *027/50456* ⊕ *www.manningsemporium.ie.*

Glengarriff

14 km (8 miles) northwest of Bantry.

One of the jewels of Bantry Bay is Glengarriff, the "rugged glen" much loved by the writers William Thackeray and Sir Walter Scott. The drive from Bantry along the cliff top, with views of the islands of the bay and its shelter belt of mountains, is one of the scenic highlights of West Cork. The descent into the sheltered wooded village reveals yet another landscape: thanks to the Gulf Stream, it's mild enough down here for subtropical

plants to thrive. Trails along the shore are flanked by rhododendrons and offer beautiful views of the nearby inlets, loughs, and lounging seals. You're very much on the beaten path, however, with crafts shops, tour buses, and boatmen soliciting your business by the roadside.

GETTING HERE AND AROUND
Glengarriff is a 10-minute drive, 14 km (8 miles) from Bantry on the N71. There is a large public parking lot at Quill's Woolen Mills; on-street parking is easily found, too. Buses from Cork City stop here, and some continue to the Beara Peninsula. There is no public transportation locally, but you can take a boat trip around the harbor, where huge seals bask in fine weather.

Blue Pool Ferry
TRANSPORTATION SITE (AIRPORT/BUS/FERRY/TRAIN) | Buy a ticket at the kiosk beside the Quill's Woolen Mills car park, and follow the trail to an enchanting hidden harbor that's surrounded by rocks and overhanging trees. Boats leave from here for Garnish Island and Illnacullin Gardens,

traveling via Seal Island. No need to land—you can take a round-trip tour and enjoy the wildlife of the bay, which includes a colony of comical basking seals. Cameras at the ready! ✉ *N71* ☎ *027/63333* ⊕ *www.bluepoolferry.com* ✈ *€10* ☉ *Closed Nov.–mid-Mar.*

Sights

★ Ilnacullin

GARDEN | Many visitors head to Glengarriff because of that Irish Eden, Ilnacullin. On Garnish Island, offshore from Glengarriff and beyond islets populated by comical-looking basking seals, you can find one of the country's horticultural wonders. In 1910 a Belfast businessman, John Annan Bryce, purchased this rocky isle, and, with the help of famed English architect Howard Peto and Scottish plantsman Murdo Mackenzie, transformed it into a botanical wonderland. The main showpiece is a wisteria-covered "Casita"—a roofed-over viewing point that overlooks a sunken Italian garden and pool. The modest Bryce family home is open to visitors, presented as it would have been in the early 20th century.

You get to Ilnacullin by taking a Blue Pool ferry (10 minutes), which departs for the island from Glengarriff. George Bernard Shaw found Ilnacullin peaceful enough to allow him to begin his *St. Joan* here; maybe you'll find Garnish inspiring, too. ■ **TIP→ Credit cards are not accepted on island.** ✉ *Garnish Island* ☎ *027/63040* ⊕ *www.garinishisland.ie* ✈ *Gardens €5, ferry €10 round-trip* ☉ *Closed Nov.–Mar.*

★ Ring of Beara

SCENIC DRIVE | Glengarriff is the gateway to this 137-km (85-mile) scenic drive that circles the Beara Peninsula on R572. One of the main attractions is the **Beara Way,** a 196-km (120-mile) marked walking route that takes in prehistoric archaeological sites. **Dursey Island** is a birder's paradise that you reach by cable car. From Dursey Island, head for tiny **Allihies,** the former site of a huge copper mine, celebrated in its own museum. The area is now the home of several leading Irish artists, some of whom invite studio visits (watch for signs). Continue along a breathtaking coastal road to **Eyeries**—a village overlooking Coulagh Bay—and then up the south side of the Kenmare River to Kenmare. ✉ *R572.*

Hotels

Glengarriff Eccles

$$ | HOTEL | Fronted by a massive wrought-iron balcony, this stately landmark has looked out over the calm water of Glengarriff's harbor since before the Victorian novelist William Thackeray passed through. **Pros:** water's edge location; great sense of history; locals use the bar. **Cons:** five-minute walk from village; a bit eerie when not busy. ⑤ *Rooms from: €120* ✉ *Harbour* ☎ *027/63003* ⊕ *www.eccleshotel.com* ☉ *Closed Nov.–mid-Mar.* ⇆ *66 rooms* ❙⊙❙ *Free breakfast.*

Glengarriff Park Hotel

$ | HOTEL | Smack-dab in the middle of the scenic and busy village of Glengarriff, this small, family-run hotel is an excellent base for touring, with some great scenic walks on the doorstep, and sits alongside its sister establishments MacCarthy's Bar and the Park Bistro. **Pros:** great value; knowledgeable local staff; handy one-stop shop for bed, food, and drink; popular destination for Irish people on short breaks. **Cons:** views from bedrooms are disappointing; in high season the village is busy with tourists and tour buses en route to Killarney and the Ring of Kerry. ⑤ *Rooms from: €89* ✉ *Village Center* ☎ *027/63000* ⊕ *www.glengarriffpark.com* ⊟ *No credit cards* ⇆ *26 rooms* ❙⊙❙ *Free breakfast.*

THE SOUTHWEST

Updated by
Alannah Hopkin

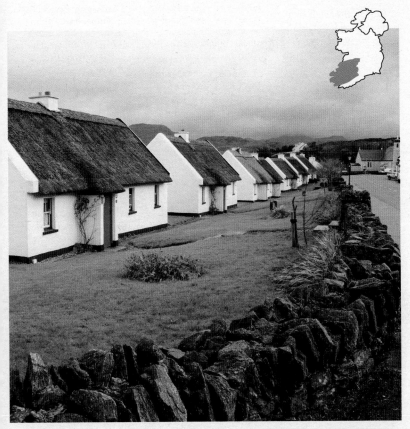

◉ Sights	🍴 Restaurants	🏨 Hotels	🛍 Shopping	🍸 Nightlife
★★★★★	★★★★★	★★★★★	★★★★★	★★★☆☆

WELCOME TO THE SOUTHWEST

TOP REASONS TO GO

★ **The Ring of Kerry:**
The most brazenly scenic coastal drive in Ireland might have been designed with the visitor in mind—cameras and videos at the ready!

★ **Skellig Michael:** Take a wet and wonderful ride out to Ireland's most spectacular island, whose twin peaks, crowned with a medieval monastery, beckon to you along the Ring of Kerry.

★ **The Gap of Dunloe:** A half-day tour lets you walk or ride horseback through the heart of Killarney's purple mountains and cross the glittering blue lake by rowboat.

★ **Adare:** Discover Ireland's prettiest village by taking a walk past its cute thatched cottages to the banks of the River Maigue, where the remains of priories established by medieval monks still stand.

★ **"Castle Country":** Limerick is studded with top attractions like King John's Castle on the banks of the Shannon.

1 Killarney and Nearby. Nineteenth-century visitors found the views of Killarney every bit as romantic and uplifting as the mountains of Switzerland; the unique combination of glacial landscape and abundant subtropical vegetation, studded by the bright blue waters of the lakes, creates an unforgettable vista—and it smells good, too, with peat-fire smoke mingling with fresh mountain air.

2 Kenmare. A lively little town, its streets lined with restaurants and boutiques, Kenmare is a natural stopping place where the roads from Bantry and Killarney intersect.

3 Sneem. This small, lively village with different-colored houses is a highlight of the lush, sheltered southern route of the Ring of Kerry.

4 Waterville. Popular with golfers and anglers, and boasting spectacular sea views on its eastern approach, this is a popular holiday spot for outdoors types.

5 The Skelligs and Valentia. An extension to the Ring of Kerry, highlights include sheltered Valentia Island, and the wild offshore vista of the rocky, twin-peaked Skelligs of Star Wars fame.

6 Cahirciveen. Its main market town, Cahirciveen has the Ring's only sizeable supermarket and an interesting heritage center.

7 Glenbeigh. Blink and you miss the village it's so tiny, but follow the signs for Rossbeigh on its outskirts for a walk on its superb wild, sandy beach.

8 Killorglin. Famous for the annual Puck Fair in August, this little market town on the River Laune is especially lively in summer.

9 Annascaul. The wide road in this quiet little village is a relic of its importance as a cattle-trading center in the past century; most visitors today seek out the pub once owned by Polar explorer Tom Crean.

10 An Daingean (Dingle Town). Beware, this little Irish-speaking town on a sheltered harbor backed by mountains and abounding in friendly pubs and restaurants just might steal your heart away.

11 Ceann Tra (Ventry). More a village than a town, Ventry is chiefly known for its long, sandy beach.

12 Ceann Sléibhe (Slea Head). The rocky southwest extremity of the peninsula boasts dramatic coastal scenery and deserted beaches.

CLARE

N24

Limerick City

Patrickswell
Adare

N21

N20

LIMERICK

N20

Kilrush

Loop
Head

Shannon Estuary

Glin

Listowel

15

KERRY

N21

Tralee

14

Castleisland

CORCA DHUIBHNE
(DINGLE PENINSULA)

An Daingean
(Dingle Town)

N70

Farranfore

Mallow

10

9

Annascaul

Ceann Trá
(Ventry)

R561

8

Killorglin

R562

Killarney

11

N70

N72

12

Ceann Sléibhe
(Slea Head)

Aghadoe

1

13

Glenbeigh

Lake Leane

Blasket
Islands

Gap of Dunloe

CORK

Ring of Kerry

7

Dingle Bay

Cahirciveen

6

N71

N22

Valentia Island

5

IVERAGH PENINSULA

Portmagee

Sneem

Tahilla

2

Kenmare

The Skelligs

Waterville

4

3

N71

5

Ring of Kerry

Skellig Michael

N70

Kenmare Bay

Glengarriff

BEARA PENINSULA

Dursey
Island

Bere
Island

Bantry Bay

Timoleague

0   20 mi

0   20 km

Skibbereen

13 Great Blasket Island.
The nimble-footed will
enjoy an excursion to this
rocky offshore island,
which was inhabited by
hardy souls until 1954.

14 Tralee. The largest
town in County Kerry is
the county's the main
business and shopping
destination, worth visiting
chiefly for its folk theater
and excellent museum.

15 Listowel. This sleepy
little north Kerry town is
famous for its literary
festival in late May, its
writers' museum, and its
castle.

16 Adare. The thatched
cottages make this one of
Ireland's prettiest villages,
but don't miss the monas-
tic remains and imposing
manor house, now a
luxury hotel.

17 Limerick City. Ireland's
third-largest city, and the
nearest to Shannon
Airport, is located on the
wide River Shannon, and
has a riverside walk that
visits most of its historic
attractions.

Ever since Killarney was first "discovered" by William Thackeray and Sir Walter Scott, visitors have been searching for superlatives to describe the deep blue lakes, dark green forests, and purple mountainsides of this romantic region. While modern-day tour-bus traffic and increased visitor numbers have slightly diminished the experience, the appeal of small-scale lake and mountain scenery, the ever-changing light, and the unusual flora and fauna persists—along with the lingering aroma of turf smoke—and the old tales resurrected by the tour guides continue to cast a unique spell.

To be in a hurry in the Southwest is to be ill-mannered. To truly enjoy the amazing array of scenic delights found here, remember that the locals of the Southwest—the region stretches from the Ring of Kerry in the south, the Dingle Peninsula in the west, through Killarney and north to Adare, and Limerick City—are unusually laid-back, even by Irish standards. They still remember what attracted tourists in the first place: uncrowded roads, unpolluted beaches and rivers, easy access to golf, unspoiled scenery, and, above all, time to stop and talk. So take your cue from them and venture onto the back roads. Meander along at your own pace, sampling wayside delights. Before you know it, you'll be far from Killarney town's crowds and in the middle of the region's tranquil and incredibly stunning landscapes.

MAJOR REGIONS

The Ring of Kerry. One of Europe's great scenic drives, a highlight of the Wild Atlantic Way, the route runs around the edge of this rocky peninsula, passing from the subtropical splendor of **Sneem,** on the sheltered Kenmare River, past Waterville, where the twin-peaked Skellig rocks hover on the horizon, to the starker views of Dingle Bay to the north. Stunning mountain and coastal views are around almost every turn. The only drawback: on a sunny day, it seems like half the nation's visitors are traveling along this two-lane road, packed into buses, riding bikes, or backpacking. The route is narrow and curvy, and the local sheep think nothing of using it for a nap: take it slowly.

The gorgeously scenic **Dingle Peninsula** stretches for some 48 km (30 miles) between **Tralee** (pronounced "tra- *lee*") in the east and **Ceann Sléibhe (Slea Head)** in the west. Often referred to by its Irish name, Corca Dhuibhne (pronounced "cor-kah-guy-nay"), the peninsula is made up of rugged mountains, seaside cliffs, and softly molded glacial valleys and lakes. Long, sandy beaches and Atlantic-pounded cliffs unravel along the coast. Drystone walls enclose small, irregular fields, and exceptional prehistoric and early Christian remains dot the countryside. As you drive over its mountain passes, looking out past prehistoric remains to the wild Atlantic sea, Dingle can be a magical destination that makes you feel as if you're living in an ancient legend. Unfortunately, Dingle is notorious for its heavy rainfall and impenetrable sea mists, which can strike at any time of year. If they do, sit them out in **An Daingean (Dingle Town)** and enjoy the friendly bars, cafés, and crafts shops. ■**TIP→ West of Annascaul, the peninsula is Irish-speaking: English is considered a second language. A good Irish-English map can prove handy.**

Until several decades ago, Shannon meant little more to most people—if it meant anything at all—than the name of the longest river in Ireland and Great Britain, running from County Cavan to Limerick City in County Clare. But mention Shannon nowadays and people think immediately of the airport, which has become western Ireland's principal gateway. In turn, what also comes to mind are many of the glorious sights of **North Kerry and Shannonside**: **Adare,** sometimes called "Ireland's Prettiest Village" with its charming thatched cottages (and the neighboring Adare Manor, a grand country-house hotel); and **Limerick City,** which attracts visitors tracing the memories so

movingly captured in Frank McCourt's international best seller, *Angela's Ashes.* Limerick City bears the scars of history from the 1691 Siege of Limerick—a confrontation with the English.

Planning

Getting Here and Around

AIR TRAVEL

The Southwest can be accessed from two international airports: Cork (ORK) on the southwest coast, and Shannon (SNN) in the west (26 km [16 miles] west of Limerick City). Cork Airport is about two hours' drive from both Killarney and Kenmare. Shannon Airport is 135 km (84 miles) from Killarney via Limerick, a journey that takes about two hours. Kerry County Airport (KIR) at Farranfore, 16 km (10 miles) from Killarney, has daily flights from Dublin, London (Stansted and Luton), and Frankfurt (Hahn) operated by Ryanair.

AIRPORT INFORMATION Kerry County Airport. ✉ *N23, Farranfore, Killarney* ☎ *066/976–4644* ⊕ *www.kerryairport.ie.*

AIRPORT TRANSFERS

Bus Éireann runs a 40-minute bus route (€5) between Shannon Airport and Limerick City between 8 am and midnight.

CONTACTS Bus Éireann. ☎ *061/313–333* ⊕ *www.buseireann.ie.*

BUS TRAVEL

Bus Éireann operates express services from Dublin to Limerick City and Tralee. Most towns in the region are served by the provincial Bus Éireann network. The main Bus Éireann bus stations in the region are at Limerick and Tralee, and there is also a bus station in Killarney. The bus stations are located outside the railway stations. Buses tend to stop running in the early evening, which is fine if you want to stay overnight and leave the next morning, but it rules out many day trips—unless you want to spend most of the day on the bus. As a general rule, the smaller the town, and the more remote, the less frequent its bus service: some of the smaller villages on the remote Corca Dhuibhne (Dingle Peninsula) have bus service only one day a week in winter. Bus Éireann runs a regular bus service around the Ring of Kerry between mid-June and mid-September, but there are only two buses a day, leaving Killarney at 8:45 am or 1:45 pm.

CONTACTS Bus Éireann. ☎ 01/836–6111 in Dublin, 061/313–333 in Limerick, 066/716–4700 in Tralee ⊕ www.buseireann.ie.

CAR TRAVEL

A car is the ideal way to explore this region, packed as it is with scenic routes, attractive but remote towns, and a host of out-of-the-way restaurants and hotels that deserve a detour. Road upgrades have not kept up with the increased usage; as a result, prepare for peak-hour traffic jams.

The main driving route from Dublin is N7, which goes 192 km (120 miles) directly to Limerick City. If you land at Shannon Airport, access to the Southwest is also via Limerick City; from there, pick up the N21 to Killarney. From Limerick it is about two hours to Killarney (111 km [69 miles]), and another half hour to Kenmare. An alternate, more scenic, route from Dublin leaves the N7 at Naas to join the N8 at Portlaoise, turning off the main Dublin–Cork road at Mitchelstown and following the N72 to Killarney. Both journeys from Dublin take about four hours; many people prefer to fly from Dublin to Kerry Airport (40 minutes) and pick up a rental car there.

TAXI TRAVEL

A taxi from Shannon Airport to Limerick City costs about €35. It costs €4.10 to hire a taxi on the street (€4.45 at night); add €2 to book one by phone, and €1.03 per kilometer. Full details of fares and conditions are on the National Transport Authority's website.

Taxis are also found at train stations in Tralee, Killarney, and Limerick, and at Shannon and Kerry airports. Otherwise, they must be prebooked by phone: ask for the number of the local company at your hotel or bed-and-breakfast.

CONTACTS Killarney Cabs. ☎ 087/228–8822 ⊕ www.killarneycabs.com. **National Transport Authority.** ☎ 01/879–8300 ⊕ www.transportforireland.ie/taxi. **Tralee Radio Taxis.** ☎ 066/712–5451 ⊕ www.traleeradiotaxis.com.

TRAIN TRAVEL

The region is accessible by train from Dublin Heuston Station and from Cork's Kent Station. From Dublin the region is served by two direct rail links, to Limerick Junction (where you change trains for Limerick City), and on to Tralee (via Mallow and Killarney). The rail network is mainly useful for moving from one touring base to another.

⇨ *For more information on getting here and around, see "Travel Smart Ireland."*

Hotels

For accommodations, the Southwest has some of the great country houses, including Adare Manor in County Limerick; Kenmare's unique duo of the magnificent Sheen Falls Lodge and the stately Park Hotel; the Cahernane House, which recalls Killarney's Victorian heyday; and finally the rambling landmark resort, the Parknasilla Resort in Sneem, a great place for a family break. At the other end of the spectrum is the uniquely Irish experience of a farmhouse bed-and-breakfast, such as Lakelands Farm Guesthouse in Waterville, with rowboats bobbing on Lough Currane at the bottom of the garden. In between is a range of excellent family-owned and-run traditional hotels, such as the Brook Lane Hotel in Kenmare, the Butler Arms in Water-ville, and the secluded Carrig Country House at Glenbeigh near Killorglin. *Hotel reviews have been shortened. For full information, visit Fodors.com.*

Restaurants

Kenmare, Dingle, and Killarney all have a high density of restaurants and gastro-pubs serving locally raised meat, artisanal cheeses, and local seafood. Kerry mountain lamb has a unique flavor imparted by the wild herbs and grasses that those sheep you see on every hillside are busy munching. Adare also has an array of tempting restaurants: choose between the low-ceilinged charm of the tiny rooms in the thatched-cottage restaurant, the Wild Geese, and the genuine old-world hospitality at the blissfully comfortable Dunraven Arms, an old coaching inn still with some of its original antiques, which is now one of Ireland's leading hotels. *Restaurant reviews have been shortened. For full information, visit Fodors.com.*

What It Costs in Euros			
$	$$	$$$	$$$$
RESTAURANTS			
under €19	€19–€24	€25–€32	over €32
HOTELS			
under €120	€120–€170	€171–€210	over €210

Tours

BUS TOURS
Many of the tours listed here can be booked through the Killarney Tourist Office.

Bus Éireann
BUS TOURS | A range of daylong and half-day guided tours are offered from June to September. You can book them at the bus station in Killarney, or at any tourist office. The memorable Gap of Dunloe Tour includes a coach or vintage bus and boat trip; you can add on a horse-drawn jaunting car ride through the Gap. More conventional day trips can also be made to the Ring of Kerry, An Daingean (Dingle), and Ceann Sléibhe (Slea Head), and to Caragh Lake and Rossbeigh. Full-day tours depart at 10:30 am and return at 5 pm, and the price does not include lunch and refreshments. ☎ *061/313–333 in Limerick, 066/716–4700 in Tralee, 064/663–0011 in Killarney* ⊕ *www.buseireann.ie* ✉ *From €25.*

Keating Coaches
BUS TOURS | Day trips and half-day tours of the Shannon region from Limerick City (book in advance; minimum of four people required) include themes such as "castles and gardens," "highways and byways," and "flying boats, monks, and dolphins." ☎ *086/811–6258* ⊕ *www.limericktours.com* ✉ *From €16.*

SPECIAL-INTEREST TOURS

Adams & Butler
SPECIAL-INTEREST | This company provides customized self-driven or chauffeur-driven group tours with accommodations in private country houses and castles. It also conducts special-interest tours on themes like gardens, architecture, ghosts, and golf. ☎ *01/288–9355* ⊕ *www.adamsandbutler.com* ✉ *Prices on request.*

Go Visit Ireland
SPECIAL-INTEREST | This Killorglin-based company offers comprehensive packages (including accommodations and meals) for walking, cycling, fishing, and golfing holidays on the Ring of Kerry and the Dingle Peninsula with experienced local guides. ✉ *Killorglin* ☎ *066/976–2094* ⊕ *www.govisitireland.com* ✉ *From €710.*

Hidden Ireland Tours
SPECIAL-INTEREST | Two knowledgeable Ireland-based guides, Con Moriarty of Killarney and Ann Curran of Dingle, will tailor a package to suit your interests for

Walking Tours

Gap of Dunloe. You can customize your tour with this company, and walk, hire a pony and trap (a horse-drawn carriage), or ride on horseback for the central 11-km (7-mile) off-road stretch of the Gap. A vintage bus takes you to the starting point at Beaufort, and you can choose to cross the lake in an open boat, landing at Ross Castle, a short walk from the center of Killarney town. ⊠ *O'Connor's Pub, 7 High St., Killarney* ☎ *064/663–0200* ⊕ *www. gapofdunloetours.com* 🖾 *From €16.*

Ireland Walk Hike Bike. A variety of walks and bike tours on the Ring of Kerry are available through this company; some include accommodations and evening meals. ☎ *066/718– 6181* ⊕ *www.irelandwalkhikebike.com* 🖾 *Prices on request.*

Irish Ways Walking Tours. Customized walking tours for two or more can explore Dingle, Killarney, and the Ring of Kerry and include seven nights of accommodation in farmhouses and country homes. ☎ *01/260–0749* ⊕ *www. irishways.com* 🖾 *From €760.*

Killarney Guided Walks. Run by Richard Clancy, a noted historian, these tours feature a two-hour walk in Killarney National Park daily at 11 am; departures are from O'Sullivan's Bike Shop opposite the cathedral in Killarney; phone ahead to book November through April. ⊠ *New St., Killarney* ☎ *087/639–4362* ⊕ *www.killarneyguid-edwalks.com* 🖾 *€10.*

Outdoors Ireland. Hill walking and rock climbing in the Kerry hills and kayaking on the lakes of Killarney are the specialty of this tour company based in Beaufort, Killarney. They also lead tours of the Kerry Way. ⊠ *Beaufort, Killarney* ☎ *086/860–4563* ⊕ *www. outdoorsireland.com* 🖾 *From €60.*

groups of 2 to 16 people, and upward. Consider an eight-day walking tour with bases in Killarney and Dingle, or a luxurious car tour staying in some of the region's best country-house hotels. Slow food, painting, literary tours, or antiques tours can also be arranged. ☎ *087/221– 4002* ⊕ *www.hiddenirelandtours.com* 🖾 *Prices on request.*

When to Go

The best times to visit the Ring of Kerry, Killarney, and Dingle are mid-March to June, and September and October. In July and August it's the peak holiday period, meaning roads are more crowded, prices are higher, and the best places are booked in advance. March can be chilly, with daily temperatures in the 40s and 50s. The average high in June is 65°F (18°C), which is about as hot as it gets. May and June are the sunniest months, while May and September are the driest months. The farther west you go, the more likely you'll get rain. The weather is not such a crucial factor in Adare and the Limerick area, but from November to mid-March daylight hours are short, the weather is damp, and many smaller places on the Kerry coast and in Killarney are closed.

Festivals and Events

Dingle Food Festival

On the first weekend in October, this increasingly popular festivals showcases the Peninsula's flavors through tastings, cooking demonstrations, and market stalls. You can sample local produce on the "Taste Trail" at more than 70 venues across town, enjoy special menus, a craft beer and cider trail, or follow the progress of the Great Dingle Bake-Off. And, of course, there's live music, too. ✉ *Dingle* ☏ *087/998–0554* ⊕ *www. dinglefood.com.*

Listowel Writers' Week

Big names and beginners rub shoulders at this major event on the Irish literary calendar, which takes over the small North Kerry town for five days in late May and early June. Workshops for all levels combine with readings and prize-giving events for a range of competitions, including the National Poetry Award. ✉ *Listowel* ☏ *068/21074* ⊕ *www.writer- sweek.ie.*

★ Other Voices

MUSIC FESTIVALS | The first weekend in December, with its short, cold days, is not everyone's idea of the best time to visit Dingle, but fans of this offbeat music festival have other things on their mind than weather. An eclectic assortment of names from the popular music world, big and upcoming, perform in Dingle's tiny church, St. James's, while more than 20 other acts perform live all over town. Your €30 registration fee for the three-day festival gives you a chance in the lottery draw for much-coveted church seats, as well as giving you entrance to all the oth- er gigs. Those without church tickets can watch the live performances, which are live streamed into the town's bars and nightclubs. ✉ *St. James's Church, Dingle* ⊕ *www.othervoices.ie.*

Portmagee Set Dancing and Music Weekend

Maybe not high profile on a national scale, but certainly high on local flavor and fun, this is a friendly festival that keeps alive the old traditions of Irish music and dance. Held on the first weekend of May (a holiday weekend), it's based in the local community hall and the Bridge Bar and features dance workshops, traditional music sessions, and the Saturday night

"Mighty Céili." ✉ *Portmagee* ☏ *066/947– 7108* ⊕ *www.moorings.ie.*

Puck Fair

Expect big crowds at one of Ireland's oldest fairs—it celebrated its 405th year in 2018. It's held over three days starting August 10 in the streets of Killorglin. On day one, a goat is crowned King Puck, and horses are traded in the traditional manner. All three days feature street stalls, a fun fair (midway), and free entertainment, including traditional music and dancing. ✉ *Killorglin* ☏ *066/976–2366* ⊕ *www.puckfair.ie.*

Rose of Tralee International Festival

The town of Tralee is en fête for five days in mid-August with street theat- er, parades, fireworks, and big-name concerts. The highlight is a televised two- evening show in which young women from the Irish diaspora compete for the title of Rose, as they have done since 1959. ✉ *Tralee* ☏ *066/712–1322* ⊕ *www. roseoftralee.ie.*

Planning Your Time

If you're here for a short stay—three or fewer days—you'd do well to base yourself in Killarney and devote your time to exploring the surrounding area, then heading out to the Ring of Kerry or the Dingle Peninsula. With more time at your disposal, consider a half-day trip to Skellig Michael, an unforgettable remote, rock-hewn monastery, or Adare, one of Ireland's prettiest villages.

You also want to pick your peninsula, for two of Ireland's most scenic destinations sit side by side on the map: the Iveragh Peninsula (also known as the Ring of Kerry, for its scenic drive) and the Dingle Peninsula (also known by its Irish name, Corca Dhuibhne). If you like wild, rugged scenery, archaeological remains, and Irish music, Dingle is for you. In contrast, the Ring of Kerry is a longer drive with more varied scenery, ranging from lush subtropical vegetation to rocky coves and long sandy beaches near Glenbeigh. The scenery is punctuated by a series of small villages, all much quieter than Dingle.

IF YOU HAVE THREE DAYS

Spend the first day driving the Ring of Kerry, pausing often to take in the varied coastal scenery. Spend the night in Kenmare or Killarney, then head out the next morning to explore Killarney National Park either on a boat trip or in a horse-drawn jaunting car. Next head for Dingle and drive the Slea Head loop, before enjoying fresh seafood and live traditional music in Dingle Town, a good overnight stop. On your third morning, drive the Conor Pass to Tralee, heading away from the rugged coast to rich farmlands and a short walk around historic Adare. Finish the day with a riverside walk and overnight stay in Limerick City.

Visitor Information

Fáilte Ireland (⊕ www.failteireland.ie) provides a free information service; its tourist information offices (TIOs) also sell a selection of tourist literature. Fáilte Ireland's TIOs will book accommodations for you anywhere in Ireland. Seasonal TIOs in Waterville, Cahirciveen, and Valentia are open from June to September; the TIO in Kenmare is open Easter to October. All of the seasonal TIOs are generally open Monday to Saturday 9–6; in July and August they are also open Sunday 9–6. Year-round TIOs can be found in Adare, An Daingean/Dingle, Killarney, Limerick, Shannon Airport, and Tralee. These offices are usually open Monday to Saturday 9–6 and also Sunday 9–6 in July and August.

Killarney and Nearby

87 km (54 miles) west of Cork City, 19 km (12 miles) southeast of Killorglin, 24 km (15 miles) north of Glengarriff.

One of Southwest Ireland's most attractive locales, Killarney is also the most heavily visited town in the region (its proximity to the Ring of Kerry and to Shannon Airport helps to ensure this).

Killarney is famous for its lakes, not for the town, a point to bear in mind in order to avoid disappointment. Killarney town was one of the first places in Europe to owe its existence almost entirely to the tourism industry. Visitors started seeking out the region's dramatic lake scenery in the early 19th century, and the arrival of the railroad ensured its growing popularity. Today Killarney is a small, low-key town lined with shops and eateries firmly targeted at the numerous visitors, but it's also a popular holiday destination for Irish visitors, and retains the traditional friendliness of less famous towns. There's a lively restaurant scene, and some good crafts and clothing shops, but you may want to limit time spent there if nightclubs, Irish cabarets, and singing pubs—a local specialty—aren't your thing.

The nightlife is at its liveliest from May to September. At other times, particularly from November to mid-March, when many of the hotels are closed, the town is quiet to the point of being eerie. Given the choice, go to Killarney in April, May, or early October.

GETTING HERE AND AROUND

Killarney is about 2 hours from Cork on the N22, about 3 hours from Shannon Airport via Limerick, and 2½ hours from Limerick on the N21/23/22. From Shannon Airport be sure to take the tunnel (toll €1.80) route when approaching Limerick, rather than driving through the center of the city. The main car park in Killarney is near the tourist information office in the town center, and there are others around the town, all operated on a "pay-and-display" basis during business hours. The town is well served by Expressway buses and has a rail link to Dublin (3 hours, 20 minutes) and Cork (2 hours, 20 minutes). The bus and train stations are adjacent to each other, in the center of town, with taxi ranks. Most B&Bs and hotels offer a pickup service. Elsewhere, taxis should be prebooked by phone.

There is no local bus service in Killarney town; the traditional way to get around, especially if you plan to visit the car-free Muckross Park, is to hire one of the famous ponies and traps, known as "jaunting cars." The leading jaunting, bus, and boat tour operator is Killarney Jaunting Cars. An hour's "jaunt" for four people costs about €40. Jaunting cars can be prebooked and will collect you at your hotel (see below for booking information) or hired at the junction of Main Street and East Avenue. From April to October a shuttle bus service operates from the Killarney Tourist Office, and is a good way to see out-of-town sights including Muckross House and Farms, the Gap of Dunloe, and Ladies' View.

■ **TIP**→ **From mid-March to September you can view the national park by taking a water-coach cruise on the Lily of Killarney boat from Ross Castle (one hour, €12); book at the Killarney Tourist Office.**

CONTACTS Killarney Bus and Train Station. ⊠ *East Ave.* ☎ *064/663–0011 bus station, 064/663–1067 train station.* **Killarney Jaunting Cars Ltd/Tangney Tours.** ⊠ *Gilhuys, 10 B Muckross Close* ☎ *064/663–3358* ⊕ *www.killarneyjauntingcars.ie.* **Killarney Shuttle Bus.** ⊠ *Beech Rd.* ☎ *087/138–4384* ⊕ *www.killarneyshuttlebus.com.*

VISITOR INFORMATION
CONTACTS Discover Ireland Centre. ⊠ *Aras Fáilte, Beech Rd.* ☎ *064/663–1633* ⊕ *www.killarney.ie.*

Sights

With its glacial landscape enhanced by subtropical vegetation, the views found in and around Killarney are legendary. Yes, the lakes really are sapphire blue (at least when the sun is out), and seen from a distance, the MacGillicuddy's Reeks really are purple. Add a scattering of large gray rocks (large, as in big as a car), and acres of lush green flowering shrubs and trees, and you're starting to get the picture.

Aghadoe
ARCHAEOLOGICAL SITE | This is an outstanding place to get a feel for what Killarney is all about: lake and mountain scenery. Stand beside Aghadoe's 12th-century ruined church and Round Tower, and watch the shadows creep gloriously across Lower Lake, with Innisfallen Island in the distance and the Gap of Dunloe to the west. ⊠ *Killarney* ✛ *5 km (3 miles) west of Killarney on Beaufort–Killorglin road.*

★ Gap of Dunloe
NATURE SITE | **FAMILY** | Massive, glacial rocks form the sides of this narrow mountain pass that stretches for 6½ km (4 miles) between MacGillicuddy's Reeks and the Purple Mountains. The rocks create strange echoes: give a shout to test it out. Five small lakes are strung out beside the road. Cars are banned from the gap, but in summer the first 3 km (2 miles) are busy with horse and foot traffic, much of which turns back at the halfway point. The entrance to the Gap is 10 km (7 miles) west of Killarney at Beaufort on the N72 Killorglin Road. If you drive or are on a tour bus, stop here and either hire a pony and trap or opt to walk. One advantage to an organized tour—and a popular option—is that, without the need to get back to your car, you can amble through the parkland as far as Lord Brandon's Cottage, then get a prebooked boat back to Killarney town. ⊠ *N72 (Killorglin Rd.), Beaufort.*

Innisfallen Island
ISLAND | The monastic ruins on Innisfallen Island include a Celtic cross and date from the 6th or 7th century. Between AD 950 and 1350 the *Annals of Innisfallen* were compiled here by monks. (The book survives in the Bodleian Library in

Oxford.) There is a rough walking trail around the island, a wishing stone, and wild deer, but don't expect any facilities. On a sunny day, this is a charming place to take a picnic. From Ross Castle, row yourself over or let a boatman-guide take you out to the island (both options €12), or you can join a cruise (€12) from the castle, in a covered, heated launch. ⊠ *Killarney.*

Kate Kearney's Cottage

RESTAURANT—SIGHT | At the entrance to the Gap of Dunloe, Kate Kearney's Cottage is a good place to rent a jaunting car or pony. Kate was a famous beauty who sold illegal *poitín* (moonshine) from her home, contributing greatly, one suspects, to travelers' enthusiasm for the scenery. Appropriately enough, Kearney's is now a pub and restaurant, and a good place to pause for an Irish coffee. ⊠ *Gap of Dunloe, Beaufort* ☎ *064/664–4146* ⊕ *www.katekearneyscottage.com* ⊘ *Closed 2 wks from Jan. 6.*

★ Killarney House

GARDEN | FAMILY | Hidden away behind tall walls in the center of town for many years, Killarney House and its formal gardens are now open to the public as a visitor center and introduction to Killarney National Park. The house was originally the stable block of a more imposing manor that burned down in 1913, and now contains a museum with information about Killarney Town and the flora and fauna of Killarney National Park, as well as changing art exhibits relating to the area. The long-established formal gardens are enhanced by the natural backdrop of Killarney's wild mountains under a huge, ever-changing sky. There are easily accessible walks laid out in the grounds, and free guided tours every half hour. ⊠ *Killarney House, Dromhale , Killarney National Park* ⊹ *Enter by Countess Gates beside Kenmare Pl. (where pony and traps wait), or 2 smaller gates on Mission Rd. (R877)* ☎ *085/801–9773* ⊕ *www. killarneynationalpark.ie.*

Killarney National Park

NATIONAL/STATE PARK | The three Lakes of Killarney and the mountains and woods that surround them make up this beautiful national park. It extends to nearly 25,000 acres, which includes oak holly and yew woodlands, and is populated by red deer. The **National Park Visitor Centre** at Muckross House offers an audiovisual presentation that is a good introduction to what you can explore on the signposted self-guiding trails that thread the park.

At the park's heart is the **Muckross Demesne,** known locally as Muckross Park, the entrance to which is 4 km (2½ miles) from Killarney on N71. Cars aren't allowed in this part of Muckross Park; you can either walk, rent a bicycle, or take a traditional jaunting car (pony and a cart).

The air here smells of damp woods and heather moors. The red fruits of the Mediterranean strawberry tree (*Arbutus unedo*) are at their peak in October and November, which is also about the time when the bracken turns rust color, contrasting with the evergreens. In late April and early May, the purple flowers of the rhododendron *ponticum* put on a spectacular display. ⊠ *Muckross Rd.* ⊕ *www. killarneynationalpark.ie* ⊠ *Free.*

★ Ladies' View

VIEWPOINT | This famed viewpoint, with a stunning panorama of the three lakes and the surrounding mountains, is especially glorious on a sunny day but worth a visit in any weather. The name goes back to 1861, when Queen Victoria was a guest at Muckross House. Upon seeing the view, her ladies-in-waiting were said to have been dumbfounded by its beauty. You may find yourself speechless, too, so be sure to bring your camera. ⊹ *19 km (12 miles) southwest of Killarney on N71 in Kenmare direction.*

Lord Brandon's Cottage

RESTAURANT—SIGHT | The Gap of Dunloe's southern end, 7 km (4½ miles) west of Killarney, is marked by Lord Brandon's

Cottage, a basic tea shop serving soup and sandwiches. From here, a path leads to the edge of Upper Lake, where you can journey onward by rowboat (a traditional wooden boat with a motor)—but only if you have booked it in advance. It's an old tradition for the boatman to carry a bugle and illustrate the echoes. The boat passes under Brickeen Bridge and into Middle Lake, where 30 islands are steeped in legends, many of which your boatman is likely to recount. Look out for caves on the left-hand side on this narrow stretch of water. ⊠ *Gap of Dunloe, Beaufort* ☉ *Closed Oct.–Apr.*

Muckross Friary

ARCHAEOLOGICAL SITE | The monks were driven out of this 15th-century Franciscan friary by Oliver Cromwell's army in 1652, but it's amazingly complete (rare among Irish ruins), although roofless. An ancient yew tree rises above the cloisters and breaks out over the abbey walls. Three flights of stone steps allow access to the upper floors and living quarters, where you can visit the cloisters and what was once the dormitory, kitchen, and refectory. ⊠ *Muckross Rd. (N71)* ⊹ *4 km (2½ miles) south of Killarney* ☎ *064/667–0144* ⊕ *www.heritageireland.ie* ⬚ *Free.*

★ Muckross House

FARM/RANCH | FAMILY | Hero of 1,001 travel posters, the ivy-covered 19th-century Elizabethan-style manor known as Muckross House, 6½ km (4 miles) south of Killarney within the Killarney National Park, now houses the Kerry Folklife Centre. Downstairs, bookbinders, potters, and weavers demonstrate their crafts. Upstairs, elegantly furnished rooms portray the lifestyle of the landed gentry in the 1800s; in the basement you can experience the conditions of servants employed in the house. Next door you'll find the Killarney National Park Visitor Centre.

The informal grounds are noted for their rhododendrons and azaleas, the water garden, and the outstanding limestone rock garden. In the park beside the

house, the Muckross Traditional Farms comprise reconstructed farm buildings and outbuildings, a blacksmith's forge, a carpenter's workshop, and a selection of farm animals. It's a reminder of the way things were done on the farm before electricity and the mechanization of farming. Meet and chat with the farmers and their wives as they go about their work. The visitor center has a shop and a restaurant. ⊠ *Muckross Rd. (N71)* ☎ *064/667–0144* ⊕ *www.muckross-house.ie* ⬚ *House €10, farms €10, farms and house €16, visitor center free* ☉ *Farms: closed Nov.–Feb.; Mar., Apr., and Oct., closed weekdays.*

Ross Castle

CASTLE/PALACE | A fully restored 15th-century stronghold of the O'Donoghue Ross clan, sited on the lower lake 2 km (1 mile) south of town, this castle was the last place in the province of Munster to fall to Oliver Cromwell's forces in 1652. You can see its curtain walls, towers, and display of 16th- and 17th-century furniture on a 40-minute guided tour. ⊠ *Knockreer Estate, Muckross Rd. (N71)* ☎ *064/663–5851* ⊕ *www.killarneynationalpark.ie* ⬚ *€5* ☉ *Closed Nov.–Feb.*

Torc Waterfall

BODY OF WATER | FAMILY | You reach this roaring cascade by a footpath that begins in the parking lot outside the gates of the Muckross Park, 8 km (5 miles) south of Killarney. After your first view of the Torc, which will appear after about a 10-minute walk, it's worth the climb up a long flight of stone steps to the second, less-frequented clearing. ⊠ *Muckross Rd. (N71).*

🍴 Restaurants

Bricín

$ | IRISH | Candles and an open fire cast a warm light on Persian-style rugs and dark red walls hung with antique engravings of Killarney at this cozy little eatery set above a ground-floor craft emporium on the main street, while simple country-style wooden tables and stick-back chairs are set within "snug" areas created by stained-glass panels. The good-value menu features boxty (Irish potato pancake) with a choice of fillings, including vegetarian. Other options include baked salmon stuffed with crabmeat, char-grilled beef fillet, and roast rack of lamb. And, in the unlikely event you didn't hit a craft shop in Killarney, you can browse the shelves before making your way to the restaurant. **Known for:** boxty (Irish potato pancake); baked salmon stuffed with crabmeat; craft shop downstairs. $ *Average main: €18* ✉ *26 High St.* ☎ *064/663–4902* ⊕ *bricin.ie* ▭ *No credit cards* ⊗ *Closed Jan. 7–mid-Mar., Mon. Easter–Oct., and Mon.–Wed. Nov.–Dec.*

Gaby's Seafood

$$$ | SEAFOOD | Old-fashioned in the best sense of the word, and long established, this is a special-occasion venue where you can expect the best seafood and steak in Killarney. Local turbot, salmon, langoustine, and lobster are served in classic style on white table linens in a low-lit, timbered dining room. Behind the rustic exterior is a little bar beside an open fire; steps lead up to the main dining area, where ornate wooden stick-back chairs match a huge wooden dresser. In summer you can sip an aperitif in the small garden. Try the seafood platter (seven or eight kinds of local seafood) or lobster Gaby (shelled, simmered in a cream-and-cognac sauce, and served back in the shell). Regular menu items also include a selection of beef fillet and sirloin steaks, au poivre or with garlic butter, and herb-scented rack of lamb. **Known for:** lobster "Gaby"; special-occasion dining; excellent steaks. $ *Average main: €32* ✉ *27 High St.* ☎ *064/663–2519* ⊕ *www.gabys.ie* ⊗ *Closed Sun., and Mon.–Wed. in Jan. and Feb. No lunch.*

Robertino's

$$ | ITALIAN | Both rustic and romantic, with beamed ceilings and witty touches like a full-size marble statue, Robertino's is a Killarney landmark, cheerfully serving superior Italian cuisine—from pizza and pasta to fresh seafood and steaks and a tapas menu—since 1993. The tables are candlelit, and there is a choice of the quiet interior or a lively front area with plate-glass windows on to the main street. **Known for:** flame-grilled sirloin or fillet steaks; coda di rispo—panfried monkfish with prawns and Parma ham; authentic Spanish tapas. $ *Average main: €21* ✉ *9 High St.* ☎ *064/663–4966* ⊕ *www.robertinosrestaurant.com.*

Treyvaud's

$$$ | EUROPEAN | FAMILY | Step behind the Victorian arched facade here and you'll discover a buzzing contemporary restaurant, masterminded by the two Treyvaud brothers, that features classic Irish dishes (e.g., fish cakes, sausages, or bacon and cabbage) with a Continental twist. The interior is simple—pine floorboards, wood-beam ceiling, lines of red-back chairs—so the food takes center stage. To start try the local smoked salmon, or deep-fried calamari. Follow with bacon and cabbage Treyvaud-style (smoked loin with buttered cabbage and whole-grain mustard sauce), or half a roast guinea fowl with wild forest mushrooms, or the renowned homemade fish cakes with whole-grain mustard, chives, and garlic aioli. In winter this place is famous for its wide selection of game, including rabbit, wild boar, pheasant, and quail. **Known for:** panfried medallions of venison; bacon and cabbage; roast guinea fowl with forest mushrooms. $ *Average main: €25* ✉ *62 High St.* ☎ *064/663–3062* ⊕ *www. treyvaudsrestaurant.com.*

 ## Hotels

While the immediate region of Killarney has a vast array of accommodations, visitors should consider staying in hotels in Glenbeigh (about 20 minutes' drive away) if they really want to savor the region's peace and quiet.

The beauty gauge buries the needle at the Gap of Dunloe, considered by many to be the scenic star of the Lakes of Killarney region.

Aghadoe Heights

$$$$ | HOTEL | Once inside this large, modern hotel you'll soon forget its blocklike external appearance, as the entrancing panorama of Killarney's lakes casts its spell. **Pros:** memorable views; excellent spa; easy access to great hiking trails. **Cons:** 4 km (2½ miles) out of town; its size can make it feel impersonal; frequented by large tour groups. $ *Rooms from: €230* ✉ *Off N22* ☎ *064/663–1766* ⊕ *www.aghadoeheights.com* ⤳ *74 rooms* ⦿ *Free breakfast.*

★ Cahernane House Hotel

$$$$ | HOTEL | Dating from 1877, this imposing gray-stone house, once the residence of the earls of Pembroke, sits at the end of a long private avenue through a tunnel of trees—a refuge from the touristy buzz of Killarney town. **Pros:** great old-world atmosphere; very luxe; fantastic views. **Cons:** standard rooms are disappointingly plain; lots of weddings; rooms in new wing lack character of those in main house. $ *Rooms from: €220* ✉ *Muckross Rd.* ☎ *064/663–1895* ⊕ *www.cahernane.com* ⊘ *Closed Nov.– mid-Mar.* ⤳ *38 rooms* ⦿ *Free breakfast.*

Earls Court House Hotel

$$ | B&B/INN | In a quiet suburb within walking distance of Killarney's center, this spacious family-run hotel is furnished with interesting antiques collected by Emer Moynihan, who likes to greet her guests with home-baked goods by an open fire. **Pros:** quiet location; plenty of parking; spacious rooms with Jacuzzi baths. **Cons:** long walk or short taxi ride to town center; no bar or restaurant; old rooms smaller than newest ones. $ *Rooms from: €130* ✉ *Woodlawn Jct., Muckross Rd.* ☎ *064/663–4009* ⊕ *www. killarney-earlscourt.ie* ⊘ *Closed mid-Nov.– mid-Mar.* ⤳ *30 rooms* ⦿ *Free breakfast.*

Friars Glen

$$ | B&B/INN | Set in its own 28 acres within Killarney National Park, this stone house is a dream retreat for nature lovers, where it's not uncommon to spot deer in the colorful flower beds. **Pros:** beautiful gardens; pleasantly rural peace; traditional in style, but with modern comforts. **Cons:** remote from town; limited choice of restaurants nearby; fills up quickly, so book well in advance. ⑤ *Rooms from: €130* ⊠ *Mangerton Rd.* ☎ *064/663–7500* ⊕ *www.friarsglen.ie* ⊙ *Closed Nov.–Feb.* �753 *10 rooms* ⊺⊙⊦ *Free breakfast.*

Killarney Park Hotel

$$$$ | HOTEL | FAMILY | This luxurious hotel, a distinctive yellow-painted building in landscaped grounds, is a few minutes' walk from the train station, shops, and restaurants, making it an excellent base, with or without a car. **Pros:** central location; excellent dinner at the Park Restaurant; leisure center with a 20-meter pool. **Cons:** no lake or mountain views; popular wedding venue; sells out well in advance July and August. ⑤ *Rooms from: €320* ⊠ *East Ave. (N71)* ☎ *064/663–5555* ⊕ *www.killarneyparkhotel.ie* ↜ *68 rooms* ⊺⊙⊦ *Free breakfast.*

Loch Lein Country House Hotel

$$ | HOTEL | A perfect rural retreat combining warm hospitality with a scenic location, this spacious country house is 3 km (2 miles) out of town near Killarney's famous golf courses. **Pros:** excellent value; short walk from Loch Lein; spacious rooms with lake or mountain views. **Cons:** distance from town; closed off-season; no nearby pubs or coffee shops. ⑤ *Rooms from: €155* ⊠ *Off N72, Fossa* ☎ *064/663–1260* ⊕ *www.lochlein.com* ⊙ *Closed mid-Oct.– mid-Apr.* ↜ *23 rooms* ⊺⊙⊦ *Free breakfast.*

★ The Mills Inn

$ | B&B/INN | If you wince at tour-bus crowds, consider heading to the Irish-speaking village of Ballyvourney, where this historic coaching inn beside the rapid-flowing River Sullane has old castle ruins, a stable yard, and gardens on its grounds. **Pros:** lively local trade in bar; village location with peaceful country walks; live Irish music on Friday evening. **Cons:** 15-minute drive to Killarney; on busy main road (but quiet at night); not much else happening in village. ⑤ *Rooms from: €100* ⊠ *N22, Baile Bhuirne*

☎ *026/45237* ⊕ *www.millsinn.ie* ↜ *20 rooms* ⊺⊙⊦ *Free breakfast.*

 ## Nightlife

BARS AND PUBS

Buckley's Bar

MUSIC CLUBS | Located in the Arbutus Hotel, this popular spot has traditional Irish entertainment nightly from around 10 pm from June through September, and on Sunday from 1 to 3 pm and weekend evenings year-round. ⊠ *Arbutus Hotel, College St.* ☎ *064/663–1037.*

★ Courtney's Bar

BARS/PUBS | Famous for its selection of more than 30 Irish and Scottish whiskeys, this family-run traditional bar in the town center hosts live traditional music on Thursday and Friday and is a magnet for visiting musicians. ⊠ *24 Plunkett St.* ☎ *064/663– 2689* ⊕ *www.courtneysbar.com.*

The Danny Mann

BARS/PUBS | Live Irish music is provided by local bands in this friendly hotel bar. Visitors are encouraged to sing along or offer a solo, or even just tell a joke. It's impossible to resist joining in. ⊠ *Eviston House Hotel, New St.* ☎ *064/663–1640.*

★ JM Reidy's

BARS/PUBS | Informally known as "the sweetshop Pub" this much-loved Killarney landmark, bang in the center of town, dates from 1870 and was recently given an inspired makeover. The sweets are still there in jars, but one side of the pub now serves coffee, cakes, and light snacks, while the other is a regular pub. Both sides of the establishment are decorated with a fascinating collection of memorabilia. It's a great place to meet the locals. ⊠ *4 Main St.* ☎ *066/663–2456* ⊕ *reidyskillarney.com.*

Performing Arts

CABARET

Gleneagles

CABARET | The place for big-name Irish cabaret—from comedian Brendan Grace to the High Kings to Daniel O'Donnell— at the Irish National Events Centre (INEC) within the hotel. Gleneagles also has a night club. ⊠ *Muckross Rd.* ☎ *064/667–1555* ⊕ *www.inec.ie.*

🛍 Shopping

CLOTHING

Aran Sweater Market

CLOTHING | Traditional fisherman's knitwear, designed and knitted in the Aran Islands, can be purchased here. You can acquire an heirloom-quality piece or buy knitting wool and patterns and make your own. ⊠ *College St.* ☎ *064/663–9756* ⊕ *www.aransweatermarket.com.*

Kerry Woollen Mills

CLOTHING | This mill was established here in the 17th century and still uses the original buildings. Its traditional woolen products, from knitting yarns to hats and capes, make great gifts. The property is signposted off the main road between Killarney and Killorglin. ⊠ *Off N72, Beaufort* ☎ *064/664–4122* ⊕ *www.kerrywoollenmills.ie.*

MacBee's

CLOTHING | This modern boutique stocks the best of Irish and international high fashion. ⊠ *26 New St.* ☎ *064/663–3622* ⊕ *macbees.ie.*

Quills Woollen Market

CLOTHING | Stop here for the town's largest selection of Irish woolen goods. Quills carries knitwear, tweeds, linens, and Celtic jewelry. ⊠ *Market Cross, 79 High St.* ☎ *064/663–2277* ⊕ *www.irishgiftsandsweaters.com.*

CRAFTS

Bricín Craft Shop

CRAFTS | Interesting handicrafts here include candles, ceramics, and woolens. ⊠ *26 High St.* ☎ *064/663–4902.*

The Kilkenny Shop

CRAFTS | Peruse this shop's stock of contemporary Irish pottery, ironwork, woodwork, crystal, and jewelry. ⊠ *3 New St.* ☎ *064/662–3309* ⊕ *www.kilkennyshop.com.*

Mary Neeson Ceramics

CERAMICS/GLASSWARE | Her gallery is near the main entrance to Muckross House, and most of her finely textured pieces cost between €20 and €80 and can be shipped worldwide. ⊠ *The Bluepool Studio and Gallery, Muckross Rd.* ✛ *On Killarney town side of N71 approaching Muckross House* ☎ *064/662–9049* ⊕ *www.maryneesonceramics.com.*

Mucros Craft Shop

CRAFTS | Adjacent to Muckross House, the craft center has a wide range of gifts and clothing, as well as a resident weaver, a bookbindery, and Mucros Pottery. Margaret Phelan works on-site producing tableware in attractive blue and honey-color glazes. ⊠ *Muckross House, N71* ☎ *064/667–0147* ⊕ *www.muckross-house.ie.*

MUSIC

Variety Sounds

MUSIC STORES | Visit this specialist music shop for Irish music and songbooks and a collection of Irish musical instruments including tin whistles and bodhrans. ⊠ *7 College St.* ☎ *064/663–5755.*

Activities

BICYCLING

O'Sullivan's Cycles

BICYCLING | A bicycle is the perfect way to enjoy Killarney's mild air, whether within the confines of Muckross Park or farther afield in the Kerry Highlands, and O'Sullivan's (opposite the tourist office) is a top place to rent bicycles for either the day or the week. ✉ *Lower New St.* ☎ *064/663–1282* ⊕ *www.killarneyrentabike.com.*

FISHING

Salmon and brown trout populate Killarney's lakes and rivers.

O'Neill's

FISHING | To bag your own salmon or brown trout in Killarney's wondrous lakes and rivers, check out this longtime outfitter of fishing tackle, bait, and licenses. ✉ *6 Plunkett St.* ☎ *064/663–1970.*

GOLF

★ Killarney Golf and Fishing Club

GOLF | This club is set amid a stunning mixture of mountains, lakes, and forests. There are two courses: Mahony's Point, along the shores of Lough Leane, and— the jewel in the crown—water-feature-packed Killeen. Despite the abundance of seaside links, many well-traveled golfers name Killarney their favorite place to play in Ireland. Freshwater fishing is also available here. ✉ *Mahony's Point, N72* ✛ *3 km (2 miles) west of Killarney on Kilorglin road* ☎ *064/663–1034* ⊕ *www. killarneygolfclub.ie* ✉ *Mahony's Point €60 mid-Apr.–mid Oct.; €40 mid-Oct.–mid-Apr.; Killeen €100 mid-Apr.–mid-Oct.; €75 mid-Oct.–mid-Apr.* ⚐ *Mahony's Point: 18 holes, 6780 yards, par 72; Killeen: 18 holes, 7178 yards, par 72.*

HIKING

Cronin's Yard

CLIMBING/MOUNTAINEERING | Drive out to Beaufort, 10 km (7 miles) west of Killarney on the N72 Killorglin road, and follow signs to this famed gateway to the MacGillicuddy's Reeks—the traditional starting point for the ascent of Ireland's highest mountain, Carrauntoohil (3,406 feet). Outdoors types will definitely fall in love with Killarney here. Parking at the yard is €2 for the whole day. You can prebook a guide for the ascent, which is about six hours round-trip. For a less strenuous outing, there is a self-guided, signposted 8-km (5-mile) loop of sandy paths and mountain tracks. On your return, enjoy a hot bowl of soup in the tearoom and, especially if the Irish weather has not been kind, luxuriate in a hot shower (small fee). Those with sleeping bags can avail of their wooden "sleeping pods," and wake up to a stunning view. ✉ *Mealis, Beaufort* ☎ *064/662–4044* ⊕ *www.croninsyard.com.*

Kerry Way

HIKING/WALKING | This long-distance walking route—it takes about eight days, start to finish—passes through the Killarney National Park on its way to Glenbeigh. You can get a detailed leaflet about the route from the Kerry tourist information office. ⊕ *www.kerryway.com.*

Mangerton Mountain

HIKING/WALKING | The 2,756-foot summit of Mangerton can be reached on foot in about two hours—less if you rent a pony. It's perfect if you want a fine, long hike with good views of woodland scenery.

Mangerton Walking Trail

HIKING/WALKING | You can reach the small tarred road leading to this scenic trail that circles Mangerton Lake (aka Devil's Punch Bowl) by turning left off N71 midway between Muckross Friary and Muckross House (follow the signs).

Muckross Park

HIKING/WALKING | A car-free zone frequented by pony and traps, this park within the Killarney National Park has four signposted nature trails for walkers. Try the 4-km (2½-mile) Arthur Young's Walk, which passes through old yew and oak woods frequented by Sitka deer. For a longer hike, take an open boat from Ross Castle to the head of the Upper Lake, then walk back along the lakeside to Muckross House, about 10 km (6 miles). ✉ *Killarney* ⊕ *www.killarneynationalpark.ie.*

HORSEBACK RIDING

Killarney Riding Stables

HORSEBACK RIDING | Book a day or half day of horseback riding on a quiet cob in Killarney National Park, or embark on a three- or six-day Reeks Trail ride through the mountains and woodlands of MacGillicuddy's Reeks. ✉ *N72, Ballydowney* ☎ *064/663–1686* ⊕ *www.killarney-riding-stables.com.*

Kenmare

34 km (21 miles) south of Killarney, 336 km (209 miles) southwest of Dublin.

Located slightly inland without a clear view of Kenmare Bay, Kenmare is a natural stopover for Ring of Kerry buses and travelers as it is the closest town to Killarney. Set at the head of the sheltered Kenmare River estuary, this small but bustling market town makes a lively touring base for those who wish to skip hectic Killarney altogether. The town was founded in 1670 by Sir William Petty (Oliver Cromwell's surveyor general, a multitasking entrepreneur), and most of its buildings date from the 19th century, when it was part of the enormous Lansdowne Estate—itself assembled by Petty.

Kenmare offers an amazing number of stylish little restaurants, tearooms, and cafés for a town its size, as well as top-notch fine dining in the Park Hotel and Sheen Falls Lodge. It also boasts the top-rated Kenmare Market, with purveyors of organic goods and foodstuffs (March to December, Wednesday 10–5). The shopping is pretty good, too, with Irish high fashion, crafts, and original art vying for your attention.

GETTING HERE AND AROUND
Kenmare is at the intersection of the N71 road that links Bantry and Glengarriff with Killarney, and the N70, which continues around the perimeter road known as the Ring of Kerry. Killarney and Glengarriff are both about 40 to 45 minutes away on scenic mountain roads. Kenmare is a natural stopover between Glengarriff (21 km [13 miles] south) and Killarney (34 km [21 miles] to the north). The mountain

pass (N71) from Kenmare to Killarney via Ladies' View is a scenic highlight, offering a stunning first view of the lakes. There is ample parking in Kenmare town center.

A bus route, operated by Bus Éireann, connects Killarney to Kenmare; it continues on around the Ring of Kerry, stopping in all the villages between Kenmare and Killorglin before returning to Killarney. Otherwise, there is no public transportation in this area.

TOURS
Kenmare Coach and Cab
You can opt to base yourself in Kenmare and take a guided tour of the Ring by minibus (June to August) with this local taxi company. Its minibuses depart from the square for the Ring on Monday, Wednesday, and Friday at 10 am. Other destinations include the Ring of Beara and Glengarriff (Tuesday and Thursday). It is best to reserve by 10 pm the night before. ☎ *064/664–1491* ⊕ *www.kenmarecoachandcab.com.*

VISITOR INFORMATION
CONTACTS Kenmare Tourist Office. ✉ *The Square* ☎ *064/664–1233* ⊕ *kenmare.ie.*

Sights

Kenmare Heritage Centre
INFO CENTER | Come to this center in the tourist office to learn about the town's history. They can outline a walking route to Kenmare's places of interest. ✉ *The Square* ☎ *064/664–1233* 🎫 *Free* ⊗ *Closed Nov.–Easter; Easter–Oct., closed Sun.*

Kenmare Market
MARKET | About 15 outdoor vendors offer local organic produce and a few exotic imports to an appreciative local clientele. Look out for Knockatee cheese (from Tuosist down the road), Olivier's smoked trout from Killorglin, organic veggies, homemade pâtés, fresh fish, and French soaps and sweets. ✉ *The Square*

Killarney and
The Ring of Kerry

N2

N2

N70

Aghadoe

Killarney

Ross Castle

Lake Leane

Innisfallen Island

Muckross Friary

Muckross House

Muckross

Torc Waterfall

Ladies' View

N71

R569

Kenmare

Killarney National Park

Gap of Dunloe

Reeks

MacGillicuddy's Reeks

Black Valley

Muckross Lake

Upper Lake

Carrauntoohill 1,038 m 3,414 ft

R568

R569

N70

Ring of Kerry

Blackwater Bridge

N70

Ring of Kerry

BEARA PENINSULA

Killorglin

Caragh Lake

Kerry Bog Village Museum

Glencar

Blackstone Bridge

Caragh River

Glenbeigh

Rossbeigh Strand

Ring of Kerry

I V E R A G H   P E N I N S U L A

Sneem

Kenmare Bay

Dingle Bay

Kells

Ring of Kerry

Mastergeehy

Lough Currane

Staigue Fort

N70

Derrynane National Park

Derrynane House

Caherdaniel

Canglass Point

Doulus Head

Cahirciveen

N70

R567

Waterville

Abbey Island

Deenish Island

Knightstown

Chapeltown

R565

Portmagee

Cill Rialaig

R566

Ballinskelligs

Ballinskelligs Bay

Hog's Head

Scariff Island

Valentia Island

Skellig Experience

St Finian's Bay

St Finian's Bay

Puffin Island

Bolus Head

Little Skellig

The Skelligs

Skellig Michael

5 mi

5 km

0

5 km

0

Bright Waters and Dark Skies

When planning a day out on the water, bear in mind the long days of the Irish summer. In May the sun rises at 5:40 am and doesn't set until 9:21 pm, while by July the sun is rising at 5:33 and setting at 9:47. The light will linger for another hour or so on clear evenings.

Once the sun has set, you will be beneath some of the clearest night skies in Europe—providing the mist holds off. Southwest Kerry is recognized as the Kerry International Dark Sky Reserve due to the lack of light pollution in the area, and in 2014 the reserve achieved Gold Tier status, representing the highest level of darkness and greatest visibility of night-sky features. Over the Ring of Kerry an unusual array of phenomena are visible, including a great view of the Milky Way. Anyone with even a slight knowledge of astronomy will be thrilled at the array of stars.

⊘ *Closed Jan. and Feb.; Mar.–Dec., closed Thurs.–Tues.*

Stone Circle

ARCHAEOLOGICAL SITE | Perhaps the town's most notable historic sight is this 3,000-year-old monument that dates from the early Bronze Age. Sometimes called the Druid Circle, it is within five minutes' walk of the village square (head down Market Street in front of the tourist office). It consists of 15 large stones arranged in a circle around a huge central boulder, which marks a rare Bronze Age burial site. ⊠ *Market St.*

🍴 Restaurants

★ Lime Tree

$$$ | **EUROPEAN** | An open fire, stone walls, and a minstrel's gallery above the main room lend considerable character to this restaurant, while the chef-owner's imaginative ways with local produce result in memorable fare. Built in 1823 as a schoolhouse, it is located in its own leafy gardens near the Park Hotel (where many of its staff trained). The food is elegantly plated and served on plain wooden tables set with white Irish-linen napkins.

In the long summer evenings light streams in from tall windows. Try one of the creative vegetarian options, such as goat's cheese croquettes with beetroot chutney, or roast rack of Kerry lamb, with warm crepes with vanilla ice cream and butterscotch sauce to finish. Reservations are advisable. **Known for:** creative use of local produce; high professional standards of service; quaint country ambience. $ *Average main: €28* ⊠ *Shelburne St.* ☎ *064/664–1225* ⊕ *www. limetreerestaurant.com* ⊘ *Closed Mon.–Thurs. Nov.–early Mar. No lunch.*

Mulcahy's

$$ | **ECLECTIC** | Previously a pub, the wood-clad restaurant is stylish and contemporary with brown leather seats at small wooden tables, and a menu starring fresh Irish produce and Asian influence. Start with sushi and sashimi, or wild-mushroom pearl-barley risotto with aged Parmesan, and follow with roast halibut with mussel, bacon, and clam cream or pork belly with salt-baked celeriac, chorizo, and puffed crackling. The food is plated with flamboyance and highly Instagrammable. Chef Bruce Mulcahy runs a relatively modest operation, but many people in the know reckon he is one of Ireland's most talented chefs. **Known for:** authentic sushi and sashimi; superb presentation; friendly, widely traveled owner-chef. $ *Average main: €24* ⊠ *Main St.* ☎ *064/664–2383* ⊕ *www.mulcahyskenmare.ie* ⊗ *Closed Tues. and Wed. Oct.–May and last 2 wks in Jan. No lunch.*

Packies

$$$ | EUROPEAN | For many returning visitors, a meal at this busy little bistro-style restaurant is a quintessential Kenmare experience. Chef Martin Hallissey leases it from his mentor—and original owner—Maura Foley, who jump-started the Kenmare restaurant scene back in the 1980s. Wooden tables and chairs of different shapes and sizes are crammed into a former high-street shop, the tables set with black place mats. Stone floors and rough-plaster walls are warmed by colorful local paintings and the buzz of expectation among the closely packed diners. The fresh-tasting, strongly flavored food rises far above the rustic setting. The contemporary Irish menu may feature ray wing with caper butter, roast lobster with garlic butter, or the house-special Irish stew. Desserts include homemade crème brûlée and a memorable sticky toffee pudding. **Known for:** freshest local fish, served Mediterranean style; Thai crab cakes; sticky toffee pudding. $ *Average main: €30* ⊠ *Henry St.* ☎ *064/664–1508* ⊗ *Closed mid-Jan.–mid-Mar., Sun. mid-Mar.–Sept., and Sun.–Thurs. Oct.–Dec. No lunch.*

Tom Crean Fish & Wine

$$ | IRISH | Owner Aileen d'Arcy named her restaurant after her grandfather, the Antarctic explorer Tom Crean, and you can learn his story while browsing the menu, which is dominated by local produce, with an emphasis on vegan options as well as local seafood. Top bets include Sneem black pudding with apple and tomato chutney, baked in phyllo pastry, and local duck breast, panfried and served with roasted root vegetables and Puy lentils, or Sneem lobster, grilled or poached. Known for her warm welcome, Aileen learned her trade at Kenmare's famed Park Hotel, and shares the chef duties with her two sons. Ask them about their attempt to follow in Tom Crean's footsteps in the Antarctic: it's a great story. There are four simple rooms above the restaurant that can be booked for B&B. **Known for:** imaginative salads; chefs who have tales of Antarctic travels; Sneem black pudding with chutney. $ *Average main: €23* ⊠ *25 Main St.* ☎ *064/664–1589* ⊕ *www.tomcrean. ie* ▭ *No credit cards* ⊗ *Closed mid-Dec.–late Mar., Tues. and Wed. No lunch.*

Hotels

Brook Lane Hotel

$$ | HOTEL | Located about a mile outside the village on the road to Sneem, the decor at this small boutique hotel is lively, thanks to the bright abstract art on the walls and bold, striking color schemes that are an interesting contrast to the Victorian-style furniture and heavy brocade drapes. **Pros:** bar, restaurant, and parking on-site; excellent breakfast; bathrooms especially luxurious. **Cons:** an uninspiring mile-long walk into village; bar can get very busy after 9 in summer; books up well in advance on weekends. $ *Rooms from: €160* ⊠ *Sneem Rd.* ☎ *064/664–2077* ⊕ *www.brooklanehotel. com* ⇥ *20 rooms* ⊚ *Free breakfast.*

★ Park Hotel Kenmare

$$$$ | HOTEL | One of Ireland's premier country-house hotels, this 1897 stone château has spectacular views of the Caha Mountains and its 11-acre parkland, where every tree seems manicured. **Pros:** great amenities including spa and movie theater; immaculate decor; one of Kenmare's best restaurants. **Cons:** a bit like living in a museum; basic room rates are quite steep; extra charge for Jacuzzi and thermal suite. $ *Rooms from: €390* ⊠ *Shelburne Rd.* ☎ *064/664–1200* ⊕ *www.parkkenmare.com* ⊗ *Closed late*

Oct.–mid-Dec. and mid-Jan.–early Mar.
🛏 *43 rooms* ❚◎❘ *Free breakfast.*

Sallyport House

$$ | **B&B/INN** | Across the bridge on the way into Kenmare, this 1932 family home has been enlarged to serve as a comfortable B&B, with spotless rooms and harbor or mountain views. **Pros:** interesting antiques; impeccable housekeeping; quiet location. **Cons:** no credit cards; short opening season; only five rooms. $ *Rooms from: €145* ✉ *Shelbourne St. (N71)* ☎ *064/664–2066* ⊕ *www. sallyporthouse.com* ☐ *No credit cards* ⊘ *Closed Oct.–Apr.* 🛏 *5 rooms* ❚◎❘ *Free breakfast.*

Sea Shore Farm

$$ | **B&B/INN** | Mary Patricia O'Sullivan offers a warm but professional welcome to her spacious farmhouse on Kenmare Bay. In fair weather there are views across the sea to the hills on the Beara Peninsula, and although the place is very close to Kenmare, you can walk across her farmland to the deserted seashore and view its plentiful wildlife. **Pros:** quiet rural spot with views of calm estuary; personal attention from owner-manager; oodles of old-fashioned charm. **Cons:** a mile out of town; no bar or restaurant; farm no longer active. $ *Rooms from: €120* ✉ *Off N70* ☎ *064/664–1270* ⊕ *www.seashorekenmare.com* ⊘ *Closed Nov.–mid-Mar.* 🛏 *6 rooms* ❚◎❘ *Free breakfast.*

★ Sheen Falls Lodge Kerry Hotel

$$$$ | **HOTEL** | The magnificence of this bright-yellow, slate-roof stone manor is matched only by its setting on 300 secluded acres of lawns, gardens, and forest between Kenmare Bay and the falls of the River Sheen. **Pros:** rooms have bay or river views; good sport amenities on-site; Skellig Island trips (boat or helicopter) by arrangement. **Cons:** modern interiors lack traditional character; 2 km (1 mile) from the village; spa gets busy: book in advance. $ *Rooms from: €350* ✉ *Off N71* ☎ *064/664–1600* ⊕ *www.*

Ring Strategy 👁

Tour buses tend to start in Killarney and head for Killorglin to ply the Ring counterclockwise, so consider jumping ahead and starting in Killorglin ahead of the Killarney buses, or following the route clockwise, starting in Kenmare (although this means you risk meeting tour buses head-on on narrow roads). Either way, bear in mind that most of the buses leave Killarney between 9 and 10 am.

sheenfallslodge.ie ⊘ *Closed Jan. 3–Feb. 6* 🛏 *66 rooms* ❚◎❘ *Free breakfast.*

🛍 Shopping

Avoca Handweavers

CLOTHING | At this scenic spot, midway between Kenmare and Killarney, you'll find wool clothing, mohair throws, and rugs in remarkable palettes and a variety of weaves. ✉ *Moll's Gap (N71)* ☎ *064/663–4720* ⊕ *www.avoca.ie.*

The Cashmere Shop

CLOTHING | Here you'll find Irish-made knitwear in lambswool and cashmere. ✉ *20 Henry St.* ☎ *064/664–8986* ⊕ *cashmereireland.com.*

Kenmare Bookshop

BOOKS/STATIONERY | A good selection of books of local interest and all the best sellers can be found here. ✉ *Shelburne St.* ☎ *064/664–1578.*

Norman McCloskey Photography

ART GALLERIES | Norman has been photographing this area since 1992. He has created some breathtakingly beautiful images, many of them large-scale landscapes that can be seen and purchased here. ✉ *3 Henry St.* ☎ *087/274–4879* ⊕ *www.normanmccloskey.com.*

Gifts From Kerry

You will soon notice that parts of County Kerry have more sheep than people. Sheep mean wool, and in this part of Ireland wool means sweaters, socks, and wool hats. All three will come in very useful during your stay, and make great gifts, too.

Louis Mulcahy Pottery. Ceramics are a strong point, too, with the Louis Mulcahy Pottery ceramics workshop and showrooms on Slea Head being the most western pottery in Europe. ⊠ *Clogher, Ballyferriter, Dingle, Co. Kerry* ☎ *066/915–6229* ⊕ *www.louis-mulcahy.com.*

Quills Woollen Market. This top gifts-and-souvenirs resource has outlets in Killarney, Kenmare, Sneem, and Dingle. Look out for "blackthorns": a traditional, craggy walking stick made from branches of the blackthorn tree, a handy accessory to have while you're here, and a great souvenir to take home. ⊠ *Market Cross, Killarney, Co. Kerry* ☎ *064/663–2277.*

Paul Kelly Jewellers
JEWELRY/ACCESSORIES | Striking, modern jewelry in gold and silver is made and sold here. ⊠ *33 Henry St.* ☎ *064/664–2590* ⊕ *www.pfk.ie.*

Skyline Gallery
ART GALLERIES | Stunning landscape images by international award-winning Irish photographer Eoghan Kavanagh are showcased here. ⊠ *27 Henry St.* ☎ *064/664–8621* ⊕ *www.skyline.ie.*

The White Room
TEXTILES/SEWING | Irish lace and linen, both new and antique, are the specialty here. ⊠ *21 Henry St.* ☎ *064/664–0600* ⊕ *www.thewhiteroomkenmare.com.*

Activities

BICYCLING
Finnegan's Bicycle Hire
BICYCLING | Pick up a free copy of the Ring of Kerry Cycle Route brochure from the tourist information office on the Square, and then explore the Ring using quiet country roads. The full trip is a blister-inducing 213 km (133 miles). Bikes are available for rent at this shop in town. ⊠ *Henry St.* ☎ *064/664–1083.*

WILDLIFE-WATCHING
Seafari Seal and Eagle Watching Cruises
WILDLIFE-WATCHING | FAMILY | With complimentary tea and coffee for adults, plus lollipops (suckers) for the kids, Seafari features fun two-hour ecotours with regular sightings of seals and white-tailed sea eagles. Reservations are essential, and there are special family rates. They are also an outfitter for kayaking, sailing, and windsurfing. ⊠ *Kenmare Pier, 3 Pier Rd.* ☎ *064/664–2059* ⊕ *www.seafariireland.com* ⊠ *From €20.*

Sneem

27 km (17 miles) southwest of Kenmare.

The pretty little village of Sneem (from the Irish for "knot") is settled around an English-style green on the Ardsheelaun River estuary, and its streets are filled with houses washed in different colors. The effect has been somewhat diminished by a cluster of new holiday home developments. The town's souvenir shops play Irish music over loudspeakers when the Ring of Kerry tour buses stop here.

The Ring of Kerry—one of Ireland's most popular scenic routes—is also one of Europe's great drives.

GETTING HERE AND AROUND

It takes about 15 minutes to reach Sneem from Kenmare on N70. There's plenty of free street parking in the town's main square. ■TIP→ **To see the best of Sneem, park near the Blue Bull pub, and walk down the narrow road beside it, signposted "Pier." This quiet byway leads past a carefully tended community garden, terminating about 300 yards farther on at the village pier. Take a seat and look back toward the village to appreciate Sneem's unique location, nestled amid lush subtropical growth between the sea and the hills.**

Sights

★ Derrynane House

HOUSE | The Ring of Kerry has very few beautiful and historic country houses, so many visitors here enjoy making a special excursion to Derrynane House. Famed as the home of Daniel O'Connell ("The Liberator," 1775–1847), the mansion comes complete with a lovely garden and 320-acre seaside estate, now called the Derrynane National Park. The house's

south and east wings—which O'Connell himself remodeled—are decorated with much of the furniture and other items associated with the man who campaigned for Catholic Emancipation (the granting of full rights of citizenship to Catholics), which became a reality in 1829. Take a self-guided tour: every piece has a genuine connection to O'Connell. ⊠ *Off N70 ✛ 30 km (18 miles) west of Sneem, near Caherdaniel* ☎ *066/947–5113* ⊕ *www.derrynanehouse.ie* 🖾 *€4* ⊘ *Closed mid-Dec.–mid-Mar.; Mon. and Tues. Oct.; weekdays Nov.–mid-Dec.*

Derrynane National Park

HIKING/WALKING | FAMILY | The 320-acre estate of Derrynane House is freely accessible and has trails running through mature woodland, bordering on rocky outcrops that lead to wide sandy beaches and dunes. At low tide you can walk to Abbey Island offshore. ⊠ *Sneem.*

Staigue Fort

ARCHAEOLOGICAL SITE | Take a 4-km (2½-mile) detour off the N70 Ring of Kerry road to visit Staigue Fort. Approximately

2,500 years old, the mortar-free stone fort is almost circular and about 75 feet in diameter, with a single south-side entrance. From the Iron Age (from 500 BC to the 5th century AD) and early Christian times (6th century AD), such "forts" were, in fact, fortified homesteads for several families of one clan and their cattle. The walls at Staigue Fort are almost 13 feet thick at the base and 7 feet thick at the top; they still stand 18 feet high on the north and west sides. Within them, stairs lead to narrow platforms on which the lookouts stood. ■TIP➔ **Private land must be crossed to reach the fort, and a "compensation for trespass" of €1 is often requested by the landowner.** The site has free parking and is freely accessible, but has no facilities. ⊠ *Sneem* ✛ *Signposted 4 km (2½ miles) inland at Castlecove.*

Hotels

★ Parknasilla Resort

$$$$ | **RESORT** | **FAMILY** | For more than a century Parknasilla, a towering, gray-stone mansion on a stunningly beautiful inlet of the Kenmare estuary, has been synonymous with old-style resort luxury, attracting guests like George Bernard Shaw, Princess Grace, and Charles de Gaulle. **Pros:** excellent sports amenities and spa; sheltered coastal location; great family destination. **Cons:** grounds and hotel big enough to get lost in; busy in July and August; weather can be fickle (rainy) on this coast. ⑤ *Rooms from: €220* ⊠ *N70* ☎ *064/667–5600* ⊕ *www. parknasillaresort.com* ✆ *Closed Nov.–early Mar.* ➫ *83 rooms* ⦿| *Free breakfast.*

Sneem Hotel

$$ | **HOTEL** | Meet the locals and enjoy spacious accommodations at this waterfront hotel and apartment complex on Goldens Cove, a rocky, sheltered spot with views of distant mountains. **Pros:** great sea views; popular with locals; good value for the Ring of Kerry. **Cons:** some new development detracts from the views;

10-minute walk from the village; no pool. ⑤ *Rooms from: €150* ⊠ *Goldens Cove* ☎ *064/667–5100* ⊕ *www.sneemhotel. com* ➫ *69 rooms, 28 apartments* ⦿| *Free breakfast.*

Waterville

35 km (22 miles) west of Sneem.

Waterville, a seaside village facing Ballinskelligs Bay, is famous for its sportfishing, its 18-hole championship golf course (adopted as a warm-up spot for the British Open by Tiger Woods), and for the fact that Charlie Chaplin and Charles de Gaulle spent summers here. The village, like many others on the Ring of Kerry, has a few restaurants and pubs, but little else. There's excellent salmon and trout fishing at nearby Lough Currane, and the area offers challenging hikes with stunning vistas.

GETTING HERE AND AROUND

Waterville, part of the Ring of Kerry driving loop, is a short half-hour drive from Sneem on the N70. You approach the town driving through the dramatically rocky Coomakesta Pass and Hog's Head. Stop at one of the viewing areas to take in the panoramic sea views, which look out at the distinctive Skellig Rocks. There is plenty of free parking in the village.

VISITOR INFORMATION

CONTACTS Waterville Tourist Office. ⊠ *Town Center* ☎ *066/947–8818* ⊕ *www. visitwaterville.ie.*

Sights

Cill Rialaig

MUSEUM | West of Waterville and 1 km (½ mile) before the Irish-speaking village of Ballinskelligs is the Cill Rialaig Arts Centre. This is the best place in Kerry to see Irish and international art, along with fine crafts and gifts. Its attractive, thatched, beehive-shape roof is hard to miss. There's also a café with wholesome homemade food and a wood-burning pizza oven. ⊠ *R566* ☎ *066/947–9277* ⊕ *www.cillrialaigartscentre.com* ⊠ *Free* ⊙ *Café closed Mon. and Tues.*

 Hotels

Butler Arms Hotel
$$ | HOTEL | Charlie Chaplin loved it here—the connection is now commemorated by a mini film festival here in late August—and a whole host of families return year after year to this rambling old-world landmark, with its white-castellated-corner tower. **Pros:** charmingly old-fashioned; the hub of village life; new wing rooms have sensational sea views. **Cons:** public rooms very busy on weekends; has some shabby corners; old wing has small, plain rooms. $ *Rooms from: €145* ⊠ *N70* ☎ *066/947–4144* ⊕ *www. butlerarms.com* ⊙ *Closed Nov.–Mar.* ⊱ *36 rooms* ⊙ *Free breakfast.*

Lakelands Farm Guesthouse
$ | B&B/INN | Amid rocky hills, this spacious, Dutch-gable modern house enjoys a stunning location about a mile off the Ring on the shore of Lough Currane (boats for hire) and is hosted by an angling/shooting guide and his wife. **Pros:** good location for game anglers, golfers, and hikers; great scenery; huge bedrooms. **Cons:** nearly 3 km (2 miles) outside village; well maintained, but not stylish; no bar. $ *Rooms from: €90* ⊠ *Lake Rd.* ✦ *Look for signpost on N70 on south side of village* ☎ *066/947–4303* ⊕ *www.lakelandswaterville.com* ⊙ *Closed mid-Oct.–Apr. 3* ⊱ *12 rooms* ⊙ *Free breakfast.*

 Nightlife

Inny Tavern
BARS/PUBS | For live Irish music, head to this traditional country pub that's popular among locals. ⊠ *Inny Bridge* ☎ *066/947–4512.*

 Shopping

★ Skelligs Chocolate
FOOD/CANDY | FAMILY | The wild coastal road between Waterville and Portmagee is an unusual location for a chocolate factory, café, and shop, but then this is unusual chocolate, handmade in small batches, and acclaimed by connoisseurs for its excellence. A visit to the chocolate factory is also the perfect rainy-day treat: taste the freshly made samples, buy some to take home, then sip a hot chocolate in the café while enjoying the stormy sea view. ⊠ *The Glen, Skellig Ring (R566), Ballinskelligs* ☎ *066/947–9119* ⊕ *www.skelligschocolate.com.*

 Activities

GOLF
★ Waterville Golf Links
GOLF | Famously adopted by Tiger Woods and Mark O'Meara to practice their swings for the British Open, this 18-hole championship links course remains one of the toughest and most scenic in Ireland or Britain, and as one of Ireland's top five courses, it is considered to be among the best in the world. Consisting of sand dunes, gorse, native grass, and sod-faced bunkers linked by firm fairways and carefully tended greens, Waterville is bordered by the wild Atlantic on two of its three sides. Gary Player described the 11th hole, which runs for 500 yards through majestic dunes, as "the most beautiful and satisfying par-5 of them all." Caddies must be booked in advance. ⊠ *N70, on Cahirciveen side of village* ☎ *066/947–4102* ⊕ *www.watervillegolflinks.ie* ⊠ *Apr.–Oct., weekdays €210, weekends €230; Nov.–Mar., €75* ⚑ *18 holes, 7355 yards, par 72.*

The Kerry Way, Waterville
HIKING/WALKING | For a great day trip, hike the 12-km (7-mile) coastal section of the Kerry Way signposted walking route from Waterville to Caherdaniel, which has great views of small islands and rocky

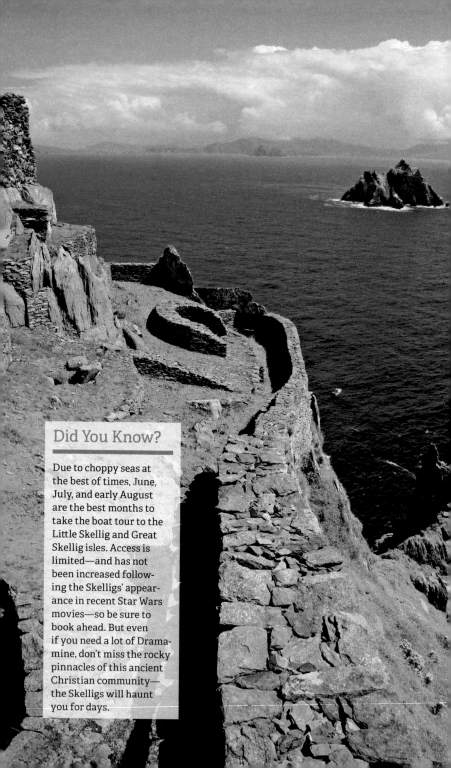

Did You Know?

Due to choppy seas at the best of times, June, July, and early August are the best months to take the boat tour to the Little Skellig and Great Skellig isles. Access is limited—and has not been increased following the Skelligs' appearance in recent Star Wars movies—so be sure to book ahead. But even if you need a lot of Dramamine, don't miss the rocky pinnacles of this ancient Christian community— the Skelligs will haunt you for days.

coves. ⊠ *Waterville* ⊕ *www.kerryway.com.*

The Skelligs and Valentia

Islands off the coastal town of Port-magee, 21 km (13 miles) northwest of Waterville; Valentia Island is across a road bridge from Portmagee.

In the far northwestern corner of the Ring of Kerry, across Portmagee Channel, lies scenic Valentia Island, reached by leaving the Ring of Kerry on the R565 to Portmagee, then crossing the road bridge to the island. Valentia where the eastern end of the first transatlantic telegraph cable was sited, and also known for its well-preserved tetrapod fossil trackways. Visible from Valentia, and on a clear day from Waterville and other points along the coast, are the Skelligs, one of the most spectacular sights in Ireland. Sculpted as if by the hand of God, the islands of Little Skellig, Skellig Michael (or the Great Skellig), and the Washerwoman's Rock are distinc-tively cone-shape, surrounded by blue swirling seas. The largest island, Skellig Michael, distinguished by its twin peaks and ancient monastic site, rises 700 feet from the Atlantic. During the journey to these islands you'll pass Little Skellig, the breeding ground of more than 22,000 pairs of gannets. Puffin Island, to the north, has a large population of shear-waters and storm petrel. Puffins nest in sand burrows on the Skellig Michael in the month of May. Skellig Michael can be visited by boat, but it is an arduous journey that should be booked in advance and attempted in good weather. ■TIP➜ **In spite of the Skelligs' increased fame following the last two Star Wars movies, visitor access is limited by law: consider a cruise around the islands, without landing, which provides some great photo ops, or if weather prohibits, opt for a visit to the Skellig Experience Visitor Centre instead.**

GETTING HERE AND AROUND

To visit the Skelligs, you can take a half-day trip in an open boat—perfect for adventurers who pack plenty of Dramamine. The entire visit takes 3 to 4 hours, with 1½ hours on Skellig Michael, where visitors are supervised by resi-dent guides, and the remaining time in transit (the duration varies depending on the weather and tides). There are no facilities on the island. Note that the waters are choppy at the best of times, and trips are made when the weather permits. Even in fine weather, it can be a rough, white-knuckle ride (at least 45 minutes) as you cross the swell of the open sea, and it's not suitable for small children. One worthy outfitter to the Skelligs is Sea Quest, on Valentia Island. ■TIP➜ **From April to October the Valentia Island Car and Passenger Ferry operates a daily shuttle for cars and foot passengers between Knightstown on Valentia Island and Renard Point near Cahirciveen. The five-minute ferry ride saves a round-trip of about 25 km (15 miles) by land.**

CONTACTS Sea Quest. ⊠ *The Pier, Portmagee* ☎ *066/947–6214* ⊕ *www.skelligsrock.com.* **Valentia Island Car and Passenger Ferry.** ⊠ *Renard Point, Cahir-civeen* ☎ *066/947–6141.*

VISITOR INFORMATION
CONTACTS Skelligs Tourist Office. ⊠ *Skellig Experience, Valentia Island* ☎ *066/947–6306* ⊕ *www.skelligexperi-ence.com.*

Sights

Skellig Experience
MUSEUM | FAMILY | Located on Valentia Island, just across the bridge from Portmagee, the Skellig Experience offers an alternative for the less adventurous traveler. This center contains exhibits on local birdlife, the history of the lighthouse and keepers, and the life and work of the early Christian monks. There's also a 15-minute audiovisual show that allows

you to "tour" the Skelligs without leaving dry land—although the center does offer a 90-minute nonlanding cruise around the islands. But if you're up for it, don't miss the boat ride from Portmagee that lets you land on the rocks; Skellig Michael is something you won't soon forget. ✉ R565, Valentia Island ☎ 066/947–6306 ⊕ www.skelligexperience.com ☒ €5, cruise €35 ⊗ Closed Dec.–Feb.

★ Skellig Michael

ISLAND | The masterpiece of the Skellig Islands is the phenomenal UNESCO World Heritage site of Skellig Michael, with its amazing remains of a 7th- to 12th-century village of monastic beehive dwellings that were home to a group of early Christian monks. In spite of a thousand years of battering by Atlantic storms, the church, oratory, and living cells are surprisingly well preserved. The site is reached by climbing more than 600 increasingly precipitous steps, offering vertigo-inducing views. The Skelligs boat trip includes 1½ hours on Skellig Michael. Despite the publicity following the island's brief but pivotal appearance in the movie *Star Wars: The Force Awakens,* access to this fragile site is still limited to 180 visitors a day, so book in advance and hope for good weather. Because of the choppy seas, stiff climb, and lack of facilities, the trip is not recommended for small children or those with mobility issues. ✉ Skellig Islands ⊕ www.heritageireland.ie ☒ Free (charge for boat trip) ⊗ Closed Oct.–mid-May.

🍴 Restaurants

★ Bridge Bar

$ | IRISH | The dramatic location of this simple bar on the windswept waterfront of the tiny fishing village of Portmagee has led the Bridge to feature in ads as "the quintessential Irish pub." A simple menu with the emphasis on local seafood, fish-and-chips, and lamb is served in the low-beamed bar's rustic pine interior. From May to September

the pretty, adjoining Moorings restaurant serves a more ambitious, pricier menu most evenings. There are also 14 rooms overhead and an ace craft shop next door, as well as set dancing every Tuesday evening. **Known for:** local seafood chowder; unpretentious hospitality; popularity with locals. ⑤ Average main: €15 ✉ Main St., Portmagee ☎ 066/947–7108 ⊕ www.moorings.ie.

Hotels

★ Atlantic Villa

$ | B&B/INN | This substantial detached house was built in 1873 for the cablemaster who was in charge of the transatlantic cable station that put this sheltered inshore island on the map. **Pros:** characterful Victorian house; dedicated owner-chef; guests welcome to enjoy garden. **Cons:** gets booked up fast; limited choice of pubs and restaurants nearby; island very busy July and August. ⑤ Rooms from: €90 ✉ Farranreagh, Knight's Town, Valentia Island ☎ 087/212–6798 ⊕ www.atlanticvilla. ie ⊗ Closed Christmas–Feb. 🛏 5 rooms ⦾ Free breakfast.

Shealane Country House Bed & Breakfast

$ | B&B/INN | A large, modern house on Valentia Island, beside the bridge to the mainland, Shealane is easily reached but also affords views of cows grazing in the adjoining field and a breakfast room with ocean views. **Pros:** great views; quiet rural location; handy base for boat trips to Skellig Michael. **Cons:** outside the village; rooms book far in advance for July and August; limited choice of nearby restaurants. ⑤ Rooms from: €90 ✉ Corha-Mor, Valentia Island ☎ 087/630–1547 ⊕ www. valentiaskelligs.com ☒ No credit cards ⊗ Closed mid-Oct.–Mar. 🛏 5 rooms ⦾ Free breakfast.

Activities

HIKING

Valentia Island

HIKING/WALKING | Even in high summer, Valentia Island is a peaceful spot for walking, with little traffic. Walk the 3-km (2-mile) road from Knightstown to the historic Slate Quarry, 900 feet above the sea, with views of the Skellig Islands offshore. A signpost on the return journey will direct you to the lighthouse at Cromwell Point and more great sea views. A longer hike in this corner of the island will take you to the tetrapod trackway: footsteps left by dinosaurs some 350 million years ago. Hiking maps are freely available. ⊕ www.valentiaisland.ie.

Cahirciveen

18 km (11 miles) north of Waterville.

Cahirciveen (pronounced "cah-her-si-veen"), at the foot of Bentee Mountain, is the gateway to the western side of the Ring of Kerry and the main market town for southern Kerry. Following the tradition in this part of the world, the modest, terraced houses are each painted in different colors (sometimes two or three)—the brighter the better.

GETTING HERE AND AROUND

Cahirciveen is about a 15-minute drive from Waterville on N70, double that if you choose to detour to Portmagee for a visit to the Skellig Rock and Valentia Island. In summer you can return from Knightstown on Valentia Island to Cahirciveen by ferry. There is free parking on the side streets off the main road and outside the tourist office. ■TIP→ **If the tourist office is closed, contact the Barracks Heritage Centre with any questions as it's run by helpful local people who know everything that's going on in and around Cahirciveen.**

VISITOR INFORMATION

CONTACTS Cahirciveen Tourist Office.
⊠ *Church St.* ☎ *066/947–1300.*

◉ Sights

Cahirciveen Parish Daniel O'Connell Memorial Church

RELIGIOUS SITE | This large, elaborate, neo-Gothic structure dominates the main street. It was built in 1888 of Newry granite and black limestone to honor local hero Daniel O'Connell—the only church in Ireland named after a layman. ⊠ *Main St.* ☎ *066/947–2210.*

Old Barracks Heritage Centre

MUSEUM | The converted former barracks of the Royal Irish Constabulary, an imposing, castlelike structure (built after the Fenian Rising of 1867 to suppress further revolts) now houses this museum. Well-designed displays depict scenes from times of famine, the life of Daniel O'Connell, and the restoration of this fine building from a blackened ruin. ⊠ *The Barracks, Brendan's Terr.* ☎ *066/401–0430* ⊕ *www.theoldbarrackscahersiveen.com* ⊠ *€4* ☉ *Mar., Apr., and Nov., closed weekends.*

❖ Restaurants

O'Neill's The Point Seafood Bar

$ | SEAFOOD | FAMILY | O'Neill's is a pub on the pier from which the ferry departs from Cahirciveen for the five-minute trip to Knightstown on Valentia Island. It has been in the same family since the 1800s, and serves only the freshest local seafood, simply prepared. It is decorated with nautical bric-a-brac and historical local photos. Try and get a seat in one of two bay windows to watch the sun setting over the Atlantic—a memorable and very romantic sight. If you are staying on Valentia, hop on the car ferry and take the five-minute crossing as a foot passenger for your meal to add to the special atmosphere. At lunch try fresh crabmeat on home-baked soda bread, or strips of hake fried in a light batter. The monkfish casserole on diced potatoes with garlic and parsley is renowned, as are the prawns or crab claws *al pil pil*—tossed in hot olive oil with garlic and chili. Most main courses come with salad, and there is a small dessert menu. **Known for:** fresh crabmeat on home-baked soda bread; monkfish casserole; fresh lobster salad. $ *Average main: €12* ⊠ *Renard Point* ✛ *Follow signs on N70 south of Cahirciveen for the car ferry* ☎ *066/947–2165* ⊕ *www.oneillsthepoint.ie* ⊗ *Closed Dec.–mid-Mar.*

Glenbeigh

27 km (17 miles) northeast of Cahirciveen.

The road from Cahirciveen to Glenbeigh is one of the Ring's highlights. To the north is Dingle Bay and the jagged peaks of the Dingle Peninsula, which will, in all probability, be shrouded in mist. If they aren't, the gods have indeed blessed your journey. The road runs close to the water here, and beyond the small village of Kells it climbs high above the bay, hugging the steep side of Drung Hill before descending to Glenbeigh. Note how different the stark character of this stretch of the Ring is from the gentle, woody Kenmare Bay side.

On a boggy plateau by the sea, the block-long village of Glenbeigh is a popular holiday base—the hiking is excellent in the Glenbeigh Horseshoe, as the surrounding mountains are known, and the trout fishing exceptionally good in Lough Coomasaharn. The area south of Glenbeigh and west of Carrantouhill Mountain, around the shores of the Caragh River and the village of Glencar, is known as the Kerry Highlands. The scenery is wild and rough but strangely appealing. A series of circular walks have been signposted, and parts of the Kerry Way pass through here. The area attracts serious climbers who intend to scale Carrantouhill, Ireland's highest peak (3,408 feet).

GETTING HERE AND AROUND

The tiny roadside village of Glenbeigh is about 40 minutes from Cahirciveen on N70. There's free parking on the streets.

Sights

Caragh Lake

BODY OF WATER | A signpost to the right outside Glenbeigh points to Caragh Lake, a tempting excursion south to a beautiful expanse of water set among gorse- and heather-covered hills and majestic mountains. The road hugs the shoreline much of the way. ⊠ *Glenbeigh.*

Kells Bay Gardens

BODY OF WATER | **FAMILY** | The subtropical gardens teeming with ferns and exotic plants date from 1838, and have been fully restored and greatly improved by the present owners, Billy and Penn Alexander. The Skywalk rope bridge is the longest in Ireland and takes half an hour to walk. The front-gate waterfall and the giant Chilean wine palm compete for your attention with carved wooden dinosaurs and giant Dicksonia antarctica (Tasmanian fern trees) dating from the 1890s, so allow at least an hour for the rest of the garden. Penn, a former chef, has opened a Thai restaurant that is very popular locally and opens for lunch, dinner, and takeaway. Do not let the rain put you off visiting: Kells receives more than 60 inches of rain annually, and it actually enhances the plants and the waterfall. But do wear sensible shoes as it is usually damp underfoot. ⊠ *Kells Bay Gardens, Cahirciveen* ✛ *Signposted off N70 13 km (8 miles) north of Cahirciveen* ☎ *066/947–7975* ⊕ *www.kellsbay.ie.*

Kerry Bog Village Museum

MUSEUM VILLAGE | **FAMILY** | Worth a quick look, this museum, between Glenbeigh and Killorglin on the Ring of Kerry, is a cluster of reconstructed, fully furnished cottages that vividly portray the daily life of the region's agricultural laborers in the early 1800s. The adjacent Red

Fox Bar is famous for its Irish coffee. ⊠ *N70, Shronowen Bog* ☎ *066/976–9184* ⊕ *www.kerrybogvillage.ie* 🖺 *€7.*

Beaches

Rossbeigh

BEACHES | FAMILY | On the coast, Rossbeigh consists of a tombolo (sand spit) of about 3 km (2 miles) backed by high dunes. It faces Inch Strand, a similar formation across the water on the Dingle Peninsula. Popular with families for its safe swimming, it also attracts walkers. **Amenities:** food and drink; lifeguards; parking (no fee). **Best for:** swimming; walking. ⊠ *Rossbeigh Rd.* ✛ *2 km (1 mile) west of Glenbeigh.*

Hotels

Blackstones House

$ | B&B/INN | FAMILY | Padraig and Breda Breen's farmhouse is a rambling old building on the Caragh River in Lickeen Wood, where a gentle stretch of rapids leads to a salmon pool. **Pros:** genuine farmhouse hospitality; peaceful, off the beaten track; great value. **Cons:** very simple, not a frill in sight; rustic riverside location not to all tastes; 15 minutes from nearest town, Killorglin. ⑤ *Rooms from: €80* ⊠ *Glencar* ☎ *066/976–0164* ⊕ *www.blackstoneshouse.com* ⊘ *Closed Nov.–mid-Mar.* 🖙 *6 rooms* ⦿⊦ *Free Breakfast.*

★ Carrig Country House

$$$ | HOTEL | A rambling two-story Victorian house covered in flowering creepers and set on 4 acres of lush gardens along the secluded shore of Caragh Lake, this comes pretty close to most people's dream rural retreat. **Pros:** lovely secluded location; real country-house atmosphere; excellent restaurant. **Cons:** tricky to find first time; only croquet and fishing on-site; no air-conditioning. ⑤ *Rooms from: €195* ⊠ *Caragh Lake, off Ring of Kerry, Killorglin* ✛ *From Killorglin, take Ring of Kerry toward Glenbeigh. After*

4 km (2½ miles) turn left, signposted "Caragh Lake"; at Caragh Lake School and Shop, turn sharp right and continue to hotel. From Glenbeigh, turn right near Red Fox Inn onto Caragh Lake road (signposted) ☎ *066/976–9100* ⊕ *www.carrighouse.com* ⊘ *Closed Nov.–early Mar.* 🖙 *16 rooms* ⦿⊦ *Free breakfast* ⚲ *Restaurant open daily May–Sept.; closed Sun.–Tues. Oct.–Apr.*

Activities

BICYCLING

Caragh Lake Cycling Route

BICYCLING | Cyclists love this circuit, which is about a 35-km (22-mile) round-trip from Glenbeigh. It is relatively traffic-free compared to the Ring of Kerry, and runs through truly remote bog and mountain landscape that's rich in wildlife. You might spot a herd of long-bearded wild goats, or a peregrine falcon soaring above. But bring your own drinks and snacks: retail outlets are scarce in these parts. ⊠ *Glenbeigh.*

Glenross Caravan & Camping Park

BICYCLING | Rent a bike here to explore the coast around Glenbeigh and follow the scenic route around Caragh Lake, one of the most peaceful places on earth. ⊠ *Ring of Kerry (N70)* ☎ *066/663–1282* ⊕ *www.campingkerry.com.*

GOLF

Dooks Golf Club

GOLF | On the second tier of courses in Ireland's Southwest, Dooks doesn't quite measure up to the world-class clubs, but offers, nonetheless, a completely worthwhile day of golf if you're touring the area. The scenery is spectacular, including views of the majestic Macgillicuddy's Reeks. Built in the old tradition of seaside links, it's shorter and a bit gentler, although the greens are small and tricky. ⊠ *Glenbeigh* ☎ *066/976–8205* ⊕ *www.dooks.com* 🖺 *Nov.–Mar., €60; Apr. and Oct., €100; May–Sept. €140*

🏌 *18 holes, 6586 yards, par 71* ⊘ *Closed to nonmembers on weekends.*

HIKING

Blackstones Bridge

HIKING/WALKING | **FAMILY** | In this partially wooded area near Glencar, in the shadow of Carrauntuohill, Ireland's highest mountain, and the MacGillicuddy Reeks, a series of looped walks from 3 km (2 miles) upward, are mapped out on picture boards in the parking areas. ⊠ *Off N70* ✛ *About 12 km (7 miles) southeast of Glenbeigh* ⊕ *www.irishtrails.ie.*

Cappanalea Outdoor Education Centre

CANOEING/ROWING/SKULLING | Canoeing, rock climbing, and orienteering are among the outdoor activities available (book in advance) at this center, located between Caragh and Cappanalea lakes, and can be arranged to meet the needs of all comers. ⊠ *Oulagh West, Caragh Lake, Killorglin* ☎ *066/976–9244* ⊕ *www. cappanalea.ie.*

HORSEBACK RIDING

Burke's Horse Trekking Center

HORSEBACK RIDING | **FAMILY** | Gallop a 5-km (3-mile) stretch of Rossbeigh Strand, or take a trek around quiet country roads on a horse from this long-established family business. They use mainly quiet colored cobs (black-and-white long-haired all-rounders). Hats and boots are included in the price. Book 24 hours in advance to avoid disappointment. ⊠ *R564* ☎ *087/237–9100* ⊕ *www.beachtrek.ie* 🖃 *From €20.*

Killorglin

14 km (9 miles) east of Glenbeigh, 22 km (14 miles) west of Killarney.

Killorglin is on top of a hill beside the River Laune. At the "top of the town" is a Continental-style piazza, with outdoor tables in good weather and free entertainment in summer. (This is also the location of the tourist information office.)

Venture down the hill to find an old-style traditional pub where you can savor a pint.

Killorglin is famed as the scene of the Puck Fair, three days of merrymaking during the second weekend in August. A large billy goat with beribboned horns, installed on a high pedestal, presides over the fair. The origins of the tradition of King Puck are lost in time. Horse dealing takes place in an open field on the first morning of the fair. In the village the main attractions are fun fair rides, street traders, street performers, free outdoor concerts, and extended drinking hours. The crowds can be huge, so avoid Killorglin at fair time if you've come for peace and quiet. On the other hand, if you intend to join in the festivities, be sure to book accommodations well in advance.

GETTING HERE AND AROUND

The town is a 10-minute drive on the R70 from Glenbeigh. Street parking is available, and there is a free parking lot near the tourist information office.

VISITOR INFORMATION

CONTACTS Killorglin Tourist Office. ⊠ *Iveragh Rd.* ☎ *066/976–1451* ⊕ *www. reeksdistrict.com.*

🍴 Restaurants

The Bianconi

$$ | **IRISH** | This busy Victorian-style pub (with guest rooms) was once the coaching inn for the national network of horse-drawn coaches known as Bianconis; today, it serves local seafood and traditional Irish food. Its dark-wood interior has a rambling barroom with a tile floor, leatherette banquettes, and ancient stuffed animals above the booths. The menu includes such favorites as Dingle Bay prawns, local oak-smoked salmon, a steaming mussel pot in garlic sauce, and braised shank of Kerry lamb. **Known for:** hearty portions of bistro-style food; Kerry lamb; Dingle Bay seafood. 💲 *Average main: €21* ⊠ *Lower Bridge*

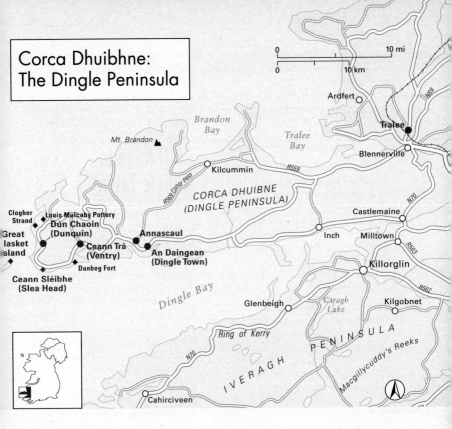

Corca Dhuibhne: The Dingle Peninsula

Corca Dhuibhne (Dingle Peninsula)

Brandon Bay

Mt. Brandon ▲

Tralee Bay

Ardfert

Tralee

Blennerville

Kilcummin

R559

R559 Conor Pass

CORCA DHUIBHNE
(DINGLE PENINSULA)

Castlemaine

N70

Clogher Strand

Louis Mulcahy Pottery

Dún Chaoin
(Dunquin)

Annascaul

Inch

Milltown

R563

Great Blasket Island

Ceann Trá
(Ventry)

An Daingean
(Dingle Town)

Killorglin

Dunbeg Fort

R562

Ceann Sléibhe
(Slea Head)

Dingle Bay

Glenbeigh

Caragh Lake

Kilgobnet

Ring of Kerry

N70

IVERAGH PENINSULA

Macgillycuddy's Reeks

Cahirciveen

0   10 mi
0   10 km

St. ☏ 066/976–1146 ⊕ www.bianconi.ie
☾ No lunch Sun.

The Ring of Kerry

The Ring of Kerry is a 179 km circular route around Kerry's Iveragh Peninsula. It takes in the towns of Killarney, Beaufort, Killorglin, Glenbeigh, Caherciveen, Waterville, Caherdaniel, Sneem, and Kenmare.

⇨ *For more on the Ring of Kerry, see the feature in this chapter.*

★ The Ring of Kerry

SCENIC DRIVE | Along the perimeter of the Iveragh Peninsula, the dramatic coastal road from Kenmare to Killorglin known as the Ring of Kerry is probably Ireland's single most popular tourist route. Stunning mountain and coastal views are around almost every turn. The only drawback: on a sunny day, it seems like half the nation's visitors are traveling along this two-lane road, driving, packed into buses, riding bikes, or backpacking. The route is narrow and curvy, and the local sheep think nothing of using it for a nap; take it slowly. Tour buses tend to start in Killarney and ply the Ring counterclockwise, so consider jumping ahead and starting in Killorglin or following the route clockwise, starting in Kenmare (although this means you risk meeting tour buses head-on on narrow roads). Either way, bear in mind that most of the buses leave Killarney between 9 and 10 am. The trip covers 179 km (111 miles) on N70 (and briefly R562 and N71) if you start and finish in Killarney; the journey will be 40 km (25 miles) shorter if you only venture between Kenmare and Killorglin. Because rain blocks views across the water to the Beara Peninsula in the east and the Dingle Peninsula in the west, hope for sunshine. It makes all the difference.

Annascaul

47 km (30 miles) northwest of Killarney.

An important livestock center until the 1930s, this village near the junction of the Castlemaine and Tralee roads has a wide road, as cattle trading was once carried out in the streets. The town also has many pubs. It is a popular base for walkers tackling the Dingle Way (179 km [111 miles]) or the shorter (57-km [35-mile]), three-day Kerry Camino (⊕ *www. kerrycamino.com*).

GETTING HERE AND AROUND

Annascaul is about one hour from Tralee on the N86, just over an hour from Killarney (take N70 then R561), and less than half-an-hour's drive from Dingle Town continuing on the main N86. There is abundant free parking in town.

 ## Sights

The South Pole Inn

HISTORIC SITE | This fascinating landmark was built by local hero Tom Crean (1877–1938). Crean enlisted in the English navy at the age of 15, and served on three expeditions to Antarctica—the *Discovery* (1901–04) and the *Terra Nova* (1910–13), both under the command of Captain Robert Falcon Scott, and the *Endurance* (1914–16), where he was second officer to Ernest Shackleton. Crean himself failed to reach the South Pole on any of these expeditions, and named his pub so that in his retirement he could go to work at the South Pole every day.

Memorabilia at the pub fill in the details of Crean's Antarctic adventures. Famed for his amazing strength and resilience, he walked 56 km (35 miles) through an Antarctic blizzard to bring help to his colleagues, with only two bars of chocolate and three cookies for sustenance. For this he received the Albert Medal for Bravery. On another occasion he survived a 15-day journey across 1,280 km (800 miles) of ocean in an open boat. ⊠ *Off N86, Anascaul* ☎ *066/915–7388.*

An Daingean (Dingle Town)

18 km (11 miles) west of Annascaul, 67 km (42 miles) west of Killarney, 45 km (28 miles) west of Killorglin.

Backed by mountains and facing a sheltered harbor, An Daingean, the chief town of its eponymous peninsula, has a year-round population of 1,400 that more than doubles in summer. Although many expect Dingle (to use its English name) to be a quaint and undeveloped Gaeltacht village, it has many crafts shops, seafood restaurants, and pubs.

Still, you can explore its main thoroughfares—the Mall, Main and Strand Streets, and the Wood—in less than an hour. Celebrity hawks, take note: off-season Dingle is favored as a hideaway by the likes of Julia Roberts, Paul Simon, and Dolly Parton. These and others have their visits commemorated on Green Street's "path of stars."

The latest addition to the annual calendar is the **Dingle Food and Wine Festival.**

GETTING HERE AND AROUND

Dingle Town is about an hour and 15 minutes' drive from Tralee on the N86, and about two hours west of Killarney via Killorglin and Castlemaine. There are daily buses from Tralee, which also has the nearest train station.

There is no public transportation west of Dingle Town, around Slea Head, where the best scenery is found. If you don't have a car, the 30-km (18-mile) circuit can be toured by minibus. If you are driving, bear in mind that there are no gas stations and no ATMs west of Dingle Town, so load up on supplies before you leave.

Most boats to the Blasket Islands leave from Dunquin, 21 km (13 miles) west of town, but Dingle Bay Charters leaves from the Dingle Town marina.

TOURS

Coastline Tours

If you don't have a car, this company offers minibus tours (€25 per person for a three-hour tour) of the 30-km (18-mile) route around Slea Head. ☎ *087/998–2230* ⊕ *www.coastline-tours.com.*

Dingle Bay Charters

The boats of Dingle Bay Charters leave from the marina in Dingle Town, making ecotours of the Blasket Islands daily between May and September, weather permitting (from €40). They also run a harbor cruise (€10 for one hour) several times daily between April and September, and a 3½-hour cruise around the Skellig Rocks (€100 per person). ⊠ *Dingle Marina, Dingle* ☎ *066/915–1344* ⊕ *www. dinglebaycharters.com.*

VISITOR INFORMATION

CONTACTS An Daingean (Dingle Town) Tourist Office. ⊠ *Strand St., Dingle* ☎ *066/915–1188* ⊕ *www.dingle-penin-sula.ie.*

Sights

Fungie

MARINA | FAMILY | Since 1985, Dingle's central attraction, apart from its "trad" music scene, has been a winsome bottlenose dolphin who has taken up residence in the harbor. The Dingle dolphin, or Fungie, as he has been named, will play for hours with swimmers (a wet suit is essential) and scuba divers, and he follows local boats in and out of the harbor. It's impossible to predict whether he will stay, but boatmen have become so confident of a sighting that they offer trippers their money back if Fungie does

not appear. Boat trips (€10) leave the pier hourly in July and August between 11 and 6, weather permitting. ⊠ *The Pier, Dingle* ☎ *066/915–2626* ⊕ *www. dingledolphin.com.*

🍴 Restaurants

Ashe's

$$$ | SEAFOOD | This pub has been sitting here since it opened in 1949 as a drapery with a liquor license, and its history over the years has included its location as the unofficial base for the cast of *Ryan's Daughter,* which filmed in the town in 1968. In fact, it was for this crew that Ashe's first started serving food, and while the bar has expanded to accommodate more visitors with two additional cozy, no-frills rooms, the fare served up on the plain wooden tables remains the freshest seafood, cooked to order, and a small selection of meat and vegetarian dishes—all hearty and good. Reservations are advised. **Known for:** good-value early menu from 5:30–6:30 (booking advised); Blasket Island lobster, steamed with lemon or garlic butter; Glenbeigh mussels in Thai-style broth. ⑤ *Average main: €27* ⊠ *6 Main St., Dingle* ☎ *066/915–0989* ⊕ *ashesbar.ie* ⊘ *Closed Sun. and Mon. Nov.–Apr.*

★ Chart House

$$$ | IRISH | Host Jim McCarthy is often found in the early evening leaning over the red half door of this low, cabinlike stone building. The atmosphere is pleasantly informal (nautical artifacts complement the rusty-red walls and matching tablecloths), but both food and service are polished and professional. Top choices include Dingle Bay crabmeat salad with ginger mayonnaise and mango salsa, or rack of Kerry mountain lamb. Finish the meal with a selection of Irish cheeses, served with a glass of port, or choose from a range of homemade desserts. **Known for:** cottage-style dining room; Annascaul black pudding; roast rack of Kerry lamb. ⑤ *Average main:*

Continued on page 379

THE RING OF KERRY

When you travel Ireland's most popular scenic route, leaving your car behind makes all the difference. Here's how to get far from the madding crowd.

The Ring of Kerry is one of Europe's great drives. The common wisdom, though, is that it suffers from its own popularity: tour buses dominate the road from sunup to sundown. There's more than a grain of truth to this reputation, but that doesn't mean you should scratch the Ring from your itinerary. Instead, plan to turn off the main road and get out of your car. You'll make a blissful discovery: the Iveragh Peninsula—one of the most beautiful locations in all of Ireland—remains largely unspoiled. It's full of fabulous places to hike, bike, and boat—and best of all, there are views the tour bus passengers can only dream of.

Top, Elevated coastal view from the Ring of Kerry; Below left, on horseback in Rossbeigh Strand, Kerry; Below right, cycling around the Ring

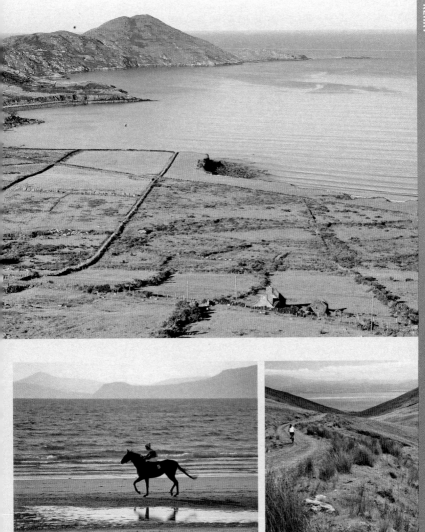

AROUND THE RING BY FOOT AND BY BIKE

HIKING THE RING

Option number one for getting outdoors around the Ring of Kerry is to go by foot. There are appealing walking options for every degree of fitness and experience, from gentle, paved paths to an ascent up Ireland's tallest mountain.

THE KERRY WAY

The main hiking route across the peninsula is the Kerry Way, a spectacular 133-mile footpath that's easily broken down into day-trip-size seg-

ments. The path winds from Killarney through the foothills of the MacGillicuddy's Reeks and the Black Valley to Glencar and Glenbeigh, from where it parallels the Ring through Cahirciveen, Waterville, Caherdaniel, and Sneem, before ending in Kenmare. The route, indicated by way markers, follows grassy old paths situated at higher elevations than the Ring—meaning better, and more tranquil, views. Hiking the entire Kerry

Way can take from 10 to 12 days. Numerous outfitters organize both guided and unguided tours. For a great day trip, hike the 10 km (6 miles) section from Waterville to Caherdaniel, which has great views of small islands and rocky coves. In the Glencar area near Blackstones Bridge, a series of shorter signposted walks, from 3 km (2 miles) upward, put you in the shadow of Carrauntuohill, Ireland's highest mountain.

TAKING IT EASY: THREE GENTLE STROLLS

Muckross Park in Killarney is a car-free zone with four signposted nature trails. Try the 4 km (2½ miles) Arthur Young's Walk through old yew and oak woods frequented by sika deer. You can also take an open boat from Ross Castle to the head of the Upper Lake, then walk back along the lakeside to Muckross House—about 10 km (6 miles).

The trails in **Derrynane National Park**, a 320-acre estate, run through mature woodland, bordering on rocky outcrops that lead to wide sandy beaches and dunes. At low tide, you can walk to Abbey Island offshore.

Even in high summer, **Valentia Island** is a peaceful spot for walking, with little traffic. Walk the road from Knightstown through the sub-tropical vegetation of the Knight of Kerry's estate, to the historic **Slate Quarry** (3 km/2 miles), 900 ft above the sea, with views of the Skelligs offshore.

CYCLING THE RING

The Ring of Kerry Cycle Route follows the main road for about a third of its 134 miles, but the rest is on deserted roads, including a long, scenic loop through Ballinskelligs, Portmagee, and Valentia Island. There are significant climbs and strong winds along the way, so good fitness is a prerequisite.

EASY RIDES

From Killarney, the N71 road past **Muckross Park** and the **Upper Lake** takes you through ancient woodlands to Ladies' View (about 12 km/7.5 miles). From here you have one of the area's best panoramas, with the sparkling blue lakes backed by purple mountains. The scene will be in front of you as you make the ride back.

From **Glenbeigh**, escape the traffic by riding inland to peaceful Caragh Lake through a bog and mountain landscape that's rich in wildlife. You might spot a herd of long-bearded wild goats, or a peregrine falcon hovering above its prey. The full circuit of the lake, returning to Glenbeigh, is about 35 km (22 miles).

KEY

- 🚣 *Boating*
- 🚲 *Cycling*
- 🎣 *Fishing*
- 🚶 *Hiking*
- 🐎 *Horseback Riding*

RING ACTIVITIES

BOATING AROUND THE RING...

Kenmare Bay is the best spot for boating expeditions, on which you can see castles, seals, dolphins, and salmon farms. Boats can take up to 10 people.

...AND SWIMMING

Swimming off the beaches around the coast is confined to July and August, when the water temperatures reach 55 to 60 degrees. There are dive centers at **Caherdaniel**, **Kenmare**, and **Valentia Island**.

...AND FISHING

There's good fishing here, both inland and at sea. **Portmagee** and **Waterville** are the main deepsea angling centers; outings are generally from small open boats carrying up to 10 rods and run about €30 per person per day. Wreck and reef fishing promises pollock, ling, cod, conger, monkfish, and shark. Inshore there are bass, turbot, dogfish, flounder, and tope.

The **Caragh Lake** and the rivers **Laune**, **Inny**, **Roughty**, and **Caragh** are all excellent for wild salmon—and all are beautiful wilderness locations. **Lough Currane** near Waterville is one of the great sea trout fisheries. The season runs from March to September, and fishing permits are available locally from hotels. You'll find tackle shops in Killarney and Waterville. For detailed information before you go, check out the website of the Inland Fisheries Ireland (⊕ www.fishinginireland.info).

...AND EQUITREKKING

Horses hold a special place in the hearts of the Irish. Horsemanship and breeding are sources of national pride. If you share the Irish passion for all things equine, there's no better way to see the Ring than from the back of a horse. You can gallop along the 3mile stretch of **Rossbeigh Strand**, or take a trek around quiet country roads.

Top left, horses at the Lakes of Killarney; Right, trout fishing; Bottom left, fishing boats in the Dingle harbor

WEATHER, FLORA, AND TOURING TIPS

Swimming at the Ring

THANKS TO
THE GULF STREAM...

The warm waters flowing from the Gulf of Mexico across the Atlantic, known as the Gulf Stream, give Ireland a mild climate, and the effects are particularly felt along the Ring of Kerry. The area is frost-free year round, with temperatures averaging 45 degrees Fahrenheit in winter and 60 in summer. But rain is a constant threat, brought in from the Atlantic by the prevailing southwesterly winds. Console yourself with this though: it may be wet, but it is never freezing.

Don't bother touring the Ring in heavy sea mist: you won't see a thing. But don't let other forms of rain deter you. Part of the attraction of the Ring is the interplay of light with sea, mountain, and distant horizons. Rain often enhances the view, and can give delightful effects. The sun is often shining before the rain has finished, so rainbows abound. Any weather, good or bad, seldom lasts more than half a day: if it's wet in the morning, it will probably be sunny in the afternoon, and vice versa.

SOCK IT TO ME

Bring a rain jacket and a warm fleece or sweater: sea winds can be chilly. Above all, wear sensible footwear. If you're venturing off-road, even in summer, you will be glad of strong, waterproof shoes. And bring plenty of socks. There's nothing more miserable than wet feet!

LAND OF EXOTIC PALMS

With no frost, Killarney and the Iveragh Peninsula are havens for subtropical vegetation. The New Zealand fern tree and the banana tree thrive. The "palm trees" you see here are usually yuccas that have been allowed to grow tall. Flax also grows to enormous size, and is often used as a shelter belt. The leaves of the gunnera can grow to the size of a compact car—look for them in Muckross Park. The lakes of Killarney are surrounded by luxuriant woods of oak, arbutus, birch, holly, and mountain ash, with undergrowth of ferns, saxifrages, and mosses. Rhododendron and azaleas thrive on pockets of acid soil, and are at their best from mid-April to May.

Valentia Island

THE ICE AGE COMETH, AND GOETH

Some 60 million years ago, the great rias, or drowned rivers, that became the bays of Bantry, Kenmare, and Dingle were formed. The sea penetrated far inland, forming the peninsulas of Beara, Iveragh, and Dingle. A million years ago, these lands were gripped by the Ice Age. When the ice receded, some 10,000 years ago, it left corries (or glacial hollows) gouged out of the mountains, great rocks scattered on the landscape (giving rise to legends of giants throwing stones), and outcrops of ice-smoothed sandstone.

THE TWIN PEAKS OF YOUR TRIP

Above and below left, ancient monastic site on Skellig Michael with Little Skellig in the background.

The distinctive conical **Skellig Rocks** hover offshore at the western end of the Iveragh Peninsula, surrounded by swirling blue sea. They're a haunting presence that seems to follow along as you travel the mainland from Valentia to Waterville and Caherdaniel.

A venture out to the twin peaks of **Skellig Michael** (shown above, also known as Great Skellig) is a truly awesome experience. Boats leave from Waterville, Ballinskelligs, and Portmagee for a white-knuckle ride lasting about 45 minutes. Along the way you pass Michael's companion, **Little Skellig,** where people aren't allowed but gannets flourish.

Skellig Michael rises steeply for 700 feet; you reach the summit by climbing 600 steps cut into the rockface. Once there, you find, amazingly, the remains of a monastery, occupied by hermit monks from the 7th to 12th century.

Looking back to the mainland and out at the wild expanse of open sea, you get an inkling of the monks' isolation from all things worldly. A visit to Skellig Michael may not be the most comfortable outing of you trip, but it will probably be the most memorable.

BIRDS OF THE SKELLIGS
The Ring of Kerry is one of the best places in Europe for observing seabirds, and the Skelligs are a particular treasure for birders. The gannet, with a wing span of 2 yards, is Ireland's largest seabird and up to 22,000 nesting pairs reside on Little Skellig, where they dive for food from heights of up to 120 feet.

If you are lucky enough to get out to Skellig Michael in May, you'll be warned to watch out for comical-looking **puffins** (*below*) nesting in burrows underfoot.

Below, two puffins standing on Skellig rocks

The coastal tip of the Dingle Peninsula provides a dramatic seascape whatever the weather.

€28 ✉ The Mall, Dingle ☎ 066/915–2255 ⊕ www.thecharthousedingle.com ☉ Closed Jan. 2–mid-Feb., and Mon. and Tues. in Apr., May, and mid-Sept.–Dec. (call to confirm). No lunch.

★ Out of the Blue

$$$ | SEAFOOD | Every fishing port should have a simple waterfront bistro like this one, serving the best seafood (the owner won't open up if there's no fresh-caught seafood available—which is almost never). Lobster, scallops, and crayfish are specialties, but also expect turbot, black sole, plaice, brill, monkfish, and even the humble pollack on the daily blackboard menu of this unpretentious shack. There's a short but well-chosen wine list, and basic dessert selection. **Known for:** serving only fresh seafood; modern twists on classics; the bargain "Fish Deal" set menu. ⑤ Average main: €27 ✉ The Pier, Dingle ☎ 066/915–0811 ⊕ www.outoftheblue.ie ☉ Closed mid-Nov.–mid-Mar. No lunch Mon.–Sat.

Pantrí

$ | CAFÉ | A small, friendly café in the center of Dingle with a large outdoor seating area, Pantrí offers delicious meals equally suitable to those that are easily pleased and those with food sensitivities. It's a popular breakfast spot, offering the traditional "full Irish" with local artisanal pork products, or vegan alternatives, as well as home baking and buckwheat pancakes. At lunch, there is always a freshly made soup of the day using locally sourced, seasonal ingredients. The veggie burger is a popular option, or try local seafood in a Thai fish soup. The food is beautifully presented, garnished with edible flowers, and obviously prepared with unusual attention to detail. **Known for:** local artisanal sausages and bacon; an excellent veggie burger; homemade carrot cake. ⑤ Average main: €8 ✉ Lower Main St., Dingle ☎ 086/103–2399 ☉ Closed Tues. Jan.–mid-Apr. No dinner Apr.–Oct.

Hotels

Dingle Skellig Hotel and Peninsula Spa

$$ | **HOTEL | FAMILY** | This rambling modern hotel's setting on Dingle Bay offers great views of the water, notably from the restaurant and the spa's outdoor hot tub. **Pros:** waterfront location; outdoor hot tub with sea view; separate floors for child-free guests. **Cons:** some undistinguished architecture; on the edge of town; bar very busy on weekends. Ⓢ *Rooms from: €170* ⊠ *Dingle Harbor, Dingle* ☎ *066/915–0200* ⊕ *www.dingleskellig.com* ⊘ *Closed Jan., and Mon.–Thurs. in Nov. and Dec.* ⇨ *113 rooms* ⦿ *Free breakfast.*

★ Greenmount House

$$ | **B&B/INN** | More like a modern boutique hotel than a B&B, the combination of comfort and elegance in the lobby sets the tone, as do the wonderful views of the town and harbor. **Pros:** rooms both stylish and comfortable; wine license; wonderful breakfasts. **Cons:** new developments mar an otherwise great view; short walk uphill from town center; can fill up quickly: book well ahead. Ⓢ *Rooms from: €130* ⊠ *Upper John St., Dingle* ☎ *066/915–1414* ⊕ *www.greenmounthouse.ie* ⊘ *Closed Christmas Day and mid-Jan.–mid-Feb.* ⇨ *12 rooms* ⦿ *Free breakfast.*

Heaton's Guesthouse

$$ | **B&B/INN** | On the Slea Head edge of Dingle Town, but just a short walk to the center, this traditional-style yellow house is right on the water's edge. **Pros:** spacious, stylish house; outstanding breakfast; only a short walk from town. **Cons:** if it rains you'll be driving, not walking, to nearest bars and restaurants. Ⓢ *Rooms from: €132* ⊠ *The Wood, Dingle* ☎ *066/915–2288* ⊕ *www.heatonsdingle.com* ⊘ *Closed Dec. 1–27 and Jan. 7–31* ⇨ *16 rooms* ⦿ *Free breakfast.*

ⓨ Nightlife

Nearly every bar on the Corca Dhuibhne (Dingle Peninsula), particularly in the town of An Daingean, offers live music nightly in July and August.

An Droichead Beag (The Small Bridge)

MUSIC CLUBS | For a lively nighttime spot, try this large, busy pub in the town center, known for live Irish music. ⊠ *Main St., Dingle* ☎ *066/915–1723.*

★ Dick Mack's

MUSIC CLUBS | Part cobbler's shop, part bar, this tiny pub is a quintessential Dingle experience, with music nightly and a big selection of whiskeys. Anything can and does happen. ⊠ *Green St., Dingle* ☎ *066/915–1707.*

O'Flahertys

BARS/PUBS | An Daingean's pubs are well known for their music, but among them O'Flaherty's, a simple, stone-floor bar at the entrance to town, is something special and a hot spot for traditional musicians. Spontaneous sessions occur most nights in July and August, less frequently at other times. Even without music, this pub is a good place to compare notes with fellow travelers. ⊠ *Bridge St., Dingle* ☎ *066/915–1983* ⊕ *www.oflahertysbardingle.com.*

⬤ Shopping

Greenlane Gallery

ART GALLERIES | The gallery shows a cross section of contemporary artists, most of them influenced by the local landscape. ⊠ *Holy Ground, Grey's La., Dingle* ☎ *066/915–2018* ⊕ *www.greenlanegallery.com.*

Leác a Ré

CRAFTS | For handmade Irish crafts, check out this noted emporium. ⊠ *Strand St., Dingle* ☎ *066/915–1138.*

Murphy's Ice Cream

FOOD/CANDY | One of Ireland's more unusual culinary success stories, Murphy's has won international awards. Find out why at this flagship parlor. ⊠ *Strand St., Dingle* ☎ *066/915–2644* ⊕ *www.murphysicecream.ie.*

★ **Original Kerry Gift Shop and Craft Center**

CRAFTS | This is a co-operative venture that provides a retail outlet for 32 Kerry-based craft workers. From jewelry to soap to wood turning to rain hats, glass, and ceramics, you will find all things handmade here. ⊠ *Upper St., Dingle* ☎ *083/852–0705* ⊕ *www.originalkerry.shop.*

Weaver's Shop

CLOTHING | Lisbeth Mulcahy sells outstanding handwoven, vegetable-dyed woolen wraps and mufflers, in an attractive range of colors. ⊠ *Green St., Dingle* ☎ *066/915–1688* ⊕ *www.lisbethmulcahy.com.*

Activities

BICYCLING

Dingle Electric Bike Experience

BICYCLING | You'll remember your bike ride around Slea Head for a long time, but given gradients and head-winds in this area, you might be inclined to remember it more favorably with the benefit of an electric bike. Dingle Electric Bike Experience will deliver to your lodgings, provide luggage transfers on request, self-guiding maps, free helmets, locks, and high-visibility gear, plus a choice of electric or conventional bike to suit your needs. ⊠ *Dingle* ☎ *086/084–8378* ⊕ *www.dinglebikes.com.*

HORSEBACK RIDING

Dingle Horse Riding

HORSEBACK RIDING | Up in the hills behind Dingle Town, this stable offers some unforgettable treks. The two-hour rides (€65) follow mountain tracks then proceed through the town to visit the dolphin Fungie before galloping back along the beach. The half-day trek (€100) goes to Ventry Strand. Six-day trail rides with accommodations are also available.

⊠ *Baile na Buaile, Dingle* ☎ *086/821–1225* ⊕ *www.dinglehorseriding.com.*

Ceann Trá (Ventry)

8 km (5 miles) west of An Daingean (Dingle Town) on R561.

The next town after An Daingean along the coast, Ceann Trá has a small outcrop of pubs and small grocery stores (useful, since west of Dingle Town you'll find few shops of any kind), and a long sandy beach. Between Ventry and Dún Chaoin (Dunquin) are several interesting archaeological sites on the spectacular cliff-top road along Ceann Sléibhe (Slea Head).

GETTING HERE AND AROUND

It takes about 10 minutes to reach Ventry by car on R561 from Dingle Town. Take extra care when driving these narrow scenic roads, which can be busy with cyclists, walkers, and sometimes sheep, as well as many other drivers unfamiliar with the locality.

Sights

Dunbeg Fort

ARCHAEOLOGICAL SITE | Perched on the very edge of a Dingle Bay cliff, and set in the small district of Fahan (which is part of the larger township of Ventry), this small, well-weathered fort was an important Iron Age defensive promontory site, inhabited from about AD 800 until around 1200. It was badly damaged by storms in the winter of 2017–18, and it is unlikely full access will be restored, but you can still view it from above. Its drystone mound was defended against cattle raiders by four earthen rings—note the *souterraine* (underground) escape route, by the entrance. In addition, there are a number of archaeological artifacts here to interest the time traveler.

There is a 10-minute audiovisual show in the adjacent visitor center, but just as fascinating is the building itself, a modern replica of the drystone construction of the clocháns (pronounced "cluk- *awns*"), the famous prehistoric "beehive" cells first used by hermit monks in the early Christian period. Beside it is a typical *naomhóg* (pronounced "na- *vogue*"), a tarred canvas canoe, resting upside down.

About 1 km (½ mile) farther on is another parking lot, and an interesting group of clocháns can be visited (€2 fee to resident farmer), built of drystone and set on the southern slopes of Mt. Eagle looking out directly across the sea to Skellig Michael. Far from being only prehistoric relics, as the signposts claim, clocháns were being built until a century ago; wood was scarce and stone abounded, so you'll find more than 400 of them between Ceann Sléibhe and Dún Chaoin. ⊠ *Fahan, Ventry* ✛ *8 km (5 miles) west of Ventry* ☎ *066/915–9070* ⊠ *€3*.

 Beaches

Ventry Beach

BEACHES | Ventry Beach (or Ventry Strand) is just southwest of the village of Ceann Trá (Ventry). This lovely stretch of golden sand, said by many to be one of Ireland's most beautiful beaches, runs for 8 km (5 miles) and is part of the Dingle Way walking route. There is a dune system with a small lake, wetlands, and a reed swamp, and abundant wildlife. In July and August it attracts families and swimmers. **Amenities:** food and drink; lifeguards; parking (no fee); toilets; water sports. **Best for:** surfing; swimming; walking; windsurfing. ⊠ *Ventry*.

Ceann Sléibhe (Slea Head)

16 km (10 miles) west of An Daingean (Dingle Town), 8 km (5 miles) west of Ceann Trá.

From the top of the towering cliffs of Ceann Sléibhe (pronounced "kyeown *shla*-va") at the southwest extremity of the Dingle Peninsula, the view of the Blasket Islands and the Atlantic Ocean is guaranteed to stop you in your tracks. Alas, Slea Head—to use its English name—has become so popular that tour buses, barely able to negotiate the narrow road, are causing traffic jams, particularly in July and August. Coumenole, the long, sandy strand below, looks beautiful and sheltered, but swimming here is dangerous. This treacherous stretch of coast has claimed many lives in shipwrecks—most recently in 1982, when a large cargo boat, the *Ranga,* foundered on the rocks and sank. In 1588 four ships of the Spanish Armada were driven through the Blasket Sound; two made it to shelter, and two sank. One of these, the *Santa Maria de la Rosa,* is being excavated by divers.

GETTING HERE AND AROUND
Slea Head is a 10-minute drive from Ventry on R559.

 Beaches

Clogher Strand

BEACH—SIGHT | This dramatic, windswept stretch of rocks and sand visible below the coast road to the north of Slea Head is not a safe spot to swim, but it's a good place to watch the ocean dramatically pound the rocks when a storm is approaching or a gale is blowing. It may be familiar from David Lean's 1970 film *Ryan's Daughter.* **Amenities:** none. **Best for:** walking. ⊠ *Dunquin* ✛ *On left as you travel from Dunquin to Ballyferriter on R559, across from Louis Mulcahy Pottery.*

Dún Chaoin (Dunquin)

13 km (8 miles) west of Ceann Trá, 5 km (3 miles) north of Ceann Sléibhe (Slea Head).

Once the mainland harbor for the Blasket islanders (when there *were* islanders, as the Blaskets are deserted now), Dún Chaoin is at the center of the Gaeltacht, and attracts many students of Irish language and folklore.

GETTING HERE AND AROUND
Dunquin is on R559 at the western end of the Dingle Peninsula. Bus Éireann's Dingle–Ballyferriter service (Monday and Thursday only) calls at Dunquin.

 Sights

★ **Blasket Centre**
INFO CENTER | FAMILY | The Blasket Islands (An Bhlascaoid Mhóir) are among Ireland's most extraordinary islands. The largest visible from Ceann Sléibhe is the Great Blasket, inhabited until 1953. The Blasket islanders were great storytellers and were encouraged by Irish scholars to write their memoirs. The Blasket Centre explains the heritage of these islanders and celebrates their use of the Irish language with videos and exhibitions. ⊠ *Dunquin* ☎ *066/915–6444* ⊕ *www.heritageireland.ie* ⊡ *€5* ⊗ *Closed Nov.–mid-Mar.*

Dún Chaoin Pier
MARINA | Signposted from the main road, Dún Chaoin pier is surrounded by cliffs of colored Silurian rock, more than 400 million years old and rich in fossils. Down at the pier you can see *naomhóga* (open fishing boats traditionally made of animal hide stretched over wooden laths and tarred) stored upside down. Three or four men walk the curraghs out to the sea, holding them over their heads. Similar boats are used in the Aran Islands, and when properly handled they're extraordinarily seaworthy. ⊠ *R559, Dunquin.*

Kruger's Pub
RESTAURANT—SIGHT | Long frequented by artists and writers, including Brendan Behan, Kruger's Pub is known as Dunquin's social center. ⊠ *Dunquin* ⊹ *Signposted on left about 1 km (½ mile)* beyond Dunquin Pier ☎ *066/915–6127* ⊕ *www.krugers.ie.*

★ **Louis Mulcahy Pottery**
STORE/MALL | Overlooking the beach is the pottery studio of one of Ireland's leading ceramic artists. Louis Mulcahy produces large pots and urns that are both decorative and functional. You can watch the work in progress and buy items at workshop prices. There's also a coffee shop. ⊠ *Clogher Strand, Ballyferriter* ☎ *066/915–6229* ⊕ *www.louismulcahy. com.*

Great Blasket Island

★ The Great Blasket, which measures roughly 3 km by 1 km (2 miles by ½ mile), has no traffic, no pub, no hotel, and no electricity. Yet this island—centerpiece of the An Bhlascaoid Mhóir (Blasket Islands)—is one of the most memorable places in Ireland to visit.

Until 1954 a small community of hardy fisherfolk and subsistence farmers eked out a living here.

Today, visitors are usually attracted by the literary heritage of the island—the Irish-language writings of Tomás Ó Criomhthain, Muiris Ó Suilleabhain (also known in English as Tomás O'Crohán and Maurice O'Sullivan), and Peig Sayers—but what makes people return is something else: a rare quality of light and an intense peace and quiet in beautiful, unspoiled surroundings.

The inadequacy of the existing piers limits visitors to the island to a maximum of about 400 per day, a figure that is reached only rarely, with the average less than 200. Most visitors stay for three or four hours, walking, sketching, or taking photographs.

The silence strikes you at once. The seabirds, stonechats, and swallows sound louder than on the mainland; sheep graze silently on the steep hillside. The simple domestic ruins are very touching; you do not need to know the history to work out what happened to their owners (most departed for other places, with many settling in Springfield, Massachusetts).

■TIP→ Before you go, read Maurice O'Sullivan's *Twenty Years a-Growing*, a fascinating account of a simple way of life that has only recently disappeared on the Blaskets. For an overview of the island's more recent history, read *Hungry for Home: Leaving the Blaskets—A Journey from the Edge of Ireland* by Cole Moreton.

GETTING HERE AND AROUND

These days it takes only 15 minutes from Dún Chaoin (Dunquin) Pier to make the 3-km (2-mile) crossing of the Blasket Sound, but even on a calm day the swell can be considerable. In summer the island is usually accessible most days; in winter the island can be cut off for weeks.

CONTACTS **Blasket Island Ferry.** ☎ 085/775–1045 ⊕ www.blasketisland. com. **Dingle Bay Charters.** ☎ 066/915–1344 ⊕ www.dinglebaycharters.com.

Tralee

50 km (31 miles) northeast of An Daingean (Dingle Town) on R559.

County Kerry's capital and its largest town, Tralee (population 24,000) is the main shopping and business destination for North and West Kerry, with a large student population. It's also the transportation hub of the region. As such, people used to joke that the only good things to come out of Tralee were the buses shuttling travelers elsewhere. To a certain extent, that is still the case: apart from some Georgian town houses near the museum there is not much of architectural or antiquarian interest. Modern renovations, including concrete piazzas (which attract crowds of drinkers on weekends) have done little to ameliorate

Tralee's medium-size-town-with-little-character feel. Accordingly, however, there are no tourists, so the local folk have been fashioning some worthwhile sights, including the town museum, and the Siamsa Tíre—the National Folk Theatre of Ireland—which stages impressive dances and plays based on Irish folklore.

The town has long been associated with the popular Irish song "The Rose of Tralee," the inspiration for the annual Rose of Tralee International Festival. The second week of August, Irish communities worldwide send young women to join native Irish competitors; one of them is chosen as the Rose of Tralee. Visitors, musicians, and entertainers pack the town then. A two-day horse-racing meet—with seven races a day—runs at the same time, which contributes to the crowds.

GETTING HERE AND AROUND

Tralee is at the junction of the N21 from Limerick (about 1½ hours away), the N21 and N22 from Killarney (about a half-hour away), and the N86 from Dingle (an hour and 15 minutes away). It's also the terminus for the train from Dublin (the trip takes 3 hours and 45 minutes) and is well served by buses from Shannon Airport, Limerick, Killarney, and Dingle. There's a bus service that circles the town every hour, mainly to facilitate students; visit the tourist information office for details.

CONTACTS **Tralee Bus Station.** ⊠ John Joe Sheehy Rd. ☎ 066/716–4700. **Tralee Rail Station.** ⊠ Casement Station, John Joe Sheehy Rd. ☎ 066/712–3522 ⊕ www. irishrail.ie.

VISITOR INFORMATION
CONTACTS **Tralee Tourist Office.** ⊠ Ashe Memorial Hall, Denny St. ☎ 066/712–1288 ⊕ www.discoverireland.ie/traleetio.

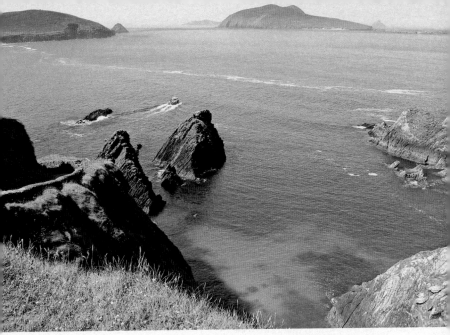

Almost as memorable as the boat ride to the Skellig isles is the excursion out to the unspoiled Blasket Islands, a favorite escape for poets and writers.

Sights

Kerry County Museum

MUSEUM | FAMILY | Tralee's major cultural attraction traces the history of Kerry's people since 5000 BC, using dioramas and an entertaining audiovisual show. There is an excellent display on Roger Casement, the celebrated humanitarian activist whose brief sojourn in Kerry during Ireland's Easter Rising had a huge impact locally and internationally. You can also walk through a life-size reconstruction of a Tralee street of the Middle Ages. ⊠ *Ashe Memorial Hall, Denny St.* ☎ *066/712–7777* ⊕ *www.kerrymuseum. ie* ☒ *€5* ⊘ *Sept.–May, closed Sun. and Mon.*

Tralee Bay Wetlands Center

BODY OF WATER | FAMILY | Get to know the birdlife of the area before venturing on to Kerry's many beaches by visiting this small but effective center, just a short drive from town. The trail offers bird hides, and the nature zone will help you identify the many wading birds of the area, while the viewing tower reveals the vast expanse of Tralee Bay and the Slieve Mish mountains. It is also one of the best lunch places in town, with wholesome, homemade, hot daily specials, salads, wraps, and paninis. ⊠ *Ballyard Rd* ⊹ *Off main N86 Dingle road on Wild Atlantic Way* ☎ *066/712–6700* ⊕ *www.tralee-baywetlands.org* ☒ *€6, café free* ⊘ *Last admission 4:30, 6:30 July and Aug.*

Restaurants

Bella Bia

$$ | ITALIAN | Bia is Irish for food, so as the name suggests, the idea here is to combine Irish hospitality with Italian cuisine. The busy restaurant is just across the road from Siamsa Tíre (the Irish Folk Theatre), on the ground floor of a characterful slate-fronted town house. Pine-top tables are candlelit, and informally set with red paper napkins. Turnover here is brisk, and advance booking is advisable. The three-course set menu is good value at €22. Local prawns feature with garlic, tomato, and brandy in a fettucine dish, while lamb chops with mushrooms, rosemary, and white wine sauce makes a successful Irish-Italian combo. Vegan and vegetarian specials are also available. In summer, you are encouraged to end your meal by lingering over an Irish coffee in the heated garden. **Known for:** good value set menu; wide variety of meat and fish dishes; heated garden for lingering over a drink in summer. $ *Average main: €22 ⊠ 1 Ivy Terr. ⊹ Across road from Siamsa Tire (Folk theater)* ☎ *066/714–4896.*

The Daily Grind

$ | CAFÉ | In the heart of Tralee's pedestrianized town center, this place is known for the best barista coffee in town. Grab a freshly baked scone while you can (they sell out early) or choose from the simple daytime menu, which features lasagna, quiche of the day, homemade soup, and gourmet sandwiches. There are three interconnecting rooms around a central patio, with daily newspapers and Wi-Fi supplied for free. **Known for:** freshly baked scones; excellent lasagna; best coffee in town. $ *Average main: €8 ⊠ 33 The Mall* ☎ *066/712–8728.*

Hotels

★ Ballygarry House Hotel

$$ | HOTEL | A mile and a half outside town, this family-run hotel with 6 acres of gardens and supremely stylish guest rooms is an excellent choice if you're touring by car. **Pros:** next to a woodland amenity area for runners; free access to spa and outdoor hot tub; Brooks Restaurant is highly reputed. **Cons:** no shops or cafés within walking distance; older "classic" rooms a bit plain, worth upgrading to "superior"; often hosts large weddings. $ *Rooms from: €160 ⊠ Leebrook* ☎ *066/712–3322* ⊕ *www.ballygarryhouse.com* ⊷ *64 rooms* ⦿*| Free breakfast.*

Brook Manor Lodge

$$ | B&B/INN | Set against a dramatic backdrop of the Slieve Mish Mountain, this large double-gable country house is a nice option, both as a touring base and for avoiding Tralee's notoriously snarled-up traffic and late-night noise. **Pros:** quiet and spacious; nearby beaches and golfing; delicious breakfast. **Cons:** no nearby village; no pub in walking distance. $ *Rooms from: €120 ⊠ Fenit Rd. (R558)* ☎ *066/712–0406* ⊕ *www.brookmanorlodge.com* ⊘ *Closed mid-Nov.–mid-Mar.* ⊷ *8 rooms* ⦿*| Free breakfast.*

Nightlife

The Abbey Inn

BARS/PUBS | Slap-bang in the middle of the town center, this two-story inn stays open late up to seven nights a week, and has live music and DJs, big-screen sports, and poker classics. ⊠ *Bridge St.* ☎ *066/712–3390.*

Performing Arts

National Folk Theater of Ireland (Siamsa Tíre)

THEATER | Language is no barrier to the supremely colorful entertainment offered by this theater, which re-creates traditional rural life through music, mime, and dance. ⊠ *Town Park* ☎ *066/712–3055* ⊕ *www.siamsatire.com.*

Activities

GOLF
★ Ballybunion Golf Club

GOLF | President Bill Clinton will be eternally associated in Irish golfers' minds with this revered course. In fact, there's even a brass statue of him teeing off in the nearby village, to commemorate his visit here in 1999. On the shore of the Atlantic where the Shannon Estuary meets the open sea, Ballybunion has the huge dunes of County Clare's Lahinch courses without the blind shots. It's no pushover, but every hole is pleasurable. Watch out for "Mrs. Simpson," a double fairway bunker on the 1st hole, named after the wife of Tom Simpson, the architect who remodeled the course in 1937. (Tom Watson did the same in 1995.) The Cashen Course, which opened in 1985, was designed by Robert Trent Jones Sr. and currently is available at a bargain rate if you've paid for a round on the Old Course. ⊠ *Sandhill Rd., Ballybunion* ☎ *068/27146* ⊕ *www.ballybuniongolfclub.ie* ✍ *Old Course: mid-Apr.–early Oct. €230; Cashen Course: mid-Apr.–early Oct. €80; €210 to play both on same day* ⅄ *Old Course: 18 holes, 6568 yards, par 72; Cashen Course: 18 holes, 6306 yards, par 70.*

Tralee Golf Club

GOLF | Tralee is what all modern golf-course architects *wish* they could do in the States: find unspoiled, seaside links and route a course on it that's designed for the modern game. This is an Arnold Palmer–Ed Seay design that opened in 1984, and the location is fantastic—cliffs, craters, dunes, and the gale-blowing ocean. Don't let the flat front 9 lull you to sleep—the back 9 can be a ferocious wake-up call. ⊠ *West Barrow, Ardfert* ☎ *066/713–6379* ⊕ *www.traleegolfclub.com* ✍ *May–Sept. €230, Apr. and Oct. and Nov.–Mar. €160* ⅄ *18 holes, 6975 yards, par 72* ⊘ *Closed to nonmembers Wed. and Sun. Sept.–May.*

Adare

19 km (12 miles) southwest of Limerick City, 82 km (51 miles) northeast of Tralee.

On the banks of the River Maigue, this once-upon-a-time-ified village dotted with thatch cottages is famed as one of Ireland's prettiest spots. It was given a beauty makeover by a rich Anglo lord, the 3rd Earl of Dunraven, in the 1820s and 1830s, in an effort to create the "perfect rustic village." To a great extent, he succeeded.

Few local feathers were ruffled since Dunraven won goodwill by restoring many villagers' houses. Playing into the mid-19th-century vogue for romantic rusticity, the earl "picturesquely" restored many of the town's historic sights, including the remains of two 13th-century abbeys, a 15th-century friary, and the keep of the 13th-century **Desmond Castle** (now the centerpiece of a private golf course). Adjacent to the Adare Heritage Centre you'll find the **Trinitarian Priory**, founded in 1230 and now a convent. From the main bridge (where you can best view the castle), head to the **Augustinian Priory** and its gracious cloister. The most fetching time-burnished allure is provided by Adare's stone-built, thatch-roof cottages, often adorned with colorful, flower-filled window boxes and built for the earl's estate tenants. Some now house boutiques selling Irish crafts and antiques, along with a fine restaurant called the Wild Geese. Adare Manor, an imposing Tudor–Gothic Revival mansion, which was once the grand house of the Dunraven peerage, is now a celebrated hotel; on its grounds you can view two 12th-century ruins, the **St. Nicholas Chapel** and the **Chantry Chapel**.

GETTING HERE AND AROUND
Adare is on the main road (N21) between Tralee and Limerick, just over an hour from Tralee and about 20 minutes from Limerick. The parking lot is in the center of town behind the Adare Heritage Centre; parking here is free. Buses on the Limerick–Tralee route stop at the Heritage Centre.

Sights

Adare Heritage Centre
INFO CENTER | This center is home to an array of helpful facilities, including a restaurant and three retail outlets (one sells sweaters, another crafts, and the third heraldry items). There is also an exhibition on Adare's history since 1223, complete with a 15-minute audiovisual display, but some may feel it is not worth the extra fee. Guided tours of Desmond Castle (June–September; €6) can be booked in advance online, and leave the center by bus. ⊠ Main St. ☎ 061/396–666 ⊕ www.adareheritagecentre.ie 🖼 Heritage center free, exhibition €5.

🍴 Restaurants

★ The Wild Geese
$$$ | MODERN EUROPEAN | There's a charming, old-world atmosphere in the series of small dining rooms in this low-ceiling thatched cottage, one of the prettiest in a village famed for its fairy-tale looks. Co-owner and chef David Foley uses the best local produce to create imaginative and seriously good dishes (try the pan-seared scallops with slow-cooked pork belly). **Known for:** sophisticated modern Irish food; inventive mains; great value three-course Sunday lunch. ⑤ Average main: €26 ⊠ Rose Cottage, Main St. ✛ Opposite Dunraven Arms ☎ 061/396–451 ⊕ www.thewild-geese. com ⊗ Closed Mon., and 3 wks in Jan. No dinner Sun.; no lunch Tues.–Thurs.

Hotels

★ Adare Manor Hotel
$$$$ | HOTEL | Play king or queen for a day at this spectacular, recently overhauled, Victorian Gothic mansion, once the abode of the earls of Dunraven and still a wonderland, thanks to 840 well-manicured acres outside and the 36-foot-high, 100-foot-long Minstrels' Gallery with its decorated ceiling and stained-glass

As cute as a Fisher-Price toy village, Adare is a thatched-roof jewel laid out with characteristics that conjure up the English rather than the Irish countryside.

windows inside. **Pros:** fully updated Gothic mansion; one of Ireland's best golf courses; excellent amenities including a cinema, spa, and pool. **Cons:** off the beaten track as a touring base; expensive. ⑤ *Rooms from: €595* ✉ *Limerick Rd.* ☎ *061/396–566* ⊕ *www.adaremanor. ie* ↪ *108 rooms* ⦿ *Free breakfast.*

Dunraven Arms Hotel

$$$ | HOTEL | Charles Lindbergh stayed here in Room 6 while he advised on the nearby Shannon Airport's design, and he might still cotton to this tranquil, antiques-adorned landmark, established as a coach stop in 1792, even though it is now somewhat overrestored and generic. **Pros:** the staff make it a memorable Irish experience; in a pretty village; very relaxing ambience. **Cons:** interior design verges on bland; expensive for what it is; Adare itself a small village of limited appeal. ⑤ *Rooms from: €180* ✉ *Main St.* ☎ *061/605–900* ⊕ *www.dunravenhotel. com* ↪ *86 rooms* ⦿ *Free breakfast.*

Fitzgeralds Woodlands House Hotel and Spa

$$ | HOTEL | FAMILY | On 44 acres of landscaped grounds on the Limerick side of the village, this former B&B has evolved into a thriving modern hotel in the energetic, capable hands of the Fitzgerald family. **Pros:** young, enthusiastic staff; jolly and unpretentious; good sports amenities. **Cons:** a sprawling, undistinguished modern building; about 3 km (2 miles) outside the village; no elevator. ⑤ *Rooms from: €130* ✉ *Knockanes* ☎ *061/605–100* ⊕ *www.woodlands-hotel.ie* ↪ *98 rooms* ⦿ *Free breakfast.*

★ Mustard Seed at Echo Lodge

$$ | B&B/INN | This is the small country hotel of your dreams: a Victorian yellow-stucco jewel set atop a small hill overlooking Ballingarry, a village that time forgot, deep in rural Ireland, yet only 13 km (8 miles) southwest of Adare. **Pros:** stylish flair; extremely comfortable; acclaimed restaurant. **Cons:** in the middle of nowhere; rooster crows at dawn. ⑤ *Rooms from: €140* ✉ *Village Center, Ballingarry* ☎ *069/68508* ⊕ *www.*

mustardseed.ie ⊘ *Closed last 2 wks in Jan.* ⇌ *16 rooms* ⦿ *Free breakfast.*

Shopping

Draiocht Art Gallery
ART GALLERIES | *Draiocht* means "magic" in Irish, and this gallery is described by its owner as "a magical store of crafts and gifts." Many of the crafts and ceramics are Irish-made, and the colorful paintings in its large gallery come from all over Ireland. ⊠ *Station Rd., Blackabbey, across side road from Heritage Centre* ☎ *061/395–539* ⊕ *www.draiochtadare.ie.*

George & Michelina Stacpoole
ANTIQUES/COLLECTIBLES | Head here to find a nice selection of antiques large and small, plus books, and knitwear designed by Michelina. ⊠ *Main St.* ☎ *061/396–409.*

Lucy Erridge's
JEWELRY/ACCESSORIES | This cottage boutique has Irish-made jewelry and fine ladies' wear from Irish designer labels. ⊠ *Main St.* ☎ *061/396–898.*

Activities

GOLF

Adare Manor Golf Course
GOLF | Connected with the celebrated Adare Manor luxury hotel, this parkland stretch is on the ancestral estate of the Earl of Dunraven. Its immediate success was virtually guaranteed by the international profile of its designer, Robert Trent Jones Sr. The front 9 are dominated by an artificial 14-acre lake with a $500,000 polyethylene base. It's in play at the 3rd, 5th, 6th, and 7th holes. The dominant hazards on the homeward journey are the River Mague and the majestic trees, which combine to make the par-5 18th one of the most challenging finishing holes imaginable. ⊠ *Adare* ☎ *061/395–044* ⊕ *www.adaremanor.com* ⊠ *June–Sept. €360 (€250 hotel guests), Oct.–May €290 (€250 hotel guests)* ⅃ *18 holes, 7453 yards, par 72.*

Limerick City

19 km (12 miles) northeast of Adare, 198 km (123 miles) southwest of Dublin.

Before you ask, there's *no* direct connection between Limerick City and the facetious five-line verse form known as a "limerick," which was first popularized by the English writer Edward Lear in his 1846 *Book of Nonsense.* The city, at the head of the Shannon Estuary and at the intersection of a number of major crossroads, is an industrial port and the republic's third-largest city (population 75,000). If you fly into or out of Shannon Airport, and have a few hours to spare, do take a look around. The attractions around the cathedral and the castle are linked by a riverside footpath, while the western part of the town center is dominated by mid-18th-century buildings with fine Georgian proportions. What's more, the city has undergone considerable revitalization since the days recounted in Frank McCourt's famed childhood memoir, *Angela's Ashes.* Limerick was Ireland's first national City of Culture in 2014, resulting in ongoing intensified activity in the arts sector.

GETTING HERE AND AROUND
Limerick is a major gateway to the Southwest and the West of Ireland, and is linked to Dublin by the M7 motorway (the drive is about 2½ hours). Cork is two hours south on the N20. A tunnel under the city links the Cork road with the road to Shannon Airport (N19) and the N18 to Galway (about 1½ hours). There are excellent express bus links to these cities and to Killarney. Limerick has a rail link to Dublin via Limerick Junction, and a smaller commuter line travels via Ennis to Galway (two hours). Citylink buses, bookable online only, serve Dublin, Shannon, and Cork airports.

Within the city, there is a regular bus service for shoppers connecting the historic center with the newer Crescent

Looming over Adare's Desmond Castle is the regal Adare Manor Hotel, once home to the town's lord of the manor, the Earl of Dunraven.

Shopping Centre at Dooradoyle. If driving, it's advisable to use a multistory parking garage, as on-street parking can be hard to find. If you do get lucky, you'll have to become familiar with "disk" parking regulations, which involve buying a ticket (or disk) for around €2 an hour from a machine or a shop and displaying it. Beware: car-clamper officers are active!

CONTACTS Limerick Bus Station. ✉ Colbert Station Forecourt, Parnell St. ☎ 061/313–333 ⊕ www.buseireann.ie. **Limerick Rail Station.** ✉ Colbert Station, Parnell St. ☎ 061/315–555.

TOURS

Limerick Civic Trust

To appreciate Limerick's long and eventful history, take a 45-minute guided tour of medieval Limerick and the Masonic Lodge with Limerick Civic Trust. Advance booking is required. ✉ Church St. ☎ 061/313–399 ⊕ www.limerickcivictrust. ie.

Shannonside Tours

City walks are scheduled from May to mid-October and can be booked at the tourist office, the departure point. Choose between Georgian Limerick, including Frank McCourt's *Angela's Ashes,* and medieval Limerick. At other times of the year small groups can book in advance directly with Noel Curtin. ✉ Limerick City Tourist Office, Arthur's Quay ☎ 087/235–1339 Noel Curtin (mid-Oct.–Apr.), 061/317–339 Limerick Tourist Office (May–mid-Oct.).

VISITOR INFORMATION
CONTACTS Limerick City Tourist Office. ✉ Arthur's Quay ☎ 061/317–522 ⊕ www. discoverireland.ie.

Sights

There has been a huge investment in Limerick's inner city in recent years, and it is finally starting to pay off. The snarled-up traffic that used to bedevil the city center has been eased by the opening of an east–west tunnel that takes much of the heavy traffic along with its noise and pollution under the River Shannon instead of across it. An attractive riverside walk now leads visitors past the Hunt Museum to the city's medieval center, which is sited, as in Paris, on a small island surrounded by rushing water. Bars and restaurants have started to colonize the quiet riverside quays between the Hunt Museum and the Absolute Hotel, while the Georgian Quarter now has a focal point in One Pery Square, an elegant 18th-century town house converted into a popular hotel, spa, and bistro. The good-natured sporting passion of Limerick's rugby supporters is legendary, and if you are in town on a match day it will never be forgotten. At any time of year, Limerick's reputation for friendliness is a genuine phenomenon: total strangers will engage you in conversation on the street—relax and enjoy!

Cruises Street

NEIGHBORHOOD | An inviting pedestrian thoroughfare, this street has chic shops and occasional street entertainers. ☒ *Opposite side of O'Connell St. from Arthur's Quay Shopping Centre.*

The Frank McCourt Museum

MUSEUM | FAMILY | This imposing redbrick building dating from 1814 was once the school attended by American-Irish author, Frank McCourt (1930–2009), best known for his "misery memoir" (later a movie) *Angela's Ashes,* the story of his impoverished Limerick childhood. See the actual classroom in use in the 1930s, posters and photographs of the Pulitzer Prize–winning author, and a replica of the McCourt home in this modest but oddly touching tribute. ☒ *Hartstonge St.* ☎ *061/319–710* ⊕ *frankmccmuseum. wixsite.com/frankmccourtmuseum* ☎ *€5* ⊘ *Closed weekends Nov.–Mar.*

Hunt Museum

MUSEUM | In the Old Customs House on the banks of the Shannon in the city center, the Hunt Museum has the finest collection of Celtic and medieval treasures outside the National Museum in Dublin. Ancient Irish metalwork, European objets d'art, and a selection of 20th-century European and Irish paintings—including works by Jack B. Yeats—are on view. A café overlooks the river. ☒ *Rutland St.* ☎ *061/312–833* ⊕ *www. huntmuseum.com* ☎ *€5 (free Sun.).*

King John's Castle

CASTLE/PALACE | FAMILY | First built by the Normans in the early 1200s, King John's Castle still bears traces on its north side of a 1691 bombardment. If you climb the drum towers (the oldest section), you'll have a good view of the city and the Shannon. Inside, a 22-minute audiovisual show illustrates the history of Limerick and Ireland; an archaeology center has three excavated, pre-Norman houses; and two exhibition centers display scale models of Limerick from its founding in AD 922. ☒ *King's Island* ☎ *061/360–788* ⊕ *www.shannonheritage.com/KingJohnsCastle* ☎ *€11.*

Limerick City Gallery of Art

ART GALLERIES—ARTS | With its home in the historic Carnegie Building, this has now been converted into one of Ireland's finest galleries of contemporary art. Along with a small but charming permanent collection of Irish art, it also mounts exhibits of international contemporary art. The café has excellent home baking and coffee, and is a hub of the local community. ☒ *Carnegie Bldg., Pery Sq.* ☎ *061/310–633* ⊕ *gallery.limerick.ie* ☎ *Free.*

O'Connell Street

NEIGHBORHOOD | Here you can find Limerick City's main shopping area, which consists mostly of modest chain stores. However, the street lies one block inland from (east of) the Arthur's Quay Shopping Centre, through which it can be reached. Along with the futuristic tourist information center, this was part of a successful campaign to develop the Shannonside quays. ☒ *Limerick City.*

St. Mary's Cathedral

RELIGIOUS SITE | Limerick is a predominantly Catholic city, but the Protestant St. Mary's Cathedral is the city's oldest religious building. Once a 12th-century palace—pilasters and a rounded Romanesque entrance were part of the original structure—it dates mostly from the 15th century. The black-oak carvings on misericords in the choir stalls are from this period. ✉ *Bridge St.* ☎ *061/310–293* ⊕ *www.cathedral.limerick.anglican.org* ☞ *€5.*

 ## Restaurants

★ Sash

$$ | **IRISH** | Housed in an elegant Georgian room complete with sash windows (hence the name), this relaxed, modern bistro is the see-and-be-seen destination for Limerick's movers and shakers. It is also known for its robust, brasserie-style cooking, its daily specials chosen according to market availability. **Known for:** vegetables from their own garden; grilled rib-eye steak; interesting wine list featuring small vineyards. ⑤ *Average main: €24* ✉ *1 Pery Sq.* ☎ *061/402–402* ⊕ *www.oneperysquare.com/sash-restaurant* ⊗ *No dinner Sun.–Thurs., but bar menu available in Park Room.*

Hotels

Absolute Hotel

$$ | **HOTEL** | Conveniently located on a riverbend in Limerick's medieval center, this boat-shape hotel, marked by its pronounced architecture and design, is a great base for city sightseeing, dining, and shopping. **Pros:** museums and bars within 100 yards; short walk to shopping area; reasonably priced food and drink. **Cons:** secure private parking is limited (€5 for nearby public parking); not easy to find. ⑤ *Rooms from: €120* ✉ *Sir Harry's Mall, Island Rd.* ☎ *061/463–600* ⊕ *www.absolutehotel.com* ⌑ *99 rooms* ⦿ *Free breakfast.*

Limerick City Hotel

$ | **HOTEL** | **FAMILY** | Clean, airy, and in good shape (unlike some of Limerick's other inner-city lodgings), this big, well-run hotel has recently been refurbished. **Pros:** good value for couples and families; central location, 30 minutes to Shannon Airport; adjacent to riverside walks. **Cons:** nothing exciting about the experience; no free parking, but good rates offered at adjacent multistory car park. ⑤ *Rooms from: €110* ✉ *Lower Mallow St.* ☎ *061/207–000* ⊕ *www.limerickcityhotel.ie* ⌑ *141 rooms* ⦿ *Free breakfast.*

One Pery Square

$$ | **HOTEL** | One of Limerick's finest Georgian houses—a tall redbrick structure with classical cut-stone portico, overlooking leafy People's Park—has been converted into a sumptuous boutique hotel with a reputation for attentive service. **Pros:** genuinely stylish; private parking; excellent service. **Cons:** you need to book well in advance; no air-conditioning. ⑤ *Rooms from: €140* ✉ *1 Pery Sq.* ☎ *061/402–402* ⊕ *www.oneperysquare.com* ⌑ *20 rooms* ⦿ *Free breakfast.*

 ## Nightlife

Curragower Pub

BARS/PUBS | Across the river from King John's Castle, this is a favorite haunt of music students from Limerick University. You can hear good traditional music nightly from May through September, and Wednesday through Saturday in winter. ✉ *Clancy's Strand* ☎ *061/321–788* ⊕ *www.curragower.com.*

Dolan's Pub

BARS/PUBS | A lively waterfront spot, Dolan's has traditional Irish music every night, and dancing classes from September to May. Dolan's Warehouse, under the same management and in the same location, is a live-music venue with top national and international acts. ✉ *3–4 Dock Rd.* ☎ *061/314–483* ⊕ *www.dolans.ie.*

The Locke Bar & Oyster House

BARS/PUBS | Set on the riverside, this is one of Limerick's oldest bars, dating from 1724, and has live music every night. It's also a great place for outdoor drinking in summer, or a simple bar food meal ⊠ *3 George's Quay* ☎ *061/413–733* ⊕ *www. lockebar.com.*

Nancy Blake's Pub

BARS/PUBS | There's traditional music at this busy pub year-round on Sunday night from 9 pm, and also on Wednesday and Thursday. ⊠ *19 Denmark St.* ☎ *061/416–443.*

W.J. South's Pub

BARS/PUBS | An old-fashioned pub, this one is typical of the age of Frank McCourt's *Angela's Ashes*. There's no music, but drop by for hearty bar food or a drink after visiting the nearby Frank McCourt Museum. ⊠ *4 Quinlan St.* ☎ *061/318–850.*

 # Shopping

MALLS AND SHOPPING CENTERS

Arthur's Quay Shopping Centre

CLOTHING | A small indoor shopping mall near the tourist office, Arthur's Quay has a fine choice of Irish crafts and knitwear. ⊠ *Patrick St.* ☎ *061/419–888* ⊕ *www. arthursquay-shopping.com.*

The Milk Market

OUTDOOR/FLEA/GREEN MARKETS | Occupying a historic site two blocks east of Arthur's Quay (ask at the tourist information office), the Milk Market is a vibrant weekend market selling virtually everything but milk. On Friday the emphasis is on fashion and crafts, Saturday is the big food day, featuring many local artisanal producers, and Sunday adds antiques and a flea-market ambience into the mix of food and handicrafts. ⊠ *Cornmarket Row* ☎ *061/214–782* ⊕ *www.milkmarketlimerick.ie.*

O'Mahony's

BOOKS/STATIONERY | Known for its good selection of Irish interest, this shop has been selling books since 1902. ⊠ *120 O'Connell St.* ☎ *061/418–155* ⊕ *www. omahonys.ie.*

COUNTY CLARE, GALWAY CITY, AND THE ARAN ISLANDS

Updated by
Vic O'Sullivan

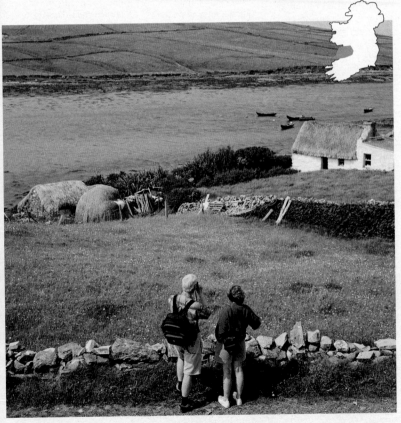

⊙ Sights	🍴 Restaurants	🛏 Hotels	🛍 Shopping	🍸 Nightlife
★★★★★	★★★★★	★★★★☆	★★★★☆	★★★★★

WELCOME TO COUNTY CLARE, GALWAY CITY, AND THE ARAN ISLANDS

TOP REASONS TO GO

★ **Atlantic Coast:** County Clare's slice of the Wild Atlantic Way driving route is 75 miles of mind-blowing seascapes, which peaks, literally, with the colossal Cliffs of Moher.

★ **Galway City:** With great restaurants, bars, shopping, and a vibrant arts scene throughout its cobbled medieval quarter, Galway is a lively city that loves to celebrate.

★ **Dun Aengus, Aran Islands:** Rivaling the Cliffs of Moher for its edge-of-the-world setting, Dun Aengus fort on Inis Mór, the largest of the Aran Islands, stands 100 meters high and barrier-free above the Atlantic Ocean.

★ **The Burren Food Trail:** Artisanal chocolatiers, cheese makers, confectioners, farmers, and beekeepers are harnessing the Burren's unique landscape using age-old techniques, putting this UNESCO Global Geopark at the helm of Ireland's emerging food scene.

Without ever passing beyond the perimeter of this region, visitors get to sample the best of Ireland's attributes like a well-thought-out tasting menu. The west coast of County Clare and the Aran Islands offer cinematic seascapes, music, age-old Irish traditions, and, of course, the giant Cliffs of Moher and mysterious rocky Burren Park. The rural villages, country castles, lakes, and pastures of Clare match every preconception of Ireland's varied green landscape while Galway City is easily the liveliest city in Ireland after Dublin.

1 Bunratty Village. A medieval village and Durty Nelly's Pub hugging Bunratty Castle.

2 Quin. A rural village home to a worth-visiting abbey, fort, early-Celt dwellings, and a stunning castle-hotel.

3 Ennis. The lively county town with good pubs and live music.

4 Killaloe. A good base to explore the River Shannon by boat.

5 Kilkee. A quiet seaside town with a crescent-shape beach and the stunning Loop Head Peninsula.

6 Lahinch. A popular seaside town for surfers and walkers and a good base to explore area attractions.

7 The Cliffs of Moher. One of Ireland's top attractions.

8 Doolin. A tiny fishing village known for its live music and pubs and a launch pad to the Aran Islands.

9 The Burren. A dramatic landscape home to forts, megalithic tombs, and rare flora and fauna.

10 Ballyvaughan. A pretty village on the water and good base for exploring the Burren.

11 Kinvara. Set on a pretty harbor and known for its good pubs, festivals, and oysters.

12 Coole Park. A nature reserve and popular haunt for W.B. Yeats fans.

13 Galway City. Ireland's liveliest city, named European Capital of Culture 2020.

14 The Aran Islands. A short ferry ride from Galway or Doolin, these rocky isles are home to prehistoric sites and beautiful scenery.

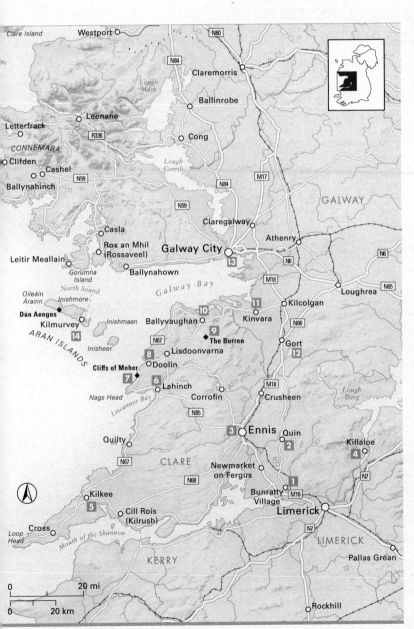

Clare Island

Westport

CONNEMARA

Letterfrack

Clifden

Cashel

Ballynahinch

N59

Leenane

R336

Cong

Lough Mask

N84

Claremorris

N60

Ballinrobe

Lough Corrib

M17

N84

N59

Casla

Ros an Mhíl (Rossaveel)

Leitir Meallain

Gorumna Island

North Sound

Ballynahown

Claregalway

Galway City

Athenry

GALWAY

N6

N6

Oileáin Árainn

Inishmore

Dún Aengus

Kilmurvey

14

ARAN ISLANDS

Inishmaan

Inisheer

Galway Bay

Ballyvaughan

10

The Burren

9

11

Kinvara

Kilcolgan

M18

N66

Loughrea

N65

Nags Head

N67

Lisdoonvarna

8

Doolin

Cliffs of Moher

7

6

Lahinch

Corrofin

Liscannor Bay

Gort

12

M18

Crusheen

Lough Derg

N85

Quilty

N67

CLARE

N68

Kilkee

5

Cill Rois (Kilrush)

Cross

Loop Head

Mouth of the Shannon

KERRY

Newmarket on Fergus

Ennis

3

Quin

2

Killaloe

4

N7

Bunratty Village

1

M18

Limerick

N7

LIMERICK

Pallas Green

Rockhill

0   20 mi

0   20 km

The West of Ireland is the most westerly seaboard in Europe, and the part of Ireland least influenced by its neighbor to the east, England. Galway and West Clare are where the Irish go to reconnect with their heritage, whether by practicing their jigs at the Fleadh Nua folk festival, enjoying "the craic" at the Lisdoonvarna Matchmaking Festival, visiting the ancient megalithic tombs of the Burren, or trading news with a Gaeltacht (Irish-speaking) resident. Wherever you go in the West, you'll not only see, but more important hear, how the best of traditional Ireland survives.

This area is distinctly different from the rest of Ireland and is bent on retaining its unspoiled, rugged way of life. With much of nature's magnificence on display—the majestic Cliffs of Moher, the rocky Burren, and the sublime Aran Islands—it's easy to see why. Visitors continue to relish the unique thrill of standing high above the pounding Atlantic, watching seabirds reel below, as the numerous Cliffs of Moher posts on social media demonstrate.

West Clare, in fact, is the guardian of Ireland's musical traditions, where people still flock to learn new dance steps and fiddle riffs. The hub of the area remains Galway, the city that loves to celebrate. Saunter through its naturally festive, pedestrianized center and the city's many pubs, and you will find proof of Galway's reputation for good times. Not far away is the town of Ennis, and villages like Doolin and Kinvara, also noted as trad-music hot spots.

Visitors will find, particularly in western County Galway, the highest concentration of Gaeltacht communities in Ireland, with roughly 40,000 native Irish speakers and the country's first Irish-language TV station based in tiny An Spidéal (Spiddle), a suburb of Galway City. You'll see plenty of signs printed in Irish only. This is especially the case on the isolated Oileáin Árainn (Aran Islands), where many Irish schoolchildren have their first experience of a place where Irish is the main language during summer camps. These limestone islands are actually geological extensions of the mainland expanse known as the Burren, a craggy landscape rich in megalithic remains, unique geological formations, rare flora and fauna, and a rich history of myth and legend.

MAJOR REGIONS

County Clare claims two of Ireland's unique natural sights: the awesome **Cliffs of Moher** and the stark, mournful landscape of **the Burren,** which hugs the coast from Black Head to the Cliffs of Moher. In fact, the county's entire Atlantic coastline offers magnificent views from **Ballyvaughan** in the north to beyond **Kilkee** in the south. Venture inland to discover the medieval charms of **Bunratty, Killaloe, Quin,** or the county's lively capital town of **Ennis.** Whether you're looking for inimitable countryside scenery, the perfect wave in **Lahinch,** the challenging hiking trails in the Burren, or just a guaranteed Irish music session any night of the week in **Doolin,** you can find it in Clare. Just beyond the county border in South Galway is the heartland of the Irish literary revival which took place in **Kinvara,** with its famous bay side tower house and **Coole Park.**

Galway City. Just an hour's drive north from Ennis in County Clare, the walkable harbor city of Galway, is one of Ireland's prettiest cities and definitely one of its liveliest. The short drive to Clare and surrounding Galway attractions like Connemara, makes Galway City a great base for exploring the West of Ireland.

The Aran Islands. An hour or less from the mainland via ferry are the ageless Aran Islands. Once famed for their isolation, they are now disturbed a bit by some 60,000-plus curious visitors every summer, but even so they retain a distinctive identity, with traditional communities where Irish is still the daily language. Swap the car for a bike to discover the drystone walls and gigantic ocean views from the deserted lanes of these three islands, **Inis Mor (Inishmore), Inis Meain (Inishmaan),** and **Inis Oirr (Inisheer).**

Planning

Getting Here and Around

AIR TRAVEL

Shannon Airport, 93 km (55 miles) south of Galway in County Clare, is the most accessible point of entry for international travelers to this region. Flying time from Dublin is about 30 minutes. Aer Arann services all three Aran Islands from Connemara Airport at Inverin, which is 27 km (16 miles) west of Galway on R336. Ask about transport to the airport when buying your ticket: there is usually a courtesy bus from the center of Galway City.

Dublin Airport offers a wider range of international routes and is 216 km (134 miles) east of Galway by motorway.

AIRLINE CONTACTS Aer Arann Islands. ☎ *091/593–034* ⊕ *www.aerarannislands. ie.*

AIRPORTS Aerfort Chonamara/Connemara Airport. ✉ *Caislean Inveran Inverin, Co. Galway* ✈ *30 km (19 miles) due west on R336* ☎ *091/593–034* ⊕ *www.aeraran-nislands.ie.* **Shannon Airport.** ✈ *235 km (149 miles) west of Dublin Airport on M7* ☎ *061/712–000* ⊕ *www.shannonairport. ie/.*

AIRPORT TRANSFERS

With all the major car rental companies in its concourse and frequent bus transport on-site, Shannon Airport is well connected to Galway, Limerick, and Ennis by road. The M18 opened in late 2017, cutting the drive from Shannon Airport to Galway to just one hour. The airport is 25 km (16 miles) south of Ennis, 84 km (52 miles) south of Galway, and 64 km (40 miles) southeast of Doolin, the seasonal port for the Aran Islands.

BOAT AND FERRY TRAVEL
FROM KERRY TO CLARE

The Tarbert–Killimer Ferry leaves every hour on the half hour and takes 20 minutes to cross the Shannon Estuary from North County Kerry to West County Clare. Alternatively, the Shannon tunnel, which bypasses Limerick City, is a quicker route to north Clare from Dingle and Killarney. The ferry runs every day of the year except Christmas and costs €20 one-way, €30 round-trip. Cyclists, pedestrians, and motorcyclists pay €5 one-way. (Ferries return from Killimer every hour on the hour.)

CONTACTS Clare Island Ferry Company.
☎ 098/23737 ⊕ www.clareislandferry.com. **Corrib Cruises.** ☎ 087/994–6380 ⊕ www.corribcruises.com. **Killary Cruises.** ✉ Nancy's Point ☎ 091/566–736 ⊕ www.killaryfjord.com/.

TO THE ARAN ISLANDS

The spell of the famed Oileáin Árainn (Aran Islands) is such that many travelers can't resist their siren call and make for the first ferry leaving from Doolin, which offers rates of €10 one-way. There are two ferry operators on the pier. A new boat in 2018, the M.V. *Doolin Express,* cuts the transfer time from Doolin to the islands in half to 20 minutes.

Departures from Doolin to Inis Oirr are at 10, 11, 1, 4, and 5:30. The last ferry back to Doolin leaves at 4:45. In Doolin, you can book your trip in advance online or just walk down to the pier and book a seat. Sailing season is generally March to early November.

Day trips from Galway City leave the city at 9:30 or noon and return by 6:30. Various licensed, escorted tours are available at Galway Tourist Information Office in Forster Place.

The standard ferry deal in Galway City costs €25 round-trip and €9 for bus transfer to the ferry port at Ros an Mhíl (Rossaveal). Look out for money-saving offers that may include bed-and-breakfast accommodations, free transfers to Ros an Mhíl or Connemara Airport (both 40 minutes away), bicycle rental on the islands, or a ferry-out, flight-back plan. There are three different ferry operators, and tickets are not transferable, so check the return sailing times of your operator when you get on board. If you opt for the five-minute flight, for safety reasons, you (yes, you—not your bags) will be weighed at check-in, and allocated an appropriate seat. There are similar combo tickets available from Doolin, with options that include a cruise of nearby Cliffs of Moher, interisland transfers, and overnight stays.

CONTACTS Aran Island Ferries. ✉ Aran Island Ferries, 37–39 Forster St., Galway, Center ☎ 091/568–903 ⊕ www.aranislandferries.com. **Bill O Brien's Doolin Ferry Co.** ✉ No. 1 Doolin Pier, Doolin ☎ 065/707–5555 ⊕ www.doolinferry.com. **Doolin2Aran Ferries.** ✉ Doolin Pier, Doolin ☎ 065/707–5949 ⊕ www.doolin2aranferries.com.

BUS TRAVEL

Shannon Airport, Ennis, and Galway City have excellent connections to and from other regions in Ireland. Bus Éireann has the greatest network of bus routes in Ireland. Its Expressway 20 service connects Galway to Dublin, while its Expressway 51 service connects Cork to Galway via Limerick City, Shannon Airport, and Ennis.

Bus Éireann's regional services can take you from Ennis and Galway to smaller towns and villages throughout the district. Regional service 343 connects Shannon Airport to Limerick and Ennis. For those heading to the coast, regional service 350 connects Ennis and Galway via Lahinch, Doolin, the Cliffs of Moher, and Kinvara.

Dublin Coach's M7 Express brings passengers to Bunratty and Ennis from Dublin and Kerry. City Link connects Galway to Dublin, Cork, and Limerick.

BUS CONTACTS Bus Éireann. ☎ 01/836–6111 in Dublin ⊕ www.buseireann.ie. **Citylink.** ☎ 091/564–164 ⊕ www.citylink. ie. **Dublin Coach.** ☎ 01/465–9972 ⊕ www. dublincoach.ie. **GoBus.ie.** ✉ Gobus Unit 8, Forster Ct., Center ☎ 091/564–600 ⊕ www.gobus.ie.

BUS STATIONS Ennis Bus Station. ✉ Station Rd., Ennis ☎ 065/682–4177 ⊕ www. buseireann.ie/. **Galway Bus Station.** ✉ Station Rd., Galway City ☎ 091/562–000.

CAR TRAVEL
A car is the best mode of transport to navigate all that this region has to offer. Irish airports (Shannon, Dublin, Cork, and Belfast) have an ample supply of car rentals available.

There are three main access points to this area by car from anywhere in Ireland. The M6 (expressway) connects the region to the north and east, including Dublin. The N18 (highway) filters in traffic to South County Clare from the south through a tunnel under the River Shannon (bypassing Limerick City) and onward to Galway by the M18. For those following the Wild Atlantic Way driving route, Shannon Ferries offer an hourly ferry service from Tarbert in County Kerry to Killimer, near the Loop Head peninsula in County Clare. A series of coastal roads lead to the N67 and onward to Galway City. ■TIP→ Time permitting, pull off the M18 at the N85 exit and meander through the Burren.

ROAD CONDITIONS
The West has good, wide main roads (National Primary Routes) and better-than-average local roads (National Secondary Routes), both known as "N" routes. Since late 2017 the M18 has connected the M6 to Galway City, bypassing all towns in between. If you follow the Wild Atlantic Way touring trail on the smaller Regional (R) routes particularly in West Clare, you may encounter some challenging roads. Narrow and twisty, they are also used by hikers and cyclists from April to October, as well as local traffic (which can take the form of huge trucks serving the local agricultural co-ops, school buses, and tractors). The speed limits on these Regional routes is 80 kph (50 mph), even for trucks and buses, so use your common sense and adjust your speed accordingly. ■TIP→ If traffic builds up behind you, it is customary to signal to the left and slow down or pull over to let the locals fly by. Your kind gesture will usually be acknowledged with a flash of lights, nod, or a wave.

TAXI TRAVEL
Taxis operate on the meter for journeys of up to 30 km (22 miles). For longer journeys, agree on the fare in advance. A Shannon Airport to Galway City journey will cost you about €120.

CONTACTS AAA Taxis. ☎ 065/689–2999 ⊕ aaataxisennis.ie. **Big O Taxis.** ✉ 17 Eyre Sq.,, Center ☎ 091/585–858 ⊕ www. bigotaxis.com. **Burren Taxis.** ✉ Fergus Row, Ennis ☎ 065/682–3456. **Galway Taxis.** ✉ 57 Dominick St. Lower, Galway City ☎ 091/561–111 ⊕ www.galwaytaxis. com.

TRAIN TRAVEL
The region's main rail stations are in Galway City and Ennis. Trains for Galway and Ennis leave from Dublin's Heuston Station (on different lines). Fares vary depending on time and season; tickets are generally cheaper if purchased online. Trains run direct to Galway via Athlone, taking about three hours. The cost of an adult one-way ticket from Dublin to Galway is €36.60 (adult same-day return is €39.10; an adult open return costs €51.40) from the booking office or ticket vending machine (TVM). For Ennis—which is reached via the Cork and Tralee line—you must change twice. The cost of an adult one-way ticket from Dublin Heuston to Ennis is €59.90 (adult same-day return is €73.40; an adult open return is €80.60).

The Limerick-to-Galway train stops at Sixmilebridge and Ennis in County Clare and Gort, Ardrahan, Craughwell, Athenry, Oranmore in County Galway before arriving at its destination. Limerick Station connects the region to the south, while Galway connects to Dublin. ■TIP→ **Check out the deeply discounted online fares on Irish Rail's website, which also allows for a free seat reservation. Online tickets go on sale 60 days before the date of travel.**

CONTACTS Ennis Station. ✉ *Quin Rd., Ennis* ☎ *065/684–0444* ⊕ *www.irishrail. ie/.* **Galway Station–Ceannt Railway Station.** ✉ *Eyre Sq., Center* ☎ *091/537–528* ⊕ *www.irishrail.ie.* **Irish Rail–Iarnod Éire-ann.** ✉ *Iarnród Éireann HQ, Connolly Station, Amien St., Dublin 1* ☎ *01/836–6222* ⊕ *www.irishrail.ie.*

Hotels

Since the arrival of Airbnb, a host of quirky properties from medieval tower houses to thatched coastal cottages are now available to rent in this region. Still, some of Ireland's finest country-house and castle hotels are in this area and worth a stay. Indoor pools and tennis courts are the exception rather than the rule in this region, where business is largely seasonal and the emphasis is on outdoor pursuits. Guesthouse properties are in abundance on the Aran Islands and in rural areas, while the region also has its fair share of luxurious retreats. Festivals and events can have an impact on occupancy and rates. Booking ahead for popular locations like Doolin or Galway in July and August is always a good idea. ■TIP→ **Many properties use a popular tourist destination as their address, but these are often miles away from the main drag, on pathless roads. Every building in Ireland has an Eircode (***www.eircode. ie***), which you should ask for to get an exact location before booking.** *Hotel reviews have been shortened. For full information, visit Fodors.com.*

Restaurants

Although some restaurants in remote areas close off-season, the larger towns and main tourism centers offer year-round service. Galway City has one of Ireland's finest dining scenes, which is gaining recognition nationally and around the globe. But some places are culinary landmarks in the region, including the award-winning Wild Honey Inn in Lisdoonvarna, County Clare, where the fare is simple but leaps from the sea to your plate. At the other extreme are more dazzling experiences, like Bunratty's Castle's medieval banquet or the superb formal restaurant at Dromoland Castle. For impromptu dining, wander the towns of Ennis or Galway and you will easily find satisfying and hearty pub fare to restore you.

Restaurant reviews have been shortened. For full information, visit Fodors. com.

What It Costs in Euros			
$	$$	$$$	$$$$
RESTAURANTS			
under €19	€19–€24	€25–€32	over €32
HOTELS			
under €120	€120–€170	€171–€210	over €210

Tours

Galway City Walking Tours
WALKING TOURS | Fiona Brennan meets visitors at Eyre Square for an introduction to Galway, then walks with them to Shop Street, taking in the "Two Wildes," Lynch's Castle, Lynch's window, and St. Nicolas Church before continuing to the King's Head Pub and Kirwins Lane, finishing at the Spanish Arch. The walk lasts about 90 minutes and offers an excellent introduction to the city. Tours are available

year-round and can accommodate visitor schedules. ✉ Center ☎ 087/290–3499 ⊕ www.galwaywalkingtours.com ⚐ From €12.

Heart of Burren Walks

WALKING TOURS | Heart of Burren Walks has a 2½-hour guided walk with author Tony Kirby in June, July, and August (Tuesday to Saturday). The trail starts at Cassidy's pub in Carran at 10:30 am each day except Friday, when it starts at 2:15 pm. Highlights include the region's rare global landform (limestone pavement), the renowned Burren wildflower mix, and several archaeological monuments. ☎ 087/292–5487 ⊕ www.heartofburren-walks.com ⚐ From €20.

Lally Tours

BUS TOURS | A vintage double-decker bus departs every 45 minutes from Eyre Square in June, July, and August (every 90 minutes in spring and fall). Lally offers hourly tours of Galway City from 10:30 am until 4:30 pm from mid-March to October. It also offers daily tours to the Cliffs of Moher and the Burren, returning to Galway around 4:30. ✉ Eyre Sq., Galway City ☎ 091/562–905 ⊕ www.lallytours.com ⚐ From €12.

When to Go

Like everywhere in Ireland, the weather in this region is unpredictable but rarely extreme. A downpour can last a week in July, while October can offer crisp blue skies ideal for trekking the Burren. Rainproof gear, layers of clothing, and hiking boots are the key to enjoying the great outdoors. From November to February the days are short, road conditions unreliable in remote areas, and many of the attractions, hotels, restaurants, and ferry services are scaled back or closed. July and August are peak travel times, justifiably so, and with 17 hours of daylight and an abundance of festivals, the opportunities to explore and experience Ireland are endless. If you don't want to contend with crowds and high hotel rates, like during Galway Race week at the beginning of August when demand outstrips supply for hotel rooms, then try the shoulder seasons from March to June or September and October instead. Mid-spring and early summer is when the Burren is in full bloom and service in the region is unhurried. Most attractions open for St. Patrick's Day, when days begin to stretch. In September and October the pace slows, and landscapes are ablaze with color. ■ TIP➔ To catch a flavor of local community and team sport passion, catch one of the planet's fastest field games—a hurling match—during your stay. Check ⊕ www.gaa.ie.

Festivals and Events

For visitors and locals alike, festivals provide both free entertainment and a chance to meet people from all backgrounds who share a common interest.

APRIL
Galway Food Festival

FESTIVALS | Galway's diverse dining scene displays its wares in an extended food village on the banks of the Corrib every Easter, showcasing the best of indigenous produce. Traditional and ethnic dishes reflect the city's growing international community. Expect beer workshops, restaurant trails, and more than 70,000 people engaging with the area's finest chefs while exploring the intriguing tapestry of Ireland's new food movement. ✉ Center ⊕ www.galwayfoodfestival.com.

MAY
Fleadh na gCuach

During the first weekend in May, the scenic harbor village of Kinvara hosts the hugely popular three-day traditional music festival, Fleadh na gCuach (the Cuckoo Fleadh), attracting musicians from far and wide. ✉ Main St., Galway City.

★ Fleadh Nua

FESTIVALS | Ennis comes alive with the beat of the bodhrán for eight days at the end of May in one of Ireland's greatest traditional music festivals. It offers workshops, concerts, trad sessions, parades, and street performances, as well as the opportunity to mix with locals. ■TIP➔ **Book ahead to avoid staying in the periphery.** ✉ *Fleadh Nua Office, The Market, Ennis* ☎ *065/682–4276* ⊕ *www. fleadhnua.com.*

JULY

Galway Arts Festival

Held the middle two weeks of July, the Galway Arts Festival hosts an international array of the best of contemporary theater, film, rock, jazz, traditional music, poetry readings, comedy acts, and visual arts exhibitions. ☎ *091/566–577* ⊕ *www. giaf.ie.*

The Galway Races

Known as the place where shady deals took place between politicians and developers during the boom times, the Galway Races is a high-profile event that brings the city to a standstill and brings out all of Ireland's aspiring socialites, horse-racing enthusiasts, and ostentatious hats. Room rates skyrocket around this festival so plan accordingly. ✉ *Galway City* ⊕ *www. galwayraces.com.*

★ The Willie Clancy Summer School

The sleepy town of Miltown Malbay has woken up every July since 1973 to the sound of harps, tin whistles, and uilleann pipes. The weeklong Willie Clancy Summer School, named after the legendary piper, is the largest of its kind in Ireland, with 135 daily workshops and a full program of recitals, concerts, and dances open to the public. ☎ *065/708–5107* ⊕ *www.scoilsamhraidhwillieclancy.com.*

AUGUST

Cruinniú na mBád Festival

Kinvara's Cruinniú na mBád, meaning "the gathering of the boats," in late August commemorates a time when the Galway Hookers—red-sailed, black-hulled timber boats—hauled turf to trade in Galway. It's a great opportunity to see restored craft in all their glory and remember a time gone by. ✉ *Kinvara* ⊕ *www.galwaytourism.ie.*

SEPTEMBER

Galway International Oyster and Seafood Festival

Ireland's significance as the cradle of fresh oysters might have gone under the radar if it weren't for this late-September festival, culminating in a masquerade ball with flowing Guinness and champagne. ✉ *Center* ☎ *091/394–637* ⊕ *www. galwayoysterfestival.com.*

Lisdoonvarna Matchmaking Festival

Held in September in the spa town of Lisdoonvarna in the Burren, Europe's largest matchmaking fest is a monthlong festival of music, dancing, craic, and—if you're lucky—love. The last weekend of the festival turns into "The Outing," an LGBT-focused spin on Europe's biggest singles' event. ✉ *Lisdoonvarna* ⊕ *www. matchmakerireland.com.*

OCTOBER

★ Galway Aboo Halloween Festival

Galway's Latin Quarter hosts Ireland's biggest Halloween event on the last weekend of October. The highlight is the Sunday parade performed by the theatrical troupe Macnas, who add vibrant color in the early-evening darkness. ✉ *Center* ⊕ *www.macnas.com.*

Planning Your Time

There's much to see between Clare and Galway, so prioritizing your time means prioritizing your interests: if you want quintessential Irish castles, scenery, music, and history, spend all three days in Clare, allowing yourself time to stop and explore everything from Bunratty to the Burren and Craggaunowen to the Cliffs, as well as a night on the Aran Islands. If you want a little city buzz with your scenery, save the third day for vibrant Galway City—rich in history and buzzing with artistic activity and festivals—and plan to spend the night so that you can sample the lively pub and music scenes.

IF YOU HAVE 3 DAYS

With three days in this region, start with the Cliffs of Moher, the region's most breathtaking attraction, best enjoyed early in the day. Allow the rest of the day for exploring the Burren Park. Your first stop should be the pretty village of Kilfenora where you will find an unrivalled collection of High Crosses and the Burren Center Museum, the place for an overview of the park's evolution. Then head north along Corkscrew Hill, a road that's etched into a mountainside with panoramic views of the Burren's karst landscape. From here drive the short distance to Ailwee Cave and the Burren's famous landmark, the Poulnabrone Dolmen—an ancient portal tomb. Settle down for the night in Ballyvaughan, a quiet village on Galway Bay.

On Day 2, take the coastal route south with the Burren's rocky contours to the left and the blue ocean to the right, and pause by the roadside as the Cliffs of Moher come into view. Move onto Doolin Pier to catch the first ferry to the Aran Islands, which departs at 10 am. The boats sail to all three islands, but for a day trip, Inis Oírr is the closest, which gives you the most island time to seek out its hidden beaches and meandering pathways that carve through the neat stonewalled fields. Upgrade your ferry ticket to stay on board to cruise the Cliffs of Moher from the ocean, where you can fully appreciate their vast scale. Spend the evening in Doolin, where there's a guaranteed opportunity for a lively traditional music session in any of the pubs.

On Day 3, head to Galway City. It's Ireland's most charming city, with a bohemian attitude, fine dining, and an invigorating pub scene. Stay anywhere between the Quays and Eyre Square and explore the city's medieval quarter on foot, before selecting one of its fine restaurants to round off the evening.

Visitor Information

Fáilte Ireland provides free information service, tourist literature, and an accommodations booking service at its TIOs (tourist information offices). The following offices are open all year, generally weekdays 9–6 (daily during the high season): Aran Islands (Inis Mór), Ennis, and Galway City. Other TIOs that operate seasonally, generally weekdays 9–6 and Saturday 9–1, include: Cliffs of Moher (April–October; a concession within the main visitor center, which opens year-round) and Salthill (May–September).

Information on Kinvara, Galway City, and the Aran Islands can be found at Discover Ireland (⊕ www.discoverireland.ie/places-to-go/galway). Information on the main sights in County Clare—Ennis, the Burren, and the Cliffs of Moher—can be found at Shannon Region Tourism (⊕ www.discoverireland.ie/places-to-go/clare).

CONTACTS Ennis Tourist Information Office. ⊠ Arthur's Row, Ennis ☎ 065/682–8366 ⊕ www.discoverireland.ie/Activities-Adventure/ennis-tourist-office/70922. **Galway City Discover Ireland Centre.** ⊠ Forster St., Center ☎ 091/537–700 ⊕ www.discoverireland.ie/places-to-go/galway.

Bunratty Village

18 km (10 miles) west of Limerick City on N18 road to Shannon Airport.

Bunratty was a thriving village until its population was decimated by the great famine in the middle of the 19th century. A hundred years later, Bunratty returned to prosperity with the development of nearby Shannon Airport, and that's when

Bunratty Castle became one of Ireland's first major tourist attractions. The Celtic Tiger economy brought back the population with the construction of high-end housing and hospitality properties, but its medieval castle still takes center stage. The village has become the entertainment hub for the wider area, with a good mix of restaurants and pubs. The original Durty Nelly's Pub close to Bunratty Castle attracts older characters and tourists, while locals head down to Gallagher's Restaurant on the weekends.

GETTING HERE AND AROUND
Bunratty is about 15 minutes from Limerick's center on the N18 Galway road. Most Bus Éireann buses to Shannon Airport also stop at Bunratty: confirm when boarding. Dublin Coach offers an M7 Express service that links Bunratty directly to Dublin and Killarney.

Sights

★ Bunratty Castle and Folk Park
CASTLE/PALACE | FAMILY | Fifteenth-century Bunratty Castle, once the stronghold of the Earls of Thomond who would leave Ireland in the 17th century for a cozier lifestyle in England, is the park's highlight. It's now fully restored to its former glory, including everything from its carefully chosen period furniture to its "murder holes" that allowed defenders to pour boiling oil on attackers below. The views across the Shannon River from over the battlements is very impressive. Bunratty Folk Park is a carefully planned reconstruction of a typical 19th-century village, which comes complete with school, haberdashery, and, of course, a fully stocked Mac's Pub. Other highlights scattered about the park include the Shannon Farmhouse, the park's first exhibit, which was transported stone by stone from a site earmarked for Shannon Airport's main runway and the 1898 Hazelbrook House, which was the home of Ireland's most famous ice-cream producers. A new café and high-end gift store at the entrance to the park has good-quality lunch bites. ■ **TIP** → **Visit Bunratty Castle first as it is the earliest attraction to close (at 4 pm, to facilitate the evening banquets).** ⊠ *Bunratty* ☎ *061/360–788* ⊕ *www.shannonheritage.com* ⊠ *From €12.*

Restaurants

★ Gallagher's Seafood Restaurant
$$ | SEAFOOD | In the village's only thatched cottage outside the folk park, Gallagher's Restaurant has been wowing for the last two decades, with a strong focus on local, straight-from-the-sea catches. After a recent renovation the nooks and crannies are gone, with a more open layout and a new-found bustle. **Known for:** seafood; thatched cottage setting close to Bunratty Castle; nightly specials. ⑤ *Average main: €20* ⊠ *Old Bunratty Rd., Bunratty* ☎ *061/363–363* ⊕ *www.gallaghersofbunratty.com.*

Noel's at the Manor
$$$ | MODERN IRISH | This fine little eatery packs a punch in the local dining scene, harvesting the best of local produce from the sea and land. Operated by the Wallace family in a modern, stone-and-plaster inn on the western perimeter of the village, the style and presentation of the food comes with five-star finesse. **Known for:** seafood chowder; local produce; warm, relaxed atmosphere. ⑤ *Average main: €25* ⊠ *Bunratty Village, Bunratty* ☎ *61/707–984* ⊕ *www.bunrattymanor.ie/ eat* ⊗ *Closed Sun. and Mon.*

Hotels

Carrygerry Country House
$$ | B&B/INN | Modest and gabled, this 1793 country house is only 8 km (5 miles) from Shannon Airport and just 12 km (7 miles) from Bunratty (so a convenient first stop for visitors who want to sample the castle's medieval banquet), but it is also a world apart, with views across the plains where horses calmly graze,

as they have done for centuries, to the distant Shannon Estuary. **Pros:** real Irish character; abundant wildlife, birdsong, peace and quiet; excellent restaurant. **Cons:** tricky to find; bar menu only some nights. $ *Rooms from: €140* ⊠ *Carrygerry, Shannon, Newmarket on Fergus* ☎ *061/360–500* ⊕ *www.carrygerryhouse. com* ⊙ *Call to confirm dinner Sun.–Tues. (bar menu only when quiet)* ⚲ *11 rooms* ‖○‖ *Free breakfast*.

Nightlife

Durty Nelly's Pub

BARS/PUBS | Brimming with character, the low ceilings and stone flooring of this popular haunt next to Bunratty's Castle draw back to earlier centuries. The pub was formerly known as "the Pike" (short for "turnpike") due to its role as the toll gate for the arched stone bridge that connects it to the other side of the Ratty River. Clients clamor at the small bar for service where bar food and heartier restaurant-style portions are available. ■**TIP**→ **Durty Nelly's is bang in the middle of the well-beaten tourist trail, so expect as many visitors as locals.** ⊠ *Bunratty Village, Bunratty* ☎ *061/364–861* ⊕ *www. durtynellys.ie*.

Performing Arts

Bunratty Castle Medieval Banquets

THEATER | Filled with music and story telling, Bunratty Castle's medieval banquets have been entertaining guests since 1963. Guests are heralded over a drawbridge by a kilt-wearing bagpiper before being ushered by courtiers and ladies-in-waiting to a banquet featuring spare ribs and mead, a honey wine produced locally. The congregation sits on benches while two unsuspecting guests are crowned Earl and Lady Thomond and allotted the responsibility of tossing someone into the great hall's dungeon. Banquets are held subject to demand at 5:30 and 8:45 nightly. ⊠ *Bunratty Castle & Folk Park, Low Road, Bunratty Village, Bunratty* ✛ *Car park is on access road between castle and Durty Nelly's Pub* ☎ *061/711–222* ⊕ *www.bunrattycastle.ie/ medieval-banquet* ⚲ *€63*.

Folkpark's Traditional Irish Night

DANCE | The pomp and pageantry at Bunratty Castle's great hall is high-kicked aside for less formal shenanigans in the Folk Park's barn. Bodhráns players, fiddlers, and traditional dancers (male and female) perform jigs and reels for guests who are offered Irish stew, spuds, and other 19th- (pre- and postfamine) century staples. ⊠ *Corn-Barn, Bunratty Folk Park, Bunratty* ☎ *061/711–222* ⊕ *www.bunrattycastle.ie/folk-park/traditional-night* ⚲ *€43*.

Shopping

Blarney Woolen Mills

GIFTS/SOUVENIRS | Tweeds, caps, rain-proof gear, and a sizeable selection of contemporary clothing make this a good one-stop shop for gifts or to buy gear without the garish hues in other tourist-centric stores. Next door (or by upstairs annex) Meadow's and Byrne offers tasteful home furnishing and appliances. A daytime restaurant upstairs offers sandwiches and reasonably priced mains. ⊠ *Bunratty Village, Bunratty* ☎ *061/364–321* ⊕ *www.blarney.com*.

Bunratty Winery

WINE/SPIRITS | Less than a kilometer past the entrance to Bunratty Castle and Folk Park on the Low Road is this unexpected find, which sells unique Irish liquor such as mead (the beverage of choice at the castle banquets) and *poitín* (or potcheen). The latter is a potent liquor that was legalized in 2008 in a somewhat diluted form; however, its original ingredients of potatoes (of course), molasses, and beets remain. ⊠ *Low Rd., Bunratty E, Bunratty* ✛ *1 km (½ mile) past Bunratty heading north on Low Rd.* ☎ *061/362–222* ⊕ *www.bunrattymead.net*.

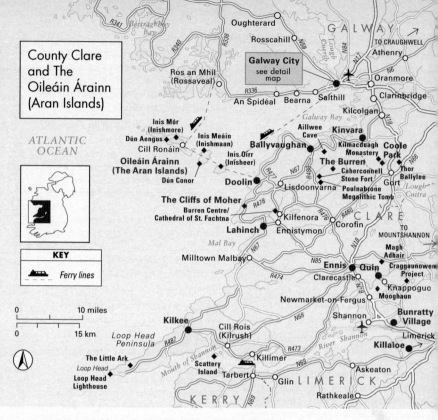

County Clare and The Oileáin Árainn (Aran Islands)

ATLANTIC OCEAN

KEY

Ferry lines

0 — 10 miles
0 — 15 km

Quin

21 km (13 miles) north of Bunratty.

Quin Village has retained the essence of old Ireland despite the fact that it is only a 20-minute drive from Shannon Airport and less than 6½ km (4 miles) from iconic Dromoland Castle. "Blow ins" have infiltrated village life with the development of smaller units in the village center, but little else has changed in Quin over the last century. Dominated by its 14th-century Franciscan abbey, its line of vernacular low-rise buildings is broken only by a narrow bridge over the Rine River. A plaque plays tribute to the village's only celebrity, Paddy Hannan. He was accredited with Australia's Kalgoorlie gold rush and subsequent prosperity of the area, where he lends his name to a main street.

● Sights

The Craggaunowen Project

BUILDING | It's a strange experience to walk across the little wooden bridge above reeds rippling in the lake into Ireland's Celtic past as a jumbo jet passes overhead on its way into Shannon Airport—1,500 years of history compressed into an instant. But if you love all things Celtic, you'll have to visit the Craggaunowen Project. The romantic centerpiece is Craggaunowen Castle, a 16th-century tower house restored with furnishings from the period. It was a retreat for "Honest" Tom Steele, a local squire who famously canvassed Pope Pius VII to change his religion before he had a change of heart and became a key figure in Catholic emancipation. Look for Steele's initials carved into a stone quoin outside the castle. Huddling beneath its battlements are two replicas of early Celtic-style dwellings. On an island in the lake, reached by a narrow footbridge, is a clay-and-wattle *crannóg*, a fortified lake dwelling; it resembles what might have been built in the 6th or 7th century, when Celtic influence still predominated in Ireland. The reconstruction of a small ring fort shows how an ordinary soldier would have lived in the 5th or 6th century, at the time Christianity was being established here. Characters from the past explain their Iron Age (500 BC–AD 450) lifestyle, show you around their small holding stocked with animals, and demonstrate crafts skills from bygone ages. Be sure to check out the Brendan boat, a hide vessel used by explorer Tim Severn to test, and prove, the legend that Irish St. Brendan discovered America in a curragh boat almost a millennium before Christopher Columbus. ■TIP→ **The park is hilly in parts, particularly near the wild boar compound. Bring comfortable walking shoes.** ⊠ *Craggaunowen, Kilmurry* ☎ *061/711–222* ⊕ *www.shannonheritage.com/craggaunowen* ⊠ *From €10* ⊘ *Closed Sept.–Mar.*

Magh Adhair

ARCHAEOLOGICAL SITE | Wander off the beaten path to discover the inauguration site of Ireland's greatest king, Brian Boru. Weaving through narrow country lanes, Magh Adhair appears to the left like a grass-coated mound of earth just past a small stone bridge that crosses Hell River. The mound is in fact a natural amphitheater where a lone voice could cut through large crowds during important regional ceremonies. It's one of the most sacred druid sites in Munster and believed to be the final resting place of Adhar, whose brother, Aengus, built Dun Aengus—a giant hill fort overlooking the ocean in the Aran Islands. Watch out for the bullaun (basin) stone altar, which looks like a giant's molar with a smooth, bowl-shape top. The druids believed that this altar captured hallowed water that protected their chieftains during and after

life. ■TIP→ **Park the car before reaching the site as the road is very narrow.** ⊕ *About 6 mins northwest on R469 from Quin village* ⊠ *Free.*

Mooghaun Hill Fort

ARCHAEOLOGICAL SITE | This prehistoric hill fort, once populated with the most powerful aristocrats in the region, is the largest of its kind in Ireland. It commands a sweeping view of the Shannon, Ireland's longest river, which made it the perfect outlook for enemies navigating the main transport artery into the region. Today, a series of sturdy concentric walls set into a deep hilly thicket that hugs the northern territory of Dromoland Estate are what remain of this former chieftain stronghold, constructed around 1000 BC. Information markers guide visitors past significant landmarks over the 27 acres, and a timber tower at the summit of the hill offers a rewarding view over the countryside. While much of the experience here is in your imagination (as in, imagining what would have once taken place on this very ground), the site makes for a truly beautiful and serene woodland walk, and it is particularly attractive in early autumn when the oak, horse chestnut, and beech trees turn every shade of crimson and amber. ■TIP→ **Turn to the left on leaving Mooghaun, and heading toward Quin, cast an eye over a humped-back bridge. It was the site of Europe's greatest gold find, many pieces of which are on display in Dublin and at the British Museum in London. The hoard belonged to the residents of Mooghaun.** ⊠ *Mooghaun Hill Fort* ⊕ *6 km (4 miles) south of Quin* ⊠ *Free.*

Quin Abbey

ARCHAEOLOGICAL SITE | Set in a meadow by a crystal clear river in the heart of the village and beside the ruin of St. Mary's Church, Quin Abbey is one of Ireland's finest ancient monasteries. Legend has it that a McNamara chieftain built the abbey in 1402 in gratitude to God for saving his son, who had survived a tumble into the icy river at the site of construction. The choice of location was most likely due to the sturdy retaining walls and turrets of an old Norman castle that had remained intact, forming a practical foundation for the abbey. The bumpy terrain in the surrounding fields gives an insight to the old castle's scale. Despite Quin Abbey's desecration and damage during the turbulent 17th century, its bell tower, cloisters, and lady's chapel are well maintained. Take time to inspect the south-facing wall of the church: the shape of a crucifix will appear, etched onto the charred masonry after a Cromwellian visit. The founder of the monastery is interred here, while his descendant, "Fireball" McNamara, is buried around the corner in the lady's chapel. Other notable eternal guests of the abbey include the Dunboyne family from nearby Knappogue Castle, and the Blood Family, relatives of the great crown jewel thief, Thomas Blood. ⊠ *Quin Abbey* 🎫 *Free* ⊘ *Closed Nov.–Mar., but grounds open all year.*

Hotels

★ Dromoland Castle Hotel and Country Estate

$$$$ | **HOTEL** | **FAMILY** | With structures that date back to the 11th and 16th centuries, and now one of Ireland's grandest hotels, Dromoland Castle's picture-perfect setting and lavish finishes offer a classic fairy-tale feel but with modern comforts, thanks to a just-completed multimillion-euro restoration. **Pros:** old-fashioned luxury with modern amenities; high standard of service; beautiful grounds. **Cons:** in part, the grounds double as a golf course; some Queen Anne–section bedrooms have small windows facing a courtyard; lake-view rooms are in high demand and difficult to reserve. 💲 *Rooms from: €454* ⊠ *15 km (9 miles) southeast of Ennis via M18, Newmarket on Fergus* 🕾 *061/368–144* ⊕ *www.dromoland.ie* 🛏 *98 rooms* 🍽 *Free breakfast.*

 Activities

GOLF

Dromoland Golf Course

GOLF | Dromoland Golf Club is set in a 450-acre estate of rich woodland and rolling open pasture on the grounds of the famed Dromoland Castle hotel. The parkland course has a natural lake that leaves little room for error on a number of holes. Beginners, take note: a state-of-the-art golf academy can help you to improve your swing. ⊠ *Newmarket on Fergus* 🕾 *061/368–444* ⊕ *dromolandgolf.com* 📧 *Apr.–Oct. €110, Nov.–Mar. €70, twilight and early-bird €70* 🏌 *18 holes, 6824 yards, par 72.*

Ennis

9½ km (6 miles) north of Newmarket-on-Fergus on M18.

Ennis is Clare's main town, with a medieval layout that follows the River Fergus with a network of narrow lanes and a one-way road system. Offload the car at the first opportunity and explore on foot. The brightly painted facades of its shop fronts are vibrant, even on the dullest day. That liveliness is echoed later in the evening with a guaranteed trad music session in one the town's myriads of pubs. A sculpture trail adds a novel way to navigate the lanes and alleys with anything from braying cattle in the marketplace to giant outstretched hands outside Ennis Cathedral.

GETTING HERE AND AROUND

Ennis is best served by Exit 12 from the M18 Limerick–Galway motorway. Dublin Coach M7 Express connects Dublin to Ennis. Bus Éireann connects Ennis to Cork, Limerick, Shannon Airport, and Galway. From Ennis there are two Bus Éireann buses a day to the Cliffs of Moher Visitor Centre (50 minutes); the same bus also calls at Lisdoonvarna and Doolin. Ennis Railway Station can be accessed from Limerick City and Galway on the Irish Rail commuter route linking Limerick and Galway; the trip to Limerick takes 40 minutes, and Galway is one hour, 20 minutes.

TOURS

Limerick-based bus company Barratt Tours (⊕ barrattstours.ie) offers a guided tour of the Cliffs of Moher and the Burren leaving from the tourist information office in Ennis (€27; Saturday only from March 21 to early May, then Saturday–Thursday from early May to mid-September). Or opt for taxis, whose rates for long trips can be affordable if shared by four people.

VISITOR INFORMATION

CONTACTS Ennis Tourist Office. ✉ Arthur's Row, Town Center ✛ On narrow lane off O'Connell St. ☎ 065/682–8366 ⊕ www. discoverireland.ie/places-to-go/clare.

Restaurants

The Cloister Restaurant and Bar

$$ | EUROPEAN | Nestled by 13th-century Ennis Friary, this landmark restaurant's contemporary flair contrasts with its old open-stone walls and timber joists, and it offers a great wine list. It has a pared-back menu that will keep any carnivore satisfied, with fresh local catch and game among the mains. **Known for:** great character; good wine list; modern Irish menu. ⑤ Average main: €23 ✉ Abbey St., Ennis ☎ 065/686–8198 ⊕ www.cloisterrestaurant.ie.

Food Heaven

$ | IRISH | Commanding a prime location in the town's market, Food Heaven is one of the best places to eat breakfast in Ennis, with standouts including a goat cheese–and–cherry tomato omelet and the requisite full Irish breakfast. The light menu throughout the day attracts locals with its selection of quiche and sandwiches, until the early evening, when you'll see panfried hake or risotto. **Known for:** breakfast; light bites; freshly baked

desserts. ⑤ Average main: €13 ✉ 21 Market St. ☎ 065/682–2722 ⊕ www. food-heaven.ie ⊗ Closed Sun.

Souper Cafe

$ | CAFÉ | For soup lovers, this modest, brightly painted café on a square in the heart of Ennis will hit all the right notes. With daily changing specials and a range of paninis and sandwiches, it's the perfect pit stop for a quality snack or budget lunch. **Known for:** daily soup specials; full Irish breakfast; French onion soup. ⑤ Average main: €9 ✉ 10 Merchants Sq. ☎ 065/682–3901 ⊗ Closed Sun. No dinner.

Hotels

Old Ground Hotel

$$ | HOTEL | Understated modern bedrooms and a cornerstone location on O'Connell Street, right in the town center, is the key to the enduring success of this 18th-century ivy-clad landmark hotel. **Pros:** central location; great pub; comfortable rooms. **Cons:** extremely busy bar; finding parking can be a challenge; no leisure facilities. ⑤ Rooms from: €120 ✉ O'Connell St. ☎ 065/682–8127 ⊕ www.oldgroundhotelennis.com ▭ No credit cards ⤶ 83 rooms ❍❍ Free breakfast.

Nightlife

Ennis is one of the West's traditional-music hot spots. You're likely to hear sessions at many pubs, but keep in mind that sessions don't necessarily take place every night and that the scene is constantly changing.

★ Brogans Bar and Restaurant

BARS/PUBS | Enter through a side alley door to this large landmark pub that has served and entertained locals for over 35 years, right in the town center. Musicians appear to crawl out of the handsome woodwork nightly and perform impromptu to an appreciative audience. Quality

Where to Hear Traditional Irish Music

If you're interested in "trad" music, the beat of a *bodhrán* or the tap of a shoe will likely lead you to Galway and County Clare's great folk *fleadhs* (festivals) and pub *seisiúns* (sessions).

Doolin

The seaside village of Doolin hosts regular sessions in the pubs along the length of its short, ribbon layout. The best chance to catch a quality performance is at the **Russell Festival Weekend** (⊕ www.michorussellweekend.ie) at the end of February.

East Clare

East Clare takes its rich legacy of trad music seriously from Ennis to Killaloe, with some of the most powerful performances held in small rural villages. In Feakle check out **Peppers** (⊕ www.peppersoffeakle.com) or **Short's Bar**, which holds the title of the longest unbroken Thursday musical performance in Ireland: they haven't missed a beat in more than 45 years. **The Feakle Festival** (⊕ www.feaklefestival.ie) has five unbroken days of trad music on the Wednesday that follows the first weekend in August.

Ennis

During the last week in May, the pleasant country town of Ennis hosts the **Fleadh Nua** (⊕ www.fleadhnua.com), a massive eight-day-long celebration of dancing and song, with concerts, workshops, and competitions. Many of the events are open-air and free, and there is a great festive buzz. Ennis is home to a growing cadre of musicians: the Custys, Siobhán and Tommy Peoples, flute player Kevin Crawford, and accordion whiz kid Murty Ryan. Check out **Knox's Pub** (✉ Abbey St. ☎ 065/682–9264) and **Cruise's Bar** (✉ Abbey St. ☎ 065/684–1800) for lively evening sessions.

Miltown Malbay

Held during the first week in July, the **Willie Clancy Summer School** (⊕ www.willieclancyfestival.com) is Ireland's biggest traditional music summer school. Classes, lectures, and recitals attract around 1,500 students from 42 countries to this tiny village on the west coast of Clare near Spanish Point. Set dancing is a big draw here, and a surefire way to make friends.

bar food is available. ✉ 24 O'Connell St. ☎ 065/684–4365 ⊕ www.brogansbarandrestaurant.com.

Knox's Pub & Storehouse Restaurant
MUSIC CLUBS | This Victorian-style bar, close to Ennis Friary, with a traditional plate-glass shop front with brick, timber, and bric-a-brac finishes, serves bar food in its Storehouse until 9 pm and offers live traditional music regularly from 9:30 pm. ✉ 18 Abbey St. ☎ 065/682–2871 ⊕ www.knoxs.ie.

McHugh's Bar
BREWPUBS/BEER GARDENS | Behind one of the most charming facades in Ennis is McHugh's Bar, the town's hub for craft beer. Order a pint of its own brand, Western Herd, and settle in for the occasional, impromptu music session. ✉ 78 Parnell St. ☎ 087/393–4545 ⊕ westernherd.com/our-bar.

★ Nora Culligans Whiskey Bar
BARS/PUBS | Behind the subtle, light-yellow timber-front entrance, this whiskey and tequila bar is a long warren of Victorian-bar idiosyncrasies, with lofty ceilings,

barrel tables, two-story-high whiskey cabinets that manifest like the lovechild of an old west saloon and a traditional Irish pub. The evening entertainment reflects the same hybrid, with jazz, blues, acoustic sessions, and the occasional bit of reggae offered back-to-back with trad music sessions. It's the best place in town for a refreshing cocktail, and the antidote to an overindulgence in ballads and fiddles. ✉ *26 Abbey St.* ☎ *065/682–4954* ⊕ *www.noraculligans.com.*

The Poet's Corner

BARS/PUBS | The O'Connell Street door to the Old Ground Hotel leads directly to the Poet's Corner, a spacious, popular bar with pub grub in the day, and regular traditional music sessions on weekends from 9:30. ✉ *Old Ground Hotel, Main St., 58–60 O'Connell St.* ☎ *065/682–8127* ⊕ *www.oldgroundhotelennis.com/poets-corner-bar.html.*

Preachers Pub

MUSIC CLUBS | As you'd expect from the name, this hotel bar has a church theme and was formerly a chapel. That does not inhibit the devoted musicians who congregate here from 9:30 pm on weekends to play traditional music. ✉ *Temple Gate Hotel, The Square* ☎ *065/682–3300* ⊕ *www.templegatehotel.com/preachers-pub.html.*

🎭 Performing Arts

Glór—Irish Music Centre

CONCERTS | Ennis's venue for large concerts, Glór hosts popular touring acts, art-house cinema, stand-up comedy, and competitions of Irish music, song, and dance—including May's hectic Fleadh Nua. There's also an art gallery, a café, and free parking. ✉ *Causeway Link* ☎ *065/684–3103* ⊕ *www.glor.ie.*

💼 Shopping

The Belleek Shop

GIFTS/SOUVENIRS | A wide array of top names in Irish design is featured here, including Belleek china, throws, capes, Waterford crystal, Newbridge silverware, and Donegal Parian china, as well as Stephen Pearce, Nicholas Mosse, and other collectible ceramics. ✉ *36 Abbey St.* ☎ *065/686–7891* ⊕ *www.belleek-shop.com/.*

Carraig Donn

CLOTHING | A popular spot with locals for its own line of knitwear as well as its mix of Irish and international brands, Carraig Donn is also a sure thing for visitors looking for some contemporary Irish fashion, jewelry, crystal, and pottery. ✉ *Bank Pl.* ☎ *065/689–3433* ⊕ *www.carraigdonn.com.*

Custy's Traditional Music Shop

MUSIC STORES | This is where Ennis's traditional musicians stock up on sheet music, specialist books, and musical instruments. ✉ *Cooke's La.* ☎ *065/682–1727* ⊕ *www.custysmusic.com.*

Ennis Bookshop

BOOKS/STATIONERY | This long-established bookstore carries a wide range of local history and Irish-interest titles along with new publications. ✉ *13 Abbey St.* ☎ *065/682–9000* ⊕ *www.ennisbookshop.ie.*

Scéal Eile Books

BOOKS/STATIONERY | This little find on the heart of the town's market square is living proof that there is still a heartbeat thumping in the traditional, independent book store. Every book is hand chosen by a member of staff or requested by a customer, with a selection of new, out-of-print, or secondhand books available on-site. Scéal Eile (translated as "another story") doubles as a performance theater, and is popular as a book-signing venue. ✉ *16 Lower Market St.* ☎ *065/684–8648* ⊕ *www.scealeilebooks.ie.*

Seoidín

JEWELRY/ACCESSORIES | Stop here for a good selection of gold and silver jewelry as well as some lovely Irish-made gifts. ⊠ *52 O'Connell St.* ☎ *065/682–3510* ⊕ *www.seoidin.com.*

Tony Honan Antiques

ANTIQUES/COLLECTIBLES | Established in 1966 and specializing in antique clocks as well as Irish and internationally sourced antiques, this old gem of a shop is handily located in the town center. ⊠ *14 Abbey St.* ☎ *065/682–8136* ⊕ *www.tonyhonanantiques.com.*

Activities

BICYCLING

Tierney Cycles

BICYCLING | Follow the scenic Burren Cycleway (69 km [43 miles]) to the famous Cliffs of Moher, or join the Clare 250 Mile Cycle charity event in May, on a bike rented from family-run Tierney Cycles & Fishing. ⊠ *17 Abbey St.* ☎ *065/682–9433* ⊕ *www.clarebikehire.com.*

Killaloe

50 km (31 miles) east of Ennis.

Killaloe is separated from its sister town Ballina by an impressive 13-arch bridge across the River Shannon and a county border; a trek across the bridge is worthwhile for superior dining options. Killaloe—once the hometown of Ireland's greatest king, Brian Boru—is a good base from which to begin navigating the Shannon by boat.

TOURS

★ Killaloe River Cruises

BOAT TOURS | For an overview of the lake's significance from the birth of Brian Boru to the harnessing of its waters to create the greatest edifice of Ireland, the Ardnacrusha Power Station, take "the Spirit of Killaloe" tour out onto Lough Derg. It's an hour of fresh lake air and sweeping views. ⊠ *Killaloe* ✛ *On Ballina side of Killaloe Bridge* ☎ *086/814–0559* ⊕ *killaloerivercruises.com.*

Sights

St. Flannan's Cathedral

RELIGIOUS SITE | Built by the O'Brien clan in the early 13th century, Killaloe Cathedral is the most prominent landmark in the town's streetscape. Inside the cathedral you can see rare carvings including a Kilfenora Cross and the Thorgrim Stone, which has unique runic and ogham inscriptions. ■ **TIP→ Capture the cathedral's beauty from across the lake in Ballina.** ⊠ *Royal Parade, Killaloe* ⊕ *cathedral.killaloe.anglican.org.*

Restaurants

Flanagans on the Lake

$ | INTERNATIONAL | This lakeside restaurant, convenient for a bite before or after a River Shannon cruise, serves up international fare with breezy service. Locally produced standards like beef and Guinness pie as well as its reputable hamburgers, are favorites. **Known for:** hamburgers; summer barbecues; lakeside setting. Ⓢ *Average main: €17* ⊠ *Killaloe* ☎ *061/622–790* ⊕ *www.flanagansonthelake.com.*

Goosers

$ | IRISH | One of the most famous landmarks in town, complete with thatched roof, turf fire, and stone flooring, this classic Irish pub is a cozy a retreat from the lake in winter and a popular spot for alfresco dining in summer. Goosers is directly across the lake from St. Flannan's Cathedral and close to the town bridge that links County Tipperary to County Clare (Goosers is technically on the Tipperary side, but just barely), and serves traditional fare from Irish stew to bacon and cabbage. **Known for:** lakeside setting; traditional Irish fare; lively weekend trade. Ⓢ *Average main: €16* ⊠ *Ballina Rd.,*

Killaloe ☎ *061/376–791* ⊕ *www.goosers. ie.*

 Hotels

Lakeside Hotel and Leisure Centre

$ | **HOTEL** | **FAMILY** | The trip across the Shannon on the one-way lane bridge is worth it for this stunningly appointed property with full-on lake views back over the town's historic 13-arch bridge. **Pros:** lake views; leisure facilities. **Cons:** some rooms need an upgrade. ⑤ *Rooms from: €110* ⊠ *Killaloe* ☎ *061/376–122* ⊕ *www. lakesidehotel.ie* ⊙ *Closed Dec. 21–27* ⊐ *43 rooms* ⦿ *No meals.*

Kilkee

56 km (35 miles) southwest of Ennis.

Kilkee is the access point to Loop Head and the only major town on the peninsula. Its faded Victorian lure is still recognizable behind the shabby facades along its promenade. Back in its 19th-century heyday the town was connected to Limerick City by steamboat, horse and carriage, or train service, which facilitated its growth and reputation as a bathing spot across Britain and Ireland. It attracted the literati like Charlotte Brontë, Alfred Tennyson, and Aubrey de Vere along with tragic Empress Sissi of Austria and, in more recent decades, ocean explorer Jacques Cousteau.

The transport between Limerick City and Kilkee is confined to the annals of history, but there's still a strong presence of Shannonsiders visiting the town, and with good reason. It has a pristine, horseshoe-shape beach and an epic cliff-side walk from Diamond Rock, passing the Pollock holes, natural swimming pools encased in stone.

Kilkee's main attraction is its convenient location on the eastern ridge of the Loop Head Peninsula. Loop Head is County Clare's most southwesterly point and an extension of the Wild Atlantic Way driving route. This wild and rugged coastline enjoyed relative obscurity for more than a century until the Star Wars film crew arrived to capture its end-of-world coastline in *The Last Jedi*.

Further into Loop Head Peninsula there's a white-knuckle coastal drive with stopovers that include the Bridges of Ross, a coastal rock formation with blowholes, dolphin-watching tours, and deep-sea fishing.

 Sights

The Little Ark

RELIGIOUS SITE | In a small annex at the Church of the Little Ark, just outside the tiny village of Kilbaha, is a wonderfully quirky slice of local history. During penal times Roman Catholic parishioners were restricted access to church, so Father Michael Meehan came up with the idea of holding mass in "no man's land" or rather, no man's *sea*, much to the frustration of local landlords. The little ark was the size of a carriage and fully assembled by 1852, when it was pulled into the shallow waters of a local cove, where locals could worship uninterrupted. ⊠ *Church of the Little Ark, Kilbaha* ⊹ *20 km (12 miles) southwest of Kilkee on R487* ⊠ *Free; doors to church remain open throughout the day.*

Loop Head Lighthouse

LIGHTHOUSE | Loop Head Lighthouse has kept navigators on the right watery path since its construction in 1670. The current, pint-size white tower house was built in 1854 and is open for tours. On a fine day, views from the balcony encompass the Blaskets in the south to the 12 Pin Mountains in Connemara. There's a lighthouse exhibition in the light keeper's cottage. ⊠ *Kilbaha South* ⊕ *www.loophead.ie/what-to-see-in-ireland-loop-head-lighthouse* ⊠ *€5, cash only* ⊙ *Closed Nov.–mid-Mar.*

Scattery Island

HISTORIC SITE | Once a community, this remote island where the mouth of the Shannon River touches the Wild Atlantic Way is a time capsule of days gone by. St. Senan set up a monastery here in the 6th century believing that the remoteness of the island brought him closer to God. The six churches on the island today date from the 14th century, and its Round Tower at 120 feet is one of the tallest in Ireland. Drop by Kilrush Marina for a frequent ferry service to the island. ⊠ *Kilrush Marina, Merchants Quay, Kilrush* ☎ *085/250–5512* ⊕ *www. scatteryislandtours.com* ⊠ *€20* ☉ *Closed Oct.–Apr.*

 Beaches

Kilkee Beach

BEACHES | This wide, sweeping, crescent-shape, sandy beach is cradled by the town's rocky contours and slopes down gently to the ocean. The absence of a strong current means that it's one of the safest swimming spots on the west coast. **Amenities:** none. **Best for:** swimming, walking.

 Restaurants

The Long Dock

$ | **SEAFOOD** | Carrigaholt Village, with its crumbling medieval tower house perched on the coast, is home to this almost-200-year-old pub and restaurant, one of County Clare's great culinary finds. Seafood is sourced from the local pier for chowder, as are oysters, mussels, and lobsters, and served in the warmth of an open-hearth fireplace and Liscannor stone flooring. **Known for:** seafood chowder; historical paraphernalia; open fire. $ *Average main: €17* ⊠ *West St., Carrigaholt* ☎ *065/905–8106* ⊕ *www. thelongdock.com/* ☉ *Closed Mon.–Wed. Nov.–Mar.*

Morrissey's Seafood Bar and Grill

$ | **IRISH** | Set on a bend in the river a short drive north of Loop Head Peninsula, this unpretentious town house has gained a national reputation. The key to its success is simplicity, with a menu that keeps in season whether it's a heartwarming casserole in winter or fruit crumbles in late summer. **Known for:** homemade scampi and chips; crab claws; simple, seasonal dishes. $ *Average main: €17* ⊠ *Main St., Doonbeg* ✛ *9½ km (6 miles) north of Kilkee on N67* ⊕ *www.morrisseysdoonbeg.ie* ☉ *Closed Mar.*

Murphy Blacks Restaurant

$ | **SEAFOOD** | Set in modest Victorian quarters on the main thoroughfare into Kilkee, Murphy Blacks is operated by a duo with a vast experience in hospitality and the local fishing trade. Order the seafood pie, filled with mussels, prawns, salmon, and cod. **Known for:** seafood; daily specials; authentic Victorian building. $ *Average main: €18* ⊠ *O'Connell St.* ✛ *Just off promenade, close to Stella Maris Hotel* ☎ *085/875–4886* ⊕ *www.murphyblacks. ie* ☉ *Closed Sun.; hrs vary off-season.*

 Hotels

Loop Head Lightkeeper's House

$$$$ | **RENTAL** | With 300 degrees of coastal views and little else but ocean between this retreat and New York, Loop Head Lighthouse is the place to rewind and charge batteries. **Pros:** wood-burning stove in the living room; sea views; privacy. **Cons:** no water-main supply, so guests should bring bottled water for drinking; cliff-side location requires supervision for kids; two-night minimum stay. $ *Rooms from: €225* ✛ *The tip of Loop Head Peninsula* ☎ *01/670–4733* ⊕ *www. irishlandmark.com/property/loop-head-lightkeepers-house* ☉ *Closed Jan.* ⫧ *3 rooms* �‖ *No meals.*

Stella Maris Hotel

$$$ | B&B/INN | If a town the size and scale of Kilkee can have a grande dame property, then the Stella Maris is the place; it's a handsome, charming little hotel close to the sea, with a contemporary country style. **Pros:** sea views; close to the beach; free Wi-Fi. **Cons:** lack of street parking; in a busy part of the town; few leisure facilities on-site. ⑤ *Rooms from: €190* ✉ *O'Connell St., Kilkee* ☎ *065/905–6455* ⊕ *www.stellamarishotel.com* ↪ *12 rooms* ⑩ *Free breakfast.*

Lahinch

6 km (4 miles) south of the Cliffs of Moher, 29 km (18 miles) northwest of Ennis.

Lahinch's promenade is milling with a mix of locals and visitors out to inhale the fresh Atlantic air at all times of year. Its golf course consistently ranks in the world's top 100 links, but it's the surfers in search of the big one that have put this busy beach resort on the global map. Aileen's Wave is the product of the ocean pitted against the Cliffs of Moher, resulting in the perfect aquatic colossus.

The sandy beach backed by dunes brings a tenfold increase in population during summer months, when parking is a challenge and lines spill out the doors of its restaurants.

GETTING HERE AND AROUND

Lahinch (also spelled Lehinch, on maps and GPS) is a seaside resort 29 km (18 miles) northwest of Ennis on the N85. Pay for parking on the seafront. It can be reached by bus from Ennis (½ hour).

 Beaches

Lahinch Beach

BEACHES | FAMILY | At the first hint of sunshine, locals drop everything and flock to Lahinch's Blue Flag beach, a wide, sandy crescent about 2½ km (1 mile)

long, facing southwest onto the Atlantic Ocean. The most popular beach in County Clare, it has a good selection of facilities (even off-season), but it can get crowded (the trick is to arrive early). The beach has long been a family favorite, offering safe bathing, and ideal conditions for beginner surfers. **Amenities:** food and drink; lifeguards; parking (fee); toilets; water sports. **Best for:** sunset; surfing; swimming; walking. ✉ *Lahinch Beach* ✛ *Arriving from Ennistymon on N85, ignore right-hand turn at village entrance for Cliffs of Moher (R478), and continue straight for about 50 meters to reach promenade and car park* ➠ *Parking fee.*

 Restaurants

O'Looney's Waves Restaurant

$ | MODERN IRISH | Travelers come here to get up close and personal with the surf from behind a bowl of steaming Atlantic seafood chowder. Floor-to-ceiling windows capture the breath of the bay from a cozy distance, except in storm season when it can be a little too close for comfort. **Known for:** ocean views; seafood; drawing crowds. ⑤ *Average main: €15* ✉ *Promenade* ☎ *065/708–1880* ⊕ *www. olooneys.ie* ⊘ *Closed Nov.–Mar. 16 and weekdays Mar.–June 1.*

 Hotels

★ Moy House

$$$ | B&B/INN | Built for Sir Augustine Fitzgerald, this enchanting, 18th-century Italianate-style lodge sits amid 15 private acres on an exhilarating, Wuthering Heights–like windswept cliff top that's a three-minute drive from Lahinch. **Pros:** romantic cliff-top location; ocean views; dining room with tasting menu. **Cons:** outside town; the entrance is on a busy narrow road, walk beyond with caution; lack of leisure facilities. ⑤ *Rooms from: €195* ✉ *Miltown Malbay Rd.* ☎ *065/708–2800* ⊕ *www.moyhouse.com* ⊘ *Closed Nov.–Mar.* ↪ *9 rooms* ⑩ *Free breakfast.*

Nightlife

Cornerstone Bar

BARS/PUBS | On the corner of the main street, this sandstone cottage, with its low roof, is the place to cozy up for a postsurf pint. Traditional food is served until 9 pm, and there's live Irish music on weekends. ⊠ *Main St.* ☎ *065/708–1277.*

O'Looney's

MUSIC CLUBS | Known as Lahinch's surfers' pub, O'Looney's has a spacious oceanfront location and live music most nights in summer. ⊠ *The Promenade* ☎ *065/708–1414* ⊕ *www.olooneys.ie.*

Shopping

Lahinch Surf Shop

SPORTING GOODS | Tom and Rosemary Buckley's surf shop, the first in Ireland, dates from 1989, and is a landmark on Lahinch's Promenade. You'll find top-quality boards, wet suits, and accessories, as well as lots of local tips and advice. Check their website for daily surf reports and a live webcam. ⊠ *The Promenade* ☎ *065/708–1543* ⊕ *www.lahinchsurf-shop.com.*

Activities

GOLF

Lahinch Golf Club

GOLF | It's known as "the St. Andrews of Ireland," and with good reason: Lahinch links architect Old Tom Morris also worked on the St. Andrew's course design and hailed from the town. The busy R478 (main road to the Cliffs of Moher) splits Lahinch's two 18-hole courses. The old course is littered with blind spots (particularly the 5th) and large bunkers. The more recent Castle Course, named after the castle ruin at hole 7, is flatter. Goats have lifelong membership of the course, and are free to wander at will. They have even infiltrated the club's emblem. ⊠ *The Seafront* ☎ *065/708–1003* ⊕ *www.lahinchgolf.com*

⌑ *May–Sept., Old Course, €210, Castle Course €35. Mid-Mar.–late Apr. and Oct. 1–26, Old Course €160, Castle Course €35* ⚲ *Old Lahinch: 18 holes, 6950 yards, par 72; Castle Course: 18 holes, 5700 yards, par 69* ☞ *Lahinch is a walking-only course.*

SURFING

Lahinch Surf School

SURFING | Surfing champion John McCarthy was one of the first to harness the west of Ireland's Atlantic waves; his unmissable kiosk near the promenade houses a surf school for budding surfers of all stages and ages. ⊠ *Promenade* ☎ *087/960–9667* ⊕ *www.lahinchsurf-school.com* ⌑ *€35 (2-hr lessons).*

The Cliffs of Moher

10 km (6 miles) northwest of Lahinch.

One of Ireland's most breathtaking natural sights, the majestic Cliffs of Moher rise vertically out of the sea in a wall that stretches over a long, 8-km (5-mile) swath and in places reaches a height of 710 feet. On a clear day you can see the Aran Islands and the mountains of Connemara to the north, as well as the lighthouse on Loop Head and the mountains of Kerry to the south. Get up close and you can study the stratified deposits of five different rock layers visible in the cliff face. But most visitors prefer to take in the grand distant vistas, especially as they open up every turn of the trail along the famous Burren Way that runs from Doolin to the cliffs.

GETTING HERE AND AROUND

Head north and west from Lahinch through Liscannor on the R478 for 19 km (12 miles)—or west from Lisdoonvarna for about the same distance on the R478—and you will come to the visitor center, a lone feature dominating the otherwise empty landscape, and its huge car park (fee), which is the only parking option. The parking fee includes entrance to the visitor center.

There is a bus service to the Cliffs of Moher Visitor Centre from both Ennis and Galway City. A bus from Ennis to the cliffs takes about 50 minutes. The bus trip from Galway City takes about one hour, 50 minutes.

CONTACTS Cliffs of Moher Cruises.
☎ *065/707–5968* ⊕ *www.cliffs-of-moher-cruises.com.* **Ennis Bus Station.** ⊠ *Station Rd., Ennis* ☎ *065/682–4177.* **O'Brien Line.** ⊠ *Doolin Pier, Doolin* ☎ *065/707–5555* ⊕ *www.obrienline.com.*

TOURS

One of the most popular ways of viewing these natural wonders is by heading to Doolin (alternative port of departure: Liscannor) to sail on one of the Cliffs of Moher cruises. Take either of the two operators from Doolin Pier. Doolin2Aran Ferries and O'Brien Line offer one-hour cruises (€15) departing every day from noon, weather permitting, from "the first fine day in March" to early November.

◉ Sights

★ Cliffs of Moher
VIEWPOINT | FAMILY | Though not the tallest cliffs in Ireland, these giant bastions of Irish tourism are on the bucket list of everyone's visit to Ireland because of one undeniable fact; they're magnificent. Reaching a colossal height of 700 feet and looming over 8 km (5 miles) of County Clare's jagged coastline, they offer panoramic views across the seaboard from County Kerry to County Galway. Numerous colonies of seabirds, including puffins and guillemots, make their homes in the shelves of rock on the cliffs.

The **Cliffs of Moher Visitor Experience**—a grass-roof, subterranean visitor center built into the cliff face—is a good refuge from passing rain squalls. The interior imitates the limestone caves of County Clare and contains a gift shop, public

toilets, and a tearoom. The *Atlantic Edge* exhibition features information panels and interactive consoles for children; the highlight is the Ledge, a vertiginous virtual reality tour of the cliffs from a bird's-eye view. Outside the center, extensive hiking paths (some with elevated viewing platforms) give access to the real thing, including O'Brien's Tower, a 19th-century folly built on the cliffs' highest point (€2 extra for access to upper levels and O'Brien exhibit) at the northern extremity. Parking is on the opposite side of the R478; access is by pedestrian crossing. ■**TIP**→ **Take the Cliffs of Moher cruise from Doolin or Liscannor for a different perspective of the cliffs below the giant stacks.** ⊠ *Cliffs of Moher Visitor Centre (signposted on R478 north from Liscannor), Lahinch* ⊕ *6½ km (4 miles) north of Liscannor on R478* ☎ *065/708–6141* ⊕ *www.cliffsofmoher.ie* 🎫 *€8.*

Doolin

6 km (4 miles) north of the Cliffs of Moher.

Once an enchanting backwater of colorful fishermen's cottages, this tiny village—set at the point where the Cliffs of Moher flatten out and disappear into the sea as limestone plateaus—now seems to consist almost entirely of B&Bs, hostels, hotels, holiday homes, pubs, and restaurants. Built on a flat, low-lying plain that follows the River Aille a short walk from the pier, it's hard to identify where the village begins and ends. The frenzy of bank lending during Ireland's Celtic Tiger economic boom years is responsible for the explosion in development, making the little bridge that leads into Fisher Street almost impassable during peak-season travel. Doolin's frequent trad sessions and its seasonal ferry service to the Aran Islands draw the crowds.

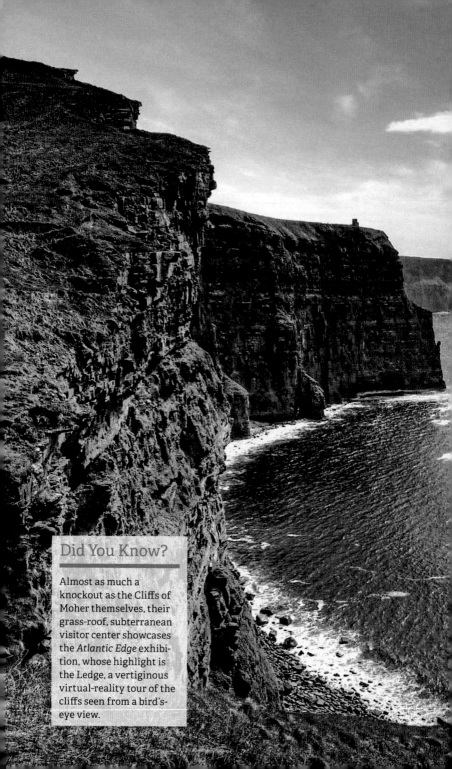

Did You Know?

Almost as much a knockout as the Cliffs of Moher themselves, their grass-roof, subterranean visitor center showcases the *Atlantic Edge* exhibition, whose highlight is the Ledge, a vertiginous virtual-reality tour of the cliffs seen from a bird's-eye view.

GETTING HERE AND AROUND

Doolin is on the R479 about 6 km (4 miles) north of the Cliffs of Moher visitor center. There is one bus a day from Ennis and five from Galway. Doolin is not on the express route: be sure to take a local bus.

At the pier, the two local ferry services with a plethora of online presence vie loudly for passing trade in front of their cabins. Both offer similar services, which include tours beneath the Cliffs of Moher. While visitors flock to O'Connor's, McDermott's, and McGann's pubs to catch a trad session, the village regains some of its old essence in the quieter months. *Car parking fees are now payable at Doolin harbor. Expect to pay €1 for up to 2 hrs; €5 for up to 30 hrs; and €15 for a wk.*

TOURS

Doolin2Aran Ferries

BOAT TOURS | Doolin2Aran Ferries offers transport to all the Aran Islands, with the option to cruise beneath the Cliffs of Moher. ⊠ *Doolin Pier* ☎ *065/707–5949* ⊕ *www.doolin2aranferries.com* ✉ *From €15.*

O'Brien Line

BOAT TOURS | O'Brien offers daily sailing from March to November to the three Aran Islands and an optional cruise beneath the Cliffs of Moher. The newest ship in the fleet, the *Doolin Express,* gets you from Doolin to the closest island in 15 minutes. ⊠ *O'Brien Line Ferries, Doolin Pier* ☎ *065/707–5618* ⊕ *www. obrienline.com* ✉ *From €15.*

Sights

★ Cliffs of Moher Walking Trail

TRAIL | Avoid the tourist buses and take the lesser-seen view of the Cliffs of Moher by following the trail from Doolin to Liscannor. From Fisher Street in Doolin, climb up the steep, narrow road by the village's low stone wall and follow the trail through a meadow, which leads to a cliff-hugging pathway with Ireland's most dramatic seascape as its constant companion. Between Doolin and the Cliffs of Moher the terrain is hilly, with views over a giant slab of rock that creates a surf swell called Aill na Searrach. Stop and enjoy the staggering panorama of Galway Bay and the Aran Islands from the highest point of the Cliffs of Moher. The final leg of the trail brings Hag's Head into view before descending into Liscannor Village, the home of submarine inventor John P. Holland. The trail is 14 km (8½ miles) and it takes on average 3½ hours to complete. The trail is challenging, with features that include road walking on uneven surface, exposed, rail-free cliff-top paths, and steep flagstone steps. Organized walks from Doolin leave from O'Connor's pub at 10 am daily.

Doolin Cave

CAVE | Formed from a drop of water thousands of years ago, Doolin Cave's Great Stalactite hangs from the ceiling like a giant rocky sword. The 24-foot feature is one of the world's longest known free-hanging stalactites, and the cave's star attraction. Tours of the cave run on the hour, and outside there's a walking trail around a working farm. ⊠ *Doolin Cave, Craggycoradon E ✛ 4 km (2½ miles) from Doolin on R479* ☎ *65/707–5761* ⊕ *www.doolincave.ie.*

Hotels

Ballinalacken Castle Hotel

$$ | B&B/INN | Not actually a castle, Ballinalacken is rather a mustard-color Victorian lodge in the shadow of medieval tower-house ruins, a few miles from Doolin Village; its hilly location, set back from the road in a 100-acre wildflower meadow, offers panoramic coastal views and enough distance from Doolin's busy nightlife to guarantee a peaceful night's sleep. **Pros:** coastal views; warm, old-fashioned welcome from the O'Callaghan family. **Cons:** not in fact a castle. ⑤ *Rooms from: €130* ⊠ *Coast Rd.* ✛ *5*

Did You Know?

Volumes have been
written on the diverse
animal and plant species
that thrive among the
karst stones of the
Burren, and the best
way to discover them is
on foot along dozens of
signposted walks. A good
book on the subject is
Burren Country (Collins
Press, 2011) by Paul
Clements.

km (3 miles) outside Doolin on Lisdoonvarna Rd. ☎ 086/361–3719 ⊕ www.
ballinalackencastle.com ⊘ Closed Nov.–
mid-Apr. No dinner Tues. ↵ 10 rooms, 2
suites ⌁ Free breakfast.

Cullinan's Guesthouse

$ | B&B/INN | A short walk from Fisher
Street, this well-established guesthouse overlooking the River Aille offers
brightly furnished rooms at competitive
rates. **Pros:** within easy walking distance to entertainment. **Cons:** views are
inconsistent across rooms; no restaurant. $ Rooms from: €110 ⊠ Doolin
☎ 065/707–4183 ⊕ www.cullinansdoolin.
com ↵ 8 rooms ⌁ Free breakfast.

Nightlife

Famous for their traditional-music
sessions, Doolin's three traditional pubs
can squeeze in big crowds, which means
compromising comfort on busy nights.
All pubs are furnished simply with timber
benches and well-worn bar stools, and
they serve simple bar food from midday
until 9 pm. As you might imagine, the
word is out about Doolin's trad scene—
the pubs regularly overflow with crowds
(and the video cams can get really annoy-
ing). Purists often hightail it to East Clare
for serious trad sessions, except at the
end of February when the **Micho Russell
Festival** draws the best talent to Doolin.

Gus O'Connor's

MUSIC CLUBS | Set in the village's main
(and only) street, popular Gus O'Connor's
has tables outside near a stream and live
music every night after 9:30 in the summertime. ⊠ Fisher St. ☎ 065/707–4168
⊕ www.gusoconnorsdoolin.com.

McDermott's

MUSIC CLUBS | Popular with locals, McDer-
mott's is a great spot for soul-warming
live music and traditional fare. Live music
nightly early spring to late autumn,
and weekends in winter. Note: it's
sometimes closed during the day in

low season. ⊠ R479 ☎ 065/707–4328
⊕ www.mcdermottspub.com.

McGann's Pub & Restaurant

MUSIC CLUBS | Across the road from
McDermott's, McGann's is the smallest of Doolin's three famous pubs and
has been run by the same family for
70 years. Breakfast is a highlight, so
luckily, McGann's offers B&B, too (must
book ahead). ⊠ R479 ☎ 065/707–4133
⊕ www.mcgannspubdoolin.com.

The Burren

*Extends throughout western County
Clare from the Cliffs of Moher in the
south to Black Head in the north, and as
far southeast as Corofin.*

★ As you travel north toward Ballyvaughan, the landscape becomes rockier
and stranger. Instead of the seemingly
ubiquitous Irish green, gray becomes the
prevailing color. You're now in the heart of
the Burren, a 300-square-km (116-square-
mile) expanse that is one of Ireland's
strangest landscapes. With dramatic
ocean-edge frontier land, *turloughs* (dis-
appearing lakes), underground rivers, and
a smooth lunar landscape that's scarred
with ancient portal tombs, the Burren
and the Cliffs of Moher are collectively
designated a UNESCO Global Geopark
site. Locals speculate that *Lord of the
Rings* author J.R.R. Tolkien drew inspiration from the park's ruggedness when he
imagined Middle Earth while working as
an external examiner at nearby University
College Galway.

The Burren is aptly named: it's an
Anglicization of the Irish word *bhoire-
ann* (a rocky place). Stretching off in all
directions, as far as the eye can see, are
vast, irregular slabs of fissured limestone, known as karst, with deep cracks
harboring plant life that's as alien as the
setting. Corkscrew Hill on the N67, a
winding road carved into the landscape,
offers the best overview of the Burren.

Pull over onto one of its viewing areas to capture the rocky pavements and silver limestone hills framed by the cerulean Atlantic to the north.

Late spring is when plant life is most vibrant and it heralds the Burren in Bloom festival, with organized walks from mid-May to early June.

Human life on the barren landscape is equally fascinating, though almost paradoxical, because on first inspection it appears as though its terrain is too harsh to sustain life. However, locals harnessed the land and sea, and thrived. Their habits and customs stretching back thousands of years can be seen at the Burren Centre in Kilfenora.

Burial sites like the iconic Poulnabrone Dolmen or Roughan Hill's extensive network of homes, walls, and wedge tombs dating back more than 5,000 years identify a lifestyle that changed very slowly in the millennia that followed, up until the 17th century. ⚠ **Burren Park is fragile. Do not pick rare flowers, enter portal tombs, or toss cigarette butts on the roadside, as this leaves an indelible mark on this incredible landscape.**

GETTING HERE AND AROUND
Take the R476 from Ennis (look for road signs for Corofin) when approaching the Burren from the south, or N67 from Galway when coming from the north. The Burren has roads and lanes that weave through the landscape like a spider's web, so mapping a route is the best way to explore this rich tapestry of natural beauty, fascinating wildlife, and archaeological sites. Park only in designated car parks (free), which have been built adjacent to the major sites, and proceed by foot to avoid damaging the delicate ecology. The main bus stop for travelers to the Burren area is Ballyvaughan or Lisdoonvarna.

◉ Sights

Burren Centre
INFO CENTER | Along with a café and a crafts shop with good maps and locally published guides, the tiny Burren Centre has a modest audiovisual display and other exhibits that explain the Burren's geology, flora, and archaeology. ✉ *8 km (5 miles) southeast of Lisdoonvarna on R476, Kilfenora* ☎ *065/708–8030* ⊕ *www. theburrencentre.ie* 🎫 *€6* ⊘ *Closed Nov.–mid-Mar.*

★ The Burren Way
TRAIL | You can explore the Burren area by car, from a bike, or from the back of a bus, but the very best way to soak in the raw beauty of this craggy landscape is on foot. The Burren Way is a 123-km (82-mile) way-marked hiking trail, its highlight being the stretch from Lahinch to Ballyvaughan on the shores of Galway Bay, a distance of 35 km (22 miles). If you're short on time/breath, you may want to focus on the most spectacular and popular section, which runs along the top of the Cliffs of Moher from Doolin to the coast near Lisdoonvarna, a distance of about 5 km (3 miles). The trail continues through the heart of the Burren's gray, rocky limestone landscape, with ever-changing views offshore of the Aran Islands and Galway Bay. Buy a map locally. ⊕ *www.burrengeopark.ie.*

Caherconnell Stone Fort
ARCHAEOLOGICAL SITE | There are several stone forts in the Burren thought to have been in use between AD 400 and 1200, but Caherconnell—1 km (½ mile) south of Poulnabrone—is the best preserved, and the only one excavated and made accessible to visitors. The visitor center has an audiovisual display on the chief archaeological features of the area, including burial places marked by dolmens or cairns. Ongoing excavations continue to fill in the blanks of this impressive structure's history. Be sure to check out the sheepdog demonstrations

Burren Driving Tour

Even locals find the Burren's labyrinthine network of narrow lanes and famine roads a challenge to navigate. With flaky phone signals, setting out with a plan (and map!) is best.

■ From Ballyvaughan to Fanore Beach (16 km [10 miles]): Heading south along the R477 is always a good idea for taking advantage of County Clare's dramatic coastline, rather than catching a glimpse of it in the rearview mirror. Fanore is a blink-and-miss-it village that ribbons along the road with unimposing architecture. Fanore means "ring of gold," an effective description of the curving, sandy contour of its beach, which is located south of the village. It's an intimate beach, with a decked pathway down to the fine sand, which has ocean views that are interrupted only by the Aran Islands. ■TIP→ Photo op: midway to Fanore Beach, watch out for Black Head Lighthouse for panoramic views of Galway Bay.

■ From Fanore Beach to Kilfenora (18 km [11 miles]): The small village of Kilfenora is also known as the "city of the crosses," due to the multitude of intricately inscribed High Crosses housed under the glass roof of **St. Fachtna's Cathedral.** This small village also has the **Burren Center**, a modest museum dedicated to Ireland's most fascinating landscape. ■TIP→ Photo op: slip off onto the R478 via Lisdoonvarna and head for Doonagore for panoramic Aran Island views over Doolin Village.

■ From Kilfenora to Ailwee Caves (18 km [11 miles]): Head north via the R478, N67, and R480 to discover underground passages at **Ailwees Cave.** River stalactites and waterfalls lead to the core of the mountain that was once occupied by bears. Their remains are still visible today in the cave. There is also a birds-of-prey center on-site. ■TIP→ Photo op: Corkscrew Hill, a series of steep, winding bends accurately described by its name provides staggering contrasting views of the Atlantic's deep blue water against the stark, gray contours of the Burren.

■ From Ailwee Cave to the Burren Perfumery (16 km [10 miles]): Heading south on the R480, the **Caherconnell Stone Fort** has a visitor center and café. The ringfort dates back to the 11th century, and remained inhabited for more than 500 years. The **Burren Perfumery** on the L1014 captures fragrances from the Burren's unique foliage. ■TIP→ Photo op: the most iconic landmark in the Burren is the Poulnabrone megalithic tomb, 8 km (5 miles) south of Ailwee Cave on the R480.

■ From Burren Perfumery to Corcomroe Abbey (14 km [9 miles]): Heading north on the L1014, **Corcomroe Abbey** was coined St. Mary of the Fertile Rock by the Cistercian community who lived there centuries ago. Inside, an effigy of an O'Brien chieftain reclines in peace by a retaining wall. For a sweet diversion, head over to the **Hazel Mountain Chocolate Factory** five minutes away by car. ■TIP→ Photo op: head off the radar to the remote Oughtmama, with abandoned churches and cairns that lie in the shadow of a bald limestone hill. It's a mesmerizing 9½-km (6-mile) coastal drive back to Ballyvaughan.

and café. ✉ *Kilfenora* ☎ *065/708–9999* ⊕ *www.caherconnell.com* 🍴 *From €6* ⊘ *Closed Nov.–mid-Mar.*

Cathedral of St. Fachtna

RELIGIOUS SITE | Beside the Burren Centre in Kilfenora, the ruins of a small 12th-century church, once the Cathedral of St. Fachtna, have been partially restored as a parish church. Over the transept a glass ceiling protects High Crosses and effigies from the harsh elements. There are some interesting carvings in the roofless choir, including an unusual, life-size human skeleton. In a field about 165 feet west of the ruins is an elaborately sculpted High Cross that is worth examining, though parts of it are badly weathered. ✉ *Kilfenora*.

★ Poulnabrone Megalithic Tomb

MEMORIAL | The biggest and most famous of the Burren's megalithic tombs, Poulnabrone ("the hole of sorrows") is a portal grave/dolmen with a massive capstone and a majestic presence amid the craggy limestone fields shouldering the moody gray Burren skies. The monument was built around 4,500 years ago. Stand downwind and you might hear ancient whispers. There is a designated car park nearby with a historical time line, and a short gravel walkway to the dolmen (freely accessible). It's open and windy here, so grab an extra layer. ✉ *On R480, 8 km (5 miles) south of Ballyvaughan, Kilfenora*.

Restaurants

Hazel Mountain Cafe

$ | **CAFÉ** | This surprising find in a cottage on the northern ridge of the Burren is not only a refreshing place for a soup-and-sandwich break, it's also home to the boutique **Hazel Mountain Chocolate Factory,** which produces chocolate using the same techniques employed by the monks who once occupied nearby Corcomroe Abbey. Vegetables are grown on-site and the cakes baked star in their own cookbook. **Known for:** chocolate; hearty soup with homegrown vegetables; cottage farmhouse setting. **$** *Average main: €10* ✉ *Oughtmama Bellharbour County Clare, Oughtmama* ☎ *065/707–8847* ⊕ *www.hazelmountain-chocolate.com* ⊘ *Closed winter*.

★ Wild Honey Inn

$$ | **MODERN IRISH** | Owner-chef Aidan McGrath and wife Kate's modest Victorian premises on the outskirts of Lisdoonvarna have become something of a culinary landmark by being Ireland's first pub to be awarded a Michelin star in 2017. A brief, well-thought-out menu showcases the best of local produce, which includes hake, lamb, rib-eye steak, and pork. **Known for:** award-winning restaurant; excellent seafood; inn is a good base for Burren. **$** *Average main: €24* ✉ *Kincora Rd., Lisdoonvarna* ☎ *065/707–4300* ⊕ *www.wildhoneyinn.com* ⊘ *Closed Nov.–Feb.*

Nightlife

Roadside Tavern

BREWPUBS/BEER GARDENS | Husband-and-wife team Birgitta and Peter Curtain offer their own craft beer and innovative food sourced from their neighboring Burren Smokehouse store in the quirky Roadside Tavern just off the main street of Ireland's matchmaking capital, Lisdoonvarna. The pub, owned by generations of Curtains, has regular trad sessions and guaranteed banter from Peter. Hobbit enthusiasts are particularly welcome, as the premises is home to the Burren Tolkien Society. ✉ *Kincora Rd., Lisdoonvarna* ☎ *065 /707–4084* ⊕ *roadsidetavern.ie*.

Vaughan's Pub

MUSIC CLUBS | Known for its traditional-music sessions in a village famed for its céilí band, Vaughan's has been a local favorite for years. Its claim to fame is a cameo appearance in the television series *Father Ted*. Set-dancing sessions are held in the barn every Sunday at 9:30

pm. ✉ *Main St., Kilfenora* ☎ *065/708–8004* ⊕ *www.vaughanspub.ie* 🎟 *€5 dancing sessions.*

🛍 Shopping

Burren Perfumery

PERFUME/COSMETICS | Shopping opportunities are not abundant in this rocky terrain, so don't miss the chance to buy Burren-inspired organic perfumery products at this delightful spot. The Burren is known for its wildflowers, and the perfumery is committed to its conservation: all the products on sale are sourced from ethical specialist growers, and made on-site, in small batches. As well as perfume there are soaps, creams, and balms, and you can visit the workshops to see them being made (April to September). There is also an organic herb garden, and a flower-bedecked tearoom (April to September) selling delicious organic home baking and light lunches. ✉ *The Burren Perfumery , Carron, Ballyvaughan* ☎ *065/708–9102* ⊕ *www.burrenperfumery.com.*

🏃 Activities

BICYCLING

West Ireland Cycling

BICYCLING | Either take an organized or self-guided Burren tour or hire a top-of-the-range bike from this Galway-based outfit. They can also deliver up to 80 bikes by trailer for groups, from €20 a day or €120 a week. ✉ *Earl's Island, Galway City* ☎ *087/176–8480* ⊕ *www.westirelandcycling.com.*

Ballyvaughan

37 km (23 miles) north of Ennis on R476 and R480.

A pretty little waterside village and a good base for exploring the Burren, Ballyvaughan attracts walkers and artists who enjoy the views of Galway Bay and access to the Burren.

👁 Sights

Aillwee Cave

CAVE | **FAMILY** | A vast 2-million-year-old cave, Aillwee is the biggest and most impressive chamber in the region accessible to those who aren't spelunkers. Illuminated for about 3,300 feet, the cave contains an underground river and waterfall. Aboveground, there are a big crafts shop, cheese-making demonstrations, a café, and the **Burren Birds of Prey Centre,** which puts on flying displays from eagles, falcons, hawks, and owls daily at noon and 3 pm (weather permitting). Discounts available if you book online. ✉ *5 km (3 miles) south of Ballyvaughan on R480* ☎ *065/707–7036* ⊕ *www.aillweecave.ie* 🎟 *From €15.*

🍴 Restaurants

★ Linnane's Lobster Bar

$$$ | **IRISH** | It doesn't get much better than this 300-year-old, slated, white-washed cottage with a turf fire and full-length windows that open out onto a terrace overlooking Galway Bay. The specialty is seafood; clams, scallops, salmon, crab claws, and lobster—the restaurant's cornerstone dish. **Known for:** fresh lobster; beautiful sea views; traditional setting and music. 💲 *Average main: €25* ✉ *Cartron, New Quay, Oughtmama* ✛ *12 km (7 miles) northeast on N67 of Ballyvaughan* ☎ *65/707–8120* ⊕ *www.linnanesbar.com* ⊙ *Restaurant closed Mon.–Thurs. Nov.–Mar.*

Monk's Pub

$ | **MODERN IRISH** | **FAMILY** | This landmark dining pub a stone's throw from Ballyvaughan Pier has changed hands and fortunes over the past few years, but all you need to know is that it is back on its game with a freshly renovated interior and menu. The welcoming fire and friendly service remain, as does the signature seafood chowder that lures locals and visitors from miles around. **Known for:** seafood chowder; cozy atmosphere. ⑤ *Average main: €15* ⊠ *Ballyvaughan* ⚓ *Near pier* ☎ *065/707–7059* ⊕ *www. monks.ie* ⊙ *Closed Oct.–May. No food Mon.–Thurs.*

 Hotels

Drumcreehy Country House
$ | **B&B/INN** | The pretty gabled facade with dormer windows is traditional in style, but, in fact, Bernadette Moloney and her German husband, Armin Grefkes, designed and built this house specifically as a B&B. **Pros:** big bedrooms for a B&B; nice waterfront location; peaceful nights. **Cons:** a long (1-mile-plus) walk down a narrow busy road to village. ⑤ *Rooms from: €100* ⊠ *Bishop's Quarter* ☎ *065/707–7377* ⊕ *www.drum-creehyhouse.com* 🛏 *12 rooms* ⦿ *Free breakfast.*

Gregans Castle Hotel
$$$ | **HOTEL** | Miles from the nearest town, this handsome ivy-clad Georgian retreat lies in the heart of the Burren, its turf fires and antique furnishings a draw back to a simpler time. **Pros:** fine dining; perfect for anyone who wants to get away from it all; scenic location. **Cons:** not a castle but a fine, rustic Georgian farmhouse; TV-free zone, only one in-house; very remote, car essential. ⑤ *Rooms from: €210* ⊠ *Base of Corkscrew Hill* ☎ *065/707–7005* ⊕ *www.gregans.ie* ⊙ *Closed Dec. 2–mid-Feb.* 🛏 *15 rooms, 6 suites* ⦿ *Free breakfast.*

Hyland's Burren Hotel
$ | **HOTEL** | A turf fire greets you in the lobby of this unpretentious coaching inn, in the heart of the Burren, which dates from the early 18th century and has become a cheerful, welcoming spot with a reputation for friendliness and good entertainment. **Pros:** central location; bar and restaurant on-site; pleasant staff. **Cons:** won't win any style contests;

bar and restaurant very busy July and August. ⑤ *Rooms from: €99* ⊠ *Main St.* ☎ *065/707–7037* ⊕ *www.hylandsburren. com* 🛏 *32 rooms* ⦿ *Free breakfast.*

 Nightlife

O'Lochlainns Bar
BARS/PUBS | No Ballyvaughan trip would be complete without this old-timer's pub, with its epic collection of whiskey brands. Set in a tidy building near the village square, with one eye on Galway Bay, O'Lochlainn's is a family business that opens every night from 8 until late. Its intimate dark-wood interior is a throwback to the 1930s, when it was a store and local tea blender. ⊠ *Ballyvaughan* ☎ *065/707–7006.*

Kinvara

18 km (11 miles) north east of Ballyvaughan, 29 km (17½ miles) south of Galway City.

Kinvara, with its pretty harbor and iconic ocean-edge tower house, makes for a leisurely break along the busy tourist trek between the Cliffs of Moher and Galway City. Its quayside cafés and brightly painted pubs entice visitors to linger and toss aside the itinerary. Kinvara is home to the annual Fleadh na gCuach (Cuckoo Fleadh), a traditional music festival held the first weekend of May, as well as the long-standing early-August sailing event, Cruinniú na mBád (Festival of the Gathering of the Boats), in which traditional brown-sail Galway hookers laden with turf race across the bay.

GETTING HERE AND AROUND
The N67 coast road, a narrow but scenic route, follows the shore of Galway Bay from Ballyvaughan to Kinvara. From Kinvara, N67 joins the busy national route, the M18, at Clarenbridge and continues into Galway City (29 km [17 miles]). There is free but limited parking in Kinvara. Bus

Éireann runs buses between Kinvara and Galway City; the journey takes about 30 minutes. The same bus continues to the Cliffs of Moher, Lisdoonvarna, and Doolin.

 Sights

Dunguaire Castle
CASTLE/PALACE | Like a chess piece flung onto a windswept rock a short stroll from the village of Kinvara, Dunguaire Castle has braced the Atlantic for 400 years, replacing the king of Connaught's 6th-century palace upon its construction. Built in 1520 by the O'Hynes clan, the tiny storybook castle takes its name from the fabled king of Connaught, Guaire. In 1924 it was purchased by Oliver St. John Gogarty, the noted surgeon, man of letters, and model for Buck Mulligan, a character in James Joyce's *Ulysses*. To his outpost came many of the leading figures of the 19th-century Celtic revival in Irish literature. Today Dunguaire is used for a medieval banquet that honors local writers and others with ties to the West, including Lady Gregory, W.B. Yeats, Seán O'Casey, and Pádraic Ó Conaire. ■TIP→ Book in advance for the medieval banquet. ⊠ Kinvara ☎ 061/711–222 ⊕ www.shannonheritage.com ☜ €8 ۞ Closed Oct.–Mar.

 Restaurants

★ Moran's Oyster Cottage
$$$$ | SEAFOOD | This small thatched cottage is just upstream from where the Dunkellin River flows into Dunbulcaun Bay, the epicenter of Ireland's fresh oyster trade. The local oysters make a regular appearance, straight from bay to plate, though Atlantic seafood chowder, smoked salmon, seafood cocktail, lobster with boiled potatoes and garlic butter, and fresh crab salad are also on offer. **Known for:** fresh oysters; pretty waterside setting; landmark restaurant for generations. ⑤ *Average main: €33* ⊠ *The Weir,*

Kilcolgan ✠ Signposted off main road on south side of Clarinbridge ☎ 091/796–113 ⊕ *www.moransoystercottage.com.*

The Pier Head
$$ | IRISH | Once the village pub, the Pier Head is still a bar, but it sells more food than pints these days. The location is idyllic, at the top (head) of the village's pier. **Known for:** views across Kinvara Bay; fresh seafood; hearty, local food. ⑤ *Average main: €24* ⊠ *Kinvara* ☎ 091/638–188 ▤ *No credit cards* ۞ *Closed Mon. and Tues. Nov.–mid-Mar.*

 Hotels

The Merriman Hotel
$ | HOTEL | Don't let its traditional cottage looks deceive you: this whitewashed, thatched inn on the shores of Galway Bay is, in fact, a midsize hotel, decorated with locally made, well-designed furniture, and original crafts, paintings, and sculpture. **Pros:** village center location; free and secure car parking; good restaurant. **Cons:** bar gets very busy on weekends; small windows in bedrooms. ⑤ *Rooms from: €80* ⊠ *Main St.* ☎ 091/638–222 ⊕ *www.merrimanhotel.com* ۞ *Closed Jan.–Mar.* ⇄ *32 rooms* ☉ *Free breakfast.*

Coole Park

24 km (15 miles) northeast of Corofin on M18.

This nature reserve attracts William Butler Yeats fans and those seeking pleasant and easy walking trails.

 Sights

Coole-Garryland Nature Reserve
NATIONAL/STATE PARK | Coole Park was once the home of Lady Augusta Gregory (1859–1932), patron of W.B. Yeats and cofounder with the poet of Dublin's Abbey Theatre. Yeats visited here often, as did almost all the other writers who

contributed to the Irish literary revival in the first half of the 20th century. The house became derelict after Lady Gregory's death and was demolished in 1941; the grounds are now a wildlife park with a herd of deer and 6 km (4 miles) of nature trails. Picnic tables make this a lovely alfresco lunch spot. There's also a visitor center with displays on Lady Gregory and W.B. Yeats. Don't miss the park's only reminder of its literary past, the Autograph Tree, a giant copper beech, on which many of Lady Gregory's famous guests carved their initials. ⊠ *R458 (well signposted), Gort* ☎ *091/631–804* ⊕ *www.coolepark.ie* ⊠ *Free* ◷ *Visitor center and tearooms closed Oct.–Easter.*

Kilmacduagh Monastery

ARCHAEOLOGICAL SITE | Kilmacduagh's 110-foot-high (33.5-meter-high) Round Tower, reputedly the tallest in the world, tilts 1 meter (3 feet) from the vertical over the monastery below. Arguably more impressive than the famous tower at Glendalough and without the backdrop of tour buses, Kilmacduagh is peaceful apart from the mournful lowing of cattle. The monastery was founded in the 7th century, but the tower, cathedral, churches, and abbot's home were built more than three centuries later. St. Colman, who founded the monastery, is buried behind the cathedral. Lying on his grave is believed to relieve back pain. The key to the site can be obtained across the street at the Tower View Guesthouse with a €5 deposit. ⊠ *Kilmacduagh, Gort* ✛ *6 km (4 miles) southwest on R460 from Gort* ⊠ *Free.*

★ Thoor Ballylee (Yeats's Tower)

CASTLE/PALACE | W.B. Yeats wrote some of his finest poetry, including "The Tower" and "The Winding Stair" in Thoor Ballylee, a small castle just an eight-minute drive from Gort. You can take the winding staircase that led the famous poet up to his writer's garret. A tablet with the words "I, the poet William Yeats, With old mill boards and sea-green slates, And smithy work from the Gort forge, Restored this tower for my wife George. And may these characters remain, When all is ruin once again" is mounted outside as a testament to the time he spent in his summer retreat. ⊠ *Gort* ✛ *1½ km (1 mile) off R458* ⊕ *www.yeatsthoorballylee.org/visit* ⊠ *€7* ◷ *Closed Nov.–Apr.*

🍴 Restaurants

Gallery Cafe

$ | MODERN IRISH | A chilled-out café in the middle of town, Gallery Cafe has heaps of character with local artist exhibitions and the occasional live performance providing an ever-changing setting. The seasonal menu often features local catch, stews, and braised venison as well as sandwiches. **Known for:** hearty winter menu; quirky art exhibitions; town square setting. ⑤ *Average main: €15* ⊠ *The Square, Gort* ☎ *091/630–630* ⊕ *www.thegallerycafegort.com* ◷ *Closed Mon. and Tues.*

Galway City

The harbor city of Galway is the unofficial capital of the west of Ireland and the stronghold of traditional Irish ways, from its rapturous music scene to its artisanal restaurants that reap the local seafood harvest.

Its streets, with their famed boho bars and cafés that spill out onto its cobbled medieval lanes, are basking in international recognition having scored the title of both European City of Gastronomy in 2018 and European Capital of Culture for 2020. Despite being Ireland's fourth-largest city, it has retained the essence of a much smaller town, particularly in its compact and very walkable nucleus. The city's beating heart lies within this short thoroughfare and the twisting labyrinth of alleys that flow into it.

Galway City

City of the Tribes

Galway's urban elite was confined to 14 families of Anglo-Norman and Irish origins who controlled the city for the greater part of the second millennium, until the arrival of Oliver Cromwell's troops in the 17th century.

The families lived within Galway's city walls and built up their wealth through international trade, while the native Irish lived in the hinterlands.

Their names are still common in Galway and elsewhere in Ireland: Athy, Blake, Bodkin, Browne, D'Arcy, Dean, Font, French, Kirwan, Joyce, Lynch, Morris, Martin, and Skerret.

The city's medieval heritage, a fusion of Gaelic and Norman influences, is apparent in the intimate two- and three-story stone buildings, winding streets, narrow passageways, and cobblestones underfoot.

It's most alive later in the evening when street lights come on and the sound of uilleann pipes, harps, and bodhráns filters through the air. It's a vibrancy that's fueled both by the fact it's a university town and the epicenter of western Ireland, which ensures that it glows until the early hours.

While Galway has more than its fair share of Michelin stars, the foodie experience predictably balances the finest organic, locally sourced food with a chilled-out service in most restaurants.

Druid Lane Theatre just off Quay Street hosts traveling and homegrown productions, while Macnas, a troupe of avant-garde performers and puppeteers, add drama and color to city highlights from St. Patrick's Day to the Galway Halloween Parade.

Galway's growth and popularity mean that at its busiest moments, its narrow, one-way streets are jam-packed with pedestrians, while cars are gridlocked.

GETTING HERE AND AROUND

Galway is connected to Dublin by motorways M6–M4–M50 (four-lane highways with concrete dividers, some tolls), 208 km (129 miles) with a journey time of about two hours, 20 minutes. There is a

similarly good road to Limerick, the M18/N18 (100 km [62 miles]), with a journey time of one hour.

Express bus services to Galway from Dublin are available from both Bus Éireann and Citylink. Both take about three hours, 40 minutes from Dublin City Center. Bus services to Galway from Cork call at Limerick and Shannon Airport. Journey time from Cork is 4½ hours. There are also daily buses from Galway to Westport (1½ hours), Ballina (2½ hours), Sligo (2½ hours), and Belfast (6½ hours). For quick hops around the city, use a taxi, such as those of Big O.

Irish Rail–Iarnrod Éireann trains run from Dublin's Heuston Station to Galway City via Athlone. The journey takes two hours, 10 minutes. There are trains from Limerick City via Ennis on the new commuter route, a two-hour journey.

CONTACTS Big O Taxis. ☎ *091/585–858* ⊕ *www.bigotaxis.com.* **Ceannt (Bus) Station.** ✉ *Eyre Sq.* ☎ *091/562–000.* **Ceannt (Rail) Station.** ✉ *Eyre Sq.* ☎ *091/564–222* ⊕ *www.irishrail.ie.* **Citylink.** ✉ *17 Forster St.* ☎ *091/564–164* ⊕ *www.citylink.ie.*

TOURS

Lally Tours

BUS TOURS | While Galway's historic center is compact and can be explored on foot, many visitors enjoy a quick orientation. Hop aboard Lally Tours' vintage double-decker bus for an hour-long Old Galway City Tour. Every 90 minutes (every 45 minutes from June to August) buses leave from the tourist office in Forster Place on the corner of Eyre Square. ☒ *4 Forster St.* ☎ *091/562–905* ⊕ *www. lallytours.com* ☑ *From €12.*

VISITOR INFORMATION

CONTACTS Galway Discover Ireland Centre. ☒ *Forster St., Eyre Sq.* ☎ *091/537–700* ⊕ *www.discoverireland.ie/places-to-go/ galway.*

 ## Sights

Most of the city's sights, aside from the cathedral and the university campus, can be found in a narrow sector of the medieval town center that runs in a southwesterly direction from Eyre Square to the River Corrib. Not only is the city center compact, but it's also largely pedestrian-friendly, so the best way to explore it is on foot. It takes only five minutes to walk straight down Galway's main shopping street, the continuation of the north side of Eyre Square, to the River Corrib, where it ends (note that the name of this street changes several times).

Eyre Square

PLAZA | The largest open space in central Galway and the arrival and departure point by train and bus, this is a favorite chill-out spot on a sunny day for students, visitors, and lunching locals. Eyre Square on the east side of the River Corrib incorporates a sculpture garden and children's play area on its east side, while its west side is bound by a heavily traveled road. In the center is **Kennedy Park,** a patch of lawn named in honor of John F. Kennedy, who spoke here when he visited the city in June 1963. At the

north end of the park, a 20-foot-high steel sculpture standing in the pool of a fountain represents the brown sails seen on Galway hookers, the area's traditional sailing boats. Now a feature of Kennedy Park, the **Browne Doorway** was taken in 1905 from the Browne family's town house on Upper Abbeygate Street; it has the 17th-century coats of arms of both the Browne and Lynch families (two of Galway's 14 founding families). ☒ *Galway City.*

Galway Cathedral

RELIGIOUS SITE | Dominating Galway City's skyline for more than half a century with its massive, green, copper dome, Galway Cathedral's hulking brick exterior has had a mixed reception from critics since its construction. Inside, the limestone walls draw the eye up, while the stained-glass windows and the dome's light-filled contour add a heavenly perspective. ☒ *Nun's Island* ☎ *091/563–577* ⊕ *www.galwayca-thedral.ie* ☑ *Free.*

Galway City Museum

MUSEUM | The city's civic museum, housed in a modern building behind the Spanish Arch, contains materials relating to local history: old photographs, antiquities (the oldest is a stone ax head carbon-dated to 3500 BC), and a full-scale Galway hooker (turf-carrying boat) in the stairwell, as well as information on the city's involvement in Ireland's 1916 Rising. On the top floor, there's a child-friendly ocean-life museum with panoramic Corrib River views. Its café, the Kitchen, is a lively lunch and coffee spot. ☒ *Spanish Parade, Spanish Arch* ☎ *091/532–640* ⊕ *www.galwaycitymu-seum.ie* ☑ *Free* ⊙ *June–Sept., closed Mon.; Oct.–Easter, closed Sun. and Mon.*

The Hall of the Red Earl

HOUSE | Galway's Custom's House discovered a hoard of artifacts in its foundation, which revealed the site's significant past, as the palace of Ricard de Burgo, an earl who was the grandson of the city's founding father. The floodlit foundation of the building can be explored from a gangway through a glass partition that surrounds the dig, unveiling city life in Galway in the 13th century, before the 14 tribes ruled the city. ⊠ *Druid La., Center* ⊠ *Free.*

Katie's Claddagh Cottage and Claddagh Arts Centre

ARTS VENUE | On the west bank of the Corrib Estuary, this district was once an Irish-speaking fishing village outside the walls of the old town. The name is an Anglicization of the Irish *cladach,* which means "marshy ground." It retained a strong, separate identity until the 1930s, when its traditional thatched cottages were replaced by a conventional housing plan and its unique character and traditions were largely lost. One thing has survived: the claddagh ring, composed of two hands clasped around a heart with a crown above it (symbolizing love, friendship, and loyalty), was designed some 400 years ago by a goldsmith in this village, and is still used by many Irish, and Irish diaspora, as a wedding ring. Reproductions in gold or silver are favorite Galway souvenirs. Katie's Cottage, a replica of a typical claddagh home, is open as a café and exhibition center. ⊠ *Upper Fairhill Rd., The Claddagh* ⊠ *From €3.*

Lynch's Castle

CASTLE/PALACE | Lynch's Castle, once the stronghold of Galway's ruling family, dates back to 1600. These days it's occupied by a branch of a local bank, making its stone fireplace accessible to the public. Check out the gargoyles peering from its facade before heading around the corner to find Lynch's window. According to legend, magistrate and mayor James Lynch FitzStephen hanged his son from its sturdy Gothic frame as punishment for the murder of a Spanish sailor. ⊠ *Shop St., Center.*

NUI Galway

COLLEGE | Thanks in part to its central location, NUI Galway has become an inextricable part of Galway life since its construction in 1845, as only a handful of other universities, such as Oxford, have done. In fact its Tudor Gothic–style quadrangle was modeled on Christ Church in Oxford. It houses Galway's "hidden museum," the **James Mitchell Geology Museum,** which has a collection of 15,000 rocks, gemstones, and fossils. ⊠ *Newcastle Rd., University* ☎ *091/524–411* ⊕ *www.nuigalway.ie* ⊠ *Free.*

Salmon Weir Bridge

BRIDGE/TUNNEL | The bridge itself is nothing special, but in season—from mid-April to early July—shoals of salmon are visible from its deck as they lie in the clear river water before making their way upstream to the spawning grounds of Lough Corrib. ⊠ *West end of St. Vincent's Ave., Center.*

Salthill

NEIGHBORHOOD | FAMILY | A lively, hugely popular seaside resort, Salthill is beloved for its old-fashioned seaside promenade—the traditional place "to sit and watch the moon rise over Claddagh, and see the sun go down on Galway Bay," as Bing Crosby used to croon in the most famous song about the city. Today locals use it for a routine run from the city center or weekend leap into the ocean from its diving boards. The main attraction of the village, set 3 km (2 miles) west of Galway, is the long sandy beach along the edge of Galway Bay and the promenade above it. New hotels, trendy restaurants, and craft beer pubs along the seafront have nevertheless left plenty of room for the traditional amusement arcades (full of slot machines), seasonal cafés, and a fairground.

Spanish Arch

MEMORIAL | Built in 1584 to protect Spanish ships that were unloading cargoes of wines and brandies at the quays, this impressive stone arch is now the central feature of the newly restored Spanish Parade, a riverside piazza that draws a gathering of buskers and leisure seekers. ⊠ *Spanish Parade, Spanish Arch.*

St. Nicholas' Collegiate Church Galway

RELIGIOUS SITE | Built by the Anglo-Normans in 1320 and enlarged by member of the 14 tribes when they were at their most powerful during the 16th century, the church contains many fine carvings of lions, mermaids, and gargoyles dating from the late Middle Ages, and it's one of the best-preserved medieval churches in Ireland. Columbus prayed here on a visit to Galway in 1477. On Saturday morning, a street market, held in the pedestrian way beside the church, attracts dozens of vendors and hundreds of shoppers. ✉ *Mainguard St. and Lombard St., Center* ☎ *091/564–648* ⊕ *www.stnicholas.ie* 🎫 *Free.*

Restaurants

★ Aniar Restaurant

$$$$ | IRISH | J. P. McMahon has caused quite a stir in the Galway dining scene with his tapas at Cava Bodega and the recently opened casual spot Tartare, but award-winning Aniar (meaning "from the west") is his flagship restaurant. A minimalist Nordic decor provides an unfussy backdrop for the chef's equally unfussy approach to food. **Known for:** seaweed ice cream; minimalist furnishings; locally sourced food. ⑤ *Average main: €65* ✉ *53 Lower Dominick St., Center* ☎ *091/533–947* ⊕ *aniarrestaurant.ie.*

Ard Bia at Nimmo's

$$ | EUROPEAN | Expect to wait in line at this city-center restaurant set in an old stone house, with tables overlooking the Corrib. Ard Bia serves budget-conscious, freshly baked and sourced food, with a menu that changes according to what is in season. Jumbled furnishings from dressers to crockery in a casual setting contrasts the more spacious, timber-floored restaurant upstairs. **Known for:** all-day brunch; river views; seasonal menu. ⑤ *Average main: €21* ✉ *The Long Walk, Spanish Arch, Spanish Arch* ✦ *Head for Spanish Arch and restaurant*

is right behind it ☎ *091/561–114* ⊕ *www.ardbia.com.*

Cupán Tae

$ | IRISH | For anyone seeking an authentic tea-drinking experience, à la the Irish grandma who serves tea as an art form, the Cupán Tae ("the cup of tea" in Irish) serves it up with fussy crockery and much nostalgia. Breakfast is top-notch, and the popular afternoon tea comes complete with fresh-baked pastries served on a tiered china stand (of course). **Known for:** afternoon tea; breakfast; nostalgic setting. ⑤ *Average main: €14* ✉ *8 Quay La., Center* ☎ *091/895–000* ⊕ *cupantae.eu.*

★ Kai Cafe and Restaurant

$$ | CONTEMPORARY | Tucked inside a renovated cottage in the shadow of St. Ignatius's limestone belfry is one of Galway's best restaurants. The bare stone walls and floors are brightened by a pop of color from thrifted chairs and a skylight that draws in natural light, but what really shines is the reasonably priced and locally sourced organic food. **Known for:** creative menu; excellent wine list; reservations in demand. ⑤ *Average main: €23* ✉ *20 Sea Rd., Center* ⊕ *kaicaferestaurant.com.*

★ Loam

$$$$ | IRISH | The industrial facade and simply furnished interior of this award-winning restaurant and wine bar just off Eyre Square betray nothing of head chef Enda McEvoy's daily creations; he scours, forages, and travels the coast for the finest and most offbeat indigenous ingredients like reindeer moss or trout caviar. Plates are imaginatively presented, and the tasting menu has a cult following across the country (but is fairly priced at €60). **Known for:** award-winning chef; mostly organic, biodynamic wines; foraged local and all-Irish ingredients. ⑤ *Average main: €60* ✉ *Geata na Cathrach, Fairgreen, Center* ☎ *091/569–727* ⊕ *www.loamgalway.com* ⊘ *Closed Sun. and Mon.*

Pedestrian alleys and high-style boutiques help make Galway into a stroller's paradise—keep your eye out for the many 19th-century footscrapers.

McDonagh's Fish and Chips

$ | SEAFOOD | The humble fish-and-chip is king at this stalwart restaurant, serving deep-fried cod, whiting, haddock, and hake for decades. The reasonably priced fish is served with a heap of fabulous, freshly cooked chips (which have won a nationwide competition for the best in Ireland) and eaten at communal tables—a great way to meet the locals. **Known for:** Quay Street location; popularity with locals; prize-winning chips. $ *Average main: €10* ✉ *22 Quay St., Spanish Arch* ☎ *091/565–001* ⊕ *mcdonaghs.net.*

Oscar's Seafood Bistro

$$ | MODERN IRISH | Taking full advantage of Galway's fish-rich waters, Oscar's offers a daily changing menu based on the availability of the straight-from-trawler catch at the local market. Its warm interior with a ruby red backdrop, billowing fabric, and pine furnishings in close quarters has the essence of a seafaring vessel, with mackerel from the Aran Islands, and monkfish and scallops. **Known for:** oysters; great-value early-bird meals; fresh

catch. $ *Average main: €20* ✉ *Dominick St. Lower, Center* ☎ *91/582–180* ⊕ *www. oscarsseafoodbistro.com* ⊙ *Closed Sun.*

The Pie Maker

$ | CAFÉ | This quirky little slice of Galway harbors some of the city's best sweet and savory treats behind its maroon, ivy-clad facade, and a visit is the antidote for a misty Galway day. Beef and craft beer or chicken-and-mushroom pies are savory favorites, while sweet tooths will love the banoffee. **Known for:** intimate space in the city center; heartwarming pies. $ *Average main: €9* ✉ *10 Cross St. Upper, Center* ⊕ *www.thepiemaker.ie.*

★ The Pullman Restaurant

$$$$ | MODERN IRISH | Stationed on the grounds of Glenlo Abbey Hotel, over-looking Lough Corrib in the outskirts of Galway, is Ireland's most unique restaurant: two intricately restored train carriages that starred in Sidney Lumet's 1974 film, *Murder on the Orient Express*, starring Ingrid Bergman. Fully equipped with brass luggage racks and mahogany paneling, the carriages are as

Galway's Emerging Food Scene

Ever since a local hotelier created Galway's oyster festival more than 50 years ago to celebrate the region's legacy of producing the world-famous delicacy, the city has become one of Ireland's leading food hubs. Major annual food events have helped to create a citywide culinary environment that connects to the wider region. Each year Galway kicks off the season with its Food Festival at Easter, followed by the oyster festival in September and the Food On the Edge Festival a month later. By the end of the year, Eyre Square turns into a maze of timber kiosks selling artisanal food at Galway's Christmas market.

More recently, the city has placed itself firmly on the international culinary map with top-notch restaurants like Loam, Aniar, and Kai, and by becoming a European Region of Gastronomy for 2018, an award that recognizes the region's integration of gastronomy into tourism, culture, and economy.

Good food has also become part of everyday Galway life. The Saturday food market brings in the best of local food producers into the city center to set up their stalls behind the Collegiate Church of St. Nicholas as far as Sheridan's Cheesemongers. It attracts locals into the city in the early morning. New restaurants look to local food producers using age-old cooking methods to draw out indigenous flavors in inventive ways, giving the city more than its fair share of Michelin-starred restaurants. ⊕ *www.galwaymarket.com.*

impressive as the menu, which highlights wild game, fish, and beef. **Known for:** train carriages from the movie; lake views; wild game. ⑤ *Average main: €57* ✉ *Glenlo Abbey Hotel, Kentfield Bushy Park* ☎ *091/519–600* ⊕ *www.glenloabbeyhotel.ie/en/pullman-restaurant-galway* ⊗ *Closed weekdays Nov.–Feb.*

The Seafood Bar at Kirwan's

$$$ | SEAFOOD | Nestled into a lamp-lit corner of Kirwan's Lane near the Quays, this slim, two-story oasis has served quality local seafood for more than 20 years. Its selection reads like a travel guide from the highlights of the Wild Atlantic Way: Burren smoked salmon, Dingle prawns, and Connemara mussels. **Known for:** local seafood; daily specials; Kirwan's Lane location. ⑤ *Average main: €25* ✉ *Kirwan's La., Spanish Arch* ☎ *091/568–266* ⊗ *No lunch Sun. Nov.–Apr.*

🛏 Hotels

The G Hotel

$$$$ | HOTEL | *G* is for "glamour"—or for "good grief" (depending on your taste for over-the-top decor)—at this flamboyant player at the top end of Galway's hotel scene, whose architects worked with star hat designer Philip Treacy (a native of Galway) to create an interior that is every bit as fanciful as Treacy's hats. **Pros:** spa is the best pampering spot in the city; views of Lough Atalia; flamboyant decor. **Cons:** walk from city center; style may not appeal to everyone. ⑤ *Rooms from: €240* ✉ *Wellpark* ☎ *091/865–200* ⊕ *www.theghotel.ie* ⤳ *101 rooms* ⑩ *Free breakfast.*

Hotel Meyrick Galway

$$ | HOTEL | Galway's grande-dame hotel was built to accommodate train passengers to the heart of Galway in the middle of the 19th century, but even after an expensive makeover, the hotel has

managed to retain its Victorian character and restrained opulence with black-and-white-checkered tiles, sash windows, solid oak fixtures, and crystal chandeliers. **Pros:** location on Eyre Square; rooftop hot tub. **Cons:** not all bedrooms have a/c; limited parking. ⑤ *Rooms from: €155* ⊠ *Eyre Sq., Center* ☎ *091/564–041* ⊕ *www.hotelmeyrick.ie* ⇨ *99 rooms* ❖*◎❖ Free breakfast.*

⭐ **The House Hotel**

$ | **HOTEL** | Sheltered from noise on a one-way street with views overlooking the River Corrib, the House Hotel is arguably Galway's best-appointed property, just a stone's throw from the best of the city's vibrant restaurant and pub scene and a two-minute walk from the Quays. **Pros:** excellent city-center location; river views; trendy bar. **Cons:** remote car parking. ⑤ *Rooms from: €99* ⊠ *Spanish Parade, Spanish Arch* ☎ *091/538–900* ⊕ *www.thehousehotel.ie* ⇨ *40 rooms* ❖*◎❖ Free breakfast.*

Jurys Inn Galway

$ | **HOTEL** | Expect good-quality budget accommodations at this four-story hotel set beside the historic Spanish Arch and the river. **Pros:** reliable Irish budget hotel chain; great location for pubs, clubs, and river views. **Cons:** rates subject to demand, so book early; favorite for large bachelor/bachelorette parties. ⑤ *Rooms from: €89* ⊠ *Quay St., Spanish Arch* ☎ *091/566–444* ⊕ *www.jurysinn.com/hotels/galway* ⇨ *130 rooms* ❖*◎❖ Free breakfast.*

Park House Hotel

$$$$ | **HOTEL** | Even though this is a large, luxury hotel in central Galway, snazzily converted from a 200-year-old warehouse, it feels like a home away from home, thanks to attentive owner-managers. **Pros:** friendly, professional staff; a haven of quiet. **Cons:** tricky to find vehicle entrance first time. ⑤ *Rooms from: €230* ⊠ *Forster St., Center* ☎ *091/564–924* ⊕ *www.parkhousehotel.ie* ⇨ *84 rooms* ❖*◎❖ Free breakfast.*

Sea Breeze Lodge Bed and Breakfast

$$$$ | **B&B/INN** | Not your typical West of Ireland bolthole, this B&B has the elegance of a luxurious, small, boutique hotel with the charm and warm welcome of a bed-and-breakfast. **Pros:** modern bathrooms and rooms; views of Galway Bay; quiet location. **Cons:** not in the city center; walk to pubs and restaurants; two-night minimum stay required. ⑤ *Rooms from: €240* ⊠ *9 Cashelmara, Salthill* ☎ *091/529–581* ⊕ *www.sea-breezelodge.org* ☉ *Closed Nov.–mid-Mar.* ⇨ *6 rooms* ❖*◎❖ Free breakfast.*

🍸 Nightlife

Galway has more of a late-night pub scene than a club scene. And, being a music center, Galway regularly hosts top-notch performances in its impressive selection of theaters. Because of its small size and concentration of pubs and restaurants, Galway can seem even livelier at 11 pm than it does at 11 am. On weekends, when there are lots of students and other revelers in town, Eyre Square and environs can be rowdy after pub-closing time—2 am on Friday and Saturday. On the plus side, if you've been staying out in the country and you're ready for a little nightlife, you're certain to find plenty of it here.

The best pub scene is the area between Eyre Square and the Spanish Arch, where many bars stay open until 2 am on weekends.

CLUBS

Electric Garden & Theatre

DANCE CLUBS | Galway's liveliest nightclub has several different spaces including Electric, the main room, and the indoor-outdoor Glasshouse. The cocktails are great, as are the sounds, ranging from Balearic beats to house anthems to hip-hop Brooklyn Beats night. ⊠ *36 Upper Abbeygate St., Center* ☎ *091/565–976* ⊕ *www.electricgalway.com.*

Galway's Craft Beer Scene

There's a quiet taste revolution taking place in Galway City, with a growing amount of taps dedicated to craft beer. To discover the city's earliest craft beer pub, head out to Salthill Promenade to the **Oslo Microbrewery and Gastro Bar** (⊕ www.galwaybaybrewery.com/oslo). It's home to the Galway Bay Brewery, which has spawned a plethora of new pubs in Galway City and beyond. With 21 craft beers on tap, including six on rotation, **The Salt House** (⊕ www.galwaybaybrewery.com/salthouse) in Raven Terrace, across the Corrib from the Quays, offers a further range of 120 bottled brands. Other bars have moved in for a slice of the action, pairing food with their beers. For somewhere intimate with a rotating selection of beers and bespoke burgers, try **Caribou** (⊕ thisisgalway.ie/drink-galway/caribou) in Woodquay (near McSwiggan's). **Bierhaus** (⊕ www.bierhausgalway.com), at the bottom of Henry Street, has more than 60 craft beers available (20 on tap) with a new sandwich bar on-site.

Halo Nightclub

DANCE CLUBS | This sophisticated spot for dressy over-23-year-olds has live entertainment in five bars on two floors and two dance floors, as well as quiet booths. It's open Friday, Saturday, and bank-holiday Sundays from 11 pm. ✉ *36 Upper Abbeygate St., Center* ☎ *091/565–976* ⊕ *halonightclub.com.*

Hyde Bar and Gin Parlour

BARS/PUBS | Gin is having a moment in Ireland right now and nowhere is that more evident or celebrated than Hyde Bar and Gin Parlour, where you will find over 500 brands of gin, featuring flavors from potato to rhubarb to "Unicorn Tears." The bold interior, with electric-blue and shocking-pink furnishings and larger-than-life wall murals, comes as a surprise after entering the classic ivy-clad doorway. There's also a good selection of craft beer and the old reliable beverages. By day, this is a hugely popular brunch spot. ✉ *The Forster Court Hotel, Forster St., Center* ☎ *91/564–111* ⊕ *www.hydebargalway.ie.*

PUBS

Áras na nGael

BARS/PUBS | Cross O'Brien Bridge and take the first left to find this Irish-speaking social club–pub, which is a great place to hear traditional music, watch (or join) dancing and language classes, and hear the Irish language in use. Non–Irish speakers are very welcome. Open weekdays only. ✉ *45 Dominick St.* ☎ *091/567–824* ⊕ *www.arasnangael.ie.*

The Crane Bar

BARS/PUBS | Arrive early to get a seat at this tiny bar to the west of Claddagh; its two floors can get crammed during nightly trad sessions. ✉ *2 Sea Rd.* ☎ *091/587–419* ⊕ *www.thecranebar.com.*

The Dáil Bar

BARS/PUBS | While it looks traditional with its dark-wood decor, the Dáil is actually a recent arrival on the pub scene, and very popular with a younger crowd. ✉ *42–44 Middle St., Center* ☎ *091/563–777.*

★ King's Head

BARS/PUBS | With the most eye-catching facade on High Street, if not Galway City, the King's Head is dripping with 800 years of history with its association to the execution of King Charles I. There are trad music sessions nightly. ✉ *15 High St., Center* ⊕ *thisisgalway.ie/drink-galway/the-kings-head* ☒ *Free.*

McSwiggan's

BARS/PUBS | A popular Galway City pub with a restaurant upstairs, McSwiggan's has everything from church pews to ancient carriage lamps contributing to its eclectic character. ✉ *3 Eyre St., Wood Quay, Center* ☎ *091/568–917* ⊕ *mcswiggans.ie.*

Monroe's

BARS/PUBS | A large and sociable pub, Monroe's has free music nightly from 9 pm and regularly hosts impressive rock acts. ✉ *20 Dominick St., just across bridge from Claddagh, Center* ☎ *091/583–397.*

Nova Bar

BARS/PUBS | Cocktails, beer, and wine are served in this tiny bar, which has a DJ and live entertainment, plus student night on Wednesday. ✉ *1 William St. W, Center* ☎ *091/725–693* ⊕ *novabargalway.com.*

★ O'Connor's

BARS/PUBS | Fans of musician Ed Sheeran will instantly recognize the interior of this landmark pub as the location of his "Galway Girl" music video with actress Saoirse Ronan. Trading since 1942 this generous-size tavern in Salthill, is a firm favorite with visitors who browse through the pub's vast collection of paraphernalia, from farmyard tools and grandma's garters (hanging over a hearth) to a life-size statue of the "Quiet Man," John Wayne. Its impressive collection of whiskey is showcased on an imposing shelf behind the bar counter. ✉ *Salthill House, Upper Salthill Rd., Salthill* ☎ *091/523–468* ⊕ *www.oconnorsbar.com.*

The Quays

BARS/PUBS | Behind the simple facade, this Gothic bar is a surprising labyrinth of rooms across three stories, kitted out with furnishings from a medieval church, including pews, a giant organ, and altar. There are regular rock and country sessions. ✉ *Quay St., Center* ☎ *091/568–347* ⊕ *www.louisfitzgerald.com/quaysgalway.*

★ The Róisín Dubh

BARS/PUBS | A legend in its own right and a serious venue for stand-up comics, silent discos, emerging rock and traditional bands, the Róisín Dubh often showcases big, if still-struggling, talents. ✉ *Dominick St., Spanish Arch* ☎ *091/586–540* ⊕ *roisindubh.net.*

Taaffe's

BARS/PUBS | Open for 150 years, Taaffe's is bang in the city center and hosts regular trad music sessions that start from 5:30 pm. ✉ *19 Shop St., Center* ☎ *091/564–066.*

★ Tigh Neachtain

BARS/PUBS | This bright-blue, mural-scarred pub is in the hub of Galway's medieval center and the core of its beating heart. For more than 120 years its mahogany snugs and alcoves have given patrons refuge from the city's infamous mist and rain while its stock of more than 130 brands of whiskey has fueled heat through their veins. Predictably, it's buzzing on the weekends. ✉ *17 Cross St., Spanish Arch* ☎ *091/568–820* ⊕ *www.tighneachtain.com.*

🎭 Performing Arts

GALLERIES

NUI Galway

ART GALLERIES—ARTS | The art gallery at University College has a number of intriguing exhibitions each year on painting, sculpture, and photography. ✉ *University* ✛ *Downstairs in Quadrangle* ☎ *091/495–098* ⊕ *www.nuigalway.ie* ☞ *No step-free access.*

THEATER

An Taibhdhearc Theatre

THEATER | Founders of the Gate Theatre in Dublin, partners Hilton Edwards and Micheál Mac Liammóir created the national Irish-language theater, An Taibhdhearc (pronounced "*on tie*-vark") to produce first-class Irish works in both English and Irish languages. ⊠ *Middle St., Center* ☎ *091/562–024* ⊕ *www. antaibhdhearc.com.*

Druid Theatre Company

THEATER | Ireland's theatrical hub outside the capital, the Druid has pioneered Galway's identity as a center for the arts. Playwright Martin McDonagh debuted here along with many other playwrights. The Druid showcases 20th-century Irish and European plays and is considered a pioneer in the development of Irish theater. Its players have toured extensively and performed at Lincoln Center in New York, and several London venues. The Druid regularly presents a production at Galway Arts Festival in late July. ⊠ *Druid La., Center* ☎ *091/568–660* ⊕ *www. druid.ie.*

★ Macnas

PUPPET SHOWS | An internationally renowned, roving Galway-based troupe of performance artists, Macnas has raised street theater in Ireland to new levels. While their participation in the July Arts Festival's parade is always much anticipated, it's their broody, giant-scale procession at the Galway Aboo Halloween parade that's the annual highlight. ⊠ *Fisheries Field, Salmon Weir Bridge, Center* ☎ *091/561–462* ⊕ *www.macnas. com.*

🛍 Shopping

BOOKS

★ Charlie Byrne's Bookshop

BOOKS/STATIONERY | Take extra time to leaf through this treasure trove of literature. Heaving with 10,000 publications, the flagship store has new, discounted, and out-of-print titles, and an unrivaled range of Irish-interest books. Check in on Saturday for good old children's storytelling sessions. ⊠ *The Cornstore, Middle St.,* *Center* ☎ *091/561–766* ⊕ *www.charlieb-yrne.com.*

CLOTHING

Faller's Sweater Shop

CLOTHING | The choicest selection of Irish-made sweaters can be found here, and all competitively priced. ⊠ *25 High St., Center* ☎ *091/564–833.*

O'Máille's

CLOTHING | O'Máille's is popular for its selection of Aran sweaters and hand-woven tweeds. ⊠ *16 High St., Center* ☎ *091/562–696* ⊕ *www.omaille.com.*

CRAFTS AND GIFTS

Cloon Keen Atelier

GIFTS/SOUVENIRS | The candles, body-care products, and perfumes stocked here are produced in nearby Spiddal by dedicated artisans. ⊠ *21a High St., Center* ☎ *091/565–736* ⊕ *www.cloonkeenatelier. com.*

Galway Irish Crystal

CERAMICS/GLASSWARE | A factory outlet on the city's ring road, Galway Irish Crystal sells hand-cut Irish glass, Belleek pottery, and other fine porcelain. ⊠ *Dublin Rd., Merlin Park* ☎ *091/757–311* ⊕ *www. galwaycrystal.ie.*

★ Judy Greene Pottery

CRAFTS | Ceramics by Judy Greene—a local potter specializing in hand-thrown ceramics depicting landscapes and Irish flora—as well as handmade jewelry and knitwear can be found in this two-story store in atmospheric Kirwan's Lane. ⊠ *Kirwan's La., Center* ☎ *091/561–753* ⊕ *www.judygreenepottery.com.*

Kilkenny Shop

CRAFTS | Synonymous with good modern design in Ireland, the Kilkenny Shop stocks the best ceramics, crystal, leatherware, clothing, and other craft items from around the country. ⊠ *6–7 High St., Center* ☎ *091/566–110* ⊕ *www.kilkenny-shop.com.*

FOOD
★ Sheridan's Cheesemongers
FOOD/CANDY | Together, Seamus and Kevin Sheridan know all of Ireland's artisanal-cheese makers personally and stock the widest possible range of delectable cheeses in their aromatic store to the rear of St. Nicholas' Collegiate Church. Italian charcuterie and home branded chutneys along with the fine selection from the wineshop upstairs will complete your picnic. ⊠ *16 Churchyard St., Center* ☎ *091/564–829* ⊕ *www.sheridanscheesemongers.com.*

JEWELRY
Cobwebs
JEWELRY/ACCESSORIES | Phyllis MacNamara's cute two-story boutique is filled with an irresistible selection of antique jewelry (real and costume) and collectibles for men and women, all with a witty twist. A selection of jewelry from local goldsmiths is also available. ⊠ *7 Quay La., Spanish Arch* ☎ *091/564–388* ⊕ *www.cobwebs.ie.*

Thomas Dillon's Claddagh Gold
JEWELRY/ACCESSORIES | Dating from 1750, Thomas Dillon's claims to be the original maker of Galway's famous claddagh ring. In the back of the crimson shop the Claddagh Ring Museum has a small but interesting display of antique claddagh rings and old Galway memorabilia. ⊠ *1 Quay St., Spanish Arch* ☎ *091/566–365* ⊕ *www.claddaghring.ie.*

MUSIC
Kieran Moloney
MUSIC STORES | A display case of the craft of Irish luthiers, this lovely old-world shop stocks acoustic stringed instruments and some wind instruments, including Irish handmade uilleann pipes, Irish bouzoukis and, more tempting for the traveler, pocket-size tin whistles. ⊠ *Olde Malt Arcade, 17 High St., Center* ☎ *091/566–488* ⊕ *www.moloneymusic.com.*

⚲ Activities

BICYCLING
Bike Hire Ireland
BICYCLING | Prebook your bike of choice from a wide range of brands if you have strong preferences, and just hit the road. Or opt for a self-guided tour: the company has handy drop-off points in Connemara, the Burren, and Kerry. ⊠ *Westside Business Centre, Seamus Quirke Rd.* ☎ *091/525–007* ⊕ *www.bikehireireland.com* ☞ *Rates from €10 a day.*

FISHING
Anglers have a choice of freshwater fishing and deep-sea fishing from collection points throughout the city.

Duffy's Fishing
FISHING | A good range of clothing, gear, and tackle for anglers is for sale here. ⊠ *5 Mainguard St., Center* ☎ *091/562–367.*

GOLF
Galway Bay Golf Resort
GOLF | An 18-hole parkland course near the village of Renville, 16 km (10 miles) from the city, Galway Bay Golf Resort is on the shores of Galway Bay, opposite the city, and was designed by former Ryder Cup and World Cup golfer, Christy O'Connor Jr. The Atlantic Ocean forms a dramatic backdrop to a course featuring mature trees, concealed bunkers, and highly praised putting surfaces. ⊠ *Renville, Oranmore* ☎ *091/790–711* ⊕ *www.galwaybaygolfresort.com* ☔ *Oct.–Mar. €95; Apr.–Sept. €135* ⚑ *18 holes, 7308 yards, par 72.*

Galway Golf Club
GOLF | Galway Golf Club was established in 1895, and moved to its present location in suburban Salthill in 1925. At that point it was redesigned by course architect Alister McKenzie, who was also responsible for Augusta, home of the U.S. Masters. It has been the home base of two famous Irish pros, Christy O'Connor Sr., and his nephew, Christy O'Connor Jr. In spite of its proximity to the

Aran Rediscovered

During the 1800s, the islands, wracked by famine and mass emigration, were virtually forgotten by mainland Ireland. At the turn of the 20th century, however, the books of J. M. Synge (1871–1909)—who learned Irish on Inishmaan and wrote about its people in his famous play *Riders to the Sea*—prompted Gaelic revivalists to study and document this isolated bastion of Irish culture. To this day, Synge's travel book *The Aran Islands*, first published in 1907, and reissued by Penguin with a brilliant introduction by artist and mapmaker Tim Robinson in 1992, remains the best book ever written about the islands. Liam

O'Flaherty became one of the most famous sons of Inishmore through his novels, such as *Famine*. And in 1934, American director Robert Flaherty filmed his classic documentary *Man of Aran* on Inishmore, recording the islanders' dramatic battles with sea and storm, and bringing the islands into the world spotlight. The film is still highly esteemed by the islanders, and there are frequent showings on Inishmore during the summer months. Flaherty, incidentally, continues to be a common surname on the islands; it is hard to visit the islands *without* meeting a Flaherty.

city, there are excellent views of Galway Bay, the Burren, and the Aran Islands. It has an abundance of trees, prickly gorse bushes in the rough, and some tricky fairways that run close to the ocean. ⊠ *Blackrock, Salthill* ☎ *091/522–033* ⊕ *www.galwaygolf.com* ✉ *May–Sept. €100, Oct.–Apr. €35–€50* 🏌 *18 holes, 2995 yards, par 70.*

RIVER CRUISING

Corrib Princess

BOATING | A lovely way to spend a fine afternoon is to take a Corrib Cruise from Wood Quay, behind the Town Hall Theatre, at the Rowing Club; it lasts 1½ hours and travels 8 km (5 miles) up the River Corrib and about 6 km (4 miles) around Lough Corrib. There's a bar on board, tea and coffee, and a commentary. The trip costs €17, and boats depart daily at 12:30 and 2:30 from May through September, with an additional departure at 4:30 July through August (except Saturday). You can also rent the boat for an evening. ⊠ *Wood Quay* ☎ *091/563–846* ⊕ *www. corribprincess.ie.*

The Oileáin Árainn (Aran Islands)

No one knows for certain when the Aran Islands—Inis Mór (Inishmore), Inis Meáin (Inishmaan), and Inis Oírr (Inisheer)—were first inhabited, but judging from the number of Bronze Age and Iron Age forts found here (especially on Inis Mór), 3000 BC is a safe guess.

Each island has a hotel, and there's no shortage of guesthouses, campsites, hostels, and B&Bs, many in simple family homes. Each island has at least one wine-licensed restaurant serving plain home cooking. Most B&Bs will provide a packed lunch and an evening meal on request. For general information about visiting the Aran Islands and useful links, try ⊕ *www.aranislands.ie.*

Once the day-trippers leave, the islands regain a mellowness that's lost in the flurry to see everything. From spring to autumn the days are long, so the islands can be enjoyed at a leisurely pace while

As you arrive by plane over the Aran Islands, their famous stone-wall fences—built by medieval farmers to clear lands for farms—come into view.

locals hit the pubs later in the evening and place drink orders in a mishmash of English and Irish.

GETTING HERE AND AROUND

The two main transport arteries to the Aran Islands are via Doolin in County Clare or Connemara in County Galway.

Aer Arann Islands offers 10-minute flights to the Aran Islands. The nonislander fare is €49 round-trip, leaving from Connemara Airport near Inverin, 30 km (19 miles) west of Galway.

In Connemara, regular ferries service all three islands. Park at Rossaveal (Ros an Mhíl), 37 km (23 miles) west of Galway City. or book a shuttle bus from the city when buying your ticket. There are at least two sailings a day, and four or more in high season, timed to facilitate day trips. Ask when boarding about interisland ferries if you intend to visit more than one island. Inis Mór, the biggest island, is the only one with organized transport. Book a tour or taxi in advance (through the TIO in Galway), or hire a

bicycle (including electric bikes) or pony and trap on landing.

The Doolin ferry crossing is seasonal from March to early November. The pier has recently increased in size, facilitating larger vessels such as the Doolin Express, which offers a quick and even sailing to the islands.

CONTACTS Aer Arann Islands. ☎ *091/593–034* ⊕ *www.aerarannislands.ie.* **Galway Tourism.** ✉ *Forster St., Eyre Sq., Galway City* ☎ *091/537–700* ⊕ *www.galwaytourism.ie.*

Inis Mór (Inishmore)

20 km (12 miles) southwest of Rossaveal Ferry Port, 24 km (15 miles) north of Doolin Pier.

Dún Aengus Hillfort is the main draw to Inis Mór, the largest and most populated of Aran's three islands. Stretching more than 16 km (10 miles) long and about 2 km (1 mile) wide at most points, with an area of 7,640 acres, it's too large to fully explore on foot on a day trip, so hire a bicycle near the pier to navigate its lanes.

If time permits, head for the less frequented west of the island, visiting Dún Dúchathair, a dramatically sited, freely accessible promontory fort.

VISITOR INFORMATION
CONTACTS Oileáin Árainn (Aran Islands)–Inis Mór (Inishmore) Tourist Office. ⊠ *Beside Inis Mór Bicycle Hire, Cill Ronáin [Kilronan]* ☎ *099/61263* ⊕ *www.discoverireland.ie.*

Sights

★ Dún Aengus
ARCHAEOLOGICAL SITE | Even if you have only a few hours to explore Inis Mór, rent a bike (next to the pier) and head straight for Dún Aengus. Set at the edge of a 300-foot precipice towering over the ocean, this semicircular fortress is one of the finest prehistoric monuments in Europe and the main draw to Inis Mór. The purpose of its construction more than 3,000 years ago is a matter of conjecture, and also irrelevant to the legions of seabirds who occupy its scenic Atlantic perch looking out on Connemara and the 12 Pin Mountains. Allow 1–1½ hours for a visit. ⚠ **In order to protect this fragile monument from erosion, you should approach it only through the visitor center, which gives access to a 1-km (½-mile) uphill walk over uneven terrain—wear sturdy footwear.** ⊠ *8 km (5 miles) east of Cill Ronáin (Kilronan), Kilmurvy* ☎ *099/61008* ⊕ *www.heritage-ireland.ie/en/west/dunaonghasa* ⊠ *€5.*

Hotels

Aran Camping and Glamping
$$ | **RENTAL** | Aran's glamping units, or *clocháns,* are igloo shaped (inspired by monks' medieval beehive huts that made a guest appearance in *Star Wars: The Last Jedi*) and fully heated, with en suite and cooking facilities. **Pros:** unique units; atmospheric setting on beach;

heated, with cooking facilities. **Cons:** no concierge service; groups discouraged; no TV. $ *Rooms from: €125* ⊠ *Inis Mor, Frenchman's Beach, Aran Islands* ☎ *086/189–5823* ⊕ *www.irelandglamping.ie* ⊠ *9 units* ⊠ *No meals.*

Ard Einne Guesthouse
$ | **B&B/INN** | The rambling 80-year-old house on Inishmore, with its distinctive dormer windows, is close to both the beach and the town; many guests base themselves here for two or three nights, to make a thorough exploration of the island. **Pros:** great location for getting away from it all; near the airport; sea views. **Cons:** one of the island's biggest guesthouses; no elevator; a walk from the island's main hub. $ *Rooms from: €80* ⊠ *Cill Ronáin [Kilronan]* ☎ *099/61126* ⊕ *www.ardeinne.com* ⊙ *Closed Nov.–Jan.* ⊠ *8 rooms* ⊠ *Free breakfast.*

Kilmurvey House
$ | **B&B/INN** | This rambling 200-year-old stone farmhouse, once the family home of the O'Flahertys—one of whom was Oscar Wilde's godfather—whose descendants include the famed writers Liam and Robert, is the first choice of many visitors to the island thanks to its location at the foot of Dún Aengus fort, a three-minute walk from the beach, and about 6½ km (4 miles) from the quay and the airport (accessible by minibus). **Pros:** lovely warm welcome; courtesy minibus to and from restaurants; memorable location adjacent to historic fort. **Cons:** 6½ km (4 miles) from village, pubs, and restaurants; public minibus costs €5 each way; no elevator. $ *Rooms from: €90* ⊠ *Cill Ronáin [Kilronan]* ☎ *099/61218* ⊙ *Closed mid-Oct.–Mar.* ⊠ *12 rooms* ⊠ *Free breakfast.*

Nightlife

Joe Mac's
BARS/PUBS | Located right off the pier, Joe Mac's is a good place for a fireside pint

Who Was Father Ted?

Although the last episode of Channel 4's sitcom series *Father Ted* aired 20 years ago, the program, which features the unorthodox antics of three priests, has left its mark on County Clare and the Aran Islands, which doubled up as the infamous Craggy Island throughout three years of filming. Today this cult classic has resulted in a series of festivals, the most notable being **TedFest** (⊕ *www.tedfest.org*), which occurs in February on Inis Mór. It's a weekend of mayhem, with a hefty price tag of €150, which doesn't include transport, food, or accommodation. Independent Ted Heads can go to Inis Oirr to see the rusty shipwreck of the MV *Plassy* used in the series' opening credits or head back to the mainland for a spot of tea at Ted's old **Parochial House** (⊕ *www.fathertedshouse.com*) in the Burren. For a little context, and to understand the phenomenon of *Father Ted*, the series can be found on Amazon or BBC America.

while waiting for the ferry home. ⊠ *Cill Ronáin [Kilronan]* ☎ *099/61248.*

Joe Watty's

BARS/PUBS | Located on the hill outside the village, Joe Watty's is the hub of Inis Mór's entertainment, with regular music sessions and reliable food. ⊠ *Main Rd., Cill Ronáin [Kilronan]* ☎ *086/049–4509* ⊕ *www.joewattys.ie.*

Ostán Oileáin Árainn

MUSIC CLUBS | Fans in the know say this is the place to head for the best in traditional music on the Aran Islands. ⊠ *Cill Ronáin [Kilronan], Aran Islands* ☎ *099/61104* ⊕ *www.aranislandshotel.com.*

Inis Meáin (Inishmaan)

3 km (2 miles) east of Inis Mór (Inishmore).

The middle island in both size and location, Inis Meáin has a population of about 300 and its empty beaches and breathtaking scenery can be explored on foot or bicycle with relative ease.

Sights

You have no alternative to walking if you want to reach the island's major antiquities: **Dún Conor (Conor Fort),** a smaller version of Dún Aengus; the ruins of two **early Christian churches**; and a chamber tomb known as the **Bed of Diarmuid and Grainne,** dating from about 2000 BC. You can also take wonderful cliff walks above secluded coves.

Traces the author of *The Playboy of the Western World,* John Millington Synge, who stayed here more than a hundred years ago, dot the island—from his thatched residence to Synge's Chair, a collection of rocks on the isolated westerly side of the island where the writer honed his craft on a limestone cliff edge high above the ocean

It's on Inis Meáin that the traditional Aran lifestyle is most evident. Most islanders still don hand-knitted Aran sweaters, though nowadays they wear them with jeans and sneakers.

Aran Island Woolens

Made of plain, undyed wool and knit with distinctive crisscross patterns, sometimes referred to as *báinín* sweaters or "ganseys," the Aran sweater is a combination of folklore and fashion.

Since harsh weather made warmth and protection vital out in the Atlantic Ocean, the women of Aran long ago discovered the solution to this problem in this strong, comfortable, hand-knit sweater. Indeed, these Arans can hold 30% of their weight in water before they even start to feel wet. The reason? Traditionally, the wool used was unwashed and retained its water-repellent natural sheep's lanolin.

Look for the Pattern

Not so long ago, these pullovers were worn by every County Donegal fisherman, usually made to a design belonging exclusively to his own family. It's said that a native can tell which family the knitter belongs to from the patterns used in a genuine Aran sweater. Often the patterns used religious symbols and folk motifs, such as the Tree of Life, the Honeycomb (standing for thrift and thought to be lucky), the SeaHorse, the Blackberry—all are patterns in the almost sculptured, deeply knitted work that characterizes the Aran method. Their famous basket stitch represents the fisherman's basket, a hope for a *curragh* (fishing boat) heavy with catch. A colorful belt called a *crios* (pronounced "criss") is handcrafted in many traditional designs as a useful accessory.

Making Your Purchase

Most of the Aran sweaters you'll see throughout Ireland are made far north of the islands themselves, in County Donegal, an area most associated with high-quality, handwoven textiles. The best are painstakingly knitted by hand, a process that can take weeks. As a result, prices are not cheap, and if you think you've found a bargain, check the label before buying—it's more likely a factory copy. Still, the less expensive, lighter-weight, hand-loomed sweaters (knitted on a mechanical loom, not with needles) are less than half the price, and more practical for most lifestyles. But the real McCoy is still coveted: some of the finest examples woven by Inis Meáin are sold at luxury stores like Bergdorf Goodman and Wilkes Bashford. And young Irish designers like Liadain De Buitlear are giving the traditional Aran a newer-than-now spin, highly popular in Dublin boutiques.

🛏 Hotels

★ Inis Meáin Restaurant and Suites

$$$$ | **HOTEL** | A remote, luxurious restaurant-hotel with sweeping sea views and a minimalist interior, Inis Meáin Restaurant and Suites offers a unique, modern-monastic retreat in a stunning, low-lying stone and glass building that blends with the stonescape of the island. **Pros:** excellent restaurant has a cult following; exquisite views; private and peaceful. **Cons:** off-the-grid feel not for everyone; two-night minimum stay; books up far in advance and no waitlist. $ *Rooms from: €350* ✉ *Aran Islands* ☎ *086/826–6026* ⊕ *inismeain.com* ⊘ *Closed Oct.–late Mar.* 🛏 *4 rooms, 1 suite apartment* ⦿ *Free breakfast.*

🛍 Shopping

Inis Meáin Knitting

OUTLET/DISCOUNT STORES | Inis Meáin Knitting is a young company producing quality knitwear in luxury fibers (a slick twist on the standard Aran sweater) for the international market, including Barneys New York and Bergdorf Goodman. The factory showroom has an extensive selection of garments at discount prices. ⊠ *Carrown Lisheen, Aran Islands* ✛ *From pier, walk 5 mins due west* ☏ *099/73009* ⊕ *www.inismeain.ie.*

Inis Oírr (Inisheer)

4 km (2½ miles) east of Inis Meáin (Inishmaan), 8 km (5 miles) northwest of Doolin Docks.

Inis Oírr, the smallest island, can be explored on foot in an afternoon, though if the weather is fine you may be tempted to linger on the long, sandy beach between the quay and the airfield. Only one stretch of road, about 500 yards long, links the airfield and the sole village; after that it's hilly pathways with panoramic views back to the mainland and the Cliffs of Moher. A cycle to the island's lighthouse offers rich views across the island's maze of stone walls, framed by the ocean.

To the east of the village there is a holy well and seal colony.

For guests that linger for the night, Tigh Neds (Ned's House) near the pier is the place for an aperitif accompanied with the sound of the ocean, while Tigh Ruairi in the village offers hearty fare. The island has a campsite, hostel, self-catering, and a selection of guesthouses.

👁 Sights

Church of Kevin

RELIGIOUS SITE | Signposted to the southeast of the quay, the Church of Kevin is a small, early Christian church that gets buried in sand by storms every winter. Each year the islanders dig it out of the sand for the celebration of St. Kevin's Day on June 14. ⊠ *Inis Oirr.*

MV *Plassy* Shipwreck

LOCAL INTEREST | The hulking, rusty wreck lying on the island's west coast has gained a cult following ever since it appeared in the opening credits of the acclaimed Irish television show, *Father Ted.* Horses and traps stop by to explain its fleeting fame and cyclists stop here to take a selfie break. ⊠ *Aran Islands* 🎟 *Free.*

O'Brien's Castle

ARCHAEOLOGICAL SITE | This ruined 15th-century tower house (also referred to as *An Tur Faire* or "the tower ruin") dominates the island from the top of a steep rocky hill; a martello tower keeps it company. ⊠ *Inis Oirr* 🎟 *Free.*

🍴 Restaurants

Teach an Tae (Cafe Aran Tea Rooms)

$ | IRISH | Michael and Alissa Donoghue do not have to travel far to get the ingredients for their little cottage café that overlooks the pier. Their flock of chickens

Island Nights

To appreciate the fierce loneliness of the Aran Islands you must spend the night on one. Because all the islands, especially Inishmore, crawl with day-trippers, it's difficult to let their rugged beauty sink into your soul until 10 pm, when the sky is dark and the pubs fill with the acrid smell of peat smoke and Guinness. Once the day-trippers clear out, the islands' stunningly fierce and brooding beauty is disturbed only by the bleat of the sheep and the incessant rush of the wind.

provide eggs, and the vegetable and herb garden—nurtured with seaweed throughout the year—furnishes their salads. **Known for:** lemon poppy-seed cake; pretty cottage setting; made-from-scratch menu; free Wi-Fi. $ *Average main: €5* ⊠ *Lurgan Village, Aran Islands* ☎ *099/75092* ⊕ *www.cafearan.ie.*

Hotels

Hotel Inisheer

$ | **HOTEL** | A basic low-rise in the middle of the island's only village, a few minutes' walk from the quay and the airstrip, this simple whitewashed building with a slate roof and tile flooring has bright, plainly furnished rooms, with pine-frame beds, pine floors, and white bed linen. **Pros:** very clean; good location between pier and airstrip; larger rooms upstairs are good for families. **Cons:** basic standard of comfort (certainly no frills); noise from the pub. $ *Rooms from: €89* ⊠ *Inis Oirr* ☎ *099/75020* ⊕ *www.hotelinisoirr.com* ⊙ *Closed Oct.–Mar.* ⇋ *14 rooms* ⦿| *Free breakfast.*

Activities

BICYCLING
Rothaí Inis Oírr (Inisheer Bike Hire)

BICYCLING | Just up from the pier, this small stone cabin rents bicycles and is a good place to stop for general advice. While horse and carriage rides offer an easier tour of the island, there is no more rewarding way to discover this little wind-swept corner of the Atlantic Ocean than by bike. ■**TIP➜ If it's your first time here and you only have the day, manage your time: only explore the west of the island, saving time for the beach near the pier.** ⊠ *Aran Islands* ☎ *099/75049* ⊕ *www.rothai-inisoirr.com* ⊠ *€10.*

CONNEMARA AND COUNTY MAYO

Updated by
Vic O'Sullivan

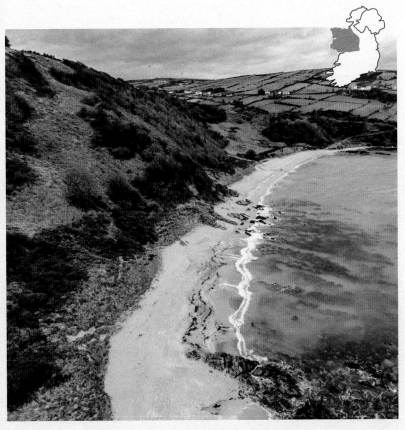

⊙ Sights	🍴 Restaurants	🛏 Hotels	🛍 Shopping	🍸 Nightlife
★★★★★	★★☆☆☆	★★★★★	★★☆☆☆	★☆☆☆☆

WELCOME TO CONNEMARA AND COUNTY MAYO

TOP REASONS TO GO

★ **Captivating Connemara:** An almost uninhabited landscape of misty bogland, studded with deep blue lakes under huge Atlantic skies: painters have strived for generations to capture the ever-changing light.

★ **The Great Western Greenway:** Cycle this historical railway line from the alluring market town of Westport, past Newport's handsome high arched bridge to Achill Island with Clew Bay's islands as a constant companion.

★ **The Erris Peninsula:** Sheltering the western seaboard from the full brunt of the Atlantic's force, this forlorn and off-radar Gaeltacht (Irish-speaking region) is speckled with secret coves, enormous cliff edges, and breathtaking views.

★ **Clifden and the Sky Road:** Walk the Sky Road to take in its breathtaking scenery—sea views on one side, the Twelve Bens Mountains on the other—from the compact village of Clifden, the liveliest spot for miles around.

With the most westerly seaboard in Europe, this region is one of the wildest stretches of the Wild Atlantic Way. While just to the west and north of hip Galway City, this area is famed for its remoteness and rural character. Connemara sits in the northwest corner of County Galway. County Mayo is Ireland's third-largest county, with coast on three of its four sides, and the River Moy and the huge expanse of Lough Conn and Lough Cullin on the fourth. Bright lights are to be found in Clifden and Westport, both lively small towns of great charm.

1 Roundstone. This charming Connemara fishing village has an especially scenic setting, which makes it popular with artists and photographers.

2 Clifden. With the Twelve Bens Mountains backdrop and the Atlantic Ocean in the foreground, Clifden is a beautiful base for exploring the Connemara region.

3 Letterfrack. The gateway village to Connemara National Park and a convenient base for local hiking and spending time at Kylemore Abbey.

4 Kylemore Valley. A beautiful stretch of Connemara that contains the lakeside Kylemore Abbey.

5 Leenane. A tiny, idyllic village that is home to Killary Harbour and a cool food truck.

6 Cong. Hugging Ashford Castle, this small village is known as the setting for 1950s movie, *The Quiet Man.*

7 Westport. On an inlet of Clew Bay, this attractive town is a great base for exploring Achill Island and Croagh Patrick.

8 Castlebar. Not as pretty as Westport but Mayo's capital town is a lively town and home to the Museum of Country Life.

9 Foxford. A pretty village and home to Foxford Woollen Mills and showroom and its heirloom woollen blankets and throws.

10 Belmullet. This under-the-radar town is the perfect access point to the rugged and unspoiled Mullet Peninsula.

11 Killala. A pretty bay-side village and the gateway to Mayo's rugged northern coast.

HIKING THE WEST

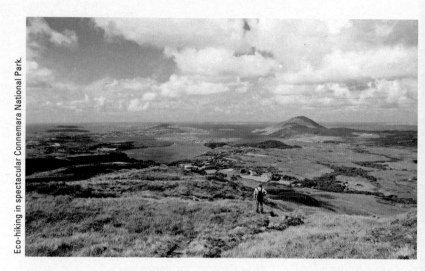

Eco-hiking in spectacular Connemara National Park.

More and more, travelers are discovering that Ireland's western regions are hiking heaven. In fact, hikes or guided walks through Connemara or County Mayo are the best ways to explore these territories at first hand, or rather, foot.

Why hike the West? It has some of the finest rugged scenery and dramatic indented coastline in all Ireland. In Connemara serried ranks of heather-clad mountains, interspersed with bright blue lakes, beckon to the walker as dramatic cloud formations scud across huge Atlantic skies. In County Mayo, the huge conical bulk of Croagh Patrick spectacularly looms above Clew Bay. Or what about earning some blisters among the free-range sheep of the Doolough Valley, set in the shadow of Mweelrea Mountain? The attraction lies in the terrific views nearly everywhere you look. Coastal views alternate with mountain vistas, often topped by a perfect rainbow. A daily highlight is the spectacular sunset over the Atlantic, at its biggest and best in late August.

PACK TO HIKE

You can't hike Connemara and Mayo in sneakers, due to the combination of bog, rocky terrain, and frequent showers. Wear waterproof hiking boots, quick-drying trousers rather than denim, and carry lightweight, waterproof rainwear (preferably breathable). Because of the wind, most Irish walkers wear knitted or fleece hats, so pack accordingly.

Hiking buffs are glad to know that the last decade has seen the completion of various "way-marked" (signposted) walking routes, which can be sampled in easy one- or two-hour "loops," or, for more serious walkers, made the focus of a visit.

KNOW WHERE YOU'RE GOING

Walkers on way-marked trails are advised to buy an Ordnance Survey map of the area, which is sold locally. Most tourist offices also have free maps of less ambitious walks on roads and local footpaths.

TOP HIKING DESTINATIONS

The Western Way's County Galway section extends from Oughterard on Lough Corrib through the mountains of Connemara to Leenane on Killary Harbour, a distance of 50 km (30 miles). Its 177-km (110-mile) County Mayo section, known as the Western Way (Mayo), continues past Killary Harbour to Westport on Clew Bay to the Ox Mountains east of Ballina. This trail should be the first choice of serious walkers, as it includes some of the finest mountain and coastal scenery in Ireland. The Great Western Green-way is a traffic-free 42-km (26-mile) cycling and walking trail that follows the line of Mayo's Westport–Mulranny Railway (closed since 1937) along the

Many way-marked hikes go past beautiful lakes like Lough Corrib.

northern shore of Clew Bay and has scenic walking and cycling with very few inclines, suitable for moderately fit people. Another perfect hiking destination is Connemara National Park, which consists of some 5,000 acres of untamed mountain wilderness in and around the Twelve Bens peaks. Allow an hour or two to hike the Diamond Hill Loop, along 7 km (4 miles) of gravel tracks and paved mountain paths, to a 1,493-foot peak, with a 360-degree vista taking in the distant sea, the tur-rets of Kylemore Abbey, and the higher peaks in the south. The nearby visitor center (March–October, free) has dis-plays on the flora, fauna, and geology of Connemara.

WALKING IN COMPANY

Walking festivals are highly popular. Achill Island in County Mayo hosts the **Achill Walks Festival** (⊕ *www.achilltourism.com*) in early April, to tempt people out again after the long dark winter, while the **Four Seasons Walking Festival** features excursions from Clifden guided by an archaeologist four times a year.

Stop and smell the heather.

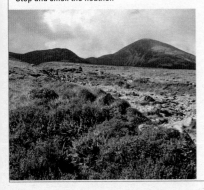

A landscape where the thundering Atlantic forms the pounding backbeat to the most westerly seaboard in Europe, this most distinct area of Ireland has been an escape from urban stress since its vast empty landscapes and rocky indented coast was "discovered" by writers and artists in the 19th century. While Mayo's bustling town of Westport has assumed the identity of hip destination to a younger, more confident Ireland, the surrounding countryside still attracts the traditional anglers, golfers, and seekers of rural solitude, along with savvy hikers, cyclists, and birders.

It is a landscape richly endowed with magnificent views: Connemara's combination of rugged coastline, mountains, moorland, and lakes; the distinctive cone-like shape of Croagh Patrick, towering over the 365 islands of Clew Bay, and the rippling waters of Lough Corrib, Lough Conn, and many smaller lakes. The Irish people are well aware of what a jewel they have in the largely unspoiled wilderness, grazed by sheep and herds of wild ponies, that is the 5,000-acre Connemara National Park, the result of a successful lobby for landscape preservation. Peat lands—or bogs, as they are called around here—are at last being valued for their unique botanical character.

Unlike most of Ireland where the marks of Viking, Norman, and English invaders blotted out much of the rich heritage of the ancient Irish kingdoms, these western counties retained, by virtue of their remoteness, those essential Celtic characteristics of rebellion and individuality, and the accompanying graces of unstinting hospitality and courtly good manners. These traits survive, despite the purges of Cromwell's English armies and the all-pervasive trauma of the Great Famine (1845–49). That era started a tradition of emigration that continued to deprive the area of the majority of its youth well into the 1960s. The growth of tourism since the 1970s, the building of fine new hotels and the upgrading of traditional ones has helped to provide jobs for the local population. Another boost has come from the development of fish farming, and the fostering of local artisanal food producers, whose farmhouse cheese and smoked salmon enhances the menus of the West.

MAJOR REGIONS

Connemara. Bordered by the long expanse of Lough Corrib on the east and the jagged coast of the Atlantic on the west is the rugged, desolate region of western County Galway known as Connemara. Like the American West, it's an area of spectacular, almost myth-making geography—of glacial lakes; gorgeous, silent mountains; lonely roads; and hushed, uninhabited boglands. **Roundstone,** a pretty harbor village that lies in the shadows of the glacially carved Twelve Bens mountain range lures artists and visitors all year, while Connemara's "capital" town, **Clifden,** is the gateway to the panoramic Sky Road. Beyond the small towns and villages there are few people, since Connemara's population is sparse even by Irish standards. Especially in the off-season, you're far more likely to come across sheep strolling its roads than another car.

South County Mayo. County Mayo has long empty roads that stretch for miles. **Castlebar,** the county town, has been overshadowed by its neighbor **Westport,** an elegantly laid-out 18th-century town with quays on the shore of island-studded Clew Bay, under the towering conical peak of St. Patrick's holy mountain, Croagh Patrick. Not only does Westport have scenery, it also has some excellent hotels and bars, some a legacy of the boom years that brought metropolitan chic to the heart of the West.

North County Mayo. The land between Castlebar and Ballina is rugged, sparsely populated, and leads to one of the most dramatic coastlines in Ireland. Lough Conn and Lough Cullin are two great fishing lakes divided by a land bridge,

Pontoon, under which their waters meet. The slopes of Mt. Nephin tower over untilled acres teeming with wildlife, including snipe and woodcock. Mayo's rugged **North Mayo Coast** has a number of sights worth exploring by car.

Planning

Getting Here and Around

A car is almost essential in Connemara and Mayo. Trains arrive from Dublin to Westport and Ballina, with Manulla Junction connecting these towns. The bus network is more flexible, but there are not many services each day, and the entire bus system goes into semihibernation during the winter months, so plan accordingly. If a rental car is out of the question, one option is to make Westport your base, and take a day trip to Connemara and Kylemore Abbey. Then get an Expressway bus to Ballina, and explore the north coast on local buses. The hardy can always consider making a biking trip through the region, even though it does get periods of strong rain.

AIR TRAVEL

Ryanair flies to Ireland West Airport Knock daily from London's Stansted Airport and Luton Airport; flying time is 80 minutes. Aer Lingus flies to Knock from Gatwick daily. Flybe and Ryanair have regular services to Knock from other major U.K. cities.

CONTACTS Aer Lingus. ☎ *1890/800–600* ⊕ *www.aerlingus.com.* **Flybe.** ☎ *44 1392/683–152 outside U.K.* ⊕ *www.flybe. com.* **Ryanair.** ☎ *1520/444–004* ⊕ *www. ryanair.com.*

AIRPORTS

The West's only airport with a transatlantic service is Shannon, 25 km (16 miles) south of Ennis.

Ireland West Airport Knock, at Charlestown—near Knock, in County Mayo—has direct services to London's Stansted, Luton, and Gatwick, and to Manchester and East Midlands.

CONTACTS Ireland West Airport Knock.
☎ 094/936–8100 ⊕ www.irelandwestairport.com. **Shannon Airport.** ☎ 061/712–000 ⊕ www.shannonairport.ie.

BOAT AND FERRY TRAVEL

Corrib Cruises runs daily trips on Lough Corrib at 11:15 am year-round from the public pier at Cong, with great views of Ashford Castle and the Connemara mountains, and an optional visit to the monastic ruins on Inchagoill Island. The boat has indoor and outdoor seating and a licensed bar. From April to October you can board either at Cong or at Oughterard, on the opposite side of the lake. You can use the cruise as a ferry service from one village to the other, or opt for a historic cruise with guide (€20 from Cong, €28 from Oughterard).

The Inisbofin Ferry Company offers a regular, year-round, 30-minute service from Cleggan to Inisbofin for €20 round-trip.

Clare Island in Clew Bay and its smaller neighbor, Inishturk Island, are increasingly popular day-trip destinations with hikers and natural historians. Clare Island Ferry Company sails to Clare Island and Inishturk between May and September, leaving the mainland at 9:30 am (10:45 Monday and weekends) with last ferry returning at 6:15 pm (€17 round-trip). There is a scaled-down service from February to April and October; check the website for details. O'Malley Ferries is a year-round operator serving Inishturk. Both leave from Roonagh Pier at Louisburgh, a 35-minute drive west of Westport. Tickets can be bought at the Westport Tourist Office.

From April through October, Killary Cruises runs 90-minute trips around Killary Harbour (€21), Ireland's only fjord, in an enclosed catamaran launch with seating for 150 passengers, plus a bar and restaurant.

CONTACTS Clare Island Ferry Company.
☎ 098/23737 ⊕ www.clareislandferry.com. **Corrib Cruises.** ☎ 087/994–6380 ⊕ www.corribcruises.com. **Inisbofin Ferry.** ✉ Inishbofin Island Discovery Ltd., Cloonamore, Inishbofin Island, Connemara ☎ 095/45819 ⊕ inishbofinislanddiscovery.com. **Killary Cruises.** ✉ Nancy's Point ☎ 091/566–736 ⊕ www.killaryfjord.com/. **O'Malley Ferries.** ☎ 098/25045 ⊕ www.omalleyferries.com.

BUS TRAVEL

Bus Éireann runs several Expressway buses into the region from Dublin, Cork City, and Limerick City to Galway City (change for Connemara) and Westport, the principal depots in the region. Bus Éireann also has two services an hour from Shannon Airport to Galway City. A one-way trip costs €9.50.

Citylink operates frequent buses, with up to 17 departures daily, between Clifden, Galway City, and Dublin and Dublin Airport. The trip costs €18 one-way.

Within Connemara and Mayo, bus routes are often slow and circuitous, and service can be erratic. The national transport website has an integrated journey planner that is useful for long cross-country trips, for example, Westport to Ballina. To plan local journeys, use the Bus Éireann website or phone the bus station (they are always very helpful).

Bus Éireann local buses travel from Galway City to Cong, Clifden, and Westport. There are no buses linking Cong, Clifden, and Westport: you must return to Galway City and take a different bus line out again to visit each place.

BUS CONTACTS Bus Éireann. ☎ 01/836–6111 in Dublin ⊕ www.buseireann.ie. **Citylink.** ✉ Unit 1, Forster Ct., 17 Forster St., Galway City ☎ 091/564–164 ⊕ www.citylink.ie. **National Travel Website.** ⊕ www.transportforireland.ie.

BUS DEPOTS Ballina Bus Station.
☎ *096/71800* ⊕ *www.buseireann.ie.*
Galway City Bus Station (*Ceannt Station*).
☎ *091/562–000* ⊕ *www.buseireann.ie.*

CAR TRAVEL

The 207-km (129-mile) Dublin–Galway City trip is on a motorway (four-lane expressway) and takes about two hours, 20 minutes. The 196-km (122-mile) drive from Cork to Galway City (opt for the toll tunnel under Limerick) takes about three hours, and another 45 minutes to Oughterard, where the Connemara scenery begins. From Killarney, the shortest route to cover the 193 km (120 miles) to Galway (three hours) is to take N22 to Tralee, then N69 through Listowel to Tarbert and ferry across the Shannon Estuary to Killimer (⇨ *see Chapter 9: County Clare, Galway City, and the Aran Islands*). From here, join N68 in Kilrush, and then pick up the M18.

ROAD CONDITIONS

Connemara and Mayo have good, wide main roads (National Primary Routes) and better-than-average local roads (National Secondary Routes), both known as *N* routes. If you stray off the beaten track on the smaller Regional (*R*) or Local (*L*) routes, you may encounter some hazardous mountain roads. Narrow, steep, and twisty, they are also frequented by untended sheep, cows, and ponies grazing "the long acre" (as the strip of grass beside the road is called) or straying in search of greener pastures. If you find a sheep in your path, just sound the horn, and it should scramble away. A good maxim for these roads is: "You never know what's around the next corner." Bear this in mind, and adjust your speed accordingly. Hikers and cyclists constitute an additional hazard on narrow roads. Within the Connemara Irish-speaking area, signs are in Irish only. The main signs to recognize are Gaillimh (Galway), Ros an Mhíl (Rossaveal), An Teach Dóite (Maam Cross), and Sraith Salach (Recess).

TAXI TRAVEL

Within Westport, taxis operate on the meter. Outside the town, agree on the fare in advance.

TRAIN TRAVEL

The region's main rail stations are in Galway City, Westport, and Ballina. Trains leave from Dublin's Heuston Station. The journey time to Galway is three hours; to Westport and Ballina, 3½ hours. Rail service within the region is limited. The major destinations of Galway City and Westport/Ballina are on different branch lines. Connections can be made only between Galway and the other two cities by traveling inland for about an hour to Athlone.

CONTACTS Ballina Station. ☎ *096/71820* ⊕ *www.irishrail.ie/travel-information/ballina.* **Dublin Heuston Station.** ☎ *01/836–6222* ⊕ *www.irishrail.ie/travel-information/dublin-heuston.* **Galway Station.** ☎ *091/537581* ⊕ *www.irishrail.ie/travel-information/galway-ceannt.* **Westport Station.** ☎ *098/26939* ⊕ *www.irishrail.ie/travel-information/westport.*

⇨ *For more information on getting here and around, see* Travel Smart Ireland.

Hotels

Accommodations in the area tend to the traditional; outside Westport there are few with indoor pools and gyms. Instead there are informal, friendly places where you will probably end up comparing notes with other travelers over a huge cooked breakfast. Add variety by alternating rural isolation with the lively towns. Both Clifden in Connemara and Westport in Mayo have lively pub scenes. Clifden attracts a younger, mainly single, crowd, especially in July and August, so be prepared: the music might be rock rather than Irish. *Hotel reviews have been shortened. For full information, visit Fodors.com.*

Restaurants

Pubs and informal hotel restaurants are the main places to eat in this sparsely populated rural area, though there are also some fine-dining options. The only places with a choice of stand-alone restaurants are Clifden, the "capital" of Connemara (in fact a small village), and Westport, the chief resort in County Mayo. From Easter into the summer months, many menus feature Connemara lamb: the sheep graze on wild herbs on the mountain slopes, which gives the meat a distinctive flavor. The other star is local seafood, including crab and lobster in summer, and superb Atlantic salmon all year round, fresh or smoked. For seafood try the Tavern Bar and Restaurant near Westport, or Mitchell's in Clifden; for country house–style elegance go to Rosleague Manor in Letterfrack, or Mount Falcon near Ballina. *Restaurant reviews have been shortened. For full information, visit Fodors.com.*

What It Costs in Euros

	$	$$	$$$	$$$$
RESTAURANTS				
	under €19	€19–€24	€25–€32	over €32
HOTELS				
	under €120	€120–€170	€171–€210	over €210

Tours

All TIOs (tourist information offices) in the West provide lists of suggested cycling tours. The only guided bus tours in the region, which take in the main sights of Connemara (€20), start from Galway and Westport and run between June and September only. Book at the bus station or tourist office.

Clew Bay Bike Hire and Outdoor Adventures

GUIDED TOURS | Cycling breaks and guided daylong cycle tours in the Westport area are available, as well as sea kayaking, and the opportunity to finish the day with a mini cruise across Clew Bay. The most popular product, however, is day hire of electric bicycles that take the hard work out of cycling. The company also has a free drop-off and pickup service via minibus and cycle trailer—invaluable if the weather takes a turn. ✉ *Distillery Rd., Westport* ☎ *098/37675* ⊕ *www.clewbaybikehire.ie* ⬚ *From €20.*

Connemara Adventure Tours

SELF-GUIDED | Self-guided or customized tours for walkers, cyclists, golfers, and horseback riders are available from this company. Groups of 8 to 16 people participate in three-, four-, or seven-day programs, staying in a comfortable B&B near Westport, or traveling to a new destination each night with luggage transfer. Walk Clare Island, climb Diamond Hill, or gallop along a sandy beach on Clew Bay. ✉ *Killary Adventure Centre, Leenane* ☎ *095/42276* ⊕ *www.connemaraadventuretours.com* ⬚ *From €395 for 3 days.*

Connemara Safari Walking Holidays

WALKING TOURS | Choose between three and five-day residential walking holidays starting in either Clifden or Westport. The company specializes in "island hopping" and remote-island hikes. ✉ *Sky Rd., Clifden* ☎ *095/21071* ⊕ *www.walkingconnemara.com.*

Croagh Patrick Walking Holidays

WALKING TOURS | This company runs week-long walking holidays at various dates between April and September, based in B&B accommodations near Westport; contact Gerry Greensmyth. ✉ *Belclare, Westport* ☎ *098/26090* ⊕ *www.walkingguideireland.com* ⬚ *From €800.*

Galway Tour Company

GUIDED TOURS | This Galway-based company runs a Connemara tour that takes in Clifden, Kylemore Abbey, and Cong, the famed location of the classic movie *The Quiet Man*. Tickets can be purchased from the Galway Tourist Information Office or on the tour bus. ☎ 091/566–566 ⊕ *www.galwaytourcompany.com* ☒ *From €30.*

Lally Tours

GUIDED TOURS | Galway City–based Lally Tours runs a €30 day tour through Connemara and County Mayo. ☒ *4 Forster St., Galway City* ☎ *091/562–905* ⊕ *www. lallytours.com* ☒ *From €20.*

Michael Gibbons Walking Ireland

GUIDED TOURS | This Clifden-based company organizes everything from daylong mountain treks to weeklong holidays, with an emphasis on archaeology. ☒ *Island House, Market St., Clifden* ☎ *095/21379* ⊕ *www.walkingireland. com.*

When to Go

There is a local saying in the Westport area: if you can't see the summit of Croagh Patrick, then it is raining; if you can see it, it is about to rain. Avoid visiting between November and February, when many places close for the winter, and the days are short and overcast. In fact, you could have your umbrellas out constantly during all times but the warmest months, July and August, when the average temperatures are around 15°C (60°F).

Festivals

Clifden Arts Festival

CULTURAL FESTIVALS | Held annually in mid-September since 1977, the Clifden Arts Festival has a great selection of music, arts, and poetry in a friendly, informal atmosphere and scenic environment, making it an excellent time to tune in to local culture. ⊕ *www.clifdenartsfestival.ie.*

Croagh Patrick Heritage Trail Walking Festival

CULTURAL FESTIVALS | This is a three-day guided walking festival along 61 km (38 miles) of one of the most beautiful trails in the country. The accredited route takes you through lush farmland, forest paths, and remote boglands, past historic houses and archaeological remains, en route to Croagh Patrick, Ireland's most famous pilgrimage site. The trail includes moderate to hard walking and is held on the second weekend of March. ☎ *094/903–0687* ⊕ *croi.ie/tc-events/her-itage-trail/* ☒ *€20 per day, or €50 for all three days.*

Planning Your Time

Visitors are often geared to a faster pace, but they should allow at least two days for exploring the region, four to six days if you intend to do some serious hiking or cycling, take a boat trip on Lough Corrib, visit an island, and enjoy the village (and pub) life of Clifden and Westport. Although distances between sights are not great, you may want to take scenic—meaning slower—national secondary routes. Covering 80 to 112 km (50 to 70 miles) per day on these roads is a comfortable target.

If you love the outdoors, dramatic scenery, empty roads, and deserted coves, then you'll be in heaven in Connemara and Mayo. If you're a city lover, and tend to fade without daily doses of caffeine and retail therapy, then base yourself in Clifden for the first night, where there is coffee aplenty and surprisingly good shopping for a very small town (Irish designer wear, locally made tweed, traditional hand-knits, and wackier handcrafted knitwear).

IF YOU HAVE 3 DAYS

Allow a full day to meander slowly from Galway City to Clifden, perhaps stopping by Roundstone, a charming fishing village, to hike heather-clad Errisbeg

Mountain or idle on the white sandy dunes of Dog's Bay. Next morning, take a stroll along the Sky Road before heading to the lovely Kylemore Abbey and its gardens. Drive the scenic Doolough Valley to Westport for your second night. Next day, hire a bike to cycle on the traffic-free coastal path, the Great Western Greenway, or drive across the bridge to Achill Island for some magnificent coastal scenery. If the weather grounds you, head up to Turlough and the nostalgic Museum of Country Life (allow two hours), but if it is fine, push on to the North Mayo coast, where you can walk in the footsteps of Stone Age farmers, and test your nerve on rugged Downpatrick Head.

Visitor Information

Discover Ireland provides free information service, tourist literature, and an accommodations booking service at its TIOs (tourist information offices). Oughterard, Castlebar, Ballina, Belmullet and Westport TIOs are open all year, generally weekdays 9–6 during the high season. Other TIOs that operate seasonally, generally weekdays 9–6 and Saturday 9–1, include Clifden (March–October) and Cong (May–mid-September). Information on Connemara and Mayo can be found at ⊕ *www.discoverireland.ie/places-to-go*. In addition to this main website, we sometimes also list a town website in individual town sections; this is occasionally an ad-supported site that is unofficial, but still helpful. Generally speaking, tourism has been carefully nurtured in this region. Ferry services to the islands and on Lough Corrib have been upgraded, while walking and cycling holidays are a big growth area.

Roundstone

18 km (10 miles) south of Clifden.

The vibrantly colored vernacular facades that follow the hilly terrain of this ocean-harbor village, nestled in the shadows of the Twelve Bens Mountains, make for the most photogenic streetscape in the West of Ireland. Art, crafts, and custom-made musical instruments workshops line the street along with inviting restaurants and pubs. The village's terraced buildings overlook a deep blue bay, which is peppered with small fishing trawlers, traditional currachs (large, tar-lacquered canoes) and rowboats. Roundstone featured as the main setting for the 1997 romantic comedy movie *The Matchmaker*, starring Janeane Garofalo and Milo O'Shea.

GETTING HERE AND AROUND
Roundstone is located 18 km (10 miles) south of Clifden on the coastal road R341 and 76 km (47 miles) northwest from Galway City. Bus Éireann offers an irregular service from Galway and Clifden on bus No. 419.

 ## Sights

Dog's Bay Beach
BEACH—SIGHT | Dog's Bay Beach lies back to back with Gurteen Beach, forming a tombolo that juts out into the ocean. Unlike other local limestone beaches, Dog's Bay's brilliant white sand was formed from seashells, and it horse shape stretches for a mile along the Connemara coast. Its clear, blue water is sheltered from currents, making it popular with swimmers and kitesurfers. **Amenities:** none. **Best for:** swimming; watersports; walking.

 ## Restaurants

★ O'Dowds Seafood Bar and Restaurant
$$ | **MODERN IRISH** | This fourth-generation establishment sits in the heart of

Roundstone overlooking the harbor. It attracts year-round guests with its fresh-from-the-boats lobster, mussels, prawns, and crab, or other local produce such as Connemara lamb, and homey, open-fire setting. **Known for:** seafood chowder; harbor views; dillisk rice. $ *Average main: €16* ✉ *Main St.* ☎ *095/35809* ⊕ *www. odowdsseafoodbar.com.*

 Hotels

★ **Ballynahinch Castle Hotel**
$$$$ | HOTEL | More like a rambling country house than a castle, this magnificent crenellated mansion sits beside a river amid 700 wooded acres with a rugged mountain backdrop. **Pros:** genuine Irish country-house experience; lived-in luxury; stunning surroundings. **Cons:** authentic doesn't come cheap; car needed to explore the greater area; some rooms do not have river views. $ *Rooms from: €320* ✉ *Ballynahinch Castle, Connemara* ✛ *After Recess, take R341 turn to your left, signposted Roundstone. The hotel is 5 km (3 miles) up this road on right* ☎ *095/31006* ⊕ *www.ballynahinch-castle. com* ⇆ *45 rooms* ❑ *Free breakfast.*

Clifden

66 km (41 miles) southwest of Cong, 79 km (49 miles) northwest of Galway.

★ With roughly 2,600 residents, Clifden would be called a village by most, but in these parts it's looked on as something of a metropolis. Clifden's first attraction is its location—perched high above Clifden Bay on a forested plateau, its back to the spectacular Twelve Bens mountains. The tapering spires of the town's two churches add to its alpine look.

Clifden is a popular base thanks to its selection of small restaurants, lively bars with music most summer nights, pleasant accommodations, and excellent walks. It's quiet out of season, but in July

and August crowds flock here, especially for August's world-famous Connemara Pony Show. Year-round, unfortunately, Clifden's popularity necessitates a chaotic one-way traffic system, and on summer Sunday afternoons loud techno music blasts out of certain bars. So if you're looking for a sleepy country town that time forgot, this may not be the place for you.

GETTING HERE AND AROUND
Clifden is 66 km (41 miles) southwest of Cong: travel via Maam Cross and take the N59 westward. The town is 79 km (49 miles) northwest of Galway City on the N59 and takes about 1½ hours to reach. It is a busy main road with only one lane in each direction, and delays can occur. Follow signs to find the car parks (and free parking).

Bus Éireann and Citylink have daily bus service from Galway Bus Station. Bus Éireann's route takes two hours (at least half of that through great scenery), while Citylink's service takes 1½ hours and continues from Galway to Dublin and Dublin Airport. Some of these services continue to Letterfrack (about 20 minutes) and Leenane (about an hour). Check with Galway Bus Station on day of travel.

VISITOR INFORMATION
CONTACTS Clifden Tourist Office.
✉ *Galway Rd.* ☎ *095/21163* ⊕ *www. discoverireland.ie/Activities-Adventure/ clifden-tourist-information-centre/48273.*

 Sights

Clifden Castle
CASTLE/PALACE | Clifden Castle was built above the town in 1815 by John D'Arcy, the town's founder and High Sheriff of Galway, who wished to establish a center of law and order in what he saw as the lawless wilderness of Connemara. Before the founding of Clifden, the interior of Connemara was largely uninhabited, with most of its population clinging to the

seashore. Wear appropriate footwear as there is a lovely, fifteen-minute winding walk from the nearest carpark. ⊠ *Sky Rd.*

The Derrigimlagh Walking Loop

HIKING/WALKING | In June 1919, pilot John Alcock and navigator Arthur Whitten Brown entered the annals of navigation history by taking the first transatlantic flight from Newfoundland to a bumpy crash-landing in the heart of Derrigimlagh Bog, close to Guglielmo Marconi's groundbreaking wireless station. Both the bog and the wireless station are noted in the staggeringly beautiful 5-km (3-mile) Derrigimlagh trail that passes miniature lakes, peat bogs, and rare flora and fauna. ⊠ *Ballyconneely* ⊕ *www. discoverireland.ie/Arts-Culture-Heritage/ derrigimlagh/91306.*

★ Sky Road

SCENIC DRIVE | Drive the aptly named Sky Road to really appreciate Clifden's breathtaking scenery. Signposted at the west end of town, this high, narrow circuit heads west, giving views of several offshore islands, before looping back to the N59 after about 10 km (6 miles) alongside phenomenal views of Clifden Bay's precipitous shores. The Sky Road loops beneath to the Beach Road, where hikers can enjoy the Connemara shoreline. ⊠ *Clifden.*

Restaurants

Mitchell's Seafood

$ | SEAFOOD | A town-center shop has been cleverly converted into a stylish, two-story eatery. Beyond the plate-glass windows, there's a welcoming open fire, and you can eat at the bar or at one of the polished wood tables. **Known for:** cozy ambience with an open fire; fresh seafood; braised whole sea bass with fennel butter. ⑤ *Average main: €18* ⊠ *Market St.* ☎ *095/21867* ⊕ *mitchellsrestaurantclif-den.com* ⊘ *Closed Nov.–Feb.*

🛏 Hotels

Abbeyglen Castle Hotel

$$ | HOTEL | Creeper covered, as if under a Sleeping Beauty spell, the gorgeous Victorian castle-manor of Abbeyglen sits framed by towering trees on a height above Clifden town—if time hasn't completely stopped here, it has certainly slowed down, but that's just the way the relaxed guests want it. **Pros:** complimentary tea and scones; pleasantly homey rather than luxurious; nice old-fashioned touches, like real room keys. **Cons:** uphill walk back from Clifden; more of a manor house than a castle; not a romantic hideaway: guests are expected to mingle. ⑤ *Rooms from: €156* ⊠ *Sky Rd.* ☎ *095/21201* ⊕ *www.abbeyglen. ie* ⊘ *Closed Jan. and Feb.* ⊷ *42 rooms* ❑ *Free breakfast.*

Dún Rí

$ | B&B/INN | An old town house in the lower, quieter part of Clifden has been extended and converted into a comfortable guesthouse with private parking. **Pros:** hotel-grade rooms at B&B prices; quiet yet central location; homemade breads and jams at breakfast. **Cons:** bland design; parking lot is effectively on-street, not secured. ⑤ *Rooms from: €100* ⊠ *Hulk St.* ☎ *095/21625* ⊕ *www.dunri.ie* ⊷ *13 rooms* ❑ *Free breakfast.*

★ The Quay House

$$ | B&B/INN | Nineteenth-century time travelers would feel right at home in this three-story, town center Georgian house, Clifden's oldest building (1820) that once housed the harbor master. **Pros:** fetching decor; quiet location; harbor views. **Cons:** uphill walk into town; rooms in new wing less attractive than those in the main house; you'll need to book well in advance. ⑤ *Rooms from: €160* ⊠ *The Quay* ☎ *095/21369* ⊕ *www.thequay-house.com* ⊘ *Closed Nov.–mid-Mar.* ⊷ *14 rooms* ❑ *Free breakfast.*

President Reagan, Brad Pitt, Rory McIllroy … and now you? Lucky travelers call Ashford Castle their Cong home-away-from-home.

 Nightlife

J Conneely's Bar

BARS/PUBS | Irish music is played every night in the summer from 6:30 pm at this popular town-center bar. It gets livelier after 9 pm, when it stops serving food. ✉ *Market St.* ☎ *095/22733.*

Lowry's Bar Lounge

BARS/PUBS | This central pub is famed for its traditional Irish music, played from 10 until late on weekdays, and on Sunday from 6 to 8:30. Lowry's also has a wide range of whiskeys and decent pub grub. ✉ *Market St.* ☎ *095/21347* ⊕ *www. lowrysbar.ie.*

Shopping

All Things Connemara

CRAFTS | This friendly boutique is a showcase for crafts and artisanal products made in Connemara, from marble jewelry and seaweed-based cosmetics to Irish whiskey, knitwear, and handmade pottery. Electric bikes are also available for hire, and there's information about outdoor activities and guided tours. ✉ *Market St.* ☎ *095/22630* ⊕ *www. allthingsconnemara.ie.*

The Clifden Bookshop

BOOKS/STATIONERY | As well as selling books of local interest, the bookshop also stocks artists' supplies and is an informal meeting point for visiting poets, writers, artists, and photographers. ✉ *Main St.* ☎ *095/22020* ⊕ *www.clifdenbookshop. com.*

The Connemara Hamper

FOOD/CANDY | A small but well-stocked specialty food shop, this is an ideal place to pick up picnic fare, with its excellent Irish farmhouse cheeses, pâtés, smoked Connemara salmon, and handmade Irish chocolates. ✉ *Market St.* ☎ *095/21054* ⊕ *www.connemarahamper.com.*

Millar's Connemara Tweeds

CRAFTS | This long-established emporium sells a good selection of traditional tweeds, hand-knitted items, housewares, and gifts. ✉ *Main St.* ☎ *095/21038* ⊕ *www.millarsconnemara.ie/.*

Station House Courtyard

CRAFTS | Set around a cobbled courtyard, the Station House has crafts studios, antiques dealers, and designer-wear outlets. ✉ *Old Railway Station, Bridge St.* ☎ *095/21699* ⊕ *www.clifdenstation-house.com.*

 Activities

BICYCLING
Mannion Bike Hire

BICYCLING | Explore Connemara by renting a bike from this handy outfitter. ✉ *Bridge St.* ☎ *095/21160* ⊕ *www.clifdenbikes.com.*

GOLF
Connemara Golf Links

GOLF | On a dramatic stretch of Atlantic coastline, the links course masterminded by Eddie Hackett, Ireland's finest course designer, is sited between the Twelve Bens and the rugged coast, with unforgettable views of the sea, hills, and huge western sky. The opening hole has a challenging dogleg, while the back 9 make for a memorable golfing experience, considered equal to any in the world. ✉ *9 km (5½ miles) south of Clifden on R341, Ballyconneely* ☎ *095/23502* ⊕ *www.connemaragolflinks.com* ✉ *Nov.–Mar. €60, Apr.–Oct. €110* ⚹ *18 holes, 7055 yards, par 72.*

HORSEBACK RIDING
Errislannan Manor Connemara Pony Stud and Riding Centre

HORSEBACK RIDING | Ride a sure-footed Connemara pony in its native habitat at this long-established riding center, where these sturdy ponies are also bred. Treks are tailored to your ability, and the views of coast and hills from the mountain trails are unforgettable. ✉ *6½ km (4 miles) from Clifden on Ballyconneely road (R341), Ballyconneely* ☎ *095/21134* ⊕ *www.errislannanmanor.com.*

Letterfrack

14 km (9 miles) north of Clifden.

This is the gateway village to the famous Connemara National Park. It also makes a handy base for those visiting spectacular Kylemore Abbey, one of Ireland's grandest ancestral estates.

GETTING HERE AND AROUND
Letterfrack is 14 km (9 miles) north of Clifden on the N59. The journey takes about 15 minutes. There is plenty of free parking in the village center. Bus Éireann has daily routes linking Letterfrack and Clifden, a 20-minute journey. The nonexpress service originates in Galway, and takes about two hours, 30 minutes to reach Letterfrack. Citylink also operates between Letterfrack and Clifden (continuing to Galway).

 Sights

★ Connemara National Park
NATIONAL/STATE PARK | The 5,000-acre Connemara National Park lies southeast of the village of Letterfrack. Its visitor center covers the area's history and ecology, particularly the origins and growth of peat—and presents the depressing statistic that more than 80% of Ireland's peat, 5,000 years in the making, has been destroyed in the last 90 years. You can also get details on the many excellent walks and beaches in the area. The misleadingly named "park" is, in fact, just rocky or wooded wilderness territory, albeit with some helpful trails marked out to aid your exploration. It includes part of the famous **Twelve Bens** mountain range, which is for experienced hill walkers only. An easier hike is the Lower Diamond Hill Walk, at about 3 km (less than 2 miles). Ask for advice on a hike suited to your abilities and interests at the Park and Visitor Centre, which is on the N59 as you arrive in Letterfrack from Clifden, on your right, clearly signposted, not too far southeast of the center of Letterfrack.

Few landscapes are as quintessentially Irish as the ravishing ones found in Connemara National Park.

✉ *Park and Visitor Centre, on N59 near Letterfrack* ☎ *095/41054* ⊕ *www.connemaranationalpark.ie* 🖾 *Free* ⊘ *Visitor center closed Nov.–mid-Mar.*

★ Inishbofin

BEACH—SIGHT | Cleggan is the ferry port for this stark and unsettlingly beautiful outpost of Connemara. The island is a hiker's paradise, with loop routes that lead to a plethora of fine sandy beaches by the Atlantic's pristine water. Just 5 km (3 miles) by 3 km (2 miles), it was once a stronghold of the pirate queen Grainne O'Malley, and the crumbling ruin of a Cromwellian barracks is a stark reminder for visitors of the clergy held captive by troops before they were shipped afar. The island is now a holiday retreat dotted with small pubs and inns for those who want quiet time. The ferry costs €20 round-trip for an adult. ⊹ *14 km (8 miles) west of Letterfrack is Cleggan, the ferry port with 3 daily sailings to Inisbofin* ☎ *95/45819* ⊕ *inishbofinislanddiscovery. com.*

 ## Restaurants

Veldon's Seafarer

$ | **IRISH** | Ship's wheels, fishing nets, and sculpted stone sharks leave little doubt that the Atlantic's catch takes center stage in this small, whitewashed cottage inn right in the heart of Letterfrack. Stuffed with timber nooks and crannies, and with an open fire, it's the place to warm up after a Connemara coastline hike. **Known for:** seafood chowder; local catch; posthike spot. ⑤ *Average main: €14* ✉ *Letterfrack* ☎ *095/41046* ⊕ *www. veldons.ie.*

 ## Hotels

★ Renvyle House Hotel

$$ | **HOTEL** | **FAMILY** | A lake at its front door, the Atlantic Ocean at the back, and the mountains of Connemara as a backdrop form the enthralling setting for this hotel 8 km (5 miles) north of Letterfrack, home to the Long Room, one of the most eminently civilized salons in Ireland—Arts and Crafts–style polished wood, original art, and red geraniums. **Pros:** secluded end-of-the-world location; history, character, and charm; excellent restaurant. **Cons:** driving distance to anywhere else; bar and restaurant very busy at peak times; rooms are well maintained but a little dated. $ *Rooms from: €160* ⊠ *Renvyle* ☎ *095/46100* ⊕ *www.renvyle.com* ⊘ *Closed Jan. 6–mid-Feb.* ⇆ *65 rooms, 3 apartments* ⊙ *Free breakfast.*

Rosleague Manor

$$$ | HOTEL | This pink, creeper-clad, two-story Georgian house occupies 30 lovely acres and has a jaw-dropping view: a gorgeous lawn backdropped by Ballinakill Bay and the dreamy mountains of Connemara. **Pros:** quiet and elegant; mesmerizing views; excellent restaurant. **Cons:** can be very quiet off-season; usually fully booked from mid-July to end of August; closed to the public when hosting a wedding. $ *Rooms from: €210* ⊠ *Rosleague Bay* ☎ *095/41101* ⊕ *www.rosleague.com* ⊘ *Closed Nov.–mid-Mar.* ⇆ *20 rooms* ⊙ *Free breakfast.*

�️ Nightlife

The Clover Fox

MUSIC CLUBS | For traditional music, the best option in this region is the Clover Fox, formerly the Bards Den. The cottage also houses informal dining, an arts and crafts shop, and hostel. ⊠ *Main St.* ☎ *095/41042.*

Paddy Coyne's Pub

BARS/PUBS | One of the most popular and long-established pubs in County Galway, where traditional musicians meet every Wednesday, is 3 km (2 miles) west of Letterfrack on the scenic Renvyle Peninsula. It's a good bet for music any night in summer. ⊠ *Tully Cross* ☎ *095/43499* ⊕ *paddycoynespub.com/.*

🛍️ Shopping

Avoca Letterfrack Store

CRAFTS | An extensive selection of crafts and women's fashions made by the stellar Avoca Handweavers is showcased here, along with delicious food products from the Avoca Pantry range. ⊠ *Rosleague, Letterfrack,* ⊕ *N59, west of village* ☎ *095/41058* ⊕ *www.avoca.com/en/stores-and-cafes/letterfrack.*

Letterfrack Country Shop

FOOD/CANDY | A great place to put together a picnic, this is the biggest supermarket for miles around (but still very small by city standards), and has a special line in local, artisanal foods, including smoked Connemara salmon, locally grown salads, handmade breads, and local cheeses. ⊠ *N59, village center* ☎ *095/41850.*

Kylemore Valley

Runs for 6½ km (4 miles) between Letterfrack and intersection of N59 and R344.

One of the more conventionally beautiful stretches of road in Connemara passes through Kylemore Valley, which is between the Twelve Bens to the south and the naturally forested Dorruagh Mountains to the north. Kylemore (the name is derived from *Coill Mór,* Irish for "big wood") looks "as though some colossal giant had slashed it out with a couple of strokes from his mammoth sword," as artist and author John Fitz-Maurice Mills once wrote.

👁️ Sights

★ Kylemore Abbey

CASTLE/PALACE | One of the most magical "castles" in all of Europe, much-photographed Kylemore Abbey is set on a reedy lake with a backdrop of wooded hillside. The storybook Gothic Revival, gray-stone mansion was built as a private

Did You Know?

To best savor spectacular Kylemore Abbey, book a guided hike up the hill to the life-size statue of Jesus, usually surrounded by grazing sheep. The resident nuns will tell you that the view over the lake is well worth the effort.

home between 1861 and 1868 by Mitchell Henry, a member of Parliament for County Galway, and his wife, Margaret, who had fallen in love with the spot during a carriage ride while on their honeymoon. The Henrys spared no expense—the final bill for their house is said to have come to £1.5 million—and employed mostly local laborers, thereby abetting recovery from the famine (this area was among the worst hit in all of Ireland). Adjacent to the house (a short walk from the Abbey) is a spectacular neo-Gothic chapel, which, sadly, became the burial place for Margaret, who died after contracting "Nile fever" on a trip to Egypt. In 1920, nuns from the Benedictine order, who fled their abbey in Belgium during World War I, sought refuge in Kylemore and ran a girls' boarding school here until 2010. Three reception rooms and the main hall are open to the public, as are a crafts center and cafeteria. You can prebook a guided hike and nature walk (€3) uphill to the life-size statue of Jesus for an unforgettable view of the tranquil abbey and lake from above. There's also a 6-acre walled Victorian garden; a shuttle bus (free with admission) from the abbey to the garden departs every 15 minutes during opening hours. An exhibition and video explaining the history of the house can be viewed year-round at the abbey, and the grounds are freely accessible most of the year. ■TIP→ Be sure to visit the "Ironing Stone," a short walk from the chapel. Legend has it that this massive stone was tossed here by Irish mythical warrior Cú Chulainn. If you stand with your back to the rock and throw a pebble over the stone three times, your wish will be granted. ⊠ Entrance off N59 about 8 km (5 miles) east of Letterfrack, Letterfrack ☎ 095/52001 ⊕ www.kylemoreabbey.com ⊠ €13.

Leenane

18 km (11 miles) east of Letterfrack.

Nestled idyllically at the foot of the Maamturk Mountains and overlooking the tranquil waters of Killary Harbour, Leenane is a tiny village noted for its role as the setting for the film *The Field,* which starred Richard Harris.

GETTING HERE AND AROUND

Leenane is 18 km (11 miles) east of Letterfrack on the N59. The journey takes just over 15 minutes. There is free parking in the village, on the streets, and in designated car parks. Leenane has at least one Bus Éireann schedule a day, traveling to Galway via Clifden, taking about one hour, 15 minutes to Clifden. In summer there is also a bus to Westport, a 45-minute journey.

TOURS

Killary Cruises

Take a 90-minute trip (€21) around Killary Harbour in an enclosed Killary Cruises catamaran launch with seating for 150 passengers, bar, and restaurant. ⊠ Nancy's Point ☎ 091/566–736 ⊕ killaryfjord.com/ ⯈ Closed Nov.–Mar.

⊙ Sights

★ Killary Harbour

BODY OF WATER | Beyond Kylemore, N59 travels for some miles along Killary Harbour, a narrow fjord that runs for 16 km (10 miles) between County Mayo's Mweelrea Mountain to the north and County Galway's Maamturk Mountains to the south. The dark, deep water of the fjord reflects the magnificent steep-sided hills that border it, creating a haunting scene of natural grandeur. The harbor has an extremely safe anchorage, 78 feet deep for almost its entire length, and is sheltered from storms by mountain walls. The rafts floating in Killary Harbour belong to fish-farming consortia that raise salmon and trout in cages beneath the water. This is a matter of some controversy all over the West. Although some people welcome the employment opportunities, others bemoan the visual blight of the rafts. ⊠ *Killary.*

The Sheep and Wool Centre

FACTORY | The Sheep and Wool Centre, in the center of Leenane, focuses on the traditional industry of North Connemara and West Mayo. Several breeds of sheep graze around the house, and there are demonstrations of carding, spinning, weaving, and the dyeing of wool with natural plant dyes. ⊠ *Leenane* ☎ *095/42323* ⊕ *www.sheepandwool-centre.com* ⌨ *Museum €5* ⊗ *Closed Nov.–mid-Mar.*

Restaurants

★ Misunderstood Heron

$ | **MODERN IRISH** | Gaining a steady following from locals and visitors, Misundersood Heron is serving some of the finest local produce from unlikely quarters—the back of a food truck usually parked in Killary Loop Trail—and confusing the occasional guest in seach of the more standard truck fare like a humble kebab or burger. Instead, fresh salmon with pickles, sourdough roast chicken wrap with harissa mayo and red onion, or mussels and lamb are all served at good value. **Known for:** fresh produce. **$** *Average main: €12* ⊠ *Killary Loop Trail* ☎ *087/991–5179* ⊕ *www.facebook.com/ MisunderstoodHeron* ⊗ *Closed Nov.– Mar. Hrs vary seasonally, so call ahead to confirm* ⊟ *No credit cards.*

Hotels

★ Delphi Lodge

$$$$ | **B&B/INN** | In the heart of what is arguably Connemara's most spectacular mountain and lake scenery, 13 km (8 miles) north of Leenane off R335, this

Leenane and the Arts

Martin McDonagh's *Leenane Trilogy*, featuring a cast of tragicomic grotesques, presents an unflattering view of rural Irish life. An international hit, the plays brought a renown Leenane presumably could have done without. The plot thickened with Kevin Barry's "Fjord of Killary," a hilariously black short story set in a hotel in Leenane and published in the *New Yorker* in February 2010, and in Barry's collection *Dark Lies the Island* (2012).

attractive Georgian sporting lodge heavily stocked with fishing paraphernalia has a lovely lakeside setting. **Pros:** beautiful secluded location; abundant peace and quiet; good base for touring west Connemara and south Mayo. **Cons:** you've got to like fishing or walking; communal dining table seating up to 40 people; no in-room TVs, only one communal set. **$** *Rooms from: €265* ⊠ *Leenane* ☎ *095/42222* ⊕ *www.delphilodge.ie* ⊗ *Closed mid-Oct.–mid-Mar.* ⌦ *13 rooms, 5 cottages* ⏐⊙⏐ *Free breakfast.*

Leenane Hotel

$$ | **HOTEL** | Built in the 1790s at the entrance to Leenane village as a coaching inn, this hotel is only separated from Killary Fjord by the main road. **Pros:** comfortable and atmospheric one-stop base; beautiful views; therapeutic seaweed baths. **Cons:** some of the older bedrooms very small; lighting rather dim in bar and lounge. **$** *Rooms from: €120* ⊠ *Leenane* ☎ *095/42249* ⊕ *www.leenanehotel. com* ⊗ *Closed mid-Nov.–mid-Mar.* ⌦ *66 rooms* ⏐⊙⏐ *Free breakfast.*

En Route

Doolough Valley. You have two options for traveling onward from Leenane to Westport. The first is to take the direct route on N59. The second is to detour through the Doolough Valley between Mweelrea Mountain (to the west) and the Sheeffry Hills (to the east) and on to Westport via Louisburgh (on the southern shore of Clew Bay), passing through the hauntingly beautiful Doolough Valley with its stark stone cross that commemorates a particularly shameful chapter in Ireland's potato famine. The latter route adds about 24 km (15 miles) to the trip, but devotees of this part of the West claim that it takes you through the region's most impressive, unspoiled stretch of scenery. If you opt for the longer route, turn left onto R335 1½ km (1 mile) beyond Leenane. Just after this turn, you can hear the powerful rush of the Aasleagh Falls. You can park over the bridge, stroll along the river's shore, and soak in the splendor of the surrounding mountains. ⊠ *Doolough Valley (R335)*.

Cong

23 km (14 miles) northeast of Maam Cross.

Set on a narrow isthmus between Lough Corrib and Lough Mask on the County Mayo border near Maam Cross, the pretty, old-fashioned village of Cong is still as camera-ready as it was when John Ford filmed *The Quiet Man* here in 1951. Dotted with ivy-covered thatch cottages with a cookie-cutter cuteness that may appear somewhat contrived, this tiny village still provides a wonderful photo backdrop.

Just two blocks long, and bisected by the chocolate-brown River Cong, the village is surrounded on all sides by thickly forested hills. Besides the much-vaunted *Quiet Man* connections, which may be puzzling to those who are not fans of the classic movie, you can walk among the riverside remains of the 12th-century abbey, and discover its Monks' Fishing House. Information boards in the village will guide you to a stone circle and the richly carved Market Cross. Almost larger than the village itself is the celebrated luxury hotel found here, Ashford Castle,

much beloved by billionaires and off-duty celebrities. It was once the country estate of the powerful Guinness family. A footpath runs from Cong Abbey to Ashford Castle, and out its gates is a pleasant walk of about 3 km (2 miles). There is now a €10 admission fee to the grounds of Ashford Castle unless you have prebooked lunch, dinner, or afternoon tea. A still more romantic way to see the castle is on a boat trip run by the local Corrib Cruises from the public pier in Cong.

GETTING HERE AND AROUND

Cong is 23 km (14 miles) northeast of Maam Cross on the N59, a scenic drive skirting the shores of Lough Corrib. The main car-parking area is on the edge of the village, a three-minute walk, and is clearly signposted. There is very limited parking in the village itself.

There is a limited Bus Éireann service from Galway Bus Station to Cong—be sure to get a bus that goes to Ryan's, the bus stop in the village center. The journey takes just over an hour. You can also take a delightful day trip to Cong by Corrib Cruises boat from Oughterard between April and October.

VISITOR INFORMATION

CONTACTS Cong Tourist Office. ✉ *Abbey St.* ☎ *094/954–6542* ⊕ *www. discoverireland.ie/Activities-Adventure/ cong-tourist-office/48280.*

👁 Sights

Augustine Abbey

ARCHAEOLOGICAL SITE | Cong is surrounded by many stone circles and burial mounds, but its most notable ruins are those of the Augustine Abbey, overlooking a river. Dating from the early 12th century when it was founded by Turlough O'Connor, the High King of Ireland, this Abbey is an impressive example of ancient Irish architecture and still retains some finely carved details and a cloister and served as a hospital and college in its day. Don't miss the fishing hut, an ingenious invention to keep fishermen dry. ✉ *Abbey St.*

Quiet Man Museum and Gift Shop

MUSEUM | Cong's 15 minutes of fame came in 1952, when John Ford's *The Quiet Man,* one of his most popular films, was released to a global audience. John Wayne plays a prizefighter who goes home to Ireland and courts the fiery Maureen O'Hara. The Quiet Man Museum, in the village center, is an exact replica of the cottage used in the film, with reproductions of the furniture and costumes, a few original artifacts, and pictures of actors Barry Fitzgerald and Maureen O'Hara on location. Margaret and Gerry Collins host *Quiet Man* walking tours, leaving the cottage at 11 am daily and exploring such Cong village sites as the river fight scene, the "hats in the air" scene, and Pat Cohan's Bar. There is also a chauffeur-driven tour option. ✉ *Circular Rd., Cong Village Center* ☎ *094/954–6089* ⊕ *www.quietmanmuseum.com* 🖾 *€5, walking tour €15* ⊗ *By appointment only Nov.–Mar.*

🛏 Hotels

★ Ashford Castle

$$$$ | **HOTEL** | **FAMILY** | Massive and flamboyantly turreted, this famed mock-Gothic baronial showpiece, dating from the 13th century, and rebuilt in 1870 for the Guinness family, has been wowing visitors like President Reagan, John Travolta, Brad Pitt, and Pierce Brosnan—who got married here, as did Rory McIlroy—ever since. **Pros:** epitome of a romantic Irish castle; excellent facilities and activities; regal grounds. **Cons:** so luxurious you are cut off from the normal hubbub of Irish life; activities and dining options book up quickly at peak times; does not come cheap. 💲 *Rooms from: €625* ✉ *Cong* ☎ *094/954–6003* ⊕ *www.ashfordcastle. com* 🛏 *82 rooms, 1 cottage* 🍽 *Free breakfast.*

The Lodge at Ashford Castle

$$$$ | **HOTEL** | A white Victorian house set on the exquisite grounds of Ashford Castle and overlooking Lough Corrib, the Lodge is Ashford Castle's fun and funky sister property, its bold and witty decor freely combining Warhol and hunting prints, more like a pal's mildly eccentric home than a hotel. **Pros:** access to outdoor activities on Ashford estate for half the (lodging) price; good restaurant and bar food on-site; secluded lakeside location. **Cons:** popular wedding venue; 2½-km (1½-mile) walk or drive to main estate; least expensive rooms in courtyard lack view and wow factor. 💲 *Rooms from: €320* ✉ *Lisloughrey Pier* ☎ *094/5400* ⊕ *www.thelodgeac. com* ⊗ *Closed midweek Nov.–Feb.* 🛏 *64 rooms* 🍽 *Free breakfast.*

Ryan's Hotel

$ | **B&B/INN** | With framed fishing ties and specimen fish given pride of place on the lobby wall, you know you are in a hostelry favored by anglers. **Pros:** affordable alternative to Ashford Castle; central to village; good area for walkers and anglers. **Cons:** uninspiring views from

The village of Cong is world-famous as the setting for John Ford's Oscar-winning *The Quiet Man,* and the Quiet Man Museum takes you behind the scenes.

most rooms. $ *Rooms from: €90* ⊠ *Main St.* ☎ *094/954–6243* ⊕ *www.ryanshotel-cong.ie* ⤵ *12 rooms* ⎆ *Free breakfast.*

Westport

32 km (20 miles) north of Leenane.

★ By far the most attractive town in County Mayo, Westport is on an inlet of Clew Bay, a wide expanse of sea dotted with islands and framed by mountain ranges. It's one of the most attractive heritage towns in Ireland, its Georgian origins clearly defined by the broad streets skirting the gently flowing river and, particularly, by the lime-fringed central avenue called the Mall. Built as an O'Malley stronghold, the entire town received a face-lift when the Brownes, who had come from Sussex in the reign of Elizabeth I, constructed Westport House and much of the modern town, which was laid out by architect James Wyatt when he was employed to finish the grand estate of Westport House.

GETTING HERE AND AROUND

Westport is 32 km (20 miles) north of Leenane on the R335, and 78 km (48 miles) north of Clifden, a journey of about an hour. It is 80 km (50 miles) northwest of Galway on the N84 and R334 via Headford, picking up the N84 again before taking the R330 at Partry. The journey takes about one hour, 18 minutes. There is ample parking in the town center, on the streets, and in designated lots, with a nominal charge during business hours. There is more parking down on the quays.

There are Bus Éireann schedules daily from Westport (the Octagon monument) to Galway City, traveling on the nonscenic N17 via Claremorris. The express takes one hour, 50 minutes, while the nonexpress bus takes more than two hours. There are also direct buses from Westport to Ballina, a journey of about an hour. There is no bus station in Westport. Irish Rail trains travel from Dublin's Heuston Station to Westport, a journey of 3½ hours.

VISITOR INFORMATION

CONTACTS Croagh Patrick Visitor Centre.
⊠ *Teach na Miasa, Murrisk* ☎ *098/64114*
⊕ *www.croagh-patrick.com.* **Westport Tourist Office.** ⊠ *Fáilte Ireland, Discover Ireland Centre, Bridge St.* ☎ *098/25711* ⊕ *www.discoverireland.ie/places-to-go/ westport.*

◉ Sights

★ Achill Island

BEACH—SIGHT | Achill Island is only 20 feet from the mainland and has been connected by a bridge since 1887, the latest (2008) being a €5 million swing bridge, known locally as "our Calatrava-style bridge." At 147 square km (57 square miles), it is Ireland's largest offshore island, with a population of 2,700. The main reason for visiting is to enjoy the wild open spaces of its unspoiled bogs and long empty beaches, plus abundant flora, especially wild heather and, in May and June, rhododendrons. Fuchsia blooms later in the summer.

Keem Bay on the island's western coastline is the showstopper in this remarkably beautiful, windswept corner of Ireland. Accessible by car on a twisting road carved into a cliff top, the bay is an uninhibited sandy retreat from modern civilization. The beach is hugged by two enormous cliffs, creating a dazzlingly white valley that spills into the ocean. High over Keem Bay is a 1½-km (1-mile) cliff-edge walk, onward to Croaghaun (668m) with the island's most westerly peak where, at its summit, visitors can see peregrine falcons in their habitat or spot whales far below in the Atlantic Ocean. The best introduction to Achill is to follow signs for the 20-km (12-mile) Atlantic Drive. The road runs through Keel, which has a 3-km-long (2-mile-long) beach with spectacular rock formations in the eastern cliffs. Dugort, on the north shore, is a small village with a beautiful golden strand. Above it is the 2,204-foot Slievemore, the island's highest summit.

At its base is the Deserted Village, a settlement of 80 ruined one-room stone houses, abandoned since the 1845 famine.

Clare Island

ISLAND | Clew Bay is said to have 365 islands, one for every day of the year. The biggest and most interesting to visit is Clare Island, at the mouth of the bay. In fine weather the rocky, hilly island, which is 8 km (5 miles) long and 5 km (3 miles) wide, has beautiful views south toward Connemara, east across Clew Bay, and north to Achill Island. About 150 people live on the island today, but before the 1845–47 famine it had a population of about 1,700. A 15th-century tower overlooking the harbor was once the stronghold of Granuaile, the pirate queen, who ruled the area until her death in 1603. She is buried on the island, in its 12th-century Cistercian abbey. Today most visitors seek out the island for its unusual peace and quiet, golden beaches, and unspoiled landscape. A singles' adventure festival, which involves outdoor activities, locally sourced food, and music, is held twice a year in May and September, and is proving very popular with the unattached. There are two ferry services to the island, one year-round, the other seasonal; both depart from Roonagh Pier, near Louisburgh, a scenic 19-km (12-mile) drive from Westport on R335 past several long sandy beaches. The crossing takes about 15 minutes. Dolphins often accompany the boats on the trip, and there are large populations of seals under the island's cliffs. ⊠ *Clew Bay* ☎ *098/25045 for ferry info, 098/23737* ⊕ *www.clareisland.ie* ⊠ *Ferry €17 round-trip (discounted online)* ☞ *Two ferry companies serve Clare Island. Your return ticket will only be valid on a ferry belonging to the company you came out with.*

★ Croagh Patrick

MOUNTAIN—SIGHT | Look out as you travel north for the great bulk of 2,500-foot-high

Croagh Patrick; its size and conical shape make it one of the West's most distinctive landmarks. On clear days a small white oratory is visible at its summit (it stands on a ½-acre plateau), as is the wide path that ascends to it. The latter is the Pilgrim's Path. Each year about 25,000 people, many of them barefoot, follow the path to pray to St. Patrick in the oratory on its peak. St. Patrick, who converted Ireland to Christianity, spent the 40 days and nights of Lent here in 441. The traditional date for the pilgrimage is the last Sunday in July. In the past, the walk was made at night, with pilgrims carrying burning torches, but that practice has been discontinued. The climb involves a gentle uphill slope, but you need to be fit and agile to complete the last half hour, over scree (small loose rocks with no trail). This is why most climbers carry a stick or staff (traditionally made of ash, and called an ash plant), which helps you to stop sliding backward. These can sometimes be bought in the parking area. The hike can be made in about three hours (round-trip) on any fine day and is well worth the effort for the magnificent views of the islands of Clew Bay, the Sheeffry Hills to the south (with the Bens visible behind them), and the peaks of Mayo to the north. The climb starts at Murrisk, a village about 8 km (5 miles) before Westport on the R335 Louisburgh road. ⊠ *Westport.*

Octagon

PLAZA | Westport's streets radiate from its central Octagon, where an old-fashioned farmers' market is held on Thursday morning; look for work clothes, harnesses, tools, and children's toys for sale. Presiding over the square at the top of the tall fluted column is a statue of St Patrick, which replaced an earlier statute of a faceless banker (his face was removed by pellets during Civil War target practice,) Traditional shops—ironmongers, drapers, and the like—line the streets. ⊠ *Westport.*

Westport House

HOUSE | FAMILY | Westport House and Country Park, a stately home built on the site of an earlier castle (believed to have been the home of the 16th-century warrior queen, Grace O'Malley) is the town's most famous landmark. Set right on the shores of a lake, the house remained the property of the Browne family from the 17th century until recent years, when a local businessman purchased it. Architect Richard Cassels (who also designed Powerscourt in County Wicklow and the Irish government's nerve center, Leinster House) masterminded the design of the house, which was constructed in 1730 and added to in 1778, and then finally completed in 1788 by architect James Wyatt with a lavish budget from the Browne's trading history with Jamaica. The rectangular, three-story house is furnished with late-Georgian and Victorian pieces. Family portraits by Opie and Reynolds, a huge collection of old Irish silver and old Waterford glass, plus an opulent group of paintings—including *The Holy Family* by Rubens—are on display. A word of caution: Westport isn't your usual staid country house. The old dungeons now house interactive games, and the grounds have given way to an amusement park for children and an adventure center offering zip rides, laser combat games, and archery. In fact, the lake is now littered with swan-shape "pedaloes," boats that may be fun for families but help destroy the perfect Georgian grace of the setting. If these elements don't sound like a draw, arrive early, when it's less likely to be busy. There is also a 1½-km (1-mile) riverside walk, a tree trail, a gift shop, and a coffee shop. ⊠ *Off N59, south of Westport, clearly signposted from Octagon* ☎ *098/27766* ⊕ *www.westporthouse. ie* ⊠ *House and gardens €14, activities from €3; 10% discount online.*

Connemara's Wild Ponies

As you drive through Connemara, you will not only see sheep roaming the hillsides (more sheep than people) but also herds of wild ponies, usually gray (the proper term for white horses) or dun (buckskin) in color.

Connemara ponies are strong, hardy, companionable, highly intelligent, and surprisingly elegant. Averaging around 13 to 14 hands, they are much sought after for riding and show jumping. They are assumed to be a cross between a native Irish breed and Spanish-bred Arab horses imported in Elizabethan times.

The breed was only recognized in the early 20th century and is now celebrated on the third weekend in August at the Connemara Pony Show in Clifden. The whole town takes on a festive air, with parties long into the night, as breeders and competitors from all over Ireland revel in the annual get-together. The show-jumping competitions are pretty nifty, too.

Restaurants

★ Cronin's Sheebeen

$ | **MODERN IRISH** | Overlooking Clew Bay on the outskirts of Westport, this whitewashed, thatched cottage-pub is the stuff of dreams, and so is the food offered by the father-and-son team who own it. The fresh salmon, hake, turbot, or mussels from nearby Rossaveal or the Corrib give the menu a sea-hopping freshness, providing balance to the bolder, more colorful choices, like chicken marinated in mojito. **Known for:** warm ginger and banana cake; fresh Newport langoustine with wild garlic and lovage butter; Clew Bay seafood chowder. $ *Average main: €15* ⊠ *Rosbeg, Westport* ⊹ *4 km (2½ miles) west on L5840 from Westport* ☎ *98/26528* ⊕ *www.cronins-sheebeen.com* ⊗ *No food Mon.–Thurs. Nov.–Mar.*

The Tavern Bar and Restaurant

$ | **SEAFOOD** | **FAMILY** | The emphasis is firmly on seafood and fresh local produce at this traditional family-run tavern in the village of Murrisk beneath Croagh Patrick. Hearty portions of Clew Bay seafood, Connemara lamb, and local farmhouse cheeses are served all day, and kids can get half portions or order from their own menu. **Known for:** seafood chowder with homemade brown bread; lobsters in summer; fresh oysters. $ *Average main: €14* ⊠ *Murrisk* ⊹ *5 km (3 miles) from Westport* ☎ *098/64060* ⊕ *www.tavernmurrisk.com* ⊗ *Bar food daily. Restaurant upstairs closed Nov.–mid-Mar., and some weeknights mid-Mar.–Oct.; call to confirm.*

Hotels

Clew Bay Hotel

$ | **HOTEL** | In Westport's town center, this hotel welcomes guests with a traditional wooden facade but inside, a contemporary glass-roofed lobby becomes the centerpiece of a stylish modern interior decorated with original artwork. **Pros:** central location, adjacent to bars and shops; bespoke walking and cycling activity breaks; good value. **Cons:** risk of late-night noise in front rooms; no private parking; bathrooms a bit old-fashioned; popular with stag and hen parties. $ *Rooms from: €100* ⊠ *James St.* ☎ *098/28088* ⊕ *www.clewbayhotel.com* ⇗ *40 rooms* ❍ *Free breakfast.*

Knockranny House Hotel & Spa

$$ | HOTEL | Built on a bluff just outside town, with a commanding view of Croagh Patrick, Knockranny's modern-day mock-Tudor facade comes as a surprise, but inside guests are drawn by the inviting aroma of an open fire in the spacious lobby. **Pros:** peaceful haven with high standard of comfort; upgrade to a more spacious room for only €10; nice views. **Cons:** a 10-minute walk into town; lots of corridors to negotiate; design of public rooms a little bland. ⑤ *Rooms from: €158* ⊠ *Castlebar Rd. (N5)* ☎ *098/28600* ⊕ *www.knockrannyhousehotel.ie* ⤴ *97 rooms* ⦿ *Free breakfast.*

Mulranny Park Hotel

$$ | HOTEL | FAMILY | Perched on a cliff overlooking a vast, sandy beach on the northern side of Clew Bay, 25 minutes' drive from Westport, this is one of Ireland's best-loved "bucket and spade" hotels, built in 1897 for holidaymakers arriving by train. **Pros:** that huge beach on your doorstop and panoramic sea views; indoor pool and leisure center; Great Western Greenway walking/cycling route on-site. **Cons:** very popular with groups and extended families; must reserve evening meal in advance to ensure a place; village of Mulranny does not have much else to offer. ⑤ *Rooms from: €150* ⊠ *Mulranny* ☎ *098/36000* ⊕ *www.mulrannyparkhotel.ie* ⦿ *Closed Jan. 7–31* ⤴ *41 rooms, 20 apartments* ⦿ *Free breakfast.*

Westport Plaza Hotel

$$ | HOTEL | With all the hallmarks of Ireland's Celtic Tiger boom time, this swish and stylish boutique hotel has a vast marble lobby with a double-sided gas fire and huge guest rooms with large, veneered, Art Deco–style furniture and bathrooms with Jacuzzi tubs and modern showers. **Pros:** some rooms have balconies overlooking roof garden; great amenities; quiet but central. **Cons:** avoid the few bedrooms with street views; you might forget you're in Ireland; guests have to walk outside to the pool. ⑤ *Rooms from: €158* ⊠ *Castlebar St.* ☎ *098/51166* ⊕ *www.westportplazahotel.ie* ⤴ *85 rooms, 3 suites* ⦿ *Free breakfast.*

Nightlife

Matt Molloy's

MUSIC CLUBS | In Westport's town center try this favorite spot; Matt Molloy is not only the owner but also a member of famed musical group the Chieftains. Traditional music is, naturally, the main attraction. ⊠ *Bridge St.* ☎ *098/26655* ⊕ *www.mattmolloy.com.*

The Towers Bar & Restaurant

MUSIC CLUBS | A good spot for traditional music from 9 pm, the Towers is also known for its tasty pub grub. In summer there are outdoor tables set up beside the bay. Children are welcome up to 7 pm. ⊠ *The Quay* ☎ *098/24844* ⊕ *www.thetowersbar.com.*

Shopping

Carraig Donn

CLOTHING | A good selection of crystal, jewelry, and ceramics are the main temptations here, along with Carraig Donn's own line of knitwear. ⊠ *Bridge St.* ☎ *098/50300* ⊕ *www.carraigdonn.ie.*

McCormack's

ART GALLERIES | Downstairs is a traditional butcher shop, but climb one flight up to find the Andrew Stone gallery, with work by local artists for sale and a café serving homemade recipes. ⊠ *Bridge St.* ☎ *098/25619.*

O'Reilly/Turpin

GIFTS/SOUVENIRS | Head here for the best in contemporary Irish design for knitwear, ceramics, jewelry, and other decorative items. ⊠ *Bridge St.* ☎ *098/28151* ⊕ *www.oreillyturpin.ie.*

Thomas Moran's

GIFTS/SOUVENIRS | It's worth a visit to Thomas Moran's just to see the cluttered, quirky facade that has welcomed customers through its doors for well over a century. Inside, take some time to rummage through the irresistibly unique gifts: locally made blackthorn sticks, bargain umbrellas, and high-kitsch souvenirs. ⊠ *Bridge St.* ☎ *098/25562.*

 ## Activities

BICYCLING
Clew Bay Bike Hire

BICYCLING | Explore the scenic bike trails of Clew Bay, including the Great Western Greenway, on a top-of-the-range bike, available by the hour, day, or multiday. The minibus and bike trailer provide a free drop-off and collection service for an extra fee. In addition, kayak hire and escorted trips are available. ⊠ *Distillery Rd.* ☎ *098/37675* ⊕ *www.clewbaybikehire.ie.*

Electric Escapes

BICYCLING | Take the hard work out of cycling and rent an electric bike to explore the Great Western Greenway, or join a guided cycle tour along the Bangor Trail, amid 1,000 square miles of wilderness. ⊠ *Distillery Rd.* ☎ *098/56611 landline, 087/745–1155 mobile* ⊕ *www.electricescapes.ie.*

★ Great Western Greenway

BICYCLING | FAMILY | This 42-km (26-mile) off-road cycling and walking trail follows the route of the railway line that ran along the edge of Clew Bay through Newport and Mulranny from 1895 until 1937, connecting Westport to Achill Island. It passes through some of the most spectacular scenery in the West of Ireland, and has given a major boost to tourism in the area. The birdsong and the sound of the wind are praised as highly as the great coastal scenery. It is just as enjoyable to drive out along the N59 and walk a short section as it is to walk or cycle the whole path. ⊠ *Great Western Greenway (N59)* ⊕ *www.greenway.ie.*

GOLF
Westport Golf Club

GOLF | Twice this inland 18-hole course hosted the Irish Amateur Championship. It lies in the shadows of the mountain Croagh Patrick, which gives the course a stunning backdrop. ⊠ *Westport* ☎ *098/28262* ⊕ *www.westportgolfclub. ie* 🗓 *May–Sept. €75, Oct.–Apr. €50* ⚐. *18 holes, 7000 yards, par 73.*

Castlebar

18 km (11 miles) east of Westport on N5.

The capital of Mayo, situated on its central limestone plain, once the biggest town for miles around, Castlebar is now a commercial and shopping hub for the region, overshadowed by its more scenic neighbor, Westport. Park in one of the many pay-and-display car parks, and proceed on foot.

GETTING HERE AND AROUND
Castlebar is 18 km (11 miles) east of Westport on the N5 and 40 km (25 miles) west of Knock Airport. The journey takes about 15 minutes by car. There are plenty of pay-and-display parking lots in the town center, which has a one-way traffic system and is compact and walkable. Bus Éireann has regional links from here to Galway City in the South (3 hours, 30 minutes via Westport) and Ballina in the North (one hour). Dublin Airport is a meandering five-hour ride by bus; rail is a better option. The rail connection to Westport in the West takes 18 minutes, and it is three hours to Dublin Heuston in the East; change at Manulla Junction for the one-hour trip to Ballina.

VISITOR INFORMATION
CONTACTS Castlebar Tourist Information Office. ⊠ *Linenhall St.* ☎ *094/902–1207* ⊕ *www.mayo-ireland.ie.*

Sights

Ballintubber Abbey

BUILDING | The only church in Ireland founded by an Irish king and still in daily use, Ballintubber's has greeted its faithful flock since 1216, when Cathal O'Connor built it on the site of St. Patrick's church, which was built some 800 years earlier, a replica of which can be found on the grounds. In the 1960s the 15th-century cloister was unearthed by excavators in surprisingly good condition, given Cromwell had left his mark on the abbey, and it now creates a serene space alongside the abbey. Scan the gardens for Seán na Sagart's (Sean the priest hunter's) Tree. He escaped the gallows indebted to local sheriff Bingham—to be repaid by bringing him one head of a priest yearly. After Sean's death the tree grew from his grave and splintered in half, creating a fitting epitaph for a black soul. In more recent times, 007 actor Pierce Brosnan's marriage to Keely Shaye Smith occurred in the abbey. ⊠ *Castlebar* ✛ *14 km (9 miles) south of Castlebar on N84* ☎ *094/903–0934* ⊕ *www.ballintubberabbey.ie* ⊠ *Free* ☞ *Abbey: daily, 9 am–midnight. Guided tours available 9:30–5 by arrangement.*

The Linenhall Arts Centre

ARTS VENUE | The town's arts center has a calendar of exhibitions, concerts, and performances, a crafts shop, and a handy coffeeshop with home baking. It occupies an imposing gray limestone building dating from 1790, when the town had a thriving linen industry. ⊠ *Linenhall St.* ☎ *094/902–3733* ⊕ *www.thelinenhall.com* ⊠ *Free; event ticket prices vary.*

The Mall

NATIONAL/STATE PARK | At the center of Castlebar is the pleasant tree-lined Mall, with some good 18th-century houses. A memorial honors the French soldiers who died during the 1798 uprising when Castlebar was briefly the capital of "the Provisional Republic of Connaught." The Mall was once a cricket pitch belonging to the local landlord, Lord Lucan, and is now a town park. ⊠ *Castlebar.*

Museum of Country Life

MUSEUM | To understand the forces that have led to such dramatic changes in Turlough, pay a visit to the Museum of Country Life, which focuses on rural Ireland between 1860 and 1960—a way of life that remained unchanged for many years, then suddenly came to an end within living memory. At this highly acclaimed museum, the only branch of the National Museum of Ireland outside Dublin, you're invited to imagine yourself back in a vanished world, before the internal combustion engine, rural electrification, indoor plumbing, television, and increased education transformed people's lives and expectations. For many, this is a journey into a strange place, where water had to be carried from a well, turf had to be brought home from the bog, fires had to be lighted daily for heat and cooking, and clothes had to be made painstakingly by hand in the long winter evenings. Among the displayed items are authentic furniture and utensils; hunting, fishing, and agricultural implements; clothing; and objects relating to games, pastimes, religion, and education.

The museum experience starts in Turlough Park House, built in the High Victorian Gothic style in 1865 and set in pretty lakeside gardens. Just three rooms have been restored to illustrate the way the landowners lived. A sensational modern four-story, curved building houses the main exhibit. Cleverly placed windows afford panoramic views of the surrounding park and the distant Round Tower, allowing you to reflect on the reality beyond the museum's walls. Temporary exhibitions, such as *Romanticism and Reality,* help illustrate the divide between the dreamy image of old rural life and its actual hardships. The shop sells museum-branded and handcrafted gift items as well as a good selection of books on related topics. A café with indoor and outdoor tables is in the stable yard, and you can take scenic lakeside walks in the park. Like all branches of the National Museum of Ireland, admission is free, making it a great rainy-day resource. ⊠ *Museum of Country Life, Turlough Park House, Castlebar* ✛ *7 km (4 miles) south of Castlebar on N5* ☎ *094/903–1755* ⊕ *www.museum.ie/Country-Life.*

🍴 Restaurants

Café Rua

$ | **MODERN IRISH** | **FAMILY** | This friendly, boho-chic café with its traditional red shop front (*rua* is Irish for red) is a showcase for fresh, locally produced foods, simply served. There's an imaginative children's menu, and at lunch there are three daily specials—roast meat, fish, and vegetarian—while many opt for the homemade soup and sandwich (served in a traditional soft roll known as a *blaa*), or a salad. **Known for:** fresh, simply prepared dishes; local produce; home baking. $ *Average main: €10* ⊠ *New Antrim St.* ☎ *094/902–3376* ⊕ *www. caferua.com* ▱ *No credit cards* ⊘ *Closed Sun. No dinner Mon.–Wed.*

Dining Room

$ | **MODERN IRISH** | A modern intimate dining room with rustic brickwork makes a fitting setting for chef Kevin Stirzaker's seasonal menu that offers the best of local produce, simply prepared to let the quality produce speak for itself. Menu highlights include black pudding with seared scallops or fire-roasted tomato and barley risotto. **Known for:** local produce; early-bird special; excellent service. $ *Average main: €18* ⊠ *Main St.* ☎ *094/902–1861* ⊕ *www.diningroomcastlebar.com* ⊘ *Closed Mon. and Tues.*

🍸 Nightlife

John McHale's Pub

BARS/PUBS | This classic Irish pub is one of the oldest in town, and the best place for a bit of traditional local banter. It's known as the home of the "meejum" (or medium—a glass that measures somewhere between a half pint and pint) of Guinness and for the high quality of its stout. ⊠ *Newline , Chapel St. Lower* ☎ *094/902–1849.*

Foxford

As you travel from Turlough northeast to Ballina, you have a choice of two routes. The longer and more scenic is via the tiny, wooded village of Pontoon, skirting the western shore of Lough Conn and passing through the rough bogland of the Glen of Nephin, beneath the dramatic heather-clad slopes of Nephin Mountain (2,653 feet) to Crossmolina and Ballina. The shorter route follows N5 and N58 to Foxford, a pretty village with several crafts and antiques shops.

GETTING HERE AND AROUND

Take N5 and N58 from Turlough.

Sights

★ Foxford Woolen Mills

INFO CENTER | A good place for a break is the Foxford Woolen Mills Visitor Centre, where you can explore the crafts shop and grab a bite at the restaurant. Few first-time visitors leave without buying an heirloom-quality Foxford blanket. The *Foxford Experience* tells the story of the wool mill, famous for its tweeds and blankets, from the time of the famine in the mid-19th century—when it was founded by the Sisters of Charity to combat poverty—to the present day. ⊠ *Lower Main St., Foxford* ☎ *094/925–6104* ⊕ *www.foxfordwoollenmills.ie.*

Belmullet

80 km (50 miles) northwest of Westport.

Belmullet's unconventional streetscape skirts its waterfront and the town harbors a friendly, unpretentious attitude that harks back to an earlier time. Nestled in a quiet, northwest corner of the Irish coast, it's the place to go off-radar from the convoy of rental cars that blast their way along the Wild Atlantic Way, the popular trail that connects Ireland's western seaboard. Belmullet's real lure is its location as the capital and access point to the Mullet (or Erris) Peninsula, a windswept playground crammed with abandoned islands, ocean-carved blow holes, endless miles of beaches, rugged coastal trails, and an enormous skyline that lights up the night when the clouds retreat.

GETTING HERE AND AROUND

A car or hiking boots are the best methods of transport in this area. Bus Éireann bus No. 446 offers a twice-daily service between the larger town of Ballina and Belmullet as far as Blacksod.

 ## Sights

Blacksod Lighthouse

LIGHTHOUSE | Few would believe that the modest, sandstone lighthouse on the southeast tip of the Mullet Peninsula could have had a pivotal role in history, but a weather report issued by the lighthouse keeper on June 3, 1944, convinced General Dwight D. Eisenhower to delay the D-Day invasion of Normandy by 24 hours. This delay saved the Allies from a catastrophic fate. Blacksod Lighthouse dates from 1864 and embraces the full brunt of the Atlantic Ocean's extreme weather. ⊠ *Blacksod, Erris, Belmullet* ✛ *21 km (13 miles) south of Belmullet on R313* ⊘ *Closed fall–spring. Contact ahead.*

Wild Nephin Ballycroy National Park

NATIONAL/STATE PARK | Located in the southern territory of the Mullet Peninsula and covering 42½ square miles of Atlantic bogland and mountainous wilderness, Ballycroy is one of only six national parks in Ireland and utopia for the outdoor adventurer. Marked looped trails offer staggering views across Blacksod Bay and the Achill Islands. Once the sun sets, the area becomes a "dark-sky park," where visitors arrive with flashlights to witness the uninterrupted view of the heavens. The park is equipped with a visitor center and café. To camp, contact the park manager. ⊠ *Ballycroy Village, Belmullet* ☎ *098/49888* ⊕ *www.ballycroynationalpark.ie* ⊠ *Free* ⊘ *Closed Nov.–mid-Mar.*

 ## Hotels

Talbot Hotel

$ | **HOTEL** | The quirky, modern-boutique-hotel hallmarks and bold color scheme and decor are a little at odds with the town's otherwise plain offerings, but the focus on style here does not in any way divert attention from comfort. **Pros:** town-center location; reliable pub food every night; large suites with spacious bathrooms. **Cons:** street parking; main restaurant closed Monday to Thursday ; modern decor may not suit those seeking more traditional Irish country style. ⑤ *Rooms from: €90* ⊠ *Barrack St., Belmullet* ☎ *097/20484* ⊕ *www.thetalbothotel.ie* ⥬ *21 rooms* ⑩ *Free breakfast.*

 ## Nightlife

McDonnells

BARS/PUBS | The perfect antidote to a day hiking the peninsula, this cozy, open-fire pub is known locally as the "lobster pot," because once you're there, there's no getting out. It's the heart of the community where guests linger longer than planned, and where tourists only stand out if they don't join in with the conversation, dancing, or trad music session. Owned by the McDonnell family since 1942, the pub, in true rural Irish fashion, is adjacent to the family's other business—an undertaker's—and so it has been the location of an occasional wake. ⊠ *Lower Barrack St., Belmullet* ☎ *097/81194.*

Activities

Carne Golf Links

GOLF | Overlooking Blacksod Bay, with breathtaking views of Inis Géidhe and Inis Glóire, the final island home to the legendary "Children of Lir," Carne is in the sandy heartland of the peninsula and features in the top 50 courses in both Britain and Ireland. Currently in the process of expanding an extra 9 holes to bring the course to 27, it was the last course designed by Eddie Hackett, and many critics believe that it was his finest design. ⊠ *Carne, Belmullet ✛ 4 km (2½ miles) west of Belmullet on the R313* ☎ *97/82292* ⊕ *www.carnegolflinks.com* ⚐ *18 holes, 6706 yards, par 72* ☞ *Nov.– Feb., €50; Mar. €65; Apr.–Oct. €110.*

Cross Loop Walk

HIKING/WALKING | With a dramatic trailhead at Cross Abbey and its hilltop Termoncarragh graveyard that has defied the force of the Atlantic for centuries, this trail weaves it way past sand dunes and the crystal-blue setting of the Iniskea Islands, where the Atlantic air swirls through the houses in an abandoned village. Start your hike at low tide to take advantage of the trail's 2½ km (1½ miles) of strand. Note that the beach has strong undercurrents and is not safe for swimming. A black post leads hikers across sandy dunes, then turns to curve around a lakeshore filled with wild swans. Cast an eye back to the Atlantic coast to see Inis Glóire, the tiny island where the fabled Children of Lir spent the last three centuries of their lives as swans. Stop by Ionad Deirbhile, a nearby visitor center

and café in Blacksod, to get your bearings. ⊠ *Belmullet ✛ Follow R313 west as far as Binghamstown, indicated by small church. Veer right to coastal road. Parking available at trailhead* ☎ *97/85727* ⊕ *www. ionaddeirbhile.ie.*

Killala

64 km (40 miles) northeast of Westport and 64 km (40 miles) east of Belmullet.

When a modest fleet of French military ships landed in this pretty bay-side village to aid the Irish in their quest for freedom back in 1798, Killala would forever mark its place in history as the point of the first failed Irish Rebellion, with countless heartfelt ballads like *Minstrel Boy* or *The Wind that Shakes the Barley* inspired by the bloodshed spilled by the conquerors. Dominating the village's narrow, twisting lanes is an impressive 12th-century limestone Round Tower. The 84-foot-high structure is visible from the surrounding countryside, and it's one of the finest examples of its kind in the country. Killala is also the gateway to Mayo's rugged northern coast, a dramatic, windswept stretch of cliffs, where the wind howls in from the Atlantic directly from Iceland, the nearest landmass. The cliffs at Downpatrick have spectacular blowholes and have weathered dramatically since Stone Age farmers built Céide Fields, now a unique visitor center showcasing one of the oldest known field systems in the world.

GETTING HERE AND AROUND

A car is the best way to explore this area. There is a commuter bus twice a day from Ballina, Route 445, as far as Ballycastle. Between May and mid-September there is a private bus service visiting Killala, Ballycastle, and the Céide Fields; get details from Ballina Tourist Information Office.

Sights

Ballycastle

TOWN | Anywhere else in Ireland this tiny one-street village would be unremarkable, but out on this wild windswept coast, its brightly painted houses in the relatively sheltered valley of the Ballinglen River are a welcome sign of normal life and coziness. Mary's Tea Rooms gives a warm welcome, while within shouting distance, Ballinglen Arts Foundation puts on art exhibitions between May and September. ⊠ Ballycastle.

Céide Fields

ARCHAEOLOGICAL SITE | Buried below North Mayo's wild boglands is the most extensive Stone Age monument on Earth. The Céide Fields' megalithic tombs, dwelling sites, field system, and vast, stone-walled meadows stretch back 6,000 years and were unearthed in the 1930s when a local teacher noticed stone formation when cutting turf. The visitor center is housed under a glass-and-steel-pyramid and has a magnificent 4,300-year-old Scotch pine that looms alongside the staircase, which alone makes the visit worthwhile. Meander along the ancient pathways at leisure, and stop by the viewing platform to see the ocean over a 110-meter-high cliff. Guided tours are also worthwhile; check ahead for times. Admission includes an optional guided walk through an excavated section of the stones; wet-weather gear is provided when necessary. The Céide Fields are on R314, 5 km (3 miles) west of Ballycastle. ⊠ Ballycastle ☎ 096/43325 ⊕ www.ceide-fields.com ☜ €5 ⏱ Closed Nov.–Mar.

Downpatrick Head

BEACH—SIGHT | On a clear day you can see the dramatic sea stack at Downpatrick Head in the distance from the Céide Fields Visitor Centre. It is worth getting closer. This rivals the far more famous (and bigger) Cliffs of Moher as an experience of nature in the wild. Wild Atlantic Way signposts lead you to a gravel car park a short walk across rough grass from the cliffs. Keep a tight hold on your kids: the unfenced cliffs rise 126 feet above the sea, and the wind can be strong. The sea stack, known in Irish as Dun Briste (the Broken Fort) is 262 feet offshore and rises to a height of about 164 feet. The sea has undermined the headland and spouts up to great heights through impressive blowholes, which are fenced off for safety. The sea stack was inhabited until the 14th century when nature rendered it an island. In May and June the cliffs are covered in sea pinks and nesting seabirds.

Hotels

Mount Falcon Estate

$$$$ | **HOTEL** | **FAMILY** | About 19 km (12 miles) south of Killala and set in a 100-acre estate between Ballina and Foxford, this baronial 1876 cut-stone house is the centerpiece of a family-owned property with 45 luxury self-catering houses, a lake and river fishery, indoor pool, and spa. **Pros:** spacious, restful surroundings; high standard of comfort; excellent restaurant. **Cons:** busy with families during Irish school holiday; rooms in the new wing are a little plain; two-night minimum stay in summer. ⑤ *Rooms from: €270* ⊠ *Foxford Rd. (N26), Ballina, Ballina* ✛ *20 mins south of Killala via N26 and R314* ☎ *096/74472* ⊕ *www.mountfalcon.com* ⇗ *32 rooms* ⑴⊙⑴ *Free breakfast.*

Stella Maris Country House Hotel

$$$ | **HOTEL** | This former coast-guard station and convent has a stunning waterside location looking across a wide bay to local landmark Downpatrick Head. **Pros:** high standard of comfort; talented owner-chef; unforgettable sea views. **Cons:** 3 km (2 miles) from nearest village; visited by some spectacular sea storms. ⑤ *Rooms from: €175* ⊠ *Ballycastle* ✛ *Drive west through Ballycastle village on R314 and after about 2 km (1¼ miles) look for fingerpost pointing to right* ☎ *096/43322* ⊕ *www.stellamarisireland.com* ⏱ *Closed mid-Oct.–mid-Apr.* ⇗ *12 rooms* ⑴⊙⑴ *Free breakfast.*

THE NORTHWEST

Updated by
Paul Clements

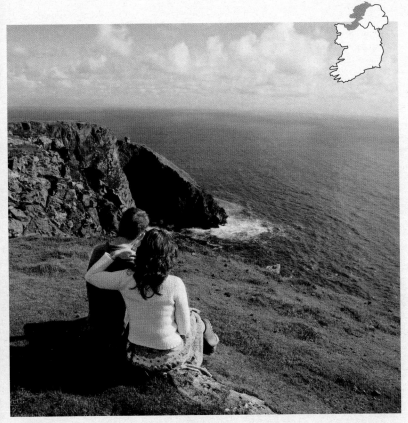

● Sights	⏸ Restaurants	⊟ Hotels	⊟ Shopping	⍟ Nightlife
★★★★★	★★★☆☆	★★★☆☆	★★★☆☆	★★★☆☆

WELCOME TO THE NORTHWEST

TOP REASONS TO GO

★ **Gaeltacht Country:** Venture to the seaside village of Ard an Rátha to listen to the seductive rhythms of locals conversing in full Irish (Gaelic) flight. Don't worry: everyone has English at the ready for lost visitors.

★ **Follow in the Yeatses' Footsteps:** From Sligo Town's museums head out to the majestic Ben Bulben peak to seek out places special to the famous brother duo, W.B. Yeats, the great poet, and Jack B. Yeats, one of Ireland's finest 20th-century painters.

★ **Garbo's Castle:** The legendary screen actress was just one of the many notables who enjoyed a stay at Glenveagh Castle.

★ **Hiking the Slieve League Cliffs:** To truly humble yourself before ocean, cliff, and sky, hike these fabled headlands, the highest sea cliffs in Europe.

★ **Lissadell House:** A magnificently restored ancestral home on the shores of Drumcliff Bay, not far from the grave of W.B. Yeats.

1 Sligo. What the poet William Butler Yeats would say about his native Sligo Town—a once-idyllic spot now overrun with modern shopping malls—can only be imagined, but it makes a great jumping-off point for exploring Yeats Country: the Lake Isle at Innisfree, the cairn-crowned Knocknarea (a peak often painted by brother Jack), and Drumcliff, where W.B. lies buried under the shadow of Ben Bulben.

2 Lough Gill. A freshwater lake shared between Sligo and Leitrim and a place of serene beauty.

3 Lake Isle of Inisfree. Famed in the poetry of W.B. Yeats, this island is on most visitors' itinerary.

4 Carrick-on-Shannon. A bustling town filled with characterful shops and pubs, and a launching place to see the River Shannon.

5 Rosses Point. Small village at the entrance to Sligo Harbour, which features in the paintings of Jack B. Yeats.

6 Drumcliff. At the foot of Ben Bulben mountain, the church graveyard is a place of pilgrimage as the burial place of W.B. Yeats.

7 Mullaghmore. A long-established holiday village with a superb beach and ocean views.

8 Ballyshannon. One of Ireland's oldest towns on the banks of the River Erne and good base for exploration.

9 Donegal Town. A vibrant town noted for its historic 15th-century castle and excellent shopping.

10 Killybegs. This fishing town is one of Ireland's busiest ports and a regular stop for cruise liners.

11 Gleann Cholm Cille (Glencolumbkille). Wild and remote, Glencolumbkille is a get-away-from-it-all destination by the ocean.

12 Ard an Rátha (Ardara). A laid-back, old-fashioned town noted for its weaving shops and time-burnished pubs.

13 Letterkenny. A large modern town with many historic buildings, well suited for exploring the Wild Atlantic Way.

14 Gartan Lough. Home to Glebe House and Gallery.

15 Glenveagh National Park. The wildest part of Donegal is home to a fairytale castle and nature trails.

Malin Head

Toraigh
(Tory Island)

ROSGUILL
PENINSULA

Lough
Swilly

Tory Sound

Sheephaven
Bay

FANAD PENINSULA

INISHOWEN PENINSULA

Carrigart

N56

Creeslough

Rathmullan

Glenveagh
National Park   15

DERRYVEAGH MOUNTAINS

Ramelton

Ariann Mhor
(Aranmore
Island)

R257

THE ROSES
(NA ROSA)

R245

♦ Glenveagh
Castle
14   ♦ Glebe House
and Gallery

N13

Derry

A5

Gweebarra
Bay

N56

Letterkenny   13

Pluck

DONEGAL

N56

N14

Loughros More
Bay

Ard an Ratha
(Ardara)   12

N15

A5

Gleann Cholm Cille
(Glencolumbkille)   11

Newtownstewart

NORTHERN
IRELAND

ieve League
Mountains

N56

Donegal
Town   9

Omagh

Killybegs   10   Bruckless

Clanabogan

0   10 mi

N15

A5

0   10 km

Donegal Bay

Ballyshannon

Irvinestown

Dromore

TYRONE

7   Bundoran   8

Mullaghmore

Lower
Lough Erne

A32

Lough
Melvin

Lissadell House   N15   Ben Bulben

LEITRIM

Trory

Enniskillen

Drumcliff   6

FERMANAGH

Sligo Bay

5   Sligo Town

Culkey

Knocknarea   1   N16   Manorhamilton

Lough Gill

3   2

Mackan

Lisnaskea

N59

Lake Isle of Innisfree

Ballysadare

Derrylin

N17   N4

SLIGO

Kilconny

Cloverhill

4

With its towering cliffs, secluded expanses of golden beaches, and sun-tinted waters, the Northwest is an untamed and wild part of Ireland—shaped, influenced, and tormented by the sea. Wide skies make it the perfect place to appreciate the shape-shifting light, slowly moving cloud formations, and crimson sunsets. As you drive around counties Sligo, Leitrim, and Donegal, you will discover roads curve this way and that, following the course of the indented coastline, a mountain valley, glen, or stream. But the only traffic jam you're likely to encounter will be a herd of heifers, reducing you to cow speed.

A place of nature on a grand scale, the Northwest should be appreciated in a leisurely way. Catch a cloudless evening and you may be enchanted by a night sky display of the aurora borealis, the northern lights; and amid this celestial light show, or even an astonishing star-filled sky, you will find a silence that kindles the imagination.

Like nowhere else, this region influenced the writer William Butler Yeats and his brother Jack Butler Yeats, a painter. Both immortalized this splendidly lush and rugged countryside in their work, and "Yeats Country" still attracts fans. Twenty-first-century Sligo pulses not only in the present but also with the charge of history, for it was the Yeatses' childhood home, the place that, more than any other, gave rise to their particular geniuses—or, as Jack B. put it: "Sligo was my school and the sky above it."

Northwest Ireland is overwhelmingly rural and underpopulated. That's not to say there isn't a bit of action here, with plenty to experience. Sligo Town, with its winding streets and Italian Quarter is as busy as Galway—an amazing feat for a town of only 18,000.

After you've drunk in the best views in Europe, washed by the Atlantic Ocean at Slieve League, you can pick up unique tweeds in Donegal, look out for golden eagles at fairy-tale Glenveagh Castle, delve into the past at Glencolumbcille Folk Village, or sample burstingly fresh local seafood. Savor the boating town of Carrick-on-Shannon in Leitrim, a place full of architectural delights, or stroll through the county's glens and hillsides—a completely undiscovered part of the country.

MAJOR REGIONS

Donegal Bay. As you drive north to Donegal Town, the glens of the Dartry Mountains (to which Ben Bulben belongs) gloriously roll by to the east. Look across coastal fields for views of the waters of Donegal Bay to the west. In the distant horizon the Donegal hills beckon. This stretch, dotted with numerous prehistoric sites, has become Northwest Ireland's most popular vacation area. There are a few small and unremarkable seashore resorts, and in some places you may find examples of haphazard and fairly tasteless construction that detracts from the scenery. In between these minor resort developments, wide-open spaces are free of traffic. The most intriguing area lies on the north side of the bay—all that rocky, indented coastline due west of Donegal Town. Here you enter the heart of away-from-it-all: County Donegal.

Northern Donegal. Traveling on northern County Donegal's country roads, you've escaped at last from the world's hurry and hassle. There's almost nothing up here but scenery, and plenty of it: broad, island-studded loughs of deep, dark tranquillity; unkempt, windswept, sheep-grazed grasses on mountain slopes; ribbons of luminous greenery following sparkling streams; and the mellow hues of wide boglands, all under shifting and changing cloudscapes. This trip begins in Letterkenny, the largest town in the county (population 19,500), and makes a beeline to the Irish Xanadu of Henry P. McIlhenny's Glenveagh Castle. Just one word of warning: don't be surprised if you

find a sheep standing in the middle of a mountain road looking as though you, rather than it, are in the wrong place.

Sligo and Nearby. Just as James Joyce made Dublin his own through his novels and stories, Sligo and its environs, known locally as Yeats Country, are bound to the work of W.B. Yeats (1865–1939), Ireland's first of four Nobel laureates, and to the work of his brother Jack B. Yeats (1871–1957), one of Ireland's most important 20th-century painters, whose Expressionistic landscapes and portraits are as emotionally fraught as his brother's poems are lyrical and plangent. The brothers intimately knew and eloquently celebrated in their art not only **Sligo Town** itself, but also the surrounding countryside, with its lakes, farms, woodland, and dramatic mountains that rise up not far from the center of town. On the Sligo-to-Drumcliff route, you will often see glimpses of Ben Bulben mountain, which looms over the western end of the Dartry range. The areas covered here are the most accessible parts of Northwest Ireland, easily reached from Galway.

Planning

Getting Here and Around

AIR TRAVEL

The principal international air-arrival point to Northwest Ireland is Ireland West Airport Knock, 55 km (34 miles) southwest of Sligo Town. City of Derry Airport, a few miles over the border, receives flights from London Stansted, Liverpool, Edinburgh, and Glasgow. City of Derry (also called Eglinton) is a particularly convenient airport for reaching northern County Donegal. Donegal Airport, in Carrickfinn, typically receives flights from Dublin. Ryanair has daily flights to Ireland West Airport Knock from London Stansted and London Gatwick, and also serves City of Derry Airport daily from London.

AIRPORTS City of Derry Airport.
☎ 028/7181–0784 ⊕ www.cityofder-ryairport.com. **Donegal Airport.** ✉ Car-rickfinn, Kincasslagh ☎ 074/954–8232 ⊕ www.donegalairport.ie. **Ireland West Airport Knock.** ✉ Knock ☎ 094/936–8100 ⊕ www.irelandwestairport.com.

AIRLINES Aer Lingus. ☎ 1890/800–600 ⊕ www.aerlingus.com. **British Airways City Express.** ☎ 0844/493–0787 ⊕ www.britishairways.com. **Ryanair.** ☎ 0871/246–0000 ⊕ www.ryanair.com.

AIRPORT TRANSFERS

If you aren't driving, Ireland West Airport Knock becomes less attractive; there are no easy public transport links, except the once-a-day (in season) local bus to Charlestown, 11 km (7 miles) away. You can get taxis—both cars and minibus-es—right outside Ireland West Airport Knock. The average rate is around €1.50 per kilometer. If you're not flying into Knock, you may have to phone a taxi company. Phone numbers of taxi compa-nies are available from airport information desks and are also displayed beside pay phones.

BUS TRAVEL

Getting around by bus is easy enough if you plan to visit only the larger towns. Bus Éireann's routes are regular and reliable and there are also several pri-vately run local bus companies, including McGeehan Coaches.

Bus Éireann helpfully offers a flexible Open Road bus pass ideally suited for travelers in the Northwest. A three-day tourist travel pass costs €60 and €16.50 for each additional day up to a maximum of six days. You can go anywhere in the republic on the nationwide network of services with this pass, but it is not valid across the border in Northern Ireland. For arrival and departure information with Bus Éireann, log on to ⊕ www.whens-mybus.ie.

CONTACTS Bus Éireann. ☎ 01/836–6111 in Dublin, 071/916–0066 in Sligo,

074/912–1309 in Letterkenny ⊕ www.buseireann.ie. **Bus Feda.** ☎ 074/954–8114 ⊕ www.feda.ie. **McGeehan Coaches.** ☎ 074/954–6150 ⊕ www.mcgeehan-coaches.com. **North West Busways.** ☎ 074/938–2619 ⊕ www.foylecoaches.com.

CAR TRAVEL

There is only one way to fully explore the rural Northwest of Ireland and that's by car. Once here, you can always rent a car at Ireland West Airport Knock or Sligo Town. But if coming from Dublin, many opt to rent from one of the bigger com-panies at the larger airports. If arriving from Northern Ireland, there are rental agencies aplenty in Derry or Belfast, but be sure to tell your agency if you are planning to cross the border.

The roads between the larger towns are fairly well maintained and signposted, but go slightly off the beaten track and con-ditions can vary from bad to dirt track. As long as you're not in a mad rush, this can add to the delight of your journey. This is rural Ireland, and if the scenery doesn't make this blissfully clear, then the sus-pension on your rented car certainly will!

In the Irish-speaking areas, signposts are written only in the Irish (Gaelic) language, which can be confusing. Make sure that your map gives both English and Irish place-names.

TRAIN TRAVEL

Sligo Town is the northernmost direct rail link to Dublin. If you want to get to Sligo Town by rail from other provincial towns, you must make some inconvenient con-nections and take roundabout routes. The rest of the region has no railway service.

CONTACTS Irish Rail. ☎ 01/836–6222, 071/916–9888 for Sligo train station ⊕ www.irishrail.ie.

The Wild Atlantic Way

The Wild Atlantic Way, Ireland's first long-distance driving route, runs from northern Donegal down to West Cork, traversing isolated headlands, inlets, and little-visited peninsulas. The route follows the tortuous twists of roads that hug this indented coastline for more than 2,500 km (1,500 miles), but is arguably at its most dramatic in the Northwest. Donegal, with nearly 30% of all Ireland's sandy beaches, has the lion's share of golden strands. Malinbeg beach or Rossnowlagh are places to get out of the car, listen to the booming breakers, and absorb the tingling fresh air that has crossed 4,828 km (3,000 miles) of sea.

All along the coast "Discovery Points" showcase areas of interest (including bars and restaurants), provide information on heritage and culture, and suggest viewpoints at which to breathe in the dramatic scenery and watch the interplay of light. Secret places to visit along the way are said to be "where the locals go," and generally speaking, local knowledge is the best advice to go on. The driving route, which is well signposted with new information boards pointing you in the right direction, has created a wave of regeneration throughout the area. Information is also available from tourist offices in Sligo, Donegal, and Letterkenny where you can pick up copies of the Fáilte Ireland *North West Tourist Pocket Guide,* which includes details of the route. Each of the west of Ireland areas that make up the route from Donegal to Cork also has its own pocket guide, which are available in local tourist information offices. In the Northwest, highlights include the following favorite stopping points:

■ Start your journey at **Malin Head,** the most northerly point of the route and at the headland known as Banba's Crown, named after a mythical queen. Call into the Seaview Tavern where the owner Michael Doherty will direct you to local beauty spots. The spectacular stretch of coastline from **Bunbeg to Carrigart** includes Horn Head where squabbling seabirds converge, while across Sheephaven Bay, the rugged splendor of the Rosguill peninsula is ideal for a short looped walk or bike ride.

■ Famed for its musical connection and walls filled with memorabilia, Leo Crolly's Tavern at **Meenaleck** in western Donegal is the home of musicians Enya, Clannad, and Moya Brennan. It is the place to see dancers kick their heels in the air. (⊕ www. leostavern.com).

■ A narrow strip of Atlantic coastline at **Streedagh Beach** in northern County Sligo provides unique access to rocks encrusted with fossils as well as the site of three Spanish Armada shipwrecks. (⊕ www.seatrails.ie).

■ Fancy a hearty gallop on a young horse along a deserted beach? Then canter along on your own private island that crosses an Atlantic channel to O'Connor's and Dernish Islands at **Grange** near Sligo. (⊕ www. islandviewridingstables.com).

■ One of Ireland's original coastal thatched pubs, the Beach Bar at **Aughris** in County Sligo is the place for a warming bowl of chowder surrounded by 300 years of maritime history. It's a pub where locals will happily spin you a yarn in exchange for a pint. (⊕ www.thebeachbarsligo. com).

Hotels

True, it's the farthest-flung corner of Ireland, but thanks to the area's popularity, good bed-and-breakfasts and small hotels are abundant. In the two major towns—Sligo Town and Donegal Town—and the small coastal resorts in between, many traditional provincial hotels have been modernized (albeit not always elegantly). Yet most manage to retain some of the charm that comes with older buildings and personalized service. Away from these areas, your best overnight choice is usually a modest guesthouse that includes bed, breakfast, and an evening meal, though you can also find first-class country-house hotels with that gracious professionalism found elsewhere in Ireland. Consider staying in an Irish-speaking home to get to know some of the area's Gaeltacht population. Glencolumbkille's excellent Oideas Gael cultural center specializes in this; the local tourist information office (TIO) can be helpful in making a booking with an Irish-speaking family. *Hotel reviews have been shortened. For full information, visit Fodors.com.*

Restaurants

Donegal mountain spring lamb, Glen Bay crab, Donegal Bay oysters and mussels, Lough Swilly wild salmon, Enniscrone lobster, freshly baked scones, crusty homemade brown bread, and Guinness cake are just some of the delicious reasons why you will not go hungry traveling through the Northwest. Sligo Town has established itself as a sort of last stop for food lovers, with a number of tempting shops promoting local produce that are well worth a visit. The Sligo Food and Cultural Festival, held each May, is filled with activities, from live music and dancing to seaweed collecting, art tours, and cooking competitions, all the while promoting local goods and artisanal delicacies.

You're likely to find the finest food at the higher-quality country houses, where chefs elegantly prepare local meat, fish, and produce in a hybrid Irish-French haute cuisine. *Restaurant reviews have been shortened. For full information, visit Fodors.com.*

What It Costs in Euros			
$	$$	$$$	$$$$
RESTAURANTS			
under €19	€19–€24	€25–€32	over €32
HOTELS			
under €120	€120–€170	€171–€210	over €210

Tours

Bus Éireann
Bus Éireann has budget-price, guided, one-day bus tours of the Donegal Highlands and to Glenveagh National Park; they start from Bundoran, Sligo Town, Ballyshannon, and Donegal Town. ☎ 01/836–6111 ⊕ www.buseireann.ie.

When to Go

When it rains, it really pours. Forget about the winter months, when inclement weather and a heavy fog swing in from the Atlantic and settle in until spring, masking much of the beautiful scenery. But in all seasons remember to pack a warm and waterproof coat (especially if you're headed to the coast) and bring a good pair of walking shoes. It's not all doom and gloom: the weather can be glorious in the summer months—just don't bet your house on it.

Festivals and Events

Sligo Live Music and Arts Festival
FESTIVALS | If you're visiting in the fall, don't miss the Sligo Live Music and Arts

Festival, held at various venues around town. Established in 2005, the festival runs over the bank-holiday weekend at the end of October and has links with North America, particularly with WGBH in Boston. It's elbow-room only, as hotels, pubs, and cafés are crammed with scores of live sessions while fiddlers, dancers, jugglers, and puppeteers fill the streets. For dates and details of gigs, visit the website, where you can buy tickets. ⊠ *Sligo* ⊕ *www.sligolive.ie.*

Yeats Festivals

CULTURAL TOURS | There's no getting away from events linked to the illustrious Yeats family. The Yeats International Summer School, which marked its 60th anniversary in 2019, is a permanent fixture and a prestigious academic talking shop. It runs for 12 days from the end of July. The Yeats Winter School is held over a weekend in January and includes lectures and tours (details at ⊕ *www.yeatssociety. com*). W.B.'s brother, Jack B., the painter, is now in the limelight, with his work fetching high prices in auction houses. Tread Softly, a mix of theater, music, film, art, and readings, takes place at the same time as the summer school and explores the link between the brothers (⊕ *www.treadsoftly.ie*). June 13 has been designated Yeats Day, when costumed actors take to the streets for poetry readings and a host of other events. ⊠ *Sligo* ⊕ *www.yeatssociety.com, www. treadsoftly.ie.*

Planning Your Time

The Northwest is one of Ireland's most compact regions, and beautifully designed so that you can see the best of it with a three- or five-day trip. The best starting place is the gateway town where all the trains deposit you: Sligo, an excellent base thanks to its first-class hotels and facilities.

Try to plan your visit around one of the many festivals held in the Northwest.

Each village tends to have its own *féile* (festival) during the summer months, and it's often worth the money and effort to attend. Music festivals abound, from the traditional Irish Sligo Feis Ceoil in mid-April, to the chamber-music festival in May, Music in Drumcliff, to the country-and-western Bundoran Music Festival in June, to the jazz-and-blues weekend féile in Gortahork, County Donegal, in April. But in this Irish-speaking stronghold, the emphasis is on Irish traditional music. Every summer weekend you are guaranteed a bit of *craic* (fun) with lively sessions in most pubs. Sligo Town, Ard an Rátha (Ardara), Ballyshannon, and Letterkenny are all hot spots. There are village festivals dedicated to hill walking, fishing, poetry, art, and food—as the saying goes, "any excuse for a féile."

IF YOU HAVE 3 DAYS

Start your tour with Sligo's walking trail, a signposted trail of the town with a free tourist-board booklet to help you identify the important buildings and architectural surprises. Whatever else you do, don't forget to call into Hargadons time-burnished bar—unchanged since 1868—for some fresh mussels and a glass of stout. You can drive or take an organized tour in the afternoon to the Lake Isle of Innisfree, south of Sligo Town. Start early on Day 2 for a short trip out to catch the sea breezes at Strandhill, Rosses Point, or Mullaghmore, followed by an onward drive north to Donegal. Stop en route at Drumcliff churchyard to pay your respects at W.B. Yeats's grave. West of Drumcliff, just off the Wild Atlantic Way driving route, take a short detour to the restored Lissadell House and gardens; you will need at least two hours to do justice to this historic estate. Donegal Town, with its Irish tweed stores, is good for a spot of shopping followed by a tour of the 15th-century Donegal Castle. After an hour's drive west over twisting roads and amid glorious mountain scenery via the fishing port of Killybegs, you will come to the "back of the beyonds," aka

Donegal's Gaeltacht

County Donegal was part of the ancient kingdom of Ulster, not conquered by the English until the 17th century. By the time the British withdrew in the 1920s, they had still not eradicated rural Donegal's Celtic inheritance. It thus shouldn't come as a surprise that it contains Ireland's largest Gaeltacht (Irish-speaking) area. Driving in this part of the country, you may either be frustrated or amused when you come to a crossroads whose signposts show only the Irish place-names, often so unlike the English versions as to be completely incomprehensible. To make things more confusing, some shop and hotel owners have opted to go with the English, not Irish, variant for their establishment's name. All is not lost, however, as maps generally give both the Irish and English names.

And locals are usually more than happy to help out with directions (in English)—often with a colorful yarn thrown in.

Glencolumbkille, where you can happily putter around the Folk Village Museum. You can overnight here or drive north to Letterkenny, a modest-size town with decent hotels, cafés, and restaurants. After a morning exploring Letterkenny's streets, you should devote the entire afternoon to Glenveagh: tour the castle and rhododendron-filled gardens, follow one of the short nature trails in search of the golden eagles that are found here, or join a ranger-guided hill walk and take a picnic with you.

Visitor Information

The tourist information office (TIO) in Sligo Town provides a 24-page booklet detailing a signposted walking tour of Sligo, information about bus tours of Yeats Country, and details of boat tours of Lough Gill. It's also the main visitor information center for Northwest Ireland. Open hours are September to mid-March, weekdays 9–5; mid-March to August, weekdays 9–6, Saturday 10–4, and Sunday 11–3. If you're traveling in County Donegal in the north, try the TIO at Letterkenny, about 1½ km (1 mile) south of town. It's open September to May, weekdays 9–5; June to August, Monday–Saturday 9–6 and Sunday noon–3. The office at Bundoran is open all year, weekdays 9:30–5.

Sligo Town

60 km (37 miles) northeast of Ballina, 138 km (86 miles) northeast of Galway, 217 km (135 miles) northwest of Dublin.

Sligo is the best place to begin a tour of Yeats Country. Squeezed on to a patch of land between Sligo Bay and Lough Gill, Sligo Town is clustered on the south shore between two bridges that span the River Garavogue, just east of where the river opens into the bay. Thanks to the pedestrian zone along the south shore of the river (between the two bridges), you can enjoy vistas of the river while right in the center of town.

Sligo was often a battleground in its earlier days. It was attacked by Viking invaders in AD 807; later, it was invaded by a succession of rival Irish and Anglo-Norman conquerors. In 1642 the British soldiers of Sir Frederick Hamilton fell upon Sligo, killing every visible inhabitant, burning the town, and destroying the interior of the beautiful medieval abbey. Between 1845 and 1849, more than a million people throughout Ireland died in the potato famine or fled to escape it.

The Sligo of the 21st century is as lively and crowded as its considerably larger neighbor to the southwest, Galway, with locals, students from the town's college, and tourists bustling past its historic buildings and along its narrow sidewalks and winding streets.

They certainly enjoy their music in Sligo. Organized by the umbrella group Con Brio, event highlights encompass chamber music in Drumcliff in May, the Baroque Festival of Music at the end of September, the weeklong Sligo Live Music Festival at the end of October, and the annual Choral Festival in November. Informal musical offerings include the Rosses Point Wild Atlantic Sea Shanty Festival held in mid-June with its hub at Austies Bar, a place filled with maritime memorabilia and redolent of the sea. If you want some social lubricant, try traditional music in pubs such as Shoot the Crows, Hargadons, or the Harp Tavern.

GETTING HERE AND AROUND

Sligo's two main pay car parks are on Wine Street and in the Quayside Shopping Centre. Prices are between €1 and €1.20 per hour. In other parts of the town, such as Temple Street (by the cathedral), you pay €3 for the day if you park before 11 am. In the morning, school runs and store deliveries can cause congestion, but the town is mostly free of any serious traffic problems. Sligo is two hours north of Galway on the N17 and three hours' driving time to Dublin on the N4.

Trains are in short supply in the Northwest region, but buses are plentiful. From Sligo Town, buses spider out frequently in all directions, serving rural towns and villages in counties Sligo, Leitrim, and much farther afield.

The main service is operated by Bus Éireann, which has 47 departures daily from its McDiarmada Station at Lord Edward Street to many points of the Irish geographical compass. Five daily express services link Sligo with Dublin Airport and Dublin city center's Busáras Station. There are daily services south to Ballina and Westport in County Mayo. Galway City is a 2½-hour journey. Main bus corridors north of Sligo run to Bundoran, Donegal Town, Letterkenny, and Derry. There are also four daily services between Sligo and Belfast, a trip that takes about three hours, although you will have to change buses in Enniskillen.

Iarnród Éireann, the Irish Rail company, operates efficient intercity train connections from Sligo to Dublin. However, other towns in County Donegal are not served by trains, nor are other nearby cities in Ireland: even if you're traveling to Galway or Belfast, you must transfer in Dublin first. Eight services run on weekdays to and from Dublin's Connolly Station, taking three hours and five minutes to reach Sligo, with reduced service on weekends. ■ TIP→ **Standard-class round-trip fares are considerably cheaper if booked online.** Sligo's McDiarmada Station is a 10-minute walk to the city center (walk downhill and turn left).

CONTACTS Sligo Railway Station. ✉ *Lord Edward St., Sligo* ☎ *071/916–9888* ⊕ *www.irishrail.ie.*

TOURS
SLIGO TOWN TOURS

In the summer a good way to get your bearings is to join one of the guided walking tours of Sligo that leave from the tourist office on O'Connell Street. During June, July, and August these free two-hour tours (Tuesday–Friday 11 am–1 pm) are led by a knowledgeable guide and cover cultural history as well as stopping at many architectural highlights.

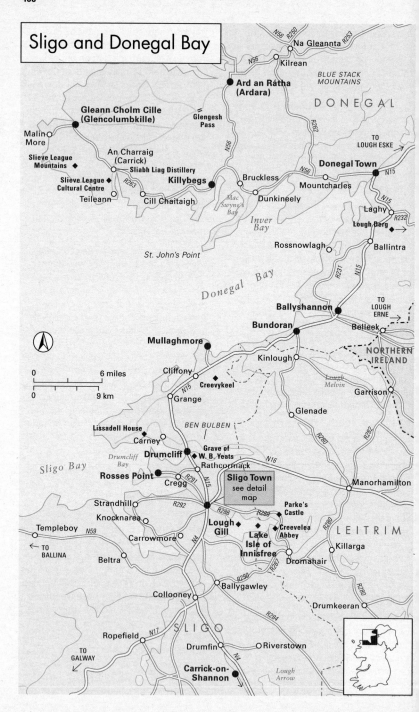

Sligo and Donegal Bay

★ Seatrails Walks and Horse Treks

GUIDED TOURS | Auriel Robinson is a maritime archaeologist with a wealth of knowledge about the coastal heritage and history of Sligo. She leads fascinating tours visiting such sites as Carrowmore megalithic cemetery, the majestic landscape surrounding Carrowkeel tombs, and Knocknarea Mountain, where you will hear stories of the fiery Queen Maeve. Other tours, lasting up to three hours, focus on the Spanish Armada shipwrecks at Streedagh Beach in 1588, a Coney Island walk, and a scenic coastal trek called Heritage on Horseback, which leads to a secluded beach. Customized daylong tours can also be organized. ⊠ Sligo ☎ 087/240–5071 ⊕ www. seatrails.ie ⌖ From €25.

Sligo Food Trail

SELF-GUIDED | A wide range of restaurants, cafés, street markets, and bars make up this culinary trail, which extends through both the town and county. One of the highlights is the Oyster Experience, run through WB's Coffee House in Stephen Street, where you can learn the correct way to shuck and eat oysters. Pick up a detailed booklet on the trail at the tourist office and devise your own route, whether it's walking through town, driving, or cycling in the lush countryside. You will find everything from crepes, seafood, and tapas bursting with flavor to Mammy Johnston's delectable ice-cream parlor at Strandhill. ⊠ Sligo town and county, Sligo ☎ 185/023–0330 ⊕ www.sligofoodtrail.ie.

BIKING IN COUNTY SLIGO

For those who prefer two wheels, you can hire bicycles in Sligo Town—a fun way to explore the streets or venture into the surrounding countryside on a short ride to the coast. A top-class route is the 40-km (25-mile) signposted cycle loop of Lough Gill that passes through some of Sligo's most scenic areas and is mainly flat and on quiet roads. Hire bicycles from Chain Driven Cycles (⊠ 23 High St. ⊕ www.chaindrivencycles.com).

WALKING IN COUNTY SLIGO

Sligo's environs, made up of coast, mountains, forest, and lakes, offer some of the best walking anywhere in the Northwest. A detailed website featuring a series of suggested local walks covers everything from the long-distance Sligo Way to the magical and mysterious limestone caves at Keshcorran (25 minutes south of Sligo Town by car) or the Miners' Way & Historical Trail. It includes information on Sligo's flowers and fauna, and what to look out for when you pull on your walking boots. View a PDF of the color brochure online at ⊕ www. sligowalks.ie.

VISITOR INFORMATION

CONTACTS County Sligo Tourism. ⊠ Old Bank Bldg., O'Connell St., Sligo ☎ 185/023–0330 ⊕ www.sligotourism.ie.

◉ Sights

★ The Model: Home of the Niland Collection

GARDEN | The main attraction at the Model, housed in a school built in 1862, is one of Ireland's largest collections of works by 20th-century artists from home and abroad, as well as a stunning new collection of artwork acquired by the gallery in 2018. Each year, the Model displays six curated exhibitions from its collection, frequently featuring work by famed Irish painter Jack B. Yeats, who once said, "I never did a painting without putting a thought of Sligo in it." At the heart of the collection is the work amassed by the woman whose name the gallery now bears, Nora Niland, who was the Sligo librarian from 1945 until the late 1970s, and who recognized the importance of Jack B.'s work. Only a small selection of this work is on display at any time, but you can view the whole collection on the Model's website. Paintings such as *The Funeral of Harry Boland* and *A Political Meeting (In the West of Ireland)* by John Yeats (father of Jack B. and W.B.), who had a considerable reputation

Sligo Town

KEY

① Exploring Sights

① Restaurants

① Hotels

as a portraitist, also hang here on a rotating basis, as does work by Sean Keating and Paul Henry. Free informal curators' tours are held along with talks by the artist-in-residence. In 2018 a mystery donor, who bought items from a Yeats family collection auction in London, donated eight artworks—six paintings and two sketches—to the gallery. It includes what is regarded as John Yeats's masterpiece, his oil on canvas, *Self-Portrait, New York*, which at £87,500 was the most valuable item in the auction. The donation also included drawings and portraits by the artist of his children, William, Susan, Elizabeth, and Jack. The Model also has a 180-seat cinema with a program run in conjunction with the Irish Film Institute, and a good café. In 2015 the Yeats Secret Garden, an enclosed wildflower area behind the gallery, opened to the public. It represents W.B. Yeats's vision of a

secret hideaway and comes complete with a makeshift mud cabin. ⊠ *The Mall, Sligo* ☎ *071/914–1405* ⊕ *www.themodel. ie* ✉ *Free* ⊗ *Closed Mon.*

Sligo Abbey

RELIGIOUS SITE | A massive stone complex famed for its medieval tomb sculptures, Sligo Abbey is the town's only existing relic of the Middle Ages. Maurice FitzGerald erected the structure for the Dominicans in 1253. After a fire in 1414, it was extensively rebuilt, only to be destroyed again by Cromwell's Puritans under the command of Sir Frederick Hamilton, in 1642. Today the abbey consists of a ruined nave, aisle, transept, and tower. Some fine stonework remains, especially in the 15th-century cloisters. In the cloister east ambulatory, you'll find a love knot, which is said to represent the bond between earthly and spiritual love.

Local custom holds that it is a wishing stone so be sure to touch it and make a wish as you pass. The visitor center is the base for 30-minute guided tours, which are included with admission. ⊠ *Abbey St., Sligo* ☎ *071/914–6406* ⊕ *www.heritageireland.ie* ⊠ *€5* ⊘ *Closed Nov.–Mar.*

Sligo County Museum

MUSEUM | The showpiece of this museum is its Yeats Hall, which houses a collection of W.B. Yeats's writings from 1889 to 1936, various editions of his plays and prose, and the Irish tricolor (flag) that draped his coffin when he was buried at nearby Drumcliff. His letters to James Stephens and Oliver St. John Gogarty offer insight into W.B.'s obsessive love for Sligo, the landscape of his poetic imagination. After Sligo Borough Council was dissolved in 2014, two solid silver maces, which were used to accompany the mayor during public ceremonies, were presented to the museum. Now on display in a glass cabinet, they bear the Irish hallmark for the years 1702–03 and depict the emblems of Ireland (harp), England (rose), Scotland (thistle), and France (fleur-de-lis). ⊠ *Stephen St., Sligo* ☎ *071/911–1850* ⊕ *www.sligolibrary.ie* ⊠ *Free* ⊘ *Closed Sun. and Mon.*

St. John's Church

RELIGIOUS SITE | Designed in 1730 by Richard Castle—the architect who gave us the spectacular Powerscourt and Russborough stately houses in County Wicklow—this Church of Ireland structure has a handsome square tower and fortifications. In the north transept is a copper bronze memorial plaque to Susan Mary Yeats, mother of W.B. and Jack B. A beautiful stained-glass window commemorates William and Elizabeth Pollexfen, the Yeatses' maternal grandparents. Next door is the larger and newer Roman Catholic Cathedral of the Immaculate Conception (with an entrance on Temple Street), consecrated in 1874. Tours of St. John's can be arranged through the Yeats Society Memorial Building. ⊠ *John St., Sligo.*

Yeats Memorial Building

LIBRARY | The Yeats Society made major updates to its imposing memorial building on Hyde Bridge in 2018, reinventing the displays for a fresh new experience. A stylish permanent exhibition, *Yeats and the Western World,* honors the poet, providing an insight into the influence that both the Irish west and North America played in W.B. Yeats's life and work. The poet visited Canada and the United States on four occasions, lunching with President Theodore Roosevelt in Washington and speaking to members of the Press Club, Authors' Club, and the Arts Club. The exhibition also features a mock-up of an Edwardian drawing room, including the desk owned by the Yeatses' sister Elizabeth, known as Lolly.

The society remains an active hub for lectures, poetry readings, discussion, and literary events, and is home to the Yeats International Summer School conducted here every August since 1959. On the first floor, a gallery hosts a rotating exhibition of contemporary art. Research scholars can explore the Yeats Reference Library, which has more than 3,000 titles. On the ground floor, drink in the essence of the great man at the delightful Lily's & Lolly's Café, rededicated in honor of the Yeats sisters, or dine alfresco at tables overlooking the River Garavogue. ⊠ *Hyde Bridge, Sligo* ☎ *071/914–2693* ⊕ *www.yeatssociety.com* ⊠ *€3* ⊘ *Closed Sun.*

🍴 Restaurants

★ Bistro Bianconi

$ | ITALIAN | In the heart of Sligo's busy Italian Quarter, Bistro Bianconi has built on its long-established reputation for top-class pizzas baked in a wood-burning oven. Inventive gourmet pizzas include the Michelangelo (goat cheese, caramelized onions, pepperoni, and a sprinkling of Parmesan), the Vegetariano, and the perennial favorite, Quatro Formaggi. **Known for:** irresistible pizzas; affordable prices; chicken bocconcini (with glazed

ham and cheese). $ *Average main: €17*
✉ *Tobergal La., Sligo* ☎ *071/914–1744*
⊕ *www.bistrobianconi.ie.*

★ Coach Lane Restaurant

$$ | MODERN IRISH | This bustling eatery—deservedly one of Sligo's most popular—divides itself into two culinary halves: a relaxed downstairs bar (from 3 pm daily) with red-check tablecloths, serving fish pie and steaming bowls of beef-and-Guinness stew; and a more formal (and expensive) upstairs dining room (5:30–10 pm), where lamb, duck, and steak share space on the menu with pasta and seafood platters. Reservations are required for both bar food and the dining room. **Known for:** fresh fish; monster tomahawk steaks; relaxed bar. $ *Average main: €23* ✉ *1–2 Lord Edward St., opposite bus and train station and across busy main road, Sligo* ☎ *071/916–2417* ⊕ *www.coachlane.ie.*

Eala Bhán

$$ | MODERN IRISH | Preening swans (the name means "White Swan") are visible from the dining-room window of this modern, comfortable restaurant, serving Irish food starring local produce. Steak and seafood are prominent on the evening dinner menu, as well as vegetarian dishes. **Known for:** fish-based casseroles; luxurious riverside dining; afternoon tea. $ *Average main: €23* ✉ *Rockwood Parade, Sligo* ☎ *071/914–5823* ⊕ *www.ealabhan.ie.*

Osta Café & Wine Bar

$ | IRISH | Osta Café's philosophy is straightforward: serve locally sourced food, preferably organic, simply prepared. Come for light bites, lunch, or Sunday brunch; the "30-km breakfast" is named for the proud fact that all ingredients are from within that distance—with the exception of the fair-trade, organic Mexican and Peruvian arabica coffee (ethically sourced). **Known for:** local produce; crowd-pleasing brunches; Victoria sponge cake. $ *Average main: €10* ✉ *Garavogue Weir, Stephen St., Sligo* ☎ *071/914–4639* ⊕ *www.osta.ie.*

 Hotels

★ Coopershill

$$$$ | HOTEL | Step beyond the elegant, symmetrical stone facade with its central Palladian window, and wander through an appealing mix of antique bureaus, marble busts, mounted deer heads, and 19th-century paintings that fill the large reception rooms of this three-story Georgian farmhouse. **Pros:** peaceful and luxurious; free papers and mineral water; eco-friendly. **Cons:** rooms can be chilly on cold days; quite a trek to the nearest pub or shops; prices are a bit inflated. $ *Rooms from: €224* ✉ *Off N4, 17 km (11 miles) southeast of Sligo, Riverstown* ☎ *071/916–5108* ⊕ *www.coopershill.com* ⊗ *Closed Nov.–Mar.* ↳ *8 rooms* ⊚ *Free breakfast.*

★ The Glasshouse

$$ | HOTEL | Cosmopolitan modernists will love this funky, six-story riverside hotel—it elevates accommodations in Sligo to a brash new level: just take a look at the towering exterior, which has been designed to resemble a ship docked at the harbor. **Pros:** excellent location—Sligo's bustling heart is around the corner; minigym; stylish restaurant. **Cons:** decor may be too vibrant for some; inconsistent service; charge for car parking. $ *Rooms from: €160* ✉ *Swan Point, Sligo* ☎ *071/919–4300* ⊕ *www.theglasshouse. ie* ↳ *116 rooms* ⊚ *Free breakfast.*

Sligo Park Hotel & Leisure Club

$$$ | HOTEL | Ideally located for those touring Yeats Country, this hotel was refurbished in 2018, bringing a refreshed glow to the bar, restaurant, and lobby while bedrooms, many with views of the parkland gardens, countryside, or Sligo Bay, were reimagined in restful, neutral shades. **Pros:** functional rooms with a view; good facilities include a fitness center, swimming pool, and ample car parking; evening entertainment. **Cons:** it's a 30-minute walk into town; the dining focus is on pub grub rather than

Sligo's most famous native son, poet W.B. Yeats, is honored by many memorials and statues found throughout the town.

restaurant meals; pricey for the neighborhood. $ Rooms from: €199 ⊠ Pearse Rd. off N4, Sligo ☎ 071/919–0400 ⊕ www. sligoparkhotel.com 🛏 136 rooms ⟆Ol Free breakfast.

Nightlife

★ Hargadons Bar

BARS/PUBS | Part of the social fabric of Sligo since 1868, Hargadons Bar preserves its unique historic character and maintains high standards in a much-loved institution. Wood paneling, cozy snugs (small booths) for private powwows, marble-top counters, and little glass doors on hinges make this place especially conducive to that intangible Irish element, the craic. Check out the walls, covered with historical black-and-white photos as well as fading invoices from the bar's early days. Hearty food at great prices is served at lunchtime (12:30–3:30 pm) and the evening dinner menu (4–9 pm), featuring oysters, mussels, salmon, venison, steak sandwiches, or chicken wings, lists local suppliers. The bar specializes

in Irish craft beers with Andersons from Sligo and the White Hag from Ballymote among a wide selection. On Friday night musicians often hold center stage with a range of country-rock, pop, folk, and Irish traditional. Walk through the bar and in separate premises at the back you will find the well-stocked Hargadons Wine Shop in Johnston Court. ⊠ 4–5 O'Connell St., Sligo ☎ 071/915–3709 ⊕ www. hargadons.com.

Performing Arts

THEATER

Hawk's Well Theatre

THEATER | With a jam-packed calendar year-round, Hawk's Well Theatre hosts amateur and professional companies from all over Ireland (and occasionally from Britain) in an eclectic mix of shows. Tickets run €14–€30; the box office is open weekdays 10–5:30, Saturday 2–5, and on Sunday from two hours before the performance. ⊠ Temple St., Sligo ☎ 071/916–1518 ⊕ www.hawkswell.com.

Strandhill Detour

A short 8-km (5-mile) detour west of Sligo Town is Strandhill, a bustling little gem of a village, sitting on the Coolera peninsula. The skyline is dominated by the bulk of the majestic Knocknarea mountain, and this spot has become seriously chichi with good reason, including excellent surfing (and surfing schools), the Queen Maeve hiking trail, great pubs, and local seaweed baths. Locals will tell you to be sure to take in the tame jet-black crows along the beachfront who follow visitors around, posing for photo ops. The charming Shells Café, on the shorefront, bears all the hallmarks of a Cape Cod café and has become a bit of a destination-dining sensation. A 10-minute drive from Strandhill Village lies the townland of Carrowmore, which has become famous as one of Ireland's most extensive prehistoric cemeteries.

🛍 Shopping

Sligo Town has Northwest Ireland's most thriving shopping scene, with lots of food-related, crafts, and hand-knits shops. Two useful websites are ⊕ *www. sligotourism.ie* and the excellent Sligo Craft Trail ⊕ *www.madeinsligo.ie*; leaflets can also be picked up from the tourist office.

Carraig Donn

GIFTS/SOUVENIRS | In addition to Irish knitwear, Carraig Donn carries pottery, glassware, linens, and Aran knits for children. ⊠ *41 O'Connell St., Sligo* ☎ *071/914–4158* ⊕ *www.carraigdonn.com.*

The Cat & the Moon

CRAFTS | The Cat & the Moon specializes in eclectic and stylish Irish-made crafts, jewelry, pottery, ironwork, and scarves; it's named after the play by W.B. Yeats. Upstairs is the Hamilton Gallery, featuring work by contemporary Irish artists. ⊠ *4 Castle St., Sligo* ☎ *071/914–3686* ⊕ *www.thecatandthemoon.ie.*

Cosgrove and Son

FOOD/CANDY | The upscale deli Cosgrove and Son, now in the fifth generation, sells everything from Parma ham to carrageen moss boiled in milk (a local cure for upset stomachs). Stock up here for a picnic with excellent muesli, boiled ham, local cheeses, salads, and peanut rayu sauce. ⊠ *32 Market St., Sligo* ☎ *071/914–2809.*

Tír na nÓg

FOOD/CANDY | Irish for "land of the ever-young," Tír na nÓg sells organic foods, including local cheeses and honeys, and other health-oriented items. A sister store across the street sells cards and posters. ⊠ *Grattan St., Sligo* ☎ *071/916–2752.*

Lough Gill

1½ km (1 mile) east of Sligo Town.

Lough Gill means "lake of brightness." In fine weather, the beautiful river-fed lough and its surroundings are serenity itself: sunlight on the meadows, lough-side cottages, the gentle sound of water, salmon leaping, a yacht sailing by.

GETTING HERE AND AROUND

To get to the lake from Sligo Town, take Stephen Street, which turns into N16 (signposted to Manorhamilton and

Enniskillen). Turn right almost at once onto R286. Within minutes you can see gorgeous views of the lake so adored by the young W.B. Yeats.

Sights

Creevelea Abbey

RELIGIOUS SITE | Founded by the Franciscans in 1508, Creevelea was the last community to be established before the suppression of the monasteries by England's King Henry VIII, and the abbey now lies in handsome ruins. Like many other decrepit abbeys, the place still holds religious significance for the locals, who revere it. One curiosity here is the especially large south transept; notice, too, its cloisters, with well-executed carvings on the pillars of St. Francis of Assisi. The abbey is located a 10-minute walk from Dromahair by following a flower-filled path alongside the Bonet River. ⌧ *R288, Dromahair* ⌖ *On outskirts of Dromahair, 16 km (10 miles) southeast of Sligo.*

Parke's Castle

CASTLE/PALACE | This fortified house was built on the eastern shore of Lough Gill in the 17th century by an English Planter (a Protestant colonist settling on Irish lands confiscated from Catholic owners) who needed the strong fortifications to defend himself against a hostile populace. His relations with the people were made worse by the fact that he obtained his building materials mainly by dismantling a historic fortress on the site that had belonged to the clan leaders, the O'Rourkes of Breffni (once the name of the district). Don't miss the blacksmith's forge, which has been rebuilt and the nearby tiny circular sweathouse (an early druid sauna). In 2017 new steel battlements replaced wooden ones along the walkways of the Bawn area of the castle, improving visitor access. The entrance fee includes a short video show on the castle and local history; guided tours are available on the hour and last 45 minutes. In summer, boat tours of the lough leave from here. ■TIP➔ **For a breathtaking view of the nearby Lough Colgagh, drive west from Parke's Castle keeping the lake on your left. You will find a small car park from where you can drink in the spectacular views.** ⌧ *R288, Fivemilebourne* ☎ *071/916–4149* ⊕ *www.heritageireland. ie/en/north-west/parkescastle* ⛅ *€5* ⊙ *Closed Oct.–Mar.*

Hotels

Stanford Village Inn

$ | B&B/INN | With a 200-year-old pedigree and in the same family for six generations, this former stone-front mill, rustic inn is one of the few stops for sustenance near Lough Gill. **Pros:** blissful, pastoral location; log fires, slate floors add to the sense of history; traditional music on weekends. **Cons:** limited choice of food; accommodation could do with an update; basic amenities in rooms. ⑤ *Rooms from: €80* ⌧ *7 km (5 miles) from Parke's Castle, 19 km (12 miles) from Sligo Town, off R288, Dromahair* ☎ *071/916–4140* ⇥ *9 rooms* ⦿ *Free breakfast.*

Lake Isle of Innisfree

15 km (9 miles) south of Sligo Town via Dromahair.

In 1890 W.B. Yeats was walking through the West End of London when, seeing in a shop window a ball dancing on a jet of water, he was suddenly overcome with nostalgia for the lakes of his Sligo home. It was the moment—and the feeling—that shaped itself into his most famous poem, "The Lake Isle of Innisfree":

I will arise and go now, and go to Innisfree,

And a small cabin build there, of clay and wattles made:

Nine bean-rows will I have there, a hive for the honey-bee,

And live alone in the bee-loud glade.

And I shall have some peace there, for peace comes dropping slow.

Although there's nothing visually exceptional about Innisfree (pronounced "*in-nish*-free"), the "Lake Isle" is a must-see if you're a W.B. fan. To reach Innisfree from Dromahair, take R287, the minor road that heads back along the south side of Lough Gill, toward Sligo Town. Turn right at a small crossroads, after 4 or 5 km (2 or 3 miles), where signposts point to Innisfree. A little road leads another couple of miles down to the lakeside, where you can see the island just offshore.

Carrick-on-Shannon

31 km (24 miles) south of Sligo Town.

Carrick-on-Shannon grew up around the river that still plays an important role in the town's confidence. Its original Irish name, Cora Droma Rúisc, means "the stony ford of the ridge in the marsh." Today's prosperous town, with a population of 3,500, takes pride in its past and is full of architectural surprises. In the first decade of the 21st century many old buildings were given life again, in some cases being turned into cultural or arts centers, offices, or restaurants. Bistro bars, stylish hotels, delis, and boutiques sit cheek by jowl with old-world pubs and family-run shops. In 1613 King James I granted the town a Royal Charter by which it became a Royal Borough with a corporation made up of a Provost, Burgesses, and Commonalty. It had the right to send two members to the Irish Parliament and continued to do so up to the Act of Union in 1800 when the Parliament voted itself out of existence.

GETTING HERE AND AROUND

The main N4 Sligo–Dublin road that skirts Carrick-on-Shannon carries heavy traffic throughout the day, but the town avoids serious congestion. There is ample free car parking in the Townspark

area, between the Bush and Landmark hotels. An hourly metered charge applies for parking on the main street where a one-way traffic system operates. Sligo is an hour's drive west while Dublin is just over two hours southeast on the N4.

Seven daily Bus Éireann departures leave Carrick-on-Shannon for Dublin (airport and city center); journey time is 2½–3 hours, and the fare is €19.50 round-trip to the city center. Sligo is an hour's bus journey with seven departures in each direction Monday–Saturday (five on Sunday) and costs €13 one-way. Regular daily services from Carrick also run to Boyle, Longford, Mullingar, and Athlone. There is no bus station in Carrick, so the pickup point is at the waterfront near the Landmark Hotel.

Carrick-on-Shannon is well served by Irish Rail. The town is on the main Dublin–Sligo intercity rail line and eight trains run weekdays with a restricted service on weekends. From Dublin, trains take just over two hours to reach Carrick (€33 one-way, €37 round-trip). From Sligo, the journey takes 44 minutes and costs €16.20 one-way, €19 round-trip. The small station is on the outskirts of town, so if you're laden with luggage, you'll need a cab for the final leg into town. You can also catch a train from Carrick to neighboring towns such as Ballymote, Collooney, Boyle, Longford, and Mullingar. Fares are cheaper if booked online one week in advance at ⊕ *www.irishrail.ie*.

VISITOR INFORMATION

CONTACTS Fáilte Ireland Tourist Information Office. ⊠ *Old Barrel Store, The Quays* ☎ *071/962–0170* ⊕ *www.leitrimtourism. com.*

 Sights

Attic Memorial at Carrick Workhouse
CEMETERY | Follow the stylized footprints of a mother and child from St. George's Heritage Centre to the Attic Memorial at Carrick Workhouse to step back into

tragic Leitrim. This workhouse opened in 1842 to accommodate hundreds who sought refuge here from the Great Famine. With bare floorboards and whitewashed walls it looks pretty much as it did in the 1840s. Wexford artist Alanna O'Kelly's multimedia installation, *No colouring can deepen the darkness of truth,* brings a fresh dimension to this thought-provoking place, which also houses a reading room. In 2019 a new 15-minute DVD on the history of the workhouse was added. Nearby is a Great Famine Commemoration Graveyard. ⊠ *Summerhill* ☎ *071/962–1757* ⊕ *www. carrickheritage.com* 🖾 *€5.*

Costello Memorial Chapel
RELIGIOUS SITE | Ask at the tourist office for a copy of the signposted historical walking-town-trail booklet and accompanying map (€2). A top sight is one of Ireland's tiniest: the Costello Memorial Chapel, built in 1879, is the smallest church in Ireland and a testament to a man's love for his wife. Built by local businessman Edward Costello in memory of Mary Josephine, its tiny dimensions are a mere 16 feet long, 12 feet wide, and 30 feet high. The church is open during daytime hours and admission is free. ⊠ *Bridge St.*

Shannon Blueway
TRAIL | FAMILY | Developed by Waterways Ireland, the Shannon Blueway—the first recreational trails of its kind in Ireland—runs along the Lough Allen Canal and follows the river from Drumshanbo to Leitrim village and on to Carrick-on-Shannon. Cycle along the 23½ km (14½ miles) of leafy trails, kayak on the lake, or walk along the newly opened boardwalk, known locally as the "snake in the lake" for the way it twists along the lakeside for 525 feet. Maps and details of the trails are available at the visitor center (April–October, Monday–Saturday 10–6). Electric bikes are available from **Electric Bike Trails** in Leitrim village (⊕ *www.electricbiketrails. com*). ☎ *086/828–8747, 071/964–1522 for visitor center* ⊕ *www.bluewaysireland.org.*

★ St. George's Heritage & Visitor Centre
MUSEUM | Restored by a local heritage group, St. George's Heritage & Visitor Centre occupies St. George's (Church of Ireland), built in 1827. The bright interior houses the Telford Organ (built in 1846), the magnificent altarpiece entitled *The Adoration of the Shepherds* (painted in 1831 by the Swedish artist Carl Gustave Plagemann), and dazzling displays of ecclesiastical silver. But many eyes will be focused on the array of motorized banners choreographed to rise and fall to classical organ music, as they unfurl the names of more than 270 Leitrim men killed during World War I. A central theme is "Twin Traditions," the mingling of Gaelic and Planter cultures entwined for the past 400 years. Next door, the story of Leitrim is told in a lyrical 10-minute film, *Leitrim: Enduring and Enchanting,* in the visitor center. ⊠ *St. Mary's Close* ☎ *071/962–1757* ⊕ *www.carrickheritage. com* 🖾 *€5* ⊗ *Closed weekends Oct.–Apr.*

🍴 Restaurants

The Oarsman Bar & Restaurant
$$ | IRISH | A Carrick institution, this gastropub is very popular, so advance reservations for dinner are usually needed. Main-course dishes may include rack of lamb, Hereford steak, pork loin, or sustainable fish such as ling. **Known for:** mussels; superb range of craft beers; live music. ⑤ *Average main: €21* ⊠ *Bridge St.* ☎ *071/962–1733* ⊕ *www.theoarsman. com.*

★ St. George's Terrace
$$$ | IRISH | An unlikely find in a small country town, this sophisticated newcomer to the Carrick culinary scene is set in a handsome Victorian redbrick building that was formerly the National Irish Bank. The elegant dining room has abstract artwork on the denim blue, forest green, and gray walls; a huge chandelier; sash windows; linen on the tables; and superb service. **Known for:** locally sourced food; Thornhill duck with rhubarb and parsnip;

Sunday lunch has become an institution. $ *Average main: €27* ✉ *St. George's Terrace, 100 meters from Dock Arts Center* ☎ *071/961–6546* ⊕ *www.stgeorgesterrace.com* ⊘ *Closed Mon. and Tues.*

Hotels

Bush Hotel

$$ | **HOTEL** | With roots stretching back to 1794, this historic and convivial hotel enjoys a central location in the heart of Carrick. **Pros:** superb breakfast; relaxing place to appreciate the layers of Irish history; comfortable rooms. **Cons:** room lights slow to warm up but all in an eco-friendly cause; noisy revelers on main street; not many amenities. $ *Rooms from: €129* ✉ *Main St.* ☎ *071/967–1000* ⊕ *www.bushhotel.com* ⊅ *54 rooms* ❑ *Free breakfast.*

★ The Landmark Hotel

$$ | **HOTEL** | If you want to watch the River Shannon cast its calming spell as you sip the best cocktails in Leitrim, head to this waterfront landmark where guest rooms are sleek, spacious, spotlessly well-appointed, and most have riverside views. **Pros:** top location; riverside views; resident mixologist. **Cons:** service slow at peak times; traffic noise from busy bypass road; frequent bachelor and bachelorette parties. $ *Rooms from: €170* ✉ *The Waterfront* ☎ *071/962–2222* ⊕ *www.thelandmarkhotel.com* ⊅ *60 rooms* ❑ *Free breakfast.*

Performing Arts

Dock Arts Centre

ARTS CENTERS | Carrick's impressive Dock Arts Centre is a former courthouse and now a happening place to take in a concert, play, or arts event. Sympathetically restored as Leitrim's first integrated arts center, it houses a chic theater with seating for more than 100 and the Jury Room café bar. Shows run €12–€35. ✉ *St. George's Terr.* ☎ *071/965–0828* ⊕ *www.thedock.ie.*

Shopping

Leitrim Design House

CRAFTS | In the same building as the Dock Arts Centre you'll find the Leitrim Design House, which promotes modern Irish craftsmanship. It sells bespoke fine art, original prints, jewelry, ceramics, glass, textiles, and natural cosmetics as well as stationery and greetings cards, all helping to conserve the rich cultural identity of Leitrim. ✉ *St. George's Terr.* ☎ *071/965–0550* ⊕ *www.leitrimdesignhouse.ie.*

Market Yard Centre

FOOD/CANDY | Carrick's architectural gem, the Market Yard Centre is in the heart of the town; known in 1839 as the Shambles, it is now home to a popular weekly farmers' market (Thursday 10–2) where you can buy everything from freshly picked vegetables and French breads to succulent cuts of organic meats. ✉ *Main St., under Clock Tower* ☎ *071/965–0816* ⊕ *www.themarketyardcentre.com.*

Trinity Rare Books

BOOKS/STATIONERY | Hidden-away Trinity Rare Books is run by a garrulous Canadian with a depth of knowledge of both the Irish and international book market. The shop is also helping revive the vinyl record market and stocks many 1970s and '80s pop classics. ✉ *Bridge St.* ☎ *071/962–2144.*

Rosses Point

8 km (5 miles) northwest of Sligo Town.

It's obvious why W.B. and Jack B. Yeats often stayed at Rosses Point during their summer vacations: glorious pink-and-gold summer sunsets over a seemingly endless stretch of sandy beach. Coney Island lies just off Rosses Point. Local lore has it that the captain of the ship *Arathusa* christened Brooklyn's Coney Island after this one, but there's probably more legend than truth to this, as it's widely agreed that New York's Coney Island was named after the Dutch word *konijn* (wild rabbits, which abounded there during the 17th century).

GETTING HERE AND AROUND
Rosses Point is an 8-km (5-mile) drive west of Sligo Town on the R291 around the northern arm of Sligo Harbour. There's a free car park with dramatic views overlooking Drumcliff Bay. Bus Éireann operates a service from Sligo bus station to Rosses Point and drops you off at the Catholic church. The bus serves Rosses Point beach only in July and August.

 Activities

GOLF
★ **County Sligo Golf Club**
GOLF | Founded in 1894 on land leased from an uncle of W.B. Yeats, and one of Ireland's grand old venues, the popular County Sligo coastal links course is situated in the heart of Yeats Country at Rosses Point, a seaside village 8 km (5 miles) north of Sligo Town. Ominous Ben Bulben mountain (best viewed from the par-5 3rd hole) dominates the northern views on this infamously windy course, which will test any player's ability to keep the ball low off the tee. The third green was extended in 2015 to add an extra challenge, and improvements in 2017 led to the strategic repositioning of eight bunkers on the championship course. The 17th is the signature hole—a long par-4 with a steeply uphill green, which was flattened a little in 2018 and extended to make it more player-friendly. Another feature of the course is the array of wildlife; it teems with flora and fauna, a wonderful distraction for visitors. Big-hitting names in the golfing world, including Sir Nick Faldo, Padraig Harrington, and Rory McIlroy, are honorary members. On weekends the course is open to members only until 11 am, after which time visitors may play. ✉ *Rosses Point, Sligo* ☎ *071/917–7134* ⊕ *www.countysligogolfclub.ie* ✉ *Apr.–Oct., Sun.–Fri. 18 holes €175, Sat. €195; 9 holes €25* ⚐ *18 holes, 7095 yards, par 71.*

Drumcliff

15 km (9 miles) northeast of Rosses Point, 7 km (4½ miles) north of Sligo Town.

W.B. Yeats lies buried with his wife, Georgie, in an unpretentious grave in the cemetery of Drumcliff's simple Protestant church, where his grandfather was rector for many years. W.B. died on the French Riviera in 1939; it took almost a decade for his body to be brought back to the place that more than any other might be called his soul-land. It is easy to see why the majestic Ben Bulben (1,730 feet), with its sawed-off peak (not unlike Yosemite's Half Dome), made such an impression on the poet: the mountain gazes calmly down upon the small church, as it does on all of the surrounding landscape—and at the same time stands as a sentinel facing the mighty Atlantic.

Drumcliff is where St. Columba, a recluse and missionary who established Christian churches and religious communities in Northwest Ireland, is thought to have founded a monastic settlement around AD 574. The monastery that he founded before sailing off to the Scottish isle of Iona flourished for many centuries, but all that is left of it now is the base of a Round Tower and a carved High Cross (both across N15 from the church) dating from around AD 1000, with scenes from the Old and New Testaments, including Adam and Eve with the serpent and Cain slaying Abel.

GETTING HERE AND AROUND
Follow the main N15 north of Sligo Town, taking the signposts for Donegal, and you will come to Drumcliff. There is ample parking at the church. It's a 15-minute drive from Sligo to Drumcliff. The Sligo–Donegal Town bus stops at Drumcliff and sets down passengers at the post office from where it's a five-minute walk to the

grave of W.B. Yeats. Journey time is 15 minutes and a round-trip costs €7.30.

Sights

Drumcliff Tea House and Craft Shop

STORE/MALL | A good place to buy local crafts, books of W.B. Yeats's poetry, and books about the poet's life, the Drumcliff Tea House and Craft Shop also sells light lunches and snacks, including soup, sandwiches, sausage rolls, and panini, as well as baked goods. ⊠ *Next to Protestant church* ☎ *071/914–4956* ⊕ *www. drumcliffeteahouse.ie.*

★ Lissadell House

HOUSE | Standing beside the Atlantic waters of Drumcliff Bay, on the peninsula that juts out between Donegal and Sligo bays, Lissadell is an austere but classical residence built in 1834 by Sir Robert Gore-Booth. After a prolonged legal dispute, the lavishly restored house (to the tune of €9 million) reopened to visitors and has reestablished itself as the leading attraction in the Northwest and highlight of the Wild Atlantic Way coastal driving route. The house was designed by the London architect Francis Goodwin. Two of its most notable features are a dramatic 33-foot-high gallery, with 24-foot-tall Doric columns, clerestory windows, and skylights. Lissadell was the ancestral home of the Gore-Booth family, whose members Eva and Constance were close friends of W.B. Yeats. The house became a holiday retreat for the poet, and a copy of his poem "In Memory of Eva Gore-Booth and Con Markievicz" is on display. Constance Gore-Booth, who later became Countess Markievicz, fought in the 1916 Easter Rising in Dublin. She was the first woman to be elected to the House of Commons (although she did not take her seat) and later became the first female member of the Dáil (Irish Parliament). A fascinating exhibition features her paintings and letters. The Yeats Gallery contains first editions, letters, paintings,

drawings, and photographs relating to the work of W.B., his brother Jack, father John, and sisters Lily and Lolly. Among the recent acquisitions is a table from Coole Park in County Galway where W.B. dined with Lady Gregory. The walled Victorian kitchen garden, created in 1841, now showcases heritage vegetables and fruit similar to those grown in its heyday. A staggering 180 varieties of potatoes—one was first grown here in the 19th century—are lovingly tended. ⊠ *Lissadell, Ballinfull, 11 km (7 miles) north of Sligo Town, Sligo* ✛ *Take N15 north for 5 km (3 miles), then turn left after Drumcliff and follow road to Carney for 6 km (4 miles). The Lissadell entrance is 3rd road on left after Carney* ☎ *071/916–3150* ⊕ *www.lissadellhouse.com* ⊠ *€14 includes guided tour of house.*

Mullaghmore

37 km (24 miles) north of Sligo Town.

In July and August, the sleepy fishing village of Mullaghmore becomes congested with tourists. Its main attractions: a 3-km-long (2-mile-long) sandy beach, and the turreted, fairy-tale Classie Bawn—the late Lord Louis Mountbatten's home. (He, his grandson, and a local boy were killed when the IRA blew up his boat in the bay in 1979; the castle is still privately owned and not open to the public.) A short drive along the headland is punctuated by unobstructed views beyond the rocky coastline out over Donegal Bay. When the weather is fair, you can see all the way across to St. John's Point and Drumanoo Head in Donegal.

GETTING HERE AND AROUND
Mullaghmore is a 30-minute drive from Sligo along the N15 main road to Donegal. Look for the turnoff signpost at the village of Cliffony; from there it's a five-minute drive along a narrow country road to reach Mullaghmore. There is a large free car park.

 ## Sights

Creevykeel
ARCHAEOLOGICAL SITE | One of Ireland's best megalithic court-tombs, Creevykeel contains a burial area and an enclosed open-air court where rituals were performed around 3000 BC. Bronze artifacts found here are now in the National Museum in Dublin. The site (signposted from N15) lies off the road, just beyond the edge of the village of Cliffony. ⊠ *3 km (2 miles) southeast of Mullaghmore off N15.*

 ## Hotels

Beach Hotel
$ | HOTEL | If there's a chill in the air, you can warm up at the roaring fires in the restaurant and residents' lounge of this large harborside Victorian hotel. **Pros:** sea views; acclaimed seafood restaurant; packages include excursions with local fishermen. **Cons:** the single beds are pretty tight; extra charge of €10 per night for a sea view room; no elevator. ⑤ *Rooms from: €110* ⊠ *The Harbour* ☎ *071/916–6103* ⊕ *www.beachhotelmullaghmore.com* ⊘ *Closed Nov.–mid-Mar.* 🛏 *28 rooms* ⑩ *Free breakfast.*

Bundoran

17 km (11 miles) northeast of Mullaghmore, 35 km (22 miles) northeast of Sligo Town.

Resting on the south coast of County Donegal, Bundoran is one of Ireland's most popular seaside resorts, a favorite haunt of holidaymakers from both sides of the border. Somewhat ambitiously, the tourist board labels Bundoran "Ireland's Capital of Fun." The place has worked hard to sell its big draw, the quality of its surfing waves, and in recent years it has attracted water warriors from Hawaii, South Africa, Brazil, Australia, and Germany—they can't all be wrong about this surf hot spot.

GETTING HERE AND AROUND
The coastal town of Bundoran is on the main N15 Sligo–Donegal route. From April to September you pay at a meter for hourly parking on the main street. It's €3 to park all day at Waterworld or €2 for parking at the main supermarkets. Over in the west end of town, opposite the Allingham Arms Hotel, car parking is free. Driving time south to Sligo is 45 minutes and it's 30 minutes north to Donegal Town.

VISITOR INFORMATION
CONTACTS **Bundoran Tourist Office.** ⊠ *Main St.* ☎ *071/984–1350* ⊕ *www. discoverbundoran.com.*

 ## Sights

To escape Bundoran's souvenir shops and amusement arcades, head north of the center to the handsome beach at Tullan Strand, washed by giant surfing waves. Between the main beach and Tullan, the Atlantic has sculpted cliff-side rock formations that the locals have christened with whimsical names such as the Fairy Bridges, the Wishing Chair, and the Puffing Hole (which blows wind and water from the waves pounding below). The surf here is regarded as not just the best in Ireland, but on a par with the best in the world. Storms produce huge and highly dangerous swells—perfect surfing conditions for extreme wave chasers.

Bundoran Waterworld

AMUSEMENT PARK/WATER PARK | FAMILY |
When the weather closes in, retreat indoors at Bundoran's Waterworld and Seaweed Baths along the seafront. The bathing facilities are open only to adults and have individual and dual seaweed bathing rooms, steam cabinets, and Relaxarium for 15 minutes of total mind and body calm. An individual seaweed bath is €22.50. Kids' attractions include a pirate galleon ship, along with new speed-drop slides and a toddler pool, combining to create one of Ireland's top water parks. Neptune's snack bar, open July and August, sells sandwiches, wraps, salads, and drinks. ⊠ *The Promenade* ☎ *071/984–1172* ⊕ *www.waterworldbundoran.com* 🎟 *€14* ⊗ *Closed early Sept.–early Apr.*

 Hotels

Holyrood Hotel

$$ | HOTEL | With the mountains on one side and the sea on the other, the Holyrood, part of the fabric of Bundoran for more than 60 years, is delightfully hemmed in and conveniently placed along Main Street. **Pros:** central location with sea views; leisure center and spa; free car parking. **Cons:** few frills; can be noisy in summer with families; not much to do in the area unless you're a surfer. ⑤ *Rooms from: €140* ⊠ *Main St.* ☎ *071/984–1232* ⊕ *www.holyroodhotel.com* ⇨ *91 rooms* ⦿*⦿ Free breakfast.*

Ballyshannon

23 km (15 miles) north of Mullaghmore, 42 km (26 miles) northeast of Sligo Town.

The former garrison town of Ballyshannon rises gently from the banks of the River Erne and has good views of Donegal Bay and the surrounding mountains. Come early August, this quiet village springs to life with a grand fest of traditional music, the **Ballyshannon Folk Festival** (☎ 086/252–7400 ⊕ *www.ballyshannonfolkfestival.com*), Ireland's longest-running music gathering. The town is a hodgepodge of shops, arcades, and hotels. Its triangular central area has several bars and places to grab a snack. The town was also the birthplace of the prolific poet William Allingham. Another son of Ballyshannon, the legendary rock guitarist Rory Gallagher, who died in 1995, is also honored with an annual summer musical tribute. More than 10,000 visitors pour into the town to ensure his spirit lives on in the hearts of many fans years after his death. **The Rory Gallagher International Tribute Festival** (⊕ *www.rorygallagherfestival.com*) is held over the June bank holiday week. A newly established website to what is classified as Ireland's oldest town is worth exploring: ⊕ *www.discoverballyshannon.ie.*

GETTING HERE AND AROUND

Ballyshannon is on the main N15 Sligo–Donegal route, about 20 minutes south of Donegal Town. There are several free car parks around the town, but parking on the main street is metered.

 Sights

Belleek Pottery Ltd.

FACTORY | For generations the name Belleek has been synonymous with much of Ireland's delicate ivory porcelain figurines and woven china baskets (sometimes painted with shamrocks). In 2017 Belleek celebrated its 160th anniversary, producing a limited range of products from each decade since it was established in 1857. The main factories are in Northern Ireland (which is why their prices are quoted in pounds sterling, not euros)

Some of Ireland's most delicate woven porcelain baskets are made by Belleek, just across the border from Ballyshannon in Northern Ireland.

just down the road from Ballyshannon. Watch the introductory film, take the 30-minute tour, stop by for refreshment in the tearoom, or just head to the on-site shop. The factory-museum-store is near the border with Northern Ireland. Company products can also be found in the shops of Donegal and Sligo. ⊠ 6 km (4 miles) east of Ballyshannon, 3 Main St. ☎ 028/6865–9300 in Northern Ireland ⊕ www.belleek.ie ⊠ £5 ⏀ Closed weekends in Jan. and Feb.

Lough Derg

RELIGIOUS SITE | From Whitsunday to the Feast of the Assumption (June to mid-August), tens of thousands beat a path to the shores of Lough Derg, ringed by heather-clad slopes. In the center of the lake, Station Island—known as St. Patrick's Purgatory (the saint is said to have fasted here for 40 days and nights)—is one of Ireland's most popular pilgrimage sites and a haven for those seeking spiritual renewal. It's also the most rigorous and austere of such sites in the country. Pilgrims stay on the island for three days without sleeping, and ingest only black tea and dry toast. They pay €75 to walk barefoot around the island, on its flinty stones, and pray at a succession of shrines. Nonpilgrims may not visit the island from June to mid-August. You can also visit the island for a "Quiet Day" trip (10–4) that costs €45 including the boat journey and lunch. In the Basilica of St. Patrick's Purgatory look out for the astonishing work of the Irish stained-glass artist Harry Clarke, whose 14 windows feature the apostles, St. Paul, and the Virgin Mary. To find out how to become a pilgrim, write to the Reverend Prior or visit the website for more details. To reach the shores of Lough Derg, turn off the main N15 Sligo–Donegal road in the village of Laghy on to the minor R232 Pettigo road, which hauls itself over the Black Gap and descends sharply into the border village of Pettigo, about 21 km (13 miles) from N15. From here, take the Lough Derg access road for 8 km (5 miles). During pilgrim season, buses connect Pettigoe with Bally-shannon and Enniskillen from Thursday

Traditional Irish Crafts

While the entire country is blooming with craftsworkers, the Northwest region offers some seventh-level shopping, thanks to hand-knit Aran sweaters, fine Parian china, and handwoven tweeds. Those who want to make browsing—and buying—easy will find the famous multidealer town cooperatives (such as Midleton's Courtyard Crafts or Doolin's Celtic Waves) tempting. But, in general, the more interesting craftspeople are found outside the main cities, and intrepid consumers should head for smaller towns where overheads are lower (and the scenery is better). Don't buy the first blackthorn walking stick you see. Take a good look around and visit any number of crafts shops—you'll probably end up with a bogwood paperweight and basketweave china tureen as well!

Belleek China

China has been made in Belleek, a village just on the border with County Fermanagh, Northern Ireland, since 1857. This local product is a lustrous fine-bone china with a delicate green or yellow-on-white design and often incorporates weave-effect pottery. Americans love it. Old Belleek is an expensive collector's item, but modern Belleek is more reasonably priced and very likely to appreciate in value over the years (according to some experts).

Claddagh Rings

Born in the Claddagh area of Galway during the 17th century, the claddagh ring incorporates three symbols: a heart (for love), a pair of hands (for friendship), and a crown (for loyalty). Worn on the right hand, with crown and heart facing out, it symbolizes the wearer is still "free"; worn on the left, with symbols tucked under, indicates marriage.

Irish Lace

Traditional Irish crochet and lace making use a fine cotton and date back to the 1840s when they originated in the cottage homes and lace schools of Carrickmacross.

Spongeware Pottery

One of Ireland's most beautiful collectibles, Irish spongeware first appeared in 18th-century potteries. With the use of a cut sponge, patterns and images—often "rural" in flavor, like plants and sheep—are applied to the lovely cream-colored surface.

Waterford Crystal

Founded in 1783, Waterford crystal is noted for its sparkle, clarity, and heft. Thicker glass means that each piece can be wedge-cut on a diamond wheel to dramatic effect (as you can see during the famous factory tour held at the Waterford factory in Southeast Ireland). Waterford artisans apprentice for eight years.

to Monday. There are no services on Tuesday or Wednesday. It's a 30-minute journey from both towns and the round-trip taxi fare is €40. There is also a direct Bus Éireann service in the Pilgrim Season from Dublin to Lough Derg from Thursday to Monday. Journey time is just over four hours. ✉ *Ardara* ☎ *071/986–1518* ⊕ *www.loughderg.org.*

▼ Nightlife

Dicey Reilly's

BREWPUBS/BEER GARDENS | "Dicey's," as the locals call it, has been selling beer in a variety of forms since 1856. Also noted for its selection of quality wines from around the world, the company has branched into handcrafted beers and opened a microbrewery beside the bar. It's no surprise that Donegal Blonde, with the merest hints of biscuit and malt, and a fine balance of hop flavors, is one of its most popular beers. Another favorite is the Atlantic Amber ale with fruity hops. If these aren't to your liking, there are a staggering 450 world beers from which to choose. Glass cabinets hold a veritable social and cultural history of Ballyshannon, with old bus timetables and drama and music festival programs from the 1960s, while tins of Old Holborn Blended Virginia, Campbell's Tea, and Grate Polish sit side by side on shelves. Guided tours of the brewery lasting 40 minutes are held by appointment. ✉ *Market St.* ☎ *071/985–1371* ⊕ *www.donegalbrewingcompany.com.*

Seán Óg's

BARS/PUBS | One of the biggest and most popular pubs, Seán Óg's, has a DJ playing hits on Saturday evening. ✉ *Market St.* ☎ *071/985–8964.*

Donegal Town

21 km (13 miles) north of Ballyshannon, 66 km (41 miles) northeast of Sligo Town.

With a population of about 3,000, Donegal is Northwest Ireland's largest small village—marking the entry into the back-of-the-beyond of the wilds of County Donegal. The town is centered on the triangular Diamond, where three roads converge (N56 to the west, N15 to the south and the northeast) and the mouth of the River Eske pours gently into Donegal Bay. You should have your bearings in five minutes, and seeing the historical sights takes less than an hour; if you stick around any longer, it'll probably be to do some shopping—arguably Donegal Town's top attraction.

The town of Donegal was previously known in Irish as Dún na nGall, or "fort of the foreigners." The foreigners were Vikings, who set up camp here in the 9th century to facilitate their pillaging and looting. They were driven out by the powerful O'Donnell clan (originally Cinel Conail), who made it the capital of Tyrconail, their extensive Ulster territories. Donegal was rebuilt in the early 17th century, during the plantation period, when Protestant colonists were planted on Irish property confiscated from its Catholic owners.

The Diamond, like that of many other Irish villages, dates from this period. Once a marketplace, it has a 20-foot-tall obelisk monument (1937), which honors the town monks who, before being driven out by the English in the 17th century, took the time to copy down a series of old Irish legends in what they called *The Annals of the Four Masters.*

GETTING HERE AND AROUND

Donegal is a 60-minute drive from Sligo north along the N15. The main pay car park is at the quay beside the tourist information office on the approach road from the south. Catch the wrong day in the height of summer and Donegal Town is a bottleneck. Fortunately, that doesn't occur very often—the reason may be a local wedding, a festival, a funeral, or a Gaelic football match. The main delays focus on the one-way system operating around the Diamond. Try to avoid this area around 5 pm.

Public transport throughout Donegal is limited to buses. Bus Éireann operates direct daily services from Donegal Town to Dublin Airport and the city center, which also stop in the nearby towns of Ballyshannon and Belleek. It runs regular services between the bigger towns linking Donegal Town with Bundoran, Letterkenny, and west to Killybegs, Glencolumbkille, Glenties, and Dungloe. There is no bus station, but buses stop outside the Abbey Hotel in the Diamond. A raft of smaller independently run buses crisscrosses Donegal's roads—including McGeehan Coaches, Patrick Gallagher Coaches, Feda O'Donnell Coaches, John McGinley Coach Travel, and Donegal Coaches—and these companies pick up and drop off in Quay Street.

VISITOR INFORMATION

CONTACTS Discover Ireland Centre, Donegal Town. ☒ *The Quay* ☎ *074/972–1148* ⊕ *www.discoverireland.ie.*

 Sights

Donegal Castle

CASTLE/PALACE | Donegal Castle was built by clan leader Hugh O'Donnell in the 1470s. More than a century later, this structure was the home of his descendant Hugh Roe O'Donnell, who faced the might of the invading English and was the last clan chief of Tyrconail. In 1602 he died on a trip to Spain while trying to rally reinforcements from his allies. Its new English owner, Sir Basil Brooke, modified the little castle in 1610, fitting Jacobean towers and turrets to the main fort and adding a Jacobean mansion (which is now a ruin). Inside, you can peer into the garderobe (the restroom) and the storeroom, and survey a great banquet hall with an exceptional vaulted wood-beam roof. Also of note is the gargantuan sandstone fireplace nicely wrought with minute details. Mind your head on the low doorways and be careful on the narrow trip stairwell. The small, enclosed grounds are pleasant. ☒ *Tirchonaill St., near north corner of Diamond* ☎ *074/972–2405* ⊕ *www.heritageireland. ie* ☒ *€5* ⊘ *Closed Tues. and Wed. in Oct.–Mar.*

A Taste of Donegal

If you happen to be in town over the last weekend in August, you will inevitably come across a huge food festival called a Taste of Donegal. Celebrity chefs flaunt their skills in cooking demonstrations and host master classes in gin, beer, and cocktail making, while more than 120 exhibitors showcase their products and tantalize your taste buds. Alongside it all, music and street entertainment is guaranteed, and the weekend culminates in a thrilling fireworks display over Donegal Bay. ⊕ *www.atasteofdonegal.com*

Franciscan Abbey

RELIGIOUS SITE | The ruins of the Franciscan Abbey, founded in 1474 by Hugh O'Donnell, are a five-minute walk south of town at a spectacular site perched at the end of the quay above the Eske River, where it begins to open up into Donegal Bay. The complex was burned to the ground in 1593, razed by the English in 1601, and ransacked again in 1607; the ruins include the choir, south transept, and two sides of the cloisters, between which lie hundreds of graves dating to the 18th century. The abbey was probably where *The Annals of the Four Masters,* which chronicles the whole of Celtic history and mythology of Ireland from earliest times up to the year 1618, was written from 1632 to 1636. The Four Masters were monks who believed (correctly, as it turned out) that Celtic culture was doomed by the English conquest, and they wanted to preserve as much of it as they could. At the National Library in Dublin, you can see copies of the monks' work; the original is kept under lock and key. ☒ *Off N15, at end of quay* ☒ *Free.*

Restaurants

Blueberry Tea Room and Restaurant

$ | CAFÉ | Proprietors Brian and Ruperta Gallagher serve breakfast, lunch, afternoon tea, and a light early evening meal—always using homegrown herbs in this congenial but unassuming tearoom. Daily specials—Irish lamb stew, pasta dishes, and turkey or chicken—are served from 9 to 7. **Known for:** pasta; sandwiches; chocolate steam pudding. $ *Average main: €10* ⌧ *Castle St.* ☎ *074/972–2933* ⊙ *Closed Sun.*

Hotels

★ The Central Hotel

$$$ | HOTEL | With its bright white shutters and boldly red facade, this family-run pretty-as-an-Irish-picture inn sits smack on Donegal's central square, the Diamond. **Pros:** convenient location; views of Donegal Bay and the River Eske; suites with spacious lounge areas. **Cons:** no frills; relentless surge of taxis and motorbikes circling the Diamond; street-facing rooms can be noisy. $ *Rooms from: €174* ⌧ *The Diamond* ☎ *074/972–1027* ⊕ *www.centralhoteldonegal.com* ➥ *117 rooms* ⋈ *Free breakfast.*

★ Harvey's Point Country Hotel

$$$$ | HOTEL | Set in a remote and breathtaking location in landscaped gardens on the shores of Lough Eske at the foot of the Blue Stack Mountains, Harvey's Point has, since 1989, been a spirit-lifting escape. **Pros:** timeless grandeur; peaceful surroundings; Sunday lunch buffet. **Cons:** older rooms lack the opulence of new ones; long walk to ATM; books up quickly in summer. $ *Rooms from: €270* ⌧ *6 km (4 miles) northwest of Donegal Town, off N15, Lough Eske* ☎ *074/972–2208* ⊕ *www.harveyspoint.com* ➥ *64 rooms* ⋈ *Free breakfast.*

★ Lough Eske Castle

$$$$ | HOTEL | Most guests gasp as they come down the sweeping drive through ancient woodland and arrive at this magnificent Tudor-style baronial castle—complete with Sleeping Beauty tower and crenellations and a suitably regal backdrop of Lough Eske and the Blue Stack Mountains. **Pros:** stunning location; gracefully furnished bedrooms; despite size, still feels intimate. **Cons:** lines form at busy breakfast times; limited choice on the dinner menu; pricey afternoon tea. $ *Rooms from: €325* ⌧ *3 km (2 miles) north of Donegal Town, Lough Eske* ☎ *074/972–5100* ⊕ *www.lougheskecastlehotel.com* ➥ *97 rooms* ⋈ *Free breakfast.*

Nightlife

The Abbey Hotel

MUSIC CLUBS | Visit for music every night in July and August and live bands every Saturday night throughout the year. ⌧ *The Diamond* ☎ *074/972–1014* ⊕ *www.abbeyhoteldonegal.com.*

The House Gastro Pub

PIANO BARS/LOUNGES | On Friday night during the spring and summer months, acoustic guitarists entertain drinkers at the House, a 2018 addition to the town's bar and restaurant scene. Wine, beer, and cocktails are on the drinks menu, and small plates feature dishes such as dynamite shrimp, crab pancakes, and Tso chicken. ⌧ *The Diamond* ☎ *074/972–1049* ⊕ *www.thehousegastropub.ie.*

Activities

BICYCLING

Wild Atlantic Cycles

BICYCLING | Based in Donegal Town, this bike-rental company offers suggested routes around the area for all levels of cycling enthusiasts. Most routes are loops, while some are along scenic coastal roads around Donegal Bay, varying in distance. A half-day bike rental costs €15 and full day €20. ⌧ *Donegal Town* ☎ *074/972–3513* ⊕ *www.wildatlanticcycles.com.*

GOLF

Donegal Golf Club

GOLF | Highly rated by both local and visiting golfers, this course, on the Murvagh peninsula on the shores of Donegal Bay, is approached through a forest. The windswept links are shadowed by the Blue Stack Mountains, with the Atlantic as a dramatic backdrop. The greens are large, but the rough is deep and penal, and there's a constant battle against erosion by the sea. The par-3 5th, fittingly called the "Valley of Tears," begins a run of four of the course's biggest challenges, which could have you discreetly hiding your scorecard by the time you reach the 18th. In 2016 the course was enhanced with extra bunkers added at the 16th while the 17th was extended by more than 150 meters. Keep an eye out for rare flora on the course including pyramidal orchids as wells as scarlet pimpernel and dog violet. ⊠ *Murvagh, Laghy* ☎ *074/973–4054* ⊕ *www.donegalgolfclub.ie* ⌚ *May–Sept. €130; Apr. and Oct. €100; Nov.–Mar. €50* 🏌 *18 holes, 7400 yards, par 73.*

🛍 Shopping

Long the principal marketplace for the region's wool products, Donegal Town has several smaller shops with local hand weaving, knits, and crafts.

Donegal Craft Village

CRAFTS | Explore this small cluster of workshops where you can buy hand-woven goods, jewelry, and glass from young, local craftspeople. You can even watch the items being made Monday to Saturday 9:30–5:30. The Aroma Café in the Craft Village is a top-class spot for homemade cakes and breads, and also serves dishes with a Mexican twist. The Village is closed on Sunday. ⊠ *N15, 1½ km (1 mile) south of town* ☎ *074/972–2225* ⊕ *www.donegalcraftvillage.com.*

Four Masters Bookshop

BOOKS/STATIONERY | For the best selection of local history books on Donegal and Ireland in general, Ordnance Survey maps, and travel guides, as well as music and Celtic jewelry, the Four Masters Bookshop is a great place to browse. ⊠ *The Diamond* ☎ *074/972–1526.*

Magee's

CLOTHING | The main hand-weaving store in town, trading for more than 150 years, Magee's carries renowned private-label tweeds for both men and women (jackets, hats, scarves, suits, and more), as well as pottery, linen, crystal, and Irish-made jams, preserves, and chocolates. An upstairs café, the Weaver's Loft, serves hot food at lunchtime as well as snacks, teas, and coffees. ⊠ *The Diamond* ☎ *074/972–2660* ⊕ *www.magee1866.com.*

Simple Simon's

FOOD/CANDY | The only health-food shop hereabouts, Simple Simon's sells whole food, essential oils, and other whole-earth items, as well as breads and cakes from the kitchen on the premises. A small café serves herbal teas and coffee. ⊠ *The Diamond* ☎ *074/972–3690.*

Killybegs

28 km (17 miles) west of Donegal Town.

Trawlers from Spain, Portugal, and Norway are moored in the harbor at Killybegs, one of Ireland's busiest fishing ports. Though it's one of the most industrialized places along this coast, it's not without some charm thanks to its waterfront location. Killybegs once served as a center for the manufacture of Donegal hand-tufted carpets, examples of which are in the White House and the Vatican.

GETTING HERE AND AROUND

Killybegs is a 45-minute drive west of Donegal Town along the N56. It's a busy fishing and tourist port in the summer months but there are plenty of parking spaces at the harbor front or along the side roads off the main street, which is a one-way system. Regular daily bus connections link Killybegs with Donegal Town or north to Ardara. Services west to Glencolumbkille along the narrow and twisty R263 are much less frequent.

Sights

Killybegs International Carpet Making and Fishing Centre

FACTORY | High-quality hand-knotted and hand-tufted carpets are produced at this factory to order: a square foot costs around €200. Visitors are welcome to commission a piece, but examples of the carpets are not sold off the peg. In the fishing center interpretative panels take you through a detailed history of the fishing industry in Killybegs; local fishermen (when not hauling in the catch) will show you how to mend nets and recount some fishy tales. For €1 you can play with the Ship Simulator and steer your own boat through the tricky waters of the harbor. ⊠ *Kilcar Rd.* ☎ *074/974–1944* ⊕ *www. visitkillybegs.com* ⊠ *€5* ⊗ *Closed weekends, unless cruise ships are in port.*

Sliabh Liag Distillery

GUIDED TOURS | The Sliabh Liag Distillery (pronounced "Slieve league") began producing rich, smoky, and peaty whiskeys in 2014, tapping into a renaissance of interest in a long-forgotten Donegal heritage. Illicit distilling of *poitín* (pronounced "potcheen") in this area goes back hundreds of years; its capital was in nearby Glen Lough. More than 170 years after the last official production in the county, the company now produces the Silkie, a smooth whiskey said to have a gentle butteriness and flavor inspired by the folktales of the Donegal Gaeltacht's legendary shapeshifters, called "selkies." It also produces An Dúlamán, a maritime gin made from carrageen moss and dulse harvested from the sea. Guided tours, lasting up to 60 minutes, are held daily at noon, 2, and 4, and the price includes two tastings. ⊠ *Line Rd., Carrick*

En Route

As you travel west on N56, which runs slightly inland from a magnificent shoreline of rocky inlets with great sea views, it's worthwhile to turn off the road from time to time to catch a better view of the coast. About 6 km (4 miles) out of Donegal Town, N56 skirts Mountcharles, a bleak hillside village that looks back across the bay.

☎ *074/973–9875* ⊕ *www.sliabhliagdistillery.com* ⊠ *€10.*

Slieve League Cultural Centre

INFO CENTER | Stop off in Tí Linn at the Slieve League Cultural Centre for some Italian Illy coffee, and sample the home-baked cakes that include Tunisian orange cake, coffee cake with Baileys Irish cream liqueur, teacakes, or homemade scones; you can also stock up on information about the cultural history of the region. Paddy Clarke runs the center and is a rich source of information about the area, especially the archaeological heritage. The center is ideally located for exploration of this part of the Wild Atlantic Way driving route through southwest Donegal. You can buy maps here that will help pinpoint walking, driving, and cycling routes of the whole area. ⊠ *Cliffs Rd., Carrick* ✛ *20 km (12½ miles) from Killybegs* ☎ *074/973–9077* ⊕ *www. sliabhliag.com.*

★ Slieve League Mountains

MOUNTAIN—SIGHT | The dramatic Slieve League cliffs and mountains have become the starting point for the Irish leg of the International Applachian Trail, an extension to the original route stretching from Georgia to Maine and then on to Newfoundland. And what more spectacular setting could you have for such a renowned trail linking two pieces of land separated by thousands of kilometers of ocean?

Make no mistake, the landscape hereabouts is awe-inspiring. The narrows and twists of R263 afford terrific views of Donegal Bay before descending into pretty Cill Chartaigh (Kilcar), a traditional center of tweed making. Signposted by its Irish name, the next village, An Charraig (Carrick), clings to the foot of the Slieve League Mountains, whose color-streaked ocean cliffs are, at 2,000 feet, the highest in Ireland. Slieve League (Sliah Liec, or Mountain of the Pillars) is a ragged, razor-back rise bordered by the River Glen. To see the cliffs, follow the little road to the Irish-speaking village of Teileann, 1½ km (1 mile) south from Carrick. Then take the narrow lane (signposted "Bunglass Cliffs") that climbs steeply to the top of the cliffs. The mountain looks deceptively easy from the back (the inaccessible point borders the Atlantic), but once the fog rolls in, the footing can be perilous. If you want to take in this thrilling perspective—presuming you're hardy and careful—walk along the difficult coastal path from Teilann: not for the dizzily squeamish. The cliffs have been made more accessible by widening the road to the top and enhancing it with parking lots, turnouts, fencing, and an information panel as part of the Donegal Interpretative Project, the first of its kind anywhere in Ireland. A viewing point over the sea cliffs ensures visitors can appreciate one of the finest panoramas in Europe in safety. The designation of the Slieve League Cliffs as one of the leading Signature Discovery Points on the Wild Atlantic Way means you may have to share the stunning views.

If you've a mind for a hike, then follow the Appalachian Trail through County Donegal, head eastwards along the Bluestacks Way, cross the Irish border on to the Ulster Way and end up on the Causeway Coast Way, finishing your trek at Ballycastle in the far north of County Antrim. Now that's a walk that'll require a certain amount of advance training—never mind a little stamina and some planning. And, if you feel like an even grander challenge, then Scotland—just a few miles across the sea—has also signed up for the trail. ⊠ *Teilin ⊕ 20 km (12½ miles) from Killybegs.*

🍴 Restaurants

★ Kitty Kelly's

$$ | IRISH | About 10 minutes by car from Killybegs, this much-loved bistro in a restored 200-year-old farmhouse got a thorough face-lift in 2017, with new fireplaces and seating against calming lilac and gray decor. Renowned chef Remy Dupuy, whose pedigree stretches back to training at Claridge's in London, reestablished it as a celebrated Donegal eatery serving lunch and dinner, conjuring up such delights as a prawn and monkfish starter, panfried black sole, and guinea fowl. **Known for:** panfried fish; good-value Sunday lunches; renowned French chef. ⑤ *Average main: €24 ⊠ Largy ⊕ 10-min drive from Killybegs town* ☎ *074/973–1925* ⊙ *Hrs vary Sept.–early Nov. and Feb.–June.*

Mellys Café

$ | IRISH | With more than 60 years in business—it opened in 1956 and you get the impression that very little has changed since then—Mellys is a family-run Killybegs institution with a focus on consistently superb fish. Haddock, plaice, hake, and calamari are all staples served with generous portions of tasty chips (fries). **Known for:** simple, well-done seafood; local banter; enduring warmth. ⑤ *Average main: €11 ⊠ Main St.* ☎ *074/973–1093.*

🛏 Hotels

★ Bay View Hotel

$ | HOTEL | One of Ireland's most historic hotels, Bay View is well placed for seeing Donegal Bay and the nearby Slieve League Cliffs; its shiny guest rooms

To make the Slieve League mountains—Ireland's highest—more accessible, a viewing station allows access to one of Europe's grandest sea vistas.

and lively bar and restaurant are all part of the sceney package. **Pros:** excellent rooms; ideal base for exploring southern Donegal; free car parking. **Cons:** sea-view rooms cost extra; smells from the harbor can be strong; lacks amenities. ⑤ *Rooms from: €99* ⊠ *Main St., Carrick* ☎ *074/973–1950* ⊕ *www.bayviewhotel.ie* ⇨ *40 rooms* ⑩ *Free breakfast.*

Tara Hotel

$$ | HOTEL | This modern, bright, and airy harborside hotel—an ideal base to explore this alluring corner of southern Donegal—has 32 well-equipped guest rooms tastefully decorated in warm colors with dark-red carpets and teakwood; most have expansive harbor vistas, and some come with small balconies. **Pros:** rooms with harbor views; excellent seafood restaurant; convenient location. **Cons:** no pool; noisy during big sporting events; no fancy frills. ⑤ *Rooms from: €145* ⊠ *Harbor front* ☎ *074/974–1700* ⊕ *www.tarahotel.ie* ⇨ *32 rooms* ⑩ *Free breakfast.*

Gleann Cholm Cille (Glencolumbkille)

27 km (17 miles) west of Killybegs on R263, 54 km (27 miles) west of Donegal Town.

"The back of beyond" at the far end of a stretch of barren moorland, the tiny hamlet of Gleann Cholm Cille clings dramatically to the rockbound harbor of Glen Bay. Known alternatively as Glencolumbkille (pronounced "glen-colm- *kill*"), it remains the heart of County Donegal's shrinking Gaeltacht region and retains a strong rural Irish flavor, as do its pubs and brightly painted row houses. The name means St. Columba's Glen; the legend goes that St. Columba, the Christian missionary, lived here during the 6th century with a group of followers before many of them moved on to find greater glory by settling Scotland's Isle of Iona. Some 40 prehistoric cairns, scattered around the village, have become connected locally with the St. Columba myths. The village has a website (⊕ *www.gleanncholmcille. ie*) where hopeful overnighters can track down one of the village B&Bs. There are no hotels in town, but walking lodges, friendly inns that cater to hikers, are worth checking out.

Cliffs surrounding Gleann Cholm Cille rise up to more than 700 feet, including Glen Head; many cliffs are studded with ancient hermit cells. Also of note is a squat martello tower, built by the British in 1804 to protect against an anticipated French invasion that never happened. Another good walk is the 8-km (5-mile) trek to Malinbeg, reached by the coast road running past Doon Point. Look for the ruins of no less than five burial cairns, a ring fort, a second martello tower, and one of the best beaches in Ireland, renowned for its calm waters, dramatic scenery, and lovely golden sand.

GETTING HERE AND AROUND

It's a roller-coaster mountain road to Glencolumbkille, and you need your wits about you on the R263 from Killybegs. The journey time is 30 minutes (at a top speed of 65 kph [40 mph]). Once you get to Glencolumbkille, car parking is not a problem. Ardara, to the northeast along the R230, is a 45-minute drive (but it'll take much longer if you stop to drink in the stunning scenery).

The main Donegal Town–Dungloe Bus Éireann service does not go to Glencolumbkille, but there is twice-daily Bus Éireann service (at 9:30 am and 6:15 pm, Monday–Saturday) that leaves Donegal Town for Glencolumbkille year-round. There is also a Monday–Saturday bus from Glencolumbkille to Donegal Town at 7:20 am. There are four buses each day from Donegal Town to Dungloe; the service goes via Killybegs, Ardara, and Glenties.

For buses to Teelin or Glenveagh National Park it is best to check online or directly

with the bus station in Stranorlar as there are frequent changes to the service.

CONTACTS Stranorlar Bus Station.
☎ *074/913–1008.*

Sights

★ Glencolmcille Folk Village Museum

MUSEUM | Walk through the beachfront Folk Village Museum to explore rural life. This *clachan,* or tiny village, comprises eight cottages, all of which are whitewashed, thatch-roofed, and extremely modest in appearance. Three showcase particular years in Irish culture: 1720, 1820, and 1920; pride of place goes to the 1881 schoolhouse and the re-created *shebeen* (pub). You'll also find an interpretive center, tea shop, regular demonstrations of hand weaving, and crafts shop selling local handmade products. Three small cottages, with bare-earth floors, represent the basic living conditions over three centuries. The signposted circular nature and history trail is a tranquil and reflective place that includes a sweat house (early Irish sauna), replica lime kilns, and mass rocks. Standing in the car park at 15 feet tall is a unique stone map of Ireland, Clocha na hEireann, which is made up of a stone from all 32 counties. It was erected in 2016 to commemorate the 100th anniversary of the Easter Rising in 1916. ⊠ *Near beach, Glencolumbkille* ☎ *074/973–0017* ⊕ *www.glenfolkvillage.com* ⊠ *€6* ⊗ *Closed Nov.–Easter.*

House of St. Columba

RELIGIOUS SITE | Atop the cliff rising north of the village, House of St. Columba is a small oratory said to have been used by the saint himself. Inside, stone constructions are thought to have been his bed and chair. Every year on June 9, starting at midnight, local people make a 3-km (2-mile) barefoot procession called An Turas (The Journey) around 15 medieval crosses and ancient cairns, collectively called the stations of the cross. ⊠ *Glencolumbkille.*

To step back in time, just head to Gleann Cholm Cille—if you're lucky you'll catch the locals rethatching their roofs.

Oideas Gael: Sport & Culture

COLLEGE | If you fancy expanding your mind and horizons, both from a sporting and cultural point of view, then Oideas Gael has an excellent selection of courses for the culturally curious holidaymaker. Since it was formed in 1984, Oideas Gael has run acclaimed Irish-language classes, as well as programs on hill walking, archaeology, landscape, and the environment. Other activities include painting, traditional music, dance, digital photography, and even tapestry hand weaving—one of Donegal's renowned crafts. The courses, which attract thousands of participants from all over the world, run from March to October. Accommodations are based in self-catering hostels or with local families. For a rundown on the schedule and prices, check the website. ⊠ Glencolumbkille ☎ 074/973–0248 ⊕ www.oideas-gael.com.

Silver Strand Beach

BEACHES | An Trá Bhán lives up to its name: it's a beautifully enclosed small silvery-white sandy beach, quiet and hidden from view and visitor traffic. Peaceful solitude is the name of the game here, but if your hair is standing on end it's because you're being watched; there are a few peeping sheep on the surrounding hillsides. ■ TIP→ When you've had your fill of sand and serenity, explore the ruined promontory fort, Dun Allt, directly above the beach. It was built around 300 BC, and archaeologists believe it was used as a defensive fortification when the community was in danger of attack. **Amenities:** parking (no fee). **Best for:** swimming; walking. ⊠ Gleann Cholm Cille, Glencolumbkille.

Hotels

Ionad Siúl Walking Lodge

$ | B&B/INN | Not a hotel per se—there is no bar, pool, or meal plan—Ionad Siúl has clean, comfortable, and spacious rooms, all en suite (bathroom included), with a handy kitchen for those who can whip up their own breakfasts. **Pros:** set in spectacular countryside; place to meet fellow travelers; good value. **Cons:** rooms are basic; limited facilities; little dining choice

Donegal Tweed

When it comes to Donegal tweed, weavers—inspired by the soft greens, red rusts, and dove grays of the famed Donegal landscape—have had centuries of experience. In long-gone days, crofters' wives concocted the dyes to give Donegal tweed its distinctive flecks, and their husbands wove the cloth into tweed. Traditional Donegal tweed was a salt-and-pepper mix, but gradually weavers began adding dyes distilled from yellow gorse, purple blackberries, orange lichen, and green moss. Today most tweed comes from factories. However, there are still about 25 local craftsmen working from their cottages. Chic fashion designers such as Armani, Ralph Lauren, and Burberry all use handwoven Donegal tweed—obviously, more fashionable than ever. As with Aran sweaters, Donegal tweed is today regarded as a badge of iconic chic—a 21st-century symbol of Irish folk art.

nearby. $ *Rooms from: €70* ✉ *Glencolumbkille* ☎ *074/973–0302* ⊕ *www. ionadsiul.ie* ➟ *12 rooms* ⦿| *No meals.*

Ard an Rátha (Ardara)

28 km (17 miles) northeast of Gleann Cholm Cille, 40 km (25 miles) northwest of Donegal Town.

At the head of a lovely ocean inlet, the unpretentious, old-fashioned hamlet of Ard an Rátha (Ardara) is built around the L-shape intersection of its two main streets. (If you come from Glencolumbkille, expect a scenic drive full of hairpin curves and steep hills as you cross over Glengesh Pass.) For centuries, great cloth fairs were held on the first of every month; cottage workers in the surrounding countryside still provide Ard an Rátha (and County Donegal) with high-quality, handwoven cloths and hand knits. The village was thrust into the spotlight on St. Patrick's Day 2012 when it set a record for the most St. Patricks gathered in one place. A total of 229 such saints turned up with their crosiers, including visiting saint clones from Europe.

GETTING HERE AND AROUND

Three main roads from the north, east, and south converge on Ardara, which really only gets busy in the summer months. There is ample, free street parking in the town. It's 30 minutes from Killybegs and 75 minutes from Donegal Town to the south and east. Letterkenny is a 75-minute drive north along the N56 to Glenties, followed by the narrower R250.

TOURS

Dylan Thomas Footsteps Walking Tours
WALKING TOURS | Peter Alexander is a knowledgeable guide who runs walking tours in the footsteps of Welsh poet, Dylan Thomas, who lived in a cottage north of Glencolmcille for two months in the summer of 1935. He takes small groups into the remote and spectacular valley of Glenlough, where the derelict cottage still stands hemmed in on all sides by mountains. Thomas was told by his doctor in London to take a complete rest and keep off alcohol. But with the cheap availability of the locally distilled poitín, he was led astray and became self-absorbed. He did manage to write several poems and a vampire

Northern Donegal

ATLANTIC OCEAN

Fanaid Head

Fanaid Ligthouse ◆

0 ___ 5 miles

0 ___ 7.5 km

Toraigh
(Tory Island)

Horn Head

Ross Gull
Peninsula

Fanaid
Peninsula

Portsalon

Tory
Sound

Na Dunaibh

Sheephaven
Bay

Carraig Airt
(Carrigart)

Mulroy
Bay

Bloody Foreland Head

Dun Fionnachaid
(Dunfanaghy)

N56

Kerrykeel

Meenlaragh

R257

Muckish
Mountain

Creeslough

R245

R246

Gortahork

An Fal
Carrach

Milford

Gaoth Dobhair
(Gweedore Headland)

**Glenveagh
National
Park**

N56

R247

Bun Beag
(Benbeg)

Gweedore

N56

Errigal
Mountain

R251

Lough
Beagh

◆ **Glenveagh Castle
and Gardens**

Ramelton

R259

Arainn Mhor
(Aranmore)

Croithshli

Dun Luiche

**Gartan
Lough**

Church Hill

D O N E G A L

River Swilly

The Rosses
(Na Rosa)

Loughanure

R254

Tropical World ◆

R245

R259

D E R R Y V E A G H
M O U N T A I N S

R251

Letterkenny

An Chlochán Liath
(Dungloe)

N56

An Dubhcharaid
(Doocharry)

R250

N56

N13

Pluck

N14

story during his stay here. The tour guide recounts fascinating details of the landscape and cultural history of the area over three hours. Tours start from Ardara by car or minibus and must be booked in advance. Make sure you bring walking boots and wet-weather clothes. ⊠ *Main St., Ardara* ☎ *086/177–7043* ↻ *Prices vary* ↻ *Tours leave from outside Ulster Bank.*

 Restaurants

Ramblers Restaurant

$$ | IRISH | Huge steaks and fresh, locally sourced fish dominate the dinner menu in the renovated restaurant in the Nesbitt Arms Hotel. Decor still harks back to the days when Ardara was Donegal's foremost weaving and wool center; tweed throws and blankets will keep you warm on a night of wild Atlantic weather.

Known for: great steaks; quality lunch on the go; local whiskeys. ⑤ *Average main: €22* ⊠ *Main St., Ardara* ☎ *074/954–1103* ⊕ *www.nesbittarms.com.*

 Hotels

★ Woodhill House

$$ | B&B/INN | High ceilings, marble fireplaces, and stained glass adorn the interior of this spacious Victorian manor house; bedrooms have superb views of the Donegal mountains, and some guest rooms overlook the garden. **Pros:** quiet location; beautifully maintained house and gardens; in-house bar. **Cons:** complaints about poor TV reception; long, dark walk from town at night; few extra frills. ⑤ *Rooms from: €120* ⊠ *Wood Rd., Ardara* ☎ *074/954–1112* ⊕ *www.woodhill-house.com* ⊗ *Closed Christmas wk* ⇆ *13 rooms* ⑪ *Free breakfast.*

Nightlife

For a small, old-fashioned village, Ard an Rátha has a surprising number of pubs, many of which have traditional music in the evening.

The Corner Bar

PIANO BARS/LOUNGES | You'll likely find this place packed, as it features music almost every night from May to September and on weekends the rest of the year. It's a great place to mix with locals as well. ⊠ *Main St., Ardara* ☎ *074/954–1736.*

Nancy's Pub

BARS/PUBS | With its glowing fire, Nancy's, now in its eighth generation of the same family, makes you wonder if you've wandered into the owner's sitting room. The walls are filled with framed black-and-white photographs of the family and of old Ardara. Seafood, in the form of chowder, oysters, prawns, and mussels, dominates the menu served noon to 9 year-round. Ask for the Louis Armstrong sandwich, which consists of "jazzed-up" smoked salmon with grilled cheese on wheat bread. To accompany your food, try the old-fashioned, naturally fermented farmyard cider—a big hit with visitors. Between March and November there's a mix of pop and contemporary music on Saturday night. ⊠ *Front St., Ardara* ☎ *074/954–1187* ⊕ *www.nancysbarardara.ie.*

Shopping

Many handwoven and locally made knitwear items are on sale in Ard an Rátha. Some stores commission goods directly from knitters, and prices are about as low as anywhere. Handsome, chunky Aran hand-knit sweaters (€80–€130), cardigans (similar prices), and scarves (€25) are all widely available.

Campbells Tweed Shop

CLOTHING | Stores such as Campbells are treasure troves of ready-to-wear tweeds—sports jackets can run up to €120. ⊠ *Front St., Ardara.*

C. Bonner and Son

CLOTHING | Factory knitwear from €30 to €150 is for sale here, as well as pottery, tweeds, jewelry, and gifts. There's also a good selection of hand-knit Aran sweaters and cardigans available. ⊠ *Front St., Ardara* ☎ *074/954–1303.*

E. Doherty (Ardara) Ltd

CLOTHING | Through the work of one of the last weavers in Donegal this store showcases handwoven tweeds, from scarves and caps for €25 to capes for €225, from Ard an Rátha and other parts of the country. ⊠ *Front St., Ardara* ☎ *074/954–1304* ⊕ *www.handwoventweed.com.*

John Molloy

CLOTHING | High-quality handwoven Donegal tweed and hand-knit Aran sweaters are on sale at this factory shop, on the Killybegs Road, on the outskirts of town. After a 10-minute factory tour during which you can watch the hand-weaving and knitting processes, the Weavers coffee shop is an ideal place for a break. ⊠ *Killybegs Rd., Ardara* ☎ *074/954–1133* ⊕ *www.johnmolloy.com.*

Letterkenny

55 km (34 miles) northeast of Ard an Rátha, 51 km (32 miles) northeast of Donegal Town, 35 km (21 miles) west of Derry.

Letterkenny, like Donegal to the south, is at the gateway to the far Northwest; you're likely to come through here if you're driving west out of Northern Ireland. Letterkenny's claim to fame has been that it has the longest main street in the whole country, but it's also a bustling, modest-size Irish town with family-run shops, and a good place to get a sense of the warm local identity.

GETTING HERE AND AROUND

Standing at the intersection of the main roads linking Derry and Donegal Town, Letterkenny is at the southern end of Lough Swilly and serves as a handy refueling stop for many drivers. Parking along the main street is free for the first 30 minutes only; use the pay-and-display ticketing system at €1 per hour when your free time is up. There are three main car parks that also have a metered charge, but you can park free in the grounds of the cathedral.

Derry is just 30 minutes away along the N13 on a wide fast road, while Donegal is 60 minutes south. The area's major tourist attraction, Glenveagh National Park, is a 30-minute drive northwest along the N56 and then R256.

Bus Éireann runs nine daily services to and from Dublin city center (via Dublin Airport) and Letterkenny with a journey time of four hours. This part of Donegal is served well by independent operators, with many routes connecting with Derry and the Inishowen Peninsula. Most buses leave Derry city's bus station in Foyle Street.

VISITOR INFORMATION

CONTACTS Fáilte Ireland Northwest Tourism Office. ✉ *Neil T. Blaney Rd.* ☎ *074/912–1160* ⊕ *www.discoverireland. ie/northwest.*

 Sights

An Grianán Theatre

DANCE | The 380-seat An Grianán Theatre hosts a wide variety of cultural and artistic events. The program includes drama, comedy, music, and dance, while changing exhibitions feature the work of local artists and photographers. An Grianán also hosts, along with several other venues, the Letterkenny trad week held in January, which features traditional groups and singers as well as bluegrass bands from the United States. The Eatery Café serves light meals and drinks

---

Fields of Gold

In June 2018 farmers digging in a wet corner of a field in Tullydonnell near Convoy, 15 km (9 miles) south of Letterkenny, made an astonishing find of historical significance. After removing a stone boulder they saw flashes of light and uncovered four overlapping rings of gold in perfect condition. The rings have been described as wrist or arm bands because of their size. Dating to the Bronze Age, they are among the heaviest prehistoric gold objects ever found in Ireland. Known as the Tullydonnell Hoard, they are now on permanent display at the National Museum in Dublin. For now, these fields are indeed just fields to the naked eye, but they are worth stopping to admire if only to ponder the recent yield and perhaps, other yet-to-be-discovered treasures of Ireland's ancient past.

---

from 9:30 am to 3:30 pm. ✉ *Port Rd.* ☎ *074/912–0777* ⊕ *www.angrianan.com.*

St. Eunan's Cathedral

RELIGIOUS SITE | With its 212-foot-high spire St. Eunan's Cathedral is the most outstanding building in Letterkenny, dominating the town, especially when illuminated at night. This striking, ornate Gothic Revival structure was finally finished in 1901, and is the only cathedral in the county. Designed by William Hague of Dublin and built of white Donegal sandstone, the exterior of the building is said to be in perfect classical-rule proportion. Inside, the intricate decorative ceilings and ceramic floor mosaics are the work of Italian artist Signor Amici of Rome. The main and side altars are carved from the finest Italian marble, while the great nave arch depicts in a series of panels in bas-relief the lives of St. Eunan and St.

Columba in meticulous detail. ⊠ *Cathedral Sq., Convent Rd.* ☎ *074/912–1021* ⊕ *www.steunanscathedral.ie.*

Tropical World

ZOO | FAMILY | Drama from the world of nature, in the form of an amazing butterfly house, is on display at Alcorn's Tropical World and mini zoo, near Letterkenny. You will also find an eclectic collection of lizards, lemurs, geckos, squirrel monkeys, bearded dragons, and even snakes—who said St. Patrick banished them all from Ireland's fair shores? The addition of a Jurassic Land and a Bug World in 2017 brought added dimensions of color. There's a covered play area for children as well as a café and garden center. ⊠ *Loughnagin* ☎ *074/912–1541* ⊕ *www.tropicalworld.ie* ⊠ *€9* ⊙ *Closed Oct.–Mar.*

Restaurants

The Quiet Moment Tea Rooms

$ | IRISH | This delightful, old-fashioned tearoom with granite tables and mahogany paneling serves light bites and more substantial fare for breakfast and lunch. Try the filling QM minigrill for breakfast or, at lunchtime, beef lasagna or quiche. **Known for:** awesome breakfasts; sweet chili deluxe triple sandwich; flavored lattes. ⑤ *Average main: €9* ⊠ *94–96 Upper Main St.* ☎ *074/912–8382* ⊕ *www.quietmoment.ie.*

Hotels

Ardeen Country House

$ | B&B/INN | Overlooking Lough Swilly and the River Lennon and set at the edge of Ramelton, 13 km (8 miles) north of Letterkenny, Ardeen Country House makes an ideal base for exploring the region, especially Glenveagh National Park. **Pros:** homey B&B atmosphere; finely appointed rooms; great breakfast and afternoon tea. **Cons:** one bathroom is private but not en suite; no bar, but try Conway's thatched pub where you're likely to stumble across a music session; long way from town. ⑤ *Rooms from: €90* ⊠ *Ramelton* ☎ *074/915–1243* ⊕ *www.ardeenhouse.com* ⊙ *Closed Oct.–Mar.* ⇨ *8 rooms, 3 self-catering* ⑩ *Free breakfast.*

Clanree Hotel

$ | HOTEL | Formerly a Holiday Inn, this hotel has reinvented itself with flair, and the spacious entrance hall—with framed tweed pieces hung on walls, reflecting the area's connection to the industry—strikes a distinctive and welcoming note. **Pros:** fully equipped health and fitness center; excellent value bar food; superb location for touring countryside. **Cons:** room service can be slow; queues for the breakfast buffet; not many extra frills. ⑤ *Rooms from: €119* ⊠ *Derry Rd.* ☎ *074/912–4369* ⊕ *www.clanreehotel.com* ⇨ *120 rooms* ⑩ *Free breakfast.*

Gartan Lough

21 km (13 miles) northwest of Letterkenny on R251.

Gartan Lough and the surrounding mountainous country are astonishingly beautiful. St. Columba was supposedly born here in AD 521, and the legendary event is marked by a huge cross at the beginning of a footpath into Glenveagh National Park. (Close to Church Hill village, Gartan Lough is technically within the national park and is administered partly by the park authorities.)

Sights

Glebe House and Gallery

HOUSE | On the northwest shore of Gartan Lough just off R251 is Glebe House and Gallery, a sweetly elegant redbrick Regency manor with 25 acres of gardens. For 30 years, Glebe House was the home of the distinguished landscape and portrait artist Derek Hill, who furnished the house in a mix of styles with art from around the world and who died in 2000; in 1981 he gave the house and its contents, including his outstanding art collection, to the nation. Highlights include paintings by Renoir and Bonnard, lithographs by Kokoschka, ceramics and etchings by Picasso, and the paintings *Whippet Racing* and *The Ferry, Early Morning* by Jack B. Yeats, as well as Donegal folk art produced by the Toraigh Islanders and paintings by Louis Le Brocquy. The decoration and furnishings of the house, including original William Morris wallpaper, are also worth a look. Everything Hill collected is still here, including his cobra-skin slippers on the wooden floor under his bed. The house is accessed only by guided tour (45 minutes) with a maximum of 15 people. ⊠ Church Hill ☎ 074/913–7071 ⊕ www. glebegallery.ie ☎ €5 house tour; gallery free ⊗ Closed Nov.–May, and Fri. in June, Sept., and Oct.

Glenveagh National Park

21 km (13 miles) northwest of Letterkenny.

GETTING HERE AND AROUND

Glenveagh National Park is 30 minutes northwest of Letterkenny along the N56 through Kilmacrenan and then left on to the R255, a road that leads on to Gweedore on the western Donegal coastline. There is a free car park at the visitor center.

 Sights

★ Glenveagh National Park

NATIONAL/STATE PARK | Bordered by the Derryveagh Mountains (Derryveagh means "forest of oak and birch"), Glenveagh National Park encompasses 24,000 acres of wilderness—mountain, moorland, lakes, and woods—that has been called the largest and most dramatic tract in the wildest part of Donegal. Within its borders, a thick carpet of russet-color heath and dense woodland rolls down the Derryveagh slopes into the broad open valley of the River Veagh (or Owenbeagh), which opens out into Glenveagh's spine: the long and narrow, dark and clear Lough Beagh.

The lands of Glenveagh (pronounced "glen- *vay*") have long been recognized as a remote and beautiful region. Between 1857 and 1859, John George Adair, a ruthless gentleman farmer, assembled the estate that now makes up the park. In 1861 he evicted the estate's hundreds of poor tenants without compensation and destroyed their cottages. Nine years later Adair began to build **Glenveagh Castle** on the eastern shore of Lough Veagh, but he soon departed for Texas. He died in 1885 without returning to Ireland, but his widow, Cornelia, moved back to make Glenveagh her home. She created four gardens, covering 27 acres; planted luxuriant rhododendrons; and began the job of making this turret-and-battlement-laden 19th-century folly livable. At the end of a dramatic 3-km-long (2-mile-long) entryway, perched over the lake waters, this is a true fairy-tale castle. Like a dollhouse Balmoral, its castellated, rectangular keep, battlemented ramparts, and a Round Tower enchantingly conjure up all the Victorian fantasies of a medieval redoubt.

Beyond the castle, footpaths lead into more remote sections of the park, including the **Derrylahan Nature Trail,** a 1½-km (1-mile) signposted trail where you may suddenly catch sight of a soaring golden eagle or chance upon a shy red deer. More than 400 deer are spread out around the moorland and mountains. Take time to visit the 2½-acre Pleasure Grounds, a sunken garden at the heart of the estate with a sinuous lawn and Japanese maples.

■**TIP**➔ **A shuttle bus runs from the visitor center to the castle, and on weekends a bus service drops you off at the start** of a 90-minute walking route. One of the highlights for hikers is the Lough Inshagh Path, a quiet stony dirt track, which will take 2½ hours to walk one way. ✉ *R251, Church Hill* ☎ *076/100–2551* ⊕ *www. glenveaghnationalpark.ie* ⧉ *Castle tour €7, shuttle bus €3, weekend bus €3.*

Hotels

Fanad Lighthouse

$$$$ | **RENTAL** | One of the brand-new attractions along the Wild Atlantic Way, Fanad Lighthouse offers accommodations in a remote and spectacular area, as well as a unique tour for visitors. **Pros:** outstanding views; unique accommodation; the waters are famed for cetaceans. **Cons:** long way from nearby towns; make your own meals; two-night minimum stay. ⑤ *Rooms from: €280* ✉ *Fanad Head Lighthouse, Fanad Head, Kincasslagh* ⊕ *Fanad Head is at northern tip of Fanad peninsula, about 35 km (22 miles) north of Letterkenny at mouth of Lough Swilly* ☎ *083/809–1199* ⊕ *www.fanadlighthouse.com* ⤳ *3 houses* ⍾ *No meals.*

Rathmullan House

$$$$ | **HOTEL** | There is an otherworldliness to Lough Swilly, which is mirrored in the classic country-house comfort of Rathmullan where log fires roar in antiques-filled surroundings in a place that drips with character. **Pros:** dream location at the water's edge; good on-site restaurants; ideal for exploring the Wild Atlantic Way route to Fanad Head. **Cons:** popular for noisy family gatherings; restaurant very busy at peak times; pricey rooms. ⑤ *Rooms from: €250* ✉ *Coast Rd., Rathmullan* ⊕ *34 km (21 miles) from Glenveagh* ☎ *074/915–8188* ⊕ *www. rathmullanhouse.com* ⊘ *Closed Jan., and weekdays in Dec., Feb., and Mar.* ⤳ *34 rooms* ⍾ *Free breakfast.*

NORTHERN IRELAND

Updated by Paul
Clements

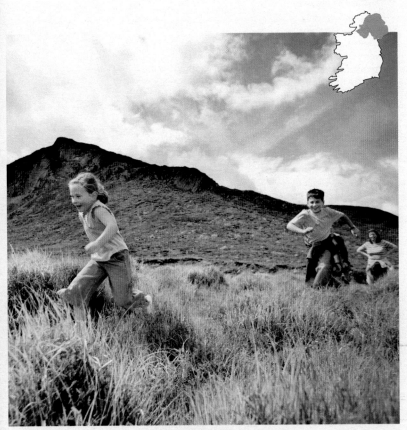

⊙ Sights	🍴 Restaurants	🛏 Hotels	🛍 Shopping	🍸 Nightlife
★★★★★	★★★★★	★★★★☆	★★★☆☆	★★★★☆

WELCOME TO NORTHERN IRELAND

TOP REASONS TO GO

★ **Belfast, Gateway City:**
A bustling city that bristles with Victorian shop fronts, hip restaurants, and the Titanic Belfast Visitor Centre.

★ **The Giant's Causeway:**
This spectacular remnant of Ireland's volcanic period steals you away from the 21st century and transports you to a time when the giant Finn MacCool roamed the land.

★ **Nine Glens of Antrim:**
Fabled haunt of "the wee folk," the glacier-carved valleys have a beauty that has become synonymous with Irishness. Don't miss Glenariff, dubbed "Little Switzerland" by Thackeray.

★ **The Dark Hedges:** An atmospheric road tunnel of 250-year-old beech trees near Ballymoney in North Antrim that is attracting thousands of fans of the TV series Game of Thrones.

★ **Ulster-American Folk Park:** A tale of two countries joined by a common people is told at this museum, which re-creates a 19th-century Tyrone village and boasts the Mellon Centre for Migration Studies.

North of the vibrant Victorian city of Belfast, ageless wonders of the Causeway Coast step from the sea, while south of the inspiring skyline of Derry lie the border counties, where tiny "Ulster" towns dot the scenic landscapes around the Lakes of Fermanagh and Mountains of Mourne.

1 Belfast. Northern Ireland's capital and home to Titanic Belfast.

2 Day Trips From Belfast. An hour's drive from Belfast, you'll find incredible castles and museums.

3 Carrickfergus and Larne. Home to Carrickfergus Castle.

4 Glens of Antrim. Lush and scenic coastline.

5 Ballycastle. Popular seaside town.

6 Giant's Causeway. One of Ireland's top attractions.

7 Bushmills. Home to the world-famous distillery.

8 Dunluce Castle. The north's most evocative ruins.

9 Limavady. The inspiration for "Danny Boy."

10 Bellaghy. Nobel laureate Seamus Heaney put

this rural village on the map.

11 Derry. A vibrant and storied walled city.

12 Omagh. The county town of Tyrone.

13 Belleek. Known the world over for its pretty pottery.

14 Enniskillen. Fermanagh's charming county town.

Carrick-a-Rede rope bridge

Benbane Head 6

Bushmills 5

Dunluce Castle 8 7 Giant's Causeway

Ballycastle

Coleraine

Lough Foyle

A2

9 Limavady

11 Derry

DERRY

A6

A29

4 Glenariff

GLENS OF ANTRIM

A26

ANTRIM

Ballymena

Larne

A36

Island Magee

North Channel

Maghera 10 Bellaghy

A26

A6

Antrim

A8

3 Carrickfergus

Belfast Lough

Ulster-American Folk Park

A505

Cookstown

Lough Neagh

A26

2

1 Belfast

A2

A20

A2

ARDS PENINSULA

A2

12 Omagh

TYRONE

A5

A4

A29

A3

Lisburn

A1

DOWN

Castle Ward

Portaferry

A4

A3

Armagh

A27

Banbridge

A24

19 Downpatrick

20

17

A28

A1

N2

N54

ARMAGH

A25

Mountains of Mourne

Dundrum Bay

A2

CAVAN

IRELAND

N2

Newry

18

0   20 mi

0   20 km

N1

Kilkeel

15 Florence Court. An early Irish Georgian house.

16 Castle Coole. A picture-perfect castle with remarkably preserved interiors.

17 Armagh. Ireland's spiritual capital just one hour from Belfast.

18 The Mountains of Mourne. Gorgeous countryside and great hiking.

19 Downpatrick. Famous for its County Museum and ancient High Cross.

20 Castle Ward. Home to a regal and stately 1760 castle on pretty grounds.

ALL ABOUT IRISH WHISKEYS

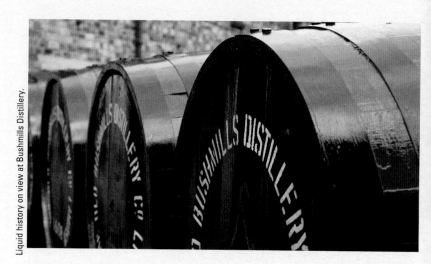

Liquid history on view at Bushmills Distillery.

Located on the Antrim coast, the small town of Bushmills lays claim to the world's oldest distillery. Today, its name is synonymous with the best in whiskey. Taste one drop and you may never drink Jim Beam or Jack Daniels again.

Some 135 years ago, Ireland had 28 whiskey distilleries in what was a great industry. Today, the Irish distilling industry is undergoing a revival with a rapid growth in new distilleries. A young generation of whiskey makers is operating, and there are now more than 40 new or proposed distilleries throughout Ireland. Four of the newest are on the Powerscourt estate in County Wicklow, on the Slane Castle estate in County Meath, the Liberties distillery in Dublin, and Echlinville in County Down—the first new distillery in the North in over 125 years. The Irish boxer Conor McGregor has even launched his own celebrity brand whiskey label, Proper No. Twelve, a triple-distilled premium spirit. For some, Bushmills is the best, literally, and has the titles to prove it. It is also the only distillery in Ireland to make triple-distilled single malt whiskey.

OLD BUSHMILLS

✉ 2 Distillery Rd., Bushmills, Co. Antrim
☎ 028/2073–3218
⊕ www.bushmills. com ✉ £8 ⊙ Tours Apr.–Oct., Mon.–Sat. 9:15–5, Sun. noon–5; Nov.–Mar., weekdays 9:30–3:30, weekends 12:30–3:30.

WHAT TO DRINK

Some prefer the classic melt-in-your-mouth Black Bush (drunk neat) to the more expensive malt. Other delights include the limited-edition 1608, the Original, and four single malts: aged 10 years, 12 years, 16 years, and 21 years.

THE "WATER OF LIFE"

Whiskey is a word that comes from the Irish *uisce beatha,* meaning "water of life." Water is a major factor influencing the flavor of any whiskey. For Bushmills, it flows from the crystal clear St. Columb's Rill, taking its character from the basalt and turf bed of the River Bush. Another key ingredient is malted barley, which is here ground into grist in the mash house and added to boiling water in vats to become wort. Yeast is then added to the mix, and the fermentation turns the sugars to alcohol. The wash goes into a copper pot and is distilled three times, each distillation making the alcohol purer. By comparison, American whiskey is distilled only once. The spirit is diluted, then matured in oak casks, and seasoned by sherry, bourbon, or port. A small portion, about 2% of the distillate, evaporates and is affectionately known as the "angels' share." Remember to first try Bushmills neat and then add water in teaspoonful increments, as a soupçon of water unlocks the flavor while knocking a little fire out of the whiskey—there's a crucial tipping point, so don't dilute too much!

WHAT'S IRISH ABOUT WHISKEY?

First off, it is spelled with an "e," to distinguish it from Scotch whisky.

Drink Bushmills neat.

Learn how malted barley and yeasts are alchemized into whiskey.

"Irish" has a characteristic flavor that distinguishes it from Scotch, bourbon, or rye; try it straight or with water, as it is best without a mixer. And don't go chasing after *poitín* (pronounced "potcheen"), the famed Irish moonshine. Any attempts by a "stranger" to procure it results either in meeting a brick wall or a wild goose chase. Just as well: it produces one of the worst hangovers known to man or woman.

TOURING THE DISTILLERY

Set in an area of natural beauty a short distance from the Giant's Causeway, Bushmills was granted its first license in 1608, although records refer as far back as 1276. Visitors to the distillery are shown around a jumbled collection of redbrick and whitewashed buildings that include 20 warehouses brimming with 350,000 barrels of whiskey. Look out for the long rows of Oloroso sherry casks, where the drink is aged in some instances for more than 25 years (they favor a generous gestation here). Tours run regularly, and it's worth signing up for the premium tasting tour (£37 per person) in which you get to taste seven whiskeys; if you wish to have a tour of the distillery as well this costs £8. Tasting sessions all take place in the 1608 pub where American troops were once billeted during World War II.

Never in its history has Northern Ireland enjoyed such peace, stability, and investment, all of which is making it the envy of Europe. Once a region torn apart by civil strife and sectarian violence, today it has changed beyond recognition. A dizzying rate of regeneration has led to the glossy rebirth of its two major cities, Belfast and Derry, bursting with confidence and contemporary cool. A creative and cultural renaissance has brought an astonishing surge of interest from many parts of the world, and new superluxury hotels, trendy bars, and chic restaurants have created a huge number of opportunities for holidaymakers.

The Six Counties that make up Northern Ireland cover less than 14,245 square km (5,500 square miles)—the country is about half the size of Delaware and less than one-fifth the size of the Republic of Ireland, its neighbor to the south. But within Northern Ireland's boundaries are some of the most unspoiled scenery you could ever hope to find on this earth: the granite Mountains of Mourne; the Giant's Causeway, made of extraordinary volcanic rock; more than 320 km (200 miles) of coastline beaches and hidden coves; and rivers and leaf-sheltered lakes, including Europe's largest freshwater lake, Lough Neagh, that provide fabled fishing grounds. Ancient castles and Palladian-perfect 18th-century houses are as numerous here as almost anywhere else in Europe, and each has its own tale of heroic feats, dastardly deeds, and lovelorn ghosts.

Present-day Northern Ireland, a province of just 1.8 million people that along with Great Britain composes the political entity of the United Kingdom, retains its sense of separation, both in the vernacular of the landscape and, some would say, in the character of the people. For all that, the border between north and south is of little consequence if you're just here to see the country, and though political divisions still exist, peace reigns in Northern Ireland today. There are no border checkpoints, no one is stopped or questioned, no passports are checked, and there isn't even a sign announcing you are passing from the north into the south.

It's also a golfing powerhouse, with some of the world's best courses (and golfers); its young bands are renowned; its writers and poets have been internationally acclaimed; and Belfast is home to the Titanic Belfast, one of Europe's leading visitor attractions. The "peace dividend" has led to massive investment and revitalization in many towns and cities, and the North is truly open for business as never before.

MAJOR REGIONS

Belfast's city center is made up of three roughly contiguous areas that are easy to navigate on foot. From the south end to the north, it's about an hour's leisurely walk. The arrowhead-shape district extending from Howard Street in the north to Shaftesbury Square at the southern tip, and bordered on the west by Great Victoria Street and the east by Bedford Street and Dublin Road, is known as the **Golden Mile** and is a great area from which to begin an exploration of Belfast. The **Central District,** immediately north of the Golden Mile, extends from Donegall Square north to St. Anne's Cathedral. **University Area** in Belfast's southern end around Queen's University, is the center of student life and the hub of the city's nightlife. Within the city boundary, **East Belfast** covers Ballyhackamore on the Newtownards Road and up to the Stormont Parliament while in **West Belfast,** the physical scars of the Troubles are still evident, from the peace line that divides Catholic and Protestant West Belfast to the murals on gable walls. For **daytrips,** the sights along the Ards Peninsula, mid County Down, and the north coast are an hour or less drive from Belfast.

Starting in Belfast and stretching 80 km (50 miles) along Northern Ireland's Atlantic shore, **the Giant's Causeway Coast** holds many of the province's don't-miss attractions. The man-made brilliance of the castle at Dunluce, the endless string of whitewashed fishing villages along the sea, and the world-famous natural wonder that is the Giant's Causeway are just some of the delights to be discovered here. Once your car or mountain bike (ideal for the Causeway's flat terrain) makes it past some fair-size towns, you'll enter the splendid Glens area—one of the more "gentle" (an Irish turn of phrase for supernatural) places in all Ireland. Here, ageless villages, still inhabited by descendants of the ancient Irish and the Hebridean Scots who hailed from across the narrow Sea of Moyle, are set in peaceful, old-growth forests that have become synonymous with Irishness. Nearer the Giant's Causeway more cosmopolitan pleasures are to be found, including Bushmills—the oldest licensed distillery in the world—and the old walled city of Derry. The hot new attractions along the Causeway Coast are the locations used for the *Game of Thrones* TV series, in particular the Dark Hedges, a road tunnel of ancient beech trees.

While blissfully off the beaten track, the **Border Counties** region contains some dazzling sights: the Ulster American Folk Park; the great stately houses of **Castle Coole** and **Florence Court**; the pottery town of **Belleek**; the breathtaking **Mountains of Mourne**; and the blessed St. Patrick sites in **Armagh** and **Downpatrick.** During the worst of the Troubles, the counties of Armagh and Down, which border the republic, were known as "bandit country," but now you can enjoy a worry-free trip through the calm countryside and stop in at some very "Ulster" towns—delightfully distinct from the rest of Ireland.

Planning

Getting Here and Around

Because Northern Ireland is so small, one option is to simply base yourself in the two main cities, Belfast and Derry, and make day trips out. However, one of the real glories is the endless supply of spectacular rural scenery. The good news is that bus travel is both quick and fairly priced, with express buses operating on all the high-traffic routes. The bad news is that rail options are somewhat limited: there are just three main routes out of Belfast. That said, you can easily access much of the country by bus or train, though in some areas, including the wildly popular Causeway Coast, you may end up on smaller bus routes such as the Causeway Coast Express if you don't drive a car.

AIR TRAVEL
AIRPORTS

Belfast International Airport at Aldergrove is the North's principal airport, 30½ km (19 miles) north of town. George Best Belfast City Airport is the secondary airport, 6½ km (4 miles) east of the city. It receives flights from U.K. provincial airports, from London's Gatwick and Heathrow, and from Stansted and Luton (both near London). City of Derry Airport is 8 km (5 miles) from Derry and receives flights from Glasgow, Edinburgh, Liverpool, and London. United Airlines and several Europe-based airlines are the major carriers serving Northern Ireland's airports.

CONTACTS Belfast International Airport at Aldergrove . ☎ 028/9448–4848 ⊕ www. belfastairport.com. **City of Derry Airport .** ☎ 028/7181–0784 ⊕ www.cityofderryairport.com. **George Best Belfast City Airport .** ☎ 028/9093–9093 ⊕ www.belfastcityairport.com.

FLIGHTS

Scheduled services from the United States and Canada are mostly routed through Dublin, Glasgow, London, or Manchester. Frequent services to Belfast's two airports are scheduled throughout the day from London Heathrow, London Gatwick, and Luton (all of which have fast coordinated subway or rail connections to central London) and from 17 other U.K. airports.

CONTACTS Aer Arann Islands. ☎ 091/593–034 ⊕ www.aerarannislands.ie. **Aer Lingus.** ☎ 0333/004–5000 ⊕ www.aerlingus.com. **British Airways.** ☎ 0844/493–0787 ⊕ www.ba.com. **EasyJet.** ☎ 033/0365–5000 ⊕ www.easyjet.com. **Flybe.** ☎ 0371/700–2000 ⊕ www.flybe.com. **Jet2.** ☎ 0800/408–1350 ⊕ www.jet2.com. **Ryanair.** ☎ 0330/100–7838 ⊕ www.ryanair.com. **United.** ☎ 0845/607–6760 ⊕ www.united.com.

AIRPORT TRANSFERS

Ulsterbus, a branch of Translink, operates Airport Express 300 buses (one-way £8, round-trip £11) several times an hour between Belfast International Airport and Belfast city center (6:50 am–6:15 pm), and Airport Express 600 buses between George Best Belfast City Airport and the city center (one-way £2.50; every 20 minutes, weekdays 6 am–10:05 pm). From the City Airport, you can also travel into Belfast by train from Sydenham Halt to Lanyon Place Station or catch a taxi from the airport to your hotel. Value Cabs serves both Belfast airports. The fare from Belfast International to Belfast city center is around £32; from Belfast City Airport to the city center is around £8.

If you arrive at the City of Derry Airport, you may need to call a taxi to get to your destination. The fare for Foyle cabs is about £12 to the city center. A direct bus service, the Airporter, links Derry with both Belfast International and George Best Belfast City airports (one-way £20, round-trip £30).

CONTACTS Airporter. ☎ 028/7126–9996 ⊕ www.airporter.co.uk. **City Cabs.** ☎ 028/7126–4466 ⊕ www.citycabsderry. com. **Foyle Taxis.** ✉ Newmarket St., Derry ☎ 028/7127–9999 ⊕ www.foyletaxis. com. **The Taxi Company.** ☎ 028/7126–2626 ⊕ www.thetaxi-co.com. **Translink Airport Services.** ☎ 028/9066–6630 ⊕ www.translink.co.uk/services/other-translink-services. **Value Cabs.** ☎ 028/9080–9080 ⊕ www.valuecabs. co.uk.

BIKE TRAVEL

Belfast Bikes

BICYCLE TOURS | Scattered around the city are more than 45 docking stations from where you can rent your own bike, a low-cost way to travel for a few hours or half day. The bikes are free for the first 30 minutes, up to two hours is £1.50, and four hours is £3.50. Download the app in advance to register. ✉ City Hall, Donegal Sq. N, Central District ☎ 034/3357–1551 ⊕ www.belfastbikes.co.uk.

BOAT AND FERRY TRAVEL

P&O Ferries has a one-hour sailing from Cairnryan, Scotland, to Larne, and a two-hour ferry, both with train (more convenient) or bus connections to Belfast, 35½ km (22 miles) to the south. Stena Line has eight-hour daytime or overnight car ferries that connect Belfast with the English west-coast port of Liverpool every day. Stena Line also operates a fast catamaran (1½ hours) between Belfast and Stranraer, Scotland.

CONTACTS P&O Ferries. ☎ 0871/664–4777 ⊕ www.poferries.com. **Stena Line.** ✉ Victoria Terminal 2, W. Bank Rd., Belfast ☎ 028/9088–4013 ⊕ www.stenaline. co.uk.

BUS TRAVEL

Northern Ireland's main bus company, Ulsterbus, operates direct Goldline service—superior express buses with modern, comfortable seats—between Dublin and Belfast. Bus Éireann runs direct service to Belfast from Dublin, calling

at Dublin Airport. The ride takes three hours; both company's buses arrive at Belfast's Europa Buscentre, just behind the Europa Hotel. The Aircoach operates a direct service every hour from Belfast to Dublin airport and takes two hours. If you are planning a trip to the Giant's Causeway from Belfast by bus then Translink operates a special daily Goldline coach service (No 221) on this route from April to October for £12.50.

You can take advantage of frequent and inexpensive Ulsterbus links between all Northern Ireland towns. If you want to tour the North by bus and train, contact Translink: an iLink ticket allows unlimited travel on bus or train (£16 per day, or £58 per week; it costs £1 to buy the card). Best buy: the Sunday Rambler Ticket, from 9:30 am for £9.50 for unlimited travel on all scheduled Ulsterbus services.

CONTACTS Bus Éireann. ☎ 01/836–6111 in Dublin ⊕ www.buseireann.ie. **Europa Buscentre.** ✉ Great Victoria St., Golden Mile ☎ 028/9066–6630 ⊕ www.translink. co.uk. **Translink Ulsterbus.** ✉ Glengall St., Belfast ☎ 028/9066–6630 ⊕ www. translink.co.uk/ulsterbus.

CAR TRAVEL

The fast N1/A1 road connects Belfast to Dublin in 160 km (100 miles) with an average driving time of two hours. When in Belfast, it's best to avail yourself of the many parking garages. If you opt for street meter-ticket parking, check the posted regulations because many spots become no-parking during rush hours. Throughout Northern Ireland, there are plenty of parking lots in the towns, and you should use them.

TAXI TRAVEL

Most taxis operate on the meter; ask for a price for longer journeys. You can order in advance. The minimum fare is usually £2.40 plus £1.15 per mile thereafter. Uber is also available in Northern Ireland but taxis are much more abundant.

CONTACTS FonaCAB. ☎ 028/9033–3333 ⊕ www.fonacab.com. **Foyle Taxis.** ✉ 10a Market St., Derry ☎ 028/7126–3905 ⊕ www.foyletaxis.com. **Value Cabs.** ☎ 028/9080–9080 ⊕ www.valuecabs. co.uk.

TRAIN TRAVEL

The Dublin-to-Belfast Enterprise Service, run jointly by Northern Ireland Railways (a company operated by Translink) and Irish Rail–Iarnród Éireann (which only services the Republic of Ireland), operates trains, the fastest of which take about two hours, between Dublin and Belfast's Central Station. A single journey costs £30; a same-day return is £34. You can change trains at Lanyon Place Station for the city-center Great Victoria Street Station, which is adjacent the Europa Buscentre.

Northern Ireland Railways (NIR) runs four rail routes from Belfast's Lanyon Place Station: northwest to Derry via Coleraine; east to Bangor along the shore of Belfast Lough; northeast to Larne (for the P&O European ferry to Scotland); and south to Dublin. Nine daily weekday trains operate between Belfast and Derry, with seven trains on Saturday and five on Sunday. The journey time is about two hours, and a round-trip ticket costs £19. If you travel after 9:30 am, you'll get a third off the standard fare, reducing it to £12.70. Best buy: the £7.50 Sunday Day Tracker gives you unlimited travel on all scheduled train services within Northern Ireland.

There are frequent connections to Lanyon Place Station from the city-center Great Victoria Street Station and from Botanic Station in the university area. If you want to tour the North by train, contact Northern Ireland Railways–Translink: an iLink ticket allows unlimited travel on bus or train (£16 per day, or £58 per week; it costs £1 to buy the card).

CONTACTS Enterprise Service. ✉ Lanyon Place Station, E. Bridge St., Belfast ☎ 028/9066–6630 ⊕ www.translink. co.uk/enterprise. **Iarnród Éireann.**

☎ 00353/836–6222 timetables ⊕ www. irishrail.ie. **Northern Ireland Railways.** ✉ Lanyon Place Station, East Bridge St. ☎ 028/9066–6630 ⊕ www.translink. co.uk/services/ni-railways.

TRAIN STATIONS Botanic Station. ✉ Botanic Ave., Belfast ☎ 028/9089–9400. **Lanyon Place Station.** ✉ E. Bridge St., Belfast ☎ 028/9089–9400 ⊕ www.translink. co.uk.

Hotels

Major hotel chains have invested in Northern Ireland's cities. In Belfast's surrounding area, you can also choose from the humblest terraced town houses or farm cottages to the grandest country houses. Dining rooms of country-house lodgings frequently match the standard of top-quality restaurants. All accommodations in the province are inspected and categorized by the Northern Ireland Tourist Board Information Centre, which publishes hostelry names, addresses, and ratings in the free guidebooks *Hotel and Guest House Guide* and *Bed & Breakfast Guide,* also available online. Hundreds of excellent-value specials—single nights to weekend deals, the most intimate bed-and-breakfasts to Belfast's finest hotels—become available in the low season, from October to March. *Hotel reviews have been shortened. For full information, visit Fodors.com.*

Restaurants

Belfast has experienced an influx of au courant and internationally influenced restaurants, bistros, wine bars, and—as in Dublin—European-style café-bars where you can get good food most of the day and linger over a drink. Local produce and seasonal creativity are the order of the day with top-quality fresh local meat and experimental chefs constantly trying out new ideas. Traditional dishes still dominate some menus and include

Biking Belfast

The center of Belfast is flat, with well-marked cycle lanes, although it may appear that buses and taxis dominate the roads. Two of the most prominent docking stations are in front of City Hall and at the rear of the building in Linenhall Street. One of the most relaxing routes is along the riverside embankment leading to Ormeau Park, just a 20-minute ride from the center. It is a pleasant way to explore the surroundings, especially midmorning or early afternoon when there is less traffic. The tranquil Lagan Valley towpath, full of history and wildlife, is also worth cycling, and can be accessed from Stranmillis. It provides 17 km (11 miles) of continuous off-road cycling or walking on Belfast's doorstep. For more details check ⊕ www.laganvalley.co.uk.

Guinness-and-beef pie; steak, chicken, and pork; champ (creamy, buttery mashed potatoes with scallions); oysters from Strangford Lough; Ardglass herring; mussels from Dundrum; and smoked salmon from Glenarm. By the standards of the United States, or even the rest of the United Kingdom, restaurant prices can be surprisingly moderate. A service charge of 10% may be added to the bill; it's customary to pay this, unless the service was bad. *Restaurant reviews have been shortened. For full information, visit Fodors.com.*

What It Costs in Pounds Sterling			
$	$$	$$$	$$$$
RESTAURANTS			
under £15	£15–£18	£19–£22	over £22
HOTELS			
under £82	£82–£115	£116–£160	over £160

Money

Unlike Ireland, Northern Ireland uses British currency. Euros are accepted in some shops along the border areas and in some shopping centers in Belfast. You may sometimes be given bank notes, drawn on Ulster banks. Be sure not to get stuck with a lot of these when you leave, because they're accepted with reluctance, if at all, in the rest of the United Kingdom and are difficult to change at banks back home.

Tours

BIKE TOURS

Belfast City Bike Tours

BICYCLE TOURS | Join guided bike rides of many areas with Belfast City Bike Tours. Cycle lanes are provided on most main roads and excellent paths link up all sections of the towpath and riverbank with signposted trails. ⊠ *Belfast* ☎ *077/8049–6969* ⊕ *www.belfastcitybiketours.com* 🚲 *From £25.*

Iron Donkey Bicycle Touring

BICYCLE TOURS | Some of the most scenic parts of Northern Ireland are opened up by Iron Donkey Bicycle Touring, which organizes multiday tours. Itineraries include the Mourne Mountains, Glens of Antrim, Causeway Coast, the Sperrin Mountains, and other destinations. ☎ *029/2089–1650* ⊕ *www.irondonkey. com.*

Game of Thrones

Parts of the Northern Irish landscape have become a location backdrop for the blockbuster TV series *Game of Thrones*. Top wow-factor sites that are big hits with Instagrammers include the Dark Hedges, an eerie road tunnel of enormous 18th-century beech trees near Ballymoney (known in the series as Kingsroad), through which Arya Stark made her escape from King's Landing; nearby Slemish Mountain is the setting of Shillanavogy Valley, while the dramatic headland, Fair Head in County Antrim, is where Davos Seaworth was shipwrecked after the battle of King's Landing.

■ TIP→ **Thousands of visitors are now converging on the Kingsroad, so avoid the crowds by going at first light or later in the day. Free parking is available at the Hedges Hotel, a five-minute walk from the trees.** When several of the Dark Hedges beech trees came down in a fierce storm in 2016, the wood from two of them was salvaged and transformed into 10 ornately carved wooden doors, each depicting moments inspired by the show. These "Doors of Thrones" hang in pubs, restaurants, and other venues across Northern Ireland, near filming locations, giving visitors a brand-new *Game of Thrones* trail to follow.

At tourist offices you can pick up a "Journey of Doors" passport, which outlines all 10 locations, then collect stamps from each one; more details are available at ⊕ *www.discovernorthernireland.com/gameofthrones*. There is an environmental order to ensure the preservation of the beech trees. For more information on their story, visit the website of the Causeway Coast & Glens Heritage Trust (⊕ *www.ccght.org/darkhedges*). In County Down, the historic mansion Castle Ward doubles as the castle of Winterfell, home of the Stark family. Another major film location in south Down is Tollymore Forest Park, in the Mourne Mountains, where you can sign up for an immersive guided tour, with Stark cloaks provided at no extra cost. This tour, the Belfast Winterfell Day Tour, costs £40 (⊕ *www.gameofthrones-tours.com*). All told, there are more than 40 sites throughout Northern Ireland with some form of connection to the blockbuster series and, consequently, there are a large number of tour companies vying for your business. One of the best themed tours is a McComb's Coaches day tour, which takes in key geographical locations along the Antrim coast and costs £35 (⊕ *www.mccombscoaches.com*).

BUS TOURS
Allens Tours

BUS TOURS | Allens Tours operate day tours from Belfast to the Giant's Causeway with stops at Carrickfergus and the Dark Hedges in County Antrim, the scene of some of the filming for *Game of Thrones*. Check the website for special deals. ⊠ *Belfast* ☎ *028/9091–5613* ⊕ *www.allensbelfastbustours.com* ✉ *£25 for a 1-day tour.*

Ulsterbus Tours

BUS TOURS | Half- or full-day trips are available during the summer from Belfast to the Glens of Antrim, the Fermanagh lakes, Lough Neagh, the Mountains of Mourne, Strangford Lough in the Ards Peninsula, and northwest Donegal. Prices range from £20 to £45, which may include, in the case of the Fermanagh excursion, lunch and a river cruise. ⊠ *Belfast* ☎ *028/9066–6630* ⊕ *www.ulsterbustours.com* ✉ *From £20.*

When to Go

If the weather is good—and most of the year it isn't—touring Northern Ireland can be a real pleasure. But the place is so green for a reason: lots of rain, which means you should certainly pack your raincoat. Because you're on the coast, even on bright summer days you can feel the chill from the sea, so it's best to wear layers. The weather from May to September is a little friendlier to tourists.

Planning Your Time

Though Northern Ireland may not look that big on paper, tackling a fair share of its many attractions in less than a week isn't possible without exhausting yourself in the process. If your time is limited, choose the eastern half (Belfast, the Antrim Coast, and the Mountains of Mourne) or the western half (Derry and the border counties). The cities are small enough to tour in a day or two. But remember that the rural wonders—the Antrim Coast, the Fermanagh lakes, the Mountains of Mourne—cast their spell easily. You may head out to enjoy them for a day trip and find yourself wishing that you'd factored in more time to explore the endless string of postcard-worthy villages, misty glens, and rugged mountains. Distances are not great, but neither are the roads—you'll spend most of your time traveling smaller roads, not major express highways. If you have three days, spend an extra night and day in Derry. A half-day side trip should also be made to the top-class Ulster American Folk Park at Omagh, where the contribution of Northern Irish people to American history is traced.

FESTIVALS AND EVENTS

When planning your visit, remember that Northern Ireland is a great place for festivals: almost every town has its own theme festival of some sort. The Belfast International Arts Festival,

held in October, is one of the biggest, with a packed program of arts, music, and literature. Belfast's Cathedral Arts Quarter Festival, held late April to early May, uses established, new, and unusual venues throughout the oldest part of the city center for two weeks of music, theater, and visual arts. In early April the Titanic Festival commemorates the anniversary of the sinking in 1912 of RMS *Titanic*, built in Belfast. Early in May, tens of thousands of revelers flock to Derry for an annual five-day extravaganza, the City of Derry Jazz and Big Band Festival (⊕ *www.cityofderryjazzfestival.com*), held at various venues. Féile an Phobail, the West Belfast Festival (⊕ *www.feile-belfast.com*), held in early August, is a 10-day schedule of events with a political and international theme.

Arts Council of Northern Ireland
ARTS FESTIVALS | The country's main arts agency supports a range of cultural events, including many Belfast festivals, and has information about them. ✉ *The Sidings, Lisburn* ☎ *028/9262–3555* ⊕ *www.artscouncil-ni.org*.

Belfast International Arts Festival
FESTIVALS | This long-established Belfast festival lasts for three weeks in October and is the city's major arts festival. ☎ *028/9033–2261* ⊕ *www.belfastinternationalartsfestival.com*.

Cathedral Quarter Arts Festival
FESTIVALS | This early-May festival, always buzzing with energy, attracts local, national, and international visual and performing artists. Its base of operations is the Black Box on Hill Street, at the heart of the Cathedral Quarter, where a café serves snacks during the day and light lunches. The same organization runs the very successful Out to Lunch festival in January. ☎ *028/9023–2403* ⊕ *www.cqaf.com*.

Festival of Fools
FESTIVALS | This vibrant three-day street-theater event coinciding with the

Cathedral Quarter Arts Festival spills into public spaces across Belfast the first weekend in May. The popular event has been running since 2003 and features world-class entertainers in the form of acrobats and visiting artistes. ⊠ *Cathedral Quarter* ☎ *028/9023–6007* ⊕ *www.foolsfestival.com.*

The Ould Lammas Fair

FESTIVAL | Every year since 1606, on the last Monday and Tuesday in August, Ballycastle has hosted the Ould Lammas Fair, a modern version of the ancient Celtic harvest festival of Lughnasa (Irish for "August"). Ireland's oldest fair, this is a very popular two-day event with entertainers, several hundred shopping stalls, and even a pony show. Treat yourself to the fair's traditional snacks, dulse (sun-dried seaweed; also known as dillisk) and yellowman (rock-hard yellow toffee). ⊠ *Ballycastle* ⊕ *www.discovernorthernireland.com.*

Visitor Information

Tourism Northern Ireland provides information about attractions, accommodations, and activities online and at its central and regional tourist information offices (TIOs). The offices in Belfast and Derry are open year-round; other useful TIOs are in Enniskillen, Armagh, Newcastle, Carrickfergus, and at the Giant's Causeway on the North Antrim coast.

CONTACTS Tourism Northern Ireland. ⊠ *Linum Chambers , Bedford Sq., Bedford St., 10th fl.–12th fl., Belfast* ☎ *028/9023–1221* ⊕ *www.discovernorthernireland.com.*

Belfast

Before English and Scottish settlers arrived in the 1600s, Belfast was a tiny village called Béal Feirste ("sandbank ford") belonging to Ulster's ancient O'Neill clan. With the advent of the Plantation period (when settlers arrived in the 1600s), Sir Arthur Chichester, from Devon in southwestern England, received the city from the English Crown, and his son was made Earl of Donegall. Huguenots fleeing persecution from France settled near here, bringing their valuable linen-work skills. In the 18th century, Belfast underwent a phenomenal expansion—its population doubled every 10 years, despite an ever-present sectarian divide. Although the Anglican gentry despised the Presbyterian artisans—who, in turn, distrusted the native Catholics—Belfast's growth continued at a dizzying speed. The city was a great Victorian success story, an industrial boomtown whose prosperity was built on trade, especially linen and shipbuilding. Famously (or infamously), the *Titanic* was built here, giving Belfast, for a time, the nickname "Titanic Town." Having laid the foundation stone of the city's university in 1845, Queen Victoria returned to Belfast in 1849—she is recalled in the names of buildings, streets, bars, monuments, and other places around the city—and in the same year, the university opened under the name Queen's College. Nearly 40 years later, in 1888, Victoria granted Belfast its city charter. Today its population is nearly 300,000, tourist numbers have increased, and this dramatically transformed city is enjoying an unparalleled renaissance.

The city has restored most of its major public buildings such as museums, churches, theaters, City Hall, Ulster Hall—and even the glorious Crown Bar—spending millions of pounds on its built heritage. A jail that at the height of the Troubles held some of the most notorious murderers involved in paramilitary violence is now a major visitor attraction.

GETTING HERE AND AROUND
BUS TRAVEL
Pink-and-white Metro buses are the best way to get around. Fares range from £1.40 to £2, depending on the

Tracing your Roots

A staggering 3 million documents are stored in the archives of the **Public Record Office of Northern Ireland** (PRONI), with 900,000 official government files and 300,000 maps—a wonderful place to stir the imagination of researchers and visitors. Most records date from around 1600 to the present. For those interested in roots tourism, or anyone with ancestors from the northern third of Ireland, it is an amateur genealogist's dream; those precious transcripts could provide a vivid piece of the family jigsaw. ⊠ *Titanic Blvd., Queen's Island, Titanic Quarter, Belfast* ☎ *028/9053–4800* ⊕ *www.nidirect.gov.uk/proni.*

The Ulster Historical Foundation has a skilled team to help with genealogical research. In recent years, with many more records available online, there is greater access to them, and the staff are adept at unearthing information about those elusive Irish or Scots-Irish ancestors. The UHF offers personal consultation, assessment, and research, as well as document retrieval. Its research offices are in Belfast's Cathedral Quarter at ⊠ *Corn Exchange, 31 Gordon St., Belfast* ☎ *028/9066–1988* ⊕ *ancestryireland. com.*

For a different take on Ulster-Scots history and language, it's worth calling into the **Ulster-Scots Visitor Centre**. This government-funded agency promotes the study of Ulster-Scots as a living language as well as its culture and history. You can tour the Discover Ulster-Scots Centre and view exhibition panels on dialect and heritage. ⊠ *Ulster-Scots Agency, Corn Exchange, 31 Gordon St., Belfast* ☎ *028/9023–1113* ⊕ *ulsterscotsagency. com.*

---

zone. If you're staying a few days, buy a Smartlink Travel Card for more than five journeys, which is a 30% saving; a weekly card is £15, plus £1 for the card. A Metro day ticket costs £4 and takes you anywhere on the network. Most bus routes start from Donegall Square or adjoining streets. The new Glider is a rapid-bus cross-city transit system that links west and east Belfast and takes in the Titanic Quarter via the city center. The service, which has two routes, G1 and G2, is operated by Translink and connects with the wider bus and rail network. The G1 runs from the Twinbrook area in the west of the city, via the center, to the east as far as Dundonald. The G2 operates from Wellington Place in the city center to Titanic Quarter. You can buy a ticket for the Glider at the Metro Kiosk at Donegall Square West or in the Visit Belfast Tourist Office, Donegall Square North, both of which are just a few yards from where the bus starts from at Wellington Place (or they can be bought at main bus stations). A single journey is £2. You must have a ticket before you board. One-day unlimited travel on all Glider and Metro services costs £4.

CAR TRAVEL

Belfast is 167 km (104 miles) north of Dublin. Motorways, or dual carriageways, lead into Belfast's city center from the main airports and seaports, and the fast N1/A1 motorway links the city with Dublin. The trip takes about two hours. The drive from Derry takes 90 minutes. The main arterial routes into central Belfast are busy only at peak commuter times, between 8 and 9 am and 5 and 6 pm.

Street parking costs £1.30 per hour for a pay-and-display ticket from a meter. The maximum parking time is two hours

Sights ▼

1 Albert Memorial
   Clock Tower E4
2 Botanic Gardens........ D9
3 City Hall E5
4 Crown Liquor Saloon... D6
5 Crumlin Road Gaol....... C2
6 Europa Hotel D6
7 First
   Presbyterian Church E4
8 Grand Opera House D5
9 High Street E4
10 Knockbreda
   Parish Church G9
11 Lagan Boat
   Company N.I. Ltd....... F4
12 Linen Hall Library D5
13 Metropolitan
   Arts Centre (MAC)...... E3
14 Northern Ireland
   War Memorial............ E4
15 Queen's
   University Belfast............ D8
16 St. Anne's
   Cathedral E4
17 St. Malachy's
   Church E6
18 St. Peter's
   Cathedral B4
19 Sinclair
   Seamen's Church........ F3
20 Titanic Belfast.......... H2
   Titanic's Dock And
21 Pump-House Tour I1
22 Ulster Hall D6
23 Ulster Museum.......... D9
24 W5:whowhat
   wherewhenwhy G3

Restaurants ▼

1 Café Parisien............. E5
2 Coppi...................... E3
3 Deanes Restaurant..... D5
4 Established Coffee E4
5 The Ginger Bistro....... D6
6 The Great Room......... E4
7 James Street
   and Co.................... D5
8 John Long's.............. C5
9 Made in Belfast:
   Cathedral Quarter E4
10 The Morning Star....... E4
11 Mourne Seafood Bar... D4
12 Neill's Hill Cafe &
   Brasserie I5
13 The Northern Whig..... E4
14 Ox Restaurant........... F5
15 Red Panda............... D6
16 Wolf and Whistle
   Restaurant............... A6
17 Yard Bird................. E4
18 Zen E6

Hotels ▼

1 Benedict's of Belfast ... D7
2 Bullitt Hotel E4
3 Clayton Hotel Belfast... D6
4 Culloden Estate & Spa ...I4
5 Dukes at
   Queens Hotel........... D8
6 Dunadry Hotel........... A1
7 Grand Central Hotel ... D5
8 Jurys Inn Belfast....... D5
9 Malmaison................ E4
10 The Merchant Hotel..... E4
11 The Old Inn I4
12 The Old Rectory
   Guesthouse.............. C9
13 Rayanne House...........I4
14 Roseleigh House........ F9
15 Ten Square D5
16 Titanic Hotel............. H3

KEY

① Exploring Sights

① Restaurants

① Hotels

The Troubles

Northern Ireland's historic conflict between Catholic and Protestant, Irish and English, had its roots in the first Norman incursions in the 12th century, when the English endeavored to subdue the potential enemy they saw in Ireland. The northern province of Ulster proved the hardest to conquer, but in 1607, its Irish nobility fled, their lands then given by the English to "the Planters"—staunch Protestants from England and Scotland.

Fast-forward through three centuries of smoldering tensions and religious strife to the overwhelming 1918 Nationalist vote across Ireland for Sinn Féin ("Ourselves Alone"), the party that believed in independence for all of Ireland. In Ulster, however, 22 (out of 29) seats went to the Unionists, who believed in maintaining British rule. After 50 years of living with a Unionist majority, students in Belfast's Queen's University launched a civil rights protest in 1968, claiming equal rights in jobs, housing, and opportunity. They were met by brutal British suppression, which, in turn, awoke the Irish Republican Army (IRA), dormant for decades. Britain then imposed Direct Rule. This struggle tragically came to a head on Bloody Sunday, January 30, 1972, when British paratroopers opened fire on people participating in a nonviolent protest in Derry against the British policy of internment without trial. When the smoke cleared, 13 people—all Catholic and unarmed—had been killed.

Decades of guerrilla conflict ensued between the IRA, the UDA/UVF (Protestant/Loyalist paramilitaries), and the British government and continued until 1998's Good Friday Agreement, which finally gave the province its own parliament. But a mere two months later, the province's fragile peace was shattered when a massive car bomb exploded in the quiet market town of Omagh on August 15. A minority of dissident Republicans had succeeded in killing 31 people. Despite this appalling act, the peace process continued, and Unionists eventually entered government proceedings with Sinn Féin at the end of 1999.

In September 2005, the IRA decommissioned all its weapons. In 2009, the Loyalist paramilitaries—the Ulster Volunteer Force and its splinter group, the Red Hand Commando—destroyed their weapons. By 2010, the biggest Loyalist paramilitary group, the Ulster Defence Association, decommissioned all weapons and was closely followed by two Irish Republican paramilitary groups—the extreme Irish National Liberation Army and the Official IRA—who also announced they had put weapons beyond use. The endorsement of what everyone had hoped to be a "final political deal" culminated in the Hillsborough Castle Agreement (2010), securing the stability of the Northern Ireland Assembly.

For many nationalists, the icing on the political cake came in June 2010 from the British government: an apology for Bloody Sunday saying it had been "unjustified and unjustifiable."

for such street spaces. Be careful not to overstay, as zealous clamping wardens operate. Multistory car-park garages are at the Victoria Square and Castle Court shopping centers. Some, but not all, hotels have parking. If you need it, ask a hotel or inn prior to booking.

TRAIN TRAVEL

As the capital city of Northern Ireland, Belfast is well served by an efficient train network. Most trains arrive and leave from Lanyon Place Station, a 15-minute walk from the city center.

CONTACTS Belfast Metro Service. ⊠ *Donegall Sq. W* ☎ *028/9066–6630* ⊕ *www.translink.co.uk/metro.* **Lanyon Place Rail Station.** ⊠ *E. Bridge St.* ☎ *028/9089–9400.*

TOURS
BUS TOURS
★ Belfast City Sightseeing

BUS TOURS | Belfast City Sightseeing runs the most comprehensive open-top tour through Belfast. The Belfast City Tour covers the City Hall, University Quarter, Shipyard, Titanic Quarter, Stormont, Shankill and Falls Roads, peace lines, Crumlin Road Gaol, and the Grand Opera House on Great Victoria Street. You can hop off and hop on as you please at any of the 23 stops. The entire route, without stops, takes about an hour and a half. The combo ticket allows discounted entry prices to some visitor attractions. The full-day *Game of Thrones* Tour takes in locations in North Antrim and runs daily throughout the year. ⊠ *City Tour departs from outside National Grand Cafe in High St.; Game of Thrones Tour departs daily from Glengall St., Central District* ☎ *028/9032–1321* ⊕ *www.belfastcitysightseeing.com* ⊠ *City Tour from £13; Game of Thrones Tour £39, includes Giant's Causeway.*

Giants Causeway Coastal Tours

DRIVING TOURS | Historical walking and driving tours that come with tales of myths and legends are the specialty of Giants Causeway Coastal Tours. The company also runs excursions outside Belfast to some of Northern Ireland's major tourist attractions. The owner tailors his tours to suit individual interests and requirements. ⊠ *Central District* ☎ *079/1229–0935* ⊕ *www.giantscausewaycoastaltours.com* ⊠ *Full-day tour for 6 people £300.*

McComb's Coach Travel

BUS TOURS | As well as the standard open-top bus tours of Belfast and trips to the Giant's Causeway, McComb's also organizes more specific tours, such as a *Game of Thrones* tour costing £35 per person. As part of the *Game of Thrones* tour, optional tickets can also be purchased for visiting the Giant's Causeway and cost an extra £12.50. Parts of the series were filmed in Belfast, County Antrim, and other areas of Northern Ireland. ⊠ *22 Donegall Rd., Central District* ☎ *028/9031–5333* ⊕ *www.mccombscoaches.com/tours.*

TAXI TOURS
The Official Black Taxi Tours

DRIVING TOURS | All the main political highlights and trouble spots of the 1970s and '80s, such as the Falls and Shankill roads, are covered by the comprehensive Official Black Taxi Tours. They also run day tours to the Giant's Causeway and Antrim coast. Pickups are available from your hotel or B&B, or from bus and train stations. ⊠ *Belfast* ☎ *028/9064–2264* ⊕ *www.belfasttours.com* ⊠ *£40 up to 2 passengers, plus £17 per additional person.*

TaxiTrax Tours

DRIVING TOURS | The itinerary of the popular TaxiTrax Tours provides a balanced history lesson covering the Troubles and includes the peace wall and the city's famed murals. ⊠ *King St.* ☎ *028/9031–5777* ⊕ *www.taxitrax.com* ⊠ *£35 up to 3 passengers, plus £12 per additional person.*

Titanic Tours Belfast

SPECIAL-INTEREST | For an in-depth *Titanic* tour—one that also takes in the *Nomadic,* the *Titanic*'s dock and pump house, as well as several other locations—consider Titanic Tours Belfast, a tour by taxi, run by Susie Millar, the great-granddaughter of an assistant deck engineer who sailed on the ill-fated liner. Tours are by appointment and can accommodate up to four people. They last nearly three hours. Pickup is arranged from your accommodations. ⊠ *Belfast* ☎ *078/5271–6655* ⊕ *www.titanictours-belfast.co.uk* ✉ *From £25.*

WALKING TOURS
Hidden Belfast

WALKING TOURS | Focusing on buildings and history, Hidden Belfast walking tours last one hour and meet at the front gates of Belfast City Hall; look for the Hidden Belfast umbrella. Tours leave twice a day, at 11 am and 1 pm in July and August. Check website for departure times and phone in advance to confirm. ⊠ *Meet outside front gates of City Hall, Donegall Sq. N, Central District* ☎ *077/7164–0746* ⊕ *www.experiencebelfast.com* ✉ *£10 (includes tea/coffee).*

Parliament Buildings Tour

PERSONAL GUIDES | Free tours of Parliament Buildings are held twice every weekday at 11 and 2. Take a stroll around the home of the Northern Ireland Assembly to see one of the city's most striking pieces of architecture. The restaurant is open to the public for morning coffee, lunch (£17.75 for three courses), or afternoon tea (£15), from where you can enjoy a view overlooking the Stomont estate and the rolling Castlereagh hills of east Belfast. It is open 10–4 weekdays, and booking is advisable via its website or by telephone (☎ *028/9052–1041*). ⊠ *Upper Newtownards Rd., Stormont, East Belfast* ☎ *028/9052–1802* ⊕ *www. parliamentbuildings.org.*

Titanic Walking Tours

WALKING TOURS | Colin Cobb holds fascinating guided tours of Queen's Island, which explores all things *Titanic.* Tours last 90 minutes and visitors are taken through the highlights of the main buildings associated with the liner. The meeting point is outside the main entrance of Titanic Belfast on Queen's Road in the Titanic Quarter. From the city center you can take the Glider bus, G2, which leaves from Wellington Place close to the City Hall. ⊠ *Titanic Quarter* ☎ *075/4648–9875* ⊕ *www.titanicwalk.com.*

VISITOR INFORMATION
Visit Belfast Welcome Centre

Directly opposite City Hall, this is the first stop to find out what's on, to buy tickets for events and tours, or to book accommodations and travel. Multimedia information touch-screens and self-service kiosks provide a signposting service for more than 400 attractions throughout Northern Ireland. A Translink desk helps plan and organize travel within Northern Ireland and further afield. There's also free Wi-Fi access, a currency exchange, and left luggage facilities. It costs £4 to leave your luggage for four hours, and £6 for more than four hours. Ask about the Belfast Visitor Pass, which allows discounts of between 10% and 40% on some visitor attractions and tours as well as savings offering unlimited travel on bus and train routes. An adult day pass costs £6, two days £11, and three days £14.50. ⊠ *8–9 Donegall Sq. N, Central District* ☎ *028/9024–6609* ⊕ *www. visit-belfast.com.*

Golden Mile

Although it doesn't glow in quite the way the name suggests, the bustling Golden Mile and its immediate environs harbor noteworthy historic buildings. In addition, the area is filled with hotels and major civic and office buildings, as well as some restaurants, cafés, and shops.

Even if you don't end up staying here, you're likely to pass through it often.

Sights

★ Crown Liquor Saloon

LOCAL INTEREST | Belfast is blessed with some exceptional pubs but the Crown is one of the city's glories. Owned by the National Trust (the U.K.'s official conservation organization), it's an ostentatious box of delights and immaculately preserved. Opposite the Europa Hotel, it began life in 1826 as the Railway Tavern and is still lighted by gas; in 1885 the owner asked Italian craftsmen working on churches in Ireland to moonlight on rebuilding it, and its place in Irish architectural pub history was assured. Richly carved woodwork around cozy snugs (cubicles—known to regulars as "confessional boxes"), leather seats, color tile work, and an abundance of mirrors make up the decor. But the pièce de résistance is the embossed ceiling with its swirling arabesques and rosettes of burnished primrose, amber, and gold, as dazzling now as the day it was installed. The Crown claims to serve the perfect pint of Guinness—so no need to ask what anyone's drinking. When you settle down with your glass, note the little gunmetal plates used by the Victorians for lighting their matches as well as the antique push-button bells for ordering another round. Ageless, timeless, and classless—some would say the Crown is even priceless. If you wish to eat, choose the upstairs dining room, which has a much wider and better selection of food. ⊠ *46 Great Victoria St., Golden Mile* ☎ *028/9024–3187* ⊕ *www.nicholsons-pubs.co.uk.*

★ Crumlin Road Gaol

JAIL | FAMILY | Designed by Charles Lanyon, and opened in 1846, this jail held more than 500 prisoners at its peak; today it is one of Belfast's hottest tourist tickets. Throughout its 150-year lifetime, around 25,000 convicts passed through its doors. During the worst years of the Troubles, between 1969 and 1996 (when the prison closed), it held some of the North's most notorious prisoners, including many involved in paramilitary violence. The building has undergone a £10 million restoration, and, with its cream-walled corridors and black railings, has been transformed to reflect the way it looked in Victorian days. The engrossing 75-minute tour takes in the holding, punishment, and condemned cells—the latter where the prisoners were held before being taken to the gallows for execution. The highlight is the execution chamber, hidden behind a moving bookcase where the guide explains the gory details of how the long-drop method was used to break the prisoner's neck. Exhibits in the museum include handcuffs, uniforms, a flogging rack with the birch used for punishment, photographs, and maps. The jail is said to be one of the most haunted buildings in Belfast, and paranormal tours are held occasionally. The Crum Café sells daytime snacks, while Cuffs Bar and Grill is open for evening dining. ⊠ *53–55 Crumlin Rd., North Belfast* ☎ *028/9074–1500* ⊕ *www.crumlinroad-gaol.com* ⊠ *£12.*

Europa Hotel

HOTEL—SIGHT | A landmark in Belfast, the Europa is seen as a monument to the resilience of the city in the face of the Troubles. The most bombed hotel in Western Europe, the hotel was targeted 11 times by the IRA starting in the early 1970s and refurbished every time; today it shows no signs of its explosive history after a £1 million renovation in 2016. President Bill Clinton and First Lady Hillary Clinton chose the hotel for an overnight visit during their 1995 visit—for 24 hours the phones were answered with "White House Belfast, can I help you?" The former president's room is now called the Clinton Suite and contains memorabilia from the presidential stay. ⊠ *38 Great Victoria St., at Glengall St., Golden Mile* ☎ *028/9027–1066* ⊕ *www.hastingshotels.com.*

What's Next for the North?

Since the peace process and the Good Friday Agreement of 1998 considerable change has come about in Northern Ireland. Another political accord, the Stormont House Agreement, was endorsed in 2014 and facilitated with a £2 billion financial package from the British government. This brought a newfound business confidence, driven by tourism, that generated millions for the economy. The deal was seen as a political breakthrough but since 2016 the two main parties—the Democratic Unionists (representing Union within the U.K.) and the Republican Sinn Fein—have been at odds, plunging the power-sharing assembly at Stormont into crisis. Some of the disputed issues, such as the legal recognition of the Irish language in the North—anathema to most Unionists—tensions over Brexit, the United Kingdom's exit from the European Union, and other political bickering, have led to the suspension of the assembly for more than two years.

Against this background, the legacy of the "Troubles" continues to present a problem in terms of how best to deal with it. Sporadic outbursts of violence occur and murders have continued such as that of 29-year-old journalist Lyra McKee in April 2019. She was killed by an organization styling itself as the New IRA, a dissident Republican group who see the Good Friday Agreement as a barrier to a united Ireland. McKee was struck by a stray bullet as she reported on a riot in the Creggan area of Derry. In the international media there was fear that this outrage would rupture the relative peace that has existed for 21 years but the reality is different. Northern Ireland is enjoying the greatest prosperity and longest period of stability in its history and few commentators forecast a return to the "Troubles." That said, it is a place in transformation with some seemingly intractable problems and a refusal on the part of politicians to compromise.

Since 1998 more than 160 murders have taken place. However, these have been on a completely different pattern from the harrowing days of the 1970s and 1980s. (In the worst single year, 1972, a total of 476 people were killed.) The incidents are mostly localized within communities and involve paramilitary drug-related gang feuds on both the Republican and Loyalist sides. The sectarianism that marked the worst years of violence has all but disappeared from the streets and in particular has no bearing on tourists visiting the North. Clearly, the past still echoes in the present, and it has been a longer road to peace than many anticipated when the Good Friday Agreement was signed.

Grand Opera House

ARTS VENUE | Belfast's opera house, which regularly hosts musicals, plays, and concerts, exemplifies the Victorians' fascination with ornamentation, opulent gilt moldings, and intricate plasterwork, and will celebrate its 125th anniversary in December 2020. The renowned theater architect Frank Matcham beautifully designed the building in 1894. Facilities include bars on all floors, a café on the ground floor, and party room. Contemporary Irish artist Cherith McKinstry's exquisite angel-and-cherub-laden fresco floats over the auditorium ceiling. During 2020 the opera house is planning a once-in-a-generation multimillion-pound restoration project, which promises to return the matchless building to its former glory and will enhance the public areas. It will also lead to its closure for several months in the early part of the year. Structural surveys began in 2019 and historical paint specialists started peeling back the layers of paint, varnish, and gilding from 21 locations around the auditorium, analyzing them to examine the decorative schemes of the past. As yet, there has been no trace of the ghost that has reportedly been seen on the stage down through the decades. ⚠ **During the refurbishment early in 2020 the theater is expected to go dark for a number of months, so it is best to check in advance with the box office about specific shows.** ✉ *2 Great Victoria St., Golden Mile* ☎ *028/9024–1919* ⊕ *www.goh.co.uk.*

🍴 Restaurants

★ The Ginger Bistro

$$ | **MODERN IRISH** | Modern Irish classics with an international twist attract the foodie crowd to this cheerful bistro just off Great Victoria Street, which was extended in 2018 to become a 70-seat bistro. A short but perfectly balanced menu emphasizes locally sourced seafood and lean meats. **Known for:** best-selling squid and dips; outstanding wine and beer menu; lively atmosphere. ⑤ *Average main: £17* ✉ *68–72 Great Victoria St., Golden Mile* ☎ *028/9024–4421* ⊕ *www.gingerbistro.com* ⊗ *Closed Sun. and Mon.*

John Long's

$ | **IRISH** | Hearty eaters adore this long-standing institution, which has served fish-and-chips for more than 100 years. The completely basic Athol Street premises, close to the city center, welcomes garbage collectors, business execs, schoolboys from the nearby Royal Belfast Academical Institution, and patrons from every sector, who flock here for the secret-batter-recipe fish. **Known for:** classic fish-and-chips; local favorite; best value in town. ⑤ *Average main: £8* ✉ *39 Athol St., Golden Mile* ☎ *028/9032–1848* ⊕ *www.johnlongs.com* ⊗ *Closed Sun. No dinner.*

Red Panda

$$ | **CHINESE** | The £9.90 two-course lunch on Thursday and Friday is an exceptional value at this long-established central eatery. It includes a starter of fresh fruit or salad, along with a main-course dish of your choice with rice. **Known for:** honey chili chicken; super seafood selection; stuffed chitterlings with salt. ⑤ *Average main: £16* ✉ *60 Great Victoria St., Golden Mile* ☎ *028/9080–8700* ⊕ *www.thered-panda.co.uk* ⊗ *No lunch Sat.*

🍸 Nightlife

The glorious Crown Liquor Saloon is far from being the only old pub in the Golden Mile area—some, but by no means all, of Belfast's evening life takes place in bars and restaurants here. At several replicated Victorian bars, more locals and fewer visitors gather.

Brennan's Bar

BARS/PUBS | A noisy, modern pub, this bar jams on up-to-the-minute music. It can get a bit boisterous, so some may prefer a quiet snug (booth) across the road in the more serene Crown Liquor Saloon. Food is served from noon daily (Monday through Thursday until 8, weekends until 7). ✉ *48 Great Victoria St., Golden Mile* ☎ *028/9024–2986.*

Robinsons

BARS/PUBS | A popular pub encompassing four venues under one roof, Robinsons draws a young crowd with folk music in its Fibber Magees bar on Sunday and funk in the trendy BT1 karaoke bar on weekends. Food is served daily from 12:30 to 9 pm. ✉ *38–42 Great Victoria St., Golden Mile* ☎ *028/9024–7447* ⊕ *www.robinsonsbar.co.uk.*

Performing Arts

★ Grand Opera House

THEATER | Shows from all over Ireland and Britain—and sometimes farther afield—play at this beautifully restored Victorian theater. Though it has no resident company of its own, major West End musicals and plays pass through, plus the occasional opera or ballet. It's worth attending a show just to enjoy the gigantic and splendid opera house itself. The Baby Grand—a theater-within-a-theater—hosts comedy, live music, and educational workshops as well as film and special events. On the second floor you can peruse a theater-history exhibition. Guided backstage tours are available, mostly on alternate Saturday mornings (10:30–11:30) and cost £8.50; check the website for details. Be aware also that the theater is undergoing renovation during the early months of 2020, so check with the box office about shows. ⊠ *2 Great Victoria St., Golden Mile* ☎ *028/9024–1919* ⊕ *www.goh.co.uk.*

Central District

Belfast's Central District, immediately north of the Golden Mile, is not geographically the center of the city, but it's the old heart of Belfast. It's a frenetic place, where both locals and visitors shop. Cafés, pubs, offices, and shops of all kinds occupy the redbrick, white Portland stone, and modern buildings that line its narrow streets. Many streets are pedestrian-only, so it's a good place to take a leisurely stroll, browse the windows, and see some sights to boot. It's easy to get waylaid shopping and investigating sights along the river when taking this walk, so give yourself at least two hours to cover the area comfortably.

The Central District contains what locals call the Cathedral Quarter: radiating out from the new, mock neo-Palladian development of St. Anne's Square. Small

Victorian Grisly

Most of Belfast's landmarks were built during the reign of Queen Victoria. Once considered unappealing—"Victorian Grisly" was the epithet used by more than one critic—today they are marvelous remnants of an age that considered show, pomp, and circumstance paramount. Most of these buildings are found within 20 blocks of each other and a time-travel walk can hit many of them, including City Hall, the Grand Opera House, Crown Liquor Saloon, Ulster Hall, St. Malachy's Church, and St. Anne's Cathedral.

privately owned art galleries, alongside the Black Box—a major performance venue—line the side streets and are crammed in alongside a new wave of bars and lively bistros, making it the new restaurant central. Crowning it all is the dramatic Metropolitan Arts Centre, Northern Ireland's flagship location for the arts.

Sights

Albert Memorial Clock Tower

MEMORIAL | Tilting a little to one side—not unlike Pisa's more notorious leaning landmark—this clock tower was named for Queen Victoria's husband, Prince Albert. The once-dilapidated Queen's Square on which it stands has undergone a face-lift, and a restoration has brought the clock back to its original glory. The tower itself is not open to the public. ⊠ *Queen's Sq., Central District.*

★ City Hall

TOUR—SIGHT | Built of Portland stone between 1898 and 1906 and modeled on St. Paul's Cathedral in London, this

Renaissance revival–style edifice—the cynosure of central Belfast—was designed by Brumwell Thomas (who was knighted but had to sue to get his fee). Before you enter, take a stroll around Donegall Square to see statues of Queen Victoria and a column honoring the U.S. Expeditionary Force, which landed in the city on January 26, 1942—the first contingent of the U.S. Army to arrive in Europe during World War II. A monument commemorating the *Titanic* stands in the grounds, and in 2012 a granite memorial was unveiled in a *Titanic* memorial garden opened for the 100th anniversary of the ship's sinking. The memorial, on the east side of the grounds, lists the names of everyone who died in the tragedy. Enter the building under the porte cochere at the front. From the entrance hall (the base of which is a whispering gallery), the view up to the heights of the 173-foot-high Great Dome is a feast for the eyes. With its complicated series of arches and openings, stained-glass windows, Italian-marble inlays, decorative plasterwork, and paintings, this is Belfast's most ornate public space—a veritable homage to the might of the British Empire. After an £11 million restoration, the modernized building has been brought into the 21st century and is home to the Bobbin café. In 2017 a permanent self-guided interactive exhibition on the history of Belfast spanning 16 rooms was installed, covering six theme zones including cultural heritage, sporting celebrities, and laureates of the arts. Look out for the exhibit of ceremonial keys presented by visiting dignitaries from 10 U.S. towns and cities, reflecting the close ties between Northern Ireland and America. In the courtyard a 60-jet fountain has been dedicated to Belfast City Council members killed during the Troubles. Free, one-hour guided tours of the building are available or you can rent headphones for £3.50. Tours are held weekdays at 11, 2, and 3, and weekends at noon, 2 and 3. ⊠ *Donegall Sq., Central District* ☎ *028/9027–0456* ⊕ *www.belfastcity.gov.uk* ✉ *Tours free.*

First Presbyterian Church

RELIGIOUS SITE | The First Presbyterian Church dates from 1783 and has an interesting elliptical interior. It hosts free lunchtime concerts in July and August. Guided tours, lasting 45 minutes, are held on weekday mornings at 11 and are free. ⊠ *Rosemary St., Central District* ☎ *078/4140–8222.*

High Street

NEIGHBORHOOD | Off High Street, especially down to Ann Street (parallel to the south), run narrow lanes and alleyways called entries. Though mostly cleaned up and turned into chic shopping lanes, they still hang on to something of their raffish character, and have distinctive pubs with little-altered Victorian interiors. Among the most notable are the Morning Star (Pottinger's Entry off High Street), with its large windows and fine curving bar; White's Tavern (entry off High Street), Belfast's oldest pub, founded in 1630, with plush seats and a big, open fire; and the delectable Muriel's Café Bar in Church Lane, with its damask drapes and velvet seats, themed on a 1920s hat shop. Look into St. George's Church, at one end of High Street, a beautiful building with a magnificent portico transported by canal from the house of the eccentric Earl Bishop of Derry. ■ TIP→ Don't miss Kelly's Cellars, a 200-year-old pub in Bank Street, not far from High Street. The bar was the meeting place of the militant Nationalist group, the Society of United Irishmen, whose leader Wolfe Tone is remembered as the founder of Irish Republicanism. A colorful wall mural erected in the upstairs bar in 2018 features the poet Seamus Heaney, writers such as Oscar Wilde, Brendan Behan, and Samuel Beckett, and musicians including Phil Lynott and Sinéad O'Connor. At lunchtime they serve tasty bowls of filling beef stew, but get there early as stocks are limited (☎ *028/902–6058.* ✉ *High St., Central District.*

Knockbreda Parish Church

RELIGIOUS SITE | Belfast has so many churches you could visit a different one nearly every day of the year and still not make it to them all. The oldest house of worship is the Church of Ireland Knockbreda Parish Church. This dark structure was built in 1737 by Richard Cassels, who designed many of Ireland's finest mansions. It quickly became *the* place to be buried—witness the vast 18th-century tombs in the churchyard. ✉ *Church Rd., off A24, Belfast* ☎ *028/9064–5372* ⊕ *www.knockbredaparish.org.*

Lagan Boat Company N.I. Ltd

TOUR—SIGHT | To see the city from a different perspective, board the *Titanic* harbor tour, which takes in the shipyard where the famous liner was built. The 65-minute tour leaves daily (March–October) from Donegall Quay at noon, 2, and 3:30 pm near the *Big Fish* sculpture (a gigantic salmon covered in tiles and printed with text and imagery about Belfast). Weekend tours are held in the winter months. Tickets can be bought in the Maritime Emporium shop beside the Obel tower at Donegall Quay. ✉ *66 Donegall Quay, Central District* ☎ *028/9024–0124* ⊕ *www.laganboatcompany.com* 🍽 *Tours £12.*

★ Linen Hall Library

LIBRARY | With its distinctive grayish-yellow brick, this library—the oldest subscription library in Ireland—is a comfortable place to escape the bustle of the city streets. The library, which was awarded museum status, has an unparalleled collection of tens of thousands of documents and books relating to the Troubles, regarded as the definitive archive and attracting scholars from all over the world. A digital archive launched in 2018, *Divided Society,* features a wide range of material relating to the peace process of the 1990s resulting in the Belfast Agreement on Good Friday in 1998. One early librarian, Thomas Russell, was hanged

Poor Philomena

One of the largest private collections of *Titanic* memorabilia in Ireland is on display in Robinson's Bar in Great Victoria Street (opposite Europa Hotel, at Great Victoria and Glengall Streets). It includes letters and postcards written on board the ship and poignant items such as "Philomena," the doll recovered floating at the wreck site.

in 1803 for supporting an Irish uprising; another early user, Henry Joy McCracken, a founding member of the United Irishmen, went to the scaffold owing the library £1.30 in subscriptions arrears, a debt that was eventually paid by a descendant in 2001. American visitors in particular like to see one extremely rare item: the original document recording the first ever acts passed by the American Congress in New York on March 4, 1789. On the walls are paintings and prints depicting Belfast views and landmarks. Much of this artwork is for sale. Look out for the beautiful stained-glass windows on the first floor featuring portraits of men eminent in literature and science. It's an ideal hideaway for relaxing with a newspaper, enjoying the library's café, and falling into conversation. Guided 45-minute tours are held at 10:30 am weekdays. ✉ *17 Donegall Sq. N, Central District* ☎ *028/9032–1707* ⊕ *www.linenhall.com* 🍽 *Free, tours from £5* ⏱ *Closed weekends.*

Metropolitan Arts Centre (MAC)

ARTS VENUE | Eye-catchingly beautiful, and flooded with light, the Metropolitan Arts Centre (MAC) is Northern Ireland's flagship home for the arts and energizer of the Cathedral Quarter's flourishing creative scene. Six stories tall, and with two theaters, three art galleries, and artists' studios—along with a café, bar, and restaurant—the MAC is the centerpiece of the neo-Palladian St. Anne's Square development. The MAC makes an astonishing statement with redbrick and dark basalt, oak furnishings, Danish fabric panels, steel balustrades, bronze window frames, and dark-gray terrazzo flooring. Downstairs is a 350-seat auditorium, while upstairs is a 120-seat studio. The galleries present up-and-coming Northern Irish artists as well as attention-grabbing temporary exhibitions incorporating the works of world-renowned artists. Ushers, known as "MACtivists," are on hand to help point you in the right direction. ☒ St. Anne's Sq., Exchange St., Cathedral Quarter ☎ 028/9023–5053 ⊕ www. themaclive.com 🖾 Galleries free.

Northern Ireland War Memorial

MEMORIAL | Alongside St. Anne's Cathedral, the memorial building houses an interactive exhibition about World War II. During the April 1941 Belfast blitz, this area was bombed by the Luftwaffe, resulting in more than a thousand deaths. The memorial's American Wall of Friendship contains a copper frieze perpetuating the wartime bonds created between the people of Northern Ireland and the United States. ☒ 21 Talbot St., Cathedral Quarter ☎ 028/9032–0392 ⊕ www.niwarmemorial.org 🖾 Free.

Sinclair Seamen's Church

RELIGIOUS SITE | By the riverfront is one of the most appealing churches, Presbyterian Sinclair Seamen's Church. Designed by Charles Lanyon, the architect of Queen's University, it has served the seafaring community since 1857. The pulpit is shaped like a ship's prow; the bell is from HMS Hood, a Royal Navy battleship sunk in Portland Harbor on the south coast of England in 1914; and even the collection plates are shaped like lifeboats. Tours are offered between March and December on Wednesday from 2 to 4:30. ☒ Corporation Sq., off Donegall Quay, Central

District ☎ 028/9031–9931 ⊗ Closed Jan. and Feb.

St. Anne's Cathedral

RELIGIOUS SITE | At the center of the eponymous Cathedral Quarter, St. Anne's is a turn-of-the-20th century edifice in the Irish neo-Romanesque style. Lord Carson (1854–1935), who was largely responsible for keeping the six counties inside the United Kingdom, is buried here by virtue of a special Act of Parliament. His is the only tomb. The 175-foot stainless-steel Spire of Hope atop the cathedral's roof adds to the city's skyline and shines brightly as a beacon of newfound optimism for the future. The German Luftwaffe bombed this section of Belfast during World War II; on the cathedral's Talbot Street side, at No. 21, the Northern Ireland War Memorial has an interactive exhibit about the war. ☒ Donegall St., Cathedral Quarter ☎ 028/9032–8332 ⊕ www.belfastcathedral.org 🖾 £5, includes tour and guidebook.

St. Malachy's Church

RELIGIOUS SITE | Opened in 1844, this is one of the most impressive redbrick Tudor revival churches in Ireland. One of the interior highlights is the densely patterned fan-vaulted ceiling, a delightfully swirling masterpiece of plasterwork—whose inspiration was taken from the chapel of Henry VII at Westminster Abbey in London—tastefully repainted in cream. The painting over the high altarpiece, Journey to Calvary, was carried out by portraitist Felix Piccioni, whose family were refugees from the Austrian region of Italy. In 1868 the largest bell in Belfast was added to the church, but after complaints that its deafening noise was interfering with the maturing of whiskey in the nearby Dunville distillery, it was wrapped in felt to soften its peal and vibration. Along the southeast wall of the church gazing out in contemplative mood with his brown eyes and torn chocolate brown coat is the delicate Statue of the Ragged Saint. St. Benedict Joseph Labre, the patron saint of the unemployed, welcomes visitors into the ethereal elegance of one of Belfast's most architecturally romantic buildings. ✉ *Alfred St., Central District* ☎ *028/9032–1713* ⊕ *www.saint-malachysparish.com* 💷 *Free.*

St. Peter's Cathedral

RELIGIOUS SITE | The elegant neo-Gothic "twin spires" of St. Peter's Cathedral dominate the skyline of West Belfast. Finding this Roman Catholic cathedral is difficult, but worth the effort. Built in 1866, when the Catholic population was rapidly increasing, St. Peter's acted as a focal point for the community. ✉ *St. Peter's Sq., West Belfast* ☎ *028/9032–7573.*

★ Titanic Belfast

TOUR—SIGHT | **FAMILY** | This world-class attraction headlines a "Titanic Experience" exhibition along with showcasing nine linked interpretative galleries that outline the *Titanic*'s dramatic story as well as the wider theme of Belfast's seafaring and industrial heritage. The stunning bow-shape facade of the six-story building reflects the lines of the great ship, the shardlike appearance created from 3,000 different-shape panels each folded from silver anodized aluminum sheets into asymmetrical geometries. The ultimate, startling effect is of light caught by a cut diamond. As you wander through Titanic Belfast you learn about the thriving boomtown at the turn of the 20th century; the ride through the reconstruction of the shipyards echoes with the sounds and sensations of more than 100 years ago. In one of the galleries, the ship's saga is brought up to the present with the discovery of the wreck and into the future with live links to contemporary undersea exploration. Also on-site is a movie theater designed by the *Titanic* explorer Robert Ballard (he discovered the wreck in 1985), which shows films about the ship. From time to time new exhibits are added; one of these is the original plan used during the British Titanic Inquiry held one month after the sinking. The historic plan was a vital reference tool and contains markings indicating where the liner struck the iceberg. The inquiry concluded that the loss of the liner had been brought about by "excessive speed." Tours are self-guided; audio guides are available in seven languages and cost £3. The one-hour Discovery Tour (£9) explores the symbolism of the Titanic building and incorporates the new Titanic Hotel, the converted former drawing offices of Harland & Wolff shipyard. The admission price to Titanic Belfast includes access to the nearby *SS Nomadic*, *Titanic's* original tender ship and the last remaining White Star Line vessel. Following a stint as a Parisian restaurant and nightclub, *Nomadic* was restored and visitors can experience a permanent and tangible piece of maritime heritage at Hamilton Dock. You can separately book a visit to the *Nomadic* on its own. Tickets are £7, more details at ⊕ *www.nomadicbelfast.com.* You can also buy a White Star Premium Pass (£30) for daylong benefits such as discounts in the bistro and in the Titanic Store, as well as access to SS *Nomadic* and a personalized souvenir photograph of your visit. Tickets for Titanic Belfast are based on a timed ticketing, with slots available every 15 minutes throughout opening times; last admission is one hour, 45 minutes before closing time. ■**TIP➔ On selected Sundays, afternoon tea is hosted by the grand staircase in the Titanic Suite, but must be booked in advance. The cost is £27.50, £33 with a glass of prosecco, or £36 with a glass of Heidsieck Monopole Champagne, the official champagne of the RMS Titanic.** ✉ *Olympic Way, 6 Queen's Rd., Titanic Quarter, Titanic Quarter* ☎ *028/9076–6386* ⊕ *www.titanicbelfast.com* 💷 *£19 includes Titanic Experience tour at Titanic Belfast and entrance to SS Nomadic; discovery tour £9.*

★ Titanic's Dock and Pump-House Tour

MARINA | The atmospheric 900-foot-long dock where the *Titanic* was built—in its time the biggest in the world—is open to the public and ranks as one of *the* great attractions in Northern Ireland. Since 2012, and the events held for the 100th anniversary, *Titanic*'s Dock—officially known as the Thompson Dry Dock—has been accessible to visitors. Steps lead deep down 44 feet to the floor of the dock, where you can bask in the evocative spirit of this remarkable place well below sea level. In its heyday in the early 20th century, the dock could hold 21 million gallons of water. Today it is Belfast's outstanding relic of the *Titanic*'s legacy and strikingly represents the ship's physical footprint. Built by 500 men over a period of seven years, it was the beating heart of the shipyard's operation during the construction of the great White Star Liners—*Britannic*, *Olympic*, and *Titanic*. But it was a tight squeeze; the *Titanic* barely fit in. The original steel-casing gate (now showing some signs of rust) that enclosed the dock and kept ships watertight weighs a staggering 1,000 tons. You can access the dock via the Pump House Café 1404. The tour, which is self-guided, costs £3. The café serves snacks, coffees, and lunches, and if you are driving, car parking is free when you spend £5 or more in it. ■TIP→ **The easiest way to reach the Dock and Pump House is to board the G2 Glider bus at Wellington Place, near the City Hall, and alight at the Titanic Belfast stop on Queen's Road, home to the SSE Arena and W5 science center; you can also take a train to the Titanic Quarter stop or opt for a 20-minute walk from Belfast city center.** ✉ *Queen's Rd., Titanic Quarter* ☎ *028/9040–9951* ✆ *£3.*

Ulster Hall

ARTS VENUE | It has hosted Charles Dickens, the Rolling Stones, and Rachmaninov as well as a diverse range of Irish politicians from Charles Stewart Parnell to Ian Paisley. Built in 1862 as a ballroom, the Ulster Hall, affectionately known as the Grand Dame of Bedford Street, is still thriving. Much of W. J. Barre's original decor has been restored

and 13 historic oil paintings reflecting the history and mythology of Belfast by local artist Joseph Carey are on display in their original magnificence in the Carey Gallery. Another highlight is an interpretative display featuring poetry, pictures, and sound telling the history of the hall through personal reminiscences. During World War II the building was used as a dance hall by U.S. troops based in Northern Ireland. The hall is also the permanent home of the Ulster Orchestra. Drink in some of Belfast's colorful history, and reflect on the fact that it was here in March 1971 Led Zeppelin debuted "Stairway to Heaven" on stage. At the box office you can buy tickets for all upcoming events at both Ulster Hall and Waterfront Hall. ✉ *Bedford St., Central District* ☎ *028/9033–4400* ⊕ *www. ulsterhall.co.uk.*

W5: whowhatwherewhenwhy

MUSEUM | **FAMILY** | A staggering 250 hands-on exhibits allow children to explore the world through games and activities. Part of the Odyssey complex in Belfast's docks, the W5 science discovery center takes a high-tech approach to interpreting science and creativity for adults and children. Video displays and flashing lights enhance the futuristic feel, and you can do everything from exploring the weather to building houses, bridges, and robots. The Discovery exhibits for children under eight cover subjects such as spying, forensics, and nature. A huge multistory climbing structure called Climbit, a cross between a maze and a jungle gym, is a fun feature in the atrium for kids three and up. ■TIP→ **Make your way to the upper floors for spectacular views over the city and beyond.** ✉ *2 Queen's Quay, Titanic Quarter* ☎ *028/9046–7700* ⊕ *www.w5online. co.uk* ✆ *£10.*

The Titanic Belfast is a modern, world-class museum and experience center that takes a deep dive into the ship and its tragic maiden voyage.

🍴 Restaurants

Café Parisien

$ | FRENCH | Taking its name from the eponymous first-class café on RMS *Titanic*, Café Parisien divides itself into a downstairs creprerie and a stylish upstairs restaurant in a landmark six-story sandstone building opposite City Hall. Choose from an array of savory or sweet crepes and galettes or head upstairs for main courses at lunch or dinner, which may include beef bourguignon or bouilla-baisse, the celebrated stew of Provence. **Known for:** unmissable savory crepes; Belfast's best bouillabaisse; stunning views of City Hall. ⑤ *Average main: £14* ✉ *Cleaver House, 1–3 Donegall Sq. N, Central District* ☎ *028/9590–4338* ⊕ *www.cafeparisienbelfast.com.*

Coppi

$$ | ITALIAN | The small dishes known as *cicchetti,* beloved of Venetian bars and a counterpart to tapas, draw the crowds to Coppi in the ever-popular Cathedral Quarter. Named after a world-champion Italian racing cyclist, Angelo Fausto Coppi, it serves flavorful Mediterranean cuisine amid modern industrial decor. **Known for:** duck ragù; sharing dishes; best tiramisu in town. ⑤ *Average main: £15* ✉ *St. Anne's Sq., Cathedral Quarter* ☎ *028/9031–1959* ⊕ *www.coppi.co.uk.*

★ Deanes Restaurant

$$$ | EUROPEAN | For more than 20 years Michael Deane has been the leader of the Belfast culinary pack, and his flagship operation has three distinct restaurants in one building. The Meat Locker is a beef-driven grill room and steak house; Eipic is an upscale, one–Michelin star restaurant and opulent champagne bar serving a variety of multicourse menus; and Love Fish is a less formal seafood restaurant with a Hamptons vibe. **Known for:** locally sourced beef at the Meat Locker; elegant food at Eipic; great value seafood at Love Fish. ⑤ *Average main: £19* ✉ *28–40 Howard St., Central District* ☎ *028/9033–1134* ⊕ *www.michaeldeane. co.uk* ⊗ *Eipic closed Sun.–Tues.*

Established Coffee

$ | IRISH | In a world of behemoth coffee chains it is heart-warming to find an independent store creating a funky vibe serving freshly ground beans from plantations in Kenya, Ethiopia, and Guatemala. Right in the heart of the Cathedral Quarter, this unpretentious café with its minimalist surroundings, communal wooden tables, and cement floor attracts a crowd of MacBook and smartphone lovers, as well as those gasping for a caffeine hit. **Known for:** espresso filter coffee; luxurious cinnamon swirls; cool place to hang out. $ *Average main: £9* ⊠ *54 Hill St., Cathedral Quarter* ✛ *Hill St. is one of main thoroughfares in Cathedral Quarter and café is a short walk from St Anne's Cathedral* ☎ *028/9031–9416* ⊕ *www.established.coffee.*

★ The Great Room

$$$$ | EUROPEAN | Inside the lavish Merchant Hotel, beneath the grand dome of this former bank's great hall and Ireland's biggest chandelier, find the perfect setting for a memorable dinner of adventurous European fare. Exceptional dishes include wild Irish venison loin, lamb saddle, or, for vegetarians, pappardelle pasta with black truffles and olive oil. **Known for:** venison and duck; first-class service; luxurious dining in opulent surroundings. $ *Average main: £24* ⊠ *35 Waring St., Cathedral Quarter* ☎ *028/9023–4888* ⊕ *www.themerchanthotel.com.*

James Street and Co

$$ | MODERN IRISH | The mainstay of this classy city-center big hitter with an epic reputation is County Tyrone sirloin, rib-eye, or beef fillet steaks as well as prime cuts cooked to your liking on a charcoal grill. Based in a former linen mill, exposed brick walls and leather banquettes set the scene for a terrific meal. **Known for:** charcoal grill steaks; buttery potatoes; heavenly Baked Alaska. $ *Average main: £16* ⊠ *21 James St. S, Central District* ☎ *028/9560–0700* ⊕ *www.jamesstandco.com.*

★ Made in Belfast: Cathedral Quarter

$$ | MODERN IRISH | This self-styled "restolounge" in the happening Cathedral Quarter is one of Belfast's buzziest bistros. Decorated in a giant mishmash of vintage lamps and fabrics, 1950s collectibles, and drawings from local artists, this outlet follows the Cuisinart school of restaurant design, mixing and matching all sorts of antiques and upcycled objects, including a ceiling covered in glossy magazine photographs. **Known for:** flatiron steaks; eccentric decor; impressive range of cocktails. $ *Average main: £16* ⊠ *23 Talbot St., Cathedral Quarter* ☎ *028/9545–8120* ⊕ *www.madeinbelfast-ni.com.*

★ The Morning Star

$ | IRISH | Halfway down a narrow lane is the 19th-century Morning Star, one of the city's most historic pubs, first built as a coaching stop for the Belfast-to-Dublin post. There's a traditional bar downstairs and a cozy velvet and wood-panel restaurant upstairs serving locally sourced food. **Known for:** grass-fed beef from family farm; local mussels; artisanal breads. $ *Average main: £13* ⊠ *17–19 Pottinger's Entry, Central District* ☎ *028/9023–5986* ⊕ *www.themorningstarbar.com.*

Mourne Seafood Bar

$$ | SEAFOOD | Connoisseurs of fresh fish and shellfish love Mourne Seafood, hidden down a side street and established as a firm favorite. Mussels are from Strangford Lough while oysters are sourced from shellfish beds in Carlingford Lough. **Known for:** seafood casserole; chunky chowder; truffle fries. $ *Average main: £16* ⊠ *34–36 Bank St., Central District* ☎ *028/9024–8544* ⊕ *www.mourneseafood.com.*

The Northern Whig

$ | EUROPEAN | Housed in an elegant former newspaper building in Belfast's historic Cathedral Quarter, the Northern Whig is spacious and stylish. In the evenings, one wall slides away so you can watch a jazz band, or a DJ playing folk and pop. **Known for:** brasserie-style food; traditional wooden bar; cocktails. $ *Average main: £12* ☒ *2–10 Bridge St., Central District* ☎ *028/9050–9888* ⊕ *www.thenorthernwhig.com.*

★ Ox Restaurant

$$$ | MODERN IRISH | You'd be hard-pressed to eat this well, for so little money, in such relaxed surroundings anywhere else in Northern Ireland or indeed the whole island. Lunches are either two courses (£22) or three (£28) with choices such as flatiron steak, or cod and lemongrass, and to cap it all, views through the large windows stretch over the River Lagan to the glowing 56-foot-tall Ring of Thanks-giving beacon by the Scottish artist Andy Scott. **Known for:** multicourse tasting menus; delicate white chocolate parfait; top-quality seasonal ingredients. $ *Average main: £22* ☒ *1 Oxford St., Central District* ☎ *028/9031–4121* ⊕ *www.oxbelfast.com* ☽ *Closed Sun. and Mon.*

Yard Bird

$$ | BRITISH | The humble chicken is the raison d'être of Yard Bird, on the site of a linen warehouse built in the 1750s. Start your visit with an aperitif in the Dirty Onion bar downstairs (ask the bartender about the pub's name), which retains the original, evocative tree-trunk-size beams, bare floors, and walls of the 18th century. **Known for:** tender rotisserie chicken; fast service; authentic pub with live music. $ *Average main: £16* ☒ *3 Hill St., Cathedral Quarter* ☎ *028/9024–3712* ⊕ *www.thedirtyonion.com.*

Zen

$$ | JAPANESE | The standout dishes at Belfast's finest Japanese restaurant are the sea bass and sole, or the Zen monkfish. Among the discerning diners who frequent this lively spot, the delicious assorted mushroom teppanyaki is also a big hit. **Known for:** sea bass and sole; monkfish in tangy sauce; sushi bar menu. $ *Average main: £16* ☒ *55–59 Adelaide St., behind City Hall, Central District* ☎ *028/9023–2244* ⊕ *www.zenbelfast.co.uk* ☽ *No lunch Sat.*

Hotels

Bullitt Hotel

$$$ | HOTEL | This new centrally located hotel takes its trendy vibes (and name) from the "King of Cool," Steve McQueen, and delivers a no-frills experience with compact rooms. **Pros:** stylish with a sense of humor; central location; meet the locals in the bar. **Cons:** rooms are small; not many facilities; traffic noise from busy street. $ *Rooms from: £120* ☒ *40A Church La., Central District* ☎ *028/9590–0600* ⊕ *www.bullitthotel.com* ⇌ *74 rooms* ⦿ *No meals.*

Clayton Hotel Belfast

$$$ | B&B/INN | A short stroll from the city center, the Clayton has bright new decor from a 2018 renovation and is the only hotel in the area with a leisure club and swimming pool, plus an endless choice of restaurants on its doorstep. **Pros:** value deals; health club and facilities are top-notch; excellent breakfasts. **Cons:** lines at busy times; no car-parking spaces available; surrounding streets can be noisy at night. $ *Rooms from: £140* ☒ *22 Ormeau Ave., Central District* ☎ *028/9032–8511* ⊕ *www.claytonhotelbelfast.com* ⇌ *170 rooms* ⦿ *Free breakfast.*

Grand Central Hotel

$$$$ | HOTEL | Echoing the name of a grand 20th-century hotel that stood on downtown Royal Avenue until the 1970s, this swish 23-floor venue is part of the Hastings portfolio and boasts the highest bar in Ireland. **Pros:** top location; lavish furnishings and fittings; panoramic views from top-floor bar. **Cons:** expensive rooms; no gym, pool, or parking; pricey cocktails. $ *Rooms from: £200* ☒ *Bedford St., Central District* ⊹ *City center, 5-min walk from City Hall* ☎ *028/9023–1066* ⊕ *www.grandcentralhotel.com* ⇌ *300 rooms* ⦿ *Free breakfast.*

Jurys Inn Belfast

$$$$ | HOTEL | Step inside this city-center hotel and you will feel the refreshing glow of a place that has been given a £9 million makeover and upped its game. But it's the new 80-bedroom extension that steals the show, where pebble-gray decor and burnt-orange furnishings set the scene. **Pros:** plush new extension with spacious rooms; speedy self-check-in; central location. **Cons:** extra charge for superior rooms; no parking, but discounted rates in two local car parks; large coach parties can take over. ⑤ *Rooms from: £250 ⊠ Fisherwick Pl., at Great Victoria St., Central District* ☎ *028/9053–3500* ⊕ *www.jurysinns.com* ➤ *270 rooms* ⦿*❙ Free breakfast.*

★ Malmaison

$$$$ | HOTEL | Living up to its claim to be "a hotel that dares to be different," this transformed 19th-century grain ware-house incorporates trendy decor choices, modern facilities, and elegant finishes, all the while retaining original details like cast-iron pillars, wood beams, and giant portholes (inside) and gargoyles (out-side). **Pros:** trendy decor; fantastic central location; lively bar and good restaurant. **Cons:** lack of car parking; dark bar not for everyone; service can be inconsistent. ⑤ *Rooms from: £195 ⊠ 34–38 Victoria St., Central District* ☎ *028/9022–0200* ⊕ *www.malmaison.com* ➤ *62 rooms* ⦿*❙ No meals.*

★ The Merchant Hotel

$$$$ | HOTEL | A mix of Victorian grandeur and Art Deco–inspired modernity, this hotel—regarded by some as Ireland's most spectacular—was built as the headquarters of Ulster Bank in the mid-19th century and still leads the way in style and sophistication. **Pros:** opulent guest rooms; a byword for glamour and cocktails; history and architecture buffs love it. **Cons:** noisy pubs nearby; breakfast room service is pricey; can be difficult to get a reservation in Great Room. ⑤ *Rooms from: £359 ⊠ 16 Skipper St.,* *Cathedral Quarter* ☎ *028/9023–4888* ⊕ *www.themerchanthotel.com* ➤ *67 rooms* ⦿*❙ Free breakfast.*

Roseleigh House

$$ | B&B/INN | This Victorian guesthouse on a tree-filled avenue in residential South Belfast, about 20 minutes south of the city center, is a friendly option. **Pros:** the breakfasts are healthy and robust; terrific suburban location away from city noise and just a 15-minute bus ride into town; owners eager to please. **Cons:** no bar, but around the corner are plenty; about 20 minutes from city center; no amenities. ⑤ *Rooms from: £105 ⊠ 19 Rosetta Park, Belfast ⊹ By car from city center follow signs to Newcastle and take Ravenhill Rd. to Rosetta roundabout; or board No. 78 Metro bus from City Hall along Ravenhill Rd. and alight at round-about at Rosetta, which is a 2-min walk from house* ☎ *028/9064–4414* ⊕ *www. roseleighhouse.co.uk* ➤ *7 rooms* ⦿*❙ Free breakfast.*

Ten Square

$$$$ | HOTEL | You don't get much more downtown or contemporary than this fashionable boutique hotel (a former post office) right behind City Hall, especially after a £1.5 million overhaul in 2017 added 70 bedrooms and modernized all rooms with smart technology. **Pros:** luxurious surroundings; attention to detail in the attractive rooms; super-king beds. **Cons:** few amenities; outside seating gets traffic fumes; no car parking. ⑤ *Rooms from: £170 ⊠ 10 Donegall Sq. S, Central District* ☎ *028/9024–1001* ⊕ *www. tensquare.co.uk* ➤ *130 rooms* ⦿*❙ Free breakfast.*

★ Titanic Hotel

$$$ | HOTEL | The former drawing office headquarters of Harland & Wolff shipyard where the RMS *Titanic* plans were cre-ated has been repurposed with panache (and £28 million), and 30 years after it closed, given a new lease on life as a lux-ury hotel that honors its nautical heritage without kitsch. **Pros:** excellent location

and views; skylights run length of bar; museum-worthy artifacts on display. **Cons:** modern bathrooms but can be cold; Titanic tourists everywhere; hallways a little dark. ⑤ *Rooms from: £from 130* ✉ *8 Queens Rd., Titanic Quarter ✛ Next door to Titanic Belfast Visitor Centre* ☎ *028/9508–2000* ⊕ *www.titanichotelbelfast.com* ⤵ *119 rooms* ⑪ *Free breakfast.*

Nightlife

Bittles Bar

BARS/PUBS | Colorful drawings of political, cultural, and social life hang on the walls of this triangular Victorian pub on the fringes of the Cathedral Quarter. The drawings are by talented local artist Joe O'Kane, a pub patron. From a selection of rotating taps, Bittles serves local craft brews such as Farmageddon cider, Hilden ales, Cute Hoor, and Chieftain IPA from Franciscan Well Brewery, Cork. It also stocks a large range of craft gins, including Gunpowder from Drumshanbo in Leitrim, and two local ones, Shortcross and Belfast 1912. ✉ *70 Upper Church La., Cathedral Quarter.*

The Duke of York

BARS/PUBS | Along a narrow cobblestone alleyway bang in the heart of the Cathedral Quarter, the Duke of York specializes in rare antique whiskeys. With its ancient mirrors, vintage signage, and other memorabilia, it is a glittering shrine to long-forgotten distilleries—but more importantly it's also the best whiskey bar in Belfast, if not all of Ulster. It's said they have a better selection of rare Bushmills whiskeys than the famous distillery itself. One of the most popular is 12-year-old Redbreast, while their Powers John Lane is a classy single-pot-still whiskey, also 12 years, with a combination of bourbon- and oloroso-sherry-cask-matured spirits. ✉ *7–11 Commercial Ct., Cathedral Quarter ✛ Cathedral Quarter* ☎ *028/9024–1062* ⊕ *www.dukeofyorkbelfast.com.*

Hell Cat Maggies

BARS/PUBS | This first-floor New York–inspired bar beside City Hall is named after a formidable character who was born in Ireland and raised hell with the Dead Rabbit street gang, part of the infamous Gang of New York in the 1800s. Drinks, such as the Bowery Brawler and the New York Freeze, reflect the connection. The food, served from noon, includes mussels with Guinness and garlic, falafal burgers, chicken stack, waffle fries, or shrimp cocktail. ✉ *2 Donegall Sq. W, Central District* ☎ *028/9050–9777* ⊕ *www.hellcat-maggies.com.*

The John Hewitt Bar

BARS/PUBS | A must for every traveler, this bar named after one of Ulster's most famous poets (who ironically wasn't a big drinker) is traditional in style with a marble counter, waist-high wooden paneling, high ceilings, and open fire. It channels Hewitt's socialist sensibility, as it's owned by the Belfast Unemployed Centre (which it helps fund with its profits)—top pub grub is served from noon to 4 pm and live music is featured most nights. Irish artisanal cider and bottled craft beers are the most popular. ✉ *51 Donegall St., Cathedral Quarter* ☎ *028/9023–3768* ⊕ *www.thejohnhewitt.com.*

Kremlin

BARS/PUBS | A massive statue of Lenin above the front door greets patrons of the city's oldest gay club. The over-the-top Soviet theme continues inside. Superstar DJs regularly fly in to perform. ✉ *96 Donegall St., Cathedral Quarter* ☎ *028/9031–6060* ⊕ *www.kremlin-belfast.com.*

Madden's Bar

BARS/PUBS | A popular locals' favorite near the Castle Court mall, Madden's has live music nightly and traditional tune fests with set dancing on Wednesday night. ✉ *74 Berry St. behind Castle Court, Central District* ☎ *028/9024–4114.*

McHugh's

BARS/PUBS | In Belfast's oldest building (1711), McHugh's has three floors of bars and restaurants, and live music Thursday to Sunday. Food is served from lunchtime in the downstairs bar, while dinner—including special "on the hot rock" steaks, cooked to your liking—is available 6 pm–9 pm in the upstairs restaurant. McHugh's retains the character of an early-18th-century dockside inn and exudes a homey feel with open fires. ⊠ 29–31 Queen's Sq., Central District ☏ 028/9050–9999 ⊕ www.mchughsbar. com.

★ The National Grande Café

CAFES—NIGHTLIFE | Named after its former bank occupant, the National underwent an eco-friendly face-lift in 2019 to enhance the overall experience at this café as well as food and drink offerings. The £425,000 renovation included a new retractable roof, energy-efficient natural-gas heating in the popular beer garden, and the introduction of a closed-loop system enabling all parts of the fruit to be used in cocktails without waste. Ingredients in the food are sourced within 64 km (40 miles) of Belfast and, to cut down the amount of glass or plastic, the bar filters and carbonates its own tap water. Quality deluxe sandwiches with beef brisket, chicken, or pulled pork, along with tapas, croques, and salads span the menu throughout the day; to wash your food down choose from hangover cures, low-alcohol gin, or bracing cocktails such as the National Spritz, Nitro Espresso martini, or Irish coffee made with Powers whiskey (all £10). The nightclub has also been rebranded and renamed Upstairs at The National. ⊠ 62–68 High St., Central District ☏ 028/9031–1130 ⊕ www.thenationalbelfast.com.

Union Street Pub

BARS/PUBS | A gay-friendly bar near the Cathedral Quarter, Union Street is housed in a converted 19th-century shoe factory. The three-story redbrick Victorian is one of the city's few gastropubs, with a more formal upstairs restaurant that's popular with local foodies. ⊠ 8–14 Union St., Central District ☏ 028/9031–6060 ⊕ www.unionstreetbar.com.

White's Tavern

BARS/PUBS | A roaring fire greets you as soon as you enter White's Tavern, which claims to be the oldest public house in Belfast. Friendly staff serve pub grub until 8 pm, including the famous creamy, buttery, cholesterol-laden potato champ served as a side dish with pork burgers, battered chicken, steak, or fish. Live-music sessions are held in the downstairs bar on weekend evenings. When the weather cooperates, catch a free movie outside in the courtyard cinema. ⊠ 2–12 Winecellar Entry, Central District ☏ 028/9031–2582 ⊕ www.whitesbelfast. com.

Performing Arts

Belfast Waterfront

CONCERTS | This world-class performance venue, which doubled its exhibition space in 2015, houses a 2,235-seat concert hall (for ballet and classical, rock, and Irish music) and a 500-seat studio space (for modern dance, jazz, and experimental theater). The Arc Brasserie (5–7:30) and two bars make the Waterfront a convenient place to eat, have a pint, and enjoy the river views before or after your culture fix. The main box office for booking events here is based at the Ulster Hall in Bedford Street. ⊠ 2 Lanyon Pl., East Bridge St. ☏ 028/9033–4400 ⊕ www.waterfront.co.uk.

Ulster Hall

CONCERTS | The historic Ulster Hall (it once hosted Rachmaninov) is the permanent home of the Ulster Orchestra. The classical music season runs here from September through April. Concerts are mostly held on Friday, but you can call or check online (⊕ www.ulsterorchestra. com) to learn about other dates and

Get your perfect pint of Guinness at the Crown Liquor Saloon, a Victorian extravaganza of embossed ceilings, gilded arabesques, and carved woodwork.

free open rehearsals and 50-minute lunchtime concerts. Apart from classical, the hall presents rock, folk, traditional Irish, blues, jazz, and other forms, along with comedy and cabaret acts. With its superb acoustics, Ulster Hall provides the perfect listening and foot-tapping experience. ⊠ *Bedford St., Central District* ☎ *028/9033–4455* ⊕ *www.ulsterhall. co.uk.*

 ## Shopping

FOOD

Sawers Deli

FOOD/CANDY | From feta cheese to foie gras, there's a dazzling selection of artisanal foods from local and international suppliers at this deli, founded in 1897. The new sensation is Irish Black Butter, which is not actually a dairy product but a delicious spread made from cider, brandy, spices, and treacle for toast or local soda bread. Browse the shelves for a trip through some of the finest Northern Irish produce. Find Robert Ditty's Irish oatcakes rolled with County Armagh oats; salty and flavor-filled Kearney blue cheese from the Ards Peninsula; the lemony, zesty bolie log, a soft goat cheese from the famed Fivemiletown creamery in County Tyrone; and a raft of jams and spiced apple chutney from Erin Grove Preserves in Fermanagh—all set alongside a selection of wheat and focaccia breads. Don't forget the Suki tea made by the Belfast Brew company, which specializes in loose-leaf teas and old-fashioned teapots. ⊠ *Fountain Centre, 5–6 College St., Central District* ☎ *028/9032–2021* ⊕ *www.sawersbelfast. com.*

GALLERIES

Artcetera Studio

ART GALLERIES—ARTS | Opened in 2016, Artcetera displays painting and photography by local artists and hosts occasional lunchtime or evening music events. The gallery also presents art by students from the nearby Ulster University. ⊠ *43b Rosemary St., Central District* ☎ *028/9573–8500.*

Belfast Exposed

ART GALLERIES—ARTS | A photography gallery, Belfast Exposed also has a large digital archive of images. Talks by local artists and exhibitions are held regularly. ✉ *23 Donegall St., Cathedral Quarter* ☎ *028/9023–0965* ⊕ *www.belfastexposed.org.*

Golden Thread Gallery

ART GALLERIES—ARTS | One of Belfast's best arts venues, the Golden Thread has exhibited at the Venice Biennale and the International Symposium for Electronic Art. The gallery presents visual art from paintings on canvas to the latest digital arts. Their two key objectives are to increase public access to the contemporary visual arts and generate support for Northern Irish art and artists. ✉ *84–94 Great Patrick St., Cathedral Quarter* ☎ *028/9033–0920* ⊕ *www.goldenthreadgallery.co.uk.*

Space Craft

ART GALLERIES—ARTS | Unique gifts are for sale in this shop that is the new retail branch of Craft Northern Ireland, a collective of local artists and designers. Here you will find traditional-frame-weaving baskets made from willow, terra-cotta plates, ceramic figurines, pewter jewelry, hand-carved papier mâché dolls, machine-stitched maps, bespoke furniture, and much more. The shop hosts exhibitions as well as the Arts Council craft collection each year. ✉ *Fountain Centre, College St., 1st fl., Central District* ☎ *028/9032–9342* ⊕ *www.craftni.org* ⊠ *Free.*

GIFTS
Utopia

JEWELRY/ACCESSORIES | Stocked with everything from toys to costume jewelery, Utopia sells intricate silver pendants and earrings made by local designer Alpha Zed. Also worth a look are the wooden, alabaster, and metal chess sets. ✉ *Fountain Centre, College St., Central District* ☎ *028/9024–1342.*

The Wicker Man

GIFTS/SOUVENIRS | Aficionados of *Game of Thrones* love this shop, which specializes in merchandise from the hit TV series. Offerings linked to local locations from the program include coasters, calendars, mugs, notebooks, shot glasses, mats, badges, posters, and postcards. Shelves and cabinets are filled with quality Irish crafts including knitwear, pottery, linen, and jewelry such as claddagh rings, as well as mini sods of Irish-turf incense and tea towels bearing colloquial Belfast and Ulster phrases. ✉ *18 High St., Central District* ☎ *028/9024–3550* ⊕ *www.thewickerman.co.uk.*

JEWELRY
The Steensons

JEWELRY/ACCESSORIES | A major draw of the superb handcrafted and locally designed jewelry in this goldsmiths is a new range of products inspired by the *Game of Thrones* TV series. Display cabinets showcase sterling silver cuff links, necklaces, earrings, and a range of pins and pendants connected to the series costing between £95 and £145. Pieces include crowns, Margaery's "Purple Wedding," Cersei's lion pendant, and Littlefinger's mockingbird pin. The shop also stocks the work of more than 50 European and local designers. ✉ *Bedford House, Bedford St., Central District* ☎ *028/9024–8269* ⊕ *www.thesteensons.com.*

MARKETS AND MALLS
Castle Court

SHOPPING CENTERS/MALLS | The city's second-largest shopping mall is euro-friendly, with most shops accepting it alongside the pound sterling. Many international stores, gift shops, and cafés can be found under Castle Court's glass roof, next to British clothing chains such as Miss Selfridge and Dorothy Perkins. For one-stop shopping, head for Debenham's department store, which has everything from cosmetics to kitchenware. ✉ *10 Royal Ave., Central District*

☏ *028/9023–4591* ⊕ *www.castlecourt-uk. com.*

★ St. George's Market

OUTDOOR/FLEA/GREEN MARKETS | For an authentic blast of Belfast life, make your way to the enormous indoor St. George's Market on Friday, Saturday, and Sunday. When it opened in the 1890s, this historic market sold butter, eggs, poultry, and fruit. Today it is a vibrant place with 150 traders selling everything from organically grown produce to zippers and antiques to local art and curios. The Friday Variety Market starts at 6 am and runs until 2 pm; the Saturday City Food and Garden Market, 9–3; and the Sunday Food, Craft, and Antique market, 10–4. There's an international culinary flavor with Cuban sandwiches, savory crepes, paella, tapas, pizzas, and Thai dishes. Foodies love the treats at Aunt Sandra's Candy Factory stall, with its fudge and flavored sweets, and the 25 terrific breads at Piece of Cake Bakery. Next door is S. D. Bell's coffee stand; the company is older than the market, as it was set up in 1887 and has been brewing nonstop ever since. ✉ *12–20 E. Bridge St., Central District* ☏ *028/9043–5704* ⊕ *www.belfastcity. gov.uk/stgeorgesmarket.*

★ Victoria Square

SHOPPING NEIGHBORHOODS | Occupying an eight-block site in central Belfast, this shopping center has changed the Belfast skyline. The flagship 800,000-square-foot shopping complex, all glittering steel, is presided over by a vast geodesic glass dome eight stories high. The House of Fraser department store is the main anchor tenant and designer shops such as Cruise, Hugo Boss, and Michael Kors provide shoppers their fix of happiness. Coffee shops, fast-food restaurants, and an eight-screen cinema are also on-site. The complex paints a delightful architectural contrast, incorporating noted Victorian landmarks such as the McErvel's Seed Warehouse and the Royal Belfast Ginger Ale Manufactory. ■TIP➔ Make your way

up to the viewing gallery for great views of Belfast; admission is free and a guide can show you the sights. The **Q-Park** (⊕ *www.q-park.co.uk*) provides 1,000 parking spaces and is open 24/7. ✉ *1 Victoria Sq., at Chichester, Montgomery, Ann, and Victoria Sts., Central District* ☏ *028/9032–2277* ⊕ *www.victoriasquare.com.*

University Area

At Belfast's southern end, the part of the city around Queen's University is dotted with parks, botanical gardens, and leafy streets with fine, intact, two- and three-story 19th-century buildings. The area evokes an older, more leisurely pace of life. The many pubs and excellent restaurants make this area the hub of the city's nightlife. However, remember that Belfast is a student town and this is the main university area—the pace of life here can be fast (and sometimes a little furious) during school-term weekends.

 ## Sights

Botanic Gardens

GARDEN | In the Victorian heyday it was not unusual to find 10,000 of Belfast's citizens strolling about here on a Saturday afternoon. These gardens are a glorious haven of grass, trees, flowers, curving walks, and wrought-iron benches, all laid out in 1827 on land that slopes down to the River Lagan. The curved-iron and glass Palm House is a conservatory marvel designed in 1839 by Charles Lanyon. Inside, the hot "stove wing" is a minijungle of exotic plants such as the bird-of-paradise flower and heavily scented frangipani. The Tropical Ravine House reopened in 2018 after extensive restorations, which allow visitors to experience it as it would have looked when it was built between 1877 and 1902. In the main grounds you can wander around the arboretum and the 100-year-old rockery, or in summer savor the colors and scents of the herbaceous borders. ■TIP➔ A fun

Fern Madness

One of the highlights of a visit to Belfast's Botanic Gardens is the Tropical Ravine House, a lush cathedral of greenery, restored during 2018 at a cost of £3.8 million, and an internationally significant building. Victorians brought many specimens back to Ireland from their travels in the mid-19th century that natural history experts labeled pteridomania, or "fern madness." Through pictorial signboards, information panels, microscopes, audio and hands-on displays, visitors can explore close up the life cycle of these exotic plants against a background of birdsong. Old features such as the waterfall,

cascade, and pool have been reinstated and are home to the giant lily Victoria amazonica. Walk around the upper canopy and cast-iron columns and you will be astounded at the smells and the scale of the ferns and trees. Some, such as the firewheel tree, are native to the Australian rain forest, while the custard tree, which blends the taste of banana, pineapple, papaya, peach, and strawberry, is from Central and South America. Hour-long guided tours are held at 11 on Tuesday and Thursday morning and at 2 on Wednesday afternoon. Advance booking is essential. ⊕ www.belfastcity.gov.uk/events

challenge is to follow the Tree Trail, which leads you around 20 trees, many planted in the 19th century, with specimens such as the Tree-of-Heaven, Japanese red cedar, and the wonderful Ginkgo biloba from China. ⊠ Stranmillis Rd., University Area ☎ 028/9031–4762 ⊕ www.belfastcity.gov.uk ⊠ Free.

Queen's University Belfast

COLLEGE | Dominating University Road is Queen's University. The main buildings, modeled on Oxford's Magdalen College and designed by the ubiquitous Charles Lanyon, were built in 1849 in the Tudor Revival style. The long, handsome, redbrick-and-sandstone facade of the main building features large lead-glass windows, and is topped with three square towers and crenellations galore. University Square, really a terrace, is from the same era. The Seamus Heaney Library is named after the Ulster-born 1997 Nobel Prize–winning poet who died in 2013. The McClay Library in College Park features a multistory open atrium, 1.5 million volumes, and the Brian Friel Theatre, named in honor of one of

Ireland's most illustrious playwrights. The C. S. Lewis reading room on the first floor has a replica of the wardrobe door used in the film *The Lion, the Witch, and the Wardrobe*. The Queen's Welcome Centre hosts a program of exhibitions and serves as a visitor information point. Guided tours are available but must be booked in advance. ⊠ University Rd., University Area ☎ 028/9097–5252 ⊕ www.qub.ac.uk ⊠ Free.

★ Ulster Museum

MUSEUM | FAMILY | Next door to the Botanic Gardens, the rejuvenated Ulster Museum is a big hit with visitors for its spacious light-filled atrium and polished steel. The museum's forte is the history and prehistory of Ireland, using exhibitions to colorfully trace the rise of Belfast's crafts, trade, and industry. In addition, the museum has a large natural history section, with a famed skeleton of the extinct Irish giant deer and a trove of jewelry and gold ornaments recovered from the Spanish Armada vessel *Girona*, which sank off the Antrim Coast in 1588. Take time to seek out the *Girona*'s stunning gold salamander studded with

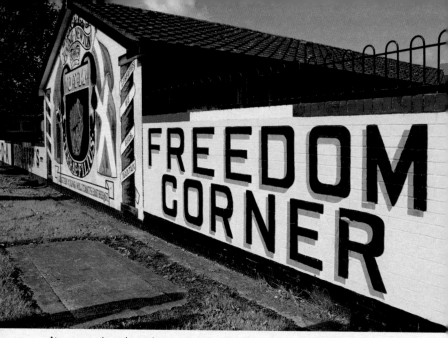

At a conservative estimate, there are more than 70 wall murals throughout the city.

rubies and still dazzling after 400 years in the Atlantic. The museum includes a first-rate collection of 19th- and 20th-century art from Europe, Britain, and America. The Modern History gallery tells the story of Ulster from 1500 to 1968 and shows a remarkable range of objects from the history collection, many on display for the first time. A new permanent exhibition installed in 2018 presents a somber look at the history of the civil and political conflict in Northern Ireland. "The Troubles and Beyond" recounts in a graphic way the story of three decades of communal violence covering the 1970s, '80s, and '90s. Through a wide variety of images, including reproduction of wall murals, maps, photographs, and propaganda ephemera, as well as videos, listening posts, and screens, the harrowing story of the conflict, which claimed more than 3,000 lives is told in an engaging way. Look out for two poignant wall exhibits: the Peace Quilt, a red fabric with white birds representing the dove of peace and a teddy bear as a reminder of the children who suffered the loss of loved ones;

and a powerful oil painting by the artist Jack Pakenham, *Peace Talks,* completed in 1992 as Northern Ireland moved slowly towards a resolution of the Troubles. The art, history, and nature discovery zones are packed with hands-on activities for children. Kids enjoy the Peter the Polar Bear exhibit and the famed Egyptian mummy, Takabuti. There's an innovative 360-degree light-and-sound immersive experience, museum shop, café, and restaurant. ■ TIP→ **Sunday morning is the quietest time to visit, but go early before the crowds. Afterward, lay out a picnic in the Belfast Botanical Gardens next door.** ⊠ *Stranmillis Rd., University Area* ☎ *028/9044–0000* ⊕ *www.nmni.com/um* ✉ *Free* ⊙ *Closed Mon., except for Northern Irish holidays.*

 Hotels

Benedict's of Belfast
$$ | HOTEL | Friendly, lively, and convenient, Benedict's looms large on Bradbury Place in the heart of the action beside the bright lights of Shaftesbury Square.

Pros: triple glazing in rooms; great inexpensive dining; 10-minute walk from the city center. **Cons:** guests have experienced late check-in due to rooms not being ready; not many extras; service can be inconsistent. ⓢ *Rooms from: £85* ✉ *7–21 Bradbury Pl., University Area* ☎ *028/9059–1999* ⊕ *www.benedictshotel.co.uk* ⌐ *32 rooms* ⦿ *Free breakfast.*

Dukes at Queens

$ | HOTEL | Although it retains its distinguished redbrick Victorian facade, the inside of this handsome hotel on bohemian Botanic Avenue has been revamped in a cool contemporary style with chic, modern guest rooms. **Pros:** stylish; good value for the price; five-minute walk from Queen's University and the Botanic Gardens. **Cons:** noisy, busy area; bar can get very crowded; on-street parking difficult. ⓢ *Rooms from: £80* ✉ *65–67 University St., University Area* ☎ *028/9023–6666* ⊕ *www.dukesatqueens.com* ⌐ *32 rooms* ⦿ *Free breakfast.*

The Old Rectory Guesthouse

$$ | B&B/INN | Upscale breakfasts are the big draw at Mary and Jerry Callan's well-appointed South Belfast house built in 1896 as a Church of Ireland rectory. **Pros:** beautifully prepared, hearty breakfasts; suite-size rooms; historic house. **Cons:** hard to find; no bar; few amenities. ⓢ *Rooms from: £98* ✉ *148 Malone Rd., University Area* ☎ *028/9066–7882* ⊕ *www.anoldrectory.co.uk* ⌐ *7 rooms* ⦿ *Free breakfast.*

 Nightlife

Alibi

BARS/PUBS | On Friday and Saturday nights, Alibi comes alive upstairs for clubbers and local nighthawks. Downstairs, from 5 to 10 pm, the bar serves pizzas or chips. There's a cinema club on Tuesday night and the prosecco flows on Friday. ✉ *23–31 Bradbury Pl., University Area* ☎ *028/9023–3131* ⊕ *www.alibibelfast. com* ⌐ *£10 Sat.*

★ Belfast Empire Music Hall

BARS/PUBS | Inside a deconsecrated church, the Music Hall has been one of the city's leading music venues for more than 30 years. Most nights are devoted to concerts from groups such as local heroes Snow Patrol. Stand-up comedy nights are usually on Tuesday—Patrick Kielty was a regular until he hit the big time in London. The Rab McCullough blues nights on Thursday are popular, as is the long-running Ken Haddock's supper club on Sunday night. ✉ *42 Botanic Ave., University Area* ☎ *028/9024–9276* ⊕ *www.thebelfastempire.com.*

Botanic Inn

BARS/PUBS | Known as "the Bot" to its student clientele, the Botanic is a big, popular disco-pub. ✉ *23–27 Malone Rd., University Area* ☎ *028/9050–9740* ⊕ *www.thebotanicinn.com.*

Chelsea Wine Bar

BARS/PUBS | Packed with affluent professionals determined to prove that life begins at 30, the Chelsea serves reasonably priced contemporary gastropub cuisine and has 100-plus wines on its list. There's live music on Friday and Saturday evening in the downstairs bar. ✉ *346 Lisburn Rd., University Area* ☎ *028/9068–7177* ⊕ *www.chelseawinebar.com.*

Cutters Wharf

BARS/PUBS | Down by the river south of the university, this bar and upstairs restaurant is at its best on summer evenings and during music performances on Sunday after 6. Spacious and light inside, it rarely gets too packed; if seating is limited, try the picnic tables and chairs on the wooden deck outside. ✉ *4 Lockview Rd., University Area* ☎ *028/9080–5100* ⊕ *www.cutterswharf.co.uk.*

The Playwright

BARS/PUBS | Moody black-and-white framed portraits of famous Irish novelists, poets, and playwrights such as Oscar Wilde and George Bernard Shaw adorn the walls of this liquor lounge and taphouse, popular with students and visitors. Sip a glass of wine or beer and reflect on the words of Wilde, who said, "Alcohol, taken in sufficient quantities, may produce all the effects of drunkenness." A much sought-after drink here is the smooth-flavored Pogues whiskey—named in honor of the legendary band—which has an aroma of malts and cracked nuts. Live bar entertainment features acoustic acts from Thursday to Sunday, while the huge Time nightclub on the first and second floors is open Friday and Saturday nights with music from local DJs. ⊠ *5–6 Lower Crescent, University Area* ☎ *028/9031–2742.*

Town Square Bar

BARS/PUBS | Gin is top of the bill at the newly styled Town Square, which offers a sparkling collection of cocktails. The local Jawbox gin is paired with ginger ale, lime, and coriander, while the Aviation cocktail comes with star anise, berries, and tonic—all alongside a range of rotating taps of beer and cider. Try the Irish Noir cocktail, made up of Black Bush, vermouth, toffee tincture, and Peychaud's bitters. As part of the restyle, a gin bar was added, as well as newly created space for concerts, wine tastings, and fund-raising events. ⊠ *13 Lower Crescent, University Area* ☎ *079/3824–4851* ⊕ *www.townsquarebelfast.com.*

 Performing Arts

The Crescent Arts Centre

ART GALLERIES—ARTS | Based in a beautifully restored rambling stone building—a former girls' high school—the Crescent presents an all-year-round series of events. Experimental dance and theater, concerts, and workshops are all part of the program. The center also hosts the Belfast Book Festival (in the second week of June) during which writers participate in lively talks, lectures, and readings. Exhibitions are held in the upstairs gallery. Light meals and snacks are available at lunchtime in the Pantry Café, where storyboards tell the history of the building and famous locals connected to it. ■**TIP**➔ **Nature note: between May and July, common swifts fly in from southern Africa to nest above the center's stone walls. Special "swift bricks" have been installed to provide nesting sites.** ⊠ *2 University Rd., University Area* ☎ *028/9024–2338* ⊕ *www.crescentarts. org.*

★ Lyric Theatre

THEATER | One of Northern Ireland's most prized cultural organizations, the Lyric presents a diverse repertory of classical, popular, and contemporary drama, frequently showcasing the work of local playwrights. With its angular brick bulk topped by three distinctive sloping roofs, the theater is an impressive Modernist achievement. The Lyric's famed patron Liam Neeson made his 1976 stage debut here in Brian Friel's *Philadelphia, Here I Come!* Strong emphasis is placed on the use of natural light, with a glass-walled Long Hall running the length of the first floor and looking out over the River Lagan. The main auditorium is lined with iroko wood and has 33 different styles of brick, all specially fired so each one is complete and uncut. In addition to the main 390-seat venue, presided over by the Danske Bank Stage, the Naughton Studios, a theater space, holds up to 125 people. In the foyer look out for the stunning wall portraits of local actors, playwrights, and poets painted by the renowned Belfast artist Colin Davidson. ⊠ *55 Ridgeway St., University Area* ☎ *028/9038–1081* ⊕ *www.lyrictheatre. co.uk.*

Queen's Film Theatre (QFT)

FILM | Belfast's main art cinema shows domestic and foreign movies on its two screens. ⊠ *20 University Sq., University Area* ☎ *028/9097–1097* ⊕ *www.queens-filmtheatre.com.*

🍽 Shopping

No Alibis

BOOKS/STATIONERY | For more than 20 years, No Alibis has been specializing in Irish, British, and American crime thrillers, as well as general fiction and nonfiction, plus a smattering of the work by local novelists and poets. All in all, it's a bibliophile's delight with knowledgeable staff and regular book launches and literary readings, some of which are held in the nearby Ulster Museum. The shop hosts jazz, blues, and other music events on Friday night. ⊠ *83 Botanic Ave., University Area* ☎ *028/9031–9601* ⊕ *www. noalibis.com.*

East Belfast

A number of excellent restaurants and cafés have sprung up in East Belfast. These are a handy stopping-off point, especially if you are visiting Parliament Buildings at Stormont for a tour or a walk around the grounds, or are exploring sights along the coast leading down to Strangford Lough. The main suburban area to focus on is Ballyhackamore, on the Upper Newtownards Road, and because of a proliferation of new restaurants, cafés, and bars, the area has become known to locals as "Bally-snack-amore."

If you are driving, you can park in some of the area's side streets or hop on the new Glider bus (G1), a rapid-transit service connecting the east and west of the city, which leaves from close to City Hall and takes about 20 minutes to reach the area.

🍴 Restaurants

Neill's Hill Cafe & Brasserie

$ | EUROPEAN | Named after a long-forgotten railway station in East Belfast, this casual brasserie has established itself as a calming spot in buzzy Ballyhackamore,

Dormant Ed Isn't Dead

The Ulster Museum's showstopper, *Edmontosaurus,* is the most complete dinosaur fossil on display in Ireland. "Ed," as he's affectionately known, roamed America about 70 million years ago and would have looked a bit like a plucked turkey. At 20 feet long, Ed has settled into his 21st-century home and is now a big attraction.

where lunchtimes can get crowded. Dishes change monthly, but typical main courses for dinner are burgers, steaks, pork fillet, prawns, lemon sole, and sea bass from Walter Ewing, Belfast's top fish supplier. **Known for:** local Portavogie prawns; awesome weekend brunches; Sunday roast carvery dinner. $ *Average main: £12* ⊠ *229 Upper Newtownards Rd., East Belfast* ☎ *028/9065–0079* ⊕ *www.neillshill.com.*

🎬 Performing Arts

SSE Arena

CONCERTS | The Belfast Giants hockey team is the main tenant of the 10,000-seat SSE Arena, but Northern Ireland's biggest indoor venue also hosts rock, pop, and classical concerts. The adjacent SSE Pavilion complex has bars, restaurants, shops, and nightclubs. ⊠ *2 Queen's Quay, Titanic Quarter* ☎ *028/9076–6000* ⊕ *www.ssearenabelfast.com.*

West Belfast

The self-contained, village-y feel of Andersonstown (known to locals as Andy-town) bustles with shops, restaurants, bars, and takeaways. If you are on a tour of the murals of the area, the Falls

Road is a 20-minute walk away. You can reach the area on the new Glider G1 bus service or Metro bus, or simply hail one of the many taxis that operate around the roads. During the height of the Troubles in the 1970s and '80s, this area experienced some of the worst violence, but is now a safe place to visit.

Restaurants

Wolf and Whistle Restaurant

$ | IRISH | Beside Casement Park—home ground of the Antrim Gaelic Athletic Club—this popular restaurant is just the place to catch your breath after taking a Black Taxi tour of the nearby political murals. The menu focuses on steaks and burgers, but you can also enjoy a wide selection of salads. **Known for:** well-dressed burgers; extensive salad selection; large portions. $ *Average main: £13* ⊠ *67–71 Andersonstown Rd., West Belfast* ☎ *028/9060–2210* ⊕ *www. wolfandwhistlebar.co.uk.*

Performing Arts

Cultúrlann McAdam Ó Fiaich

ART GALLERIES—ARTS | Celebrating *Gaeilge* (Irish language) and culture, this cosmopolitan arts center hosts exhibitions, book launches, concerts, theater, and poetry readings. Two choirs—one from a children's drama school and the other from resident theater company Aisling Ghéar—are based here. For travelers interested in the Gaeltacht experience, this is a great place to start. On the ground floor, the Dillon Gallery, named after the Falls Road artist Gerard Dillon, who spent much time painting in Connemara in the West of Ireland, mounts shows by top local and international artists. A shop sells Irish-language and English books as well as crafts and the all-important West Belfast Mural Map. Also here are a tourist information point, Wi-Fi access, and Restaurant Bia. Ask for information about the Gaeltacht Way, a 4-km (2½-mile) walking route that takes in the major Irish language-related sites of the area. ⊠ *216 Falls Rd., West Belfast* ☎ *028/9096–4180* ⊕ *www.culturlann.ie.*

East of Belfast

The area that lies East of Belfast covers North County Down and the towns of Holywood, Bangor and Newtownards, all within a 10-mile radius of the city. This area is locally known as the "Gold Coast" since it is the home of several lavish hotels and Northern Ireland's most expensive and secluded privately owned houses. The main one that is open to the public is Mount Stewart, owned by the National Trust, on the shores of Strangford Lough and well worth a day trip from Belfast. The Ulster Folk and Transport Museum at Cultra, near Holywood, showcases the social history of Northern Irish life.

Hotels

★ Culloden Estate & Spa

$$$$ | HOTEL | This imposing, grand vision in Belfast stone presides over the forested slopes of the Holywood hills and the busy waters of Belfast Lough. **Pros:** mansion is rich in character; comfy Egyptian-cotton bedding; fairy-tale setting with great views. **Cons:** restaurant can get busy; massages, manicures, and vintage champagne don't come cheap; 10-minute drive from city center. $ *Rooms from: £280* ⊠ *142 Bangor Rd., 8 km (5 miles) east of Belfast on A2, Holywood* ☎ *028/9042–1066* ⊕ *www.hastingsho-tels.com/culloden-estate-and-spa* ⇝ *98 rooms* ❍ *Free breakfast.*

★ The Old Inn

$$ | B&B/INN | Set in the village of Crawfordsburn, this 1614 coach inn—reputedly Ireland's oldest—certainly looks the part: it's pure 17th century, with a sculpted thatch roof, half doors, and leaded-glass windows. **Pros:** a proverbial

step back in time; lots of 17th-century character; comfortable rooms. **Cons:** slow service; breakfasts not always up to snuff; public transport limited so a car is necessary. $ *Rooms from: £110* ✉ *15 Main St., 16 km (10 miles) east of Belfast on A2, Crawfordsburn* ⊹ *The Old Inn is in center of Crawfordsburn, just off main A2 road to Bangor County Down* ☎ *028/9185–3255* ⊕ *www.theoldinn.com* ⤷ *33 rooms* ❄❄ *Free breakfast.*

Rayanne House

$$$ | **B&B/INN** | Since the 100th anniversary of the sinking of the RMS *Titanic* in 2012, this country house has enjoyed unparalleled success by re-creating the liner's "last meal," a highlight of any stay here. **Pros:** bright, airy rooms with garden views; handsome furnishings; sumptuous nine-course menu. **Cons:** Holywood nightlife is limited to a few bars; bit of a trek to city center; few amenities. $ *Rooms from: £145* ✉ *60 Demesne Rd., Holywood* ⊹ *Follow A2 east of Belfast to town of Holywood, approx 8 km (5 miles) by car on main road to Bangor, County Down* ☎ *028/9042–5859* ⊕ *www. rayannehouse.com* ⤷ *11 rooms* ❄❄ *Free breakfast.*

Day Trips from Belfast

The sights along the Ards Peninsula, mid County Down, and the north coast are a short drive from Belfast—an hour or less, perfect for day trips.

Sights

★ Belfast Castle

CASTLE/PALACE | In 1934 this spectacularly baronial castle, built for the Marquess of Donegall in 1865, was passed to the Belfast Corporation. Although the castle functions primarily as a restaurant, it also houses, in the cellar, the Cave Hill Visitor Centre, which provides information about the castle's history and its natural surroundings in Cave Hill Country

Carbing Up

When it comes to food, Northern Ireland is most famed (or notorious) for its Ulster yry, a fried-up carbohydrate blowout of a breakfast that is a cardiologist's nightmare. Sausage, bacon, eggs, black pudding, fried soda bread, and potato bread (and perhaps a grilled tomato or fried mushrooms) all make a meal that sounds as dangerous to your health as bungee jumping without a harness. After a night on the Guinness, however, you'll understand why this breakfast is so popular: it makes a great cure for a hangover.

Park. Tours are self-guided and take in the reception rooms built by the Earls of Shaftesbury. For a fine introduction to the castle and park, check out the excellent eight-minute video *Watching over Belfast*. In fact, the best reason to visit the castle is to stroll the ornamental gardens and then make the ascent to McArt's Fort. This promontory, at the top of sheer cliffs 1,200 feet above the city, affords an excellent view across Belfast. Take the path uphill from the parking lot, turn right at the next intersection of pathways, and then keep left as you journey up the steep-in-places hill to the fort. ■ **TIP**→ **After your walk, the Tavern Bar is a great place for drinks, snacks, and meals.** ✉ *Antrim Rd., 4 km (2½ miles) north of Belfast, North Belfast* ☎ *028/9077–6925* ⊕ *www.belfastcastle.co.uk* ✉ *Free.*

Belfast Zoo

ZOO | **FAMILY** | From the superstar Chilean flamingos and a silverback gorilla to spot-necked otters, West African chimps, and Goodfellow's tree kangaroos, you can enjoy the spectacle of more than 150 types of the world's most exotic creatures on a visit to Belfast Zoo. Great strides have transformed this place into a friendly environment for the animals. Note that it's on the steep side of Cave Hill and getting around the zoo involves a strenuous uphill walk for even the most energetic (not ideal for anyone with mobility problems)—a stroller would be advisable for small children. A popular attraction at the Rainforest House, a walk-through exhibition with dense tropical landscaping, is the toco toucan, with its huge, bright, yellow-orange bill. The zoo is also noted for its children's farm and underwater views of the resident penguins and sea lions. An Adventurers' Learning Centre includes sculptures linked to the zoo's animals as well as themed areas such as a giraffe plain, meerkat mound, crocodile creek, hippo haunt, and gorilla glade. New arrivals since 2017 include turquoise dwarf geckos, the Madagascar tree boa, a female panther chameleon from Madagascar, a breeding pair of Fijian banded iguana, and critically endangered frogs, while the new Buzz Stop became home to more than 2,000 Irish black honeybees. ■TIP→ **The Treetops Tearoom (at the top of the Cave Hill site) affords the perfect view over Belfast Lough and is surrounded by the Malayan sun bear and cheetah.** ⊠ *Antrim Rd., North Belfast* ☎ *028/9077–6277* ⊕ *www.belfastzoo. co.uk* ✉ *£13.*

★ **Hillsborough Castle**

CASTLE/PALACE | This Georgian palace—the only royal residence in Ireland and that for 50 years was the official home of the Governor of Northern Ireland—opened its doors to the public for the first time in 2015, and has since become a leading attraction. It was built in the 1770s by Wills Hill, the 1st Marquess of Downshire, Ireland's largest landowner and

Secretary of the American Colonies. Benjamin Franklin's five-day stay here is said to have contributed directly to the American War of Independence, such was the animosity between Franklin and Hill. Other visits included that of President George W. Bush and the historic meeting in 2005 between the Queen and Mary McAleese, then president of Ireland. The building was the location for talks during the recent Northern Ireland peace process, and is still the current home of the Secretary of State for Northern Ireland. Guided 45-minute castle tours are held hourly from 10 am to 4 pm. Visitors are brought through elegant state rooms, still used by the royal family, including the throne room and graceful drawing room; look out, too, for impressive royal portraits and paintings by Old Masters such as Gainsborough and Van Dyck. A new café opened in 2019, which means that for the first time in the castle's 250-year history the public can enjoy snacks, lunches, or afternoon tea in royal surroundings. ■TIP➔ Explore the 100 acres of beautiful gardens by following signposts through peaceful woods, waterways, and neatly manicured lawns. ⌧ The Square ☎ 028/9268–1308 ⊕ www.hrp.org.uk/hillsborough-castle ⌧ £13.

★ **Montalto Estate**

SELF-GUIDED | The elegant beauty of this centuries-old estate transports visitors into a different realm to explore a historic demesne, which opened to the public in 2018. The Montalto Estate, near Ballynahinch in mid County Down, was built in the 1750s and inherited by the Earl of Moira, who made the Georgian mansion his permanent home, bringing exotic plants from all over the world. The estate played a leading role in the Battle of Ballynahinch, fought during the Irish Rebellion in June 1798, when it suffered severe damage. The army, which lost 40 troopers, was victorious, but during the battle up to 100 insurgents were killed. After falling into neglect, the estate has now been revitalized with a visitor

center, gift shop, and café, as well as three wonderful walking trails: the lake walk, the garden walk, and the woodland walk. A huge amount of attention has been lavished on the landscape with the planting of thousands of trees and the creation of six new gardens, an orchard, and wildflower meadow, alongside dazzling additions including a summer house, witch's cottage, tree house, and boathouse. ■TIP➔ **Montalto house and grounds are in private ownership, and although the house is not open to the public, private tours may be prearranged. It is worth booking to see the original plastered ceiling created in 1758 by Robert West, as well as art and antiques. Tickets for the house tour cost £30 and include afternoon tea.** ⌧ Montalto Estate, Spa Rd., Ballynahinch, Belfast ✛ The entrance is on Spa Rd., about 2 km (1 mile) south of Ballynahinch town, which is 24 km (15 miles) south of Belfast ☎ 028/9756–6100 ⊕ www.montaltoestate.com ⌧ £8 for grounds only.

★ **Mount Stewart**

HOUSE | A dynamic £7.5 million makeover opened a new chapter in the history of Mount Stewart, the stately Neoclassical home near Belfast. Now in the care of the National Trust, it was formerly the country estate of the marquesses of Londonderry, whose fame, or infamy, became known around the world thanks to the historical role played by the 2nd Marquess. Known as Castlereagh, this Secretary of Ireland put down the Rising of 1798, helped forge the Act of Union, and killed himself by cutting his own throat. Mount Stewart was constructed in two stages where an earlier house had stood: George Dance designed the west facade (1804–05), and William Vitruvius Morrison designed the Neoclassical main part of the building (1845–49), complete with an awe-inspiring Grecian portico facade. The 7th Marchioness, Edith, managed to wave her wand over the interior—after a fashion: Chinese vases, Louis-Philippe tables, and Spanish oak chairs do their worst to clutter up the rooms here. Still, the house does have some noted 18th-century interiors, including the central hall and the grand staircase hung with one of George Stubbs's most famous portraits, that of the celebrated racehorse Hambletonian, after he won one of the most prominent contests of the 18th century—this is perhaps the greatest in situ setting for a painting in Ireland. As part of the restoration program, and with the help of 18 people to take it down, the painting was rehung and reframed with a traditional gilt frame at a cost of £35,000 and now has pride of place on the west stairs. Hambletonian was the most famous Thoroughbred horse in Britain in the late 1700s and early 1800s; art experts regard it as the most important equestrian painting in the world and describe its value as priceless. Elsewhere, a team of builders, conservation architects, specialist engineers and joiners, and more than 40 local volunteers carried out important repair and restoration work on the building, the stone floor in the central hall, and its valuable treasures. The result is that eight new rooms previously unseen are now open to the public. A guided tour of the house, lasting 40 minutes, is held in the morning and included with admission.

On the grounds, don't miss the octagonal folly Temple of the Winds (Sunday 2–5 only), a copy of a similar structure in Athens, and the remarkable bathhouse and pool at the end of the wooded peninsula just before the entrance to the grounds. There are no fewer than 18 named garden walks—you'll need more than one day to explore all of them. The exotic plants have survived because of Strangford Lough's mild microclimate. During 2017 four new walking trails,- covering up to 10 km (7 miles) in the demesne grounds were also opened to the public and can take between 30 minutes and one hour. A restoration project in 2018, led by rangers, has resulted in a red squirrel colony numbering more

The Greening of Belfast

It was due to Edith, the 7th Marchioness of Londonderry, that Mount Stewart was transformed into a garden showplace in the 1920s. Taking advantage of the salubrious microclimate of the Ards Peninsula, she created, in short order, a Shamrock Garden, Dodo Garden (note the stone figures that honor her close circle of friends— the "Warlock" is Winston Churchill), and Lady Mairi's Garden, complete with a "Mary, Mary, Quite Contrary" statue surrounded with silver bells and cockleshells.

than 50 and the establishment of a squirrel lookout. ■ TIP➔ A delightful 3-km (2-mile) stroll around the grounds takes in rare tree species, the lake, rock-garden terraces, the famed statue of a white stag, and spectacular views over the house to Strangford Lough where there is a thriving seal population. Opening times change here—phone ahead or check the website for the complete schedule. ⬜ Portaferry Rd., Newtownards ✛ Ulsterbus 10 on Belfast to Portaferry route stops near front entrance ☎ 028/4278–8387 ⊕ www.nationaltrust.org.uk/mount-stewart ⬜ £12.

★ **Ulster Folk and Transport Museum**
MUSEUM | Devoted to the province's social history, the excellent Ulster Folk and Transport Museum vividly brings the past to life. The museum first invites you to visit Ballycultra—a typical Ulster town of the early 1900s—which comes alive thanks to costumed guides who practice such regional skills as lace making, sampler making, spinning, weaving, wood turning, forgework, printing, open-hearth cooking, carpentry, basket making, and needlework. The setting is evocative: a

score of reconstructed buildings moved here from around the region, including a traditional weaver's dwelling, terraces of Victorian town houses, an 18th-century country church, a village flax mill, a farmhouse, and a rural school. The museum also houses special collections and archives of interest to researchers on topics such as folklife, Ulster dialect, an oral history of linen, and radio and television archives of BBC Northern Ireland. Across the main road (by footbridge) is the beautifully designed Transport Museum, where exhibits include locally built airplanes and motorcycles, as well as the iconoclastic car produced by former General Motors whiz kid John DeLorean in his Belfast factory in 1982. The Transport Museum also houses the *TITANICa* exhibition, which tells the story of the liner's construction in Belfast and what life was like on board. The museum is on the 70 acres of Cultra Manor, encircled by a larger park and recreation area. ⊠ *153 Bangor Rd., 11 km (7 miles) east of Belfast on A2, Cultra* ☎ *028/9042–8428* ⊕ *www.nmni.com/uftm* ⊠ *From £9* ☉ *Closed Mon.*

Carrickfergus and Larne

16 km (10 miles) northeast of Belfast.

Carrickfergus, on the shore of Belfast Lough, grew up around its ancient castle. When the town was enclosed by ramparts at the start of the 17th century, it was the only English-speaking town in Ulster. Not surprisingly, this was the loyal port where William of Orange chose to land on his way to fight the Catholic forces at the Battle of the Boyne in 1690. However, the English did have one or two small setbacks, including the improbable victory in 1778 of John Paul Jones, the American naval hero, over the British warship HMS *Drake*. Although a long way from home, this stands as the first naval victory of America's fledgling fleet. After this battle, which was waged in Belfast Lough, the inhabitants of Carrickfergus stood on the waterfront and cheered Jones when his ship passed the town castle, demonstrating their support for the American Revolution. Carrickfergus's past can still be seen in some of its old buildings. St. Nicholas's Church, built by John de Courcy in 1205 (remodeled in 1614), and the North Gate in the town's medieval walls are worth checking out. Dobbins Inn on High Street has been a hotel for more than three centuries and is a popular local watering hole.

GETTING HERE AND AROUND

A 15-minute drive northeast of Belfast on A2, Carrickfergus is an easy town to negotiate. There's a huge free parking lot beside the castle, and parking on the main streets is free, though limited to one hour. Pay-and-display lots, costing £0.40 per hour, operate at Joymount, Bride, and Lancastrian Streets.

Trains run by Northern Ireland Railways from Belfast on this section of the Antrim Coast go only as far as the 40 km (25 miles) to Larne. Daily service stops at a number of towns, including Carrickfergus, Whitehead, and Glynn. A round-trip ticket from Belfast's Yorkgate or Central Station to Carrickfergus costs £6.80 (£4.40 after 9:30 am); from Belfast to Larne, it's £11.50 (£7.70 after 9:30 am).

VISITOR INFORMATION
CONTACTS Carrickfergus Tourist Information Center. ⊠ *Carrickfergus Castle, Marine Hwy.* ✛ *Located in Carrickfergus Castle* ☎ *028/9335–8262* ⊕ *www.midandeastantrim.gov.uk.*

Sights

Andrew Jackson Cottage and U.S. Rangers Museum
MUSEUM | The museum tells the tale of the seventh U.S. president, whose parents emigrated from here in 1765. This thatch cottage, reroofed in 2019 with the addition of underfloor heating, is just outside town and is a reconstruction

of an 18th-century structure thought to resemble their home. Interpretive panels, illustrating Jackson's story as well as Ulster–Scots history, have been added. The cottage is open year-round, but access from Monday to Wednesday is by arrangement through Carrickfergus tourist office. ⊠ *Larne Rd., 1½ km (1 mile) northeast of Carrickfergus, 2 Boneybefore* ☎ *028/9335–8262* ⊕ *www.midandeastantrim.gov.uk* ⊠ *Free.*

★ Carrickfergus Castle

CASTLE/PALACE | Built atop a rock ledge in 1180 by John de Courcy, provincial Ulster's first Anglo-Norman invader, Carrickfergus Castle is still in good shape and has sparked renewed visitor appeal with the opening of its dungeons. Apart from being captured briefly by the French in 1760, the castle—one of Ireland's largest—stood as a bastion of British rule until 1928, at which time it still functioned as an English garrison. Walk through the 13th-century gatehouse into the Outer Ward and continue into the Inner Ward, the heart of the fortress, where the four-story keep stands, a massive, sturdy building with walls almost 8 feet thick. Make sure you venture down the steps into the dark stone dungeons along with an ammunitions room. The town's tourist information center is also here in the reception. ⊠ *Off A2, Marine Hwy.* ☎ *028/9335–1273* ⊕ *www.midandeastantrim.gov.uk* ⊠ *£6.*

Carrickfergus Museum and Civic Centre

MUSEUM | As one of the most archaeologically excavated towns in Northern Ireland, Carrickfergus is home to many fascinating finds on display in this museum, exploring life in the town from medieval times to the present. Tourist visitor information is available at the nearby Carrickfergus Castle. ⊠ *11 Antrim St.* ☎ *028/9335–8241* ⊕ *www.midandeastantrim.gov.uk.*

Gobbins Cliff Path

HISTORIC SITE | Thrill seekers love this newly revived dramatic cliff walk in east County Antrim. Cut into the towering rock on the eastern side of Islandmagee Peninsula, the path is linked with a new metal staircase and is one of Northern Ireland's best-kept secrets. Originally built in 1902 by the railway magnate Berkeley Deane Wise, in its heyday it was as popular as the Giant's Causeway but fell into disrepair and closed to the public after World War II. Today it merits a government-approved acronym, ASSI, for Area of Special Scientific Interest, and is noted for its noisy colonies of puffins, razorbills, fulmars, peregrine falcons, and guillemots. On a clear day panoramic views across the North Channel stretch from the Scottish Outer Hebrides in the north to the English Lake District in the south. Legends associated with the Gobbins include mythical figures such as Gobbin Saor, a giant who lived in the cliffs. An exhibition room with interpretation, a café and crafts shop, and a tourist information point are located at the site. ⚠ **On occasion, due to stormy weather, the path is closed to visitors. Call in advance to make sure it is fully operational.** ⊠ *68 Middle Rd., Islandmagee, Larne* ☎ *028/9337–2318* ⊕ *www.thegobbinscliffpath.com* ⊠ *£15.*

Glens of Antrim

Beginning 24 km (15 miles) north of Carrickfergus at Larne.

North of Carrickfergus after Larne, the coast of County Antrim becomes spectacular—wave upon wave of high green hills, dotted with lush glens, curve down to the hazy sea among valleys carved out by glaciers at the end of the last Ice Age. Before you tackle the Glens, though, it's worth considering a short detour from Larne to the nearby peninsula of Islandmagee where the Gobbins path is a dramatic cliff-face walk cut into the towering rock. Nine wooded river valleys occupy the 86 km (54 miles) between Larne and Ballycastle, the two largest

In the early 20th century, the Marchioness of Londonderry remade her Mount Stewart estate into the horticultural showplace of Northern Ireland.

towns in the Glens of Antrim. Until the building of the narrow coastal road in 1834, the Glens were home to isolated farming communities, whose residents adhered to the romantic, mystical Celtic legends and the everyday use of the Irish language. Steeped in Irish mythology, the Glens were first inhabited by small bands of Irish monks as early as AD 700. Some residents proudly note that Ossian, the greatest of the Celtic poets, is supposedly buried near Glenaan. The Glens are famed beauty spots and popular destinations: for tourist offices, head to the larger towns such as Larne, Ballymena, and Ballycastle. Cushendall's tourist information office opens all day during the summer months and mornings only in the winter (✉ Mill St. ☎ 028/2177–1180), but Cushendun and Carnlough are extremely small and can't support tourist offices even in high season. McKillop's (✉ 14–16 Main St. ☎ 028/2888–5236), a shop in Carnlough, has leaflets describing local attractions, and the folks there are happy to give tips about the Glens. Also helpful is the Causeway Coast and Glens website, ⊕ www.visitcauseway-coastandglens.com.

GETTING HERE AND AROUND
The scenic Antrim Coaster Goldline buses from Larne to Ballycastle traverse part of the coastline—a 110-km (68-mile), three-hour journey. It is best to buy a Rambler ticket at £9. The service operates Monday through Sunday, from early July to mid-September. Because reservations are not accepted, arrive early in summer to be assured a window seat. To start the journey from Belfast you must first take a bus or train to Larne.

Oft lauded as one of Ireland's most scenic drives—on a clear day you can see Scotland—the A2 Antrim coastal route is a delightful, narrow, winding, two-lane road that hugs the slim strip of land between the hills and sea, bringing you to the magnificent Glens of Antrim. In most towns, cars park free of charge on the main street or in lots overlooking the harbor. The road is busy in summer, so allow extra travel time.

Giant's Causeway Coast

VISITOR INFORMATION

CONTACTS Ballymena Visitor Information Centre. ✉ *The Braid, Ballymena Town Hall Museum and Arts Centre, 1–29 Bridge St., Ballymena* ☎ *028/2563–5010* 🌐 *www.midandeasttrim.gov.uk.* **Larne Tourist Information.** ✉ *96 Main St., Larne* ☎ *028/2826–0395* 🌐 *www.midandeasttrim.gov.uk.*

⊙ Sights

The Glens merit several days of serious exploration. Supernarrow B-roads curl west off A2, up each of the beautiful glens, where trails await hikers. You need a full week and a rainproof tent to complete the nine-glen circuit (from south to north: Glenarm, Glencloy, Glenariff, Glenballyeamon, Glenaan, Glencorp, Glendun, Glenshesk, and Glentaisie); or you could just head for Glenariff Park, the most accessible glen.

Carnlough

TOWN | A little resort made of white limestone, Carnlough overlooks a small harbor surrounded by stone walls. The harbor can be reached by crossing over the limestone bridge from Main Street, built especially for the Marquess of Londonderry. The small harbor, once a port of call for fishermen, now shelters pleasure yachts. Carnlough is surrounded on three sides by hills that rise 1,000 feet from the sea. McKillop's shop serves as a tourist information point and dispenses maps and local literature. The owners also run a first-floor self-catering apartment, which sleeps up to six people. ✉ *14–16 Harbor Rd., 24 km (15 miles) north of Larne on A2, Carnlough* ☎ *028/2888–5236* 🌐 *www.mckillops.co.uk.*

Cushendall

INFO CENTER | Turnley's Tower—a curious, fortified square tower of red stone, built in 1820 as a curfew tower and jail for "idlers and rioters"—stands at a crossroads in the middle of Cushendall, called the capital of the Glens because it has a few more streets than the other villages nearby. The road from Water-foot to Cushendall is barely a mile long and worth the stroll or cycle out to see the coastal caves (one of which had a resident for many years, a local woman named Anne Murray) that line the route. The tourist information center, based in the Old School House in Mill Street, is well stocked with maps, information on local attractions, and a wide selection of books for sale on local history, heritage, and culture. ⊠ *3 km (2 miles) north of Glenariff on A2, Cushendall* ☎ *028/2177–1180* ⊕ *www.visitcausewaycoastandglens.com.*

★ Cushendun

TOWN | Off the main A2 route, the road between Cushendall and Cushendun turns into one of a Tour-de-France hilliness, so cyclists beware. Your reward, however, is the tiny jewel of a village, Cushendun, which was designed in 1912 by Clough Williams-Ellis (who also designed the famous Italianate village of Portmeirion in Wales) at the request of Ronald John McNeill, Baron Cushendun. Up sprang a series of cottages and a village square of seven houses, all done up in the Cornish taste courtesy of the Penzance-born wife of the baron. To top it all off, the baron had Glenmona House built in the regal neo-Georgian style. From this part of the coast you can see the Mull of Kintyre on the Scottish mainland. Hikes along the beachy strand have inspired poets and artists, including John Masefield. ⊠ *2 km (1½ miles) north of Cushendall on Coast Rd., Cushendun.*

★ Glenariff Forest Park

BODY OF WATER | Head to this natural preserve to explore the most beautiful and unsettled of Antrim's glens. Glenariff was christened "Little Switzerland" by Thackeray for its spectacular combination of rugged hills and lush vales. The main valley opens on to Red Bay at the village of Glenariff (also known as Waterfoot). Inside the park are picnic facilities and dozens of good hikes. Bisecting the park are two lovely rivers, the Inver and the Glenariff, which help sculpt the rocky gorges here and culminate in the famous 5½-km (3½-mile) **Waterfall Trail**, marked with blue arrows, which passes outstanding views of Glenariff River, its three waterfalls, and small but swimmable loughs. Escape from the summer crowds by taking one of the longest trails, such as the **Scenic Hike**. Pick up a detailed trail map at the park visitor center, which also has a small cafeteria. ⊠ *98 Glenariff Rd., 7 km (4.3 miles) north of Carnlough, off A2, Glenariff* ☎ *028/7034–0870* ⊠ *Vehicles £5.*

Hotels

Ballygally Castle

$$$$ | HOTEL | Connoisseurs of sea views love this baronial castle, built by a Scottish lord in 1625 to rise dramatically beside Ballygally Bay, and which is playing host to waves of *Game of Thrones* fans due to filming in the area. **Pros:** deluxe rooms have coastal views; handy stopover en route to the Giant's Causeway; good location for Game of Thrones fans. **Cons:** busy at peak holiday times; somewhat bland, if comfortable furnishings; service can be hit-or-miss. ⑤ *Rooms from: £190* ⊠ *274 Coast Rd., Ballygally* ☎ *028/2858–1066* ⊕ *www.hastingshotels.com* ⮡ *54 rooms* ⫶◎⫶ *Free breakfast.*

★ Galgorm Resort & Spa

$$$$ | RESORT | The original Italianate house dates from the 1850s, but the completion of a £10 million renovation in 2015 pushed this manor house resort into the premier league. **Pros:** an elegant mix of cozy and luxurious; access to sports, fishing, and golf; relaxing spa. **Cons:** if not a golfer, swimmer, or spa fan, there's not a lot to do in the immediate area; somewhat remote and a long walk to shops; pricey food and beverages. ⑤ *Rooms from: £200* ✉ *136 Fenaghy Rd., 40 km (25 miles) east of Larne on A36, Ballymena* ☎ *028/2588–1001* ⊕ *www.galgorm.com* ☞ *122 rooms, 6 riverside cottages, 6 fishermen's cottages* ❙◎❙ *Free breakfast.*

The Hedges Hotel

$$ | **HOTEL** | Cashing in on the international appeal of *Game of Thrones,* the Hedges hotel is as close as you can get to staying beside one of the most photogenic film locations, the Dark Hedges, known in the series as Kingsroad, and famed for its ancient beech trees. **Pros:** pleasant country hotel; idyllic countryside on doorstep; practical base for exploring Causeway Coast. **Cons:** a little basic; bedrooms are somewhat plain; area can get seriously crowded. ⑤ *Rooms from: £109* ✉ *139a Ballinlea Rd., Stranocum, Ballycastle* ✛ *In north Antrim countryside, hotel is 11 km (7 miles) north of Ballymoney and 19 km (12 miles) south of Ballycastle* ☎ *028/2075–2222* ⊕ *www.thehedgeshotel.com* ☞ *16 rooms* ❙◎❙ *Free breakfast.*

★ The Londonderry Arms Hotel

$$ | **HOTEL** | What awaits at this lovely traditional inn are ivy-clad walls, gorgeous antiques, regional paintings, prints and maps, and lots of fresh flowers—all time-burnished accents well befitting an estate once inherited by Sir Winston Churchill. **Pros:** fine historic vibe; on a peaceful bay at the foot of Glencloy; spacious rooms. **Cons:** chattering birds in the ivy sometimes provide unscheduled early wake-up call; old-fashioned hotels (and creaky floorboards) aren't to everyone's taste; service moves at a slow pace. ⑤ *Rooms from: £110* ✉ *20 Harbor Rd., Carnlough* ☎ *028/2888–5255* ⊕ *www.londonderryarmshotel.com* ☞ *35 rooms* ❙◎❙ *Free breakfast.*

En Route

The precipitous Antrim Coast Road cuts off from A2 and heads north from Cushendun past dramatically beautiful Murlough Bay to Fair Head and on to Ballycastle. In this area are Drumnakilly, a renowned pagan site; Torr Head, a jutting peninsula; and three state parks that allow for some fabulous hikes, fine hill walking, and great views of Scotland from Fair Head. Or you can rejoin A2 at Cushendun via B92 (a left turn). After a few miles the road descends, passing ruins of the Franciscans' 16th-century Bonamargy Friary, into Ballycastle.

Ballycastle

86 km (54 miles) northwest of Larne.

Ballycastle is the main resort at the northern end of the Glens of Antrim. People flock here in summer, but apart from peak season, this is a quiet town. Ballycastle is shaped like an hourglass, with its strand and dock on one end, its pubs and chippers on the other, and the 1-km (½-mile) Quay Road in between. Beautifully aged shops and pubs line its Castle, Diamond, and Main Streets.

GETTING HERE AND AROUND

Regular bus services link Ballycastle with the main towns of Bushmills, Coleraine, Ballymoney, and Ballymena. Translink buses run daily between the towns. The Antrim Coaster 252 also stops in Ballycastle.

Ballycastle is an hour's drive north of Belfast on the M2, which leads on to A26 before branching off to the narrower A44. You can park free along the seafront and at the marina. Other car parks are on Quay Road and Ann Street.

VISITOR INFORMATION
CONTACTS Ballycastle Visitor Information Centre. ✉ *Portnagree House, 14 Bayview Rd.* ☎ *028/2076–2024* ⊕ *www.visitcausewaycoastandglens.com.*

 Sights

★ Carrick-a-Rede
BRIDGE/TUNNEL | Adrenaline junkies love the rope bridge—off the coast at Ballintoy in Larrybane—which spans a 60-foot gap between the mainland and tiny Carrick-a-Rede Island. The island's name means "rock in the road" and refers to how it stands in the path of the salmon that follow the coast as they migrate to their home rivers to spawn. The bridge is open to the public daily, weather permitting. More than 430,000 visitors cross it (or at least take a look at it) each year, looking down on heart-stopping views of the crashing waves 100 feet below. For an exhilarating cliff-top experience, the rope bridge walk is hard to beat. The island's small two-roomed Fishermen's Cottage, where they mended nets and kept materials, has been restored and opened to the public on selected dates on weekends once a month. The whole area is designated a Site of Special Scientific Interest because of its unique geology, flowers, and fauna. The area has also been identified as a dark-sky discovery site and with the absence of any light pollution is the ideal place to view the stars. If you need warming up after your walk, the Weighbridge tearoom serves snacks and hot drinks. ■TIP→ **It is strongly advised to book in advance online; there may be up to a three-hour wait at peak times.** ✉ *119a White Park Rd., 8 km (5 miles) west of Ballycastle on B15, Ballintoy* ☎ *028/2076–9839* ⊕ *www.nationaltrust.org.uk/carrick-a-rede* 🎟 *£9.*

Rathlin Island
ISLAND | There's a sense of dreamy loneliness about this spot, rising 8 km (5 miles) offshore beyond the tide rip of Sloch na Marra (Valley of the Sea) and across Rathlin Sound. About 140 people still live on Northern Ireland's only offshore island, amid the twin delights of history and wildlife. The postman doubles as the lighthouse keeper and the school has just eight children. In 1306 the Scottish king Robert the Bruce took shelter in a cave (under the east lighthouse) and, according to the popular legend, was inspired to continue his armed struggle against the English by watching a spider patiently spinning its web. It was on Rathlin in 1898 that Guglielmo Marconi set up the world's first cross-water radio link, from the island's lighthouse to Ballycastle. Hiking and bird-watching—look out for the Atlantic nomads: thousands of choughs, puffins, guillemots, and razorbills nesting on the cliffs and sea stacks in the summer—are the island's main activities.

The **Rathlin West Light Seabird Centre and lighthouse** (☎ *028/2076–0062*) is the best place to head for spectacular close-ups of the birds, an awesome sight, which is known as Northern Ireland's largest seabird city. It is more than 6½ km (4 miles) from the harbor at Church Bay, so it's best to take the privately run Puffin Bus (£5 round-trip). Eight waymarked walking trails covering 45 km (27 miles)

Cave Dwelling 👁

The coastal caves of Cushendall have been used for various purposes, including housing. One of the more colorful residents was a lady called Anne Murray who lived in one cave for 50 years, supplementing her income as one of the region's best *poitín* brewers. The damp and windy conditions obviously agreed with her—as did perhaps a taste of her own brew?—for she lived to the ripe old age of 100.

have been given quality status, meaning they are among the best available. You can download the maps to these Rathlin walks at ⊕ *www.walkni.com*.

The **Boathouse Visitor Centre** (☎ *028/2076–2225*) houses a collection of photographs, tools, and implements from the island's past. The center is open from April through mid-September. A high-speed double-decker catamaran, the M.V. *Rathlin Express,* cuts the 10-km (6-mile) journey time crossing over the Sea of Moyle to 25 minutes; from July to September it runs six round-trips daily (£12; reservations 24 hours ahead essential). Unless the sea is extremely rough, the M.V. *Spirit of Rathlin* ferryboat also makes four daily round-trips (£12, reservations also essential). This more leisurely trip can take up to 45 minutes; be mindful of the weather to ensure that you can return on the same day. The last return to Ballycastle is at 4:15 pm for the *Rathlin Express* and 5:30 pm for the *Spirit of Rathlin.* The Rathlin Sound Maritime Festival is a 10-day annual celebration of the area's rich natural history, culture, and music held at the end of May and beginning of June and offers an inspiring mix of activities including a regatta, talks, and tours. For further information on events on Rathlin check the local community development's website (⊕ *www. rathlincommunity.org*). ■ TIP→ **If you want lunch, the best place is the historic Manor House with outdoor tables by the water's edge. The former residence of the island laird, this elegant, whitewashed, Georgian building is now in the care of the National Trust** (⊕ *www.manorhouserathlin.com*). ✉ *Rathlin Island, 9½ km (6 miles) from Ballycastle* ☎ *028/2076–9299* ⊕ *www. rathlinballycastleferry.com* ✉ *Lighthouse £5; Boathouse Visitor Centre free.*

Giant's Causeway

19½ km (12 miles) west of Ballycastle.

★ Northern Ireland's most scenic seascape is a natural wonder that no visitor to the area should miss.

GETTING HERE AND AROUND
BUS TRAVEL
The Antrim Coaster 252 bus (£9 round-trip) is a great way to take in the dramatic coastline. The bus departs at 9:05 am for the Giant's Causeway from Belfast's Europa Buscentre. The Coaster stops on the Nook Main Road, where you can catch a shuttle bus (£2 round-trip) down to the causeway itself. The Translink Causeway Rambler high-frequency service (from June to mid-September) hits all the main visitor attractions, including Bushmills Distillery, Giant's Causeway, and the Carrick-a-Rede rope bridge. An all-day Rambler ticket allows you to hop on and off as many times as you like. It costs £9 per adult and £4.50 for a child and is valid only the day of purchase, available at the Europa Buscentre in Belfast or at any Translink station. For a more direct bus between Belfast and Coleraine, catch the Translink Goldline Express service for £19 before 9:30 or £12.67 after.

CAR TRAVEL
The causeway is just off the A2 coast road. The nearest towns are Coleraine (a 20-minute drive), Ballycastle (10 minutes), and Ballymoney (35 minutes). In summer, the roads are congested, particularly on bank holidays and festival weekends. You can park your car at the center itself, which has 400 spaces (the parking fee is included in the admission price), or leave it in nearby Bushmills, where a park-and-ride service operates. The National Trust, which runs this site, has introduced a Green Travel Admission Ticket for visitors arriving by park and ride or public transportation, knocking £1.50 off the standard adult admission price.

TRAIN TRAVEL

No regular public trains serve the Giant's Causeway, but a fun passenger link is provided on a narrow-gauge train running from Bushmills. The Giant's Causeway and Bushmills Railway leaves Runkerry Road, Bushmills, for the 3-km (2-mile) journey along the track bed of the former causeway tram. The train operates every weekend from Easter until the end of June, and daily in July and August. The nearest Translink train stations are 21 km (14 miles) away in Portrush or 18 km (11 miles) west in Coleraine, where the main Belfast–Derry train stops (£19 round-trip, after 9:30 am £12.70). If you buy a one-day iLink ticket, you can ride buses and trains to get to and from the Giant's Causeway.

CONTACTS Giant's Causeway and Bushmills Railway. ☎ *028/2073–2844* ⊕ *www.free-webs.com/giantscausewayrailway.*

TOURS

Two bus tours from Belfast (among many) are the Giant's Causeway Tour by Allen's Tours and a same-named offering from McComb's. Both cost £17.50.

Allen's Giant's Causeway Tour

Allen's Tours operates day tours to the Giant's Causeway as well as to the nearby Carrick-a-Rede rope bridge (£25). ☎ *028/9091–5613* ⊕ *www.allensbelfast-bustours.com.*

McComb's Giant's Causeway Tour

McComb's/MiniCoach operates day tours of Belfast to the Giant's Causeway (£25) and *Game of Thrones* tours (£35). ✉ *Belfast* ☎ *028/9031–5333* ⊕ *www.mccombscoaches.com.*

VISITOR INFORMATION

CONTACTS Giant's Causeway Tourist Office. ✉ *Visitor Centre, Giant's Causeway Centre, 44 Causeway Rd., Bushmills* ☎ *028/2073–1855* ⊕ *nationaltrust.org.uk/giants-causeway.*

◉ Sights

★ Giant's Causeway

NATURE SITE | FAMILY | Northern Ireland's only UNESCO World Heritage site, the Giant's Causeway is a mass of almost 40,000 mostly hexagonal pillars of volcanic basalt, clustered like a giant honeycomb and extending hundreds of yards into the sea. This "causeway" was created 60 million years ago, when boiling lava, erupting from an underground fissure that stretched from the north of Ireland to the Scottish coast, crystallized as it burst into the sea. As all Ulster folk know, though, the truth is that the giant Finn MacCool, in a bid to reach a giantess he'd fallen in love with on the Scottish island of Staffa (where the causeway resurfaces), created the columns as stepping-stones. Unfortunately, the giantess's boyfriend found out, and in the ensuing battle, Finn pulled out a huge chunk of earth and flung it toward Scotland. The resulting hole became Lough Neagh, and the sod landed to create the Isle of Man. In the peak summer months it can be very busy—get here early or leave your visit until late afternoon, when it's generally quieter.

To reach the causeway, you can either walk 1½ km (1 mile) down a long, scenic hill or take the Causeway Coaster minibus. A popular option with many visitors is to take the 20-minute walk downhill to the main causeway and catch the shuttle bus back uphill (£2 return).

A good place to start is the **Giant's Causeway Visitor Experience,** made of locally quarried basalt from the very same lava flows that formed the causeway. The glass front ensures spectacular coastal views, and the building is sunken into the ground, blending so effectively into the landscape that the indigenous grasses on the roof restore the natural ridgeline and provide a habitat for wildlife.

Inside the building, a stunning exhibition, complete with the 21st-century commercialization of Finn MacCool, is made up of five parts: coastal map, geological history, people and their stories, natural life, and the power of the landscape. Exhibition panels along with 3-D displays showcase detail on the geological and scientific nature of the area. Guided one-hour tours of the stones are included in the admission price, and visitors are issued a hand-held device with recorded snippets of oral history. Tours leave every hour during the day. Kids love the center, so make sure you allow enough time on your visit to let them take in everything.

Outside, be aware that not all stones are created equal. Be sure to take a seat in the "Wishing Chair" and also look out for the "Giant's Boot," "Camel," "Harp," and the "Giant's Organ Pipes." Heading west, keep an eye out for Port-na-Spania, the spot where the 16th-century Spanish Armada galleon *Girona* went down on the rocks. The ship was carrying an astonishing cargo of gold and jewelry, some of which was only recovered in 1967. Beyond this, Chimney Point is the name given to one of the causeway structures on which the Spanish fired, thinking that it was Dunluce Castle, which is 8 km (5 miles) west.

You can park at the center—the fee is included in the admission price—or use the park-and-ride service between Bushmills and the causeway. Visitors who opt for the park and ride, or who arrive by public transportation, save £1.50 on the standard adult admission price (£3.75 per family) as part of a Green Travel Admission Ticket. Booking online in advance is recommended and saves you £1.50 on the adult admission price. ⊠ *44 Causeway Rd., Bushmills* ☎ *028/2073–1582* ⊕ *www.nationaltrust.org.uk/giantscauseway* ⊠ *£13.*

Bushmills

3 km (2 miles) southwest of Giant's Causeway.

The pleasant town of Bushmills is world-famous for its centuries-old distillery.

GETTING HERE AND AROUND
Bushmills is on the A2 coastal route and an ideal stopping place for refueling. It has the best parking facilities for exploring the Giant's Causeway. A park-and-ride service operates from the town to the visitor center and saves you the trouble of finding a space. If visiting Bushmills Distillery, there's a large free car park out front. Parking is free in the town along main streets.

 Sights

★ **Bushmills**
WINERY/DISTILLERY | Reputedly the oldest licensed distillery in the world, Bushmills was first granted a charter by King James I in 1608, though historical records refer to a distillery here as early as 1276. Bushmills produces the most famous of Irish whiskeys—its namesake—and a rarer black-label version, Black Bush, widely regarded as the best of the best. On the guided tour, discover the secrets of the special water from St. Columb's Rill, the story behind malted Irish barley, and learn about triple distillation in copper stills and aging (which happens for long years in oak casks). You begin in the mashing and fermentation room, proceed to the maturing and bottling warehouse, and conclude, yes, with the much anticipated, complimentary shot of *uisce beatha,* the "water of life." Try to join a less crowded early-morning tour. Separate tours include a one-hour nosing and tasting tour at £30, and a premium tour at £37, which includes tasting five Bushmills whiskeys and two others for comparison (75 minutes). In 2017 the company launched its first

If you summon up the nerve to cross the famous 60-foot-long Carrick-a-Rede rope bridge, which sways over a rocky outcrop and the turbulent sea, be mindful that you have to do it again to get back to the mainland.

new domestic whiskey for five years. Bushmills Red Bush was matured in first-fill, medium-char bourbon casks, which soften the spirit, producing a blend of single-malt and grain whiskey said to deliver a sweet and smooth taste, a steal at £24 a bottle. The following year saw the debut of Bushmills Distillery Exclusive, a single malt aged in acacia casks and priced at £74, which, according to connoisseurs, delivers "sweet vanilla and accentuated dried fruit flavors." You can also have a light lunch in the Distillery Kitchen Restaurant or buy souvenirs in the distillery gift shop. ⚠ **During July coppersmiths and distillers carry out annual maintenance work and, while tours are still held, you may not be able to access all the production areas.** ⊠ *2 Distillery Rd., off A2* ☎ *028/2073–3218* ⊕ *www.bushmills. com* ✉ *Tours from £8; children under 8 not permitted on tour.*

 Hotels

The Bushmills Inn

$$$$ | B&B/INN | A perfectly enchanting old coach inn dating from the 1600s that welcomes with peat fires, a dazzlingly inventive dinner menu, and cozy rooms; the master distiller's suite even comes with fluffy slippers and bathrobes. **Pros:** close to distillery and the Giant's Causeway; comfortable rooms; easy to chat with locals in the bar. **Cons:** if you're tall, look out for the low timber beams; deluxe rooms are more expensive; no amenities. ⑤ *Rooms from: £220* ⊠ *9 Dunluce Rd.* ☎ *028/2073–3000, 028/2073–2339* ⊕ *www.bushmillsinn. com* ➦ *41 rooms* ⦿ *Free breakfast.*

Causeway Hotel

$$$$ | HOTEL | Owned by England's National Trust and flaunting a stunning location overlooking the Atlantic Ocean, this 1840s hotel is less than a half mile from the celebrated Giant's Causeway. **Pros:** good location for bracing coastal walks; many rooms updated in 2018; as close as it gets to the Giant's Causeway. **Cons:** too many family parties; service can be a tad churlish; coastal area is often chilly, even in summer. $ *Rooms from: £180* ✉ *40 Causeway Rd.* ☎ *028/2073–1210* ⊕ *www.thecausewayhotel.com* 🛏 *28 rooms* ⊠ *Free breakfast.*

Dunluce Castle

3 km (2 miles) west of Bushmills.

Dunluce is midway between Bushmills and Portrush, and its photogenic castle makes it a worthy stop.

GETTING HERE AND AROUND

There is a small, free car park at the castle but it isn't big enough to accommodate large numbers at busy times. ■ TIP→ **Park free in Bushmills or Portrush, both a 10-minute drive away, and hop on the Causeway Rambler bus, which operates in summer along the A2 coastal route and drops you at the castle.** Coleraine is the nearest big town. Derry is an hour's drive west.

Sights

Dunluce Castle

CASTLE/PALACE | FAMILY | Dramatically perched on a 100-foot-high basalt-rock cliff, halfway between Portrush and the Giant's Causeway, Dunluce Castle is one of the north's most evocative ruins. Even roofless, this shattered bulk conjures up a strength and aura that is quintessentially Antrim. Originally a 13th-century Norman fortress, Dunluce was captured in the 16th century by the local MacDonnell clan chiefs—the so-called Lords of the Isles. They enlarged it, in part using profits from salvaging the Spanish galleon *Girona,* and made it an important base for ruling northeastern Ulster. Perhaps the MacDonnells expanded the castle a bit too much, for in 1639 faulty construction caused the kitchens (with all the cooks) to plummet into the sea during a storm.

Between 2009 and 2012, archaeologists uncovered belt buckles, thimbles, dress fastenings, jewelry, clay pipes, animal bones, and shards of pottery that are now on display in the Discovery Room. An eight-minute introductory film explores the castle's history. Audio guides are available in seven languages. Guided tours are held every day at 11 and 2 in the summer months and last 45 minutes. ■ TIP→ **Children love the sand pit where they can handle tools and dress up.** ✉ *87 Dunluce Rd.* ☎ *028/2073–1938* ⊕ *www.discovernorthernireland.com* 🎟 *£6.*

Portstewart Strand

BEACHES | Signposted as "The Strand" at all major junctions in town, this magnificent 3-km (2-mile) stretch of golden sand is one of the north coast's finest beaches, suitable for all ages. Owned by the National Trust, well maintained, and clean, it's the ideal spot for picnics, swimming (though the water can be quite chilly), or long walks among sand dunes that are a haven for wildflowers such as bird's foot trefoil, wild pansy, and thyme, and butterflies including common blue, meadow brown, and dark green fritillary. Lifeguards are on duty at Easter and from June to August. The beach has an undertow at certain points and small sections have seaweed, but it's not a big nuisance. Two-hour guided butterfly safaris aimed at families are held on weekends during the summer. On warm days the beach fills with cars, but its size ensures that it is never completely crowded. ■ TIP→ **To cool down take the delightful 20-minute walk along the cliff-top path into Portstewart for an ice-cream sundae at the famed Morelli's shop along the promenade. Amenities:** food and drink; parking; showers; toilets. **Best for:** surfing; swimming; walking. ✉ *118 Strand Rd., Portstewart* ☎ *028/7083–6396* ⊕ *www.nationaltrust.org.uk/portstewartstrand* 🎟 *£7 per car (£3 in winter).*

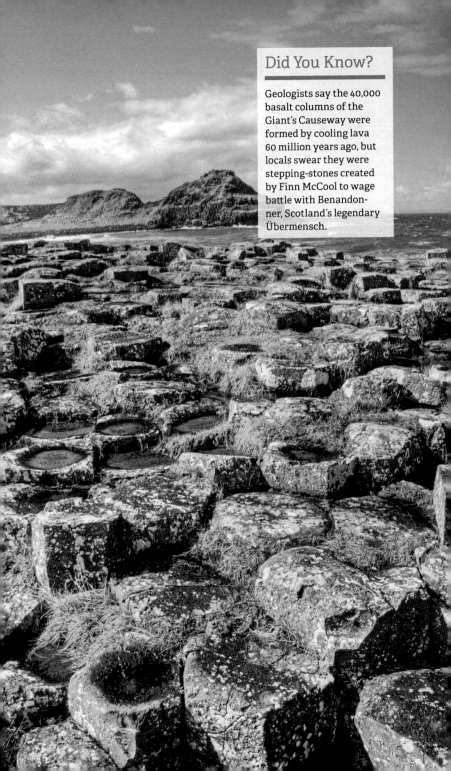

Did You Know?

Geologists say the 40,000 basalt columns of the Giant's Causeway were formed by cooling lava 60 million years ago, but locals swear they were stepping-stones created by Finn McCool to wage battle with Benandonner, Scotland's legendary Übermensch.

Restaurants

★ Harry's Shack

$$ | IRISH | With its raw wooden tables, wood-burning stove, sand on the floor, and outdoor terrace, this beachside restaurant in Portstewart, about 20 minutes from Dunluce, is *the* destination restaurant par excellence of the north coast. Brunches might consist of pancakes with maple syrup, mackerel fish cakes, or pasta. **Known for:** fresh, tasty lobster; local pale ale; on-the-beach dining with outdoor bar. ⑤ *Average main: £15* ⊠ *118 Strand Rd., Portstewart* ☎ *028/7083–1783.*

Ramore Restaurants

$ | ECLECTIC | FAMILY | Creative, moderately priced fare, alongside panoramic views in an elegant setting, attract locals and tourists to this popular restaurant and wine bar complex with multiple venues. The light-filled Mermaid Kitchen and Bar, serving seafood, conjures up a beachside feel evocative of coastal Maine, except you're looking out on Portrush's West Strand (although admittedly Belfast is only 100 km [60 miles] south); the more informal Harbour Bistro serves wood-fired steaks and burgers; Neptune and Prawn serves Asian-inspired fare; and the Tourist Restaurant has a Mexican theme with burritos, nachos, and tacos and specializes in pizzas and burgers. **Known for:** multiple venues; wood-fired burgers and grilled fish; sea and sunset views. ⑤ *Average main: £13* ⊠ *The Harbor, Portrush* ☎ *028/7082–4313* ⊕ *www. ramorerestaurant.com.*

🏃 Activities

GOLF

Castlerock Golf Club

GOLF | The Mussenden Course underwent major reconstruction during 2018, which resulted in six holes being altered, although there was no change to one of its most unusual, "Leg o' Mutton," a 200-yard par-3 with railway tracks to the right and a burn to the left. The course has bedded well and is regarded as having the best greens in Ireland. The finish is spectacular: from the elevated 17th tee, where you can see the shores of Scotland, to the majestic 18th, which plays uphill to a plateau green. The club also boasts the equally scenic 9-hole Bann Course. ⊠ *65 Circular Rd., Derry* ☎ *028/7084–8314* ⊕ *www.castlerockgc. co.uk* ☒ *Mussenden: weekdays £80, weekends £95; Bann: weekdays £15, weekends £20* ⚐ *Mussenden: 18 holes, 6747 yards, par 73; Ban: 9 holes, 4892 yards, par 68.*

Portstewart Golf Club

GOLF | More than 120 years old, Portstewart may scare you with its opening hole, known as "Tubber Patrick," generally regarded as the toughest starter in Ireland. Picture a 425-yard par-4 that descends from an elevated tee to a small green tucked between the dunes. The Strand Course is affectionately called "The Sleeping Giant," and the manicured greens are known for uniformity and speed. Eight of the holes have been redesigned to toughen the course and two have been lengthened. From its rolling fairways and undulating dunes the views stretch across the Atlantic Ocean to north Donegal. In 2017 the club hosted the Irish Open, and the winner, Jon Rahm, a Spanish professional, described it as an amazing course, saying "it is one of the most beautiful I have ever seen." If you want a break from the grand scale of the Strand championship links, there's the Old Course and the Riverside, 36 holes of downsize, executive-style golf. A modern clubhouse has a bar and restaurant. ⊠ *117 Strand Rd., Portstewart* ☎ *028/7083–2015* ⊕ *www.portstewartgc. co.uk* ☒ *The Strand: daily £175; Old Course: summer weekdays £15, winter £10, weekends £15 all year; Riverside: weekdays £25, weekends £29* ⚐ *The Strand: 18 holes, 7118 yards, par 72; Old Course: 18 holes, 4730 yards, par 64; Riverside: 18 holes, 5725 yards, par 68.*

While cliff erosion has played havoc with what's left of its battlements, Dunluce Castle still remains one of Northern Ireland's most intensely beautiful sights.

★ Royal Portrush Golf Club

GOLF | One of the leading courses in the United Kingdom or Ireland, Royal Portrush raised its profile hosting the world's best golfers for the British Open in summer 2019, only the second time in its 150-year history it was held outside of Scotland or England. The Open left a considerable legacy that boosted the reputation, not only of the club, but of the north Irish coast as a premier destination for international events, and has left a satisfying afterglow. A series of upgrades included new 7th and 8th holes that replaced the 17th and 18th, freeing up land for spectators, and the course length has increased by nearly 200 yards. The championship Dunluce course is named for the ruins of the nearby castle and is a sea of sand hills and curving fairways all routed through rugged links land, constantly changing in both direction and elevation. Despite its understated appearance, the course poses many challenges. "White Rocks," the par-4 5th hole, is quite literally a cliffhanger. It's a wicked dogleg with the green perched on the edge of a cliff. "Calamity," formerly the 14th hole, is now the 236-yard par-3 16th hole demanding total precision to carry the ball over the green and a yawning chasm. The Valley Course is a less exposed, tamer track. Both are conspicuous for their lack of bunkers. In a poll of Irish golf legends, Dunluce was voted the best in Ireland—among those who have graced the greens here are Gary Player, Arnold Palmer, Jack Nicklaus, and Ernie Els. Darren Clarke plays his golf here when he's home, and it's where Graeme McDowell, former U.S. Open champion, learned his golf at an early age. ⊠ *Dunluce Rd., Portrush* ☎ *028/7082–2311* ⊕ *www.royalportrushgolfclub.com* ✉ *Dunluce: Apr.–Oct., £220; Nov.–Mar., £90, excluding Sun. Valley: Apr.–Oct., £50; Nov.–Mar., weekdays only £25* ⛳ *. Dunluce: 18 holes, 7317 yards, par 72; Valley: 18 holes, 6336 yards, par 75.*

Limavady

27 km (17 miles) east of Derry.

In 1851, at No. 51 on Limavady's Georgian main street, Jane Ross wrote down the tune played by a traveling fiddler and called it "Londonderry Air," better known now as "Danny Boy." While staying at an inn on Ballyclose Street, William Thackeray (1811–63) wrote his rather lustful poem "Peg of Limavady" about a barmaid. Among the many Americans descended from Ulster emigrants was President James Monroe, whose relatives came from the Limavady area.

GETTING HERE AND AROUND

Translink buses leave Limavady every hour during the day for Derry; journey time is 35 minutes. There is no train station, but you can connect with the train to Belfast by taking a bus to Coleraine or Ballymena.

On the main route between Derry and Coleraine, Limavady is well served with car parking. Motorists park free on the main street with a one-hour time limit. Pay-and-display parking, costing £0.40 per hour, is available at Newtown Square (off Linenhall Street) and on Connell Street.

VISITOR INFORMATION

CONTACTS Limavady Tourist Office.
✉ *Roe Valley Arts Centre, 24 Main St.*
☎ *028/7776–0650* ⊕ *www.visitcauseway-coastandglens.com.*

Hotels

Roe Park Resort

$$$$ | RESORT | A country estate serves as the model for this modern deluxe resort on 155 acres straddling the banks of the River Roe—the place is relatively large and impersonal, although the lobby is welcoming and guest rooms have simple, clean-line beds in woods and rich earth tones. **Pros:** ideal location for golfers and spa lovers; lively bars; family-friendly. **Cons:** can be noisy with evening wedding parties; new suites are expensive; limited public transport, you need a car. $ *Rooms from: £258* ✉ *Roe Park* ☎ *028/7772–2222* ⊕ *www.roeparkresort.com* 🛏 *118 rooms* ⏷ *Free breakfast.*

Bellaghy

32 miles (51 km) south of Dunluce Castle and 20 miles (32 km) north of Belfast International Airport.

In the rural heartland of South Derry, close to the River Bann that divides Counties Derry and Antrim lies the small town of Bellaghy (pop. 1,100). Halfway between Belfast and Derry (making it an easy stop on a drive between both), Bellaghy is on the fringe of Lough Neagh—Ireland's biggest inland lake and a place memorialized in the poetry of Seamus Heaney.

Sights

★ Seamus Heaney HomePlace

TOUR—SIGHT | Dedicated to the memory of the prize-winning poet and Nobel laureate Seamus Heaney, this £4.25 million arts center in his home village of Bellaghy explores his life and work, arranged over two floors with displays, touchscreens, and interactive exhibits. Heaney, whose lyrical poetry is rooted in the land of his birth but speaks to people around the world, won the Nobel Prize for Literature in 1995. Everyone from Bill Clinton to local schoolchildren have expressed their high esteem for Heaney; Robert Lowell called him the greatest Irish poet since Yeats. Through words, images, artifacts, and powerful voice recordings, his distinctive accent and rhythm come alive. Highlights include the Poetry Wall, where visitors can engage with the building blocks, tools, and methods he employed and an Attic Study, where you can see how his original manuscripts were revised and rewritten. A substantial library houses his poetry and translations of his work in more than 20 languages. There's also a 190-seat theater with a regular series of readings, music, and talks. Guided bus tours of Heaney Country are organized by Eugene Kielt, who also runs Laurel Villa, a superb Victorian B&B in nearby Magherafelt with a strong poetry slant (⊕ *www. laurel-villa.com*). ⊠ *45 Main St.* ⊹ *Equidistant between Belfast and Derry, a 45-min drive from both cities* ☎ *028/7938–7444* ⊕ *www.seamusheaneyhome.com* ⊠ *£7* ⊗ *Closed Sun. morning.*

Derry

Wrapped in historic walls and hilly cobbled streets, Derry (or Londonderry, as it's also known) oozes character. It's a small city on the rise, with the imprint of the past around every corner, proud of its 400-year-old walls and architectural heritage as well as the multimillion-pound beautification project that has seen landmark buildings emerge in recent years. Derry's remarkable history is told in expressive visual terms: walls and stained glass, a compelling open-air gallery of 21st-century political murals, the rejuvenated Guildhall, and a spectacular Peace Bridge across the River Foyle. The bridge links the city center with Ebrington Square, a redeveloped military parade ground now turned into a spacious playground filled with concerts and tai chi practitioners. The base figured in World War II's Battle of the Atlantic, and its developers are slowly building a gallery, art center, studios, bars, shops, and a maritime museum.

Collectively, the changes of recent years are viewed as progress born of the peace process, and there is great desire to continue to build on this message that this city's communities, so long divided, now desire to work together.

GETTING HERE AND AROUND
BUS TRAVEL
In 2017 Translink introduced 12 new double-decker Goldline express coaches on its fast route between Belfast and Derry over the Glenshane Pass. At peak times services operate every 15 minutes and include nine direct daily services between the two cities (£12.50 single, £19 same-day return, £22 open return). Journey time is one hour and 40 minutes. Weekend service, especially on Sunday, is less frequent. An alternative, slightly longer route, operated by Translink Goldline between Belfast and Derry, travels along the M1 motorway and through County Tyrone—it takes about two hours. Translink buses run from Derry to neighboring towns, with fares averaging about £16.50 round-trip. You can also catch a bus from City of Derry Airport into the Foyle Street bus station in the city center (£6.30 round-trip). The Airporter Coach, which leaves from Bay Road, operates between Derry and Belfast International Airport and George Best Belfast City Airport. Tickets to both airports cost £30 round-trip. If you're traveling across the border from Derry into Donegal, then you have a choice of using Bus Éireann or the Lough Swilly Bus Company.

CAR TRAVEL
The city's two main shopping centers, Foyleside and Quayside, have multistory car parking garages. Collect a ticket on entry and pay at a machine on departure. Other main car parks, which are mostly pay-by-the-hour via metered ticket machines, are located at Foyle Street, Carlisle Road, William Street, Society Street, Queens Quay, Alfred Street, and Victoria Market. Derry is a 75-minute drive from Belfast; A6 takes you over the mountainous Glenshane Pass. Roads lead south to Strabane and Omagh on A5 and on to Dublin (about four hours away, depending on road conditions and traffic). Derry is also the jumping-off point for exploring the Inishowen Peninsula by

Dangling mobiles of words from Seamus Heaney's poems invite visitors to HomePlace to play with language.

car and the beautifully remote northern Donegal region.

TRAIN TRAVEL

One of the most relaxing ways to arrive in Derry is by train. Frequent daily services on Northern Ireland Railways link it with Coleraine, Ballymena, Antrim, and Belfast. For the final 20-minute section of the journey—along the County Derry coastline—the track runs parallel to the sea and is one of Ireland's most stunning routes. The journey time from Belfast to Derry is about two hours (£19 round-trip, £12.70 after 9:30 am; trains run at 20 minutes past the hour from 6 am until 9 pm). The main station is in the Waterside area of the city; catch a free 10-minute shuttle bus across Craigavon Bridge to get to the West Bank, where most attractions are concentrated.

CONTACTS Airporter Coach. ☎ 028/7126–9996 ⊕ www.airporter.co.uk.

TOURS

Bogside History Tours

WALKING TOURS | Paul Doherty's Bogside tours come with personal knowledge since his father, Patrick, was one of a group of civilians killed by British soldiers during a civil rights march on January 30, 1972. His one-hour tour provides an educational, and at times emotional, insight into the era and retraces parts of the original march stopping at places where the dead and injured fell. The company also offers a city walls tour. Tours are held all year at 11 and 1, with an additional tour at 3 from May through August. The meeting point is at the Guildhall in the city center. ✉ Guildhall St., Bogside ☎ 077/3145–0088 ⊕ www.bogsidehistorytours.com ☎ £6.

Martin McCrossan City Walking Tours

WALKING TOURS | These walks leave daily at 10, noon, 2, and 4 year-round. The departure point is 11 Carlisle Road (just show up; reservations not necessary). Tours last one hour and incorporate not only history and centuries-old stories but also architecture and engaging bits of local lore and humor. ⊠ *11 Carlisle Rd., West Bank* ☎ *028/7127–1996* ⊕ *www. derrycitytours.com* 🎫 *£4.*

VISITOR INFORMATION
CONTACTS Visit Derry. ⊠ *44 Foyle St., West Bank* ☎ *028/7126–7284* ⊕ *www. visitderry.com.*

Sights

Derry's name shadows its history. Those in favor of British rule call the city Londonderry, its old Plantation-period name: the "London" part was tacked on in 1613 after the Flight of the Earls, when the city and county were handed over to the Corporation of London, which represented London's merchants. The corporation brought in a large population of English and Scottish Protestant settlers, built towns for them, and reconstructed Derry within the city walls (which survive almost unchanged to this day). Derry's sturdy ramparts have withstood many fierce attacks—they have never been breached, which explains the city's coy sobriquet, "The Maiden City." The most famous attack was the siege of 1688–89, begun after 13 apprentice boys slammed the city gates in the face of the Catholic king, James II. Inhabitants, who held out for 105 days and were reduced to eating dogs, cats, and laundry starch, nevertheless helped to secure the British throne for the Protestant king, William III. Whatever you choose to call it—and the latest name is Derry/Londonderry—the city is no longer an underrated place.

Centre for Contemporary Art (CCA)
MUSEUM | Contemporary Irish and international artistic collaborations are part of the credo of this cutting-edge gallery. It has featured shows by emerging Irish artists and enjoys connections with galleries in India and France, as well as London and Dublin. There's a free public library where you can browse books on art. ⊠ *10–12 Artillery St., West Bank* ☎ *028/7137–3538* ⊕ *www.cca-derry-londonderry.org.*

Derry City Walls
PROMENADE | Established under a charter by James I in 1613, Derry is among a small but distinctive coterie of places throughout Europe that have preserved their ancient ramparts. Built between 1614 and 1618, the walls today allow you to get a feel for Derry's deep history by strolling along the parapet walkway and pausing on a platform. Pierced by eight gates (originally four) and as much as 30 feet thick, the gray-stone ramparts are only 1½ km (1 mile) all around. On your walk, take a break at a strategically placed café or simply drink in the atmosphere of this most photogenic of cities. In summer when the walls are awash with tourists, "ambassadors" are on hand to point you the right way. The program will feature music, dance, theater, films, workshops, and archaeological demonstrations. For events see: ⊕ www.walledcity400.com. ⊠ *West Bank* ⊕ *www.visitderry.com.*

Derry Girls Mural
PUBLIC ART | Since it was erected in 2019, the Derry Girls mural has become the talk of the town and a must-see sight for tourists. The extensive 3-meter-high artwork, based on the cast of a hit British comedy TV series, *Derry Girls,* has been spray-painted on to the gable wall of Badgers bar in Orchard Street. The eye-catching wall of fame in the city center can be clearly seen from a walk on the walls and is a contrast to some murals elsewhere. The sitcom, which has earned critical acclaim—the *Holywood Reporter*'s reviewer declared it her favorite comedy of the year—features the adventures of five Derry teenagers navigating their way around the late-Troubles era of the early 1990s. It has been picked up by Netflix and turned into a second series, which ends with the re-creation of Bill Clinton's visit to Derry

in 1995. ⊠ *18 Orchard St., Central District*
☏ *028/7136–3306.*

Derry Wall Murals

PUBLIC ART | Dramatic wall murals
throughout Derry testify to the power
of art as historical document, while also
serving as a reminder of painful pasts.
Symbolic of the different communities,
the murals attract considerable curiosity
from tourists. The Bogside Gallery of
Murals, painted by William Kelly, Kevin
Hasson, and Tom Kelly, are made up
of 12 wall paintings known collectively
as "The People's Gallery." They include
the *Bloody Sunday Commemoration,
The Death of Innocence, Civil Rights,
The Hunger Strikes,* and a poignant one
featuring the Nobel peace prize–winning Derry politician John Hume along
with Martin Luther King Jr., Nelson
Mandela, and Mother Teresa—all beside
the Brooklyn Bridge. In 2015 a mural
featuring John Hume and Ivan Cooper,
founding members of the civil rights
movement, was restored. The paintings
span the length of Rossville Street in the
heart of the Bogside. Some of the guided
walking tours that leave from the tourist
information center include the story of
the murals. On the other side of the
political divide, close to the city walls, the
Protestant Fountain estate is home to
one of the oldest King Billy murals along
with other colorful ones linked to the
siege of Derry. ⊠ *Rossville St., Bogside*
☏ *028/7126–7284.*

Ebrington Square

PLAZA | Since its reincarnation as a venue
for open-air concerts and other outdoor
events, Ebrington Square, a former
military barracks on the River Foyle's east
bank, has become an established cultural
hub. It was named for Lord Ebrington,
the Lord Lieutenant of Ireland during the
years 1839–41 when many of the military
buildings here were erected, including
the Star Fort, one of the architectural
highlights. During World War II, the
barracks became part of a naval base
that later functioned as an antisubma-
rine training school for the Allied navies
operating from the city. Derry's contribution to the Battle of the Atlantic was
acknowledged with the unveiling in
2013 of the *International Sailor,* a bronze
statue in the square, which pays tribute
to seamen from the 12 Allied nations
who protected shipping convoys. It is a
replica of the *Mariner* statue in Halifax,
Nova Scotia. The base closed in 2004 and
is being slowly redeveloped. There are
two restaurants, the Walled City Brewery
and Ollie's Cafe, and a maritime museum
is planned. ⊠ *Ebrington Sq., East Bank*
🎫 *Free.*

Garden of Reflection

GARDEN | An imaginative *rus in urbe,* this
small city-center oasis of calm features
a courtyard, amphitheater, and gallery
space where travelers can escape the
bustle of traffic and noise. A paved "river" runs through the garden, symbolic
of life's journey, while artistic features
include a crystal healing wall and special-
ly commissioned artworks. In the words
of the new era, it is "a shared space"
that can be enjoyed by all sections of the
community in a historic part of the walled
city. Lunchtime events are sometimes
held. ⊠ *16 Bishop St.* ☏ *028/7126–1941*
🎫 *Free.*

★ Guildhall

MUSEUM | **FAMILY** | The rejuvenated Victo-
rian Guildhall is an outstanding example
of the city's ornate architecture. It has
been refashioned as a visitor center with
interactive exhibits telling the story of the
Plantation of Ulster and the construction
of the walled city, and how these events
shaped present-day Derry. Touch-screen
displays explain the building's special
features, like the elaborate ceilings, baronial wood paneling, and a magnificent
organ. For children, hands-on displays
include a puzzle of a 1598 map of Ulster,
and a wheel they can spin to find out
about the different London companies
and how land was divided. Kids can also

An annual bluegrass music festival at the Ulster American Folk Park reaffirms the strong links between Northern Ireland and the United States.

build a *bawn,* stone house, or castle using wooden blocks, or dress up in the clothes of Planters or Irish people of the period. Look out, too, for the delightful scale model of the city in 1738 showing just a few thatched cabins outside the perimeter wall. A conserved page (a folio) from the Great Parchment Book of 1639 detailing the account of the Plantation is also on display. With the gleaming restoration, one of the most famous of all Derry's local sayings, "You've more faces than the Guildhall clock"—not a compliment—has renewed resonance. ■ TIP➔ **Enjoy an alfresco coffee in the Guild Café at the harbor square entrance overlooking the Foyle, an ideal spot to catch the riverine light and reflect on 400 turbulent years of history.** ⊠ *Guildhall Sq., West Bank* ☎ *028/7137–6510* ⊕ *www. derrystrabane.com/guildhall* ✉ *Free.*

Museum of Free Derry

MUSEUM | At Free Derry Corner stands the white gable wall where in 1969 Catholics defiantly painted the slogan "You are now entering Free Derry" as a declaration of a zone from which police and the British Army were banned until 1972, when the army broke down the barricades. The black lettering became instantly recognizable as a symbol of resistance, and 50 years later the words are still there but have taken on much wider significance. They also now represent social and international themes, including marriage equality, gay pride, or medical issues such as cancer, when for several weeks the wall is painted a different color. On January 30, 1972, 13 civil rights marchers were shot and killed by British soldiers. Thirty-eight years later, the British government released its official report on the shootings, which resulted in a hugely significant official apology from Prime Minister David Cameron, saying that he was "deeply sorry" for what happened on Bloody Sunday and that it "had been unjustified and unjustifiable." The £2.2 million, two-story museum built on the same site tells the complete story of that day and the many years of campaigning for an apology. Saved sections of the front face

Northern Irish Food: Baking Crazy

The sweet aroma of freshly baked cakes will distract you during a visit to Northern Ireland. It is famed for its bakeries, producing calorie-laden handmade fancies and traditional breads using age-old recipes. In family-run shops, shelves heave with fresh cream cakes, pastries, scones, and local specialties such as chocolate caramel squares or "fifteens"—made of 15 digestive biscuits, 15 marshmallows, and 15 glacé cherries—once tasted never forgotten. Local breads to try include the floury "Belfast Bap," often turned into a sandwich with artery-clogging fillings of Irish bacon, cheese, and sausage, and the soda "farl," cooked on the griddle rather than in the oven and most often found at breakfast time on either side of an Ulster fry.

of the old building retain the bullet scars from that fateful day. ■ TIP➜ **Visitors will find a real-time recording of the event and a viewing room, as well as newspaper reports, photographs, and posters about the "Battle of the Bogside." The National Civil Rights Archive is also held here and research facilities are available on the first floor. One-hour Free Derry Walking Tours (£5) leave from the museum at 10, noon, and 2 each day.** ✉ *Bloody Sunday Centre, 55 Glenfada Park, off Rossville St., West Bank* ☎ *028/7136–0880* ⊕ *www.museumoffreederry.org* 🍴 *£6.*

The Siege Museum and Apprentice Boys Hall

MUSEUM | Imposing in its Scottish Baronial fortified grandeur, this is a meeting place for the exclusively Protestant organization set up in 1715 to honor 13 Apprentice Boys who slammed the city gate in the face of the Catholic King James in 1688, sparking the Siege of Derry. The Memorial Hall was renovated in 2015, and next door to it stands a £2 million center that tells the fascinating story of the 105-day siege and chronicles the history of the Apprentice Boys. A look-alike sandstone scale model of Walker's Pillar—blown up by the IRA

in 1973—has been re-created. During excavation work in 2014, before the new museum was built, archaeologists unearthed Derry's oldest building, believed to date to at least 1602. The brick-and-wood structure perished during the O'Doherty Rebellion of 1608—predating the historic city walls by several years. Excited archaeologists also uncovered musket balls, a cannonball, pottery shards, clay pipes, and even some intact centuries-old wine bottles—although their drinking maturity has yet to be established. ✉ *13 Society St., West Bank* ☎ *028/7126–1219* ⊕ *www.thesiegemuseum.org* 🍴 *£4.*

St. Augustine's Church

RELIGIOUS SITE | This small jewel of a church is wedged just inside the ramparts of the walls. In the ancient graveyard a large board map registers the location of 163 gravestones in alphabetical order. The site was known as "God's Little Acre," indicating a much larger graveyard, but now sits in an area of a quarter of an acre. It has been a sacred spot since St. Columba founded his first abbey here in AD 546. The oldest gravestone—in the church porch—is that of Richard Carrec, an Elizabethan soldier, dating from circa 1609. Immerse yourself in the serenity of the graveyard under the shadow of the cherry trees, tune into the birdsong, a world away from the tour groups being corralled around the walls. Visitors can tour the church and adjoining graveyard from May to October and are welcome at worship on Sunday or at morning communion on Tuesday at 10:30 am. ⊠ *Palace St., West Bank* ☎ *028/7136–6041.*

★ **St. Columb's Cathedral**
RELIGIOUS SITE | The first Protestant cathedral built in the United Kingdom after the Reformation, this houses the oldest and largest bells in Ireland (dating from the 1620s). It's a treasure house of Derry Protestant emblems, memorials, and relics from the siege of 1688–89; most visitors come to see the keys that locked the four main gates of the city during the siege. The church was built in 1633 in simple Planter's Gothic style, with an intricate corbeled roof and austere spire. In the vestibule is the 270-pound mortar ball that was fired over the wall during the Siege of Derry, with an invitation to surrender sent by King James. Legend has it that when it was read, every man, woman, and child in the city rushed to the walls and shouted, "No surrender!"—a Protestant battle cry to this day. The attached Chapter House Museum has the oldest surviving copy of a map of Derry (from 1600) and the Bible owned by Governor George Walker during the siege. View the information panels and artifacts in display cases that include the original keys to the city and other relics. In recent years the tower and spire have been restored and the stonework and stained-glass windows repaired. A new LED lighting system reveals the beauty of the elegant Canadian pine ceiling. Knowledgeable tour guides are on hand. ⊠ *London St., off Bishop St., West Bank* ☎ *028/7126–7313* ⊕ *www.stcolumbscathedral.org* 🎫 *£2 suggested donation.*

Tower Museum
MUSEUM | The history of Derry is chronicled in this tall, medieval, and magical granite tower that houses the Tower Museum. The original building was constructed in 1615 by the O'Dohertys for their overlords, the O'Donnells, in lieu of tax payments. The museum has excellent information celebrating the life and legacy of St. Columba, with a Discovery Zone on the first floor. The vivid *Story of Derry* covers the city's history, from its origins as a monastic settlement in an oak grove up to the Troubles, which began in 1969 after years of institutionalized discrimination in jobs and public housing. There's also an exhibition—spread over four floors—on the Spanish Armada, thanks to the fact that its fourth-largest ship, *La Trinidad Valencera*, foundered in Kinnagoe Bay, in County Donegal, in 1588. ⊠ *Union Hall Pl., West Bank* ☎ *028/7137–2411* ⊕ *www.derrystrabane.com/towermuseum* 🎫 *£4.*

Verbal Arts Centre
ARTS VENUE | You might expect to see it in Dublin, but the complete manuscript of James Joyce's *Ulysses* has been handwritten on the walls of the Verbal Arts Centre by Colin Dark. You don't, of course, have time to read all of it, but while you're here, admire the marble floor designed by celebrated Irish artist Louis le Brocquy. The center is a hotbed of literary activity promoting the spoken and written word, and presents storytelling re-created in the old Irish tradition of fireside tales. ⊠ *Stable La. and Mall Wall, Bishop St., West Bank* ☎ *028/7126–6946* ⊕ *theverbal.co.*

🍴 Restaurants

Browns in Town
$$ | **IRISH** | The owner, Ian Orr, a former maestro chef who has handed over the cooking to others, has put Derry on the culinary map and in particular this ubercool spot. Candles on tables and leather upholstered horseshoe booths

Derry

St. Columb's Park

EBRINGTON

River Foyle

Browning Dr.

Asylum Rd.

Clarendon St.

Princes St.

Queen St.

Patrick St.

Strand Rd.

Great James St.

Francis St.

Sackville St.

William St.

Little Diamond

Frederick St.

Abbey St.

Rossville St.

Chamberlain St.

Tourist Information Centre

Waterloo Place

Custom House St.

Waterloo St.

High St.

Magazine St.

Fahan St.

Listannon Pk.

Free Derry Corner

Fahan St.

Butcher St.

Society St.

Palace St.

Bishop Street Within

London St.

Pump St.

Ferryquay St.

Linenhall St.

Market St.

Artillery St.

Shipquay St.

Union Hall

Bank Pl.

Water St.

Orchard St.

Whitaker St.

Carlisle Rd.

Bridge St.

Foyle St.

Westland St.

Lecky Rd.

St. Columb's Walls

Long Tower St.

Barrack St.

Bishop Street Without

Upper Bennett St.

Harding St.

The Fountain

Aubrey St.

Wapling Ln.

Hawkin St.

John St.

Foyle Rd.

Peace Bridge

Waterside Link

Train Station

Bellvue Ave.

Maureen St.

Ivy Terrace

Ferguson St.

Lower Bennett St.

Abercorn Rd.

Foyle Rd.

Craigavon Bridge

Foyle Park

Spencer Rd.

Fountain Hill

Moore St.

Duke St.

KEY

1 *Exploring Sights*
1 *Restaurants*
1 *Hotels*

Sights ▼

1 Centre for Contemporary Art (CCA) **C5**
2 Derry City Walls **A5**
3 Derry Girls Mural **C5**
4 Derry Wall Murals **A4**
5 Ebrington Square **E3**
6 Garden of Reflection ... **B5**

7 Guildhall **C3**
8 Museum of Free Derry . **A4**
9 The Siege Museum and Apprentice Boys Hall... **B4**
10 St Augustines Church.. **A5**
11 St Columb's Cathedral.. **B5**
12 Tower Museum **C4**
13 Verbal Arts Centre...... **A5**

Restaurants ▼

1 Browns in Town **B3**
2 Claudes Café **B4**
3 Entrada Restaurant...... **C3**
4 The Exchange............ **C3**
5 Fitzroy's **C5**
6 Primrose **B2**

7 Thompson's Restaurant. **C2**
8 The Warehouse.......... **C3**

Hotels ▼

1 Beech Hill Country House Hotel.... **D7**
2 Bishop's Gate Hotel **A6**
3 Maldron Hotel **B4**
4 The Merchant's House **B1**

with calming cream and brown timber shades set a stylish scene, where the three-course dinner menu at £25 is a hit. **Known for:** Greencastle seafood chowder; chicken wings; banoffee profiterole. [$] *Average main: £17* ⊠ *23 Strand Rd., Central District* ☎ *028/7136–2889* ⊕ *www.brownsrestaurant.com.*

Claudes Cafe

$ | **CAFÉ** | "Say nothin' till ye see Claude," was a famous old Derry saying in the days when Claude Wilton, a solicitor and civil rights campaigner represented all classes and creeds. Although he died in 2008, his name lives on T-shirts in this central, bike-theme café. **Known for:** chicken panini; freshly roasted Segafredo coffee; homemade scones. [$] *Average main: £7* ⊠ *4 Shipquay St., Central District* ☎ *028/7127–9379* ⊕ *www.claudescafederry.co.uk.*

Entrada Restaurant

$$ | **EUROPEAN** | A Spanish theme dominates the food in this newly refashioned brasserie (once the Custom House Restaurant), which opened in 2017. Starters may include tapas or spiced beef croqueta followed by main courses of sirloin, fillet, or rib-eye steak, all cooked in a Spanish charcoal-burning oven and served with *patatas bravas* or heavenly garlic aioli skinny fries. **Known for:** Spanish-style cooking; sirloin steaks; classic cocktails. [$] *Average main: £17* ⊠ *Custom House St., Queen's Quay, Central District* ☎ *028/7137–3366* ⊕ *www.the1876.co.uk* ��� *Closed Mon. and Tues.*

The Exchange

$$ | **IRISH** | Standout dishes at this busy eatery include Louisiana chicken with chorizo cream sauce and tobacco onions, ribs and steaks, and locally caught seafood such as panfried salmon, smoked haddock, or grilled sea bass. Service is superefficient but can be a touch brisk. **Known for:** Louisiana chicken; natural smoked haddock; freshly made cheesecake. [$] *Average main: £15* ⊠ *Exchange House, Queen's Quay, Central District*

Walking Derry

It's easy to find your own way around Derry's streets and riverside. Walkers and cyclists can explore the new traffic-free Waterside Greenway, a 3½-km (2-mile) route through parkland from the east bank of the Foyle over the Peace Bridge to the Foyle Bridge. Or follow the Pathway to Peace, an initiative that emerged after the unveiling of Ireland's first peace flame in Derry by Martin Luther King III in 2013. Ask at the tourist office for details.

☎ *028/7127–3990* ⊕ *www.exchangerestaurant.com* ��� *No lunch Sun.*

Fitzroy's

$ | **EUROPEAN** | **FAMILY** | Great-value portions of burgers, steaks, fish, and Caesar salads are dinner favorites at this popular city-center brasserie that has chalked up a quarter century satisfying the Derry palate. The lunch dishes may include seafood chowder or the delectable chicken melter, made up of cheese, tobacco onions, and bacon with Mexican spices. **Known for:** seafood chowder; chicken melter; malteaser meringue. [$] *Average main: £13* ⊠ *2–4 Bridge St., Central District* ☎ *028/7126–6211* ⊕ *www.fitzroysrestaurant.com.*

★ Primrose

$ | **MODERN IRISH** | Part restaurant, part cocktail bar, part French-style patisserie, Primrose has become a firm favorite with Derry foodies since opening on Strand Road in 2017. Main courses may include roasted cod loin with parsnips and butter sauce, bacon loin with choucroute, wild mushroom and leek risotto, or haddock with buttermilk batter, best washed down with local craft beers such as Northbound's Oak Smoked Beer or Milk Stout from the Walled City brewery. **Known for:** roasted cod loin; lemon meringue pie; sensational pastries made from scratch. ⑤ *Average main: £14* ✉ *53–5 Strand Rd., Central District* ☎ *028/7137–3744* ⊕ *www.primrose-ni. com.*

Thompson's Restaurant

$$ | IRISH | On the banks of the River Foyle, this airy and cool main restaurant of the City Hotel, taking its name from the old Thompson's Mill that once occupied this site, is a fine place to chill while taking in some great river views. The menu might include pork belly, oven-baked salmon, or supreme of chicken with an herb stuffing. The Wine and Dine menu (available every night except Saturday), based on two people sharing two courses, is £39 for two. **Known for:** delicious chicken supreme; impressive, inexpensive wine list; river views. ⑤ *Average main: £15* ✉ *City Hotel on Queen's Quay, Central District* ☎ *028/7136–5800* ⊕ *www.cityhotelderry.com* ⊗ *No lunch Mon.–Sat.*

The Warehouse

$ | IRISH | Right next door to the Guildhall, the Warehouse constitutes a harmonious commingling of café, bistro, art gallery, and shop—but most come to sample the food. The café's breakfasts include dry-cured bacon and toasted sourdough or Kilbeggan organic porridge with apple syrup; lunch specials may be spiced bean stew followed by soothing desserts of Porter cake or macaroons. **Known for:** legendary Scotch eggs; Hannan steaks; Terry's orange cheesecake. ⑤ *Average main: £13* ✉ *1 Guildhall St.* ☎ *028/7126–4798* ⊕ *www.thewarehousederry.com.*

 Hotels

Beech Hill Country House Hotel

$$$ | HOTEL | Journey past a fairy-tale gatehouse amid clumps of beech trees, streams, and a duck pond to reach this grand 1729 country home in 32 acres of woodland. **Pros:** steeped in history; pretty

---

The High and the Flighty

Aviation fans, take note: Derry was where Amelia Earhart touched down on May 21, 1932, after her historic solo flight across the Atlantic. Local lore has it that the first man to reach her airplane greeted her in typically unfazed Derry fashion: "Aye, and what do you want, then?"

---

grounds for walks; walled garden with herbs, veggies, and fruit. **Cons:** not many frills; creaky floors and squeaky doors; long walk from city center. ⑤ *Rooms from: £150* ✉ *32 Ardmore Rd., 3 km (2 miles) southeast of town off A6, Beech Hill* ☎ *028/7134–9279* ⊕ *www.beech-hill. com* ⇥ *28 rooms* ⑩| *Free breakfast.*

★ Bishop's Gate Hotel

$$$$ | HOTEL | Restored from a historic city-center building that was once a gentleman's club, Bishop's Gate Hotel has kept its Edwardian craftsmanship and original architectural details but the plush rooms with velvet furnishings are all fit for the 21st century; just for fun, the guest rooms have retained their antique telephones with rotary dials—and yes, they do work. **Pros:** elegant restoration; central location; valet parking available. **Cons:** surrounding streets can be noisy at night; short on amenities; slow service at busy times. ⑤ *Rooms from: £189* ✉ *24 Bishop St. Within, Central District* ☎ *028/7114–0300* ⊕ *www.bishopsgate-hotelderry.com* ⇥ *31 rooms* ⑩| *Free breakfast.*

Maldron Hotel

$$ | HOTEL | A long-established hotel within the historic walls, the Maldron is ideally suited for exploration of the city center and for guided walking tours. **Pros:** top-notch location for exploring Derry's

walls, sights, and shops; tastefully decorated rooms with modern facilities; lively bar. **Cons:** limited parking available; standard rooms adequate but small; few amenities. $ *Rooms from: £109 ⊠ Maldron Hotel, Butcher St., Central District* ☎ *028/7137–1000* ⊕ *www.maldronhotelderry.com* ⇥ *93 rooms* ⏃ *Free breakfast.*

★ The Merchant's House

$ | **B&B/INN** | Originally a Victorian merchant's family home built to Georgian proportions, No. 16 Queen Street was then a rectory and bank, before Joan Pyne turned it into the city's grandest B&B—garnet-color walls, elaborate plasterwork, and a fireplace make the parlor warm and cheerful. **Pros:** graceful and elegant; great value; owners are knowledgeable about local sights. **Cons:** rooms next to kitchen noisy in morning; small bathrooms; no amenities. $ *Rooms from: £75 ⊠ 16 Queen St., West Bank* ☎ *028/7126–9691* ⊕ *www.thesaddlershouse.com* ⇥ *8 rooms in Merchant's House; 7 rooms with shared bath in Saddler's House* ⏃ *Free breakfast.*

Nightlife

Peadar O'Donnell's Bar

BARS/PUBS | Traditional Irish and folk music sessions are held most nights in the main downstairs bar. There's a different musical personality in the nightclub Gweedore Upstairs, where you're likely to hear everything from indie and house music to rock and chart disco. ⊠ *59–63 Waterloo St., West Bank* ☎ *028/7126–7295.*

Sandinos Cafe Bar

LOCAL INTEREST | For a funky afternoon pit stop, try Sandinos, a haunt of radicals and writers (posters of Che Guevara and Nicaraguan writers decorate the walls). Sample the dozen or so world beers, or try the Dubliner Irish whiskey, a blend of honeycomb and caramel flavors, or The Pogues Irish Whiskey, named after

the famed band. There's traditional Irish music on Sunday from 3 to 9. ⊠ *Water St., West Bank* ☎ *028/7130–9297* ⊕ *www.sandinoscafebar.com.*

Sugar Nightclub

BARS/PUBS | This nightclub is above the popular Quays Bar and many night owls consider this *the* place for dance music in Derry. The club is open only on Wednesday, Friday, and Saturday. ⊠ *33 Shipquay St., West Bank* ☎ *028/7126–6017.*

Performing Arts

If there's one thing about Derry, it certainly knows how to throw a good party. A maelstrom of creative energy was released by the city's role in 2013 as the U.K. City of Culture, and through that cultural transformation the city strengthened its musical mojo. Long celebrated as a place of music, Derry has always expressed its soul in words and songs. Phil Coulter, its most famous musical son, wrote "Ireland's Call," the politically neutral anthem played at Irish rugby, cricket, and hockey internationals, and composed a new song, "Bright, Brand New Day," to celebrate the cultural year. Other celebrated musical offspring of the city include Feargal Sharkey and his band the Undertones, and Nadine Coyle from Girls Aloud.

Music festivals take pride of place in the annual calendar of events. During the City of Derry Big Band Jazz Festival in May, it's a case of boogie all over town: R&B, swing, jive, soul, and blues singers, as well as tribute acts, take over bars, cafés, hotels, restaurants, and community centers. Music also tops the bill at the Foyle Folk Festival, the Walled City Music Festival, and the Maiden City Festival. Literature, drama, and film are all given prominence throughout the year. On October 31, the Banks of the Foyle Halloween Carnival morphs into what the tourism bureau calls "the largest street party in Ireland." The city has also reinvented itself with cultural centers and new galleries sprouting up—excellent places for visual snacking.

Millennium Forum

CONCERTS | This catch-all venue hosts everything from boy bands and comedians to plays, musicals, tattoo conventions, and even weddings (invitations required). The Arbutus at the Forum restaurant on the ground floor offers discounts on show nights and snacks during the day from noon. ⊠ *Newmarket St., West Bank* ☎ *028/7126–4455, 028/7137–2492 for reservations* ⊕ *www.millenniumforum.co.uk.*

Playhouse

CONCERTS | With its impressive auditorium and workshop spaces, the Playhouse stages traditional and contemporary plays and holds concerts. ⊠ *5–7 Artillery St., West Bank* ☎ *028/7126–8027* ⊕ *www.derryplayhouse.co.uk.*

🛍 Shopping

Although the major retail department stores are here, shopping is generally low-key. There are some upscale examples of Irish craftsmanship to be found, however. Stroll up Shipquay Street to discover small arts-and-crafts stores and an indoor shopping center. Walk through the Craft Village (just off Shipquay Street) to see the way the city used to look. The Village, with its glass canopy, re-creates life between the 16th and 19th centuries and sells Derry crystal, handwoven cloth, ceramics, jewelry, and books. Not to be outdone by Belfast, Derry has set up its own Cathedral Quarter. In the heart of the old city, streets leading from the cathedral—Pump Street, Artillery Street, and Bishop Street—are busy with craft workers, goldsmiths, and jewelers; art galleries sit cheek by jowl with nail bars, solariums, and treatment spas. Bedlam, a maze of rooms on Bishop Street, is a humming nest of traders under one roof. Vintage clothes, antiques, retro furnishings, and New Age products are on sale.

To appreciate the beauty and scale of the area's Georgian architecture, walk slowly along Pump Street, with a copy of *City of Derry,* an excellent historical gazetteer to the built heritage—it has a wealth of information and color about each individual building. As you wander around the streets, look out for the Golden Teapot—a 19th-century trade sign in the shape of a gilded copper teapot—restored in 2013 and hanging outside Faller's jewelers on Strand Road; catch the right moment and a plume of environmentally friendly smoke is discharged from its spout. The only other one in the world is in Boston.

BOOKS

Foyle Books

BOOKS/STATIONERY | Derry's largest selection of secondhand and antiquarian titles can be found here. The specialties include English lit, Irish-language books, criticism, poetry, biography, local history, heritage and culture, travel, music, and sports. For further browsing check the website, where it is known as Walled City Books accessible through the Abe Books site. ⊠ *12 Magazine St., West Bank* ☎ *028/7137–2530.*

CRAFTS, GIFTS, AND JEWELRY

Faller The Jeweller

JEWELRY/ACCESSORIES | It's worth calling in to hear the history of the restored Victorian golden teapot hanging outside this long-established family-run shop. Faller's specializes in brooches and charms reflecting local landmarks in its Drop of Derry range; you can even buy a small replica of the famed teapot. The city's cultural history, music, and sporting life are featured in designs as well as Roaring Meg cannon, the Peace Bridge, Guildhall, and city walls. Even more popular are the High Crosses of Inishowen in nearby Donegal; ancient Celtic crosses such as St. Mura, Donagh, and Cooley are all available as pendants. ⊠ *12 Strand Rd.,*

West Bank ☏ *028/7136–2710* ⊕ *www. faller.com.*

Occasions

GIFTS/SOUVENIRS | This remains one of Derry's best showcases for Irish crafts, cards, and gifts. ✉ *48 Spencer Rd., East Bank* ☏ *028/7132–9595.*

Thomas the Goldsmith

JEWELRY/ACCESSORIES | Head here for exquisite work by international jewelry designers. Ask about their Peace Bridge Collection, handcrafted and individually designed in the workshop. ✉ *7 Pump St., West Bank* ☏ *028/7137–4549* ⊕ *www. thomasgoldsmiths.com.*

Omagh

55 km (34 miles) south of Derry.

Omagh, the county town of Tyrone, lies close to the Sperrin Mountains, with the River Strule to the north. The playwright Brian Friel was born here. Sadly, it's better known as the scene of the worst atrocity of the Troubles, when an IRA bomb killed 31 people in 1998. On the 10th anniversary of the bombing, the **Garden of Light,** a touching memorial by artist Sean Hillen and landscape architect Desmond Fitzgerald, was opened. A heliostatic mirror in the memorial park tracks the sun and directs a beam of light onto 31 small mirrors, each etched with the name of a victim. They in turn bounce the light via another hidden mirror onto a heart-shape crystal in an obelisk at the bomb site in Market Street. An entire room in Omagh Library, housing 800 books of condolence and reflecting worldwide media coverage, is dedicated to the memory of the attack. Ask about access to this archive at the tourist office, which is in the Strule Arts Centre, a good place for a relaxing snack or meal, and where you may also find out about any events or shows being held. Pick up a voucher booklet, Explore Omagh, which offers discounts in many shops

and restaurants, as well as two-for-one entrance deals to the Ulster American Folk Park (⊕ *www.exploreomaghsperrins. com*).

GETTING HERE

The Translink Goldline service operates buses between Derry and Belfast and traverses delightfully mellifluous-sounding Tyrone towns, from Strabane to Ballygawley, and thence along the M1 into Belfast. Journey time is just under two hours (£19 round-trip, or £12.70 after 9:30 am). Services in both directions stop on request at the popular Ulster American Folk Park.

Omagh, 55 km (34 miles) south of Derry on A5, is a busy hub. Free car parking on the town's two main central streets, High and Market, is available for one hour. Pay-and-display ticket machines, costing £0.40 per hour, operate in car parks at Mountjoy Road (beside the bus station) and Kevlin Avenue. You can also park free for two hours in the retail park at the Showgrounds, on Sedan Avenue.

Sights

⭐ **Ulster American Folk Park**

MUSEUM | The excellent Ulster American Folk Park re-creates a Tyrone village of two centuries ago, a log-built American settlement of the same period, and the docks and ships that the emigrants to America would have used. The center-piece is an old whitewashed cottage, now a museum, which is the ancestral home of Thomas Mellon (1813–1908), the U.S. banker and philanthropist. Another thatch cottage is a reconstruc-tion of the boyhood home of Archbishop John Hughes, founder of New York's St. Patrick's Cathedral. There are full-scale replicas of Irish peasant cottages, a New York tenement room, immigrant transport ship holders, plus a 19th-century Ulster village, complete with staff dressed in period costumes. The **Mellon Centre for Migration Studies** contains 16,000 books and periodicals, an Irish emigration database including passenger lists from 1800 to 1860, emigrant letters, and maps of geographical regions of both Ireland and America. Other notable exhibits include William Murray's drapery store and W. G. O'Doherty's original candy store on the bustling Ulster Street, where visitors can explore the world of retail therapy in the early 1900s. ✉ *Mellon Rd., Castletown, 10 km (6 miles) north of Omagh on A5* ☎ *028/8224–3292* ⊕ *www.nmni.com/uafp* 🎫 *£9* ⊘ *Closed Mon. Mellon Centre closed Sun. and Mon.*

Belleek

42 km (25 miles) southwest of Omagh.

World-famous Belleek Pottery is made in the old town of Belleek, on the northwestern edge of Lower Lough Erne, at the border with Northwest Ireland. Other porcelain-ware makers are a couple of miles across the border.

GETTING HERE AND AROUND

Belleek is on A46, a scenic route running along the southern shore of Lower Lough Erne between Enniskillen (a 30-minute drive), in County Fermanagh, and Ballyshannon (15 minutes), in County Donegal. There is ample car parking at the pottery factory—the reason most people come here—with no time restrictions. You can also park free along main or side streets.

Sights

★ Belleek Pottery

TOUR—SIGHT | On the riverbank stands the visitor center of Belleek Pottery Ltd., producers of Parian china, a fine, eggshell-thin, ivory porcelain shaped into dishes, figurines, vases, and baskets. There's a factory, showroom, exhibition, museum, and café. You can watch a 20-minute audiovisual presentation or join a 30-minute tour of the factory,

where you can get up close and talk to craftspeople—there's hardly any noise coming from machinery in the workshops. Everything here is made by hand just as workers did back in 1857. The showroom is filled with beautiful but pricey gifts: a shamrock cup-and-saucer set costs about £59, and a bowl in a basket-weave style (typical of Belleek) runs £100 and up. The company has a jewelry portfolio called Belleek Living featuring designs inspired by the Irish landscape. ✉ *3 Main St.* ☎ *028/6865–8501* ⊕ *www.belleek.ie* 🎫 *£6.*

Restaurants

The Thatch

$ | **CAFÉ** | Housed in a lovely building dating to the 18th century, this simple café is worth a visit—not just for the excellent soups, sandwiches, baked potatoes, and similarly light fare—but also because it's the only thatch-roof establishment in the entire county. Full of locals and the sounds of easy banter, it's the perfect place to glean insider knowledge and gossip about the surrounding area. 💲 *Average main: £10* ✉ *20 Main St.* ☎ *028/6865–8181* ▭ *No credit cards* ⊘ *Closed Sun.*

Enniskillen

5 km (3 miles) south of Devenish Island, Lower Lough Erne.

Enniskillen is the pleasant, smart-looking capital of County Fermanagh and the only place of any size in it. The town center is, strikingly, on an island in the River Erne between Lower and Upper Lough Erne. The principal thoroughfares, Townhall and High Streets, are crowded with old-style pubs, family-run shops, and rows of red-brick Georgian flats. The tall, dark spires of the 19th-century St. Michael's and St. Macartin's Cathedrals, both on Church Street, tower over the leafy town center.

Beautiful Belleek

The origins of Belleek china are every bit as romantic as the Belleek blessing plates traditionally given to brides and grooms on their wedding day—that is, if you believe the legends. The story goes that in the mid-1800s, John Caldwell Bloomfield, the man behind the world-famous porcelain, accidentally discovered the raw ingredients necessary to produce china. After inheriting his father's estate in the Fermanagh Lakelands on the shore of the Erne River, he whitewashed his cottage using a flaky white powder dug up in his backyard. A passerby, struck by the luminescent sheen of the freshly painted cottage, commented on the unusual brightness of the walls to Bloomfield, who promptly ordered a survey of the land, which duly uncovered all the minerals needed to make porcelain. The venture was complete when

Bloomfield met his business partners, London architect Robert Armstrong and wealthy Dublin merchant David McBirney. They decided to first produce earthenware, and then porcelain. The rest, as they say, is history. The delicate, flawless porcelain (Bloomfield declared that any piece with even the slightest blemish should be destroyed) soon attracted the attention of Queen Victoria and other aristocrats. Other companies tried to mimic the china's delicate beauty, but genuine Belleek porcelain is recognizable by its seashell designs, basket weaves, and marine themes. It has become a favored tradition in Ireland to give a piece of Belleek china at weddings, giving rise to a saying: "If a newly married couple receives a piece of Belleek, their marriage will be blessed with lasting happiness."

GETTING HERE AND AROUND

Translink's Goldline express buses connect Enniskillen with Belfast, 145 km (90 miles) east. Buses run from early morning to late evening, with a two-hour journey time (£19 round-trip). Enniskillen also has a slew of cross-border services in many directions. Bus Éireann operates expressway routes west to Sligo.

Enniskillen is 85 km (52 miles) south of Derry on A32 and A5. The town has many car parks, including ones at East Bridge, Eden, Market, and Townhall Streets. Be warned: parking attendants clamp down on all drivers lacking a ticket for the required duration of their stay. On the street there are few free spaces, so be careful where you park.

TOURS

Erne Tours

BOAT TOURS | Fancy a dreamy boat tour on Lough Erne? This company operates tours, about 100 minutes long on the lower lough, aboard the *Kestrel,* a 56-seat water bus. The boat leaves from Round O Pier at Enniskillen. Each day it stops for 45 minutes at Devenish Island. From early May to the end of September, the company also has a Saturday-evening dinner cruise departing at 6:30. The three-course meal costs £33 (two-course £28), and the cruise, which leaves from the Killyhevlin Hotel near Enniskillen, lasts two hours. ✉ *Round O Pier* ☎ *028/6632–2882* ⊕ *www.ernetours.com* ☞ *100-min tour £10.*

VISITOR INFORMATION

Fermanagh Visitor Information Centre
Your first stop should be the tourist information office on Wellington Road—based at Castlebarracks—for an excellent array of leaflets, maps, and guidebooks. Pick up brochures on History and Heritage Trails, Natural Heritage Trails, and shopping and arts and crafts throughout County Fermanagh. The Fermanagh Genealogy Centre is also based in this building and assists visitors in finding their family history connections in Fermanagh by providing a free 30-minute consultation. The center is open for appointments on Monday, Wednesday, and Thursday afternoon 2–5 (⊕ www.fermanaghgenealogy.org). ⊠ *Castlebarracks, Wellington Rd.* ☎ *028/6632–5000* ⊕ *www.enniskillencastle.co.uk.*

 Sights

Blakes of the Hollow

RESTAURANT—SIGHT | Among the several relaxed and welcoming old pubs in Enniskillen's town center, the one with the most appeal is Blakes, a place hardly altered since it opened in 1887. Its name derives from the fact that the heart of the town lies in a slight hollow and the pub's landlord is named William Blake. Traditional music sessions are held on Friday night in the front bar, which is also the best place for local gossip and stories. If the *druth*—a Fermangh word for thirst—is on you, then it's worth trying the craft beer, Inishmacsaint, from an island in Lough Erne that reflects an ancient tradition established by monks 900 years ago; or you could try the exclusive Midleton Single Cask Irish Whiskey, 26 years in the making. Bottled exclusively for Blake's, it went on sale in 2019, although you can't buy it by the glass—only by the bottle—and for a cool £690. The bar displays one of the doors from the *Game of Thrones* TV series filmed in parts of Northern Ireland. The door was salvaged from beech trees that came down in a storm in 2016 and were transformed into unique works of art. This one, Door 4, depicts House Targaryen's return to power. Lunch and dinner are served in the adjoining Café Merlot. ⊠ *6 Church St.* ☎ *028/6632–2143* ⊕ *www.blakesofthehollow.com.*

Buttermarket

STORE/MALL | More than 20 wonderful arts-and-crafts shops selling Fermanagh pottery, jewelry, and paintings are gathered at the Buttermarket, a restored dairy market built in 1835. The organically run skin-care shop, Natures Inspiration, sells biodegradable products, free of artificial coloring or fragrances and not tested on animals. The center also has a café. ⊠ *Down St.* ☎ *028/6632–3117* ⊕ *www.fermanaghenterprise.com.*

Enniskillen Castle

CASTLE/PALACE | Strategically sited overlooking the River Erne, Enniskillen's 600-year-old waterfront castle is one of the best-preserved monuments in the north, and has undergone a multimillion-pound redevelopment, which has seen the tourist office merging with the castle complex, creating a new gateway to the region. Built in the early 15th century by the Gaelic Maguires to command the waterway, the castle was of tremendous importance in guarding one of the few passes into Ulster and the crossing point between Upper and Lower Lough Erne. After a yearlong program of work costing £3.3 million, four new galleries spread over two floors are now in place in the restored barrack coach house. Fermanagh's unique lakeland history is interpreted in the galleries. Exhibitions highlight life from prehistoric times to the present day, from *crannógs* (man-made island settlements) to early Christian stone sculpture, Belleek pottery, and rural crafts and traditions. A new building, in the shape of the original armory, links the visitor center with the coach house, allowing tourists a glimpse of the original castle wall. The center, styling itself as a "history hub," combines tourism, genealogy, archive, and heritage services alongside a café and shop. The Camp Commander's garden has also been re-created. The polished paraphernalia of the Inniskillings Museum, which includes weapons, badges, medals, and engravings, is held in the castle keep. Pride of place is given to the bugle sounded at the charge of the regiment at the Battle of the Somme in 1916. There are interactive displays, and a Roll of Honor contains the names of the 9,100 people from all over Ireland who died in World War II. ⊠ *Castlebarracks, Wellington Rd.* ☎ *028/6632–5000* ⊕ *www.enniskillencastle.co.uk* ✉ *£5.*

Enniskillen Royal Grammar School

ARTS VENUE | Beyond the West Bridge is Enniskillen Royal Grammar School, formerly Portora Royal School (it became co-ed in 2017), established in 1608 by King James I. On the grounds are some ruins of Portora Castle. Writers educated here included Samuel Beckett and Oscar Wilde, the pride of the school (until his trial for homosexuality). The life and writings of Beckett, the droll existentialist and arch-modernizer born near Dublin in 1906, is celebrated at the Happy Days International Beckett Festival; some festival events are held at the school, as well as other locations around Fermanagh over the bank holiday weekend at the end of August. The multidisciplinary festival incorporates literature, theater, visual arts, film, and comedy, and offers a chance to savor some of Beckett's killer lines, such as this one from *Waiting for Godot*: "Let us not then speak ill of our generation, it is not any unhappier than its predecessors." ⊠ *Derrygonnelly Rd.* ☎ *028/6632–2658* ⊕ *www.happy-days-enniskillen.com.*

Water Gate

MILITARY SITE | At the Erne riverside, the 16th-century Water Gate, between two handsome turrets, protected the town from invading armies. The flag of St.

George flies over the building, a tradition that dates back to the 17th century, when local soldiers of the Inniskilling Regiments fought for the Protestant William of Orange against the Catholic James II. ⊠ *Enniskillen.*

Hotels

★ Lough Erne Resort

$$$$ | **RESORT** | Set between two serene lakes on the small island of Ely, the manicured lawns of the Lough Erne Resort, with its backdrop of shimmering Castle Hume Lough, is a special property with a country-house feel in a mix of reconstituted sandstone and Danish timber. **Pros:** handsome rooms with great amenities; Thai spa and pool; two championship golf courses. **Cons:** luxury comes at a steep price; no loungers for swimming pool users; service slow at busy times. Ⓢ *Rooms from: £180* ⊠ *Belleek Rd., 5 km (3 miles) north of Enniskillen* ☎ *028/6632–3230* ⊕ *www.lougherneresort.com* ➪ *120 rooms* ⦿ *Free breakfast.*

Florence Court

11 km (7 miles) south of Enniskillen.

When it comes to Early Irish Georgian houses, there are few as magical as Florence Court. There are 15 km (9 miles) of signposted walking and biking trails in the grounds, ranging from short walks to three-hour hikes. The longer ones link up with the Ulster Way and Cuilcagh Way long-distance routes.

GETTING HERE AND AROUND

There is no direct bus service, but the main Enniskillen–Swanlinbar Translink bus pulls over on request to allow you to hop off at the Creamery Corner stop. From there, it's a 3-km (2-mile) walk to the estate's entrance, and a rather long walk along the avenue to reach the main house.

Take A4 south from Enniskillen and continue south on A32 (also signed as Swanlinbar Road) to reach Florence Court. The drive takes 10 minutes. There is ample car parking at Florence Court, and in summer an overflow car park operates. The admission price to the house and grounds includes parking.

◉ Sights

★ Florence Court

HOUSE | FAMILY | Less known than some showier estates, this three-story Anglo-Irish mansion was built around 1730 for John Cole, father of the 1st Earl of Enniskillen. Topped off about 1760 with its distinctive two flanking colonnaded wings, the central house contains a surfeit of Palladian windows, keystones, and balustrades—thanks to, as one architectural historian put it, "the vaingloriousness of a provincial hand." Even more impressive is its bucolic, baroque setting, as the Cuilcagh Mountains form a wonderful contrast to the shimmering white-stone facade. Showstoppers in terms of design are the rococo plasterwork ceilings in the dining room; the Venetian Room; and the famous staircase—all ascribed to Robert West, one of Dublin's most famous *stuccadores* (plasterworkers). For a peek at the "downstairs" world, check out the restored kitchen and other service quarters. You can browse a gift shop and secondhand bookstore; holiday accommodations are available at the Butler's Apartment. During 2019 two greenhouses were restored and produce from them is available to buy in the shop. A new visitor center, opposite the walled garden, with an outdoor shop sells takeaway snacks. ✉ *11 km*

(7 miles) south of Enniskillen on A4 and A32, Enniskillen ☎ 028/6634–8249 ⊕ www.nationaltrust.org.uk/florence-court ✉ £12 for house, park, and grounds.

Castle Coole

3 km (2 miles) east of Enniskillen.

This "uncommonly perfect" mansion (to quote the eminent architectural historian Desmond Guinness) is on its own landscaped oak woods and gardens at the end of a long tree-lined driveway.

GETTING HERE AND AROUND
There is no bus service to Castle Coole. You can request the driver to stop on the Translink Enniskillen–Clones route only. The main express bus service heading for Belfast does not stop here.

A five-minute drive from Enniskillen on A4, Castle Coole has a car park (£2.50 per car) that overflows in the summer.

 Sights

Castle Coole
CASTLE/PALACE | Although the Irish architect Richard Johnston made the original drawings in the 1790s, and was responsible for the foundation, the castle was, for all intents and purposes, the work of James Wyatt, commissioned by the 1st Earl of Belmore. One of the best-known architects of his time, Wyatt was based in London but visited Ireland only once, so Alexander Stewart was drafted as the resident builder-architect. The designer wasn't the only imported element; in fact, much of Castle Coole came from England, including the main facade, which is clad in Portland stone and was hauled here by bullock carts. And what a facade it is—in perfect symmetry, white colonnaded wings extend from either side of the mansion's three-story, nine-bay center block, with a Palladian central

portico and pediment. It is perhaps the apotheosis of the 18th century's reverence for the Greeks.

Inside, the house is remarkably preserved; most of the lavish plasterwork and original furnishings are in place. The saloon is one of the finest rooms in the house, with a vast expanse of oak flooring, gilded Regency furniture, and gray scagliola pilasters with Corinthian capitals. One-hour tours are held daily, with the last one at 4:15 pm, and include Life Below Stairs, which explores the servants' rooms and service quarters; above stairs is the present Earl of Belmore, who still lives on the estate. During the day the Tallow House tearoom serves lunches and snacks. ✉ *Dublin Rd., A4, Enniskillen ☎ 028/6632–2690 ⊕ www.nationaltrust.org.uk/castle-coole ✉ House and grounds £11; grounds only £4; car £10 (per adult).*

Armagh

75 km (42 miles) east of Enniskillen.

The spiritual capital of Ireland for 5,000 years, and the seat of both Protestant and Catholic archbishops, Armagh is the most venerated of Irish cities. St. Patrick called it "my sweet hill" and built his stone church on the hill where the Anglican cathedral now stands. On the opposite hill, the twin-spire Catholic cathedral is flanked by two large marble statues of archbishops, who look across the land. Despite the pleasing Georgian terraces around the elegant mall east of the town center, Armagh can seem drab. It suffered as a trouble spot in the sectarian conflict, though it's now the scene of some spirited and sympathetic renovation.

GETTING HERE AND AROUND
Buses link Armagh with neighboring towns as well as Belfast, an 80-minute journey. You can catch a Translink

Fabled haunt of "the little people," the stately abode of Florence Court sits in a vale reputedly populated by leprechauns and fairies.

Goldline express from the Buscentre on the Lonsdale Road in Armagh (£17 round-trip, one-third discount after 9:30 am). Cross-border buses also operate out of Armagh—you can hop aboard the Belfast–Galway Bus Éireann bus that runs via Cavan Town and Athlone. Round-trip to Galway is £35.15. Bus Éireann expressway connections run from Dublin to Portrush on the north coast and stop in Armagh. The Armagh–Dublin bus journey (three times each day at 8 am, noon, and 8 pm) takes 2¾ hours and costs £21.65 round-trip.

Armagh is a one-hour drive from Belfast along A3 before joining the M1 at Portadown. Dublin is just over two hours south via Newry on A28 and A1, before crossing the Irish border to join the motorway for the rest of your journey. There are several pay-and-display parking lots in Armagh city center. The main one is next to the tourist office, on English Street. You can also park at the mall, and there is free parking on side streets.

VISITOR INFORMATION

CONTACTS Armagh Visitor Information Centre. ✉ *40 English St.* ☎ *028/3752–1800* ⊕ *www.visitarmagh.com.*

Sights

Armagh Planetarium

OBSERVATORY | FAMILY | Displayed here in all its nickel-iron glory is Ireland's largest meteorite, an astonishing 4.5 billion years old and weighing 336 pounds. Elsewhere, find a spaceship, satellite models, a moon map on which you can walk, and the Digital Theater with Digistar 5—sit back and navigate the night sky in the company of experts. Weekend children's activities include building and launching rockets. Outside, stroll through the solar system and the Milky Way at the huge scale model of the universe. ✉ *College Hill* ☎ *028/3752–3689* ⊕ *www.armagh-planet.com* 🎟 *£8.*

Off The Beaten Path

Marble Arch Caves Global Geopark. This geopark—one of Europe's finest show caves—has an interpretative center and trail walking routes in the surrounding mountainous uplands, including Cuilcagh, the highest point shared between counties Fermanagh and Cavan. The only UNESCO geopark in Northern Ireland, it's an ideal half-day underground activity, especially if it's a wet day in Fermanagh. Stalactites glisten above streams as you admire fragile mineral veils and cascades of calcite-coated walls and waterfalls. Guided boat tours, run by knowledgeable tour guides, last 75 minutes but may not be available after heavy rain. The show cave requires climbing 150 steps so it is not accessible for wheelchairs or strollers. ▣TIP→ **Bring walking shoes and a warm sweater. Tours begin at Marlbank Scenic Loop Centre, Florencecourt. There are frequent events that are suitable for children, such as fossil fun days and wildlife walks—check the website for details. There's also a restaurant and souvenir shop.** ✉ *43 Marlbank Rd., Legnabrocky, Florencecourt, Enniskillen* ✛ *The geopark is in south Fermanagh, 19 km (12 miles) south of Enniskillen and about 3 km (2 miles) from village of Florencecourt. It also lies 8 km (5 miles) on northern side of Irish border separating Cavan from Fermanagh* ☎ *028/6634–8855* ⊕ *www.marblearchcavesgeopark.com* ✉ *£11* ⊘ *Closed Nov.–mid-Mar.*

Navan Centre and Fort

ARCHAEOLOGICAL SITE | FAMILY | Just outside Armagh is Ulster's Camelot—the region's ancient capital. Excavations date activity to 700 BC. The fort has strong associations with figures of Irish history. Legend has it that thousands of years ago this was the site of the palace of Queen Macha; subsequent tales call it the barracks of the legendary Ulster warrior Cuchulainn and his Red Branch Knights. Remains dating from 94 BC are particularly intriguing: a great conical structure, 120 feet in diameter, was formed from five concentric circles made of 275 wooden posts, with a 276th, about 12 yards high, situated in the center. In a ritual whose meaning is not known, it was filled with brushwood and set on fire. Young children can dig into the past in the Archeo Pit, dress up as a Celt, and touch history with "feely boxes." In the summer guided tours are held every two hours and last 40 minutes. Ecology trails bring the environmental aspects of Navan to life. There's a bug hotel, listening posts, bird boxes, a viewing hide, and Armagh's only "bug and beastie" viewer. ✉ *81 Killyleagh Rd., 3 km (2 miles) west of Armagh on A28* ☎ *028/3752–9644* ⊕ *www.navan.com* ✉ *Apr.–Sept. £7, Oct.–Mar. £6.*

St. Patrick's Anglican Cathedral

RELIGIOUS SITE | Near the city center, a squat battlement tower identifies the cathedral, in simple, early-19th-century low-Gothic style. On the site of much older churches, it contains relics of Armagh's long history. Brian Boru, the High King (King of All Ireland) is buried here. In 1014, he drove the Vikings out of Ireland but was killed after the battle was won. Some memorials and tombs here are by important 18th-century sculptors such as Roubiliac and Rysbrack. The cathedral's atmospheric crypt is also open to visitors by prior arrangement. Dating from the Middle Ages, this sanctuary was where law-abiding citizens safely stored their valuable goods. A few archbishops are buried here, too. ✉ *43*

Abbey St., Cathedral Close ☎ *028/3752–3142* ⊕ *www.stpatricks-cathedral.org* 🎫 *£3.*

St. Patrick's Roman Catholic Cathedral

RELIGIOUS SITE | The pale limestone St. Patrick's, the seat of a Roman Catholic archdiocese, rises above a hill to dominate the north end of Armagh. The cathedral's rather gloomy interior is enlivened by a magnificent organ, the potential of which is fully realized at services. Construction of the twin-spire structure started in 1840 in the neo-Gothic style, but the Great Famine brought work to a halt until 1854, and it wasn't completed until 1873. An arcade of statues over the main doorway on the exterior is one of the cathedral's most interesting features. The altar is solid Irish granite, and the woodwork is Austrian oak. ✉ *Cathedral Rd.* ☎ *028/3752–2802* ⊕ *www.armagharchdiocese.org/st-patricks-cathedral.*

The Mountains of Mourne

52½ km (32½ miles) southeast of Armagh on A28, 51 km (32 miles) south of Belfast.

Subjects of a song that is sung on every Irish occasion from baptisms to funerals, the Mountains of Mourne must surely qualify as one of Ireland's best-known ranges. According to those lyrics by Percy French, the Mountains of Mourne "sweep down to the sea," from 2,000-foot summits. East of the unprepossessing border city of Newry, this area was long considered ungovernable, its hardy inhabitants living from smuggling contraband into the numerous rocky coves on the seashore. Much of the Mourne range is still inaccessible except on foot. The countryside is gorgeous: high, windswept pasture and moorland threaded with bright streams, bound by a tracery of drystone walls, and dotted with sheep and whitewashed farmhouses snuggled in stands of sycamore. It's the perfect landscape for away-from-it-all walkers, cyclists, and serious climbers.

GETTING HERE AND AROUND
Newcastle bus station on Railway Street is the arrival and departure point for all routes to one of the most scenic parts of Northern Ireland. Ulsterbus service leaves Belfast regularly for the 48-km (30-mile) trip to Newcastle (70 minutes, £15 round-trip). If you wish to appreciate the panoramic glory of the Mountains of Mourne, take a bus from Newcastle along the coast to the foothill towns of Annalong and Kilkeel (£8.30 round-trip). To truly get an up-close feel for the mountains, board the Mourne Rambler (info found on Rambler Services on the Translink website), a 23-seat rural bus that transports you to the heart of Mourne country. A complete circuit on the Rambler, which runs in July and August and during school holidays over Easter, takes 90 minutes (£9). You can also catch a bus from Newcastle to Dublin. This service starts from Downpatrick and runs from Newcastle to Castlewellan, Newry, and across the border to Dublin (£22.60 round-trip).

Newcastle is a 45-minute drive south of Belfast on A24 through Ballynahinch. A one-way system operates through the town and is especially crowded during summer. Car parks are at the seafront near the Slieve Donard Hotel, beside the bus station, and at Donard Park. The nearest city is Newry, a 35-minute drive west on A25.

Sights

Castlewellan Forest Park

NATIONAL/STATE PARK | A huge maze, grown to symbolize Northern Ireland's convoluted path to peace, comprises 1,150 acres of forested hills running between the Mourne Mountains and Slieve Croob. There are also signposted

Thackeray admired the Church of Ireland's St. Patrick's Cathedral, which, with St. Patrick's Roman Catholic Cathedral, jointly presides over Armagh.

mountain-biking trails, ranging from short routes of 4 km (2½ miles) up to 19 km (12 miles), and 7½ km (5 miles) of walking trails. Look out for the multistemmed sequoia, a giant redwood in the walled garden, which, in 2018, was named as Northern Ireland's Tree of the Year by the Woodland Trust, a conservation charity. With the maze, lake, secluded arbors, and arboretum, the park makes an excellent introduction to the area. Bike and canoe rental is available at the center starting from £18 for three hours. ☒ Castlewellan ☎ 028/4377–8664 ⊕ castlewellancastle.org ☒ Free, vehicles £5.

Newcastle

INFO CENTER | A disarmingly subtle resort, Newcastle offers cool restaurants, art galleries, independent shops, antique emporia, chic cafés, and ice-cream boutiques on its 3-km-long (2-mile-long) energizing stretch of waterfront. But you will still find old-fashioned amusement arcades, fun fairs, and children's play areas to serve up a little seaside resort nostalgia. Sculptures, named by local

schoolchildren, are arranged close to the beach and reflect the town's maritime connection. The visitor information center, at 10–14 Central Promenade, is well stocked with details on local attractions, and books and maps of walking and biking trails in the Mourne Mountains and forest parks. A mountain-biking trail map is available for £2; if you intend to cycle, ask for the "Make Your Day Cycle Routes" brochure. ☒ Newcastle ☎ 028/4372–2222 ⊕ www.visitmourne-mountains.co.uk.

Silent Valley

VIEWPOINT | The road to Silent Valley Reservoir Park leads to mountain views and excellent photo ops. Also here is a visitor center with an informative exhibition explaining the history of Silent Valley. Look into the Locals Room, which celebrates the men who worked on the building of the reservoir as well as the Mourne Wall. You can also pick up information on a walking and heritage trail of 1.8 km (just over 1 mile) or the more strenuous Ben Crom Dam Walk, which

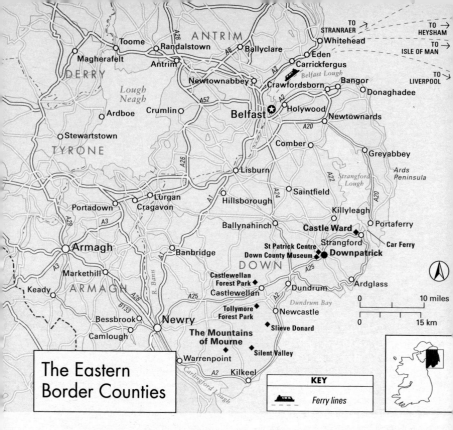

The Eastern Border Counties

KEY

Ferry lines

is 10 km (6 miles). ✉ *Kilkeel ⌖ 6 km (4 miles) north of Kilkeel off B27, right turn* ☎ *028/9035–4716* ⊕ *www.niwater.com/silent-valley* ✍ *£2, vehicles £5.*

Slieve Donard

MOUNTAIN—SIGHT | Looming above Newcastle is Slieve Donard, its panoramic, 2,796-foot-high summit grandly claiming views into England, Wales, and Scotland "when it's clear enough"—in other words, "rarely," say the pessimists. It's not possible to drive up the mountain, so leave your car in the Donard parking lot and follow signs for the Slieve Donard Trail. It should take roughly three hours to climb to the summit and no longer than two hours to descend. Experienced hikers should not find it difficult, but if you prefer an easier trek, follow the trails signposted in Tollymore Forest Park or follow the Mourne Coastal Footpath.

Hiking boots are essential and, as the weather can be unpredictable, it's advisable to take an extra layer of clothing, even in summer. ✉ *Mourne Mountains, Newcastle.*

Tollymore Forest Park

NATIONAL/STATE PARK | Covering 1,300 acres and entered through Gothic gateways, Tollymore Forest Park has been thrust into the spotlight because of its starring role in the TV series *Game of Thrones*. The forest extends up the valley of the River Shimna, which was the place where the Starks discovered the dire wolf pups in Westeros. It was also used for the Haunted Forest north of the wall, the Wolfswood near Winterfell, and the Kings Road near Castle Black. The arboretum at Tollymore has the widest range of tree species of any park in Ireland. Apart from the better-known oak, birch, beech, and Sitka spruce, the eucalyptus from Australia and Tasmania stand out and bring a cheerful note. *Game of Thrones* fans can book a Tollymore guided locations trek held at 10 and 3 each day for £10 (this does not include the entrance fee to the forest park). The tour, lasting 1 hr and 45 minutes, is an immersive experience; Stark cloaks are provided at no extra cost. Alternatively, you can do the trek yourself without an official guide. Details are at ⊕ *www.gameofthrones-tours.com*, or for more information ☎ *028/9568–0023.* ✉ *Tullybrannigan Rd., Mourne Mountains* ☎ *028/4372–2428* ⊕ *www.walkni.com* 🚗 *Vehicles £5.*

Restaurants

Brunel's

$$ | MODERN IRISH | A huge mural on brick walls features a top-hatted Isambard Kingdom Brunel, this relaxed seafood restaurant's namesake and a famous figure in engineering history with connections to the area. The food philosophy here means using seasonal and local produce, and the menu features wild ingredients freshly foraged from nearby Dundrum Bay or Strangford Lough. **Known for:** outstanding roast beef; hay-smoked venison; white chocolate crème brûlée. ⑤ *Average main: £16* ✉ *32 Downs Rd, Mourne Mountains* ⊹ *The restaurant overlooks seafront a few minutes' walk from Slieve Donard Hotel* ☎ *028/4372–3951* ⊕ *www.brunelsrestaurant.co.uk.*

★ Carrick Cottage Café

$ | IRISH | Venture a few miles south of Newcastle and a 10-minute drive toward Annalong to Head Road where hedgerows are replaced by stone walls to find a 100-year-old traditional whitewashed building that has been refashioned as a cozy café against the backdrop of Slieve Bingian mountain. Set amid the timeless wide-angle landscape of undulating countryside and green fields unspooling to the distant horizon of coast and sea, this is the place for those hungry for

scenery as much as tray bakes, sandwiches, and salads. **Known for:** delicious homemade snacks and cakes; Illy coffee adds perfection; jaw-dropping vistas of mountains and sea. ⑤ *Average main: £10* ✉ *204 Head Rd., Mourne Mountains* ⊹ *Drive south from Newcastle along A2 road to Annalong and turn right to signpost for Carrick Little where you can park and walk to café a few minutes away* ☎ *075/9592–9307.*

Niki's Kitchen Café

$ | IRISH | Famed for its huge rhubarb and ginger scones (one may well satisfy two) as well as its breakfasts, this split-level café pulls in the crowds and is a beloved spot of hikers. Lunch may be lasagne, feta cheese, cured meat sandwiches, or specials such as salt and chili chicken wings, while for salad lovers, vegan and gluten-free dishes are available. **Known for:** gargantuan tasty scones; laid-back lunches; free car parking in Donard Park. ⑤ *Average main: £11* ✉ *107 Central Promenade, Mourne Mountains* ⊹ *At one end of main promenade overlooking seafront* ☎ *028/4372–6777.*

🛏 Hotels

Briers Country House

$$ | B&B/INN | An elegant 18th-century country house with mature gardens, this is the ideal place to feel the fresh sea breezes and sample the delights of Newcastle and the surrounding mountainous countryside. **Pros:** scenic location; delightful gardens; close to many amenities. **Cons:** some rooms slightly cramped; gets very busy in high season; few facilities. ⑤ *Rooms from: £100* ✉ *39 Middle Tollymore Rd., Newcastle* ⊹ *400 yards from front entrance to Tollymore Forest Park* ☎ *028/4372–4347* ⊕ *www.thebriers.co.uk* 🛏 *9 rooms, 1 3-bedroom cottage* ⍥ *Free breakfast.*

★ Slieve Donard Resort & Spa

$$$$ | RESORT | A lavish redbrick monument to Victoriana, this turreted hotel, built in 1898, stands like a palace on green lawns at one end of Newcastle's 6½-km (4-mile) sandy beach; the traditional furnishings help make it feel like stepping back in time to the town's turn-of-the-20th-century heyday as an elegant seaside resort, though the bright guest rooms have modern comforts. **Pros:** appealing mix of luxury, history, and style; fireplaces in lobby welcome on chilly days; breakfasts are top-notch. **Cons:** housekeeping slow with requests; occasional noise from wedding receptions; sea-view rooms are pricey. ⑤ *Rooms from: £209* ⊠ *Downs Rd., Newcastle* ☎ *028/4372–1066* ⊕ *www. hastingshotels.com/slieve-donard-resort-and-spa* ⌁ *181 rooms* ⎮⚭⎮ *Free breakfast.*

 ## Activities

BICYCLING
Bicycling

BICYCLING | The Mournes and surrounding area are renowned for spectacular walking countryside, but increasingly have also become noted for top-class bike trails, seaside rides alongside beaches, tracks through sylvan forests, and cross-country cycle routes. Nine magnificient cycling tours through the region have been created and range from gentle cycling mainly on quiet, flat roads to longer routes with steep ascents. For details of these trails pick up the free leaflet from tourist board office, "Make Your Day Cycle Routes," which includes a map and information on distance, grade, and points of interest. The tourist office can also supply details on bike rental. ⊠ *Central Promenade, Mourne Mountains* ☎ *028/4372–2222* ⊕ *visitmourne-mountains.co.uk.*

GOLF
★ Royal County Down

GOLF | With a stunning backdrop of mountains and sea, Royal County Down is a links course with craterlike bunkers and small dunes; catch it on the right day at the right time, and you may think you're on the moon. For better players, every day is the right one. Back in his day, Harry Vardon labeled it the toughest course in the Emerald Isle, and if you can't hit your drive long and straight, you may find it so. No visitors are allowed on Wednesday or Saturday. ⊠ *36 Golf Links Rd., Newcastle* ☎ *028/4372–3314* ⊕ *www. royalcountydown.org* ⎘ *Championship: weekdays £240 am, £230 pm, weekends £250. Annesley: £50* ⚐. *Championship: 18 holes, 7204 yards, par 71; Annesley: 18 holes, 4617 yards, par 66.*

HIKING AND WALKING
Tollymore National Outdoor Centre

CLIMBING/MOUNTAINEERING | If you need advice on mountain climbing, canoeing, and hiking trails, this impressive center is the place to head. ⊠ *Bryansford, Newcastle* ☎ *028/4372–2158* ⊕ *www. tollymore.com.*

Downpatrick

21 km (14 miles) northeast of Newcastle.

Downpatrick once was called plain and simple "Down" but had its name changed by John de Courcy, a Norman knight who moved here in 1176. De Courcy set about promoting St. Patrick, the 5th-century Briton who was captured by the Irish and served as a slave in the Down area before escaping to France, where he learned about Christianity and bravely returned to try to convert the local chiefs. Although it's not true that Patrick brought a new faith to Ireland—there was already a bishop of Ireland before Patrick got here—he must have been a better missionary than most because he did indeed win influential converts. The clan chief of the Down area gave him land at the village of Saul, near Downpatrick, to build a monastery. You could happily spend a morning here visiting a trio of top-class sites: Down Cathedral, Down County Museum (now housing the ancient High Cross of

A four-hour ascent of the Slieve Donard peak—queen of the magnificent Mountains of Mourne—offers vistas that reach as far as Scotland and the Isle of Man.

Down), and the Saint Patrick Centre are all clustered within a few minutes' walk of each other.

GETTING HERE AND AROUND

Buses arrive at the main station in Downpatrick from many points of County Down and beyond. Frequent Translink Goldline express services run to and from Belfast. The journey time is one hour (£10.50 round-trip or £7 after 9:45 am). Some services link up with the Belfast Metro network of suburban routes. To visit Strangford, there are daily services from Downpatrick (£6.10 round-trip); to visit Castle Ward, ask the driver to stop by the roadside. Buses also leave Downpatrick for Dublin; the journey takes just over three hours (£20.85 round-trip; £19.50 to Dublin Airport).

Downpatrick is 21 km (14 miles) east of Newcastle on A2 and A25 and 30 km (22 miles) south of Belfast on A24. On-street parking is free but restricted to either 30 or 60 minutes. The car park at the Grove shopping center is pay-and-display and costs £0.40 per hour. There is free parking on English and Market Streets and beside the bus station.

VISITOR INFORMATION

CONTACTS Downpatrick Visitor Information Centre. ⊠ *53A Market St.* ☎ *028/4461–2233* ⊕ *www.visitstrangfordlough.co.uk.*

 Sights

Down Cathedral

RELIGIOUS SITE | The Cathedral of the Holy Trinity, or Down Cathedral as it's commonly known, is one of the disputed burial places of St. Patrick. In the churchyard, a somber flat stone slab inscribed "Patric" is supposedly the saint's tomb. It might be here, at Saul, or, some scholars argue, more likely at Armagh. The stone was quarried in 1990 at Slievena-Largie near Castlewellan and took 12 men 14 days to cut from the quarry. The church, which lay ruined from 1538 to 1790 (it reopened in 1818), preserves parts of some of the earlier churches and monasteries that have stood on this site, the oldest of which dates to the 6th century. Even by then, the cathedral site had long been an important fortified settlement: Down takes its name from the Celtic word *dun*, or fort. Information panels tell the history of the building through a timeline, showing the connection with St. Patrick, and give details on the war memorials. In the summer of 2018 a replica of St. Patrick's Cross was installed in the grounds of the cathedral, just yards from where he is said to be buried. The reproduction, sculpted from Mourne granite, is on the Hill of Down where the original cross once stood. There's also a shop selling souvenirs. ⊠ *35 English St.* ☎ *028/4461–4922* ⊕ *www.downcathedral.org* ⊡ *£2.*

★ **Down County Museum**

MUSEUM | With the transfer of the 1,100-year-old Mourne granite High Cross as the centerpiece of an elaborate extension in 2015, this museum, housed in an 18th-century jail, has gained serious cachet. The Downpatrick High Cross had stood in front of nearby Down Cathedral since the late 19th century, but had suffered deterioration through weather damage—never mind the Viking pillagers—and has been moved permanently indoors. The original location of the intricately patterned cross, carved around AD 900 as a "prayer in stone," is believed to have been the early medieval monastery on the Hill of Down. The extension now houses a display, *Raising the Cross in Down,* alongside two new galleries reflecting the maritime and agricultural history of the area. Elsewhere, look into the small cells in the jail along a narrow whitewashed corridor. The other main exhibition is *Down through Time,* while frequent photographic exhibitions and artwork are on display in other rooms. Behind the building, a short signposted trail leads to an example of a Norman motte and bailey known as the Mound of Down or "Dundalethglas." A large

egg-shape enclosure, this is one of Northern Ireland's most impressive earthen fortifications and may have been a royal stronghold of the Dál Fiatach, the dynasty that ruled this part of County Down in the first millennium AD. The Cathedral View Tearoom serves homemade lunches and snacks. ⊠ *The Mall, English St.* ☎ *028/4461–5218* ⊕ *www.downcountymuseum.com* ⊡ *Free.*

The Saint Patrick Centre

MUSEUM | FAMILY | The interactive exhibits here bring the ancient myths and stories of early Christian Ireland to life. You can explore how St. Patrick's legacy developed in early Christian times, examine the art and metalwork that were produced during this golden age, and listen to modern debates about Ireland's patron saint. Interpretative boards outline local sites connected with the saint. Self-guided tours of sites linked with St. Patrick last about 70 minutes and take you across a bridge over the River of Words. If time is short, you can opt to watch the IMAX cinema presentation, a 17-minute, 180-degree audiovisual flight that whizzes you around relevant Irish sites—a highlight of the entire exhibition. The center includes a café, the Grove gift store, an art gallery, terraced gardens, and a well-stocked tourist information office. ⊠ *St. Patrick's Sq., 53A Lower Market St.* ☎ *028/4461–9000* ⊕ *www. saintpatrickcentre.com* ⊡ *£6* ⊙ *Closed Sun.*

St. Patrick's Trail

TOUR—SIGHT | After returning to Ireland in the year AD 432, Ireland's patron saint seems to have popped up everywhere on his peregrinations. You can explore places associated with him along St. Patrick's Trail, a 92-mile signposted driving route linking 15 historic and ecclesiastical sites across the beautiful drumlin hills of counties Down and Armagh. Pick up a trail map at the tourist office in Armagh or Downpatrick, and at major attractions on the route you qualify for 2-for-1 entry. ⊠ *Downpatrick* ☎ *028/4461–2333* ⊕ *www.discovernorthernireland.com.*

Restaurants

Denvir's Coaching Inn Restaurant

$ | **IRISH** | In this atmospheric, white-washed coaching inn dating to 1642, noted for its architectural merit, exposed oak beams, stone floors, and a large open fireplace testify to the antiquity; the Snug bar top was crafted from timbers of ships wrecked in Lough Foyle. On the menu, solid traditional dishes dominate—fish from Ardglass, chargrilled steaks, burgers, chicken, and spring lamb. **Known for:** creamy chowder; homemade chargrilled burgers; gin garden. ⑤ *Average main: £13* ⊠ *14–16 English St.* ☎ *028/4461–2012* ⊕ *www.denvirs.com.*

🛏 Hotels

★ Dufferin Coaching Inn

$ | **B&B/INN** | An elegant Georgian inn dating from 1803, this historic building sits next to picture-perfect, grandly gracious Killyleagh Castle—reputedly the longest-inhabited castle in Ireland and arguably the country's prettiest. **Pros:** ideal for exploring Strangford Lough attractions; good value for the money; graceful period house. **Cons:** far from the bright city lights; no elevator; lacks amenities. ⑤ *Rooms from: £70* ⊠ *33 High St., 10 km (6 miles) north of Downpatrick, Killyleagh* ☎ *028/4482–1134* ⊕ *www.dufferincoachinginn.com* ⤳ *7 rooms* ◎❘ *Free breakfast.*

Castle Ward

11 km (7 miles) northeast of Downpatrick, 3 km (2 miles) west of Strangford village on A25; on southern shore of Strangford Lough, entrance by Ballyculter Lodge.

GETTING HERE AND AROUND
CAR TRAVEL

Castle Ward is a 40-minute drive south of Belfast along A24 and the narrower A25. The nearest big town is Downpatrick (10 minutes by car). Strangford is a five-minute drive east on A25 and connects with an idyllic car and passenger ferry service to Portaferry (five minutes), from where you join A20 and the scenic Ards Peninsula back to Belfast via Newtownards.

👁 Sights

★ Castle Ward

CASTLE/PALACE | With a 500-acre park, an artificial lake, a Neoclassical temple, and a vast house in Bath stone magically set on the slopes running down to the Narrows of the southern shore of Strangford Lough, Castle Ward must have been some place to call home. About 3 km (2 miles) from the village of Strangford, off the road to Downpatrick, this regal stately home was designed around 1760 in, rather famously, two differing styles. Bernard Ward, 1st Viscount Bangor, could rarely see eye to eye (gossip had it) with his wife, Lady Anne, and the result was that he decided to make the entrance and salons elegant exercises in Palladian Neoclassicism, while milady transformed the garden facade and her own rooms using the most fashionable style of the day, Strawberry Hill Gothic. His white-and-beige Music Room is picked out in exquisite plasterwork, while her Boudoir has an undulating fan-vaulted ceiling that conjures up the "gothick" medievalisms of King Henry VII's chapel at Westminster. Tours are held every hour. ■TIP→ **There are walking and cycling trails of the grounds from where you can look out over the lough shore and see the location of Winterfell used for the TV series Game of Thrones.** A weekly *Game of Thrones* archery experience is held from March. In the spring and summer months sea safaris, as well as high tea and sea voyages around Strangford Lough, are organized at Castle Ward and leave from the pier at Strangford; these should be booked directly via email through Strangford Sea Safaris. ✉ *3 km (2 miles) west of Strangford on Downpatrick Rd. (A25), Downpatrick* ☎ *028/4488–1204* ✉ *fun@strangford-seasafari.com for Strangford Sea Safaris* ⊕ *www.national-trust.org.uk/castle-ward* 💷 *£11.*

Index

Photo Credits

Front Cover: SIME / eStock Photo [Description: UK, Northern Ireland, Ballymoney, Dark Hedges.] **Back cover, from left to right:** Patryk Kosmider/shutterstock, SAKhanPhotography/istockphoto, yktr/istockphoto. **Spine:** nhtg/Shutterstock. Interior, from left to right: elementals/istockphoto (1). Mustang_79/istockphoto (2). clu/iStockphoto (5). **Chapter 1: Experience Ireland:** Bart_Kowski/istockphoto (8). Aervisions (10-11). Ruth Medjber (11). Nataliya Hora/Shutterstock (11). Victoriasky1/Dreamstime.com (12). jamegaw/shutterstock (12). Chris Hill/Tourism Ireland (12). Sue Burton PhotographyLtd/shutterstock (12). Guinness Storehouse (13). Macmillan Media/Courtesy of Tourism Ireland (13). Tourism Ireland (14). Gardiner Mitchell/Courtesy of Ireland Tourism (14). Stefano_Valeri/shutterstock (15). All Rights Reserved (16). Stefan Missing/shutterstock (16). Chris Bellew/Fennell Photography (16). Courtesy of Asford Castle (16). Courtesy of Jerpoint Glass (17). Tourism Ireland (17). 4kclips/shutterstock (17). Rihardzz/Dreamstime.com (17). Douglas Gray/shutterstock (18). Nhtg/Dreamstime.com (18). Christopher Hill/Tourism Ireland (19). Alison Crummy/Fáilte Ireland (20). Courtesy of Tourism Ireland (20). Courtesy of Historic Royal Palaces (20). Courtesy of Tourism Ireland (20). Chris Hill Photographic (21). Chris Hill/Courtesy of Tourism Ireland (22) (All). Fáilte Ireland/Courtesy of Tourism Ireland (23) (All). Courtesy of Dromoland Castle (24). Courtesy of Hayfield manor (24). Courtesy of Ashford Castle (24). Courtesy of Adare Manor (24). Courtesy of Ballynachin Castle (25). Courtesy of Lough Eske Castle (25). Barry Murphy (25). Courtesy of Bellingham Castle (25). Natalia Ruedisueli/shutterstock (26). Ireland Tourism (27). Courtesy of MourneTextiles (28). Courtesy of Celtic Whiskey Shop (29). Jed Niezgoda (30). DON MACMONAGLE (30). Fáilte Ireland/Courtesy of Tourism Ireland (30). Clare Keogh (31). David Ribeiro/Dreamstime (31). **Chapter 3: Dublin:** IIC / age fotostock (71). Nico Tondini/age fotostock (74). Ye/Shutterstock (75). Antonio V. Oquias/Shutterstock (75). Rob Wilson/Shutterstock (92). Hochgeladen von Tormod/wikipedia.org (106). Beinecke Rare Book and Manuscript Library, Yale University (108). clu/iStockphoto (108). Arrow Books (109). Macmillan (109). wikipedia.org (109). Jean-Pierre De Mann/age fotostock (109). si_arts/Shutterstock (110). janetmck/Flickr (111). Library of Congress Prints and Photographs Division (112). National Portrait Gallery, London/wikipedia.org (112). Georgios Kollidas/iStockphoto (112). Lebrecht Music and Arts Photo Library / Alamy (113). Ida Kar Collection/Mary Evans Picture Library (113). wikipedia.org (113). Jack_Dawkins/Flickr (114). Homer Sykes/age fotostock (114). Wikipedia (114). Razvan Stroie/Shutterstock (117). Martin Child/age fotostock (126). Bartkowski/shutterstock (135). **Chapter 4: Dublin Environs:** fineartfotography/Shutterstock (157). Stbernardstudio/Dreamstime.com (160). Pyma/Shutterstock (161). Amanda Bullock (161). UnaPhoto/Shutterstock (170). Gail Johnson/Shutterstock (175). Eireann/Shutterstock (184). Warrenfish/wikipedia.org (186). The Irish Image Colle/age fotostock (190). Joe Cornish/Dorling Kindersley (192). Department of the Environment, Heritage and Local Government, Ireland. (192). Joe Cornish/Dorling Kindersley (193) (All). Russborough (194) (All). Russborough (195). Web Gallery of Art (195). Lokono/Dreamstime.com (196). **Chapter 5: The Midlands:** MNStudio/istockphoto (201). The Irish Image Colle/age fotostock (204). The Irish Image Colle/age fotostock (205). ARCO/Krieger C/age fotostock (205). The Irish Image Colle/age fotostock (219). The Irish Image Colle/age fotostock (225). Javier Mediavilla Ezquibela/wikipedia.org (234). **Chapter 6: The Southeast:** Kai Loos/age fotostock (241). Kevin Galvin/age fotostock (251). Kevin Galvin/age fotostock (255). Martin Moos/age fotostock (262). Terry Murphy/Tourism Ireland (272). Richard Cummins/age fotostock (278). walshphotos/Shutterstock (280). George Munday/age fotostock (283). Irish Typepad/Flickr (284). Patryk Kosmider/Shutterstock (284). Patryk Kosmider/Shutterstock (286). Christian Handl/age fotostock (286). Danilo Donadoni/age fotostock (287). Marc C. Johnson/Shutterstock (287). The Irish Image Colle/age fotostock (288). Marc C. Johnson/Shutterstock (289). **Chapter 7: County Cork:** The Irish Image Colle/age fotostock (293). Gubbeen Farmhouse Products (296). Jaroslaw Grudzinski/Shutterstock (297). Rick Senley / age fotostock (297). Richard Cummins / age fotostock (305). RIEGER Bertrand / age fotostock (310, 313). walshphotos/Shutterstock (318-319). IIC/age fotostock (327). Christian Handl/age fotostock (333). **Chapter 8: The Southwest:** Ramon Mascaró/istockphoto (335). walshphotos/Shutterstock (349). Magann/Dreamstime.com (359). ARCO/Ludaescher/age fotostock (362). Joe Gough/iStockphoto (372-373). John Brennan/iStockphoto (373). Jonathan Hession/Tourism Ireland (373). Rambling Traveler/Flickr (374). Bertrand Collet/Shutterstock (375). Giovanni Rinaldi/iStockphoto (376). Insuratelu Gabriela Gianina/Shutterstock (376). Cork Kerry Tourism (376). Jonathan Hession/Tourism Ireland (377). nagelestock.com/Alamy (377). Ariel Cione/iStockphoto (378). ingmar wesemann/iStockphoto (378). Stephan Hoerold/iStockphoto (378). Michelle Nadal, Fodors.com (379). Justin James Wilson/Shutterstock (385). David Mason/iStockphoto (389). Jack Hardy (391). **Chapter 9: County Clare, Galway City, and the Aran Islands:** IIC / age fotostock (395). Patryk Kosmider/Shutterstock (420-421). Jordache/Dreamstime.com (423). rejflinger/Flickr (437). Chris Hill/Tourism Ireland (445). **Chapter 10: Connemara and County Mayo:** Shawn Williams/istockphoto (451). Ivica Drusany/Shutterstock (454). LaRsNoW @/Flickr (455). Holger Leue/Tourism Ireland (455). Kelvin Gillmor (466). Roger Kinkead/Tourism Ireland (468). Wiltilroeotte/Dreamstime.com (470-471). The Irish Image Colle/age fotostock (476). **Chapter 11: The Northwest:** Holger Leue/Tourism Ireland (487). Ken Welsh/age fotostock (503). Red/Dreamstime.com (513). Holger Leue/Tourism Ireland (521). The Irish Image Colle/age fotostock (523). **Chapter 12: Northern Ireland:** Brian Morrison/Northern Ireland Tourist Board (531). Martin Bobrovsky/age fotostockv (534). yvescosentino/Flickr (535). David Cordner/Northern Ireland Tourist Board (535). Titanic Belfast (560). IIC/age fotostock (566). Joe Fox/age fotostock (570). Brian Morrison/Tourism Ireland (581). traveling, Fodors.com member (589). Josemaria Toscano/Shutterstock (591). Nahlik/Dreamstime (593). Paul McErlane/Alamy Stock Photo (596). Geray Sweeney/Tourism Ireland (599). Brian Morrison/Northern Ireland Tourist Board (614). Tony Pleavin/Northern Ireland Tourist Board (617). Tony Pleavin/Northern Ireland Tourist Board (621). **About Our Writers:** All photos are courtesy of the writers except for the following: Alannah Hopkin, courtesy of Nelius Buckley; Anto Howard, courtesy of William Hederman.

*Every effort has been made to trace the copyright holders, and we apologize in advance for any accidental errors. We would be happy to apply the corrections in the following edition of this publication.

Notes

Notes

Fodor's ESSENTIAL IRELAND 2020

Publisher: Stephen Horowitz, *General Manager*

Editorial: Douglas Stallings, *Editorial Director*; Margaret Kelly, Jacinta O'Halloran, Amanda Sadlowski, *Senior Editors*; Kayla Becker, Alexis Kelly, Teddy Minford, Rachael Roth, *Editors*

Design: Tina Malaney, *Design and Production Director*; Jessica Gonzalez, *Graphic Designer*; Mariana Tabares, *Design & Production Intern*

Production: Jennifer DePrima, *Editorial Production Manager*; Carrie Parker, *Senior Production Editor*; Elyse Rozelle, *Production Editor*; Jackson Pranica, *Editorial Production Assistant*

Maps: Rebecca Baer, *Senior Map Editor*; David Lindroth, Mark Stroud (Moon Street Cartography), *Cartographers*

Photography: Jill Krueger, *Director of Photo*; Namrata Aggarwal, Ashok Kumar, Carl Yu, *Photo Editors*; Rebecca Rimmer, *Photo Intern*

Business & Operations: Chuck Hoover, *Chief Marketing Officer*; Robert Ames, *Group General Manager*; Tara McCrillis, *Director of Publishing Operations*; Victor Bernal, *Business Analyst*

Public Relations and Marketing: Joe Ewaskiw, *Senior Director Communications & Public Relations*; Esther Su, Senior *Marketing Manager*; Ryan Garcia, Thomas Talarico, Miranda Villalobos, *Marketing Specialists*

Fodors.com Jeremy Tarr, *Editorial Director*; Rachael Levitt, *Managing Editor*

Technology: Jon Atkinson, *Director of Technology*; Rudresh Teotia, *Lead Developer*; Jacob Ashpis, *Content Operations Manager*

Writers: Paul Clements, Alannah Hopkin, Anto Howard, Vic O'Sullivan

Editor: Jacinta O'Halloran

Production Editor: Elyse Rozelle

3rd Edition

ISBN 978-1-64097-170-7

ISSN 2471–9188

Library of Congress Control Number 2019938168

All details in this book are based on information supplied to us at press time. Always confirm information when it matters, especially if you're making a detour to visit a specific place. Fodor's expressly disclaims any liability, loss, or risk, personal or otherwise, that is incurred as a consequence of the use of any of the contents of this book.

SPECIAL SALES

This book is available at special discounts for bulk purchases for sales promotions or premiums. For more information, e-mail SpecialMarkets@fodors.com.

PRINTED IN THE UNITED STATES OF AMERICA

10 9 8 7 6 5 4 3 2 1

About Our Writers

Paul Clements is a writer, broadcaster, and journalist, and former BBC news editor who lives in Belfast. He writes travel, nature, and cultural heritage features for a range of Irish newspapers and a monthly local history column for the *Irish Times*. Paul is the author of four discursive travel books about Ireland: *Irish Shores; A Journey Round the Rim of Ireland*, based on a hitchhiking trip around the coast; the best-selling *The Height of Nonsense: The Ultimate Irish Road Trip*, which is the story of a quirky quest for the highest geographic point in each of Ireland's 32 counties; *Burren Country: Travels Through an Irish Limestone Landscape*, a collection of essays about the unique Burren region of County Clare, and *Wandering Ireland's Wild Atlantic Way: From Banba's Crown to World's End*, a journey along this 2,500 km route. In addition, his biography, *Romancing Ireland*, on the travel writer Richard Hayward was adapted for BBC television.

Alannah Hopkin grew up in London but spent most of her childhood summers on her uncle's farm near Kinsale, where she learned two of the most important things in life: how to ride a horse and how to sail a boat. After graduate studies in Irish literature, she worked as a writer in London, but ancestral voices were calling her home, and she spent more and more time in County Cork, where horses and boats were easier to find. After publishing her first novel, she made the big leap and moved to Kinsale for a trial six months … and is still there 30 years later. Another novel was followed by an acclaimed book about the cult of St. Patrick, which will be reissued in 2020. She

has written on travel and the arts for the *Sunday Times,* the *Guardian,* and the *Financial Times* in London, and contributes regularly to the *Irish Examiner* and the *Irish Times*. Recent books include, *The Dogs of Inishere* (Dalkey Archive Press), and *Eating Scenery: West Cork, the People and the Place* (The Collins Press, Cork). Alannah updated County Cork and the Southwest.

For our coverage of Dublin, **Anto Howard** has checked every fact, burnished every metaphor to the fine gleam of ancient brogues, and has so lovingly described the towns and villages found in the Dublin Environs and Southeast chapters that even their natives will leave for the pleasure of coming back. Six postgraduate years of living in New York City recently convinced Anto of the charms of his native Ireland, and he duly returned to take up residence in Dublin. He has written and edited books and articles about such far-flung places as Costa Rica, Las Vegas, and Russia, and has contributed to such publications as *National Geographic Traveler* and *Budget Travel*. Anto (christened Anthony—Dubliners have a habit of abbreviating perfectly good names) is also a playwright, and his shows have been produced in Dublin and in New York. He has also written the book *Slow Dublin*, a manual for living life to the full in his home city.

Vic O'Sullivan spent his early years in Toronto before moving to County Clare in Ireland. He graduated as a Chartered Certified Accountant and worked in aircraft finance and the hospitality sector before returning to the University of Limerick to study journalism. He has written on travel for the *LA*

About Our Writers

*Times,*the *Chicago Tribune, Guardian, Daily Mail, Irish Examiner, Lonely Planet,* and the *Sunday Business Post,* and contributes regularly to the *Sunday Times* and the *Irish Times.* He has traveled extensively, is a fair weather runner and avid reader, and lives with his family and a cocker spaniel called Anakin Skywalker in Bunratty Village, County Clare. Vic updated the County Clare, Galway City, and the Aran Islands chapter along with Connemara and County Mayo. Find Vic on Twitter @VicBunratty.